International Business

BS0037 International Business:
Globalisation and Trade

BS0038 International Business and
Multinational Enterprise

We work with leading authors to develop the strongest educational materials bringing cutting-edge thinking and best learning practice to a global market.

Under a range of well-known imprints, including Financial Times/Prentice Hall, Addison Wesley and Longman, we craft high quality print and electronic publications which help readers to understand and apply their content, whether studying or at work.

Pearson Custom Publishing enables our customers to access a wide and expanding range of market-leading content from world-renowned authors and develop their own tailor-made book. You choose the content that meets your needs and Pearson Custom Publishing produces a high-quality printed book.

To find out more about custom publishing, visit www.pearsoncustom.co.uk

A Pearson Custom Publication

International Business

BS0037 International Business: Globalisation and Trade

BS0038 International Business and Multinational Enterprise

Compiled from:

International Business: Strategy, Management and the New Realities
by S. Tamer Cavusgil, Gary Knight and John R. Riesenberger

International Business Fifth Edition
by Alan M. Rugman and Simon Collinson

The World Economy: Resources, Location, Trade, and Development Fifth Edition
by Frederick P. Stutz and Barney Warf

International Business Sixth Edition
by Ricky W. Griffin and Michael W. Pustay

The Business of Tourism Eighth Edition
by J. Christopher Holloway
with Claire Humphreys and Rob Davidson

International Business: The Challenges of Globalization
Fifth Edition
by John J. Wild, Kenneth L. Wild and Jerry C. Y. Han

Innovation Management and New Product Development
Fourth Edition
by Paul Trott

PEARSON
Custom
Publishing

Pearson Education Limited
Edinburgh Gate
Harlow
Essex CM20 2JE

And associated companies throughout the world

Visit us on the World Wide Web at:
www.pearsoned.co.uk

First published 2010

This Custom Book Edition © 2010 Published by Pearson Education Limited

Compiled from:

International Business: Strategy, Management and the New Realities
by S. Tamer Cavusgil, Gary Knight and John R. Riesenberger
ISBN 978 0 13 173860 7
Copyright © 2008 by Pearson Education, Inc., Upper Saddle River, New Jersey, 07458.

International Business Fifth Edition
by Alan M. Rugman and Simon Collinson
ISBN 978 0 273 71654 9
Copyright © Pearson Education Limited 2000, 2006, 2009

The World Economy: Resources, Location, Trade, and Development Fifth Edition
by Frederick P. Stutz and Barney Warf
ISBN 978 0 13 506846 2
Copyright © 2007, 2005, 1998 by Pearson Education, Inc.

International Business Sixth Edition
by Ricky W. Griffin and Michael W. Pustay
ISBN 978 0 13 507227 1
Copyright © 2010, 2007, 2005, 2002, 1999 by Pearson Education, Inc.,
publishing as Prentice Hall, One Lake Street, Upper Saddle River, New Jersey

The Business of Tourism Eighth Edition
by J. Christopher Holloway with Claire Humphreys and Rob Davidson
ISBN 978 0 273 71710 2
Copyright © Pearson Education Limited 1983, 2002, 2006, 2009

International Business: The Challenges of Globalization Fifth Edition
by John J. Wild, Kenneth L. Wild and Jerry C. Y. Han
ISBN 978 0 13 609520 0
Copyright © 2010, 2008, 2006, 2003, 2000 by Pearson Education, Inc.,
publishing as Prentice Hall, One Lake Street, Upper Saddle River, New Jersey

Innovation Management and New Product Development Fourth Edition
by Paul Trott
ISBN 978 0 273 71315 9
Copyright © Pearson Professional Limited 1998
Copyright © Pearson Education Limited 2002, 2005, 2008

ISBN 978 1 84776 728 8

Printed and bound by in Great Britain by Henry Ling Limited at the Dorset Press,
Dorchester, DT1 1HD.

Contents

SEMESTER 1   **INTERNATIONAL BUSINESS: GLOBALISATION AND TRADE**   **1**

Section 1   Institutional Perspective   3

Globalization of Markets and the Internationalization
of the Firm   4
Chapter 2 in *International Business: Strategy, Management and the New Realities*
S. Tamer Cavusgil, Gary Knight and John R. Riesenberger

International Trade   37
Chapter 6 in *International Business*
Fifth Edition
Alan M. Rugman and Simon Collinson

Regional Economic Integration   72
Chapter 8 in *International Business: Strategy, Management and the New Realities*
S. Tamer Cavusgil, Gary Knight and John R. Riesenberger

International Culture   105
Chapter 5 in *International Business*
Fifth Edition
Alan M. Rugman and Simon Collinson

Section 2   Firm Perspective   135

International Trade Patterns   136
Chapter 13 in *The World Economy: Resources, Location, Trade, and Development*
Fifth Edition
Frederick P. Stutz and Barney Warf

Section 3   National Level   177

Development and Underdevelopment in the Developing World   178
Chapter 14 in *The World Economy: Resources, Location, Trade, and Development*
Fifth Edition
Frederick P. Stutz and Barney Warf

Section 4   Industry Level and Corporate Issues   225

Ethics and Social Responsibility in International Business   226
Chapter 5 in *International Business*
Sixth Edition
Ricky W. Griffin and Michael W. Pustay

Resources and Environment   256
Chapter 4 in *The World Economy: Resources, Location, Trade, and Development*
Fifth Edition
Frederick P. Stutz and Barney Warf

Manufacturing   298
Chapter 7 in *The World Economy: Resources, Location, Trade, and Development*
Fifth Edition
Frederick P. Stutz and Barney Warf

The Era of Popular Tourism: 1950 to the Twenty-First Century   332
Chapter 3 in *The Business of Tourism*
Eighth Edition
J. Christopher Holloway with Claire Humphreys and Rob Davidson

The Economic Impacts of Tourism   347
Chapter 5 in *The Business of Tourism*
Eighth Edition
J. Christopher Holloway with Claire Humphreys and Rob Davidson

SEMESTER 2   **INTERNATIONAL BUSINESS AND THE MULTINATIONAL ENTERPRISE**   **375**

Section 1   FDI Theory   377

Foreign Direct Investment   378
Chapter 7 in *International Business: The Challenges of Globalization*
Fifth Edition
John J. Wild, Kenneth L. Wild and Jerry C. Y. Han

Consumption   402
Chapter 11 in *The World Economy: Resources, Location, Trade, and Development*
Fifth Edition
Frederick P. Stutz and Barney Warf

Section 2   Market Entry Strategies   417

Marketing in the Global Firm   418
Chapter 17 in *International Business: Strategy, Management and the New Realities*
S. Tamer Cavusgil, Gary Knight and John R. Riesenberger

Licensing, Franchising, and Other Contractual Strategies   450
Chapter 15 in *International Business: Strategy, Management and the New Realities*
S. Tamer Cavusgil, Gary Knight and John R. Riesenberger

Global Market Opportunity Assessment   482
Chapter 12 in *International Business: Strategy, Management and the New Realities*
S. Tamer Cavusgil, Gary Knight and John R. Riesenberger

Section 3   Strategies and Structures   519

Global Strategy and Organization   520
Chapter 11 in *International Business: Strategy, Management and the New Realities*
S. Tamer Cavusgil, Gary Knight and John R. Riesenberger

Section 4   International Collaborations   553

International Strategic Alliances   554
Chapter 13 in *International Business*
Sixth Edition
Ricky W. Griffin and Michael W. Pustay

Section 5   International Production Networks   579

Organizational Participants that make International
Business Happen   580
Chapter 3 in *International Business: Strategy, Management and the New Realities*
S. Tamer Cavusgil, Gary Knight and John R. Riesenberger

Global Sourcing   612
Chapter 16 in *International Business: Strategy, Management and the New Realities*
S. Tamer Cavusgil, Gary Knight and John R. Riesenberger

Production Strategy   645
Chapter 10 in *International Business*
Fifth Edition
Alan M. Rugman and Simon Collinson

Section 6   International Knowledge Networks and Technology   679

Innovation Management: An Introduction   680
Chapter 1 in *Innovation Management and New Product Development*
Fourth Edition
Paul Trott

Transportation and Communications   720
Chapter 9 in *The World Economy: Resources, Location, Trade, and Development*
Fifth Edition
Frederick P. Stutz and Barney Warf

Managing Intellectual Property   756
Chapter 5 in *Innovation Management and New Product Development*
Fourth Edition
Paul Trott

Semester 1

International Business: Globalisation and Trade

Section 1
Institutional Perspective

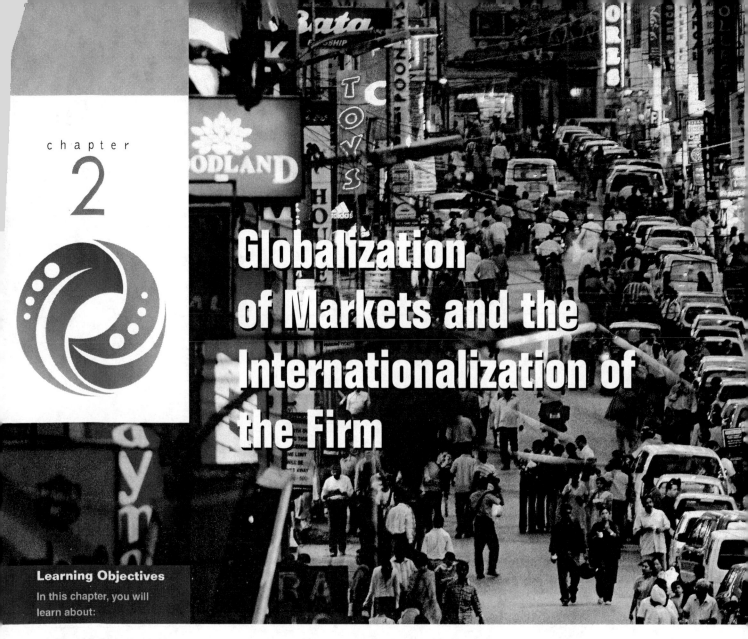

chapter

2

Learning Objectives

In this chapter, you will learn about:

1. Why globalization is not a new phenomenon

2. An organizing framework for market globalization

3. Dimensions of market globalization

4. Drivers of market globalization

5. Technological advances as a driver of market globalization

6. Societal consequences of market globalization

7. Firm-level consequences of market globalization: internationalization of the firm's value chain

Globalization of Markets and the Internationalization of the Firm

> ## Bangalore: The New Silicon Valley

Weekday evenings in Bangalore, thousands of young men and women commute by bus to the call centers that characterize this city, the fifth largest in India. As the business day begins in Eastern Canada and the United States, these young Indians put on their telephone headsets to begin the overnight shift. They assist North American customers with service problems regarding credit cards, product purchases, and Internet transactions. Over 100,000 people are employed in Bangalore writing software, designing chips, running computer systems, reading X-rays, processing mortgages, preparing tax forms, and tracing lost luggage for firms in Australia, China, Europe, Japan, and North America. You can observe the same pattern in Delhi, Chennai, Hyderabad, and other emerging high-tech centers across India. Accenture, AOL, Intel, Cisco, Oracle, Philips, and Ernst & Young all have located operations in the country.

The number of people working in outsourced information technology (IT) services in India surpassed one million in 2008. What is the attraction? First, Indians are paid roughly one-quarter of what Westerners receive for similar work, and in many cases they do a better job. Second, India is home to several million highly

4   International Business

educated knowledge workers. Third, English is widely spoken. Finally, being located in a different time zone from Europe and the United States allows the Indians to take advantage of time-sharing. When North Americans are ending their workday, Indians are arriving at the office to start their day. Because of instant data transmission via the Internet, Europeans and North Americans can e-mail the projects they are working on to their Indian counterparts, who then submit the completed work by the next morning. For companies in the knowledge economy, welcome to the 24-hour workday.

Infosys is the leading software firm in India. Infosys CEO Nandan Nilekani boasts of his global video conference room with a wall-size flat screen TV. Infosys regularly holds virtual meetings with its key global value-chain players on the super-size screen. The company's American designers can be on the screen speaking with their Indian software writers and their Asian manufacturers, simultaneously. "That's what globalization is all about today," says Nilekani. Above the screen are eight clocks that sum up the Infosys workday: 24/7/365. The clocks are labeled U.S. West, U.S. East, London, India, Singapore, Hong Kong, Japan, and Australia.[1]

Nilekani explains that computers are becoming cheaper and commonplace around the world, and there is an explosion of e-mail software and search engines like Google. Proprietary software can chop up any piece of work and send one part to Boston, one part to Bangalore, and one part to Beijing, making it easy for anyone to do remote development. "When all these things came together, they created a platform for intellectual work that could be delivered from anywhere. It could be disaggregated, delivered, distributed, produced and put back together again. What you see in Bangalore today is really the culmination of all these things coming together." Emerging markets like India, Brazil, and China can compete equally for global knowledge work as never before.[2]

Ravi Patel is typical of the knowledge workers Bangalore IT firms employ. He drives a Suzuki car, uses a Sony Ericsson mobile phone, and banks with Citibank. He hangs out with friends drinking Starbucks coffee, or Bacardi and Sprite. He watches American movies on a Samsung TV, brushes his teeth with Colgate, and owns a pair of Reeboks. At work Ravi uses an Acer computer with Microsoft software, a Lucent telephone, a Mita copy machine, and drinks Coca-Cola.

Ravi's life illustrates the phenomenon of *globalization*. Globalization has several implications:

- It is increasingly difficult to distinguish where you are in the world based on the products and services that you consume.

- The most important technologies can be developed in most locations worldwide.

- Jobs in the knowledge sector are being performed wherever the firm can extract maximal advantages, anywhere in the world.

- In the long run, by emphasizing free trade and global sourcing, globalization allows consumers worldwide to receive maximum quality at minimum price. Buyers in both producer and consumer nations increase their discretionary income and quality of life.[3]

Sources: John Heilemann (2004). "In Through the Outsourcing Door." *Business 2.0*, November; (2003). "Where Is Your Job Going?" *Fortune*, November; Friedman, Thomas. (2005). "It's a Flat World, After All." *The New York Times Magazine*, April; Siegel, Jeremy. (2005). *The Future for Investors*. New York: Crown Business.

Globalization of markets
The gradual integration and growing interdependence of national economies.

The opening vignette highlights two megatrends that, more than any other, have altered the business environment: the globalization of markets and technological advances. As we discussed in Chapter 1, **globalization of markets** refers to the gradual integration and growing interdependence of national economies. Globalization allows firms to view the world as an integrated marketplace. Initially, scholars used the term *market globalization* to refer to the emergence of global markets for standardized products and services and the growth of world-scale companies that serve those markets. However, the term has a broader meaning, and also refers to the interconnectedness of national economies and the growing interdependence of buyers, producers, suppliers, and governments in different countries. Market globalization is manifested by the production and marketing of branded products and services worldwide. Declining trade barriers, and the ease with which international business transactions take place due to the Internet and other technologies, are contributing to a gradual integration of most national economies into a unified market.

Ongoing technological advances characterize the other megatrend that has transformed contemporary business. Developments in information, manufacturing, and transportation technologies, as well as the emergence of the Internet, have facilitated rapid and early internationalization of countless firms, such as Neogen (www.neogen.com). The firm's founders developed diagnostic kits to test for food safety. Compared to test kits then available from other firms, Neogen's products were more accurate, more efficient, and easier to use. As word spread about the superiority of the products Neogen was able to internationalize quickly, and acquired a worldwide clientele. Farmers use Neogen test kits to test for pesticide residue; veterinarians use them for pharmaceuticals, vaccines, and topicals; and the USDA's Food Safety Inspection Service has used Neogen's rapid test for E. coli. Today, Neogen is a highly successful international firm.

Modern technology is promoting a higher level of international business activity than ever before. For example, many companies in software, gaming, or entertainment maintain a presence only on the Web. Advances in transportation and communication technologies have greatly aided express delivery service providers such as DHL, UPS, and FedEx to serve clients around the world.

The twin trends of market globalization and technological advances now permit firms to more readily engage in both marketing and *procurement* activities on a global scale. Companies increasingly sell their offerings throughout the world. More firms source raw materials, parts, components, and service inputs from suppliers located around the globe. These trends also serve to transform national economies. Growing world trade and foreign direct investment, coupled with the spread of technology, provide consumers and industrial buyers with a much greater choice of products and services. The competitive and innovative activities of internationally active firms are helping to reduce the prices that consumers and firms pay for products and services. Job creation by internationally active firms is contributing to higher living standards for people around the world. At the same time, preferences for some consumer products appear to be converging across markets, exemplified by the universal popularity of certain music, entertainment, consumer electronics, and food. Globalization is helping to disseminate values from liberalized economies about free trade and respect for intellectual property rights to an ever-widening international audience.[4]

 # Why Globalization Is Not a New Phenomenon

Advanced technologies, such as the Internet and modern transportation systems, have accelerated the pace of globalization. However, globalization is not a new phenomenon; it has simply accelerated and gained complex character in recent decades. Early civilizations in the Mediterranean, Middle East, Asia, Africa, and Europe have all contributed to the growth of cross-border trade over time. Globalization evolved out of a common, shared international heritage of all civilizations, no matter where they developed, to reach out and touch one another.[5] It is a culmination of the wonders of difference and discovery that people recognized thousands of years ago. Exchange with others gave societies the opportunity to expand and grow. Trade through the ages fostered civilization; without it, we would be a world of warring tribes bent on getting what we need through combat.[6] Cross-border trading opened the world to innovations and progress.

Phases of Globalization

Since the 1800s, we can identify four distinct phases in the evolution of market globalization. Each phase is accompanied by revolutionary technological developments and international trends. These are illustrated in Exhibit 2.1. Let's briefly review these stages.

The first phase of globalization began about 1830 and peaked around 1880.[7] International business became widespread during this period due to the growth of railroads, efficient ocean transport, and the rise of large manufacturing and trading companies. Invention of the telegraph and telephone in the late 1800s facilitated information flows between and within nations, and greatly aided early efforts to manage companies' supply chains.

Phase of Globalization	Approximate Period	Triggers	Key Characteristics
First phase	1830 to late 1800s, peaking in 1880	Introduction of railroads and ocean transport	Rise of manufacturing: cross-border trade of commodities, largely by trading companies
Second phase	1900 to 1930	Rise of electricity and steel production	Emergence and dominance of early multinational enterprises (primarily European and North American) in manufacturing, extractive, and agricultural industries
Third phase	1948 to 1970s	Formation of General Agreement on Tariff and Trade (GATT); conclusion of World War II; Marshall Plan to reconstruct Europe	Concerted effort on the part of industrializing Western countries to gradually reduce barriers to trade; rise of multinational companies from Japan; cross-border trade of branded products; cross-border flow of money paralleling the development of global capital markets
Fourth phase	1980s to present	Radical advances in information, communication, manufacturing, and consultation technologies; privatization of state-owned enterprises in transition countries; remarkable economic growth in emerging markets	Unprecedented rate of growth in cross-border trade of products, services, and capital; participation in international business of small and large companies originating from many countries; focus on emerging markets for export, FDI, and sourcing activities

Exhibit 2.1 Phases of Globalization Since the Early 1800s

The second phase of globalization began around 1900 and was associated with the rise of electricity and steel production. The phase reached its height just before the Great Depression, a worldwide economic downturn that began in 1929. In 1900, Western Europe was the most industrialized region in the world. Europe's colonization of countries in Asia, Africa, the Middle East, and beyond led to the establishment of some of the earliest subsidiaries of multinational firms. European companies such as BASF, British Petroleum, Nestlé, Shell, and Siemens had established foreign manufacturing plants by 1900.[8] In the years before World War I (pre-1914), many firms were already operating globally. The Italian manufacturer Fiat supplied vehicles to nations on both sides of the war.

The third phase of globalization began after World War II. At war's end, in 1945, substantial pent-up demand existed for consumer products, as well as for input goods to rebuild Europe and Japan. The United States was least harmed by the war and became the world's dominant economy. Substantial government aid helped stimulate economic activity in Europe. Before the war, tariffs and other trade barriers had been high, and there had been strict controls on currency and capital movements. Several industrialized countries, including Australia, Britain, and the United States, systematically sought to reduce barriers to international trade. The result of this effort was the *General Agreement on Tariffs and Trade* (GATT). Emerging from the Bretton Woods Conference of 23 nations in 1947, the GATT served as a global negotiating forum for liberalizing trade barriers.

The GATT marked the beginning of a series of annual negotiating meetings aimed at reducing barriers to international trade and investment. Participating governments recognized that liberalized trade would stimulate industrialization, modernization, and better living standards. The GATT eventually transformed into the World Trade Organization (WTO) as more countries joined this multinational agency. The **World Trade Organization** is a multilateral governing body empowered to regulate international trade and investment. The WTO aims to ensure fairness and efficiency in international transactions. Some 149 nations are now members of the WTO. Additional global cooperation in the post-war era gave birth to other international organizations such as the International Monetary Fund and the World Bank.

World Trade Organization A multilateral governing body empowered to regulate international trade and investment.

Early multinationals from this third phase of globalization originated from the United States, Western Europe, and Japan. The Europeans often expanded into former colonies. Firms like Unilever, Philips, Royal Dutch-Shell, British Petroleum, and Bayer organized their businesses by establishing independent subsidiaries in each of the foreign countries where they did business. Numerous companies developed internationally recognized trade names, including Nestlé, Kraft, John Deere, Kellogg, Lockheed, Caterpillar, Coca-Cola, Chrysler, Pepsi-Cola, Singer (sewing machines), and Levi's. American multinationals such as IBM, Boeing, Texas Instruments, Xerox, and McDonnell Douglas spread out across the globe on the strength of technological and competitive advantages. Gillette, Kodak, and Kellogg succeeded by offering unique products. Foreign subsidiaries of these firms were formed along a clone model, wherein they produced and sold the same products as the parent firm and operated miniature, autonomous versions of those firms. Gradually, multinational firms began to seek cost advantages by locating factories in developing countries with low labor costs.

Growing MNE activities and early efforts at trade liberalization resulted in substantial increases in international trade and investment beginning in the 1960s. Recovered from World War II, MNEs in Europe and Japan began to challenge the global dominance of U.S. multinationals. With the easing of trade barriers and currency controls, capital began to flow freely across national borders, leading to integration of global financial markets.[9]

The fourth and current phase of globalization began in the early 1980s. This period witnessed enormous growth in cross-border trade and investment. The current phase was triggered by key trends, including the commercialization of the personal computer, the development of the Internet and the Web browser, advances in communication and manufacturing technologies, the collapse of the Soviet Union and ensuing market liberalization in central and Eastern Europe, and the industrialization and modernization efforts of East Asian economies, including China.

Growing international prosperity began to reach emerging markets such as Brazil, India, and Mexico. The 1980s witnessed huge increases in FDI, especially in capital- and technology-intensive sectors. Technological advances in information, communications, and transportation made it feasible for managers to organize far-flung operations around the world, geographically distant yet electronically interconnected. These technologies also facilitated the globalization of the service sector in areas such as banking, entertainment, tourism, insurance, and retailing. The merger of major firms once viewed as strongholds of national corporate power exemplified the growing integration of the world economy. For example, GM acquired Saab in Sweden, Ford acquired Mazda in Japan, and Daimler Benz bought Chrysler in the United States.

In the contemporary era, countless firms configure and coordinate trade and investment activities in a giant global marketplace. In their own way, globalization and technological advances are resulting in the "death of distance."[10] That is, the geographic and, to some extent, cultural distances that separate nations are shrinking. Exhibit 2.2 reveals the progression of this trend. The ensuing phases of globalization have gradually shrunk the world into a manageable global marketplace.

Exhibit 2.2

The Death of Distance

SOURCE: Adapted from P. Dicken (1992), *Global Shift*. New York: Guilford, p. 104.

In this time period...	Fastest transportation was via...	At a speed of...
1500 to 1840s	• Human-powered ships and horse-drawn carriages	10 miles per hour
1850 to 1900	• Steamships • Steam locomotive trains	36 miles per hour 65 miles per hour
Early 1900s to today	• Motor vehicles • Propeller airplanes • Jet aircraft	75 miles per hour 300–400 miles per hour 500–700 miles per hour

 ## An Organizing Framework for Market Globalization

Exhibit 2.3 presents an organizing framework for examining market globalization. The exhibit makes a distinction between the: (1) drivers or causes of globalization; (2) many dimensions or manifestations of globalization; (3a) societal consequences of globalization; and (3b) firm-level consequences of globalization—factors compelling companies to proactively internationalize. The exhibit's double arrows point to the interactive nature of the relationship between market globalization and its consequences. For example, as market globalization intensifies, individual business enterprises are compelled to respond to challenges and exploit new advantages. Keep in mind, however, that firms do not pursue internationalization strategies solely as a reaction to market globalization. As we discussed in Chapter 1, firms seek internationalization proactively also as a result of various internal forces (e.g., pursuit of growth, customers, or to minimize dependence on the domestic market through geographic diversification). Often adverse conditions in the home market, such as regulation or declining industry sales, compel firms to proactively seek international expansion.

Given the intensity of global competition, many firms proactively pursue internationalization as a strategic move. That is, they display a more aggressive attitude toward identifying foreign market opportunities, seeking partnerships with foreign firms, and building organizational capabilities to enhance their competitive advantage. Firms with such a proactive stance tend to be more successful in global competition than those firms that engage in international business as a reactive move.

Vodafone, one of the leading wireless phone services providers, is a good example of firms pursuing internationalization as a strategic growth alternative. The firm's main offerings include telecommunications and data services, multimedia portals, cellular operations, satellite services, and retail shops. Vodafone has annual sales of over $40 billion and some 200 million customers in 30 countries. Founded in 1982 in Britain, by 1993 Vodafone had interests in mobile phone networks in Australia, Greece, Hong Kong, Malta, and Scandinavia. The firm launched or bought stakes in operations throughout Europe, the Americas, and parts of Asia and Africa. Vodafone has internationalized mainly through foreign direct investment by drawing funds from global capital markets.

Vodafone took advantage of other important trends in the globalization era, including harmonization of communications technologies, converging buyer characteristics, and reduced trade and investment barriers. As emerging markets develop economically, they leapfrog older telecom technologies (typically landline systems) and embrace cell phone technology instead—a boon to Vodafone. In

```
┌─────────────────────────────────────────────────┐
│  1. Drivers of Market Globalization               │
│                                                    │
│   • Worldwide reduction of barriers to trade and investment │
│   • Transition to market-based economies and adoption of free │
│     trade in China, former Soviet Union countries, and elsewhere │
│   • Industrialization, economic development, and modernization │
│   • Integration of world financial markets         │
│   • Advances in technology                          │
└─────────────────────────────────────────────────┘
                        ▼
┌─────────────────────────────────────────────────┐
│  2. Dimensions of Market Globalization            │
│                                                    │
│   • Integration and interdependence of national economies │
│   • Rise of regional economic integration blocs    │
│   • Growth of global investment and financial flows │
│   • Convergence of buyer lifestyles and preferences │
│   • Globalization of firms' production activities   │
└─────────────────────────────────────────────────┘
```

```
┌──────────────────────────────────────┐   ┌──────────────────────────────────────────────┐
│ 3a. Societal Consequences of Market   │   │ 3b. Firm-level Consequences of Market          │
│     Globalization                      │   │     Globalization:                             │
│                                        │   │     Internationalization of the Firm's Value Chain │
│  • Loss of national sovereignty        │   │                                                 │
│  • Offshoring and the flight of jobs   │   │  • Countless new business opportunities for internationalizing firms │
│  • Effect on the poor                  │   │  • New risks and intense rivalry from foreign competitors │
│  • Effect on the natural environment   │   │  • More demanding buyers, who source from suppliers worldwide │
│  • Effect on national culture          │   │  • Greater emphasis on proactive internationalization │
│                                        │   │  • Internationalization of firm's value chain   │
└──────────────────────────────────────┘   └──────────────────────────────────────────────┘
```

Exhibit 2.3 The Drivers and Consequences of Market Globalization

Turkey, Vodafone acquired Telsim, the country's second biggest mobile phone operator. In 2007, Vodafone acquired much of India's cell phone business, a move that leverages the country's rapid economic growth and need for modern telephony.

Vodafone's proactive global strategy emphasizes selling standardized products and services and pursuing standardized marketing programs across the globe. To minimize costs and project a global image, many of Vodafone's cell phones are largely identical worldwide, with adaptations made to accommodate local regulations and telephone standards. Vodafone spends considerable resources on advertising every year, with a focus on developing and maintaining a global brand that people recognize everywhere. The convergence of buyer lifestyles and economic levels worldwide help facilitate the global approach. Management coordinates operations on a global scale and strives to implement common business processes in procurement and quality control. The strategies of product standardization, global branding, and maximizing sales to customers worldwide owe much of their success to the globalization of markets. Vodafone's strategic internationalization allows the firm to benefit from economies of scale, which helps make its products more price-competitive.[11]

 Dimensions of Market Globalization

As a broad phenomenon, globalization has been investigated from the perspective of various disciplines, including economics, history, anthropology, political science, sociology, and technology. In terms of international business, market globalization can be viewed simultaneously as a: (1) consequence of economic, technological, and government policy trends; (2) driver of economic, political, and social phenomena; and (3) driver and consequence of firm-level internationalization. Globalization of markets is a multifaceted phenomenon, with five major dimensions:

Value chain The sequence of value-adding activities performed by the firm in the process of developing, producing, marketing, and servicing a product.

1. **Integration and interdependence of national economies.** Internationally active firms devise multicountry operations through trade, investment, geographic dispersal of company resources, and integration and coordination of **value chain** activities—the sequence of value-adding activities performed by the firm in the process of developing, producing, marketing, and servicing a product. The *aggregate* activities of these firms give rise to *economic integration*. Governments contribute to this integration by various means. First, they gradually lower barriers to international trade and investment (for example, by negotiating trade agreements). Second, they increasingly harmonize their monetary and fiscal policies within *regional economic integration blocs* (also known as *trade blocs*), such as the European Union. Third, they devise and supervise *supranational* institutions—such as the World Bank, International Monetary Fund, and the World Trade Organization—that seek further reductions in trade and investment barriers.

2. **Rise of regional economic integration blocs.** Closely related to the previous trend is the emergence since the 1950s of regional economic integration blocs. Examples include the North American Free Trade Agreement area (*NAFTA*), the Asia Pacific Economic Cooperation zone (*APEC*), and *Mercosur* in Latin America. These regional economic blocs incorporate groups of countries within which trade and investment flows are facilitated through the reduction of trade and investment barriers. In more advanced arrangements, such as the "common market," barriers to the cross-border flow of factors of production (mostly labor and capital) are removed. The European Union, in addition to adopting free trade among its members, is harmonizing fiscal and monetary policies and adopting common business regulations.

3. **Growth of global investment and financial flows.** In the process of conducting international transactions, firms and governments buy and sell large volumes of national currencies (such as dollars, euros, and yen). The free movement of capital around the world— the globalization of capital— extends economic activities across the globe and is fostering interconnectedness among world economies. Commercial and investment banking is a global industry. The bond market has gained worldwide scope, with foreign bonds representing a major source of debt financing for governments and firms. Information and communications networks facilitate heavy volumes of financial transactions every day, integrating national markets. Nevertheless, widespread integration can have negative effects. For example, when Thailand and Malaysia experienced a monetary crisis in 1997, it quickly spread to South Korea, Indonesia, and the Philippines, causing prolonged recession in most East Asian economies.

The French supermarket Carrefour is one of many multinational enterprises that contribute to convergence of consumer lifestyles and preferences.

4. **Convergence of consumer lifestyles and preferences.** Around the world, many consumers are increasingly similar in how they spend their money and time. Lifestyles and preferences are converging. Consumers in Tokyo, New York, and Paris demand similar household goods, clothing, automobiles, and electronics. Teenagers everywhere are attracted to iPods, Nokia cell phones, and Levi's jeans. Major brands have gained a worldwide following. The trend is encouraged by greater international travel, movies, global media, and the Internet, which expose people to products, services, and living patterns from around the world. Hollywood films such as *Kill Bill* and *Lord of the Rings* receive much attention from a global audience. Convergence of preferences is also occurring in industrial markets, where professional buyers source

raw materials, parts, and components that are increasingly *standardized*—that is, very similar in design and structure. Yet, while converging tastes facilitate the marketing of highly standardized products and services to buyers worldwide, they also promote the loss of traditional lifestyles and values in individual countries.

5. **Globalization of production.** Intense global competition is forcing firms to reduce the cost of production and marketing. Companies strive to drive down prices through economies of scale and by standardizing what they sell. They seek economies in manufacturing and procurement by shifting these activities to foreign locations in order to take advantage of national differences in the cost and quality of factor inputs. Firms in the auto and textile industries, for example, have relocated their manufacturing to low labor-cost locations such as China, Mexico, and Eastern Europe. Production on a global basis is occurring in the service sector as well, in such industries as retailing, banking, insurance, and data processing. As an example, the real estate firm RE/MAX has established more than 5,000 offices in over 50 countries. The French firm Accor operates hundreds of hotels worldwide.

 Drivers of Market Globalization

Various trends have converged in recent years as causes of market globalization. Five drivers are particularly notable:

1. **Worldwide reduction of barriers to trade and investment.** The tendency of national governments to reduce trade and investment barriers has accelerated global economic integration. For example, tariffs on the import of automobiles, industrial machinery, and countless other products have declined nearly to zero in many countries, encouraging freer international exchange of goods and services. Reduction in trade barriers is greatly aided by the WTO. China joined the WTO in 2001 and has committed to making its market more accessible to foreign companies. Reduction of trade barriers is also associated with the emergence of regional economic integration blocs, a key dimension of market globalization.

2. **Market liberalization and adoption of free markets.** Built in 1961, the Berlin Wall separated the communist East Berlin from the democratic West Berlin. The collapse of the Soviet Union's economy in 1989, the tearing down of the Berlin Wall that same year, and China's free-market reforms all signaled the end of the 50-year Cold War between autocratic communist regimes and democracy, and smoothed the integration of former command economies into the global economy. Numerous East Asian economies, stretching from South Korea to Malaysia and Indonesia, had already embarked on ambitious market-based reforms. India joined the trend in 1991. These events opened roughly one-third of the world to freer international trade and investment. China, India, and Eastern Europe have become some of the most cost-effective locations for producing goods and services worldwide. Privatization of previously state-owned industries in these countries encouraged economic efficiency and attracted massive foreign capital into their national economies.

3. **Industrialization, economic development, and modernization.** Industrialization implies that emerging markets—rapidly developing economies in Asia, Latin America, and Eastern Europe—are moving from being low value-adding commodity producers, dependent on low-cost labor, to sophisticated competitive producers and exporters of premium products such as electronics, computers, and aircraft.[12] For example, Brazil has become a leading producer of private aircraft, and the Czech Republic now excels in the production of automobiles. As highlighted in the opening vignette, India is now a leading supplier of computer software. Economic development is enhancing standards of living and discretionary income in emerging markets. Perhaps the most important measure of economic development is *Gross National Income (GNI)* per head.[13] Exhibit 2.4 maps the levels

Exhibit 2.4

Gross National Income in U.S. Dollars

SOURCE: World Bank (2006) World Bank Development Indicator database. Numbers are based on the Atlas Methodology of the World Bank, a three-year average of the official exchange rate, adjusted for inflation.

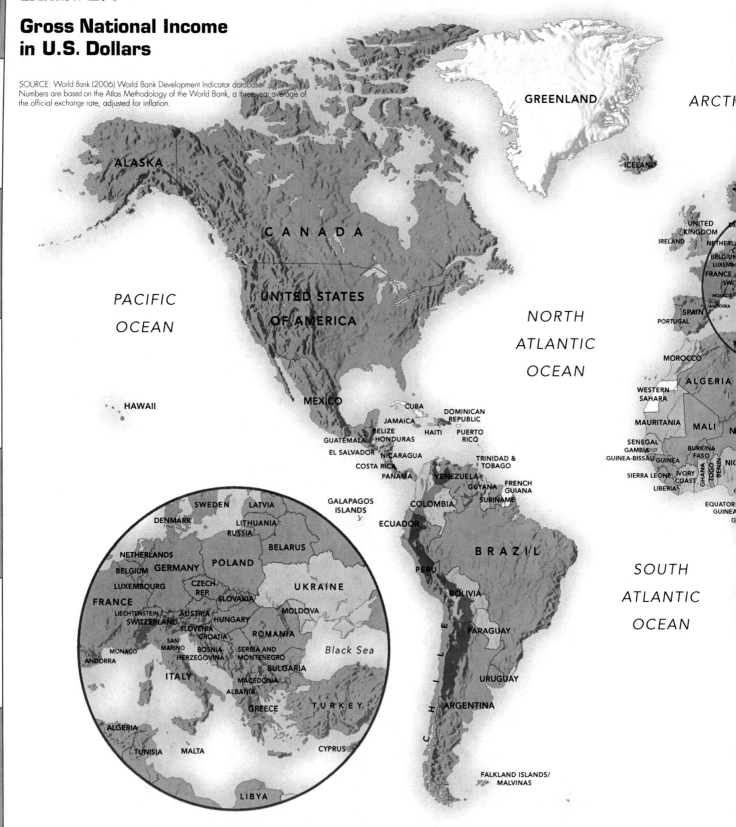

GNI in U.S. Dollars Per Capita, 2005

- 7,490 or more
- 2,350 - 7,490
- 1,110 - 2,350
- 430 - 1,110
- less than 430
- No data

of GNI worldwide. The exhibit reveals that Africa is home to the lowest-income countries, along with India and a few other countries in Asia and Nicaragua. These areas are also characterized by low levels of market globalization. The adoption of modern technologies, improvement of living standards, and adoption of modern legal and banking practices are increasing the attractiveness of emerging markets as investment targets and facilitating the spread of ideas, products, and services across the globe.

4. Integration of world financial markets. Integration of world financial markets makes it possible for internationally active firms to raise capital, borrow funds, and engage in foreign currency transactions. Financial services firms follow their customers to foreign markets. Cross-border transactions are made easier partly as a result of the ease with which funds can be transferred between buyers and sellers, through a network of international commercial banks. For example, as an individual you can transfer funds to a friend in another country using the Society for Worldwide Interbank Financial Telecommunication (SWIFT) network. Connecting over 7,800 financial institutions in some 200 countries, SWIFT facilitates the exchange of financial transactions. The globalization of finance contributes to firms' ability to develop and operate world-scale production and marketing operations. It enables companies to pay suppliers and collect payments from customers worldwide.

5. Advances in technology. Technological advances are a remarkable facilitator of cross-border trade and investment. Let's elaborate on this important driver of globalization and company internationalization in greater detail.

 ## Technological Advances as a Driver of Market Globalization

Perhaps the most important drivers of market globalization since the 1980s have been technological advances in communications, information, manufacturing, and transportation. While globalization makes internationalization an imperative, technological advances provide the *means* for internationalization. Initially, technological advances have greatly eased the management of international operations. Firms now interact more efficiently with foreign partners and value-chain members than ever before. Firms transmit all variety of data, information, and vital communications that help ensure the smooth running of their operations worldwide. In addition, companies use information technology to improve the productivity of their operations, which provides substantial competitive advantages. For example, information technology allows firms to more efficiently adapt products for international markets, or produce goods in smaller lots to target international niche markets.

In addition, technological advances have made the cost of international operations affordable for all types of firms, explaining why so many small- and medium-sized enterprises (SMEs) have internationalized during the past two decades. Panel (a) of Exhibit 2.5 shows how the cost of international communications has plummeted over time. Panel (b) shows how the number of Internet users has grown dramatically in recent years.

Technological advances have also spurred the development of new products and services that appeal to a global audience. Leading examples include Walkman, PlayStation 3, and personal digital assistants (PDAs). Emerging markets and other developing country economies also benefit from technological advances, due in part to technological leapfrogging. For instance, Hungary and Poland went directly from old-style analog telecommunications (with rotary dial telephones) to cell phone technology, bypassing much of the early digital technology (push-button telephones) that characterized advanced economy telephone systems.

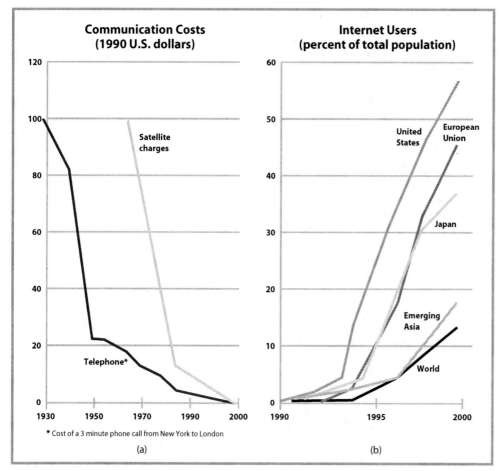

Communication Costs
(1990 U.S. dollars)

Satellite charges

Telephone*

* Cost of a 3 minute phone call from New York to London

(a)

Internet Users
(percent of total population)

United States

European Union

Japan

Emerging Asia

World

(b)

Exhibit 2.5

Declining Cost of Global Communication and Growing Number of Internet Users

SOURCE: IMF (2005), *World Economic Outlook*. Washington, DC: International Monetary Fund, from *World Economic Outlook*, 2005, Washington DC: International Monetary Fund. Copyright © 2005. Used with permission.

China and India are the new beachheads of technological advances. The opening vignette revealed how India has become a focus of global Internet- and knowledge-based industries. Top management at Intel and Motorola, two of the world's premier technology companies, agree that China is the place to be when it comes to technological progress. Both firms receive a substantial portion of their revenue from sales in China. Management predicts double-digit increases in demand for technology products in China far into the future. Intel's CEO commented, "I come back from visiting China and feel as if I've visited the fountain of youth of computing."[14]

The most important activity underlying technological advances is *innovation*. Societies and organizations innovate in various ways, including new product designs, new production processes, new approaches to marketing, and new ways of organizing or training. Innovation results primarily from research and development.[15] Today, more scientists and engineers are engaged in R&D activities worldwide than ever before. For example, the Japanese introduced quartz technology in clock making. The technology allowed greater accuracy and significantly lowered production costs, allowing Japanese manufacturers to establish their leadership in the clock-making industry within a few years. Among the industries most dependent on technological innovation are biotechnology, information technology, new materials, pharmaceuticals, robotics, medical equipment and devices, lasers and fiber optics, and various electronics-based industries.

Technological advances have had the greatest impact in several key areas: information technology, communications, manufacturing, and transportation.

Information Technology

The effect of information technology (IT) on business has been nothing short of revolutionary. IT is the science and process of creating and using information resources. The cost of computer processing fell by 30 percent *per year* during the past two decades, and continues to fall. The remarkable performance of the U.S. economy in the 1990s was due in large part to aggressive integration of IT into firms' value-chain activities, which accounted for 45 percent of total business investments at the time. IT alters industry structure and, in so doing, changes the rules of competition. By giving companies new ways to outperform rivals, IT creates competitive advantage.[16] For example, geographically distant country subsidiaries of a multinational company can be interconnected via intranets, facilitating the instant sharing of data, information, and experience across the firm's operations worldwide.[17] MNEs also use collaboration software that connects global product development teams scattered around the world, enabling them to work together. IT provides benefits for smaller firms as well, allowing them to design and produce customized products they can target to narrow, cross-national niches.

IT has spawned new products, such as cell phones, and new processes, such as automated factory controls. Online search engines such as Google and Yahoo allow anyone access to unlimited data in order to research markets, customers, competitors, and countries' economic conditions. At a higher level, IT supports managerial decision making—such as selection of qualified foreign business partners—based on accessing key information and intelligence.

Communications

It took five months for Spain's Queen Isabella to learn about Columbus' voyage in 1492; two weeks for Europe to learn of President Lincoln's assassination in 1865; and only seconds for the world to witness the collapse of New York's World Trade Center towers in 2001. The most profound technological advances have occurred in communications, especially telecommunications, satellites, optical fiber, wireless technology, and the Internet. At one time, people and companies used expensive phone calls, slow postal service, and clunky telex machines to communicate with foreign suppliers. In 1930, a 3-minute phone call between New York and London cost $3,000. By 1980, the cost had fallen to $6. Today, the call costs only a few cents. Scanners and fax machines send documents worldwide practically for free. Banking transactions are relatively costly when performed via ATM machines or telephones, but are virtually free when handled via the Internet.

The Internet, and Internet-dependent communications systems such as intranets, extranets, and e-mail, connect millions of people across the globe. The dot-com boom of the 1990s led to massive investment in fiber optic telecommunications. Today, the widest range of products and services—from auto parts to bank loans—is marketed online. Transmitting voices, data, and images is essentially costless, making Boston, Bangalore, and Beijing next door neighbors, instantly. South Korea, where Internet access is nearly 100 percent, is leading the way. South Korea's broadband networks for home are among the fastest in the world. Korean schoolchildren use their cell phones to get homework from their teachers and play games online with gamers worldwide. Adults use their phones to pay bills, do banking, buy lottery tickets, and check traffic conditions.

Widespread availability of the Internet and e-mail makes company internationalization cost-effective. For instance, Amdahl, a manufacturer of large-scale computers, uses the Internet to order circuit boards from factories in Asia and to arrange international shipments of parts and components via firms like DHL and Federal Express. Search engines, databases, reference guides, and countless government and private support systems assist managers to maximize knowledge and skills for international business success. The Internet opens up the global marketplace to companies that would normally not have the resources to do international business, including countless SMEs. By establishing a presence on the Web, even tiny enterprises take the first step in becoming multinational firms. Thanks to the Internet, services as diverse as designing an engine, monitoring a security camera, selling insurance, or secretarial work have become easier to export than car parts or refrigerators. The *Global Trend* feature highlights the emergence of e-commerce and its effect on international company operations and performance.

The Internet is stimulating economic development and a massive global migration of jobs, particularly in the services sector.[18] As Netscape cofounder Marc Andreesson observed, "A 14-year-old in Romania or Bangalore or Vietnam has all the information, all the tools, all the software easily available to apply knowledge however they want. Communications and information technology are now in the process of connecting all of the knowledge pools in the world together."[19] In the not-too-distant future, much of what has ever been written and recorded on paper, tape, or film will be accessible online.

> GLOBAL TREND

Globalization and E-Business in the Online World

Information technology and the Internet are transforming international business by allowing firms to conduct e-commerce online, as well as integrate e-business capabilities for activities such as sourcing and managing customer relations. E-business drives the firm's globalization efforts by helping it beat geography and time zones. The modern firm, small or large, does business around the world all day, every day. E-business levels the playing field for all types of firms. Thanks to e-technologies, even new companies can be active abroad. Born-global firms are among the most intensive users of the Web for global selling, procurement, and customer service.

E-business provides at least three types of benefits. First, it *increases productivity* and *reduces costs* in worldwide value-chain activities through online integration and coordination of production, distribution, and after-sale services. Second, it

creates value for existing customers and uncovers new sales opportunities by increasing customer focus, enhancing marketing capabilities, and launching entrepreneurial initiatives. A key benefit is the ability to implement marketing strategy on an international scale and integrate customer-focused operations worldwide. Virtual interconnectedness facilitates the sharing of new ideas and best practices for serving new and existing international markets. Third, it *improves the flow of information and knowledge throughout the firm's worldwide operations*. The Internet allows the firm to move information quickly throughout its operations worldwide, and to interact more effectively with customers, suppliers, and partners. Managers can make instantaneous changes to strategies and tactics in the firm's value-chain activities. The firm can accommodate real-time changes in market conditions almost as quickly as they occur.

For example, Cisco uses e-business solutions to minimize costs and maximize operational effectiveness in its international supply chain. The firm uses the Internet to remain constantly linked to suppliers and distributors. This helps Cisco manage inventory, product specifications, and purchase orders, as well as product life cycles. *E-procurement* systems help Cisco save money on transaction processing, reduce cycle times, and leverage supplier relations.

Customer relationship management is especially critical in foreign markets where buyers often favor local vendors. Internet-based systems provide real-time information, forecast shifting short- and long-term market needs, and increase the effectiveness of after-sales service. E-commerce enhances the means for firms to achieve competitive advantages and performance objectives in a global marketplace.

Low freight costs are one driver of market globalization.

Manufacturing

Computer-aided design (CAD) of products, robotics, and production lines managed and monitored by microprocessor-based controls are transforming manufacturing, mainly by reducing the costs of production. Revolutionary developments now permit low-scale and low-cost manufacturing. Firms can produce products in short production runs cost effectively. These developments benefit international business by allowing firms to more efficiently adapt products to individual foreign markets, profitably target small national markets, and compete more effectively with foreign competitors who already have cost advantages.

Transportation

Managers consider the costs of transporting raw materials, components, and finished products when deciding to either export or manufacture abroad. For example, if transportation costs to an important market are high, management may decide to manufacture its merchandise in the market by building a factory there. Beginning in the 1960s, technological advances led to the development of fuel-efficient jumbo jets, giant ocean-going freighters, and containerized shipping, often through the use of high-tech composites and smaller components that are less bulky and lightweight. As a result, the cost of transportation as a proportion of the value of products shipped internationally has declined substantially. Lower freight costs have spurred rapid growth in cross-border trade. Technological advances have also reduced the costs of international travel. Until 1960, it was common to travel by ship. With the development of air travel, managers quickly travel the world.

 # Societal Consequences of Market Globalization

Our discussion so far has highlighted the far-reaching, positive outcomes of market globalization. Nevertheless, globalization has produced some harmful consequences as well. While major advances in living standards have been achieved in virtually all countries that have opened their borders to increased trade and investment, the transition to an increasingly single, global marketplace poses challenges to individuals, organizations, and governments. Low-income countries have not been able to integrate with the global economy as rapidly as others. Poverty is especially notable in Africa and in populous nations such as Brazil, China, and India. Let's now turn to some of the unintended consequences of globalization.

Loss of National Sovereignty

Sovereignty is the ability of a nation to govern its own affairs. One country's laws cannot be applied or enforced in another country. The sovereignty of nations is a fundamental principle that governs global relations. Globalization can threaten national sovereignty in various ways. MNE activities can interfere with the sovereign ability of governments to control their own economies, social structures, and political systems. Some corporations are bigger than the economies of many nations. Indeed, Wal-Mart's internal economy—its total revenues—is larger than the GDP of most of the world's nations, including Israel, Greece, and Poland. Large multinationals can exert considerable influence on governments through lobbying or campaign contributions. It is not unusual for large corporations to lobby their government, say, for devaluation of the home currency, which gives them greater price competitiveness in export markets. MNEs can also influence the legislative process and extract special favors from government agencies.

At the same time, even the largest firms are constrained by *market forces*. In countries with many competing companies, one company cannot force customers to buy its products or force suppliers to supply it with raw materials and inputs. The resources that customers and suppliers control are the result of free choices made in the marketplace. Company performance depends on the firm's skill at winning customers, working with suppliers, and dealing with competitors. Corporate dominance of individual markets is rare. In reality, market forces dominate companies. Indeed, gradual integration of the global economy and increased global competition, combined with privatization of industries in various nations, are making some companies *less* powerful within their national markets.[20] For instance, Ford, Chrysler, and General Motors once completely dominated the U.S. auto market. Today many more firms compete in the United States, including Toyota, Honda, Hyundai, Kia, Nissan, and BMW. Indeed, in annual sales, Toyota now rivals General Motors in GM's home market.

Today, globalization creates incentives for governments to pursue sound economic policies and for managers to manage their firms more effectively. To minimize globalization's harm and reap its benefits, governments should strive for an open and liberalized economic regime: freedom to enter and compete in markets; protection of persons and intellectual property; rule of law; and voluntary exchange imposed by markets rather than through political processes. Transparency in the affairs of businesses and regulatory agencies is critical.

Occasionally, governments need to scrutinize corporate activities. An example from the United States is the Sarbanes-Oxley Act of 2002 (also known as the Public Company Accounting Reform and Investor Protection Act of 2002). The legislation resulted from a decline in public trust of financial reporting practices in the wake of a series of corporate and accounting scandals involving firms such as Enron, Tyco International, and WorldCom. The legislation introduced new or enhanced standards for all U.S. public company boards, management, and public accounting firms.

Offshoring and the Flight of Jobs

Globalization has created countless new jobs and opportunities around the world, but it has also cost many people their jobs. For example, Ford, General Motors, and Volkswagen all have transferred thousands of jobs from their factories in Germany to countries in Eastern Europe. This occurred partially because mandated shorter working hours (often just 35 hours per week) and generous benefits made Germany less competitive, while Eastern Europe offers abundant low-wage workers. Recognizing this, the German government is loosening Germany's labor laws to conform to global realities. But these changes have disrupted the lives of tens of thousands of German citizens.[21] General Motors and Ford have also laid off thousands of workers in the United States, partly the result of competitive pressures posed by carmakers from Europe, Japan, and South Korea.

Offshoring is the relocation of manufacturing and other value-chain activities to cost-effective locations abroad. For example, the global accounting firm Ernst & Young has much of its support work done by accountants in the Philippines. Massachusetts General Hospital has its CT scans and X-rays interpreted by radiologists in India. Many IT support services for customers in Germany are based in the Czech Republic and Romania.[22]

Offshoring has resulted in job losses in numerous mature economies. The first wave of offshoring began in the 1960s and 1970s with the shift of U.S. and European manufacturing of cars, shoes, electronics, textiles, and toys to cheap-labor locations such as Mexico and Southeast Asia. The next wave began in the 1990s with the exodus of service sector jobs in credit card processing, software code writing, accounting, health care, and banking services. High-profile plant closures and relocation of manufacturing facilities to low-cost countries have received ample media attention in recent years. Critics have labeled many MNEs as "runaway" or "footloose" corporations—quick to relocate production to countries that offer more favorable access to inputs. For example, Electrolux, a Swedish manufacturer of home appliances, moved its Greenville, Michigan, refrigerator plant to Mexico in 2005. Electrolux had provided 2,700 jobs in this western Michigan community of 8,000. Despite repeated appeals by the local community, the labor union, and the state of Michigan, Electrolux went with its decision to shift manufacturing to Mexico. One can imagine the devastation to the economic livelihood of this community.

Effect on the Poor

Multinational firms are often criticized for paying low wages, exploiting workers, and employing child labor. Child labor is particularly troubling because it denies children educational opportunities. The International Labor Organization (www.ilo.org) estimates there are as many as 250 million children at work around the world, many working full time. Nike has been criticized for paying low wages to shoe factory workers in Asia, some of whom work in sweatshop conditions. Critics complain that while founder Phil Knight is a billionaire and Nike sells shoes for $100 or more, Nike's suppliers pay their workers only a few dollars per day.

Labor exploitation and sweatshop conditions are genuine concerns in many developing economies.[23] Nevertheless, consideration must be given to the other choices available to people in those countries. Finding work in a low-paying job may be better than finding no work at all. Recent studies suggest that banning products made using child labor may produce negative, unintended consequences.[24] Eliminating child labor can worsen living standards for children. Legislation that reduces child labor in the formal economic sector (the sector regulated and monitored by public authorities), may have little effect on jobs in the informal economic sector (sometimes called the underground economy). In the face of unrelenting poverty, abolishing formal sector jobs does not ensure that children leave the workforce and go to school.

In many developing countries, work conditions tend to improve over time. The growth of the footwear industry in Vietnam has translated into a five-fold increase in wages in recent years. While still low by advanced economy standards, increasingly higher wages are improving the lives of millions of workers and their families. For most countries, globalization tends to support a growing economy. Exhibit 2.6 on pages 48–49 shows the GDP growth rate worldwide from 1997 to 2006. Note that most nations experienced significant, positive growth. As shown in the map, the world's fastest growing large economies are China and India. Chile, Ireland, and Vietnam are also on the fast growth track. The former Soviet Union countries in Eastern Europe suffered setbacks in the 1990s as they transitioned to market-based economic systems. Most African countries continue to suffer low or negative GDP growth and alarming poverty.

Wages and sweatshop conditions are slowly improving in developing economies, such as those in Central America.

Critics insist that such workers be provided a decent wage. However, legislation to increase minimum wage levels can also reduce the number of available jobs. That is, countries that attract investment due to low-cost labor gradually lose their attractiveness as wages rise. More broadly, the evidence suggests that globalization is associated with higher wage growth over time. Exhibit 2.7 on page 50 reveals that countries that liberalize international trade and investment enjoy faster per capita economic growth. The exhibit shows how, during the 1990s, developing economies that emphasized integration with the rest of the world had faster per capita GDP growth than already integrated advanced economies, which, in turn, grew faster than nonintegrating developing economies.

Governments are responsible for ensuring that the fruits of economic progress are shared fairly, and that all citizens have access to improved welfare, living standards, and higher-value-adding, higher-paying jobs. Developing countries can engage in a number of proactive measures to reduce poverty. They can improve conditions for investment and saving, liberalize markets and promote trade and investment, build strong institutions and government to foster good governance, and invest in education and training to promote productivity and ensure worker-upward mobility. Advanced economies can play a role in reducing poverty by making their markets more accessible to low-income countries, facilitating the flows of direct investment, other private capital, and technology into low-income countries, and providing debt relief to heavily indebted nations.

Effect on the Natural Environment

Globalization can harm the environment by promoting increased manufacturing and economic activity that result in pollution, habitat destruction, and deterioration of the ozone layer. For instance, economic development in China is attracting much inward FDI and stimulating the growth of numerous industries. The construction of factories, infrastructure, and modern housing can spoil previously pristine environments. As an example, growing industrial demand for electricity led to construction of the Three Gorges Dam, which flooded agricultural lands and permanently altered the natural landscape in Eastern China.

While it is generally true that globalization-induced industrialization produces considerable environmental harm, the harm tends to decline over time. The evidence suggests that environmental destruction diminishes as economies develop, at least in the long run. To the extent that globalization stimulates rising living standards, people focus increasingly on improving their environment. Over time, governments pass legislation that promotes improved environmental conditions. For example, Japan endured polluted rivers and smoggy cities in the early decades of its economic development following World War II. But as Japan's economy grew, the Japanese passed tough environmental standards aimed at restoring natural environments.

Evolving company values and concern for corporate reputations also lead most firms to reduce or eliminate practices that harm the environment.[25] For example, with rising affluence in Mexico, big American automakers like Ford and GM have gradually improved their environmental standards. Benetton in Italy (clothing), Alcan in Canada (aluminum), and Kirin in Japan (beverages), are examples of firms that embrace practices that protect the environment, often at the expense of profits.[26] Conservation Coffee Alliance, a consortium of companies, has committed approximately $2 million to environmentally friendly coffee cultivation in Central America, Peru, and Colombia.

Effect on National Culture

Globalization exerts strong pressures on national culture. Market liberalization leaves the door open to foreign companies, global brands, unfamiliar products,

Exhibit 2.6

The Growth of World GDP, Average Annual Percent Change, 1998–2007

SOURCE: International Monetary Fund, World Economic Outlook Database

GREENLAND

ARCTI

ALASKA

ICELAND

CANADA

PACIFIC OCEAN

UNITED STATES OF AMERICA

NORTH ATLANTIC OCEAN

UNITED KINGDOM
IRELAND
NETHERLA
G
BELGIUM
LUXEMBO
FRANCE
SWIT
MONACO
ANDORRA
SPAIN
PORTUGAL

MOROCCO

HAWAII

MEXICO

CUBA
DOMINICAN REPUBLIC
JAMAICA
BELIZE
HAITI
PUERTO RICO
GUATEMALA
HONDURAS
EL SALVADOR
NICARAGUA
COSTA RICA
PANAMA

TRINIDAD & TOBAGO

VENEZUELA
GUYANA
FRENCH GUIANA
SURINAME

GALAPAGOS ISLANDS

COLOMBIA

ECUADOR

PERU

BRAZIL

WESTERN SAHARA
ALGERIA
MAURITANIA
MALI
SENEGAL
GAMBIA
GUINEA-BISSAU
GUINEA
SIERRA LEONE
IVORY COAST
LIBERIA
BURKINA FASO
GHANA
TOGO
BENIN
NIG
EQUATORI
GUINEA
G

SOUTH ATLANTIC OCEAN

SWEDEN
DENMARK
LATVIA
LITHUANIA
RUSSIA
NETHERLANDS
GERMANY
POLAND
BELARUS
BELGIUM
LUXEMBOURG
CZECH REP.
UKRAINE
FRANCE
LIECHTENSTEIN
SWITZERLAND
AUSTRIA
SLOVAKIA
HUNGARY
MOLDOVA
SLOVENIA
CROATIA
ROMANIA
SAN MARINO
MONACO
BOSNIA-HERZEGOVINA
SERBIA AND MONTENEGRO
Black Sea
ANDORRA
BULGARIA
ITALY
MACEDONIA
ALBANIA
GREECE
TURKEY
ALGERIA
CYPRUS
TUNISIA
MALTA
LIBYA

BOLIVIA

PARAGUAY

URUGUAY

ARGENTINA

CHILE

FALKLAND ISLANDS/ MALVINAS

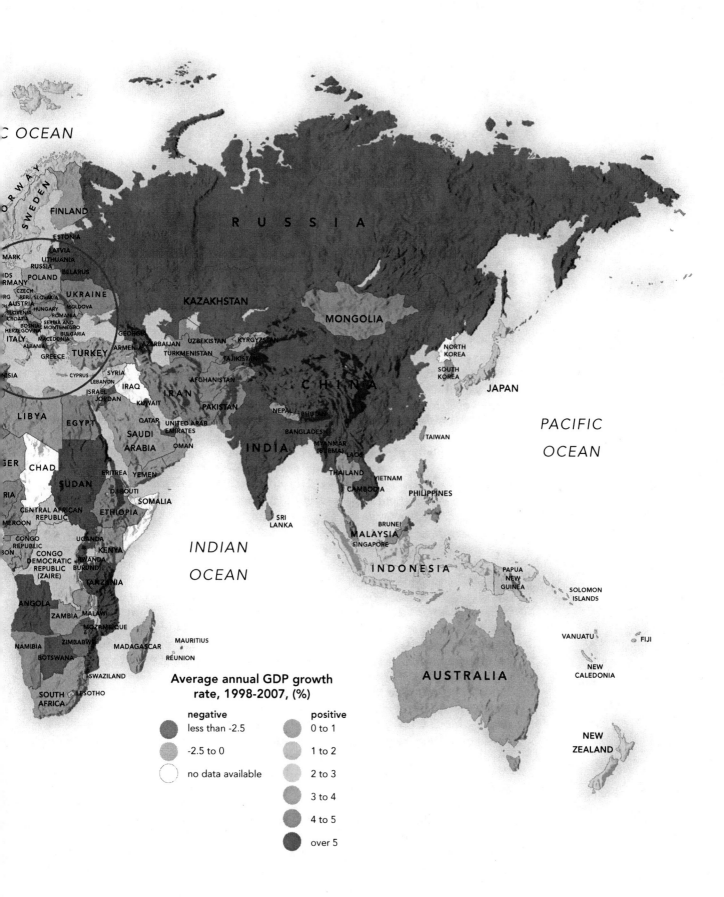

Average annual GDP growth rate, 1998-2007, (%)

negative
- less than -2.5
- -2.5 to 0
- no data available

positive
- 0 to 1
- 1 to 2
- 2 to 3
- 3 to 4
- 4 to 5
- over 5

Exhibit 2.7

Relationship Between Globalization and Growth in Per Capita Gross Domestic Product, 1990s, (adjusted for purchasing power parity)

SOURCE: Dollar, D. (2004) "Globalization, Poverty and Inequality since 1980," World Bank Policy Research Working Paper 3333, June 2004, Washington, DC: World Bank. © 2004 World Bank.

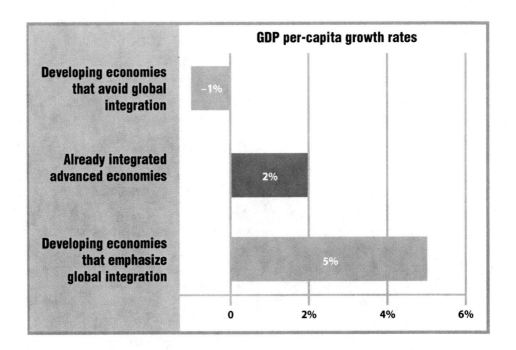

and new values. Consumers increasingly wear similar clothing, drive similar cars, and listen to the same recording stars. Advertising leads to the emergence of societal values modeled on Western countries, especially the United States. Hollywood dominates the global entertainment industry. In this way, globalization can alter people's norms, values, and behaviors, which tend to homogenize over time.

Critics call these trends the "McDonald-ization" or the "Coca-Colonization" of the world. To combat such trends, governments try to block cultural imperialism and prevent the erosion of local traditions. In Canada, France, and Germany, the public sector attempts to prevent U.S. ideals from diluting local traditions. Hollywood, McDonald's, and Disneyland are seen as Trojan horses that permanently alter food preferences, lifestyles, and other aspects of traditional life. In a globalizing world, for better or worse, such trends appear to be inevitable.

Information and communications technologies promote the homogenization of world cultures. People worldwide are exposed to movies, television, the Internet, and other information sources that promote lifestyles of people in the United States and other advanced economies. Appetites grow for "Western" products and services, which are seen to signal higher living standards. For example, despite low per-capita income, many Chinese buy consumer electronics such as cell phones and TV sets. Global media have a pervasive effect on local culture, gradually shifting it toward a universal norm.

At the same time, the flow of cultural influence often goes both ways. For instance, Advanced Fresh Concepts is a Japanese food company that is transforming fast food by selling sushi and other Japanese favorites in supermarkets throughout the United States. It sells some $250 million worth of sushi to U.S. buyers every year.[27] As the influence of the Chinese economy grows over time, Western countries will likely adopt cultural norms from China as well. Chinese restaurants and some Chinese traditions are already a way of life in much of the world outside China. Similar influences can be seen from Latin America and other areas in the developing world.

In addition, cultural anthropologists note that cultural values change at a glacial pace. Even if people from different nations appear similar on the surface, they usually hold traditional attitudes, values, and beliefs rooted in the

International Business

history and culture of the country where they live. Although some tangibles are becoming more universal, people's behavior and mindsets remain stable over time. Religious differences are as strong as ever. Language differences are steadfast across national borders. While a degree of cultural imperialism may be at work, it is offset by the countertrend of nationalism. As globalization standardizes superficial aspects of life across national cultures, people are resisting these forces by insisting on their national identity and taking steps to protect it. This is evident, for example, in Belgium, Canada, and France, where laws were passed to protect national language and culture.

 ## Firm-Level Consequences of Market Globalization: Internationalization of the Firm's Value Chain

Western companies such as McDonald's can influence people's food preferences, but cultural values remain stable over time.

The globalization of markets has opened up countless new business opportunities for internationalizing firms. At the same time, globalization implies that firms must accommodate new risks and intense rivalry from foreign competitors. Globalization results in buyers who are more demanding and who shop for the best deals from suppliers worldwide. A purely domestic focus is no longer viable for firms in most industries. Companies need to proactively internationalize their value chain in order to profit from new opportunities and reduce the harm of potential threats. Managers must increasingly adopt a worldwide orientation rather than a local focus. Internationalization may take the form of global sourcing, exporting, or investment in key markets abroad. The more proactive firms seek a simultaneous presence in all major trading regions, especially Asia, Europe, and North America. They concentrate their activities in those countries where they can achieve and sustain competitive advantage.

The most direct implication of market globalization is on the firm's value chain. Market globalization compels firms to organize their sourcing, manufacturing, marketing, and other value-adding activities on a global scale. As noted earlier, a value chain is the sequence of value-adding activities performed by the firm in the process of developing, producing, marketing, and servicing a product. In a typical value chain, the firm conducts research and product development (R&D), purchases production inputs, and assembles or manufactures a product or service. Next, the firm performs marketing activities such as pricing, promotion, and selling, followed by distribution of the product in targeted markets and after-sales service. Value chains vary in complexity and across industries and product categories. The value chain concept is useful in international business because it helps clarify what activities are performed *where* in the world. For instance, exporting firms perform most "upstream" value-chain activities (R&D and production) in the home market and most "downstream" activities (marketing and after-sales service) abroad.

Exhibit 2.8 illustrates a typical international firm's value chain. Each value-adding activity is subject to internationalization; that is, it can be performed abroad instead of at home. As the examples in Exhibit 2.8 suggest, companies have considerable latitude regarding where in the world they locate or *configure* key value-adding activities. The most typical reasons for locating value-chain activities in particular countries are to reduce the costs of R&D and production or to gain closer access to customers. The practice of internationalizing the value

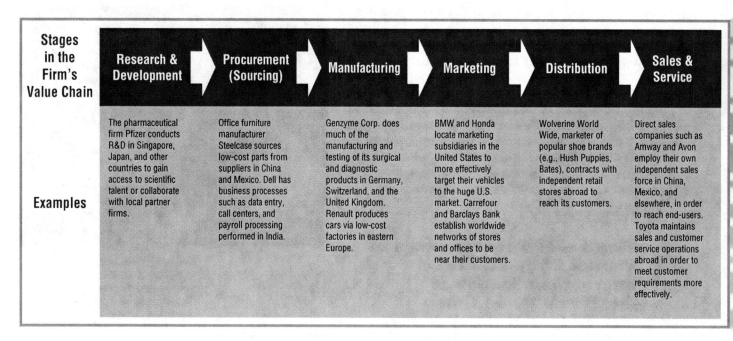

Stages in the Firm's Value Chain	Research & Development	Procurement (Sourcing)	Manufacturing	Marketing	Distribution	Sales & Service
Examples	The pharmaceutical firm Pfizer conducts R&D in Singapore, Japan, and other countries to gain access to scientific talent or collaborate with local partner firms.	Office furniture manufacturer Steelcase sources low-cost parts from suppliers in China and Mexico. Dell has business processes such as data entry, call centers, and payroll processing performed in India.	Genzyme Corp. does much of the manufacturing and testing of its surgical and diagnostic products in Germany, Switzerland, and the United Kingdom. Renault produces cars via low-cost factories in eastern Europe.	BMW and Honda locate marketing subsidiaries in the United States to more effectively target their vehicles to the huge U.S. market. Carrefour and Barclays Bank establish worldwide networks of stores and offices to be near their customers.	Wolverine World Wide, marketer of popular shoe brands (e.g., Hush Puppies, Bates), contracts with independent retail stores abroad to reach its customers.	Direct sales companies such as Amway and Avon employ their own independent sales force in China, Mexico, and elsewhere, in order to reach end-users. Toyota maintains sales and customer service operations abroad in order to meet customer requirements more effectively.

Exhibit 2.8   Examples of How Firms' Value-Chain Activities Can Be Internationalized

chain is often referred to as *offshoring*, where the firm relocates a major value-chain activity by establishing a factory or other subsidiary abroad. A related trend is global sourcing, in which the firm delegates performance of the value-adding activity to an external supplier or contractor located abroad. We discuss offshoring and global sourcing in Chapter 16.

As German carmaker BMW launched a new factory in South Carolina, Jackson Mills, an aging textile plant a few miles away, closed its doors and shed thousands of workers in the same month. In both cases, globalization had created a new reality for these firms. By establishing operations in the United States, BMW found it could manufacture cars cost-effectively while more readily accessing the huge U.S. market. In the process, BMW created thousands of high-paying, better-quality jobs for U.S. workers. Simultaneously, Jackson Mills had discovered it could source textiles of comparable quality more cost-effectively from suppliers in Asia. Globalization drove these firms to relocate key value-adding activities to the most advantageous locations around the world.

Diverse Perspectives on Globalization of Markets

Recently, a major university sponsored a roundtable on the broader implications of international business. The participants were an anti-international business activist, a business executive with extensive international dealings, and a trade official from the U.S. government. Each of these individuals expressed varying views. Excerpts from the exchange present the diverse perspectives of market globalization held by different interest groups.

Activist

"One problem with international business is that it often ignores human rights and basic labor standards. Low-wage factories abroad create substandard working conditions. The activities of multinational companies result in not only job losses here at home, but also in low wages and exploited workers around the world. Just think of the sweatshops in Asia that make imported clothing. Think of the auto workers in Mexico who live in horrible conditions and make only a few dollars a day."

Business Executive

"Our country needs to participate in the global economy. Companies that export provide better-paying jobs, have more profits, pay higher taxes, and stimulate purchases from local suppliers. Foreign companies that invest here create new jobs, enhance local living standards, and pressure our firms to stay competitive in a challenging global marketplace. Exporters pay higher wages and provide better benefits than nonexporting firms. Many companies need access to foreign markets because of the huge, upfront research and development costs they accumulate. One more pill is cheap; it's the cost of research to find a cure for AIDS that is prohibitive. I think it's a pretty strong argument for the human basis of doing international business. Companies need big markets to amortize the costs of big projects. Africa is getting decimated by AIDS. But pharmaceutical firms can't do the necessary R&D unless they can amortize those costs over much larger potential markets. In the long run, uninterrupted international commerce is good."

Trade Official

"The current administration believes strongly in the value of free trade. The President strongly supported NAFTA, and this has already had a positive effect on the U.S. economy through increasing exports to Mexico, creating jobs for Americans, and leading to improved investment opportunities. Countries are forging ahead with international trade ties. Canada has completed a free trade agreement with Chile. Economic ties lead to cultural ties and more peaceful relations. Also, it is hard for our government to promote freedom and democracy around the world if we are not promoting free trade."

Activist

"We cannot overlook the detrimental effects of globalization on the natural environment. The more we trade internationally, the more irreparable harm will be done to the environment. International business means more environmentally damaging development. Companies internationalize so they can become more efficient. But if countries have weak environmental standards, then factories will be built with minimal environmental standards."

Business Executive

"If we trade internationally, then living standards will increase everywhere. As living standards rise, awareness of and care for the environment will also increase. In other words, international business is good for the world because it creates wealth. The more affluent the people, the more they will care about their environment and pass laws to protect it. Right here at home, we have shown that a good economy and a clean environment are not mutually exclusive. We can have it both ways: a clean planet and a better economic quality of life."

Trade Official

"I think part of the solution is to negotiate trade agreements that take environmental factors into account. International trade that runs roughshod over legitimate environmental concerns is counterproductive and defeats the political agendas of most governments around the world. It is clear that international trade must take environmental concerns into account."

Activist

"International trade interferes with the sovereignty of national governments. When General Motors is the nation's biggest company, like it is in Canada, it is harder for governments to manage policies regarding taxes, monetary policy, social issues, and exchange rates. And who are we, trying to impose our own cultural standards on the world? When I am in Europe or Asia, I see McDonald's all over the place. They see the United States as a dominating power that uses globalization to its own advantage, harming the economic, cultural, and environmental interests of the rest of the world."

"Global companies claim that they spread modern technologies around the world. But technology is good only if you have access to it. In most of Africa, you have no on-ramp to the Internet. To access the Internet, you need access to a computer; awfully difficult or impossible in countries where people make only a few dollars a day. When you're paid such a low wage, how can you afford technology? How can you afford to go see a doctor, even if he has the technology? Globalization is widening the gap between rich and poor. As inequality grows, people have less and less in common. Multinational companies have weakened poor countries and are exposing poor people to harmful competition. Infant industries in developing economies can't make it when they're confronted with the power of giant multinational firms."

Business Executive

"Companies increasingly recognize the importance of being good global citizens. Motorola has profited from its business in China, but it has also contributed to the development of educational systems in that country. There are a lot more literate people, especially literate women, in China than ever before. Japanese MNEs have done a great job of investing in the communities where they do business. Businesses are not all evil; they do a lot of good for the world, too. Bill Gates is going to do more than any government to get people computers and get them hooked up on the Internet. He has created the world's largest fund to combat diseases of the poor. He and Warren Buffett are tackling many of these diseases in a systematic way. GlaxoSmithKline is working with the World Health Organization to find a cure for Elephantiasis, which is a terrible disease that afflicts people in Africa."

Trade Official

"Globalization is complex and it is hard to tease out what is bad and what is good. Globalization has made rapid progress since the 1980s, a period during which global poverty has actually declined. Social indicators for many poor countries show improvement over several decades. It is true that income disparities have increased dramatically over the last 50 years while international trade has integrated the world economy. The world has experienced a generally rising tide in terms of peoples' standard of living. People everywhere today are better off than they were 50 years ago. There are some exceptions to this, of course, but it's better to live in a world in which 20 percent of the people are affluent

and 80 percent are poor, than a world in which nearly 100 percent of the people are poor, as was the case throughout most of human history. There is a strong role for government in all this. Countries benefit from trade, but governments are responsible for protecting citizens from the negative or unintended consequences that trade can bring."

AACSB: Reflective Thinking, Ethical Reasoning

Case Questions

1. Do you think globalization and MNE activity are creating problems for the world? What kinds of problems can you identify? Are there some unintended consequences of international business?

2. Summarize the arguments in favor of globalization made by the business executive. What is the role of technology in supporting company performance in a globalizing business environment?

3. What are the roles of state and federal governments in dealing with globalization? Do you believe that government has a responsibility to protect its citizens from the potential negative effects of foreign MNEs conducting business in their countries? What kinds of government actions would you recommend?

4. What is the role of education in: addressing some of the problems raised in the previous discussion; creating societies in which people can deal effectively with public policy issues; creating citizens who can compete effectively in the global marketplace?

Sources: Bernard, Andrew, and J. Bradford Jensen. (1999). *Exporting and Productivity.* Cambridge, MA: National Bureau of Economic Research; International Monetary Fund. (2002). *Globalization: Threat or Opportunity?* Retrieved from www.imf.org/external/np/exr/ib/2000/041200. Washington, DC: International Monetary Fund; Lechner, Frank. (2004). *Does Globalization Cause Poverty?* Retrieved from www.sociology.emory.edu/globalization/issues03.html (Atlanta, GA: Emory University Globalization Web site); Lechner, Frank, (2004). *Does Globalization Diminish Cultural Diversity?* Retrieved from www.sociology.emory.edu/globalization/issues05.html (Atlanta, GA: Emory University Globalization Web site); Lechner, Frank, Deborah McFarland, Thomas Remington, and Jeff Rosensweig. (2004). *Is a Globalization Backlash Occurring?* Retrieved from www.emory.edu/ACAD_EXCHANGE/1999/mayjune99/global.html (Atlanta, GA: Emory University Globalization Web site); McCarty, William, Mark Kasoff, and Doug Smith. (2000). "The Importance of International Business at the Local Level," *Business Horizons* (May–June, 2000), 35–42.

Key Terms

globalization of markets   value chain   World Trade Organization (WTO)

Summary

In this chapter, you learned about:

1. **Why Globalization is not a new phenomenon**

   Globalization of markets refers to the gradual integration and growing interdependence of national economies. Early civilizations in the Mediterranean, Middle East, Asia, Africa, and Europe have all contributed to the growth of cross-border trade over time. Bursts of cross-border trade have been triggered by world events and technological discoveries. The first distinct phase of market globalization ran from about 1830 to the late 1800s and was spurred by the growth of railroads, efficient ocean transport, and the rise of large manufacturing and trading firms. The second phase coincided with the rise of electricity around 1900 and peaked in the 1930s with the coming of World War II. The third phase emerged in 1945, along with the rise of economic powers such as the United States and Japan, pent-up demand, and efforts to rebuild war-torn areas. The fourth and current phase began in the 1980s and was stimulated particularly by the rise of IT, the Internet, and other advanced technologies. The **World Trade Organization** is a multilateral governing body empowered to regulate international trade and investment.

2. **An organizing framework for market globalization**

   Market globalization can be modeled in terms of its drivers, dimensions, societal consequences, and firm-level consequences. As market globalization intensifies, firms are compelled to respond to challenges and exploit new advantages. Many firms proactively pursue internationalization as a strategic move. They become more aggressive at identifying foreign market opportunities, seeking partnerships with foreign firms, and building organizational capabilities in order to enhance their competitive advantage.

3. **Dimensions of market globalization**

   Market globalization refers to the growing integration of the world economy from the international business activities of countless firms. It represents a growing global interconnectedness of buyers, producers, suppliers, and governments. Globalization has fostered a new dynamism in the world economy,

the emergence of *regional economic integration blocs*, growth of global investment and financial flows, the convergence of buyer lifestyles and needs, and the globalization of production. At the business enterprise level, market globalization amounts to reconfiguration of company **value chains**—the sequence of value-adding activities including sourcing, manufacturing, marketing, and distribution—on a *global* scale.

4. **Drivers of market globalization**

   Market globalization is driven by several factors, including falling trade and investment barriers, market liberalization and adoption of free market economics in formerly closed economies, industrialization and economic development, especially among emerging markets, integration of world financial markets, and technological advances.

5. **Technological advances as a driver of market globalization**

   Advances in technology are particularly important in driving market globalization. The most important advances in technology have occurred in information technology, communications, the Internet, manufacturing, and transportation. These systems help create an interconnected network of customers, suppliers, and intermediaries worldwide. They have made the cost of international business affordable for all types of firms.

6. **Societal consequences of market globalization**

   There is much debate about globalization's benefits and harm. Critics complain that globalization interferes with national *sovereignty*, the ability of a state to govern itself without external intervention. Globalization is associated with *offshoring*, the relocation of value-chain activities to foreign locations where they can be performed less costly by subsidiaries or independent suppliers. Globalization tends to decrease poverty, but may widen the gap between the rich and the poor. Unrestricted industrialization may harm the natural environment. Globalization is also associated with the loss of cultural values unique to each nation.

7. Firm-level consequences of market globalization: Internationalization of the firm's value chain

Market globalization compels firms to organize their sourcing, manufacturing, marketing, and other value-adding activities on a global scale. Each value-adding activity can be performed in the home country or abroad. Firms choose where in the world they locate or configure key value-adding activities. Firms internationalize value-chain activities to reduce the costs of R&D and production, or to gain closer access to customers.

Test Your Comprehension

1. Define market globalization. What are the underlying dimensions of this megatrend?

2. Is globalization a recent phenomenon? Describe the four phases of globalization.

3. Summarize the five dimensions of globalization. Which of these do you think is the most visible manifestation of globalization?

4. Describe the five drivers of globalization.

5. What is the role of the World Trade Organization?

6. In what areas have technological advances had their greatest effect on facilitating world trade and investment?

7. What are the pros and cons of globalization?

8. What effect does globalization have on national sovereignty, employment, the poor, the natural environment, and national culture?

9. What are the implications of globalization for firm internationalization?

Apply Your Understanding AACSB: Communication, Reflective Thinking, Ethical Reasoning, Use of Information Technology, Analytical Skills

1. Imagine you are studying for your international business class at a local coffee shop. The manager spies your textbook and remarks: "I don't get all that foreign business stuff. I don't pay much attention to it. I'm a local guy running a small business. Thank goodness I don't have to worry about any of that." The manager's comments make you think. Despite the manager's comments, you realize there is much more to business than just local concerns. What is the likely value chain of a coffee shop? For example, how did the varieties of coffee beans get there? What is the likely effect of market globalization on coffee shops? Do technological advances play any role in the shop's value chain? Does globalization imply any negative consequences for the worldwide coffee industry? Justify your answer.

2. Suppose you get a job at Fossil Fuel, Inc., an oil company that has been severely criticized for global business practices that are seen to exacerbate economic, political, and social phenomena in some countries. Your boss directs you to increase your familiarity with market globalization, with a view to developing company strategies that are more sensitive to the firm's globalization critics. In your investigation, you discover that there are five major dimensions associated with market globalization. What are these dimensions? What are the drivers of market globalization? Structure and elaborate your answer in the form of a memo to your boss.

3. Globalization provides numerous advantages to businesses and consumers around the world. At the same time, some critics believe that globalization is harming various aspects of life and commerce. In what ways is globalization good for firms and consumers? In what ways is globalization harmful to firms and consumers?

4. Thinking in terms of the global value chain, what role does technology play in each of the value chain stages? Structure your answer by thinking about each stage of the value chain (R&D, procurement, manufacturing, marketing, distribution, sales, and service) and each major type of international technology (information technology, communications, manufacturing, and transportation). For example, today many firms use global teams to conduct R&D for new product development. The teams are linked together via intranets and other communications technologies that facilitate instantaneous interaction on daily R&D activities with team members worldwide.

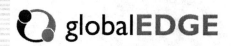
AACSB: Reflective Thinking, Ethical Reasoning, Use of Information Technology, Analytical Skills

Refer to Chapter 1, page 27, for instructions on how to access and use globalEDGE™.

1. *Foreign Policy* magazine, together with *A.T. Kearney, Inc.*, prepares an annual *Globalization Index* (enter "globalization index" at globalEDGE™), which ranks the 20 most globalized nations. The index uses four different dimensions to measure globalization:

   ▪ *Economic integration with the rest of the world* (such as trade and FDI levels),

   ▪ *Personal contact with the rest of the world* (such as international travel and tourism, telephone traffic),

   ▪ *Political engagement with the rest of the world* (such as memberships in international organizations, concern about world poverty and other global issues),

   ▪ *Technological integration with the rest of the world* (such as Internet users, hosts, secure servers).

   Visit globalEDGE™ and explain why each of these dimensions is important for a nation to have a substantial presence in the global economy and international business.

2. Service sector jobs are increasingly outsourced to lower-cost locations abroad. globalEDGE™ has various resources that detail the nature and location of jobs that have been transferred abroad. Some experts believe that the resulting foreign investment and increased demand in lower-cost countries will cause wages to rise in those countries, eliminating cost advantages from offshoring and narrowing the income gap between developed economies and low-cost countries. In other words, offshoring will help to reduce global poverty. Others believe that manufacturing jobs will be consistently moved to low-cost countries, making China and India the world's center of innovation and production. What do you think? Find three articles on outsourcing at globalEDGE™ by doing a search using the keywords "global outsourcing" or "offshoring," and write a report on the most likely consequences of these trends for your country, its workers, and consumers.

3. A key characteristic of globalization is the increasingly integrated world economy. Multinational enterprises (MNEs) and many nations have a vested interest in maintaining the globalization trend. If the trend were somehow reversed, participants in international business, such as exporters, would likely suffer big economic losses. In many ways, globalization's role in the world economy is critical. But just how big is the global economy? What is the extent of international trade relative to the size of the global economy? What is the proportion of international trade in the GDPs of each of the following countries: Australia, Canada, Sweden, United Kingdom, and the United States? Use globalEDGE™ to address these questions.

CKR Cavusgil Knight Riesenberger

Management Skill Builder©

What is a C/K/R Management Skill Builder©?

A C/K/R MSB© is a practical exercise designed to help you become familiar with key managerial challenges or decisions that entry-level professionals working in international business are likely to encounter. Completing the C/K/R MSBs© in this book will enable you to acquire practical, real-world skills that will help you perform well in your career. Each C/K/R MSB© presents:

- A managerial challenge in the context of a real-world scenario
- The skills that you will acquire in solving the challenge
- A methodology and resources to use in solving the challenge

For each *C/K/R MSB©*, the following sections are featured in the textbook:

1. Introduction
2. Managerial Challenge
3. Background
4. Managerial Skills You will Gain
5. Your Task

Each C/K/R MSB© is then continued on the C/K/R Knowledge Portal©, and features the following additional sections:

1. Expanded Background
2. Your Task and Methodology
3. Suggested Resources for this Exercise
4. Template

In order to complete each C/K/R MSB©, you need to visit the C/K/R Knowledge Portal© at **www.prenhall.com/cavusgil**.

Management Skill Builder©

Corporate Social Responsibility: Coffee, Ethiopia, and Starbucks

Corporate social responsibility refers to a management practice of making business decisions that have a positive effect on society and the environment. Management should make decisions that properly balance the business goal of profit and social issues such as education, diversity, poverty, the treatment of workers, and stewardship of the environment.

AACSB: Communication, Reflective Thinking, Ethical Reasoning, Use of Information Technology, Analytical Skills

Managerial Challenge

In international settings, the firm must establish itself as a global citizen. It must be a socially responsible corporate player. This may imply sacrificing a degree of profitability in order to make a contribution to the broader needs of the host country.

How managers resolve this trade-off between optimizing business decisions with meeting the expectations of its stakeholders (customers, employees, suppliers, taxpayers, community groups, and shareholders) is critical. The managerial challenge is one of achieving social responsibility while simultaneously meeting revenue and profitability goals.

Background

Starbucks, the international coffee vendor, contracts with farmers in Ethiopia to grow coffee beans. Acting on behalf of its coffee growers, the Ethiopian government has argued that Starbucks keeps too much of the profits from these operations: Starbucks sells coffee for $26 per pound, while it seems to overlook the fact that coffee growers in developing countries such as Ethiopia are not receiving a fair price.

Consider that many coffee experts and many coffee drinkers believe Ethiopian coffee to be the best in the world. Starbucks certainly wants to offer Ethiopian coffee, which enjoys such a great reputation, to its customers. For example, Starbucks sells a coffee called Harer, which is the name of a particular Ethiopian coffee bean. Starbucks can charge customers a premium for the experience. But Ethiopian coffee sellers cannot charge Starbucks for using that name. By seeking registered trademark status for Harer and other Ethiopian coffee beans in the United States, the Ethiopian government believes it can bargain for better export prices on behalf of some 15 million Ethiopians who depend on coffee growing for their livelihood. The Ethiopian government has received much support in this highly publicized conflict from Oxfam, a non-governmental organization concerned with global poverty issues (http://www.oxfamamerica.org).

For its part, Starbucks has resisted actions that would reduce its bargaining power with Ethiopian

coffee growers. The firm has also argued that trademarking coffee beans might introduce legal complexities that will force coffee buyers to turn to other countries. Starbucks management said that it favors a geographic certification model (similar to Florida Orange Juice or Napa Valley Wines), which provides a point of origin and establishes standards of quality.

Managerial Skills You Will Gain

In this C/K/R/ Management Skill Builder©, as a prospective manager, you will:

1. Learn the complexity of appropriately balancing the needs for corporate profitability and social responsibility.

2. Research the power of activist groups such as Oxfam.

3. Develop a systematic process through which a firm can reconcile competing demands of corporate and societal objectives.

Your Task

In this C/K/R Management Skill Builder©, assume that you are a manager at Starbucks assigned to advise senior management on whether to proceed with the endorsement of trademark rights in the United States.

In light of recent negative publicity and actions of activist groups, should Starbucks maintain its position that trademarking coffee beans might compel coffee buyers like itself to turn to alternative coffee growing nations?

Your assignment is to research the issue of Starbucks's corporate social responsibility with regard to coffee profit sharing in Ethiopia. What actions should Starbucks take in this regard?

Go to the C/K/R Knowledge Portal©

www.prenhall.com/cavusgil

Proceed to the C/K/R Knowledge Portal© to obtain the expanded background information, your task and methodology, suggested resources for this exercise, and the presentation template to use.

INTERNATIONAL TRADE

Contents

Introduction
International trade theory
Barriers to trade
Non-tariff barriers to trade
Other economic developments
Appendix to Chapter 6:
Balance of payments

■ **Active Learning Case**
Trade of the triad and China

■ **International Business Strategy in Action**
Microsoft shows the world is not flat
The courier wars

■ **Real Cases**
Job losses and offshoring to China
Dumping on trade complaints

Objectives of the chapter

An understanding of international trade is critical to the study of international business. The primary objective of this chapter is to examine key economic theories that help to explain why nations trade. In addition, the role and importance of a country's barriers to trade will be studied and discussion will focus on why most nations use trade barriers despite vigorous international efforts to eliminate them.

The specific objectives of this chapter are to:

1 *Define* the term *international trade* and discuss the role of mercantilism in modern international trade.
2 *Contrast* the theories of absolute advantage and comparative advantage.
3 *Relate* the importance of international product life cycle theory to the study of international economics.
4 *Explain* some of the most commonly used barriers to trade and other economic developments that affect international economics.
5 *Discuss* some of the reasons for the tensions between the theory of free trade and the widespread practice of national trade barriers.

Active Learning Case

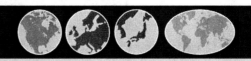

Trade of the triad and China

Over the last three decades, new entrants into the world export market have transformed the economies of industrialized countries and the types of products they export. At the beginning of this time period, the Japanese were a growing force in the international arena. They dominated the 1980s and were able to make substantial gains at the expense of such dominant exporters as the UK and the United States. Indeed, between 1980 and 1990, both these countries lost worldwide market share to the Japanese in such industries as automotive products, office machines, telecom equipment, machinery and transport equipment, chemicals, and textiles.

In the late 1980s, however, the world economy began to see major changes. Asia, South Korea, Singapore, Taiwan, Thailand, and China were growing much more competitive on the world stage. South Korea, for example, started expanding its automotive industry, while China's market share of office and telecom equipment rose from zero to about 1 percent of the market in 1990 to 4.5 percent by 2000. Meanwhile, thanks to NAFTA—which decreased barriers to trade within North America—Mexico and Canada were increasing their market share of automotive products, machinery, and transport equipment. Such competition spurred the United States to radically restructure many of its industries; invest billions in new technology, plant, equipment, and information technology; and introduce improvement programs, such as Six Sigma, that allowed it to match the quality offerings of worldwide competitors. As a result, the US share of the world's export market in areas such as automotive products, machinery and transport equipment, chemicals, and textiles somewhat recovered. The big loser was Japan, which saw its export market share decline in most of these areas.

Today the biggest challenge to the export markets of industrialized countries is China. Between 2000 and 2005, China's share of the world's exports merchandise more than doubled—from 4.7 percent to 9.8 percent (see Table 1). This increase comes at the expense of exports by triad countries over the same period. By 2005 the core triad's share of world exports was 42.3 percent, with the EU accounting for over half of this (see Table 2). The United States and Japan were the hardest hit.

China's expansion is particularly evident in the clothing and textile markets. Today the country holds 26.9 percent and 20.2 percent of each market, respectively (see the first table). More impressive, however, are China's improvements in exports of office and telecom equipment and of

Table 1 China's share of the world's market for exports of manufactures

Industry	2000	2005
All manufactures	4.7	9.6
Iron and steel	3.1	6.1
Chemicals	2.1	3.2
Machinery and transport equipment	3.1	na
Automotive products	0.3	1.1
Office and telecom equipment	4.5	17.7
Textiles	10.5	20.2
Clothing	18.3	26.9

Note: Manufactures are a subcategory within merchandise exports. These data include intra-regional EU exports.

Source: Authors' calculations based on data from World Trade Organization, *Statistics Database*.

Table 2 The triad's share of merchandise world exports

	1995	2001	2005	2005 − 1995
US	15.3	16.1	11.7	−3.6
EU	26.2	22.2	22.9	−3.3
Japan	11.6	8.9	7.7	−3.9
Triad	53.1	47.2	42.3	−10.8
Non-triad	46.9	52.8	57.7	10.8

Note: Data are calculated using world trade minus intra-regional EU trade.

Source: Authors' calculations based on data from World Trade Organization, *International Trade Statistics, 2004 and 2007*.

machinery and transport equipment, both of which require significant technology know-how.

As can been seen in the tables, China's rise as a world exporter has decreased the share of the triad's share of world exports in manufactures. In response to China's increased competitiveness, triad countries are trying to balance the need to integrate this new player into the international business arena with the negative short-term effects to their economies.

Japan's attitude toward China took a turn from protectionism when it realized that this new trade partner could help it overcome some of the problems associated with its rigid economic system. Large amounts of inexpensive, low-skilled labor now allowed Japanese companies to outsource some of their manufacturing operations overseas, within its own region, while more skilled Japanese workers took care of the more specialized areas of the production process. In addition, China eased Japan's long dependence on the US economy for its industrial and consumer products.

While US and EU companies have also moved operations to Japan, the governments are reacting more aggressively to pressure from special interest groups that see China as a threat to US businesses and jobs. The United States, which runs a large trade deficit with China, has argued that the yuan is undervalued, creating an unfair advantage for Chinese producers. The United States is threatening to impose tariffs on Chinese products. Japan has joined this wagon and is pressuring China to move to a more flexible exchange rate. Yet, critics argue that no one truly knows the market value of the yuan and that a fall on its price after deregulation could only worsen matters. For its part, the EU has reacted by asking China to curtail exports of textiles into the union after exports of clothing increased by 534 percent in less than six months in 2005.

An increase in exports by any nation does not necessarily mean that other countries are losing out. In terms of trade alone, any new entrant to the world exports market, other things being equal, will decrease the share of world exports of all other countries. This, however, does not mean that other countries are exporting less. They could be exporting, in value terms, a significantly higher amount because a new trade partner also means a new market to which they can export. More specifically, however, trade creates losers and winners. Triad economies are being forced to specialize. While those with most to lose pressure their governments to impose trade barriers, those with most to win—high-skilled industries—are expanding to serve the Chinese market. Further, customers' real incomes increase when they can purchase the same products at lower prices.

The data on this case help to reinforce an important principle of international trade: specialize in those products in which you can achieve an advantage. Over time, of course, competitors may erode this advantage by developing even better offerings for the export market. In this case, it is important either to counterattack by improving your own offering to win back this market share, or to find other markets where the country's skills and resources will allow it to compete effectively. In light of the emergence of more and more industrial countries in Asia, the growing competitiveness of Latin America, and the emerging industries of Eastern Europe and the former Soviet Union, triad managers have their work cut out for them.

Sources: "Chinese Urged to Curb EU Exports," BBC.co.uk, May 12, 2005; "China's Yuan under Fresh Pressure," BBC.co.uk, May 6, 2005; "The Halo Effect," *The Economist*, September 30, 2004.

1 How does the process of the UK's finding market niches help illustrate the theory of comparative advantage?

2 How does an EU manager's desire to buy domestic products illustrate the importance of consumer taste in international markets?

3 In what way could the EU use trade barriers to protect its markets from foreign competitors? Who can be affected by these trade barriers?

INTRODUCTION

International trade
The branch of economics concerned with the exchange of goods and services with foreign countries

International trade is the branch of economics concerned with the exchange of goods and services with foreign countries. Although this is a complex subject, we will focus on two particular areas: international trade theory and barriers to trade.

Some international economic problems cannot be solved in the short run. Consider the US balance of trade deficit. US trade with Japan and China heavily affects its overall imbalance. Moreover, this trade deficit will not be reduced by political measures alone; it will require long-run economic measures that reduce imports and increase exports. Other nations are also learning this lesson—and not just those that have negative balances. After all, most countries seem to want a continual favorable trade balance, although this is impossible, since a nation with a deficit must be matched by a nation with a surplus.[1]

International trade has become an even more important topic now that so many countries have begun to move from state-run to market-driven economies.[2] Inflation and, in many cases, unemployment are severe problems for these nations. Fortunately, enhanced international trade is one way to address a weak macroeconomy.[3] International commitment to a free market will bring prosperity to the world economic system. Since the time of Adam Smith in 1790, economists have shown that free trade is efficient and leads to maximum economic welfare. In this chapter we will discuss the economic rationale for free trade and the political impediments to it.

INTERNATIONAL TRADE THEORY

To understand the topic of international trade, we must be able to answer the question: why do nations trade? One of the earliest and simplest answers to this question was provided by mercantilism, a theory that was quite popular in the eighteenth century, when gold was the only world currency. **Mercantilism** holds that a government can improve the economic well-being of the country by encouraging exports and stifling imports. The result is a positive balance of trade that leads to wealth (gold) flowing into the country.

Neo-mercantilism, like mercantilism, seeks to produce a positive balance of trade but without the reliance on precious metals. Most international trade experts believe that mercantilism is a simplistic and erroneous theory, although it has had followers. For example, under President Mitterrand in the late 1970s and early 1980s, France sought to revitalize its industrial base by nationalizing key industries and banks and subsidizing exports over imports. By the mid-1980s the French government realized that the strategy was not working and began denationalizing many of its holdings.[4] More recently, China has proven to be a strong adherent of mercantilism, as reflected by the fact that it tries to have a positive balance with all of its trading partners.

A more useful explanation of why nations trade is provided by trade theories that focus on specialization of effort. The theories of absolute and comparative advantage are good examples.

Theory of absolute advantage

The **theory of absolute advantage** holds that nations can increase their economic well-being by specializing in the production of goods they can produce more efficiently than anyone else. A simple example can illustrate this point. Assume that two nations, North and South, are both able to produce two goods, cloth and grain. Assume further that labor is the only scarce factor of production and thus the only cost.

Labor cost (hours) of production for one unit

	Cloth	Grain
North	10	20
South	20	10

Thus lower labor-hours per unit of production means lower production costs and higher productivity per labor-hour. As seen by the data in the table, North has an absolute advantage in the production of cloth since the cost requires only 10 labor-hours, compared to 20 labor-hours in South. Similarly, South has an absolute advantage in the production

Mercantilism
A trade theory which holds that a government can improve the economic well-being of the country by encouraging exports and stifling imports to accumulate wealth in the form of precious metals

Neo-mercantilism
A trade theory which holds that a government can improve the economic well-being of the country by encouraging exports and stifling imports

Theory of absolute advantage
A trade theory which holds that nations can increase their economic well-being by specializing in goods that they can produce more efficiently than anyone else

of grain, which it produces at a cost of 10 labor-hours, compared to 20 labor-hours in North.

Both countries gain by trade. If they specialize and exchange cloth for grain at a relative price of 1:1, each country can employ its resources to produce a greater amount of goods. North can import one unit of grain in exchange for one unit of cloth, thereby paying only 10 labor-hours for one unit of grain. If North had produced the grain itself, it would have used 20 labor-hours per unit, so North gains 10 labor-hours from the trade. In the same way, South gains from trade when it imports one unit of cloth in exchange for one unit of grain. The effective cost to South for one unit of cloth is only the 10 labor-hours required to make its one unit of grain.

The theory of absolute advantage, as originally formulated, does not predict the exchange ratio between cloth and grain once trade is opened, nor does it resolve the division of the gains from trade between the two countries. Our example assumed an international price ratio of 1:1, but this ratio (P_{cloth} to P_{grain}) could lie between 2:1 (the pretrade price ratio in South) and 1:2 (the pretrade price ratio in North). To determine the relative price ratio under trade, we would have to know the total resources of each country (total labor-hours available per year), and the demand of each for both cloth and grain. In this way we could determine their relative gains from trade for each country.

Even this simple model of absolute advantage has several important implications for international trade. First, if a country has an absolute advantage in producing a product, it has the potential to gain from trade. Second, the more a country is able to specialize in the good it produces most efficiently, the greater its potential gains in national well-being. Third, the competitive market does not evenly distribute the gains from trade *within* one country. This last implication is illustrated by the following example.

Prior to trade, the grain farmers in North work 20 hours to produce one unit of grain that could be exchanged for two units of cloth. After trade, those who remain can exchange one unit of grain for only one unit of cloth. Thus, the remaining grain producers are worse off under trade. Cloth producers in North, however, work 10 hours, produce one unit of cloth, and exchange it for one unit of grain, whereas previously they received only half a unit of grain. They are better off. If grain producers in North switch to cloth production, then 20 hours of labor results in the production of two units of cloth, which they can exchange for two units of grain. Thus, international trade helps them. As long as North does not specialize completely in cloth, there will be gainers (cloth producers and grain producers who switched to cloth) and losers (those who continue as grain producers).

Because the nation as a whole benefits from trade, the gainers can compensate the losers and there will still be a surplus to be distributed in some way. If such compensation does not take place, however, the losers (continuing grain producers) would have an incentive to try to prevent the country from opening itself up to trade. Historically, this problem has continued to fuel opposition to a free trade policy that reduces barriers to trade. A good example is Japanese farmers who stand to lose their livelihood if the government opens up Japan to lower-priced agricultural imports.

A more complicated picture of the determinants and effects of trade emerges when one of the trading partners has an absolute advantage in the production of both goods. However, trade under these conditions still brings gains, as David Ricardo first demonstrated in his theory of comparative advantage.

Theory of comparative advantage

Theory of comparative advantage
A trade theory which holds that nations should produce those goods for which they have the greatest relative advantage

The **theory of comparative advantage** holds that nations should produce those goods for which they have the greatest relative advantage. In terms of the previous example of two countries, North and South, and two commodities, cloth and grain, Ricardo's model can be illustrated as follows:

Labor cost (hours) of production for one unit

	Cloth	Grain
North	50	100
South	200	200

In this example North has an absolute advantage in the production of *both* cloth and grain, so it would appear at first sight that trade would be unprofitable, or at least that incentives for exchange no longer exist. Yet trade is still advantageous to both nations, provided their *relative* costs of production differ.

Before trade, one unit of cloth in North costs (50/100) hours of grain, so one unit of cloth can be exchanged for half a unit of grain. The price of cloth is half the price of grain. In South, one unit of cloth costs (200/200) hours of grain, or one grain unit. The price of cloth equals the price of grain. If North can import more than half a unit of grain for one unit of cloth, it will gain from trade. Similarly, if South can import one unit of cloth for less than one unit of grain, it will also gain from trade. These relative price ratios set the boundaries for trade. Trade is profitable between price ratios (price of cloth to price of grain) of 0.5 and 1. For example, at an international price ratio of two-thirds, North gains. It can import one unit of grain in return for exporting one and a half units of cloth. Because it costs only 50 hours of labor to produce the unit of cloth, its effective cost under trade for one unit of imported grain is 75 labor-hours. Under pretrade conditions it costs North 100 labor-hours to produce one unit of grain. Similarly, South gains from trade by importing one unit of cloth in exchange for two-thirds of a unit of grain. Prior to trade, South spent 200 labor-hours producing the one unit of cloth. Through trade, its effective cost for one unit of cloth is $\frac{2}{3} \times 200$, or 133 labor-hours—cheaper than the domestic production cost of 200 labor-hours. Assuming free trade between the two nations, North will tend to specialize in the production of cloth, and South will tend to specialize in the production of grain.

This example illustrates a general principle. There are gains from trade whenever the relative price ratios of two goods differ under international exchange from what they would be under conditions of no trade. Such domestic conditions are often referred to as *autarky*, which is a government policy of being totally self-sufficient. Research shows that free trade is superior to autarky. In particular, free trade provides greater economic output and consumption to the trade partners jointly than they can achieve by working alone. By specializing in the production of certain goods, exporting those products for which they have a comparative advantage, and importing those for which they have a comparative disadvantage, the countries end up being better off.

The general conclusions of the theory of comparative advantage are the same as those for the theory of absolute advantage. In addition, the theory of comparative advantage demonstrates that countries jointly benefit from free trade (under the assumptions of the model) even if one has an absolute advantage in the production of *both* goods. Total world efficiency and consumption increase.

As with the theory of absolute advantage discussed previously, Ricardo's theory of comparative advantage does not answer the question of the distribution of gains between the two countries, nor the distribution of gains and losses between grain producers and cloth producers within each country. No country will lose under free trade, but in theory at least all the gains could accrue to one country and to only one group within that country.

Factor endowment theory
A trade theory which holds that nations will produce and export products that use large amounts of production factors that they have in abundance and will import products requiring a large amount of production factors that they lack

Heckscher–Ohlin theory
A trade theory that extends the concept of comparative advantage by bringing into consideration the endowment and cost of factors of production and helps to explain why nations with relatively large labor forces will concentrate on producing labor-intensive goods, whereas countries with relatively more capital than labor will specialize in capital-intensive goods

Leontief paradox
A finding by Wassily Leontief, a Nobel Prize-winning economist, which shows that the United States, surprisingly, exports relatively more labor-intensive goods and imports capital-intensive goods

International product life cycle (IPLC) theory
A theory of the stages of production of a product with new "know-how": it is first produced by the parent firm, then by its foreign subsidiaries, and finally anywhere in the world where costs are the lowest; it helps explain why a product that begins as a nation's export often ends up as an import

Factor endowment theory

In recent years more sophisticated theories have emerged that help clarify and extend our knowledge of international trade. The **factor endowment theory** holds that countries will produce and export products that use large amounts of production factors that they have in abundance, and they will import products requiring large amounts of production factors that they lack. This theory is also known as the **Heckscher–Ohlin theory** (after the two economists who first developed it). The theory is useful in extending the concept of comparative advantage by bringing into consideration the endowment and cost of production factors. The theory also helps explain why nations with relatively large labor forces, such as China, will concentrate on producing labor-intensive goods, whereas countries like the Netherlands, which has relatively more capital than labor, will specialize in capital-intensive goods.

However, the factor endowment theory has some weaknesses. One weakness is that some countries have minimum wage laws that result in high prices for relatively abundant labor. As a result, they may find it less expensive to import certain goods than to produce them internally. Another weakness is that countries like the United States export relatively more labor-intensive goods and import capital-intensive goods, an outcome that appears surprising. This result, discovered by Wassily Leontief, a Nobel Prize-winning economist, is known as the **Leontief paradox** and has been explained in terms of the quality of labor input rather than just labor-hours of work. The United States produces and exports technology-intensive products that require highly educated labor. The Leontief paradox not only shows one of the problems with factor endowment theory, but also helps us understand why no single theory can explain the role of economic factors in trade theory. Simply put, the subject is too complex to be explained with just one or two theories.

International product life cycle theory

Another theory that provides insights into international theory is Vernon's **international product life cycle (IPLC) theory**, which addresses the various stages of a good's life cycle. In particular, the theory helps explain why a product that begins as a nation's export often ends up becoming an import. The theory also focuses on market expansion and technological innovation, concepts that are relatively de-emphasized in comparative advantage

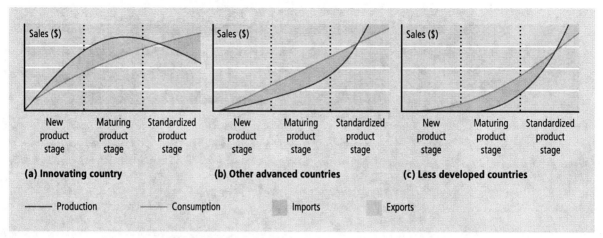

Figure 6.1 The international product life cycle

Source: Raymond Vernon and Louis T. Wells, Jr., *The Manager in the International Economy* (Englewood Cliffs, NJ: Prentice Hall, 1991), p. 85.

theory. IPLC theory has two important tenets: (1) technology is a critical factor in creating and developing new products; and (2) market size and structure are important in determining trade patterns.

Product stages

The IPLC has three stages: new product, maturing product, and standardized product. A new product is one that is innovative or unique in some way (see Figure 6.1a). Initially, consumption is in the home country, price is inelastic, profits are high, and the company seeks to sell to those willing to pay a premium price. As production increases and outruns local consumption, exporting begins.

As the product enters the mature phase of its life cycle (see Figure 6.1b), an increasing percentage of sales is achieved through exporting. At the same time, competitors in other advanced countries will be working to develop substitute products so they can replace the initial good with one of their own. The introduction of these substitutes and the softening of demand for the original product will eventually result in the firm that developed the product now switching its strategy from production to market protection. Attention will also be focused on tapping markets in less developed countries.

As the product enters the standardized product stage (see Figure 6.1c), the technology becomes widely diffused and available. Production tends to shift to low-cost locations, including less developed countries and offshore locations. In many cases the product will end up being viewed as a generic, and price will be the sole determinant of demand.

Personal computers and the IPLC

In recent years a number of products have moved through the IPLC and are now in the standardized product stage. Personal computers (PCs) are a good example, despite their wide variety and the fact that some versions are in the new product and maturing product phases. For example, the early version of PCs that reached the market in the 1984 to 1991 period were in the standardized product stage by 1995 and sold primarily on the basis of price. Machines that entered the market in the 1996 to 1998 period were in the maturing stage by 1999. PCs with increased memory capability that were in the new product stage in 1999 quickly moved toward maturity, and by 2002 they were being replaced by even better machines with faster processors and more multimedia capabilities. Today, diskettes are standardized and rarely used while standard components include CD writers, DVD ROMs,

DSL and wireless Internet connectors, USB ports, advanced graphics and sound, flat LCD monitors, digital photography capabilities, etc.

Desktop computers have been replaced by laptop models that are lighter, faster, more sophisticated, and less expensive than their predecessors. In turn, these machines are being replaced by notebooks with advanced Pentium chips, long-term battery capability, and storage capable of holding billions of bytes complete with wireless equipment and serve as a complete communications center from which the international executive can communicate anywhere in the world. These machines will first be manufactured locally and then in foreign markets. This is largely because IBM (the inventor of the PC) computers became a commodity, and IBM's PC division was sold to the Chinese firm Lenovo in 2005. Lenovo has the benefit of low labor costs and it is better able to manufacture the laptops of today. Thus, computers will continue to move through an IPLC.

The IPLC theory is useful in helping to explain how new technologically innovative products fit into the world trade picture. However, because new innovative products are sometimes rapidly improved, it is important to remember that one or two versions of them may be in the standardized product stage while other versions are in the maturing stage and still others are in the new product phase.

Other important considerations

Many factors beyond those we have considered greatly influence international trade theory.[5] One is government regulation. Countries often limit or restrict trade with other countries for political reasons. For example, despite the benefits of international trade, the EU does not always see eye to eye with the United States on regulatory matters. As a result there are different government regulations affecting business in Europe, than in North America. For example, EU competition policy differs from US antitrust policy, see the box **International Business Strategy in Action: Microsoft shows the world is not flat**. Other important factors include monetary currency valuation and consumer tastes.

Monetary currency valuation

Monetary exchange rate
The price of one currency stated in terms of another currency

When examining why one country trades with another, we need to consider the **monetary exchange rate**, which is the price of one currency stated in terms of another currency. For example, from 1995 to 1998 the value of the Japanese yen declined significantly over the value of the US dollar. As a result, many Japanese businesses found their products becoming much more competitive in the US market. Thereafter, the Japanese government announced that because the yen was again getting too strong, it wanted to weaken its value, thus ensuring that Japanese businesses could maintain their international competitiveness. Another reason why monetary currency valuation is important is because a foreign firm doing business will report its revenues and profits in home-country currency. So if a British firm sold $10 million of machinery in Canada and the value of the Canadian dollar declined against the British pound, the UK company would report less revenue (in terms of British pounds) than if the Canadian dollar had remained stable or, better yet, increased in value against the pound. In mid-2005, the euro became so strong compared to the dollar that Volkswagen reported a 63 percent decline in pre tax profits.[6] In the next chapter we will discuss exchange rates in more detail.

Consumer tastes

International trade is not based solely on price; some people will pay more for a product even though they can buy something similar for less money. This willingness to pay more may be based on prestige, perceived quality, or a host of other physical and psychological reasons. Personal tastes dictate consumer decisions.

Microsoft shows the world is not flat

The dispute between Microsoft and the European Commission demonstrates that the world is not flat. Microsoft is a company that has ridden the wave of worldwide Internet access and software applications. Yet, it has run into a brick wall in Brussels. There the EU Directorate General for Competition and State Aid (DG Comp) has imposed large fines for breaking its competition rules.

In March 2004, the DG Comp ruled that Microsoft is abusing its dominant market position with its Windows operating system. Since then the DG Comp has been threatening to impose large daily fines because it says Microsoft is failing to comply with that ruling. On September 17, 2007, Microsoft lost an appeal to the European Court of First Instance ending a nine-year battle with the EU. It paid fines to the EU of over $1.2 billion. In January 2008 the EU launched a new antitrust investigation against Microsoft.

This case illustrates that even the world's most successful Internet-based software company does not have unrestricted global market access for its products. Instead, the world is divided into a 'triad' with strong barriers for entry into the key regional markets of the EU, North America, and Asia–Pacific. Microsoft is simply the latest large MNE to misread the world marketplace. Today, business activity is organized mainly within each region of the triad, not globally. For US firms, going to a foreign triad market in Europe and Asia is fraught with peril.

The world's 500 largest firms, on average, sell 72 percent of their goods and services in their home region. Very few firms are truly global, defined as selling a significant percent of their products in each triad region. For example, the world's largest firm, Wal-Mart, has 94 percent of its sales in North America. Unfortunately, Microsoft does not reveal the geographic dispersion of its sales, but it is likely that a majority of them are also in North America. Firms like Wal-Mart and Microsoft need to understand that a business model developed for North America will need to be adapted when going to Europe and Asia.

In the case of Microsoft the key difference is in the way that the EU regulatory system operates. In Europe competition policy can be used as a barrier to entry. An individual firm (in this case, Sun Microsystems) can signal an EU-wide investigation. In this process the deck is stacked against the foreign firm. In 2001 the US firm General Electric also made a similar mistake in its planned acquisition of Honeywell which was disallowed by the EU.

While the United States has somewhat similar antitrust provisions, the application of these is more business friendly than in Europe. US antitrust aims to help

Source: Getty Images/AFP/Jean-Christophe Verhaeagen/Stringer

consumers, whereas EU law helps competitors. Microsoft was able to settle its antitrust case with the Bush administration, but it failed to do so with the EU. The regulatory climate in Europe is harsher than in North America. Multinational firms like Microsoft which assume free trade, worldwide market entry, and the other aspects of flat earth thinking are learning expensive lessons. In addition to differences in regulatory standards across the triad, there are major cultural, social, and political differences that deny globalization.

In terms of regulatory differences antitrust is but one of an array of market-entry barriers. Even worse are antidumping and countervailing duty laws which are used to keep out foreign rivals. The United States itself administers its antidumping and countervailing duty laws in favor of the home team. In 2006, on security grounds, the US Congress overturned the executive branch decision to allow Dubai Ports International to acquire the US ports owned by P&O, a British firm. The Europeans perceive that the US commitment to free trade is weak; this is stiffening their spine with regard to Microsoft. The end result is typical triad-based economic warfare, where market entry is denied by the local bureaucrats and politicians.

While the US system is transparent, the EU investigation of unfair trade law cases, as well as antitrust, can be opaque and self-serving. The EU bureaucrats have continued the case against Microsoft even after Sun Microsystems and other business rivals in Europe, like Novell and RealNetworks, have settled their disputes. So now we can see the EU, as an institution, fighting a foreign multinational. Not exactly a flat world.

The lessons of the Microsoft case are the following. First, globalization is a myth; instead world business is conducted mainly on an intra-regional basis within each part of the triad. Second, it is unlikely that the regulatory standards across the triad will be harmonized; thus, multinationals must be prepared to adapt their business models when they enter foreign regions of the triad. Third, even in high-tech areas such as software Internet applications, the technology itself does not guarantee the flat promise of worldwide market access. The world is not flat; rather, there are very strong regional fault lines.

Sources: Indiana University CIBER Director's Message, May 1, 2006; *Financial Times*, September 18, 2007; *Wall Street Journal*, September 18, 2007; *Financial Times*, January 15, 2008.

✔ Active learning check

Review your answer to Active Learning Case question 2 and make any changes you like. Then compare your answer to the one below.

 How does an EU manager's desire to buy domestic products illustrate the importance of consumer taste in international markets?

This example shows that people often buy goods based on personal preference, rather than only on such characteristics as low price, high quality, or improved productivity. Of course, this "Buy EU" focus will often come into play only when all other factors are approximately equal. The manager is unlikely to turn down a China-made product that is 30 percent less expensive in favor of one that is made domestically. So there are limits to the effects of consumer taste on purchase decisions, though it is certainly one variable that has proven very important in international trade.

BARRIERS TO TRADE

Why do many countries produce goods and services that could be purchased more cheaply from others? One reason is trade barriers, which effectively raise the cost of these goods and make them more expensive to local buyers.

Reasons for trade barriers

One of the most common reasons for the creation of trade barriers is to encourage local production by making it more difficult for foreign firms to compete there. Another reason is to help local firms export and thus build worldwide market share by doing such things as providing them with subsidies in the form of tax breaks and low-interest loans. Other common reasons include:

1 Protect local jobs by shielding home-country business from foreign competition.
2 Encourage local production to replace imports.
3 Protect infant industries that are just getting started.
4 Reduce reliance on foreign suppliers.
5 Encourage local and foreign direct investment.
6 Reduce balance of payments problems.
7 Promote export activity.
8 Prevent foreign firms from *dumping* (selling goods below cost in order to achieve market share).
9 Promote political objectives such as refusing to trade with countries that practice apartheid or deny civil liberties to their citizens.

Commonly used barriers

A variety of trade barriers deter the free flow of international goods and services.[7] The following presents six of the most commonly used barriers.

Price-based barriers

Imported goods and services sometimes have a tariff added to their price. Quite often this is based on the value of the goods. For example, some tobacco products coming into the United States carry an ad valorem tariff (see below) of over 100 percent, thus more than doubling their cost to US consumers. Tariffs raise revenues for the government, discourage imports, and make local goods more attractive.

Quantity limits

Quota
A quantity limit on imported goods

Embargo
A quota set at zero, thus preventing the importation of those products that are involved

Quantity limits, often known as **quotas**, restrict the number of units that can be imported or the market share that is permitted. If the quota is set at zero, as in the case of Cuban cigars from Havana to the United States, it is called an **embargo**. If the annual quota is set at 1 million units, no more than this number can be imported during one year; once it is reached, all additional imports are turned back. In some cases a quota is established in terms of market share. For example, Canada allows foreign banks to hold no more than 16 percent of Canadian bank deposits, and the EU limits Japanese auto imports to 10 percent of the total market.

International price fixing

Cartel
A group of firms that collectively agree to fix prices or quantities sold in an effort to control price

Sometimes a host of international firms will fix prices or quantities sold in an effort to control price. This is known as a **cartel**. A well-known example is OPEC (Organization of Petroleum Exporting Countries), which consists of Saudi Arabia, Kuwait, Iran, Iraq, and Venezuela, among others (see Table 6.1). By controlling the supply of oil it provides, OPEC seeks to control both price and profit. This practice is illegal in the United States and Europe,[8] but the basic idea of allowing competitors to cooperate for the purpose of meeting international competition is being endorsed more frequently in countries such as the United States.[9] For example, US computer firms have now created partnerships for joint research and development efforts.

Non-tariff barriers

Non-tariff barriers
Rules, regulations, and bureaucratic red tape that delay or preclude the purchase of foreign goods

Non-tariff barriers are rules, regulations, and bureaucratic red tape that delay or preclude the purchase of foreign goods. Examples include (1) slow processing of import permits, (2) the establishment of quality standards that exclude foreign producers, and (3) a "buy local" policy. These barriers limit imports and protect domestic sales.

Table 6.1 Members of the Organization of Petroleum Exporting Countries (OPEC), 2007

Member country	Quotas (barrels per day)
Algeria	810
Indonesia	1,396
Iran	3,861
Iraq	na
Kuwait	2,105
Libya	1,398
Nigeria	2,164
Qatar	676
Saudi Arabia	8,561
United Arab Emirates	2,301
Venezuela	3,028
Total	26,300

Source: Adapted from www.opec.org.

Financial limits

Exchange controls
Controls that restrict the flow of currency

There are a number of different financial limits. One of the most common is **exchange controls**, which restrict the flow of currency. For example, a common exchange control is to limit the currency that can be taken out of the country; for example, travelers may take up to only $3,000 per person out of the country. Another example is the use of fixed exchange rates that are quite favorable to the country. For example, dollars may be exchanged for local currency on a 1:1 basis; without exchange controls, the rate would be 1:4. These cases are particularly evident where a black market exists for foreign currency that offers an exchange rate much different from the fixed rate.

Foreign investment controls

Foreign investment controls
Limits on foreign direct investment or the transfer or remittance of funds

Foreign investment controls are limits on foreign direct investment or the transfer or remittance of funds. These controls can take a number of different forms, including (1) requiring foreign investors to take a minority ownership position (49 percent or less), (2) limiting profit remittance (such as to 15 percent of accumulated capital per year), and (3) prohibiting royalty payments to parent companies, thus stopping the latter from taking out capital.

Tariff
A tax on goods shipped internationally

Import tariff
A tax levied on goods shipped into a country

Export tariff
A tax levied on goods sent out of a country

Transit tariff
A tax levied on goods passing through a country

Specific duty
A tariff based on the number of items being shipped into a country

Ad valorem duty
A tax which is based on a percentage of the value of imported goods

Compound duty
A tariff consisting of both a specific and an ad valorem duty

Such barriers can greatly restrict international trade and investment. However, it must be realized that they are created for what governments believe are very important reasons. A close look at one of these, tariffs, helps to make this clearer.

Tariffs

A **tariff** is a tax on goods that are shipped internationally. The most common is the **import tariff**, which is levied on goods shipped into a country.[10] Less common is the **export tariff**, for goods sent out of the country, or a **transit tariff** for goods passing through the country. These taxes are levied on a number of bases. A **specific duty** is a tariff based on units, such as $1 for each item shipped into the country. So a manufacturer shipping in 1,000 pairs of shoes would pay a specific duty of $1,000. An **ad valorem duty** is a tariff based on a percentage of the value of the item, so a watch valued at $25 and carrying a 10 percent duty would have a tariff of $2.50. A **compound duty** is a tariff consisting of both a specific and an ad valorem duty, so a suit of clothes valued at $80 that carries a specific duty of $3 and an ad valorem duty of 5 percent would have a compound duty of $7.

Governments typically use tariffs to raise revenue and/or to protect local industry. At the same time, these taxes decrease demand for the respective product while raising the price to the buyer. This is illustrated in Figure 6.2, which shows how the quantity demanded

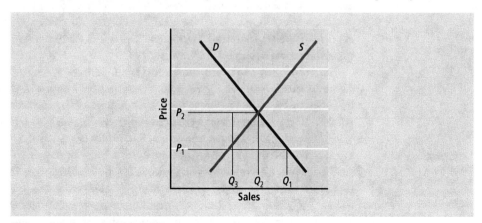

Figure 6.2 Impacts of a tariff

Source: Raymond Vernon and Louis T. Wells, Jr., *The Manager in the International Economy* (Englewood Cliffs, NJ: Prentice Hall, 1991), p. 85.

declines from Q_1 to Q_2 when a tariff drives the price of a good from P_1 to P_2 (the world price plus the tariff). This price increase allows local producers to sell Q_3Q_2 and thus take market share away from foreign firms that were exporting Q_3Q_1 into the country. However, the figure shows this is done at the price of charging the consumer more money *and* reducing the number of buyers who purchase the product. At new price P_2, there are no longer any imports.

There are numerous reasons for using tariffs, such as to protect domestic industries or firms. The US government has used them to prevent foreign companies from selling goods at lower prices in the United States than back home. US auto makers have often accused their overseas rivals of using this tactic. In the case of Japanese car manufacturers, this was a particularly troublesome area when the value of the yen rose sharply in the early 1990s. As a result, argued the US car companies, imported parts and cars had to reflect the increased value of the yen or be subjected to tariffs.[11] Others have made similar arguments. Eastman Kodak, for example, asked the US Commerce Department to impose steep tariffs on the Fuji Photo Film Company. Kodak's argument was partially based on the rising yen. However, it also reflected a concern with **dumping**, which is the selling of imported goods at a price below cost or below that in the home country. In this case Kodak argued that Fuji sold color photographic paper for less than 20 cents a square foot in the United States, while charging almost 60 cents a square foot in Japan.[12] For an example of a protectionist tariff, see the box International Business Strategy in Action: The courier wars.

Dumping
The selling of imported goods at a price below cost or below that in the home country

Another reason for using tariffs is to raise government revenue. Import tariffs, for example, are a major source of revenue for less developed countries. A third reason is to reduce citizens' foreign expenditures in order to improve the country's balance of payments.

Tariffs continue to be one of the most commonly used barriers to trade, despite the fact that they often hurt low-income consumers and have a limited impact, if any, on upper-income purchasers. In recent years most industrialized countries have tried to reduce or eliminate the use of these trade barriers and to promote more free trade policies.[13] The United States is a good example. (The trade policies of the EU are discussed in Chapter 16 and those of Japan in Chapter 17.)

US trade policy

Despite being a highly protectionist nation in its early years, the United States has a policy today that generally strives to lower tariffs and trade barriers through the use of multilateral agreements. Since the protectionist disaster of the Depression years, the United States has sought to minimize the use of tariffs. It supported the General Agreement on Tariffs and Trade (GATT), and now it supports the 1994 World Trade Organization (WTO), which exists to liberalize trade and investment. Today US tariffs average only 2 to 3 percent ad valorem to most countries of the world.[14]

The move away from tariffs does not mean US trade policy is completely open.[15] The US government employs a variety of approaches to promote or discourage international trade. For example, to encourage trade, there is the **North American Free Trade Agreement (NAFTA)**, which eliminates most trade restrictions (such as tariffs) among the United States, Canada, and Mexico and extends national treatment to foreign investment, and the **Caribbean Basin Initiative**, which eliminates tariffs on many imports from the Caribbean and Central American regions. Yet the **Trading-with-the-Enemy Act** disallows trade with countries judged to be enemies of the United States, including North Korea and Cuba. The US administration has the authority to prevent sales of goods to foreign governments when they are not deemed to be in the best interests of the United States. These goods can range from computers to chemicals to materials used for making nuclear weapons.[16]

Caribbean Basin Initiative
A trade agreement that eliminates tariffs on many imports to the United States from the Caribbean and Central American regions

The courier wars

Local businesses have many reasons for encouraging their governments to erect barriers to trade. One of the most common is when an industry is not competitive on a worldwide basis and foreign competition could bring about the bankruptcy of local firms. The US steel industry is a good example. The efficiencies of both West European and Japanese steelmakers have brought new challenges to the US steel industry, which asked President George W. Bush to protect it from foreign imports.

Sometimes, however, local firms will seek protection from foreign competition even though they are profitable. Why? Because they don't want to give up any of their local market share—which will happen if more entrants are allowed into the industry. A good example is found in the courier wars now being fought in the United States. The three firms involved are FedEx, UPS, and DHL. The first two are US companies that collectively control 80 percent of the US market. The other is a German company that holds very little of the market. The total sales in 2006 of UPS are $47.5 billion; for FedEx, $32 billion; while for DHL there are no data except for its parent firm, Deutsche Post, at $79.5 billion.

FedEx operates out of Memphis, Tennessee, where it has a major distribution hub and a large number of aircraft to help meet its commitment of one-day delivery. UPS's airport hub is in Atlanta, Georgia, while DHL's hub is near Miami, Florida. All three firms do business in Europe, where they are also profitable. FedEx and UPS have been trying to prevent DHL from building an air fleet business in the United States to deliver packages and mail just like they do. Moreover, the two giant US firms have been receiving support from the Department of Transportation, which they have lobbied to prevent DHL from getting an air license.

One of the arguments made by FedEx and UPS is that although DHL Airways is 100 percent US owned, the parent company is controlled through an agreement by German owners with DHL's US subsidiary. This latter arrangement might seem a little strange, but a similar situation exists in Canada. The largest courier service in that country is Purolator, which is owned by the Canadian Post Office, a Crown monopoly. Yet despite this monopoly, both FedEx and UPS do quite well in Canada. US law, however, does not allow foreign entities to own more than 49 percent of the equity and 25 percent of the voting stock of a US air carrier.

Deutsche Post circumvented these regulations by selling a controlling stake of DHL Airways to an American

with large stakes in DHL's international operations. Critics claimed that DHL Airways had entered into an agreement with Deutsche Post to be a captive vendor and that in practical terms Deutsche Post owned DHL. The Department of Transportation then forced DHL Airways to expand its contracts outside of DHL. To this date, however, 90 percent of DHL Airways' business continues to be with DHL.

In 2003, DHL sought to expand its airline capacity by integrating Seattle-based Airborne's airline fleet. FedEx and UPS once again appealed to the Department of Transportation and to US politicians claiming that despite the new company being 100 percent owned by public shareholders, it would follow the same strategy that DHL Airways always did: working under an exclusive agreement with DHL. The Dutch TNT (with worldwide sales of $17 billion) is emerging in 2007 as another foreign competitor with its US hub in Chicago.

In 2003 John Bartholdi, a Georgia Tech logistics professor, and his 60 students began the annual Great Package Race to determine which carrier is most efficient in delivering packages to worldwide locations. DHL is frequently the winner.

Websites: www.fedex.com; www.dhl.com; www.ups.com; www.purolator.com.

Sources: "A Tricky Business," *The Economist*, June 30, 2001, pp. 55–56; "Transportation Labor Urges US Government to Revoke DHL's Air Freight Forward License," *TTD News*, January 30, 2001; Gene G. Marcial, "DHL Could Help Airborne Take Off," *Business Week*, July 9, 2001; Brian O'Reilly, "They've Got Mail," *Fortune*, February 7, 2000; "A Package with Strings Attached," *Economist.com*, March 27, 2003; "Airborne Fires Back at UPS, FedEx 'Duopoly'," *Puget Sound Business Journal*, April 7, 2003.

Foreign Sales Corporation Act
Legislation designed to allow US exporters to establish overseas affiliates and not pay taxes on the affiliates' income until the earnings are remitted to the parent company

Trade adjustment assistance
Assistance offered by the US government to US businesses and individuals harmed by competition from imports

The United States has also used negotiated agreements to limit the type or number of products entering the country. For example, a voluntary agreement with Japan restricts the number of cars imported to the United States. At the same time, exports are encouraged through legislation such as the **Foreign Sales Corporation Act**, which allows US exporters to establish overseas affiliates and not to pay taxes on the affiliates' income until the earnings are remitted to the parent company. The government also offers **trade adjustment assistance** to US businesses and individuals who are harmed by competition from imports. This aid takes such forms as loans for retooling and job counseling for those seeking alternative employment.

 Active learning check

Review your answer to Active Learning Case question 3 and make any changes you like. Then compare your answer to the one below.

3 In what way could the EU use trade barriers to protect its markets from foreign competitors? Who can be affected by these trade barriers?

The EU could take a number of steps to protect its markets from foreign competitors. Examples include establishing or increasing ad valorem tariffs, placing quantity limits on various imports, and limiting foreign direct investment. Of course, other countries could retaliate and take similar action against EU-produced goods, so the use of these trade barriers must be selective and should not be undertaken unless efforts at negotiated agreements prove fruitless.

NON-TARIFF BARRIERS TO TRADE

The economic effects of non-tariff barriers (NTBs) to trade are roughly similar to those of tariffs. They are inefficient distortions that reduce potential gains from trade. Table 6.2 lists a wide range of NTBs.

NTBs have gained prominence and importance in recent years as nations have begun resorting to them more frequently for protection. Sometimes they are not imposed by countries to interfere deliberately with trade.[17] Rather, they arise out of domestic policy and economic management. Examples include tax breaks to reduce regional income disparities or regulations designed to increase local purchasing or employment. These, in turn, result in a type of indirect export subsidy. Other NTBs are more blatant devices that restrict imports or foster exports.

Quotas

The most important NTBs are quotas that restrict imports to a particular level.[18] When a quota is imposed, domestic production generally increases and prices rise. As a result, the government usually ends up losing tariff revenues.

Historically, the GATT and WTO have prohibited import quotas except on agricultural products, as emergency measures, or when a country has short-run balance of payments problems. Countries have circumvented this regulation most notably for textiles, footwear, and automobiles by negotiating voluntary export restraint agreements that are useful in preventing retaliatory action by the importing country. In general, business would rather be protected by quotas than by tariffs. Under quotas, if future domestic demand is known,

Table 6.2 Common non-tariff barriers to trade

Specific limitation	Customs administrative rules	Government participation	Import charges
Quotas (including voluntary)	Valuation systems	Procurement policies	Import deposits
Import licenses	Antidumping rules	Export subsidies and incentives	Supplementary duties
Supplementary incentives	Tariff classifications	Countervailing duties	Import credits
Minimum import limits	Documentation needed	Domestic assistance programs	Variable levies
Embargoes	Fees	Trade diverting	Border levies
Sectoral bilateral agreements	Disparities in quality and testing standards		
Orderly marketing agreements	Packaging, labeling, and marketing standards		

companies can determine their future production levels. Under tariffs, domestic producers must estimate the elasticity of the demand curve for imported products and the future movements in world prices, which is a more difficult challenge.

"Buy national" restrictions

"Buy national" regulations require governments to give preference to domestic producers, sometimes to the complete exclusion of foreign firms. In Europe, for example, many of the telephone, telegraph, electric utility, airline, and railroad industries are government owned and buy from national firms only, thus closing a large market to exporters. On the other hand, countries like the United States have a similarly wide range of inefficient "Buy American" regulations at the national and state levels that discriminate against foreign suppliers. During the 1970s Tokyo Round of the GATT negotiations, a mild code to open up government contracts to foreign suppliers was negotiated. Only 28 governments have agreed to the WTO's Government Procurement Agreement and these must now publicize large procurement contracts to make public the winner's bid price or the basis for selecting the winning bid.

Customs valuation

Also during the GATT Tokyo Round, considerable progress was made in the area of customs valuation for the payment of duties. In the United States, there were nine valuation systems prior to the Tokyo Round. Value for duty is now generally based on the invoice cost, and the latitude of US customs to reclassify products has been reduced.

Technical barriers

Product and process standards for health, welfare, safety, quality, size, and measurements can create trade barriers by excluding products that do not meet them. Testing and certification procedures, such as testing only in the importing country and conducting on-site plant inspections, are cumbersome, time consuming, and expensive. The costs must be borne by the exporter prior to the foreign sale. National governments have the right and duty to protect their citizens by setting standards to prevent the sale of hazardous products. But such standards can also be used to impede trade. For example, at one point Japan excluded US-made baseball bats from the market because they did not meet the country's standard. No product produced outside Japan (even products made by foreign subsidiaries of Japanese MNEs) could bear the certification stamp of the Japanese Industrial Standard (JIS) or the Japanese Agricultural Standard (JAS), and selling in Japan without the JIS or JAS logo was difficult. Similarly, at one time the new regulations for automobile safety in the United States required that bumpers be above the height practical for imported sub-compact cars, thus creating a technical barrier for these car manufacturers. Today the new code on technical barriers to trade requires consultation between trading partners before a standard that impedes trade is put in place. The code also requires that testing and certification procedures treat imports and domestic goods equally and that the importing country accept certification testing conducted in the exporting country.

Antidumping legislation, subsidies, and countervailing duties

The GATT and WTO allow importing countries to protect their producers from unfair competition, such as "dumping" goods at extremely low prices in an effort to gain market share and to drive out local competition. Importing countries are allowed to impose additional duties on products that have received export subsidies or are "dumped." Before the duties are imposed, however, the country must show that its domestic industry has suffered "material" injury from dumped or subsidized imports. Although products at these artificially low prices provide consumers in the importing country with a "good buy," such competition is thought to be unfair to domestic producers who object to dumping (and also to subsidized imports that can be offset by "countervailing" duties) if the domestic market of the exporting country is closed to them. A good example is the US auto industry, which claims that some Japanese cars are cheaper in the US market than at home, while Japan continues to impede exports of US cars into Japan.

The GATT and the WTO have developed a code on countervailing duties and antidumping duties that now expedites the process of determining whether exports have been dumped or subsidized and whether the domestic industry has been injured. This subject is exceedingly complex. Here are some examples (and answers):

If the EU remits value-added taxes on exports by EU producers, is this a subsidy? (No)

If Canada subsidizes production in a specific sector in one of its depressed regions for domestic purposes, are the exports of a subsidized firm subject to countervailing action? (Yes)

If the British government subsidizes the British steel industry and its losses incurred by selling at home and abroad at prices below full cost, are its exports subject to antidumping or to countervailing duties? (Maybe, sometimes)

The problem is complex because of the difficulty in determining what material injury is and how it should be measured. This area is likely to be a point of contention for years to come.

Agricultural products

Trade in agricultural products is highly regulated by both quotas and fixed and variable tariffs. Domestic producers in most industrialized countries are often highly subsidized both directly and by artificially high domestic prices. Agricultural exports are often subsidized as well. And the EU flatly refused to discuss its Common Agricultural Policy (CAP) at the

Tokyo Round. The CAP sets variable tariffs on imports to maintain high domestic prices by excluding or impeding imports. Major reforms in the CAP are now underway that will see continuing support for farmers but independently of production volumes. This is expected to improve the EU's negotiating position at the WTO. The United States is not without guilt in this area, however, since it also subsidizes the export of many agricultural products. The countries most affected by these subsidies are less developed countries with abundant and inexpensive labor and land and thus a competitive advantage in agricultural products. Agricultural subsidies have often stalled trade talks as these countries refused to further liberalize while developed countries continued to subsidize agriculture.

Export restraints

Over the vigorous objections of countries exporting natural resources, the GATT (and WTO) rounds have moved to tighten the conditions under which exports could be restrained. In general, world tariffs increase with the level of processing; for example, import duties increase as copper is processed from concentrate to blister, to refined copper, to copper wire and bars, to copper pots and pans. This tariff structure makes upgrading of natural resources in the producing country difficult. During the Tokyo Round, natural resource-producing countries were largely unsuccessful in their attempts to harmonize tariffs on a sectoral basis in order to increase their ability to upgrade prior to export. However, they did argue successfully for their right to restrict exports to induce further domestic processing.

OTHER ECONOMIC DEVELOPMENTS

In addition to the above, other economic developments warrant consideration. These include countertrade, trade in services, and free trade zones.

Countertrade

Countertrade
Barter trade in which the exporting firm receives payment in products from the importing country

Countertrade is essentially barter trade in which the exporting firm receives payment in terms of products from the importing country. Countertrade is important to the airline industry (for example, the purchase of Boeing 747s by British Airways if Boeing uses Rolls Royce engines) and in defense (for example, the purchase of US jet fighters by Canada if some of the parts are locally sourced in Canada). Barter sometimes takes the form of a buyback in which the exporter agrees to take products that are locally produced.

Countertrade tends to decrease the efficiency of world trade because it substitutes barter for the exchange of goods by the price system. For example, a US exporter of machinery to Indonesia may have to take payment in an "equivalent value" of palm oil or rattan. The exporting firm will then either have to sell these products, in which it has no expertise itself, or sell them through a broker or other firm. Some party to the trade—exporter, importer, or consumer—must bear these additional costs. Despite such obvious inefficiencies, countertrade appears likely to continue as an increasingly important factor in the international trade environment of the twenty-first century.

In one type of situation, however, countertrade may be beneficial. For example, if a US producer of textile machinery exports to China and agrees to take payment in the form of textile products, importers in the United States may perceive a lower risk of variability in product quality and delivery schedules (as a result of US technology and management), and the Chinese may perceive a lower risk of product failure in buying the machinery since the selling firm will not be "paid" unless the machinery performs to specifications.

Trade in services

International trade in services has received relatively little attention from governments or trade economists during trade negotiations. Reliable statistics are seldom collected. However, as high-income countries move toward a service economy, trade in services has grown and become a significant component of the current accounts of many countries.

In 2006, the United States exported goods worth $1.024 trillion and imported goods worth $1.860 trillion, which left a deficit of $836 billion on merchandise trade. In services it exported $413 billion and imported $342 billion for a trade surplus of $71 billion that partly offset its merchandise trade deficit. And, it had a deficit of $7.3 billion in the net income receipts from US FDI abroad. Thus, the net deficit on these three accounts for the United States in 2006 was $856.7 billion. Details of the US goods, services, and FDI accounts appear in Table 6.3. (The balance of payments account will be explained in the Appendix of this chapter.)

The flow of services across/among countries is highly regulated. Internationally traded services such as banking, investment income, insurance, media, transportation, advertising, accounting, travel, and technology licensing are subject to a host of national and international regulations for economic, social, cultural, and political reasons. In 1995, the General Agreement on Trade in Services (GATS) came into effect. It covers all services except those provided by the government and those related to air traffic. Member countries are not forced to open all their service industries but can choose those areas for which they want to guarantee access to foreigners and, within a framework, how much access they want to provide. For example, a host nation might limit the scope of a foreign bank's operation through the use of licenses or by setting a maximum number of allowable branches. As of January 2000, more than 140 WTO members started negotiating to further liberalize services.

Whatever forum is used, negotiating reductions in service trade barriers will be difficult, complex, and lengthy. The barriers are often difficult to list, much less quantify for purposes of negotiation. And the issues are often highly charged and not subject to rational

Table 6.3 Overview of the US balance of current account, 2006, preliminary

Items	Credits (1) (billions of US $)	Debits (2) (billions of US $)	Balance (1) – (2)
Trade of goods and services	1,436.8	2,202.1	(765.3)
Goods, balance of payments basis	1,023.7	1,859.7	(836.0)
Services	413.1	342.4	70.7
Direct defense expenditures	16.7	31.2	(14.5)
Travel	85.7	73.3	12.4
Passenger fares	22.1	27.3	(5.2)
Other transportation	48.2	65.6	(17.4)
Royalties and license fees	62.1	26.5	35.6
Other private services	177.3	114.5	62.8
US government miscellaneous services	1.1	4.0	(2.9)
Income receipts	622.0	629.3	(7.3)
FDI income	619.1	619.9	(0.8)
Direct investment receipts/payments	295.9	145.6	150.3
Other private receipts	320.8	329.2	(8.4)
US government receipts	2.4	145.1	(142.7)
Compensation of employees	2.9	9.4	(6.5)
Unilateral current transfers, net		84.1	(84.1)
Total	2,058.8	2,915.5	(856.7)

Source: Adapted from BEA, *Survey of Current Business*, June 2007, Table 2 International transactions.

analysis. For example, Canada imposes Canadian content requirements on television, radio, and print media to foster a "national cultural identity," to protect its cultural heritage, and to protect the domestic arts, theater, and movie industries. A government that reduced these trade barriers or even agreed to negotiate them would be in trouble with the (protected) Canadian media, as well as with the general public.

Free trade zones

Free trade zone
A designated area where importers can defer payment of customs duty while further processing of products takes place (same as a foreign trade zone)

A **free trade zone** is a designated area where importers can defer payment of customs duty while products are processed further (same as a foreign trade zone). Thus, the free trade zone serves as an "offshore assembly plant," employing local workers and using local financing for a tax-exempt commercial activity. The economic activity takes place in a restricted area such as an industrial park, because the land is often being supplied at a subsidized rate by a local host government that is interested in the zone's potential employment benefits.

To be effective, free trade zones must be strategically located either at or near an international port, on major shipping routes, or with easy access to a major airport. Important factors in the location include the availability of utilities, banking and telecom services, and a commercial infrastructure.

More than 400 free trade zones exist in the world today, often encompassing entire cities, such as Hong Kong and Singapore. More than two-thirds are situated in developing countries, and most of their future growth is expected to occur there.

The advantages offered by free trade zones are numerous and mutually beneficial to all stakeholders. For private firms, the zones offer three major attractions. First, the firm pays the customs duty (tariff) only when the goods are ready to market. Second, manufacturing costs are lower because no taxes are levied. Third, while in the zone the manufacturer has the opportunity to repackage the goods, grade them, and check for spoilage. Secondary benefits to firms take the form of reduced insurance premiums (since these are based on duty-free values), reduced fines for improperly marked merchandise (since the good can be inspected in a zone prior to customers' scrutiny), and added protection against theft (resulting from security measures in the bonded warehouses).

At the state and local levels, advantages can be realized in terms of commercial services. On a more global level, free trade zones enable domestic importing companies to compete more readily with foreign producers or subsidiaries of MNEs, thereby increasing participation in world trade. Favorable effects are felt on the balance of payments because more economic activity occurs and net capital outflow is reduced. Finally, the business climate is improved due to reduced bureaucracy and resultant savings to business capital, currently inaccessible because of the delay in paying duties and tariffs. A free trade zone is a step toward free trade and can be an important signal by government to business that the economy is opening up. Opportunity replaces regulation, and growth of economic activity should result.

Before the establishment of more free trade zones becomes fully accepted and encouraged, governments must be convinced of their many economic benefits. Free trade zones are a vital necessity if nations are to remain competitive on an international scale. Not only will existing companies benefit from their use, but new industries will be attracted, keeping up the same benefits of world trade.

Maquiladora **industry**
A free trade zone that has sprung up along the US–Mexican border for the purpose of producing goods and then shipping them between the two countries

The *maquiladora* **industry** along the US–Mexican border is an excellent example of a free trade zone. The low wage rate in Mexico and the NAFTA of 1994 make the *maquiladora* region both accessible and important to labor-intensive firms in the United States and Canada. From only 12 *maquiladora* plants in 1965, approximately 3,000 existed in 2000. The *maquiladora* industry has been so successful that only oil earns Mexico more foreign currency today.

No Mexican taxes are paid on goods processed within the *maquiladoras*. Foreign companies doing such processing can benefit from lower wages and land costs than those in the United States as they increase the value added to their products. In return, Mexico attracts FDI into permanent plants, creates jobs, and collects taxes on any final products sold to the foreign firms, or within Mexico. Even though the United States has several hundred free trade zones of its own, many near seaports or airfields, these lack the low-wage workers of their Mexican counterparts.

Canada does not have free trade zones, but the federal government allows duty drawbacks, which arguably offer many of the same advantages. Unfortunately, these drawbacks, which are repayments of customs duties, apply retroactively and involve enough paperwork to discourage all but the largest or most dedicated organizations. As such, NAFTA and the lower-wage labor in Mexico have attracted Canadian firms producing labor-intensive products. Free trade zones exist in many other parts of the world than North America, and the advantages of these zones are enjoyed by businesses worldwide.[19]

KEY POINTS

1 International economics is the branch of economics concerned with the purchase and sale of foreign goods and services. This includes consideration of areas such as international trade, balance of payments, and barriers to trade.

2 A number of international trade theories help to explain why nations trade. These include the theory of absolute advantage, the theory of comparative advantage, the factor endowment theory, the Leontief paradox, and the international product life cycle theory. While no one theory offers a complete explanation of why nations trade, they collectively provide important insights into the area. Other key considerations that offer explanations for why nations trade include monetary currency valuation and consumer tastes.

3 There are a number of barriers to trade. Some of the most common include price-based barriers, quantity limits, international price fixing, non-tariff barriers, financial limits, and foreign investment controls.

4 Although tariffs are often introduced to maintain local jobs and assist infant industries, they are inefficient. This economic inefficiency results in higher prices of imported goods for the consumers. The redistribution of resources from more efficient industry further adds to the cost of a tariff. Such costs do not occur under free trade.

5 Non-tariff barriers (NTBs) provide similar economic inefficiencies to tariffs. Unlike tariffs, however, NTBs are not imposed by nations to interfere deliberately with trade; they arise out of domestic policy. There are several types of NTBs, including quotas, "Buy national" restrictions, technical barriers, and export restraints.

6 Countertrade is a form of barter trade in which the exporting firm receives payments in terms of products produced in the importing country. It is most pronounced in East–West trade, and although it may be beneficial to the trading partners, it increases the inefficiencies in the world trade system, which in turn raises costs and decreases trade volume.

7 Services are an important but somewhat misunderstood component of trade. Despite the trade of services in the billions of dollars among high-income countries, regulation has been outside the mandate of GATT. As services increase in importance, future discussion will take place concerning whether an international organization like GATT will carry the mandate to regulate this type of trade.

8 A free trade zone is a designated area where importers can defer payment of customs duty while further processing of products takes place. In essence, it is an offshore assembly plant. The majority of these areas exists in developing countries and handles approximately 20 percent of worldwide trade. Free trade zones are advantageous to all because they provide benefits such as increased employment and lower business costs.

Key terms

- international trade
- mercantilism
- neo-mercantilism
- theory of absolute advantage
- theory of comparative advantage
- factor endowment theory
- Heckscher–Ohlin theory
- Leontief paradox
- international product life cycle (IPLC) theory
- monetary exchange rate
- quotas
- embargo
- cartel
- non-tariff barriers
- exchange controls
- foreign investment controls
- tariff
- import tariff
- export tariff
- transit tariff
- specific duty
- ad valorem duty
- compound duty
- dumping
- Caribbean Basin Initiative
- Foreign Sales Corporation Act
- trade adjustment assistance
- countertrade
- free trade zone
- *maquiladora* industry

Review and discussion questions

1 Why is it difficult to solve international economic problems in the short run?

2 What is the supposed economic benefit of embracing mercantilism as an international trade theory? Are there many disadvantages to the use of this theory?

3 How is the theory of absolute advantage similar to that of comparative advantage? How is it different?

4 In what way does factor endowment theory help explain why nations trade? How does the Leontief paradox modify this theory?

5 If an innovating country develops a new technologically superior product, how long will it be before the country begins exporting the product? At what point will the country begin importing the product?

6 Of what value is the international product life cycle theory in helping to understand why nations trade?

7 How does each of the following trade barriers work: price-based barriers, quantity limits, international price fixing, non-tariff barriers, financial limits, and foreign investment controls?

8 What are some of the reasons for trade barriers? Identify and describe five.

9 How does the United States try to encourage exports? Identify and describe two ways.

10 Non-tariff barriers have become increasingly predominant in recent years. Describe a non-tariff barrier, and list four types, explaining how the United States does or could use such a device.

11 How does countertrade work? Is it an efficient economic concept?

12 What is a free trade zone? Is it an efficient economic concept?

13 What are two future problems and challenges that will have to be addressed by the international monetary system? Describe each.

14 What is meant by the term *balance of payments*?

15 What are the three major accounts in the balance of payments?

16 How would the following transactions be recorded in the IMF balance of payments?
   a IBM in New York has sold an $8 million mainframe computer to an insurance company in Singapore and has been paid with a check drawn on a Singapore bank.
   b A private investor in San Francisco has received dividends of $80,000 for stock she holds in a British firm.
   c The US government has provided $60 million of food and medical supplies for Kurdish refugees in Turkey.
   d The Walt Disney Company has invested $50 million in a theme park outside Paris, France.

Real Case

Job losses and offshoring to China

It was not a difficult choice to make. Over the last 10 years, US imports of manufactured goods from China shot up. Cheap labor—Chinese labor is six times lower than Mexican labor—accounts for this. Continuing manufacturing operations in the United States and remaining price competitive is simply not feasible. When jobs are outsourced across national borders, e.g. from the United States to China, this is called offshoring.

Competition on quality, which can shelter domestic manufacturing from outsourcing to developing countries, was not an alternative because Chinese products for export are usually as good (although not in toys as Mattel found in 2007). When high labor intensity is tied to quality, the Chinese can outdo Western industrialized countries. Another factor is that the Chinese have a combination of highly skilled management and low-skilled labor, ensuring that production is efficient and that quality standards are met. This ability to produce high-quality goods is also what allows China to move from export manufacturing of Christmas decorations, toys, footwear, and clothing to household, consumer appliances, and, increasingly, the IT manufacturing sector.

National Presto, a US firm that makes high-quality pressure cookers and electric frying pans, had a difficult decision to make in the early 2000s. It could either offshore its production to China or see its market share continue to deteriorate. In 2002, the company closed plants in Mississippi and New Mexico, reducing its US workforce to less than half, and expanded its production in China. By 2003, all significant products marketed by the company were made in China.

Like many other US, European, and Japanese companies, National Presto uses an agent in Hong Kong to subcontract production to manufacturing plants in mainland China. Larger companies like Motorola, Philips, IBM, Toshiba, and GE have more control over their manufacturing plants in China. Kyocera of Japan, for example, invested $90 million in the early 2000s to construct a high-tech industrial park in Shilong Town of Dongguan City, Guangdong Province. Only 20 years ago Guangdong was dominated by paddy fields; today it is China's largest manufacturing cluster.

Proponents of free trade argue that political rhetoric against trade with China is meant to appease US fears of job losses. Yet, as seen in the following table, under 2 percent of all job losses in the United States in the first quarter of 2007 were the result of overseas relocation. While some argue that this percentage is undervalued because it does not take into consideration potential job gains that never materialized, others argue that given economic conditions there was no assurance that firms that created new jobs in China would have chosen to create these jobs in the United States if offshoring to China had not been a possibility.

International Business

Outsourcing and job losses in the United States, first quarter of 2007

Reasons for job losses	Losses	% of total
Overseas relocation	1,830	1.8
Domestic relocation	5,506	5.4
Other	95,431	92.9
Total, private non-farm sector	102,767	100.0

Note: Data only cover layoffs in companies with at least 50 workers, who have filed for unemployment insurance, for at least 50 workers, and where unemployment lasted more than 30 days.

Source: US Bureau of Labor Statistics, "Extended Mass Layoffs Associated with Domestic and Overseas Relocations," May 16, 2007.

China has become the world's largest manufacturer, ahead of the United States, Japan, and Germany. It has outpaced Japan to become the country having the largest trade surplus with the United States. US politicians and lobby groups blame Chinese protectionist practices for the growing trade deficit between the two nations, which in 2003 was estimated at $124 billion. Among the barriers the United States claims prevent a free flow of its goods to China are import barriers, unclear legal provisions applied in a discriminatory manner against US imports, and an undervalued yuan. The last one has generated the most controversy in the last few years. The Chinese yuan has been fixed at 8.28 to the dollar since 1994, a rate that critics argue to be up to 40 percent undervalued. Yet economists do not all agree that the yuan is undervalued. Some fear that a sharp deterioration would hurt not only the Chinese economy but also those trading partners that are most heavily dependent on Chinese imports.

Sources: "Chinese Trade Reform 'Is Failing'," *BBC News*, April 1, 2004; "China Defiant on Currency Exchange," *BBC News*, September 2, 2003; Mary Hennock, "China: The World's Factory Floor," *BBC News*, November 11, 2002; www.worldbank.com; "Kyocera to Build High-Tech Industrial Park in Dongguan," *People's Daily*, September 13, 2000.

1 Does the theory of comparative advantage apply to China's trade with industrialized countries? How?

2 How does the factor endowment theory apply to China's trade with industrialized countries?

3 Are any of the countries mentioned operating in autarky?

4 How can distribution of gains from free trade cause much of the political debate regarding trade with China?

Real Case

Dumping on trade complaints

One of the biggest problems in international trade is the ability of domestic producers to lobby their home governments to erect barriers to trade. In the past, the textile, apparel, and shoe industries were able to obtain protection from cheaper imports through tariffs, quotas, and special measures. Now multilateral trade agreements under the GATT and WTO (and also regional and bilateral agreements such as NAFTA and the emerging Asian Pacific Economic Cooperation forum) outlaw such blatant instruments of protection. However, these agreements have been re-placed by more subtle ones.

Prominent as a new type of protectionist device is the use of "unfair trade laws," especially antidumping (AD) and countervailing duty (CVD) actions. The economic logic of AD and CVD makes some sense. It is unfair for a foreign producer to "dump" a product in your country below its price in the home country, or below the cost of producing it. Similarly, subsidized foreign products should be offset by a CVD of equivalent effect. The problem, however, lies with the administration of the trade laws, which is subject to political lobbying.

A variety of studies have found that the bureaucrats who administer AD and CVD laws are subject to capture by the home industries, who then use AD and CVD cases as harassment tools against often economically efficient foreign rival producers. For example, Rugman and Anderson (1987) found that the US administration of AD and CVD was used in a biased manner against Canadian producers, especially in resource-based industries such as softwood lumber, fishing, and agriculture. Thus, in the Canadian–US Free Trade Agreement of 1989, and again in NAFTA, five-person binational panels of trade law experts were set up to review the decision of the US (and Canadian) trade law agencies.

In a subsequent study, Rugman and Anderson (1997) found that these binational panels were able to remand back (i.e. successfully challenge) the decision of the US agencies twice as often in cases involving Canada as in AD and CVD cases involving the rest of the world. In related work researchers have found that the EU is just as bad as the United States when it comes to taking questionable AD measures, especially against Asian countries. Indeed, one of the unresolved problems is how smaller countries can secure access to the protected markets of triad economies such as the United States and the EU. In Japan's case, there are similar arguments (including those from its triad rivals) that it has entry barriers in place preventing market access.

Website: www.wto.org.

Sources: Andrew D. M. Anderson, *Seeking Common Ground: Canada–US Trade Dispute Settlement Policies in the Nineties* (Boulder, CO: Westview Press, 1995); Alan M. Rugman, *Multinational Enterprises and Trade Policy* (Cheltenham: Edward Elgar, 1996); Alan M. Rugman and Andrew D. M. Anderson, *Administered Protection in America* (London and New York: Routledge, 1987); Alan M. Rugman and Andrew D. M. Anderson, "NAFTA and the Dispute Settlement Mechanisms," *The World Economy*, December 1997, pp. 935–950; Alan M. Rugman and Michael Gestrin, "EC Anti-Dumping Laws as a Barrier to Trade," *European Management Journal*, vol. 9, no. 4 (December 1991), pp. 475–482.

1 Why are AD and CVD measures brought and imposed?

2 What is the impact on a firm from a non-triad country if it faces an AD or CVD case in its major market?

3 What is the solution to the abusive use of AD and CVD measures by triad economies?

ENDNOTES

1 Asra Q. Nomani and Douglas Lavin, "US and Japan Nearing Accord in Trade Dispute," *Wall Street Journal*, March 10, 1994, p. A3; and Richard McGregor, "Beans are on the Beijing Menu as Bush Prepares to Talk Trade," *FT.com*, February 21, 2002.

2 Douglas Harbrecht et al., "Tough Talk," *Business Week*, February 20, 1994, pp. 26–28.

3 See, for example, Dana Weschler Linden, "Dreary Days in the Dismal Science," *Forbes*, January 21, 1991, pp. 68–71.

4 Also see Steven Greenhouse, "French Shift on State-Owned Sector," *New York Times*, April 8, 1991, p. C2.

5 For additional insights into trade theory, see Nicolas Schmitt, "New International Trade Theories and Europe 1991: Some Results Relevant for EFTA Countries," *Journal of Common Market Studies*, September 1990, pp. 53–74.

6 "Tested by the Mighty Euro," *Economist.com*, May 18, 2004.

7 See Richard W. Stevenson, "East Europe Says Barriers to Trade Hurt Its Economies," *New York Times*, January 25, 1993, pp. A1, C8.

8 Lucy Walker, "Sir Leon's Cartel Busters Take to the Road Again," *The European*, April 12–14, 1991, p. 25.

9 Edmund Faltermayer, "Is 'Made in the USA' Fading Away?" *Fortune*, September 24, 1990, p. 73.

10 Edward Alden and Robert Shrimsley, "EU Set to Retaliate if US Imposes Steel Tariffs," *Financial Times*, March 4, 2002.

11 See, for example, Doron P. Levin, "Honda to Hold Base Price on Accord Model," *New York Times*, September 2, 1993, p. C3.

12 Keith Bradsher, "Kodak Is Seeking Big Tariff on Fuji," *New York Times*, September 1, 1993, pp. A1, C2.

13 See, for example, Robert Cohen, "Grumbling over GATT," *New York Times*, July 3, 1993, p. 13.

14 Ed Gresser, "Tariffs Biggest US Tax on the Poor," *Reuters*, September 10, 2002.

15 See, for example, Chris Adams, "Ailing Steel Industry Launches a Battle Against Imports," *Wall Street Journal*, October 1, 1998, p. B4; and "Steel Vice," *Wall Street Journal*, October 1, 1998, p. A22.

16 As an example, see Clyde H. Farnsworth, "US Slows Computer for Brazil," *International Herald Tribune*, April 13–14, 1991, p. 5.

17 Claude Barfield, "Nerves of Steel," *Financial Times*, March 1, 2002.

18 Sometimes these are voluntary quotas, as seen in Andrew Pollack, "Japan Takes a Pre-emptive Step on Auto Exports," *New York Times*, January 9, 1993, pp. 17, 26.

19 Anthony DePalma, "Trade Pact Is Spurring Mexican Deals in the US," *New York Times*, March 17, 1994, pp. C1, 3.

ADDITIONAL BIBLIOGRAPHY

Anderson, Andrew D. M. *Seeking Common Ground: Canada–US Trade Disputes* (Boulder, CO: Westview Press, 1995).

Baggs, Jen and Brander, James A. "Trade Liberalization, Profitability, and Financial Leverage," *Journal of International Business Studies*, vol. 37, no. 2 (March 2006).

Baldauf, Artur. "Examining Determinants of Export Performance in Small Open Economies," *Journal of World Business*, vol. 35, no. 1 (Spring 2000).

Brewer, Thomas L. and Young, Stephen. *The Multinational Investment System and Multinational Enterprises* (Oxford: Oxford University Press, 2000).

Brewer, Thomas L. and Young, Stephen. "Multilateral Institutions and Policies: Their Implications for Multinational Business Strategy," in Alan M. Rugman and Thomas L. Brewer (eds.), *The Oxford Handbook of International Business* (Oxford: Oxford University Press, 2001).

Buckley, Peter J. "Government Policy Responses to Strategic Rent Seeking Transnational Corporations," *Transnational Corporations*, vol. 5, no. 2 (August 1996).

Deutsch, Klaus Gunter and Speyer, Bernhard (eds.). *The World Trade Organization Millennium Round* (London: Routledge, 2001).

Dunning, John H. and Mucchielli, Jean-Louis (eds.). *Multinational Firms: The Global-Local Dilemma* (London: Routledge, 2002).

Hennart, Jean-François. "Some Empirical Dimensions of Countertrade," *Journal of International Business Studies*, vol. 21, no. 2 (Second Quarter 1990).

Koka, Balaji R., Prescott, John E. and Madhavan, Ravindranath. "Contagion Influence on Trade and Investment Policy: A Network Perspective," *Journal of International Business Studies*, vol. 30, no. 1 (Spring 1999).

Markusen, James R. "International Trade Theory and International Business," in Alan M. Rugman and Thomas L. Brewer (eds.), *The Oxford Handbook of International Business* (Oxford: Oxford University Press, 2001).

Miller, Janice S., Hom, Peter W. and R. Gomez-Mejia, Luis. "The High Cost of Low Wages: Does Maquiladora Compensation Reduce Turnover?" *Journal of International Business Studies*, vol. 32, no. 3 (Fall 2001).

Neale, Charles W., Shipley, David D. and Dodds, J. Colin. "The Countertrading Experience of British and Canadian Firms," *Management International Review*, vol. 31, no. 1 (First Quarter 1991).

Ostry, Sylvia. *The Post-Cold War Trading System* (Chicago: University of Chicago Press, 1997).

Ostry, Sylvia. "The Multilateral Trading System," in Alan M. Rugman and Thomas L. Brewer (eds.), *The Oxford Handbook of International Business* (Oxford: Oxford University Press, 2001).

Ramstetter, Eric D. "Export Performance and Foreign Affiliate Activity in Japan's Large Machinery Firms," *Transnational Corporations*, vol. 6, no. 3 (December 1997).

Robin, Donald P. and Sawyer, W. Charles. "The Ethics of Antidumping Petitions," *Journal of World Business*, vol. 33, no. 3 (Fall 1998).

Robock, Stefan H. "The Export Myopia of US Multinationals: An Overlooked Opportunity for Creating US Manufacturing Jobs," *Columbia Journal of World Business*, vol. 28, no. 2 (Summer 1993).

Rugman, Alan M. *Multinational Enterprises and Trade Policy* (Cheltenham: Edward Elgar, 1996).

Rugman, Alan M. and Anderson, Andrew. *Administered Protection in America* (London: Croom Helm and New York: Methuen, 1987).

Rugman, Alan M. and Boyd, Gavin (eds.). *The World Trade Organization in the New Global Economy* (Cheltenham: Edward Elgar, 2001).

Rugman, Alan M. and Gestrin, Michael. "US Trade Laws as Barriers to Globalization," in Tamir Agmon and Richard Drobnick (eds.), *Small Firms in Global Competition* (New York: Oxford University Press, 1994).

Rugman, Alan M. and Verbeke, Alain. *Global Corporate Strategy and Trade Policy* (London and New York: Routledge, 1990).

Rugman, Alan M. and Verbeke, Alain. "Strategic Trade Policy Is Not Good Strategy," *Hitotsubashi Journal of Commerce and Management*, vol. 25, no. 1 (December 1990).

Rugman, Alan M. and Verbeke, Alain. "Location, Competitiveness, and the Multinational Enterprise," in Alan M. Rugman and Thomas L. Brewer (eds.), *The Oxford Handbook of International Business* (Oxford: Oxford University Press, 2001).

Sampson, Gary P. (ed.). *The Role of the World Trade Organization in Global Governance* (Tokyo, New York, Paris: United Nations University Press, 2001).

Zhang, Chun, Cavusgil, S. Tamer and Roath, Anthony, S. "Manufacturer Governance of Foreign Distributor Relationships: Do Relational Norms Enhance Competitiveness in the Export Market?" *Journal of International Business Studies*, vol. 34, no. 6 (November 2003).

How well do we keep track of the millions of transactions that take place annually among exporters and importers, international banks, and multinational companies? The bankers who tabulate the foreign exchange dealings of their own banks are only a part of the picture. How well can we account for the part of direct investment that occurs through overseas borrowing, yet affects the home country's international economic position? Even more simply, how well can we measure "international" transactions that are simply transfers of funds from the account of an importer to the account of a foreign exporter in the same bank?

The realistic answer to these questions is: not very well. National governments create elaborate accounts for the transactions between their residents and foreign residents, but it is often very difficult to obtain full and accurate information. Putting that problem aside for the moment, let us consider the methods that governments use to record each country's international transactions.

Balance of payments (BOP)
The value of all transactions between a country's residents and the rest of the world; the three broad BOP categories are the current account, capital account, and official reserves

The most widely used measure of international economic transactions for any country is the **balance of payments (BOP)**. This record attempts to measure the full value of the transactions between residents of one country and residents of the rest of the world for some time period, typically one year. The balance of payments is a flow concept, in that it records flows of goods, services, and claims between countries over a period of time, rather than a stock of accumulated funds or products. It is a value concept, in that all the items recorded receive a monetary value, denominated in the given country's currency at the time of those transactions. *The balance of payments thus is a record of the value of all the economic transactions between residents of one country and residents of all other countries during a given time period.*

Why do we worry about measuring these transactions? We do so because if a country records a substantial imbalance between inflows and outflows of goods and services for an extended period of time, some means of financing or adjusting away the imbalance must be found. For example, if the Eurozone countries record a persistent trade deficit with China for several years, there will be pressure either to devalue the euro relative to the Chinese currency, the renminbi, or for Chinese investors to place large and continuing investments into euro-denominated securities. This pressure presents both a political outcome (pressure on the Chinese government to revalue the renminbi) and an economic outcome (pressure on the euro to devalue and on European producers to lower their costs, perhaps by producing in China).

So, the importance of the balance of payments is not only macroeconomic, in the domain of government accountants, but also managerial, since an imbalance provides guidance to managers about expected government policies as well as about opportunities to take advantage of currency opportunities. Since the relatively open foreign exchange markets of many countries today leave the exchange rate substantially to supply and demand, the balance of payments is an indicator of exactly that supply and demand for a country's currency that will lead to changes in the exchange rate.

The supply and demand for a currency come from both trade flows (exports and imports) and capital flows (investments and borrowing). So, the balance of payments implications for exchange rates must include both sides of the story, the "real" flows and the financial flows.

Balance of payments accounting

There is no such thing as the balance of payments, since the accounts are organized in a double-entry bookkeeping system, and for every debit entry there is a credit entry of equal value. There are half a dozen BOP measures, which group some international transactions together and leave others in a second, "everything else" category. In each case the intent is to place the fundamental economic causes of transactions in the first group and leave the payments for them in the second group. In the actual accounts, the former transactions are listed "above the line," and the payments are left "below the line."

Current account

The **current account** consists of merchandise trade, services, and unilateral transfers. (See Table 6A, parts A and B.)

Merchandise trade is typically the first part of the current account. It receives more attention than any of the other accounts because this is where the imports and exports of goods are reported, and these are often the largest single component of all international transactions. In this account, sales of goods to foreigners (exports) are reported as credits

Table 6A Balance of payments: IMF presentation

	Debits	Credits
I Current account		
A Goods, services, and income:		
1 Merchandise	Imports from foreign sources (acquisition of goods)	Exports to foreign destinations (provision of goods)
Trade balance		
2 Shipment and other transportation	Payments to foreigners for freight and insurance on international shipments; for ship repair, stores, and supplies; and international passenger fares	Receipts by residents from foreigners for services provided
3 Travel	Expenditures by residents (including internal transportation) when traveling in a foreign country	Receipts by residents for goods and services (including internal transportation) sold to foreign travelers in reporting country
4 Investment income	Profits of foreign direct investments in reporting country, including reinvested earnings; income paid to foreigners as interest, dividends, etc.	Profits of direct investments by residents in foreign countries, including reinvested earnings; income received by residents from abroad as interest, dividends, etc.
5 Other official	Foreign purchases by government not included elsewhere; personal expenditures of government civilian and military personnel stationed in foreign countries	Expenditures of foreign governments for goods and services, not included elsewhere; personal expenditures of foreign civilian and military personnel stationed in reporting country
6 Other private	Payments to foreigners for management fees, royalties, film rentals, construction, etc.	Receipts from foreigners for management fees, royalties, film rentals, construction, etc.
Goods, services, and income balance		
B Unilateral transfers:		
1 Private	Payments in cash and kind by residents to foreigners without a quid pro quo such as charitable gifts and gifts by migrants to their families	Receipts in cash and kind by residents from foreigners, individuals, or governments without a quid pro quo
2 Official	Transfers by government of reporting country for pensions, reparations, and grants for economic and military aid	Transfers received by government from foreigners in the form of goods, services, or cash as gifts or grants. Also tax receipts from non-residents
Current account balance		

	Debits	Credits
II Capital account		
C Capital, excluding reserves:		
1 Direct investment	(a) Increased investment in foreign enterprises controlled by residents, including reinvestment of earnings	(a) Decreased investment in foreign enterprises controlled by residents
	(b) Decreases in investment by residents in domestic enterprises controlled by foreigners	(b) Increases in investment in domestic enterprises by foreigners
2 Portfolio investment	(a) Increases in investment by residents in foreign securities	(a) Decreases in investments by residents in foreign securities
	(b) Decreases in investment by foreigners in domestic securities such as bonds and corporate equities	(b) Increases in investment by foreigners in domestic securities
3 Other long-term, official	(a) Loans to foreigners	(a) Foreign loan reductions
	(b) Redemption or purchase from foreigners of government securities	(b) Sales to foreigners of government securities
4 Other long-term, private	(a) Long-term loans to foreigners by resident banks and private parties	(a) Long-term loans by foreigners to resident banks or private parties
	(b) Loan repayments by residents to foreign banks or private parties	(b) Loan repayments by foreigners to residents
5 Other short-term, official	(a) Short-term loans to foreigners by central government	(a) Short-term loans to resident central government by foreigners
	(b) Purchase from foreigners of government securities, decrease in liabilities constituting reserves of foreign authorities	(b) Foreign sales of short-term resident government securities, increases in liabilities constituting reserves of foreign authorities
6 Other short-term, private	(a) Increases in short-term foreign assets held by residents	(a) Decreases in short-term foreign assets held by residents. Increase in foreign liabilities of residents
	(b) Decreases in domestic assets held by foreigners, such as bank deposits, currencies, debts to banks, and commercial claims	(b) Increase in domestic short-term assets held by foreigners or decrease in short-term domestic liabilities to foreigners
III Reserves		
D Reserves:		
1 Monetary gold	Increases in holdings of gold, SDRs, foreign convertible currencies by monetary authorities; decreases in liabilities to IMF or increase in IMF assets position	Decreases in holdings of gold, SDRs, foreign convertible currencies by monetary authorities; increases in liabilities to IMF or decrease in IMF assets position
2 Special drawing rights (SDRs)		
3 IMF reserve position		
4 Foreign exchange assets		
E Net errors and omissions:	Net understatement of recorded debts or overstatement of recorded credits	Net understatement of recorded debts or overstatement of recorded credits
Balances:		
Balances on merchandise trade	A-1 credits minus A-1 debits	
Balance on goods, services, and income	A-1 through A-6 credits minus A-1 through A-6 debits	
Balance on current account	A and B credits minus A and B debits	

because they are a source of funds or a claim against the purchasing country. Conversely, purchases of goods from overseas (imports) are recorded as debits because they use funds. This payment can be made by either reducing current claims on foreigners or increasing foreign liabilities.

Merchandise trade transactions can affect a country's BOP in a number of ways. Assume that Nissan Motor of Japan has sold General Motors in the United States $600,000 worth of engines and these engines will be paid for from GM's account in a Detroit bank. In this case the imports are a debit to the current account (A-1) and a credit to the "other short-term, private" capital account (C-6b). Here is how the entry would be recorded:

		Debit	Credit
A-1	Merchandise imports	$600,000	
C-6b	Increase in domestic short-term assets held by foreigners		$600,000

The result of this purchase is that the United States has transferred currency to foreigners and thus reduced its ability to meet other claims.

Services

The services category includes many payments such as freight and insurance on international shipments (A-2); tourist travel (A-3); profits and income from overseas investment (A-4); personal expenditures by government, civilians, and military personnel overseas (A-5); and payments for management fees, royalties, film rental, and construction services (A-6). Purchases of these services are recorded as debits, while sales of these services are similar to exports and are recorded as credits. For example, extending the earlier example of Nissan and GM, assume that the US auto maker must pay $125,000 to Nissan to ship the engines to the United States. The transaction would be recorded this way:

		Debit	Credit
A-2	Shipment	$125,000	
C-6b	Other short-term private capital		$125,000

GM purchased a Japanese shipping service (a debit to the current account) and paid for this by increasing the domestic short-term assets held by foreigners (a credit to the capital account).

Unilateral transfers

Unilateral transfers are transactions that do not involve repayment or the performance of any service. Examples include the American Red Cross sending $10 million in food to refugees in Somalia; the United States paying military pensions to residents of the Philippines who served in the US Army during World War II; and British workers in Kuwait shipping money home to their families in London. Here is how the American Red Cross transaction would appear in the US BOP:

		Debit	Credit
B-1	Unilateral transfers, private	$10 million	
A-1	Merchandise exports		$10 million

Capital account

Capital account items are transactions that involve claims in ownership. Direct investment (C-1) involves managerial participation in a foreign enterprise along with some account that involves degree of control. The United States classifies direct investments as those investments that give the investor more than 10 percent ownership. Portfolio investment (C-2) is investment designed to obtain income or capital gains. For example, if Exxon shipped $20 million of equipment to an overseas subsidiary the entry would be:

		Debit	Credit
C-1	Direct investment	$20 million	
A-1	Exports		$20 million

"Other long-term" capital accounts are differentiated based on whether they are government (C-3) or private (C-4) transactions. These transactions have a maturity of over one year and involve either loans or securities. For example, Citibank may have loaned the government of Poland $50 million. "Other short-term" capital accounts are also differentiated based on whether they are governmental (C-5) or private (C-6). Typical short-term government transactions are short-term loans in the securities of other governments. Private transactions often include trade bill acceptances or other short-term claims arising from the financing of trade and movements of money by investors to take advantage of interest differentials among countries.

Official reserves

Official reserves are used for bringing BOP accounts into balance. There are four major types of reserves available to monetary authorities in meeting BOP deficits (D1 through D4 in Table 6A). These reserves are analogous to the cash or near-cash assets of a private firm. Given that billions of dollars in transactions are reported in BOP statements, it should come as no surprise that the amount of recorded debits is never equal to the amount of credits. This is why there is an entry in the reserve account for net errors and omissions. If a country's reporting system is weak or there are a large number of clandestine transactions, this discrepancy can be quite large.

US BOP

The official presentation of the US BOP is somewhat different from the IMF format presented in Table 6A. Because the United States plays such a dominant role in the world economy, it is important to examine the US system. Table 6B presents US international transactions for two recent years.

A number of select entries in Table 6B help to highlight the US BOP. Lines 2 and 19 show that in 2006 exports of goods and services were $765.3 billion (line 73) less than imports. This trade deficit was greater than that in 2002 when it stood at $421.7 billion, and 2003 when it was $496.5 billion, showing that the United States continues to have trade deficit problems.

To assess the trade situation accurately, however, we need to examine the data in more depth. This information is provided in Table 6C. The table shows that although US exports are strong in areas such as capital goods and industrial supplies and materials, the country also imports a large amount of these products. In addition, the United States is a net importer of foods, feeds, and beverages, automotive vehicles and parts, consumer goods, and petroleum and products.

Table 6B US international transactions, 2006

Line	(Credits +; debits −)	2006 (in millions of US $)
	Current account	
1	Exports of goods and services and income receipts	2,056,836
2	Exports of goods and services	1,436,816
3	Goods, balance of payment basis	1,023,689
4	Services	413,127
5	Transfers under US military agency sales contracts	16,682
6	Travel	85,697
7	Passenger fares	22,060
8	Other transportation	48,208
9	Royalties and license fees	62,051
10	Other private services	177,284
11	US government miscellaneous services	1,145
12	Income receipts	622,020
13	Income receipts of US-owned assets abroad	619,085
14	Direct investment receipts	295,884
15	Other private receipts	320,796
16	US government receipts	2,405
17	Compensation of employees	2,935
18	Imports of goods and services and income payments	−2,831,369
19	Imports of goods and services	−2,202,083
20	Goods, balance of payment basis	−1,859,655
21	Services	−342,428
22	Direct defense expenditures	−31,180
23	Travel	−73,299
24	Passenger fares	−27,306
25	Other transportation	−65,611
26	Royalties and license fees	−26,523
27	Other private services	−114,485
28	US government miscellaneous services	−4,024
29	Income payments	−629,286
30	Income payments on foreign-owned assets in the US	−619,862
31	Direct investment payments	−145,561
32	Other private payments	−329,231
33	US government payments	−145,070
34	Compensation of employees	−9,424
35	Unilateral current transfers, net	−84,122
40	US-owned assets abroad, net (increase/financial outflow (−))	−1,045,760
55	Foreign-owned assets in the US, net (increase/financial inflow (+))	−1,764,909
71	Balance on goods (lines 3 and 20)	−835,966
72	Balance on services (lines 4 and 21)	70,699
73	Balance on goods and services (lines 2 and 19)	−765,267
74	Balance on income (lines 12 and 29)	−7,266
75	Unilateral current transfers, net (line 35)	−84,122
76	Balance on current account (lines 1, 18, and 35 or lines 73, 74, and 75)	−865,655

Source: US Department of Commerce, *Survey of Current Business*, June 2007, p. D-59.

In the early 1980s US trade deficits were offset by large amounts of income generated by direct investments abroad. Later in the decade massive international borrowing offset these deficits. More recently the situation has improved somewhat, and dollar devaluation has helped to generate stronger demand for US exports, thus partially reducing the growth rate of its annual trade deficit. However, more concerted action will be needed if the United States is to continue on this course. One way is to continue to increase US competitiveness

Table 6C US merchandise trade, 2006

	2006 (billions of US $)
Exports	1,023,109
Foods, feeds, and beverages	65,962
Industrial supplies and materials	276,045
Capital goods, except automotive	413,894
Automotive vehicles, engines, and parts	107,161
Consumer goods, except automotive	129,982
Other	43,589
Imports	1,861,380
Foods, feeds, and beverages	74,938
Industrial supplies and materials	601,988
Capital goods, except automotive	418,271
Automotive vehicles, engines, and parts	256,660
Consumer goods, except automotive	442,595
Other	59,487

Source: US Dept of Commerce, *Survey of Current Business*, June 2007, p. D-59.

in the international market. Another way is to get other countries to reduce their trade barriers and to make international markets more open.

When a country suffers a persistent balance of trade deficit, the nation will also suffer from a depreciating currency and will find it difficult to borrow in the international capital market. In this case there are only two choices available. One is to borrow from the IMF and be willing to accept the restrictions that the IMF puts on the country, which are designed to introduce austerity and force the country back on to the right economic track. The other approach is for the country to change its fiscal policy (tariffs and taxes), resort to exchange and trade controls, or devalue its currency. To prevent having to undertake austerity steps, the United States will have to continue working very hard to control its trade deficit.

Chapter 8: Regional Economic Integration

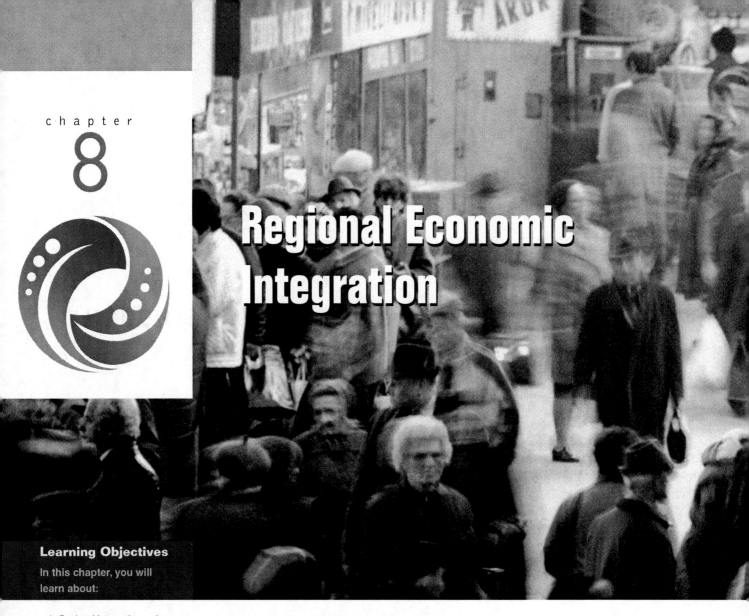

chapter

8

Regional Economic Integration

Learning Objectives

In this chapter, you will learn about:

1. Regional integration and economic blocs
2. Types of regional integration
3. Leading economic blocs
4. Why countries pursue regional integration
5. Success factors for regional integration
6. Drawbacks and ethical dilemmas of regional integration
7. Management implications of regional integration

> ## The European Union

At the end of World War II, Europe was economically and physically devastated. The war resulted in the destruction of much of Europe's industry and infrastructure. Soon after, at the onset of the Cold War between the United States and the Soviet Union, the European continent was physically and politically divided between Western and Eastern Europe. Many Europeans feared for their future.

To help address these concerns and generally promote peace and harmony in Europe, six western European countries—Belgium, France, Italy, Luxemburg, the Netherlands, and West Germany—formed an alliance in 1957, the European Economic Community. Its successor is the European Union (EU), which was established in 1992 and today includes 27 countries. Because the original bloc was founded in 1957, the EU in 2007 celebrated its 50th anniversary, making it one of the world's oldest regional economic blocs. A regional economic integration bloc (economic bloc) is an alliance of two or more countries that agree to eliminate tariffs and other restrictions to the cross-border flow of products, services, capital, and, occasionally, labor. Presently, the EU is the world's most advanced and largest economic bloc, with nearly a half billion people and about $14 trillion in annual GDP.

While the EU's original members were all Western European nations, it now includes Eastern European countries as well. Thirteen EU countries have adopted the

euro as their common currency, helping to lower business transaction costs and increase the transparency of pricing throughout the European area.

Trade and investment within Europe have become much easier since the 1950s. The member states allow investors from other member countries to freely establish and conduct business and transfer capital and earnings. Gradual elimination of bureaucracy at Europe's national borders has cut delivery times and reduced transportation costs. For example, the EU eliminated the need for volumes of customs clearance documents.

The EU is home to the headquarters of some of the world's most important firms. One such firm is Allianz, an insurance company founded in Germany. Allianz offers a range of insurance products and services, including life, health, and casualty insurance. In terms of market targeting and strategy development, Allianz management at one time viewed Europe as a collection of disparate countries. Since the creation of the EU, however, Allianz treats Europe increasingly as one large marketplace. Management attempts to devise pan-European strategies, an approach that reduces costs and increases the efficiency of Allianz's operations throughout Europe.

Development of the EU has allowed Allianz to internationalize faster than other insurers. The firm is present in all the new EU countries—such as Poland, Hungary, and the Czech Republic—which are proving to be among Allianz's most profitable markets. In 2006, Allianz changed its legal status from a German company to that of a Societas Europaea (SE), a company based and regulated in the EU as a whole. The legal groundwork for SE status was put in place in 2004, with passage of EU legislation that allows such firms to operate seamlessly across all 27 EU countries. By transforming into a European firm, Allianz is becoming more European than German.

Today, the EU is at a crossroads. Member countries signed the European Constitution in 2004—a treaty that aimed to improve the functioning of the EU's governing institutions. The goal of the constitution is to clarify the distribution of powers and legitimize the EU's federal authority, in much the same way the U.S. Constitution did for the United States. However, in a referendum held in 2005, France and the Netherlands rejected the constitution, which caused other countries to postpone or halt ratification. At present, the constitution's future and longer-term political integration of the EU are in limbo. Meanwhile, in the decade through 2007, performance of the EU economy was sluggish. GDP growth and productivity stagnated and the unemployment rate hovered between 8 and 12 percent. Many Europeans are dissatisfied with the EU and are opposed to the entry of additional countries into the bloc.

The challenges facing the EU today might be typical of economic blocs in the most advanced stages of development. Nevertheless, economic blocs have become typical of the emerging landscape of international trade and investment. Today, there are roughly 200 agreements for regional trade integration around the world, some more active than others. Such alliances represent a long-term trend and are likely a stepping-stone to the emergence of worldwide free trade. ◀

Sources: *Economist*. (2005). "Business: Limited appeal; Pan-European companies." Sept 17, p.72; *Economist*. (2007). "Fit at 50? A Special Report on the European Union." March 17, Special Section; European Commission. *The Internal Market—Ten Years without Frontiers*. Retrieved from *www.ec.europa.eu*; *Hoovers.com*. (2007). Corporate profile of Allianz at *www.hoovers.com*; U.S. Commercial Service. (2006). *Doing business in the European Union*. Washington, DC: U.S. and Foreign Commercial Service and U.S. Department of State.

 ## Regional Integration and Economic Blocs

Regional economic integration The growing economic interdependence that results when two or more countries within a geographic region form an alliance aimed at reducing barriers to trade and investment.

The opening vignette highlights one of the most remarkable features of contemporary international business: the worldwide trend to **regional economic integration**. Also known as *regional integration,* regional economic integration refers to the growing economic interdependence that results when two or more countries within a geographic region form an alliance aimed at reducing barriers to trade and investment. Since the end of World War II, most nations have sought to collaborate, with the aim of achieving some degree of economic integration. It is estimated that about 40 percent of world trade today is under some form of preferential trade agreements signed by groups of countries. The trend is based on the premise that, by cooperating, nations within a common geographic region connected by historical, cultural, linguistic, economic, or political factors can gain mutual advantages.[1] The free trade that results from economic integration helps nations attain higher living standards by encouraging specialization, lower prices, greater choices, increased productivity, and more efficient use of resources.

To better understand regional integration, think of international business as existing along a continuum where, at one extreme, the world operates as one large free-trade area in which there are no tariffs or quotas, all countries use the same currency, and products, services, capital, and workers can move freely among nations without restriction. At the other extreme of this continuum is a world of prohibitive barriers to trade and investment where countries have separate currencies and have very little commercial interaction with each other. Regional integration is an attempt to achieve freer economic relations. Two of the most well-known examples of this trend are the European Union (EU) and the North American Free Trade Agreement area (NAFTA). The EU is composed of 27 member countries in Europe. NAFTA is composed of Canada, Mexico, and the United States.

Regional integration results from the formation of a **regional economic integration bloc**, or simply, an economic bloc, a geographic area that consists of two or more countries that agree to pursue economic integration by reducing tariffs and other restrictions to cross-border flow of products, services, capital, and, in more advanced stages, labor. (In this text, we follow the convention of using the French term, "bloc," instead of "block.") At minimum, the countries in an economic bloc become parties to a **free trade agreement**, a formal arrangement between two or more countries to reduce or eliminate tariffs, quotas, and other barriers to trade in products and services. The member nations also undertake cross-border investments within the bloc.

More advanced economic blocs, such as the EU, permit the free flow of capital, labor, and technology among the member countries. The EU is also harmonizing monetary and fiscal policies and gradually integrating the economies of its member nations. For example, in light of the faster pace of economic activity in the EU, the European Central Bank recently tightened its monetary policy by raising interest rates on the money that it loans to European banks, in an effort to reduce inflation. Cross-border merger and acquisition deals increased markedly between Austria, France, the United Kingdom, the Netherlands, and other member countries in recent years.

Why would a nation opt to be a member of an economic bloc instead of working toward a system of worldwide free trade? The primary reason is that such blocs involve a smaller number of countries and, therefore, are much easier to negotiate than a system of worldwide free trade composed of all the nations in the world. This helps explain why roughly 200 economic integration agreements have been negotiated, presenting both opportunities and challenges to internationalizing firms.

Note that the proponents of free trade on a global scale are disappointed about the proliferation of regional trade agreements. Since 1947, the General Agreement on Tariffs and Trade (GATT) and the World Trade Organization (WTO) have achieved great success in fostering economic integration on a *global* scale. The WTO recognizes that regional integration can play an important role in liberalizing trade and fostering economic development. However, existing WTO rules have been less effective in dealing with groups of countries, and the world body has failed to ensure compliance with WTO rules by all members of an economic bloc. Slow progress to liberalize trade, especially in agricultural products, has prompted many developing countries to seek alternatives to the multilateral trading system favored by the WTO. Today, the WTO remains in negotiations with economic blocs, with the aim of exercising better control over their evolution and of minimizing risks associated with regional economic integration.[2]

Types of Regional Integration

Regional integration involves processes by which distinct national economies become economically linked and interdependent through greater cross-national movement of products, services, and factors of production. Economic integration allows member states to use resources more productively. The total output of the integrated area becomes greater than that achievable by individual states.

Exhibit 8.1 identifies five possible levels of regional integration. Regional integration is best viewed as a continuum, with economic interconnectedness progressing from a low level of integration—the free trade area— through higher levels to the most advanced form of integration—the political union. The *political union* represents the ultimate degree of integration among countries, which has not yet been achieved. The **free trade area** is the simplest and most common arrangement, in

Regional economic integration bloc A geographic area consisting of two or more countries that have agreed to pursue economic integration by reducing barriers to the cross-border flow of products, services, capital, and, in more advanced states, labor.

Free trade agreement A formal arrangement between two or more countries to reduce or eliminate tariffs, quotas, and barriers to trade in products and services.

Free trade area A stage of regional integration in which member countries agree to eliminate tariffs and other barriers to trade in products and services within the bloc.

Level of Integration	Free Trade Area	Customs Union	Common Market	Economic and (sometimes) Monetary Union	Political Union
Members agree to eliminate tariffs and non tariff trade barriers with each other but maintain their own trade barriers with non member countries. *Examples: NAFTA, EFTA, ASEAN, Australia and New Zealand Closer Economic Relations Agreement (CER)*					
Common external tariffs *Example: MERCOSUR*					
Free movement of products, labor, and capital *Example: Pre-1992 European Economic Community*					
Unified monetary and fiscal policy by a central authority *Example: The European Union today exhibits common trade, agricultural, and monetary policies*					
Perfect unification of all policies by a common organization; submersion of all separate national institutions *Example: Remains an ideal; yet to be achieved*					

Exhibit 8.1 Five Potential Levels of Regional Integration among Nations

which member countries agree to gradually eliminate formal barriers to trade in products and services within the bloc, while each member country maintains an independent international trade policy with countries outside the bloc. NAFTA is an example. The free trade area emphasizes the pursuit of comparative advantage for a group of countries rather than individual states. Governments may impose local content requirements, which specify that producers located within the member countries provide a certain proportion of products and supplies used in local manufacturing. If the content requirement is not met, the product becomes subject to the tariffs that member governments normally impose on nonmember countries.

The next level of regional integration is the **customs union**, which is similar to a free trade area except that the member states harmonize their trade policies toward nonmember countries. Unlike a free trade area, in which individual countries have their own external trade policies, the members of a customs union adopt *common* tariff and nontariff barriers on imports from nonmember countries. MERCOSUR, an economic bloc consisting of Argentina, Brazil, Paraguay, and Uruguay, is an example of this type of arrangement. Use of a common tariff system means that an exporter outside MERCOSUR faces the *same* tariffs and nontariff barriers by *any* MERCOSUR member country. Determining the most appropriate common external tariff is challenging,

Customs union A stage of regional integration in which the member countries agree to adopt common tariff and nontariff barriers on imports from nonmember countries.

because member countries must agree on the tariff level. In addition, governments must agree on how to distribute proceeds from the tariff among the member countries.

At the next stage of regional integration, member countries may establish a **common market** (also known as a single market), in which trade barriers are reduced or removed, common external barriers are established and products, services, and *factors of production* such as capital, labor, and technology are allowed to move freely among the member countries. As with a customs union, the common market also establishes a common trade policy with nonmember countries. The EU is a common market. It has gradually reduced or eliminated restrictions on immigration and the cross-border flow of capital. A worker from an EU country has the right to work in other EU countries, and EU firms can freely transfer funds among their subsidiaries within the bloc.

Common markets are hard to create because they require substantial cooperation from the member countries on labor and economic policies. Moreover, because labor and capital can flow freely inside the bloc, benefits to individual members vary, because skilled labor may move to countries where wages are higher and investment capital may flow to countries where returns are greater. In the EU, for example, Germany has seen a sharp influx of workers from Poland and the Czech Republic, because workers from the latter countries can earn substantially higher wages in Germany than they can in their home countries.

An **economic union** is a stage of regional integration in which member countries enjoy all the advantages of early stages, but also strive to have common fiscal and monetary policies. At the extreme, each member country adopts identical tax rates. The bloc aims for standardized monetary policy, which requires establishing fixed exchange rates and free convertibility of currencies among the member states, in addition to allowing the free movement of capital. This standardization helps eliminate discriminatory practices that might favor one member state over another. Through greater mobility of products, services, and production factors, an economic union enables firms within the bloc to locate productive activities in member states with the most favorable economic policies.

The EU has made great strides toward achieving an economic union. For example, 13 EU countries have established a *monetary union* in which a single currency, the euro, is now in circulation. Monetary union and the euro have greatly increased the ease with which European financial institutions establish branches across the EU and offer banking services, insurance, and savings products.

Economic unions have additional characteristics. To achieve greater economic integration, member countries strive to eliminate border controls, harmonize product and labeling standards, and establish regionwide policies for energy, agriculture, and social services. An economic union also requires its members to standardize laws and regulations regarding competition, mergers, and other corporate behaviors. To facilitate free trade in services, member countries harmonize procedures for licensing of professionals so that a doctor or lawyer qualified in one country can practice in any other country.

In describing an economic union, the United States provides a good analogy. Imagine that each of the fifty states is like an individual country, but joined together in a union. The members have a common currency and a single central bank with a uniform monetary policy. Trade among the members takes place unobstructed and both labor and capital move freely among them, in pursuit of optimal returns. The federal government applies a uniform tax and fiscal policy. However, just as would occur in an economic union, the individual U.S. states also govern themselves in such areas as education, police protection, and local taxes, thereby maintaining some local autonomy. Nevertheless, the analogy only goes so far. The United States *is* a country and, unlike a real economic union, the U.S. states cannot withdraw from the union.

Common market A stage of regional integration in which trade barriers are reduced or removed, common external barriers are established, and products, services, and factors of production are allowed to move freely among the member countries.

Economic union A stage of regional integration in which member countries enjoy all the advantages of early stages, but also strive to have common fiscal and monetary policies.

Leading Economic Blocs

Examples of regional integration can be found on all continents. Leading economic blocs are illustrated in Exhibit 8.2 on pages 230–231. In this section, we discuss notable blocs in Europe, the Americas, Asia, the Middle East, and Africa.

Europe has the longest experience with regional integration and is home to several economic blocs. The most important of these are the European Union and the European Free Trade Association. Exhibit 8.3 on page 232 shows these two blocs in detail.

The European Union (EU)

Exhibit 8.4 highlights the notable features of the member countries in the European Union—the world's most integrated economic bloc. "PPP terms" in the exhibit refers to *purchasing power parity* (PPP), which means that per capita GDP figures have been adjusted for price differences. The EU traces its roots to the years following World War II, when six war-weary countries—Belgium, France, Germany, Italy, Luxembourg, and the Netherlands—sought to promote peace and prosperity through economic and political cooperation (www.europa.eu). These countries signed the Treaty of Rome in 1957, eventually leading to the formal creation of the EU in 1992. The EU has taken the following steps toward becoming a full-fledged economic union:

* *Market access.* Tariffs and most nontariff barriers have been eliminated for trade in products and services, and rules of origin favor manufacturing that uses parts and other inputs produced in the EU.

* *Common market.* The EU removed barriers to the cross-national movement of production factors—labor, capital, and technology. For example, an Italian worker now has the right to get a job in Ireland and a French company can now invest freely in Spain.

* *Trade rules.* The member countries have largely eliminated customs procedures and regulations, which streamlines transportation and logistics within Europe.

* *Standards harmonization.* The EU is harmonizing technical standards, regulations, and enforcement procedures that relate to products, services, and commercial activities. Thus, where British firms once used the imperial measurement system (that is, pounds, ounces, and inches), they have converted to the metric system, used by all the EU. Where German merchants once had a unique standard for the quality of meat and produce, they now follow procedures prescribed by the EU.

In the long run, the EU is seeking to adopt common fiscal, monetary, taxation, and social welfare policies. The 2002 introduction of the euro—the EU's common currency and now one of the world's leading currencies—simplified the process of cross-border trade and enhanced Europe's international competitiveness. Its introduction eliminated exchange rate risk in much of the bloc and forced member countries to improve their fiscal and monetary policies. Psychologically, the single currency allows consumers and businesses to think of Europe as a single national entity. Instituting the euro meant that national governments had to cede monetary power to the European Central Bank, which is based in Luxembourg and oversees EU monetary functions.

The EU has four additional institutions that perform its executive, administrative, legislative, and judicial functions. The *Council of the European Union*, based in Brussels, is the EU's main decision-making body. Composed of representatives from each member country, it makes decisions regarding economic policy, budgets, and foreign policy, as well as admission of new member countries. The *European Commission*, also based in Brussels, is similarly composed of delegates from each member state and represents the interests of the EU as a whole. It proposes legislation and policies and is responsible for implementing the decisions of the *European Parliament* and the Council of the EU. The European Parliament consists of elected representatives that hold joint sessions each month. By common agreement, the Parliament meets in three different cities (Brussels, Luxembourg, and Strasbourg, France) and can have up 732 total representatives. The Parliament has three main functions: (1) form EU legislation, (2) supervise EU institutions, and (3) make decisions about the EU budget. Finally, the *European Court of Justice*, based in Luxembourg, interprets and enforces EU laws and settles legal disputes between member states.[3]

The Global Trend feature discusses specific challenges of integrating new member states into the EU. Since 2004, 12 new states have joined the EU. The more recent addition of Bulgaria and Romania brings the total number of member countries to 27. The new member countries are important, low-cost manufacturing sites for EU firms.[4] For example, Peugeot and Citroën now produce cars at a plant in the Czech Republic. At full capacity, the factory turns out 300,000 vehicles per year. South Korea's Hyundai now produces the Kia brand of cars at a plant in

> GLOBAL TREND

Integrating Eastern Europe and Turkey into the EU

Germany's per capita GDP is $32,684. By comparison, Romania's is $10,152, Bulgaria's is $10,844, and Poland's is $14,609 (all are 2007 figures). These Eastern European countries, with their low-wage workers, make excellent manufacturing sites for firms from Western Europe and elsewhere. Just as these and other Eastern European countries have recently joined the European Union (EU), officials in Germany, France, and other long-established EU members fear losing jobs and investment to the new EU members. These same officials are reluctant to allow other low-wage countries, such as Turkey or the Ukraine, to join the EU.

In population terms, Turkey (with 71 million people) is about the same size as the 12 Eastern European countries that joined the EU since 2004. However, Turkey poses additional challenges because of cultural differences, its Islamic heritage, and historically high inflation. Some oppose Turkey joining the EU because the country is seen as too remote from current EU countries in cultural and geographic terms. Suc-

cessive Turkish governments have long sought EU membership, in part because it will help maintain economic reform in their country.

Proponents of EU enlargement are optimistic. They argue that low wages in the bloc's newest members are more an opportunity than a threat. Why? One reason is that Poland, Hungary, and other recent entrants are attracting substantial business investment that might go to China and other low-wage countries on the opposite side of the world.

The Eastern European countries will not maintain their low-cost labor advantages indefinitely. These satellites of the former Soviet Union are much richer today than they were after the collapse of communism in 1989, when Poland's per capita GDP was just $2,000. Starting from a much lower income level, these countries are relatively new to free-market economics and, as such, are growing their economies far faster than their affluent Western EU neighbors. The reason relates partly to the incremental value of inward investment in poorer countries versus richer countries. The profitability

of using additional capital or better technology is greater in an emerging market like Poland than in a high-income country like Germany. For example, while replacing an existing computer with a new, faster computer has a relatively small payoff for a German firm, installing a new computer in a Polish firm where records are kept by hand has an enormous payoff.

Rapid economic growth spurred by affiliation with the European Union implies that the newest EU members may reach economic parity with the rest of Europe within a few decades, a short time span in the life of a nation. When that day arrives, Germans, French, British, and other venerable members of the EU bloc will no longer worry about the competitive threat of their new low-wage neighbors.

Sources: *Business Week.* (1999). "How Far, How Fast? Is Central Europe Ready to Join the EU," Nov. 8, pp. 64–66; *Economist.* (2005). "Transformed: EU Membership has Worked Magic in Central Europe." June 25, pp. 6–8; *Economist.* (2004). "The Impossibility of Saying No." Sept. 18, 30–32; *Financial Times.* (2005). "Why Turks are Changing Tack on Foreign Ownership." June 28. Special report.

Exhibit 8.2

The Most Active Economic Blocs

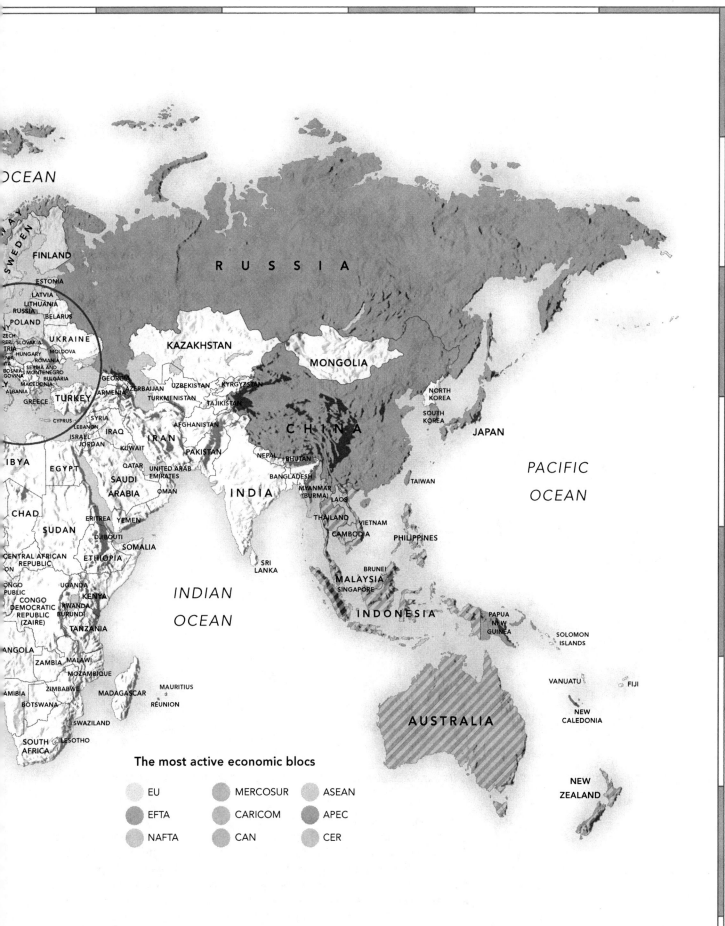

The most active economic blocs

- EU
- EFTA
- NAFTA
- MERCOSUR
- CARICOM
- CAN
- ASEAN
- APEC
- CER

Exhibit 8.3

Economic Integration in Europe

Slovakia, while Japan's Suzuki makes cars in Hungary. Output of automobiles in the eastern region is growing rapidly.[5] Most of the newest EU entrants are one-time satellites of the former Soviet Union, and have economic growth rates far higher than their 15 Western European counterparts. They are poised to achieve per capita income levels similar to the EU's wealthier countries within a few decades. However, their ascension poses special challenges. Less-developed economies such as Romania, Bulgaria, and Lithuania may require decades of developmental aid to catch up.[6]

The EU faces other challenges as well. There is a tension in Europe between the forces for regional integration and the forces for retaining national identity. EU countries recognize that relinquishing autonomy in certain key areas and combining resources across national borders are necessary steps. However, some EU members, particularly Britain, are reluctant to surrender certain sovereign rights. They insist on maintaining their ability to set their own monetary and fiscal policies, and to undertake their own national military defense.

Finally, the Common Agricultural Policy (CAP) has long been a fixture of the European bloc. The CAP is a system of agricultural subsidies and programs that guarantees a minimum price to EU farmers and ranchers.

Members	Population (millions)	GDP (U.S.$, billions, PPP terms)	GDP per capita (U.S.$; PPP terms)	Exports as a percentage of GDP
Austria	8	$299	$36,189	29%
Belgium	10	353	33,908	52
Bulgaria	8	83	10,844	16
Cyprus	1	20	23,419	7
Czech Republic	10	210	20,539	44
Denmark	5	204	37,398	26
Estonia	1	26	19,243	36
Finland	5	179	34,162	29
France	63	1,988	31,377	17
Germany	83	2,699	32,684	26
Greece	11	274	24,733	3
Hungary	10	190	18,922	42
Ireland	4	192	45,135	53
Italy	59	1,791	30,383	17
Latvia	2	34	15,062	21
Lithuania	3	57	16,756	36
Luxembourg	0.5	35	76,025	28
Malta	0.4	8	21,081	44
The Netherlands	17	550	33,079	44
Poland	38	557	14,609	24
Portugal	11	218	20,673	18
Romania	22	219	10,152	51
Slovakia	5	101	18,705	67
Slovenia	2	49	24,459	38
Spain	42	1,203	28,810	16
Sweden	9	297	32,548	30
United Kingdom	61	2,004	32,949	14
	Total: 491	Total: $13,840		

Exhibit 8.4 Key Features of the European Union Member Countries, 2007

SOURCE: International Monetary Fund at www.imf.org

Original goals of the CAP were to provide a fair living standard for agricultural producers and food at reasonable prices for consumers. In reality, however, the CAP has increased food prices in Europe and consumes over 40 percent of the EU's annual budget. It complicates negotiations with the World Trade Organization for reducing global trade barriers. The CAP imposes high import tariffs that unfairly affect exporters in developing economies, such as Africa, that rely heavily on agricultural production. The EU has been working in recent years to reform the CAP, but progress has been slow. Meanwhile, entry into the EU of new member countries since 2004 has increased the number of bloc farmers from 7 to 11 million and increased crop production by 10 to 20 percent.

European Free Trade Association (EFTA)

The second largest free trade area in Europe is the European Free Trade Association (EFTA; see www.efta.int), which was established in 1960 by Austria, Britain, Denmark, Norway, Portugal, Sweden, and Switzerland. However, most of these countries eventually left the EFTA to join the EU. The current EFTA members are Iceland, Liechtenstein, Norway, and Switzerland. The bloc promotes free trade and strengthens economic relations with other European countries and the world. The EFTA Secretariat, headquartered in Geneva, has negotiated trade agreements with several non-European countries. EFTA members cooperate with the EU via bilateral free trade agreements, and, since 1994, through the European Economic Area arrangement, which allows for free movement of people, products, services, and capital throughout the combined area of the EFTA and the EU.

North American Free Trade Agreement (NAFTA)

Consisting of Canada, Mexico, and the United States, NAFTA is the most significant economic bloc in the Americas (see www.nafta-sec-alena.org). Exhibit 8.5 highlights key features of the NAFTA countries. The concept suggests that, in the long run, exchange rates should move toward levels that would equalize the prices of an identical basket of goods and services in any two countries. Since prices vary greatly among countries, economists adjust ordinary GDP figures for differences in purchasing power. Adjusted per capita GDP more accurately represents the amount of products that consumers can buy in a given country, using their own currency and consistent with their own standard of living.

Members	Population (millions)	GDP (U.S.$ billions, PPP terms)	GDP per capita (U.S.$; PPP terms)	Exports as a percentage of GDP
Canada	33	$1,225	$37,321	29%
Mexico	108	1,192	10,993	18
United States	302	13,678	45,257	6
	Total: 443	Total: $16,095		

Exhibit 8.5 North American Free Trade Agreement (NAFTA), 2007

SOURCE: International Monetary Fund at www.imf.org

Comparable in size to the EU, NAFTA was launched in 1994. Its passage was smoothed by the existence, since the 1960s, of the *maquiladora* program. Under this program, U.S. firms have been able to locate manufacturing facilities in an area just south of the U.S. border and access low-cost labor and other advantages in Mexico without having to pay significant tariffs.

For its member countries, the NAFTA agreement increased market access. The agreement eliminated tariffs and most nontariff barriers for products and services traded in the bloc, and made it possible for member country firms to bid for government contracts. NAFTA established trade rules and uniform customs procedures and regulations, while prohibiting the use of standards and technical regulations as trade barriers. The member countries agreed to rules for investment and intellectual property rights. NAFTA also provides for dispute settlement in areas such as investment, unfair pricing, labor issues, and the environment.

What did NAFTA accomplish for its members? Since the bloc's inception, trade among the members has more than tripled and now exceeds one trillion dollars per year. In the early 1980s, Mexico's tariffs averaged 100 percent and gradually decreased over time, eventually disappearing under NAFTA. In the 10 years following NAFTA's launch in 1994, U.S. exports to Mexico grew from about $40 billion to more than $110 billion. U.S. exports to Canada nearly doubled, to nearly $200 billion. Canada's exports to Mexico and the United States also more than doubled. In 1994, Mexican exports to the United States averaged about $50 billion per year, compared to over $160 billion by 2005.[7]

Mexico benefited greatly from NAFTA. Access to Canada and the United States helped launch numerous Mexican firms in industries such as electronics, automobiles, textiles, medical products, and services. For instance, Mexico gave birth to a $100 million-per-year dental supply industry, in which entrepreneurs export labor-intensive products such as braces, dental wax, and tools used in dental work to the United States. Annual foreign investment in Mexico rose from $4 billion in 1993 to nearly $20 billion by 2006 as United States and Canadian firms invested in their southern neighbor. In the years following NAFTA's passage, Mexico's per capita income rose substantially, to about $11,000 in 2007, making Mexico the wealthiest country in Latin America in terms of per capita income.[8]

Compared to the days before NAFTA, the member countries now trade more with each other than with former trading partners outside the NAFTA zone. Both Canada and Mexico now have some 80 percent of their trade with, and 60 percent of their FDI stocks in, the United States.[9] By increasing Mexico's attractiveness as a manufacturing location, firms like Gap Inc. and Liz Claiborne moved their factories from Asia to Mexico during the 1990s. IBM shifted much of its production of computer parts from Singapore to Mexico.

NAFTA also stimulated some restructuring in the North American labor market. Falling trade barriers triggered job losses in the North as factories were "exported" to Mexico to profit from its low-cost labor. Nevertheless, increased purchasing power of Mexican consumers meant that they could afford to buy imports from Canada and the United States. As part of the accord, the member countries were also required to strengthen their labor standards. Workers in the NAFTA zone gained the right to unionize. The accord helped to improve working conditions and compliance with labor laws. NAFTA also includes provisions that promote sustainable development and environmental protection.

Let's turn now to a collection of lesser known economic blocs, often composed of developing economies. Compared to the EU or NAFTA, the remaining blocs are less stable and have been less successful. These blocs are located in Latin America, Asia, the Middle East, and Africa.

Members	Population (millions)	GDP (U.S.$ billions, PPP terms)	GDP per capita (U.S.$; PPP terms)	Exports as a percentage of GDP
Argentina	39	$599	$15,509	6%
Brazil	189	1,758	9,286	5
Paraguay	6	32	5,264	9
Uruguay	3	38	12,012	4
Venezuela	28	182	6,614	18
Bolivia *	10	28	2,858	7
Chile *	17	225	13,588	12
Colombia *	48	380	7,975	5
Ecuador *	14	62	4,591	13
Peru *	29	190	6,609	6
	Total: 383	Total: $3,494		

* Associate members

Exhibit 8.6 El Mercado Comun del Sur (MERCOSUR), 2007

SOURCE: International Monetary Fund at www.imf.org

El Mercado Comun del Sur (MERCOSUR)

Established in 1991, MERCOSUR, or the *El Mercado Comun del Sur* (the Southern Common Market) has, become the strongest economic bloc in South America (see www.mercosur.int). Exhibit 8.6 provides the membership and key features of the MERCOSUR bloc. The four largest members alone—Argentina, Brazil, Paraguay, and Uruguay—account for some 80 percent of South America's GDP. Within its borders, MERCOSUR established the free movement of products and services, a common external tariff and trade policy, and coordinated monetary and fiscal policies. An additional priority is the construction of reliable infrastructure—roads, electricity grids, and gas pipelines—across a landmass larger than Mexico and the United States combined. MERCOSUR eventually aims to become an economic union.

MERCOSUR's early progress was impressive. It attracted much investment from nonmember countries, particularly in the auto industry. During its first six years, trade among the member countries tripled.[10] In addition to its regular members, MERCOSUR also has five associate members, which have access to preferential trade but not to the tariff benefits of full members. MERCOSUR has trade agreements with various nations outside the bloc. Some predict that MERCOSUR will be integrated with NAFTA and the Dominican Republic-Central American Free Trade Agreement (DR-CAFTA) as part of the proposed Free Trade Area of the Americas (FTAA), bringing free trade to the entire western hemisphere. If implemented, this integration would bring free trade to the entire western hemisphere.

The Caribbean Community (CARICOM)

Composed of roughly 25 member and associate member states around the Caribbean Sea, CARICOM was established in 1973 to lower trade barriers and institute a common external tariff (see www.caricom.org). However, the bloc has met with little success in stimulating economic development. Problems have resulted due to economic difficulties of the individual members and their inability to agree on basic issues. In recent years, the bloc has made much progress toward establishing the Caribbean Single Market, a common market that allows for a greater degree of free movement for products, services, capital, and labor, and gives citizens of all CARICOM countries the right to establish businesses throughout the region.

Comunidad Andina de Naciones (CAN)

Long called the Andean Pact, the Comunidad Andina de Naciones (CAN) was established in 1969 and includes Bolivia, Colombia, Ecuador, Peru, and Venezuela (see www.comunidadandina.org). The CAN countries have a population of 120 million and a combined GDP of $260 billion. CAN is expected to merge with MERCOSUR to form a new economic bloc that encompasses all of South America. The pact achieved little progress in its first 20 years, with intra-bloc trade reaching only 5 percent of the bloc members' total trade.[11] This low trade rate is partially due to geography: The Andes mountain range makes cross-border land transportation costly and cumbersome.

Association of Southeast Asian Nations (ASEAN)

One of the few examples of economic integration in Asia, ASEAN was created in 1967 with the goal of maintaining political stability and promoting regional economic and social development (see www.aseansec.org). Subsequently, ASEAN created a free trade area in which many tariffs were reduced to less than 5 percent. However, further regional integration has been slowed by large economic differences among the member countries. For instance, oil-rich Brunei has a per capita income of over $26,000, while Vietnam's is less than $4,000. The mass movement of workers from poor to prosperous countries that would likely result with further ASEAN integration reduces the likelihood that this bloc will become a common market or an economic union. In the long run, ASEAN aims to incorporate international trading powerhouses like Japan and China, whose membership would accelerate the development of extensive trade relationships. Exhibit 8.7 profiles the ASEAN. Note that Singapore's exports as a percent of its GDP exceed 100 percent. The reason is that Singapore is an entrepôt nation, an import-export platform for Asia, trading far more goods than it manufactures.

Asia Pacific Economic Cooperation (APEC)

Originally suggested by Australia, APEC aims for greater free trade and economic integration of the Pacific Rim countries. It incorporates 21 nations on both sides of the Pacific, including Australia, Canada, Chile, China, Japan, Mexico, Russia, and the United States (www.apec.org). Its members account for 85 percent of total regional trade, as well as one-third of the world's population and over half its GDP. APEC aspires to remove trade and investment barriers by 2020. Nevertheless, APEC has accomplished little. Progress has been slowed by economic and political turmoil in some member countries, as well as failure to agree on foundational issues. Members have varying national economic priorities, and the composition of less affluent Asian countries alongside strong international traders like Australia, Japan, and the United States makes it difficult to achieve agreement on a range of issues.

Members	Population millions	GDP (U.S.$ billions, PPP terms)	GDP per capita (U.S.$; PPP terms)	Exports as a percentage of GDP
Brunei	0.4	$10	$26,098	52%
Cambodia	15	41	2,673	6
Indonesia	225	1,146	5,097	8
Laos	6	15	2,402	3
Malaysia	27	341	12,703	47
Myanmar (Burma)	58	105	1,814	3
Philippines	88	474	5,409	9
Singapore	5	140	31,165	130
Thailand	66	626	9,427	16
Vietnam	86	300	3,503	10
	Total: 576	Total: $3,198		

Exhibit 8.7 Association of Southeast Asian Nations (ASEAN), 2007

SOURCE: International Monetary Fund at www.imf.org

Australia and New Zealand Closer Economic Relations Agreement (CER)

In 1966, Australia and New Zealand reached a free trade agreement that removed 80 percent of tariffs and quotas between the two nations, but was relatively complex and bureaucratic. In 1983, the Closer Economic Relations Agreement (CER) sought to accelerate free trade, leading to further economic integration of the two nations. The CER gained importance when Australia and New Zealand lost their privileged status in the British market as Britain joined the EU. Many believe the CER has been one of the world's most successful economic blocs. In 2005, the members began negotiating a free trade agreement with the ASEAN countries, a move that would further reduce Australia and New Zealand's dependence on trade with Britain.

Economic Integration in the Middle East and Africa

The Middle East and North Africa comprise a collection of primarily Islamic countries where oil is often the driving economic force. The Middle East's primary regional organization is the Gulf Cooperation Council (GCC; see www.gcc-sg.org.htm). Established in 1981 to coordinate economic, social, and cultural affairs, the GCC consists of Bahrain, Kuwait, Oman, Qatar, Saudi Arabia, and the United Arab Emirates. Specific GCC initiatives include coordination of the petroleum industry, abolition of certain tariffs, and liberalization of investment, as well as harmonization of banking, financial, and monetary policies. The GCC also wants to establish an Arab common market and increase trade ties with Asia. Although largely focused on political issues, the GCC has spawned agreements that allow its citizens to travel freely among, and establish businesses in, other member nations.

Elsewhere in the Middle East, efforts have been made for regional economic integration, such as the Arab Maghreb Union (composed of Algeria, Libya, Mauritania, Morocco, and Tunisia) and the Regional Cooperation for Development (RCD; composed of Pakistan, Iran, and Turkey). The Maghreb

Union is still struggling to become a viable economic bloc. The RCD was dissolved in 1979 and replaced by the Economic Cooperation Organization (ECO). The ECO is an international organization that now includes ten Middle Eastern and Asian countries, seeking to promote trade and investment opportunities in the region. Such regional groups are very early attempts at regional integration that may foster the development of inter-Arab trade and investment. Another grouping, the Arab League, is a longstanding political organization with 21 member states and a constitution that requires unanimous agreement in any decision making. It has been relatively unsuccessful in fostering regional economic development.

These workers harvest table grapes growing in Robertson, South Africa. External tariffs of NAFTA and the EU hinder African agricultural exports to Europe and North America.

Africa would like better access to European and North American markets for sales of farm and textile products. African countries believe they can gain clout to negotiate free trade with the developed world by forming economic blocs through regional integration. To this end, the continent has established at least nine economic blocs. Most notable are the Southern African Development Community, the Economic Community of West African States, the Economic Community of Central African States, and, most recently, the African Union for Regional Cooperation. However, these groups have not had much impact on regional trade. This failure is partially due to political turmoil and misunderstandings about free trade, as well as underdeveloped economic and transportation systems. Political instability, civil unrest and war, military dictatorships, corruption, and infectious diseases have prevented economic development in many African countries.

 # Why Countries Pursue Regional Integration

Economic integration contributes to corporate and industrial growth, and hence to economic progress, better living standards, and higher tax revenues for the member countries. Nations seek at least four objectives in pursuing regional integration.

Expand market size. Regional integration greatly increases the scale of the marketplace for firms inside the economic bloc. For example, while Belgium has a population of just 10 million, the absence of trade barriers with other countries in the EU gives Belgian firms easier access to a total market of roughly 490 million buyers. In a similar way, management at Allianz, the German insurance firm featured in the opening vignette, has come to view Europe as one large marketplace. When NAFTA was formed, Canadian firms gained access to the much larger markets of Mexico and the United States. In this way, consumers also gain access to a greater selection of products and services.

Achieve scale economies and enhanced productivity. Expansion of market size within an economic bloc gives member country firms the opportunity to increase the scale of operations in both production and marketing. This leads to greater concentration and increased efficiency in these activities. For instance, where a German firm may be only moderately efficient when producing 10,000 units of a product strictly for the German market, it greatly increases its efficiency by producing 50,000 units for the much larger EU market. Internationalization inside the bloc helps firms learn to compete more effectively outside the bloc as well. The firms enjoy additional benefits through increased access to factors of production that now flow freely across

Members of MERCOSUR, which include Argentina, Brazil, Paraguay, and Uruguay—seek to expand market size, achieve scale economies, attract foreign direct investment, and build defensive and political posture.

national borders within the bloc.[12] Labor and other inputs are allocated more efficiently among the member countries. More efficient use of resources should lead to lower prices for consumers.

Attract direct investment from outside the bloc. Compared to investing in stand-alone countries, foreign firms prefer to invest in countries that are part of an economic bloc because factories that they build within the bloc receive preferential treatment for exports to other member countries. For example, many non-European firms—including General Mills, Samsung, and Tata—have invested heavily in the EU to take advantage of Europe's economic integration. By establishing operations in a single EU country, these firms gain free trade access to the entire EU market.

Acquire stronger defensive and political posture. One goal of regional integration is to give the member countries a stronger defensive posture relative to other nations and world regions. This was one of the motives for creating the European Community (the precursor to the EU), whose members sought to strengthen their mutual defense against the expanding influence of the former Soviet Union. Today, some view the EU as a means for Europe to counterbalance the power and international influence of the United States. Forming an economic bloc also allows countries to obtain greater bargaining power in world affairs and thereby political power. For example, the EU enjoys greater influence with the World Trade Organization in trade negotiations than any individual member country. Broadly speaking, countries are more powerful when they cooperate together than when they operate as individual entities.

Success Factors for Regional Integration

Experience with regional economic integration suggests that the most successful economic blocs tend to possess the following characteristics.

Economic similarity. The more similar the economies of the member countries, the more likely the economic bloc will succeed. Significant wage rate differences means that workers in lower-wage countries will migrate to higher wage countries. Significant economic instability in one member can quickly spread and harm the economies of the other members. For instance, a severe recession in one country increases the likelihood that others also experience an economic slowdown. Compatibility of economic characteristics is so important that the EU requires its current and prospective members to meet strict membership conditions, ideally low inflation, low unemployment, reasonable wages, and stable economic conditions.

Political similarity. Similarity in political systems enhances prospects for a successful bloc. Countries that seek to integrate regionally should share similar aspirations and a willingness to surrender national autonomy for the larger goals of the proposed union. In the EU, for example, Sweden has encountered difficulties in revising its fiscal policy to be more in line with other EU member countries. Sweden has attempted to lower its corporate income tax rate and other taxes to improve the country's attractiveness as a place to do business in the larger EU marketplace.

Similarity of culture and language. Cultural and linguistic similarity among the countries in an economic bloc provides the basis for mutual understanding and cooperation. This partially explains the success of the MERCOSUR bloc in Latin America, whose members share many cultural and linguistic similarities. Following the passage of NAFTA, it was easier for Canadian firms to establish trade and investment relationships in the United States than in Mexico because of the similarities between the two northern countries.

Geographic proximity. Most economic blocs are formed by countries within the same geographic region; hence the name, *regional integration.* Close geographic proximity of member countries facilitates transportation of products, labor, and other factors of production. Also, neighboring countries tend to be similar in terms of culture and language.

While the four types of similarities enhance the potential for successful regional integration, economic interests are often the most important factor. Dissimilarity in one area can be overcome by similarity in the other areas. This was demonstrated in the EU, whose member countries, despite strong cultural and linguistic differences, are able to achieve common goals based on pure economic interests.

 ## Drawbacks and Ethical Dilemmas of Regional Integration

Regional integration is not a uniformly positive trend. The changes that result from regional integration can threaten firms and other constituents. Regional integration can give rise to ethical and moral concerns. These include:

Trade diversion. At least in the short run, regional integration gives rise to both trade creation *and* trade diversion. *Trade creation* means that trade is generated among the countries inside the economic bloc. This occurs because, as trade barriers fall within the bloc, each member country tends to favor trade with countries inside the bloc over trade with countries outside the bloc. At the same time, once the bloc is in place, member countries will discontinue some trade with nonmember countries, leading to *trade diversion.* The aggregate effect is that national patterns of trade are altered—more trade takes place inside the bloc, and less trade takes place with countries outside the bloc.

For example, suppose that before the formation of NAFTA, Canada and the United States were each self-sufficient in the production of wine. Suppose further that neither country imported wine from the other because of a 100 percent tariff. Now suppose that after the formation of NAFTA and elimination of the tariff, Canada began importing wine from the United States. This is an example of trade creation. Prior to NAFTA Canada had imported all its wine from France because Canada's tariff on wine imports from France was only 50 percent, making French wine cheaper than U.S. wine. Suppose that NAFTA's launch eliminated the higher U.S. tariff and made U.S. wine cheaper than French wine. Canada may then discontinue its wine imports from France in favor of imports from the United States. This is an example of trade diversion. Policymakers worry that the EU, NAFTA, and other economic blocs could turn into economic fortresses resulting in a decline in trade *between* blocs that exceeds the gains from trade *within* the blocs.

Reduced global free trade. In more advanced stages, regional integration can give rise to two opposing tendencies. On the one hand, a country that reduces trade barriers is moving toward free trade. On the other hand, an economic bloc that imposes external trade barriers is moving *away* from *worldwide* free trade. For instance, when countries form a customs union, the members impose common external trade

The European parliament meets in Strasbourg, France, where members of the EU make decisions about regional integration, including trade barriers and fiscal and monetary policy.

barriers and some member countries' external tariffs may actually *rise* relative to the tariffs in place prior to formation of the union.[13] Suppose that Germany, the EU's largest member, once had a 10 percent tariff on imported footwear. Assume that in the process of developing a common market, the EU countries collectively imposed a 20 percent tariff on footwear imports. In effect, Germany's external tariff on footwear has increased. In this way, regional integration results in *higher* trade barriers.

We addressed the harmful effects of import tariffs. Such trade barriers shield sellers inside the economic bloc from competitors based outside the bloc. However, buyers inside the bloc are worse off because they must pay higher prices for the products that they want to consume. Tariffs also counteract comparative advantages and interfere with trade flows that should be dictated by national endowments. All told, external trade barriers imposed by economic blocs result in a net loss in well-being to all the members of the bloc. Finally, because foreign firms sell less into a bloc that imposes restrictions, they are harmed as well. When external suppliers are based in developing economies, the consequences are significant. By limiting imports from such countries, trade barriers imposed by economic blocs threaten the ability of producers in these countries to improve their poor living conditions. This is the case, for example, of agricultural tariffs imposed by the EU and NAFTA blocs. These trade barriers do the most harm to farmers and ranchers in Africa, South America, and other areas characterized by substantial poverty. Governments need to consider the ethical consequences of such barriers when drafting regional integration agreements.[14]

Loss of national identity. When nations join together in an economic bloc, increased cross-border contact has a homogenizing effect; the members become more similar to each other and national cultural identity can be diluted. For this reason, member countries typically retain the right to protect certain industries vital to national heritage or security. For example, Canada has restricted the ability of U.S. movie and TV producers to invest in the Canadian film market. This is because Canada sees its film industry as a critical part of its national heritage and fears the dilution of its indigenous culture from an invasion of U.S. movie and TV entertainment programming. By enacting specific exclusions in the NAFTA accord, Canada has ensured that Canadian TV and movie interests remain largely in the hands of Canadians.

Sacrifice of autonomy. Later stages of regional integration require member countries to establish a central authority in order to manage the bloc's affairs. Each participating country must sacrifice to the central authority some of its autonomy, such as control over its own economy. In this way, nations that join an economic bloc run the risk of losing some of their national sovereignty. Concerns about national sovereignty have been a stumbling block in the development of the EU. In Britain, critics see the passage of many new laws and regulations by centralized EU authorities as a direct threat to British self-governance. Britain is a sovereign nation and the British electorate has little control over legislative efforts by EU federal authorities in continental Europe.[15] The British have resisted joining the European Monetary Union because such a move would reduce the power that they currently hold over their own currency, economy, and monetary regime.

Transfer of power to advantaged firms. Regional integration can concentrate economic power in the hands of fewer, more advantaged firms. Development of the regional marketplace attracts new competitors, from other bloc countries or from outside the bloc, into formerly protected national markets. Foreign invaders that are larger, have stronger brands, or enjoy other advantages can overwhelm local firms in their home markets. Moreover, regional integration encourages mergers and acquisitions within the bloc, leading to the creation of larger rivals. Over time, economic power gravitates toward the most advantaged firms in the bloc. Larger firms come to dominate smaller firms. For example, critics charged that as the

DR-CAFTA accord eliminated trade barriers that had protected Central American economies, U.S. firms entered these countries to manufacture and sell products. Because U.S. firms often enjoy advantages such as large size and better resources, some have come to dominate industries in Central America.

Failure of small or weak firms. As trade and investment barriers decline, protections are eliminated that previously shielded smaller or weaker firms from foreign competition. Companies typically find themselves battling new, often better-resourced rivals. New competitive pressures particularly threaten smaller firms, which may be absorbed or go out of business. The risk can be substantial for companies in smaller bloc countries, or in industries that lack comparative advantages. For example, under NAFTA, many U.S. companies in industries covered by the accord relocated their production to Mexico, the bloc member with the lowest wage rates. As a result, numerous firms in the U.S. tomato-growing industry went out of business as the industry shifted south to Mexico.

Corporate restructuring and job loss. Many firms must restructure to meet the competitive challenges posed in the new, enlarged marketplace of regional integration. Increased competitive pressures and corporate restructuring may lead to worker layoffs or re-assigning employees to distant locations. The resulting turmoil disrupts worker lives and, occasionally, entire communities. For example, MERCOSUR was a factor in the layoff of thousands of workers in Argentina's auto parts manufacturing sector. Low-priced auto parts from Brazil flowed into the MERCOSUR countries following implementation of the MERCOSUR agreement. The intense competition forced parts manufacturers in Argentina to cut costs, leading to worker layoffs.

In addition, regional integration compels many MNEs to centralize managerial control to regional or international headquarters. During this process, national managers may need to surrender some of their power and autonomy. For example, prior to EU unification, the Ford Motor Company maintained national headquarters in each of several European countries. Following EU unification, Ford reassigned some decision-making power from country heads to its European headquarters in Dagenham, England. The company centralized product design responsibilities, brought together pan-European design teams in Dagenham, and transferred financial controls and reporting to headquarters in the United States. Restructuring can prove difficult to managers, such as the head of Ford's subsidiary in Cologne, who resigned rather than lose power.

When they negotiate regional integration agreements, national governments have a responsibility to include provisions that reduce harmful effects such as job losses and the failure of small or weak firms. For example, NAFTA included various clauses aimed at softening the effects of economic restructuring that resulted from passage of the accord. NAFTA included provisions aimed at maintaining or improving labor conditions for workers in the member countries. Firms received long phase-in periods (often 10 years or more) to adjust to falling protectionist barriers. Funds were allocated to support the retraining of workers who lost their jobs due to NAFTA.

Management Implications of Regional Integration

Regional economic integration has implications for company strategy and performance. Many firms modify their strategies to take advantage of new opportunities in the enlarged marketplace or to safeguard their positions against potential threats. Choosing appropriate strategies depends largely on the firm's current position in the regional market, the characteristics of the firm's industry, and on the market's particular rules and regulations. Regional economic integration suggests at least six implications for management.

Internationalization by firms inside the economic bloc. Initially, regional integration pressures or encourages companies to internationalize into neighboring countries within the bloc. The elimination of trade and investment barriers also presents new opportunities to source input goods from foreign suppliers within the bloc. By venturing into other countries in the bloc, the firm can generate new sales and increase profits. Internationalizing into neighboring, familiar countries also provides the firm with the skills and confidence to further internationalize to markets *outside* the bloc. For example, following the formation of NAFTA, many U.S. companies entered Canada and gained valuable international experience that inspired them to launch ventures into Asia and Europe.

Rationalization of operations. Following the creation of an economic bloc, the importance of national boundaries will decrease. Instead of viewing the bloc as a collection of disparate countries, firms begin to view the bloc as a unified whole. Managers develop strategies and value-chain activities suited to the region as a whole, rather than to individual countries. *Rationalization* is the process of restructuring and consolidating company operations that managers often undertake following regional integration. When a firm rationalizes, it reduces redundancy. The goal is to reduce costs and increase the efficiency of operations. For example, management may combine two or more factories into a single production facility that eliminates duplication and generates economies of scale. Rationalization becomes an attractive option because, as trade and investment barriers decline, the firm that formerly operated factories in each of several countries reaps advantages by consolidating the factories into one or two central locations inside the economic bloc.

As an example, prior to formation of the EU, many companies operated factories in each of numerous European countries. After the EU's launch, these firms merged their plants into one or two European countries. Companies centralized plants in the EU locations that offered the lowest-cost operations and other competitive advantages. Thus, Caterpillar, the U.S. manufacturer of earth-moving equipment, was one of many companies that shifted its focus from serving individual European countries to serving the EU region. Caterpillar undertook a massive program of modernization and rationalization at its EU plants to streamline production, reduce inventories, increase economies of scale, and lower operating costs.

Companies can apply rationalization to other value-chain functions such as distribution, logistics, purchasing, and R&D. For example, following formation of the EU, the elimination of trade barriers, customs checkpoints, and country-specific transportation regulations allowed U.S. firms to restructure their EU distribution channels to make them better suited to the greatly enlarged EU marketplace. Creation of the economic bloc eliminated the need to devise separate distribution strategies for individual countries. Instead, the firms were able to employ a more global approach for the larger marketplace, generating economies of scale in distribution.

Mergers and acquisitions. The formation of economic blocs also leads to mergers and acquisitions (M&A); that is, the tendency of one firm to buy another, or of two or more firms to merge and form a larger company. Mergers and acquisitions are related to rationalization. The merger of two or more firms creates a new company that produces a product on a much larger scale. As an example, two giant engineering firms, Asea AB of Sweden and Brown, Boveri & Co. of Switzerland, merged to form Asea Brown Boveri (ABB). The merger was facilitated by regional integration of European countries in the development of the EU economic bloc. The merger allowed the new firm, ABB, to increase its R&D activities and pool greater capital funding for major projects, such as construction of power plants and large-scale industrial equipment. In the pharmaceutical industry, Britain's Zeneca purchased Sweden's Astra to form AstraZeneca. The acquisition led to the development of blockbusters such as the ulcer drug Nexium and helped transform the new company into a leader in the gastrointestinal, cardiovascular, and respiratory areas.

Regional products and marketing strategy. Regional integration can also stimulate companies to *standardize* their products and services. Companies prefer to offer relatively standardized merchandise in their various markets. The reason is that it is easier and much less costly to make and sell a few product models than dozens of models. An economic bloc facilitates the streamlining and standardization of products and marketing activities because, in more advanced stages of regional integration, the member countries tend to harmonize product standards and commercial regulations, and eliminate trade barriers and transportation bottlenecks. As conditions in the member countries become similar to each other, companies can increasingly standardize their products and marketing.[16]

For example, prior to EU unification, in order to comply with varying national regulations regarding the placement of lights, brakes, and other specifications on tractors sold in Europe, J. I. Case, a manufacturer of agricultural machinery, had produced numerous versions of its Magnum model of farm tractors. Where Case once produced 17 versions of the Magnum, the harmonization of EU product standards allowed the firm to standardize its tractor, allowing it to produce only a handful of models that were, nevertheless, appropriate for serving all the EU market.[17]

Internationalization by firms from outside the bloc. Regional integration leads to the creation of large multicountry markets, which are attractive to firms from *outside* the bloc. Such foreign firms tend to avoid exporting as an entry strategy because economic blocs erect trade barriers against imports from outside the bloc. Accordingly, the most effective way for a foreign firm to enter an economic bloc is to establish a physical presence there via FDI. By building a production facility, marketing subsidiary, or regional headquarters anywhere inside a bloc, the outsider gains access to the entire bloc and obtains advantages enjoyed by local firms based inside the bloc. As an example, since formation of the EU, Britain has become the largest recipient of FDI from the United States. U.S. firms choose Britain as the beachhead to gain access to the massive EU market. In a similar way, European firms have established factories in Mexico to access countries in the NAFTA bloc.

Collaborative ventures. Regional integration creates opportunities for cooperation among firms located inside their own bloc. For example, following creation of the European Community, the precursor to the EU, firms from France, Germany, Spain, and the United Kingdom collaborated to establish Airbus Industries, the giant commercial aircraft manufacturer. The elimination of trade and investment barriers in the EU allowed Airbus to move aircraft parts, capital, and labor among the member countries from one factory to another. In a similar way, firms from outside an economic bloc also benefit from regional integration. Outsiders ease their entry into the bloc by entering joint ventures and other collaborative arrangements with companies based inside the bloc.

In 1990, there were approximately 50 regional economic integration agreements worldwide. Today there are some 200, in various stages of development. As the growth in world trade continues apace, nations want to be part of emerging opportunities. Governments continue to liberalize trade policies, encourage imports, and restructure regulatory regimes, largely through regional cooperation. Many nations belong to several free trade agreements. Economic blocs are joining with other blocs around the world. More nations are clamoring to join the EU, which has signed trade agreements with other economic blocs worldwide. Other intercontinental blocs are underway. Empirical evidence since the 1970s suggests that regional economic integration is not slowing the progress of global free trade.[18] It is more likely that global free trade will gradually emerge as economic blocs link up with each other over time. The evidence suggests that regional economic integration is gradually giving way to a system of worldwide free trade.

CLOSING CASE

Russell Corporation: The Dilemma of Regional Free Trade

Russell Corporation is a leading manufacturer of sportswear, including sweatshirts, sweatpants, and T-shirts. Owned by Berkshire Hathaway, Russell is based in Atlanta, Georgia, in the United States, and has annual revenues of around $2 billion. Its main competitors include Adidas, Nike, Benetton, and Zara. Russell runs every step of the manufacturing process: from weaving raw yarn into fabric, to dyeing, cutting, and sewing, to selling garments through retailers. Russell's brands include JERZEES, American Athletic, Brooks, Cross Creek, Huffy Sports, Russell Athletic, and Spalding. The firm sells through mass merchandisers, department stores such as Wal-Mart, and golf pro shops. Russell sells its apparel in about 100 countries and recently restructured production. The firm closed plants, moved some manufacturing abroad, and eliminated 1,700 U.S. jobs.

Management at Russell was pleased with the passage of the Dominican Republic-Central American Free Trade Agreement (DR-CAFTA) in 2005. The pact eliminated trade barriers between the United States and six Latin American countries: Guatemala, Honduras, El Salvador, Nicaragua, Costa Rica, and the Dominican Republic. Following DR-CAFTA's passage, Central American countries experienced a significant rise in foreign direct investment (FDI) from abroad. The apparel and clothing sector—consisting of firms like Russell—were among the biggest beneficiaries.

Prior to DR-CAFTA, many North American apparel companies sourced from China and other Asian nations, where production costs are low. DR-CAFTA virtually eliminated tariffs on trade between the United States, Central America, and the Dominican Republic. Now Russell can cost-effectively source raw materials in Central America, manufacture fabric in the United States, then send the fabric to its factories in Honduras for assembly. Once the garments are completed, they are re-exported to the U.S. for distribution. Without DR-CAFTA, it would not have been cost effective to make fabric in the United States, export it to Asia, have the products manufactured there and then reexported back. Under that scenario, Russell would have shifted *all* its manufacturing to China.

Background on DR-CAFTA

In the past, Central America and the Caribbean were parties to various protectionist trade arrangements, including the worldwide Multi-Fibre Agreement (MFA) of 1974. Among its provisions, the MFA shielded the North and Central American apparel industries from foreign competition by imposing strict import quotas. When the MFA expired in 2005, many countries became exposed to the full force of cheap imports from low-cost producers in Asia. China dramatically increased its apparel exports to the United States, to the detriment of U.S. and Central American producers that long had supplied Western markets. For example, Alabama was once the world center of sock manufacturing. When the MFA expired, the sock capital shifted to Datang, China. Alabama sock workers receive an average of $10 an hour, compared to 70 cents an hour in Datang.

Since the expiration of the MFA, China has been flooding the United States with apparel. In recent years, China's share of finished clothing exports to the United States, once less than 20 percent, has leaped past 50 percent in some segments. To protect its home-grown apparel industry, the United States reimposed some trade barriers against Chinese imports. The U.S. government justified this action in part because China's currency, the yuan, is considered undervalued, which makes Chinese exports artificially cheap. However, such protection of the U.S. apparel industry is only temporary. World Trade Organization rules require the U.S. government to remove the trade barriers, at which time Chinese exports to the United States will increase.

Many in the U.S. apparel industry see DR-CAFTA as perhaps the only way to compete with China. DR-CAFTA helps maintain much apparel production in the Western Hemisphere by creating a bigger apparel market in the region and granting favorable trade status to apparel producers who manufacture their products using raw material from the DR-CAFTA region.

The United States is the biggest apparel market, importing more than $9 billion worth of apparel from the DR-CAFTA countries in each of 2004, 2005, and 2006. Honduras was the biggest shipper in dollar value, and exported products such as cotton blouses, shirts, and underwear. Meanwhile, DR-CAFTA gave U.S. producers an equal footing to sell their products to Central America. For example, the region is the second largest market for U.S. textiles and yarn, which Central American manufacturers use to produce finished apparel.

The DR-CAFTA countries are part of a large and growing trade region, and the free trade agreement is helping to improve economic conditions there. Perhaps the most important long-term benefit will be foreign investment in new technologies and a better-educated regional labor force. Some see DR-CAFTA as a further step toward development of the Free Trade Area of the Americas (FTAA), a proposed agreement that would bring free trade to all or most of North, Central, and South America.

The Situation in Honduras

Russell manufactures much of its garments in Honduras, a poor Central American country with 7 million people, one quarter of whom are illiterate. Honduras has an annual per-capita GDP of about $3,000. In 2006, the country's unemployment rate was 28 percent. The Honduras currency, the lempira, has been weakening against the U.S. dollar over time. Growth remains dependent on the U.S. economy, its largest trading partner, and on reduction of the high local crime rate. Honduras sends over 73 percent of its exported goods to the United States and receives about 53 percent of its imports from that country. The Honduran government is counting on the DR-CAFTA agreement to increase trade with the United States and the Central American region.

Few countries rely on their apparel industry more than Honduras. The Honduran government used incentives to create a large cluster of apparel firms. In addition to low-cost labor, Honduras offers a generous tax package: firms pay no income tax, value-added tax, or duties. Honduran apparel manufacturers can truck their merchandise to Puerto Cortes, Central America's biggest port, in just 30 minutes. From there, it takes only 22 hours to ship the goods to Miami by container ship. Honduras' apparel sector employs over 110,000 people, or 30 percent of the country's total industrial employment. The government is investing to improve Puerto Cortes and create a Textiles and Apparel University to train future managers and supervisors. To counter Chinese competition, the apparel industry in Honduras has begun to offer the "total package"—buying fabric, and sometimes even designing the garments, as well as final assembly.

Some Honduran apparel plants employ sophisticated technologies to increase productivity and output. For example, one supplier uses computer-aided design to cut cloth before sending it to be stitched into shirts for brands such as Jockey, Ralph Lauren, and Nautica. In 2003, the stock of U.S. FDI in Honduras was $262 million and rose to $339 million the following year. However, Honduras' legal system remains weak and corruption is a problem.

Honduran apparel producers are taking steps to survive in the evolving free trade environment. Geographic proximity to the United States is a big advantage that gives producers greater flexibility to respond quickly to rapidly evolving tastes. Honduran producers can ship finished merchandise to the United States in less than 24 hours, while similar shipments from China take up to a month.

Russell's Dilemmas

Many consumers shop for athletic clothing based on price, so even slight price increases can affect sales. Unlike Nike and Adidas, Russell does not enjoy much brand loyalty. Russell must decide whether to retain its manufacturing in Honduras or move everything to China.

An additional possibility is to establish production in Eastern Europe to gain access to the huge EU market. Meanwhile, Adidas and Nike are pursuing markets in China and other Asian countries. Labor costs for manufacturing apparel are similar in Central America and China. In both locations, workers earn around a dollar per hour and can produce over a hundred garments per day, from precut cloth. Labor costs are roughly $2 an hour in Eastern Europe, but producers are advantaged by being so close to the nearly 500 million consumers in the EU.

Management at Russell is keeping an eye on the proposed FTAA, which would widen access to the Latin American marketplace with its 500 million consumers. Maintaining a presence in Latin America would give Russell a favorable position for targeting new markets there. But progress on the FTAA has been slowed due to hostile public and governmental opposition from some South American countries. Governments in countries such as Bolivia and Venezuela argue that the FTAA will increase U.S. dominance in the region and harm local workers, subjecting them to sweatshop working conditions.

Meanwhile, regional integration is creating a larger market in the Western Hemisphere and new opportunities to source low-cost inputs from regional suppliers. While increased competition from China poses new challenges, the DR-CAFTA accord is helping to level the playing field. Russell management is concerned about manufacturing costs that are higher than competitors and is poised to consolidate much of its production into suppliers located close to its home market. At the same time, Russell is also contemplating new markets in the Americas and beyond.

AACSB: Reflective Thinking, Ethical Reasoning

Case Questions

1. Worldwide, China has the most absolute and comparative advantages in producing apparel. Free trade theory implies that retailers should import clothing from the most efficient country. Nevertheless, DR-CAFTA aims to promote Central American trade with the United States, and the United States has imposed quotas on imports from China. Given this, and the potential drawbacks of regional integration, would it be better to allow free trade to take its natural course? That is, would it be better to rescind DR-CAFTA and allow apparel retailers to import from the most cost-effective suppliers, wherever they are located worldwide?

2. What are the advantages and disadvantages of DR-CAFTA to Honduran firms? To Honduras as a nation? Should free trade be extended throughout Latin America through the proposed FTAA?

3. Honduras is a poor country that faces the loss of jobs in its apparel sector from growing foreign competition. What can the Honduran government do to help keep jobs in Honduras? The government can address some problems by attracting more foreign investment into Honduras. In what ways could foreign investment help? What steps could the government take to attract more FDI?

4. Russell Corporation is a smaller player than its formidable rivals, Adidas and Nike. What should Russell do to counter these firms? What should Russell do to counter the flood of low-cost athletic apparel now entering the United States from China? What strategic approaches should Russell follow to ensure its future survival and success?

Sources: Authers, John. (2004). "Honduras Textile Groups Hope Trade Deal Will Sew Up Future." *Financial Times*, July 27, p. 8; Authers, John. (2006). "Employment Shrinks in the Textile Sector." *Financial Times*, March 10, p. 5; Borneman, Jim. (2006). "Regional Support in a Global Fight." *Textile World*, May/June, pp. 26–32; Central Intelligence Agency. (2006). *CIA World Factbook*, entry on Honduras; Colvin, Geoffrey. (2005). "Saving America's Socks—But Killing Free Trade." *Fortune*, August 22, p. 38; *Economist*. (2004). "Textiles: Losing Their Shirts," Oct. 16, pp. 59–60; *Financial Times*. (2007). "Adidas Sets Personal best in Sports Sales." March 28, p. 17; Hoovers.com. (2006). Corporate summaries of Russell, Nike, and Adidas. Retrieved from www.hoovers.com; Lapper, Richard. (2005). "Textile groups in a bind if U.S. unravels CAFTA treaty." *Financial Times*, June 7, p.18; Millman, John. (2003). "Central America Finds Impetus for Growth." *Wall Street Journal*, Dec. 8, p. A2; Morphy, Erika. (2005). "Trade Watch: CAFTA—The Rocky Path to Regional Free Trade. *Foreign Direct Investment*, Oct. 1,p. 1; Nike, Inc. (2007). "Nike, Inc. Outlines Strategies for Global Growth and Market Leadership across Core Consumer Categories." Retrieved Feb. 6, 2007, from www.nike.com; Paulson, Henry, Jr. (2005). "CAFTA Is the American Way." *Wall Street Journal*, July 14, p. A10; *Wall Street Journal*. (2005). "Russell Corp.: Profit Estimates are Lowered Because of Katrina and CAFTA." Sept. 20, p. 1.

Key Terms

common market, p. 227
customs union, p. 226
economic union, p. 227
free trade agreement, p. 225

free trade area, p. 225
regional economic integration, p. 224

regional economic integration bloc, p. 225

Summary

In this chapter, you learned about:

1. Regional integration and economic blocs

Regional economic integration involves groups of countries forming alliances to promote free trade, cross-national investment, and other mutual goals. This integration results from **regional economic integration blocs** (or economic blocs), in which member countries agree to eliminate tariffs and other restrictions on the cross-national flow of products, services, capital, and, in more advanced stages, labor, within the bloc. At minimum, the countries in an economic bloc become parties to a **free trade agreement**, which eliminates tariffs, quotas, and other trade barriers.

2. Types of regional integration

For countries that become members of an economic bloc, there are various stages of regional integration. First is the **free trade area**, in which tariffs and other trade barriers are eliminated, and that emerge when nations sign a free trade agreement. Second is the **customs union**, a free trade area in which common trade barriers are imposed on nonmember countries. Third is the **common market**, a customs union in which factors of production move freely among the members. Fourth is the **economic union**, a common market in which some important economic policies are harmonized among the member states. A true *political union* does not yet exist.

3. Leading economic blocs

There are roughly 200 economic integration agreements in the world. The European Union (EU) is the most advanced of these, comprising 27 countries in Europe. The EU has increased market access, improved trade rules, and harmonized standards among its members. Europe is also home to the European Free Trade Association. In the Americas, the most notable bloc is the North American Free Trade Agreement (NAFTA). The bloc consists of Canada, Mexico, and the United States. NAFTA has reached only the free-trade-area stage of regional integration. Other economic blocs in the Americas include MERCOSUR, CARICOM, and CAN. In the Asia/Pacific region, ASEAN, APEC, and the Australia and New Zealand Closer Economic Relations Agreement (CER) are the leading blocs. Economic blocs in Africa and the Middle East have experienced only limited success.

4. Why countries pursue regional integration

Regional integration contributes to corporate and industrial growth, and hence to economic growth, better living standards, and higher tax revenues for the member countries. It increases market size by integrating the economies within a region. It increases economies of scale and factor productivity among firms in the member countries and attracts foreign investors to the bloc. Regional integration also increases competition and economic dynamism within the bloc, and increases the bloc's political power.

5. Success factors for regional integration

The most successful blocs consist of countries that are relatively similar in terms of culture, language, and economic and political structures. The countries should also be close to each other geographically. Countries can overcome major differences in any one of these factors if there are strong similarities in all the other factors.

6. Drawbacks and ethical dilemmas of regional integration

Regional integration simultaneously leads to *trade creation*, whereby new trade is generated among the countries inside the bloc, and *trade diversion,* in which member countries discontinue some trade with countries outside the bloc. Regional integration entails specific disadvantages. It can reduce global free trade, particularly when member countries form a customs union that results in substantial trade barriers to countries outside the bloc. When economic blocs involve many countries of various sizes, regional integration can concentrate power into large firms and large nations inside the bloc. Regional integration results in economic restructuring, which may harm particular industries and firms. When a country joins an economic bloc, it must relinquish some of its autonomy and national power to the bloc's central authority. Individual countries risk losing some of their national identity.

7. Management implications of regional integration

Regional integration leads to increased internationalization by firms inside their economic bloc. Firms reconfigure and rationalize their operations in line with the larger internal market. Management reconfigures value-chain activities on a pan-regional basis. The formation of economic blocs also leads to mergers and acquisitions because the emergence of a new, larger market favors the creation of larger firms. Managers revise marketing strategies by standardizing products and developing regional brands. Regional integration also leads firms from outside the bloc to expand into the bloc, often via direct investment and collaborations with bloc firms. But regional integration leads to competitive pressures and other challenges to firms inside the bloc, some of which may lay off workers or go out of business.

Test Your Comprehension AACSB: Reflective Thinking

1. What is a regional economic integration bloc (also called an economic bloc)?

2. What is the role of free trade agreements in the formation of economic blocs?

3. What are the different levels of economic integration?

4. Differentiate between a free trade area and a customs unions. Differentiate between a customs unions and a common market.

5. What are the world's leading economic blocs? Which blocs are most advanced in terms of regional integration?

6. Describe the major characteristics of the European Union and NAFTA.

7. Why do nations seek to join or form economic blocs? What are the advantages of such arrangements?

8. What national conditions contribute to the success of economic integration?

9. Explain the drawbacks of regional integration for nations. Explain the drawbacks for firms.

10. Distinguish between trade creation and trade diversion.

11. What strategies should companies employ to maximize the benefits of regional integration?

Apply Your Understanding
AACSB: Ethical Reasoning, Reflective Thinking, Communication

1. There are some 200 economic integration agreements in effect around the world already, far more than even a few years ago. Virtually every country is now party to one or more free trade agreements. Supporters argue that free trade is good for nations. What is the basis for their support? That is, what are the specific benefits that countries seek by joining an economic bloc? What is the main economic bloc for your country? From your perspective, what advantages has bloc membership brought to your country? What disadvantages has bloc membership produced?

2. The United States is in free trade agreements with Mexico, Canada (NAFTA), and several Central American countries (via the DR-CAFTA accord featured in the *Closing Case*), among others. Critics charge that these agreements are harmful because of the substantial wage differences with the partner countries. For example, a Mexican worker may earn one-fifth the hourly wage of a U.S. worker. Critics further argue it would be unwise for the United States to establish a common market or economic union with Latin American countries. They argue that a U.S. worker will be disadvantaged relative to a Mexican worker if he or she does not work with more or better natural resources than the Mexican, have a better skill set, and have access to better technology. What can U.S. firms do to maintain their competitiveness relative to Mexican firms, given Mexico's advantage in low wages? It is likely that some day the United States will form a common market with Mexico and other Latin American partners. In your view, what conditions should be in place before such an agreement is allowed to go forward?

3. Following implementation of free trade agreements, trade has grown *within* each of the CARICOM and CAN economic blocs. The growth of within-bloc trade implies that exports from your country to these blocs may be declining over time. Discuss strategies for counteracting such a shift. What recommendations would you make to a company for pursuing opportunities within these blocs? What is the role of international business research, market entry strategy, foreign direct investment, marketing strategy, and collaboration for maintaining or augmenting commerce with these blocs?

AACSB: **Reflective Thinking, Analytical Skills, Ethical Reasoning**

Refer to Chapter 1, page 27, for instructions on how to access and use globalEDGE™.

1. There has been much opposition to the Free Trade Area of the Americas (FTAA). For a sampling of arguments against this proposed pact, visit www.globalexchange.org; www.citizenstrade.org/stopftaa.php; and www.corpwatch.org. Also visit the official site of the FTAA at www.ftaa-alca.org, or get information on the proposed pact from globalEDGE™. Based on your reading of the chapter, evaluate the anti-FTAA arguments. What is your position? Do you agree or disagree with arguments made by the critics? Why or why not? Do you think the proposed FTAA would harm small Latin American countries? Would it be a boon only to large countries such as Brazil, Canada, and the United States?

2. Visit the Web sites of three major economic blocs. One way to do this is to enter the acronyms for each bloc into a globalEDGE™ search. Using the "Success Factors for Regional Integration" framework highlighted in this chapter, discuss the likely long-term prospects for success in each of these blocs. For each bloc, which of the success factors are strongest and which are weakest? Which bloc seems to have the best chances for long-term success? Why?

3. NAFTA is a free trade area, and the EU is a common market. Visit the Web sites of these two economic blocs, www.nafta-sec-alena.org and europa.eu.int, and explain the business strategy implications of each type of economic bloc. Small and medium-sized enterprises (SMEs) tend to be disadvantaged when it comes to competing against large corporations in regional economic blocs. What steps can SMEs in particular take to maximize prospects for success when doing business in a free trade area? What steps can SMEs take when doing business in a common market?

CKR Cavusgil Knight Riesenberger

Management Skill Builder©

Entering the Retailing Sector in the New EU Member States

Retailers expand internationally primarily through foreign direct investment. Major retailers such as Wal-Mart and Tesco have been expanding abroad since the 1970s. Recently, retailers have been targeting Eastern European countries that have joined the European Union (EU) since 2004. With a population of almost a half-billion people, the EU is an impressive potential market. However, recent enlargement of the EU from 15 to 27 members has proven difficult. Challenges have arisen due to differences in the economic conditions and the developmental stage of the new members, which are mainly Eastern European countries and former satellites of the Soviet Union.

AACSB: Reflective Thinking, Analytical Skills

Managerial Challenge

Numerous retailers are making plans to take advantage of the entry of new country markets into the EU. However, choosing the best markets to locate stores is complex because there are so many locations to consider. Managers conduct research to ensure they establish stores in locations most likely to enhance company performance.

Background

As a single unit, the EU has the largest economy in the world. The countries that joined the EU since 2004 differ in many ways from the original EU members. Most are former Soviet satellites that were under a communist command economy for several decades. New entrants such as Poland, Hungary, and the Czech Republic had to adjust their economies to qualify for EU membership. There are substantial business opportunities in these countries for large-scale retailers. Income levels in the new members are growing and the countries are excellent sites from which retailers can source manufactured goods at lower cost.

Managerial Skills You Will Gain

By completing this C/K/R Management Skill Builder©, as a prospective manager, you will:

1. Learn about the EU and its expansion to include countries in Eastern Europe.

2. Examine conditions in Eastern Europe faced by potential entrants.

3. Understand the factors to consider when locating retail stores abroad.

4. Determine how country factors relate to maximizing competitive advantage in the location of retail stores.

Your Task

Assume that you work for a large retailer, such as Wal-Mart, Tesco, or Zara. Management wants to expand into new member states of the European Union. Your task is to conduct research to determine the most attractive location for establishing a large retail store and central distribution center.

Go to the C/K/R Knowledge Portal©

www.prenhall.com/cavusgil

Proceed to the C/K/R Knowledge Portal© to obtain the expanded background information, your task and methodology, suggested resources for this exercise, and the presentation template.

Chapter 5

INTERNATIONAL CULTURE

Contents

Introduction

What is culture?

The importance of culture in different business contexts

National stereotypes and key dimensions of culture

Cross-cultural management

Culture embodied in national institutions

■ **Active Learning Case**

Culture clash at Pharmacia and Upjohn

■ **International Business Strategy in Action**

McDonald's

Danone and Parmalat—going international, staying local

■ **Real Cases**

Do not throw your *meishi*!

Sport can be local *and* global: Manchester United

Objectives of the chapter

Places and people differ. The Japanese tend to be very polite, the Australians characteristically blunt. Red means "danger" or "stop" to the British, but in Turkey it signifies death and in China, good fortune. In France getting into a *grande école* tends to guarantee good job prospects whereas in Saudi Arabia the wealth and status of your family is far more important.

Patterns of global diversity and the implications of these differences have been studied from a range of perspectives, by sociologists, psychologists, anthropologists, and political scientists. Here we are concerned with how cultural diversity and related differences in the behavior, norms, and expectations of particular groups of employees, managers, colleagues, or customers affect management decision making and corporate organizations. After an introduction to the kinds of business contexts in which cultural differences do matter, this chapter will describe some typologies of national cultural differences and discuss the implications of these for international managers.

The specific objectives of this chapter are to:

1 *Define* culture and explain the factors that underlie cultural differences.
2 *Show* where and why cultural differences matter to international managers.
3 *Explain* a number of frameworks that help identify important cultural differences.
4 *Examine* how firms can anticipate and cope with cultural differences.

Culture clash at Pharmacia and Upjohn

Despite being part of the same advanced, industrialized world, Kalamazoo (Michigan, United States), Stockholm (Sweden), and Milan (Italy) are worlds apart in many important ways. Senior managers leading the merger between two pharmaceutical firms, Upjohn Company of the United States and Pharmacia AB of Sweden (with operations in Italy), came to realize how significant these differences were after the merger took place in 1995.

Swedes take off most of the month of July for their annual vacation, Italians take off most of August. Not knowing this, US executives scheduled meetings in the summer only to have to cancel many because their European counterparts were at the beach. As the more dominant US firm began to impose its way of doing things on the newly acquired European organizations, international relationships became increasingly strained.

Neither the Swedes nor the Italians were happy with impositions such as the drug and alcohol testing policy brought in by Upjohn, or the office smoking ban. These clashed with local ways of doing things and the more informal work environment that these cultures prefer. Although Upjohn later relaxed many of these work rules, allowing some local practices and preferences to prevail, ill-feeling and a degree of resistance had already developed among European colleagues.

The additional bureaucracy and the command-and-control style imposed by the Americans created more significant problems for the 34,000 employees and managers in Pharmacia and Upjohn Company. The Swedes were used to an open, team-based style of management where responsibilities are devolved; managers are trusted and not strictly monitored or closely managed. Swedish executives also tend to build up a consensus behind big decisions, "getting everyone in the same boat" (alla aer i baten) rather than handing orders down the hierarchy. As a traditional US multinational, however, Upjohn was more used to strong leadership and a centralized command-and-control structure. Its CEO, Dr. John Zabriskie, quickly created a strict reporting system, tight budget control, and frequent staffing updates, which clashed with the Swedish organization style. Swedish managers would leave meetings disgruntled, having been overruled by US executives keen to push their vision of the merged company.

The Swedes' own ways of doing things had already clashed with the Italian style of management, following the takeover of Farmitalia (part of Montedison) by Pharmacia in 1993. Italians are used to a distinctive division between workers (and their strong unions) and managers. Their steeper hierarchies contrast the more egalitarian Swedes. Italians also place a high value on families and will leave work to tend to sick relatives or help with childcare, which the Swedes frown upon. The addition of the Americans from Upjohn to this mix created further cultural confusion. Communication problems, beyond the obvious language differences, became a real barrier to honest dialogue. "You go there thinking you're going to streamline the place," said American Mark H. Corrigan, Pharmacia and Upjohn Vice President for Clinical Development, "and you leave just having added five pounds from some wonderful meals."

These differences, many of them small but important at the local level, quickly began to have an impact on the overall performance of the merged company. In the months and years following the merger unforeseen inefficiencies and added costs began to undermine the potential synergies of bringing together two such companies in the first place. At one level the problems amounted to things like canceled meetings, new organization demands (such as monthly report writing), and a general decline in staff morale. There were also unexpected difficulties integrating the IT systems across the various parts of the merged organization. These and other changes added an estimated $200 million to the predicted costs of the restructuring, taking the total cost to $800 million. Even more seriously, for a pharmaceutical company heavily reliant on its new drugs pipeline to survive, delayed product launches and the loss of key staff (including the head of R&D at Pharmacia) had a longer-term impact. "There was probably an under-appreciation ... of these cultural differences," says Art Atkinson, former Vice President for Clinical Research and Development.

Particular problems resulted from the restructuring of the firm's global R&D structure. Prior to the merger Upjohn owned well-known names such as Rogaine and Motrin and had annual sales of around $3.5 billion, but had a weak new product pipeline and slow sales growth compared to its larger competitors. Similar-sized Pharmacia had a more promising pipeline but weak distribution and sales in the US market, the world's largest. These amounted to a strong rationale for the merger. Together they could challenge the financial power and the larger R&D programs of their competitors. However, integrating and refocusing the various parts of the new R&D structure became a major problem. Rather than place the R&D headquarters in the United States, Sweden, or Milan, a decision was made to establish a new and neutral London-based center for the R&D function. This simply added a layer of management and a more complex matrix reporting structure, which further alienated key R&D personnel.

In 1997, after the stock price of the merged corporation had fallen significantly, CEO John Zabriskie resigned. Swede Jan Ekberg, the former head of Pharmacia, took over temporarily and began to rebuild aspects of the merged organization.

After acquiring a major part of Monsanto in 2000, Pharmacia and Upjohn became Pharmacia, which was then itself acquired by the US giant Pfizer in April 2003. This made Pfizer, according to its own Annual Report, the "number one pharmaceutical company in every region of the World."

All this proves is that going global is hard work. Not all of these problems could have been foreseen, but a real lack of awareness of cultural differences did lead to many of the organization difficulties and people problems with a real impact on the bottom line.

Websites: www.accenture.com/xdoc/en/ideas/outlook/1.2000/maa2.pdf; www.pfizer.com; www.pfizer.com/are/investors_reports/annual_2003/review/index.htm.

Sources: R. Frank and T. M. Burton, "Pharmacia & Upjohn Faces Culture Clash; Europeans Chafe Under US Rules," *Wall Street Journal*, February 4, 1997; R. J. Thomas, "Irreconcilable Differences," *Accenture Outlook*, vol. 1, 2000; and Pfizer, *Annual Report*, 2003.

1 What kinds of cultural differences matter when organizations from different countries merge?

2 How well do the characteristics described in the case match the respective, stereotypical national cultures of these countries?

3 What could senior managers have done before and after the merger to alleviate some of the problems that resulted from culture clash?

4 Explain why one organization might want to impose some of its ways of doing things on another, such as an acquired firm or subsidiary.

INTRODUCTION

The number of workers employed by foreign-owned companies has grown significantly over the past 20 years as a result of the expanding activities of foreign affiliates of MNEs around the world. For many people, both employers and employees, this has brought home the realities of globalization. An estimated 73 million people globally (including 24 million in China) now work for foreign companies, nearly three times the number in 1990. Companies such as Motorola, General Motors, British Petroleum, and General Electric are among the largest private-sector employers in economies such as Malaysia and Singapore.[1]

This growing multicultural workforce, part of the increasingly global patterns of exchange and interaction discussed earlier in this book, makes it more and more important to understand how people's preferences, beliefs, and values differ. Understanding international cultural differences allows us to be aware of and adapt to the differences that matter for managers.

WHAT IS CULTURE?

Culture can be defined as "the sum total of the beliefs, rules, techniques, institutions, and artifacts that characterize human populations"[2] or "the collective programming of the mind."[3]

Socialization
The process of enculturation, or the adoption of the behavior patterns of the surrounding culture

Sociologists generally talk about the **socialization** process, referring to the influence of parents, friends, education, and the interaction with other members of a particular society as the basis for one's culture. These influences result in learned patterns of behavior common to members of a given society.

As you can see, definitions of culture vary according to the focus of interest, the unit of analysis, and the disciplinary approach (psychology, anthropology, sociology, geography, etc.).

Table 5.1 World population percentages in terms of home region, language, and religion

Home region	%	Language	%	Religion	%	
Asia	58.4	Mandarin	14.4	Christianity, including:		33
Africa	12.4	Hindi	6.0	Catholics	20	
Europe	9.5	English	5.6	Protestants	9	
Latin America	8.4	Spanish	5.6	Orthodox	4	
Former Soviet bloc	5.5	Bengali	3.4	Islam		22
North America	5.2	Russian	2.8	Hinduism		15
Australia and New Zealand	0.6	Portuguese	2.6	Non-religious		14
		Japanese	2.0	Buddhism		6
		German	1.6	Chinese traditional		4
		Korean	1.3	Primal–indigenous		3
		French	1.3	Other		3
		Other (approx. 200)	54.4			

Sources: www.census.gov; www.adherents.com.

This is significant in that studies of cultural differences adopt a specific definition and set of measurable criteria, which are always debatable. Research into culture and its impact in business and management studies is highly contentious and should not just be taken at face value, including the studies described below.

There is a strong consensus, however, that key elements of culture include language, religion, values, attitudes, customs, and norms of a group or society. Table 5.1 shows how the world's population is divided according to geography, language, and religion.

Language is perhaps the most important key to understanding culture in general and the specific values, beliefs, attitudes, and opinions of a particular individual or group. English is widely accepted as the language of business; many global institutions and companies have adopted English as their official language. For many firms, such as Toyota, NEC, Hitachi, and IBM Japan, English-speaking ability is a prerequisite for promotion.[4] However, any assumption that speaking the same language removes cultural differences is dangerous—it normally just hides them. Moreover, a reliance on English by British and American managers, and a lack of other language skills, can weaken their ability to empathize with and adapt to other cultures.

Religion, linked to both regional characteristics and language, also influences business culture through a set of shared core values. Protestants hold strong beliefs about the value of delayed gratification, saving, and investment. The sociologist Max Weber, writing in 1904, saw this Protestant work ethic as the "spirit of capitalism" during the Industrial Revolution.[5] Rather than spending, consuming, and enjoying life now, their religious beliefs prompted the Protestants to look to longer-term rewards (including those in the after-life). There are parallels with the Confucian and Shinto work ethics, which also view spiritual rewards as tied to hard work and commitment to the fruits of industry. Contrasting this, a more stoic attitude among some African populations partly explains their acceptance of the ways things are, because it is the "will of God" (*shauri ya Mungu*).

At the most general level culture can refer simply to the lifestyle and behavior of a given group of people, so **corporate culture** is a term used to characterize how the managers and employees of particular companies tend to behave. But the term is also used by human resource managers and senior management in their attempts to proactively shape the kind of behavior (innovative, open, dynamic, etc.) they hope to nurture in their organizations. Promoting a distinctive corporate culture is also expected to enhance the sense of community and shared identity that underpins effective organizations.

Corporate culture
The shared values, traditions, customs, philosophy, and policies of a corporation; also, the professional atmosphere that grows from this and affects behavior and performance

THE IMPORTANCE OF CULTURE IN DIFFERENT BUSINESS CONTEXTS

Cross-cultural management issues arise in a range of business contexts. *Within* individual firms, for example, managers from a foreign parent company need to understand that local employees from the host country may require different organization structures and HRM procedures. In cross-border mergers and acquisitions (M&As), realizing the expected synergies very often depends on establishing structures and procedures that encompass both cultures in a balanced way. Cross-border joint ventures, alliances, or buyer–supplier relationships *between* two or more firms also require a cultural compromise. Finally, for firms to sell successfully to foreign customers requires culturally sensitive adaptations to products, services, marketing, and advertising.

Figure 5.1 outlines, at the most general level, links between business contexts and particular characteristics of individuals or groups that are influenced by social and cultural norms of a particular region. At the face-to-face level in meetings the language and behavior of different peoples vary and their mutual understanding of each other's culture will influence the effectiveness and efficiency of communication between them. This influences how well multicultural workplaces operate at all levels, from strategy setting at the senior level to plant-floor operations.

Firms also tend to have different organizational and decision-making practices depending on where they have evolved and which cultures and subcultures they encompass. For firms to build successful alliances and partnerships, or for M&A activities to succeed at the company-to-company level, there needs to be an understanding of the organizational

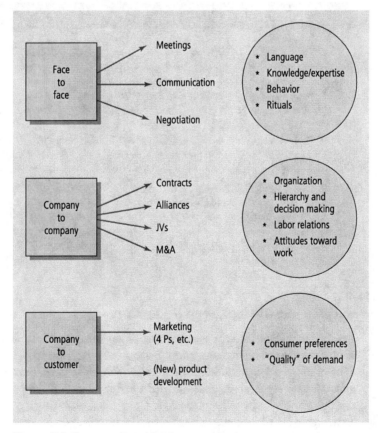

Figure 5.1 Cross-cultural business contexts

differences between them. This covers practically every element of corporate organizations from decision-making structures and systems and management–labor relationships to individual employees' attitudes toward their work and their employer.

Finally, culture influences the behavior and preferences of clients and customers. To sell successfully in a foreign market, a manager needs to adapt his or her product or service to meet the different needs of that particular group of customers. Any alteration in advertising, marketing, product or service features, after-sales support, technical back-up, documentation, etc., will be partly guided by cultural differences.

Failure to do this ends in the kinds of marketing mistakes and communication blunders that become marketing folklore. For example, Ford's low-cost truck was initially marketed as the Feira to Spanish-speaking people, but this means "ugly old woman" in Spanish. The Ford Comet, a high-end car, was sold as the Caliente in Mexico, which is local slang for "prostitute." Unsurprisingly neither model did well in these markets. This reinforces the above point about the importance of language, but also demonstrates how some of the largest and most experienced companies do not appear to do the most basic cultural due diligence (their homework!) when launching products and services in foreign markets. The chapter on marketing strategy in this book examines these kinds of issues more closely.

Ethnocentrism
The belief that one's own way of doing things is superior to that of others

Across all of the business contexts in Figure 5.1 ignorance of cultural differences represents a common stumbling block for international managers. **Ethnocentrism**, the belief that one's own way of doing things is superior to that of others, can also be a major barrier to good international management. The challenge lies in recognizing differences, combining the advantages that stem from different styles and approaches, adjusting and adapting to succeed with different people, in different partnerships, and in different markets.

 Active learning check

Review your answer to Active Learning Case question 1 and make any changes you like. Then compare your answer to the one below.

1 What kinds of cultural differences matter when organizations from different countries merge?

The definition of culture itself gives some indicators of the kinds of differences that matter. Organizations from different countries will have developed different beliefs, values, and patterns of behavior based on their underlying national culture. A wide range of differences could be important, including attitudes toward work and workplace practices, management–labor relations, the decision-making hierarchy, and division of responsibilities. Cross-border M&A often also requires changes to the marketing and branding of products and services as sales are expanded into new markets. Differences in the language, values, and preferences of customers in different countries also need to be taken into account.

Culture has always been important

Cultural convergence
The growing similarity between national cultures, including the beliefs, values, aspirations, and the preferences of consumers, partly driven by global brands, media, and common global icons

Despite the various patterns and processes of globalization, cultural differences still remain important. Even with greater common access, via various media and the Internet, to the same brands, rock icons, and sports stars, differences remain. Terms like **cultural convergence** or, simply, Americanization (the homogenization of global consumer preferences through the ubiquity of McDonald's, Coca-Cola, and Ford) overstate the similarities between groups of people around the world. (See the case **International Business Strategy in Action: McDonald's**.)

McDonald's

When José Bové, a self-proclaimed leader of France's anti-globalization movement, was sentenced for vandalizing a McDonald's restaurant in 1999, he claimed to have the backing of the French people. That might have been an overstatement, but 40,000 French people were there to show their support. It was not only the French, however; in the 1990s McDonald's restaurants were vandalized in about 50 countries. At issue is the worldwide perception that McDonald's represents a particular friendly Ronald-McDonald-type of US imperialism. Traditional lifestyles, critics say, are being eroded by McDonald's marketing practices, its value chain system, its fast-food concept, and the unhealthy food itself.

Yet, McDonald's bends over backwards to blend into local cultures. The company advertises itself to its critics as a global company owned and run by local people. Indeed, the franchise system makes it so that McDonald's Japan is run by the Japanese and Israel's McDonald's restaurants are run by Israelis. Local business owners choose their menu's offerings to fit their culture, find alternative suppliers, and create suitable marketing for their culture. An American in Saudi Arabia might seat single men with families at a McDonald's opening, but a Saudi Arabian owner would know that this is unacceptable and the restaurant will be designed to accommodate the culture.

In the land of José Bové, Asterix, a French comic-strip character who stands for individuality and ironically symbolizes local resistance to imperial forces, replaced the goofy Ronald McDonald in the company's marketing in the early 2000s. In 1999, French McDonald's went the extra mile to prove how local it was by printing advertisements making fun of US eating habits. In one ad, a large American cowboy complains that McDonald's France does not import American beef to "guarantee maximum hygienic conditions." French restaurants are more fashionably and more comfortably designed than North American ones to create an environment where customers may enjoy longer meals in accordance with French tradition. If they want, customers can order a beer from the menu.

In India, where local tastes are very different from those in the United States, the company crafted an entirely different menu that does not use beef or pork due to the mostly vegetarian population. The Indian Big Mac is made of lamb. In Israel, the locally owned McDonald's purchases over 80 percent of its ingredients from local producers, including 100 percent kosher hamburger meat, potatoes, lettuce, buns, and milkshake mix. There are no cheeseburgers in Israel's McDonald's because dairy products cannot be eaten together with meat.

On the other hand, McDonald's does bring its own culture to its foreign operations. In China, where children's birthdays are not traditionally celebrated, a successful McDonald's marketing strategy encouraged birthday parties at their establishments. Not a bad deal for children, but still a cultural effect from a foreign multinational. More mundane things, such as combo meals, are popularized through McDonald's expansion. By promoting its carbonated beverages in India, the firm is unsettling the country's tea culture. The company's presence creates a cultural exchange, not a one-sided cultural takeover.

Beyond reactionary behavior against McDonald's cultural "impositions," McDonald's has had to suffer simply for being born in the United States. Just hours after the United States began bombing Afghanistan in 2001 McDonald's restaurants were vandalized in cities in Pakistan and Indonesia and Muslim clerics asked for the boycott of US products.

For activists and cultural protectors, the most frustrating thing is that their calls go unheeded. Owners of McDonald's franchises continuously remind customers that they too are locals, that their employees are locals, and that their suppliers are mainly local. In Brazil, some anti-war protestors on their way home will stop at a McDonald's for a bite to eat.

Some of McDonald's major troubles, however, are in its most established markets in the United States, Canada, and the UK. Russian and Chinese go-getters might think that a meal in McDonald's puts them in a class above, but in its two major markets of North America and Europe, where the firm derives over two-thirds of all revenue, the food is considered unhealthy. Indeed, both Canada and the UK considered imposing a tax on fatty foods on the grounds that it was damaging to people's health and it costs the health-care system a substantial amount. The tax is unlikely to be imposed because of a strong backlash from poverty groups who argue that this tax would place an uneven burden on those who depend on cheap food for their everyday survival. In the United States, the firm is being sued over claims that it misled parents about the nutritional value of its products, leading their children to become obese and unhealthy. McDonald's in the UK reacted by eliminating supersized options from the menu. A set of healthier options has now been introduced in Europe and North America as the company fends off critics in some of its friendliest markets.

Sources: David Barboza, "When Golden Arches Are Too Red, White and Blue," *New York Times*, October 14, 2001; Tony Karon, "Adieu, Ronald McDonald," *Time.com*, January 24, 2002; Simon Romero, "War and Abuse Do Little to Harm US Brands," *New York Times*, May 9, 2004.

Cultures vary and these variations lead to real and significant differences in the ways that companies operate and people work. Moreover, *because* of globalization more and more firms are coming head to head with the added complexity of doing business globally, which stems from the huge amount of variety in the world that still exists (and arguably will always exist).

Before moving on to examine some typologies of global cultures, here is a word of warning. Much of this section will describe how various kinds of individual and group behavior can be linked to specific cultural groups and associate these cultural dispositions with different business styles and company structures. Acting on the basis of cultural stereotypes is highly sensitive and can be problematic. For example, at the simplest level a banker may be able to prove empirically that Pakistanis are more successful than Jamaicans at starting and running small businesses around the world. Using this insight as the basis for discriminating against Jamaicans wanting bank loans for business start-ups is not only unethical, but in most countries falls foul of race discrimination laws.

NATIONAL STEREOTYPES AND KEY DIMENSIONS OF CULTURE

Culture at two levels

There are traditionally two different approaches to looking at culture:

Psychic distance
A measure of the similarity or difference between two cultures; also commonly defined as the measurable distance between the home market and a foreign market resulting from the perception of cultural and business differences

- The psychic or psychological level, which focuses on the internalized norms, attitudes, and behavior of individuals from a particular culture (**psychic distance** is a measure of differences between groups).

- The institutional level, which looks at national (or group) culture *embodied* in institutions (government, education, and economic institutions as well as in business organizations).

In this chapter we will mainly discuss the first, culture as shared psychology, with a brief reference to national institutional differences at the end.

People who are born in, or grew up in, the same country tend to share similar cultural characteristics. Nordström and Valhne examined a sample of Swedish firms to understand the effects of psychic distance on market-entry strategies and costs.[6] They ranked 20 particular countries according to a range of national characteristics that contribute to psychic distance and found, as you might expect, that Denmark is closest to Sweden (1/20), the UK comes in at 6/20, Portugal at 15/20, Japan 16/20, Brazil 17/20 and Australia 20/20.

Nationality and culture tend to coincide, although nations encompass a wide variety of institutions, religions, beliefs, and patterns of behavior, and distinctive subcultures can always be found within individual countries. The only way to make sense of this wide diversity is to characterize distinct cultural groups through simplified national stereotypes.

Many studies have attempted to create these stereotypes by mapping and comparing the shared characteristics of managers and employees in different countries.[7] Researchers then examine the effects of key differences on business behavior, organization, structure, and ultimately the performance of companies from different countries. The following describes the milestone studies of this kind in the management field.

Hofstede's four dimensions of culture

Geert Hofstede is a Dutch psychologist who conducted one of the earliest and best-known cultural studies in management, on IBM's operations in 70 countries around the world.[8]

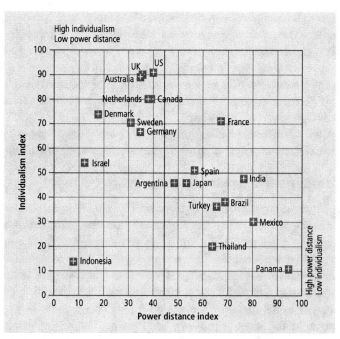

Figure 5.2 Hofstede's power distance against individualism for 20 countries

Source: Hofstede, G. (1983). The cultural relativity of organizational practices and theories, *Journal of International Business Studies*, Fall, p. 92. Copyright © Geert Hofstede.

Getting answers to 32 statements from over 116,000 questionnaires, he mapped key cultural characteristics of these countries according to four value dimensions:

1 **Power distance** is the extent to which a culture accepts that power in organizations is distributed unequally. High power distance equates with steep organizational hierarchies, with more autocratic leadership and less employee participation in decision making (see Figure 5.2 for examples).

2 **Uncertainty avoidance** is the degree to which members of a society feel uncomfortable with risk and uncertainty. High uncertainty avoidance (Japan, Argentina, France) will be reflected in the high priority placed on rituals, routines, and procedures in organizations and society in general. Countries with low uncertainty avoidance (Denmark, UK, India, US) tend to emphasize flexibility and informality rather than bureaucracy.

3 **Individualism** is the extent to which people are supposed to take care of themselves and be emotionally independent from others (see Figure 5.2 for examples).

4 **Masculinity** is the value attributed to achievement, assertiveness, and material success (Japan, Mexico, Germany, UK) as opposed to the stereotypical feminine values of relationships, modesty, caring, and the quality of life (Sweden, Netherlands, Denmark), according to Hofstede.

Figure 5.2 illustrates some of Hofstede's findings using two of the most useful dimensions, power distance against the degree of individualism/collectivism. It reflects some general stereotypes of the countries included, with clear grouping of Australia, UK and US as highly individualistic and less hierarchical (small power distance) cultures against Mexico, Thailand, and Panama at the other extreme. We will elaborate on these definitions and their practical interpretation throughout this chapter.

Among his most important contributions, Hofstede provided strong evidence for the significance of national culture over professional role, gender, or race, as a determinant of variation in employees' attitudes, values, and behaviors, accounting for 50 percent of the differences his study observed. However, his studies have come in for significant criticism, despite widespread adoption of the four-dimensional framework. Three common criticisms are: (1) that the dimensions developed from data collected between 1968 and 1973 were relevant only for that particular period; (2) that corporate cultural and other influences from this one-organization (IBM) study created significant bias; (3) that the sole use of attitude-survey questionnaires was not a valid basis for the resulting values and dimensions his study concluded with.[9]

Although Hofstede has continued to write on culture, organizations, and management[10] it is useful to look more deeply into the work of another well-known Dutch culture guru.

Trompenaars' seven dimensions of culture

Fons Trompenaars built on Hofstede's work by expanding the framework for stereotyping and comparing different national cultures and by focusing more on the management implications of cultural differences. Using initial research involving 15,000 employees in 50 countries, Trompenaars explored the "cultural extremes and the incomprehension that can arise when doing business across cultures," even when people are working for the same company.[11]

Trompenaars arrived at seven distinctive dimensions of culture and used the questionnaire responses in his study to map a wide variety of countries along a continuum from one extreme to the other within each dimension. The key to understanding this mapping approach is to identify where each country or culture is positioned *relative* to others on one or more of these dimensions.

Relative positioning gives insights into the kinds of conflicts, misunderstandings, and organizational and management problems that are likely to arise when individuals, groups, or firms from these countries interact in any of the ways described above.

1 **Universalism** *versus* **particularism.** In universalistic cultures rules and regulations are applied in all situations, regardless of particular conditions or circumstances. The example used by Trompenaars refers to a salesman who does not fulfill his monthly sales quota because he was looking after his sick son. Should he be penalized according to standard company regulations or should he be excused because of the particular circumstances?

According to Trompenaars' findings, Switzerland, Canada, and the United States are among the most universalist. Australia and the UK are also toward this end of the scale. Germany is closer to the center, as is France, but the latter sits on the particularist side of the scale. Korea, Russia, and China are the most particularist of countries. (Note that some of the countries studied by Hofstede, like the strongly particularist Yugoslavia, no longer exist.)

2 *Individualism versus* **collectivism.** This dimension, clearly building on Hofstede, centers on whether individual rights and values are dominant or subordinate to those of the collective society.

The most individualist countries are Canada, the United States, Switzerland, and the UK. Among the most collectivist are Japan, Egypt, and India (and Nepal and Kuwait).

3 **Neutral** *versus* **emotional.** This reflects how much emotions are displayed in the workplace. More importantly it indicates whether emotional or subjective (rather than objective) forms of assessment are thought to be the basis for good decision making in organizations. Some organizations emphasize reports, data, and analytical decision making by managers, whereas others feel that opinions, intuition, and gut feelings are credible or valid criteria. Predictably the most emotional countries include Italy and France and the least emotional groups (in the workplace at least) are the Japanese, Germans, Swiss, Chinese, and Indonesians.

4 **Specific** *versus* **diffuse.** Do work relationships (such as the hierarchical relationship between a senior manager and a subordinate) exist just in the workplace (are they

Universalism
The uniform application of rules and procedures, regardless of situation, context, or individuals involved

Particularism
Judging a situation and adjusting rules and procedures according to the specific situation or individuals involved

Collectivism
The tendency of people to belong to groups who look after each other in exchange for loyalty

Neutral
A preference for unemotional, objective analysis of a situation or a decision and for limited displays of emotions and feelings in the workplace

Emotional
An acceptance of emotion and subjectivity as the bases for some decision making and a preference for explicit displays of emotions and feelings in the workplace

Specific
A tendency to limit workplace relationships and obligations, including relative status and hierarchical position, to the workplace

Diffuse
A tendency for workplace relationships and obligations, including relative status and hierarchical position, to extend into social situations and activities outside of work

specific), or do they extend into the social context outside the workplace (diffuse)? Here a telling example is whether an employee is willing to help paint a senior manager's house over a weekend. Clearly Australian bosses are likely to get a characteristically blunt answer to this request! China, Japan, India, and Singapore display highly diffuse relationships, Australia and the Netherlands the most specific.

Achievement oriented
Where status is earned rather than a right; recruitment and promotion opportunities tend to be more dependent on performance, as in a meritocracy

Ascription oriented
Where status is more of a right than earned; recruitment and promotion opportunities tend to be more dependent on seniority, ethnicity, gender, religion, or birth

Sequential
Cultures that view time in a sequential or linear fashion; order comes from separating activities and commitments

Synchronic
Cultures that view events in parallel over time; order comes from coordinating multiple activities and commitments

5 **Achievement** *versus* **ascription**. This dimension refers to one's status within organizations, contrasting those cultures where status, credibility, authority, and ultimately power tend to be based on merit (achieved) against those where class, gender, education, or age tend to be the defining characteristics (status is ascribed).

Countries where status tends to be ascribed include Egypt, Turkey, and Argentina (and slightly less so, Russia, Japan, and France), and those where it is achieved include Norway, Sweden, and predictably the United States, Australia, Canada, and the UK.

6 *Attitudes toward time.* **Sequential** (time as a sequence of events) versus **synchronic** (several events juggled at the same time) views of time tend to relate to punctuality for meetings and deadlines. Swedes and other northern European cultures tend to be punctual and plan according to specific timetables. Many southern European, Latin American, and Arabic cultures see punctuality and chronological precision as far less important. They also tend to naturally cope with a range of issues simultaneously, rather than one by one.

7 *Attitudes toward the environment.* This dimension reflects the emphasis a particular culture places on people's relationship with nature and the natural environment. On the one hand some cultures emphasize control and subjugation of environmental forces, whereas others emphasize the need to work with nature, in harmony with the environment. Clearly religious and philosophical differences around the world influence differences within this dimension.

Trompenaars' seven dimensions have been used in a variety of ways to gain insights into the kinds of problems that might arise in the contexts (face to face, company to company, and company to customer) outlined in Figure 5.1. In general they indicate the organizational characteristics we can expect from firms based in particular countries or dominated by certain nationalities. They are also used to measure changes in cultural values and behavior over time. Research shows that in both Japan and China, for example, achievement orientation is on the increase alongside some elements of individualism.[12]

The Japanese are moving away from a reliance on collectivism in the form of the state, large firms, and group associations and placing more value on personal responsibility and individual performance. In China there is a shift in companies toward performance-related rewards and individual initiative, built on the changing views of the growing urban elite. But there are also wider concerns regarding the social costs as well as the benefits of self-interest.

The GLOBE project's nine dimensions of culture

More recent research has built on the Hofstede and Trompenaars research. The Global Leadership and Organizational Behavior Effectiveness (GLOBE) project began in 1992 and continues today. It has involved 150 researchers collecting data on cultural values and management and leadership attributes from 18,000 managers across 62 countries in the telecommunications, food, and banking industries.[13] In the same way as Hofstede and Trompenaars before them, the researchers place countries along a standard 1 to 7 scale. The GLOBE project, however, ends up with nine key cultural dimensions:

1 *Assertiveness.* The United States, Austria, Germany, and Greece are high; Sweden, Japan, and New Zealand are low.

2 *Future orientation.* A propensity for planning, investing, delayed gratification: Singapore, Switzerland, and the Netherlands are high; Russia, Argentina, and Italy are low.

3 *Gender differentiation.* The degree to which gender role differences are maximized: South Korea, Egypt, India, and China are high; Hungary, Poland, and Denmark are low.

4 *Uncertainty avoidance.* A reliance on societal norms and procedures to improve predictability, a preference for order, structure, and formality: Sweden, Switzerland, and Germany are high; Russia, Bolivia, and Greece are low.

5 *Power distance.* Russia, Thailand, and Spain are high; Denmark, the Netherlands, and Israel are low.

6 *Institutional collectivism (individualism vs. collectivism).* Promoting active participation in social institutions: Sweden, South Korea, and Japan are high; Greece, Argentina, and Italy are low.

7 *In-group/family collectivism.* A pride in small-group membership, family, close friends, etc.: Iran, India, and China are high; Denmark, Sweden, and New Zealand are low.

8 *Performance orientation* (much like achievement orientation). Singapore, Hong Kong, and the United States are high; Russia, Argentina, and Italy are low.

9. Humane orientation. An emphasis on fairness, altruism, and generosity: Ireland, Malaysia, and Egypt are high; Germany, Spain, France, Singapore, and Brazil are low.

Humane orientation
Cultures that emphasize helping others, charity, and people's wider social obligations

As you can see, many of these dimensions match those of Hofstede and Trompenaars, and the overall GLOBE framework is very much an extension of their approach.

The GLOBE researchers have examined the HRM implications of these cultural differences for practicing managers and looked at ways to avoid the pitfalls of ignorance and insensitivity.[14] A similar long-running study by the CRANET network has focused on European cultural differences and reports similar findings.[15]

As with the other cultural mapping studies by Hofstede and Trompenaars, GLOBE has faced some critical appraisal, which helps us understand the strengths and weaknesses of its concluding framework. A recent set of debates has usefully raised some methodological issues associated with these kinds of studies, and provides interesting points of contention we should be aware of, rather than blindly accepting the above kind of research.[16]

Applying the national culture frameworks

Different styles of communication and interaction result from the cultural differences listed above. These can lead to workplace misunderstandings, poor interpersonal and intergroup relationships, inefficiency, and higher costs. Three examples provide some insights into how we can apply the above typologies.

US managers, according to all of the above studies, are highly assertive and performance oriented relative to managers from other parts of the world (they come around the midpoint on all the other dimensions). Their interaction style is characteristically direct and explicit. They tend to use facts, figures, and logic to link specific steps to measurable outcomes, and this is the main focus of workplace interaction. Greeks and Russians are less individualistic, less performance oriented, and show lower levels of uncertainty avoidance (are less driven by procedures) than the Americans. When Russian and Greek managers, employees, customers, suppliers, or public-sector officials interact with US counterparts, they may well find their approach too direct and results focused. For them communication is likely to be more about mutual learning and an exploration of relevant issues than an explicit agreement about specific expectations and end results. Similarly, the Swedes may find the US style too aggressive and unfriendly, working against the relationship-building process that for them is a major objective of workplace interaction.

The Koreans and Japanese have highly gender-differentiated societies with males tending to dominate decision making and leading most face-to-face communication. The agenda for discussion is likely set by males, and traditional language forms differ according to whether a man is addressing a woman or an older person talking to a younger person, and vice versa. Gender- (and age-)related roles, responsibilities, and behaviors are therefore deeply embedded in language and customs.[17] Poland and Denmark lie at the other end of the continuum on the gender-differentiation dimension. Perhaps even more than other Western managers, their lack of awareness of this cultural difference runs the risk of both embarrassing female employees and offending and alienating senior Japanese male managers. This kind of clash can make negotiations and interaction of all kinds between these groups that much more difficult.

Certain kinds of HRM techniques are inappropriate for organizations that show high power distance ratings. Companies and management consultancies in the UK, the United States, and northern European countries have developed fairly participative management systems to improve productivity, based on their characteristically low power distance and flat organizational hierarchies. Techniques such as 360-degree feedback systems for developing management–employee relationships are not likely to work, however, in Mexican, Panamanian, Thai, or Russian organizations, which have high power distance and steep hierarchies. Subordinates are uncomfortable being asked to evaluate senior managers, and managers would not see subordinates as qualified to comment on their performance. More than this, to employees in some countries this kind of consultation can give the impression that senior managers do not know what they are doing! The employees may lose faith in senior management's ability and leave!

Ethnocentric
A belief in the superiority of one's own ethnic group; the dominance of the home-country culture in decision making, human resource management, and overall corporate culture in a multinational firm

None of the above examples means that international managers should (or ever could) entirely change their behavior to suit local values and practices. Like many of the challenges facing managers, cultural sensitivity and cross-cultural effectiveness come from striking a balance between one's own norms, values, and principles and those of the "foreigner." The lesson for multinational firms is that **ethnocentric** corporate cultures and completely standardized HR systems do not work. The key challenge is to adapt to get the best from local differences.

✔ Active learning check

Review your answer to Active Learning Case question 2 and make any changes you like. Then compare your answer to the one below.

2 How well do the characteristics described in the case match the respective, stereotypical national cultures of these countries?

According to the above frameworks they match reasonably well. The US culture is characterized as individualistic, achievement/performance oriented, and assertive. Most of these traits clash with the "feminine" (in Hofstede's characterization) values of relationships, modesty, caring, and the quality of life emphasized by the Swedes. Hofstede finds US managers less hierarchical than most cultures, which is not indicated in the Pharmacia–Upjohn case. However, as Figure 5.2 shows, both countries have a low power distance and high individualism rating, relative to other countries, but the United States has slightly higher power distance (steeper management hierarchy) than Sweden. Sweden also has a relatively high uncertainty avoidance ranking, preferring order, structure, and formality, which does not stand out in the case study. Swedes are also high on institutional collectivism but low on family or small-group collectivism. The Italians are the opposite. Unlike the Americans, the Italians are not at all oriented toward achievement (Trompenaars) or performance (GLOBE). They are also more emotional than the Swedes and Americans according to Hofstede and have a relatively low future orientation (GLOBE).

"The way we do things here": the implications of cultural differences for organizations and managers

Mapping out a variety of national cultural typologies using the various dimensions of culture described above gives us some insights into the kinds of differences that exist among different groups of managers, employees, and organizations.

Two key questions about the role of the individual in a firm and the role of a firm in a society from Trompenaars' study give us a starting point to explore the management implications of cultural differences. The responses in Figure 5.3 reflect the degree of support for the particular proposition A or B for each of these questions.

Americans clearly display what has been termed (originally by the sociologist Max Weber) a mechanistic and functional view of the firm as an organization (A) and a shareholder-driven, profit-oriented view of this organization in society (although more than half the US vote in Figure 5.3 was for option B). The Japanese tend to have a more organic view of the firm, emphasizing the importance of social networks and the obligation of the firm to a wider constituency of stakeholders (although this is a characteristic of traditional Japan that has been strongly tested in the recent recessionary environment).

A wide range of factors within organizations are influenced directly or indirectly by the cultural predispositions of managers and employees. We know from the above studies and a wide range of other research that these factors include:

■ The general relationship between employees and the organization: their roles and responsibilities, obligations, and loyalties and the link this has with life outside the workplace.

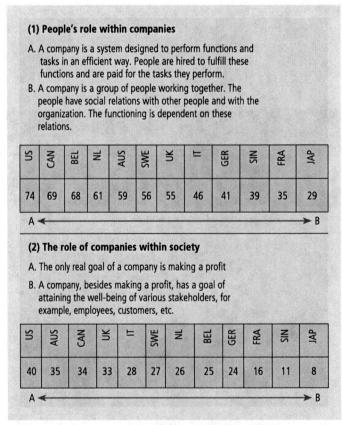

(1) People's role within companies

A. A company is a system designed to perform functions and tasks in an efficient way. People are hired to fulfill these functions and are paid for the tasks they perform.

B. A company is a group of people working together. The people have social relations with other people and with the organization. The functioning is dependent on these relations.

US	CAN	BEL	NL	AUS	SWE	UK	IT	GER	SIN	FRA	JAP
74	69	68	61	59	56	55	46	41	39	35	29

A ←————————————————————————————→ B

(2) The role of companies within society

A. The only real goal of a company is making a profit

B. A company, besides making a profit, has a goal of attaining the well-being of various stakeholders, for example, employees, customers, etc.

US	AUS	CAN	UK	IT	SWE	NL	BEL	GER	FRA	SIN	JAP
40	35	34	33	28	27	26	25	24	16	11	8

A ←————————————————————————————→ B

Figure 5.3 Excerpts from Trompenaars' cultural attitudes survey

Source: Hampden-Turner, C. and Trompenaars, F. *The Seven Cultures of Capitalism: Value Systems for Creating Wealth in the United States, Britain, Japan, Germany, France, Sweden and the Netherlands* (New York: Doubleday, 1993).

- Hierarchy, power and authority, and the accepted routes to attaining these, including factors that underpin status and credibility in different societies and organizations.
- The role of formal rules and regulations versus the informal communication, personal networks, and hidden "rules of the game."
- The accepted basis for decision making, including rationale, scientific, mechanistic, and objective versus subjective, tacit, rule of thumb, etc.
- The degree to which employees act and are treated as individuals or groups and the role of interpersonal relationships.
- Motivation and rewards systems.
- Interaction and communication mechanisms.

Work attitudes and the appropriate management of work attitudes have a significant influence on productivity and innovativeness in a company. Managers and employees who are motivated by their core social values to work hard and continually strive to improve their company's products and services and the processes by which they are produced are clearly a source of competitive advantage. It is interesting to note how social norms may drive a strong work ethic despite individual dissatisfaction with workload or job responsibilities. This has been shown in several companies between US and Japanese factory workers where the Japanese are found to be more loyal and aligned with company objectives but far less satisfied individually.[18]

Table 5.2 compares interview responses from sample workforces in seven countries. The resulting ranking of what it is that employees value most from their jobs shows that "interesting work" is what tends to engage most people, beyond everything else.

Table 5.2 Average and intra-country ranking of work goals: a seven-nation comparison

Work goals	Belgium	UK	Germany	Israel	Japan	Netherlands	United States
Opportunity to learn	5.8[a]	5.55	4.97	5.83	6.26	5.38	6.16
	7[b]	8	9	5	7	9	5
Interpersonal relations	6.34	6.33	6.43	6.67	6.39	7.19	6.08
	5	4	4	2	6	3	7
Opportunity for promotion	4.49	4.27	4.48	5.29	3.33	3.31	5.08
	10	11	10	8	11	11	10
Convenient work hours	4.71	6.11	5.71	5.53	5.46	5.59	5.25
	9	5	6	7	8	8	9
Variety	5.96	5.62	5.71	4.89	5.05	6.86	6.10
	6	7	6	11	9	4	6
Interesting work	8.25	8.02	7.26	6.75	6.38	7.59	7.41
	1	1	3	1	2	2	1
Job security	6.80	7.12	7.57	5.22	6.71	5.68	6.30
	3	3	2	10	4	7	3
Match between the people and the work	5.77	5.63	6.09	5.61	7.83	6.17	6.19
	8	6	5	6	1	6	4
Pay	7.13	7.80	7.73	6.60	6.56	5.27	6.82
	2	2	1	3	5	5	2
Working conditions	4.19	4.87	4.39	5.28	4.18	5.03	4.84
	11	9	11	9	10	10	11
Autonomy	6.56	4.69	5.66	6.00	6.89	7.61	5.79
	4	10	8	4	3	1	8

[a]First row shows average rank on a scale of 1 to 10.
[b]Second row shows ranking of work goals within each country, with a rank of 1 being *most* important and 11 being *least* important.

Source: Adapted from Itzhak Harpaz, "The Importance of Work Goals: An International Perspective," *Journal of International Business Studies*, vol. 21, no. 1 (1990), p. 81.

Three key areas capture many of the factors covered by the above typologies and cultural stereotypes, where cultural differences can make a significant difference at the company-to-company and face-to-face levels. These are organization, leadership, and communication (see Figure 5.4).

Organization

Organization styles range from organic, informal, or people oriented to systematic or mechanistic, formal, or task oriented, in keeping with some common organizational dimensions described by sociologists throughout history (such as Max Weber and Emile Durkheim). Organizations that operate very much around personal relationships and social networks contrast those that are much more functional and logical. In fact different cultures and different firms display elements of both these characteristics, but the balance varies considerably and can create tensions when groups of people or firms from different ends of the spectrum interact or try to cooperate.

As an aid to predicting differences among individuals, groups, or firms, and understanding the significance of these variations, *relative* differences among countries, organizations, and groups of people are important, rather than any absolute scores. For example, family companies are characteristically directive, individual oriented but organic. Multinational firms are usually more autocratic and mechanistic. Consulting and professional services firms are often mechanistic and emphasize individual performance and rewards but may also be fairly team oriented. Entrepreneurial new ventures will usually be organic, unsystematic, and group oriented.

Leadership

Leadership styles range from individual oriented, directive, autocratic, top down, or authoritarian to group oriented, participative, democratic, bottom up, or egalitarian. Again, cultural groups and corporations often encompass both kinds of leadership but tend to reflect one dominant style.

Individual managers from cultures that score high on the power distance or assertiveness dimensions are likely to be viewed by those from other cultures as autocratic and directive but will tend to view others as indecisive and too compromising. They will not want to spend too much time discussing issues to achieve a consensus. If they also reflect an organic

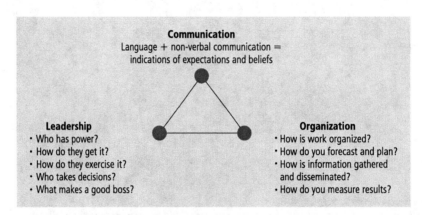

Figure 5.4 Management dimensions of culture

or informal (low uncertainty avoidance) culture, this will result in an instinctive or unsystematic decision-making and implementation style, and they might be viewed as an unpredictable autocrat. This contrasts the combination of high power distance and high uncertainty avoidance, which results in a more directive and mechanistic style. Such leaders prefer established formal routines and a command-and-control bureaucracy, while other managers are likely to see this as over-regulated and inflexible. The Pharmacia and Upjohn case demonstrates a range of these styles and the problems that result from the imposition of a new style of organization and leadership within a corporate merger.

Communication

Clearly, at the face-to-face level language differences can be the most prominent barrier to communication and therefore to cooperation and coordination. English speakers tend to have an advantage in many situations since English has emerged as the main language of business globally. However, this has led to complacency among some indigenous English speakers, notably the British and the North Americans. First, less effort is often made to learn other languages and their associated cultures, which normally limits a manager's understanding of foreign colleagues, workers, or customers. Second, the assumption is often made that once the language barrier is broken cultural differences are also removed, whereas these may remain, causing miscommunication and misinterpretation. As for much of this chapter on culture, preparation and awareness are the best starting points for minimizing differences that can create problems.

It is through efficient communication that two parties steer toward an understanding—a mutually agreed basis for doing business. The signs and signals on this route to an understanding are strongly influenced by culture. Different groups have different ways of displaying approval or of showing frustration in negotiations and different ideas of what constitutes a final agreement. The Japanese do not really have an equivalent word for the English "no" and indicate disapproval in a range of non-verbal ways. The Japanese word *hai* does mean "yes" but it often means "yes, I understand what you are saying" not "yes, I agree with what you are saying." Germans place a lot of emphasis on written communications and documented evidence rather than verbal interaction, compared to the Spanish and Italians to whom verbal interaction and agreement is recognized as binding in some contexts. The Americans prefer legal contracts and have armies of lawyers to make agreements highly specified. Other, more organic business cultures tend to work toward a relationship in which trust and understanding replace the need for legally binding contracts. Again, awareness through preparation and anticipation of differences is the best starting point for avoiding **culture clash**.

The corporate response

How have MNEs responded to the challenge of managing across cultural boundaries? What kinds of organization structures, HRM procedures, and corporate cultures have been developed to cope with the enormous differences among people and to unify this diversity toward a common purpose?

At a very general level good transnational firms develop an *awareness* and appreciation of cultural differences among their managers and employees. They also take steps to encourage *adaptation* of personal behavior or organizational practices, or products and services, to suit the changing mix of cultures within the firm, in subsidiaries and in key markets. Training programs, including a range of activities at the induction stage, when new recruits join a firm or existing personnel take up a role in a new country, are a standard way for firms to do these things. Job rotation, with a focus on developing international managers with personal experience in a variety of different countries, is also practiced by a number of firms. It is

Culture clash
When two cultural groups (national or corporate) meet, interact, or work together and differences in their values, beliefs, rules of behavior, or styles of communication create misunderstandings, antagonism, or other problems

normally very difficult to assess such practices using any form of cost–benefit analysis. The costs are usually easily identifiable, but the benefits are very often intangible. For many experienced international companies, such as Shell or Nestlé, a long-term commitment to (and investment in) cultural awareness is simply accepted as a necessary part of being global.

Beyond awareness and adaptation, the best firms aim to *leverage* the diversity of cultures within their organizations and combine the best aspects of different ways of doing things. Corporate culture, a shared identity spanning culturally diverse groups of employees, provides a way to do this. Companies can usefully invest in their own socialization mechanisms, such as social events alongside regular meetings and conferences. Company magazines, intranets, and even in-house television channels for corporate communications can all support this process. These may not only improve cross-cultural awareness, but also promote shared values, symbols, and even language to help bind employees together.[19]

Here is a list of other useful strategies for managing cultural diversity distilled from a number of research studies:[20]

1 Recognize diversity. Identify and map the various national cultures and ethnic groups within the firm and use this to understand which elements of consistency and standardization can or should be promoted.

2 Build diversity issues into recruitment, HRM planning, strategy, location decisions, alliances, and partnerships. This helps avoid clashes and inefficiency and supports cultural awareness.

3 Identify where and to what degree local divisions should be encouraged or empowered to take the lead in expressing and managing diversity. Some degree of devolution of responsibility away from the center of the firm allows local divisions to identify aspects of diversity that are most important to them and their operations.

4 Encourage cross-border discussion and interaction as well as focused training. Include specific kinds/combinations of international experience for fast-track managers.

5 Aim for a cultural balance in particular areas of strategic and tactical decision making (such as brand changes for foreign markets). Ensure a (numerically) balanced pool of managers or appropriately diverse inputs into decision making.

6 Lead from the top. Aim to match the geographic diversity of the firm's businesses with a culturally mixed senior management group and board of directors (as in the case of Sony and Unilever).

✔ Active learning check

Review your answer to Active Learning Case question 3 and make any changes you like. Then compare your answer to the one below.

 What could senior managers have done before and after the merger to alleviate some of the problems that resulted from culture clash?

A simple starting point would be to review the various frameworks (Hofstede, Trompenaars, and GLOBE, for example) to understand some generic differences between the national cultures involved in the merger and anticipate some of the likely problems. It would have also helped to examine the potential areas of organizational conflict with senior managers from each company and/or with managers with some experience of two or more of the countries and their ways of doing things. Some degree of cultural training or induction plus an investment in joint meetings and events to get to know each other could also have improved understanding and morale. However, the cost–benefit trade-off for these kinds of pre- and post-merger activity is difficult to precisely assess.

Multinational organization structures: imperialist or independent?

A key dilemma for international firms is the degree to which they promote or even impose a common, standardized corporate culture across the organization. Although this will create economies of scale and be more efficient in a number of respects, it will also stifle diversity and create clashes with local cultures and ways of doing things around the organization.

Firms respond to this dilemma in different ways, with different outcomes. At the simplest level we can map out a range of responses from what is termed *imperialist*, where a common culture is imposed wherever a company has a presence, to *federalist* or *independent* structures, where each national subsidiary bases its own culture on local norms and values. There are problems associated with either of these extremes and most firms try to steer a middle line, standardizing some elements across the whole organization to centralize and simplify some practices and unify employees, while allowing differentiation where necessary. This *transnational culture* allows for a compromise in work styles, values, and approaches, harnessing the strengths that lie in diversity.

Table 5.3 illustrates a range of organization types. In particular, it links elements of organization structure and design with cultural orientation, for example, in the relationship between headquarters and regional subsidiaries. It specifically extends the ethnocentric, **polycentric**, and **geocentric** typologies introduced by Perlmutter in the 1960s.[21]

Polycentric
Each subsidiary, division, or function reflects the culture of its host country; local managers' cultural predispositions and decision making dominate over those of home-country managers in a multinational firm

Geocentric
Neither home- nor host-country culture dominates decision making, human resource management, and overall corporate culture in a multinational firm

- *Ethnocentric* firms are where top management is dominated by home-country nationals, and procedures and management styles are transferred from the head office and imposed on regional subsidiaries in place of local ways of doing things.

- *Polycentric* firms tend to act like a federation of semi-autonomous organizations with financial controls or strict reporting structures holding them together. Subsidiaries are able to reflect the local cultural norms, and headquarters appreciates the need for different organization designs, procedural norms, rewards systems, etc., as long as profits flow to the center.

- *Geocentric* firms are seen as the ideal, collaborative, and meritocratic form of global organization. (Unilever is seen as an example based on the above statement.) An equal sharing of power and responsibility between headquarters and subsidiary; senior management promoted according to ability rather than nationality; subsidiaries that share worldwide objectives with managers focusing beyond national market interests.

In the geocentric organization the *benefits* of cultural diversity, such as knowledge of local customers and business practices, are harnessed for the good of the firm as a whole. The *costs* of diversity, such as language and communication problems, different values, and attitudes toward work, are minimized. Firms moving toward this more balanced, geocentric approach have to recognize diversity and its effects and identify which elements of consistency in regulations and values should be promoted, where and when. Local divisions must identify

Table 5.3 Organization types reflecting cultural predispositions

	Imperialist	Interventionist	Interactive	Independent
Organization	Ethnocentric	Ethnocentric	Geocentric	Polycentric
Structure	Steep hierarchy	Flat hierarchy	Network	Federation
Strategy	Dictated	Centrally decided	Jointly specified	Locally specified
Decision making	Centralized	Distributed	Shared	Devolved

aspects of diversity that are most important to them and their operations and take the lead in expressing and managing these differences. Discussion, interaction, cross-divisional teamwork and job rotation, support, awareness, and understanding go alongside training programs, language courses, and cultural assimilation.

Unilever is an example of a firm that has closely examined the range of cultures it encompassed and made a deliberate attempt to use cultural differences as a strength rather than a weakness for fulfilling its strategic aims. As part of a high-profile internal campaign the company described itself as a *multi-local multinational*, and this was used to explicitly inform employees of its cultural tolerance. According to a statement from a Unilever board chairman, one of the firm's objectives was to "Unileverize our Indians and Indianize our Unileverians."[22]

Culture clash in cross-border M&A and joint ventures

The range of organization styles in Table 5.3 also reflects the range of ways multinational firms approach the management of joint ventures or of firms acquired through merger and acquisition (M&A). They can either impose their own style of management on these organizations or allow them the independence to reflect their own cultural norms and existing corporate cultures.[23]

Cultural differences often prove to be a significant post-merger barrier for managers looking to realize the synergies and added value of pooling the resources and capabilities of two companies from different parts of the world. The Pharmacia–Upjohn case above illustrates this clearly. Culture clash and its impact on the bottom line are often complex and difficult to predict. More often failure to anticipate culture clash results from the lack of awareness on the part of senior managers and deal makers driving the M&A strategy. Financial analyses that focus the due-diligence process of counting up assets and identifying cost-cutting benefits tend to miss any estimation of cultural and organizational synergy (or lack thereof). Anticipating such problems and preparing for the development of effective relationships between people from both sides of an M&A or an alliance is central to maximizing the rewards.

Daimler-Benz ran into these problems when it merged with Chrysler. A number of senior-level US managers either were asked to leave or left because they were unhappy about the style of management imposed by Daimler. Among these early leavers were members of the design team responsible for the PT Cruiser and other Chrysler successes of the late 1990s. Many went to arch-rival General Motors, which is not an unusual outcome. One study showed that on average 20 percent of a firm's top management will leave within one year of being acquired and 70 percent will go within five years.[24]

Cultural awareness and some degree of organizational adaptation can limit the number of key people who do leave following a cross-border M&A. Understanding how to predict and mitigate the negative effects of cultural differences should be on the agenda for all managers. Despite this, in some cases an ethnocentric, imperialist approach is precisely what is needed to drive a newly merged organization forward. When Carlos Ghosn led the partial takeover of Nissan by Renault, he imposed a very non-Japanese way of doing things on the firm. In terms of the firm within its broader economic and social context, breaking *keiretsu* ties and laying off employees were radical steps to take. Internally he instituted performance-related pay and promotion and cut through a range of traditional rituals around HRM, budget control, and decision making that were underpinned by the traditional Japanese culture of the company. These were the kinds of changes that needed to be made to reverse years of losses and indebtedness. It was also, arguably, impossible for the incumbent Japanese management to make such changes. (Chapter 17, on Japan, contains the full Nissan–Renault case.)

At the other end of the spectrum, reflecting again on Table 5.3, Tata Tea Limited, owner of 54 tea estates and the second-most popular tea brand in India, provides us with an

Danone and Parmalat—going international, staying local

The dairy industry, in the main, is a local industry. Most dairy products sold at local supermarkets come from processing plants within a 500 mile (800 km) radius. However, this does not mean that these firms are all small, local operations. On the contrary, there are a small number of very large MNEs in this industry that do business worldwide and target their dairy offerings to local demand. The best known of these is Nestlé, which began operations in 1904 when it opened evaporated milk factories in both Europe and the United States. Today the company is the largest dairy company in the world and has operations in 86 countries. There are a couple of other large competitors as well, although they do not compete on as broad a scale.

One of these is Danone, a French MNE with annual revenues of €14.3 billion ($13.2 billion), which make it one of the world's 500 largest firms. The company's product line is not as broad as Nestlé, but it is just as big as the Swiss MNE in the dairy sector. Danone has operations in 120 countries and employs over 86,000 people. However, its primary base is Europe where it generates 24 percent of its revenues in France and another 35 percent throughout the rest of Europe.

Danone was originally a Spanish yogurt producer that merged with the French firm Gervais in 1967. Then in 1973 the company merged with BSN, a glass manufacturer, and adopted the packaging capability of the glass system to the food business. However, the glass business was dropped in the late 1970s, and since then Danone has focused on defining its place in the dairy industry and determining how it can better address the cultural demands of its local customers. With the decision to focus most heavily on Europe and to take advantage of the expanding EU, Danone set up centralized purchasing and research departments in order to obtain economies of scale in food distribution across that continent. At the same time the company looked to gain a greater presence in other markets, including North America, subsequently taking a 40 percent stake in Stonyfield Farm, an organic yogurt maker based in Londonderry, New Hampshire. Although Stonyfield continued to operate autonomously, the firm's strong customer relations program and its expertise in marketing fast-growing organic products provided Danone the opportunity to further increase its US market share to exploit the strengths of its new acquisition.

And to ensure that it continues to focus on its main business of dairy food, Danone has sold off its grocery business and withdrawn from brewing and packaging. Today the company's efforts are being directed most heavily

Source: Vario Images GmbH & Co KG

toward the distribution of French-made dairy products. So in both Europe and its worldwide markets, Danone is working to answer the question: how can we develop and market French-made dairy products that meet the needs of the local market?

The other major global rival to Nestlé was the Italian MNE, Parmalat. Like Danone, Parmalat marketed a wide variety of dairy products including milk, yogurt, desserts, butter, and cheese. Yet the company was best known for its development of ultra-high-temperature (UHT) pasteurized milk that allows milk to last up to six months without refrigeration. By specializing in the production and distribution of UHT milk across Europe, Parmalat was able to cut both production and distribution costs and to increase its profitability. At the same time, and unlike Danone, the company was more vigorous in its international expansion. In addition to moving into France and Germany in the 1970s, the company began expanding into North and South America soon thereafter. As a result, Parmalat earned 32 percent of its revenues in Europe, 31 percent in North and Central America, and another 29 percent from South America. Australia and Asia accounted for the remaining 8 percent.

Like its two other competitors, Nestlé and Danone, Parmalat carefully targeted its products to the local market and sought to acquire local companies that had established markets. For example, Parmalat purchased Ault Dairies, one of Canada's largest operations, as well as Beatrice Foods, another major Canadian firm. Parmalat subsequently became that country's largest dairy firm. Parmalat also had its subsidiaries employ the company's food expertise to exploit their local markets. For example, drawing on its UHT technology, Parmalat's Australian subsidiary was able to export milk products throughout the ▶

Asian market, and the company's Argentinean subsidiary, which specialized in UHT milk products, was able to create export markets in Brazil and Venezuela. In addition, in catering to local tastes the company developed a wide variety of products such as a dessert called *dulce de leche*, which it exported to a large number of countries including the United States, the UK, Russia, Spain, Uruguay, and Venezuela.

Parmalat, however, tended to maintain locally known brands, rather than replacing them with its own. In the UK, for example, Parmalat owned the Loseley yogurt brand, which was well regarded as quite an upmarket brand. Similarly, consumers in Canada and Australia may be surprised to hear that their favorite brands, such as Beatrice or Pauls, were owned by Parmalat.

Danone and Parmalat are good examples of companies that sell products that are culturally influenced. In Danone's case, it has chosen to do so by staying primarily in Europe. Parmalat, on the other hand, has been much more active in the larger international arena. Both, however, have been successful because they have been able to blend their expertise with the needs of their specific markets.

In the case of Parmalat this success now appears to have come to an end. It reached sales of $9.4 billion in 2002 and managed acquired brands in 30 different countries. But in December 2003, with talk of fraud scandals in Italy, it was revealed that Parmalat had a reported $11 billion debt and $5 billion in cash missing. By 2006, although the group still operates in the dairy industry, it is much reduced in scale and global scope. It has sold off numerous national businesses and still faces ongoing litigation.

Websites: www.danone.com; www.parmalat.net; www.nestle.com.

Sources: Danone, Annual Report, 2006; http://www.danone.com; Parmalat, Annual Report, 2006, http://www.parmalat.net; Adrian Michaels, "Judge seeks Parmalat settlement," FT.com, December 6, 2006; "A Small Town's Big Cheeses," *The Economist*, May 29, 1997; Nikhil Deogun, "Danone Groupe Scoops Up 40% Stake in Stonyfield Farm," *Wall Street Journal*, October 4, 2001, p. B9; and Deborah Orr, "Who Gets Parmalat's Milk and Cookies?" *Forbes.com*, December 24, 2003, http://www.forbes.com/2003/12/24/cz_do_1223parmalat.html.

example of a successful M&A which followed the "independent" approach vis-à-vis its newly acquired subsidiary. In March 2000 it bought one of the UK's top tea brands, Tetley Tea, some say on the basis of profits at Tata Consulting Services, the successful IT and software arm of the $9 billion Tata conglomerate. Coming more than 50 years after the end of 200 years of British colonial rule that had supported British ownership of tea estates in India, this shift of power is an appropriate symbol for the twenty-first century. But the takeover was barely noticed by the British public. In stark contrast to the imperialist approach of the British in India all those years ago, Tata took a hands-off approach, allowing the existing management, with its local knowledge and experience, to continue running Tetley. A federal structure with devolved decision making is supported by a polycentric organizational style.[25]

 Active learning check

Review your answer to Active Learning Case question 4 and make any changes you like. Then compare your answer to the one below.

4 Explain why one organization might want to impose some of its ways of doing things on another, such as an acquired firm or subsidiary.

Standardizing ways of doing things across the overall organization, to a certain extent, can be more efficient. Differences can create difficulties in communication, teamwork, motivation, or coordination, and the impact on company performance can be significant. It is important to make the distinction between the values, beliefs, and norms, plus the associated work practices and management structures that stem from the dominant national culture (the imposition can then be described as ethnocentric) or from the corporate culture. In the latter case the firm will be aiming to derive the benefits of having a shared culture that bridges the national cultural differences across the overall organization.

Cultural differences between groups of people in the one firm, or between the employees of two firms engaged in a joint venture, are not necessarily a problem. However, when they do create difficulties in terms of communication, teamwork, motivation, or coordination, the impact on company performance can be significant, despite the fact that clear cause-and-effect relationships are often difficult to identify precisely. Rather than a single "best practice" for dealing with this, the examples above suggest that solutions are context specific.

CULTURE EMBODIED IN NATIONAL INSTITUTIONS

The second level at which we can analyze cultural differences and their effects is at the institutional level, where national cultural characteristics are *embodied* in institutions from government agencies and governance mechanisms to the education system, economic institutions, and business organizations.

Firms engaging in cross-border joint ventures or M&A need to take account of the national context in which the new partner or acquired firm is situated. Similarly, when marketing and selling products in a new national market, these broader differences matter. A country's distinctive political, legal, and institutional context partly reflects its dominant national culture. Education systems, labor laws, environmental regulations, capital markets, and the relationships between private-sector businesses and public-sector organizations will vary accordingly.[26]

Trompenaars uses his findings simply to divide various countries into subgroups reflecting shared characteristics stemming from common cultural influences (Figure 5.5).

- *Western pluralism* emphasizes individual competitiveness, commonly represented by separate ventures competing in price-defined markets for success. Survival of the fittest is the catchphrase, and companies tend to be run as meritocracies.

- *Command economies* are centrally planned hierarchies with less individualism and less individual incentive. Clearly, as global politics changes, countries are tending to move out of this category. For example, Poland is now an emerging capitalist country reflecting the characteristics of Western pluralism more than a command economy.

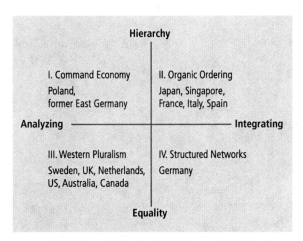

Figure 5.5 Shared characteristics stemming from common cultural influences

Source: Hampden-Turner, C. and Trompenaars, F. *The Seven Cultures of Capitalism: Value Systems for Creating Wealth in the United States, Britain, Japan, Germany, France, Sweden and the Netherlands* (New York: Doubleday, 1993).

- *Organic ordering* refers to the family-centered hierarchies of Asia, southern Europe, and Latin America. Inter- and intra-organization interaction will be based around information sharing and collaborative competition.
- *Structured networks* reflect the more equal, structured relationships between companies and with public-sector organizations that exist in some countries.

France, with some comparisons with other Western economies and organizations, provides an example, giving a snapshot of some of the main characteristics that stem from the country's cultural distinctiveness.

France: cultural and social characteristics that create a national distinctiveness

National characteristics

- Central planning, national protectionism for domestic industry, and strong government intervention in the market (compared to other European economies) lie at the heart of the French system. Civil servants are intellectual and respected as in Japan (but not the UK) and well paid (unlike Japan).
- Communication tends to be vertical (up–across–down). Bypassing official channels is not common: uncertainty reduction tends to predominate.
- Hierarchy is important, bureaucracy respected. Clear hierarchy, divisionalization, and rules and regulations guide behavior. However, this exists alongside a respect for maverick gestures and individuals or groups that overcome the obstacles and beat the system.
- Government-to-business links are formal and informal, with the elitist groups from the *grande écoles* bridging public and private sectors at the senior level. Ascription dominates over achievement compared to the UK or the United States, again with parallels with Japan.
- Competition occurs at school age when success determines assignment to a particular *cadre* or *echelon* inside and outside the workplace (depending on the school attended as much as individual performance).

Mittelstand
About 3.4 million small and medium-sized firms defined as having less than €50 million turnover that make up the heart of the German economy

- France has a large number of family-owned and managed firms. It does not have the **Mittelstand** (small technical and engineering firms) that underpin the chemical and machine tool industries in Germany.
- Capital markets are competitive but are not as "short-termist" as in the UK and the United States, with an overwhelming emphasis on share values and dividends. France does not have the strong interfirm networks that exist in Germany and Japan (*keiretsu*), which include links between financial institutions (banks, institutional shareholders) and the companies they fund.

French organizations

Esprit de corps
The spirit of a group that makes the members want the group to succeed

- French companies also tend to be hierarchical, bureaucratic, and well structured, but there is a strong view of the company as a social entity (an **esprit de corps**) with an emphasis on obligation and loyalty rather than individual gain.
- Despite moves toward a more equal relationship, French managers continue to have a supervisory role over workers. German and Japanese managers, by comparison, tend to be more collegiate and cooperative across levels of the hierarchy, including mentoring arrangements between senior and junior managers.
- Hierarchical relationships are diffuse (in Trompenaars' terminology) rather than limited to the workplace (France ranks highest among European countries along this dimension). Companies have a responsibility toward the wider society, and managers, because of their professional status, have a role to play in society.

- Scientific management techniques, termed **gestion**, dominate, which parallels German zeal for quantification and measurement to guide performance improvement.

- There is a premium on technical and on-the-job training (similar to Germany and Japan). Marketing and accountancy skills are less valued than in the UK and the United States.

- A surprise to many observers is that one-fifth of the labor force is unionized. French labor law (*Code du Travail*) is comprehensive and enforced. Companies are relatively loyal to their employees compared to British or US firms, but there is not the strong social contract that exists in Japan.

KEY POINTS

1 Culture can be defined as "the sum total of the beliefs, rules, techniques, institutions, and artifacts that characterize human populations."

2 Cultural differences can have an important effect at the face-to-face or company-to-company levels and need to be taken into account in dealing with different groups of customers around the world.

3 Culture can be analyzed at two levels: the psychic distance between groups of people, and the differences in culture embodied in national institutions and socio-economic systems.

4 Hofstede, Trompenaars, and the GLOBE researchers have constructed useful frameworks for understanding broad differences between national cultures which underpin differences in the design of organizations and the behavior of managers and employees.

5 Differences in organization, leadership, and communication can be used to measure differences in groups and individuals and help managers anticipate when and why cultures may clash.

6 Company responses to the challenges of managing diversity range from the imperialist to the independent approaches.

7 Ethnocentric firms impose a common culture on all subsidiaries, polycentric firms allow subsidiaries to reflect local ways of doing things, and geocentric firms maintain a balance between center and subsidiary.

8 When in Japan, do not throw your *meishi*!

Key terms

- *grande école*
- culture
- socialization
- corporate culture
- ethnocentrism
- cultural convergence
- psychic distance
- power distance
- uncertainty avoidance
- individualism

- masculinity
- universalism
- particularism
- collectivism
- neutral
- emotional
- specific
- diffuse
- achievement oriented
- ascription oriented

- sequential
- synchronic
- humane orientation
- ethnocentric
- culture clash
- polycentric
- geocentric
- Mittelstand
- esprit de corps
- gestion

Review and discussion questions

1 In your own words, what is meant by the term *culture*?

2 In what way do ethnocentrism and misconceptions about other cultures inhibit those doing business internationally?

3 Why is language so critical in understanding international culture? How can this problem be dealt with effectively?

4 Why are cultural differences an important factor when adapting products for new overseas markets?

5 Use Trompenaars' seven dimensions of culture to compare and contrast your own national stereotype to another.

6 Why are work attitudes of importance to MNEs? Cite and describe two examples.

7 What kinds of reward systems are likely to be effective in more individualistic and achievement-oriented cultures like the United States?

8 Explain how the GLOBE project has extended the dimensions of national culture beyond the work of Hofstede and Trompenaars.

9 In the Pharmacia–Upjohn merger how did employment practices and workplace regulations differ among the Americans, the Swedes, and the Italians, and what impact did these differences have on the operational efficiency of the merged company?

10 Show with examples how managers in multinational firms could improve their employees' awareness of the important differences among cultures.

11 What are the benefits and the problems for a polycentric MNE?

12 Why is an understanding of the institutional norms, regulations, and practices of other countries important for international firms? Give examples to illustrate your answer.

13 What does the French term *gestion* mean?

Real Case

Do not throw your *meishi*!

Some time ago the Competitiveness Division of the Department of Trade and Industry (DTI) in the British government commissioned research on British small and medium-sized enterprises (SMEs) that had managed to set up successful businesses in Japan, one of the toughest (though lucrative) global markets to break into for foreign firms (see Chapter 17). Numerous success stories from the study show how some firms managed to adapt to the differences in culture, society, and business practices that can act as barriers to foreign firms. But there are also numerous tales of the blunders that some managers made that undermined their efforts to establish themselves in Japan.

Meishi is Japanese for "business card," but has a deeper significance in Japan than elsewhere as a representation of

the employee's allegiance to and respect for his or her company. The strong emphasis placed on loyalty and obligation between employees and their firms, lifetime employment based on a moral contract (rather than a price-based contract), and a manager's position as a member of a collective all have a strong influence on his (sometimes her) behavior when interacting with others. *Kaisha-in* literally means "company person," but it also denotes the individual as a representative of "our company" in the sense of a shared group consciousness. The company name comes first, before the individual's name on the *meishi* and when making introductions. The exchange of *meishi* also establishes relative rank within the strict corporate and social hierarchy and therefore guides the correct behavior and even form of language used for interacting. Overall for the Japanese exchanging *meishi* is an important symbolic ritual.

A senior technology manager from Scotland on his first assignment to Japan was attempting to establish a strategic alliance with a local firm as a starting point for marketing and selling his firm's products locally. In his first meeting he faced six senior executives from the Japanese firm, ranged across a board room table traditionally in order of seniority. Almost the first act of the Scottish manager was to *throw* his newly printed *meishi* across the table to each of the Japanese executives in turn!

There is no way of knowing how significant this single act was in undermining this firm's market entry in Japan. It failed in its attempt to forge an alliance with this particular Japanese firm and with others, eventually leading it to abandon its attempts. What we can say for certain is that a small amount of preparation by this manager to build even a basic understanding of business etiquette in Japan would have improved this company's chances of building a successful business in Japan.

The overall study, including 30 detailed case studies of successful British firms in Japan, demonstrates very clearly that managers need to understand the cultural and social norms that underpin business practices in different countries if they are going to do business in those countries. The lesson applies to firms engaged in cross-border mergers and alliances, expanding into new markets through foreign direct investment activities, or even at the simple level, when hiring new recruits from overseas, outsourcing to foreign countries, or selling products and services abroad. Cultural awareness is critical to making business relationships work, at the face-to-face level or at the company-to-company level.

Sources: S. Collinson, *Small and Successful in Japan: A Study of 30 British Firms in the World's Most Competitive Market* (London: Avebury Press, Ashgate Publishing Group, 1996); C. Nakane, *Japanese Society* (Tokyo: Charles E. Tuttle, 1973).

1 Explain what kinds of broad cultural differences we are likely to find between the Japanese and the British.

2 What impression do you think the Scottish engineer made on the Japanese executives?

3 What steps could the Scottish firm have taken to avoid this kind of mistake?

4 How easy is it to do a simple cost–benefit analysis on investments into improved cultural awareness among employees?

Real Case

Sport can be local *and* global: Manchester United

For most sports there appears to be a natural connection with the cultures and communities of particular locations and even individual venues. Often history plays a strong role, even when sports are played internationally. St Andrews Links Course, Lord's Cricket Ground, and Wembley Stadium all have a particular symbolism to players and fans of golf, cricket, and football (soccer) in and beyond the UK.

These contrast with more "placeless" global sporting events, particularly the Olympic Games, which involve most nations of the World. Rather than creating a sense of common identity such events can reinforce national cultural identities through international competition.

Other sports remain local: Japanese Sumo Wrestling, Aussie Rules Football, and Hurling in Ireland, for example, where the connection with national culture, community and history are strongest. American football is played in several countries but only seriously in the United States. It is not only a huge commercial enterprise but, like basketball and baseball, strongly embedded in local communities through schools and colleges, as an important symbol of US cultural identity.

Source: Alamy Images/Len Grant Photography

Some sports could be defined as regional, such as baseball which is predominantly based in North America, but also popular in Japan and played little elsewhere. A few sports are marked on a global basis, although not all parts of the triad are fully involved. Golf, tennis, and soccer have global television audiences and advertising revenues. Among these, soccer is recognized as the biggest, played by an estimated 240 million people with 1.5 million teams and 300,000 clubs worldwide. Many countries, from Brazil to Cameroon, Italy to South Korea, would claim the game as an important part of popular national culture. But soccer is not a major sport in North America, where it ranks well behind American football, baseball, hockey, and car racing.

Europe hosts some of the major soccer club brands, with 52 leagues and a combined income of over $13 billion. Within this the English Premiership league is worth $3 billion. Perhaps the leading club in the Premiership is Manchester United. Not your average soccer club, but certainly one of the best illustrations in the sporting world of the evolving mix between local cultural heritage and international business.

Born in 1878, Manchester United long epitomized the connection between the local team and the local community. Its fan base was dominated for over a hundred years by local people, with Trafford Park and the Manchester Ship Canal, one of the world's first industrial centers, at its heart. The grassroots, blue-collar, working-man's passion and fierce loyalty remain at the cultural heart of the club today. Rather than symbolizing English culture it demonstrates the strength and persistence of the regional subculture of England's industrial north-west. This is reinforced by strong rivalry with other leading clubs such as Liverpool, Arsenal, and Chelsea. Now the brands of these teams are very multinational.

In the early 1990s, despite strong growth in international merchandising sales through Manchester United Merchandising, over 90 percent of revenues to the club still came from the domestic UK market. But a growing global fan club, the international spread of *Manchester United Magazine*, and the growing availability of televised games beyond the UK (particularly via Rupert Murdoch's global media networks) led to an export drive in the late 1990s and early 2000s. Countries with national teams but few big league teams, like Ireland, Scandinavia, and a range of Asian countries, where soccer is watched by millions on TV, became the club's best markets. By 2002 the global club membership had grown to 200 branches in 24 countries and with profits of over $25 million on turnover of over $100 million, it was considered the world's wealthiest club. MUTV, the club's own TV channel, and a large range of Internet sites fueled interest in the team. By 2003 Manchester United had attracted an estimated global fan base of 53 million.

Major sponsorship deals with Nike and later Vodafone (at $15 million per year) boosted its finances and its global brand footprint. The cross-border takeover by the US-based Glazer family in 2005 made the club even more international by any definition. Boosted by wins in the Premiership, the FA Cup and the European Champions League, the club's fan base had grown to an estimated 75 million worldwide. Significantly, 40 million of these were in Asia, compared to 23 million in Europe. In 2006–2007 Manchester United generated revenues of $212 million, second only to Real Madrid's $236 million. There were seven British clubs in the top twenty and four in the top ten, the others being Chelsea ($191 million), Arsenal ($177 million), and Liverpool ($134 million). The others in the top ten are Barcelona ($195 million), AC Milan ($153 million), Bayern Munich ($150 million), Inter Milan ($131 million), and AS Roma ($106 million).

By this time the club had a range of regional sponsors, with PepsiCo, Anheuser-Busch and Schick in North America, Ladbrokes in Europe, and Fuji Film and Air Asia in Asia. These were co-branding partners alongside global sponsors such as AIG, Vodafone, Nike, and Audi (and a few local partners like Dimension Data in South Africa). In some cases these have been the route to joint products and services, such as content services delivered by mobile phone to Manchester United fans through Vodafone. Pretax profits for the club reached $60 million in 2006 and turnover, including merchandising and media partnerships, was over $400 million.

Despite the fact that, on average, over half the team comprises foreign players who play against the England national team in the World Cup, and despite the fact that the clubs fan base is (in terms of pure numbers) more Asian than English, the passion for the club is still as strong as ever around Manchester. Global sports teams like Manchester United are embedded in local folklore, passionately discussed in bars and clubs around the world, part of the cultural identity of communities, but at the same time they are multinational businesses with global brands and international strategies.

Sources: A. Rugman, *The End of Globalization* (London, Random House 2001); R. Bennet and J. Blythe, *International Marketing*, 3rd ed. (London: Kogan Page, 2002); W. Manzenreiter and J. Horne, *Football Goes East: Business, Culture and the People's Game in China, Japan and South Korea* (New York: Routledge, 2004); G. P. T. Finn and R. Giulianotti *Football Culture* (New York: Routledge, 2000); "Neo-imperialism at the point of a boot", *The Economist*, March 11, 2007, p. 56; http://www.manutd.com/; "Real top Man Utd in rich league," *BBC News*, February 14, 2008, http://news.bbc.co.uk/2/hi/business/7242490.stm.

1 What makes a sport local, regional, or global?

2 What major drivers are responsible for the internationalization of Manchester United?

3 How important are Manchester United's strong local roots to its international success?

ENDNOTES

1 UNCTAD, *World Investment Report 2007*, United Nations, Geneva; http://www.unctad.org.

2 D. A. Ball and W. H. McCulloch, *International Business: The Challenge of Global Competition*, 7th ed. (Boston: Irwin McGraw-Hill, 1999), p. 258.

3 G. Hofstede, *Culture's Consequences: International Differences in Work Related Values* (Beverly Hills, CA: Sage, 1980).

4 K. Voigt, "Japanese Firms Want English Competency," *Wall Street Journal*, June 11, 2001, p. B7B.

5 M. Weber, *The Protestant Ethic and the Spirit of Capitalism*, 2nd Roxbury ed. (London: Roxbury, 1993).

6 K. A. Nordström and J.-E. Vahlne, "Is the Globe Shrinking? Psychic Distance and the Establishment of Swedish Sales Subsidiaries during the Last 100 Years," in M. Landeck, *International trade – regional and global issues* (Basingstoke: St. Martin's Press, 1994).

7 Many texts refer back to the work of Hall as one of the earliest authors in this field; E. T. Hall, "The Silent Language of International Business," *Harvard Business Review*, May–June, 1960, pp. 87–96.

8 G. Hofstede, "The Cultural Relativity of Organizational Practices and Theories," *Journal of International Business Studies*, Fall 1983, p. 92; G. Hofstede, *Cultures and Organizations; Software of the Mind: Intercultural Cooperation and Its Importance for Survival* (London: Harper Collins, 1983).

9 B. McSweeny, "Hofstede's model of national cultural differences and their consequences: a triumph of faith – a failure of analysis," *Human Relations*, vol. 55, no. 1 (2002), pp. 89–118, cites additional problems in a stronger critique of Hofstede's approach. Jowell, R. "How comparative is comparative research?" *American Behavioral Scientist*, vol. 42, no. 2 (1998), pp. 168–178, meanwhile suggests that Hofstede and other analysts' cross-national data are too concerned with "league tables of distributions showing merely 'gee whiz' national differences" rather than offering explanations and interpretations.

10 G. Hofstede, *Culture's Consequences: Comparing Values, Behaviors, Institutions and Organizations across Nations*, 2nd ed. (Thousand Oaks, CA: Sage, 2001); G. Hofstede et al., "What Goals Do Business Leaders Pursue? A Study in Fifteen Countries," *Journal of International Business Studies*, vol. 33, no. 4, (2002) pp. 785–804.

11 F. Trompenaars, *Riding the Waves of Culture: Understanding Cultural Diversity of Business* (London: Nicholas Brealey, 1993); F. Trompenaars and C. Hampden-Turner, *Riding the Waves of Culture: Understanding Cultural Diversity in Global Business* (London: Nicholas Brealey, 1998); Fons Trompenaars and Charles Hampden-Turner also run a consultancy specializing in advice and training on cross-cultural issues. The website for the firm has some useful resources for further research: http://www.7d-culture.nl/. A similar site, with a range of tools and techniques for understanding and managing differences in European cultures, is: http://www.johnmole.com.

12 C. C. Chen, "New Trends in Rewards Allocation Preferences: A Sino-US Comparison," *Academy of Management Journal*, April 1995, p. 425; Y. Ono and B. Spindle, "Japan's Long Decline Makes One Thing Rise: Individualism," *Wall Street Journal*, December 29, 2000, pp. A1, 4.

13 M. Javidan and R. J. House, "Cultural Acumen for the Global Manager: Lessons from Project GLOBE," *Organizational Dynamics*, vol. 29, no. 4 (2001), pp. 289–305.

14 D. A. Light, "Cross-cultural Lessons in Leadership", *MIT Sloan Management Review*, Fall 2003, pp. 5–6.

15 This has involved 38 universities in annual surveys of around 7,000 organizations across Europe; C. J. Brewster and H. Harris (eds.), *International Human Resource Management: Contemporary Issues in Europe* (London: Routledge, 1999); C. Brewster, "HRM Practices in Multinational Enterprises," in M. J. Gannon and K. Newman, *Handbook of Cross-cultural Management* (Oxford: Blackwell, 2001); J. Van Ommeren et al., "The Cranet Survey 1999," UK Executive Report 1999, Cranfield Network on European Human Resource Management, Cranfield, Bedford.

16 P. C. Earley, "Leading cultural research in the future: a matter of paradigms and taste," *Journal of International Business Studies*, vol. 37, no. 6 (2006), pp. 922–931; G. Hofstede, "What did GLOBE really measure? Researchers' minds versus respondents' minds," *Journal of International Business Studies*, vol. 37, no 6 (2006), pp. 882–896; P. B. Smith, "When elephants fight, the grass gets trampled: the GLOBE and Hofstede projects," *Journal of International Business Studies*, vol. 37, no. 6 (2006), pp. 915–921.

17 C. Nakane, *Japanese Society* (Tokyo: Charles E. Tuttle, 1973).

18 J. R. Lincoln, "Employee Work Attitudes and Management Practice in the United States and Japan: Evidence from a Large Comparative Survey," *California Management Review*, Fall 1989, p. 91.

19 There are many firms that offer advice and training services to help companies improve their cultural awareness and the ability of employees to adapt to cultural diversity. A useful starting point, however, is G. Wederspahn, "Do Your Employees Need Intercultural Services?" 2002, http://www.grovewell.com/pub-cultural-knowledge.html.

20 Financial Times, *Managing Global Business, Mastering Management Series* (London: Pearson, 2000); M. C. Gentile, *Managerial Excellence through Diversity: Text and Cases* (Chicago: Irwin, 1996); D. A. Thomas and R. J. Ely, "Making Differences Matter: A New Paradigm for Managing Diversity," *Harvard Business Review*, September–October 1996, pp. 79–90.

21 H. V. Perlmutter, "The Tortuous Evolution of the Multinational Enterprise," *Columbia Journal of World Business*, vol. 4, no. 1 (1969), pp. 9–18.

22 Perlmutter in Bartlett and Ghoshal, 2000, p. 77; C. A. Bartlett and S. Ghoshal, *Text, Cases and Readings in Cross-Border Management*, 3rd ed. (Boston: McGraw-Hill International Editions, 2000).

23 S. C. Collinson, "M&A as Imperialism?" in D. Angwin (ed.), *Images of M&A* (Oxford: Blackwell Publications, 2006).

24 J. P. Walsh, "Top Management Turnover Following Mergers and Acquisitions," *Strategic Management Journal*, vol. 9 (1988), pp. 173–183.

25 Collinson in Angwin, *Images of M&A*.

26 R. P. Appelbaum, W. Felstiner and V. Gessner (eds.), *Rules and Networks: The Legal Culture of Global Business Transactions*

(Oxford: Hart Publishing, 2001); R. Whitley, *Competing Capitalisms: Institutions and Economies* (Cheltenham: Edward Elgar, 2002); R. Whitley, *The Multinational Firm: Organizing across Institutional and National Divides* (Oxford: Oxford University Press, 2001); R. Whitley, *Divergent Capitalisms: the Social Structuring and Change of Business Systems* (Oxford: Oxford University Press, 1999).

ADDITIONAL BIBLIOGRAPHY

Ashkanasy, Neil M., Trevor-Roberts, Edwin and Earnshaw, Louise. "The Anglo Cluster: Legacy of the British Empire," *Journal of World Business*, vol. 37, no. 1 (2002).

Barr, Pamela S. and Glynn, Mary-Ann. "Cultural Variations in Strategic Issue Interpretation: Relating Cultural Uncertainty Avoidance to Controllability in Discriminating Threat and Opportunity," *Strategic Management Journal*, vol. 25, no. 1 (2004).

Chevrier, Sylvie. "Cross-cultural Management in Multinational Project Groups," *Journal of World Business*, vol. 38, no. 2 (2003).

Collinson, Simon C. *Small and Successful in Japan: A Study of 30 British Firms in the World's Most Competitive Market* (London: Ashgate Press, 1996).

Collinson, Simon C. and Houlden, John. "Decision Making and Market Orientation in the Internationalization Process of Small and Medium-Sized Enterprises," *Management International Review*, vol. 45, no. 4 (Fourth Quarter 2005).

Early, P. Christopher. "Leading Cultural Research in the Future: A Matter of Paradigms and Taste," *Journal of International Business Studies*, vol. 37, no. 6 (November 2006).

Fealy, Liz and Kompare, Dave. "When Worlds Collide: Culture Clash," *Journal of Business Strategy*, vol. 24, no. 4 (2003).

Friday, Ernest and Friday, Shawnta S. "Managing Diversity Using a Strategic Planned Change Approach," *Journal of Management Development*, vol. 22, no. 10 (2003).

Ghauri, Pervez. "Negotiating with the Chinese: A Sociocultural Analysis," *Journal of World Business*, vol. 36, no. 3 (Fall 2001).

Gratchev, Mikhail V. "Making the Most of Cultural Differences," *Harvard Business Review*, vol. 79, no. 9 (October 2001).

Hampden-Turner, Charles and Trompenaars, Fons. *The Seven Cultures of Capitalism: Value Systems for Creating Wealth in the United States, Britain, Japan, Germany, France, Sweden and the Netherlands* (New York: Doubleday, 1993).

Hofstede, Geert. "What Did GLOBE Really Measure? Researchers' Minds versus Respondents' Minds," *Journal of International Business Studies*, vol. 37, no. 6 (November 2006).

Holden, Nigel J. *Cross-Cultural Management: A Knowledge Management Perspective* (London: Prentice Hall, 2002).

Javidan, Mansour, House, Robert J., Dorfman, Peter J., Hanges, Paul J. and Sully de Luque, Mary. "Conceptualizing and Measuring Cultures and Their Consequences: A Comparative Review of GLOBE's and Hofstede's Approaches," *Journal of International Business Studies*, vol. 37, no. 6 (November 2006).

Kostova, Tatiana and Roth, Kendall. "Social Capital in Multinational Corporations & A Micro-Macro Model of its Formation," *Academy of Management Review*, vol. 28, no. 2 (2003).

Lenartowicz, Tomasz and Roth, Kendall. "Does Subculture Within a Country Matter? A Cross-cultural Study of Motivational Domains and Business Performance in Brazil," *Journal of International Business Studies*, vol. 32, no. 2 (Summer 2001).

Li, Ji, Lam, Kevin and Qian, Gongming. "Does Culture Affect Behavior and Performance of Firms? The Case of Joint Ventures in China," *Journal of International Business Studies*, vol. 32, no. 1 (Spring 2001).

Maddox, Robert C. *Cross-cultural Problems in International Business: The Role of the Cultural Integration Function* (London: Quorum Books, 1993).

Marshall, R. Scott and Boush, David M. "Dynamic Decision Making: A Cross-cultural Comparison of US and Peruvian Export Managers," *Journal of International Business Studies*, vol. 32, no. 4 (2001).

Martin, Joanne. *Cultures in Organizations: Three Perspectives* (New York: Oxford University Press, 1992).

McSweeny, Brendan. "Hofstede's Model of National Cultural Differences and Their Consequences: A Triumph of Faith—A Failure of Analysis," *Human Relations*, vol. 55, no. 1 (2002).

Mead, Richard. *International Management: Cross-cultural Dimensions*, 2nd ed. (Oxford: Blackwell, 1998).

Mole, John. *Mind Your Manners: Managing Business Cultures in Europe* (London: Nicholas Brealey, 1996).

Morgan, Glenn, Kristensen, Per Hull and Whitley, Richard (eds.). *The Multinational Firm* (Oxford: Oxford University Press, 2001).

Schneider, Susan C. and Barsoux, Jean-Louis. *Managing Across Cultures*, 2nd ed. (London: Prentice Hall, 2003).

Shenkar, Oded. "Cultural Distance Revisited: Towards a More Rigorous Conceptualisation and Measurement of Cultural Differences," *Journal of International Business Studies*, vol. 32, no. 3 (2001).

Simon, David G. and Lane, Peter J. "A Model of Cultural Differences and International Alliance Performance," *Journal of International Business Studies*, vol. 35, no. 4 (2004).

Sivakumar, K. and Nakata, Cheryl. "The Stampede Toward Hofstede's Framework: Avoiding the Sample Design Pit in Cross-cultural Research," *Journal of International Business Studies*, vol. 32, no. 3 (Fall 2001).

Triandis, Harry C. "The Many Dimensions of Culture," *Academy of Management Executive*, vol. 18, no. 1 (2004).

Von Glinow, Mary-Ann, Shapiro, Debra L. and Brett, Jeanne M. "Can We Talk, and Should We? Managing Emotional Conflict in Multicultural Teams," *Academy of Management Review*, vol. 29, no. 4 (2004).

West, Joel and Graham, John L. "A Linguistic-Based Measure of Cultural Distance and Its Relationship to Managerial Values," *Management International Review*, vol. 44, no. 3 (Third Quarter 2004).

Section 2
Firm Perspective

136

C H A P T E R

1 3

INTERNATIONAL TRADE PATTERNS

O B J E C T I V E S

- To describe the evolving pattern of international commerce
- To document the emerging markets for global exports
- To examine global trade flows of six major commodities groups

Containerships capable of carrying thousands of tons of cargo exemplify the importance and growth of international trade, linking far-flung economies around the world. This one, of Chinese origin, reflects the growing importance of East Asia in the world economy.

Table 13.1

Distribution of World Output ($ Billion)

Region	1980	1990	2000	Percentage of Total	Percentage Change 1980–2000
World Total	**11,982.7**	**25,442.3**	**28,854.0**	**100.00**	**240.8**
North America	3,234.1	6,495.4	8,809.4	30.5	272.4
Other Western Hemisphere	842.7	1,505.3	1,994.4	6.9	236.7
Middle East	471.4	876.2	964.7	3.3	204.6
Asia and Oceania	2,497.3	6,839.5	8,626.8	29.9	345.4
Western Europe	2,999.7	5,939.1	8,739.9	30.3	291.4
East Europe and Russia	1,399.2	2,759.4	1,784.9	6.2	127.6
Africa	538.4	1,027.3	1,089.1	3.8	202.3

Note: Figures for each region's share of world output are purchasing power parity estimates based on the UN International Comparison Project.
Source: International Monetary Fund.

As we have seen repeatedly in this book, capitalism is an economic and political system forever in flux. Incessant change is the norm in market-based societies, and this pattern continued in the late twentieth century. The focus of this chapter is largely empirical and is designed to add substance to the theoretical discussions offered in Chapter 12.

Total world output, roughly $28.8 trillion in 2000, was highly unevenly distributed among the planet's major regions (Table 13.1). The turbulent decades of the late twentieth century saw major changes in the volume and composition of international trade. World growth has averaged about 3.7 percent annually for the last three decades (Figure 13.1). World exports jumped from $2 trillion in 1980 to over $8.8 trillion in 2003, or more than 36 percent of gross world product (GWP), a clear sign of the increasing integration of national economies (Figure 13.2). Of these exports, agricultural goods comprised 7.6 percent, mining ores, fuels, and minerals another 10.8 percent, all manufactured goods 61.3 percent, and all services 20.2 percent. The growth in exports was unevenly distributed around the world. East Asian NICs led the way, with China surging to the forefront. Manufacturing exports, with the exception of a dip in the mid-1970s, continued their rapid growth and now account for about 60 percent of world exports by value.

The changing structure of trade has affected various world regions differently, leading to fluid geographies of exports (Figure 13.3). Changes in international supply and demand, prices, production and transportation technology, production techniques, and government policies all play out differently in unique local contexts. For example, OPEC countries recorded a meteoric rise in the value of their exports in the 1970s and a precipitous decline in the 1980s and 1990s; by the 2000s, oil prices had climbed again as economies around the world, including China in particular, increased their demand for energy. North America, Europe, and East Asia experienced a drop in their export earnings after the oil crisis, but as a group they recovered and now account for 80 percent of the value of world trade. With the exception of the major oil exporters, LDCs that depend

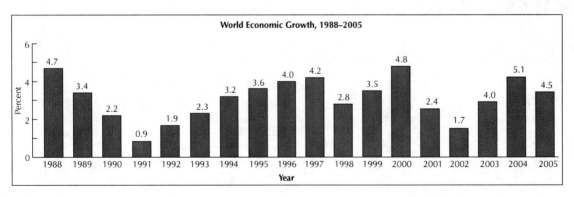

FIGURE 13.1
World economic growth, 1988–2005.

FIGURE 13.2
Postwar growth in world output and exports.

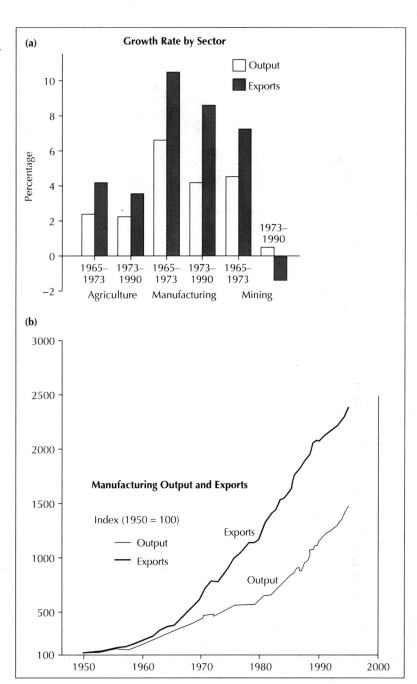

heavily on the export of a few primary commodities have fared badly. For many of them, the growth in primary commodity exports has been negative since 1980.

In addition to the expanding volume of trade, increased diversification of trade ties represents one of the most significant developments in the contemporary world economy. Advanced industrial countries still trade primarily among themselves, but the proportion has declined from more than 75 percent in 1970 to around 66 percent today. They have increased their share of exports to LDCs, and their imports from LDCs have increased still more. Another major development has been the growth of manufacturing exports from LDCs to developed countries and, to a lesser extent, to

other LDCs. Manufacturing exports now account for about 40 percent of total nonfuel exports of these countries, compared with 20 percent in 1963, and LDCs now supply 13 percent of the imports of manufactures by developed countries, compared with only 7 percent in 1973. Yet only a handful of Asian and Western Hemisphere countries are involved in this development.

EMERGING MARKETS

Exports of the industrial countries have been concentrated among the member countries of Europe, Japan, and North America. Another category of countries

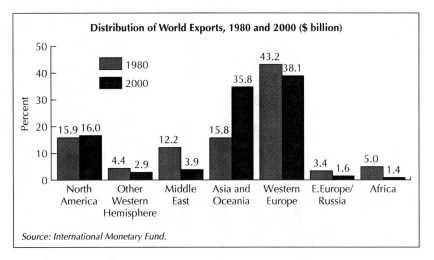

Distribution of World Exports, 1980 and 2000 ($ billion)

Source: International Monetary Fund.

FIGURE 13.3
Distribution of world exports, 1980 and 2000. Western Europe still leads the world in the distribution of world exports. Many small countries supply neighbors with manufactured goods, taking advantage of scale economies and satisfying the need for aerial specialization.

holds more promise for large increases in world exports, the emerging markets, which are generally the largest in their respective continents (Table 13.2). In Latin America, they are Argentina, Brazil, and Mexico. In Asia, they are China (including Hong Kong), Taiwan, Indonesia, Singapore, South Korea, and India. Other emerging markets include Poland, South Africa, and Turkey. Together, these 12 countries account for almost half of the world's population—3 billion people.

Emerging markets share important attributes in that they are all physically large, offering a vast array of products to serve their populations. Large internal markets allow producers to generate economies of scale and produce goods relatively cheaply. All the emerging markets are of major political importance within their world regions, where they serve as regional economic drivers. Their growth will cause further economic expansion in neighboring markets.

GDP growth rates in the emerging markets will probably enjoy growth rates above those of the industrialized countries. Thus, emerging market imports of goods and services will be important sources of growth for exporters in the developed world. In essence, emerging markets will probably become the fastest growing markets throughout the world in the twenty-first century. Such developing countries make up about 40 percent of the market for U.S. exports today.

Of the world's major regions, Asia has been growing the most quickly, experiencing 8 percent to 10 percent annual GDP growth. Since World War II, these countries, originally led by Japan and now by China, have attracted huge sums of foreign investment and industrialized at rates that compare with those of the United States in the nineteenth century. Never before in the history of humanity have so many people been raised from poverty in such a short period of time. The epitome of the newly industrializing countries in Asia are the Four Tigers (Singapore, South Korea, Taiwan, and Hong Kong). Heavily subsidized by the United States as part of its geopolitical strategy during the cold war, and often with authoritarian governments that actively shaped their growth (e.g., with export promotion strategies), the Tigers demonstrated that it was possible for some poor countries to industrialize quickly and thus rise on the ladder of economic development. Not too far behind are the achievements of Thailand, Malaysia, and Indonesia, which saw growth despite the severe Asian financial crisis of 1997. The high economic growth of these Asian countries is contrasted markedly with the economic stagnation of Pakistan, Bangladesh, and other Asian countries that pursued policies of import substitution and isolationism, producing excessive bureaucratic barriers and tariffs and fostering inefficiency and low growth. While India is changing its policies in this regard, and experiencing rapid growth, elsewhere, especially in Africa, inefficient state-run manufacturing and agricultural enterprises continue to be the dominant mode of economic activity, thus penalizing those countries' citizens.

The end of the twentieth century saw the reduction of government influence throughout the world. This conservative policy, based on a faith that only markets generate growth, is called neoliberalism, a term that harkens back to capitalism prior to the emergence of the welfare state in the 1930s. It was initiated in the United States under the Reagan administration in the 1980s, in Britain under Margaret Thatcher, and has challenged welfare states in the remainder of Europe. Globally it has been fostered by the United States, World Bank, International Monetary Fund, and the World Trade Organization. Throughout the world, neoliberal programs, implemented at the behest of the United States and the IMF, have led governments to sell off many publicly owned assets (e.g., telecommunications companies) and deregulate their economies. While such moves may generate gains in efficiency, they may also create inequality and typically penalize those who lack the resources to compete effectively in markets. Thus, economic growth is often accompanied by rising inequality and can be deleterious for the poor and unskilled.

Table 13.2

Economic Growth in the Emerging Markets, 1976–2000

| Item | Annual Percentage Change | | Average Growth in Real GDP |
	1976–1985	1987–1993	2000
World	**3.4**	**2.7**	**2.0**
Industrial countries	2.8	2.2	1.8
Developing countries	4.5	5.1	2.5
Emerging markets	6.0	6.4	2.3
China	7.8	9.3	7.5
Taiwan	8.6	8.3	4.8
India	4.6	4.1	6.0
Indonesia	5.7	6.5	−2.5
South Korea	8.0	8.1	4.5
Turkey	4.0	4.5	3.5
South Africa	2.1	0.9	1.3
Argentina	−0.5	4.4	1.5
Brazil	4.0	3.4	−1.5
Mexico	4.3	2.3	3.0
Poland	1.8	1.5	3.5
Other developing countries	0.3	1.8	3.0
East Europe and Russia	3.9	1.3	0.3

Sources: International Monetary Fund, Department of Commerce; World Economic and Social Survey 2001.

Economic growth in Latin America has varied widely among countries. Chile, which adopted neoliberal reforms under the Pinochet dictatorship, has enjoyed relatively rapid growth, including exports of wine and textiles to the United States. Argentina, in contrast, suffered an economic collapse in 2002. The low value of the peso has made Mexican goods more competitive on world markets, reversing the trend toward an increasing balance of payments and deficits for Mexico. Mexico was the only country to double its manufacturing exports in the 1990s, largely due to NAFTA.

Central Europe experienced positive but uneven growth in the last decade. Some, such as Poland, made a transition to a market-based economy relatively smoothly and had joined the European Union. These "economies in transition" remain vulnerable to external economic forces. Several, such as the Czech Republic, Hungary, and Poland, are showing modest, positive growth. Russia and the Ukraine, two leading former Soviet republics, however, suffered severe economic decline after the collapse of the Soviet Union in 1991. Caught between an old, discredited system that at least fed people and a new, corrupt, market-based one in which the government has been incapacitated by corruption and its assets sold at bargain basement prices to investors, Russia has taken much longer than expected to recover from the transition from communism to a market economy. Despite its vast resources and skilled labor force, it will be years before Russia joins the world as a fully industrialized, competitive economic power.

The economic growth in Asia over the past three decades, first in Japan, followed by the Four Tigers (newly industrialized economies of South Korea, Taiwan, Hong Kong, and Singapore), and now more recently by China, Indonesia, Malaysia, and Thailand, has brought with it a boost of international trade. It is impossible to separate increasing trade and economic growth. Economic growth leads to expanded levels of domestic consumption and investment, which result in higher levels of imports of consumer goods, raw materials, and capital goods.

WORLD PATTERNS OF TRADE

Trade simultaneously reflects economic and spatial differences in production and consumption among nations and in turn helps to generate those differences. As we saw in Chapter 12, international trade can be understood on the basis of the theory of comparative and competitive advantage and has grown more rapidly than the output of individual countries, reflecting the ways in which they are tied together by globalization. However, the volume, growth, and composition of trade vary widely among the world's major trading countries and regions.

Total World Exports of Goods and Services, 2003

	Value		*Annual Percentage Change*			
	$ Billions	*%*	*1995–2000*	*2001*	*2002*	*2003*
Agricultural products	674	7.6	−1	0	6	15
Food	543	6.1	−1	3	6	16
Raw materials	130	1.5	−3	−9	4	15
Mining products	960	10.8	10	−8	−1	21
Ores and other minerals	79	0.9	1	−4	3	24
Fuels	754	8.5	12	−8	0	23
Nonferrous metals	127	1.4	3	−9	−3	13
Manufactured goods	5,437	61.3	5	−4	5	14
Iron and steel	181	2.0	−2	−7	9	26
Chemicals	794	9.0	4	3	11	19
Other semimanufactures	529	6.0	3	−3	6	14
Machinery and transport equipment	2,894	32.6	6	−6	3	13
Textiles	169	1.9	0	−5	4	11
Clothing	226	2.5	5	−2	4	12
Other consumer goods	644	7.3	5	−2	5	15
All commercial services	1,795	20.2	4	0	7	13
Transportation	405	4.6	3	−1	5	13
Travel	525	5.9	3	−2	4	10
Other commercial services	865	9.8	6	3	10	15
Total Goods and Services	8,866	100.0				

Source: World Trade Organization.

The United States

The United States is the world's largest trading nation, accounting for more than $2 trillion worth of exports and imports in 2003. During the 1950s, the United States accounted for 25 percent of total world trade but now accounts for only 19 percent, a reflection of the growing competitiveness of other countries, particularly Europe and East Asia. From 1960 to 1970, the United States enjoyed a net trade surplus as a result of its strength in manufacturing, low oil prices, and the weak value of the dollar. However, following the petroshocks of the 1970s and deindustrialization, this surplus turned into growing trade deficits.

U.S. MERCHANDISE TRADE

Figure 13.4 shows the composition of U.S. merchandise trade with the world in 1964 and 2000. Machinery and transportation equipment accounted for the largest single proportion of exports (45%). Chemicals and other manufactures added another 31 percent, whereas agricultural products amounted to 8 percent. More than 70 percent of U.S. exports are manufactured items. Despite decades of deindustrialization, the United States remains the world's largest manufacturer today. In part this status reflects the rounds of investment that accompanied the microelectronics revolution, in which computerization dramatically raised productivity levels in steel, automobiles, and other sectors. The continued strong performance by the U.S. economy and the continuation of controlled inflation with low unemployment rates, coupled with a favorable dollar exchange rate, will ensure that U.S. goods and services remain highly competitive in world markets. U.S. firms continued to restructure and downsize to reduce costs and are continuing to reengineer with information technologies at a rapid pace.

Manufacturing goods also account for approximately 75 percent of the traded goods flowing to the United States from foreign companies. America has essentially farmed out much of its labor-intensive manufacturing to developing countries, shipping semifinished goods to countries such as Mexico for manufacturing and reimport. At the same time, it acquired an expensive taste for foreign-made items such as automobiles from Germany and Japan; shoes from Italy and Brazil;

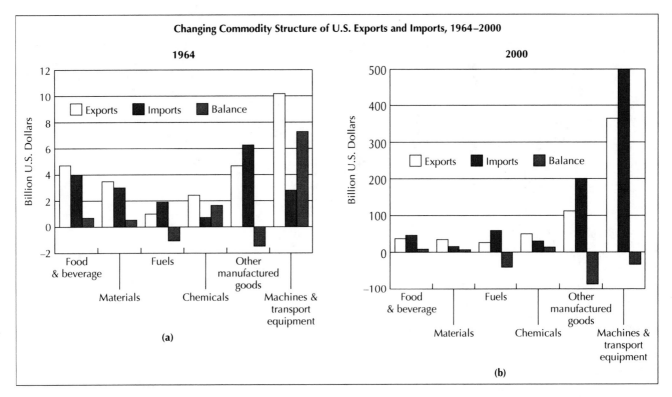

Changing Commodity Structure of U.S. Exports and Imports, 1964–2000

FIGURE 13.4
Changing structure of U.S. commodity exports and imports, 1964 and 2000. In the 1960s, the United States enjoyed a very large trade surplus in machinery and transport equipment. By 2000, however, the trade deficit was at least $230 billion because imports of manufactured goods, especially automobiles, exceeded exports.

electronic items, apparel, and toys from the Far East; and perfume and wine from France. Other imports include fossil fuels, for which the United States is not self-sufficient (Chapter 4).

The geography of U.S. merchandise trade with the world is shown in Figure 13.5. Canada, with 30 million people, represents the single largest trading partner, including 23 percent of its exports and 19 percent of its imports. U.S. trade with Canada is dominated by transportation equipment. The European Union accounts for 24 percent of U.S. exports and 21 percent of U.S. imports. The United States has a competitive disadvantage and trade deficit with Japan and China, however. During the last 30 years, the pattern of trade linkages between the United States and the world has shifted from Western Europe toward the Asian and Pacific regions. Ties with Latin America remain strong, and Mexico ranks third behind Canada and Japan as the leading trade partners of the United States, followed by China, Germany, the United Kingdom, Taiwan, France, South Korea, Singapore, Italy, Malaysia, the Netherlands, Brazil, and Belgium (Table 13.4).

The U.S. trade deficit is increasing and will remain large. In 2005, the trade deficit was $780 billion compared with $75 billion in 1993. Trade in

services includes financial and business services, as well as royalties/license fees, which include entertainment, videos, cable TV, compact disks, and recordings. Trade in services generates a surplus of revenues, but not enough to keep the trade deficit from ballooning. In 2003, the United States had a surplus of $86 billion in services trade, up from a mere $7.5 billion in 1987.

The United States has gradually undergone an important shift in the destination of its exports—away from the traditional European markets and toward Asia, Mexico, and Canada. The reasons behind this change include the rapidly growing economies of Asia, so that trans-Pacific trade now exceeds that across the Atlantic. Another reason is the progress made under the World Trade Organization in the process of liberalization of tariffs in many countries. The North American Free Trade Agreement (NAFTA) of 1994 was such a liberalization agreement and has increased trade among Mexico, the Unites States, and Canada. In addition, there have been increasing amounts of U.S. and foreign investment in the Asian economies, and this has produced rapid increases of trade in capital and intermediate goods. Investment has also come from Chinese and Japanese multinational corporations.

International Trade Patterns

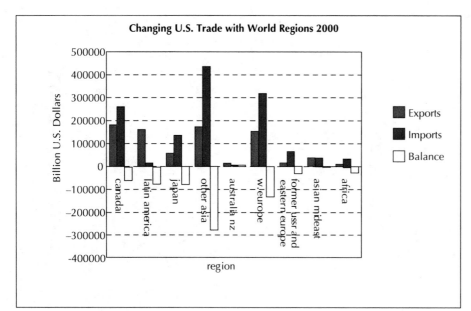

FIGURE 13.5
The changing U.S. trade with world regions, 1970 and 2000. Europe has been supplanted as the most important trade region for the United States by East Asia. Trade with Japan, especially imports, has grown rapidly, as has trade with Canada.

Table 13.4

Economic Growth in Top 20 Markets for Exports of U.S. Manufactured Goods, 1980–2000

Country	Rank 2000	Exports ($ Billion)	Share of U.S. Exports	Growth in GDP 1980–2000
Top 20 markets		556.9	81.5	3.8
Canada	1	156.3	22.9	2.8
Mexico	2	79.0	11.6	1.6
Japan	3	57.9	8.5	2.7
United Kingdom	4	39.1	5.7	2.7
Germany	5	26.6	3.9	1.9
Netherlands	6	19.0	2.8	2.5
Taiwan	7	18.2	2.7	N/A
France	8	17.7	2.6	1.9
South Korea	9	16.5	2.4	7.8
Singapore	10	15.7	2.3	7.3
Brazil	11	15.2	2.2	3.0
China	12	14.3	2.1	10.7
Belgium	13	13.9	2.0	1.8
Australia	14	11.9	1.7	3.5
Saudi Arabia	15	10.5	1.5	0.8
Italy	16	9.0	1.3	1.8
Malaysia	17	9.0	5.8	6.5
Switzerland	18	7.3	2.3	1.2
Israel	19	7.0	N/A	5.4
United States			2.5	2.7
World		683.0	3.0	2.8

Sources: International Monetary Fund, World Bank, Bank for International Settlements, United Nations, Organization for Economic Cooperation and Development, Department of Commerce.

Another shift in trade for the United States has been an expansion of the Mexican market for U.S. goods. Since 1990, Mexico has been the second largest market for U.S. manufactured goods after Canada, while Japan dropped to third in rank (but continues as the second largest partner when exports and imports are considered together). The value of U.S. manufactured goods exported to Mexico increased fourfold between 1983 and 2003. During the same period, U.S. manufactured exports to developing economies of Asia increased by 18 percent, U.S. exports bound for Europe dropped slightly, and the share exported to Japan and Canada held constant. Despite this global shift, the most important trading partners for U.S. exports remained almost unchanged from 1983 to 2003: Canada, Mexico, Japan, the United Kingdom, and Germany.

There are several sectors within manufacturing in which the United States is competitive internationally, including medical equipment, transportation equipment, and computer hardware. The medical equipment sector is one of the most competitive sectors of the U.S. economy, with export growth averaging 15 percent per year over the last five years. In 2003, exports were $17 billion, far exceeding the $6 billion of imports. Medical equipment markets are shifting, however, and industrialized countries, particularly in Europe, have traditionally been the best markets.

Two major exports of the United States are aircraft and motor vehicles. In 2003, the auto sector had a U.S. trade deficit of $120 billion, while the aircraft sector had a $20 billion surplus (Figure 13.6). Half of the motor vehicle exports are shipped outside of North America, including the three large markets of Japan,

Taiwan, and Saudi Arabia. The European markets are essentially saturated. World sales of motor vehicles grew just 1.2 percent annually over the last 10 years in the developed markets because of the prolific manufacturers.

The U.S. computer equipment industry commands more than 75 percent of the world's computer sales through global operations, but the United States has had a trade deficit in this sector since 1992 as semiconductor production and assembly of consumer electronics has moved to East Asia and Mexico. In 2003, the U.S. trade in computer equipment was a deficit of $18 billion. Foreign sales now account for more than half of the total revenues of many leading U.S. computer equipment suppliers.

U.S. SERVICES TRADE

The United States is a world leader in computer software, supplying 49 percent of the $153 billion world market for packaged software per year. The world market for software grew 35 percent annually between 1995 and 2003, benefiting world suppliers, and reached almost $180 billion in market demand by the year 2003. Asia and Latin America are expected to be the fastest growing markets for computer software. The computer software industry is moving toward *multimedia*, which combine video, animation, voice, music, and text. Implementation of *intellectual property rights* through the World Trade Organization will reduce piracy, which has been a major problem for the industry.

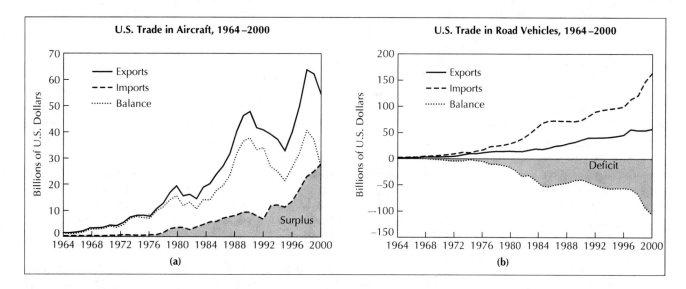

FIGURE 13.6
U.S. balance of trade in aircraft and motor vehicles, 1964–2000. The United States is the world leader in aircraft manufacturing and has maintained an important surplus since 1992. At the end of the cold war, both exports and imports dipped slightly. Road vehicles have been a bright spot in U.S. trade up until 1970. From that point onward, a trade deficit developed. Foreign auto companies sell more cars in the United States than U.S. companies sell abroad.

International Trade Patterns

The United States is also the world leader in the production, use, and export of information services and commanded 50 percent of the world market by 2003. U.S. firms produce and use the most advanced software, and exports have grown rapidly. The information industry is especially affected by government policy regarding market access, intellectual property rights, privacy protection, data security, and telecommunications services. The largest markets for U.S. information services will be the industrialized countries, especially the United Kingdom, Japan, and Canada. The most important emerging markets will be China and Korea, followed by Mexico, Brazil, and Argentina.

Services are not just food and travel, but information software, telecommunications, advertising, and entertainment. Services in North America account for about a quarter of gross domestic product and 30 percent of total exports. Canada and the United States have 150 of the world's top 500 service corporations. On the cutting edge of industry—software, information technology, and entertainment, which account for one-third of the world services sales—the United States' and Canada's position is unchallenged. For example, U.S. service exports dwarf auto exports, $266 billion to $43 billion in 2003. *Soft power* is services power, the power of Microsoft to write programs, of Hollywood to make movies, and of U.S. cultural ideals, products, and practices to become known around the world through the information revolution. Soft power gives North America the edge over every other region of the world and may replace heavy industry as the motor of the world economy of the future.

Finance is another important area of services. The U.S. stock market's gains in the 1990s rallied most equities worldwide, spurring companies to set records for mergers, acquisitions, and initial public offerings. Brighter prospects in the United States boosted trade worldwide, producing cross-border acquisitions and helping other stock markets.

The U.S. economy has reemerged as a growth magnet for the world's surplus savings because of its superior growth performance compared with other industrial nations. Japan and Europe have been so concerned about their flagging economies that they want to knock their currencies down to promote growth. Dollar-denominated assets get a boost from competitive devaluation. One reason for the better U.S. economic performance is that labor is not demanding its piece of the pie as it is in Europe and Japan. Europe's higher minimum wage, greater degree of union power, and government support for a social market economy have all put a floor under the wages of the lowest paid. To be sure, this means that income polarity is far more pronounced in the United States than elsewhere. In the United States, male wage earners in the top 10 percent of incomes make 4.4

times what those in the bottom 10 percent make, compared with 2.5 in Europe and Japan. Between 1979 and 2003, the poorest one-fifth of American families saw their income drop 11 percent, while the wealthiest one-fifth enjoyed a 28 percent increase. In the United States, capital clearly dominates labor. Overseas, that's not so, at least to the same degree. Profit ratios of publicly held U.S. companies sprinted to record levels in the 1990s, while average family incomes remained stagnant. Similarly, while U.S. public sector entitlement problems are severe, they pale in contrast to those abroad.

Canada

The United States is Canada's most significant trading partner, accounting for 82 percent of Canada's exports and 69% of its imports (Figures 13.7 and 13.8). Canada and the United States have the largest bilateral (between two countries) trade relationship in the world. Canadian exports have grown rapidly in recent years and held about $170 billion in 2000. The overall trade surplus amounts to over $10 billion annually. Trade with the United States amounted to over $290 billion in goods and services in 2003. For a country roughly one-tenth the size of the United States, Canada accounts for 21 percent of U.S. exports and 20 percent of U.S. imports. The United States runs a large merchandise deficit with Canada; in 2003, it was $20 billion.

Canada exports automobiles and transportation equipment, industrial supplies, and industrial plant and machinery parts, which combined account for 60 percent of Canada's total exports. Canada also has vast supplies of natural resources, including forest products, iron ores, metals, oil, natural gas, and coal. On the other hand, Canada imports industrial plant and machinery parts, transportation equipment, and industrial supplies from the United States. In addition, because of a longer growing season, balmy climates, and temperate agricultural territories, the United States can produce subtropical fruits and winter vegetables for colder Canada. High-tech manufactured goods are also a chief import from the United States. Canada's second most important regional partner is Asia, followed by Western Europe. Japan ranks second as an individual country, ahead of Britain, Germany, and other EU countries, which as a bloc constitute approximately 7 percent of Canadian exports and imports.

Canada's economy is more internationalized than that of the United States. Whereas the U.S. exports approximately 11 percent of its output, Canada exports approximately 20 percent of its GDP. Because of its relatively small population (30 million), Canada cannot attain the economies of scale (Chapter 5)

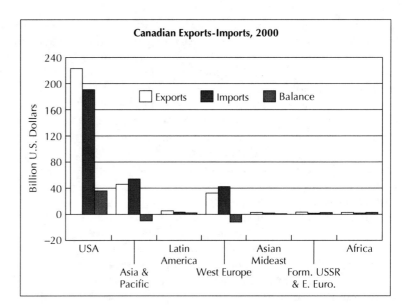

FIGURE 13.7
Canadian exports and imports by world region, 2000. Most of the foreign trade produced by the Canadian economy is with the United States. Canada enjoyed a $30 billion trade surplus with the world. The United States took 82 percent of Canadian exports and supplied 68 percent of its imports. The second most important trade partner for Canada is Asia and the Pacific, followed by Western Europe.

necessary for highly efficient plants and, therefore, must import many of its goods. As with many small countries, especially in Europe, the smaller the country, the more dependent it is on foreign markets for imports and exports.

Canada exports energy resources because of its vast amounts of hydroelectric power and its ability to manufacture hydraulic turbines and electric generators. It also produces high-tech communications equipment, including fiber-optic cables. Transportation and telecommunications equipment are required because of the vast territories that must be overcome to interconnect with the second largest country in the world. For Canada, automobiles and automobile parts represent the largest category of exports to the United States. This is a result of the U.S.-Canadian Free Trade

Agreement (FTA), which favored the export of automotive industrial goods from Canada to the United States. The FTA, enacted in 1989, lowered trade barriers between the United States and Canada as part of the 10-year phasing out process and became the nucleus for NAFTA. Today, Canadian exports and imports to the United States outpace every other world region. Free trade has come at a cost, however: Canada's competitiveness has been improved by industrial restructuring, although that process laid off many manufacturing workers. Unemployment, while declining, still remains high, at approximately 8 percent in 2003, making job creation the government's chief objective.

NAFTA sparked U.S. and Canadian merchandise trade, which saw a 14 percent increase over the first

FIGURE 13.8
Canadian-U.S. exports and imports, 1970–2000. Asia and the Pacific became the leading export destination for both Canadian and U.S. trade by 1980, following a long period of dominance by Europe and the Atlantic countries. Countries most responsible for this shift are Japan, Hong Kong, Singapore, Taiwan, and South Korea. To this list we now must add Australia, Indonesia, Malaysia, Thailand, and the Philippines.

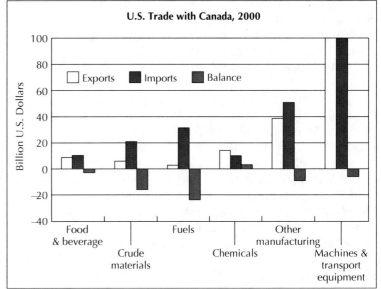

two years of its enactment in 1994. Canada's merchandise trade to the United States includes motor vehicles, motor vehicle parts, engines, office machines, timber, and newsprint. U.S. exports to Canada include primarily automobiles, trucks, special vehicles, vehicle parts, paper and paperboard, computers, and software. The best prospects for U.S. exports to Canada include computers and peripherals, automotive parts, telecommunications equipment, and automobiles. In 2003, trade between company affiliates (intracompany trade) and current companies accounted for 45 percent of U.S. exports to Canada and roughly the same proportion of U.S. imports from Canada. Canada doubled the number of cars and trucks it exports to the United States since 1989 as a result of NAFTA. Canada has overtaken Japan as the top auto exporter to the United States. Canadian labor is one-third less expensive than U.S. labor, and the quality and productivity are equal to or better than that of the United States. Automakers save $300 for each car made in Canada because of its national health care financing system, which offers for free most of the health insurance that some U.S. companies buy for their employees. (In contrast, 40 million Americans lack health care insurance.) GM spends $5,000 per year to provide health care to each current and retired employee and less than $1000 per current Canadian worker. Canada's cheap dollar ($.70 U.S.) allows the dollar of the U.S. manufacturers to go further.

A fast-growing sector of U.S.-Canadian trade is U.S. service exports, which jumped from $10 billion in 1988 to $17 billion in 2000. Canada's financial service market continues to expand as a result of the 1987 accord between the Toronto Securities Commission and the U.S. Department of Finance. This agreement allows the deregulation and integration of the financial securities industry, removing the distinctions among banks, trusts, insurance companies, and brokerages. U.S. direct foreign investment in Canada was more than $110 billion in 2003. About one-half of it was is the manufacturing sector. Canadian direct foreign investment in the United States totaled about $79 billion in 2003. Therefore, Canada's investment income balance with the United States is the single largest deficit in Canadian nonmerchandise trade.

No other market in the world is as open to U.S. goods and services as is the Canadian market. Almost 98 percent of all bilateral trade passes freely without tariff, and U.S. and Mexican products will continue to have an advantage in the Canadian market as a direct result of NAFTA. Trade between the United States and Canada is weighted heavily toward industrial goods, with 90 percent of U.S. shipment to Canada and 74 percent of Canadian exports to the United States in such goods. Machinery, transportation equipment (autos), and other manufactured products (auto parts) lead the way. Since 1960, when Canada's exports were made up of 50 percent primary products—forest, mine, and field products—Canada has shifted its emphasis toward industrial merchandise (Figure 13.9). Like the United States, Canada has found more recent trade growth with Asia and the Pacific Rim than with its traditional trading partner, Western Europe. Since 1980, the Pacific has eclipsed the Atlantic as the leading arena of North American commerce.

The European Union

Europe's trade, as a proportion of total world trade, is disproportionately large compared with its population, one-third of a billion. The EU is the largest trading block in the world, with exports totaling $2.6 trillion in 2003, about the same as imports. The EU ranks second as an export market to the United States, after Asia. Although it possesses only one-fifteenth of the world population, it accounts for 50 percent of world trade because of (1) the strength of the EU, (2) short distances and well-developed transport systems among member countries, and (3) complementary trade flows among its smaller states. Some European countries are comparable in population and size to individual U.S. states. The proximities and complementarities of Europe, with many relatively small countries close to one another, make intraregional trade ideal. This type of trade has increased from 55 percent of all European exports to 75 percent in 2003, that is, 75 percent of all exports from European nations go to other European nations. Italy, France, and the United Kingdom have populations of 60 million each, while Germany has roughly 80 million (Figure 13.10a, b, c, d). Other countries are much smaller. Some have food resources, such as Denmark and France; some have energy resources, such as Norway, the Netherlands, and the United Kingdom; some produce iron, steel, and heavy equipment, such as Italy, Germany, France, and Spain; and others produce high-value consumer goods.

As the EU grows to include new members in Eastern Europe and the Mediterranean, European intraregional trade will continue to increase. The countries that are faring worst economically are those that resist the forces of globalization. For example, France and Germany have not allowed reform of their rigid labor markets, slowing growth of their economies.

While the EU is in the midst of its economic recovery, the structural problems, such as high labor costs, economic rigidity that stalls the growth of smaller companies, industrial obsolescence, difficulty in making use of new technologies, and costly social welfare programs, tend to restrain growth below its economic potential and are keeping unemployment above 10 percent. However, the EU is the fastest growing market for U.S. high-technology exports and remains the principal

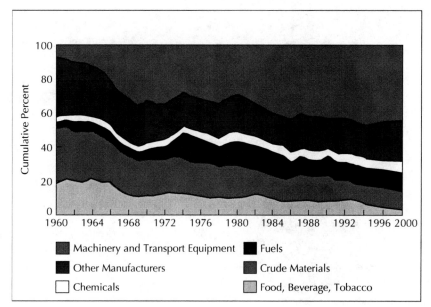

FIGURE 13.9
Canada's changing export composition, 1960–2000. In 1960, 50 percent of Canada's exports were made up of primary products: from the mine, forest, and field. Since that time, Canada has shifted its exports to industrial and manufactured products.

destination for U.S. FDI. The EU is as well the largest source area of FDI in the United States. The leading U.S. exports to the EU in 2003 were aircraft; data processing and office equipment; engines and motors; measuring, checking, and analyzing equipment; and other electronic equipment. The most promising sectors for U.S. exports to the EU include telecommunications equipment, computer peripherals, software, electronic items, pollution control, machinery, medical equipment supplies, and aircraft.

The leading economies of the EU include Germany, a major exporter as well as importer of automobiles. Britain, which has not accepted the Euro, is a significant

exporter and importer of manufactured goods. The economy of France, which is more agricultural and less productive than Germany, is nonetheless a significant producer and consumer of industrial and consumer goods. Italy, the smallest of the four, exhibits a growing strength in the exports of engineering products.

Most international trade takes the form of *intraindustry trade*—investment in foreign affiliates that produce abroad, rather than shipments of U.S.-produced goods to target export markets. These sales accounted for more than half of U.S. affiliate sales worldwide and were four times as large as U.S. affiliate sales in Canada or Asia. Consequently, Europe's overall importance for U.S. com-

FIGURE 13.10
Composition of Europe's Track.

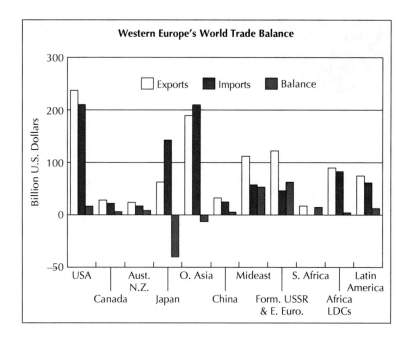

International Trade Patterns

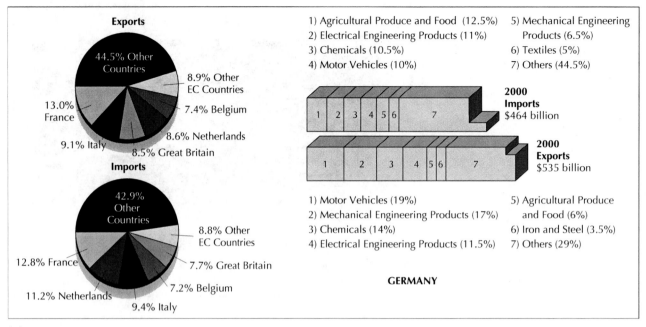

GERMANY

Exports

- 44.5% Other Countries
- 8.9% Other EC Countries
- 7.4% Belgium
- 8.6% Netherlands
- 8.5% Great Britain
- 9.1% Italy
- 13.0% France

Imports

- 42.9% Other Countries
- 8.8% Other EC Countries
- 7.7% Great Britain
- 7.2% Belgium
- 9.4% Italy
- 11.2% Netherlands
- 12.8% France

1) Agricultural Produce and Food (12.5%)
2) Electrical Engineering Products (11%)
3) Chemicals (10.5%)
4) Motor Vehicles (10%)
5) Mechanical Engineering Products (6.5%)
6) Textiles (5%)
7) Others (44.5%)

2000 Imports $464 billion

2000 Exports $535 billion

1) Motor Vehicles (19%)
2) Mechanical Engineering Products (17%)
3) Chemicals (14%)
4) Electrical Engineering Products (11.5%)
5) Agricultural Produce and Food (6%)
6) Iron and Steel (3.5%)
7) Others (29%)

(a)

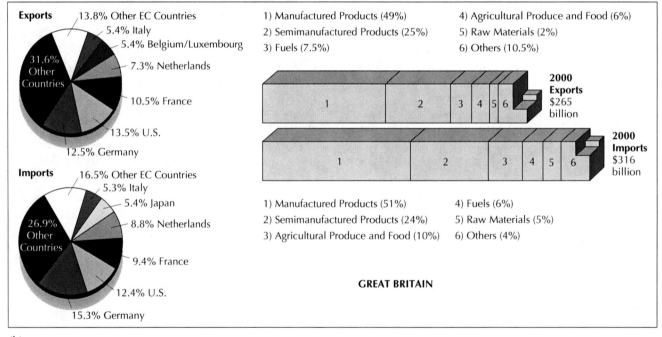

GREAT BRITAIN

Exports

- 13.8% Other EC Countries
- 5.4% Italy
- 5.4% Belgium/Luxembourg
- 7.3% Netherlands
- 10.5% France
- 13.5% U.S.
- 12.5% Germany
- 31.6% Other Countries

Imports

- 16.5% Other EC Countries
- 5.3% Italy
- 5.4% Japan
- 8.8% Netherlands
- 9.4% France
- 12.4% U.S.
- 15.3% Germany
- 26.9% Other Countries

1) Manufactured Products (49%)
2) Semimanufactured Products (25%)
3) Fuels (7.5%)
4) Agricultural Produce and Food (6%)
5) Raw Materials (2%)
6) Others (10.5%)

2000 Exports $265 billion

2000 Imports $316 billion

1) Manufactured Products (51%)
2) Semimanufactured Products (24%)
3) Agricultural Produce and Food (10%)
4) Fuels (6%)
5) Raw Materials (5%)
6) Others (4%)

(b)

FIGURE 13.10
Compostion of Europe's Trade *(cont.)*

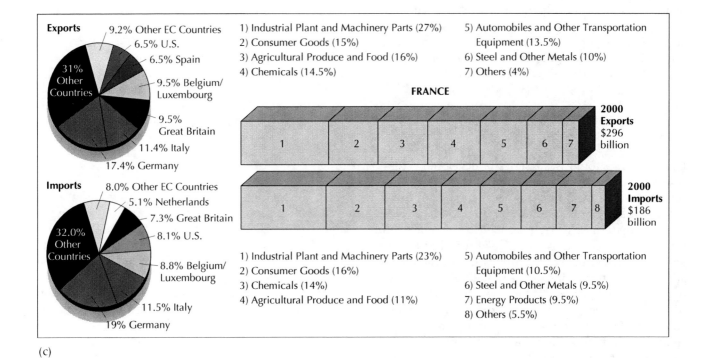

Exports

9.2% Other EC Countries
6.5% U.S.
6.5% Spain
9.5% Belgium/Luxembourg
9.5% Great Britain
11.4% Italy
17.4% Germany
31% Other Countries

1) Industrial Plant and Machinery Parts (27%)
2) Consumer Goods (15%)
3) Agricultural Produce and Food (16%)
4) Chemicals (14.5%)
5) Automobiles and Other Transportation Equipment (13.5%)
6) Steel and Other Metals (10%)
7) Others (4%)

FRANCE

2000 Exports $296 billion

Imports

8.0% Other EC Countries
5.1% Netherlands
7.3% Great Britain
8.1% U.S.
8.8% Belgium/Luxembourg
11.5% Italy
19% Germany
32.0% Other Countries

1) Industrial Plant and Machinery Parts (23%)
2) Consumer Goods (16%)
3) Chemicals (14%)
4) Agricultural Produce and Food (11%)
5) Automobiles and Other Transportation Equipment (10.5%)
6) Steel and Other Metals (9.5%)
7) Energy Products (9.5%)
8) Others (5.5%)

2000 Imports $186 billion

(c)

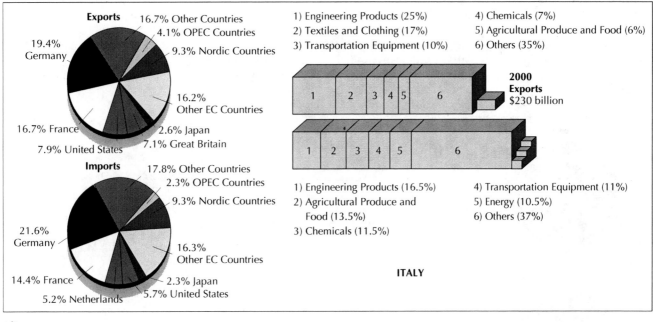

Exports

16.7% Other Countries
4.1% OPEC Countries
9.3% Nordic Countries
19.4% Germany
16.2% Other EC Countries
16.7% France
2.6% Japan
7.1% Great Britain
7.9% United States

1) Engineering Products (25%)
2) Textiles and Clothing (17%)
3) Transportation Equipment (10%)
4) Chemicals (7%)
5) Agricultural Produce and Food (6%)
6) Others (35%)

2000 Exports $230 billion

Imports

17.8% Other Countries
2.3% OPEC Countries
9.3% Nordic Countries
21.6% Germany
16.3% Other EC Countries
14.4% France
2.3% Japan
5.7% United States
5.2% Netherlands

1) Engineering Products (16.5%)
2) Agricultural Produce and Food (13.5%)
3) Chemicals (11.5%)
4) Transportation Equipment (11%)
5) Energy (10.5%)
6) Others (37%)

ITALY

(d)

FIGURE 13.10
Composition & Europes's Trade *(cont.)*

panies and the U.S. economy is much greater than trade statistics indicate. These U.S. companies' overseas affiliates are major importers of products manufactured in the United States. In 2003, sales by U.S. parent companies to the European affiliates made up 40 percent of U.S. exports to Europe.

Latin America

Latin America comprises a series of developing countries with different levels of population, income, and economic structures. For centuries, under Spanish colonialism, their traditional economic role was to provide primary materials, namely agricultural exports and mineral resources, to the developed world of Europe and North America. Latin America has economically advanced countries, including Brazil, with a population of 161 million, as well as some of the poorest countries in the world (e.g., Bolivia and Paraguay in South America, Haiti in the Caribbean, and Nicaragua and Guatemala in Central America). Latin American countries are diverse not only with regard to population and size but also with respect to development and natural resources. Some countries, such as those in the Caribbean and Central America (e.g., the Dominican Republic, Costa Rica), have agricultural surpluses. Others, as in Argentina, have grain surpluses, whereas still others, such as Venezuela and Mexico, are rich in iron ore and oil. Brazil has a wealth of minerals and is a strong producer of manufactured goods. In 2003, 62 percent of Latin America's exports, mainly food, minerals, and fuels, went to the United States. This pattern was typical for Third World nations. For a long time, Latin America had an import-substitution policy for industrialized products. However, today, Latin America's new hope to achieve wealth and a prominent place in the world economy is centered on export-led industrialization, led by Mexico, Brazil, and Chile.

Mexico

The chief trading partner of most Latin American states is the United States. Mexico's balance of merchandise trade is centered on labor-intensive manufactured products (52%), many of which flow from plants along the border that are owned by U.S., European, and Japanese MNCs (*maquiladoras*) back to the United States.

Petroleum and by-products, as well as agricultural products, account for 45 percent of Mexico's exports (Figure 13.11). Although Mexico is one of the world's largest exporters of energy, oil provided only more than 35 percent of its export revenue in 2003. Semifinished industrial supplies that act as input materials for final production compose 60 percent of Mexican imports, and manufacturing and plant equipment another 23 percent. These types of imports are necessary for Mexico to maintain its level as a newly industrializing nation. Mexico's economic woes were punctuated with the devaluation of the peso in 1995. With insufficient capital inflows to finance its account deficit, the

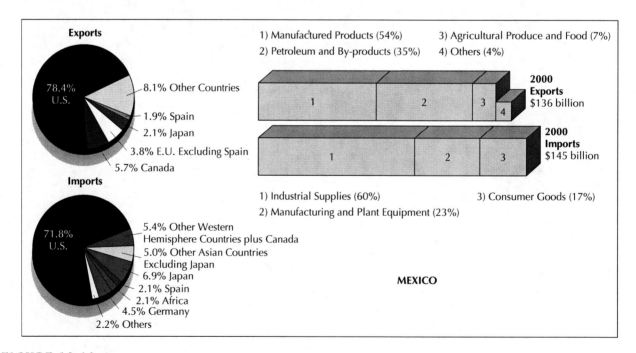

FIGURE 13.11

Composition of Mexico's world merchandise trade. The U.S. import share of the Mexican market also increased 10-fold. The United States currently dominates the Mexican market, but the Europeans and Japanese are looking at Mexico as a possible springboard to the NAFTA and South American markets.

Mexican government let the peso devalue in the face of rapidly diminishing foreign reserves. Major government programs included reduced government spending, tax and price increases, and strict control of credit. The new government programs included accelerated privatization and liberalization of key industries.

Mexican markets continued to open to foreign competition, following the enactment of the North American Free Trade Agreement (NAFTA) on January 1, 1994. NAFTA turned the Mexican economy around. Inflation dropped to about 7 percent, down from its peak at more than 150 percent in 1987. Mexico is experiencing a modernizing economy that is no longer protected from foreign competition and an improved investment environment. In 1997, rather than default on a $30 billion foreign debt, Mexico announced the return of its creditworthiness by the prepayment of the remaining $4 billion owed to the United States from the $13 billion emergency aid package negotiated in 1995. Mexico is among the fastest growing export markets for U.S. products. In 1986, Mexico became the third largest market for U.S. exports after Canada and Japan. Foreign investment opportunities are particularly strong in Mexico in infrastructure development, where the government invested $38 billion between 1995 and 2003, including airline privatization, highway construction, railroad services, and water and energy projects.

Under NAFTA, preferential duty treatment of U.S. origin goods gives them an edge over products from European or Japanese firms, which are often the principal competitors. U.S. and Canadian manufacturers must pay duty only on the value added by manufacturers in Mexico, not the products or parts shipped as semifinished or raw materials to plants in Mexico from North America. Under NAFTA, half of U.S. exports to Mexico have been eligible for no Mexican tariffs—semiconductors, computers, machine tools, aerospace equipment, telecommunication and electronic equipment, and medical supplies. Another important feature of NAFTA was the gradual phaseout of the Mexican Auto Decree, which helped the U.S. triple exports of passenger cars to Mexico since 1994. Since 1994, autos, auto parts, semiconductors, machine tools, and certain fruits and vegetables, including apples, realized export increases of between 100 percent and 10,000 percent when Mexican barriers were sharply reduced or eliminated under NAFTA.

In short, NAFTA has neither lived up to the fervent expectations of its proponents nor fulfilled the dire warnings of its opponents. It has enhanced Mexico's ability to supply U.S. manufacturing firms with low-cost parts but has not made Mexico economically independent. To some extent, Mexico's growth has been limited by American barriers to Mexican exports, including tomatoes, avocadoes, and truck drivers. Finally, it must be remembered that compared with the EU, NAFTA is a much more modest, failing to lift regulations on movements of labor, for example.

South America

South America represents a large and diverse picture of economic growth, change, and stagnation. The southern countries of Argentina, Uruguay, Chile, and Bolivia have had strong ties to Western Europe. The East Asian NICs are currently strengthening their economic ties with Latin America. Unfortunately, Latin American trade within the region is not nearly so strong as that within North America, Western Europe, or the Pacific Basin. Each country is more tied economically to Europe, the United States, and East Asia than to one another.

As a result of high indebtedness, high interest rates, and low foreign revenues, some Latin American countries can barely keep up with debt service on their international loans. Mexico, Brazil, and Argentina each owe over $100 billion to the developed world, and several other Latin American countries are close behind. Most of the loan money was put into urban infrastructures, but high world interest rates, oil prices, tariffs, and agricultural subsidies in the developed world and international recessions have minimized exports and thus foreign revenues, which are necessary to repay the debt. Brazil is a case in point. Exports are a little more than one-tenth those of the United States, but the population is approximately two-thirds that of the United States. In general, the 1990s were a disadvantageous time for Latin America because Latin American governments were forced by the International Monetary Fund (IMF) to devalue their currencies and to invoke austerity programs by restructuring their economies, raising taxes, decreasing public expenditures, and selling government-owned business enterprises, such as state banks, power companies, metal refineries, and transportation and airline companies.

Argentina, which after World War II enjoyed a standard of living comparable to Europe, suffered a steady decline in the late twentieth century. To find favor with working class voters, General Juan Peron engaged in import substitution (Chapter 11), outlawed outsourcing, developed legislation against employers dismissing employees, and strengthened unions' ability to strike, a pattern that operated in South America during the 1940s through the 1960s. The Peronist populist actions, put forward as humanistic measures to reduce the gaping inequalities in Argentine incomes, did not achieve their stated purposes: reduction of poverty and real income disparities. Instead, they resulted in hyperinflation lasting for decades. Since 1990, the government moved to correct a floundering economy hit by hyperinflation, high budget deficits, and an overcapitalized public sector. Brazilian exports to Argentina are more competitive as a result of the Mercosur Trade Agreement, which eliminated tariffs on most goods traded among the four member countries (Argentina, Brazil, Paraguay, Uruguay). The average tariff of Argentina is now 9 percent. The key sectors of import are computers, communications, and capital goods. The new export opportunities for the Argentina market include telecommunications equipment, electric power generation, transmission equipment, and medical equipment supplies and services.

In Brazil, after a surge in economic growth that averaged 5 percent during the early 1990s, the economy slowed down in the aftermath of the Asian financial crisis. Brazil is still not on sound economic footing because of erratic domestic policies and high inflation. To counterbalance high inflation, Brazil introduced a new national currency, the *real*, in 1995. With it came strict monetary controls, and consumer price increases have averaged 3 percent per month since then. Part of Brazil's policy continues to be pressured by the desire for high wages and the need to maintain high interest rates to finance domestic government debt and borrowing and to prevent capital outflows from the country.

Through all of this turmoil, Brazil maintained its trade competitiveness; imports rose almost 50 percent to $54 billion in 1996, and the EU was the most important regional market for Brazilian exports receiving 25 percent of the total. Brazil continues to export primary products, such as soybeans, iron ore, and coffee, but also exports transportation equipment and metallurgical products. Imports include industrial plant and machinery parts, fuel and lubricants, chemicals, and iron and steel. The most rapidly growing sectors in Brazil's economy include computers and peripherals (Figure 13.12). The largest single country market for Brazilian exports was the United States, accounting for $9 billion, or 20 percent, of total exports in 2000. Brazil remains the United States' largest market in South America as well, and the third largest market in the Western Hemisphere after Canada and Mexico.

Japan

The fastest growing world trade region is East Asia and the Pacific. After Europe, this region has the largest amount of internal world trade. Exports and imports in 2000 amounted to $2.9 trillion, or 23 percent of the world's total. Japan traditionally took the lead role in the development of East Asia and the Pacific. The growth of its economy after World War II is nothing short of an economic miracle. Since the 1960s, Japan has been joined by the Four Tigers of Taiwan, South Korea, Singapore, and Hong Kong. In the 1990s, however, new emerging dragons followed suit with rapidly growing economies: Thailand, Malaysia, Indonesia, and China.

While the rest of the world reeled from two major oil-price hikes in the 1970s, East Asia and the Pacific forged ahead with unprecedented growth (Chapter 12). Several factors contributed to this success, including U.S. economic and military subsidies, the Confucian culture dedicated to learning, and governments that actively promoted a shift into export promotion. In addition, Japan and other countries protected home markets with high import duties. Unlike America, where short-term profits were important to satisfy stockholders, banks, and financial institutions, Japan encouraged reinvestment and long-term growth cycles. These long cycles allowed firms time to develop products and to reinvest in the highest-quality production systems before the owners or employees could reap any of the profits. Further, many of the Asian/Pacific countries acted as resource supply centers for the United States from 1965 to 1975, during the Vietnam War, which allowed them to collect a heavy inflow of U.S. dollars.

All these factors combined allowed Japan to develop the world's second largest economy, after the United States. Japan is also tremendously more prosperous than China, which has nearly nine times the population, although China's economy is growing more quickly. Between 1960 and 2000, the combined domestic product of East Asia and the Pacific increased 25-fold, which changed their economies from developing nations to NICs. The governments initiated a switch from import substitution to export promotion, with a new emphasis on electronics, automobiles, steel, textiles, and consumer goods, whereas other developing countries in Latin America, Africa, and South Asia did not have such policies. From 1970 to 2000, foreign investment in the region, especially in Japan and the Four Tigers, grew 10-fold. This investment was led not only by United States, British, German, Canadian, and Australian firms, but also by the Japanese.

The United States plays an important role in East Asian trade. Until 1970, Western Europe was North America's chief trading partner. From 1970 to 1980, however, Asia and the Pacific had caught up with Western Europe in terms of total trade with North America, and since 1979, North American trade with Asia and the Pacific increased more rapidly than trade with Western Europe. The trade gap continued to increase, and in 2003, North American trade with Asia and the Pacific outpaced trade with Western Europe by 30 percent, nearly hitting the $450 billion mark.

Japan is the world's second leading international trading nation. Japanese exports manufactured goods and imports raw materials, food, and industrial components. Japan's economy essentially involves exchanging raw materials into high-value-added products, with high inputs of technology and labor. Unlike Western Europe and North America, Japan shows a huge export trade surplus. Although the

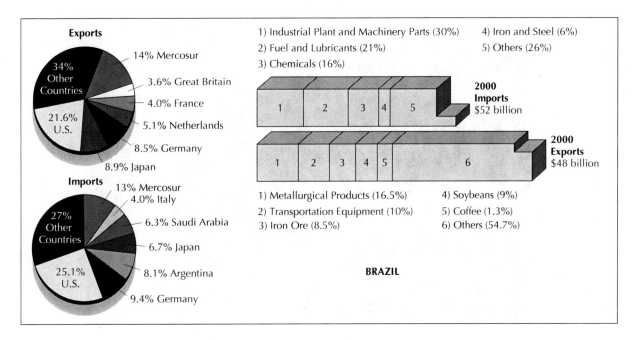

FIGURE 13.12

Composition of Brazil's merchandise trade. Computers and peripherals are the fastest-growing sectors of the Brazilian economy, followed by plastic materials and resins.

United States is its principal trading partner, both for exports and for imports, Japan has a tremendously diversified trading base, with almost 50 percent of exports and imports going to countries each composing less than 4 percent individually (Figure 13.13). The United States is by far Japan's largest trading partner, and in 2003, 30 percent of Japanese exports went to the United States and Canada, while 25 percent of imports came from Canada and the United States. After Canada, Japan has been the second largest market for U.S. exports for many years, but the U.S.-Japan trade deficit widened to $100 billion. This constituted more than one-third of the U.S. merchandise trade deficit (the other largest U.S. trade deficit was with China). The United States sells fewer exports to Japan than it imports, creating large U.S. trade deficits. The United States ships primary sector goods such as grains, feed, fruit, lumber, and non-oil commodities to Japan as a way of accounting for its imports of high-value-added manufactured items—microelectronics and automobiles, primarily. The United States does sell to Japan some high-value-added goods such as Boeing aircraft. U.S. products still account for the largest single proportion of goods imported by Japan. Indonesia, Australia, China, South Korea, and Germany follow. The United States and Indonesia fill a large need for energy that Japan cannot meet domestically. In addition, because of Japan's mountainous terrain, agricultural and food

products compose 15 percent of total imports. Chemicals, textiles, and metals are also imported.

Japan's trade surplus with Southeast Asian countries exceeded its surplus with that of the United States. As a group, Southeast Asian countries and the new industrializing countries (NICs) are now a more important export market for Japan than is the United States. To counterbalance the impact of the high-priced yen, Japanese companies have been moving labor-intensive assembly manufacturing operations to Southeast Asian countries—mostly to Thailand and Malaysia, but more recently to China.

The world dominance of Japan in the manufacture of motor vehicles is phenomenal (Figure 13.14). Fully 22 percent of its exports are motor vehicles, followed by high-tech office machinery, chemicals, electronic tubes, iron and steel products, and scientific and optical equipment. Diversification is a key word used to describe the breadth of Japanese exports. Similar to America's exportation of manufacturing jobs to Mexico and East Asia, Japan has done the same with automobile-assembly plants and autoparts firms in the United States, which now number near 400.

By 1980, Japan had become the world's leading creditor nation and a dominant player in the world financial scene. In 2003, Japanese banks accounted for 2 of the 10 largest in the world (a drop from the height of the "bubble economy," when they formed 6 out 10), although Tokyo is still one of the world's premier financial centers,

Forklifts awaiting export to America from Yokohama, Japan. Japan is the world's most prolific producer of motorized vehicles, automobiles, and commercial vehicles. More spectacular than the sheer volume of automobiles produced is the rate of industrial growth in this area. From 1960 to 2000, Japanese auto production increased by more than 5000%.

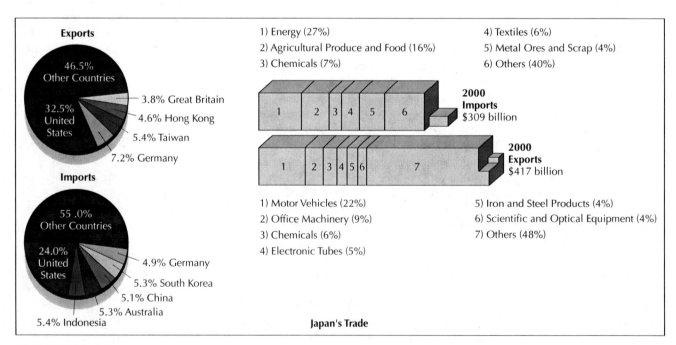

FIGURE 13.13

Composition of Japan's world merchandise trade, 2000. Japan now stands as the world's second largest economy, after that of the United States. Most important, Japan has a huge trade surplus. Japan's leading trade partner for both exports and imports is the United States.

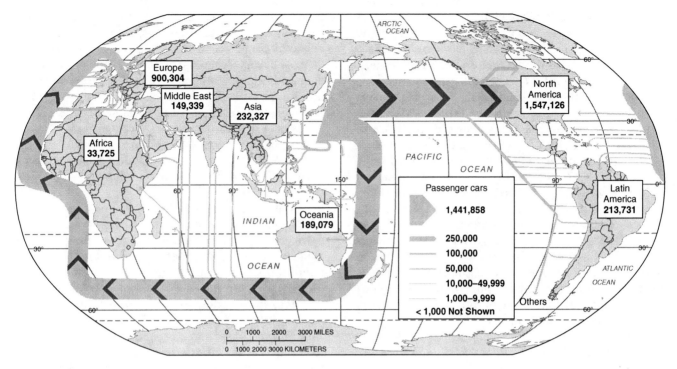

FIGURE 13.14
Geography of Japanese car exports. As the world's largest producer of automobiles, Japan controls a substantial share of the market in North America, Australia, and Europe.

alongside London and New York. Japan has managed all this with almost a total lack of food, mineral, and energy resources. It has shown the way for other East Asian and Pacific countries to follow suit. Singapore and Hong Kong are also major players in the world banking scene and have important money markets.

From 1980 to 2003, Japan attained a trade surplus of $750 billion, by far the largest in the world. It enjoyed a $100 billion bilateral trade surplus with the United States, $35 billion with Western Europe, and $25 billion with Asia and the Pacific. Both the EU, which received 15 percent of Japanese exports, and the United States, which received 28 percent, contributed to this trade surplus. As a result, protectionist voices in Europe and in America can be heard periodically accusing Japan of establishing new markets for itself by temporarily undercutting prices of foreign competitors. This monopolistic approach to competition is illegal in North America. The Japanese have also been accused of selling goods by dumping them on local markets to weaken rivals and force them to sell their market shares to Japanese firms. At the same time, the Japanese have restricted foreign firms from selling in Japan by a huge amalgam of import duties, tariffs, and regulations.

In 1985, the United States, Japan, Britain, France, and Germany began selling dollars on the world market to try to drive down the currency's value. The result was a big success, and the dollar is now quite weak, making American products competitive on world markets. The desirability of American goods has not eliminated the U.S. trade deficit yet, but movement is in that direction. At the same time, the yen soared, which caused the prices of Japanese goods in Europe and America to sky-rocket. Japanese sales dropped, and the deficit narrowed even more. However, although the American and Japanese deficits narrowed from 1988 to 2003, they still represent a huge surplus for the Japanese.

The Japanese response to the decreased demand for their goods was to establish manufacturing plants in America and in Europe to reduce the prices of their marketed items. They also established manufacturing locations in Southeast Asia, where costs were lower. Japanese multinational corporations such as Nippon erected plants in Europe, North America, and Southeast Asia. This strategy—in North America and in Southeast Asia—allowed Japan to continue trading competitively with cheaper products. Thus, Japan has relegated Southeast Asia and the United States to Third World status by using its vast amounts of inexpensive labor to produce its manufactured products.

In the 1990s, the Japanese economy endured a prolonged, serious recession prompted by the collapse of the so-called bubble economy. Equity values plunged to 50 percent of their paper value; heavy investment in North American properties tapered off to almost zero. The declining asset values left Japanese banks, which numbered seven of the largest 10 in the world, with nonperforming loans and precarious balance sheets. With a declining population, Japan experiences low rates of labor force growth. Moreover, the Japanese government, plagued by corporate scandals, has been unable to deregulate and privatize extensively. The economy is facing economic restructuring similar to that of North America (i.e., away from manufacturing and into services). The appreciation of the yen with respect to the U.S. dollar sent the price of Japanese automobiles higher in American markets.

The main contention between Japan and the United States has been closed markets. The primary policy of U.S. trade with Japan has been to open Japanese markets for imports and foreign investment. Informal obstacles such as testing standards, certification requirements, intellectual property regulations, and impenetrable distribution channels have limited U.S. exports to Japan. Although Japan has liberalized its trade relations considerably since 1990, removing many tariffs and quotas, it still has numerous nontariff barriers in place that discourage imports.

China

Following a long period of isolation in the 1950s and 1960s, China opened up to international trade and investment after the death of Mao Zedong in 1976. During the 1980s, under the policies of Deng Xiaoping, China allowed foreign companies to set up joint ventures there. *Special economic zones* (SEZs) were created along the coast to produce goods for world markets. These economic zones received tax incentives but were subject to a host of legal red tape. Today, China has become a major actor in world trade. It has a large worker base, low wages, and, because of the East Asian work ethic, relatively high levels of worker productivity. The result has been a dramatic increase in foreign trade. For example, exports increased from only $5 billion in 1976 to over $200 billion in 2003. China's primary trading partners for exports are Japan and the United States (Figure 13.15).

By all measures, however, China is a poor country. It still struggles to provide its many people with sufficient food and housing. Almost no capital is available for start-up programs; therefore, China has open doors to foreign companies, especially in the industrial sector. Foreign investment has flooded in to establish factories, to mass produce items in the areas of oil exploration, to manufacture motor vehicles, and to construct commercial buildings and hotels in the major cities. State-owned manufacturing plants account for approximately 50 percent of manufacturing exports. The other 50 percent, and an increasing proportion, are small-scale industrial plants that are owned by rural townships but leased to private individuals for profit. Textiles, clothing, and industrial products accounted for 70 percent of exports in 2003.

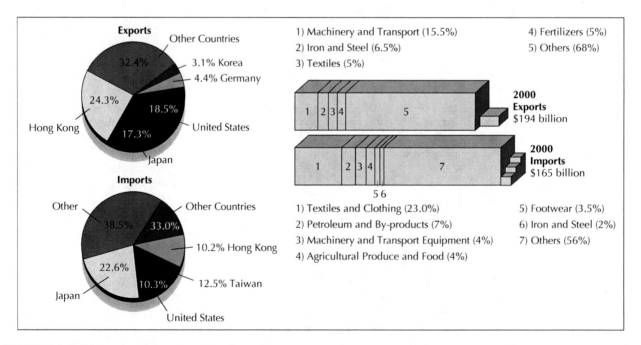

FIGURE 13.15
Composition of China's world merchandise trade. World trade is tiny compared with its population size of more than 1.2 billion people, yet it enjoys a trade surplus, exporting more than it imports, including textiles, clothing, petroleum, and by-products.

Over the last two decades, China recorded a GDP growth of 8 percent to 14 percent, continuing the surge in investment-led growth that began in 1992. Industrial output soared due in part to collectives and firms that are partially foreign owned. China's principal economic plan has been the continuation of high growth to generate jobs and to spread the benefits of economic reform from the cities to the countryside, in addition to controlling inflation.

Chinese manufactured goods lead export growth, whereas agricultural and primary products lead import growth. SEZs in southern and eastern coastal areas continue to outpace the rest of the nation in economic growth and trade. Japan continues to be China's top trading partner and source of imports. Hong Kong is the main port for exports and imports of China. Imports from the United States have been growing rapidly, but the United States ranks as the fourth largest source of Chinese imports after Japan, the EU, and Taiwan. China's major imports from the United States include cotton, fats and oils, manufactured fibers, fertilizer, aircraft, wood pulp, and leather. The most rapidly growing sectors of the Chinese economy include electrical power systems, telecommunications equipment, and automobiles (Figure 13.16). The U.S. trade deficit with China has increased steadily and stood at about $100 billion in 2003. Imports to the United States from China have grown 30 percent per year and exports 15 percent. Part of this imbalance is because China maintains an intricate system of import controls. Most products are subject to quotas, licensing requirements, or other restrictive measures.

Three out of four toys sold in America are foreign made, and 60 percent of those imports come from China. Sixty percent of all shoes sold in America come from China. In the near future, China is expected to dislodge Japan as the country giving America its biggest trade deficit. Other major goods imported into the United States from China include clothing, telephone and other telecommunication equipment, household appliances, televisions and computer chips, computers, and office equipment. China's higher trade barriers protect inefficient state-run companies that still employ two-thirds of the urban workers. China's trade patterns will change following its recent entry into the World Trade Organization (WTO).

China's transition to economic superpower status continues unabated. The economy has grown at an annual clip of about 9 percent. In 2003, China began to institute private property laws allowing home ownership of land and buildings. Real estate tycoons abound in China today, especially in coastal cities like Shanghai. China is becoming the world's factory, with growing trade surpluses to prove it. Ford and General Motors plants churn out autos for sale in East Asia. Most Chinese cannot yet afford autos, but televisions, washers, and stoves are selling well. The web of interconnections between foreign companies headed by overseas Chinese investors and a nominally communist China is growing.

Taiwan

Taiwan, with a population of 21 million and a GDP of $200 billion, has sustained a 6 percent to 7 percent economic growth rate since 1987. Long-term growth and prosperity have led to increasing land and labor costs in Taiwan and a gradual restructuring of the economy as low-wage sectors have fled. Manufacturers of

FIGURE 13.16
China's fastest growing sectors of the economy. China's fastest growing sectors include those associated with the development of power systems to produce electricity, followed by telecommunications equipment and automobile parts and service equipment. What used to be a Chinese unified national market has now separated into a number of regional markets, each pursuing its own development plan and each competing with the others to attract foreign investment and technology.

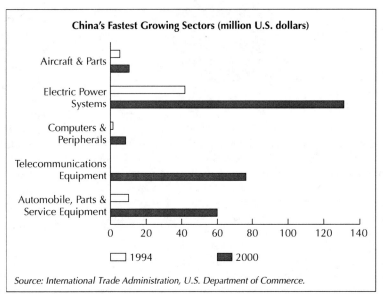

Source: International Trade Administration, U.S. Department of Commerce.

labor-intensive products such as toys, apparel and shoes, and circuit boards have moved offshore, mainly to Southeast Asia and to China. Large state-run enterprises still account for one-third of Taiwan's GDP, but major privatization efforts are underway to release power generation.

Exports account for over 35 percent of GDP in Taiwan's export-oriented economy—one of the four newly developing NICs, or Four Tigers. Manufacturing growth is now concentrated in technology-intensive industries, including petrochemicals, computers, and electronic components (Figure 13.17). In the 1990s, Taiwan's imports grew at a 14 percent annual increase. Historical trade patterns in the Pacific Rim are likely to keep Taiwan dependent on capital goods from imports from Japan. Over the last 10 years, Taiwan has made

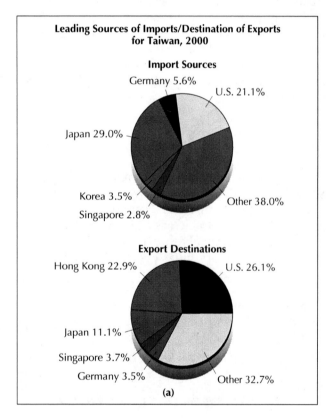

FIGURE 13.17
Taiwan's leading sources of imports and destination of exports. While Japan and the United States rank number one and two for Taiwan imports, the United States and Hong Kong are the chief destinations for Taiwanese exports. Taiwan's fastest growing sectors of the economy include computer peripherals, laboratory and scientific equipment, telecommunications, and pollution equipment. The consumer market, from cars and computers to insurance and world travel, is not only expanding in Taiwan in overall size, but also new niches continually open up as Taiwan's consumers become more discerning and more sophisticated in the world economy.

great progress in lowering trade barriers and improving market access of foreign goods.

South Korea

Another miracle of the Pacific Rim is South Korea, a country of 47 million, with a GDP of $340 billion in 2003. Its GDP growth averaged over 8 percent over the last 10 years, and its GDP per capita is $6800 (which compares favorably with the $300 GDP per capita in North Korea), putting South Korea's standard of living on a par with parts of southern Europe (e.g., Portugal). South Korea's rapid advancement has turned this nation into one of the most economically powerful in the world.

The fastest growing sectors in South Korea include transportation services and computers and peripherals (Figures 13.18 and 13.19). In 1995, South Korea opened power production to the private sector. These areas are limited to the production of electricity by coal, LNG (liquid natural gas), and water power, benefiting Canadian and U.S. companies. South Korea is implementing an ambitious transportation infrastructure development program that includes major high-speed rail and transit programs, airport development, and highway construction. Once the world's largest producer of tennis shoes, South Korea's success has driven up labor costs to the point where companies such as Nike have fled to lower-cost countries such as China, Vietnam, and Indonesia.

Australia

Australia's main trading partners are the United States, the EU, and Japan (Figure 13.20). Exports go primarily to Japan, which accounts for 20 percent. The next largest share, 10 percent, goes to South Korea, followed by New Zealand, the United States, China, and Singapore. The EU accounts for approximately another 11 percent. Because of its small population, 19 million, industrial supplies, automobiles, and industrial equipment account for more than 60 percent of imports. Japan has made its greatest market penetration into Australia and accounts for 50 percent of all vehicles purchased. The United States leads the list of importers, providing 23 percent, while EU countries supply 35 percent. Japan follows with 13 percent.

Australia is one of the leading raw-material suppliers in the world. It exports *primary products*—mainly ores and minerals, coal and coke, gold, wool, and cereals ("rocks and crops"). Almost all of its exports are from the vast wealth of land and resources that it enjoys. It is the largest exporter of iron ore and aluminum and the second or third largest exporter of nickel, coal, zinc, lead, gold, tin, tungsten, and uranium. Consequently, Australia's current problem is to withstand the declining world prices of raw

Samsung VCR assembly line in Seoul, South Korea. Foreign national corporations, like Samsung, have raised foreign exchange. Recent downturns in the global economy have slowed South Korea's progress. New problems now exist with North Korea's nuclear capability and sullen response to trade.

Pusan, South Korea is a major shipbuilding port that facilitates that country's exports of steel.

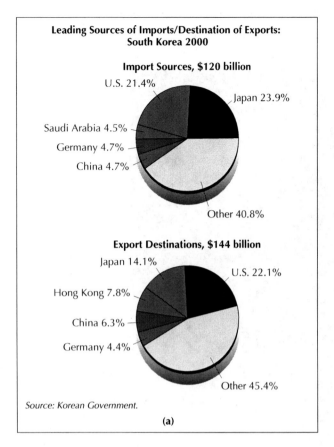

Leading Sources of Imports/Destination of Exports: South Korea 2000

Import Sources, $120 billion

U.S. 21.4%
Japan 23.9%
Saudi Arabia 4.5%
Germany 4.7%
China 4.7%
Other 40.8%

Export Destinations, $144 billion

Japan 14.1%
U.S. 22.1%
Hong Kong 7.8%
China 6.3%
Germany 4.4%
Other 45.4%

Source: Korean Government.

(a)

FIGURE 13.18
South Korea's leading sources of imports and destination of exports. Leading sources of imports included Japan and the United States, accounting for roughly 43 percent of imports. The leading export destinations included the United States and Japan, accounting for 30 percent of destinations, but a wide variety of other countries contributed to both import and export destinations for South Korea.

materials. To cushion against fluctuations in these prices, Australia needs to industrialize so that it can transform its raw materials into finished products and become an exporter of higher-value items. It has, however, become a significant exporter of wine. However, doing so is nearly impossible with a small industrial base that demands consumer products before industrial products.

India

In South Asia, India, with 1 billion people, has the world's second largest population but a relatively small economy, a reflection of the huge pools of poverty found there. Its world trade is minuscule but growing. As a result of the Green Revolution, India is self-sufficient in food production. Today, it is an exporter of primary products, gems and jewelry, textiles, clothing, and engineering goods (Figures 13.21 and 13.22). In order for its factories to operate, it must import industrial equipment and machinery, and crude oil and by-products, as well as chemicals, iron, and steel. Twelve percent of its imports include uncut gems for its expanding jewelry trade.

In international trade, India is no longer dominated by its former colonial overseer, Britain. Its leading countries of export include the United States and Japan. Britain and other EU countries account for 21 percent of total exports and 27 percent of total imports. Because India represents such a large pool of demand, most manufactured goods and consumer goods are consumed locally, not exported. Since 1990, India has also become an exporter of cereals and grains, and textiles and clothing are now the chief exports.

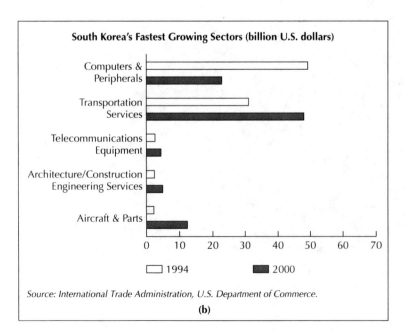

South Korea's Fastest Growing Sectors (billion U.S. dollars)

Computers & Peripherals
Transportation Services
Telecommunications Equipment
Architecture/Construction Engineering Services
Aircraft & Parts

0   10   20   30   40   50   60   70

☐ 1994   ■ 2000

Source: International Trade Administration, U.S. Department of Commerce.

(b)

FIGURE 13.19
The fastest growing sectors in South Korea include transportation services and computers and peripherals. South Korea is implementing an ambitious transportation infrastructure development program that includes major high-speed rail and transit programs, airport construction, and highway development. While South Korea's production technologies have reached nearly the level of advanced countries in key heavy and high-tech industries, they still lag somewhat behind.

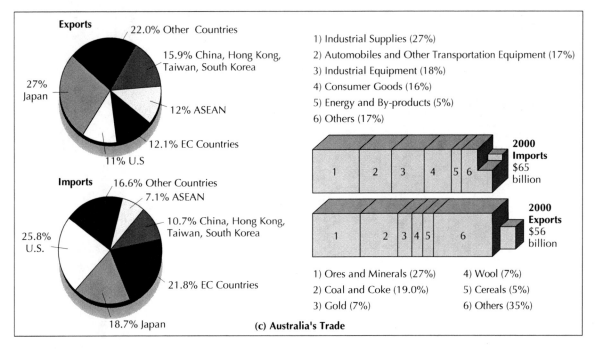

Exports

- 22.0% Other Countries
- 15.9% China, Hong Kong, Taiwan, South Korea
- 27% Japan
- 12% ASEAN
- 12.1% EC Countries
- 11% U.S

Imports

- 16.6% Other Countries
- 7.1% ASEAN
- 10.7% China, Hong Kong, Taiwan, South Korea
- 25.8% U.S.
- 21.8% EC Countries
- 18.7% Japan

1) Industrial Supplies (27%)
2) Automobiles and Other Transportation Equipment (17%)
3) Industrial Equipment (18%)
4) Consumer Goods (16%)
5) Energy and By-products (5%)
6) Others (17%)

2000 Imports $65 billion

2000 Exports $56 billion

1) Ores and Minerals (27%)   4) Wool (7%)
2) Coal and Coke (19.0%)   5) Cereals (5%)
3) Gold (7%)   6) Others (35%)

(c) Australia's Trade

FIGURE 13.20
Composition of Australia's merchandise trade.

India's GDP has continued at a 5 percent to 6 percent increase in the 1990s. Record levels of foreign capital (over $6 billion in portfolio and direct investment) stimulated a capital market over the last decade. But Indian public investment and infrastructure continue to be insufficient for a country with developmental goals.

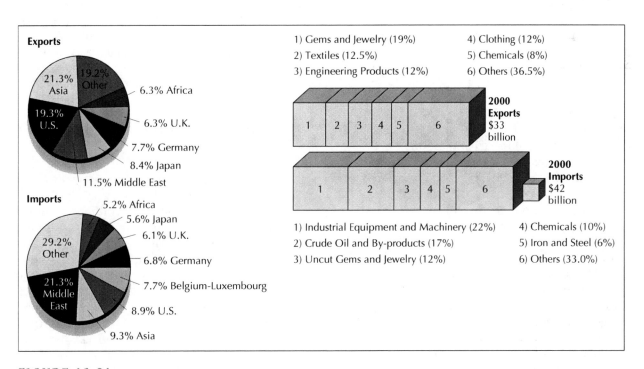

Exports

- 19.2% Other
- 21.3% Asia
- 19.3% U.S.
- 6.3% Africa
- 6.3% U.K.
- 7.7% Germany
- 8.4% Japan
- 11.5% Middle East

Imports

- 29.2% Other
- 5.2% Africa
- 5.6% Japan
- 6.1% U.K.
- 6.8% Germany
- 21.3% Middle East
- 7.7% Belgium-Luxembourg
- 8.9% U.S.
- 9.3% Asia

1) Gems and Jewelry (19%)   4) Clothing (12%)
2) Textiles (12.5%)   5) Chemicals (8%)
3) Engineering Products (12%)   6) Others (36.5%)

2000 Exports $33 billion

2000 Imports $42 billion

1) Industrial Equipment and Machinery (22%)   4) Chemicals (10%)
2) Crude Oil and By-products (17%)   5) Iron and Steel (6%)
3) Uncut Gems and Jewelry (12%)   6) Others (33.0%)

FIGURE 13.21
Composition of India's world merchandise trade, 2002. India exports gems, jewelry, and textiles. The country imports badly needed industrial equipment and machinery, as well as crude oil for fuel. Its total trade is tiny compared with its 1 billion population.

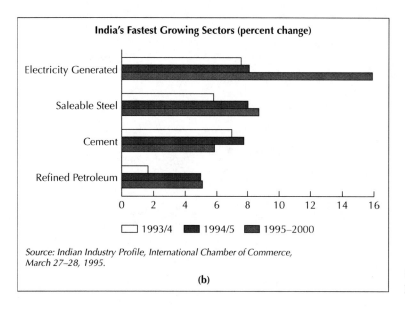

India's Fastest Growing Sectors (percent change)

Legend: ☐ 1993/4 ■ 1994/5 ▬ 1995–2000

Source: Indian Industry Profile, International Chamber of Commerce, March 27–28, 1995.

(b)

FIGURE 13.22
India's fastest growing sectors.

The Indian government began economic reforms in 1991 to liberalize the economy, privatize government-owned industry, and open India to international competition. As part of the global ascendancy of neoliberalism, the International Monetary Fund (IMF) persuaded India to turn its back on a policy of trade protection and import substitution that had been in place since the country became independent in 1949. Since 1991, India has used macroeconomic tools to improve its government deficits, inflation, and balance of payments. Import tariffs were slashed, and the government loosened its hold on business by dismantling the licensing system that governed all economic activity, moving strongly toward deregulation of the private sector.

Most economic growth, however, has been concentrated in western India, a region with a long history of trade ties. Mumbai (formerly Bombay) has become a significant financial and media center. One of the results is the accelerating development of information technology centers and industrial parks around the city of Bangalore, where companies produce software for international markets. Bangalore is India's Silicon Valley, and foreign multinationals such as IBM, Texas Instruments, Digital Equipment, Hewlett Packard, Motorola, 3M, and Qualcomm have set up operations in a huge science park.

The United States is India's single largest trading partner, and total bilateral trade was over $15 billion in 2003. Tariffs on those capital goods and equipment have been reduced from 35 percent to 25 percent, and imports of consumer goods continue to be banned. Patent protection is lacking new corporate laws, but pending trademark legislation should significantly enhance intellectual property rights protection in the near future. The biggest export opportunities to India from developed regions of the world include large electronic components. Because of increasingly stringent environmental regulations and growing industry awareness, markets for pollution control equipment are increasing at an annual rate of 40 percent. Food processing and packaging equipment is in demand as India's agricultural sector employs 70 percent of the country's workforce.

South Africa

The Republic of South Africa, with a population of 41 million and a GDP of $133 billion, is the most productive economy in all of Africa and accounts for almost 50 percent of the entire continent's output (Figure 13.23). Manufacturing now accounts for 19 percent of GDP, indicating a diversification from the traditional African dependence on gold and diamond exporting. Finance and business services account for 16 percent of the GDP as the nation moves toward the tertiary and quaternary sectors.

From World War II to 1995, South Africa practiced the policy of *apartheid*, or racial separation, that kept economic power concentrated among few large economic enterprises. The remarkable succession and peaceful transfer of power when apartheid collapsed produced an upswing in business confidence and a relaxation of foreign embargoes against South Africa. Job growth has been sluggish, however, and unemployment is 40 percent among blacks. Apartheid also caused widespread illiteracy, unemployment, and social problems that will be expensive to remedy and will take years to overcome. One-third of the population is infected with HIV. The developed countries find South Africa to be an attractive market because of the pent-up demand for goods and services. Leading U.S. exports to South Africa include aircraft and parts, industrial chemicals, computer software, pharmaceuticals, medical equipment, telecommunications equipment, and building and housing products.

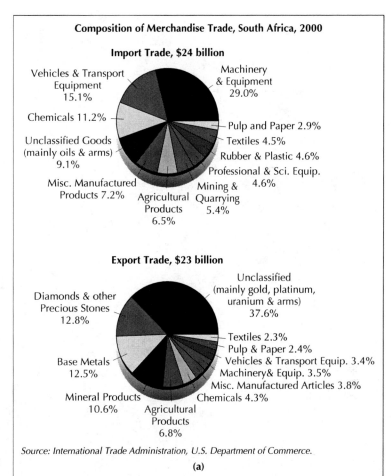

Composition of Merchandise Trade, South Africa, 2000

Import Trade, $24 billion

Vehicles & Transport Equipment 15.1%

Chemicals 11.2%

Unclassified Goods (mainly oils & arms) 9.1%

Misc. Manufactured Products 7.2%

Agricultural Products 6.5%

Mining & Quarrying 5.4%

Professional & Sci. Equip. 4.6%

Rubber & Plastic 4.6%

Textiles 4.5%

Pulp and Paper 2.9%

Machinery & Equipment 29.0%

Export Trade, $23 billion

Diamonds & other Precious Stones 12.8%

Base Metals 12.5%

Mineral Products 10.6%

Agricultural Products 6.8%

Chemicals 4.3%

Misc. Manufactured Articles 3.8%

Machinery & Equip. 3.5%

Vehicles & Transport Equip. 3.4%

Pulp & Paper 2.4%

Textiles 2.3%

Unclassified (mainly gold, platinum, uranium & arms) 37.6%

Source: International Trade Administration, U.S. Department of Commerce.

(a)

FIGURE 13.23
South Africa's composition of merchandise trade, imports and exports. U.S. and Canadian firms involved in South Africa's redevelopment will contribute to the country's revitalization process while gaining a strong commercial foothold in the new South Africa and the Africa beyond.

The United States is South Africa's largest trading partner. South Africa recently has paid attention to reorienting its own economy away from import substitution toward international competition.

Russia

The disintegration of the Soviet Union in 1991 was one of the most momentous occurrences in recent history. Russia and its former client states in Eastern Europe began a long, slow, and painful transition to market economies. While Eastern Europe, to one degree or another, has managed this transition relatively well, in Russia, transition led to economic collapse. The old central-planning systems have broken up, but the new systems that will replace them are not yet fully developed.

In 2003, the national income was 60 percent less in Russia than it was in 1990, and investment fell to pre-1970 levels. For the majority of the population, this resulted in rising unemployment, crime, and poverty. Although rich in resources such as gold, natural gas, petroleum, and timber, Russia's government and economy have been so disorganized and corrupt that the benefits of the sale of these assets have been concentrated in the

hands of a tiny, wealthy oligarchy. With the collapse of trade under the Council for Mutual Economic Assistance (COMECON), orders from nearby countries decreased by more than 50 percent, seriously hurting internal production and trade. There is a slowdown in the production of necessary raw materials, equipment, and replacement parts and a massive shortage of food, pharmaceuticals, textiles, garments, footwear, and machinery. Russia and its neighboring republics have been wrecked by inflation.

Although Russia was the basket case of the 1990s, globalization started to transform the corrupt society of postcommunism. One sign is the integration of Russia's oil industry into the world economy. In 2003, British Petroleum bought a $10 billion stake in the Russian oil giant TNK, and ExxonMobil invested $25 billion in oil development in Siberia. Russia's new oligarchies have decided that they can make more money selling shares of their fortune in global financial markets than by larceny. Russia's economic output has now reached and surpassed the level of 1991.

What does the future hold for this region with regard to international trade? There is a certain complementarity in Euro-Asia. Western Europe needs the minerals, oil, natural gas, and other raw materials that

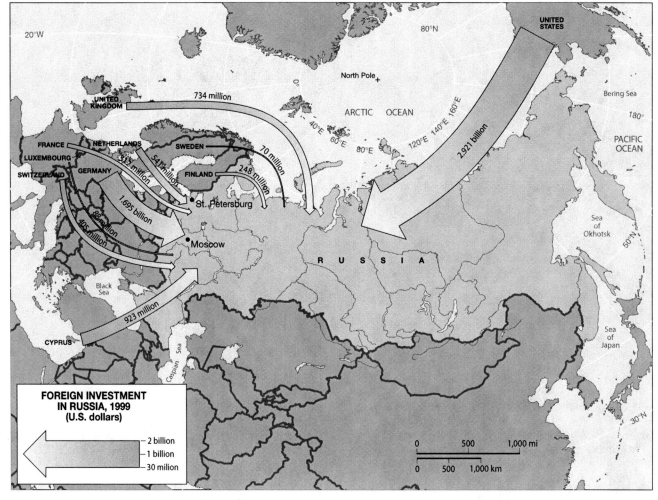

FIGURE 13.24
Foreign investment flows into Russia, 1999.

are in vast supply in Russia and the republics of the former Soviet Union. At the same time, the eastern bloc nations need foodstuffs and industrial equipment and machinery to resume their powerhouse of economic production.

Multinationals from every OECD country are investigating the potential for investment in the former Soviet Union (Figure 13.24). Automobile manufacturers from Western Europe, Japan, and the United States are also investigating their opportunities, as are consumer electronics producers. However, uncertainties still exist, and these multinationals must be cautious because of the gigantic economic uncertainties in the political and economic transformation.

Although much business and property have been privatized, agriculture remains largely in state hands as well as a third of all manufacturing plants. In 2003, Russia's population was 145 million (and falling), with a GDP of roughly $270 billion. Unemployment has leveled off, but difficult inflationary battles continue and the infrastructure is decaying. Russian privatization

has attracted investment targets, including Aeroflot, the National Electric Utility, and Gazpron (Russia's gas company).

Russia is an emerging market and constitutes one of the 10 fastest growing world markets for manufactured goods. Ordinarily, manufacturing exports to Russia continue to be infrastructure related: engineering equipment, automatic data processing, and telecommunications equipment. In 2000, the largest single export to Russia was aircraft and related equipment. Total U.S. exports to Russia have been increasing steadily and were more than $3.5 billion in 2003. Hindrances to increased world exports to Russia are substantial value added taxes, high import duties, and high excise levees. The most promising prospects for developed country exports to Russia are telecommunications equipment, computers and computer peripherals, pollution control equipment, oil and gas field machinery, construction equipment, medical equipment, electrical power systems equipment, automotive parts and services, building products, and food processing and packaging equipment.

166

The Middle East contains approximately 64 percent of the world's oil reserves, with Saudi Arabia containing 264 billion barrels, more than one-third of the world's total. Other oil producers and exporters are Bahrain, Kuwait, the United Arab Emirates, Oman, and Qatar. Four other countries—Iraq, Iran, Egypt, and Syria—have very small amounts of oil. Countries in the region without oil supplies include Egypt, Israel, Jordan, Lebanon, Turkey, Yemen, Morocco, and Tunisia.

Inexpensive oil from the Middle East fueled the world for a long time. In fact, the United States and the western European nations have enjoyed a large supply. At $4 to $5 per barrel, Middle Eastern oil helped rebuild Europe after World War II. However, in 1973 and 1979, oil supplies were interrupted by Arab boycotts of the West for its support of Israel in the 1973 Yom Kippur War, by the overthrow of the shah of Iran in 1979, and by the Iraq-Iran War, and prices climbed to $30 per barrel. OPEC's revenues reached $300 billion, and a worldwide recession was triggered. However, because of squabbling among OPEC members and because U.S.-backed Saudi Arabia decided to undercut the market to provide Western stability, oil prices decreased to less than $10 per barrel in 1986. Revenues plummeted. In the 1990s, prices declined, and OPEC nations had lost much of their stranglehold on the world market, dropping to approximately equal to OPEC's pre-1973 levels. By 2004, however, oil climbed to $40 per barrel.

While all the fluctuations in oil prices were occurring, other sources of oil, synthetic fuels, and solar, geothermal, and nuclear power sources were being explored. OPEC's largest market was Western Europe, which traditionally had poor supplies of fossil fuels. Even before the oil crises, the Middle Eastern nations fulfilled 45 percent of Western Europe's energy needs. By the 1990s, however, that proportion dropped to 20 percent as a result of not only the exploitation of the North Sea oil fields but also increased coal production in central Europe.

The region's second most important activity after oil is agriculture, but water is scarce and the few sources that do exist are heavily tapped. The Tigris and Euphrates rivers, for example, as well as the Jordan River, are argued over by countries such as Turkey, Lebanon, Syria, Israel, and Iraq. In any case, wheat, barley, vegetables, cotton, and citrus fruits can be grown and supplied to Europe, which is a short distance away. Agriculture is also the basis of Turkey's export economy. Turkey is a large exporter of wheat and mineral resources, including iron, copper, and zinc.

Egypt is now one of the world's leading exporters of cotton, yarns, textiles, and denim. Egypt has been criticized because much of its agricultural base is devoted to cotton at the expense of food crops needed to feed its people.

Israel exports cut and polished diamonds, machinery, computer software, telecommunications equipment, and is the only high-tech economy of the Middle East. Throughout the region, tourism has been impor-

Iranian oil field and peasant herder. Iran remains an important source of world oil supplies, but squabbles among OPEC members have kept world prices low.

The Suez Canal remains a vital link for distribution of oil from the Persian Gulf to Europe. Despite the fact that the Middle East was one of the early hearths of civilization and city development, it did not share in the capitalist expansion and prosperity of the last 300 years that was centered on Europe and North America. It was only with the discovery of vast oil deposits by U.S. companies in the Persian Gulf area in the second half of the twentieth century that the focus of world attention returned to the Middle East. Today, the Middle East contains the greatest extremes of wealth, versus poverty, to be found anywhere in the world, all based on whether or not a country has oil supplies.

tant; however, the continued conflict between Israel and the Palestinians has depressed the tourist industry there.

MAJOR GLOBAL TRADE FLOWS

Six major commodity groups merit further attention as fundamental to understanding international patterns of trade: microelectronics, automobiles, steel, textiles and clothing, grains and feed, and non-oil commodities.

Microelectronics

Microelectronics includes semiconductors, integrated circuits and parts for integrated circuits, and electronic components and parts. Japan and the East Asian countries, especially the Four Tigers of South Korea, Taiwan, Hong Kong, and Singapore, together account for the predominant flow of microelectronics in the world (Figure 13.25). The single largest flow from this group is from the developing countries of the Western Hemisphere other than the United States and Canada, most notably Mexico, and the countries in South Asia and East Asia, which send more than $24 billion worth of microelectronics to the United States. Japan sends another $20 billion worth of microelectronics to developing countries and more than $7 billion worth to the United States. The single largest flow of microelectronics in the world is

from the United States to developing countries and is worth $21 billion.

Although the United States no longer leads the world in the manufacture of semiconductors, it is still a major player in the global trade flow of microelectronics. Canada and the western European nations of the EU and the European Free Trade Area (EFTA) account for a much smaller proportion of overseas trade in this category. However, intra-European trade in microelectronics accounts for $15 billion.

Automobiles

Global trade within the EU accounts for the largest single flow of automobiles. More than $100 billion worth of automobiles were shipped among EU countries in 2003, and more than another $10 billion worth were sent to other European countries (Figure 13.26). The United States imported $11 billion worth as well, including Mercedes, Audis, Porsches, Volkswagens, Peugeots, Fiats, and Renaults. Japan made major inroads into the European automobile market, shipping $8 billion worth to EU. The single largest volume of flow is also accounted for by Japan and its shipment to the United States, $20 billion worth.

Japanese automobile manufacturers made major penetrations in the world automobile market between 1960 and 2000 (Figure 13.27). During the same time, the big three automakers in America scaled down operations substantially. General Motors and Ford remained

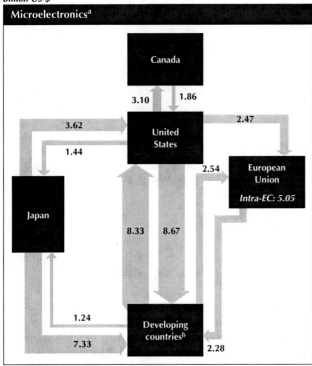

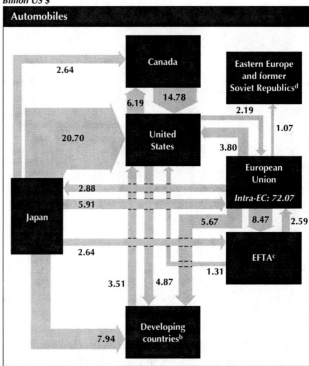

a Including integrated circuits and IC parts, semiconductors, and electronic component parts.
b Including Western hemisphere other than the United States and Canada; Africa and the Middle East; South Asia; and East Asia other than Japan, Mongolia, North Korea, Laos, and Cambodia.
Note: Width of arrows scaled to dollar volume. Trade flows less than $1 billion not shown.

FIGURE 13.25
Global trade flows of microelectronics, in billions of U.S. dollars.

c Including Austria, Switzerland, Sweden, Norway, Finland, Iceland, and Liechtenstein.
d Including Poland, Hungary, Czech Republic, Slovakia, Albania, Romania, Bulgaria, and former Soviet Republics.
Note: Width of arrows scaled to dollar volume. Trade flows less than $1 billion not shown.

FIGURE 13.26
Global trade flow of automobiles, in billions of U.S. dollars.

the world's largest automobile manufacturers in 2000, even though the Japanese captured almost 26 percent of the American automobile and light truck market. American car builders, after years of struggle, are finally turning out higher-quality competitive products. Porter (1990) described demand conditions and taste as an important factor in global comparative advantage. Given the low cost of oil, American consumers are largely bypassing passenger cars for light trucks, minivans, four-wheel drives, and sporty utility vehicles.

Japanese MNCs such as Toyota, Nissan, Mitsubishi, Mazda, and Honda have invested heavily in factories in the United States, where they escape import quotas and have access to skilled, compliant labor. Starting with the Honda plant in 1982 in Marysville, Ohio, Japanese-made vehicles that are assembled and built in America account for nearly half the Japanese car sales in the United States. Locally made Japanese cars are cheaper than those imported from Japan because they escape the high-priced parts and labor associated with the yen. Nissan's newest plants are in low-wage Smyrna, Tennessee, and produce Sentras and Ultimas.

These American-made Japanese cars are called *Japanese transplants*.

Exports of automobiles from Europe have been heavy. Germany is Europe's largest producer of cars, followed by France, Spain, and the United Kingdom. U.S. companies have diversified, so both Ford and General Motors now have substantial international automobile production (Figure 13.28).

Steel

Whereas America has lost as much as two-thirds of its steel employment in the last 20 years and now is a net importer of steel, Western Europe continues to lead the world in steel production and trade. The EU accounted for more than $44 billion worth of steel traded internally in 2000, and trade with the other European countries accounted for another $4 billion (Figure 13.29).

The single largest flow of steel was from Japan to developing countries. In addition, the EU sent $10 billion

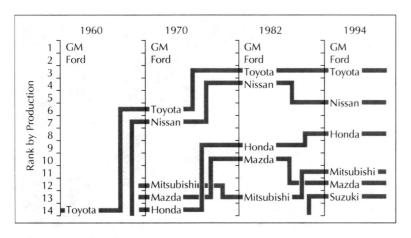

FIGURE 13.27
The rise of Japanese automobile manufacturers, 1960–1994.

worth of steel to developing countries in 2000. Steel requires large and highly efficient plants to be produced profitably, which are possible only with tremendous capital investments and large-scale economies. In the post–World War II period, steel made by traditional producers in Europe and North America became uncompetitive as new production centers began to emerge in Brazil, South Korea, Taiwan, and Japan. The migration of steel production to the Third World reflected the growing importance of labor costs, government subsidies, and taxes to the delivered cost of steel. In Chapter 7, we discussed the problems of the British and U.S. steel industries: insufficient reinvestment, reluctant unions, narrow-minded management, and lack of government support of an ailing industry. However, under the impetus of the microelectronics revolution, minimills have restored some of the efficiency of U.S. steel producers. Tariffs on European steel imports by the George W. Bush administration in 2002 threatened to provoke a trade war until the WTO forced the United States to remove them in 2003.

Textiles and Clothing

As discussed in Chapter 7, labor-intensive textile and clothing manufacture has largely shifted to developing countries (Figure 13.30), including Central America, South Asia, and parts of East and Southeast Asia (e.g., China, Thailand, Indonesia), where labor costs are much lower (Figure 13.31). Correspondingly, textile production in the last 40 years declined in the United States and Western Europe, which were the dominant producers as late as 1950. International trade in textiles reflects these shifts in production. Developing countries accounted for more than $85 billion worth of exports in 2003.

Surprisingly, Germany and Italy lead the world in textile exports, even though the main manufacturing centers of older industrialized nations have given ground to the developing world, particularly East Asia. Western Europe accounts for more than $71 billion worth of textile and clothing trade among nations within Western Europe.

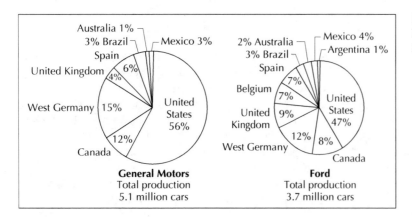

FIGURE 13.28
International automobile production by General Motors and Ford, 2000.

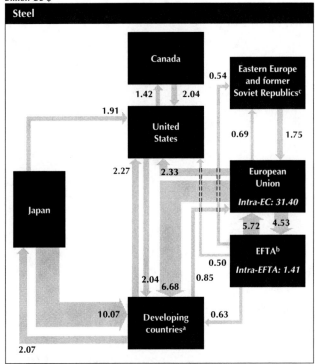

Billion US $

Steel

aIncluding Western Hemisphere other than the United States and Canada; Africa and the Middle East; South Asia; and East Asia other than Japan, Mongolia, North Korea, Laos, and Cambodia.
bIncluding Austria, Switzerland, Sweden, Norway, Finland, Iceland, and Liechtenstein.
cIncluding Poland, Hungary, Albania, Romania, Bulgaria, Czech Republic, Slovakia, and former Soviet Republics.
Note: Width of arrows scaled to dollar volume. Trade flows less than $500 million not shown.

FIGURE 13.29
Global trade flow of steel, in billions of U.S. dollars.

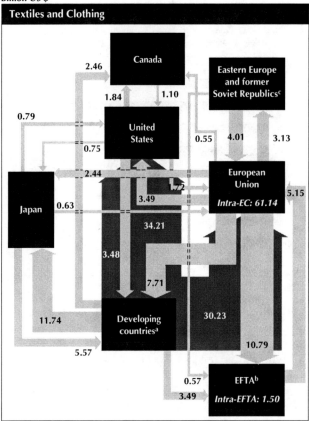

Billion US $

Textiles and Clothing

aIncluding Western Hemisphere other than the United States and Canada; Africa and the Middle East; South Asia; and East Asia other than Japan, Mongolia, North Korea, Laos, and Cambodia.
bIncluding Austria, Switzerland, Sweden, Norway, Finland, Iceland, and Liechtenstein.
cIncluding Poland, Hungary, Albania, Romania, Bulgaria, Czech Republic, Slovakia, and former Soviet Republics.
Note: Width of arrows scaled to dollar volume. Trade flows less than $500 million not shown.

FIGURE 13.30
Global trade flow of textiles and clothing, in billions of U.S. dollars. Globalizers claim that cheaper imported goods will more than compensate for the disruption and downward pressure on wages caused by increasing international trade and investment. This trade includes, of course, what is produced overseas by U.S. and Canadian multinational corporations like Nike, who pay $1.60 a day to their workers in Vietnam. But it hasn't worked out that way. A declining real wage means exactly that: Whatever benefit we have gotten from cheaper imported goods has been marginalized by other forces, including runaway factories and increased global competition.

Major gainers during the last 30 years include the East Asian countries of China, Hong Kong, South Korea, and Taiwan. By 2003, European nations accounted for 47 percent of the world trade flow, whereas East Asian countries accounted for another 43 percent. However, a much larger proportion of textiles and clothing flowed from developing countries to the United States than they did from Western Europe to the United States. Eastern Europe, Russia, Japan, and Canada are relatively small players in the world textile and clothing trade.

Grains and Feed

The primary products of wheat, corn, rice, other cereals, feed grains, and soybeans are included in the category of grains and feed. The United States exports more than $28 billion worth of feed and grains and thus is a world leader in this category (Figure 13.32). Canada is also a major exporter.

Japan, with its small base of agriculture and arable land, is a net importer, as is Eastern Europe and Russia.

Trade within the EU is large ($17 billion in 2003). Developing countries such as India, Egypt, and Argentina are some of the largest net exporting developing countries in this category.

World trade in grains, feeds, and food products had been as high as 30 percent in 1965, but these commodities slipped to less than 15 percent by 2003. Some of this reduction is because Western seeds, grains, and fertilizers are now commonplace in Third

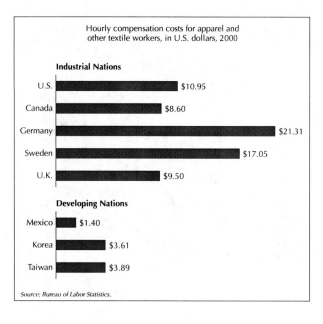

Hourly compensation costs for apparel and other textile workers, in U.S. dollars, 2000

Industrial Nations

U.S.	$10.95
Canada	$8.60
Germany	$21.31
Sweden	$17.05
U.K.	$9.50

Developing Nations

Mexico	$1.40
Korea	$3.61
Taiwan	$3.89

Source: Bureau of Labor Statistics.

FIGURE 13.31
Hourly labor costs for apparel and textile workers, 2000.

World nations, and technology from the grain revolution has taught developing countries to provide for themselves. Another portion of the reduction reflects the worsening terms of trade (Chapter 11) for primary goods, as prices of manufactures and energy rose rapidly and gave producers of feed, grains, and agricultural products less leverage in world international commerce.

Non-Oil Commodities

Non-oil commodities include copper, aluminum, nickel, zinc, tin, iron ore, pig iron, uranium ore, and alloys. Crude rubber, wood and pulp, hides, cotton fiber, and animal and vegetable minerals and oils are included in this category. The United States shows a large export potential, sending $5 billion worth to Japan, $11 billion worth to developing countries, and another $5 billion worth to the EU.

However, the developing countries of the world lead in the export of raw materials (Figure 13.33). The largest single flow of raw materials outside the more than $43 billion worth exchanged within the EU is from developing countries to Japan ($21 billion) and from developing countries to Western Europe ($24 billion). Since the early days of Europe, the international

Combined grain is off loaded on a farm near Wataga, Illinois. The United States is a world supplier of primary products, including grains, timber, and other agricultural products. Most every country in the world grows grain, and approximately a quarter of the 600 million tons of wheat produced each year enters world trade. By 1960, the Third World began to outstrip its own food production, and Europe had long been a grain importer by then. The United States and Canada became the only large grain exporters, providing 80 percent of the world's exports.

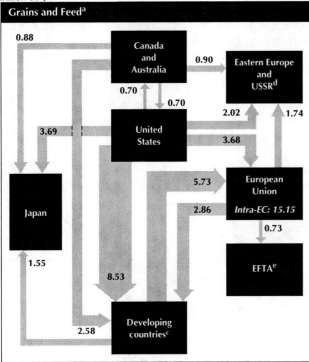

Billion US $

Grains and Feed[a]

Canada and Australia

0.88

0.90

Eastern Europe and USSR[d]

0.70

0.70

United States

3.69

2.02   1.74

3.68

5.73

European Union

2.86

Intra-EC: 15.15

Japan

0.73

EFTA[e]

8.53

1.55

Developing countries[c]

2.58

[a]Including wheat, corn, rice, other cereals, feedgrains, and soybeans.
[b]Including unwrought copper, aluminum, nickel, zinc, and tin, and ores thereof; iron ore and pig iron; uranium ore and alloys; other nonferrous ores, unwrought metals, and crude minerals; crude rubber, wood and pulp; hides; cotton fiber and other textile fibers; crude animal and vegetable materials.
[c]Including Western Hemisphere other than the United States and Canada; Africa and the Middle East; South Asia; and East Asia other than Japan, Mongolia, North Korea, Laos, and Cambodia.
[d]Including Poland, Hungary, Czech Republic, Slovakia, Albania, Romania, Bulgaria, and former Soviet Republics.
[e]Including Austria, Switzerland, Sweden, Norway, Finalnd, Iceland, and Liechtenstein.
Note: Width of arrows scaled to dollar volume. Trade flows less than $500 million not shown for grains/feed; trade flows less than $2 billion not shown for nonoil commodities.

FIGURE 13.32
Global trade flow of grains and feed, in billions of U.S. dollars.

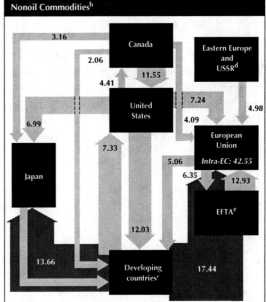

Billion US $

Nonoil Commodities[b]

3.16

Canada

Eastern Europe and USSR[d]

2.06

11.55

4.41

7.24

United States

4.98

6.99

4.09

European Union

7.33

5.06

Intra-EC: 42.55

Japan

6.35   12.93

EFTA[e]

12.03

13.66

Developing countries[c]

17.44

[a]Including wheat, corn, rice, other cereals, feedgrains, and soybeans.
[b]Including unwrought copper, aluminum, nickel, zinc, and tin, and ores thereof; iron ore and pig iron; uranium ore and alloys; other nonferrous ores, unwrought metals, and crude minerals; crude rubber, wood and pulp; hides; cotton fiber and other textile fibers; crude animal and vegetable materials.
[c]Including Western Hemisphere other than the United States and Canada; Africa and the Middle East; South Asia; and East Asia other than Japan, Mongolia, North Korea, Laos, and Cambodia.
[d]Including Poland, Hungary, Czech Republic, Slovakia, Albania, Romania, Bulgaria, and former Soviet Republics.
[e]Including Austria, Switzerland, Sweden, Norway, Finalnd, Iceland, and Liechtenstein.
Note: Width of arrows scaled to dollar volume. Trade flows less than $500 million not shown for grains/feed; trade flows less than $2 billion not shown for nonoil commodities.

FIGURE 13.33
Global trade flow of non-oil commodities, in billions of U.S. dollars.

division of labor was based on international trade. Under this unfair program, less developed countries traded their non-oil commodities—grains, feed, food stocks, and energy sources—for industrialized goods from primarily Europe and other developed nations.

S UMMARY

International trade has grown rapidly over the last 30 years and now comprises roughly one-quarter of the world's total output. As we saw in Chapter 11, trade patterns simultaneously reflect and shape the specialization of production among and within different countries. Thus, trade must be viewed within the context of national changes in the level and composition of GDP. The growth of trade has occurred more quickly than the growth in national output, meaning that countries have become increasingly interconnected. However, important shifts in production internationally have contributed to changes in trade patterns, particularly the offshoring of many low-wage, low-value-added sectors in manufacturing from developed countries to LDCs. More generally, recent changes in global trade must be seen in light of the broader dynamics of globalization, including trade deregulation under the WTO, the rise of the NICs, and changes in global finance, including currency exchange rate fluctuations.

This chapter charted several major dimensions of international trade. It noted the growth of emerging markets in some of the largest developing countries, such as China, Brazil, South Korea, and India, all of which have exhibited steady, if uneven, growth. It focused on the shifting nature and composition of U.S. exports and imports, which have become increasingly tied to East Asia, particularly Japan and China, although Canada remains the largest trading partner. NAFTA has expanded U.S. trade greatly with Mexico, as well as foreign investment such as maquilladores. The rising U.S. merchandise trade balance has been offset to some extent by a surplus in the trade balance in services. On the other side of the Pacific, the chapter pointed to the major role of trade in the growth of both the original "tigers" such as South Korea and Taiwan as well as new tigers, including Thailand and Indonesia, but, above all, China. Russia, a potential emerging giant, has remained mired in the difficult transition from communism to a market-based economy, a process fraught with corruption and inefficiency. Finally, the chapter summarized the world trade patterns in six major commodity groups, including microelectronics, automobiles, steel, textiles, grains, and non-oil commodities.

STUDY QUESTIONS

1. What has happened to the level of world trade since World War II? Why?
2. What is purchasing power parity?
3. Does the United States trade more with Europe or East Asia? Why?
4. What are Mexican maquiladoras?
5. Describe the geography of Japan's automobile exports.

KEY TERMS

capital resources
demand conditions
factor conditions
factor-driven stage
Five Little Dragons
Four Tigers
General Agreement on Tariffs and Trade (GATT)

human resources
import substitution
infrastructure
innovation drive stage
investment-driven stage
Japanese transplants
knowledge-based resources
Little Dragons

microelectronics
modernization theory
Organization of Economic Cooperation and Development (OECD)
physical resources
purchasing power parity
wealth-driven stage

SUGGESTED READINGS

Dicken, P. 2004. *Global Shift: The Internationalization of Economic Activity,* 4th ed. New York: Guilford Press.

Grant, R. 2000. "The Economic Geography of Global Trade." In *A Companion to Economic Geography.* Oxford: Blackwell.

Hiscox, M. 2001. *International Trade and Political Conflict: Commerce, Coalitions, and Mobility.* Princeton, N.J.: Princeton University Press.

Krugman, P. 1997. *The Age of Diminished Expectations.* Cambridge, Mass.: MIT Press.

Porter, M. E. 1990. *The Competitive Advantage of Nations.* New York: Free Press.

Van Marrewijk, C. 2002. *International Trade and the World Economy.* Oxford: Oxford University Press.

OFFICE OF TRADE AND INDUSTRY INFORMATION
http://www.ita.doc.gov/td/industry/otea/

WORLD BANK
http://www.worldbank.org/

TRADE STATISTICS
http://www.census.gov/indicator/www/ustrade.html

Section 3
National Level

DEVELOPMENT AND UNDERDEVELOP-MENT IN THE DEVELOPING WORLD

O B J E C T I V E S

- To outline the multiple definitions of development
- To acquaint you with the major economic problems inhibiting development in this part of the world
- To introduce major theories and perspectives on international development
- To examine the causes of poverty in the world today
- To explore the role of women in the world economy and gender roles in the workplace
- To shed light on development strategies that work and do not work

Women collecting water from a well in Ethiopia.

The modern world has its origin in the European societies of the late fifteenth and early sixteenth centuries, when capitalism began in earnest and eventually displaced feudalism throughout the continent (Chapter 2). True "modernity," however, arrived largely on the heels of the Industrial Revolution, the Enlightenment, and the massive political, social, economic, cultural, and technological changes of the nineteenth and twentieth centuries.

One of the most enduring and striking characteristics of the modern world is the division between rich and poor countries. By the nineteenth century, this division was achieved through an international system in which the wealthy minority of countries industrialized, using primary products produced by the impoverished majority of their colonies. More recently, this original global division of labor gave way to a new one: The wealthy minority is increasingly engaged in office work while parts of the developing world find hands-on manufacturing jobs on the global assembly line as well as in agriculture and raw-material production. The creation of today's world, with a rich core and a poor periphery, was not the result of conspiracy among developed countries but was the outcome of a systemic process—that process by which the world's political economy functions and, in so doing, reproduces uneven spatial development. In short, the birth of the modern world system and the schism between rich and poor countries are two sides of the same process that lies at the heart of global political economy.

This chapter deals with how this world of unequal development came about and how present structures are the result of the past. We begin by problematizing the word and idea of *development*, noting how it embodies many different concepts and measures. Next we survey the major regions of the developing world. The chapter then turns to a discussion of the characteristics of less developed countries (LDCs) and some of the barriers to their development. It compares and contrasts three major schools of thought on this issue, modernization theory, dependency theory, and world systems theory. The last part turns toward development strategies, including the central role of trade, and concludes with an examination of the potentials and pitfalls of Third World industrialization.

WHAT'S IN A WORD? "DEVELOPING"

If Europe, the United States, Australia, and Japan, all of which enjoy relatively high standards of living and material consumption, are described as developed countries, then what adjective should we use to describe the poor countries of the world? Certainly, there are many from which to choose. In the past half-century, each of the following terms has flourished in succession: *primitive, backward, undeveloped, underdeveloped, less developed, emerging,* and *developing.* Today, many people and policy makers use the word *developing* and, increasingly, the phrase *less developed countries,* but social scientists in the marxist tradition favor the term *underdeveloped.*

Underdeveloped was formerly used to describe situations in which resources were not yet developed. People and resources were seen as existing, respectively, in a traditional and "natural" state of poverty. The problem with this view is that it takes poverty to be natural and inevitable, rather than a social product, and masks the origins and historical contexts and processes that make people poor. Many scholars argue that poverty is produced, much like a building or a shirt or a TV show. Those working in the marxist tradition use the adjective *underdeveloped* to describe not an initial state but rather a condition arrived at through the agency of imperialism, which set up the inequality of political and economic dependence of poor countries on rich countries. Thus, instead of viewing underdevelopment as an initial or *passive state,* marxists view it as an *active process.*

While economic development may seem like a straightforward concept, in fact it involves several complex, even contradictory goals and concepts. Broadly speaking, development entails the growth of per capita income and the reduction of poverty. However, some countries that have experienced rapid growth of per capita income also see increases in poverty, unemployment, and inequality. Beyond income, other measures of development include income equality, nutrition, health, infant mortality, access to education, and civil liberties. In some cases, development may actually accelerate income inequality. For example, in India, the much heralded Green Revolution, which depends on fertilizer and water inputs, benefited mainly the farmers in the Punjab who were already wealthy and who owned large tracts of land. Yet other measures of development include capital inflows, the capacity to produce capital goods, trade balances, and trade reliance on one major trading partner.

Food, health, adequate shelter, and protection are essential to human well-being. When they are sufficient to meet human needs, a state of development exists; when they are insufficient, a degree of underdevelopment prevails. Even more intangible measures include life sustenance, esteem, and freedom. Mass poverty prevents people and societies from receiving due recognition or esteem. These people may even reject development. For example, if people are humiliated or disillusioned through their contacts with the "progress" introduced by foreigners, they may advocate a return to their traditional ways of life. Suspicions of western institutions that disrupt traditional lifestyles and balances of power help to fuel opposition to globalization worldwide.

More down-to-earth development goals include the following:

1. A balanced, healthful diet
2. Adequate health care

3. Environmental sanitation and disease control
4. Labor opportunities commensurate with individual talents
5. Sufficient educational opportunities
6. Individual freedom of conscience and freedom from fear
7. Decent housing
8. Economic activities in harmony with the natural environment
9. Social and political milieus promoting equality

In conventional usage, *development* is a synonym for economic growth. But growth is not development, except insofar as it enables a country to achieve the nine goals. If these goals are not the objectives of development, if modernization is merely a process of technological diffusion, and if the spatial integration of world power and world economy is devoid of human referents, that is, insensitive to people's psychological and political needs, then development should be redefined.

How Economic Development Is Measured

Geographers and other social scientists measure economic development through a number of social, economic, and demographic indexes. The principal ones are GDP per capita, the distribution of the labor force by economic sector, ability to produce consumer goods,

educational and literacy levels, the status of health of a population, and its level of urbanization.

GDP per Capita

By far the most common measure of wealth and poverty internationally is gross domestic product (GDP) per capita, that is, the sum total of the value of goods and services produced by a national economy divided by its population. As shown in Figure 14.1, GDP per capita is more than $15,000 in most highly developed nations. At the same time, the United Nations estimates that 1 billion people live on less than $2 a day, or $750 per capita per year. Japan, North America, Western Europe, Australia, and New Zealand have the highest per capita incomes in the world. The Middle East, Latin America, South Asia, East Asia, Southeast Asia, and sub-Saharan Africa have the lowest. However, GDP is a flawed measure in several respects: It does not capture nonmarket, noncommodified economic activity (e.g., barter and subsistence production or household domestic labor) and is vulnerable to fluctuations in exchange rates and the costs of living.

Per capita purchasing power is a more meaningful measure of actual income per person (Figure 14.2). The relative purchasing power in developed nations is more than $10,000 per capita per year, whereas in Africa it is much less than $1000 per capita per year. Per capita

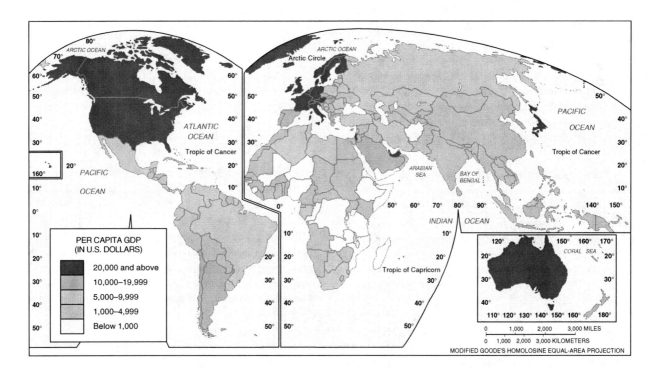

FIGURE 14.1
Annual gross domestic product (GDP) per capita. GDP per capita—the sum of a country's output divided by its population—is the most common, if flawed, measure of standards of living. GDP per capita varies from less than $250 per year in the most impoverished nations to more than $20,000 per person annually in much of Europe, Japan, and North America.

Development and Underdevelopment in the Developing World

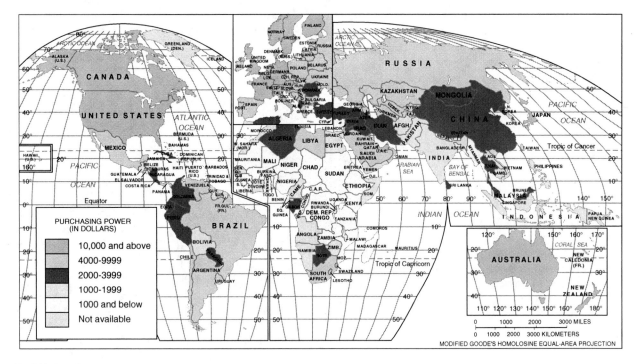

FIGURE 14.2

Per capita purchasing power. Per capita purchasing power is a better measure of a country's relative wealth than is GDP per capita because it includes the relative prices of products. For example, Switzerland, Sweden, and Japan have higher per capita GDPs than the United States. However, the United States has the world's highest per capita purchasing power because of relatively low prices for food, housing, fuel, and services.

purchasing power includes not only income, but also the price of goods in a country. The United States is surpassed by Japan, Scandinavia, Switzerland, and Germany in per capita income. However, it surpasses almost all countries in per capita purchasing power because goods and services, particularly housing, are relatively inexpensive in the United States compared with those in other industrialized nations. In other respects, however, including poverty rates and income inequality, the United States lags behind much of Europe.

Economic Structure of the Labor Force

The sectoral distribution of jobs of a country also bespeaks its economic development. Economists and economic geographers divide employment into three major categories:

1. The *primary sector* involves the extraction of materials from the earth—mining, lumbering, agriculture, and fishing.
2. The *secondary sector* includes assembling raw materials and manufacturing (i.e., the transformation of raw materials into finish products).
3. The *tertiary sector* is devoted to the provision of services—producer services (finance and business services) wholesaling and retailing, personal services, health care and entertainment, transportation, and communications.

In less developed countries, a large share of the labor force works in the primary sector, primarily as peasants and farmers (Figure 14.3). In the United States, only 5 percent of the labor force is engaged in the primary sector, including 2 percent in agriculture, whereas in certain African nations, India, and China, more than 70 percent of the laborers are in the primary sector. More than 75 percent of U.S. laborers are in the tertiary sector.

Education and Literacy of a Population

Economic development can also be measured by the extent and quality of education in a country, including the proportion of children who attend school. The *literacy rate* of a country is the proportion of people in the society who can read and write (Figure 14.4). The number of students per teacher is another measure of access to education; small classes allow more student-teacher interaction and greatly facilitate learning. Richer, First World societies generally have low student-teacher ratios, whereas poor countries have high ones (Figure 14.5). Moreover, in many developing countries, teachers' salaries are low, the buildings are decrepit, and there are insufficient funds for textbooks or scientific equipment. Notably, despite these underinvestments, many countries have ample funds for their militaries, indicating that insufficient investment in human capital is a policy choice, not a "natural" limitation.

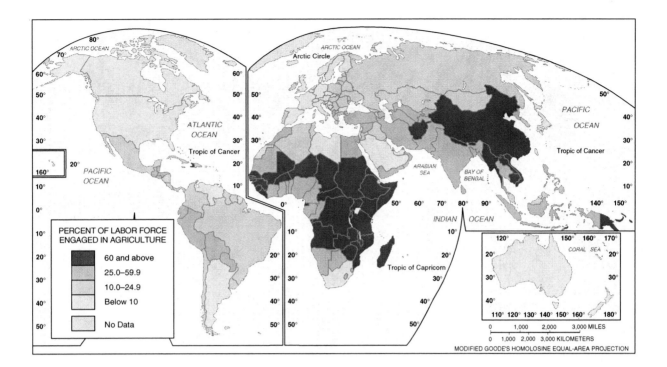

FIGURE 14.3

Percent of labor force in agriculture. Typically, poor countries have large shares of their workers in agriculture, often working in preindustrial conditions, whereas in economically advanced countries a small fraction of the labor force is so employed.

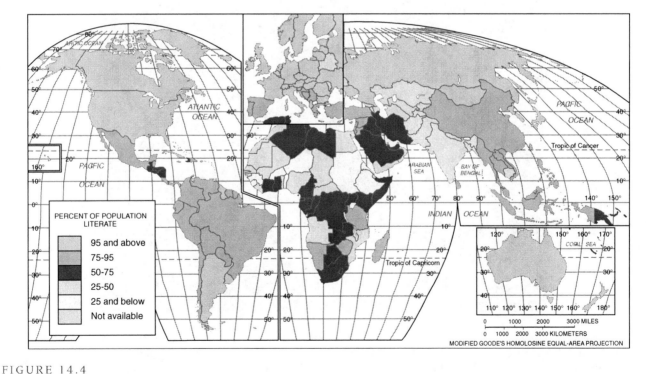

FIGURE 14.4

Literacy rates. A great disparity in literacy rates exists between inhabitants of developed countries and less developed countries. In the United States and other highly developed countries, the literacy rate is more than 98 percent. Notice the large number of countries in Africa and South Asia where the literacy rate is less than 50 percent.

Development and Underdevelopment in the Developing World

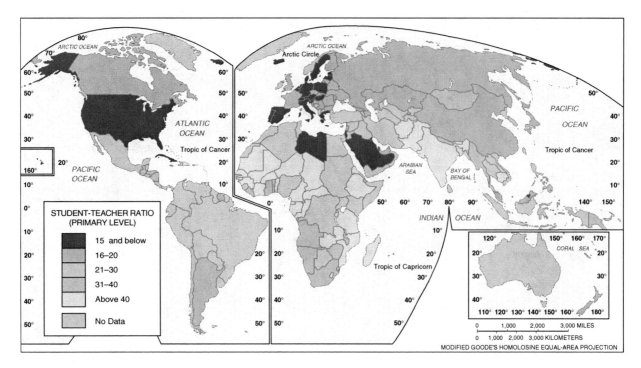

FIGURE 14.5
Students per teacher in primary school. This measure of average class size reflects the quality of each country's educational system. Small class sizes facilitate more student-teacher interaction and are one of the best measures of the resource base of a school system.

Harvesting coffee in Colombia. This woman illustrates the preindustrial types of agriculture that employ large shares of the labor force in the primary economic sector in much of the developing world. Often landless farmers, or in Latin America, *campesinos,* must sell their labor power at low wages in order to feed their families. These are the populations most vulnerable to globalization, low export prices, and exploitative local landowners. Their poverty reflects the ways in which global, national, and local forces are telescoped into places to generate both wealth and suffering simultaneously.

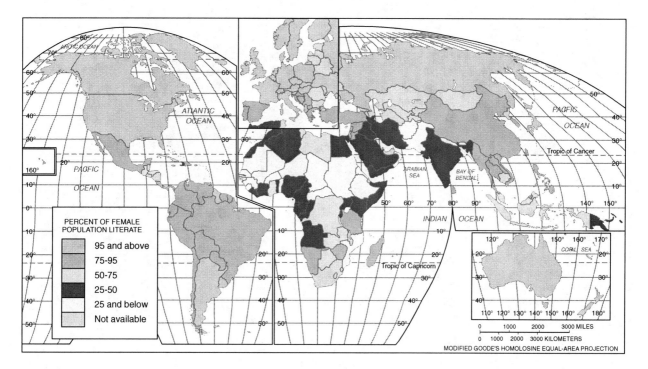

FIGURE 14.6
Literacy rate of women. The gender gap for literacy is most pronounced in the developing world, especially Africa, South Asia, and the Middle East. In most developing countries, the female literacy rate is much below the rate for men. Raising women's literacy rates is one of the most efficient means of stimulating economic and social development.

There are typically vast gender differences in literacy within developing countries. In many impoverished societies, desperately poor rural families can often only afford to send one child to school (the others are working the fields), and that child is very likely to be male. Unfortunately, worldwide, only 75 girls attend school for every 100 boys. In areas particularly disadvantageous to women, their literacy rates tend to be much lower than men's (Figure 14.6). In many nations, the literacy rate of women is less than 25 percent, whereas the literacy rate of men is between 25 percent and 75 percent. The Middle East and South Asia, where the role of women is clearly subservient to men, show the greatest disparities. However, in the highly developed world, the literacy rates of men and women are almost identical. The regions that have low percentages of women attending secondary school also generally have poor social and economic conditions for women. Indeed, raising women's literacy rates has been shown to lower fertility rates and to empower women economically and politically. In addition, because more people can read and write, a proliferation of newspapers, magazines, and scholarly journals improve and foster communication and exchange, which leads to further development by informing them of opportunities, circulating best practices, and so forth.

Health of a Population

Measures of health and welfare, in general, are much higher in developed nations than in LDCs. One measure of health and welfare is diet, typically measured as caloric consumption per capita (Figure 14.7). Most people in Africa do not receive the UN daily recommended allowance. However, in developed nations, the population consumes approximately one-third more than the minimum daily requirement and is therefore able to maintain a higher level of health. In some areas of each country, calories and food supplies are insufficient, even in the United States, where significant pockets of hunger and malnutrition exist. Conversely, an overabundance of cheap food and inadequate exercise have generated an obesity epidemic in this country, where lack of exercise and high-fat diets have caused waistlines to balloon. Obesity has become an epidemic worldwide; there are today, worldwide, more obese people than malnourished ones.

People in developed nations also have better access to doctors, hospitals, and health care providers. Figure 14.8 shows worldwide access to physicians as measured by persons per physician. For relatively developed nations, there is one doctor per 1000 people, but in developing countries, each person shares a doctor with many thousands of

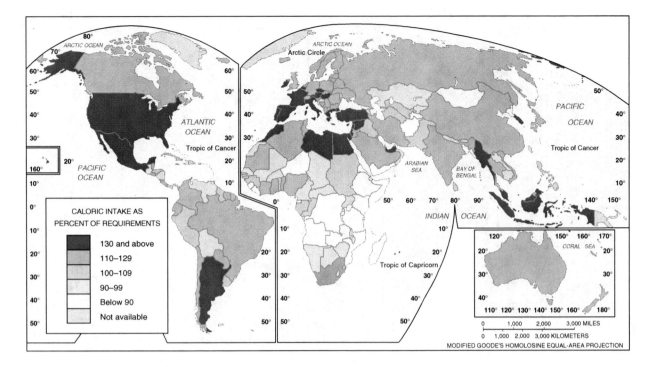

FIGURE 14.7
Daily caloric consumption per capita as a percentage of minimum nutritional requirements. Access to adequate nutrition is another measure of economic development. In many impoverished nations, malnutrition may be chronic. Conversely, many economically advanced countries, particularly the United States, suffer from an epidemic of obesity.

others. Africa by far has the worst access to health care (in some countries there are more than 15,000 people per physician, effectively meaning that most people *never* see one), followed by Southeast Asia and East Asia. Portions of the Middle East are also lacking in medical care. Everywhere, wealthier societies have better access to health care, although there are huge discrepancies within them as well, such as in the United States.

Infants and children are the most vulnerable members of any society, in part because their immunological systems are not as well developed as adults and partly because they lack effective political power to access health care resources. In developed nations, on the average, fewer than 10 babies in 1000 die within the first 100 days; in many less developed nations, more than 100 babies die per 1000 live births, the result of poor prenatal care, malnutrition, and infectious diseases. When there are economic downturns, droughts, or disruptions of the food supply brought on by war, they are generally the first to die. The geography of infant mortality (Figure 14.9)—the

An all-girls school in Kenya reflects that country's investment in human capital. The education of girls is an important means of raising standards of living and reducing birthrates, as well as providing economic opportunities for women.

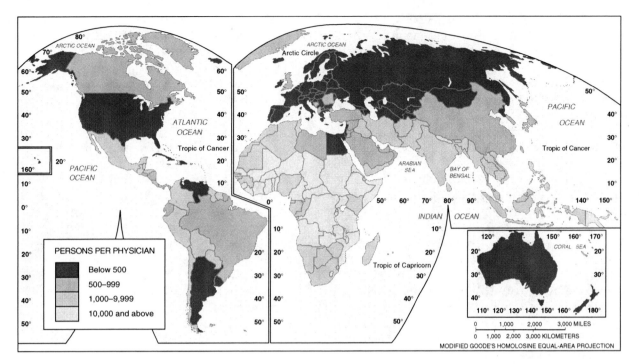

FIGURE 14.8

Persons per physician. An important measure of economic development is the number of persons per physician in a country. This measure is a surrogate for health care access, which includes hospital beds, medicine, and nurses and doctors. Most of Africa exhibits 10,000 people per physician, or more, while Europe and the United States average one doctor for every 200 people.

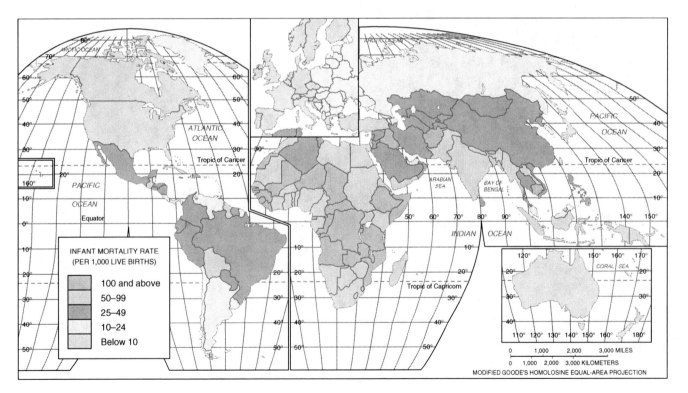

FIGURE 14.9

Infant mortality rates. Babies are the most vulnerable members of any society, and the percent who die before their first birthday is another measure of economic development and well-being. In the poorest nations, particularly Africa, more than 10 percent of babies die before their first birthday.

Development and Underdevelopment in the Developing World

proportion of babies who die before their first birthday—is thus perhaps the best measure of economic development or the lack of it. In much of Africa, more than 10 percent of infants do not live through their first year. In the developed First World, by contrast, infant mortality rates are very low. Notably, Cuba's infant mortality rate—6.0—is lower than that of the United States, which is 7.0, a discrepancy that reflects the former's investment in the health care and the latter's widespread unavailability of health insurance amid its poor.

AIDS has emerged as a significant threat worldwide. More than 23 million people have died of this disease, and an additional 45 million are infected with the HIV virus. The epicenter of the AIDS epidemic is sub-Saharan Africa (Figure 14.10), where in some countries 40 percent of the adult population is infected. The sub-Saharan region accounts for more than 60 percent of the people living with HIV worldwide, or some 25 million men, women, and children. AIDS is tightening its grip outside the United States and Europe. In India, researchers estimate that by the year 2020, 50 million people could be HIV positive. Half the prostitutes in Bombay are already infected, and doctors report that the disease is spreading along major truck routes and into rural areas, as migrant workers bring the virus home. In China, AIDS is spreading rapidly. The social consequences of this die-off are catastrophic, including millions of children who have lost their parents to the disease. Because AIDS has a long lead time in which infected people do not show symptoms, and because sexual behavior is very difficult to change, many fear that AIDS could lead to a depopulation of large parts of the world in the future comparable to the Black Death of the fourteenth century.

The reliability and quality of the food supply, access to clean drinking water, public health measures, ability to control infectious diseases, and access to health services all shape how long one lives. People in economically advanced countries have the luxury of living a relatively long time—often more than 75 years, on average—while those in poorer countries live considerably less (Figure 14.11). In parts of Africa, few adults can realistically expect to live past their fiftieth birthday. Thus, the geography of life expectancy is another measure of the health and welfare of a population.

Consumer Goods Produced

The quantity and quality of consumer goods purchased and distributed in a society is another measure of the level of economic development in that society. Easy availability of consumer goods means that a country's economic resources have fulfilled the basic human

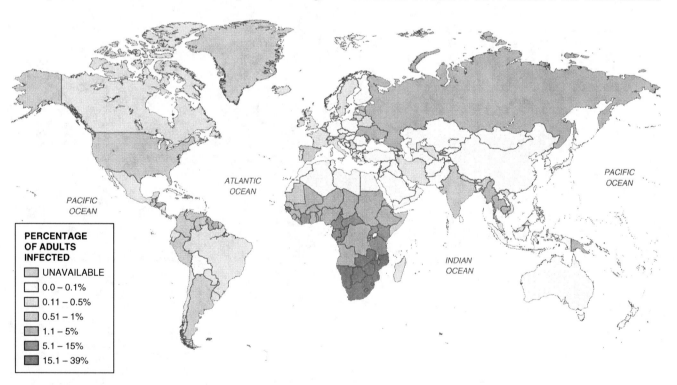

PERCENTAGE OF ADULTS INFECTED
- UNAVAILABLE
- 0.0 – 0.1%
- 0.11 – 0.5%
- 0.51 – 1%
- 1.1 – 5%
- 5.1 – 15%
- 15.1 – 39%

FIGURE 14.10

The geography of AIDS, 2005. Although AIDS does not kill as many people as malnutrition or heart disease, it ranks among the world's leading killers today, and the most rapidly growing. More than 23 million people have died of AIDS, and another 45 million are infected. The epicenter of the epidemic is Africa, where in some countries 40 percent of adults are HIV infected. The disease is only now making inroads into the huge populations of India and China and has the potential for creating a catastrophic depopulation in the future.

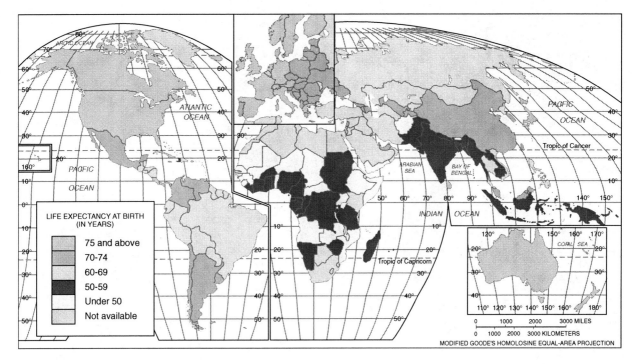

FIGURE 14.11
Life expectancy at birth. How long we can hope to live is another measure of economic development or the lack of it. In societies where people enjoy sufficient access to food, public health measures, and medical care, life expectancies are often over 75. In the poorest countries, in contrast, most people cannot expect to live beyond 50.

needs of shelter, clothing, and food, and more resources are left over to provide nonessential household goods and services. Automobiles, textiles, home electronics, jewelry, watches, refrigerators, and washing machines are some of the major consumer goods produced worldwide on varying scales. In industrialized countries, more than one television, telephone, or automobile exists for every two people. In developing nations, only a few of these products exist for a thousand people. For instance, the ratio of persons to television sets in developing countries is 150 to 1, and population to automobiles is 400 to 1. In California, the ratio for these consumer items is almost 1 to 1. The number of consumer goods such as telephones and televisions per capita is a good indicator of a country's level of economic development.

Urbanization in Developing Countries

In the industrialized West, urbanization occurred on the heels of the Industrial Revolution, that is, it was synonymous with industrialization (Chapter 2). While parts of the developing world are urbanized, in general LDCs lag behind the economically advanced countries in this regard. However, cities throughout the developing world are growing quickly, much more so than those in Europe, North America, Japan, or Australia. Today, about 56 percent of the world's people live in cities (Figure 14.12), an all-time high. However, the proportion of each country's

people that lives in cities varies widely around the globe (Figure 14.13). In parts of Latin America, urbanization rates resemble those of North America or Australia, where 75 percent or more of the people live in cities. In Asia and Africa, however, the proportions are much lower. Only 20 percent of China's people live in cities, and in wide swaths of Africa less than 20 percent do so.

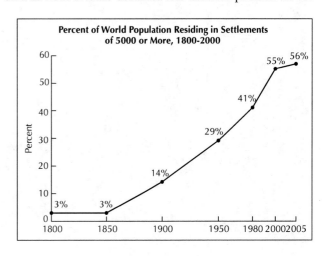

FIGURE 14.12
Percent of the world living in cities, 1800–2005. Today more than half of the planet's population lives in urban areas. Most urban growth occurs in the developing world, where large cities are fueled by waves of rural to urban migrants.

Development and Underdevelopment in the Developing World

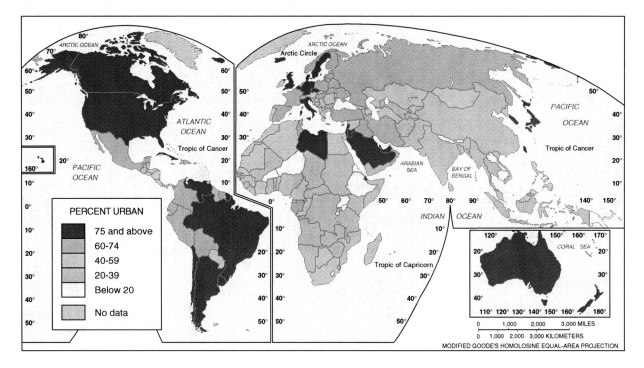

FIGURE 14.13
Urbanization rates. The proportion of people living in cities is another measure of economic development, although not a very accurate one. Generally, poor countries are less urbanized than wealthy ones. In China, for example, only 20 percent of the population lives in cities. However, in Latin America even relatively poor countries such as Brazil have high urbanization rates, where much of the poverty is clustered in large urban conurbations such as Sao Paolo and Rio de Janiero.

African children watching television. Although literacy levels increased between 1970 and 2000 in all but one country, literacy rates for women are still below 50 percent in 45 of the countries for which data are available. Literacy rates for men are below 50 percent in only 17 countries.

Urbanization in the developing world differs significantly from that in the West. Because the historical contexts of LDCs differ from that of the West, particularly through the impacts of colonialism, and because their mode of incorporation into the global division of labor was very different, the patterns of urban growth are also qualitatively different. Some countries in the developing world had well-established traditions of urbanization before the Europeans came, such as the Arab world and China. In others, powers such as Britain played a major role, constructing cities such as Calcutta in India, Rangoon in Myanmar (Burma), or Singapore; similarly, the Dutch started Batavia, Indonesia, which later became Jakarta.

Today, the vast bulk of the world's urban growth is in the developing world. The world's largest cities, for example, are found in Latin America and Asia, not Europe or North America (Table 14.1). In 2005, Mexico City and Sao Paolo, Brazil, vied for the rank of the world's largest metropolitan area, with roughly 25 million inhabitants each. Many of the others, with populations over 5 million, are located in China and India (Figure 14.14).

Moreover, cities in the developing world are growing much more rapidly than their counterparts in the developed countries. While natural growth rates in cities in the developing world is a little higher than that in the West, urbanization in LDCs is primarily due to the

Table 14.1

World's Largest Urban Areas, 1950, 1980, and 2000 (Millions)

1950		1980		2000	
New York	12.3	Tokyo	19.0	**Mexico City**	25.8
Shanghai	10.3	**Mexico City**	16.7	**Sao Paolo**	24.0
London	10.2	New York	15.6	Tokyo	22.2
Tokyo	6.7	**Sao Paulo**	15.5	**Calcutta**	16.5
Beijing	6.6	**Shanghai**	12.1	**Bombay**	16.0
Paris	5.4	**Buenos Aires**	10.8	New York	15.8
Tianjin	5.4	London	10.5	**Shanghai**	14.3
Buenos Aires	5.1	**Calcutta**	10.3	**Seoul**	13.8
Chicago	4.9	**Rio de Janiero**	10.1	**Tehran**	13.6
Moscow	4.8	**Seoul**	10.1	**Rio de Janiero**	13.3
Calcutta	4.4	Los Angeles	10.0	**Jakarta**	13.2
Los Angeles	4.0	Osaka	9.6	**Delhi**	13.2
Osaka	3.8	**Bombay**	9.5	**Buenos Aires**	13.2
Milan	3.6	**Beijing**	9.3	**Karachi**	12.0
Rio de Janiero	3.4	Moscow	8.9	**Beijing**	11.2
Philadelphia	2.9	Paris	8.8	**Dacca**	11.2
Bombay	2.9	**Tianjin**	8.0	**Cairo**	11.2
Mexico City	2.9	**Cairo**	7.9	**Manila**	11.1
Detroit	2.8	**Jakarta**	7.8	Los Angeles	11.0
Sao Paolo	2.7	Milan	7.5	**Bangkok**	10.7
Naples	2.7	**Tehran**	7.2	London	10.5
Leningrad	2.6	**Manila**	7.1	Osaka	10.5
Birmingham, U.K.	2.5	**Delhi**	7.0	Moscow	10.4
Cairo	2.4	Chicago	6.9	**Tianjin**	9.7
Boston	2.2	**Karachi**	6.2	**Lima**	9.1

Note: Cities in less developed countries are shown in boldface.
Source: National Research Council, 2003.

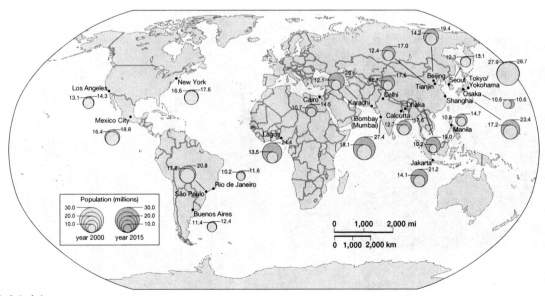

FIGURE 14.14

The location of the world's largest cities. The majority of the world's biggest cities are located not in the developed but in the developing world, particularly in China and India.

The informal economy—unregulated, untaxed, and generally consisting of low-paying service jobs—comprises a variety of occupations that employ large numbers of the urban poor in both the developing and industrialized countries. In LDCs, opportunities in the formal sector, including export-oriented multinational firms and the government, are often relatively scarce.

massive influx of rural-to-urban migrants, many of whom are displaced by agricultural mechanization, unequal land distribution, low crop prices, war, and high population growth in rural areas. To some extent, this pattern was true of cities in the developing West as well. However, because few developing countries have generated the industrial job growth that the West did during the nineteenth and early twentieth centuries, the labor markets and employment conditions in the developing world are fundamentally different. Thus, we must see LDC urban growth and rural crisis as two sides of one coin. Because many migrants move to the cities on the basis of their perceptions that there are greater opportunities to be found there (perceptions that may be erroneous due to imperfect information), they often find themselves plunged into desperate circumstances.

Assembly plants such as these in Mexico are an excellent example of a symbiotic relationship between less and more developed countries. The latter get cheap labor, while the former benefit through a boost in the local economy.

LDC urban labor markets generally do not generate sufficient employment opportunities, leading to high unemployment rates, or underemployment, in which migrants do not utilize their skills. Many find work in low-paying service jobs in the informal economy, including mining trash piles for recyclables. In Manila, the Philippines, for example, 30,000 people earn their living this way on the Payatas garbage dump, as adults and children work together, stepping over rotting debris to scavenge bits of plastic or tin cans. Others sell trinkets and food on the streets. Others find marginal incomes in prostitution, selling illegal drugs, the black market, illicit currency exchange, or as casual day laborers doing construction. Export-oriented jobs that tie cities to the global economy, such as the garment industry or electronic assembly plants—which, however exploitative they appear to Western ideas, still offer higher wages than most local opportunities—tend to be the exception, not the norm.

Residential patterns in developing countries' cities also differ from those in the West. Whereas in the developed countries the poor tend to be a minority, often consigned to the city center, in the developing world, the poor may be a majority of the city's inhabitants, depending on the overall level of economic development of that nation. Often, the relatively wealthy command the city centers, whereas the poor live in the urban periphery. In dilapidated houses, often self-made from local materials such as cinder blocks or sheets of tin, many urbanites inhabit squalid neighborhoods that go by a variety of names: slums, Brazilian *favelas*, Indonesian *kampong*, Turkish *gacekondu*, South African townships, West African *bidonvilles* (or "tin can cities"). Billions of people live today in such conditions, without adequate housing, electricity, roads, transportation systems, schools,

Most of the urban poor in the developing world live in decrepit, makeshift shelters, a reflection of their low incomes, inadequate employment opportunities, the lack of profit to lure builders of commodified housing, and their generally marginalized position within the world economy.

Favelas, or slum districts, on the outskirts of Rio de Janiero. This photo exemplifies the tendency of urban labor and housing markets in the developing world to cluster the wealthy in the center and the poor along the periphery, creating an inverse of the social geography of the American city.

clean water, or sewers. Often densities in such places are far higher than in any Western city. When migrants seize buildings or land that belongs to wealthy landowners, the government may deem such "squatter settlements" to be illegal and tear them down with bulldozers. Such communities can become more than just cesspools of misery, they can turn into breeding grounds of resentment and political activism against corrupt and uncaring governments.

Human Development Index

One measure of social and economic development that combines several types of information is the United Nation's Human Development Index (HDI), which includes life expectancy at birth, GDP per capita, and indices of schooling and literacy. Not surprisingly, the HDI varies widely among countries of the world (Figure 14.15; Table 14.2), reflecting standards of living and access to both private and public resources, which in turn are produced through various places' position in the world economy. The highest levels are found in western Europe, Japan, North America, Australia, and New Zealand, that is, the First World. sub-Saharan African countries dominate the lowest rungs of the HDI, indicative of the widespread poverty and misery found on that continent. In between lie most of Latin America, the Arab world, the former Soviet bloc, China, and South Asia. The HDI reflects the geography of human welfare and suffering, the ways in which the global economy, the legacy of colonialism, international investments (or lack thereof), and state policies shape the everyday lives of the planet's people.

Most of the world's people live in economically underdeveloped countries, and the world's largest cities are usually found there. Often the poor comprise the bulk of the population, and driven from agricultural regions by unequal land distribution and low commodity prices, flock to urban areas in chains of rural to urban migration. Within inadequate employment opportunities, low wages, and insufficient access to capital and public services, billions of people live in decrepit shantytowns without adequate water or sanitation.

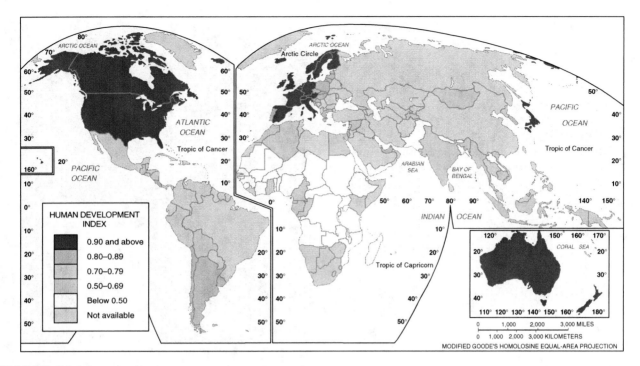

FIGURE 14.15
The Human Development Index is perhaps the best overall measure of economic development. The United Nations constructs a single index measuring life expectancy at birth, per capita purchasing power, years of schooling, and literacy rates. Note the massive difference between the First World and the Third. Western Europe is clearly distinguished from Eastern Europe and the former Soviet block. Central America and Bolivia have the lowest scores for Latin America. Sub-Saharan Africa, South Asia, and Southeast Asia have the lowest scores overall.

THE LOCATION OF UNDERDEVELOPMENT

The developed and less developed countries of the world are clearly separated on a map of the planet. A line drawn at 30° north latitude would put most of the developed countries to the north and the underdeveloped to the south, a division often known as the *North-South split.* Note that this dichotomy is not synonymous with the northern and southern hemispheres of the globe; most of the world's landmass is in the northern hemisphere, including much of the developing world (e.g., India and China). In this categorization, Australia and New Zealand, which are in the southern hemisphere, nonetheless belong economically to the North. *North* and *South* are thus shorthand terms to describe the First and Third Worlds, respectively, that is, they are social products, not referents to the world's physical geography.

The LDCs of the world—which contain the vast majority of the planet's population—include diverse societies in Latin America, East Asia (except Japan), Southeast Asia, South Asia, the predominantly Muslim world of southwest Asia and North Africa, and sub-Saharan Africa.

Latin America

Most inhabitants of this region are descendants of either Spanish or Portuguese colonists, slaves brought from Africa, and various indigenous peoples. Many people are *mestizos,* or mixed race. Even though many different native languages are still spoken by the native American peoples, Spanish and Portuguese are the dominant languages and Catholicism is the most widespread form of religion. This region shows a higher level

Table 14.2
Human Development Index, 2001

Less Developed Regions		Industrially Advanced Regions	
Latin America	.71	Japan	.98
East Asia	.61	North America	.98
Southeast Asia	.52	Australia/ New Zealand	.97
Middle East	.51	Eastern Europe	.87
South Asia	.29	Western Europe	.95
Sub-Saharan Africa	.23		

of urbanization compared with other less developed nations, as reflected in the massive conurbations of Mexico City and Sao Paulo.

Latin America's population is largely clustered along the coast, mainly the Atlantic Ocean, with the interior scarcely populated. Most of the region's economic activity is located along the south Atlantic coast, including Argentina, Uruguay, Brazil, Venezuela, and Mexico. One of the most striking characteristics of Latin America is its highly unequal distribution of wealth. A large share of the arable land is controlled by a few very wealthy families, who rent out parcels to landless tenant farmers.

Latin America is also one of the major world suppliers of raw materials. The major agricultural products of this region are tea, coffee, beef, and fruits grown for export rather than for local consumption. Many governments still practice economic policies that fail to encourage growth; the one exception is Chile, which switched to export promotion policies and has been the most rapidly growing economy in the region.

Southeast Asia

This region is a potpourri of nationalities and islands spread over a large area. Culturally, it is a mix of Buddhism and Islam, with several major languages. Indonesia is the most populous country in the region and comprises over 13,000 islands and 230 million people.

Indochina was long plagued by horrific warfare, which shattered the economies of Vietnam and Cambodia. Despite modest growth, they remain poor. Myanmar/Burma remains an isolated country trapped in poverty. Rice and plantation crops are the most common agricultural products.

The area is abundant in tin and contains substantial petroleum reserves, including Indonesia, the only Asian member of OPEC, and the tiny oil-rich sultanate of Brunei. The region's cheap labor has made it a leading manufacturer of textiles and clothing, but there are widespread discrepancies among states in terms of their economic development. Malaysia and Singapore are now major producers of electronic goods, and Singapore is a center of finance and telecommunications of worldwide significance. Thailand and Indonesia have recently joined the ranks of the newly industrializing countries (NICs), attracting foreign capital and developing a more diverse export capacity. Cities such as Bangkok have become congested with automobiles and expensive. The Philippines, in contrast, remains mired in severe poverty, a reflection of the Spanish land grant system and endemic government corruption.

Markets in Asia. Frequently, markets in the developing world are poorly developed, reflecting the partially commodified nature of social life there. Effective markets require enforced property rights and an infrastructure to work well.

East Asia (Excluding Japan)

East Asia is a vast, heavily populated region that has enjoyed the most rapid rate of economic growth in the world since World War II. Culturally, it is dominated by Buddhism.

China is the region's giant, with 1.3 billion people; despite its economic success, it still ranks among the world's poorest countries. The bulk of Chinese—80 percent—live in rural areas, including 700,000 agricultural villages. From the ascendancy of communism in 1949 to the death of Mao Zedong in 1976, China was an isolated country ruled by a Communist Party pursuing unadulterated socialism. Major events of this period include the Great Leap Forward, in which 30 million starved to death, and the Cultural Revolution of 1966–1976, a period of massive social disruption.

Since 1979, China has undergone an enormous economic and social transformation. Most communist regulations have been loosened, and market imperatives dominate in an ostensibly socialist country; farmers can now own land, control their own production, and sell their products in the marketplace. The government still has a firm grasp on the everyday lives of the citizens, but a majority of Chinese feel the country is better off today than it was several decades ago. China is the largest recipient of foreign direct investment (FDI) in the developing world, and its coastal regions have experienced rapid economic growth, including the miraculous transformation of Guangdong province in the south, which has close ties to Hong Kong.

Outside of China, Taiwan and South Korea have enjoyed rapid rates of growth since the 1960s, making them textbook examples of NICs. They benefited from being front-line states during the cold war, with massive U.S. military and economic assistance. With little arable land, they relied heavily on skilled labor and export promotion policies to advance into high-value-added goods, including steel, ships, and electronic goods, and have sizeable middle classes as a result. South Korea has become one of the most successful countries of the developing world, with a large middle class. North Korea, in contrast, suffers deepening poverty and famine.

South Asia

This area boasts the world's second largest population and some of the world's poorest people. Formerly a British colony, it split into India and Pakistan in 1947; Bangladesh seceded from Pakistan in 1971. India and Pakistan have fought several wars in the past, and continue to dispute possession of the region of Kashmir; both now possess nuclear weapons.

India is dominated by Hinduism, whereas Pakistan and Bangladesh, with roughly 160 million and 144 million people, respectively, are overwhelmingly Muslim. Population densities are high, as it is the natural rate of population increase, and the region has huge pools of poor people. India, the largest country of the region with over 1 billion people, overshadows its neighbors demographically and economically. India is the leading producer of certain world crops such as cotton. Its government long practiced policies of import substitution and protectionism that greatly slowed economic growth. Recently, as the government turned toward more export-oriented policies, western India has enjoyed modest economic growth, including the production of automobiles, movies, and software. In contrast, eastern India lags behind, as has Bangladesh.

The majority of South Asia's people live in villages and subsist directly off of the land, growing rice under quasi-feudal social relations. Many cities in the region, such as Calcutta, Madras, Delhi, Bombay, Dacca, and Karachi, contain large numbers of urban poor. Economic development is progressing slowly as most of the achievements have been erased by the rapidly growing population. Women tend to suffer harsh social and economic circumstances, and their opportunities for advancement are limited.

Middle East and North Africa

Dominated physically by deserts, this region lacks a substantial agricultural base; due to chronic shortages of water, many food products must be imported. Islam is the overriding religion, with the exception of Israel. The region's major asset is its immense petroleum reserves, the revenues from which are used to finance economic development. Culturally, this domain is dominated by Arab states, which exhibit considerable variations in economies and standards of living. Not all countries in the Middle East have large oil reserves, which are concentrated mainly in the Persian Gulf region. In general, Arab countries with large populations (e.g., Egypt) lack oil reserves, while the major petroleum exporters (e.g., Saudi Arabia, Kuwait, the United Arab Emirates) have relatively small populations. Population growth in the Arab states continues at very high levels, creating societies with large numbers of unemployed young people.

The reasons for the region's low level of development despite the presence of petroleum reserves include repressive governments that do not favor growth. Most Arab governments are repressive and at best only quasi-democratic. Some argue that the revenues from petroleum inhibit motivations to diversify their economies; in this sense, resources can be a curse rather than a blessing. Islamic traditionalism also challenges economic development in some areas; for example, women's roles in business and public life are sharply restricted, and financial markets are hindered by the Koranic prohibition against interest. The region has been severely affected by political instability. Fundamentalist Shiite Muslims took over Iran in 1979 and have promoted revolutions to cleanse the land of Westernized values and institutions elsewhere. Several wars hampered economic growth in the region, including the 1979–1989 war between Iraq and Iran, in which 1 million people died; the two American wars against Iraq (1991 and 2003), the latter of which is ongoing; civil wars in Lebanon, which decimated its banking industry; several wars between Israel and its Arab neighbors, (1948, 1956, 1967, and 1973); and constant strife between Israel and the Palestinians.

Israel is the region's only country not dominated by Muslims and its sole democracy. Israel is also the Middle East's most economically advanced state, in part because of large American subsidies, and has become a significant exporter of high-technology products and computer software. However, Israel has long been mired in conflict with the Palestinians, which has depressed the political stability of the region, including tourism and foreign investment.

Sub-Saharan Africa

Sub-Saharan Africa is by far the poorest region in the world. Despite the fact that it has a surprisingly low population density and an abundance of natural resources, most people live in poverty and suffer from poor health and a lack of education. The legacy of the long European colonial era still lives on in African countries, whose states are relatively artificial constructions wracked by tribal conflicts. Africa's artificial boundaries are the source of numerous wars, often tribal in nature. The governments of most of Africa have proved to be too corrupt and indifferent to the needs of their populations, spending most of their limited funds on the military rather than their civilian populations. Over the last 30 years, wars in Angola, Mozambique, Rwanda, Congo/Zaire, Liberia, Sierra Leone, Somalia, Ethiopia, Eritrea, and Sudan have killed over 30 million people. Famine claims the lives of another 15 million annually. Africa's economies are largely centered on the production of raw materials, including copper, uranium, diamonds, and gold. Low prices on the world resources and commodities market have contributed to the continent's economic malaise.

Africa also suffers from high rates of population growth, as its fertility rates are the highest in the world. The demand for farmland and overgrazing have stripped many agricultural areas of their potential to grow crops. Deforestation has decimated the continent's rich ecosystems and contributed to the worldwide crisis in biodiversity loss. AIDS has claimed the lives of millions, and in many countries more than one-third of all adults are infected with HIV. The epidemic has produced millions of orphans and shows little sign of slowing down. Malaria and other diseases are endemic in much of the continent. As a result of numerous wars, corrupt governments, rapid population growth, economic mismanagement, disease, drought, and lack of foreign investment, Africa is the only region in the world that has become poorer since World War II. By any measure, Africans are the poorest people in the world and the ones most in need of economic growth.

CHARACTERISTIC PROBLEMS OF LESS DEVELOPED COUNTRIES

The developing world encompasses a vast array of societies with enormous cultural and economic differences. Nonetheless, several characteristics tend to be found throughout these nations to one degree or another. Obviously, the more economically developed a country is, the less likely it is to exhibit these qualities.

Rapid Population Growth

Can we ascribe the problems of LDCs to rapid population growth? We must be careful to avoid the simplistic Malthusian error of ascribing all of the world's problems to population growth. Nonetheless, in many countries, the rate of growth does exceed productivity gains in agriculture and other sectors, diminishing the average standard of living. Many scholars argue that rapid population growth must be controlled if development is to succeed.

In many LDCs, particularly Africa, rapid population growth rates tax the available food supplies. Some LDCs (particularly in Africa) approach levels of subsistence and starvation. Rapid population growth also reduces the ability of households to save; therefore, the economy cannot accumulate investment capital (Figure 14.16). In addition, with rapid population growth, more investment is required to maintain a level of real capital growth per person. If public or private investment fails to keep pace with the population growth, each worker will be less productive, having fewer tools and equipment with which to produce goods. This declining productivity results in reduced per capita incomes and economic stagnation. Rapid population growth in agriculturally dependent countries, such as China and India, means that the land must be further subdivided and used more heavily than ever. Smaller plots from subdivision inevitably lead to overgrazing, overplanting, and the pressing need to increase food production for a growing population from a limited amount of space. Many LDCs are rapidly urbanizing. Rapid population growth generally entails large flows of rural farmers to urban areas and more urban problems. Housing, congestion, pollution, crime, and lack of medical attention are all seriously worsened by the rapid urban population growth.

Assuredly, a rapid increase in population—especially the number and proportion of young dependents—creates serious problems in terms of food supply, public education, and health and social services; it also intensifies the employment problem. However, a high rate of population growth was once a characteristic of present-day developed countries, and it did not prevent their development. This observation makes it difficult to argue that population growth necessarily leads to underdevelopment or that population control necessarily aids development. Thus it is erroneous and simplistic to blame all the LDCs' problems on population growth, which is one of several factors that contribute to poverty. Focusing on rapid population growth (i.e., the Malthusian argument laid out in Chapter 3) detracts

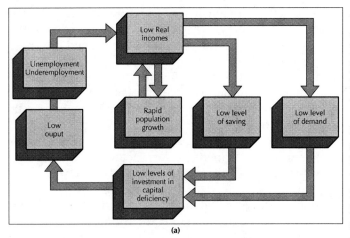

(a)

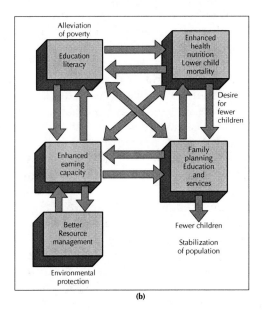

(b)

FIGURE 14.16
The cycle of poverty. Economic development means intervention in a host of intertwined variables that conspire to keep people poor. These include the historical context of a developing country and its linkages to the world system, as well as internal factors such as population growth, investment levels, and government policies.

from other, more important but politically controversial factors such as the legacy of colonialism and governments' indifference to investing in their populations and infrastructure.

Unemployment and Underemployment

Unemployment and underemployment are major problems in LDCs. Put bluntly, their economies rarely generate enough jobs for all, for a variety of reasons. *Unemployment* is a condition in which people who want to work cannot find jobs. *Underemployment* means that working people are not able to work as many hours as they would like, usually much less than 8 hours per day, and that their skills and talents are underutilized. Reliable statistics on unemployment and underemployment in LDCs are difficult to obtain, but unemployment in many developing countries often exceeds 20 percent.

Many cities in LDCs have recently experienced rapid flows of migrants from rural areas as a result of low agricultural prices and lack of land reform. Large number of migrants are attracted to cities by the expectation of jobs and higher salaries, expectations that may not be met in reality. Thus, these flows exemplify the influence of imperfect information upon spatial decision making. Once in the cities, many migrants cannot find work and contribute to the crisis of unemployment. Other migrants find limited employment as shop clerks, handicraft peddlers, or street vendors, often forming part of the unregulated, low-wage, informal economy.

Unemployment and underemployment are not the sole reasons for the problems of LDCs. Jobs are generated only when there is sufficient investment, which is lacking in most LDCs. Thus unemployment is much more complex than simply the willingness of people to work; it involves a vast, complex institutional framework in which jobs are generated, occupations and skills created and maintained, and investment capital is channeled.

Low Labor Productivity

Are the problems of LDCs a result of low labor productivity? It is true that a day's toil in a typical developing country produces very little commercial value compared with a day's work in a typical developed country. This is particularly evident in agriculture. Human productivity in a developing country may be as little as one-fiftieth of that in a developed country. Why is this?

One reason for low levels of productivity is the small scale of farming operations often found in LDCs, which generate few *economies of scale* (Chapter 5). Another is that capital investment rates are often very low, interest rates are relatively high, and most capital is generated by foreign-owned firms, whose major incentive is exports and profits, not job generation. Most developing countries lack the machines, engines, power networks, and factories that enable people and resources to produce at maximum levels of efficiency. In addition, LDCs are less able to invest in *human capital*. Investments in human capital—such as education, health, and other social services—prepare a population to be productive workers. Schools are often inadequate and literacy rates may be comparatively low.

Low labor productivity in LDCs is exacerbated by a lack of organizational skills and the absence of adequate management, both of which are necessary for increased productivity. Many of the most skilled workers immigrate to economically advanced countries, where they are more highly paid for their labor. The United States and Europe, for example, are replete with some of the best-trained labor from LDCs, including doctors, engineers, mathematicians, and scientists who have come looking for better salaries from companies or the government. This immigration has contributed to a so-called *brain drain,* whereby LDCs lose talented people to the developed world.

Although it must be acknowledged that low labor productivity is a universal attribute of LDCs, it is not a *causative* factor. The important question to consider is this: What prevents labor productivity from improving in developing countries?

Lack of Capital and Investment

Most LDCs suffer from a lack of capital accumulation in the form of machinery, equipment, factories, public utilities, and infrastructure in general. The more capital, the more tools available for each worker; thus there is a close relationship between output per worker and per capita investment and, in turn, between investment and income. If a nation hopes to increase its output, it must find ways to increase per capita capital investment.

In most cases, increasing the amount of arable land for an LDC is no longer a possibility. Most cultivable land is already in use (Chapter 6). Therefore, capital accumulation for an LDC must come from savings and investment. If an LDC can save, rather than spend, all its income and invest some of its earnings, resources will be released from the production of consumer goods and be available for the production of capital goods. But barriers to saving and investing are often high in LDCs, including high interest rates, political unrest, corruption,

Unpaved road near Kumasi, Ghana, exemplifies a transportation infrastructure suffering from insufficient investment, an obstacle to development.

and inefficient regulations. (The United States also had notable problems with low savings and investing rates.) An LDC has even less margin for savings and investing, particularly when domestic output is so low that all of it must be used to support the many needs of the country. Ethiopia, Bangladesh, Uganda, Haiti, and Madagascar save between 2 percent and 3 percent of their domestic outputs. In 2003, India and China managed to save an average of 21 percent of their domestic outputs, compared with 20 percent for Japan, 15 percent for Germany, and 5 percent for the United States.

Many LDCs suffer from *capital flight,* which means that wealthy individuals and firms in these countries have invested and deposited their monies in overseas ventures and banks in developed countries for safekeeping. They have done so for fear of expropriation by politically unstable governments, unfavorable exchange rates brought on by hyperinflation in the LDCs, high levels of taxation, and the possibility of business and bank failures. World Bank statistics suggest that inflows of foreign aid and bank loans to LDCs were almost completely offset by capital flight. In 2000, for example, Mexicans were estimated to have held about $100 billion in assets abroad. This amount is roughly equal to their international debt. Venezuela, Argentina, and Brazil also have foreign holdings between $30 and $60 billion each.

Finally, investment obstacles in LDCs have impeded capital accumulation. The two main problems with investment in LDCs are (1) lack of investment opportunities comparable to those available in developed countries and (2) lack of incentives to invest locally. Usually LDCs have low levels of domestic spending per person, so their markets are weak compared with those of advanced nations. Without domestic industries, consumers must often turn to imports to satisfy their needs, especially for high-value-added products. Factors that keep the markets weak are a lack of effective demand backed by purchasing power, a lack of trained personnel to manage and sell products at the local level, and a lack of government support to ensure stability. There is also a lack of infrastructure to provide transportation, management, energy production, and community services—housing, education, public health—which are needed to improve the environment for investment activity.

Inadequate and Insufficient Technology

Typically, LDCs lack the technologies necessary to increase productivity and accumulate wealth. Some LDCs acquire new production techniques through technology transfer that may accompany investment by multinational corporations, as happened in many of the NICs of East Asia. OPEC nations benefited from foreign technology in oil exploration, drilling, and refining. Unfortunately, for LDCs to put this available technology

The trains are crowded in Bangladesh. Typically, resources for feeding and moving the poor are inadequate. Such systems generate low rates of profit and do not attract large investors. Thus, transport systems in impoverished countries generally are provided by financially strained governments, many of which are reeling under low export prices and neoliberal programs imposed by the IMF. Thus crowding is not simply a result of population growth but reflects the political economy of public services in developing countries.

to use, they must have a certain level of capital goods (machinery, factories, etc.), which they by and large do not possess. The need is to channel the flow of technologically superior capital goods that have high levels of reliability to the developing nations so that they can improve their output.

In developed countries, technology has been developed primarily to save labor and to increase output, resulting in capital-intensive production techniques. However, in LDCs, capital intensification tends to displace workers, eliminating critically needed jobs. Thus LDCs need capital-saving technology that is labor intensive. In agriculture, much of the midlatitude technology of the developed countries (e.g., wheat harvesting combines) is unsuited for low-latitude agricultural systems with tropical or subtropical climates and soils.

Unequal Land Distribution

In most developing countries, in which a large part of the population lives in rural areas, land is a critical resource essential to survival. Unfortunately, land is often highly unequally distributed, and a small minority of wealthy landowners controls the vast bulk of arable (farmable) land. In Brazil, for example, 2 percent of the population owns 60 percent of the arable land; in Columbia, 4 percent owns 56 percent; in El Salvador,

1 percent owns 41 percent; in Guatemala, 1 percent owns 36 percent of the land; and in Paraguay, 1 percent owns an astounding 80 percent of all land suitable for farming. These numbers reflect the historical legacy of the Spanish land grant system imposed over centuries of colonialism. Wealthy rural oligarchs often control vast estates and plantations designed primarily for export crops, not domestic consumption. The majority of the rural population, consequently, is landless and must sell its labor, often at very low (below subsistence) wages, and live in serflike conditions. Shortages of land are accentuated by agricultural mechanization and high population growth. The result is frequent political turmoil, including demands for land redistribution; in much of Latin America, peasant social movements to regain control of the land are very active, and violence over land possession is frequent. Further, rural areas with high natural growth rates and widespread poverty become the source of waves of rural-to-urban migration, which often swamps cities with desperately poor people seeking jobs.

Throughout much of the developing world, land reform, which is vitally important to increased agricultural output, is lacking because the government is too inept or corrupt to redistribute the land owned by a few wealthy families. For some nations, such as the Philippines, land reform is the single most pressing problem deterring them from economic development.

In contrast, strong action taken by the South Korean government after the Korean War allowed for increased productivity and the development of an industrial and commercial middle class that made South Korea one of the success stories of the Pacific Rim.

Poor Terms of Trade

A country's terms of trade refer to the relative values of its exports and imports (Chapter 12). When the terms of trade are good, a country sells, on average, relatively high-valued commodities (e.g., manufactured goods) and imports relatively low-valued ones (e.g., agricultural products). This situation generates foreign revenues that allow the LDC to pay off debt or to reinvest in infrastructure or new technologies. Unfortunately, many LDCs, with economies distorted by centuries of colonialism, in which they became suppliers of minerals and foodstuffs, export low-valued goods, and must import expensive high-valued, manufactured ones. Many LDCs rely heavily on exports of goods such as petroleum, copper, tin and iron ore, timber, coffee, and fruits and must import items such as automobiles, pharmaceuticals, office equipment, and machine tools. The worldwide glut in raw materials, including petroleum, wheat, and many mineral ores, has depressed the prices for many LDC exports. Without indigenous manufacturing, many are forced to sell low-valued goods such as bananas for high-valued ones such as computers.

This situation makes it difficult to generate foreign revenues and exacerbates a country's debt problems. Further, poor terms of trade perpetuate a country's cycle of poverty: Low foreign revenues yield little to reinvest, which helps to create a shortage of capital, resulting in low rates of productivity.

Foreign Debt

Much of the developing world is deeply in debt to foreign governments and banks. In 2005, total world debt amounted to more than $2.6 trillion (Figure 14.17). Some nations, notably Argentina and Nigeria, have debts in excess of 100% of their annual GDPs (Figure 14.18). Having borrowed hundreds of billions of dollars, they find themselves unable to repay either the interest or the principal. Debt repayments often consume a large share of their export revenues, which might otherwise be used for development.

Debt restructuring policies imposed by the International Monetary Fund typically tie debt relief to "structural adjustment," which includes reductions in government subsidies to the poor and devaluations of currencies (which drive up the costs of imports), policies that lower the quality of life for hundreds of millions, if not billions, of people. For example, a poor mother in an LDC with a sick infant relies on imported pharmaceuticals when her country lacks a domestic industry; IMF-imposed currency devaluations will drive

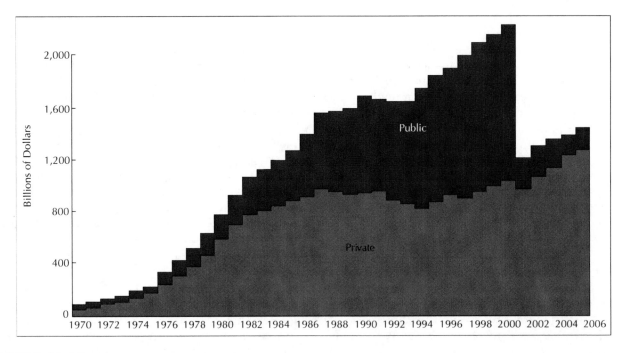

FIGURE 14.17
The external debt of all developing countries grew substantially between 1970 and 2005. It consists of two parts: the public debt, which is owed to foreign governments, and the private debt, which is owed to private banks.

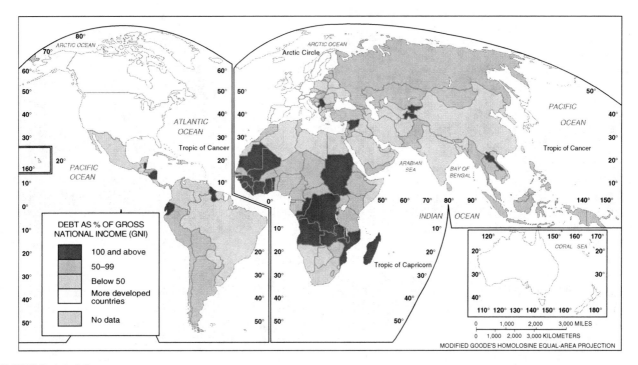

FIGURE 14.18

Debt as a percentage of gross national income, 2004. Many developing countries became indebted to finance future development, only to find themselves confronted with low prices for their exports and repatriated profits from foreign direct investment. A large share of government revenues and earnings from exports thus must pay the principal and interest of their debt. Although the poor often did not benefit from these loans, it is their taxes that are often used to pay them back.

up the costs of these necessities, often making them out of reach for the poor, who need them the most. For these reasons, scholars and politicians involved in international development often call for a debt moratorium to allow LDCs a respite from what are often crushing debt burdens.

The origins of the debt crisis lay in the 1970s and 1980s, when many LDCs took out large loans with the expectation of paying them off when their economies improved in the future. Western banks had a huge influx of petrodollars and were eager for borrowers; developing countries were happy to take advantage of this unaccustomed access to cheap loans with few strings attached. The borrowing enabled them to maintain domestic growth.

But a series of major economic changes in the world scene meant that many of these loans could not be repaid. The OPEC oil embargoes of 1973 and 1979 sent the price of crude oil skyrocketing, creating a cash-flow crisis for oil-importing LDCs. Furthermore, monies spent for oil could have been used for economic development, such as for increased infrastructure, improved education, and needed agricultural reforms. The debt of oil-importing LDCs grew from $150 billion in 1973 to $800 billion by 1985. Even oil-exporting nations such as Mexico, Libya, and Nigeria overborrowed based on

their expectations of rapidly inflated oil prices. When oil prices fell significantly in the 1980s, these nations found themselves saddled with debts that they could not afford.

The mounting debt caused concerns about the stability of the international monetary system. The cause of this instability was the overexpansion of credit, particularly through the Eurocurrency market in the 1960s and 1970s, which led to a crisis that had its roots in the overaccumulation of capital and the declining rate of profit. In 1982, Mexico ran into difficulties meeting interest and capital payments on its debts. Brazil and Argentina also appeared ready to default. A collapse of the financial system was forestalled by a series of emergency measures designed to prevent large debtor countries from defaulting on their loans. These measures involved banks, the IMF, the Bank for International Settlements, and the governments of lending countries in massive bail-out exercises that accompanied debt reschedulings.

The debt overhang persisted because debt-service ratios—annual interest and amortization payments as a percentage of total exports—remained at dangerously high levels. This factor caused a second financial crisis of global proportions in 1997 that began in Southeast Asia. The origins of the Asian crisis have been attributed to several factors, most of which revolved around the region's intersections with global finance, particularly in the domain of exchange rates. Asian financial markets suffered from insufficient regulation, leading to political considerations in credit allocation based heavily on corrupt, cronyist ties to ruling families. Often badly managed and poorly audited, banks and other lending agencies engaged in excessively risky lending practices, with assets exaggerated by inflation rates, leading to high debt-to-equity ratios. Poor recordkeeping masked a deterioration of fundamentals, the primary measures of economic health that attract or repel capital on a global basis. When exposed to sudden onsets of illiquidity or bankruptcy, the Asian financial system turned out to be highly fragile.

The crisis found its genesis in Thailand, which offers a textbook example of a small country confronted with large capital flows. In July 1997, the saturated Thai commercial property market bubble burst; the baht, pegged to the dollar (a move that had been proclaimed as providing stability), should have weakened along with the banks and property markets, but the Thai government, determined to avoid the embarrassment of devaluation, stubbornly supported the baht. Thai money market managers, knowing their currency was overvalued, sought to make a quick killing by selling baht. When Thailand's investors began buying dollars, they attracted the attention of foreign speculators, particularly foreign hedge fund speculators, who, sensing the nation's difficulty, bet heavily against the baht. Fresh from the Mexican currency crisis of 1995, American speculators in particular sought greater returns in the economically greener pastures of the Asian NICs. Determined to preserve its currency at all costs, the Bank of Thailand risked everything to protect the nation's currency against the foreign onslaught, until it was finally forced to let go, sending the baht into a free fall of devaluation.

The Thai "blood baht" soon spiraled into a vortex of financial instability that included all of East Asia except China, with secondary effects on Australia, North America, and Europe. The "Asian flu" leapfrogged in 1997–1998 from Thailand to Malaysia to Indonesia to South Korea to Taiwan to Hong Kong. A massive reversal of capital flows, which had swept into the region for decades, saw tens of billions of dollars leave for the United States and Europe; in 1997 alone, net capital flows out of Thailand were equivalent to 10.7 percent of the GDP. Interest rates rose throughout the region, stimulating a banking crisis. Decreased earnings led to deflationary shock. Corporate bankruptcies soared, especially among firms with the most debt exposure and highest debt-to-equity ratios. Stock exchanges throughout Asia suffered a repeated series of drubbings, falling as much as 75 percent by the end of 1998. Unemployment rates, generally below 5 percent before

the crisis, typically doubled or tripled. Rising poverty rates for many meant severe deprivation, including hunger and malnutrition; Indonesia, beset by 60 percent inflation in 1998 (particularly in staples such as rice and cooking oil), witnessed 40 million people, or about 20 percent of the populace, sink into poverty. Poor people, frequently peasants attracted to urban areas by the presence of foreign firms and jobs, often took the brunt of the burden, forced into deeper poverty or a return to subsistence agriculture in the hinterlands. Notably, those economies least connected to the international financial markets, such as Vietnam and the Philippines, proved to be the least susceptible. The economic turmoil also had political repercussions, leading to new, more democratic governments in South Korea and Indonesia.

Some LDCs required foreign banks to rewrite their loans and cancel or *write down* a portion of the principal and interest. The result was a loss of confidence in the future ability of many LDCs to repay. At the same time, the United States began to generate enormous federal budget deficits; to finance these, it borrowed a large portion of available investment revenue, driving up interest rates worldwide. Higher oil prices, declining prices for raw material exports, higher world interest rates, an increase in the value of the U.S. dollar, and a decline in public and private lending to LDCs because of loss of confidence all contributed to the debt crisis that prevails today.

Restrictive Gender Roles

Deeply entrenched social stratification systems work against people, especially women, in many developing countries. Gender refers to the socially reproduced differences—including both privileges and obligations—between women and men, and permeates every society's allocation of resources and people's life chances. Typically, gender roles work to the advantage of men and the disadvantage of women.

The economic, political, and social status of women around the world is spatially variable. Worldwide, nowhere can women claim the same rights and opportunities as men. Women account for most of the world's 1.3 billion people living in extreme poverty. In most countries, women do most of the field work while still being responsible for household chores such as cooking, carrying water, and raising children. In some countries with more mechanized forms of agriculture, such as most of Latin America, men assume the job of plowing, with female participation strongly diminished in the field. In these cases, women work more in the market.

Women still spend more time working than men in all regions except Anglo America and Australia, and

In Mali, women often must travel several miles a day from their villages to gather firewood. This task is usually a woman's chore in most countries and exemplifies the fact that women almost everywhere work harder and longer than do men.

their wages are lower everywhere. In Muslim areas, women are not very economically active outside of the home because of religious prohibitions. In Latin America, labor force participation of women in the economy is increasing but mostly outside of the agricultural sector. Sub-Saharan Africa, India, and Southeast Asia are highly dependent on female farm and market income as well as commodified labor in the waged labor market. At a world scale, women generally garner only 60 percent to 70 percent of what men earn, often for the same work. This ratio is remarkably widespread, including the United States, in which women comprise the bulk of the poor and where women occupy less than 3 percent of the highest levels of management and ownership.

Corrupt and Inefficient Governments

Often, LDC governments are controlled by bureaucrats whose primary interest is catering to the wealthy elite, creating governments that are at best indifferent and often outright hostile to the needs of their own populations. Many LDC public policies are ineffectual or counterproductive, frequently ignoring the rural areas in favor of cities. Government jobs are frequently allocated through patronage, not a merit system. For example, in Africa, government jobs often go disproportionately to members of the same tribe as the president. The military is often the most well-funded and well-organized institution and may be a source of

political instability, as during military takeovers of the government in coups d'état. Corruption often is endemic and may become a way of life, generating inefficiency and inequality. During the cold war, both superpowers backed oppressive regimes throughout the developing world with subsidies and arms. In poor countries, dictatorial governments often curtail their citizens' civil liberties, censoring the media and imprisoning or executing dissidents. Attacks on journalists, labor union leaders, student movements, religious groups, and ethnic minorities are often common under such situations. Thus, poor nations often have oppressive governments; widespread and well-protected civil liberties are more common with economic development. Understandably, many people feel alienated from their own governments under these conditions and may sympathize with various resistance movements, contributing to frequent political instability.

LDC governments, often with insufficient resources, frequently have great difficulty building or maintaining their nation's infrastructures. Roads, bridges, tunnels, and highways may fall into disrepair, driving up transportation costs. Dams and airports likewise may be neglected. Electrical power stations may not be maintained correctly, leading to power outages. Unsanitary water supplies become major carriers of infectious diseases such as cholera. Because the infrastructure is essential to economic development, governments that do not reinvest in their nation's transportation, water, and communication lines do not facilitate the process of economic growth.

Similarly, public services in many LDCs are often underfunded and inadequate. This means that public schools—the major avenue of upward mobility for many—may fail to educate the nation's young, leading to high illiteracy rates, especially for girls. Salaries for teachers are often too low for them to support themselves. Inadequate health care, including severe shortages of physicians and nurses, depresses the health of the labor force and lowers the productivity of labor. Underfunded transportation systems make circulation within and among cities difficult and expensive in terms of forgone time. Thus, images of crowded buses and trains in countries such as India testify to government priorities as much as population growth. Only the military tends to be a well-funded public service in much of the world.

Trends and Solutions

Worldwide, the gap between the rich and the poor is widening. The World Bank estimates that in 2004 the global poverty rate was 24 percent or about 1.5 billion people. In relative terms, the two regions of the world with the greatest proportions of people living in poverty are Latin America and sub-Saharan Africa. However, in absolute numbers, Asia is home to the greatest number of the world's poor, including vast numbers on the Indian subcontinent. There are indicators that the numbers of the poor in Asia may be declining, while the percentage of sub-Saharan Africa living in poverty is increasing quickly.

There is clearly no one-size-fits-all approach to ending poverty in poor countries. Policy analysts generally argue that poverty-reducing strategies must include the following: investing in health care and education, protecting land tenure rights for the rural poor, incorporating informal sectors of the economy into the formal sector, establishing political stability, democratizing decision making through representative government, debt relief, ending developed countries' trade restrictions against imports from less developed countries, and increasing women's decision-making power in the household. Obviously, these steps are difficult to implement, often because powerful, entrenched interests benefit from the status quo. Perhaps the best hope lies in a smoothly functioning world economy that can pull hundreds of millions of people out of poverty, as has happened in much of East Asia.

MAJOR PERSPECTIVES ON DEVELOPMENT

Theories of development have existed for many years. The earliest of them can be traced to the classical economists of the eighteenth century such as Adam Smith.

But discussion of the term *development* in the social sciences is fairly recent and flourished after World War II. Three perspectives on development in economic geography hold widely varying assumptions and conclusions, including modernization theory, dependency theory, and world-systems theory. All of these grapple with the complex question of how the global economy shapes patterns of opportunities for development in individual countries.

Modernization Theory

The first and most widely accepted theory of development is *modernization theory*. This perspective starts with the central question: Does the development of the less-developed world follow the same historical trajectory as the West? The intellectual origins of this line of thought lie with the famous sociologist Max Weber, who attributed the success of northern Europe during the Industrial Revolution to the Protestant ethic (Chapter 2). Weber's work established a precedent that viewed economic development and social change as a function of people's ideas, culture, and beliefs rather than their social relations and historical context.

Weber's ideas were enormously popular in the United States following World War II; they were translated and elaborated by Talcott Parsons. The American version tended to equate the "modern" with Western, denying the possibility of modern, non-Western cultures. Writing during a period of intense competition between the United States and the Soviet Union for influence in the developing world during the cold war, Parsonian modernization theory explicitly advocated capitalism as the best possible path any country could choose to follow (i.e., the only one that leads to modernity, wealth, and democracy). This theory argued that if LDCs adopted Western values, market relations, and government institutions, they would become affluent, democratic societies. Hence, the path to progress from traditional to modern is unidirectional. In this view, rich industrial countries, without rival in social, economic, and political development, are modern, whereas poor countries must undergo the modernization process to acquire these traits.

By changing their way of looking at the world, in particular giving up the traditions that kept them trapped in an irrational past, this theory argued that LDCs would eventually achieve the same prosperity that Europe and North America enjoyed. Modernization theory advocated stability and gradual change, not revolutionary leaps. It is worth noting that whereas Weber held that capitalism was a unique institution to Europe, modernization theorists maintained that the triumph of capitalism is inevitable worldwide.

Modernization theory posited that economic development occurred through a series of stages. At the broadest level, these include the widespread view that all economies pass through stages in which the labor force is employed first in agriculture, then manufacturing (i.e., the Industrial Revolution), then services (a postindustrial world). However, while this line of thought has some accuracy in the Western world, many developing countries witness a leapfrogging effect in which many agricultural workers plunge directly into services. This discrepancy points to the dangers of simplistically generalizing from the experience of the West to the developing world, which has a very different historical context and trajectory.

The diffusion of progress was also a major line of thought in modernization theory: New ideas, technologies, and institutions were held to flow from the core to the periphery at both the international and national scales. Internationally, diffusion occurred from the world's core, that is, the developed countries, to the global periphery as multinational corporations invested in LDCs. Investment was held to realize a country's comparative advantage and allow it to carve a niche for itself in the world economy; thus modernization theory advocated free trade. Within countries, diffusion occurred from the urban core, that is, cities, which were held to be the foci of modernity, to the rural periphery, that is, the countryside. Thus modernization theory held that urbanization was inherently a good thing, that rural areas were trapped in cycles of tradition and stagnation.

Poverty, in this conception, is held to be the result of the incomplete formation and diffusion of markets. Markets, in this view, promote an equalization of standards of living in poor and rich regions through the free flow of capital and labor. Thus modernization theory lies in direct contrast to marxist claims that capitalism inevitably generates uneven development. Economic development in this conception is likened to a race, in which the rural areas must catch up with the cities much as LDCs must catch up with the developed world.

Modernization theory also advocated major social, cultural, and political changes on the road to capitalism. Population growth, for example, must be brought under control or else the demand for resources would exceed the productivity gains of markets. Thus modernization theorists advocated family planning programs, a line of thought similar to the demographic transition (Chapter 3). During the cold war, population control policies were advocated as a means to raise standards of living and reduce the appeal of the communist bloc's alternative to capitalism. Culturally, societies (or parts of them) were divided between the traditional and the modern: Tradition was held to be synonymous with irrationality and fear of change, whereas modernity implied the belief that change is good and necessary for the sake of progress. Thus cities were alleged to be repositories of the modern, and rural areas identified with the traditional, to be transformed and brought into the modern age. The culture of modernity was to be diffused through mass education, the media, and growing literacy rates.

Politically, modernization theory equated capitalism with democracy, arguing that only market-based societies could protect civil liberties. In contrast to the centralized power of many precapitalist societies, markets tend to create multiple centers of power. The rise of a middle class was often held to be a central event in protecting civil liberties. Despotic societies tend to be poor, with a small dictatorial elite in control. By generating an educated, informed citizenry, markets were held to be antithetical to dictatorship. Modernization theorists point to countries such as South Korea as evidence of this thesis.

A major advocate of this approach was W. Rostow, an influential economist and presidential policy advisor in the 1960s who proposed a famous five-stage model of development (Figure 14.19). Rostow's model likened economic growth to an airplane taking off and proposed five stages in this process:

1. **Traditional society**—This term defines a country that has not yet started the process of development and is mired in poverty. It includes traditional societies with a very high percentage of people engaged in agriculture and a high percentage of national wealth allocated to what Rostow called "nonproductive" activities, such as the military and religion. Contemporary examples include Mali or Bhutan.

2. **Preconditions for take-off**—Under the international trade model, the process of development begins when an elite group initiates innovative economic activities. Under the influence of these well-educated leaders, the country starts to invest in new technology and infrastructure, such as water supplies and transportation systems. These projects will ultimately stimulate an increase in productivity. A culture of growth begins to take root. Examples include Thailand, Mexico, and Indonesia.

3. **The take-off**—Rapid growth is generated in a limited number of economic activities, such as textiles or food products. These few take-off industries achieve technical breakthroughs and become efficiently productive, while other sectors of the economy remain dominated by traditional practices. Examples today include China and Chile.

4. **The drive to maturity**—Modern technology, previously confined to a few take-off industries, diffuses to a wide variety of industries, which then experience rapid growth comparable to the take-off industries. Workers become more skilled and specialized. Examples include Singapore, Taiwan, and South Korea.

5. **The age of mass consumption**—The economy shifts from production of heavy industry, such as steel and energy, to consumer goods, like motor vehicles and refrigerators, and advanced services. Examples include the United States and Germany.

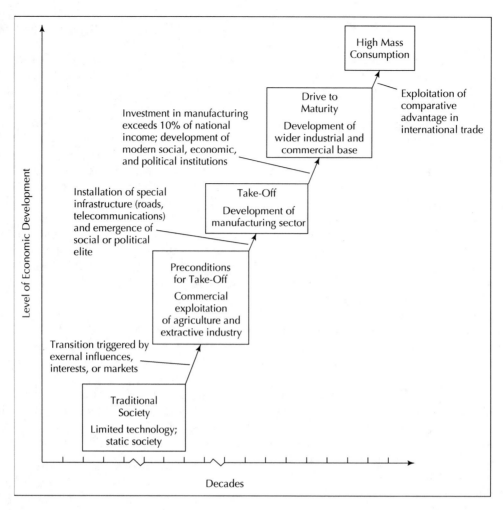

FIGURE 14.19

Rostow's five stages of the modernization process. The conventional approach to economic development viewed the process as akin to an airplane taking off, in which economies progress through a series of stages culminating in mass consumption. Others have criticized this approach for being ethnocentric (holding up the West as the only model of development) and ignoring the global and historical context of development.

Modernization theory lumped every country in the world into one of these stages. LDCs reside in the primary few stages while developed countries have passed through the preliminary stages and are now in stage 5 or beyond. It is assumed that LDCs will use this model to follow the steps of the developed countries. The international trade approach keeps countries competitive by forcing the industries to adapt and develop along world standards.

The policy implications of modernization theory are straightforward. Overall it advocates the formation of unfettered markets. Thus barriers to trade and investment should be removed, and foreign capital in the form of multinational corporations should be welcomed. Urban development should be stressed at the expense of rural areas. Internationally, this view was central in the switch from import substitution to export promotion that occurred in much of East Asia in

the 1970s and 1980s (Chapter 12). More recently, this theory is used to justify neoliberal structural adjustment policies of the International Monetary Fund, including currency devaluations and reductions in government subsidies.

Modernization theory has been soundly criticized on a number of grounds. Critics note that it is ethnocentric: It posits the history of the West as an ideal to be imitated, and everyone else's culture as inferior. It offers a simplistic, unidimensional view of history that culminates only in the experience of Europe and North America. LDCs are seen as little more than backward versions of the West, not as unique entities with their own distinct cultures and histories. Critics note that hundreds of years of colonialism produced a world economy that greatly disadvantaged the developing world; development is hardly a fair race when not all countries enjoyed the same starting point (i.e., the West has enjoyed great, deeply entrenched advantages over LDCs). Finally, by uncritically celebrating markets as mechanisms that only produce wealth and not poverty, modernization theory only celebrates the benefits but ignores the costs of capitalist development. Markets look fine to the winners, who preach free trade, but appear less rosy to those who have not benefited from them. Finally, modernization theory focuses only on the internal dynamics within countries (i.e., their cultures) and ignores the external context, the countries' colonial legacies, and the countries' position in the global division of labor. In this way it ends up blaming the victim (i.e., attributing poverty to poor people), which is politically easy but not accurate.

Dependency Theory

In the 1960s, numerous scholars from the developing world, particularly Latin America, began to question the promises and assumptions of modernization theory. What appeared as a comparative advantage and interdependence to Western scholars, for example, appeared to many in the LDCs as exploitation. Drawing from the heritage of Marxism, *dependency theorists* claimed that the development of the core countries was intrinsically dependent on the underdevelopment of the periphery countries. The theory suggests that unequal development of the world economy stems directly from the historical experience of colonialism. The development of Europe and North America, especially during the nineteenth and early twentieth centuries, relied on the systematic exploitation of underdeveloped areas by means of unequal terms of trade, abuse of low-skilled and low-paid labor, and profit extraction.

In this reading, poverty didn't just happen, but is a historic product (i.e., like a shirt or pair of tennis shoes, poverty is actively made by the dynamics of capitalism, not just something that happens to appear). This process is described as the "development of underdevelopment," which emphasizes that underdevelopment is not a static state but an active process. Dependency theorists thus argue that the LDCs were *made to be poor* by the West. Exploitation of the periphery occurs through the process of uneven exchange, in which LDCs produce low-valued goods in the primary sector and purchase high-valued goods from the core, a market mechanism that appears like an exchange of opposites but conceals the appropriation of surplus value that low-income workers in developing countries produce.

Unlike modernization theory, therefore, dependency theory focuses on external, not internal, causes of poverty. Because they occupy very different roles in the capitalist world economy, developed and underdeveloped countries are very different animals. Thus, unlike its colonies, the West was undeveloped, but not underdeveloped; LDCs do not temporarily "lag" behind West but are mired in poverty produced by the West, a situation naturalized as inevitable by the economics of comparative advantage. Dependency theorists thus argue that development and underdevelopment are two sides of global capital accumulation. The wealth of developed countries is derived from the labor and resources of the LDCs. Whereas modernization theory holds that markets eradicate uneven development, dependency theorists maintain it perpetuates it. Development and underdevelopment are therefore two sides of the same coin, a zero-sum game: Development somewhere (i.e., the West) requires underdevelopment somewhere else (i.e., its colonies). The political and social structures created under this vision of the world economy imply that independent development is impossible.

The policy implications of dependency theory, directly opposite of those espoused by modernization theorists, emphasize self-reliance; countries should exclude transnational corporations and practice import substitution to promote domestic production. Some even advocate defaulting on foreign debt.

Like modernization theory, this view is also subject to criticisms. Dependency theory tends to view the global periphery as passive and incapable of taking action; it lumps all LDCs together as if they were victimized by capitalism to the same degree. It ignores the internal causes of poverty, such as rural aristocracies that inhibit development, and its explanation for the core's wealth is simplistic. For example, dependency theory has not offered an adequate account of technological change and productivity growth. The claim that global capitalism always generates poverty in LDCs was unsustainable. Empirically, in the 1970s and 1980s, the rapid growth of the East Asian NICs in particular showed that development on the global periphery is indeed possible and that capitalism does not automatically reduce all LDCs to impoverished states.

World-Systems Theory

It is important to keep in mind that the forces driving the world economy are in a continual state of flux. The rise of the United States from a periphery to a core country, the fall of the Soviet Union, the appearance of the NICs in Asia, and the increasing importance of transnational firms exemplify the notion of permanent spatial disequilibrium. A third body of theory, *world-systems theory,* started by the sociologist Immanuel Wallerstein, takes into account this disequilibrium in explaining the changing structure of the world economy.

Unlike dependency theory, world-systems theory allows for some mobility within the capitalist world economy. Its focus is on the entire world rather than individual nation-states. Fundamentally, this view maintains that one can't study the internal dynamics of countries without also examining their external ones. Thus the boundary between foreign and domestic effectively disappears.

World-systems theory distinguishes between large-scale, precapitalist world empires, such as the Romans, Mongols, or Ottomans, which appropriate surplus from their peripheries through the state, and the capitalist world system, which arose in the "long sixteenth century" (1450–1650). Under global capitalism, there is no single political entity to rule the world (i.e., there is a single market but multiple political centers, meaning there is no effective control over the market). The political geography of capitalism is thus not the nation-state but the interstate system. Occasional attempts to reassert a world empire included the Hapsburgs, Napoleon, and Germany in World Wars I and II.

World-systems theorists maintain that capitalism takes many forms and uses labor in different ways in different regions. In the core, labor tends to be waged (i.e., organized through labor markets), while in developing countries there is considerable use of unfree labor, ranging from slavery to indentured workers to landless peasants working on plantations. The world economy structures places in such a way that high-valued goods are produced in the core and low-valued ones in the periphery. It is the search for profits through low-cost labor that drives the world system forward to expand into uncharted territories.

Unlike the bifurcation between developed and less developed countries that both modernization and dependency theories advocate, in world-systems theory there is a tripartite division among core, periphery, and semiperiphery (Figure 14.20). The core and periphery are the developed and undeveloped countries, respectively: One is wealthy, urbanized, industrialized, and democratic, the other rural, impoverished, agriculturally based, and dominated by authoritarian governments. The semiperiphery has characteristics of both core and periphery and includes states at the upper tier of the LDCs, such as the NICs, Brazil, Mexico, Thailand, and Saudi Arabia. Core processes high wages, high levels of urbanization, industrialism and postindustrialism, the quaternary sector of the economy, advanced technology, and a diversified product mix. The world periphery processes are low wages; low levels of urbanization, preindustrial, and industrial technology;

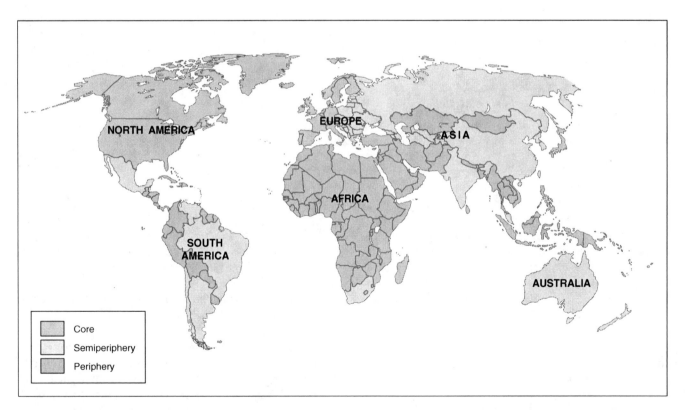

FIGURE 14.20

The geography of the world system. In world-systems theory, the global network of states and markets is dominated by a hegemonic power and a core of powerful, wealthy countries in Europe, North America, and Japan. The rest of the world is divided into an impoverished periphery, which produces raw materials, and a semiperiphery, including the newly industrialized countries, which has aspects of both the core and periphery. This approach recognizes the movement of states up and down the world system as global capitalism creates new layers of uneven development worldwide.

and a simple production mix. Consumption is low. In between are states that are part of the semiperiphery where both sets of processes coexist to a greater or lesser degree. The theory suggests that the semiperiphery countries are exploited by the core countries with regard to raw material and product flow while at the same time exploiting periphery countries.

World-systems theory pays particular attention to the role of a single hegemon that dominates the global political and economic system. The hegemon "sets the rules of the game," so to speak. During the period of Spanish dominance in the sixteenth and seventeenth centuries, for example, mercantilism was the dominant ideology. Under the Pax Britannica of the nineteenth century, free trade was the norm. And since the rise to dominance of the United States, especially since World War II, neocolonialism has been the typical pattern (although during the cold war there were two superpowers and a bifurcated world system). Hegemonic powers may overextend themselves militarily, leading to an erosion of their economic base. When powers in the core have conflicts among themselves, they open opportunities both for new hegemons and for countries on the periphery. The Napoleonic Wars of the early nineteenth century and World War II in the twentieth were thus openings for nationalist anticolonial movements worldwide, first in Latin America and later in Asia and Africa.

Hegemony exists when one core power enjoys supremacy in production, commerce, and finance and occupies a position of political leadership. The hegemonic power owns and controls the largest share of the world's production apparatus. It is the leading trading and investment country, its currency is the universal medium of exchange, and its city of primacy is the financial center of the world. Because of political and military superiority, the dominant core country maintains order in the world system and imposes solutions to international conflicts that serve its self-interests. Britain played this role in the nineteenth century, and the United States has done so since World War II. Consequently, hegemonic situations are characterized by periods of relative peace (e.g, the nineteenth century). During a power's decline from hegemony, rival core states, which can focus on capital accumulation without the burden of maintaining the political and military apparatus of supremacy, catch up and challenge the hegemonic power. Thus, in the early twentieth century, Germany challenged Britain for global leadership, with catastrophically violent results.

REGIONAL DISPARITIES WITHIN DEVELOPING COUNTRIES

In addition to the bifurcation between the developed and underdeveloped worlds, which forms the primary axis of the global economy, there are also profound spatial differences within developing countries. The geographies of colonialism, including profound rural-urban differences, are one major dimension of this predicament. Major cities of developing countries operate largely as export platforms linking the rich industrial countries and their sources of raw materials. Modern large-scale enterprises tend to concentrate in capital and port cities. Injections of capital into these urban economics attract new migrants from rural areas and provincial towns to principal cities. Migrants, absorbed by the system, are maintained at minimal levels. There is little incentive to decentralize urban economic activities. The markedly hierarchical, authoritarian nature of political and social organization retards the diffusion of ideas throughout the urban hierarchy and into rural areas.

Because economic landscapes are produced by social relations, regional inequalities within developing countries are reflections of social inequalities. The class relations in much of the less developed world are often typified by a small, powerful elite and large numbers of poor peasants, with a small middle class. Countries with highly unequal distributions of income, such as Brazil, tend to have highly unequal standards of living among their various regions. Those countries that have achieved more equality economically, such as the NICs of East Asia, tend to have fewer disparities spatially. In this way, economic landscapes mirror and contribute to social bifurcations, revealing how geographies are socially produced and socially producing.

The center-periphery concept echoes the marxist argument that the center appropriates to itself the surplus of the periphery for its own development. The center-periphery phenomenon may be regarded as a multiple system of nested centers and peripheries. At the world level, the global center (rich industrial countries) drains the global periphery (most of the underdeveloped countries). But within any part of the international system, within any national unit, other centers and peripheries exist. Centers at this level, although considerably less powerful, still have sufficient strength to appropriate to themselves a smaller, yet sizable, fraction of remaining surplus value. A center may be a single urban area or a region encompassing several towns that stand in an advantageous relation to the hinterland. Even in remote peripheral areas local, regional imbalances are likely to exist, with some areas growing and others stagnating or declining.

There are reverse flows from the various centers to the peripheries—to peripheral nations, to peripheral rural areas. Yet these flows, themselves, may further accentuate center-periphery differences. For example, World Bank, U.S. Aid for International Development (USAID), and International Development Association (IDA) loans support major infrastructure projects such as roads and power stations, which are proven money earners and reinforce the centrality and drawing power of cities and the export sectors. USAID strongly supports projects dealing with agriculture, health and family planning, school construction, and road building; industrialization projects are seldom financed.

DEVELOPMENT STRATEGIES

The economically developed countries must come to the aid of LDCs today. How can this occur peacefully? Three methods are generally cited for developed countries to help LDCs: (1) expand trade with LDCs, (2) invest private capital in LDCs, and (3) provide foreign aid to LDCs.

Expansion of Trade with Less Developed Countries

Economists suggest that expanding trade with LDCs is one way to help them. It is true that reducing tariffs and trade barriers with LDCs will improve their situation somewhat. Free trade, therefore, can have its costs. Eliminating protectionism levied against developing country producers gives them access to the large, wealthy markets in the United States, Canada, Europe, and Japan, increasing their export volumes and revenues. With the North American Free Trade Agreement (NAFTA), the United States removed all trade barriers with Mexico, for example. Mexican manufacturing flourished as a result. However, trade liberalization also opened the doors for U.S. imports, particularly heavily subsidized agricultural products, which wreaked havoc with Mexican farmers.

Private Capital Flows to Less Developed Countries

LDCs are also a destination for investments from MNCs, private banks, and large corporations. Some of these are foreign direct investment. For example, major U.S. automakers have now built numerous plants in Brazil and Mexico. In Tijuana alone, 500 U.S. labor-intensive manufacturing plants now take advantage of the low hourly wage rate. Other types of capital flows are purely financial: Citicorp and Chase Manhattan Bank have made loans to numerous LDC governments. Since the debt crisis of the 1980s and 1990s, however, investments and private capital flows have decreased substantially because of concerns about returns on investment and fears of debt default.

An international trade climate must also be supported by financial and marketing systems, a favorable tax rate, an adequately maintained infrastructure, and a reliable flow of sufficiently skilled labor. Often, however, LDCs cannot guarantee that a politically stable environment will prevail, which is difficult in many countries torn by tribal conflicts, ethnic strife, religious struggles, and civil wars. These obstacles

often thwart the major capital flows that might otherwise exist. African states in particular have not been able to tap private capital flows from large corporations and commercial banks because of problems with these conditions.

Foreign Aid from Economically Developed Nations

In order to reverse the vicious cycle of poverty, foreign aid is needed in the form of direct grants, gifts, and public loans to LDCs. Capital is necessary to finance companies, build the infrastructure, generate jobs, to increase productivity, and to retrain the labor pool.

In absolute terms, the United States has been a major world player in foreign-aid programs. U.S. foreign aid averages $15 billion per year, for example, less than 1 percent of GDP (well behind the shares of all other developed countries). The majority of this aid was administered through the State Department's USAID. Additional direct aid included food programs to needy countries under the U.S. government's Food for Peace program. Other nations have also rallied. Developed countries as a group contribute a total of $50 billion annually. In addition, OPEC nations contribute $2.5 billion. For many countries in Africa, aid can form as much as 15 percent of their national output (Figure 14.21).

Unfortunately, most U.S. aid has stipulations such as purchase requirements that make the LDCs patronize American products and services. Almost 75 percent of U.S. foreign aid is military in nature, and the vast bulk of it flows to close political allies such as Israel, Egypt, and Turkey on the basis of political ties as opposed to economic need. For example, Israel, Egypt, and Turkey each receive nearly $3 billion in aid per year. These nations are neither the most populous nor the most needy, but they occupy strategic areas of the Middle East where vast oil deposits exist and where the United States struggles against Islamic fundamentalism. In addition, the United States has guaranteed its support of Israel in its hostile environment.

Unfortunately, developed country contributions amount to only 0.5 percent of their collective GDPs. This amount is much too small to make a meaningful difference to the fortunes of the developing world. To make matters worse, Russia and eastern European nations are now making strong pleas for increased aid from the West. Many LDCs fear that aid that would normally be channeled to them will now go toward supporting privatization in former communist areas. The developed countries' fear is that the cost of failure of democratization in Russia will be far greater than the cost of foreign aid. If Europe and America agree, the larger portion of their foreign aid (through grants, loans, and direct aid) will be siphoned from the LDCs.

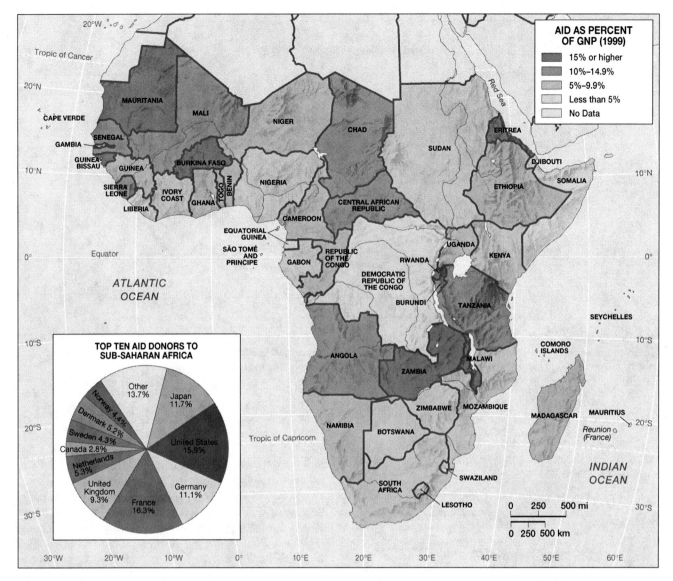

AID AS PERCENT
OF GNP (1999)
15% or higher
10%–14.9%
5%–9.9%
Less than 5%
No Data

TOP TEN AID DONORS TO
SUB-SAHARAN AFRICA

Other 13.7%
Japan 11.7%
United States 15.9%
Germany 11.1%
France 16.3%
United Kingdom 9.3%
Netherlands 5.3%
Canada 2.8%
Sweden 4.3%
Denmark 5.2%
Norway 4.4%

FIGURE 14.21
Aid dependency in Africa. In parts of sub-Saharan Africa, which lack domestic industries and export low-value primary sector goods, foreign aid comprises more than 15 percent of total output. The largest donors are France and the United States. Less than 1 percent of U.S. GDP goes to foreign aid, and most of that is military assistance to allies such as Israel.

INDUSTRIALIZATION IN THE DEVELOPING WORLD

Deindustrialization in the economically developed world did not induce widespread industrialization in the developing world. In 2004, 40 countries accounted for 70 percent of manufacturing exports from developing countries; the top 15 alone accounted for about 60 percent. Even more striking is that about one-third of all exports from the LDCs came from four Southeast Asian countries—Hong Kong, South Korea, Singapore, and Taiwan, the original "tigers" of the East Asian miracle (Figure 14.22). As the most rapidly growing economies in the world since World War II, East Asian

countries have formed a growing belt of manufacturing that may soon become the largest in the world (Figure 14.23). Most undeveloped countries saw zero or very little manufacturing growth. Industrialization occurred, therefore, only in selected parts of the developing world.

Manufacturing was slowest to take hold in the poorest countries of the periphery, most of which are in Africa. It grew fastest in the newly industrialized countries (NICs) that made a transition from an industrial strategy based on import substitution to one based on exports. The exporters can be divided into two groups. First, countries such as Mexico, Brazil, Argentina, and India have a relatively large domestic industrial base

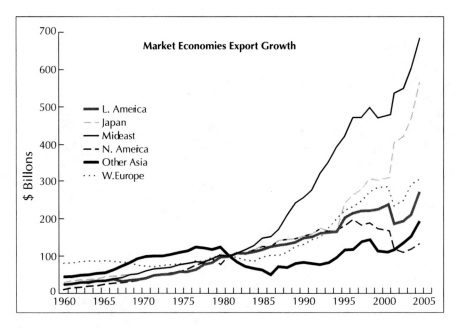

FIGURE 14.22

Market economies export growth, 1960–2004. The most spectacular rates of export growth have been in East Asia, the world's most rapidly growing area economically, where the NICs have pulled millions out of poverty.

FIGURE 14.23

Manufacturing centers in East Asia. The industrial districts of China, Korea, and Japan are becoming the largest aggregate complex of manufacturing in the world.

and established infrastructure. All four of these countries are primarily exporters of traditional manufactured goods, such as furniture, textiles, leather, and footwear. Second, countries such as Hong Kong, Taiwan, South Korea, and Singapore have few natural resources and relatively small domestic markets. But by tailoring their industrial bases to world economic needs, they have become successful exporters to developed countries. These countries emphasize exports in clothing, engineering, metal products, and light manufactures. Their success encouraged other LDCs to adopt a similar program of export-led industrialization.

Import-Substitution Industrialization

In the post–World War II period, newly independent developing countries sought to break out of their domination by, and dependence on, developed countries. Their goal was to initiate self-expanding capitalist development through a strategy of *import-substitution industrialization*. This development strategy involved the production of domestic manufactured goods to replace imports. Only the middle classes could support a domestic market; thus, industrialization focused on luxuries and consumer durables. The small plants concentrated in existing cities, which increased regional inequalities. These "infant industries" developed behind tariff walls in order to reduce imports from developed countries, but local entrepreneurs had neither the capital nor the technology to begin their domestic industrialization. Foreign multinational corporations came to the rescue. Although projects were often joint ventures involving local capital, "independent" development soon became *dependent industrialization* under the control of foreign capital. Many countries experienced an initial burst in manufacturing growth and a reduction in imports. But after a while, the need to purchase raw materials and capital goods and the heavy repatriation of profits to the home countries of the multinationals dissipated foreign-exchange savings.

Export-Led Industrialization

By the 1960s, it was apparent to many leaders of LDCs that the import-substitution strategy had failed to generate economic growth. Only countries that had made an early transition to *export-led industrialization,* such as the Asian NICs, were able to sustain their rates of industrial growth. Once again, LDC development became strongly linked to the external market. In the past, export-oriented development had involved the export of primary commodities to developed countries. Now, export-oriented development was to be based on the production and export of manufactured goods.

The growth of export-led industrialization coincided with the international economic crisis of the 1970s and 1980s. It took place at a time when the demand for imports in the advanced industrial countries was growing despite the onset of a decline in their industrial bases. It was, in short, a response to the new international division of labor. Export-oriented industrialization tends to concentrate in *export-processing zones,* where four conditions are usually met:

1. Import provisions are made for goods used in the production of items for duty-free export, and export duties are waived. There is no foreign exchange control, and there is freedom to repatriate profits.
2. Infrastructure, utilities, factory space, and warehousing are usually provided at subsidized rates.
3. Tax holidays, usually of five years, are offered.
4. Abundant, disciplined labor is provided at low wage rates.

The first export-processing zone was not established in the developing world but in 1958 in Shannon, Ireland, with the local international airport at its core. In the late 1960s, a number of countries in East Asia began to develop export-processing zones, the first being Taiwan's Kaohsiung Export-Processing Zone, set up in 1965, a strategy soon imitated across East Asia (Figure 14.24). By 1975, 31 zones existed in 18 countries. By 2001, at least 96 zones were established in developing countries. Most of them are in the Caribbean, Central and Latin America, and East Asia.

Central to the growth of LDC manufacturing exports to the developed countries are multinational corporations, which establish operating systems between locally owned companies and foreign-owned companies. The arrangement is known as *international subcontracting* or offshore assembly and *outsourcing.* Although numerous legal relationships exist between the multinational and the subcontractor, from wholly owned subsidiary to independent producer, the key point is that developing country exports to developed countries are part of a unified production process controlled by firms in the advanced industrial countries. For example, Sears Roebuck Company might contract with an independent firm in Hong Kong or Taiwan to produce shirts, yet Sears retains control over design specifications, advertising, and marketing.

Consequences of Export-Led Industrialization for Women

Export-led industrialization moves work to the workers instead of workers to the work, which was the case during the long postwar boom. In some countries this form of industrialization has generated substantial employment. For example, since their establishment, export-processing zones have accounted for at least 60 percent of manufacturing employment expansion in Malaysia and Singapore. However, in general, the number of workers in the export-processing zones' labor forces is modest. It is unlikely that these zones employ more than 1 million workers worldwide.

Much of the employment in export-processing zones is in electronics and electrical assembly or in textiles. Young, unmarried women make up the largest part of the workforce in these industries—nearly 90 percent of zone employment in Sri Lanka, 85 percent in Malaysia and Taiwan, and 75 percent in the Philippines. Explanations for this dominance of women in the workforce vary; it is often attributed to sexual stereotyping, in which the docility, patience, manual dexterity, and visual acuity of female labor are presupposed. Of more significance is the fact that women are often paid much less than men are for the same job. Thus the cheap labor so essential to the labor-intensive industries of the global assembly line also reproduces the patriarchal relations that keep many women in particularly low-paying jobs.

Export-led industrialization may lead to an imposed economic system at odds with the cultural and political institutions of the people that it exploits. Often people produce things that are of no use to them. How they produce has no relation to how they formerly produced.

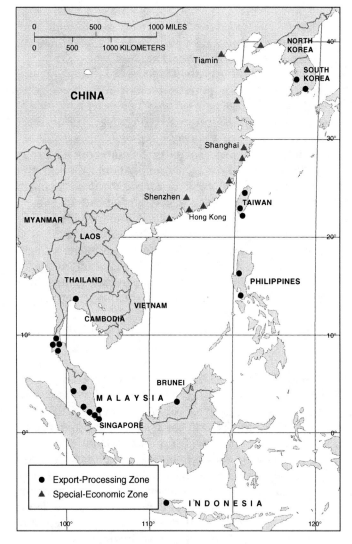

FIGURE 14.24

Export processing zones in East and Southeast Asia. These platforms, constructed by governments to attract foreign capital and facilitate exports, have become widely adopted throughout the developing world as part of the broader shift from import substitution to export-led industrialization.

Workers are often flung into an alien labor process that violates their traditional customs and codes. For example, female factory workers often pay a high price for their escape from family and home production, especially in Asia, where women's family roles have been traditionally emphasized. Because of their relative independence, Westernized dress, and changed lifestyles, women may be rejected by their clan and find it hard to reassimilate when they can no longer find employment on the assembly line.

Although export-oriented industrialization leads to growth in production and employment, as well as to increases in foreign exchange, it will not lead to the creation of an indigenous, self-expanding capitalist economy. The economic linkages between export platforms and local economies are minimal. Some scholars cite South Korea as an example of a country that has completed a successful transition to industrial capitalism. But so far Korean industrial expansion has not taken place because of domestic demand. Rather, it has occurred because the Koreans have sought to increase exports and international competitiveness. This expansion is changing, partly because of the general global tendency to stagnate.

Economic stagnation in developed countries is a major concern of developing countries that have enjoyed success with the export-led industrialization strategy. For developed countries, where production and investment are moving out, purchasing power will be lost. The resultant spiraling down of general economic activity will choke off dependent industrialization and increase poverty and suffering for workers and peasants in LDCs.

Sweatshops

Some Guess clothing is made by suppliers that use underpaid Latino immigrants in Los Angeles, sometimes working in their own homes. Mattel makes tens of millions of toys each year in China, where young female Chinese workers who have migrated hundreds of miles from home are alleged to earn less than the minimum wage of $1.99 a day. Nike is criticized for manufacturing many of its shoes in tough labor conditions in Indonesia, and some of Disney's hottest seasonal products are being made by suppliers in Sri Lanka and Haiti—countries with unsavory reputations for labor and human rights. Soccer balls are sewn together by child laborers in Pakistan, who work up to 12 hours per day. In an era of the global economy, it is impossible for consumers to avoid products made under less than ideal labor conditions. Moreover, what may appear to be horrific working environments to most citizens in the world's richest nation are not just acceptable but actually attractive to others who live overseas or even in Third World pockets of the United States. Anyone even casually familiar with how some Americans recompense their (usually immigrant) housekeepers understands their desire to work and support their families.

One icon of American culture whose manufacturing practices seem out of sync with its brand name is Disney. Disney maintains almost 4000 contracts with other companies that assume the right to manufacture Disney paraphernalia, some of which are then sold in Disney stores. These licensees go to some of the world's lowest-cost labor countries, including Sri Lanka and Indonesia, to produce stuffed animals and clothes. Disney itself rarely takes a direct hand in manufacturing. Sears, which carries 200,000 products from manufacturers operating in virtually every country, is tightening up on buying goods from suppliers with dubious records. The Gap, after enduring criticism, also has become a model for manufacturing and sourcing products abroad. In contrast to Disney, Mattel does most of its own manufacturing. It makes a staggering 100 million Barbie dolls a year in four factories, two in China and one each in Malaysia and Indonesia. The Barbie craze produced $1.4 billion in annual revenues for the firm.

Does a global economy mean consumers face no choice but to buy products made under conditions Americans don't want to think about? A number of U.S. companies say that intense global competition is no excuse for keeping working standards at the lowest possible level. Levi Strauss, for example, imposes its own "terms of engagement" on manufacturers who make its jeans products in 50 countries.

In many ways, what Americans buy is their most direct and intimate connection with the global economy. In a post–cold war era in which governments seem to be losing their power to shape the lives of people, U.S. consumer spending can be an important tool in extending American values. The silver lining is that if Americans respond to even some of these concerns, they could enjoy their shopping and improve the conditions that millions of people around the world encounter in their daily lives.

The East Asian Economic Miracle

What does it take to turn an LDC into a developed nation? Who is marching successfully forward to development? The most successful examples have been the

Making a Jackie Kennedy doll in China. The use of low-wage labor in developing countries may generate jobs for people, cheap goods for consumers in the developed world, and profits for multinational corporations, but it also frequently involves the blatant exploitation of human beings working long hours under horrendous conditions.

trading states of East Asia. South Korea, Taiwan, Singapore, and Hong Kong followed the path pioneered by nearby Japan, which began to modernize in the nineteenth century. In the 1980s and 1990s, Malaysia, Thailand, Indonesia, and the Pacific coast of China headed down the same road. After the devastation of World War II, Japan's economy was in ruins. Today, Japan's economy is the second largest in the world, two-thirds the size of that of the U.S. economy (Japan's population is only half as large). In the mid-1960s, South Korea was a land of traditional rice farmers who made up over 70 percent of the country's workforce. Its GDP per capita—$230—was the same as Ghana; today, South Korea's GDP per capita was 20 times larger, and over 70 percent of its people lived and worked in urban areas rather than on farms. South Korea's economy is now the eleventh most powerful in the world, ahead of such countries as Sweden, the Netherlands, and Australia. South Korea has become the world's largest shipbuilding nation and the world's fifth largest auto manufacturer. Its iron and steel and chemical industries are thriving, and with the largest number of PhDs per capita in the world, South Korea has become a formidable competitor in research and development of semiconductors, information processing, telecommunications, and civilian nuclear energy. Few other countries have achieved as much economically in so short a time.

How has East Asia emerged as the hub of the increasingly prosperous Pacific Rim? There are several characteristics that these societies share, which, taken together, help to explain their sustained economic growth. In addition, unique circumstances in the world political economy helped to facilitate their growth.

First, East Asian countries have exhibited an enormous commitment to education. Some of this phenomenon may be derived from the Confucian respect for learning and scholarship. East Asian educational mores encourage a docile, well-trained workforces, often consisting of easily exploited, low-wage female labor, means that they have relatively few days lost to strikes and labor unrest.

Second is a high level of national savings. East Asian governments have encouraged personal savings by restricting the movement of capital abroad, maintaining low tax rates while keeping interest rates above the rate of inflation, and limiting the importation of foreign luxury goods. The result has been the accumulation of large amounts of low-interest capital that allowed Asian countries to finance education, infrastructure, manufacturing, and commerce. Many countries in East Asia save one-third or more of their GDP (in America, in contrast, the domestic savings rate is between zero and 3 percent of the GDP).

Only recently, after economic take-off was well underway, have East Asian governments loosened financial policies to allow increased consumption and capital investment in consumer durables like new homes. Such purchases, rather than savings, may finance Asian prosperity. As Asian economies mature and their populations age, it is possible that their saving rates decline and imports may increase. Will East Asians tend more and more to consume rather than create wealth, as Americans tend to do?

Third, East Asia has enjoyed a strong political framework within which economic growth is fostered. Industries targeted for growth were given a variety of supports—export subsidies, training grants, and tariff protection from foreign competitors. Low taxes and energy subsidies assisted the business sector. Trade unions were restricted and democracy was constrained. In Japan, powerful government bureaucrats largely beyond public control promoted industrial expansion with little regard for the opinions or needs of Japanese consumers. Military governments in South Korea and Taiwan dealt harshly with industrial unrest and political dissidents. Authoritarian regimes long ruled Singapore. In no way did Asian governments follow a laissez-faire model; it is a common myth that the Asian NICs demonstrate a "free market" in operation. It is only lately that multiparty politics have been permitted outside Japan.

Fourth, the NICs engaged in widespread land reform in the 1950s. In part, this was made possible by the turmoil of the Japanese occupation and the Korean war, which dislodged the rural aristocracies that owned much of the arable land. As a result, rural land ownership in these nations is relatively egalitarian, with high rates of productivity, unlike Latin America, which still suffers from the legacy of the Spanish land grant system. Besides a thriving agricultural economy, which has dwindled in the face of rapid industrialization, the NICs have benefited from comparatively low rates of rural-to-urban migration, which helps to prevent the urban areas from being flooded by desperate peasants seeking to escape poverty.

Fifth, East Asian NIC countries exhibited a sustained commitment to exports (export-led industrialization) in contrast to the import-substitution policies that characterized India, Africa, and Latin America until very recently. Instead of encouraging industrialists with low labor costs to target foreign markets and compete there, governments in India, Latin America, and Africa decided to protect their economies rather than open them to international competition. They shielded firms from foreign competition by protective tariffs, government subsidies, and tax breaks. As a result, their products became less competitive abroad. While it was relatively easy to create a basic iron and steel industry, it proved harder to establish high-tech industries such as computers, aerospace, machine tools, and pharmaceuticals.

Most import-substituting states depend on imported manufactured goods, whereas exports still chiefly consist of raw materials such as oil, coffee, and soybeans, a condition that creates poor *terms of trade*. A country that relies on the export of raw materials—mineral and agricultural commodities, "rocks and crops"—with little or no value added to the products through finishing or manufacturing, and then has to import expensive (because of the immense value added) high-tech products, is not headed toward development unless the country commits its earnings to investment in quality exports and competitive high-tech manufacturing. Such countries need to get the fundamentals right: Keep inflation low and fiscal policies prudent, maintain high savings and investment rates, improve the educational level of the population, trade with the outside world, and encourage foreign investment.

Throughout Latin America and Africa that sort of economic strategy was often missing. Governments poured money into state-owned enterprises, large bureaucracies, and oversized armed forces, paying for them by printing money and raising loans from Western banks and international agencies. Public spending soared, price inflation accelerated, domestic capital took flight to safe deposits in American and European banks, and indebtedness skyrocketed. By the 1990s, payments on loans consumed about half of Africa's export earnings. By 1989, Argentina owed developed country banks and governments a staggering $1800 for each man, woman, and child in the country. Zambia's debt rose to 334 percent of the GDP.

Just when Latin America and Africa needed capital for economic growth, countries there found themselves overwhelmed by debt, starved of foreign funds for investment, with currencies made worthless by hyperinflation. By the 1990s, poverty in developing countries outside East Asia had increased dramatically. Lands as well as people paid the price. Forests have been recklessly logged, mineral deposits carelessly mined, fragile lands put to the plow, and fisheries overexploited in a desperate effort to escape the poverty trap.

In addition to their domestic structures, their position in the world economy also played a role in the growth of the Asian NICs. Thus, not all of the success of the NICs is due to internal, domestic factors. For example, despite the brutality of war and the untold suffering it caused, many NICs benefited from the legacy of their occupation by Japan between 1895 and 1945. Japan initiated the steel, chemicals, and textiles industries in Korea and Taiwan, as well as that in Manchuria. The Japanese also built much of the industrial infrastructure in the NICs, including roads, bridges, tunnels, ports, and airports, which, while designed to maximize the extraction of raw materials such as coal, nonetheless became important after the war. Japan also centralized the state bureaucracies of these countries, which displaced the reactionary rural aristocracies that controlled much of the economies and hindered growth. Subsequent to the war, many NICs, particularly South Korea, established imitations of the Japanese corporate zaibatsu (e.g., the Korean chaebol), many of which were closely linked to banks and obtained easy credit. Finally, Japanese foreign investment in East Asia, which exceeds that of the United States, also has accelerated the industrialization of these countries.

In addition to Japan, the United States also is responsible for much of the growth of the NICs. Throughout the cold war (1945–1991), the United States provided generous economic and military aid, freeing resources that could be harnessed for economic development. The Containment Doctrine, also known as the Truman Doctrine, positioned Japan, South Korea, Taiwan, and, to a lesser extent, other countries, as frontline states in the war against communism. The United States gave copious grants and subsidies to the NICs and awarded them preferential trade status, such as exemptions from tariffs, which allowed them easy access to the American market and significant export earnings. The roles of the United States and Japan are important in a theoretical sense as well. To some extent, the geopolitical conditions that enabled the take-off of the NICs were a unique constellation of circumstances that could not be duplicated elsewhere.

In the 1990s, the original Four Tigers of South Korea, Taiwan, Hong Kong, and Singapore were joined by a new group, including Thailand, Malaysia, and Indonesia. Each of them replicated the experience of the original NICs to one extent or another. Thailand, which long enjoyed close economic and military ties to the United States, saw a wave of investment in textiles, automobiles, toys, and tourism, propelling Bangkok into a prosperous but crowded urban center. Malaysia, under an authoritarian government, launched its "Plan 2020" to become a fully industrialized country by the year 2020. Already this strategy has succeeded, at least in the western half of the country. The country is the world's largest exporter of refrigerators and semiconductors and has close ties to banks and firms in Singapore as well. Kuala Lumpur has become a thoroughly modernized city. Indonesia, struggling to escape decades of poverty, has enjoyed some of the growth experienced in the Singapore–Kuala Lumpur corridor, including investments in textiles, shoes, electronics, and even aerospace.

Finally, no discussion of the NICs could be complete without mentioning China, the "800-pound gorilla" looming behind all of the NICs. Following decades of isolation under the communists, China began to open itself to the world economy in the late 1970s under the leadership of Deng Xiaoping. The policies implemented in the 1980s revolutionized the economy and society of the most populous nation in the world, encouraging the growth of private property and markets. Whereas the communists shunned contacts with the West, the Chinese in the last 20 years have welcomed it, making the country the single largest recipient of foreign direct investment in the developing world. The government targeted coastal areas in particular, designating them special economic zones in which investors were showered with subsidies and tax breaks. These regions include Guangdong province, located near and benefiting greatly from its ties to Hong Kong (e.g., cities such as Shenzen); Fujian province across the straits from Taiwan; and Pudong, the financial center near Shanghai (Figure 14.25). In such regions, industries such as electronics, toys, garments, and other types of light industry have exploded. Indeed, China's economy has grown an average of 8 percent annually for the last two decades, one of the highest rates in the world, and China enjoys large trade surpluses with most of the developed world. This growth has been geographically

Mumbai (Bombay), India, stock exchange provides evidence for this city's central role in the rapidly globalizing South Asian economy.

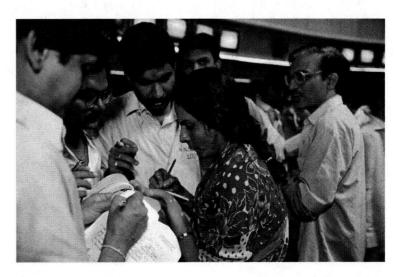

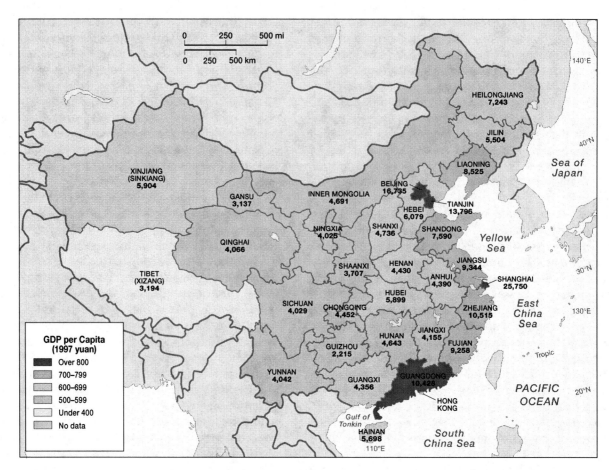

FIGURE 14.25

Unequal development in China as measured by GDP per capita. As China reentered the global economy in the late twentieth century and rapidly adopted market based economic systems, it experienced a surge in social and spatial inequality. The most rapid growth has been along the coasts, most famously in the southern province of Guangdong, while much of the country's interior remains mired in poverty. Not surprisingly, the labor force has responded to these geographic differentials by moving in large numbers to the cities, where recent migrants are often vulnerable to exploitation.

uneven (i.e., as a form of uneven spatial development), and in response it has attracted waves of peasants moving from less densely inhabited, poorer regions in the interior toward the prosperous coasts (Figure 14.25).

Although India, the world's second most populous country (with 1 billion people), lags far behind China in its level of economic development, India too has seen its pace of economic growth recently increase. Much of this growth is located on the western half of the Indian peninsula (Figure 14.26), including financial centers such as Mumbai (formerly Bombay), one of the world's largest cities, and the famous software complex in Bangalore, India's answer to Silicon Valley. Indeed, India today is the world's largest producer of software as well as films.

SUMMARY

In this chapter, we considered the issue of Third World development. We began by noting how slippery the term

development is and that there are a variety of ways to measure it. We discussed goals for development by listing objectives that are by and large universally endorsed. We then surveyed the locations of underdevelopment in various regions of the developing world. Next we explored typical characteristics and development problems of LDCs—overpopulation, lack of resources, capital shortages, insufficient foreign revenues and poor terms of trade, unequal land distribution, inadequate infrastructures and public services, and corrupt governments.

In discussing major perspectives on development, we saw how modernization theories, which stress economic growth and Westernization, have obscured important aspects of underdevelopment, particularly the long history and effects of colonialism and neocolonialism. Two major views derived from political economy—dependency theory and world-systems theory—explain why the Third World does not develop, attributing this lack of development to the role of the planet's core in dominating and exploiting its periphery.

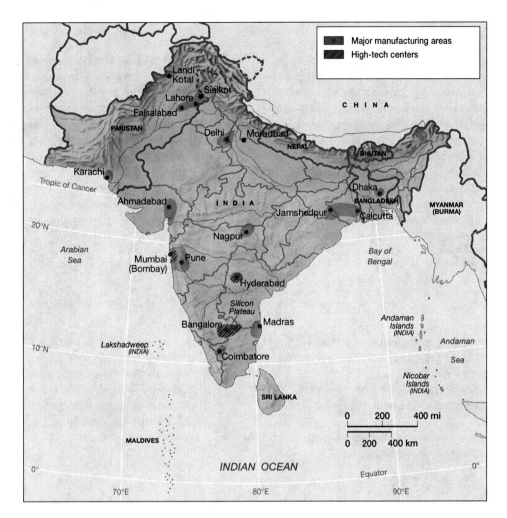

FIGURE 14.26
Uneven development in India. As India deregulated its economy and lured foreign investment, it too experienced uneven growth. The western parts of the country (including the financial and media center of Mumbai formerly Bombay) and the software district of Bangalore have done much better than the eastern half.

Bangalore, India's Silicon Plateau. With a growing population of well-educated workers, India has become the largest software producer in the world. Many of California's Silicon Valley firms use engineers and programmers in India.

Finally, we turned to several development strategies that may promote growth in the developing world. A small but growing number of countries is moving from "have-not" to "have" status, or, in the framework of world-systems theory, from the global periphery to the semiperiphery, while many more remain behind. The key factors at play here include the history of colonialism, position in the commodity chains of the global economy, cultural attitudes toward education, political stability, and capacity to carry out long-term plans, all of which shape economic performance from one country to another. The race to development will as always surely have its winners and losers. Only this time, modern communications will remind us of the growing disparity. We noted how industrialization in the developing world started under policies of import substitution, which rapidly gave way to the far more successful tactic of export promotion. This shift was most successful in the East Asian newly industrialized countries. Nonetheless, industrialization has brought with it brutal exploitation as in the case of sweatshops. The comfortable lives of many in the West often depend on the misery of workers in many poor countries.

STUDY QUESTIONS

1. Why aren't poor countries called "primitive"?
2. What are five common characteristics of less developed countries?
3. What were the origins of the world debt crises?
4. What are four ways to measure economic development?
5. Contrast modernization, dependency, and world systems theories of development.
6. How does development relate to regional disparities within countries?
7. What were the major cycles of colonialism? What did they have to do with the change in relations between world core and periphery?
8. How can the First World meaningfully assist the Third?

KEY TERMS

backwash effect
basic needs
capital flight
circular and cumulative causation
colonial division of labor
colonial organization of space
core-periphery
dependency theory
development

direct foreign aid
dual economy
export-led industrialization
import substitution
less developed countries (LDCs)
modernization theory
neocolonialism
newly industrializing countries
primary sector of the economy

privatization
secondary sector of the economy
squatter settlements
tertiary economic activity
trickle-down effects
underdevelopment
underemployment
world-systems theory

SUGGESTED READINGS

Barber, B. 1996. *Jihad v. McWorld.* New York: Ballantine.

Bhagwati, J. 2004. *In Defense of Globalization.* Oxford: Oxford University Press.

Chase-Dunn, C. 1998. *Global Formation: Structures of the World-Economy,* 2d ed. Lanham, Md.: Rowman and Littlefield.

Friedman, T. 2005. *The World Is Flat: A Brief History of the Twenty-first Century.* New York: Farrar, Straus and Giroux?

National Research Council, 2003. *Cities Transformed: Demographic Change and Its Implications in the Developing World.* Washington, D.C.: National Academies Press.

Porter, P., and Sheppard, E. 1998. *A World of Difference Society, Nature, Development.* New York: Guilford Press.

So, A. 1990. *Social Change and Development: Modernization, Dependency, and World-System Theories.* Newbury Park, Calif.: Sage.

Stiglitz, J. 2002. *Globalization and Its Discontents.* New York: W. W. Norton.

TERRA: BRAZIL'S LANDLESS MOVEMENT—NEW YORK TIMES [REALPLAYER]

http://www.nytimes.com/specials/salgado/home/

The *New York Times* has recently opened this Web special by documenting the plight of Brazil's landless in both words and pictures.

ATLAPEDIA

http://www.atlapedia.com/index.html

Atlapedia Online contains key information on every country of the world. Each country profile provides facts and data on geography, climate, people, religion, language, history, and economy, making it ideal for students of all ages.

UNITED NATIONS HUMAN DEVELOPMENT

http://www.undp.org

Report includes excellent information for developing countries.

CIA FACT BOOK

http://www.odci.gov/cia/publications/95fact/

This site includes data from every country in the world with a map.

LIBRARY OF CONGRESS

HTTP://WWW.LOC/.GOV

Astounding variety of resources and exhibits.

Section 4
Industry Level and Corporate Issues

Ethics and Social Responsibility in International Business

AFTER STUDYING THIS CHAPTER YOU SHOULD BE ABLE TO:

- Describe the nature of ethics.
- Discuss ethics in cross-cultural and international contexts.
- Identify the key elements in managing ethical behavior across borders.
- Discuss social responsibility in cross-cultural and international contexts.

- Identify and summarize the basic areas of social responsibility.
- Discuss how organizations manage social responsibility across borders.
- Identify and summarize the key regulations governing international ethics and social responsibility.

© Kathy deWitt/Alamy

> *" Many migrant workers are unaware of their legal rights, or they know they will face exploitation and bullying at work if they try to enforce those rights. "*

Migrant Workers

Globalization has brought an enormous increase in cross-border trade, along with the ability to shift investments quickly and, in areas of the world such as Europe, enormous changes in policy. Coupled with this has been the increased mobility of international labor. This factor has been driven by falling transport costs and cheaper communication. Individuals have been prepared to move across the globe in search of work and higher pay.

Migration has often been associated with poverty. In other words, people are motivated to uproot themselves and move to another country where they can be more assured of earning a livelihood. It is estimated that around 175 million people across the world live outside their own country as a result of seeking work.

Immigration is a particularly sensitive issue in certain areas, such as Europe. In many countries in the European Union there are enormous labor shortages, which are being plugged by migrant workers from central and Eastern Europe, along with new European Union members, and workers from countries that hope to soon become members of the European Union. In Britain migrant workers make up around 7 percent of the total population, or 10 percent of the working population.

Migrant workers in China are said to total as many as 150 million, or just over 11 percent of the population. The vast majority of these migrant workers are from poorer rural districts, and they have sought work in the more prosperous coastal regions.

Many migrant workers are unaware of their legal rights, or they know that they will face exploitation and bullying at work if they try to enforce those rights. In Britain there is a national minimum wage, but a research project carried out by the Trade Union Congress (TUC) in the summer of 2008 suggested that the vast majority of migrant workers, and in particular women, were likely to be paid less than the minimum wage. The majority of them were found to be working between 31 and 48 hours per week (55 percent). This compares to some 48 percent of British workers. Over 15 percent were working 48 hours or more per week, compared to 13 percent of British workers.

In 2005, the Gangmasters Licensing Authority was set up in Britain. Its goal was to protect migrant workers who were often laboring in dreadful conditions for much less than the minimum wage. In 2008, it canceled the licenses of 25 employment agents, twice as many as in 2007. The authority believed that there were still a number of unscrupulous employment agents, particularly operating in agriculture and food processing.

In 2004, a tragedy occurred in Morecambe Bay in Lancashire when 23 Chinese cockle pickers were drowned as they were caught by high tides while looking for shellfish. The Gangmaster, Lin Liang Ren, who was originally from China, was convicted of the manslaughter of 21 of the cockle pickers. He was later jailed for 14 years and will be deported to China when he has served his prison term. But despite the new legislation and the work of the authority, large numbers of Chinese, in particular, are being illegally smuggled into Britain. Many of them cannot speak English and they work and live in poor conditions. They are also under the constant threat of harassment and arrest.

Globalization offers businesses, employees, and entrepreneurs myriad new opportunities to seek new markets, broaden their product lines, and lower their cost of production. And the introduction of new products and new ways of doing business can bring major improvements in the lives of the world's poorest people, as our opening case suggests. But globalization also presents international businesses with new challenges, such as the need to define appropriate ethical standards and to operate in a socially responsible manner in all the markets and countries in which the firm does business.

Consider the case of offshore production (see "Emerging Opportunities"). Even at the extreme, the issues are not as clear as they might at first seem. For example, many people from developed countries would agree that it is unethical for a business to outsource

Emerging Opportunities

The Outsourcing Dilemma

It has long been common for firms to move production and low-skill jobs from their home country to other countries, often to capitalize on lower labor costs. But these practices sometimes result in unfavorable publicity and may even expose fundamental issues associated with potential human rights violations. Consider the following four classic examples involving fruit juices, cocoa, soccer balls, and athletic shoes.

For years, large fruit juice distributors like Minute Maid, Tropicana, and Nestlé have bought fruit juices from suppliers in South America. But a few years ago it was learned that many of these suppliers rely heavily on child labor to harvest oranges, lemons, and other fruits. Children as young as nine years old are commonly taken out of school by their impoverished parents and put to work in the citrus groves. These parents often see no problem with this behavior because they themselves had also picked fruit as children. Although some steps have been taken to address this problem, the practice nevertheless continues. A similar set of issues have been raised regarding Nestlé's, Cargill's, and Archer Daniels Midland's purchasing of cocoa from West African plantations that employ 280,000 children, some of whom are allegedly treated no better than slaves.

In San Miguelito, Mexico, 4,500 people spend their days sewing soccer balls. Workers can make a ball in about two hours, and in return they receive $1.00. The labor force includes children as young as eight years old whose smaller hands make the sewing easier. These youngsters do attend school but then put in six or more hours of sewing each evening for an average daily wage of about $3.00. Mexico's labor force includes between 4 and 5 million school-age children; 1 in 5 children work, many as field hands. Although child labor is illegal in Mexico, the law is seldom enforced.

But perhaps the most publicized example of human rights concerns involves Nike. Nike manufactures its products under contract with independent operators, mainly in Asian countries. For years there have been allegations—and some real evidence—of occasional child labor abuses, unsafe working conditions, and other violations of local regulations. Nike strenuously denies the charges and claims that the contractors, not Nike itself, are responsible for conditions in the factories. The firm also points out that these workers are often paid more than prevailing wage rates in their countries and that it clearly communicates to its suppliers that they must adhere to local labor laws. In rebuttal, some activists claim that Nike has a larger responsibility to those workers than it has been willing to accept.

These and myriad other examples have been debated and discussed for such a long time that the controversy is in some ways being clarified. Most observers agree on the fundamental issues. Firms are serving their shareholders by lowering their costs through offshore production and sourcing. And in many cases the offshore workers benefit through the creation of new jobs. The disagreements largely center on how to balance the profit-driven quest for lower labor costs against the potential exploitation of children and other low-wage earners and human rights violations.

References: "Slave Chocolate?", *Forbes,* April 24, 2006, p. 96; Pete Engardio, Aaron Bernstein, and Manjeet Kripalani, "Is Your Job Next?", *BusinessWeek,* February 3, 2003, pp. 50–60; Roger Parloff, "Can We Talk?", *Fortune,* September 2, 2002, pp. 102–110; "'Tradition' Perpetuating Poverty," *Houston Chronicle,* June 23, 2002, p. 28A; "U.S. Child-Labor Law Sparks a Trade Debate over Brazilian Oranges," *Wall Street Journal,* September 9, 1998, pp. A1, A9.

Danone SA, France's largest food conglomerate, has teamed with Bangladesh's Grameen Bank to create Shoktidoi yogurt as a means of addressing the twin problems of malnutrition and rural poverty. The fortified yogurt provides children with 30 percent of their daily nutritional needs. The company is recruiting local villagers as distribution agents, thus providing a new source of employment for the rural population.

HALEY/Sipa

Ethics and Social Responsibility in International Business

production to an offshore factory that relies on child labor and/or that maintains unsafe working conditions. But people in that country might argue that as unattractive as they might seem to outsiders, those jobs are superior to the ones that would otherwise be available.

If child labor and working conditions are not problematic, concerns may be less extreme but there remain issues of appropriate wages and the reduction of jobs in the business's home country. As an investor, a person might applaud a company that eliminates the jobs of 500 highly paid employees at home and replaces them with lower paid employees abroad. But some of those individuals who are displaced might just as vehemently argue that it is unethical for them to lose their jobs just to be replaced by someone from another country who is willing to work for less money.

This chapter explores these and other issues from an international business perspective. We first examine the nature of ethics and social responsibility in international business. We then discuss ethics in cross-cultural and international contexts. Next, we describe how firms attempt to manage ethical behavior across borders. Social responsibility in cross-cultural and international contexts is then introduced and discussed. After describing the major areas of social responsibility, we discuss how firms manage social responsibility across borders. Finally, we conclude with a summary of some of the major laws that attempt to regulate international ethics and social responsibility.

The Nature of Ethics and Social Responsibility in International Business

The fundamental reason for the existence of a business is to create value (usually in the form of profits) for its owners. Furthermore, most individuals work in order to earn income to support themselves and/or their families. As a result, the goal of most of the decisions made on behalf of a business or an individual within a business is to increase income (for the business and/or the individual) and/or reduce expenses (again, for the business and/or the individual). In most cases businesspeople make decisions and engage in behaviors, for both their personal conduct and the conduct of their organizations, that are acceptable to society. But sometimes they deviate too much from what others see as acceptable.

In recent years, it seems that the incidence of unacceptable behaviors on behalf of businesses and/or people within businesses has increased. Regardless of whether this increase is real or only illusory, such high-profile and well-documented cases as Enron, WorldCom, Tyco, and Arthur Andersen have certainly captured the attention of managers, investors, and regulators everywhere. Nor has this been a distinctly American problem. Businesses such as Royal Ahold NV (a Dutch grocery chain admitting to accounting irregularities) and Nestlé (a Swiss firm accused of violating World Health Organization codes controlling the marketing of infant formula in less developed countries) have also caught their share of attention for improprieties, real or imagined.[1] Hence, just as the business world is becoming increasingly internationalized, so too is the concern for ethical and socially responsible conduct by managers and the businesses they run.

We define **ethics** as an individual's personal beliefs about whether a decision, behavior, or action is right or wrong.[2] Hence, what constitutes ethical behavior varies from one person to another. For instance, one person who finds a 20-euro banknote on the floor of an empty room may believe that it is okay to simply keep it, whereas another may feel compelled to turn it in to the lost-and-found department and a third to give it to charity. Further, although ethics is defined in the context of an individual's belief, the concept of **ethical behavior** usually refers to behavior that conforms to generally accepted social norms. **Unethical behavior,** then, is behavior that does not conform to generally accepted social norms.

An individual's ethics are determined by a combination of factors. People start to form ethical frameworks as children in response to their perceptions of the behavior of their parents and other adults they deal with. As children grow and enter school, they are influenced by peers with whom they interact in the classroom and playground. Everyday occurrences that force the participants to make moral choices—a friend asking to copy homework, a father accidently denting a parked car when the only witness is his child, or a child who sees his mother receive too much change from the supermarket cashier—shape people's ethical beliefs and behavior as they grow into adulthood. Similarly, a person's religious training contributes to his or her ethics. Some religious beliefs, for instance, promote rigid codes of behaviors and standards of conduct, while others provide for more flexibility. A person's values also influence ethical standards. People who place financial gain and personal advancement at the top of their list of priorities, for example, will adopt personal codes of ethics that promote the pursuit of wealth. Thus, they may be ruthless in efforts to gain these rewards, regardless of the costs to others. In contrast, people who clearly establish their family and/or friends as their top priority will adopt different ethical standards.

A society generally adopts formal laws that reflect the prevailing ethical standards—the social norms—of its members. For example, because most people consider theft to be unethical, laws have been passed in most countries to make such behaviors illegal and to proscribe ways of punishing those who do steal. But while laws attempt to be clear and unambiguous, their application and interpretation still lead to ethical ambiguities. For example, most people would agree that forcing employees to work excessive hours, especially for no extra compensation, is unethical. Accordingly, laws have been passed in some countries to define work and pay standards. But applying that law to organizational settings can still result in ambiguous situations that can be interpreted in different ways. In Japan, for example, by custom a junior employee cannot leave the office until the more senior person departs, whereas in the United States the boss is often supposed to be the last to leave. These expectations are often more powerful in shaping behavior than the mere existence of a law.

These definitions suggest the following generalizations:

- Individuals have their own personal belief system about what constitutes ethical and unethical behavior. For example, most people will be able to readily describe simple behaviors (such as stealing or returning found property) as ethical or unethical.
- People from the same cultural contexts are likely to hold similar—but not necessarily identical—beliefs as to what constitutes ethical and unethical behavior. For example, a group of middle-class residents of Brazil will generally agree with one another as to whether a behavior such as stealing from an employer is ethical or unethical.
- Individuals may be able to rationalize behaviors based on circumstances. For instance, the person who finds a 20-euro banknote and knows who lost it may quickly return it to the owner. But if the money is found in an empty room, the finder might justify keeping it on the grounds that the owner is not likely to claim it anyway.
- Individuals may deviate from their own belief systems based on circumstances. For instance, in most situations people would agree that it is unethical to steal and therefore they do not steal. But if a person has no money and no food, that individual may steal food as a means of survival.
- Ethical values are strongly affected by national cultures and customs. **Values** are the things a person feels to be important. As we discussed in Chapter 3, values often center on such things as time, age, education, and status. Culture has a direct impact on the value systems of the members of that culture. Values in turn affect how those individuals define ethical versus unethical behavior. For instance, in Japan status is often reflected by group membership. As a result, behavior that helps the group is more likely to be seen as ethical, whereas behavior that harms the group is likely to be viewed as unethical.

Members of one culture may view a behavior as unethical, while members of another may view that same behavior as perfectly reasonable. An American businessman might report to the police an American customs officer who requested $100 in a envelope to clear a shipment of imported goods, whereas his Kenyan or Indonesian counterparts would likely make the payment without even being asked. These differences can create worrisome ethical dilemmas for international business practitioners when the ethical standards of their home country differ from that of the host country. Nonetheless, we want to emphasize that ethics is a distinctly individual concept, rather than an organizational one. In general, the relationship between an organization and its environment revolves around the concept of social responsibility, a topic we address later in this chapter. But as we discuss ethics per se

FIGURE 5.1

Ethics in a Cross-Cultural Context

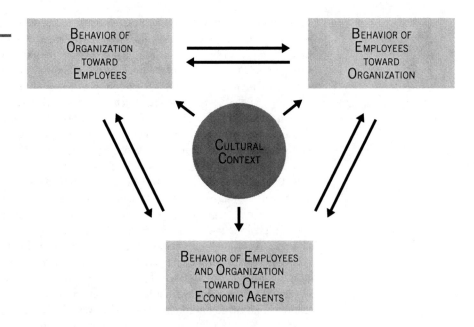

in the first part of the chapter, keep in mind that we are focusing on individuals in organizations, as opposed to the organization itself.

Ethics in Cross-Cultural and International Contexts

A useful way to characterize ethical behaviors in cross-cultural and international contexts is in terms of how an organization treats its employees, how employees treat the organization, and how both the organization and its employees treat other economic agents. These relationships are illustrated in Figure 5.1.

How an Organization Treats Its Employees

One important area of cross-cultural and international ethics is the treatment of employees by the organization. At one extreme, an organization can strive to hire the best people, to provide ample opportunity for skills and career development, to provide appropriate compensation and benefits, and to generally respect the personal rights and dignity of each employee. At the other extreme, a firm can hire using prejudicial or preferential criteria, can intentionally limit development opportunities, can provide the minimum compensation allowable, and can treat employees callously and with little regard to personal dignity.

In practice, the areas most susceptible to ethical variation include hiring and firing practices, wages and working conditions, and employee privacy and respect. In some countries both ethical and legal guidelines suggest that hiring and firing decisions should be based solely on an individual's ability to perform the job. But in other countries it is perfectly legitimate to give preferential treatment to individuals based on gender, ethnicity, age, or other non-work-related factors. Consider the case of Daslu, a São Paulo high-fashion women's clothing store catering to the wealthiest of Brazil's wealthy. Its sales staff is drawn exclusively from the same social circles as its clientele. Daslu also hires a small army of assistants—colloquially known as *aventalzinhos,* or "little aprons"—to aid the sales staff. The typical *aventalzinho* works longer hours, gets paid less, has worked for the store more years, and is more knowledgeable about the merchandise than the sales staff. Yet no *aventalzinho* has ever been promoted to a sales position, because these individuals come from the wrong social class.[3]

Wages and working conditions, while regulated in some countries, are also areas for potential controversy. A manager paying an employee less than he or she deserves, simply because the manager knows the employee cannot afford to quit and so will not risk losing his or her job by complaining, might be considered unethical. Similarly, in some countries people would agree that an organization is obligated to protect the privacy of its employees. A manager spreading a rumor that an employee has AIDS or is having an affair with a co-worker is generally seen as an unethical breach of privacy. Likewise, the manner in which an organization responds to and addresses issues associated with sexual harassment also involves employee privacy and related rights.

Managers in international organizations face a number of clear challenges with regard to these matters. The firm must deal with country-specific ethical issues regarding its treatment of employees, but must also be prepared to contend with international comparisons as well. Consider the myriad ethical dilemmas posed by the practice of outsourcing production to overseas locations. From one perspective it can be argued that firms are ethically bound to move jobs wherever they can be performed for the least cost. But some critics would argue that this practice is unethical, for it devalues the workers' numerous contributions to the firm and ignores the hardships imposed on displaced workers. In some countries, such as Japan, aggressive outsourcing that results in domestic layoffs violates the firm's implicit agreement to provide lifetime employment. The ethical issues facing the firm's managers do not end once the production is moved overseas. Contemplate the following passage from *Fortune,* a U.S. business magazine that does not have the reputation of being unsympathetic to the virtues of free markets:

> For the privilege of working 12-hour shifts seven days a week in a factory where she makes plastic casings for Motorola cellphones, Mary, 30, will be in debt for years to come. To secure work at the Motorola subcontractor, which is in Taiwan, Mary had to pay $2,400 to a labor broker in her native Philippines. She didn't have that kind of money, so she borrowed from a local money lender at an interest rate of 10% per month. That payment, however, got her only as far as Taiwan. A second labor broker met Mary at the Taipei airport and informed her of his separate $3,900 fee before delivering her to the new job.
>
> Before she left the Philippines, Mary rejoiced at the $460 she would be earning in Taiwan; it was more than five times what she could make doing similar work, if she could find it, in her own country. But once in Taiwan she began to realize that after the brokers' fees and other deductions, she would be left with almost nothing. Out of her monthly check came $215 to pay the Taiwanese broker, $91 for Taiwanese income tax, $72 for her room and board at the factory dorm, and $86 for a compulsory contribution to a savings bond she will get only if she completes her three-year contract. After 18 months she will have repaid the Taiwanese labor broker. But she still must contend with her Philippine debt and its rapidly compounding interest.[4]

Hundreds of thousands of workers have obtained their jobs in Asian factories through brokers similar to the ones used by this Philippine woman. She entered into these arrangements willingly, although out of economic desperation. However, the Philippine law that limits a broker to charging only one month's pay for his service was ignored. As the issue of debt bondage becomes more well known, the managers of the multinational corporations that outsource their production to these facilities will need to formulate their ethical responsibilities to workers, such as Mary, who are snared in debt bondage.

How Employees Treat the Organization

Numerous ethical issues also relate to how employees treat the organization. The central ethical issues in this relationship include conflicts of interest, secrecy and confidentiality, and honesty. A conflict of interest occurs when a decision potentially benefits the individual to the possible detriment of the organization. Ethical perceptions of the importance of conflicts of interest vary from culture to culture. Consider the simple example of a supplier offering a gift to a company employee. Some companies believe that such a gift can create conflicts of interest. They fear that the employee will begin to favor the supplier that offers the best gifts, rather than the supplier whose product is best for the firm. To guard against such dangers, many companies have policies that forbid their buyers from accepting gifts from suppliers. Some U.S. newspapers and broadcast media, such as the *New York Times,* even refuse to allow their employees to accept free meals for fear that their journalistic judgments and integrity might be compromised. But in other countries exchanges of gifts between a company's employees and its customers or suppliers is perfectly acceptable. In Japan, for instance, such exchanges are common (and expected) during the *ochugen* and *oseibo* gift-giving periods. *Ochugen,* which occurs in July, originally developed to pay homage to the spirit of one's ancestors, although it has evolved to reflect one's best wishes for summer. *Oseibo* gifts, which are offered in December, represent a token of gratitude for favors and loyalty shown throughout the year. Japanese department stores helpfully stock their shelves with appropriate goods at every price level during *ochugen* and *oseibo,* as well-defined cultural norms govern the level and appropriateness of the gifts to be exchanged by businesspersons, which depends upon the nature of the business relationship, its length, and the amount of business transacted. Note, however, that determining an appropriate gift by the amount of business transacted is exactly the kind of behavior that arouses suspicion of conflict of interest in many North American and European companies.

China offers a similar set of challenges to firms wishing to control conflicts of interest. Much business in China is conducted through *guanxi,* which is based on reciprocal exchanges of favors. Because of the importance of *guanxi,* North American and European firms operating in China often face a difficult task in adapting to the norms of Chinese business culture while continuing to honor company policy regarding conflicts of interest. Typically one finds that in high-context, collectivist, and power-respecting cultures, gift exchanges are a more important part of the way business is done than in low-context, individualistic, and power-tolerant cultures.

Divulging company secrets is viewed as unethical in some countries, but not in others. Employees who work for businesses in highly competitive industries—electronics, software, and fashion apparel, for example—might be tempted to sell information about company plans to competitors. Consider the plight of Durawool, an American steel-wool manufacturer. It was shocked to learn that Chinese law offered it little protection when one of its local employees left the company's Chinese subsidiary and promptly started a rival firm using Durawool's technology.[5]

A third area of concern is honesty in general. Relatively common problems in this area include such things as using a business telephone to make personal long distance calls, stealing supplies, and padding expense accounts. In some business cultures, such actions are viewed as unethical; in others, employees may develop a sense of entitlement and believe that "if I'm working here, then it's the company's responsibility to take care of my needs." The potential for conflict is clear when individuals from such divergent ethical perspectives work together.

How Employees and the Organization Treat Other Economic Agents

The third major perspective for viewing ethics involves the relationship between the firm and its employees with other economic agents. The primary agents of interest include customers, competitors, stockholders, suppliers, dealers, and labor unions. The behaviors between the organization and these agents that may be subject to ethical ambiguity include advertising and promotions, financial disclosures, ordering and purchasing, shipping and solicitations, bargaining and negotiation, and other business relationships.

For example, businesses in the global pharmaceuticals industry have been under growing criticism because of the rapid escalation of the prices they charge for their newest and most powerful drugs.[6] These firms argue that they need to invest heavily in research and development programs to develop new drugs, and higher prices are needed to cover these costs. Yet given the extent of the public health crises that plague some areas of the world—such as HIV/AIDS in sub-Saharan Africa—some activists argue that the pharmaceutical manufacturers should lower their prices and/or relax their patent protection so that patients in poorer countries can afford to purchase the drugs needed to treat such diseases. Another growing concern in recent years involves financial reporting by businesses. Because of the complexities inherent in the finances of large multinational corporations, some of them have been very aggressive in presenting their financial positions in a very positive light. And in at least a few cases some managers have substantially overstated their earnings projections and/or hidden financial problems so as to entice more investment.[7]

Differences in business practices across countries create additional ethical complexities for firms and their employees. In some countries small bribes and side payments are a normal and customary part of doing business; foreign companies often follow the local custom regardless of what is considered an ethical practice at home. In China, for instance, local journalists expect their cab fare to be paid if they are to cover a business-sponsored news conference. In Indonesia the normal time for a foreigner to get a driver's license is over a year, but it can be "expedited" for an extra $100. And in Romania, building inspectors routinely expect a "tip" for a favorable review.[8]

At times, however, the sums involved are not small. A U.S. power generating company lost a $320 million contract in the Middle East because government officials demanded a $3 million bribe. A Japanese firm paid the bribe and won the contract. Enron allegedly had a big project in India canceled because newly elected officials demanded bribes. Although such payments are illegal under U.S. law (as well as the laws of several other countries), managers nonetheless dislike losing important contracts to less ethical rivals.

Managing Ethical Behavior Across Borders

Ethics reside in individuals, but many businesses nevertheless endeavor to manage the ethical behavior of their managers and employees by clearly establishing the fact that they expect them to engage in ethical behaviors. They also want to take appropriate steps to eliminate as much ambiguity as possible about what the companies view as ethical versus unethical behavior. The most common ways of doing this are through the use of guidelines or codes of ethics, ethics training, and organizational practices and the corporate culture.

Guidelines and Codes of Ethics

Many large multinationals, including Toyota, Siemens, General Mills, and Johnson & Johnson, have written guidelines that detail how employees are to treat suppliers, customers, competitors, and other constituents. Others, such as Philips, Nissan, Daewoo, Whirlpool, and Hewlett-Packard, have developed formal **codes of ethics**—written statements of the values and ethical standards that guide the firms' actions. However, the mere existence of a code of ethics does not ensure ethical behavior. It must be backed up by organizational practices and the company's corporate culture.

A multinational firm must make a decision as to whether to establish one overarching code for all of its global units or to tailor each one to its local context. Similarly, if a firm acquires a new foreign subsidiary, it must also decide whether to impose its corporate code on that subsidiary or allow it to retain the one it may have already been following. In order for a code to have value, of course, it must be clear and straightforward, it must address the major elements of ethical conduct relevant to its environment and business operations, and it must be adhered to when problems arise. In one classic folly, Enron's board of directors was once presented with a potentially lucrative venture that contradicted the firm's code of ethics. So what did the board do? It voted to set aside the code of ethics, approved the business venture, and then reinstated the code of ethics!

Ethics Training

Some multinational corporations address ethical issues proactively, by offering employees training in how to cope with ethical dilemmas. At Boeing, for example, line managers lead training sessions for other employees, and the company also has an ethics committee that reports directly to the board of directors. The training sessions involve discussions of different ethical dilemmas that employees might face and how they might best handle those dilemmas.

Again, one decision for international firms is whether to make ethics training globally consistent or tailored to local contexts. Regardless of which approach they use, though, most multinationals provide expatriates with localized ethics training to better prepare them for their foreign assignment. BP, for instance, prepares managers at its headquarters in England for future assignments to Russia by having them undergo training in the Russian language as well as in local business customs and practices and ethics.

Organizational Practices and the Corporate Culture

Organizational practices and the corporate culture also contribute to the management of ethical behavior. If the top leaders in a firm behave in an ethical manner and violations of ethical standards are promptly and appropriated addressed, then everyone in the organization will understand that the firm expects them to behave in an ethical manner—to make ethical decisions and to do the right things. But if top leaders appear to exempt themselves from ethical standards or choose to ignore or trivialize unethical behaviors, then the opposite message is being sent—that it's acceptable to do something that's unethical if you can get away with it.

One recent survey sheds some interesting light on how these practices are implemented in various countries. The survey focused specifically on the acceptability of bribing officials when doing business in foreign countries. This survey found that Russian, Chinese, Taiwanese, and South Korean firms found bribery to be relatively acceptable. Among the countries that found bribery to be unacceptable were Australia, Sweden, Switzerland, Austria, and Canada. Italy, Japan, and the United States fell in between the extremes.[9]

Kenya is one of the countries where bribery is almost a way of life. One study estimates that as many as two-thirds of individual and business involvements with Kenyan public officials involve paying a bribe.[10] Bribery and corruption is so extensive in China that some studies estimate that the costs of corruption have wiped out the equivalent of 13 to 16 percent of the country's GDP.[11] Many of the former Soviet republics face similar problems.

Yet firms should think twice—or more than twice—before engaging in such behavior, as "Venturing Abroad" indicates. Firms that gain reputations as bribe payers are asked to pay bribes; firms with the opposite reputation often are not. As one expert in the area notes:

> Viable companies can say "no.". . . [T]he U.S. electronics group Motorola not only refused a bribe request from a Latin American official but also said it would not conduct business in that country until the regime changed. Refusal of bribe requests requires a corporate culture that supports the refusal of such requests. One of the most effective means of doing this is with a simple corporate code for managers and employees, affiliates and potential business partners. At a minimum, the code should refer to the laws that bind the company and prohibit bribery of foreign officials. The code should also describe the decision-making line for bribe requests and assure managers the company will back them when they refuse to pay a bribe.
>
> Building this into the corporate culture . . . can bring competitive advantage. The leading oil company Texaco (now part of Chevron), for example, earned such a fearsome reputation for not acceding to bribe requests that even at remote African border crossings Texaco's jeeps are sometimes waved through without any requests for a bribe.[13]

Social Responsibility in Cross-Cultural and International Contexts

As we have seen, ethics in business relate to individual managers and other employees and their decisions and behaviors. Organizations themselves do not have ethics but do relate to their environment in ways that often involve ethical dilemmas and decisions by individuals within the organization. These situations are generally referred to within the context of the organization's social responsibility. Specifically, **social responsibility** (sometimes called corporate social responsibility, or CSR) is the set of obligations an organization undertakes to protect and enhance the society in which it functions. The complexities for managers in an international business are clear—balancing the ideal of a global stance on social responsibility against the local conditions that may compel differential approaches in the various countries where the firm does business.

A classic example of this relates to the tobacco industry. In several countries, such as the United States, South Africa, and the United Kingdom, tobacco companies are limited in their ability to advertise cigarettes and are required to post health warnings

Venturing Abroad

Siemens Pays—and Pays and Pays

The saga of Siemens AG, the €87 billion Munich-based manufacturer of steam turbines, telecommunications equipment, medical scanners, and other sophisticated technology, provides a morality tale for firms pondering whether they should offer under-the-table payments to win lucrative international contracts. In October 2007, a German court fined Siemens €201 million ($284 million) for paying bribes. According to German court records, at least 77 separate bribes, totaling €12 million, were made by managers of Siemens's telecommunications equipment subsidiary to cabinet ministers and bureaucrats in Libya, Russia, and Nigeria. The court estimated the bribes generated €200 million in "unlawful economic advantages" for Siemens, which formed the basis for the magnitude of the fine. And earlier that year, another German court fined Siemens €38 million for bribes paid to Italian officials in the company's power generation subsidiary. And the worst may not be over for Siemens. The company is also under investigation by the U.S. Justice Department and the Securities and Exchange Commission for violation of the Foreign Corrupt Practices Act and securities regulations, while prosecutors in Switzerland and Liechtenstein are investigating suspicious payments funneled through their banking systems. Nor are German prosecutors finished with their investigations: in April 2008, they announced they were broadening their inquiries and contemplating criminal proceedings.

It appears that the German courts uncovered merely the tip of an iceberg. An internal investigation launched by the company after German police raided its headquarters in late 2006 has uncovered €1.3 billion in suspicious payments in 65 countries, involving six of the company's business units, made between 2000 and 2006. After the company announced an internal amnesty program, 110 of its employees stepped forward to provide additional information. Acknowledging the extent of the problem, Siemens' supervisory board replaced several of the firm's top executives with outsiders. The company's new general counsel, Peter Solmssen—like the new CEO Peter Löscher, he is a former General Electric executive—recognizes the challenges he and the company face. Notes Solmssen, "Corruption at Siemens was 'systemic' in recent years. There was a cultural acceptance that this was the way to do business around the world, and we have to change that." Among Löscher and Solmssen's first acts was an overhaul of the company's code of conduct and its compliance programs. In addition to transforming the

One of new CEO Peter Löscher's primary tasks is to change Siemens's corporate culture and eliminate its widespread use of bribery to win contracts. Siemens faces regulatory and criminal investigations in several countries, including Germany and the United States.

Siemens Corp.

Ethics and Social Responsibility in International Business

237

firm's corporate culture, they face the task of restoring the firm's external reputation and credibility. And, of course, they need to maintain Siemens's competitiveness in the marketplace: No small trick, given the distraction of the company's mounting legal problems and the ensuing drain on managerial attention and company resources. There is little doubt that Siemens will continue to pay for its misdeeds for a very long time.

References: "Siemens Power Unit Investigated," *Wall Street Journal,* April 15, 2008 (online); "Siemens Amnesty Plan Assists Bribery Probe," *Wall Street Journal,* March 5, 2008, p. A12 (includes Solmssen quote); "Siemens Internal Review Hits Hurdles," *Wall Street Journal,* January 23, 2008, p. A18; "Inside Bribery Probe of Siemens," *Wall Street Journal,* December 28, 2007, p. A4; "Siemens Ruling Details Bribery Across the Globe," *Wall Street Journal,* November 16, 2007, p. A1; "Siemens Fine Ends a Bribery Probe," *Wall Street Journal,* October 5, 2007, p. A2; "Siemens Probe Spotlights Murky Role of Consultants," *Wall Street Journal,* April 20, 2007, p. A1.

on cigarette packages. But many countries either have less restrictive limitations or no limitations whatsoever. The issue, then, is the extent to which a tobacco company should apply the most restrictive approach to all markets or else take advantage of the flexibility offered in some markets to actively promote the sale and use of tobacco products.

Areas of Social Responsibility

Organizations may exercise social responsibility toward their stakeholders, toward the natural environment, and toward general social welfare. Some organizations acknowledge their responsibilities in all three areas and strive diligently to meet each of them, while others emphasize only one or two areas of social responsibility. And a few acknowledge no social responsibility at all.

Organizational Stakeholders

Organizational stakeholders are those people and organizations that are directly affected by the practices of an organization and that have a stake in its performance.[13] Most companies that strive to be responsible to their stakeholders concentrate first and foremost on three main groups: customers, employees, and investors. They then select other stakeholders that are particularly relevant or important to the organization and then attempt to address their needs and expectations as well.

Organizations that are responsible to their customers strive to treat them fairly and honestly. They pledge to charge fair prices, to honor product warranties, to meet delivery commitments, and to stand behind the quality of the products they sell. Companies that have established excellent reputations in this area include L. L. Bean, Toyota, Land's End, Dell Computer, Daimler, BP, and Volkswagen.

Organizations that are socially responsible in their dealings with employees treat their workers fairly, make them a part of the team, and respect their dignity and basic human needs. Organizations such as 3M Company, Hoescht AG, and Honda have all established strong reputations in this area. In addition, they also go to great lengths to find, hire, train, and promote qualified minorities.

To maintain a socially responsible stance toward investors, managers should follow proper accounting procedures, provide appropriate information to shareholders about the financial performance of the firm, and manage the organization to protect shareholder rights and investments. Moreover, they should be accurate and candid in their assessment of future growth and profitability and avoid even the appearance of improprieties involving such sensitive areas as insider trading, stock price manipulation, and the withholding of financial data.

The Natural Environment

A second critical area of social responsibility relates to the natural environment.[14] Not long ago, many organizations indiscriminately dumped sewage, waste products from production, and trash into streams and rivers, into the air, and on vacant land. When Royal Dutch Shell first explored the Amazon River Basin for potential drilling sites in the late 1980s, its crews ripped down trees and left a trail of garbage in their wake. Now, however, many laws regulate the disposal of waste materials. In many instances, companies themselves have become more socially responsible in their release of pollutants and general treatment of the environment. For example, when Shell launched its most recent exploration expedition into another area of the Amazon Basin, the group included a biologist to oversee environmental protection and an anthropologist to help the team more effectively interact with native tribes.[15] Similarly, lumber retailers like Home Depot and Wickes have agreed to sell only wood products certified as having been harvested using environment-friendly techniques.[16]

Still, much remains to be done. Companies need to develop economically feasible ways to avoid contributing to acid rain and global warming; to avoid depleting the ozone layer; and to develop alternative methods of handling sewage, hazardous wastes, and ordinary garbage.[17] Procter & Gamble, for example, is an industry leader in using recycled materials for containers, while many German firms aggressively use recycled materials whenever possible. Hyatt Corporation established a new company to help recycle waste products from its hotels. Conservation Corporation of Africa, a game lodge firm based in Johannesburg, strives to make its lodges as environmentally friendly as possible. And Starbucks pays its coffee suppliers a premium of 10 cents additional per pound if they demonstrate a commitment to protect the environment. The Internet is also seen as potentially playing an important role in resource conservation. This is due to the fact that many e-commerce businesses and transactions reduce both energy costs and pollution.[18]

General Social Welfare

Some people believe that in addition to treating their stakeholders and the environment responsibly, business organizations also should promote the general welfare of society. Examples include making contributions to charities, philanthropic organizations, and not-for-profit foundations and associations; supporting museums, symphonies, and public radio and television; and taking a role in improving public health and education. Some people also believe that organizations should act even more broadly to correct the political and/or social inequities that exist in the world. For example, these observers would argue that businesses should not conduct operations in countries with a record of human rights violations, such as Myanmar (Burma) or Sudan. Recent interest by U.S. firms in oil reserves in western and central Africa have sparked concerns about human rights issues in those areas as well, an issue discussed in more depth in one of the chapter's closing cases, "A Pipeline of Good Intentions."[19] A related but distinct problem that also is receiving renewed attention is global poverty and the potential role of business in helping to address it. In Cambodia, for instance, 35 percent of the population lives below the poverty level. Fifty-nine percent lack clean drinking water, and 35 percent of children under the age of 5 are malnourished.[20] But there are also emerging signs that some countries are beginning to address poverty-related issues. Uganda, for example, is still a very poor country; foreign aid constitutes a significant portion of its national budget. But since 1993 the percentage of its population living with HIV has dropped from 33 percent to 6 percent. Primary school enrollment has jumped from 60 percent to over 75 percent of school-age children. And the proportion of its population living on less than $1 per day has fallen from 58 percent to 35 percent.[21] Yet, as illustrated in Map 5.1, numerous problem areas still exist.

Managing Social Responsibility Across Borders

As with attempts to manage ethical conduct, businesses usually make some effort to actively address social responsibility. As we will discuss, firms generally adopt one of four different basic approaches to social responsibility. The basic approach they adopt shapes how they manage issues of compliance, the informal dimensions of social responsibility, and the evaluation of their social responsibility efforts.

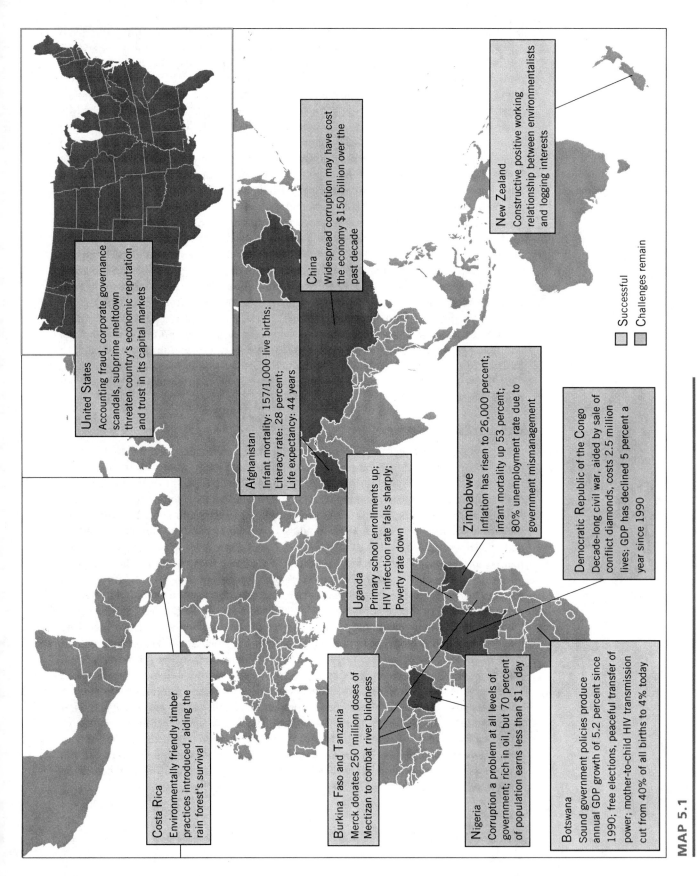

United States
Accounting fraud, corporate governance scandals, subprime meltdown threaten country's economic reputation and trust in its capital markets

China
Widespread corruption may have cost the economy $150 billion over the past decade

New Zealand
Constructive positive working relationship between environmentalists and logging interests

Afghanistan
Infant mortality: 157/1,000 live births; Literacy rate: 28 percent; Life expectancy: 44 years

Uganda
Primary school enrollments up; HIV infection rate falls sharply; Poverty rate down

Zimbabwe
Inflation has risen to 26,000 percent; infant mortality up 53 percent; 80% unemployment rate due to government mismanagement

Democratic Republic of the Congo
Decade-long civil war, aided by sale of conflict diamonds, costs 2.5 million lives; GDP has declined 5 percent a year since 1990

Costa Rica
Environmentally friendly timber practices introduced, aiding the rain forest's survival

Burkina Faso and Tanzania
Merck donates 250 million doses of Mectizan to combat river blindness

Nigeria
Corruption a problem at all levels of government; rich in oil, but 70 percent of population earns less than $1 a day

Botswana
Sound government policies produce annual GDP growth of 5.2 percent since 1990; free elections, peaceful transfer of power; mother-to-child HIV transmission cut from 40% of all births to 4% today

Successful

Challenges remain

MAP 5.1

Social Responsibility Hot Spots: Some Successes, But Many Challenges Remain

Bringing the World into Focus

Should Firms Practice Corporate Social Responsibility?

In the eyes of advocates of corporate social responsibility, the case for CSR is overwhelming. The corporate sector must be mindful of the "triple bottom line" and must continually evaluate its environmental and social performance as well as its economic achievements. The corporate sector must promote global sustainability, meeting the needs of the present without compromising the needs of the future. In short, the goal of CSR is to promote a humane and just society, and corporations must play an appropriate role in achieving this objective. After all, corporations are granted a license to operate by society; therefore they owe something to society in return. The unconstrained pursuit of profit breeds abuses, excesses, greed, and failure to consider the needs of future generations. Moreover, corporations have unique talents and resources to solve society's ills and should be expected to contribute them when necessary to address these problems.

Some experts, however, believe that the CSR movement is unethical, misguided, and inappropriate. Their case rests on a belief that in an economic system relying on shareholder capitalism, the corporate goal is (and should be) to maximize profits for shareholders. Requiring managers to promote social goals in addition to economic goals may cause managers to lose focus, thereby abandoning their fiduciary duty to shareholders. Moreover, these critics argue that the CSR movement rests on a fundamental misunderstanding of the functioning of free markets. True, firms are motivated to earn profits. But they can earn profits only by providing consumers with products that consumers are willing to buy at a price they are willing to pay; moreover, they are pressured to produce these products while using as few of society's scarce resources as possible. In a world of global competition, this is no easy task.

Approaches to Social Responsibility

As "Bringing the World into Focus" indicates, some people advocate for a larger social role for organizations, while others argue that the role is already too large. Not surprisingly, organizations themselves adopt a wide range of positions on social responsibility. The four stances that an organization can take concerning its obligations to society, as shown in Figure 5.2, fall along a continuum ranging from the lowest to the highest degree of socially responsible practices.

OBSTRUCTIONIST STANCE. Organizations that take what might be called an **obstructionist stance** to social responsibility usually do as little as possible to address social or environmental problems. When they cross the ethical or legal line that separates acceptable from unacceptable practices, their typical response is to deny or avoid accepting responsibility for their actions. For example, a few years ago top managers in several foreign affiliates of Astra, a Swedish firm, were accused of a host of improprieties ranging from sexual harassment to the diversion of company resources for personal use. When these problems first began to surface, top officials in Sweden denied any wrongdoing before they even bothered to conduct an investigation. Similarly, both Nestlé

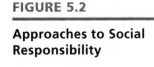

FIGURE 5.2

Approaches to Social Responsibility

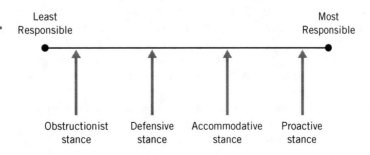

and Danone have been accused of violating international agreements signed in 1981 to control the marketing of infant formulas that serve as substitutes for breast milk. Those agreements stress the importance of breast feeding. Nestlé and Danone allegedly provided mothers in West Africa with free samples of milk powder and violated labeling standards on infant formula in the countries of Togo and Burkina Faso. The firms, however, deny any such violations and argue that their actions were all technically within the parameters of the agreements.[23] Moreover, both companies now believe that the treaties are outmoded as a result of the HIV/AIDS crisis, arguing that utilization of infant formulas may reduce the transmission of the virus from infected breastfeeding mothers to their infants.

DEFENSIVE STANCE.   One step removed from the obstructionist stance is the **defensive stance,** whereby the organization will do everything that is required of it legally but nothing more. This approach is often adopted by companies that are unsympathetic to the concept of social responsibility. Managers in organizations that take a defensive stance insist that their job is to generate profits. For example, such a firm would install pollution control equipment dictated by law but would not install higher-quality equipment even though it might limit pollution further. Tobacco companies such as R. J. Reynolds take this position in their marketing efforts. In the United States, they are legally required to include warnings to smokers on their products and to limit their advertising to prescribed media. Domestically they follow these rules to the letter of the law but use stronger marketing methods in countries that have no such rules. In many African countries, for example, cigarettes are heavily promoted, contain higher levels of tar and nicotine than those sold in the United States, and carry few or no health warning labels.[23] Firms that take this position are less likely to cover up wrongdoing than obstructionist firms and will generally admit to mistakes when they are identified and then take appropriate corrective actions.

ACCOMMODATIVE STANCE.   A firm that adopts an **accommodative stance** meets its legal and ethical requirements but will also go beyond these requirements in selected cases. Such firms voluntarily agree to participate in social programs, but solicitors have to convince the organization that the programs are worthy of their support. Some firms will match contributions made by their employees to selected charitable causes. And many organizations will respond to requests for donations to Little League baseball, youth soccer programs, and so forth. Vodafone's local affiliate, for example, sponsors a youth cricket league in Pretoria, South Africa. The point, though, is that someone generally has to knock on the door and ask—the organizations do not proactively seek such avenues for contributing.

PROACTIVE STANCE.   The highest degree of social responsibility that a firm can exhibit is the **proactive stance.** Firms that adopt this approach take to heart the arguments in favor of social responsibility. They view themselves as citizens in a society and proactively seek opportunities to contribute. An excellent example of a proactive stance is the Ronald McDonald House program undertaken by McDonald's Corp. These houses, located close to major medical centers, can be used by families for minimal cost while their sick children are receiving medical treatment nearby. Likewise, Gabrielle Melchionda owns a small skin care business in Maine called Mad Gab's. She was recently offered a $2 million contract to export her products to Turkey. But she turned the lucrative deal down when she learned that the exporter also sold weapons.[24] These and related activities and programs exceed the accommodative stance—they indicate a sincere and potent commitment to improving general social welfare in a country and thus represent a proactive stance to social responsibility. The Body Shop, Ben & Jerry's, and Timberland are three other companies widely admired for their proactive stances regarding social responsibility.[25]

Remember that these categories are not discrete but merely define stages along a continuum of approach. Organizations do not always fit neatly into one category. The Ronald McDonald House program has been widely applauded, for example, but McDonald's has also come under fire for allegedly misleading consumers about the nutritional value of its food products. And even though Astra took an obstructionist stance in the example cited above, many individual employees and managers at the firm have no doubt made substantial contributions to society in a number of different ways.

Managing Compliance

The demands for social responsibility placed on contemporary organizations by an increasingly sophisticated and educated public grow stronger every day. As we have seen, there are pitfalls for managers who fail to adhere to high ethical standards and for companies that try to circumvent their legal obligations. Organizations therefore need to fashion an approach to social responsibility the same way that they develop any other business strategy. That is, they should view social responsibility as a major challenge that requires careful planning, decision making, consideration, and evaluation. They may manage social responsibility through both formal and informal dimensions. Formal organizational dimensions used to implement a firm's social responsibility include legal compliance, ethical compliance, and philanthropic giving.

LEGAL COMPLIANCE. **Legal compliance** is the extent to which the organization conforms to regional, national, and international laws. The task of managing legal compliance is generally assigned to the appropriate functional managers. For example, the organization's top human resource executive is responsible for ensuring compliance with regulations concerning hiring, pay, and workplace safety and health. Likewise, the top finance executive generally oversees compliance with securities and banking regulations. The organization's legal department is also likely to contribute to this effort by providing general oversight and answering queries from managers about the appropriate interpretation of laws and regulations.

ETHICAL COMPLIANCE. **Ethical compliance** is the extent to which the members of the organization follow basic ethical (and legal) standards of behavior. We noted earlier that organizations have increased their efforts in this area—providing training in ethics and developing guidelines and codes of conduct, for example. These activities serve as vehicles for enhancing ethical compliance. Many organizations also establish formal ethics committees, which may be asked to review proposals for new projects, help evaluate new hiring strategies, or assess new environmental protection plans. They might also serve as a peer review panel to evaluate alleged ethical misconduct by an employee.[26]

PHILANTHROPIC GIVING. Finally, **philanthropic giving** is the awarding of funds or gifts to charities or other social programs. Giving across national boundaries is becoming more common. For example, Alcoa gave $112,000 to a small town in Brazil to build a sewage treatment plant. And Japanese firms like Sony and Mitsubishi make contributions to a number of social programs in the United States. BP has chosen to support numerous social programs in Russia and other former parts of the former U.S.S.R.

Perhaps the most significant international philanthropic program to date is that of Merck, the big U.S. pharmaceutical company, which had developed a heartworm medicine for dogs. In the affluent U.S. market Merck charged $20 to $30 for a dose of the drug. But Merck scientists discovered that their heartworm medicine could also cure onchocerciasis, a disease more commonly known as river blindness. This parasitic disease, spread by biting black flies, causes maddening itching, muscle pains, and weakness. Half of its victims suffer impaired vision, and a sixth lose their eyesight entirely. Yet the people who inhabit the lands that are plagued by river blindness are among the world's poorest. Merck decided to provide the drug, called Mectizan, for free. Since 1987, Merck has donated over 1.8 billion doses of Mectizan to people in 33 countries, sparing an estimated 69 million people annually from this terrifying disease.[27]

Unfortunately, in this age of cutbacks, many corporations have also had to limit their charitable gifts over the past several years as they continue to trim their own budgets. And many firms that continue to make contributions are increasingly targeting them to programs or areas where the firm will get something in return. For example, firms today are more likely to give money to job training programs than to the arts than was the case just a few years ago. The logic is that they get more direct payoff from the former type of contribution—in this instance, a better trained workforce from which to hire new employees—than the latter.[28]

Informal Dimensions of Social Responsibility

In addition to these formal dimensions for managing social responsibility, there are also informal ones. Leadership, organization culture, and how the organization responds to whistle-blowers each helps shape and define people's perceptions of the organization's stance on social responsibility.

ORGANIZATION LEADERSHIP AND CULTURE.   Leadership practices and organization culture can go a long way toward defining the social responsibility stance an organization and its members will adopt.[29] For example, for years Johnson & Johnson executives provided a consistent message to employees that customers, employees, communities where the company did business, and shareholders were all important—and primarily in that order. Thus when packages of poisoned Tylenol showed up on store shelves several years ago, Johnson & Johnson employees didn't need to wait for orders from headquarters to know what to do: They immediately pulled all the packages from shelves before any other customers could buy them.[30] By contrast, the message sent to Astra employees by the actions of their top managers communicates much less regard for social responsibility.

WHISTLE-BLOWING.   **Whistle-blowing** is the disclosure by an employee of illegal or unethical conduct on the part of others within the organization.[31] How an organization responds to this practice often indicates its stance toward social responsibility. In a typical North American company, whistle-blowers may have to proceed through a number of channels to be heard. Some have even been fired for their efforts, a fate that befell James Bingham, a former executive with Xerox. He attempted to blow the whistle on alleged financial mismanagement in several of the firm's foreign subsidiaries. He claimed that the firm illegally set aside $100 million when it acquired a British firm in order to use those funds to boost future earnings. He also cited a corporate culture at Xerox that, in his words, "cut bookkeeping corners to make up for deteriorating business fundamentals and to maximize short-term results." Shortly after he made his allegations, Bingham was fired.[32]

Many organizations, however, welcome the contributions of whistle-blowers. A person who observes questionable behavior typically first reports the incident to his or her boss. If nothing is done, the whistle-blower may then inform higher-level managers or an ethics committee if one exists. Eventually, the person may have to go to a regulatory agency or even the media to be heard.

Not surprisingly, attitudes toward whistle-blowing are affected by culture. Because of the traditional strong attachment of the individual to the organization in Japan, for instance, whistle-blowing is often viewed as an act of betrayal, rather than one of integrity. Back in the 1970s, one Japanese salesman discovered that his boss was engaging in price-fixing. He reported the incident to higher-ups in the organization, who told him to ignore the problem. The salesman persisted in his whistle-blowing efforts. The company's response was to exile him to a remote subsidiary, where he continued to work in a tiny office—only nine square feet—without a telephone or a pay raise for 27 years. Although whistle-blowing has become more common in Japan in the past decade, it is still frowned upon, for it disturbs the harmony of the group, or *wa*, a value much prized in Japanese culture.[33] One Japanese religious scholar notes, "Traditionally, betrayal is the biggest crime in Japan, almost worse than murder. The price was *mura hachibu,* or exile from the village."[34] A recent survey of 101 Japanese corporations indicated that only 29 have an in-house hotline for whistle-blowers. Although 20 companies replied that they were planning on installing a hotline, 49 adamantly reported they had no intention of doing so.[35]

Evaluating Social Responsibility

Any organization that is serious about social responsibility must ensure that its efforts are producing the desired benefits. Essentially this requires applying the concept of control to social responsibility. Many organizations now require current and new employees to read their guidelines or code of ethics and then sign a statement agreeing to abide by it. An organization should also evaluate how it responds to instances of questionable legal or ethical conduct. Does it follow up immediately? Does it punish those involved? Or does it use delay and cover-up tactics? Answers to these questions can help an organization diagnose any problems it might be having in meeting its social responsibilities.

Many organizations choose to conduct formal evaluations of the effectiveness of their social responsibility efforts. Some organizations, for instance, routinely conduct corporate social audits. A **corporate social audit** is a formal and thorough analysis of the effectiveness of the firm's social performance. The audit is usually undertaken by a task force of high-level managers from within the firm. It requires that the organization clearly define all its social goals, analyze the resources it devotes to each goal, determine how well it is achieving the various goals, and make recommendations about which areas need additional attention.

Difficulties of Managing CSR Across Borders

Another challenge facing corporations in establishing their policy toward corporate social responsibility is that the role of the corporation in society varies across countries. Multinational corporations, which by definition operate in multiple political and legal jurisdictions, are continually attempting to find the proper balance between the roles and behaviors expected by their home government and those expected by all of the host governments in the countries in which they operate. This is particularly complex in the case of corporate social responsibility, because corporations play very different roles in the political process of individual countries. How does an MNC please all of them? Indeed, companies are often criticized both for too much involvement in local politics and for not enough involvement. Many critics argue, for example, that oil companies play too large a role in the formulation of energy and environmental policies in the United States. Yet other critics have complained that these companies do too little to influence public policy in such countries as Nigeria or Myanmar. Shell's official policy is to support CSR "within the legitimate role of business," although that policy probably creates more questions than answers in interpreting what it means in practice.

A model developed by two Dutch CSR experts, Rob van Tulder and Alex van der Zwart, showcases this problem.[36] Their approach suggests there are three main actors in the policy formulation process:

1. The *state,* which passes and enforces laws;
2. The *market,* which through the process of competition and the pricing mechanism utilizes inputs and allocates outputs to members of the society; and
3. *Civil society,* which includes churches, charitable organizations, the Boy Scouts, labor unions, NGOs (nongovernmental organizations), and so on. Civil society in many ways manifests the cultural values of the citizens of the country.

The interplay among these three actors establishes public policy and the norms of social interaction, including, of course, accepted business behaviors. As is the case with culture, however, these social norms vary from country to country. Van Tulder and van der Zwart's model develops stereotypical behaviors in three regions of the world.

The Anglo-Saxon Approach

In van Tulder and van der Zwart's analysis, Anglo-Saxon countries view the state, the market, and civil society as separate, competitive, and antagonistic. Thus when the government must contract with the private sector to purchase goods or services, such contracting should be done through an open and competitive bidding process. When business and government fail to maintain sufficient separation, Anglo-Saxons deem that failure as corruption. Similarly, when Americans look at the relationship between civil society and government, members of the former are labeled "special interest groups." As articulated by James Madison in the *Federalist Papers,* democracy entails political competition among these special interest groups. So the U.S.–Anglo-Saxon approach focuses on competition, not cooperation, among the three groups as the means to promote social goals.

The Asian Approach

The relationship between these three actors is very different in Asia. Many Asian countries—Japan, Korea, China, and Indonesia come to mind—rely on close cooperation between the private sector and the government. Indeed, the economic clout of Japan's *keiretsu* and Korea's *chaebol* rests on their willingness to do the government's bidding and vice-versa. Many Asian leaders view this cooperation as the linchpin of their successful development strategies—the so-called "Asian Way." Note two things: First, from the perspective of the Anglo-Saxon approach, this symbiotic relationship between business and government is viewed as "crony capitalism," a polite term for corruption. Second, civil society plays a minor role in this process.

The Continental European Approach

In the European Union—particularly in continental European countries such as Austria, Germany, France, and the Netherlands—the three actors have much more cooperative ways of working with one another. In Germany, for example, large employer associations bargain with umbrella labor organizations under the watchful supervision of the government. Similarly, Germany's codetermination policy gives workers a well-defined role in the governance of large German businesses (see page 598). And, in general, the public policy process is based upon creating consensus among the three actors. Cooperation, not competition, is the hallmark of this approach.

Clearly each of the three approaches—Continental European, Asian, and Anglo-Saxon—conceptualizes the responsibilities of government, business, and civil society quite differently. This leaves MNCs that operate in all three areas with the difficult and complex task of triangulating between their own interests, the proper way of doing things according to the perspective of their home society, and the proper way of doing things according to the perspective of the society of the host countries in which they operate.

Regulating International Ethics and Social Responsibility

Not surprisingly, there have been many attempts to mandate and regulate ethical and socially responsible behavior by businesses. A detailed discussion of the myriad laws and regulations is beyond the scope of this discussion. However, we will describe a few of the more important and representative regulations.

The **Foreign Corrupt Practices Act (FCPA)** was passed by the United States Congress in 1977. The FCPA prohibits U.S. firms, their employees, and agents acting on their behalf from paying or offering to pay bribes to any foreign government official in order to influence the official actions or policies of that individual to gain or retain business. This prohibition applies even if the transaction occurs entirely outside U.S. borders. For instance, two former executives of Mobil Oil were indicted in 2003 for violating the FCPA. Allegedly they participated in an agreement to pay $78 million to several government leaders in Kazakhstan in return for control of the country's giant Tengiz oil fields; one of the executives allegedly received a $2 million kickback in the deal.[37] (See Chapter 3's closing case, "Sour Oil, Soured Deal.") Similarly, Baker Hughes, a Texas-based oilfield services provider, paid a $44 million fine to settle charges it violated the FCPA in Angola, Indonesia, Nigeria, Russia, and Uzbekistan, as well as Kazakhstan.[38] However, the FCPA does not outlaw routine payments, regardless of their size, made to government officials to expedite normal commercial transactions, such as issuance of customs documents or permits, inspection of goods, or provision of police services.

The **Alien Tort Claims Act** was passed in the United States in 1789 but has recently emerged as a potentially significant law affecting U.S. multinational corporations. Under some recent interpretations of this law, U.S. multinationals may conceivably be responsible for human rights abuses by foreign governments if the companies benefited from those abuses. For instance, the U.S. Court of Appeals for the Ninth Circuit recently allowed citizens of Burma to proceed with a case accusing Unocal of knowingly using forced labor supplied by the Burmese military. Other suits have been filed in New York and New Jersey accusing IBM, Citigroup, and other corporations of benefiting from apartheid in South Africa.[39]

The **Anti-Bribery Convention of the Organization for Economic Cooperation and Development** was developed in and first ratified by Canada in 2000; it has since been ratified by 33 other countries. The Convention is an attempt to eliminate bribery in international business transactions. Its centerpiece mandates jail time for those convicted of paying bribes.[40]

Finally, the **International Labor Organization (ILO)** has become a major watchdog for monitoring working conditions in factories in developing countries. Spurred by both Western corporations and the factories themselves, the ILO has begun to systematically inspect working conditions in countries such as Bangladesh, Cambodia, and the Philippines. Corporations find that such an independent inspection mechanism helps allay concerns from consumer activist groups; factory owners are also finding that subjecting themselves to regular ILO inspections helps them establish new business relationships with multinational corporations.[41]

There are numerous other laws and international agreements to promote socially responsible international business practices. "Emerging Opportunities" describes one such agreement, which is attempting to control trade in conflict diamonds, in order to bring peace to Sierra Leone, Congo, and other African nations.

Emerging Opportunities

Conflict Diamonds

According to Western custom, diamonds are a perfect way for a young man to demonstrate his undying love to his fiancée. But diamonds are also perfect for smuggling. They are small, easily concealed, and very valuable relative to their bulk and weight. A nasty little secret of the diamond trade is that diamond smugglers have financed some of the world's most vicious civil wars, including those that devastated Sierra Leone, Côte d'Ivoire, Congo, and Angola. Officials of nongovernmental organizations (NGOs) that are trying to aid the victims of these wars, such as CARE, Médecins sans Frontières, Global Witness, and the International Red Cross, realized that peace would be impossible unless trade in these so-called "conflict diamonds" ceased. They began publicizing the linkage between diamonds and these civil wars. Experts estimate that conflict diamonds constitute between 2 and 20 percent of the world's trade in the precious stones.

Newscom

Diamond mining is an important component of many African economies, including Sierra Leone (pictured here). Because of their high value and ease of transport, diamonds unfortunately have been used to finance some of the continent's most vicious civil wars and conflicts. The Kimberley Process is designed to reduce trade in "conflict diamonds," in the hope of bringing peace and prosperity to the region.

The diamond industry quickly realized that they faced a public relations disaster, fearing that consumers might shun diamond earrings or bracelets if they knew that their glittery purchases were helping warlords to buy bullets and machine guns. In 2000, the major countries involved in the diamond trade as producers, traders, or consumers commenced the Kimberley Process (named after the famed South African mining town) to halt trade in conflict diamonds. Seventy countries have agreed that, beginning in 2003, trade in diamonds would be limited to those stones that carry a certificate of origin from their country of production, guaranteeing that they were produced legally and outside the zones of conflict. However, the real problem is in enforcing the good intentions of the Kimberley Process. Some NGOs fear that smugglers will bribe corrupt officials to issue the certificates, or that they will devise other ways to circumvent the agreement.

(The plot of a recent James Bond movie, *Die Another Day,* involved just such a scheme.)

Other countries believe that conflict over conflict diamonds gives them an opportunity to promote their own industry. Canada, for instance, now produces 6 percent of the world's gem-quality diamonds, thanks to a discovery in the Northwest Territory in 1991. To demonstrate that their gems are produced in a conflict-free zone, one Canadian producer engraves a tiny polar bear in its diamonds, and another inscribes a maple leaf.

References: "The Dark Core of a Diamond," *Time* (Global Business bonus section), May 2006, p. A3; "Accord on Conflict Diamond Smuggling," *Financial Times,* November 11, 2005, p. 4; "Warning to 'Conflict Diamond' Traders," *Financial Times,* April 29, 2003, p. 6; "Political Correctness by the Carat," *Wall Street Journal,* April 17, 2003, p. B1; "Talks End in Agreement to Track Diamond Shipments," *Houston Chronicle,* November 30, 2001, p. 36A; "Diamond Town in the Rough," *Wall Street Journal,* July 5, 2001, p. B1; Jon Lee Anderson, "Oil and Blood," *The New Yorker,* August 14, 2000, pp. 45ff.

CHAPTERREVIEW

Summary

Ethics are an individual's personal beliefs about whether a decision, behavior, or action is right or wrong. What constitutes ethical behavior varies from one person to another. But while ethical behavior is in the eye of the beholder, it usually refers to behavior that conforms to generally accepted social norms. Unethical behavior is behavior that does not conform to generally accepted social norms. A society generally adopts formal laws that reflect the prevailing ethical standards—the social norms—of its members. Cultural differences often create ethical complications. Acceptable behavior in one culture may be viewed as immoral in another.

One important area of cross-cultural and international ethics is the treatment of employees by the organization. In practice, the areas most susceptible to ethical variation include hiring and firing practices, wages and working conditions, and employee privacy and respect. Numerous ethical issues also relate to how employees treat the organization. The central ethical issues in this relationship include conflicts of interest, secrecy and confidentiality, and honesty. A third major perspective for viewing ethics involves the relationship between the firm and its employees with other economic agents. The primary agents of interest include customers, competitors, stockholders, suppliers, dealers, and unions.

While ethics reside in individuals, many businesses nevertheless endeavor to manage the ethical behavior of their managers and employees. That is, they want to clearly establish the fact that they expect their managers and other employees to engage in ethical behaviors. They also want to take appropriate steps to eliminate as much ambiguity as possible in what the company views as ethical versus unethical behavior. The most common ways of doing this are through the use of guidelines or a code of ethics, ethics training, and organizational practices and the corporate culture.

Organizations need to define their policies toward corporate social responsibility—the set of obligations an organization has to protect and enhance the society in which it functions. Organizations may exercise social responsibility toward their stakeholders, toward the natural environment, and toward general social welfare. Some organizations acknowledge their responsibilities in all three areas and strive diligently to meet each of them, while others emphasize only one or two areas of social responsibility. And a few acknowledge no social responsibility at all.

As with attempts to manage ethical conduct, businesses usually make some effort to actively address social responsibility. This generally starts from their basic approach to social responsibility. It then extends to how they manage issues of compliance, the informal dimensions of social responsibility, and how they evaluate their efforts regarding social responsibility.

There have been many attempts to regulate ethical and socially responsible international business conduct. Four illustrative examples are the Foreign Corrupt Practices Act, the Alien Tort Claims Act, the Anti-Bribery Convention of the Organization for Economic Cooperation and Development, and the International Labor Organization (ILO).

Review Questions

1. What are ethics?
2. Distinguish between ethical and unethical behavior.
3. What role does culture play in the formation of ethics?
4. How do organizations attempt to manage ethical behavior across borders?
5. What is social responsibility?
6. What is the difference between ethics and social responsibility?
7. Identify the major areas of social responsibility for international business.
8. What are the four general approaches a firm can take with regard to social responsibility?
9. What is a whistle-blower?
10. Identify and briefly summarize representative laws and regulations that attempt to address international ethics and social responsibility.

Questions for Discussion

1. While people from the same culture are likely to have similar views of what constitutes ethical versus unethical behavior, what factor or factors would account for differences within a culture?
2. Is it valid to describe someone as having "no ethics"? Why or why not?
3. People from which countries would likely have similar ethical beliefs as people from England? Why?
4. Under what circumstances is a code of ethics most and least likely to be effective? Why?
5. What do you think is most likely to happen if the ethical behaviors and decisions of a new team of top managers of a firm are inconsistent with the firm's long-entrenched corporate culture?
6. Do you think social responsibility for a multinational corporation is something best managed locally or best managed globally?
7. Do multinational businesses ever do socially responsible things that are clearly of no benefit whatsoever to themselves?
8. What are the dangers or pitfalls that might be encountered if a multinational business attempts to be socially responsible, but only in ways that provide direct benefits to its profitability?
9. Under what circumstances, if any, might you see yourself as a whistle-blower? Under what circumstances, if any, might you keep quiet about illegal acts by your employer?
10. Do you think there should be more or fewer attempts to regulate international ethics and social responsibility? Why?
11. Consider the plight of Mary, the Philippine woman discussed on page 149. In response to the inquiries of *Fortune*'s reporter, Motorola issued a statement saying it "has a strict policy of adherence to the laws and labor practices in the countries where it operates, in addition to a rigorous code of conduct." Is this an adequate response? In your opinion, what responsibility does Motorola have to workers like Mary? Defend your answer.
12. Consider the following scenarios:
    - To assist the sale of your products in a particular foreign market, it is suggested that you pay a 10 percent commission to a "go-between" who has access to high-ranking government officials in that market. You suspect, but do not know, that the go-between will split the commission with the government officials who decide which goods to buy. Should you do it? Does it make a difference if your competitors routinely pay such commissions?
    - You have a long-standing client in a country that imposes foreign exchange controls. The client asks you to pad your invoices by 25 percent. For example, you would ship the client $100,000 worth of goods but would invoice the client for $125,000. On the basis of your invoice, the client would obtain the $125,000 from the country's central bank. The client then would pay you $100,000 and have you put the remaining $25,000 in a Swiss bank account in the client's name. Should you do it? Would it make a difference if your client is a member of a politically unpopular minority and might have to flee the country at a moment's notice?

Building Global Skills

Identify an industry that interests you personally and that has a number of major multinational companies. Potential examples include energy, automobiles, and consumer electronics. Visit the Web sites of three firms in that industry and learn as much as possible about their stances regarding ethical conduct and social responsibility. Identify commonalities and differences across the three firms. Next, develop observations about the likely effectiveness of the firms' efforts to promote ethical conduct and social responsibility based on their Web sites. Finally, respond to the following questions:

1. Symbolically, what potential role does the Internet serve in helping to promote ethical conduct and social responsibility as evidenced by the Web sites you visited?

2. Which firm has the most effective Web site vis-à-vis ethics and social responsibility? In your opinion, what makes it the best?
3. Which firm has the least effective Web site vis-à-vis ethics and social responsibility? In your opinion, what makes it the worst?

4. How do the Web sites affect your view of each company from the standpoint of a potential investor? A potential employee? A potential supplier?
5. If asked, what advice might you offer to each company to improve its attention to ethical conduct and social responsibility as reflected by its Web site?

Closing Case

A Pipeline of Good Intentions

Development economists and poverty specialists often talk about the "oil curse," a phrase reflecting the numerous instances when the discovery of oil in poor countries has paradoxically led to increases in poverty and social problems. When oil was discovered in the Doba basin in southern Chad in the 1990s, many predicted the oil curse would strike Chad as well. Chad, which is primarily desert with few natural resources, is one of the poorest countries on earth. With only a few hundred doctors to serve a population of 10 million, one-third of its children suffer from malnutrition. Since gaining independence from France in 1960, the country has been plagued by dictatorships and civil wars, as well as invasions by Libya and incursions by Sudanese rebel groups. Four times French troops have had to be sent to the former colony to restore a semblance of order.

While the Doba basin was estimated to hold 2 billion barrels of oil, Chad is landlocked. To get the oil to market, an expensive, 1,070-kilometer pipeline would have to be built from Chad to a port in Cameroon, where the oil could then be shipped from the Gulf of Guinea to world markets

(see Map 5.2). Despite a relatively low royalty rate to be paid to Chad's government—one-eighth of the value of production—the consortium of foreign companies who had discovered the oil field—Exxon Mobil, Petronas of Malaysia, and Chevron—were hesitant to develop the Doba basin because of the political risks of operating in Chad, the costliness of the pipeline, and the low quality of the oil produced there.

The consortium members and the governments of Chad and Cameroon approached the World Bank to provide financing for the $4.1 billion project. In 1999, the World Bank agreed to provide $400 million of financing; the oil companies anted up $3.5 billion. Exxon Mobil, which operates the wells, supplied 40 percent; Chevron put up 25 percent; and Petronas of Malaysia, 35 percent. The remaining funds were supplied by the European Investment Bank. The pipeline itself was to be owned and operated by two joint-venture companies, one in Chad and one in Cameroon. The two governments owned minority interests in their respective companies, with a majority stake in both taken by the consortium of oil companies.

MAP 5.2

Chad Pipeline

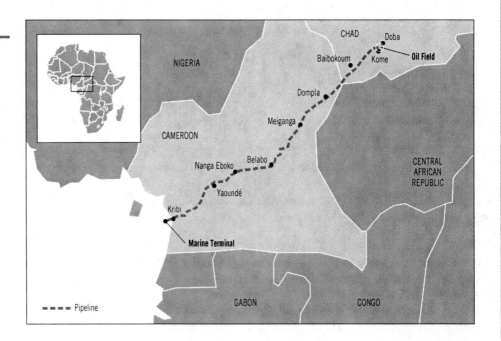

While the Bank's share of the $4.1 billion cost was small, its participation in the deal was critical. Because the World Bank had other loans outstanding to Chad, Exxon Mobil and the other oil companies believed that the World Bank's participation would lower their political risks, for Chad would be unlikely to jeopardize its relationship with the World Bank. However, the last two World Bank presidents, James Wolfensohn and Paul Wolfowitz, were growing increasingly concerned about corruption's corrosive impact on economic development. This issue was certainly germane to Chad. Transparency International, an NGO (nongovernmental organization) that annually conducts surveys of corruption, ranks Chad's government as one of the most corrupt in Africa. Facilitating corruption was the lack of accountability and transparency in the use of oil revenues by many governments. And the revenues generated by the pipeline would provide sufficient temptation: Over its estimated 25-year life, the project is expected to yield $2 billion for Chad and $500 million for Cameroon.

Given these circumstances, the World Bank agreed to lend money for the project only if it received assurances that the revenues from the oil field would be devoted to alleviating the country's poverty. To gain the World Bank's approval for the loan, Chad agreed to enact the Petroleum Revenue Management Law. Under this law, Chad's royalties were to be deposited in an escrow account at Citibank's London branch. Ten percent of the royalties were to be put in a separate fund to benefit future generations of Chad. The remaining royalty revenues were to be spent according to a formula—15 percent for general governmental needs, 80 percent for health and education services, and 5 percent in the oil-producing region, Doba.

For the first several years of the program, everything went according to plan. The oil companies drilled over 200 wells in Doba, and soon oil was flowing through the pipeline. The pipeline boosted the local economy and the government's coffers. The pipeline employs 7,300 people in Chad, 83 percent of whom are Chad nationals; the comparable figures for Cameroon are 1,100 and 90 percent. The pipeline consortium also sponsored a variety of health initiatives, including anticholera, anti-malaria, and HIV/AIDS awareness programs. Exxon has purchased more than $2 billion from local suppliers and refurbished 480 kilometers of local roads and bridges. The company also funded the construction of several local clinics, which treat more than 12,000 patients a year. In its first year of production, the pipeline generated $131 million for Chad's government, about 42 percent of its budget. By mid-2006, Chad had earned $537 million from the pipeline. Of these monies, $295 million had been directed to the priority sectors of health, education, and road rehabilitation, and $19 million had been devoted to community-development projects in the Doba region, where the oil fields were located.

Unfortunately, Chad's government began to suffer budget difficulties. President Idress Deby argued that his government could no longer honor its deal with the World Bank, in part because of the rising costs of administering to the flood of refugees fleeing the conflict in the Darfur region of neighboring Sudan. In December 2005 Chad's National Assembly voted to amend the Petroleum Revenue Management Law. The new amendments abolished the special fund that would preserve oil revenues for the benefit of future generations. In addition, the legislation doubled the percentage of oil revenues that the country could spend without outside oversight to 30 percent. It also added national security to the priority areas of education, health, and road rehabilitation.

The World Bank acted swiftly in response to this legislation, which it viewed as abandoning Chad's obligations under the agreement. In January 2006, it suspended all new grants and loans to Chad and cut off additional disbursements under existing projects with Chad. The World Bank's actions affected some $124 million in undisbursed funds in eight Bank-funded projects with Chad. To make matters worse, in April 2006, a rebel army, allegedly backed by the government of Sudan, attacked N'Djamena, Chad's capital. Although this incursion was defeated, it heightened the resolve of President Deby to relax the constraints on the oil revenues.

The Exxon-led consortium was now caught in the middle. It decided to withhold all revenues until the dispute between the World Bank and Chad's government was resolved. However, President Deby announced that if the consortium failed to deliver the funds to Chad's government, he would demand that oil production cease in Doba. Ultimately, the consortium could lose its rights to operate in the country. However, if the consortium delivered the funds to the Deby government, it faced the wrath of the World Bank and various activist groups like Transparency International.

Case Questions

1. What is the "oil curse"? Why do you think it develops?
2. Why was the World Bank's participation in the Chad-Cameroon pipeline critical?
3. Does the World Bank have a right to demand that sovereign countries like Chad spend their oil revenues in ways the World Bank deems appropriate?
4. If the World Bank and Chad's government fail to settle their dispute over amendments to the Petroleum Revenue Management Law, what should the consortium do? Should they make funds available to Chad's government in defiance of the World Bank's wishes?
5. Subsequent to the signing of the pipeline agreement, world oil prices have increased substantially. Given the abject poverty of Chad, should the oil companies offer to increase the royalties paid to Chad's government once its dispute with the World Bank is settled?

References: www.worldbank.org; "A regime saved, for the moment," *The Economist,* February 9, 2008, p. 53; "Chad Export Project: Project Update No. 22," Esso Exploration and Production Chad, Inc. (2007); "An Ill-Advised Leap into the Unknown?", *Financial Times,* March 1, 2006, p. 7; "Exxon Faces a Dilemma on Chad Project," *Wall Street Journal,* February 28, 2006, p. A4; "The 'Resource Curse' Anew: Why a Grand World Bank Oil Project Has Fast Run into the Sand," *Financial Times,* January 23, 2006, p. 13; "World Bank Pulls Chad Pipeline Loan," *Houston Chronicle,* January, 2006, p. D3; "As Exxon Pursues African Oil, Charity Becomes Political Issue," *Wall Street Journal,* January 10, 2006, p. A1; "Chad Export Project: Project Update No. 19, Annual Report 2005," Esso Exploration and Production Chad, Inc. (2006); "A Regime Change," *The Economist,* June 4, 2005, p. 65; "African Pipeline Has Yet to Deliver Lasting Benefits," *Houston Chronicle,* June 29, 2003, p. 5D; "In War on Poverty, Chad's Pipeline Plays Unusual Role," *Wall Street Journal,* June 24, 2003, p. A8.

PART 1 Closing Cases

KFC in China

KFC opened its first western-style restaurant in Beijing in 1987. It has rapidly expanded using a blend of franchising and localization strategies. It has grown from small beginnings to become China's largest foreign fast food chain. It has over 2,200 branches in 450 Chinese cities. It is a far bigger enterprise than any of the other multinational fast food chains that have tried to trade in the potentially high-risk Chinese market.

The first KFC store in China was opened close to Tiananmen Square. It is still the largest KFC outlet worldwide. Such has been the transition in fortunes for KFC and other multinational fast food outlets that initially, when they were opened, the most frequent customers were foreigners living in China. Local consumers could not afford to eat there.

Yum Brands owns the KFC and Pizza Hut brands. It quickly discovered that it is not enough to rely on a well-known foreign brand name to ensure growth. Instead, it is important to adapt to local tastes and lifestyles. KFC has, therefore, adapted its menu by adding a variety of dishes that are familiar to the Chinese.

Year on year, Yum's sales in China have increased; it was the first foreign fast food company to move into China and including the Pizza Hut stores it has 2,500 branches with annual sales of $2 billion. The nearest multinational competitor is McDonald's with just 900 branches. There is still considerable room for expansion, as China's fast food market is estimated to be worth $28 billion per year.

During 2008, with the Beijing Olympics and the higher profile that China enjoyed, Yum intended to add 425 new branches, while McDonald's aimed to top the 1,000 mark with 125 new stores. In 2007 Yum's China Division's operating profit rose by 30 percent to $375 million. This was a quarter of the entire multinationals' operating profit. The Chief Executive of Yum, David Novak, predicted that by 2017 the Chinese operation would contribute 40 percent of the overall profits.

Perceptions of Pizza Hut, in particular, are very different in China than in many other markets. In Europe and the United States, for example, Pizza Huts are regarded as being relatively inexpensive, but in China they are considered to be up-market and, therefore, Yum has targeted the estimated 250 million middle class Chinese consumers.

In a unique reverse strategy the success of Yum's Chinese business, particularly by introducing healthier products and breaking away from the notion that KFC produces junk food, Novak explained to shareholders in December 2007: "Let's learn from our most successful business. Let's learn from our China business."

The idea will be to adapt the China model across the rest of the world and increase the emphasis on breakfast and evening sales and provide broader menus.

Yum China is not content with simply taking China's fast food chicken market by storm. They are now planning the expansion of a traditional Chinese fast food chain called East Dawning.

This will take on Kung Fu Catering Management and the hotpot chain, Inner Mongolia Little Sheep. Ten East Dawning branches have been operating in Shanghai since 2005. Yum tested the Beijing market prior to the Olympics. The branches offer traditional Chinese dishes.

Initially, the novelty of KFC restaurants won over many Chinese customers. Fast food was considered to be exotic and Chinese consumers were curious. At first, KFC took advantage of the situation, charging relatively high prices. By the mid-1990s there were about 100 fast food restaurants around Beijing. It quickly became obvious that the market was not growing fast enough, as many Chinese considered that the fast food was not as good as their own Chinese cuisine. During Chinese festivals traditional Chinese restaurants were full to bursting, while KFC restaurants and McDonald's were almost empty. There were a number of reasons for this; some economic, some social and others ideological, but culture played the most important role.

The Chinese have a traditional culture of food and drink and fast food could not compare with it. Once the curiosity of the new fast food restaurants had waned, Chinese people returned to their own cuisine. In order to first survive and then to prosper, KFC had to combine the elements of the two different cuisine cultures. In other words, it had to absorb elements of Chinese cuisine.

In 2001 KFC introduced Chinese food to their menus. They started with preserved Sichuan pickle and shredded pork soup. This was a success and mushroom rice, tomato and egg soup and Peking chicken rolls were also added to the menu. McDonald's tried to follow suit and began to modify the design of the restaurants and add distinctly Chinese style soups to their menu. In effect, both KFC and McDonald's had developed intercultural management. They had retained American business culture but supplemented it with Chinese traditional culture. The businesses had used localization strategies to reinterpret American business culture.

Why then is KFC far more popular in China than McDonald's? Certainly, KFC has stressed that their own version of fast food is far healthier than other fast food options. China also is an enormous consumer of fried chicken and customers prefer it to hamburgers. KFC also has a far more Chinese-specific menu than McDonald's and, finally, KFC has made great use of deals and coupons and around 50 percent of their customers use coupons to purchase food from their branches.

On January 16, 2004, KFC had opened its one thousandth restaurant in China. The success of KFC was certainly linked to both its franchise policy and the scientific nature of its managerial operations. This was known as CHAMPS. It measures operational basics of Cleanliness, Hospitality, Accuracy, Maintenance, Product quality and Speed.

From the outset KFC took advantage of the political changes in China and the different approach of the Chinese government that began to welcome western investors. KFC certainly had a synergy with China from the very beginning.

The poultry industry in China was one of the major priorities of the agricultural modernization plans and KFC, as a predominantly poultry food chain, gained enormous support from the Chinese government.

Financially, KFC's entry into the Chinese market came at an ideal time. PepsiCo had only recently purchased the company and the business now had enormous financial muscle. The market potential in China was enormous and chicken was not only more popular, but cheaper and more widely available than beef. KFC also had the ideal image as far as the Chinese consumer was concerned; the clean branches were considered to be hygienic and KFC stressed the high levels of quality and service throughout all of their outlets.

There were, however, some weaknesses and potential threats. The Chinese government provides far more support to businesses that are bringing technology into their country and KFC was a service provider. The setting up of each new restaurant was a high-cost venture and initially KFC had problems in ensuring high quality supplies from local producers. Human resource management was difficult in a culture where family contacts are often used to obtain sought -after jobs. There was also a lack of Chinese-speaking store outlet managers and initially there were problems with the management and local employees. KFC's imposed quality standards were at variance with Chinese partners, who believed that they knew what Chinese customers wanted more than KFC.

In order to adapt and to cater for the Chinese market, KFC's strategy was to offer a blend of western style products, which would appeal to younger consumers that were eager to try foreign food, while at the same time developing traditional Chinese-style fast food. The net outcome was a blend of both east and west, with Chinese seafood and Hong Kong milk tea sitting alongside orange juice, fries and western chicken burgers. The U.S. brand image was retained, which was consistent with KFC's globalization strategy, but the incorporation of Chinese side dishes was a key localization strategy.

One of the major cultural differences between the United States and China is the perceived gulf between American individualism and Chinese collectivism. Taking this into account, it was obviously a key influence on the advertising and on the strategies used by KFC in China. Individualism emphasizes achievement, freedom, competition, pleasure and independence. On the other hand, collectivism suggests security, hierarchy, cooperation, low competition and interdependence. Harmony and conformity are also a key aspect of collectivism. KFC therefore had to adapt its advertising, in order to communicate how their products would satisfy these customer needs. The first key aspect was to become family and group orientated. Commercials promoted the KFC bucket, which could be enjoyed by the whole family; this fitted well with the value systems in China. Big families with three generations and relatives were targeted by the advertising. As far as groups were concerned, KFC commercials targeted friends having fun and work colleagues. KFC also used emotional appeals, which would find resonance in the Chinese market. They focused on patriotism, respect for the elderly, cherishing the young, friendship and romantic love.

In December 2003 KFC made a major mistake when it promoted a new chicken wrap. It featured an empty Cantonese restaurant and a packed KFC outlet and caused enormous reaction; KFC was accused of being arrogant and there was considerable backlash. KFC has since been extremely careful to avoid offending Chinese culture.

As with any foreign product or service, there is always the question of cultural imperialism and the fact that western-style fast food can be seen as an invisible cultural invasion that is trying to overwhelm traditional Chinese culture. The Chinese were particularly concerned about the influence of fast food on the young and whether it would, in effect, separate the young from their own cultural heritage. Much of this attitude has changed, as China is no longer isolationist and there is no longer a fascination for fast food just because it is foreign. KFC is a prime example of how its convenience fits in with Chinese lifestyle and the fact that it has adapted to the fast pace of modern Chinese life. Understandably, there have also been health concerns and in China there was a belief that too much fast food would cause obesity and other health problems. So far, KFC has tried to mitigate any particular problems in relation to health issues by focusing on the nutritional value.

KFC's success in China has undoubtedly been a result of understanding the country and its culture. The company has recognized that the host culture is an important consideration and cannot be overwhelmed by standardized global marketing and advertising. Undoubtedly, KFC is the most popular international brand in China. The localization strategy has certainly worked.

Yum Brands are also trying to replicate their success with KFC across their other brands. Su believes that Pizza Hut will be the next major success story. China has rising incomes and economic growth; both key drivers in helping Pizza Hut to become a major brand.

Taco Bell is also being tested in the Chinese market, with a test restaurant in Shanghai. They hope the model will work across China and if it does it will be another big success story.

Questions

1. Real Kung Fu is a Chinese fast food chain with around 200 stores across China. What are their short-term growth plans and possible problems?
2. Where is Yum Brands based and which countries does the Yum China Division cover?
3. When did KFC open its first ever drive through restaurant and how many Pizza Hut home delivery services are operating in mainland China?
4. When did KFC open its first ever drive through restaurant and how many Pizza Hut home delivery services are operating in mainland China?

Sources: China Economic Net (www.en.ce.cn), China Daily (www.chinadaily.com), The China Ex Pat (www.thechinaexpat.com), China Herald (www.chinaherald.net), People's Daily (www.english.peopledaily.com.cn), All Business (www.allbusiness.com), and Eats Online (www.eats.com)

The Oil Curse

In Chapter 5's closing case, we noted that development economists and poverty specialists often view the discovery of oil as a curse rather than a blessing. Consider the case of Nigeria.

Its 135 million citizens make it Africa's most populous country. Declared a British protectorate in 1914, it is home to more than 250 ethnic groups, although four groups—the Hausa and Fulani in northern Nigeria (29 percent), the Yoruba in the southwest (21 percent), and the Igbo (Ibo) and Ijaw in the southeast (18 percent and 10 percent, respectively)—account for the majority of the population.

Oil was first discovered in the Niger Delta in 1958, shortly before Nigeria became an independent nation in 1960. In 1967 the Ibo and other ethnic groups in the southeastern coastal region attempted to secede from Nigeria, declaring their lands the Republic of Biafra. Biafra's secession met with fierce opposition from the Hausa/Fulani and Yoruba leadership, who quickly realized that an independent Biafra would control the Niger Delta oil fields and the area's primary source of revenue. Federal troops suppressed the secession attempt in a bloody, two-year war. A cease-fire was instituted in early 1970, and Biafra was reabsorbed into Nigeria.

The Nigerian oil industry, then as now, is centered on Port Harcourt in the Niger Delta. Capable of producing 2.4 million barrels of oil a day, Nigeria is Africa's largest oil producer. Oil revenues account for 95 percent of the country's exports, 20 percent of its GDP, and 80 percent of the government's revenues. However, the country remains poor, with an estimated per capita income of $640 and a life expectancy at birth of only 47.

Unfortunately, during its brief history Nigeria has been plagued by high levels of corruption, fueled in part by the misuse of its oil revenues. Nor has Nigeria been blessed with good governments. Among the worst was the military regime of Sani Abacha, a dictator who ruled the country from 1993 to 1998. One of the low points of Abacha's reign was the sham trial and execution of Ken Saro-Wiwa, a political activist who fought to protect the environment and the human rights of the people in the Niger Delta. After 16 years of military government, in 1999 Olusegun Obasanjo was elected president of the country in what has been described as a relatively fair election by local standards. He was reelected in 2003. In 2007, he was succeeded by Umaru Musa Yar'Adua in an election that international observers characterized as tainted.

Local citizens in the Niger Delta have benefited little from the oil boom. Despite the wealth generated by the Niger Delta's oil fields, much of the local population lives in desperate poverty, lacking adequate hospitals, schools, and electricity. Pollution from drilling operations and inevitable spills have despoiled the local mangrove swamps and harmed the fisheries and the fishing industry that depends on them.

Although Presidents Obasanjo and Yar'Adua have tried to address the issues raised by community leaders in the Niger Delta, violence is increasingly supplanting political dialogue. In 2002, hundreds of Nigerian women invaded Chevron's oil processing facilities on Escravos Island, demanding that the company provide schools, clinics, and jobs for the local citizens; three months earlier a Chevron offshore drilling platform was the target of a similarly motivated raid.

In 2004, a rebel group called the Niger Delta People's Volunteer Force demanded that foreign oil companies terminate their operations in the area or face the threat of all-out war. Armed militias clashed with government forces in Port Harcourt and the surrounding Rivers State, leading to the deaths of several hundred Nigerians and making it more difficult for Shell, Chevron, and other oil companies to maintain and repair their facilities and produce and transport their products. The group's stated aim is to liberate the local Ijaw people from control of the central government and allow the Ijaws to benefit from the oil wealth that their region generates. The Nigerian government dismissed such claims, scoffing that the group was nothing more than a front for oil thieves.

There is little doubt that much oil thievery takes place in the Niger Delta. Armed gangs divert as much as 5 percent of the oil through a practice called bunkering, maneuvering small boats at night to siphon off oil from lightly guarded pipelines in remote areas. The stolen oil eventually reaches the international market, first passing through layers of middlemen. Human rights activists, however, claim the problem is not limited to local thugs, alleging that the army, the police, local politicians, and even the oil companies participate in bunkering schemes. Such lawlessness costs more than money. In May 2006, nearly 200 villagers were killed when a gasoline pipeline exploded in Inagbe, a fishing community 48 kilometers east of Lagos. Officials believe the explosion occurred because of the common practice of puncturing the pipeline to siphon off gasoline.

The security situation seems to be worsening. In early 2006, the commander of another group, the Movement for the Emancipation of the Niger Delta (MEND), declared total war on foreign oil operations. MEND wants to return control of Nigeria's oil wealth to the region where it is produced and wants the release of two ethnic Ijaw leaders being held by the central government on money laundering and treason charges. To further its goals, it has sabotaged oil-pumping stations, attacked transport barges, and kidnapped foreign oil workers, snatching them from offshore drilling rigs. MEND's actions have cut production in the Niger Delta by 455,000 barrels a day, costing the government, the industry, and the country billions of dollars of lost revenues. Shell, for example, abandoned one field in the southern Niger Delta producing 115,000 barrels per day, citing safety concerns for its employees.

Nor is the violence limited to MEND. In May 2006, three expatriate employees of ENI, the Italian oil company, were kidnapped in Port Harcourt, and an American employee of Baker Hughes was murdered in that city. In June 2006 eight foreign oil workers were kidnapped from an oil rig located 64 kilometers offshore operated by a subsidiary of Norway's Fred Olsen Energy Company. The eight were released a day later. MEND claimed it was not responsible for the murder or the kidnappings, alleging that another group had done so, motivated by the lure of ransom money. However, later in the week, MEND, the Niger Delta People's Volunteer Force, and another group, the Martyrs Brigade, launched a coordinated, 10-boat-strong attack on an oil facility in Port Harcourt, destroying a drilling rig, sinking two naval vessels, killing several soldiers, and abducting five South Korean workers. Six Chevron employees were kidnap victims in May 2007; fortunately they were released a month later unharmed.

As if this operating environment were not difficult enough, the reputation of the oil companies operating in the region has also come under attack. Royal Dutch Shell has drawn the bulk of the blame by Western activists and local citizens, although other Western companies, such as Chevron, have been targeted as well. Environmental groups and NGOs like Global Exchange and Essential Action have argued that the oil companies are taking advantage of lax enforcement of environmental laws to pollute the area and ignore the damage caused by oil and gasoline spills. Other activists have argued that Shell has alleged sabotage of the pipelines to cover up spills resulting from the company's lack of maintenance. Human rights activists claim that the foreign oil companies are complicit in human rights violations by the Nigerian government as it attempts to suppress political dissent and insurgent activity in the region.

Questions

1. Assess the political risks facing foreign oil companies operating in the Niger Delta. Should they shut down operations in the area until security improves?
2. What is the responsibility of Western oil companies like Royal Dutch Shell and Chevron to the local community?
3. What responsibility does a drilling company like Fred Olsen Energy have to its employees? In the case of kidnappings motivated by profit, should a company pay ransom?
4. Is the discovery of oil a blessing or a curse?

References: "Nigeria's Oil-Export Reliability at Risk," *Wall Street Journal,* February 11, 2008, p. A14; "Nigeria's Gang Violence Escalates," *New York Times,* November 9, 2007 (online); "In Nigeria's Violent Delta, Hostage Negotiators Thrive," *Wall Street Journal,* June 7, 2007, p. A1; "Militants Attack Nigeria Oil Field," *CNN.com,* June 7, 2006; "Nigerian Kidnappers Release Foreign Oil Workers," *Wall Street Journal,* June 4, 2006 (online); "Nigerian Gunmen Abduct 8 Workers from Oil Platform," *Wall Street Journal,* June 3, 2006, p. A5; "Gasoline Pipeline Explodes in Nigeria, Killing About 200," *New York Times,* May 13, 2006, p. A3; "Africa: Nigeria: Gunmen Kidnap 3 Foreign Oil Workers," *New York Times,* May 12, 2006 (online); "As Oil Supplies Are Stretched, Rebels, Terrorists Get New Clout," *Wall Street Journal,* April 10, 2006, p. A1; "Oil Giants to Steer Clear Until Nigeria Has a Truce," *Houston Chronicle,* April 6, 2006, p. D8; "Insecurity in Nigerian Oil Delta Here to Stay," *Houston Chronicle,* March 24, 2006, p. A19; "Nigeria Militants Threaten More Attacks," *Houston Chronicle,* March 6, 2006, p. A8; "Poverty in the Midst of Wealth," *Houston Chronicle,* March 1, 2006, p. D8; "Militants Say the Plan Is to Take More Hostages," *Houston Chronicle,* February 23, 2006, p. D3; "Nigeria Oil 'Total War' Warning," *BBC News,* February 17, 2006 (online); "SEC Widens Nigeria Bribery Probe with Shell Subpoena," *Financial Times,* October 13, 2005, p. 4; "Nigerian Army Warns Oil Rebels," *BBC News,* September 28, 2004 (online); "Nigeria's Oil Capital under Siege," *BBC News,* September 8, 2004 (online); "Women Storm Nigeria Oil Plant," *BBC News,* July 9, 2002 (online); "Nigeria Oil Rig Workers Seized," *BBC News,* April 23, 2002 (online); *The World Factbook,* www.cia.gov (online).

Market Entry Strategy Project Exercises

MESP Exercise for Part 1

This exercise is the first component of the Market Entry Strategy Project (MESP). Working with a group of your classmates, select two countries that interest you. One of these should be a relatively mature market, and the other should be an emerging market. Develop answers to each of the following questions for each country and integrate them into your completed MESP report.

1. What is the GDP of the country? What is its per capita income? How important is manufacturing in the economy? How important is agriculture? What are the primary exports and imports of the country? Who are the country's primary trading partners?
2. What is the level of foreign direct investment (FDI) in the economy? What countries are the primary suppliers of FDI to the country? How has globalization affected this economy?
3. What type of legal system does the country have? Is it generally viewed as honest and fair by local citizens? How vulnerable to political risk are foreign firms operating in the country? What types of political risk do they face?
4. What is the primary language of the country? Are other languages commonly used as well? What is the dominant religion in the country? Are there significant religious minorities in the country? If so, are their rights respected by the majority? How culturally homogenous is the country? Using Hofstede's framework, describe the culture of the country.

CHAPTER

4

RESOURCES AND ENVIRONMENT

OBJECTIVES

- To describe the nature, distribution, and limits of the world's resources
- To examine the nature of world food problems and to make you aware of the difficulties of solving them
- To describe the distribution of strategic minerals and the time spans for their depletion
- To consider the causes and consequences of the energy crisis and to examine present and alternative energy options
- To examine the nature and causes of environmental degradation
- To compare and contrast growth-oriented and balance-oriented lifestyles

"Petroleum storage facilities reflect its critical importance to the world economy."

Economic growth and prosperity depend partly on the availability of natural resources and the quality of the environment. There is growing concern that the consumption of inputs and goods in developed countries, and increasingly in developing countries, is depleting the world's stock of resources and irreparably degrading the natural environment. What can be done to effectively manage resources and protect the environment?

Optimists believe that economic growth in a market economy can continue indefinitely; they see relatively few limits in raw materials and great gains in technological productivity. In contrast, pessimists assert that there are inherent limits to growth imposed by the finiteness of the earth—by the fact that air, water, minerals, space, and usable energy sources can be exhausted or ecosystems overloaded. They believe these limits are near and, as evidence, point to existing food, mineral, and energy shortages and to areas now beset by deforestation and erosion.

Some scholars think that the long running debate on resources and the environment, which waxes and wanes over time, is counterproductive, evading practical issues that demand our immediate attention. We need to keep our purposes in mind and try to understand how to achieve our ends. If our purpose is to create a habitable and sustainable world for generations to follow, how can we redirect present and future output to serve that end? One solution is to transform our present a *growth-oriented lifestyle*, which is based on a goal of ever-increasing production and consumption, to a *balance-oriented lifestyle* designed for minimal environmental impact. A balance-oriented lifestyle would include an equitable and modest use of resources, a production system compatible with the environment, and appropriate technology. The aim of a balance-oriented world economy is maximum human well-being with a minimum of material consumption. Growth occurs, but only growth that truly benefits all people, not just the elite few. However, what societies, rich or poor, are willing to dismantle their existing systems of production to accept a lifestyle that seeks satisfaction more in quality and equality than in quantity and inequality? Are people programmed for maximum consumption by a value system constantly reinforced through advertising willing to change their ways of thinking and behaving?

This chapter, which discusses growth-oriented versus balance-oriented philosophies of resource use, deals with the complex components of the population-resources issue. Have population and economic growth rates been outstripping food, minerals, and energy? What is likely to happen to the rate of demand for resources in the future? Could a stable population of 10 billion be sustained indefinitely at a reasonable standard of living utilizing currently known technology? These are the salient, critical questions with which this chapter is concerned.

RESOURCES AND POPULATION

Popular opinion in the industrial West generally appreciates the need to reduce population growth but overlooks the need to limit economic growth that exploits resources. Most people in the economically developed world suffer from a view that holds resources are limitless and do not appreciate that our rapid consumption of them ultimately threatens our affluent way of life. The First World is, in short, liquidating the resources on which our way of life was built. The growth of some developing countries is aggravating the situation. Their growing populations put increasing pressure on resources and the environment, and many aspire to affluence through Western-style urban industrialization that depends on the intensive use of resources. Poor countries generally do not have the means for running the high-energy production and transportation systems manifest in the industrial West. Even by conservative estimates, the production of a middle-class basket of goods requires six times as much in resources as a basket of essential or basic goods. The expansion of GNP through the production of middle-class baskets means that only a minority of people in poor countries would enjoy the fruits of economic growth. Resource constraints prevent the large-scale production of consumer goods for the growing populations of the developing countries.

However, numerous measures of material well-being (e.g., per capita incomes, calories consumed, life expectancy) show that people in most, but not all, countries are better off today than their parents were. But there are problems with this optimistic assessment. These improvements are based on averages; they say nothing about the distribution of material well-being. Another difficulty is that the world may be achieving improvements in material well-being at the expense of future generations. This would be the case if economic growth were using up the world's resource base or environmental carrying capacity faster than new discoveries and technology could expand them.

Carrying Capacity and Overpopulation

The population-resources problem is much debated, particularly during periods of economic shortages and rising prices. Neo-Malthusian pessimists believe that the world will eventually enter a stationary state at *carrying capacity*, which is the maximum population that can be supported by available resources. They point to recurring food crises and famines in Africa as a result of overpopulation. However, carrying capacity, an idea borrowed from ecology, is simplistic in that it ignores the historical, political, and technological context in which the production and consumption of goods occurs. Human beings are not mindless products of an unchanging nature, and are capable of modifying their environment and altering the constraints and opportunities it presents. On the other hand, optimists believe in the saving grace of modern technology. Technological advances in the last 200 years have raised the world's carrying capacity, and future technical innovations as well as the substitution of new raw materials for old hold the promise of raising carrying capacity still further.

The answer to the population-resources problem also depends on the standard of living deemed acceptable. To give people a minimal quality of life instead of one resembling the American middle class would require vast quantities of additional resources. The establishment of an economy that provides for the basics of life—sufficient food, housing, education, transportation, and health care—depends on our capacity to develop alternatives to the high-energy, material-intensive production technologies characteristic of the industrial West. Already, there are outlines of a theory of resource use suited to the needs of a basic goods economy. Some of the main ideas are (1) the adoption of a sun-based organic agriculture; (2) the use of renewable sources of energy; (3) the use of appropriate technology, labor-intensive methods of production, and local raw materials; and (4) the decentralization of production in order to increase local self-reliance and minimize the transport of materials. These productive forces would minimize the disruption of ecosystems and engage the unemployed in useful, productive work. Typically, economies that produce essential goods for human consumption face neither excessive unemployment nor overpopulation. Moreover, secure supplies of basic goods provide a strong motivation for reducing population size, as families no longer require many children to ensure economic prosperity.

TYPES OF RESOURCES AND THEIR LIMITS

All economic development comes about through the use of human resources (e.g., labor power, skills, and intelligence). In order to produce the goods and services people demand in today's global economy, we need to obtain natural resources. What are natural resources and what are their limits?

Resources and Reserves

Natural resources have meaning only in terms of historically specific technical and cultural appraisals of nature and are defined in relation to a particular level

Some of these African mothers can do little to save their children's lives. Children are suffering the complications of undernutrition and malnutrition. Asia has managed to increase production fast enough to stay well ahead of population growth, but Latin America and Southwest Asia, the Middle East, and North Africa have barely managed to stay even with the population. The worst report is from Africa, where population growth is outstripping food production year by year. Per capita food production in Africa has been falling steadily for the last 25 years. Many factors contribute to these fluctuations, including drought, changing world prices, and civil and ethnic unrest.

of development. *Resources,* designated by the larger box in Figure 4.1, include all substances of the biological and physical environment that may someday be used under specified technological and socioeconomic conditions. Because these conditions are always subject to change, we can expect our determination of what is useful to also change. For example, uranium, once a waste product of radium mining of the 1930s, is now a valuable ore. Taconite ores became worthwhile in Minnesota only after production from high-grade, nonmagnetic iron ores declined in the 1960s.

At the other end are reserves, designated by the upper-left-hand box in Figure 4.1. *Reserves* are quantities of resources that are known and available for economic exploitation with current technologies at current prices. When current reserves begin to be depleted, the search for additional reserves is intensified. Estimates of reserves are also affected by changes in prices and technology. *Projected reserves* represent estimates of the quantities likely to be added to reserves because of discoveries and changes in prices and technologies projected to occur within a specified period, for example, 50 years.

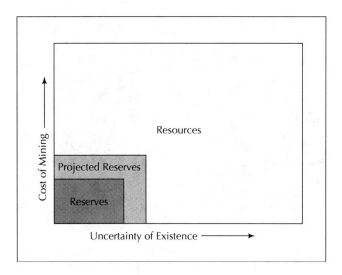

FIGURE 4.1
Classification of resources. Resources include all materials of the environment that may someday be used under future technological and socioeconomic conditions. Reserves are resources that are known and available with current technologies and at current prices. Projected reserves are reserves based on expected future price trends and technologies available.

Renewable and Nonrenewable Resources

A major distinction is between nonrenewable and renewable resources. *Nonrenewable resources* consist of finite masses of material, such as fossil fuels and metals, which cannot be used without depletion. They are, for all practical purposes, fixed in amount, or in some cases, such as soils, because they form slowly over time. Consequently, their rate of use is important. Large populations with high per capita consumption of goods deplete these resources fastest.

Many nonrenewable resources are completely altered or destroyed by use; petroleum is an example. Other resources, such as iron, are available for recycling. Recycling expands the limits to the sustainable use of a nonrenewable resource. At present, these limits are low in relation to current mineral extraction.

Renewable resources are those resources capable of yielding output indefinitely without impairing their productivity. They include *flow resources* such as water and sunlight, and *stock resources* such as soil, vegetation, fish, and animals. Renewal is not automatic, however; resources can be depleted and permanently reduced by misuse. Productive fishing grounds can be destroyed by overfishing. Fertile topsoil, destroyed by erosion, can be difficult to restore and impossible to replace. The future of agricultural land is guaranteed only when production does not exceed its maximum sustainable yield. The term *maximum sustainable yield* means maximum production consistent with maintaining future productivity of a renewable resource.

In our global environment, the misuse of a resource in one place affects the well-being of people in other places. The misuse of resources is often described in terms of the *tragedy of the commons,* a term coined by biologist Garrett Hardin in 1968. This metaphor refers to the way public resources are ruined by the isolated actions of individuals, which occurs when the costs of actions are not captured in market prices. Originally it referred to the tendency of shepherds to use common grazing land; as each one sought as much of the commons as possible, it became overgrazed. Similarly, people who fish are likely to try to catch as many fish as they can, reasoning that if they don't, others will. Thus, it exemplifies a market failure, a problem generated by individual actors who behave "rationally" but collectively create an irrational and self-destructive outcome. Similarly, dumping waste and pollutants on public waters

The Kenyan rangelands on which these herders cattle graze are in jeopardy. With growing grazing pressures, more than 60 percent of the world's rangelands and at least 80 percent of African, Asian, and Middle Eastern rangelands are now moderately to severely desertified. About 65 million hectares of once productive land in Africa have become desert during the last 50 years.

and land or into the air is the cheapest way to dispose of worthless products. Firms are generally unwilling to dispose of these materials by more expensive means unless mandated by law.

Sometimes resources are unavailable, not because they are depleted but because of politics. Resources are under the control of sovereign nation-states. Many wars in the twentieth century have been resource wars. For example, Japan invaded Korea and Taiwan in the 1890s largely in order to obtain arable land and coal. The Iraqi invastion of Kuwait in 1990 and the U.S. invasion of Iraq in 2003 were largely motivated by concerns over the region's oil supplies. In the Middle East, fierce national rivalries make water a potential source of conflict: While some parts are blessed with adequate water supplies, most of the region is insufficiently supplied. Some observers predict that political tension over the use of international rivers, lakes, and aquifers in the Middle East may escalate to war in the next few years.

Food Resources

Thanks to scientific advances in farming, world food production has been increasing faster than population (Figure 4.2). While there is sufficient food to feed everyone in the world, there are huge geographic variations in people's access to a sufficient number and quality of calories (Figure 4.3). The populations of the industrialized world are generally well fed; indeed, in the United States, the major dietary problem is an overabundance of calories and an epidemic of obesity. In the developing world, in contrast, hundreds of millions of people worldwide still go hungry daily. With demand for food expected to grow at 4 percent per year over the next 20 to 30 years, the task of meeting that need will be more difficult than ever before. A record explosion in the world's population coupled with the problem of poverty threaten the natural resources on which agriculture depends, such as topsoil. To make matters worse, environmental degradation perpetuates poverty, as degraded ecosystems diminish agricultural returns to poor people.

The gulf between the well fed and the hungry is vast. Average daily calorie consumption is 3300 in developed countries and 2650 in developing countries (Table 4.1). But these are average figures. There are people in the developed world who go hungry and some people in Africa with plenty to eat. Averages mask the extremes of *undernutrition*—a lack of calories—and overconsumption. Even with a high-calorie satisfaction, people may suffer from *chronic malnutrition*—a lack of enough protein, vitamins, and essential nutrients. The most important measure in assessing nutritional standards is the daily per capita availability of calories, protein, fat, calcium, and other nutrients. In the world today, the sharpest nutritional differences are not from country to country or from one region to another within countries. They are between rich and poor people. The poor of the earth are the hungry, and those with the least political power often suffer in terms of an insufficient food supply.

Hunger among the poor of the world is often attributed to deforestation, soil erosion, water-table depletion,

FIGURE 4.2
Trends in world food production, 1961–2001. Note the precipitous drop in food production in the former Soviet Union.

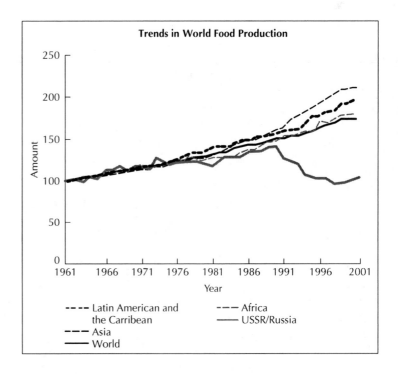

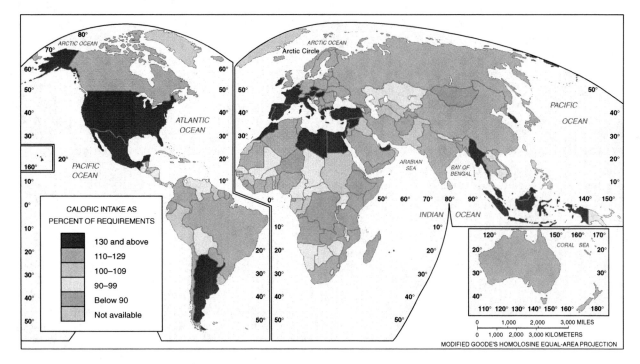

FIGURE 4.3

Caloric intake as a percentage of adult daily requirements. Highly developed regions of the world receive, on the average, 130 percent of the daily caloric requirements (2400 calories per day) set by the United Nations Food and Agricultural Organization (FAO). Some countries in South America, South Asia, and many countries in Africa receive less than 90 percent of the daily caloric requirements needed to sustain body and life. Averages must be adjusted according to age, gender, and body size of the person and by regions of the world. Although it appears from this map that the great majority of world populations are in relatively good shape with regard to calories per capita (food supply), remember that averages overshadow destitute groups in each country that receive less than their fair share. Again, the situation is most severe in the Sahel or center belt of Africa.

Table 4.1

Calorie Intake and Calorie Requirement Satisfaction, 2004.

	Highest Calorie Intake			Lowest Calorie Intake		
Country	Calorie Intake per Person per Day	Percentage of Requirements	Country	Calorie Intake per Person per Day	Percentage of Requirements	Food Aid*
United States	3699	154	Haiti	1869	79	51
Portugal	3667	153	Ethiopia	1858	77	23
Greece	3647	152	Comoros	1858	77	44
Belgium	3619	151	North Korea	1837	76	0
Ireland	3537	147	Mozambique	1832	76	33
Austria	3536	147	Congo	1755	73	486
Turkey	3525	146	Afghanistan	1745	72	51
France	3518	146	Burundi	1685	70	136
Italy	3507	146	Eritrea	1622	67	1304
Cyprus	3429	143	Somalia	1566	65	32

*In thousands of metric tons. Food and Agriculture Organization, United Nations, 2005.

the frequency and severity of droughts, and the impact of storms such as hurricanes. Although the environment does have a bearing on the food problem, it has limited significance compared with the role of social conditions such as war and a world economy whose rules are tilted against the impoverished. Subsidized agricultural exports from the United States, for example, have bankrupted millions of farmers in the developing world, reducing those countries' ability to feed themselves.

Population Growth

Population growth is one of many causes of the food problem, and Malthusian views often influence the public's opinion of this issue. However, presently, at the global level, there is no food shortage. In fact, world food production grew steadily from 1961 to 2005. Even over the next several decades, production increases, assuming continuing high investments in agricultural research, are likely to be sufficient to meet effective demand and rising world population. However, some are more pessimistic about future world food production. They argue that food production will be constrained by the limits to the biological productivities of fisheries and rangelands, the fragility of tropical and subtropical environments, massive overfishing of the world's oceans, the increasing

scarcity of fresh water, the declining effectiveness of additional fertilizer applications, and social disintegration in many developing countries.

The success of global agriculture has not been shared equally. In Africa, per capita food production has not been able to keep up with population growth. By contrast, Asia and to a lesser extent Latin America have experienced tremendous success in per capita terms. The reasons for this are complex, and have to do with the relative equality in patterns of land ownership, government policies toward farmers (e.g., price ceilings on agricultural crops), the respective ability of countries to build infrastructures and extend credit to small farmers, and the role of different states in the world economy.

The food and hunger problem is most severe in Africa. Fifteen countries are experiencing exceptional food emergencies. Of the 28 countries with food-security problems, 23 are in sub-Saharan Africa (Figure 4.4). Indeed, famine, the most extreme expression of poverty, is now mainly restricted to Africa. The fact that famine has been held at bay for decades in Latin America and Asia suggests that famine can be eliminated. But how? Certainly, bringing an end to Africa's multiple civil wars would go a long way toward eradicating famine. Africa has witnessed countless brutal conflicts that have killed tens of millions of people. Such conflicts divert resources from civilian use, interrupt the production of crops, terrorize populations, destroy the

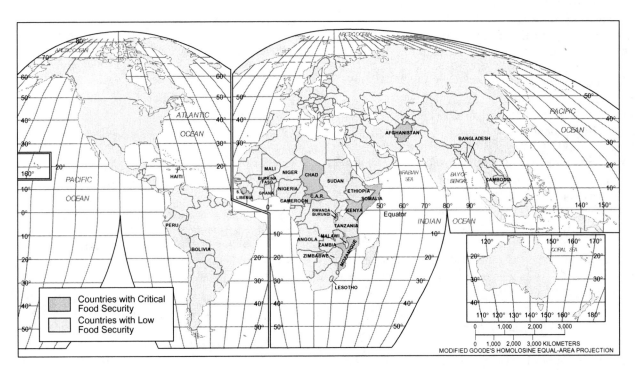

FIGURE 4.4

Developing countries with low or critical food security indexes, 2005. Africa remains the continent most seriously challenged by food shortages. Fifteen countries in the region are facing critical food emergencies. Of the 28 countries with household food security problems, 23 are in sub-Saharan Africa.

infrastructure, destabilize markets, and complicate the stability of the governments, creating famine and prohibiting the flow of developmental aid. But peace is not in itself a sufficient condition for removing acute hunger. Appropriate policies and investments are needed to stimulate rural economic growth that underpins food security and to provide safety-net protection for the absolute poor. Rural infrastructure development, credit to farmers, and land redistribution are also necessary steps in this regard. Price controls on food crops create disincentives to produce, and heavily subsidized food imports from the developed world bankrupt farmers. Often elites in the developing world care more about their foreign bank accounts than the well-being of their own populations.

The pace of urbanization in the developing countries has also contributed to the food problem. In recent decades, hundreds of millions of people who previously lived in rural areas and produced some food have relocated to urban areas, where they must buy food. As a result of urbanization, there is a higher demand for food in the face of lower supply.

Third World farmers, such as these in Indonesia, depend on high rice yields. Rice is the staple food for more than one-half the world's population. While rice and other grains supply energy and some protein, people must supplement grains with fruits, nuts, vegetables, dairy products, fish, and meat in order to remain healthy.

Poverty

The inequitable allocation of food is directly related to poverty, the single greatest cause of the hunger problem. Hungry people are inevitably poor people who lack the purchasing power to feed themselves. Under capitalism, food goes to customers who can afford it, not to where it is needed most. During famines, the prices of foods rise dramatically, with disastrous results for the poor. From the perspective of the world market, where food is produced is immaterial as long as costs are minimized and a profitable sale can be made. Thus, in the midst of hunger, food may be exported for profit. Since the populations of the developed world can afford to pay much more for food than their counterparts in less developed countries, it is not surprising that the market fails to include the poor. Solving the world food problem is ultimately a matter of alleviating poverty in developing nations. This is no easy task, and while parts of the developing world have made great economic strides over the last 40 years (e.g., East Asia), much of Africa and parts of India and Latin America remain mired in poverty and hunger. Alleviating poverty, and thus hunger, is the subject of Chapter 13, in which a host of economic development problems and strategies is discussed.

Maldistribution

The problem of world food distribution has three components. First, there is the problem of transporting food from one place to another. Although transport systems in developing countries lack the speed and efficiency of those in developed countries, they are not serious

impediments under normal circumstances. The problem arises either when massive quantities of food aid must be moved quickly or when the distribution of food is disrupted by political corruption and military conflict.

Second, serious disruptions in food supply in developing countries are traceable to problems of marketing and storage. Food is sometimes hoarded by merchants until prices rise and then sold for a larger profit. Also, much food in the tropics is lost due to poor storage facilities. Pests such as rats consume considerable quantities, and investments in concrete storage containers can help to minimize this loss.

A third aspect of the distribution problem is in the inequitable allocation of food. Only North America, Australia, and Western Europe have large grain surpluses. But food grain is not always given when it is most needed. Food aid shipments and grain prices are inversely related. Thus, U.S. food aid was low around

1973, a time of major famine in the Sahel region of Africa, because cereal prices were at a peak.

Closely associated with poverty as a cause of hunger in developing countries is the structure of agriculture, including land ownership. Land is frequently concentrated in a few hands. In Bangladesh, less than 10 percent of rural households own more than 50 percent of the country's cultivable land; 60 percent of Bangladesh's rural families own less than 2 percent. A similar situation applies in Latin America (Chapter 14). Many rural residents own no land at all. They are landless laborers who depend on extremely low wages for their livelihoods. But without land, there is often no food.

Civil Unrest and War

Political conflict is an important cause of hunger and poverty. Occasionally governments withhold food to punish rebellious populations. Devastating examples of depriving food to secessionist areas include the government in Nigeria starving the Biafrans in the 1970s and the government in Ethiopia starving the Eritreans into submission, with 6 million people dying in the process. In Sudan, the Arab government's war against the African population in Darfur has led millions to starve. In Zimbabwe, the government of Robert Mugabe denied food to his opponents in order to quash domestic opposition. Civil wars, which are frequent in developing countries whose political geographies were shaped by colonialism and which have unstable governments, devastate agricultural production. Without a stable political environment, the social mechanisms necessary to produce and distribute food to the hungry cannot operate.

Environmental Decline

As population pressure increases on a given land area, the need for food pushes agricultural use to the limits, and marginal lands, which are subject now to *desertification* and *deforestation* (Figure 4.5), are brought into production. Removal of trees allows a desert to advance, because the wind break is now absent. The cutting of trees also lowers the capacity of the land to absorb moisture, which diminishes agricultural productivity and increases the chances of drought. Desertification and deforestation are symptoms as well as causes of the food problem in developing countries. Natural resources are mined by the poor to meet the food needs of today; the lower productivity resulting from such practices is a concern to be put off until tomorrow.

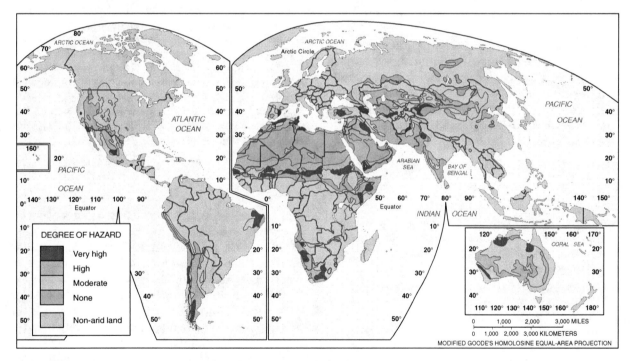

FIGURE 4.5

World desertification. The main problem is overuse by farmers and herdsmen. Approximately 10 percent of the earth's surface has lost its topsoil due to overuse of lands by humans, creating desertification. An additional 25 percent of the earth's surface is now threatened. Topsoil is being lost at a rate of approximately 30 billion metric tons per year. Approximately 20 million acres of agricultural land are wasted every year to desertification by agricultural overuse. When plants are uprooted by overplowing or by animals, the plants that stabilized shifting soil are removed. When the rains come, water erosion can wash away the remaining topsoil.

In many developing countries, government policies have emphasized investment in their militaries and cities at the expense of increasing agricultural production. In addition, some governments in Africa have provided food at artificially low prices in order to make food affordable in cities. While this practice keeps labor affordable for multinational corporations and placates the middle class, it robs farmers of the incentive to farm. Farmers cannot make a living from artificially low commodity prices.

The average debt of many developing countries runs into the billions. In 2002, the aggregate debt of African countries stood at $220 billion. Simply put, African countries have no surplus capital to invest in their infrastructure or food production systems. Instead, they have to enforce austerity, reducing levels of government services in support of economic growth, particularly agricultural growth. Debt repayments subsume a large share of foreign revenues, decreasing funds available for investment.

In recent decades, agriculture in developing countries has expanded. This expansion is in the export sector, not in the domestic food-producing sector, and it is often the result of deliberate policy. Governments and private elites have opted for modernization through the promotion of export-oriented agriculture. The result is the growth of an agricultural economy based on profitable export products and the neglect of those aspects of farming that have to do with small farmers producing food for local populations.

Imports from the developed world, particularly the United States, also exacerbate food problems. For example, after the passage of the North American Free Trade Agreement (NAFTA) in 1994, massive U.S. exports of government-subsidized corn caused the price of corn in Mexico to fall by 70 percent, bankrupting 1 million Mexican farmers.

Water for Chad. Water is an important ingredient to sustain human life. Fifty percent of the world's people do not have adequate, clean water. Villagers in Chad are delighted as the water pours out of a new water system they have worked together to construct. The system is part of an antidesertification project funded by the United Nations Development Program and the U.S. government. Acute water shortage in many parts of the world requires solutions that will be costly, technically difficult, and politically sensitive. Water scarcity contributes to the impoverishment of many countries in east and west Africa, threatening their ability to increase food production fast enough to keep pace with modern population growth.

INCREASING FOOD PRODUCTION

There is broad agreement that yield increases will be the major source of future food production growth. These can be achieved through the expansion of arable land and increased cropping intensity. The result of these methods of increasing food supply would be to put additional pressures on land and water resources and contribute significantly to human-made sources of greenhouse gases.

Expanding Cultivated Areas

The world's potentially farmable land is estimated to be about twice the present cultivated area. Vast reserves are theoretically available in Africa, South America, and Australia, and smaller reserves in North America, Russia,

and Central Asia. However, many experts believe that the potential for expanding cropland is disappearing in most regions because of environmental degradation and the high cost of developing infrastructure in remote areas. About half of the world's potentially arable land lies within the tropics, especially in sub-Saharan Africa and Latin America. Much of this land is under forest in protected areas, and most of it suffers from soil and terrain constraints, as well as excessive dryness. In Asia, two-thirds of the potentially arable land is already under cultivation; the main exceptions are Indonesia and Myanmar. South Asia's agricultural land is almost totally developed.

The expansion of tropical agriculture into forest and desert environments contributes to deforestation and desertification. Since World War II, roughly half of the world's rain forests in Africa, Asia, and Latin America have disappeared. Conversion of this land to agriculture has entailed high costs, including the loss of livelihoods for the people displaced, the loss of biodiversity, increased carbon dioxide emissions, and decreased carbon storage capacity. *Desertification*—the growth of deserts due to humanly caused factors, typically on the periphery of natural deserts—threatens about one-third of the world's land surface and the livelihood of nearly a billion people. Many of the world's major rangelands are at risk. The main factor responsible for desertification is overgrazing, but deforestation (particularly the cutting of fuel wood), overcultivation of marginal soils, and salinization caused by poorly managed irrigation systems are also important influences. Deforestation and desertification are destroying the land resources on which the development of the developing countries depends.

Raising the Productivity of Existing Cropland

The quickest way to increase food supply is to raise the productivity of land under cultivation. Remarkable increases in agricultural yields have been achieved in developed countries through the widespread adoption of new technologies. Corn yields in the United States are a good example. Yields expanded rapidly with the in-troduction of hybrid varieties, herbicides, and fertilizers. Much of the increase in yields came through successive improvements in hybrids.

The approach for increasing yields in developed countries has been adopted in developing countries. This approach is known as the *Green Revolution*, in which new high-yielding varieties of wheat, rice, and corn are developed through plant genetics, including crops that grow more quickly, perhaps yielding several harvests per year, are more pest and drought resistant, and have higher protein content. The Green Revolution has had enormous impacts in Asia and Mexico, increasing the food supply, but it is not a panacea. It depends on machinery, for which the poor lack sufficient capital to buy. It depends on new seeds, which poor farmers cannot afford. It depends on chemical fertilizers, pesticides, and herbicides, which have contaminated underground water supplies, as well as streams and lakes. It depends on large-scale, one-crop farming, which is ecologically unstable because of its susceptibility to pestilence. It depends on controlled water supplies, which have increased the incidence of malaria, schistosomiasis, and other diseases. It is confined largely to a group of 18 heavily populated countries, extending across the tropics and subtropics from South Korea to Mexico (Figure 4.6). It is also benefiting countries that include half of the world's population. This approach

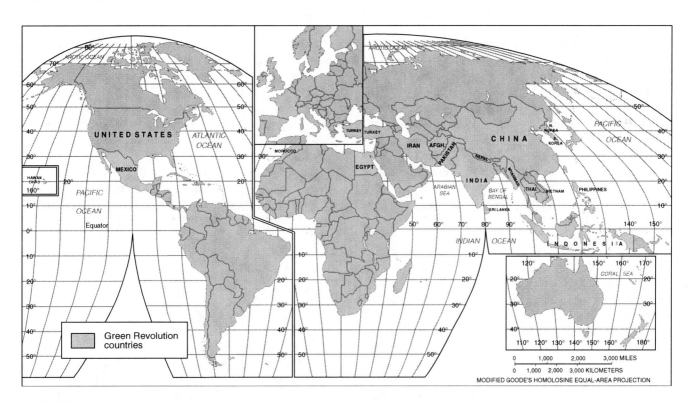

FIGURE 4.6

The chief benefiting countries of the Green Revolution. The Green Revolution was the result of plant scientists genetically developing high yielding varieties of staple food crops such as rice in East Asia, wheat in the Middle East, and corn in Middle America. By crossing "super strains" that produced high yields with more genetically diverse plants, both high yield and pest resistance were introduced.

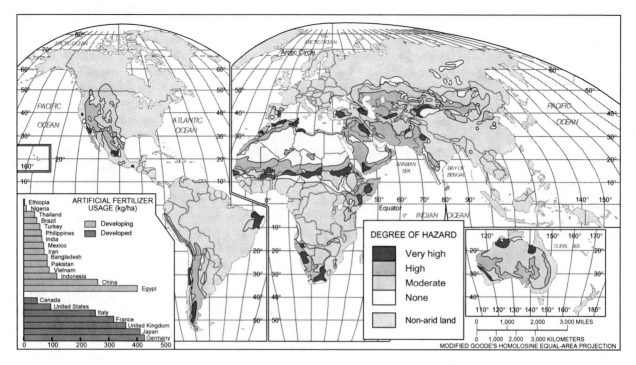

FIGURE 4.7
Artificial fertilizer usage. The application of artificial fertilizers, as opposed to natural ones obtained from people and animals, may enhance agricultural productivity but also makes economies more dependent on petroleum.

involves the widespread application of artificial fertilizers, an increasingly common practice throughout the developing world (Figure 4.7).

Politically, the Green Revolution promises more than it can deliver. Its sociopolitical application has been largely unsatisfactory. Even in areas where the Green Revolution has been technologically successful, it has not always benefited large numbers of hungry people without the means to buy the newly produced food. It has benefited mainly Western-educated farmers, who were already wealthy enough to adopt a complex integrated package of technical inputs and management practices. Farmers make bigger profits from the Green Revolution when they purchase additional land and mechanize their operations. Some effects of labor-displacing machinery and the purchase of additional land by rich farmers include agricultural unemployment, increased landlessness, rural-to-urban migration, and increased malnutrition for the unemployed who are unable to purchase the food produced by the Green Revolution.

The Green Revolution generated substantial increases in agricultural output worldwide. However, world hunger remains a serious problem, indicating that the problem is not so much one of food production, but of food demand in the economic sense (i.e., purchasing power). Unfortunately, the Green Revolution does nothing to increase the ability of the poor to buy food.

Hunger is a complex and intractable problem in large part because it is so closely tied to questions of poverty and economic development, not simply increasing agricultural productivity.

The Green Revolution has helped to create a world of more and larger commercial farms alongside fewer and smaller peasant plots. However, given a different structure of land holdings and the use of appropriately intermediate technology, the Green Revolution could help developing countries on the road toward agricultural self-sufficiency and the elimination of hunger. Intermediate technology is a term that means low-cost, small-scale technologies intermediate between primitive stick-farming methods and complex agroindustrial technical packages.

Creating New Food Sources

Expanding cultivated areas and raising the productivity of existing cropland are two methods of increasing food supply. A third method is the identification of new food sources. There are three main ways to create new food sources: (1) Cultivate the oceans, or mariculture; (2) develop high-protein cereal crops; and (3) increase the acceptability and palatability of inefficiently used present foods.

Fishing and the cultivation of fish and shellfish from the oceans is not a new idea. At first glance, the world seems well supplied with fisheries because oceans cover three-fourths of the earth. However, fish provide a very small proportion—about 1 percent—of the world's food supply.

World fish consumption in the late twentieth century increased more rapidly than did the population, and even exceeded beef as a source of animal protein in some countries. However, since 1987, fish caught by commercial fishing fleets leveled off and declined as a result of overfishing (Figure 4.8). Overfishing has been particularly acute in the North Atlantic and Pacific Oceans. Countries such as Iceland and Peru, whose economies rely heavily on fishing, are sensitive to the overfishing problem. Peru's catch of its principal fish, the anchovy, has declined by over 75 percent because of overfishing. The Peruvian experience demonstrates that the ocean is not a limitless fish resource, as did the quest for whales a century earlier.

Commercial fishing fleets employ sophisticated techniques but catch what nature has provided, much like hunters and gatherers. An alternative approach is to follow the example of animal husbandry by devising methods for commercial fish farming. *Mariculture,* or fish farming, is now expanding rapidly and accounts for 5 percent of the world's fish caught yearly. The cultivation of food fish such as catfish, trout, and salmon is big business in the United States, Norway, Japan, and other fishing countries.

Another source of future food production rests in higher protein cereal crops. Agricultural scientists seek to develop high-yield, high-protein cereal crops in the hope that development of hybrid seeds will be able to help the protein deficiency of people in developing countries who do not have available meats from which to gain their protein needs, as do people in developed countries.

Fortification of present rice, wheat, barley, and other cereals with minerals, vitamins, and protein-carrying amino acids is an approach that also deserves attention. This approach is based on the fortified food production in developed countries and stands a greater chance of cultural acceptance because individual food habits do not necessarily need to be altered. But developing countries rely on unprocessed, unfortified foods for 95 percent of their food intake. Large-scale fortification and processing would require major technological innovation and scale economies to produce enough food to have an impact on impoverished societies.

More Efficient Use of Foods

In many developing countries, foods to satisfy consumer preferences as well as religious taboos and cultural values are becoming limited. The selection of foods based on social customs should be supplemented with information concerning more efficient use of foods presently available. An effort should be made to increase the palatability of existing foods that are plentiful.

FIGURE 4.8
Global fish catch, 1950–2003. Rising demand and increasingly efficient industrial fishing methods not only have yielded dramatically higher catches, but also have increasingly depleted the world's oceans of many species. See Richard Ellis, *The Empty Ocean.*

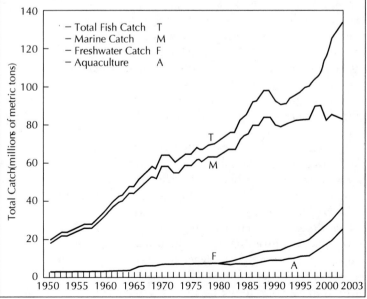

Fish meal is a good example. Presently, one-third of the world's fish intake is turned into fodder for animals and fertilizer. Fish meal is rich in the Omega 3 fatty acids and amino acids necessary for biological development. However, in many places, the fish meal is not used because of its taste and texture.

Another underused food resource is the soybean, a legume rich in both protein and amino acids. Most of the world's soybeans wind up being processed into animal feed or fertilizer and into production of nondigestible industrial materials. World demand for tofu and other recognizable soybean derivatives is not large. By contrast, hamburgers, hot dogs, soft drinks, and cooking oils made partially from soybeans are more acceptable.

A Solution to the World Food Supply Situation

As we have emphasized, there is a widely shared belief that people are hungry because of insufficient food production. But the fact is that food production is increasing faster than population, and still there are more hungry people than ever before. Why should this be so? It could be that the production focus is correct, but soaring numbers of people simply overrun these production gains. Or it could be that the diagnosis is incorrect—scarcity is not the cause of hunger, and production increase, no matter how great, can never solve the problem.

The simple facts of world grain production make it clear that the overpopulation/scarcity diagnosis is incorrect. Present world grain production can more than adequately feed every person on earth. Ironically, the focus on increased production has compounded the problem of hunger by transforming agricultural progress into a narrow technical pursuit instead of the sweeping social task of releasing vast, untapped human resources. We need to look to the policies of governments in developing countries to understand why people are hungry even when there is enough food to feed everyone. These policies influence the access to knowledge and the availability of credit to small farmers, the profitability of growing enough to sell a surplus, and the efficiency of marketing and distributing food on a broad scale.

The fact is that small, carefully farmed plots are more productive per unit area than large estates because the families that tend to them have more at stake and invest as much labor as necessary to feed themselves when they can. Yet, despite considerable evidence from around the world, government production programs in many developing countries ignore small farmers. They rationalize that working with bigger production units is a faster road to increased productivity. Often, many small farms is the answer. In the closing years of the twentieth century, many agricultural researchers, having gained respect for traditional farming systems, agree with this conclusion.

NONRENEWABLE MINERAL RESOURCES

Although we can increase world food output, we cannot increase the supply of minerals. A mineral deposit, once used, is gone forever. A *mineral* refers to a naturally occurring inorganic substance in the earth's crust. Thus, silicon is a mineral whereas petroleum is not, since the latter is of organic origin. Although minerals abound in nature, many of them are insufficiently concentrated to be economically recoverable. Moreover, the richest deposits are unevenly distributed and are being depleted.

Except for iron, nonmetallic elements are consumed at much greater rates than metallic ones. Industrial societies do not worry about the supply of most nonmetallic minerals, which are plentiful and often widespread, including nitrogen, phosphorus, potash, or sulfur for chemical fertilizer, or sand, gravel, or clay for building purposes. Those commodities the industrial and industrializing countries do worry about are the metals.

Location and Projected Reserves of Key Minerals

Only five countries—Australia, Canada, South Africa, the United States, and Russia—are significant producers of at least six strategic minerals vital to defense and modern technology (Figure 4.9). Of the major mineral-producing countries, only a few—notably the United States and Russia—are also major processors and consumers. The other major processing and consuming centers—Japan and western European countries—are deficient in strategic minerals.

How large is the world supply of strategic minerals? Most key minerals will be exhausted within 100 years, and some will be depleted within a few years at current rates of consumption, assuming no new reserves. The United States is running short of domestic sources of strategic minerals. Its dependence on imports has grown steadily since 1950; prior to that year, the country was dependent on imports for only four designated strategic minerals. When measured in terms of percentage imported, U.S. dependency increased from 50 percent in 1960 to over 82 percent in 2003. Minerals projected as future needs by the United States are unevenly distributed around the world. Many of them, such as manganese, nickel, bauxite, copper, and tin (Figure 4.9), are concentrated in Russia and Canada and in developing countries. Whether these critical

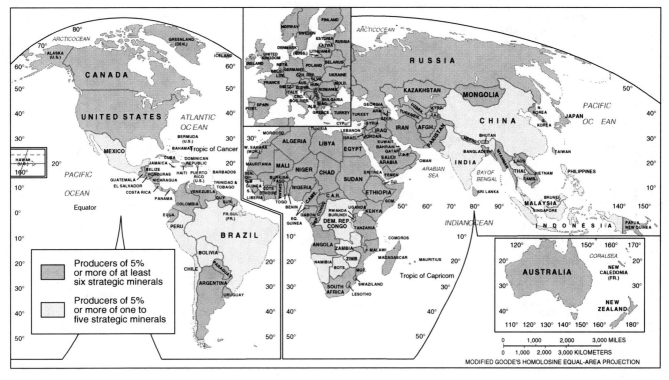

FIGURE 4.9
Major producers of strategic minerals.

substances will be available for U.S. consumption may depend less on economic scarcity and more on international tensions and foreign policy objectives.

Solutions to the Mineral Supply Problem

Affluent countries are unlikely to be easily defeated by mineral supply problems. Human beings, the ultimate resource, have developed solutions to the problem in the past. Will they in the future? Although past experience is never a reliable guide to the future, there is no need to be unduly pessimistic about the exhaustion of minerals as long as we develop alternatives.

If abundant supplies of cheap electricity ever became available, it might become possible to extract and process minerals from unorthodox sources such as the ocean. The oceans, which cover 71 percent of the earth, contain large quantities of dissolved minerals. Salt, magnesium, sulphur, calcium, and potassium are the most abundant of these minerals and amount to over 99 percent of the dissolved minerals. More valuable minerals that are also present include copper, zinc, tin, and silver. Improved efficiency of production has reduced the demand for various minerals per unit of national output (Figure 4.10). Some

minerals such as bromine and magnesium are being obtained electrolytically from the oceans at the present time.

Much more feasible than mining the oceans is devoting increased attention to improving mining technology, especially to reducing waste in the extraction and processing of minerals. Equally feasible is to utilize technologies that allow minerals to be used more efficiently in manufacturing. Also, if social attitudes were to change, encouraging lower per capita levels of resource use, more durable products could be manufactured, saving not only large amounts of energy but also large quantities of minerals.

Reusing minerals is still another option to our mineral problems. Every year in the United States and other affluent countries, huge quantities of household and industrial waste are disposed of at sanitary landfills and open dumps. These materials are sometimes called "urban ores" because they can be recovered and used again. For years, developed countries have been recycling scarce and valuable metals such as iron, lead, copper, silver, gold, and platinum, but large amounts of scrap metals are still being wasted. Although we could recover a much greater proportion of scrap, this is unlikely when prices are low or when virgin materials are cheaper than recycled ones.

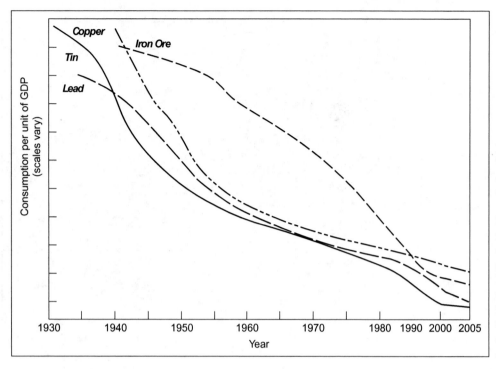

FIGURE 4.10
The consumption of lead, tin, copper, and iron ore per unit of GDP for the United States, 1930–2005. *Transmaterialization* is the process whereby natural materials from the environment are systematically replaced by higher quality or technologically more advanced materials linked to new industries—glass fibers, composites, ceramics, epoxies, and smart metals.

Environmental Impact of Mineral Extraction

Mineral extraction has a varied impact on the environment, depending on mining procedures, local hydrological conditions, and the size of the operation. Environmental impact also depends on the stage of development of the mineral—exploration activities usually have less of an impact than mining and processing mineral resources.

Minimizing the environmental impacts of mineral extraction is in everyone's best interest, but the task is difficult because demand for minerals continues to grow and ever-poorer grades of ore are mined. For example, in 1900 the average grade of copper ore mined was 4 percent copper; by 1973, ores containing as little as 0.5 percent copper were mined. Each year more and more rock has to be excavated, crushed, and processed to extract copper. The immense copper mining pits in Montana, Utah, and Arizona are no longer in use because foreign sources, mostly in the developing countries, are less expensive. As long as the demand for minerals increases, ever lower quality minerals will have to be used and, even with good engineering, environmental degradation will extend far beyond excavation and surface plant areas.

ENERGY

The development of energy sources is crucial for economic development. Today, commercial energy is the lifeblood of modern economies. Indeed, it is the biggest single item in international trade. Oil alone accounts for about one-quarter of the volume (but not value) of world trade. The U.S. economy consumes vast amounts of energy, overwhelmingly consisting of fossil fuels (Figure 4.11). These form the inputs that, along with labor and capital, run the economic machine that feeds, houses, and moves the population. As Figure 4.12 indicates, the primary uses of petroleum are transportation and industrial purposes, whereas the major uses of coal are for electrical power generation.

Until the energy shocks of the 1970s, commercial energy demands were widely thought to be unproblematic, that is, always there to generate rising affluence. Suddenly, higher prices brought energy demands in the industrial countries to a virtual standstill, generating inflation, unemployment, and accelerating deindustrialization (Figure 4.13). Thousands of factories were shut down, and more than 3 million workers were laid off. They learned firsthand that when energy fails, everything fails in an urban-industrial economy. During the 1980s and 1990s, oil prices decreased from $30 in 1981 to $14 in 1999. OPEC, once considered an invincible cartel, saw its share of world oil output drop as non-OPEC countries expanded production. Many developing countries, strapped by heavy energy debts, were relieved to see prices falling. Oil-exporting developing countries, such as Mexico, Venezuela, and Nigeria, which came to depend on oil revenues for an important source of income, were hurt the worst. By 2006, however, world spot oil prices had risen again to a nominal price of $60 per barrel.

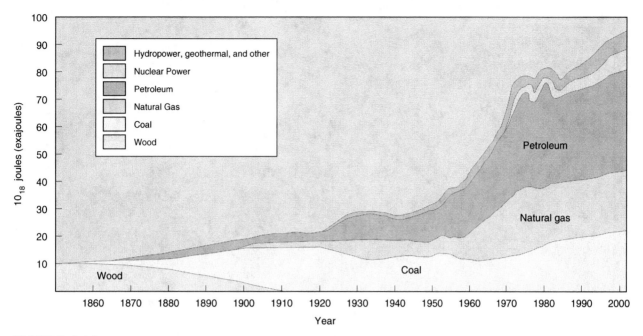

FIGURE 4.11

U.S. energy consumption in joules, 1850–2000. The U.S. economy contains 5 percent of the world's people but uses one-third of its energy. The three principal sources of fossil fuels are coal, natural gas, and petroleum. In 1850, the burning of wood provided the nation's energy supply. By 1900, wood had been supplanted by coal. After World War II, petroleum and natural gas surpasses coal as the chief source of energy in the United States. Hydro and nuclear have also increased recently.

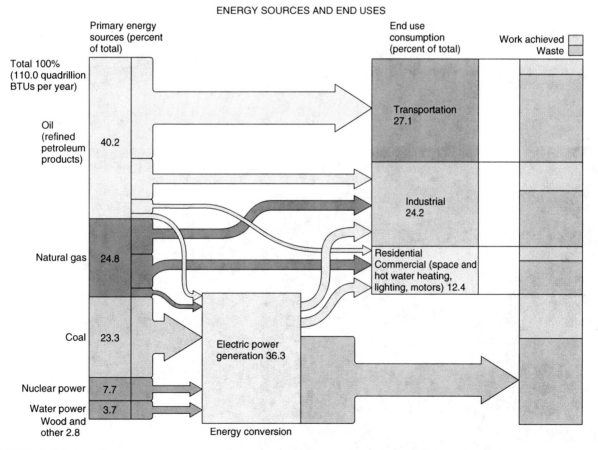

FIGURE 4.12

U.S. energy sources and end uses. Different energy inputs are applied to different uses. While coal is still widely used for electrical generation, petroleum is the most common energy source for transportation and industrial production.

Resources and Environment

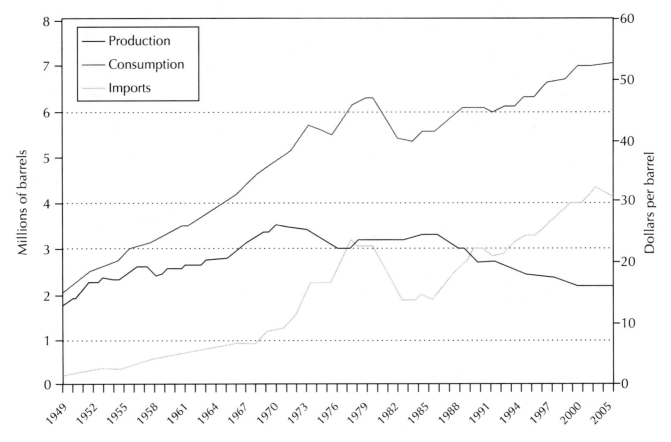

FIGURE 4.13

Oil production, consumption, and imports in the United States, 1950–2003. In the late 1970s and early 1980s, high prices created increased production and lower consumption; also, the Alaskan oil fields came into production. From 1980 onward, oil prices declined sharply due to the decline in OPEC's oligopolistic power. Imports comprise over one-half of all oil consumed in the United States.

The Persian Gulf. A satellite image of the region with the world's largest petroleum deposits.

Energy Production and Consumption

Most commercial energy produced is from nonrenewable resources. Most renewable energy sources, particularly wood and charcoal, are used directly by producers, mainly poor people in the developing countries. Although there is increasing interest in renewable energy development, commercial energy is the core of energy use at the present time. Only a handful of countries produce much more commercial energy than they consume. If we take petroleum consumption and production as an example, the main energy surplus countries include Saudi Arabia, Iraq, Mexico, Iran, Venezuela, Indonesia, Algeria, Kuwait, Libya, Qatar, Nigeria, and the United Arab Emirates. Saudi Arabia is by far the largest exporter of petroleum

and has the largest proven reserves. Nearly one-half of all African countries are energy paupers. Several of the world's leading industrial powers—most notably Japan, many western European countries, and the United States—consume much more energy than they produce, making them heavily reliant on imported oil, largely from the Middle East. This fact profoundly shapes the foreign policies of countries such as the United States.

The United States leads the world in total energy use, but leaders in per capita terms also include Canada, Norway, Sweden, Japan, Australia, and New Zealand (Figure 4.14). With 5 percent of the world's population, the United States consumes roughly one-quarter of the world's energy, largely for transportation, which consumes 40 percent of American energy

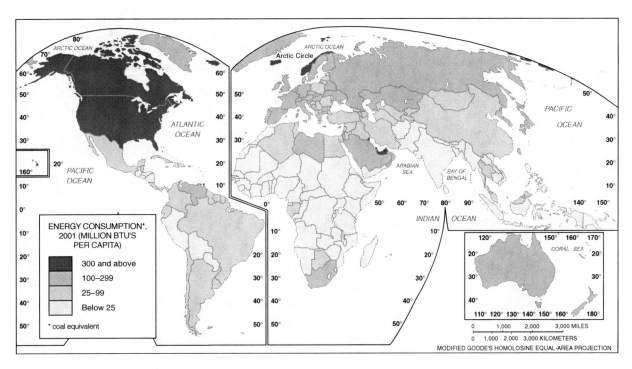

FIGURE 4.14
World per capita electricity consumption, 2001. The United States, Canada, and the Scandinavian countries consume more electricity per capita than any other countries. When the electricity usage of the United States, Canada, Europe, and Russia is combined, 75 percent of electricity usage in the world is accounted for, but only 20 percent of the people. By comparing this map to the map of crude petroleum proven reserves, the deficit areas of the world such as Europe and Japan, which have high energy needs but low fossil fuel resources, can be seen. In addition, there are areas in the world with high fossil fuel resources but low energy needs, such as the Middle East countries, Mexico, Venezuela, Indonesia, Argentina, Algeria, Nigeria, and China.

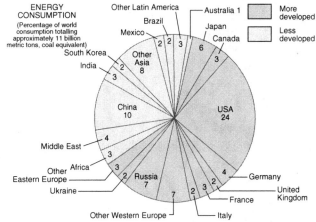

Resources and Environment

inputs. The automobile, for all the convenience it offers, is a highly energy-inefficient way to move people. In contrast, developing countries consume about 30 percent of the world's energy but contain about 80 percent of the population. Thus there exists a striking relationship between per capita energy consumption and level of development. Most developing countries consume meager portions of energy, well below levels required with even moderate levels of economic development. Commercial energy consumption in developed countries has been at consistently high levels, whereas in developing countries it has been at low but increasing levels.

Oil Dependency

Americans were seriously affected by the 1973 and 1979 Arab oil embargos, because imported oil as a proportion of total demand increased from 11 percent in the late 1960s to 50 percent in the 1970s to about 58 percent today. As a result, the administrations of the United States have repeatedly called for a national policy of oil self-sufficiency to reduce U.S. dependency on foreign supplies of petroleum, without much success. Under heavy political pressure from corporations and campaign donors, air and water pollution regulations have been relaxed, and tax credits for home energy conservation expenditures were ended. The U.S. Congress has toyed at times with the idea of imposing stricter fuel standards on new cars, but relaxed these after 2000 under pressure from automobile producers. These conflicting policies worked against federal efforts to encourage American households and companies to conserve fossil fuels. The United States imports about 58 percent of the oil it consumes, but only a small proportion comes from the Middle East. Japan, Italy, and France are much more dependent on Persian Gulf oil.

Nonetheless, U.S. industry did become more energy efficient. Manufacturing reduced its share of total U.S. energy consumption from 40 percent to 36 percent, and the burgeoning service economy consumed relatively little energy. In terms of conservation efforts, however, the United States lags behind Japan and western Europe, where energy is more expensive. Gasoline taxes in Europe, for example, help to fund more energy-efficient public transportation.

Production of Fossil Fuels

The OPEC oil embargo stimulated fossil fuel production in the United States and throughout the world. The embargo made the United States and other developed countries aware of their dependency on imported

A Shell/Esso production platform in Britain's North Sea gas field. British oil exploration was stimulated by a dramatic increase in the price of oil in the 1970s and early 1980s. Britain's North Sea oil and gas investment may keep the country self-sufficient for the foreseeable future.

oil and on the world distribution of fossil fuel reserves. The United States is richly endowed with coal but has only modest reserves of oil and natural gas. Over 65 percent of the world's oil resources are located in the Middle East. Other large reserves are found in Latin America, primarily Mexico and Venezuela, and in Russia and Nigeria. Natural gas, often a substitute for oil, is also unevenly distributed, with nearly 40 percent in Russia and central Asia and 34 percent in the Middle East (Figure 4.15).

The unevenness of the world's supply and demand for petroleum creates a distinct pattern of trade flows of petroleum (Figure 4.16), the most heavily traded (by volume) commodity in the world. Primarily, these flows represent exports from the vast reserves of the Middle East to Europe, East Asia, and North America, although the United States also imports considerable quantities from South America and Nigeria. The differences between crude oil production and consumption for each major world region are sketched in more detail in Figure 4.17.

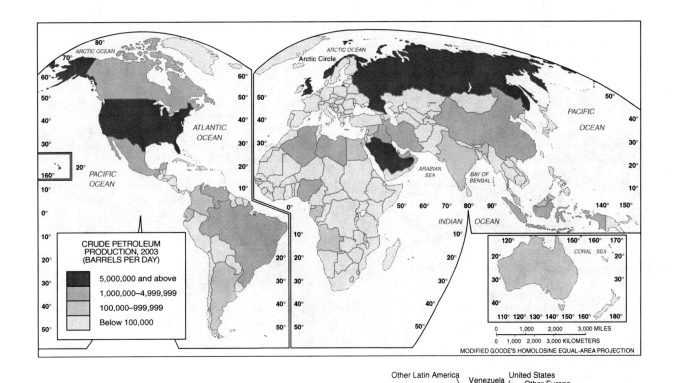

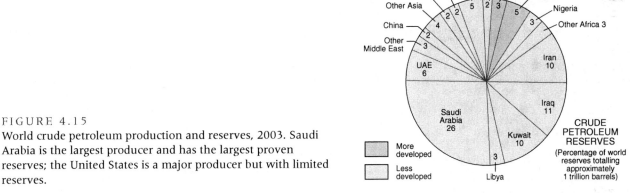

FIGURE 4.15
World crude petroleum production and reserves, 2003. Saudi Arabia is the largest producer and has the largest proven reserves; the United States is a major producer but with limited reserves.

Adequacy of Fossil Fuels

In the next few decades, energy consumption is expected to rise significantly, especially because of the growing industrialization of developing countries. Most of the future energy production to meet increasing demand will come from fossil energy resources—oil, natural gas, and coal. How long can fossil fuel reserves last, given our increasing energy requirements? Estimates of energy reserves have increased substantially in the last 20 years, and therefore there is little short-term concern over supplies; consequently, energy prices are relatively low. If energy consumption were to remain more or less at current levels, which is unlikely, proved reserves would supply world petroleum needs for 40 years, natural gas needs for 60 years, and coal needs for at least 300 years. Although the size of the world's total fossil fuel resources is unknown, they are finite, and production will eventually peak and then decline.

Oil: Black Gold

Most of the world's petroleum reserves are heavily concentrated in a few countries, mostly in politically unstable regions. Although reserves increased by 170 percent between 1978 and 2003, most of this increase is attributed to new discoveries in the Middle East. Regionally, however, reserves have been declining in important consuming countries. For example, reserves in Russia declined by 9 percent between 1991 and 2004. They also declined by 9 percent in the United States during the same period. Despite new discoveries, Europe's reserves are likely to be depleted by 2050. Moreover, exports of oil from Africa and Latin America will probably cease by 2050. The Middle East will then be the only major exporter of oil, but political turmoil (e.g., wars, revolutions) there could cause interruptions in oil supplies, creating problems for the import-dependent regions of North America, western Europe, Japan, and the East Asian newly industrializing countries (NICs).

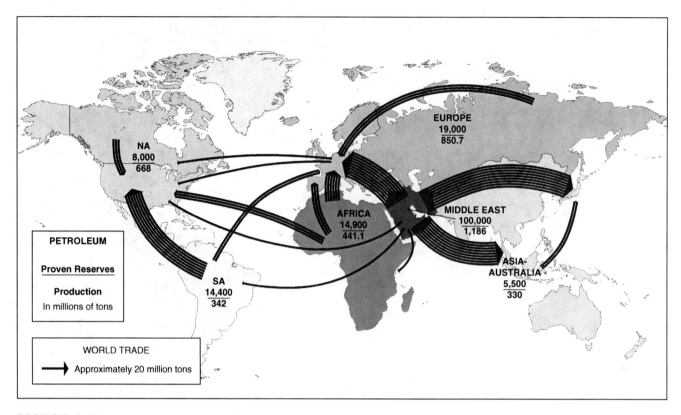

FIGURE 4.16
World trade patterns in petroleum, 2004. The major flows are from the Middle East to Europe, East Asia, and the United States, which also imports from Latin America and Nigeria.

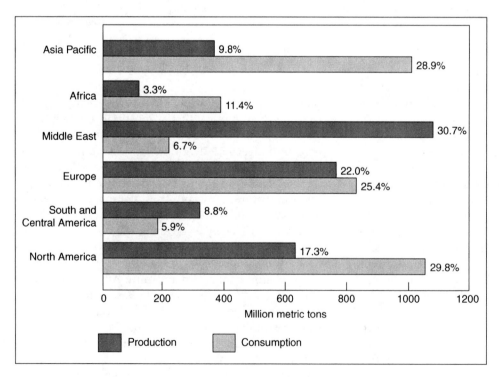

FIGURE 4.17
The production and consumption of crude oil by major world regions in millions of metric tons, 2004. The developed market economies of Europe, North America, and Asia, especially Japan, consume a far greater proportion of energy resources than they produce. Conversely, the Middle East, especially the Persian Gulf region, produces the most crude oil of any world region but consumes only one-sixth of its production. Latin America, Africa, and the former Soviet Union consume less crude oil than they produce.

Natural Gas

The political volatility of the world's oil supply has increased the attractiveness of natural gas, the fossil fuel experiencing the fastest growth in consumption. Natural gas production is increasing rapidly, and so too are estimates of proven gas reserves. Estimates of global gas reserves have increased during the last decade, primarily due to major finds in Russia, particularly in Siberia, and large discoveries in China, South Africa, and Australia. Reserves have also been increasing in western Europe, Latin America, and in North America. Gas production will eventually peak, probably in the first two or three decades of the twenty-first century. As a result, gas supplies will probably last a bit longer than oil supplies.

The distribution of natural gas differs from that of oil. It is more abundant than oil in the former Soviet Union, western Europe, and North America, and less abundant than oil in the Middle East, Latin America, and Africa. A comparison of Figures 4.18 and 4.19 shows that natural gas also differs in its pattern of production and consumption. Because of the high cost of transporting natural gas by sea, the pattern of production is similar to that of consumption.

Coal

Coal is the most abundant fossil fuel, and most of it is consumed in the country in which it is produced

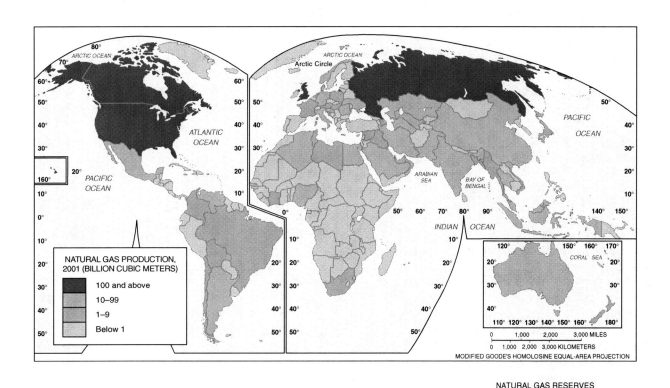

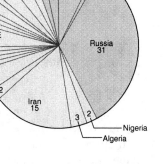

FIGURE 4.18
Production and consumption of natural gas by major world regions, 2001.

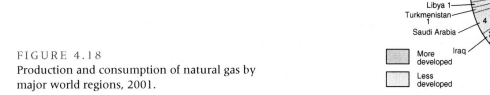

Resources and Environment

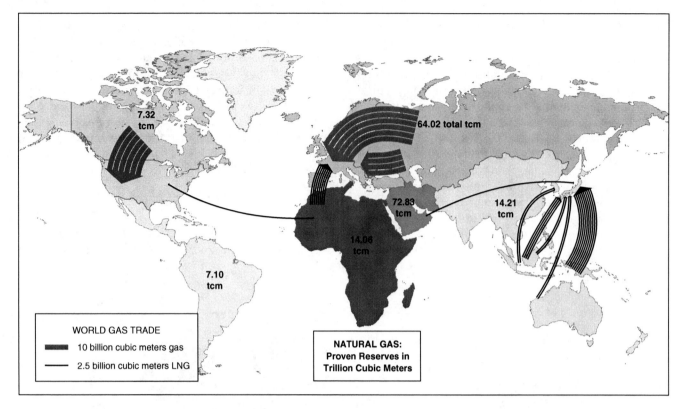

FIGURE 4.19
World trade patterns in natural gas, 2004. Russia is the world's largest exporter, primarily to Europe. Japan receives most of its gas from Southeast Asia, whereas the United States imports most from Canada.

(Figure 4.20). Use of this resource, however, has been hampered by inefficient management by the international coal industry, the inconvenience of storing and shipping, and the environmental consequences of large-scale coal burning.

China is the world's largest consumer of coal. The principal fossil fuel in North America is coal (Figure 4.21). With the exception of Russia, the United States has the largest proven coal reserves. Coal constitutes 67 percent of the country's fossil fuel resources, but only a small fraction of its energy consumption. It could provide some relief to the dependence on oil and natural gas. The use of coal, however, presents problems that the use of oil and natural gas do not, making it less desirable as an important fossil fuel. These problems are as follows:

1. Coal burning releases more pollution than other fossil fuels, especially sulfur. Low-grade bituminous coal has large amounts of sulfur, which, when released into the air from the burning of coal, combines with moisture to form acid rain (Figure 4.22).
2. Coal is not as easily mined as oil or natural gas. Underground mining is costly and dangerous, and open-pit mining leaves scars difficult to rehabilitate to environmental premining standards.

3. Coal is bulky and expensive to transport, and coal slurry pipelines are less efficient than oil or natural gas pipelines.
4. Coal is not a good fuel for mobile energy units such as trains and automobiles. Although coal can be adapted through gasification techniques to the automobile, it is an expensive conversion, and it is not, overall, well adapted to motor vehicles.

ENERGY OPTIONS

The age of cheap fossil fuels will eventually come to an end. As societies prepare for that eventuality, they must conserve energy and find alternatives to fossil fuels, especially alternatives that do not destroy the environment. How viable are the options?

Conservation

One way to reduce the gap between domestic production and consumption in the short run is for consumers to restrict consumption. Energy conservation stretches finite fuel resources and reduces environmental stress. Conservation can substitute for expensive, less environmentally desirable supply options and help to buy

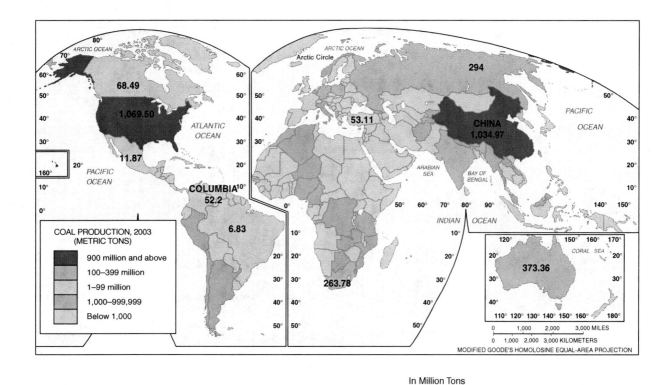

FIGURE 4.20

Coal production and reserves, 2003. The United States, China, and Russia lead the world in major coal deposits. Australia, Canada, and Europe also have major deposits.

time for the development of other more acceptable sources of energy.

Many people believe that energy conservation means a slow-growth economy; however, energy growth and economic growth are not inextricably linked. In the United States, from the early 1870s to the late 1940s, GNP per capita increased sixfold, whereas energy use per capita only slightly more than doubled. Energy efficiency, the ratio of useful energy output to total energy input, increased steadily throughout this century, partly as a result of industries installing better equipment. Even greater improvement can be expected in the new century.

Nuclear Energy

The form of nuclear energy currently in use commercially—*nuclear fission*—involves splitting large uranium atoms to release the energy within them. But nuclear fission causes many frightening issues, which became alarmingly clear after the nuclear accidents at the Three Mile Island plant in Pennsylvania in 1979 and at Chernobyl in the Ukraine in 1986. Concerns over nuclear energy range from environmental concerns caused by radiation to problems of radioactive waste disposal. Early radioactive wastes were dumped in the ocean in drums that soon began leaking. Likewise, many sites throughout the United States have contaminated groundwater supplies and leak radioactive wastes. One hotly discussed strategy currently underway is to store much of the nation's nuclear waste at Yucca Mountain, Nevada, miles away from major towns and cities. Another problem associated with the use of nuclear energy is the danger of terrorists stealing small amounts of nuclear fuel to construct weapons, which, if detonated, would wreak world havoc. Yet another is its high costs: Each plant costs billions of dollars to build and needs elaborate engineering and backup systems, as well as precautionary measures.

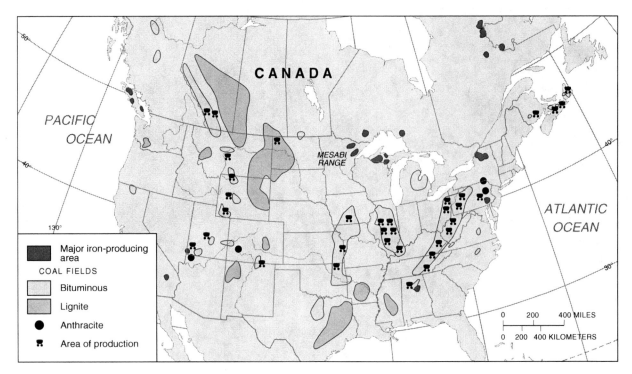

FIGURE 4.21
Major iron producing areas and coal fields of North America.

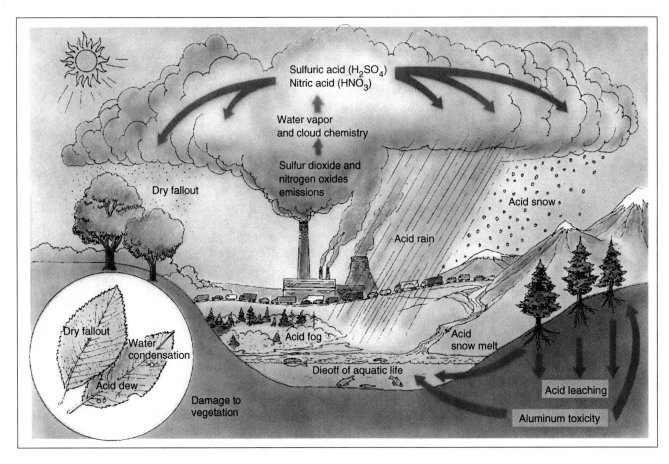

FIGURE 4.22
Acid rain creation. When sulfur is released into the atmosphere from the burning of coal and oil, it combines with moisture to create acid rain.

Nuclear power is less acceptable in North America than in some western European countries and Japan (Figure 4.23). In France, one-half of its energy comes from nuclear power; in Japan, 25 percent. Belgium, France, Hungary, and Sweden produce more than one-half of their energy from nuclear power plants, while Finland, Germany, Spain, Switzerland, South Korea, and Taiwan are also major producers and users. In the United States and Canada, countries that are less dependent on nuclear energy, the eastern portions rely on nuclear power plants more than do the western portions. For example, New England draws most of its electricity from nuclear power plants. Interestingly, some countries have decided to throw in the towel on nuclear power

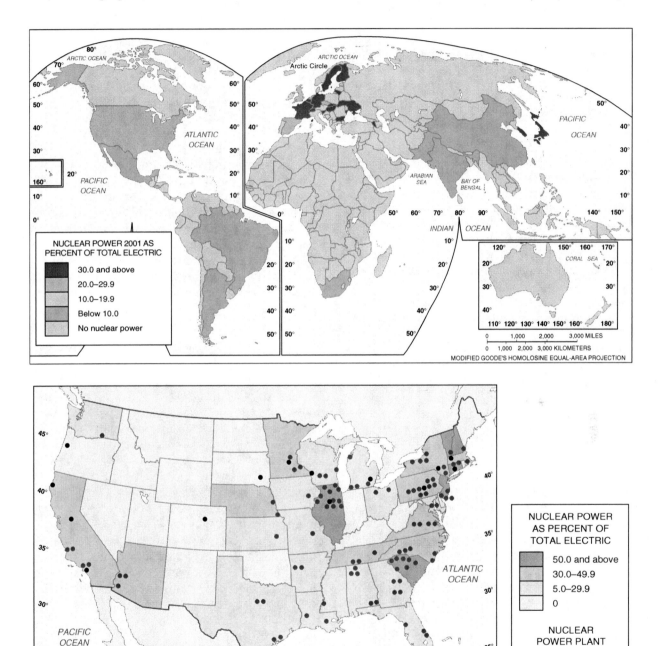

FIGURE 4.23
Nuclear power as a percentage of total energy use, 2001. The most important areas of nuclear energy production in the world include Western Europe and Japan. These are areas that have a relatively small amount of fossil fuels to satisfy local demand for energy. In Europe, for example, France, Germany, Sweden, and Finland produce more than 50 percent of their electrical energy from nuclear sources. Nuclear power is much less prevalent in the developing nations of the world because of extremely high-scale economies, or start-up costs, and the need for expensive uranium fuels.

generation because of high risk and high cost. Sweden began phasing out its nuclear plants in 1995 and is expected to be completed by 2010.

Nuclear fusion, the combination of smaller atoms to release their energy (the process that fuels the sun), has the potential to be a solution to the environmental concerns of nuclear fission because it does not release radioactive waste. The raw material for nuclear fusion is the common element hydrogen. Fusion is the process that powers the sun and can be made to occur artificially but is not yet commercially viable. If research on this technology is successful, nuclear fusion would provide limitless amounts of very cheap electricity and pose no radiation dangers.

Geothermal Power

The development of geothermal power holds promise for the future in several countries that have hot springs, geysers, and other underground supplies of hot water that can easily be tapped. The occurrence of this renewable resource is highly localized, however. New Zealand obtains about 10 percent of its electricity from this source, and smaller quantities are utilized by other countries such as Italy, Japan, Iceland, and the United States. If the interior of the earth's molten magma is sufficiently close to the surface (i.e., 10,000 feet), underground water may be sufficiently warm to produce steam that can be tapped by drilling geothermal wells. Geothermal energy is most producible in giant cracks or rifts in the earth's tectonic plate structure that occur in earthquake or active volcanic areas around the Pacific Rim. Wyoming and California are noted examples.

Hydropower

Another source of electric power, and one that is virtually inexhaustible, is hydropower—energy from rivers. Developed countries have exploited about 50 percent of their usable opportunities, Russia and Eastern Europe about 20 percent, and developing countries about 7 percent. In developed countries, further exploitation of hydropower is limited mainly by environmental and social concerns. In developing countries, a lack of investment funds and sufficiently well developed markets for the power are the main obstacles.

One of the main problems of constructing dams for hydropower is the disruption to the natural order of a watercourse. Behind the dam, water floods a large area, creating a reservoir; below the dam, the river may be reduced to a trickle. Both behind and below the dam, the countryside is transformed, plant and animal habitats are destroyed, farms are ruined, and

people are displaced. Moreover, the creation of reservoirs increases the rate of evaporation and the salinity of the remaining water. In tropical areas, reservoirs harbor parasitic diseases, such as schistosomiasis. For example, since the construction of the Aswan High Dam in the 1970s, schistosomiasis has become endemic in lower Egypt, infecting up to one-half of the population. An additional problem is the silting of reservoirs, reducing their potential to produce electricity. The silt, trapped in reservoirs, cannot proceed downstream and enrich agricultural land. The decrease in agricultural productivity from irrigated fields downstream from the Aswan High Dam has been substantial. China is completing the Three Gorges Dam on the Yangtze River, which will be the largest hydroelectric dam on the planet, and may well experience similar problems there.

The long-term hydrological, ecological, and human costs of dams easily transform into political problems on international rivers. An example is Turkey's Southeast Anatolia Project, which envisages the construction of 22 dams and 19 hydroelectric power plants. Because the project is being developed on two transboundary rivers—the Tigris and Euphrates—problems and disputes have arisen with two downstream users—Syria and Iraq—whose interests the project affects.

Solar Energy

Like river power, solar energy is inexhaustible. During the petro crises of the 1970s, solar energy caught the public imagination, including a few solar-powered homes and buildings. Large-scale utilization of solar energy, however, still poses technical difficulties, particularly that of low concentration of the energy. So far, technology has been able to convert only slightly more than 30 percent of solar energy into electricity; however, depending on the success of ongoing research programs, it could provide substantial power needs in the future. Solar energy's positive aspects are that it does not have the same risks as nuclear energy, nor is it difficult, like coal, to transport, and it is free of pollution. It is almost ubiquitous but varies by latitude and by season. In the United States, solar energy and incoming solar radiation are highest in the southwest and lowest in the northeast.

Passive solar energy is trapped rather than generated. It is captured by large glass plates on a building or house. The greenhouse effect is produced by short-wave radiation from the sun. Once the rays penetrate the glass, they are converted to long-wave radiation and are trapped within the glass panel, thus heating the interior of the structure or water storage tank. The other way of harnessing solar energy is through *solar energy,* including photovoltaic cells

The large hyperbolic cooling tower and reactor containment dome of the Trojan nuclear power plant in Rainier, Oregon. Safety issues surrounding the use of nuclear energy are fraught with turmoil. Most OECD countries expanded their nuclear energy production during the last 20 years, with France and Japan in the lead. Expansion of nuclear capacity had slowed by 1998 because of cost concerns and the chilling effects of the accidents at Three Mile Island in Pennsylvania and at Chernobyl in the Ukraine. New energy sources, such as geothermal, solar, biomass, and wind energy, have increased and now provide up to 5 percent of total primary energy requirements in Australia, Austria, Canada, Denmark, Sweden, and Switzerland.

made from silicon. A bank of cells can be wired together and mounted on the roof with mechanical devices that maximize the direct sun's rays by moving at an angle proportional to the light received. Another type of active solar energy system is a wood or aluminum box filled with copper pipes and covered with a glass plate, which collects solar radiation and converts it into hot water for homes and swimming pools.

Cost is the main problem with solar energy. High costs are associated with the capturing of energy in cloudy areas and high latitudes. But unlike fossil fuels, solar energy is difficult to store for long periods without large banks of cells or batteries. Currently, solar energy production is more expensive than other sources of fuel. To promote the development of innovative energy supplies when the Arab oil embargo hit in the 1970s, the U.S. government offered tax incentives, including tax deductions for solar units mounted on housetops. Although this tax deduction offset the high costs of constructing solar energy systems, maintenance and reliability soon become a problem. Families that move lose their investment, because most systems installed are rarely recoverable in the sale price of homes.

Wind Power

The power of the wind provides an energy hope for a few areas of the world where there are constant surface winds of 15 mph or more. The greatest majority of *wind farms* in the United States are in California. However, wind machines are an expensive investment, and the initial cost plus the unsightliness of the wind machine has ended most wind farm projects. Wind farm potential in California has never matched expectations, and wind farming stagnated; however, it is currently experiencing a revival.

Biomass

Still another form of renewable energy is biomass—wood and organic wastes. Today, biomass accounts for about 14 percent of global energy use. For Nepal, Ethiopia, and Tanzania, more than 90 percent of total energy comes from biomass. The use of wood for cooking—the largest use of biomass fuel—presents enormous environmental and social problems because it is being consumed faster than it is being replenished. Fuelwood scarcities—the poor world's energy crisis—affect 1.5 billion people and could affect 3 billion in the future unless corrective actions are taken.

With good management practices, biomass is a resource that can be produced renewably. It can be converted to alcohol and efficient, clean-burning fuel for cooking and transportation. Its production and conversion are labor intensive, an attractive feature for developing countries that face underemployment and unemployment problems. But the low efficiency of photosynthesis requires huge land areas for energy crops if significant quantities of biomass fuels are to be produced.

ENVIRONMENTAL DEGRADATION

On some days in Los Angeles, pollution levels reached what is called locally a *level three alert*, although conditions there have improved recently. People are advised to stay indoors, cars are ordered off the highways, and strenuous exercise is discouraged. In Times Beach, Missouri, which is some 50 miles south of St. Louis, dioxin levels from a contaminated plant became so high that the Environmental Protection Agency required the town to be closed and the residents to be relocated. Around Rocky Flats, nuclear wastes of plutonium have degraded the soil so that radioactivity levels are five times higher than normal. In New England, acid rain has become so bad that it has killed vegetation and fish in rivers and lakes.

Environmental problems, caused mainly by economic activity, may be divided into three overlapping categories: (1) pollution, (2) wildlife and habitat preservation, and (3) environmental equity.

Pollution

Pollution is a discharge of waste gases and chemicals into the air, land, and water. Such discharge can reach levels sufficient to create health hazards to plants, animals, and humans, as well as to reduce and degrade the environment. The natural environment has the capacity to regenerate and cleanse itself on a normal basis; however, when great amounts of gases and solids are released into it from industrial economic activity, recycling and purification needs are sometimes overwhelmed. From that point on, the quality of the environment is reduced as pollutants create health hazards for humans, defoliate forests, inundate land surfaces, reduce fisheries, and burden wildlife habitats.

Air Pollution

Air pollutants, the main sources of which are illustrated in Figure 4.24, are normally carried high into

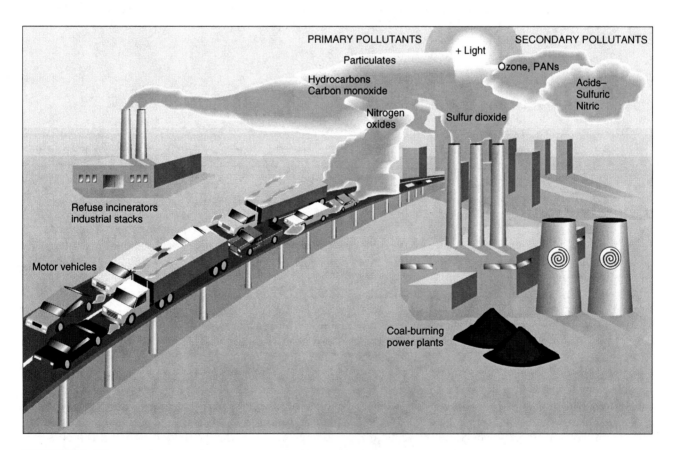

FIGURE 4.24
The primary sources of major air pollutants. Industrial processes are the major sources of particulates; transportation and fuel combustion cause the lion's share of the other pollutants.

the atmosphere, but occasionally, and in some places more than others, a temperature inversion prevents this from occurring. Inversions are caps of warm air that prevent the escape of pollutants to higher levels. Under these conditions, the inhabitants of a place are under an even greater risk. These conditions promote the formation of smog that blocks out sunshine, causes respiratory problems, stings the eyes, and creates a haze over large, congested cities everywhere.

Air pollution gives rise to different concerns at different scales. Air pollution at the local scale is a major concern in cities because of the release of carbon monoxide, hydrocarbons, and particulates. Air pollution at the regional scale is exemplified by the problem of acid precipitation in eastern North America and Eastern Europe (Figure 4.25).

At the global scale, air pollution may damage the atmosphere's *ozone layer* and contribute to the threat of *global warming*. The earth's protective ozone layer is thought to be threatened by pollutants called *CFCs (chlorofluorocarbons)*. When CFCs such as freon leak from appliances such as air conditioners and refrigerators, they are carried into the stratosphere, where they contribute to ozone depletion. As a result of the 1987 Montreal Protocol, developed countries stopped using CFCs by the year 2000 and developing countries must stop by 2010. Scientists hope that this international agreement will effectively reduce ozone depletion.

Concern about global warming centers around the burning of fossil fuels in ever greater quantities, which increases the amount of carbon dioxide in the air, which in turn makes the atmosphere more opaque, reducing thermal emission to space. Heat-trapping gases, such as carbon dioxide, warm the atmosphere, enhancing a natural *greenhouse effect* (Figure 4.26). The vast majority of these are produced by industrialized economies. Since the 1890s, the average temperature of the earth's surface has increased by 2 degrees Fahrenheit. This increase in temperature may or may not be humanly induced, however. There are divergent views on the issue. Nonetheless, even if the observed global warming is consistent with natural variability of the climate system, most scientists

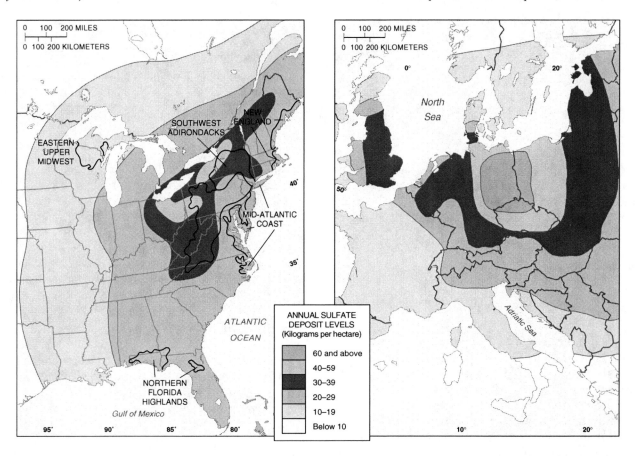

FIGURE 4.25

The worst inflicted areas of acid rain in North America occur downwind from the principal polluting regions of the industrialized Midwest. Ohio, western Pennsylvania, and northern New York State are the areas most heavily inflicted with acid rain deposits. Acid rain and snow deposits are also well documented in Europe, which is in a belt of prevailing wind coming from the west, as is the United States. Sulfur, released into the atmosphere from the burning of coal, combines with water vapor to produce sulfuric acid. Such acid creates substantial air pollution and etches away at limestone buildings, monuments, and markers on the earth. Acid precipitation can also kill plant and animal life, especially aquatic life. Literally thousands of lakes in Sweden and Norway no longer support the fish they once did.

Labels within figure: Atmosphere gets warmer; Greenhouse gases; Pollutants add to atmospheric greenhouse gases; Incoming solar radiation; Infrared is radiated back, and some is trapped by greenhouse gases; Solar radiation is absorbed and converted to infrared radiation

agree that it is socially irresponsible to delay actions to slow down the rate of anthropogenic greenhouse gas buildup. For example, continued warming would increase sea levels, disrupt ecosystems, and change land-use patterns. While agriculture in some temperate areas may benefit from global warming, tropical and subtropical areas may suffer.

Water Pollution

Although there is more than enough fresh water to meet the world's needs now and in the foreseeable future, the problem is that when we use water, we invariably contaminate it. Major wastewater sources that arise from human activities include municipal, mining, and industrial discharges, as well as urban, agricultural, and silvicultural runoff. The use of water to carry away waste material is an issue that has come into prominence, because water is being used more heavily than ever before. As populations and standards of living rise, problems of water utilization and management increase. These problems are most acute in developing countries, where some 1 billion people already find it difficult or impossible to obtain acceptable drinking water. But water is also an issue in developed countries. In the United States, for example, the major water management problem through most of the twentieth century focused on acquiring additional water supplies to meet the needs of expanding populations and associated economic activities. Recently, water management has focused on the physical limits of water resources, especially in the West and Southwest, and on water quality. Passage of the Clean Water Act in 1972 resulted in improvement in water quality of streams that receive discharges from specific locations or *point sources* such as municipal waste-treatment plants and industrial facilities. Recent efforts to improve water quality have emphasized the reduction of pollution from diffuse or *nonpoint sources* such as agricultural and urban runoff and contaminated groundwater discharges. These sources of pollution are often difficult to identify and costly to treat, and often meet with resistance from entrenched agribusiness interests.

Wildlife and Habitat Preservation

Wildlife and habitat preservation for plants and animals called *renewable natural resources* are in danger throughout the world. These natural environments are critical reserves for many species of plants and animals. Wildlife, forest lands, and wetlands, including lakes, rivers and streams, and coastal marshes, are subject to acid rain, toxic waste, pesticide discharge, and urban pollution. They are also endangered by encroachment of land development and transportation facilities worldwide. The demand for tropical hardwoods, such as teak and mahogany, has already stimulated waves of destruction in tropical rainforests. In the United States alone, expanding economic activity has consumed forests and wetlands, depleted topsoil, and polluted local ecosystems at a rapid rate. Many species of plants and animals have been reduced, including the grizzly bear, American bison, prairie dog, gray wolf, brown pelican, Florida panther, American alligator and crocodile, and a variety of waterfowl and tropical birds. All in all, the exponential growth of human beings has been closely associated with a corresponding dramatic decline in the number of species in the world (Figure 4.27), and future economic growth may threaten yet another catastrophic round of loss in the planet's biodiversity.

The problem of wildlife and habitat preservation is exacerbated by the need for economic gain and corporate profit. A variety of questions beset wildlife managers and environmental farmers. Should farmers be permitted to drain swamps in Louisiana to farm the land, thus destroying the habitat for alligators? Should forest fires started by lightning be allowed to burn themselves out, as has been the practice on western U.S. forests and rangelands? The trade-off of residential lands versus wetlands, wildlife migration versus forest management, highway safety versus habitat preservation, and conservation versus real economic development and growth of the U.S. economy are difficult issues. It is difficult to select the best alternative, and policies may reflect the power of entrenched economic interests as much as the public welfare.

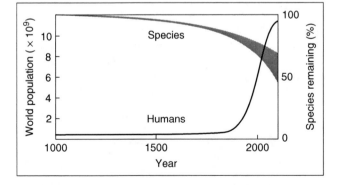

FIGURE 4.27
An inverse relationship exists between human population size and the survival of species worldwide. Uncertainty about the extent of decreasing biodiversity is reflected in the width of the species curve.

Because economic structures and change are not uniform around the world but exhibit great variation among the world's continents (as well as within them), and because population growth, cultural patterns, standards of living, and state policies regulating problems such as pollution vary widely, the environmental problems unleashed by capitalism and demographic change worldwide differ considerably.

In North America, the major environmental problems include acid rain downwind from industrial source areas (Figure 4.28). In addition, water pollution and withdrawal of groundwater are serious issues. Because the U.S. economy is so huge and energy intensive, the pollutants generated there are major sources of global problems such as the depletion of the ozone layer and global warming. Across the face of North America, other issues such as wetlands destruction, saltwater intrusion, and urban air quality are serious predicaments.

In Latin America, the primary environmental issue is deforestation, particularly in the Amazon River basin (Figure 4.29), where farmers and logging companies are stripping away the forest cover of some of the world's richest ecosystems. Further, degradation of ground cover leads to mud slides that can be lethal to thousands. Overgrazing and soil erosion are other important consequences, and in many Latin American cities, such as Mexico City, air quality is poor.

In Europe, these issues range from pollution of the Mediterranean Sea, whose coasts are populated by dense clusters of cities, as well as acid rain in Germany and Poland (Figure 4.30). Rising sea levels pose a threat to the Netherlands, much of which lies below sea level and uses dikes to hold the ocean back. Air and water pollution are constant problems requiring government intervention.

Environmental problems in Russia and its neighbors are tangled up in decades of mismanagement by the Soviet regime and an economy that collapsed in the 1990s (Figure 4.31). The Chernobyl disaster in 1985 left parts of the Ukraine polluted with nuclear waste. The extraction of water from the Aral Sea has left it nearly dead. And air pollution and acid rain take a toll on the region's enormous forests.

The predominantly Muslim world of North Africa and the Middle East has its own environmental problems (Figure 4.32). Soil erosion and overgrazing have contributed to desertification, particularly in the Sahara. Egypt's Aswan High Dam has been a mixed blessing, reducing floods on the Nile but also reducing the siltation that keeps farmlands fertile. Heavy use of river water contributes to soil salinization. All this takes place in a region with one of the world's highest rates of population growth.

Sub-Saharan Africa's environmental problems, framed in the context of extreme poverty and rapid population

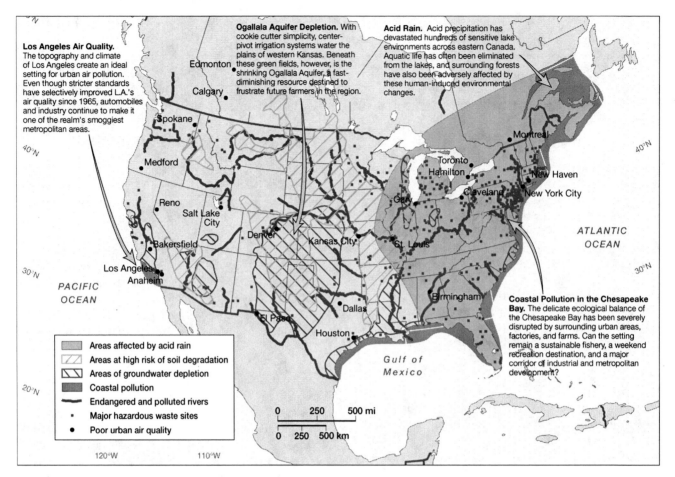

FIGURE 4.28
Environmental concerns and issues of North America.

growth, include widespread deforestation in western Africa (Figure 4.33). A continent in which islands of people were surrounded by oceans of wildlife has become one of islands of wildlife surrounded by oceans of people. Overgrazing and soil erosion threaten agricultural land as well as biodiversity, and the region is rocked by wars, drought, famines, and diseases such as AIDS and malaria.

In South Asia, the Indian subcontinent, home to more than 1.5 billion people, has seen widespread soil salinization and water and air pollution, which conspire to reduce the supply of agricultural land (Figure 4.34). Green Revolution farming accentuates these issues. Deforestation in the Himalaya mountains has increased flooding downstream in Bangladesh.

East Asia, home to 1.3 billion Chinese as well as hundreds of millions more in Korea and Japan, exhibits similar problems (Figure 4.35). The encroachment of farmers into forests has reduced the habitats of many species. Trying to stop periodic floods on the Yangtze River, the Chinese government is finishing the Three Gorges Dam, which will modify the basin and ecosystems of Asia's largest river. Japan supports 127 million people in a country with little arable land, and its dense cities exhibit severe air pollution levels,

although the rapid growth of Chinese cities has rendered the air quality there considerably worse yet.

Southeast Asia, one of three major regions in the world that sustain rainforests, has enjoyed rapid economic growth over the last two decades. Its environmental problems have grown proportionately (Figure 4.36). Deforestation in Indonesia, Malaysia, and Thailand has gone unchecked, threatening rich tropical ecosystems. Logging, farming, and international paper companies all contribute to this trend. Water pollution and soil erosion are increasingly widespread. Huge forest fires periodically carpet the region with smoke, adding to the deteriorating air quality of the region's cities, some of which are huge.

ENVIRONMENTAL EQUITY AND SUSTAINABLE DEVELOPMENT

Economic development policies and projects all too often carry as many costs as benefits. Build a dam to bring hydroelectric power or irrigation water, and fertile river bottomlands are drowned, farmers are displaced, waterborne diseases may fester in the still

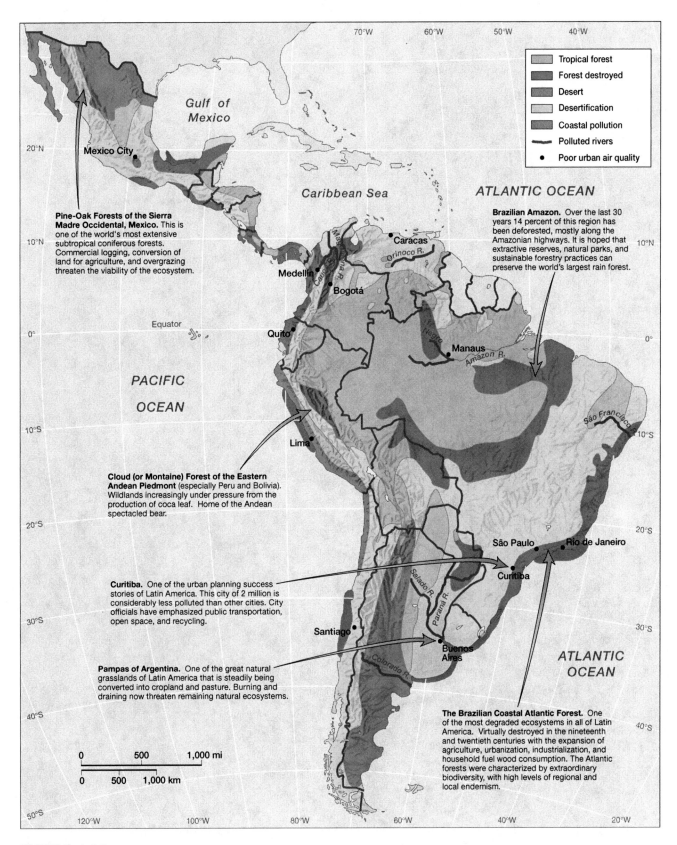

Legend:
- Tropical forest
- Forest destroyed
- Desert
- Desertification
- Coastal pollution
- Polluted rivers
- Poor urban air quality

Pine-Oak Forests of the Sierra Madre Occidental, Mexico. This is one of the world's most extensive subtropical coniferous forests. Commercial logging, conversion of land for agriculture, and overgrazing threaten the viability of the ecosystem.

Brazilian Amazon. Over the last 30 years 14 percent of this region has been deforested, mostly along the Amazonian highways. It is hoped that extractive reserves, natural parks, and sustainable forestry practices can preserve the world's largest rain forest.

Cloud (or Montaine) Forest of the Eastern Andean Piedmont (especially Peru and Bolivia). Wildlands increasingly under pressure from the production of coca leaf. Home of the Andean spectacled bear.

Curitiba. One of the urban planning success stories of Latin America. This city of 2 million is considerably less polluted than other cities. City officials have emphasized public transportation, open space, and recycling.

Pampas of Argentina. One of the great natural grasslands of Latin America that is steadily being converted into cropland and pasture. Burning and draining now threaten remaining natural ecosystems.

The Brazilian Coastal Atlantic Forest. One of the most degraded ecosystems in all of Latin America. Virtually destroyed in the nineteenth and twentieth centuries with the expansion of agriculture, urbanization, industrialization, and household fuel wood consumption. The Atlantic forests were characterized by extraordinary biodiversity, with high levels of regional and local endemism.

FIGURE 4.29
Environmental concerns and issues of Latin America.

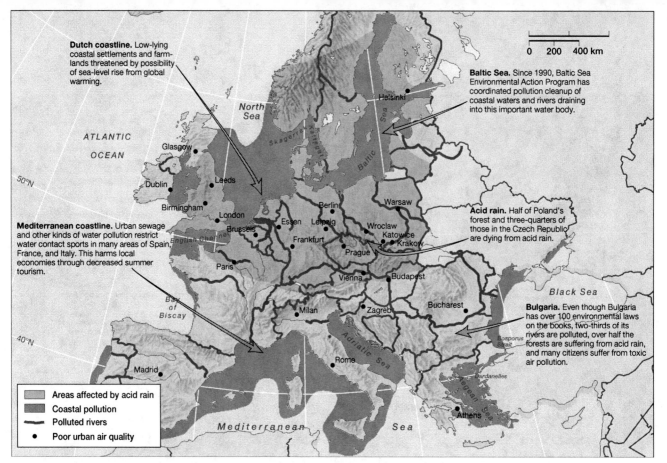

Dutch coastline. Low-lying coastal settlements and farmlands threatened by possibility of sea-level rise from global warming.

Baltic Sea. Since 1990, Baltic Sea Environmental Action Program has coordinated pollution cleanup of coastal waters and rivers draining into this important water body.

Mediterranean coastline. Urban sewage and other kinds of water pollution restrict water contact sports in many areas of Spain, France, and Italy. This harms local economies through decreased summer tourism.

Acid rain. Half of Poland's forest and three-quarters of those in the Czech Republic are dying from acid rain.

Bulgaria. Even though Bulgaria has over 100 environmental laws on the books, two-thirds of its rivers are polluted, over half the forests are suffering from acid rain, and many citizens suffer from toxic air pollution.

Legend:
- Areas affected by acid rain
- Coastal pollution
- Polluted rivers
- Poor urban air quality

FIGURE 4.30

Environmental concerns and issues of Europe.

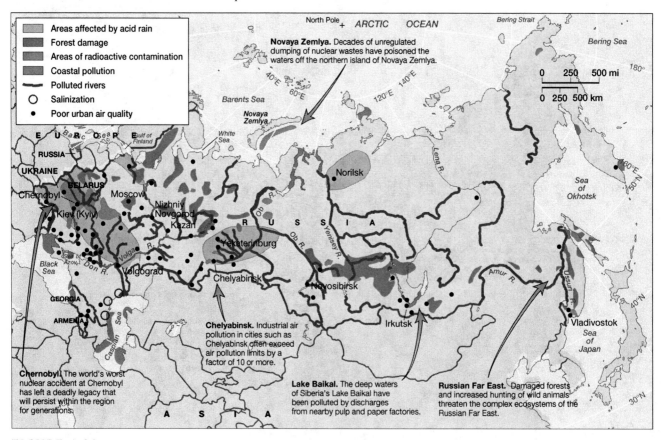

Legend:
- Areas affected by acid rain
- Forest damage
- Areas of radioactive contamination
- Coastal pollution
- Polluted rivers
- Salinization
- Poor urban air quality

Novaya Zemlya. Decades of unregulated dumping of nuclear wastes have poisoned the waters off the northern island of Novaya Zemlya.

Chelyabinsk. Industrial air pollution in cities such as Chelyabinsk often exceed air pollution limits by a factor of 10 or more.

Chernobyl. The world's worst nuclear accident at Chernobyl has left a deadly legacy that will persist within the region for generations.

Lake Baikal. The deep waters of Siberia's Lake Baikal have been polluted by discharges from nearby pulp and paper factories.

Russian Far East. Damaged forests and increased hunting of wild animals threaten the complex ecosystems of the Russian Far East.

FIGURE 4.31

Environmental concerns and issues of Russia and neighbors.

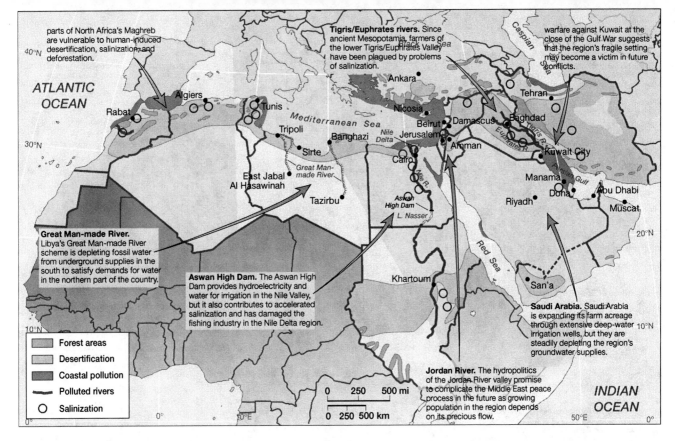

FIGURE 4.32
Environmental concerns and issues of Southwestern Asia and Northern Africa.

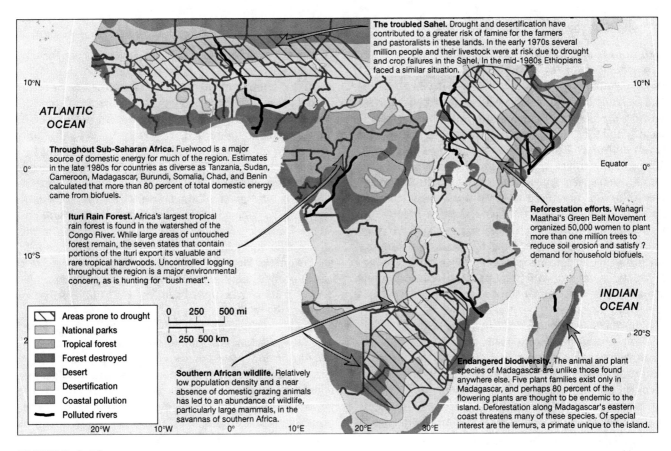

FIGURE 4.33
Environmental concerns and issues of Subsaharan Africa.

Resources and Environment

293

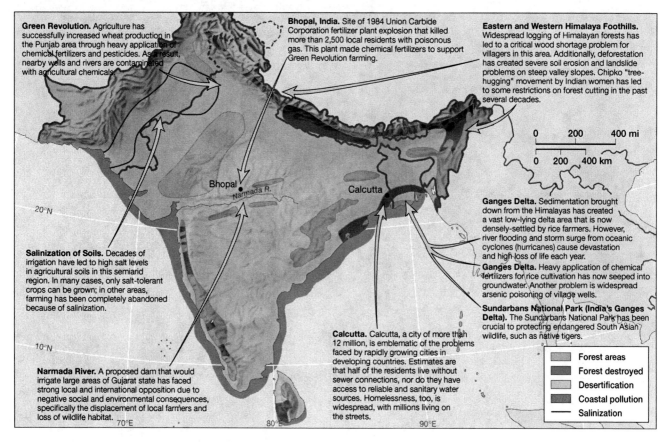

FIGURE 4.34
Environmental concerns and issues of South Asia.

Green Revolution. Agriculture has successfully increased wheat production in the Punjab area through heavy application of chemical fertilizers and pesticides. As a result, nearby wells and rivers are contaminated with agricultural chemicals.

Bhopal, India. Site of 1984 Union Carbide Corporation fertilizer plant explosion that killed more than 2,500 local residents with poisonous gas. This plant made chemical fertilizers to support Green Revolution farming.

Eastern and Western Himalaya Foothills. Widespread logging of Himalayan forests has led to a critical wood shortage problem for villagers in this area. Additionally, deforestation has created severe soil erosion and landslide problems on steep valley slopes. Chipko "tree-hugging" movement by Indian women has led to some restrictions on forest cutting in the past several decades.

Salinization of Soils. Decades of irrigation have led to high salt levels in agricultural soils in this semiarid region. In many cases, only salt-tolerant crops can be grown; in other areas, farming has been completely abandoned because of salinization.

Ganges Delta. Sedimentation brought down from the Himalayas has created a vast low-lying delta area that is now densely-settled by rice farmers. However, river flooding and storm surge from oceanic cyclones (hurricanes) cause devastation and high loss of life each year.

Ganges Delta. Heavy application of chemical fertilizers for rice cultivation has now seeped into groundwater. Another problem is widespread arsenic poisoning of village wells.

Sundarbans National Park (India's Ganges Delta). The Sundarbans National Park has been crucial to protecting endangered South Asian wildlife, such as native tigers.

Calcutta. Calcutta, a city of more than 12 million, is emblematic of the problems faced by rapidly growing cities in developing countries. Estimates are that half of the residents live without sewer connections, nor do they have access to reliable and sanitary water sources. Homelessness, too, is widespread, with millions living on the streets.

Narmada River. A proposed dam that would irrigate large areas of Gujarat state has faced strong local and international opposition due to negative social and environmental consequences, specifically the displacement of local farmers and loss of wildlife habitat.

Legend:
- Forest areas
- Forest destroyed
- Desertification
- Coastal pollution
- Salinization

waters of the reservoir, and the course of the river downstream to its delta or estuary is altered forever. Dig a well to improve water supplies in dry rangelands, and overgrazing and desertification spread outward all around the points of permanent water. Mine ore for wealth and jobs, and leave despoiled lands and air and water pollution. Build new industries, shopping malls, and housing tracts, and lose productive farmland or public open space. Introduce a new miracle crop to increase food production, and traditional crop varieties and farming methods closely synchronized to local environments disappear. Is it possible to reckon the costs and benefits of "progress"? Can we develop a humane society, one that encourages both equity and initiative, a society capable of satisfying its needs without jeopardizing the prospects of future generations? How do we go about creating a sustainable society?

The term *sustainable development* is defined as development that meets the needs of the present generation without compromising the ability of future generations to meet their own needs. Most accept its focus on the importance of long-range planning, but as a policy tool it is vague, providing no specifics about which needs and desires must be met and fulfilled and how.

In the debate on sustainable development, two different emphases have emerged. In the industrialized countries of North America, Europe, and Japan, the emphasis has been on long-term rather than short-term growth, and on efficiency. The emphasis has been on economics: If today we rely on an incomplete accounting system, one that does not measure the destruction of natural capital associated with gains in economic output, we deplete our productive assets, satisfying our needs today at the expense of our children. There is something fundamentally wrong in treating the earth as if it were a business in liquidation. Therefore, we should promote a systematic shift in economic development patterns to allow the market system to internalize environmental costs. The environmental costs of automobiles, for example, should include those associated with acid rain, primarily in the form of more expensive gasoline.

This Western emphasis on the economic aspects of sustainable development has been criticized in Africa, Asia, and Latin America. Critics from the less-developed world accuse environmentalists from the industrialized world of dodging the issues of development without growth and the redistribution of wealth. While some observers in the developing world may believe in the power of markets to distribute goods and services efficiently, they argue that social and political constraints are too severe to provide answers to all our problems. Many criticize the West's excessive consumption of resources. Many advocates in the developing world put

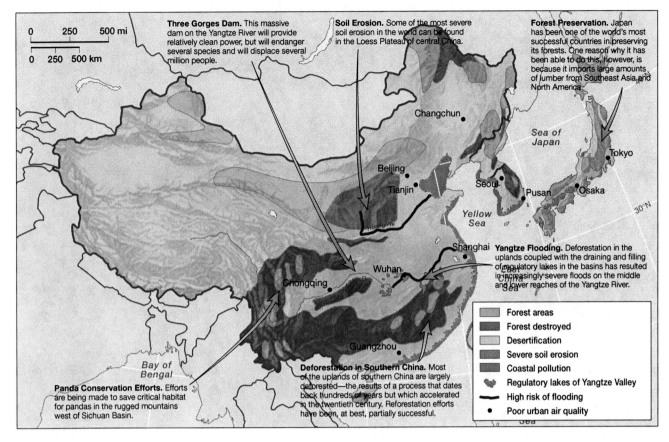

FIGURE 4.35
Environmental concerns and issues of East Asia.

The following labels appear on the map:

Three Gorges Dam. This massive dam on the Yangtze River will provide relatively clean power, but will endanger several species and will displace several million people.

Soil Erosion. Some of the most severe soil erosion in the world can be found in the Loess Plateau of central China.

Forest Preservation. Japan has been one of the world's most successful countries in preserving its forests. One reason why it has been able to do this, however, is because it imports large amounts of lumber from Southeast Asia and North America.

Yangtze Flooding. Deforestation in the uplands coupled with the draining and filling of regulatory lakes in the basins has resulted in increasingly severe floods on the middle and lower reaches of the Yangtze River.

Deforestation in Southern China. Most of the uplands of southern China are largely deforested—the results of a process that dates back hundreds of years but which accelerated in the twentieth century. Reforestation efforts have been, at best, partially successful.

Panda Conservation Efforts. Efforts are being made to save critical habitat for pandas in the rugged mountains west of Sichuan Basin.

Legend:
- Forest areas
- Forest destroyed
- Desertification
- Severe soil erosion
- Coastal pollution
- Regulatory lakes of Yangtze Valley
- High risk of flooding
- Poor urban air quality

basic human needs ahead of environmental concerns. Let us work toward a sustainable future, but let us do so by ensuring food, shelter, clean water, health care, security of person and property, education, and participation in governance for all. An extension of this sentiment is a desire to protect basic values as well—to respect nature rather than dominate it, and to use the wisdom of indigenous groups to reexamine current, mostly Western, structures of government, and the relationships that people have with the environment.

Is the consumerist West ready to listen to those with different values and priorities? Surely there are many paths to a sustainable future, each determined by individualized priorities of what is desired and therefore worthy of sustaining. Surely too, in following those paths, we must recognize that future growth will be constrained by resources that are finite or whose availability is difficult to determine. Finally, we must realize that no region can achieve sustainability in isolation. A desirable and sustainable future will be the result of many social and policy changes, some small and at the local level, others international and far reaching. If we accept that the futures of rich and poor are inextricably linked, perhaps we will achieve the humility necessary for compromise. A world that only rewards the rich, however, at the expense of the poor is doomed to social inequality and environmental destruction.

From a Growth-Oriented to a Balance-Oriented Lifestyle

Given the dynamics of the market system, it is unlikely that energy availability will place a limit on economic growth on the earth; however, ultimately, drastic changes in the rate and nature of the use of energy resources are certain. The ultimate limits to the use of energy will be determined by the ability of the world's ecosystems to dissipate the heat and waste produced as more and more energy flows through the system.

In countless ways, energy improves the quality of our lives, but it also pollutes. As the rate of energy consumption increases, so too does water and air contamination. Sources of water pollution are numerous: industrial wastes, sewage, and detergents; fertilizers, herbicides, and pesticides from agriculture; and coastal oil spills from tankers. Air pollution reduces visibility; damages buildings, clothes, and crops; and endangers human health. It is especially serious in urban-industrial areas, but it occurs wherever waste gases and solid particulates are released into the atmosphere.

Pollution is the price paid by an economic system emphasizing ever-increasing growth as a primary goal. Despite attempts to do something about pollution problems, the growth-oriented lifestyle characteristic of Western urban-industrial society continues to widen

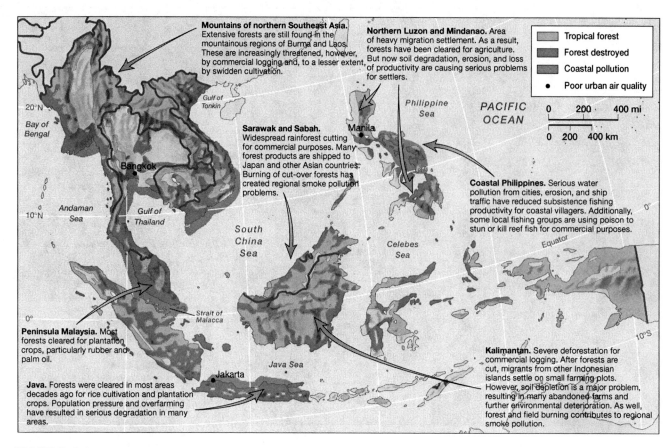

FIGURE 4.36
Environmental concerns and issues of Southeast Asia.

Mountains of northern Southeast Asia. Extensive forests are still found in the mountainous regions of Burma and Laos. These are increasingly threatened, however, by commercial logging and, to a lesser extent, by swidden cultivation.

Northern Luzon and Mindanao. Area of heavy migration settlement. As a result, forests have been cleared for agriculture. But now soil degradation, erosion, and loss of productivity are causing serious problems for settlers.

Sarawak and Sabah. Widespread rainforest cutting for commercial purposes. Many forest products are shipped to Japan and other Asian countries. Burning of cut-over forests has created regional smoke pollution problems.

Coastal Philippines. Serious water pollution from cities, erosion, and ship traffic have reduced subsistence fishing productivity for coastal villagers. Additionally, some local fishing groups are using poison to stun or kill reef fish for commercial purposes.

Peninsula Malaysia. Most forests cleared for plantation crops, particularly rubber and palm oil.

Java. Forests were cleared in most areas decades ago for rice cultivation and plantation crops. Population pressure and overfarming have resulted in serious degradation in many areas.

Kalimantan. Severe deforestation for commercial logging. After forests are cut, migrants from other Indonesian islands settle on small farming plots. However, soil depletion is a major problem, resulting in many abandoned farms and further environmental deterioration. As well, forest and field burning contributes to regional smoke pollution.

Legend: Tropical forest; Forest destroyed; Coastal pollution; • Poor urban air quality

the gap between people and nature. "Growthmania" is a road to nowhere. Many argue that we must transform our present linear or growth-oriented economic system into a balance-oriented system. A balance-oriented economy explicitly recognizes natural systems. It recognizes that resources are exhaustible, that they must be recycled, and that input rates must be reduced to levels that do not permanently damage the environment. A balance-oriented economy does not mean an end to growth but a new social system in which only desirable low-energy growth is encouraged. It requires a deemphasis on the materialistic values we have come to hold in such high esteem. If current resource and environmental constraints lead us to place a higher premium on saving and conserving than on spending and discarding, then they may be viewed as blessings in disguise.

SUMMARY

We conclude this chapter by restating the resources-population problem. It is possible to solve resource problems by (1) changing societal goals, (2) changing consumption patterns, (3) changing technology, and (4) altering population numbers. In the Western world, much of the emphasis is on technological advancement and population control.

Following a review of renewable and nonrenewable resources, we explored the question of food resources. The food "crisis" is essentially a consequence of social relations, including war and disruptions of agricultural systems. Food production is increasing faster than population growth, yet more people are hungry than ever before. In the course of transforming agriculture into a profit base for the wealthy in the developed and in the less developed worlds, the Third World poor are being forced into increasingly inhospitable living conditions. Famine, like poverty, is a social construction, not a natural event, and its origins, like its solutions, must be found in the uneven distribution of resources among and within countries.

Unlike food, which is replenishable, nonrenewable minerals and fossil fuels, once used, are gone forever. We discuss some of the alternatives to fossil fuels and point to energy conservation as a potent alternative with potential that remains to be fully exploited. Finally, the comparison between growth-oriented and balance-oriented lifestyles underscores the importance of social concerns as they relate to economic growth. Growth and inequality are inextricably linked parts of social change and environmental protection.

STUDY QUESTIONS

1. What is meant by carrying capacity?
2. Differentiate renewable from nonrenewable resources.
3. What are the major causes of Third World hunger?
4. What are three methods of expanding world food production?
5. What was the Green Revolution? Where was it largely located?
6. Summarize major flows of oil on the world market.
7. Where are the major world coal deposits located?
8. What are some alternative energy options to fossil fuels?
9. What are some environmental consequences of high energy use? Be specific.

KEY TERMS

acid rain
balance-oriented lifestyle
biomass
California Environmental Quality Act (CEQA)
carrying capacity
conservation
deforestation
depletion curves
desertification
energy
fossil fuels
geothermal energy
Green Revolution
growth-oriented lifestyle

intermediate technology
limits to growth
marine fisheries
maximum sustainable yield
minerals
mine tailings
National Environmental Policy Act (NEPA)
NIMBY and LULU effects
nonrenewable resources
normal lapse rate
Organization of Petroleum Exporting Countries (OPEC)
overpopulation
price ceiling

recycling
renewable resources
reserve
reserve deficiency minerals
resource
second law of thermodynamics
solar energy
stationary state
strategic minerals
tragedy of the commons
transmaterialization
triage
undernutrition
wind farm

SUGGESTED READING

Castree, N. and B. Braun, eds. 2001. *Social Nature: Theory, Practice, and Politics.* London: Blackwell.

Ellis, R. 2003. *The Empty Ocean: Plundering the World's Marine Life.* New York: Shearwear Books.

Falola, T. and A. Genova. 2005. *The Politics of the Global Oil Industry.* New York: Praeger.

Klare, M. 2002. *Resource Wars: The New Landscape of Global Conflict.* New York: Owl Books.

Zimmerer, K. 2006. *Globalization and New Geographies of Conservation.* Chicago: University of Chicago Press.

WORLD WIDE WEB SITES

CONSERVATION DATABASES—WCMC

http://www.unep-wcmc.org/index.html?
http://www.unep-wcmc.org/cis/~main

The World Conservation Monitoring Centre, whose purpose is the "location and management of information on the conservation and sustainable use of the world's living resources," provides five searchable databases. Users can search by country for threatened animals and plants (plants are available for Europe only), protected areas of the world, forest statistics and maps, marine statistics and maps, and national biodiversity profiles (twelve countries only at present). Information is drawn from several sources, and database documentation varies from resource to resource.

STATE OF THE WORLD'S FORESTS—FAO

http://www.fao.org/forestry/index.jsp

The United Nations Food and Agriculture Organization presents information on the current status of the world's forests, major developments over the reporting period, and recent trends and future directions in the forestry sector. SOFO provides information on global forest cover, including estimates for 1995, change from 1990, and revised estimates for forest cover change.

"MAPPING THE WORLD BY HEART"
http://www.mapping.com

Has links to worldwide geographic and educational resources, such as time zone maps and other related global information.

ENVIRONMENTAL PROTECTION AGENCY
http://www.epa.gov

This site provides everything you ever wanted to know about environment and material resources.

ATLAPEDIA
http://www.atlapedia.com/index.html

Atlapedia Online contains key information on every country of the world. Each country profile provides facts and data on geography, climate, people, religion, language, history, and economy, making it ideal for students of all ages.

AG-ECON
http://agecon.lib.umn.edu

AgEcon contains information for agricultural and applied economics.

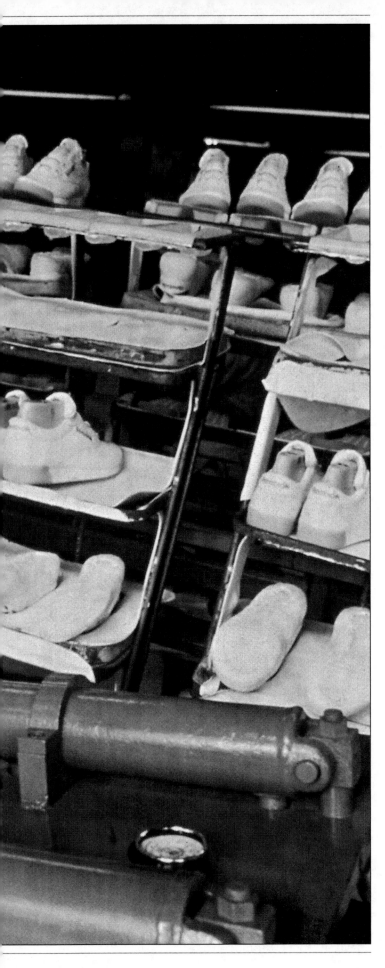

CHAPTER
7

MANUFACTURING

OBJECTIVES

- To explore the fundamental nature of the manufacturing process
- To acquaint you with the major manufacturing regions of the world
- To describe recent global shifts in the globalization of world manufacturing
- To summarize the geography of U.S. manufacturing, major industries and their changes over time
- To show the trend toward flexible manufacture, flexible labor, and the flexible economy

A maquiladora textile worker in Ciudad Juarez, Mexico.

To manufacture is to make things—to transform raw materials into goods that satisfy needs and wants. Manufacturing is crucial because it produces goods that sustain human life, provides employment, and generates economic growth. It has played this role since the Industrial Revolution in England in the late eighteenth century, when manufacturing generated the working classes of Europe, North America, and Japan.

Geographers who study manufacturing emphasize the locational behavior of firms and the structures of the places they create. First, this chapter examines the nature of manufacturing, including the basic steps involved in the transformation of raw materials into final products. Second, it turns to the major regions in the world that produce goods—North America, Europe, and Japan. Manufacturing is highly unevenly located around the world. How did these clusters come to exist? Third, it explores three crucial industries in more depth: textiles, automobiles, and electronics. Fourth, it summarizes the geography of U.S. manufacturing and the changes wrought by globalization. Fifth, it introduces the notions of flexibility, post-Fordist production, and just-in-time systems, which have revolutionized the manufacturing production and delivery process.

THE NATURE OF MANUFACTURING

Manufacturing involves deciding what is to be produced, gathering together the raw materials and semi-finished inputs at a plant, reworking and combining the inputs to produce a finished product, and marketing the finished product. These phases are called *selection, assembly, production,* and *distribution*. The assembly and distribution phases require transportation of raw materials and finished products, respectively. Industrial location theory attempts to identify the locations that will minimize these transportation costs. The production phase—changing the form of a raw material—involves combining land, labor, capital, and management, factors that vary widely in cost from place to place. Thus, each of the steps of the manufacturing process has a spatial or a locational dimension.

Changing the form of a raw material increases its use or value. Flour milled from wheat is more valuable than raw grain. Bread, in turn, is worth more than flour. This process is termed *value added by manufacturing*. The value added by manufacturing is quite low in an industry engaged in the initial processing of a raw material. For example, turning sugar beets into sugar yields an added value of about 30 percent. In contrast, changing a few ounces of steel and glass into a watch yields a high added value—more than 60 percent. The cost and productivity of labor, and the availability of skills, plays an important role in high value-added manufacturing.

CONCENTRATIONS OF WORLD MANUFACTURING

Manufacturing capacity and employment are highly unevenly distributed around the world and go far to explain the uneven spatial development that typifies the world economy. Three major areas account for approximately 80 percent of the world's manufacturing (Figure 7.1): North America, Europe (including Russia and Ukraine), and Japan.

North America

North American manufacturing is largely centered in the northeastern United States and southeastern Canada (Figure 7.2), the North American Manufacturing Belt, which accounts for one-third of the North American population and nearly two-thirds of North American manufacturing employment. This area was settled by Europeans in the seventeenth and eighteenth centuries, and grew rapidly in the nineteenth century. It was tied to the European markets and possessed the raw materials, iron ore, coal, and limestone necessary to produce the heavy machinery and manufactured items on which the industrialization of America was based. In addition, this region had many markets and a large labor pool.

The transportation system included the St. Lawrence River and the Great Lakes, which were connected to the East Coast and the Atlantic Ocean by the Mohawk and Hudson Rivers. This transportation system allowed the easy movement of bulky and heavy materials. Later, canals and railroads supplemented the river and lake system.

Within the North American Manufacturing Belt, there are several districts. The oldest is southern New England, centered on the greater Boston metropolitan area. Historically, this area was the textile and clothing manufacturing center of the early nineteenth century. Cotton was brought from the Southern states to be manufactured into garments, many of which were consumed locally and some of which were exported to Europe. As the low-wage European immigrant laborers settled and unionized, wages became higher, and the textile industry moved to the South in the early twentieth century. Today, New England manufacturing centers on electrical machinery, fabricated metals, and electronic products. The region is noted for highly skilled labor, with nearby universities—including Boston College, Boston University, Massachusetts Institute of Technology, and Harvard University—providing the chief supply (Figure 7.2).

The Middle Atlantic district includes the metropolitan areas of New York, Baltimore, Philadelphia, and Wilmington, Delaware. The Great Lakes industrial traffic terminates in New York City via the

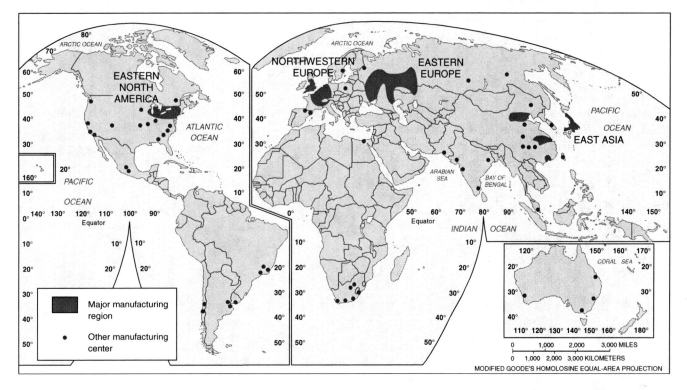

FIGURE 7.1
Worldwide distribution of manufacturing. The four main manufacturing regions include the northeastern United States and southern Great Lakes region, the northwestern European region, the eastern Soviet Union and Ukraine region, and the Japan/South Korea region. See the text for a detailed elaboration of districts within each of these regions, as well as other manufacturing regions shown as dots.

Mohawk and Hudson rivers. From New York City, foreign markets and sources of raw materials can be reached. New York City is the largest market and has the largest labor pool. Because of the enormous agglomeration economies it offers, many of the *Fortune* 500 firm headquarters are in this district. The New York district is in proximity not only to trade with the rest of the world but also to the population centers and manufacturing hubs of America (Figure 7.2). It is also near financial, communications, and news and media industries, which are important for advertising and distribution. This region produces apparel, iron and steel, chemicals, machinery, fabricated metals, and a variety of processed foods. In addition, it is the headquarters of the North American publishing industry. Many major book and magazine publishing companies are found in this region.

The central New York and Mohawk River valley district produces electrical machinery, chemicals, optical machinery, and iron and steel. These industries agglomerate along the Erie Canal and the Hudson River, the only waterway connecting the Great Lakes to the U.S. East Coast. Abundant electrical power produced by the kinetic energy of Niagara Falls provides inexpensive electricity to this district and explains the attraction of the aluminum industry, which requires large amounts of electricity. The New York industrial cities

of Buffalo, Rochester, Syracuse, Utica, Schenectady, and Albany are situated in this district.

The Pittsburgh–Cleveland–Lake Erie district, centered in western Pennsylvania and eastern Ohio, is the oldest steel-producing region in North America. Pittsburgh was the original steel-producing center because of the iron ore and coal available in the nearby Appalachian Mountains. When the iron ore became depleted, new supplies were discovered in northern Minnesota and transported in via the Great Lakes system. Besides iron and steel, electrical equipment, machinery, rubber, and machine tools are produced in this region.

The western Great Lakes industrial region is centered on Detroit in the east and Chicago in the west (Figure 7.2). In addition, Toledo, Ohio, in the east and Milwaukee in the west were long known for the production of transportation equipment, iron and steel, automobiles, fabricated metals, and machinery. Detroit and surrounding cities, of course, have the preeminent position of automobile manufacture, and Chicago has produced more railroad cars, farm tractors and implements, and food products than any other city in the United States. The convergence of railroad and highway transportation routes in this area makes it readily accessible to the rest of the country and a good distribution point to a national market.

FIGURE 7.2
Manufacturing regions and districts throughout the United States and Canada.

The following legend appears within the figure:

Anglo-American Manufacturing Region
1. New England district
   Electrical machinery
   Machinery
   Fabricated metals
   Textiles
   Electronic products
   Apparel
2. Greater New York district
   Apparel
   Printing and publishing
   Machinery
   Food processing
   Fabricated metals
   Chemicals
3. Central New York district
   Electrical machinery
   Chemicals
   Optical machinery
   Iron and steel
4. Mid-Atlantic district
   Apparel
   Iron and steel
   Chemicals
   Food processing
   Machinery
5. Pittsburgh-Cleveland district
   Iron and steel
   Machinery
   Electrical equipment
   Rubber
   Machine tools

6. Southeast Michigan district
   Automobiles
   Iron and steel
7. Lake Michigan district
   Iron and steel
   Fabricated metals
   Machinery
   Printing and publishing
   Electrical machinery
8. Southwest Ohio-Eastern Indiana district
   Iron and steel
   Fabricated metals
   Machinery
   Electrical machinery
   Paper manufacturing
9. Great Kanawha and Middle Ohio Valley district
   Chemicals
   Primary metals
   Glass
10. St. Louis district
    Transportation equipment
    Iron and steel
    Fabricated metals
    Food processing
11. Ontario Peninsula district (Canada)
    Iron and steel
    Machinery
    Chemicals
    Food processing
12. St. Lawrence Valley district (Canada)
    Pulp and paper
    Primary metals (aluminum)

Southeastern Manufacturing Region
Textiles
Apparel
Transportation equipment
Furniture
Food processing
Lumber
Primary metals
Gulf Coast Manufacturing Region
Petroleum refining
Chemicals
Primary metals (aluminum)
Electrical machinery
Electronic products
Central Florida Manufacturing Region
Food processing
Electrical machinery
Electronic products
West Coast Manufacturing Region
A Los Angeles-San Diego district
   Aircraft
   Electrical equipment
   Automobile assembly
   Apparel
   Petroleum refining
B San Francisco district
   Electronic products
   Food processing
   Shipbuilding
   Machinery

C Pacific Northwest district (Portland-Seattle, Vancouver)
   Aircraft
   Lumber products
   Food processing
Other Centers of Manufacturing
I   Kansas City
    Food processing
    Automobile assembly
II Minneapolis-St. Paul
    Food processing
    Machinery
    Fabricated metals
III Dallas-Ft. Worth
    Transportation equipment
    Food processing
IV Denver-Pueblo
    Food processing
    Chemicals
    Iron and steel
V   Phoenix
    Electrical machinery
    Electronic products

Canada's most important industrial region stretches along the St. Lawrence River Valley, on the north shore of the eastern Great Lakes (Figure 7.2). This area has access to the St. Lawrence River–Great Lakes transportation system, is near the largest Canadian markets, has skilled and plentiful labor, and is supplied with inexpensive electricity from Niagara Falls. Iron and steel, machinery, chemicals, processed foods, pulp and paper,

and primary metals, especially aluminum, are produced in this district. For example, Toronto is a leading automobile-assembly location in Canada, whereas Hamilton is Canada's leading iron and steel producer.

The southeastern manufacturing region of the United States stretches south from central Virginia through North Carolina, western South Carolina, northern Georgia, northeastern Alabama, and northeastern

New England became the first and foremost textile manufacturing region in the United States in the nineteenth century. The mills pictured here are in Lawrence, Massachusetts. By the 1940s, the textile region of southern New England had been in decline for more than 20 years. Firms left the region in search of more profitable operating conditions, and workers were forced to seek other employment. The region has experienced a revival as new industries, notably electrical engineering, have replaced the older, declining ones.

Tennessee (Figure 7.2). It wraps around the southern flank of the Appalachian Mountains because of poor transportation connections across the mountains. Textiles are the main product, the industry having moved from the Northeast to the South to take advantage of less expensive, nonunion labor. Transportation equipment, furniture, processed foods, and lumber are also produced. Aluminum manufacturers moved to this region because of the inexpensive electricity produced by the more than 20 dams built by the Tennessee Valley Authority, and Birmingham was long the iron and steel center of the southeastern United States because of the plentiful iron-ore and coal supplies nearby. Figure 7.3 shows the distribution of American textile employment today. The primary concentration is in the Southeast, particularly in North and South Carolina. Secondary concentrations are found in New England, a remnant of its heyday in the early twentieth century, as well as southern California, where sweatshops using immigrant labor are common.

The Gulf Coast manufacturing region stretches from southeastern Texas through southern Louisiana, Mississippi, and Alabama, to the tip of the Florida panhandle, including cities such as Houston, Texas; Baton Rouge, Louisiana; Mobile, Alabama; and Pensacola, Florida. Because of nearby oil and gas fields, petroleum refining and chemical production are important. The region also produces primary metals, including aluminum, and electrical machinery and electronic products.

The Los Angeles and San Diego district in southern California specializes in aircraft and aerospace manufacture and electrical equipment. In the 1930s, the airline industry chose this location because favorable weather much of the year meant unimpeded test flights and savings on heating and cooling the large aircraft plants. Federal government subsidies during World War II reinforced this advantageous location. Because of the myriad electronic parts and equipment and the associated high-tech sensing and navigational devices required in aircraft manufacture, the electronics industry was also attracted to this region and was anchored there 30 years later (Figure 7.4). Today, aircraft, apparel manufacture, and petroleum refining are important in Los Angeles, whereas San Diego also specializes in pharmaceutical production and in military and transport equipment industries.

The San Francisco Bay Area is another important West Coast manufacturing region. Electronic products, processed foods, ships, and machinery are produced in the district. *Silicon Valley*, the world's largest manufacturing area for semiconductors, microprocessors, software, and computer equipment, is located just south of San Francisco in the Santa Clara Valley.

The Pacific Northwest district includes the cities of Seattle, Washington, and Portland, Oregon. Boeing Aircraft is the single largest employer, followed closely by the paper, lumber, and food-processing industries.

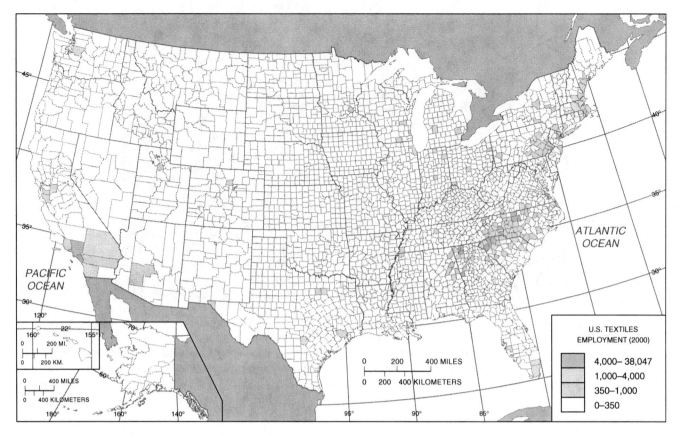

FIGURE 7.3
The distribution of U.S. textiles employment, 2000.

Europe

Europe has some of the world's most important industrial regions (Figure 7.5). They are located in a north-south linear pattern, starting from Scotland and extending through southern England, continuing from the mouth of the Rhine River valley in the Netherlands, through Germany and France, to northern Italy. Good supplies of iron ore and coal provide fuel to the countries in these industrial regions.

The Industrial Revolution started in the United Kingdom in the mid-eighteenth century. It had its basis in textile and woolen manufacture. Because many dependent nations have since learned to produce their own iron, steel, and textiles, the world currently has an oversupply of these items, and the market for British goods has decreased substantially. Britain's outmoded factories, high labor costs, slow productivity growth, and deteriorating infrastructures reduced its overall global competitiveness for products. In contrast, Germany and

San Jose, California. A $1 billion downtown renaissance has helped establish San Jose, capital of Silicon Valley, as California's third and the United States' eleventh largst city.

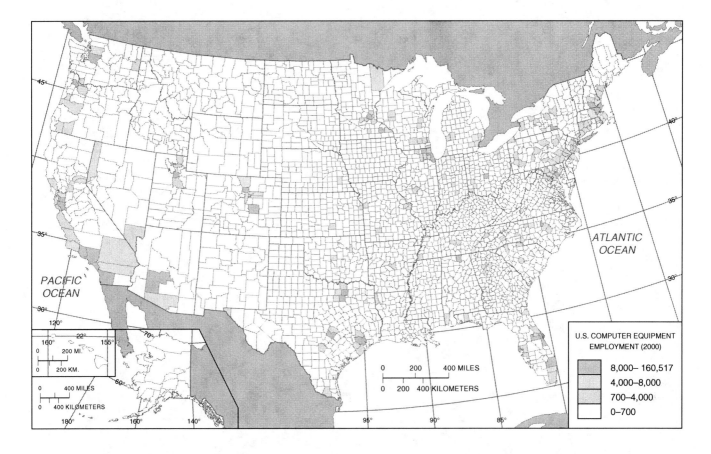

FIGURE 7.4

The distribution of U.S. computer equipment employment, 2000. California has the largest number of firms, followed by a cluster in the Northeast. Electronics manufacturing plants gravitate to highly skilled labor. The finished products are more valuable than are items of clothing, and higher wages can be paid. There is a concentration of employment in California because early electronics production was linked to the aircraft manufacturing industry centered on the West Coast; the microelectronics revolution and the rise of Silicon Valley furthered this growth.

Japan, with U.S. assistance, rebuilt after World War II, modernizing their plants and industrial processes at the same time. As a result, Germany and Japan are industrial successes in the world today, whereas Britain, more so than any other modern industrialized country, has suffered persistent industrial decline.

The largest European manufacturing region today is in the northern European lowland countries of Belgium and the Netherlands, northwestern Germany, and northeastern France. In this region, the Rhine and Ruhr Rivers meet. This region's backbone has been the iron and steel industry because of its proximity to coal and iron-ore fields. Production of transportation equipment, machinery, and chemicals helped lead Western Europe into the industrial age long before the rest of the world. The Rhine River, which is the main waterway of European commerce, empties into the North Sea in the Dutch city of Rotterdam. Consequently, because of its excellent location, Rotterdam has become the world's largest port, although it has been surpassed by those in East Asia. While exports of iron and steel are down from what they were 30 years ago, the region has been

better able to avoid the depression of the United Kingdom because of its greater internal conversion of steel into high-quality finished products, which are in demand worldwide.

The Upper Rhine–Alsace-Lorraine Region (called Mid-Rhine in Figure 7.5) is in southwestern Germany and eastern France. It is the second most important European industrial district, after the Rhine–Ruhr River valley. Because of its central location, this area is well situated for distribution to population centers throughout western Europe. The main cities on the German side include Frankfurt, Stuttgart, and Mannheim. Frankfurt became the financial and commercial center of Germany's railway, air, and road networks. Stuttgart, on the other hand, is a center for precision goods and high-value, volume, manufactured goods, including the Mercedes Benz, Porsche, and Audi automobiles. Mannheim, located along the Rhine River, is noted for its chemicals, pharmaceuticals, and inland port facilities. The western side of this district, in France, is known as Alsace-Lorraine and produces a large portion of the district's iron and steel.

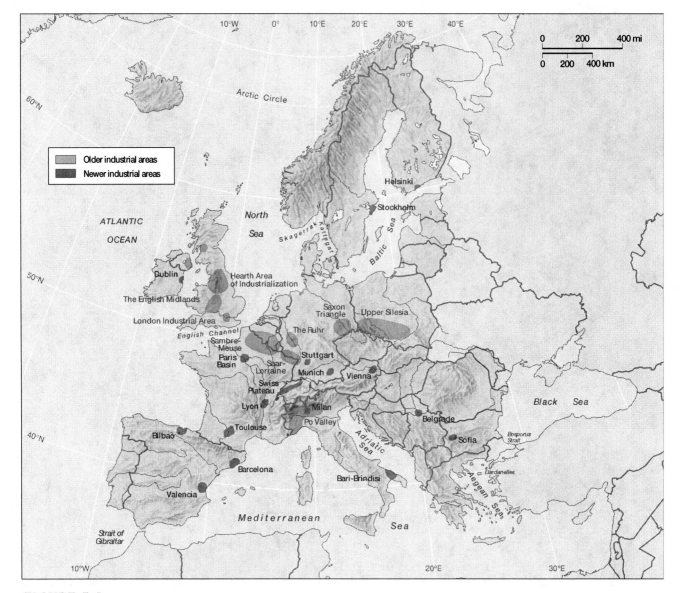

FIGURE 7.5
European manufacturing regions. Much European manufacturing exists in a linear belt from Scotland to the Midlands of Britain, to the South, including the London area. This belt continues onward from the low countries of Belgium, Luxembourg, and the Netherlands, south along the Rhine River, including portions of France and Germany, and into northern Italy. These areas became major manufacturing regions not only because of the concentration of skilled laborers but also due to the availability of raw materials, principally coal and iron ore. In addition, good river transportation was available, as well as large consuming markets for finished products.

The Po River valley in northern Italy includes Turin, Milan, and Genoa, including only one-fourth of Italy's land but more than 70 percent of its industries and 50 percent of its population. This region specializes in iron and steel, transportation equipment (especially high-value automobiles), textile manufacture, and food processing. The Emilia-Romagha region is Italy's high technology center. The Alps, a barrier to the German and British industrial regions, give the Italian district a large share of the southern European markets. The mountains also provide Italian industries with cheap hydroelectricity and therefore reduced operating costs. Compared with workers in the American Manufacturing Belt, Italian laborers are willing to work for lower wages, and thus this region attracts labor-intensive industries, such as textiles, from northern Europe.

The Ukraine industrial region relies on the rich coalfield deposits of the Donets Basin. The iron and steel industry base is the city of Krivoy Rog, with nearby Odessa as the principal Black Sea all-weather port (Figure 7.6).

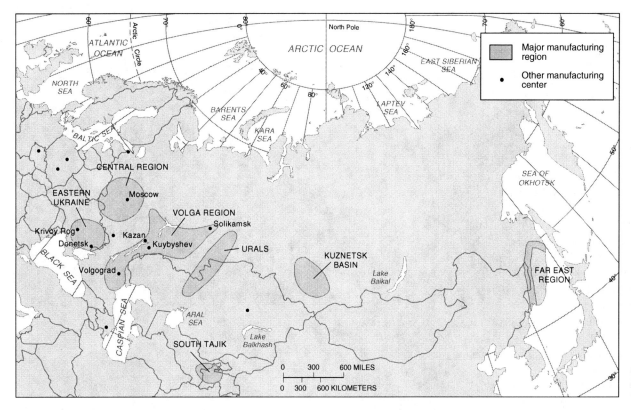

FIGURE 7.6
Manufacturing regions of Russia, Ukraine, and Central Asia.

The area is collectively known as Donbass. Like the German Ruhr area, Ukraine's industrial district is near iron-ore and coal mines, a dense population, and a large agricultural region and is served by good transportation facilities.

In Russia, the Moscow industrial region is near the population center of Russia and takes advantage of a large, skilled labor pool as well as a large market, even though natural resources are not plentiful. The largest single item produced is textiles: linen, cotton, wool, and silk fabrics. East of the Moscow industrial region is the linear Volga region, extending northward from Volgograd (formerly Stalingrad) and astride the Volga River. The Volga River, a chief waterway of Russia, has been linked via canal to the Don River and thereby to the Black Sea. This industrial region developed during and after World War II because it was just out of reach of the invading Nazi army that occupied the Ukraine. It is the principal location of substantial oil and gas production and refining. Recently, a larger oil and gas field was discovered in West Siberia. Nonetheless, the Volga district is Russia's chief supplier of oil and gas, chemicals, and related products. Recently, one of the largest automobile plants in the world opened in Toglaitti, producing Fiat automobiles.

Just east of the Volga region are the low-lying Ural Mountains that separate European Russia from Asian Russia (Figure 7.6). The Ural Mountains have the largest deposits of industrial minerals found anywhere in the former Soviet Union. Mineral types include iron, copper, potassium, magnesium, salt, tungsten, and bauxite. The central-lying Ural district was important during World War II because it also was beyond the reach of the German army. Although coal must be imported from the nearby Volga district, the Urals district provides Russia with iron and steel, chemicals, machinery, and fabricated metal.

The Kuznetsk Basin—also called *Kuzbass* and centered on the towns of Novosibirsk, along the trans-Siberian railroad, and Novokuznetsk—is the chief industrial region of Russia east of the Urals. Again, as in the case of the Ukraine and the Urals districts, the Kuznetsk industrial district relies on an abundant supply of iron ore and the largest supply of coal in the country. The Kuznetsk Basin is a result of the grand design of former Soviet city planners. These planners poured heavy investments into this region, hoping that it would become self-perpetuating and eventually the industrial supply region for Soviet Central Asia and Siberia.

In the postwar period, Japan set about the task of rebuilding itself to become a potent economic force. Japan's record of economic achievement, although tarnished by recession for the 15 years, has no equal among advanced industrial countries in the post–World War II period. In the late twentieth century, Japan's output in several manufacturing sectors increased dramatically. Today it has the second largest GNP in the world and is the world's leading producer of electronics, steel, commercial ships, and automobiles.

Compared with the United States and Britain—countries with the physical resources to sustain an industrial revolution—Japan is much less well off. Except for coal deposits in Kyushu and Hokkaido, Japan is practically devoid of significant raw materials, depending on imported raw materials for its industrial growth. Human resources, however, are not scarce. There are 127 million Japanese, one-quarter of whom are crammed into an urban-industrial core near Tokyo (Figure 7.7). When a strong work ethic is combined with a high level of collective commitment, a first-rate educational system, and government support, it produces an economy that has enjoyed significant advantages in the world economy, although Japan has suffered with the crash of the "bubble economy" in the 1990s.

Although permanent workers in large firms are well paid, especially when viewed in relation to part-time workers in small- and medium-sized firms, the relative cost of labor is lower in Japan many other industrial countries. Savings and profits are directed by the state toward whatever goals are set forth by a unique collaborative partnership between MITI—Japan's Ministry of International Trade and Industry—and private enterprise. Under MITI's guidance, Japan has relocated industries such as steel making and shipbuilding "offshore" in the newly industrializing countries (NICs), where labor costs are lower. Now, countries such as South Korea and Singapore have developed their own higher valued-added industries (e.g., consumer electronics).

THE GLOBALIZATION OF MANUFACTURING

As capitalism underwent one of its period restructurings, the new *international division of labor* asserted itself in the 1970s and 1980s, the rate of world economic growth declined, a process that coincided with the end of the long boom period after World War II. The world economic crisis started with a deep recession in 1974–1975 following the first oil shock in 1973. One of its most visible effects in the advanced economies was deindustrialization—reflected by the loss of

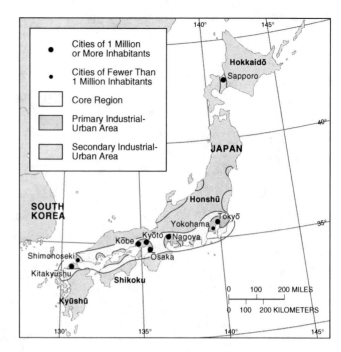

FIGURE 7.7
Japan's core region and selected cities.

manufacturing jobs. As firms restructured or went out of business in a climate of intense international competition, workers were laid off.

Dramatic changes in the geography of world manufacturing accelerated in the crisis of the 1970s and 1980s. Although the advanced countries maintained a huge share in world manufacturing output, their output grew less quickly than that of the less developed countries. The manufacturing output growth of the advanced economies slowed dramatically in the 1970s, and the number of workers in manufacturing in the advanced countries declined. Britain lost 28 percent of its manufacturing workers between 1974 and 1983; West Germany lost 16 percent; France, 14 percent; and the United States, 8 percent. The highest rate of manufacturing job loss in the United States was in the Midwest—more than 11 percent between 1975 and 1982. However, manufacturing employment increased in new industrial areas of the Sunbelt and areas successful in restructuring their industrial bases, such as New England.

Since 1960, manufacturing output has increased sharply in lower-wage industrializing periphery countries. Between 1974 and 2000, the advanced industrial countries lost 24 million jobs, whereas the newly industrializing countries gained 19 million jobs. Jobs lost in the advanced industrial countries paid from $9 to $31 an hour, but those gained in the newly industrializing countries typically paid only $8 per hour or less. The gains from expansion in the newly industrializing countries were more than offset by the losses in the advanced industrial countries. Indeed, the shift

In this textile factory in Fortaleza, Brazil, women constitute the largest part of the workforce. Brazil is a major exporter of textiles to advanced industrial countries. Despite high rates of growth in many Third World countries, only a handful of economies in East Asia actually managed to narrow the gap with the northern, industrialized countries. Moreover, increased polarization between the richer and poorer countries has been accompanied by a rising trend in income inequality within countries such as in Brazil. The income share of the richest 20 percent has grown almost everywhere, while those in the lower ranks have experienced no rise in incomes to speak of. Even the middle classes have experienced little improvement.

led to lower global wage shares that may contribute to stagnation.

The most rapid growth of manufacturing output occurred in East and South Asia, the world region with the fastest rate of economic growth since World War II. Japan, with high wages but relatively low labor militancy, set the model for much of this region, a phenomenon sometimes called the "flying geese formation." This notion compares industrialization to a flock of birds flying in a V formation, with Japan at the head, the NICs closely behind, and other countries lagging somewhat behind. Several newly industrializing countries equaled or exceeded Japan's annual growth rate in manufacturing output, including South Korea, Taiwan, Hong Kong, and Singapore.

The traditional view is that deindustrialization in some places and industrialization in others are mirror images of each other. Industrial growth and decline are offsetting tendencies, representing a zero-sum, or even a positive, global game. The shift of production processes from the industrial heartland to the periphery releases a skilled labor force for more sophisticated forms of production in developed countries and allows labor in the developing countries to move from relatively unproductive employment to more highly productive employment in industry. The shift may lead to some transitional unemployment, but job losses in the industrial heartland are of little significance compared with the enormous rewards attached to a global reallocation of production.

Nomadic capital, although it may serve individual company interests, can be socially inefficient. Those who hire labor control the work process, and distribution is always in favor of those who control the production location. Corporate allocation of production and investment is guided primarily by profitability concerns, where profitability is determined by the price of labor and the amount of work that can be extracted at this price. Nomadic capital can also be socially inefficient because giant corporations are rarely faced with the full social costs of their locational decisions. Shifting production from country to country means that the advanced industrial countries must absorb not only most of the social costs of communities that are now abandoned because they can no longer

Manufacturing Reeboks at the Lotus Plant, Philippines.

be industrially competitive but also the costs of the social infrastructure required by the newly industrializing countries.

GLOBALIZATION OF MAJOR MANUFACTURING SECTORS

Globalization occurs differently in different industries. Because various forms of manufacturing have their own specific technical, labor, and locational requirements, and because nation-states have approached different industries from a variety of regulatory perspectives, the formation of worldwide production changes is unique to each industry. Four industries—textiles and garments, steel, automobiles, and electronics—dramatize the similarities and differences that exist among manufacturing sectors as they adapt to the realities of a global market.

Textiles and Garments

The textile and garment industries dramatically reveal the globalization of manufacturing. Textile manufacture is the creation of cloth and fabric, whereas clothing manufacture uses textiles to produce wearing apparel. Textiles and garments comprise the classic low-tech industry: labor intensive, with relatively little technological sophistication, small firms, and few economies of scale. Textiles were the leading sector of the Industrial Revolution, not only in Britain but also in the remainder of Europe, the United States, and Japan. By continually looking for new sources of cheap, easily exploitable labor, this industry has exhibited a very fluid geography over time, a pattern that continues with its globalization and entry into the developing world in the late twentieth century.

Textile and garment production in the economically developed world declined steadily from the 1970s onward as the industry was confronted with cheap imports from abroad. Conversely, in the developing nations, especially in Asia, production and employment increased significantly. Today, major cotton fabric producers include China, where the garment industry has grown explosively, and India. In Asia, the industry is notorious for its exploitation of young, predominantly female labor, many of whom work long hours for very low wages. Other significant producers in the world are the United States, Russia, Brazil, and Italy (Figure 7.8).

Steel

The steel industry has played an enormously important role in the development of industrialized societies. Iron and steel production generate a wide variety of outputs essential to many other sectors as well, including, for example, parts for automobiles, ships, and aircraft; steel girders for buildings, dams, and other large projects; industrial and agricultural machinery; pipes, tubing, wire, and tools; furniture; and many others uses. The inputs into steel making are relatively simple, including iron ore, which is purified into pig iron; large amounts of energy, generally in the form of coal; and limestone, which is used in the purification process. Steel production is a very capital-intensive process, requiring huge sums of investment, and because the barriers to entry are high, it has generally been very oligopolistic. Transport costs have traditionally been high in this sector, which has made it an ideal candidate for Weberian locational analysis (Chapter 5).

The historical geography of steel production includes the important Midlands cities of Britain, such as Sheffield and Birmingham, which were critical in the early stages of the Industrial Revolution. A similar complex of steel production arose in the Ruhr region

Steel exemplifies forms of manufacturing that are highly capital intensive, relying on huge economies of scale to produce their output profitably.

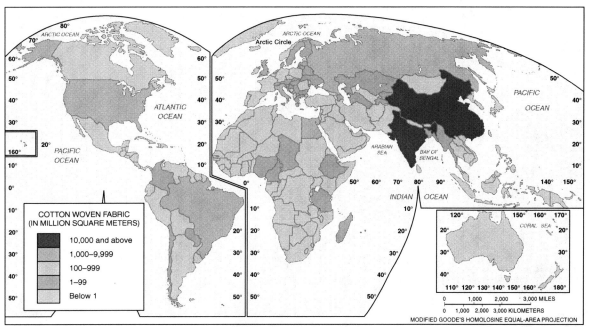

COTTON WOVEN FABRIC
(IN MILLION SQUARE METERS)

10,000 and above
1,000–9,999
100–999
1–99
Below 1

MODIFIED GOODE'S HOMOLOSINE EQUAL-AREA PROJECTION

FIGURE 7.8
Working conditions in many contemporary textile plants resemble the conditions Charles Dickens described in 19th century London.

in western Germany on the banks of the Rhine River. In the northeastern United States, the earliest iron and steel producers were very small and localized, using wood and charcoal as fuel and serving local markets. A number of changes in the third Kondratiev wave of the late nineteenth century, however, dramatically reshaped the industry. The Bessemer open hearth furnace made the production of steel relatively cheap, using huge amounts of energy in plants that were open 24 hours per day. Geographically, the industry came to center on the steel towns of the Manufacturing Belt, including, above all, Pittsburgh, but also Hamilton, Ontario; Buffalo, New York; Youngstown and Cleveland, Ohio; Gary, Indiana; and Chicago (Figure 7.9). These locations allowed easy access to coal from Appalachia, iron ore from Minnesota and upper Michigan, and

cheap transportation via the Great Lakes and the railroads. The rise of the U.S. Steel Company under Andrew Carnegie saw 30 percent of the nation's steel output in the hands of one firm in 1900.

The United States dominated the world's steel industry in the early and mid-twentieth century, producing as much as 63 percent of the world's total output after World War II. However, the rise of new competitors, first in the rebuilt factories of Europe (particularly Germany, France, and Spain) and Japan, and later in some developing countries (e.g., Brazil, South Korea) (Figure 7.10), saw a gradual decline in the share of world steel produced in the United States to 8.3 percent of the world total in 2005 (Figure 7.11).

The decline of the U.S. steel industry generated enormous problems for families living in the former steel towns. Waves of plant closures in the 1970s and

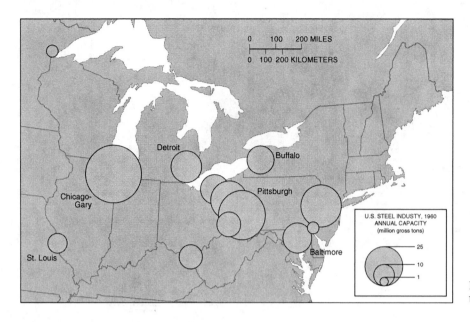

FIGURE 7.9
U.S. steel employment cities, 1950.

1980s generated high unemployment, rising poverty, depressed property values, and out-migration. Today, former giants of steel production in the Manufacturing Belt produce very little steel; Pittsburgh produces none at all. The industry's response to crisis, other than plant closures, was both to call for protectionism from imports and to restructure. The introduction of computerized technology led to widespread changes in steel production, including the emergence of highly automated "minimills" that use scrap metal as inputs (Figure 7.12), are not generally unionized, and produced specialized outputs for niche markets, all of which are symptomatic of the growth of post-Fordist production to be discussed later in this chapter.

Automobiles

From its inception at the dawn of the twentieth century, the automobile industry has unleashed major effects on cities and everyday life throughout the world. Originally Henry Ford standardized a European invention, auto production, when the industry centered upon the Detroit region, adding another layer of investment to the Manufacturing Belt. Ford introduced the moving assembly line and a highly detailed division of labor to make automobiles affordable to the middle class. He also raised wages to reduce turnover rates for his workers.

The automobile industry today comprises giant transnational corporations. Highly capital intensive, with high start-up costs, has a long history of oligopolization. Today, in no other industry do so few companies dominate the world scene. For example, the world's 10 leading automobile manufacturers produce over 70 percent of the world's automobiles. Each of these, from

General Motors and Ford to the smallest automobile producer, has foreign assembly plants in other countries. Many have full-blown vertically integrated manufacturing operations, where all parts in the final assembly are foreign supplied.

Worldwide automobile production has increased rapidly. Between 1960 and 2004, there was a worldwide increase of 400 percent. Figure 7.13 shows the 2004 world distribution of automobile production and assembly. Three major nodes of automobile production exist—Japan, the United States, and Europe. In 2004, Europe accounted for 27 percent of the world's automobiles; Japan, 20 percent; and the United States,

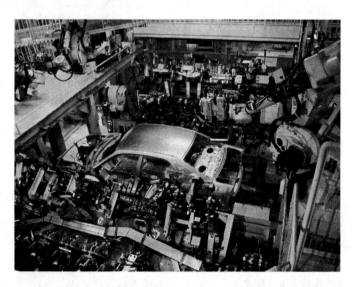

Japan utilizes one-half of all industrial robots in the world, an example of the increasing capital intensity of the production process, particularly in manufacturing.

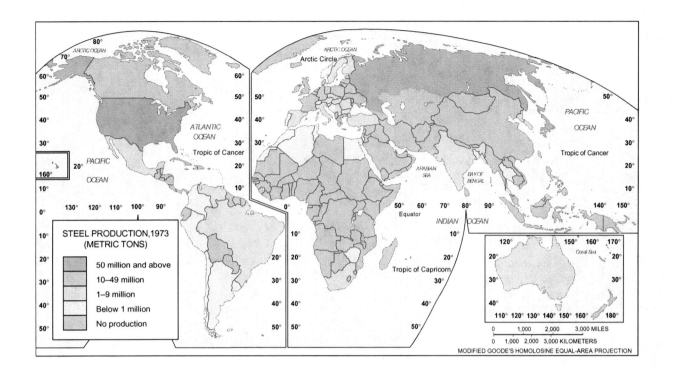

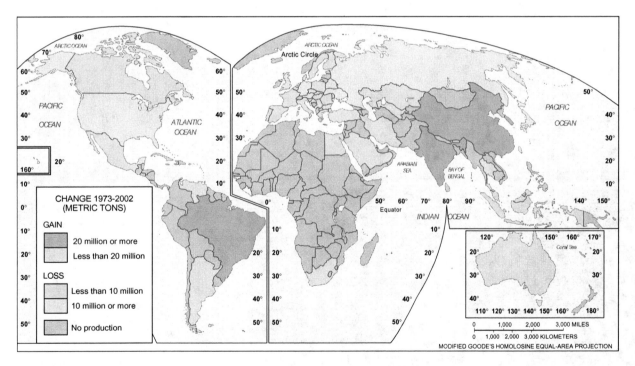

FIGURE 7.10

Worldwide steel production shifts between 1973 and 2002. In 1973, North America and Europe accounted for 90 percent of the world's steel output. Production by 2002 had shifted dramatically to developing countries in Latin American, South Asia, and East Asia. Global steel production remained approximately the same during this period.

Tracing 47 Years of Declining U.S. Share of World Crude Steel Production, 1940 - 2005

FIGURE 7.11
Decline in the U.S. share of world steel output after World War II.

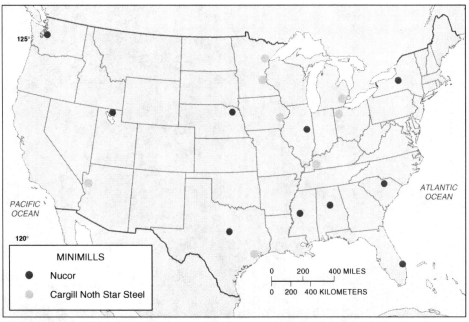

FIGURE 7.12
Minimills producing steel from scrap metal are more numerous than large integrated steel mills in the United States. They are located near markets because their main input is abundantly available there.

MINIMILLS
● Nucor
● Cargill Noth Star Steel

Firmly linked to the global economy by its reliance upon international trade, Japan's economy is heavily export-oriented as seen by these cars waiting on loading docks.

314

International Business

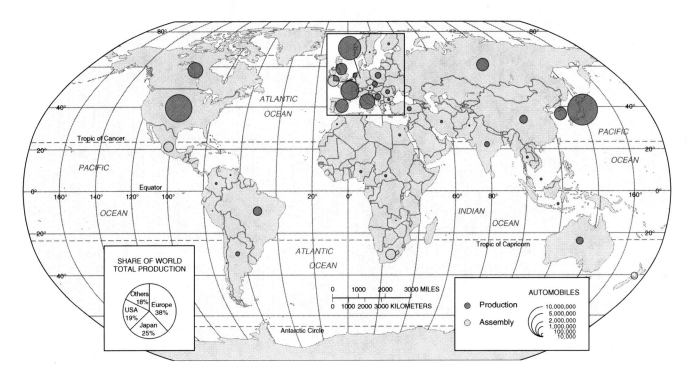

FIGURE 7.13

World distribution of automobile production and assembly. In 2002, Japan produced 10.3 million automobiles, which was 19 percent of the world's total output. In 1960, the United States produced half of the world's total automobiles, but by 2004, that proportion had dropped to 16 percent. In Europe, Germany, France, and Italy are the largest producers.

21 percent. Smaller production centers exist in Brazil, Russia, and Australia. The three developed regions of the world, East Asia, North America, and Europe, accounted for 72 percent of the automobiles produced. Unlike the trend in the textile and clothing industries, the developed countries clearly cornered the market in automobile manufacture. Only a few developing economies have shown a significant increase in automobile assembly but not in their full-scale production.

The most dramatic shift in the automobile industry was the tremendous increase in Japan's productivity between 1960 and 2000, from 165,000 to over 10 million cars annually, almost one-quarter of the world's total output, and almost surpassing U.S. output. In 1960, the United States produced more than half the world's automobiles, but by 2005, only 21 percent. Japanese firms also invested heavily in the United States in the late twentieth century, setting up factories in much of the Midwest (Figure 7.14) that allowed them access to the American market, low transport costs, and freedom from fluctuating exchange rates and threats of U.S. protectionism.

Electronics

Although its roots extend into the nineteenth century, the electronics industry underwent enormous changes with the microelectronics revolution of the late twentieth century. Microelectronic technology is the dominant technology of the present historical moment, transforming all branches of the economy and many aspects of society.

The radio was invented and produced as early as 1901, but the modern electronics industry was not born until Bell Telephone Laboratories built the transistor in the United States in 1948. The transistor supplanted the vacuum tube, which had been used in most radios, televisions, and other electronic instruments. The microelectronic transistor was a solid-state device made from silicon and acted as a semiconductor of electric current. By 1960, the *integrated circuit* was produced, which was a quantum improvement because transistors could be connected on a single small silicon chip. By the early 1970s, a computer so tiny that it could fit on a silicon chip the size of a fingernail came into production. Thus, the *microprocessor*, which could do the work of a roomful of vacuum tubes, was born. With these changes, information changed from analogue to digital format in binary code, which made it much easier for computers to use. The microprocessor made possible the microcomputer, which in turn revolutionized the collection and analysis of information, particularly office work (Figure 7.15).

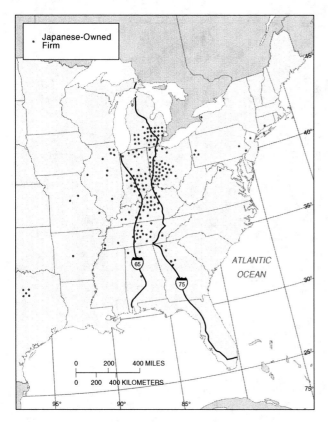

FIGURE 7.14
Distribution of Japanese-owned automobile parts manufacturing plants in the United States, 2000.

Increasing power and miniaturization progressed, and at the same time, new applications for the electronics industry were discovered, including calculators, electronic typewriters, computers, industrial robots, aircraft-guidance systems, and combat systems. New discoveries were applied to automobile construction for guidance, safety, speed, and fuel regulation. An entire new range of consumer electronics also became available for home and business use. The electronics industry, like textiles, steel, and automobiles before it, has come to be regarded as the modern touchstone of industrial success. Hence all governments in the developed market economies, as well as those in the more industrialized developing countries, operate substantial support programs for the electronics industry, particularly microprocessors and computers.

For nearly two decades, from the 1960s through the 1970s, the United States dominated the field of semiconductor manufacture. However, by the 1990s, Japan took over this role. World production of electronic components, which includes semiconductors, integrated circuits, and microprocessors, is shown in Figure 7.16. The field is dominated by Japan and the United States, with other significant production in western Europe and Southeast Asia. In 2004, Japan accounted for 40 percent of the world production of semiconductors; the United States, 21 percent; and Europe, 11 percent. In Southeast Asia, South Korea, Malaysia, Taiwan, Thailand, and Hong Kong were significant manufacturers.

The most important component of the semiconductor industry is computer memory, *RAM* (random access memory). Although the United States produced 100 percent of the world's total output in 1974, by 2004 it produced only approximately 15 percent, and Japan had claimed 70 percent. Similar to the shift in the automobile industry, there has been a tremendous global shift in the direction of East Asia, primarily to Japan, in RAM production.

The world manufacture of consumer electronics is much more widely spread than that of the semiconductor industry. Although in the semiconductor industry, the United States, Japan, and Europe account

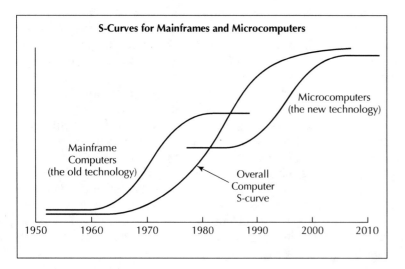

FIGURE 7.15
S-curves for mainframes and minicomputers reveal the transition of technologies within the computer industry. The microelectronics revolution had enormous effects, not only on industrial firms but also in agriculture and services, and generated much of the productivity increases of the United States in the late twentieth century.

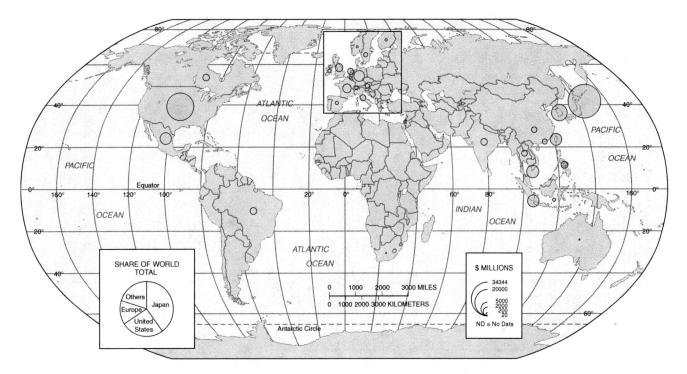

FIGURE 7.16

World production of electronic components, including semiconductors, integrated circuits, and microprocessors. In 2002, Japan produced 42 percent of the world's total electronic components, followed by the United States with 26 percent. Europe produced 12 percent of the world's total. Other leading producers included Germany, France, and the United Kingdom, with 31 percent, 19 percent, and 16 percent, respectively. Growth in the electronics industry has been greatest to the Pacific Rim with recent major centers of production developing in South Korea, Malaysia, Taiwan, and Thailand.

for 80% of the total world production, in the consumer electronics industry, these three regions account for much less. Developing countries, especially in East and Southeast Asia, are heavily involved in producing consumer electronics. Television production is an example: whereas the United States, Europe, and Japan combined produce only 30% of the world's televisions, China alone produces 26%, and South Korea produces another 14%. Singapore and Malaysia are also significant producers (Figure 7.17). As in the case of automobile and semiconductor manufacture, there has been a global shift from the developed nations to East Asia. Much of the television production that formerly occurred in the United States, Germany, and the United Kingdom now takes place in China and Malaysia. Outside Asia and North America, Brazil produces 87% of the televisions used in Latin America.

Biotechnology

Biotechnology may be defined as the application of molecular and cellular processes to solve problems, develop products and services, or modify living organisms to carry desired traits. Arising after the discovery in 1973 of recombinant DNA, biotechnology has been a rapidly growing industry worldwide, with extensive linkages to agriculture, health care, energy, and environmental sciences. In 2003, the U.S. biotech industry (excluding medical equipment firms) consisted of roughly 1,473 firms that employed 406,000 people and generated roughly $64 billion in output. There is a wide range in the size of firms in this industry, including single proprietorships and firms of more than 500 employees; the mean national annual salary in the industry is $62,500, which is well above the national average.

Pharmaceutical firms, which tend to be much larger than biotechnology companies, form the major market for biotechnology products. Large pharmaceutical firms are reliant upon biotech clusters for innovative drug solutions, and human therapeutics thus account for the vast bulk of the biotechnology industry's revenues. Other applications are found in agriculture, industry, and veterinary medicine. Many biotech firms enter into alliances with drug manufacturers, who may provide venture capital in return for marketing rights after the product is commercialized.

Manufacturing

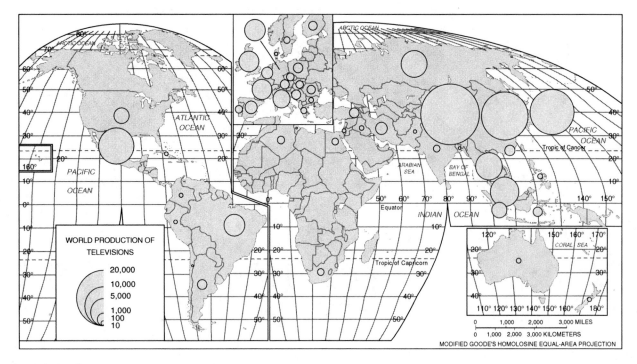

FIGURE 7.17
Worldwide television receiver production, 2000. East Asia has become the leading area in the manufacture of this commodity.

Venture capital is critical to making basic research in biotechnology commercial viable. Most small biotech firms lose money, given the high costs and enormous amounts of research necessary to generate their output and the long lag between R&D and commercial deployment (generally on the order of 12–15 years of preclinical development). Only one in 1,000 patented biotechnology innovations leads to a successful commercial product, and it may take 15 years. Venture capitalists may invest in many biotech firms, and one biotech firm may receive funding from several venture capitalists. Above all, venture capitalists look for an experienced management team when deciding in which companies they are willing to invest. Venture capitalists often provide advice and professional contacts, and serve on the boards of directors of young biotech firms. As a biotech firm survives and prospers, its relations with investors often become spatially attenuated, that is, venture capitalists gradually withdraw from day-to-day direct management.

There has been extensive state involvement in establishing biotechnology complexes since the industry began. Because of its rapid growth as well as demonstrated and potential technological advances, many national science policies target it as a national growth sector. The survival and success of biotechnology firms is heavily affected by federal research funds, primarily through institutions such as the National Science Foundation (NSF) and National Institute of Health (NIH). Other federal offices such as the Small Business Technology Transfer (STTR), Small Business Innovation Research (SBIR), Environmental Protection Agency, and the Food and Drug Administration are also significant. Federal policies regarding patents and intellectual property rights, subsidies for medical research, and national health care programs are all important. Roughly 83 percent of state and local economic development agencies have targeted the industry for industrial development. State level determinants are also critical, including regulatory policies, educational systems, taxation, and subsidies.

Biotechnology firms tend to cluster in distinct districts, and place-based characteristics are essential for the industry's success in innovation. Europe, for example, hosts the BioValley Network situated between France, Germany, and Switzerland. In Britain, Cambridge has assumed this role. Similarly, Denmark and Sweden formed Medicon Valley.

Geographically, the U.S. biotechnology industry is currently dominated by a small handful of cities, particularly Boston, San Diego, Los Angeles, San Francisco, New York, Philadelphia, Seattle, Raleigh-Durham, and

Washington, D.C., which together account for three-quarters of the nation's biotech firms and employment (Figure 7.18). All these cities have excellent universities with medical schools, state-of-the-art infrastructures (particularly fiber optics, airports), and offer an array of social and recreational environments.

Biotechnology firms tend to agglomerate for several reasons. In an industry so heavily research intensive, the knowledge base is complex and rapidly expanding, expertise is dispersed, and innovation is to be found in networks of learning rather than individual firms. This observation is at odds with the popular misconception that such firms are the products of heroic individual entrepreneurs. In a highly competitive environment in which the key to success is the rate of new product formation, and in which patent protections lead to a "winner take all" scenario, the success of biotechnology firms is closely related to their strategic alliances with universities and pharmaceutical firms. Although many biotechnology firms engage in long distance partnering, these tend to be complementary, not substitutes for, colocation in clusters where tacit knowledge is produced and circulated face to face, both on and off the job.

Because pools of specialized skills and a scientifically talented workforce are essential to the long process of research and development in biotechnology, an essential element defining the locational needs of biotech firms is the location of research universities and institutions and the associated supply of research scientists. Most founders of biotech companies are research scientists with university positions. Regional human capital may be measured by examining the prevalence of bachelor's degrees, which indicate a region's educational attainment, and the location and size of regional universities that grant Ph.D. degrees in biology and related fields. However, to a large extent local labor shortages can be mitigated through in-migration. Because knowledge is generated and shared most efficiently within close loops of contact, the creation of localized pools of technical knowledge is highly dependent on the detailed divisions of labor and constant interactions of colleagues in different and related firms. Successful biotechnology firms often revolve around the presence of highly accomplished academic or scientific "stars" with the requisite technical and scientific skills but also the vision and personality to market it. Often such individuals begin in academia and move into the private sector.

The Changing Geography of U.S. Manufacturing

The United States experienced massive industrial devolution in the 1970s and 1980s, a period during which its share of world manufacturing output decreased significantly. This trend points to a more rapid growth of manufacturing output in other countries, especially Asia. Thus, deindustrialization within the United States was

FIGURE 7.18
Major clusters of the U.S. biotechnology industry, 2004. The industry exhibits a pronounced tendency to cluster in major metropolitan areas, where access to universities and agglomeration economies is essential.

occurring at a time when American corporations were reacting to the prolonged economic crisis. Inside the United States, corporate profit rates were declining. As profit rates declined, corporations switched capital in space, going global in an effort to restore profitability. The effect of the globalization of manufacturing change has been most severe in the Manufacturing Belt, which lost millions of relatively well-paying jobs as factories closed, with devastating economic and social impacts on their communities.

North America has numerous manufacturing regions (see Figure 7.2). By far the largest is the Manufacturing Belt, which accounts for about 53 percent of the manufacturing capacity of the United States and Canada. The belt extends from the northeastern seaboard along the Great Lakes to Milwaukee, where it turns south to St. Louis, then extends eastward along the Ohio River valley to Washington, D.C. This great rectangle encompasses more than 10 districts, each with its own specialties that reflect the influences of markets, materials, labor, power, and historical forces.

The first major factories in the Belt—the textile mills of the 1830s and 1840s—clustered along the rivers of southern New England. When coal replaced water as a power source between 1850 and 1870, and when railroads integrated the Belt, factories were freed from the riverbanks. Between 1850 and 1870, many urban areas enjoyed rapidly expanding industrial production. Manufacturing employment in New York City, Philadelphia, and Chicago soared more than 200 percent between 1870 and 1900. The 10 largest industrial cities increased their share of national value added in manufacturing from less than 25 percent to almost 40 percent between 1860 and 1900.

Why did metropolitan complexes draw such a great proportion of manufacturing activity? Factories concentrated in large cities for a combination of the following reasons: (1) They could be near large labor pools, including unskilled and semiskilled immigrants; (2) they could secure easy railroad and waterway access to major resource deposits, such as the Appalachian coalfields and the Lake Superior—area iron mines; (3) they could be near industrial suppliers of machines and other intermediate products, which lowered transport costs; and (4) they could be near major markets for finished goods. In other words, *agglomeration economies* accounted for the concentration of manufacturing activity in the Manufacturing Belt. The highly concentrated pattern of industrial production served the nation (and much of the world) well for about 100 years—roughly the century between 1870 and 1970. *Inertia,* the immobility of the investment forces and social relations, ensured considerable locational stability, particularly in the capital-intensive steel industry.

However, cracks in this accumulation regime appeared as early as the late nineteenth century. Labor unrest intensified. After 1885, the number of strikes increased rapidly. Gradually, owners lost some power to labor, which allowed workers to negotiate higher wages, to organize high levels of unionization and extract better working conditions, and to command progressive welfare policies. By the early twentieth century, manufacturing started to move out of center cities to the suburbs, lured by the easy access afforded by the truck for freight transportation. But as transportation costs equalized across the nation, even the suburbs of the older manufacturing belt cities were unable to compete with more agreeable labor environments in the South and the West. The 1960s marked the start of the steady gain of manufacturing employment in the Sunbelt, including the South and parts of the Southwest. Since the early 1980s, however, there has been evidence that these areas where class conflict is low are being bypassed in favor of even cheaper labor regions in Mexico and East Asia.

The change in the location of manufacturing in the United States was particularly pronounced in the 1970s and 1980s. Virtually all states in the Manufacturing Belt experienced manufacturing job loss, and virtually all states in the South and the West registered manufacturing job gains (Figure 7.19). Labor costs in the South were often lower because it was less skilled and less unionized, in part because Southern states are "right to work" states, meaning that unions cannot force employees at an establishment to join. The migration of employment from areas of high labor costs to areas where the labor costs were less saved companies billions of dollars. From 1960 to 1980, roughly 1.7 million jobs shifted from states with high labor costs to states with low labor costs.

The expansion of manufacturing in the West is not easily explained by low labor costs. California is known for its relatively high labor costs, yet it has registered substantial increases in manufacturing employment. In California, labor costs were less important than the appeal of the physical environment and the role of the state (particularly defense spending). The West Coast manufacturing district does, however, represent an outstanding example of industrial restructuring in response to economic crisis and labor unrest. The Los Angeles–San Diego district has been extremely successful in negotiating the transition from older forms of manufacturing to newer ones. Since the 1960s, the district has shed much of its traditional, highly unionized heavy industry, such as steel and rubber. At the same time, it has attracted a cluster of high-tech industries and associated services, centered on electronics and aerospace and tied strongly to enormous defense and military contracts from the U.S. government. Additionally, it has witnessed the vigorous growth of "peripheralized" manufacturing, which resembles the industrialization of developing countries in that it depends on a highly controllable supply of cheap, typically immigrant or female labor from Mexico and East Asia.

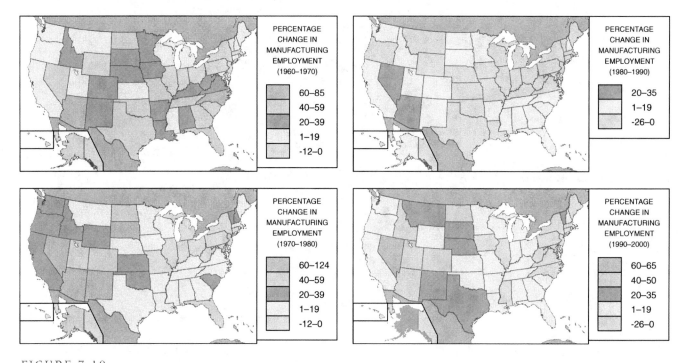

FIGURE 7.19

Changes in U.S. manufacturing employment by decade, 1960–2000. The steady losses in the northeastern Manufacturing Belt and rise of Sunbelt producers reflected the sustained impacts of globalization, technological change, and the shift into lower cost, less unionized parts of the country. The microelectronics revolution and information technology allow firms much greater locational flexibility than in the past and contribute to the low-density, decentralized landscapes of industry as well as urban areas.

Meanwhile, industrial restructuring continues to be a painful process throughout much of the Manufacturing Belt. The region contends with problems of obsolescence and reduced productivity, especially in such leading industries as steel, rubber, automobile manufacturing, and shipbuilding. Many of its inner-city areas are littered with closed factories, bankrupt businesses, depressed real estate, and struggling blue-collar neighborhoods. The effects of disinvestment on workers and their communities have been devastating. Victims of plant closings sometimes lose not only their current incomes but also often their accumulated assets as well. When savings run out, people lose their ability to respond to life crises, and often suffer depression and marital problems. Although job losses occurred in many occupations, some groups are more vulnerable than others. Unskilled workers are particularly likely to bear the costs of globalization, including job displacement. African American workers, many of them unskilled or semiskilled, were particularly hard hit, and by driving up unemployment, the deindustrialization of the inner city was in no small part responsible for the creation of the impoverished ghetto communities there.

Although the widespread manufacturing decline has produced a lasting effect on people and communities

in the Manufacturing Belt, all is not lost in the region. There have been numerous attempts to respond to the economic crisis. Some old industrial cities such as Pittsburgh successfully built new bases for employment in services, and others, such as Cleveland, indicate the potential for doing so. Southern New England, which suffered high unemployment rates throughout much of the post–World War II period, underwent a new round of industrial expansion based on electronics, one that took advantage of its pool of highly skilled workers.

The International Movement of American Manufacturing

The relocation of manufacturing within the United States is only one aspect of a wider dispersal of manufacturing capital. Foreign direct investment by American enterprises was established as early as the end of the nineteenth century. But only since World War II have American enterprises become major foreign investors. The 1940s saw heavy investment in Canada and Latin America; the 1950s in Western Europe; the 1960s and 1970s in Europe, Japan, and the Middle East; and the 1980s and 1990s in South

Manufacturing

321

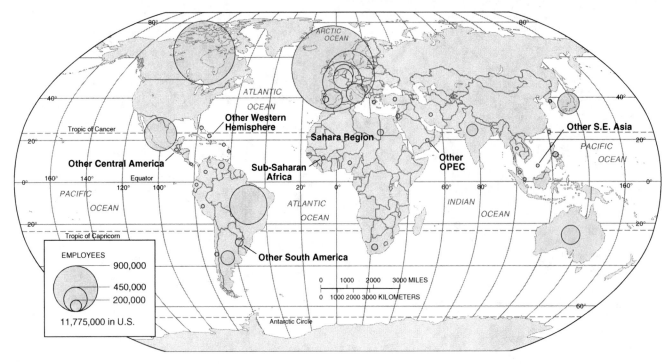

FIGURE 7.20
World employment in manufacturing of U.S.-based multinational corporations in 2000. Most MNCs invest in other developed countries.

and East Asia. Overall, most of U.S. manufacturing investments occurred in advanced industrialized countries rather than in developing countries (Figure 7.20).

Between 1945 and 1960, most U.S.-based companies were content to produce in the old industrial districts. But by 1960, western European countries and Japan had become competitors. Mounting international competition and falling profit rates at home coerced American companies to decentralize not only within the United States but also abroad. Thus domestic restructuring and internationalization can be seen as two sides of the same coin. By 1980, the 500 largest U.S.-based corporations employed an international labor force almost equivalent to the size of their labor force within the United States. Toy production, for example, has largely moved into East Asia, particularly China.

Steel offers a compelling example of the decline in industrial capacity. Between 1970 and 2005, the North American and Western European proportion of total global steel production declined from 67 percent to 42 percent, whereas developing countries' production levels increased from 10 percent to more than 30 percent. Many steel-manufacturing firms have gone out of business as the global steel-production capacity exceeds global demand. Because of government subsidies, steel mills in some countries, especially in Europe, have

remained open in the face of dwindling quotas. The U.S. government, however, has been less willing to pay unemployment compensation to displaced workers and has allowed the U.S. steel industry to decline. Since the 1970s, U.S. production has decreased 33 percent, whereas employment in the steel industry has declined 66 percent.

The dispersal of manufacturing investment to foreign lands resulted in enormous savings for American firms and enormous losses for American workers, largely due to the differences in wage rates (Table 7.1). In terms of average wages, workers in Europe, particularly Scandinavia and Germany, fare the best, with wages often one-third higher than American workers (as well as longer paid vacation periods and universal health coverage). U.S. wages are comparable to Australia, slightly higher than Ireland or Japan, and well above the developing world.

Downsizing

Downsizing (sometimes euphemistically called "right sizing") is the most critical factor inhibiting wage inflation. Once seen mainly as a component of corporate reorganization aimed at achieving a healthier bottom line, the chilling effect of downsizing on workforce wage demands has effectively kept wage inflation in check too.

International Business

Table 7.1
Hourly Wage Costs for Factory Workers,
U.S. Dollars, 2004

Norway	34.64
Denmark	33.75
Germany	32.53
Netherlands	30.76
Finland	30.67
Switzerland	30.26
Belgium	29.98
Sweden	28.42
Austria	28.29
Luxembourg	26.57
United Kingdom	24.71
France	23.89
United States	23.17
Australia	23.09
Ireland	21.94
Japan	21.90
Spain	17.10
Israel	12.18
South Korea	11.52
New Zealand	9.14
Singapore	7.45
Portugal	7.02
Taiwan	5.97
Mexico	2.50
Sri Lanka	0.51

Source: U.S. Bureau of Labor Statistics, 2004.

From 1989 through 2003 in the United States, more than 4.7 million job cuts were announced, and employees who remain are reluctant to push for pay increases. They know management has placed a ceiling on the amount allotted for wages in order to avoid the inflationary move of charging higher prices and the risk of becoming noncompetitive. The workforce is well aware that a request for a pay increase could be met with dismissal, as management turns the downsizing valve, eliminating employees deemed too costly to keep. Employees also know that any vacated position could quickly be filled by someone willing to accept the present wage. Uncertainty over when management will turn the downsizing valve has insecure employees scrambling for jobs in the most productive, high-priority areas of a company. No one wants to be targeted for dismissal simply because he or she stayed too long in an area perceived by management as too bureaucratic or obsolete. Even when employees manage to land a job in an area reasonably safe from the threat of downsizing, few are willing to ask for a raise.

Downsizing has erased the traditional bond of employer-employee loyalty, has depleted corporate memory, and in many cases has eroded the work ethic, productivity, and morale of employees. The number of executives and managers who have been laid off two or three times is growing. With each new, unexpected twist in their careers, they become more uncertain and insecure.

Downsizing has proven effective as a means of keeping inflation in check and is here to stay as a means of making companies leaner and more competitive. But how long can companies remain competitive with a disloyal, insecure workforce? Management now must ask itself if there are alternatives to turning the valve of downsizing in order to keep wages stable and inflation low. In the long run, this method of controlling inflation may not be worth the price.

Restructuring and downsizing means layoffs and hurting people at the basic survival level. Downsizing challenges people's ability to survive, to provide shelter, food, and the services needed by their families. Today white-collar as well as blue-collar jobs are being lost as globalization has extended competition from low-wage, low-skilled positions to increasingly high-skilled ones.

American Manufacturing Today

Since 1962, worldwide exports have increased from 12 percent to more than 33 percent of the world GNP, meaning roughly one-third of everything produced in the world is traded. Worldwide exports totaled $7 trillion in 2005. For manufactured goods, the proportion is much higher, ranging as high as 70 percent. Global corporations are developing a manufacturing network of decentralized plants based in large, sophisticated regional markets. Each plant will be smaller and more flexible than is typically found in today's manufacturing environment. The location of such plants will be based more on regional infrastructure, local skill levels, and government policies than on purely cost-based factors. Consider the following:

1. The development of large and sophisticated overseas markets dictates a global presence of leading manufacturers.
2. Increasing levels of nontariff barriers are forcing firms to localize production resources.
3. The evolution of a world trade system based on regional trading blocs creates incentives for firms to follow direct investment strategies that give

them a manufacturing presence in each region of significant demand.

4. Regionalization of trading economies is increasing the benefits to decentralized manufacturing organizations.
5. Exchange rates and other aspects of risks are forcing firms to be flexible in terms of capacity and location and to view their global networks in a holistic way.
6. The emergence of manufacturing technologies and methods, such as flexible manufacturing systems, just-in-time manufacturing, and total quality control, have reduced scale, increased the importance of worker education and skilled development, and placed demands on local infrastructure.
7. Large, centralized manufacturing facilities in low-cost countries with poorly skilled workers are generally not sustainable.

Traditional approaches to understanding the location of manufacturing are increasingly questionable. Large, centralized manufacturing facilities have given way to decentralized manufacturing structures, with smaller, lower scale plants serving demands and regional markets. Location depends increasingly on educational and institutional infrastructure.

To conclude, globalization, advances in technology, changes in management approach, and shifting market requirements are the new dynamics that shape manufacturing firms' organizational and locational decisions today. These trends suggest that global corporations of the future will move to networks of decentralized plants, based in large sophisticated regional markets, but linked with information technology to one another. Specific locations will be based more on local infrastructure, such as workforce capability, training programs, and government policies, than on traditional cost-base considerations. Plants will be smaller than current ones, more flexible, yet have significantly more ability to produce multiple products.

Flexible Manufacturing

In the aftermath of the turbulent 1970s—which brought on, among other things, the shift from fixed to floating exchange rates, the petrocrises, the rise of the NICs, massive deindustrialization in the West, and the microelectronics revolution—geographers and others began to recognize that capitalism in the late twentieth century was undertaking a new direction. The new world economy, characterized by mounting globalization and competition among nation-states, also included a profound shift in the nature of manufacturing, including changes in markets,

Table 7.2

Contrasts between Fordism and Post-Fordism

Fordism	*Post-Fordism*
Vertically integrated	Vertically disintegrated
Long-run contracts	Short-run contracts, JIT
Large firms	Small firms
Economies of scale	Specialized output
Competitive producers	Cooperative networks
Product price	Product quality
Mass consumption	Segmented markets
Unionized	Nonunionized
Unskilled labor	Skilled labor
Routinized work	Varied tasks
National linkages	International linkages

technologies, and location. Now, as we have seen, capitalism is a highly dynamic economy characterized by many such transformations in its history. In this sense, the creation of a new form of capitalism in the 1980s and 1990s was not particularly new. However, each age brings with it a new form of commodity production and consumption, and often a new terminology to describe these changes. A common set of terms used to sum up these epochal changes is the shift from "Fordism" to "post-Fordism," also variously known as "flexibilism" or "the flexible economy" (Table 7.2).

Fordism

Fordism, as the name indicates, is named after the American industrialist Henry Ford, who pioneered the mass production of automobiles in the early twentieth century using standardized job tasks, interchangeable parts (which date back to gun maker Eli Whitney), and the moving assembly line. Ford's methods, which were very successful, were widely imitated by other industries and soon became almost universal throughout the North American, European, and Japanese economies.

The precise moment when Fordism became the dominant form of production in the United States is open to debate. Some argue that it began as early as the late nineteenth century, during the wave of technological change in the 1880s and 1890s, when mass production first made its appearance, displacing the older, more labor-intensive (and less profitable) forms of artisanal production. For example, during this period, glass blowing, barrel making, and the production of rubber goods such as bicycle tires became steadily standardized, and the Bessemer process for fabricating steel was invented. Fordism, however, elevated this process to a whole new level, including highly refined divisions of labor within the factory, so that each worker engaged in highly repetitive tasks. Ford engaged the services of Frederick Taylor, the founder of industrial psychology, who applied time-and-motion studies to workers' jobs to organize them in the most efficient and cost-effective manner. By breaking down complex jobs into many small ones, Fordism made many tasks suitable for unskilled workers, including the waves of immigrants then arriving into the United States, and greatly increased productivity.

Others argue that Fordism was a particular kind of social contract between capital and labor, one that tolerated labor unions (such as the Congress of Industrial Organizations [CIO] that came into being in the 1930s), and so Fordism should be seen as beginning in the crisis years of the 1930s. Yet others make the case that Fordism was the backbone of the great economic boom in the three decades following World War II, when the United States emerged as the undisputed superpower in the West, and that it should only be dated back to the 1950s. Whenever its origins, Fordism is reflective of a historically specific form of capitalism that dominated most of the twentieth century.

Fordism came to stand for the mass production of homogeneous goods, in which capital-intensive companies relied heavily on economies of scale to keep production costs low and profits high. Thus, mass consumption and advertising would also come into being as the demand side of Fordism. Typically, firms working in this context were large and vertically integrated, controlling the chain of goods from raw material to final product. Ford's plants, for example, saw coal and iron ore enter one part of the factory and cars come out the other end. Well suited to large, capital-intensive production methods, this system of production and labor control was largely responsible for the great manufacturing complexes of the North American Manufacturing Belt, the British Midlands, the German Ruhr region, and the Inland Sea area of Japan.

While Fordism "worked" quite successfully for almost a century, ultimately it began to reach its social and technical limits. Productivity growth in the 1970s began to slow dramatically, and the petrocrises and rise of the NICs unleashed wave upon wave of plant closures in the United States. Because wages and salaries are often tied to the overall growth of productivity, these changes not only led to widespread layoffs, but also to declining earning power of American workers. Rates of profit in manufacturing began to drop in the 1970s and 1980s, and many firms faced the choice of either closing down, moving overseas, or reconstructing themselves with a new set of production techniques. It is in this context that Fordism began to implode, giving way to post-Fordist, flexible production techniques, which have become widespread throughout the economy today.

Post-Fordism/Flexible Production

Post-Fordism refers to a significantly different approach to the production of goods than that offered by Fordism. *Flexible manufacturing* allows goods to be manufactured cheaply, but in small volumes as well as large volumes. A flexible automation system can turn out a small batch, or even a single item, of a product as efficiently as a mass-assembled commodity. It appeared, not accidentally, at the particular historical moment when the microelectronics revolution began to revolutionize manufacturing; indeed, the changes associated with the computerization of production in some respects may be seen as capitalists' response to the crisis of profitability that accompanied the petrocrises. Post-Fordism also reflected the imperative of American firms to increase their productivity in the face of rapidly accelerating, intense international competition (Figure 7.21).

The most important aspect of this new, or lean, system is flexibility of the production process itself, including the organization and management within the factory, and the flexibility of relationships among customers, supplier firms, and the assembly plant. In contrast to the large, vertically integrated firms typical of the Fordist economy, under flexible production, firms tend to be relatively small, relying on highly computerized production techniques to generate small quantities of goods sold in relatively specialized markets. Microelectronics, in essence, circumvented the need for economies of scale.

The classic technologies and organizational forms of post-Fordism include robots and just-in-time inventory systems. The Japanese developed *just-in-time manufacturing* systems shortly after World War II to adapt U.S. practices to car manufacturing. The technique was pioneered by the Toyota Corporation (and hence sometimes called "Toyotaism"), which obviated the need for large, expensive warehouses of parts (the "just-in-case" inventory system), which saved rents in a country in which the price of land is high. Just-in-time refers to a method of organizing immediate manufacturing and supply relationships among companies to reduce inefficiency and delivery times. Stages of the manufacturing process are completed exactly when needed, according to the market, not before and not later, and parts required in the manufacturing process are supplied with little storage or warehousing time

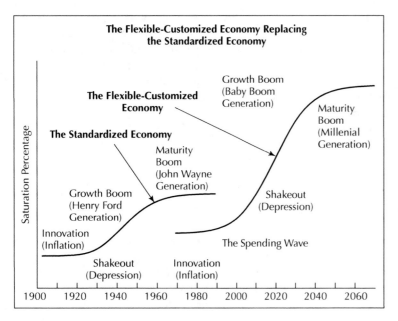

The Flexible-Customized Economy Replacing the Standardized Economy

The Flexible-Customized Economy

The Standardized Economy

Growth Boom (Baby Boom Generation)

Maturity Boom (Millenial Generation)

Maturity Boom (John Wayne Generation)

Shakeout (Depression)

Growth Boom (Henry Ford Generation)

The Spending Wave

Innovation (Inflation)

Shakeout (Depression)

Innovation (Inflation)

Saturation Percentage

1900 1920 1940 1960 1980 2000 2020 2040 2060

FIGURE 7.21

The flexible customized economy is replacing the standardized economy. Henry Ford's assembly-line approach led off the innovation phase of the standardized economy. The late twentieth century has been a comparable innovation period launched by the baby boomers. By 2000, microcomputer technology, comparable to the automobile of the early part of the century in innovation, is multiplied in its potential by powerful, flexible software. This software and hardware can revolutionize any industry, just as the assembly line revolutionized industries throughout the Fordist period of the last century. The growth boom and the spending wave create a time when innovations begin moving out of their niches into the mainstream, driven by the power of the individualist. New technologies put downward pressure on prices, but rising consumer demand from the spending wave exerts an upward pressure. A shakeout occurs, leading to survival of only the fittest companies.

and cost. This system reduces idle capital and allows minimal investment so that capital can be used elsewhere.

Occasionally machines are idle because they run only fast enough to meet output. If machines run more quickly than the market requires, they must be shut off and manufactured items warehoused. The manufacturing run proceeds only as far as the market demands, and no faster. Thus, suppliers and producers of raw materials must warehouse their inventories. Buffer stocks are very small and are only replenished to replace parts removed downstream. Workers at the end of the line are given output instructions on the basis of short-term order forecasts. They instruct workers immediately upstream to produce the part they will need just-in-time, and those workers in turn instruct workers upstream to produce just-in-time, and so on. In practice this means that buffers between workers are extremely small.

Thus, many firms in the late twentieth century engaged in significant downsizing, ridding themselves of whole divisions of their companies to focus on their core competencies. Many companies reversed their old principles of hierarchical, bureaucratic assembly-line (Fordist) processes as they switched to customized, flexible, consumer-focused processes that can deliver personal service through niche markets at lower costs and faster speeds.

In the process, the use of subcontracts accelerated rapidly. Firms always face a "make or buy" decision (i.e., a choice of whether to purchase inputs such as semifinished parts from another firm or to produce those goods themselves). Under the relatively stable system afforded by Fordism, most firms produced their own parts (i.e., decided to "make" rather than buy), justifying the cost with economies of scale, which lowered their long-run average cost curves. Large firms, for example, would have their own parts producers, trucks, or printing shops. Under post-Fordism, however, this strategy is no longer optimal: Given the uncertainty generated by the rapid technological and political changes of the late twentieth century, many firms opted to buy rather than make (i.e., to purchase inputs from specialized companies). This strategy reduces risk for the buyer by pushing it onto the subcontractor, who must invest in the capital and hire the necessary labor.

A key to production flexibility lies in the use of information technologies in machines and operations, which permit more sophisticated control over the process. With the increasing sophistication of automated processes and, especially, the new flexibility of the new electronically controlled technology, far-reaching changes in the process of production need not be associated with increase scale of production. Indeed, one of the major results of the new electronic computer-aided production technology is that it permits rapid switching from one process to another and allows the tailoring of production to the requirements of individual customers. Traditional automation is geared to high-volume standardized production; the newer flexible manufacturing systems are quite different.

As interfirm linkages grew rapidly in the 1980s, many firms found themselves compelled to enter into cooperative agreements with one another such as strategic alliances. Quality control (i.e., minimizing defect rates) became very important. Many firms succeed in this environment by entering into dense urban networks of interactions, including many face-to-face linkages, ties that the roles played by noneconomic factors such as tacit knowledge, learning, reflexivity, conventions, expectations, trust, uncertainty, and reputation in the interactions of economic actors. Post-Fordism thus highlighted the culturally embedded nature of economic linkages.

Post-Fordist approaches to production, which vary in their nature in different regions, came to dominate much of the electronics industry and automobile manufacturing, the minimills in the steel industry, and became closely associated with the new manufacturing spaces such as Silicon Valley, Italy's Emilia-Romagna region, Germany's Baden-Wurtenburg, the Danish Jutland, and the British electronics region centered around Cambridge.

The major impacts of the information and telecommunications revolution will extend well into the future. Because of the telecommunications revolution, products and services once thought to be confined to premium and niche markets will move rapidly into the mainstream. No technological innovation of the past, not automobiles, railroads, plastics, iron, or steel, ever came close to the power of the change being brought on by the information technologies. The power of 16 Cray supercomputers on a single chip is simply unprecedented in the history of the world, which will result in rapid changes in how computers increase business productivity, marking the enormous gains associated with the flexible revolution.

The flexible economy will provide an even greater innovation than the assembly line of Fordism, which in itself allowed an amazing array of standardized products to move into mass affordability and a 10-fold average wage increase for the American worker. In the coming decades, the computer will help to make customized, flexible products and services increasingly affordable. The microcomputer revolution and the innovative market demand by baby boomers will dictate the growth for decades to come and will be based on these principles: flexibility and customization to individual needs and wants, higher quality and higher value added, rapid response and delivery just-in-time, and improved personal service and follow-up.

Customization and flexibility are the watchwords of business in the immediate future. Companies that can adjust to the customized flexible economy are the ones that will prosper. The customized flexible economy means custom design of products and services around individual needs and customers. Instead of greater capital investments in infrastructure and machines, greater capital investments will come in software, allowing marketing databases to estimate needs of customers and identify niche markets. Such software will allow the production and service machinery to make "short runs" for individual and market niche needs, quickly changing markets without the setup costs and delays of the old standard assembly-line systems. The business trend of the customized flexible economy will mean that premium niche products and services of the past will move into mainstream affordability as the computer and software forces down the price and as bureaucracies become restructured and more efficient, causing a flexible labor force.

IT and Strategic/Competitive Advantage

The use of IT to increase the competitive advantage of organizations is an important issue faced by MNCs. Information technology (IT) contributes to strategic management in many ways. Consider these three:

1. IT creates applications that provide direct strategic advantage to organizations.
2. IT supports strategic changes such as reengineering. For example, IT allows efficient decentralization by providing speedy communication lines, and it streamlines and shortens product design time by using computer-aided engineering tools.
3. IT provides business intelligence by collecting and analyzing information about innovations, markets, competitors, and environmental changes. Such information provides strategic advantage because, if a company knows something important before its competitors, or if it can make the correct interpretation of the information before its competitors, then it can introduce changes and benefit from them.

Competitive strategy is the search for a competitive advantage in an industry, either by controlling the market or by enjoying larger than average profits. Such a strategy aims to establish a profitable and sustainable position against the forces that determine industry competition. The shift of corporate operations from a competitive to a strategic orientation (of which competition is only one aspect) is fundamental. IT has a significant impact on the profitability of an organization and even on its survival.

THE PRODUCT CYCLE IN MANUFACTURING

Product cycles and production systems help us to appreciate the importance of technological considerations in corporate spatial organization. The *product life cycle*, which begins with a product's development and ends when it is replaced with something better, is important geographically because products at different stages of production tend to be manufactured at different places within corporate systems. Moreover, at any given stage of the cycle, the various operations involved in the manufacture of a product such as a camera are not necessarily concentrated at a single factory. Production of a camera's complex components occurs at a different place from where the final product is assembled.

The famous economist Simon Kuznets developed the concept of the three-stage product cycle (Figure 7.22). In Stage 1, innovators discover, develop, and commercially launch a product. They also benefit from a temporary monopoly and all the special privileges—high profits—that result from it. In Stage 2, competitors buy or steal the new idea, which forces an emphasis on low-cost, standardized, mass-production technologies. Sales of the product increase for a while, but the initial high returns diminish. By Stage 3, the product begins to be superseded. Markets are lost to new products, and manufacturing capacity is reduced.

Innovation begins in an advanced industrial country. These countries have the science, the technology, and the internal market to justify R&D. As a result, they also have an international advantage, and they export their product around the world. But as the technology becomes routinized, other producers appear on the scene, first in the other advanced countries, then on the periphery. Meanwhile, back in the rich country, investment in the newest generation of sophisticated technology is the cutting edge of the economy.

There is no doubt that developed countries are the innovators of the world economy and that LDCs increasingly specialize in the laborious task of transforming raw materials into commodities. But developed countries are also engaged in activities associated with the second and third stages of the product cycle. Indeed, Britain and Canada have expressed concern about their recipient status. This concern has also been voiced in the United States.

Not all manufacturing operations are fragmented. Corporate branch plants are often *clones,* supplying identical products to their market areas. For example, medium-sized firms in the clothing industry often have this structure, as do many multiplant companies manufacturing final consumer products. Part-process structures tend to be associated with certain industrial sectors, such as electronics and motor vehicles, characterized by complex finished products comprising many individual components.

Labor is an important variable in the location of facilities making components. Manufacturers seek locations where the level of worker organization, the degree of conflict, and the power of labor to affect the actions of capital are more limited than in long-established production centers such as Detroit, Coventry, and Turin. Starting in the 1970s, Fiat began to decentralize part of the company's production away from its traditional base in Turin to the south of Italy. Compared with the workers of Turin, who were relatively strong and well organized, the workers of the south were new to modern industry and had little experience of union organization. At the international level, Ford adopted a similar tactic when it invested in Spain and Portugal in the 1970s. Ford management perceived that it could operate trouble-free plants in a region of low labor costs. The labor factor is further

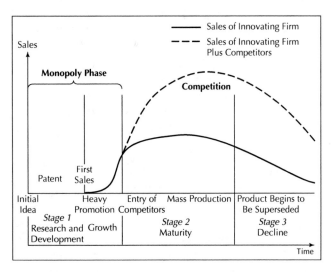

FIGURE 7.22

A typical product life cycle. Stage 1 is the monopolistic phase in which initial discovery and development are followed by the commercial launching of the product. Rapid sales ensue. The company may enjoy a monopoly during this period, at which time they attempt to improve the products. Stage 2 is characterized by the entry of competition. Emphasis is now on mass-produced, inexpensive items that are standardized and directed toward expansions of the market. Competition begins to erode a large share of the innovating firm's sales. In Stage 3, a large share of the market has been lost to new products and other companies. Overall sales of the product decline as alternative products and manufacturing processes are introduced.

International Business

emphasized by the practice of *dual sourcing*. To avoid total dependence on a single workforce that could disrupt an interdependent production system, companies such as Ford and Fiat are willing to sacrifice economies of scale for the security afforded by duplicate facilities in different locations.

Locational Adjustment

Corporate production systems undergo continuous locational adjustment. Shifts may be inspired by technical and organizational developments internal to an industry or by changes in the external environment in which they operate, such as the oil-price hikes of 1973. Particularly significant from a geographic viewpoint are adjustments in response to major shocks or stresses placed on an enterprise. For example, when faced with the challenge of competition from lower-cost regions and with a falling rate of expansion of global markets, an enterprise can adopt a number of strategies—rationalization, capital substitution, outright closure, reorganization of productive capacity associated with the closure of older plants—which all in one way or another result in losses of employment. The industrial decline of Britain provides many illustrations of painful corporate restructuring programs. The 10 largest manufacturing employers in the West Midlands reduced their British employment by 25 percent between 1978 and 1981 while increasing their overseas workforce by 9 percent. This shift in the productive base of these companies abroad undermined the economic well-being of this area. Such employment withdrawals are an aspect of the growing international integration of production and mobility of capital.

One of capital's crucial advantages over labor is geographic mobility; it can generally make use of distance and differentiation in a way that labor cannot. Corporations take advantage of such flexibility by shifting production to low-wage regions, setting up plants in areas with low levels of worker organization, or establishing plants in areas that offer incentive policies. Many LDCs offer tax relief and capital subsidies for new industries.

S UMMARY

This chapter offered an overview of the changing empirical patterns of manufacturing, the reasons that underlay them, and emphasized that manufacturing geographies are always fluid, changing over time. Four major regions of the world account for approximately 80 percent of the world's industrial production—northeastern North America, northwestern Europe, western Russia, and Japan. The textiles, clothing manufacture, and consumer electronics industries have shifted globally from the developed world to the developing world. Automobile production and semiconductor manufacture have also experienced global shifts, from North America and Europe to Japan and East Asia.

We explored the social relations that lead to industrial change, described worldwide manufacturing trends, and examined the recent history of industrial devolution in the developed world and of industrial revolution in the developing world. The processes of *deindustrialization* and *industrialization* are not temporary tendencies within the global system; rather, they constitute a zero-sum global game played by multinational nomadic capital. Multinationals switched production from place to place because of varying relations between capital and labor and new technological innovations in transportation and communications. With improved air freight, containerization, and telecommunications, multinational corporations can dispatch products faster, cheaper, and with fewer losses.

In the United States, 500,000 manufacturing jobs per year were lost between 1978 and 2002. These losses were hidden to some extent by selective reindustrialization and the migration of manufacturing from the American Manufacturing Belt to the South and the West.

The latter part of this chapter explored the ways in which manufacturing landscapes change over time. Capitalism is constantly reinventing itself through the process of "creative destruction," and one of its prime strengths is the capacity to adjust to rapid change. In the late twentieth century, as the Fordist regime of production began to collapse, the petrocrises, deindustrialization, the rise of the NICs, and the microelectronics revolution spawned the emergence of post-Fordist, flexible production techniques and organizational forms. Mounting international competition called for a restructuring of the production process in order to restore the conditions of profitability, and many firms downsizing, subcontracted many functions, and adopted technologies such as just-in-time inventory systems. Concomitantly, the business world engaged in widespread reengineering. In many sectors, these changes may be seen in light of the product cycle, a metaphorical model that encapsulates the simultaneous economic, technological, organizational, and geographic changes that confront every firm in the course of its industry's evolution.

STUDY QUESTIONS

1. What are the forces of production and the social relations of production?
2. Why are capital-labor relations a necessary starting point for studying economic geography?
3. What are four major world regions of manufacturing?
4. Summarize the historical development of the U.S. Manufacturing Belt.
5. What is inertia in industrial location?
6. When and why did the Manufacturing Belt begin to lose industry? Where, specifically, did it go?
7. Where are most U.S. multinational investments concentrated? Why?
8. What are some major world industrial problems?
9. What is the flexible economy?
10. What is the product life-cycle model?

KEY TERMS

American Manufacturing Belt
assembly costs
assembly plants
backward integration
capital-labor relations
conglomerate merger
deindustrialization
dependent industrialization
diseconomies of scale
distribution costs
diversification
dual economy
externality
flexible labor
foreign sourcing
forward integration
franchising
horizontal integration

industrial inertia
industrialization
industrial park
industrial restructuring
industry concentration
industry life cycle
inertia
information technology
integrated circuit
international subcontracting
joint venture
just-in-time manufacturing
least-cost approach
licensing venture
locational interdependence
machinofacture
microprocessor
mode of production

multinational corporations (MNCs)
multiplant enterprises
nomadic capital
offshore assembly
oligopoly
outsourcing
postindustrial
postindustrial society
product life cycle
raw-material—oriented
real-time information systems
surplus value
Taylorism
transnational corporation
value added
vertical integration
zaibatsu

SUGGESTED READINGS

Bluestone, B. and B. Harrison. 1982. *The Deindustrialization of America: Plant Closings, Community Abandonment, and the Dismantling of Basic Industry*. New York: Basic Books.

Dicken, P. 2004. *Global Shift: Industrial Change in a Turbulent World*, 4th ed. London: Guilford.

Krugman, P. 1991. *Geography and Trade*. Cambridge, Mass.: University Press.

Massey, D. 1984. *Spatial Divisions of Labor: Social Structures and the Geography of Production*. New York: Methuen.

Knox, P., Agnew, J., and L. McCarthy. 2003. *The Geography of the World Economy*, 4th ed. London: Edward Arnold.

Linkon, S. and J. Russo. 2002. *Steel-Town U.S.A.: Work & Memory in Youngstown*. Lawrence: University Press of Kansas.

WORLD FACTBOOK ON COUNTRIES
http://www.odci.gov/cia/publications/pubs.html

WORLD TRADE ORGANIZATION
http://www.wto.org/
The principal agency of the world's multilateral trading system. Its home page includes access to documents discussing international conferences and agreements, reviewing its publications, and summarizing the current state of world trade.

WORLD BANK
http://www.worldbank.org/
A leading source for country studies, research, and statistics covering all aspects of economic development and world trade. Its home page provides access to the contents of its publications, to its research areas, and to related Web sites.

BUREAU OF LABOR STATISTICS
http://stats.bls.gov/
Contains economic data, including unemployment rates, worker productivity, employment surveys, and statistical summaries.

U.S. INTERNATIONAL TRADE IN GOODS AND SERVICES HIGHLIGHTS
http://www.census.gov/indicator/www/ustrade.html

U.S. DEPARTMENT OF COMMERCE
http://www.doc.gov/
Charged with promoting American business, manufacturing, and trade. Its home page connects with the web sites of its constituent agencies.

ECONOLINK
http://www.progress.org/econolink
Econolink has selective descriptions of economic issues; many sites themselves have web links.

WEBEC: WORLD WIDE WEB RESOURCES
http://netec.wustl.edu/WebEc/WebEc.html
An extensive set of site listings concerning the economy.

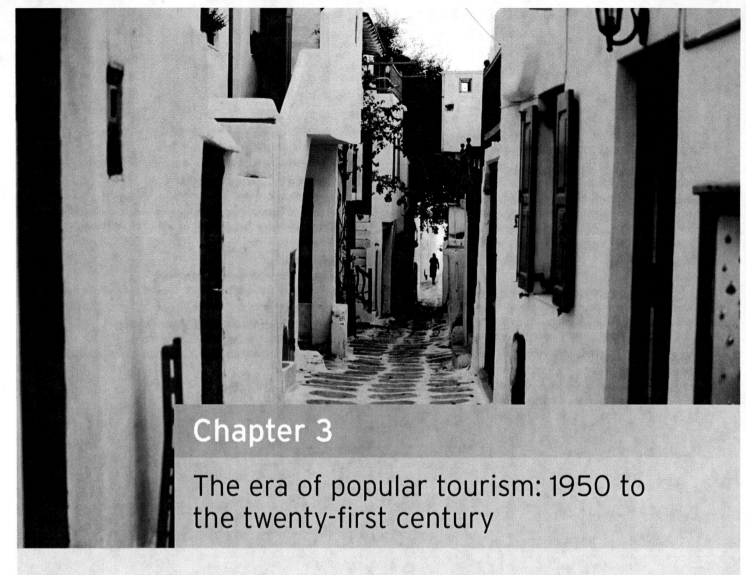

Chapter 3

The era of popular tourism: 1950 to the twenty-first century

Learning outcomes

After studying this chapter, you should be able to:

- describe the factors giving rise to mass tourism after 1950

- explain the origins and development of the package holiday

- understand the significance of rapid change in political, social and economic circumstances giving rise to the current uncertainties facing the tourism industry.

Tourism since World War II

Those who wish to see Spain while it is worth seeing must go soon.

Reverend Henry Christmas, *The Shores and Islands of the Mediterranean. Including a Visit to the Seven Churches of Asia* (1851), quoted in Löfgren, pp. 184–5

In the aftermath of World War II, the long and deprived years led to an increased desire to travel to foreign destinations, although the ability to do so was limited for many – restricted by both political barriers and inadequate finance. In Britain, as in other lands in Europe, there were also strict limits on the availability of foreign currency – a major barrier to cross-border travel. Nevertheless, the war had given rise to a curiosity among many British travellers to witness the sites of battles such as those fought on the Normandy beaches and at St Nazaire, while North Americans and Japanese alike felt similarly drawn to sites of conflict in the Pacific, such as Iwo Jima and Guadalcanal – although it was to take some 40 years or more before interest in these historic military battle sites was to approach the level of those of World War I. Interest was also limited to the sites on the western front in Europe – the horrors of warfare on the eastern front were such that neither side showed much inclination to visit the former battlefields, many of which were, in any case, banned to visitors until after the fall of the Soviet government. The extensive theatre of war had introduced the many combatants to not only new countries but also new continents, generating new friendships and an interest in diverse cultures. Another outcome of the war, which was radically to change the travel business, was the advance in aircraft technology that was soon to lead to a viable commercial aviation industry for the first time. With the ending of the war in 1945, the first commercial transatlantic flight took place between New York and Bournemouth, calling at Boston, Gander and Shannon. That flight, operated by American Overseas Airlines using a Douglas DC4, served to point the way ahead, although the cost and the time involved – a result of the frequent stops required – ensured that long-haul flights would not become popular until the advent of the jet age.

The surplus of aircraft in the immediate post-war years, a benevolent political attitude towards the growth of private-sector airlines and the appearance on the scene of air travel entrepreneurs such as Harold Bamberg (of Eagle Airways) and Freddie Laker (of Laker Airways) aided the rapid expansion of air travel after the war. More significantly for the potential market, however, aircraft had become more comfortable, safer, faster and, in spite of relatively high prices in the early 1950s, steadily cheaper by comparison with other forms of transport. The war had seen many new airports built in Europe to serve the military and these were later adapted for civilian use. This was to prove particularly valuable in opening up islands in the Mediterranean that were formerly inaccessible or time-consuming to reach by sea.

Commercial jet services began with the ill-fated Comet aircraft in the early 1950s (withdrawn from service after crashes resulting from metal fatigue), but advances in piston engine technology were already beginning to impact on price. With the introduction of the commercially successful Boeing 707 jet in 1958, the age of air travel for the masses had arrived, hastening the demise of the great ocean liners.

The number of passengers crossing the Atlantic by air exceeded those by sea for the first time in 1957 and, although the liners continued to operate across the Atlantic for a further decade, their increasingly uncompetitive costs, high fares (saddled by conference agreements on routes across the Atlantic and Pacific that banned discounting) and the length of the journey time resulted in declining load factors from one year to the next. The new jets, with average speeds of 800 to 1000 kph, compared with older propeller-driven aircraft travelling at a mere 400 kph, meant that an air traveller could reach a far more distant destination within a given time (the key New York to London route fell from 18 hours in 1949 to just 7 hours in 1969) than had been possible before. This was particularly valuable for business journeys where time was crucial.

The early 1970s saw the arrival of the first supersonic passenger aircraft, the Anglo-French Concorde. Never truly a commercial success (the governments wrote off the huge development costs), it nevertheless proved popular with business travellers and the wealthy. Travelling from London or Paris to New York in three and a half hours, it allowed businesspeople for the first time to complete their business on the other side of the Atlantic and return home without incurring a hotel stopover. The limited range and carrying capacity (just over 100 passengers) of the aircraft, and restrictions regarding sonic booms over land, acted as severe constraints on operable routes. The fatal crash near Paris of a chartered Concorde in 2000 sealed the aircraft's fate, leading to its withdrawal from service. It is thought unlikely that any further supersonic aircraft development will take place within the next 20 years (although the possibility of private supersonic jets arriving rather sooner than this is discussed in Chapter 13).

The development of the package tour

Inclusive tours by coach soon regained their former appeal after the war. The Italian Riviera was popular at first – French resorts proving too expensive – and resorts such as Rimini became affordable for the North European middle market. The inclusive tour by air – or 'package tour' as it has become known – was soon to follow.

Cheap packages by air depend on the ability of tour operators to charter aircraft for their clientele and buy hotel beds in bulk, driving down costs and allowing prices to be cut. Initially, the UK government's transport policy had restricted air charters to the movement of troops, but, as official policy became more lenient, the private operators sought to develop new forms of charter traffic. Package holidays were the outcome, as the smaller air carriers and entrepreneurs learned to cooperate.

In the late 1950s, the larger airlines began to purchase the new jets, allowing smaller companies to buy the stock of second-hand propeller-driven aircraft coming on to the market, which were then put into service for charter operations. For the first time, holiday tourists could be transported to Mediterranean destinations faster than, and almost as cheaply as, trains and coaches. These new charter services soon proved highly profitable. Meanwhile, across the Atlantic, the first stirrings of an air package holiday industry emerged as regional operators began chartering aircraft from so-called 'supplemental' carriers on routes between major cities in the USA and Canada and the Caribbean Islands.

Although there are instances of charter flights as early as the 1920s (Thomas Cook, for example, had organized an escorted charter, believed to be the first, to take fans from New York to Chicago in 1927 to see the Dempsey–Tunney heavyweight title fight) and the National Union of Students is known to have been organizing charter flights for its members as early as 1949, Vladimir Raitz is generally credited with founding the mass inclusive tour business using air charters as we know it today. In 1950, under the Horizon Holidays banner, he organized an experimental package holiday trip using a charter flight to Corsica. By chartering the aircraft and filling every seat instead of committing himself to a block of seats on scheduled air services, he was able to reduce significantly the unit cost of his air transport and, hence, the overall price to his customers. He carried only 300 passengers in the first year, but repeated the experiment the following year and was soon operating profitably. Other budding tour operators, both in Britain and on the Continent, were soon copying his ideas (Club Méditerranée being among the best-known of the early entrepreneurs) and, by the early 1960s, the package holiday to the Mediterranean had become an established product for the mass holiday market.

The Spanish coastline and the Balearic Islands were the first to benefit from the new influx of mass tourism from Britain, Germany and the Scandinavian countries, carried by the workhorse Douglas DC-3 aircraft. First, the Costa del Sol, then other coasts along the eastern seaboard, the islands of Majorca, Ibiza and, finally by the 1970s, the Canaries became, in turn, the destinations of choice for millions.

By 1960, Spain was already welcoming 6 million tourists every year and this was to grow to 30 million by 1975. Italy, Greece and other Mediterranean coastal regions all benefited from the 'rush to the sun'. Greece in particular, although slower to develop than Spain, provided a cheaper alternative as prices in the latter country rose. Only 50,000 visited in 1951, but a decade later this had grown to 500,000 and, by 1981, Greece was vying with Spain, welcoming 5,500,000.

The Nordic countries were also soon setting up their own package holiday arrangements to the Mediterranean and began to compete with Britain and their southern counterparts for accommodation along the Mediterranean coast. In Denmark, Pastor Eilif Krogager conducted a group of package tourists by coach to Spain in 1950, using the name of his village, Tjaereborg, as the company name. In 1962, Tjaereborg Travel moved into the air charter market with the formation of Sterling Airways, which soon became Western Europe's largest privately owned charter airline of the period.

In Britain, post-war difficulties in the economy forced the government to impose ever tighter controls on foreign exchange. For a brief interval in 1947, a travel ban was imposed, during which no foreign currency allowance was made. Although the ban was lifted in early 1948, severe currency restrictions remained into the late 1960s, at which point the foreign currency (V-form) allowance for travel abroad was limited to £50 per person (for business travellers, additional funds, under T-form regulations, were granted). There was, however, a silver lining to this particular cloud: it encouraged people to take package holidays rather than travel independently, so the industry continued to flourish. Also, as air transport costs were payable in sterling and as only the foreign currency element of the tour – the *net* costs of accommodation and transfers – had to be paid out of the allowance, the benefits of dealing with an operator became clear. The limits were relaxed from 1970 onwards and, with further liberalization of air transport regulations

Figure 3.1 The mass market beach holiday. Grömitz is a popular German resort in Mecklenburg Bay, North Germany.
(Photo by Chris Holloway.)

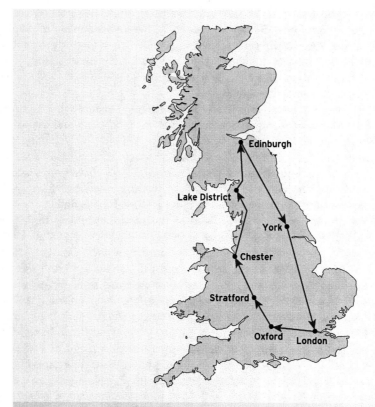

Figure 3.2 The linear tour. An example of the 'milk run' around Britain.

and longer paid holidays, which encouraged a growing number of tourists to take a second holiday abroad each year, a new winter holiday market emerged in the 1970s. With a more even spread of package holidays throughout the year, operators found that they were able to reduce their unit costs still further, so package holiday prices continued to fall, boosting off-season demand. Britain was not alone within Europe in imposing currency restrictions during these early post-war years. Indeed, exchange controls were not totally abolished in France until as recently as 1990.

A further technological breakthrough in air transport occurred in 1970, when the first wide-bodied jets (Boeing 747s), capable of carrying over 400 passengers, appeared in service. The unit cost per seat fell sharply and the result was an increased supply of seats at potentially cheaper fares. This innovation meant that, once again, the aviation industry had to unload cheaply a number of obsolescent, although completely air-worthy, smaller aircraft and these were quickly pressed into service for charter operations.

The innovation coincided with a steady increase in demand by North American visitors to Europe for basic tours of Britain and the Continent, hitting as many 'high spots' as possible in a 10- to 14-day visit. This gave rise to the concept of the 'milk run' – a popular route that would embrace the top attractions in one or more countries in a limited time-scale for the first-time visitor (see Figure 3.2). Similar short 'taster' tours around Western Europe, visiting the key cities, provided an introduction to long-haul travel for millions of Americans.

The movement to the sun

By the 1960s, it was clear that the future of mass market leisure travel was to be a north–south movement, from the cool and variable climates of North America and northern

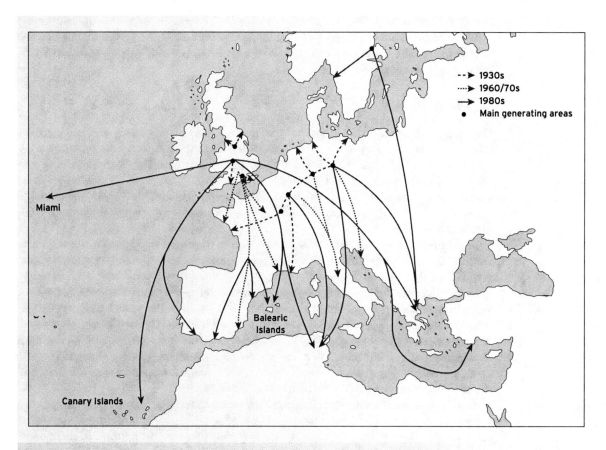

Figure 3.3 Changes in destination trends for mass market holidays, 1930s to 1980s.

Europe, where the mass of relatively well-off people lived, to the sunshine and warmth of the temperate to tropical lands in the southern part of the northern hemisphere (see Figure 3.3). These southern countries were also, for the most part, less well developed economically and so offered low-cost opportunities for the formation of a tourism industry. The new breed of tourism entrepreneurs involved with packaging tours recognized this trend very early on. Major hotel chains, too, were quick to seize the opportunities for growth in these countries and those such as Sheraton and Hyatt in the USA quickly expanded into Mexico and the Caribbean, as well as into Florida and Hawaii – the states offering the most attractive climates for tourism development. Hawaii in particular proved popular as an 'overseas' destination, following its incorporation into the USA (from 100,000 visitors in 1955, the flow of tourists increased to 2 million in 1970 and 6.5 million by 1990).

In Europe, British and German tour operators such as Thomson and TUI developed bulk inclusive tours to the Mediterranean and North Africa and, due to increasing volume, were able to charter jumbo jets for the first time, bringing prices still lower. As transport costs fell, operators were also able to attract a mass market for long-haul travel on chartered jumbo jets. Florida – boosted particularly by the attractions of the Walt Disney World Resort and Miami Beach – has become almost as popular a destination for Europeans as the major Mediterranean destinations.

By the end of the twentieth century, the expert packaging of these tours had been extended to many other types of destinations. Initially, tours to cultural and heritage sites, city breaks to major cities like London, Paris, Rome, Brussels and Amsterdam and river cruises on the Rhine or Danube were being efficiently packaged and sold to the northern

European market. The result was that, by the end of the 1960s, some 2.5 million Britons were taking packaged holidays abroad each year. By the end of the 1980s, this had grown to over 11 million, with over 70 per cent of the British population having been abroad on holiday at least once in their lives.

Identikit destinations

One important result of the growth of the mass tourism market was that those responsible for marketing tourist destinations recognized that they had to satisfy tourists sharing broadly similar aspirations, regardless of their country of origin. The destinations accepted that, apart from geographical location, there was little to differentiate one resort from another and consumers' needs were centred on good climate and beaches, reasonable standards of food and accommodation, good opportunities for entertainment and shopping and low prices.

Consumers themselves cared little which country they were in, as long as these criteria were fulfilled. The larger the mass market, the less distinctive destinations are likely to be, especially if they are small and have only recently been developed. One can find newly built 'marina'-type resorts with yachting, basins, hotel/apartment/villa accommodation, similar restaurants, cafés and shops, as well as golf, tennis, water sports, folk singers and barbecue nights in any one of a dozen countries around the Mediterranean, Caribbean, North Africa and the South Pacific. Vernacular architecture has given way to the standard monobloc development typical of all beach resorts from Miami Beach to Australia's Gold Coast, by way of Benidorm and the faceless resorts of Romania and Bulgaria (including the optimistically named 'Golden Sands' and 'Sunny Beach').

This is also true even where business travellers attending conferences abroad are concerned. A convention centre, for example, is today likely to be a multi-purpose venue containing facilities for conferences and committee/lecture rooms and including modern single or twin-bedded hotel rooms with private facilities, restaurants with banqueting rooms, bars, exhibition space, a leisure centre with pool, indoor and outdoor sports facilities and good scheduled transport links. The location may be Birmingham, Barcelona or Brisbane, but, once inside their hotel or conference centre, delegates may not even notice where they are. Indeed, one can find ubiquitous furniture of identical design (such as faux Regency chairs spray-painted in gold) in conference centres and hotels throughout the world.

The term **identikit destination** will be used to define and identify this form of resort. Each has emerged following comprehensive market research among various generating markets to find products with guaranteed mass demand. They may be contrasted with the piecemeal development of resorts two or three generations ago, the attractions at which may have been developed with very different aims and markets in mind. This is not to say that all identikit destinations are chasing identical markets. Many may be 'downmarket' in their attractiveness – that is, they may offer cheap tourism to a large number of people with the image of great popularity – while others may offer a more upmarket, but nonetheless uniform, image, offering the perception of higher quality and, thus, more expensive services to fewer visitors. In the former category we may think of Benidorm, Magaluf, Benitses in the Mediterranean, Miami Beach in Florida (see Figure 3.4) or Seefeld in Austria, while in the latter category we may think of Tahiti, Fiji, Malindi in Kenya or Barbados. Many identikit destinations have been developed through the activities of multinational tour companies, such as the all-inclusive resorts run by Sandals in the Caribbean, France's Club Méditerranée, Germany's Robinson Club or the United States' Sheraton Hotel chain. Within their establishments, the mass tourist will find a comforting degree of uniformity.

Mass tourism has therefore demanded, and been supplied with, products designed specifically for its needs, as revealed through the process of market research. Such products

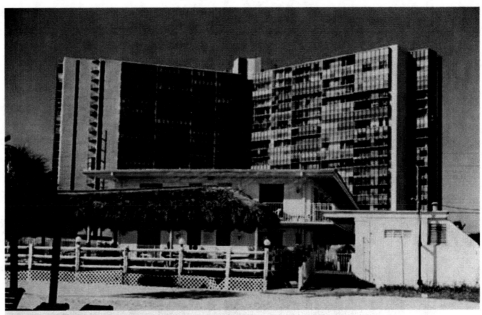

Figure 3.4 Miami Beach typifies the popular North American identikit mass holiday destination. High-rise blocks now tower over the few remaining traditional motels in Florida. *(Photo by Chris Holloway.)*

are *user-orientated* as opposed to *resource-orientated* (based on the resources available at a destination).

Many of these identikit destinations, however, are now finding themselves at a disadvantage as the world tourism market becomes more sophisticated. Research by the former English Tourism Council revealed that one of the weaknesses of many English seaside resorts has been their failure to project a unique image. Those that have succeeded – notably Blackpool and a handful of other major or minor resorts – have done so through a combination of significant investment and differentiation from other, often similar, resorts. Those resorts unable to make the investment needed to change their image are faced with the prospect of decline or have to appeal to newer, generally lower-spend markets. The later years of the last century found several of the formerly popular Mediterranean resorts attracting new tourists from the central European countries to replace the gradual decline in numbers of Western European visitors. One saving grace for those identikit destinations that developed around the core of an established town has been the ability to retain and improve the original 'old town', which is now promoted as a core attraction in its own right.

Private motoring and holidays

After a slow post-war recovery, the standard of living rose steadily in the 1950s and after. Many people could contemplate buying their first car, even if it was second-hand. For the first time, the holiday masses had the freedom to take to the roads with their families in their own private cars and, in Britain, the popular routes between London and the resorts on the south coast were soon clogged, in those pre-motorway days, with weekend traffic.

The flexibility that the car offered could not be matched by public transport services and both bus and rail lost the holiday traveller. In 1950, some two out of every three holiday-makers took the train for their holidays in Britain; this fell to one in seven by 1970. In this period, private car ownership in Britain rose from 2 million to over 11 million vehicles and, by the end of the 1980s, it had risen to some 20 million.

The Era of Popular Tourism: 1950 to the Twenty-First Century

This trend led, in turn, to a growth in camping and caravanning holidays. Ownership of private caravans stood at nearly 800,000 by the end of the 1980s (excluding static caravans in parks), while 13 million holidaymakers in the UK took their holidays in a caravan. This development was a cause for some concern, however, as the benefits to a region of private caravan tourism are considerably less than most other forms of tourism (owners can bring most of their own food with them and do not require accommodation). Also, caravans tend to clog the holiday routes in summer. Both mobile and static caravans on site are perceived as something of an eyesore, too.

The switch to private transport led to new forms of accommodation that catered for this form of travel. Britain saw the development of its first motels, modelled on the American pattern, which are the contemporary version of the staging inn for coach passengers.

The construction of a new network of motorways and other road improvements made the journeys to more distant resorts manageable for those in centres of population and, in some cases, changed both the nature of the market served and the image of the resort itself.

The ever resourceful tour operators met the private car threat to package holidays by devising more flexible packages, such as fly–drive holidays, with the provision of a hire car at the airport on arrival. Hotels, too, spurred on by the need to fill their rooms off-peak, devised their own programmes of short-stay holidays, tailored to the needs of the private motorist.

Another effect was that the demand for car rental *abroad* rose sharply, too, as the overseas holidaymaker was emboldened to move away from the hotel ghettos, so car rental businesses in popular areas profited accordingly.

The shipping business in the post-war period

By contrast with other elements of the travel business, passenger shipping companies, hit by rising prices and competition from the airlines, were struggling to survive. Forced to abandon their traditional liner routes by the 1960s, some attempted to adapt their vessels for cruising. In this, they were far from successful as vessels purpose-built for long-distance, fast, deep sea voyages are not ideally suited to cruising, either economically or from the standpoint of customer demand. Many were incapable of anchoring alongside docks in the shallower waters of popular cruise destinations such as the Caribbean islands.

Companies that failed to embark on a programme of new construction, either due to lack of resources or foresight, soon ceased trading. Others, such as the Cunard Line, were taken over by conglomerates outside the travel or transport industries. American cruise lines, beset by high labour costs and strong unions, virtually ceased to exist.

Many new purpose-built cruise liners, however, of Greek, Norwegian and, later, Russian registry, soon appeared on the market to fill the gaps left by the declining maritime powers. These vessels, despite their registry, were based primarily in Caribbean or Mediterranean waters.

British shipping was not entirely devoid of innovations at this time. Cunard initiated the fly–cruise concept in the 1960s, with vessels based at Gibraltar and Naples and passengers flying out to join their cruise in chartered aircraft.

The rapid escalation of fuel and other costs during the 1970s threatened the whole future of deep sea shipping, but, although declared dead by the pundits, this sector refused to lie down. Gradual stabilization of oil prices and control of labour costs (largely by recruiting from developing countries) enabled the cruise business to stage a comeback in the 1980s and 1990s, led by entrepreneurial shipping lines like Carnival Cruise Line, the American operator that set out to put the fun back into cruising. More informality, to appeal to more youthful family markets, helped to turn the business round, so that, by the end of the twentieth century, cruising had again become a major growth sector. Carnival absorbed many of the traditional carriers, including British companies Cunard and P&O, and had the financial backing necessary to make substantial investment in new vessels.

By contrast with the cruise business, ferry services achieved quite exceptional levels of growth between the 1950s and the end of the century. This largely resulted from the increased demand from private motorists to take their cars abroad, influencing particularly routes between Scandinavian countries and Germany, and between Britain and Continental Europe. This growth in demand was also better spread across the seasons, enabling vessels to remain in service throughout the year with respectable load factors (although freight demand substantially boosted weak passenger revenue in the winter period). Regular sailings, with fast turnarounds in port, encouraged bookings and costs were kept down by offering much more restricted levels of service than would be expected on long-distance routes. Hovercraft and jetfoil services were introduced across the Channel, although their success was limited by technical problems and being unable to sail in severe weather. Reliable, fast ferry services did not appear until the advent of the catamarans in the 1990s.

The growing importance of business travel

The growth in world trade in these decades saw a steady expansion in business travel, individually and in the conference and incentive travel fields, although recession in the latter part of the century caused cutbacks in business travel as sharp as those in leisure travel. As economic power shifted between countries, so emerging nations provided new patterns of tourism generation. In the 1970s, Japan and the oil-rich nations of the Middle East led the growth, while in the 1980s, countries such as Korea and Malaysia expanded both inbound and outbound business tourism dramatically. The acceptance of eight Eastern European nations (together with Malta and Cyprus) into the EU in May 2004 led to new growth areas in the movement of tourists during the first decade of the century, plus the rise of a new, free-spending elite within the Russian community and adjacent countries has resulted in those nationalities being among the fastest-growing sector in international tourism, albeit from a low base. Meanwhile, uncertainty in the Western world – particularly the fall and slow recovery of the stock market since the events of September 2001, followed by a deepening recession and escalating oil prices – has continued to limit the recovery of business and leisure travel well into the twenty-first century.

Nevertheless, business travel of all kinds remains of immense importance to the tourism industry, not least because the per capita revenue from the business traveller greatly exceeds that of the leisure traveller. Motivational factors involving business travel are discussed in the next chapter and the nature of business travel is explored more fully in Chapter 11, but it should be stressed here that business travel often complements leisure travel, spreading the effects of tourism more evenly in the economy. A major factor is that business travellers are not generally travelling to areas that are favoured by leisure travellers (other than in the very particular case of the conference market). Businesspeople have to go to locations where they are to conduct business, which generally means city centres, and often those cities have little to attract the leisure tourist. Travel also takes place all year round, with little peaking, and the demand for hotels occurs between Mondays and Fridays, encouraging the more attractively situated hotels to target the leisure market on weekends. Often, spouses will travel to accompany the business traveller, so their leisure needs will have to be taken into consideration, too. Thus, in practice, it becomes difficult to distinguish between business and leisure tourism.

Although business travel is less price-elastic than leisure travel, as was noted earlier, efforts to cut costs in the world of business today are ensuring business travellers no longer spend as freely as they did formerly. Fewer business travellers now travel first class or business class on airlines (many are making use of the new budget airlines to minimize costs) than before, less expensive hotels are booked and there is even a trend to travel on weekends to reduce prices. Companies are buying many more tourism products, particularly air tickets, through the Internet, where they can shop around for the cheapest tickets. These changes are not seen as short-term trends and, in future, any distinction between the two major tourist markets is likely to become less apparent.

Conference and incentive travel business

Conferences and formal meetings have become very important to the tourism industry, both nationally and internationally, with continued growth between the 1960s and the end of the century. The British conference market alone is responsible for the organization of some 700,000 individual conferences each year, the very large majority lasting just one or two days. As most of them are held in hotels, this market is vital to the accommodation sector. Low-cost carriers, having broken the traditional carriers' imposition of conditions requiring a weekend stopover to gain low fares, changed business protocol and began to win a share of those important markets.

Major conferences, such as that of the American Bar Association, which accounts for up to 25,000 delegates each year travelling all over the world (the 2000 conference was held in London), impact on all sectors of the industry, from hotels to the destination itself, which benefits from expenditure in shops, theatres, nightclubs and other centres of amusement. To serve the needs of the largest conferences, international conference centres seating up to 5000 or more delegates have been built in major cities such as London and Berlin, but the number of conferences of this size is inevitably limited, so the competition to attract them is intense.

The logistics of organizing these and other major events are generally in the hands of professional events organizers, most of whom in Britain belong to the Association of Conference Executives (ACE). As international conferences generally have English as the common language (although simultaneous translations are always available where necessary), countries such as Britain and the USA greatly benefit from this market.

Exhibitions also account for another form of business travel. Major international exhibitions can be traced to at least as far back as the Great Exhibition, held at Crystal Palace in London in 1851, and world fairs have become common events in major cities around the globe as a means of attracting visitors and publicizing a nation's culture and products. Many national events are now organized on an annual basis, some requiring little more than a field and marquees or other temporary structures – the Royal Bath & West agricultural show being one example of a major outdoor attraction, held annually in the UK's West Country. As such events have grown and become more professionally organized, so have they, too, become an important element in the business of tourism.

The all-inclusive holiday

Mention has already been made of the trend for *all-inclusive* holidays. As the term indicates, such a holiday includes everything – food, alcoholic drinks, water sports and other entertainment at the hotel. The attractions of this form of tourism are obvious – it is seen by tourists as offering better value, because they can pay up front for the holiday, know what their budget will be well in advance and be unconcerned about changes in the value of foreign currency or the need to take large sums of money abroad. For more timid foreign travellers or those who are concerned about being badgered by local souvenir sellers and 'beach salesmen', there is the added reassurance that they do not even have to leave the hotel complex to enjoy their holidays.

Critics argue that the growth of all-inclusive holidays has implications for the local economy, as local bars, shopkeepers and others no longer stand to benefit from visitors to the same extent as before. At the same time, greater profits can leak back overseas when the all-inclusive holiday sites are foreign-owned. In this sense, one may question whether or not all-inclusive tourism can be judged sustainable. Operators themselves, however, would refute this, arguing that, by keeping tourists in 'ghettos', they are in fact helping to reduce the negative impact of tourism on locals.

In its modern form, this type of tourism originated in the Caribbean and upmarket tour operators such as Sandals have promoted these programmes very successfully to the US and European markets. The concept later moved downmarket, however, and became popular in the more traditional European resorts, such as those of the Balearic Islands. Further expansion is seen as a direct threat to the livelihoods of many in the traditional coastal resorts.

Mass market tourism in its maturity

Mass market tourism to southern European resorts can be said to have entered a period of maturity by the 1980s. Although still showing steady growth, expansion was not on the scale found between the 1950s and 1970s. Short-haul travel was changing geographically, with tourists seeking new resorts and experiences. Portugal, having an Atlantic rather than a Mediterranean coast, wisely kept an upmarket image for its developments in the Algarve, while the Canaries, being within the crucial four hours' flying time from northern European airports, were the closest destinations to offer guaranteed warm winter sunshine and prospered from their year-round appeal. Other rather more exotic destinations attracted the upmarket winter holidaymaker. Tunisia, Morocco, Egypt and Israel pitched for the medium-haul beach markets. As prices rose in the traditional resorts, tourists moved on to cheaper, and less developed, destinations still close at hand. Turkey – seen as cheap, uncontested and mildly exotic – boomed in the 1980s, proving an attractive alternative to Greece. The then Yugoslavian Adriatic Coast provided charming architecture and cultural attractions in its seaside resorts, although good sandy beaches were missing. Malta had always had an appeal with the more conservative British tourist, but Crete and Cyprus began to attract larger numbers (especially following the war in Lebanon). Spain woke up to the despoliation of its resorts and made efforts to upgrade them, especially on the island of Majorca and in popular coastal towns such as Torremolinos.

By the end of the century, it was becoming clear that seaside tourism was moving in a new direction. Visitors were no longer willing simply to lie on a beach; they sought activities and adventure. For the young, this meant action, from sports to bungee jumping and discos. Taking over popular resorts on Ibiza and in Greece, they encouraged the family holiday market to move on. For the older tourist, it meant more excursions inland to cultural sites and attractive villages.

The long-haul market was changing, too. Attempts to sell some long-haul destinations as if they were merely extensions of the Mediterranean sunshine holidays failed to take into account the misunderstandings that could occur between hosts and guests, first in the Gambia, then in the Dominican Republic. Cruising, dormant for so long, suddenly found a new lease of life. Long-haul beach holidays in Kenya and Thailand, marketed at costs competitive with those in Europe, attracted Western tourists.

The American and northern European markets were joined by a rising flow of tourists from other parts of the world. The Asian market has become a leading source of business for the travel industry – in the West as well as throughout Australasia. The flow of Japanese tourists to Australia is noteworthy. Travel times to Australia are shorter than those to Europe and, equally importantly, because the travel is largely within the same longitude, there is no time change or jet lag to face. With typically only eight days of holiday, avoidance of jet lag becomes an attractive bonus for the Japanese market and makes Australia doubly attractive. Absence of jet lag is also helping to accelerate tourism to South Africa from the European nations, although uncertainty over crime and the country's political future remains.

Destinations in the Pacific began to attract Europeans in significant numbers, just as they have long attracted the Japanese and Australian markets. A large proportion of these visitors, however, were using the Pacific islands as stopover points for a night or two rather than a holiday base. The impact of technology can be seen when, for the first time, aircraft became capable of flying direct between the west coast of the USA and Australia with the introduction of the Boeing 747-400SP aircraft. Tahiti, slightly off the direct route between these continents and long established as an attractive stopover point but expensive for longer holidays, immediately suffered a sharp decline in visitors as the airlines concentrated their promotion efforts on direct non-stop services between Los Angeles and Sydney or Auckland.

The influence of information technology

The development of technology that can manage the reservation information held by tour operators, airlines and hotels has had a significant influence on the operations of such companies. Computer systems that can hold and process large amounts of data have become a key business tool for many tourism companies.

The 1970s saw the introduction of computer reservation systems (CRS) by airlines. Such systems provided them with the capability of tracking seat pricing and availability on their ever-expanding routes and schedules. By the 1980s, those systems were being installed in travel agencies, too, as the airlines realized that the agents could enter the data for the bookings, thus making them more productive for the airline. The most prominent CRSs (now known as global distribution systems (GDSs) used within the airline distribution systems) are Amadeus, Sabre, Galileo and Worldspan (the latter two merging in 2007), while regional systems also exist (such as Axess, based in Japan, and Abacus, which serves the Asia Pacific region). Often, however, the regional GDSs have links with the 'big four' GDSs. The 1990s saw the introduction and rapid growth of the Internet, allowing business to customer (B2C) systems to be developed alongside business to business (B2B) systems provided by GDS. This was coupled with the development of mass produced personal computers.

The affordability of computers and the penetration of the Internet, including the availability of broadband access, have ensured that more customers than ever before can now search for information about holiday destinations, compare travel companies (and user reviews) as well as reserve travel products online. The growth of online booking was partially fuelled by the budget airlines offering cheaper rates for online reservations, but was also encouraged by customers seeing this method of booking their travel as more convenient. The numbers of people booking their travel online has often been suggested as a threat to travel agents, but, while in some countries the high street travel agents may have declined, online travel agencies are prospering.

Furthermore, experienced travellers are prepared to book separate elements of their travel online, either direct with providers or though an intermediary, often using price comparison websites to explore the range of products open to them. Coupled with the expectation that they can book their travel online, many customers also expect short response times. They expect to have an accurate picture of the availability of their chosen product and that they will receive almost immediate confirmation of their booking, usually via e-mail. E-mail correspondence – to address questions either prior to or post booking – must therefore be dealt with quickly, usually within hours, as customers are rarely prepared to wait days for a response.

The introduction of the Internet has also led to adaptations being made to business practices. As the budget airlines encouraged booking online, customers became more comfortable with the idea of making their own reservations, which significantly impacted on the chain of distribution. Some scheduled airlines saw opportunities to sell seats direct to the customer, in the process becoming less reliant on travel agents (and, consequently, reducing levels of commission payments). More recently, travel agents have fought back, trying to make themselves indispensible to customers by offering a specialized service, creating holidays from separately selected elements, rather than offering standard packages. A further development has been the introduction of online travel intermediaries, who act as a convenient outlet for last-minute sales.

Database and Web technology has now developed to a point where companies can tailor the information they provide to customers, adjusting the Web page content according to the customer profile (determined overtly or covertly through methods such as tracking sites visited or prior bookings). Such adaptability can enhance sales by more closely matching customer needs to relevant product offers. This can also help to develop customer loyalty to particular websites.

Search engines can be an important factor for both travel companies and holiday destinations. While there are several search engines that people use to track down information, customers rarely move beyond the first few pages of results. Therefore, achieving a high ranking for key search terms can be important in ensuring that customers reach their website.

Destinations use advanced technology that allows them to offer customers detailed information about the locality, as well as providing an accommodation reservation system. Such destination management systems can help to provide a coherent link between the many small companies operating at a destination, as well as feeding information to other websites, thus further extending the marketing reach for the destination.

Back office systems have also been enhanced by the affordability of computer systems, allowing travel businesses to develop databases of customer records, which are used to enhance their marketing activities, as well as financial accounts systems and sales records. The convenience of storing customer details and sales data means that business decisions can be made that are based on analysis of this information – especially useful if there are plans to invest in activities such as new marketing campaigns.

Finally, we need to consider the impact of both wi-fi and mobile technology. Wi-fi technology has allowed many travel businesses to provide customers with convenient access to the Internet. In the past, businesses such as hotels would have charged customers to use Internet systems as they had to invest in installing network cables throughout the building. The minimal costs of installing wi-fi systems, however, as well as the wider availability of wi-fi zones in coffee shops, airports and other areas, has led to customers expecting access to the Internet as standard (and often for minimal or no charge).

Mobile technology is also increasing access to the Internet, as more phones are WAP-enabled and as the cost of accessing websites is seen to be more affordable. This allows customers to access the Web while on the move. Furthermore, the development of text messaging now allows travel companies to send booking confirmations or travel updates to a customer's mobile phone. This area of technology holds perhaps the greatest potential for changing the way travel companies interact with their customers.

Further reading

Bray, R. and Raitz, V. (2001) *Flight to the Sun: The story of the holiday revolution*, Continuum.

Brodie, A., Sargent, A. and Winterby, G. (2005) *Seaside Holidays in the Past*, English Heritage.

Franco, V. (1972) *Club Méditerranée*, Shepheard-Walwyn.

Grant, G. (1996) *Waikiki Yesteryear*, Mutual Publishing.

Löfgren, O. (1999) *On Holiday: A history of vacationing*, University of California Press.

Questions and discussion points

1. In 1984, McIntosh and Goeldner, in their classic text *Tourism Principles, Practices, Philosophies*, made a number of predictions about the future of the travel business by 2009, among which were the following:

   • red tape problems in travel would be largely eliminated
   • fast and comfortable room-to-room service would be available
   • all data of interest, and all reservations, would be made by instantaneous home video
   • consistent travel planning by weather, weeks ahead; resorts would enjoy a controlled environment
   • tourist pollution would recede as a controversial issue, largely controlled by local option and improved management
   • real-time pictures would be available from point-of-destination agencies
   • tourism and leisure would stabilize, but options would be growing, with diverse specialized tourism; extensive worldwide travel, with some space travel available
   • a typical working week would be no longer than 20 hours
   • business travel would be partly or largely superseded by new telecommunications
   • third-generation supersonic aircraft would be in operation, with many various and big jets, guided surface transport with rail services operating between 200 and 400 mph and cars with auto control operating at 100 to 200 mph.

   Now that this milestone has been reached, consider the extent to which these predictions have been fulfilled. Are those currently unfulfilled likely to come to pass within the next few years? What reasons would you give for the failure of the authors to accurately predict events at the end of the first decade of the twenty-first century?

2. The first package tours were to Corsica, a destination that has failed to fulfil its early potential and now caters largely for independent tourists or modest numbers of package holidaymakers. Suggest possible reasons for Corsica's failure to develop as a major resort destination in the manner of, for example, the Balearic Islands.

3. Offer possible explanations for the resurgence of cruising in the 1980s and the reasons for its limited appeal in the preceding decades. What lessons are to be learned from the failure of shipping managers to adapt their products to the needs of the time?

4. Critically evaluate the potential benefits and drawbacks of the popular 'taster' tours that have introduced so many North Americans to Europe.

5. With the present free currency market in Europe, it is no longer possible for a European government to restrict foreign travel as a means of aiding the balance of payments. What other steps can a government take to improve the tourism balance?

Tasks

1. Using the example of any all-inclusive holiday resort or destination known to you, draw up plans to ensure that the tourism you are attracting can be made more sustainable, both environmentally and socioculturally.

2. Prepare a talk on where you think the travel industry is going in the face of changing economic circumstances. What sectors of the industry will benefit and which will face serious challenge over the next few years? Identifying any one sector, examine how companies operating in it can best respond to the challenges faced by a faltering economy.

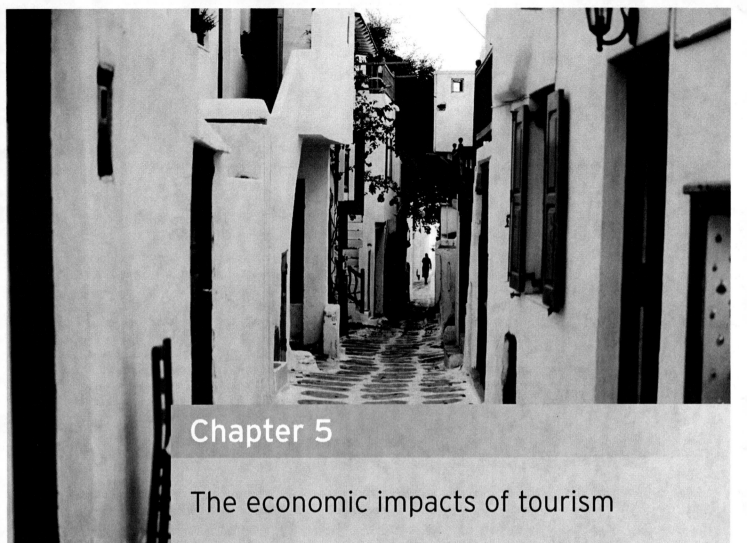

Chapter 5

The economic impacts of tourism

Learning outcomes

After studying this chapter, you should be able to:

- identify the economic benefits of tourism for a nation, both nationally and regionally

- be aware of the negative economic effects of tourism for destinations

- understand how tourism is measured statistically

- recognize the limitations of statistical measurement.

347

Introduction

> Global tourism is an $8 trillion industry. Over the past 20 years, developing countries have harnessed the rapid expansion of global tourism to promote economic growth. Through good planning, the tourism industry can powerfully transform communities, reducing poverty, protecting biodiversity, and improving gender equality, healthcare, education, and local governance.
>
> USAID, Global Development Alliance newsletter, March/April 2008

Tourism as an economic activity is important for the many countries that try to obtain a share of this $8 trillion. While it can bring in wealth and economic benefits, there are also some negative consequences for those nations and their regions. For both these reasons, it is important to understand the economic impacts of tourism.

This is a complex topic that can only be touched on in this text. Those who wish to examine the subject in depth are referred to texts designed for this purpose, such as Bull (1995). The aim of this chapter, therefore, is primarily to explore the economic impacts of tourism resulting from national and international tourist flows and the ways in which this is measured and recorded. In later chapters, the economics of the firm, the industry and its various sectors will be examined. First, however, we will look at the movement of tourists internationally and some of the economic factors influencing those flows.

The international tourist market

Tourism is probably the single most important industry in the world. According to the World Travel and Tourism Council (WTTC, 2008/2009), the global tourism industry would account for 3.4 per cent of global GDP in 2008, while the broader impacts (including the indirect effects on the economy as a result of tourism) would mean that it could be expected to account for 9.9 per cent of global GDP. Furthermore, it was estimated that the travel and tourism industry worldwide would provide 238.3 million jobs, representing 8.4 per cent of total employment.[1] According to the most recent estimate by the UNWTO,[2] 903 million international trips were taken in 2007, which represented an increase of more than 6 per cent on the previous year. The UNWTO also notes that provisional worldwide tourism receipts for 2007 suggest an increase of US$114 billion over the previous year, with a total of US$856 billion (see Table 5.1).

The rapid increase in international travel during the early post-war years – exceeding 10 per cent per annum from 1950 to 1960 – could not be permanently sustained, of course, as it reflected the pent-up demand that had built up in the war years and the slow economic recovery after the war. It is worth noting, however, that, apart from the odd hiccup, from 1970 to the 1990s, annual growth ran above 4 per cent, even in the early 1990s when there was a global recession. The WTTC has estimated that the annual growth between 2004 and 2008 averages at 4 per cent, with the tourism industry estimated as contributing US$5890 billion to global GDP in 2008. The good news for the tourism industry, therefore, is that, although the rate of increase in arrivals in some recent years has faltered – scarcely surprising, given the many turbulent world events since September 2001 – the long-term trend continues to be an upward one.

Domestic tourism

It is important to note that the data above relates to international travel and the figures do not include the vast number of people taking trips within their own countries. Often, in fact, much higher levels of domestic tourism take place. Here, Americans lead the field, with over 3.1 billion domestic trips in 2006, compared to 66 million international outbound

Table 5.1 A profile of international tourist arrivals and receipts, 1950–2007.

Year	Arrivals (m)	Receipts (US $bn)
1950	25.3	2.1
1960	69.3	6.9
1970	165.8	17.9
1980	278.2	106.5
1990	445.8	272.9
1995	544.9	410.8
2000	685.5	476.4
2001	683.8	464.4
2002	702.8	482.3
2003	689.8	524.2
2004	764.4	633.0
2005	803.4	676.5
2006	847.3	742.0
2007 (P)	903.2	855.9

Note: Excludes international fares. (P) = provisional.
Source: UNWTO, *Yearbook of Tourism Statistics*, UNWTO.

Table 5.2 A comparison of domestic trips with international tourist arrivals (2006).

Country	Domestic trips (m)	International arrivals (m)	Ratio of domestic trips to international arrivals
India	445.7	4.3	103.2
USA	3079.5	52.5	58.7
Japan	341.3	7.1	47.8
Indonesia	225.7	5.1	44.3
Brazil	225.0	6.2	36.2
Selected other countries			
China	1196.2	53.5	22.4
Australia	71.5	5.5	13.1
Germany	209.3	23.6	8.9
UK	125.8	31.2	4.0
Austria	9.8	20.0	0.5

Source: Based on Euromonitor, 2008.

trips. India, however, is the fastest-growing market for domestic tourism, with predictions of more than 1 billion domestic trips taking place by 2011. For many countries, domestic trips far exceed the level of arrivals from international tourists[3] (see Table 5.2). It is important to consider, however, that the spending of international tourists may be higher than that of domestic tourists.

Trends in international travel

As controls over the freedom of movement of populations in many countries are gradually lifted, many are seeking the opportunity to travel outside their own borders for the first time,

Table 5.3 Leading tourism-generating countries, 2006 (based on provisional tourism expenditure).

Position	Country	Expenditure (US$ billion)
1	Germany	74.8
2	USA	72.0
3	UK	63.1
4	France	32.2
5	Japan	26.9
6	China	24.3
7	Italy	23.1
8	Canada	20.5
9	Russian Federation	18.8
10	South Korea	18.2

Source: UNWTO, *Yearbook of Tourism Statistics*, UNWTO 2007.

not least residents of China, now the sixth biggest generator of overseas tourist expenditure. The UNWTO therefore continues to take an optimistic view of the long term, estimating that international tourism trips will continue to increase for the foreseeable future.

International tourism is generated, for the most part, within the nations of Europe, North America and Japan – the result of low prices, frequent flights and large, relatively wealthy populations (see Table 5.3). Japan in particular has been growing strongly as a tourism-generating country in recent years, due to its wealth and a growing willingness on the part of its population to take holidays. Traditionally, the Japanese work ethic militated against their taking all the holidays to which they are entitled, but with government encouragement and changes in attitude to work and loyalty to their firms, the Japanese have taken to travelling abroad in greater numbers and for longer periods of time. As a result, Japan is now fifth among the top ten generating countries which together are responsible for well over half the total expenditure on foreign travel.

It is interesting to note the dominance of the top three countries, which far exceed the spending levels of the rest in this list. While the half-dozen countries currently in fourth to ninth places have held positions in the top ten for several years, a new entry to this list is South Korea, which has edged out the Netherlands. The growth in the South Korean market can be attributed to a strengthening economy, which has helped to stimulate a strong business travel market. Furthermore, alongside economic growth, increased leisure time and continued enthusiasm for study abroad have fuelled expenditure on international travel. As the Chinese gain greater freedom of movement, there are expectations that its market will become more important for many destinations. With almost 40 million departures in 2006 (107,000 of whom came to Britain), predictions are that, given existing conditions, the number of Chinese travelling will have doubled by 2011.[4]

Looking at the flow of international tourism over the long term, one can conclude that the tourism business is surprisingly resilient. Whatever short-term problems emerge – acts of terrorism, medical emergencies such as SARS and bird flu, the 2004 Asian tsunami and flooding in places such as New Orleans following Hurricane Katrina in 2005 and in areas of the UK in the summer of 2007 – tourists eventually return in ever greater numbers.

Tourist destinations

While Western Europe continues to dominate, Eastern Europe has seen a growth in popularity, as expansion of the European Union and changes in the Schengen Agreement have made travel in this area easier. Also, China has experienced a rapid rise in popularity,

Table 5.4 Leading tourism-receiving countries, 2006 (based on provisional international tourist arrivals in millions) and their tourism receipts.

Position	Country	Arrivals (millions)	Receipts (US$ billion)	Per capita receipts (US$)
1	France	79.1	42.9	542.35
2	Spain	58.5	51.1	873.50
3	USA	51.1	85.7	1677.10
4	China	49.6	33.9	683.47
5	Italy	41.1	38.1	927.01
6	UK	30.7	33.7	1097.72
7	Germany	23.6	32.8	1389.83
8	Mexico	21.4	12.2	570.09
9	Austria	20.3	16.7	822.66
10	Russian Federation	20.2	7.0	34.67

Source: UNWTO, 'Tourism highlights', UNWTO, 2007.

and some researchers suggested that in the period 2006/7 it surpassed the USA to become the third most visited nation, with over 53 million visitors.[5]

Simply looking at receipts, though, will not give a sound picture of the value of tourism to an economy. It is important to consider how many tourists make up the total receipts (see Table 5.4). The countries with the highest per capita receipts are generally those where prices are highest and include countries such as Sweden, Denmark and Japan. In economic terms, the financial value of tourism to a country may be more important than the number of tourists it receives. It is vital, therefore, that the average spends of tourists from different countries are assessed, which may be influenced by the average length of time tourists from a particular country stay in a country and their average daily spend.

It is also important to take account of factors likely to lead to the growth or decline of tourism from each country. The potential for growth is high for those living in Eastern Europe, whose income, for the most part, is rising strongly since the fall of communism. The entry of several of these countries into the EU in 2004 has already boosted tourism in both directions within Europe.

The potential of Japan remains high also, as only a small proportion of its population currently travels abroad and those who do are relatively free spenders. This is partly accounted for by their high spend on shopping and souvenirs for friends and relatives.

In spite of the high revenues generated from Americans travelling abroad, only a small minority of the population actually possess a passport as most American tourists tend to travel to adjacent countries that, until recently, did not require them to carry passports. Also, because of the size and diversity of their own landscape, many are content to take holidays within their own country.

So the *propensity* to take holidays abroad is another important characteristic to take into account. The propensity to take foreign holidays varies considerably within Europe, too. It is high among the Scandinavians – no doubt this is due in part to the long winters and lack of sunshine – while only a quarter of Italians share this desire for foreign travel. Italians are surprisingly unadventurous in their travelling, with nearly half of those travelling on holiday being content to return to the same resort, and even the same hotel, every year for a decade. The French, too, prefer to travel within their own country, often to second homes in the countryside, rather than venture abroad. Although Britons have a reputation for travelling abroad, a third of the population takes no holidays at all during the year (but not necessarily the same third every year).

We should also recognize that, while tourism expenditure in aggregate will be highest for wealthy countries having large populations, the high levels of disposable income among the populations of smaller nations with a significant proportion of wealthy residents, such as Switzerland or Luxembourg, will tend to lead to higher levels of participation in international tourism. Where international borders are close to places of residence – as is the case with Switzerland and Luxembourg – this will significantly increase the propensity to travel abroad.

Propensity to travel

To help understand the travel habits of particular nations, it is possible to calculate the **travel propensity** – that is, the percentage of the population taking trips. This can be considered in two dimensions – the **net travel propensity** and the **gross travel propensity**.

Net travel propensity reflects the percentage of the population that has travelled for at least one trip (though many will have taken more). As some of the population will not have taken a trip at all, the net travel propensity will be less than 100 per cent.

Gross travel propensity reflects the total number of trips taken in relation to the total population. In areas, such as Western Europe, where the local population may take several trips, the gross travel propensity may exceed 100 per cent (as those who have been on multiple trips counterbalance those who have not travelled at all).

Example

UK travel propensity

In the case of net travel propensity, it is estimated that, 'In any given year more than a third of the UK population still does not take a holiday at all'.[6]

The gross travel propensity of the British to take a holiday – that is, the ratio of trips taken out of the total population – is high (see Table 5.5). The total number of trips is 195.79 million and, for a population of 60.59 million, this provides a gross travel propensity of 323 per cent. The propensity for international travel is lower at 115 per cent.

Table 5.5 Trips taken by the UK population, 2006.

Population (million)	Domestic trips (million)	International trips (million)
60.59	126.29	69.5

Source: *Social Trends*, 38, 2008, Office of National Statistics, 'United Kingdom Tourism Survey 2008', VisitBritain, VisitScotland, VisitWales and the Northern Ireland Tourist Board.

Other factors affecting the economic value of tourism

While there are many factors that motivate people to travel abroad, a major one is likely to be the relative cost compared with their income. Since greater demand also leads to lower prices, with transport and accommodation costs falling for each additional person booked, there is a direct relationship between cost, price and demand (see Figure 5.1). This helps to explain the vicious price wars in the travel industry, designed to capture market share and increase numbers, which have been so much a feature of competition in the travel industry over the past twenty years.

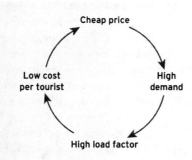

Figure 5.1 The relationship between cost, price and demand.

The continued popularity of the no frills airlines has seen an increased range of routes being offered, opening up low-cost travel to places in Eastern Europe as well as islands such as Malta. This trend is likely to continue, unless sharply curtailed by rising fuel prices or the imposition of fuel taxes to offset pollution.

Other factors to take into account include attitudes to the use of leisure time. In the USA, some 30 per cent of the workforce take less than half the holiday time to which they are entitled – and this is in a country where the average paid holiday is still only two to three weeks compared with the four to five weeks now standard throughout Europe. The Japanese, as we have seen, seldom take their full entitlement. With average holidays of 17 days, they typically take only 9.5 days. Even in the UK, roughly a quarter of the working population fails to take its full entitlement.

The value of economic data

Gathering data on tourists is a vital task for the government of a country as it is vital to its own national tourist office and the providers of tourism services. Governments need to know the contribution that tourism makes to the economy in terms of income, employment, investment and the balance of payments. Concern about regional development requires that these statistics be sufficiently refined to allow them to be broken down by region. Governments will also wish to compare their tourism performance with that of other countries, as well as to establish how well they are doing regarding attracting tourists to the country over a period of time.

Tourism organizations, whether in the public or the private sector, need such data to enable them to forecast what will happen in the future. This means identifying trends in the market, patterns of growth and changing demand for destinations, facilities or types of holiday.

On the basis of this knowledge, future planning can be undertaken. The public sector will make recommendations and decisions regarding the **infrastructure** and **superstructure** needed to support growth. Infrastructure will include, for example, the building of new airports and seaport terminals or the expansion of existing ones, the provision of new or improved roads to growing destinations and the improvement of other services, such as public utilities, including water and electricity, that will be needed to cope with the expected expansion of tourism. Some of these plans may take many years to implement. For example, the discussions surrounding the building of a fifth terminal at London's Heathrow airport took place over more than a decade, far longer than the time taken to actually construct the terminal itself. Furthermore, congestion at London airports has encouraged carriers to switch air traffic to alternative airports. Schiphol in the Netherlands is one such airport that has actively promoted itself as an alternative to Heathrow, using the hub-and-spoke system, given that it offers services to around a dozen UK airports.

Superstructure comprises the tourist amenities needed – hotels, restaurants, shops and other services that tourists take for granted when they visit. It cannot necessarily be assumed that these services will be provided by developers in the private sector. If a new destination is being developed, there will be a degree of risk involved while the destination becomes established, so developers may be reluctant to invest in such projects as hotels until there is proven demand at the destination. Governments or local authorities can themselves undertake the construction of hotels, as often occurs in developing countries, or they can encourage hotel construction by underwriting costs or providing subsidies of some kind until the destination becomes established. Similarly, private companies can use the statistics that demonstrate growth or market change, extending or adapting their products to meet the changing needs of the marketplace.

To show how this information can be used, let us take the example of a destination such as London, which attracts a high volume of overseas visitors. The flow of those visitors will be affected by a great many different factors. For example, if tourists can purchase more pounds sterling for their own currency or air fares to the destination have fallen or a major event, such as an international sports event – the Olympics – is being organized – all these factors will encourage tourists to visit the city.

Negative factors also have an effect. Terrorist activity in the capital (as in July 2005) affected decisions to come to Britain, while other global events – war in Iraq and SARS in 2003, avian flu in 2004/2005 – all influence travel plans. US tourists are particularly sensitive to the threat of terrorism and will revert to holidaying at home if they sense that the risk of foreign travel is increasing. Negative first impressions, such as air pollution in the city, extensive littering, a decaying and overcrowded public transport system, even large numbers of homeless people on the streets, can all affect tourism adversely, tourists deciding to go elsewhere or recommending to their friends that they do so.

Example

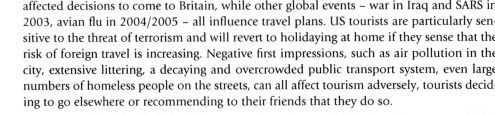

The influence of exchange rates – a UK example

Recessions may hit countries to different extents, so that, in one year, the forecast might be for a reduced number of tourists from the USA, but a growth in the number from Japan.

In the third quarter of 2000, the pound fell sharply against the dollar, while remaining relatively strong against European currencies. This encouraged Americans to travel to Britain and the British to visit the Continent, while tourists from countries such as Germany and France were dissuaded from coming to Britain and, similarly, fewer Britons visited the USA.
In 2004/2005, however, the dollar weakened against both sterling and the euro, increasing travel from Britain and the Continent to the USA (and, incidentally, further heightening the demand for second homes in Florida for the British). In 2007/2008, the dollar again weakened against the pound (at times reaching a rate of US$2 for £1). However, 2008 also saw sterling weaken by about 20 per cent on the euro, making Europe a more expensive proposition for British travellers, and, by the autumn of that year, against a background of threatening recession, sterling was falling fast against both the dollar and the euro.

This uncertainty about currency movements makes forward planning difficult, adding another element of risk to product pricing, although this can be offset to some extent by the forward purchasing of foreign currencies. If Britain does eventually join the euro, one benefit will be that it will help to stabilize their travel business with Europe. It will also allow British travellers to share with their counterparts in other EU countries the benefits of using a single currency across several countries, leading to a substantial saving on foreign exchange when calculating the costs of a holiday abroad. Such savings are less likely to be welcomed by those in the industry who provide foreign exchange facilities, however!

Companies and tourist offices will have to take all of these factors into account when drawing up their promotional campaigns – and may need to consider employing staff with the appropriate language skills to deal with any new incoming markets. On the basis of the forecasts made, organizations must decide where they will advertise, to whom and with what theme.

International tourism depends on more than merely the economic behaviour of tourists, however. As we noted in the previous chapter, it is also influenced by motivators arising from the tourists' efforts to meet their psychological or sociological needs.

The economic impacts of tourism

This chapter examines the economic effects of tourism and how these are measured. As in other industries, tourism affects the economy of those areas – whether regions, countries or continents – where it takes place. These are known as tourist **destinations**, or **receiving areas**, and many become dependent on an inflow of tourism to sustain their economy. This is especially true of developing countries, some of which are largely or almost totally dependent on tourism.

The areas from which the tourists come to visit these destinations are known as **generating areas** and, of course, as the tourists are taking their money with them to spend in other places, this represents a net loss of revenue for the generating area and a gain for the receiving area. We can say that incoming tourist spend is an **export**, while outgoing tourist spend is an **import** (as the tourist is buying services from overseas).

The flow of tourists between generating and receiving areas can be measured in four distinct ways. We must examine the effect on **income**, **employment**, the area's **balance of payments** and **investment and development**. Let us look at each of these in turn.

Income

Income is generated from pay and salaries, interest, rent and profits. In a labour-intensive industry such as tourism, the greatest proportion is likely to be derived from pay and salaries for those working in jobs either directly serving the needs of tourists or benefiting

Example

The Côte d'Azur

This resort area by the French Mediterranean sea satisfies most of the above criteria for generating a great deal of income, attracting not only many overseas visitors for a fairly long season (even through the winter some tourists will be attracted to the milder climate) but also bringing in many domestic tourists from other areas of France.

A number of upmarket resorts in the area, such as Nice, Cannes, Antibes, St Tropez and Juan les Pins, provide a good range of relatively expensive hotels. There are also expensive shops and restaurants, casinos, nightclubs and discos where the high-spend tourists can be relieved of their money, thus providing income for local businesses. There are opportunities for water-based activities, such as yachting or fishing, with marinas to attract the wealthy motor yacht owners. There are also numerous attractions nearby that bring in the day excursionists by coach or car. Finally, the area is also well served with conference and exhibition halls, which attract high-spend business tourists. All these services are labour-intensive and, thus, invaluable for providing local employment.

indirectly from the tourists' expenditure. Income will be greater in those areas that generate large numbers of tourists, where visitors tend to stay for longer periods, where the destination attracts an upmarket or more free-spending clientele and where there are many opportunities to spend.

It is essential to recognize that, while income may be greatest where levels of pay are high and there is relatively little unemployment in the area, tourism may in fact be of greater importance in those areas where there are few other opportunities for employment. Thus, tourism is the main income generator for one-third of the developing nations,[7] but is also a major income generator in the Western world. In Britain, to take one example, tourism is of prime importance in areas where there is little manufacturing industry, such as in the Scottish Highlands, western Wales and Cornwall. While tourism jobs are often seen as low-paid and seasonal, many are neither seasonal nor temporary. As to low-paid jobs, one must take into account that, without tourism, many workers would have no source of income at all, given that tourism often takes place in areas where there is little alternative work, forcing workers to move away from the area.

Income is also generated from interest, rent and profits of tourism businesses. These could include, for example, the interest paid on loans to an airline in order to buy aircraft or rent paid to a landowner for a car park or campsite near the sea. We must also count taxation on tourism activities, such as sales tax (for example, VAT), room taxes on hotel bills, duty and taxation on petrol used by tourists and other direct forms of taxation that countries may choose to levy on tourists to raise additional public income. In Austria, to give one example, there is a *Kurtaxe*, which is imposed on accommodation to raise money for the local authority. Equally, most countries levy a departure tax on all passengers travelling by air, while in the USA airline taxes are levied on both departing and arriving travellers.

Example

Tourist taxes

The Czech Republic was admitted to the EU in 2004. As a direct result, it raised VAT on restaurant meals from 5 per cent to 19 per cent; VAT on hotel accommodation also increased to the same level in the following year. The industry has argued against common VAT policies in the EU, on the grounds that it would tend to discourage international tourists, but it provides governments with a substantial tax bonus.

In 2008, the Australian government announced an increase in departure tax, expected to raise nearly half a billion dollars. The local tourism industry highlighted its concern that the tourists were being treated by government as a source of extra income, at a time when a strong Australian dollar was already impacting on the industry negatively.

In Canada, the introduction of an air travellers' security charge in 2002 increased the tax revenue earned by the government – in 2006, more than CAN$19 billion was raised. Over half of this came from taxes on products, while just under a quarter of the revenue came from taxes on income (from employment and business profits): 'Government tourism revenue rose at an annual average rate of 4.5 per cent during this period, while spending by tourists increased at an average rate of 3.8 per cent.'[8]

The sum of all incomes in a country is called the **national income** and the importance of tourism to a country's economy can be measured by looking at the proportion of national income that is created by tourism. The National Tourism Administration of the People's Republic of China forecast that, by 2020, tourism income would exceed US$439 billion, accounting for about 11 per cent of GDP.[9] Some regions of the world, particularly the Caribbean countries, are heavily dependent on the income from tourism (see Table 5.6). Some might see this as an unhealthy overdependence on one rather volatile industry.

Table 5.6 Contribution of travel and tourism to GNP, 2006.

Country	Percentage
Antigua and Barbuda	76.5
Anguilla	69.6
Aruba	69.3
Bahamas	50.8
Barbados	40.7
St Lucia	41.6

Source: WTTC, 'World key facts at a glance', WTTC, 2008.

Attempts at measuring the impact of tourism are always difficult because it is not easy to distinguish the spend by tourists from the spend by others, in restaurants or shops, for example. In resorts, even such businesses as laundromats – which we would not normally associate with the tourism industry – might be highly dependent on the tourist spend where, for instance, a large number of visitors are camping, caravanning or in self-catering facilities.

Furthermore, tourism's contribution to the income of an area is enhanced by a phenomenon known as the **tourism income multiplier**. This arises because money spent by tourists in the area will be re-spent by recipients, augmenting the total.

Tourism multiplier

The multiplier is the factor by which tourist spend is increased in this process of re-spending. This is easiest to demonstrate by way of the following fictitious example.

Example

The tourism income multiplier

A number of tourists visit Highjinks on Sea, spending £1000 in hotels and other facilities there. This amount is received as income by the hoteliers and owners of the facilities, who, after paying their taxes and saving some of the income, spend the rest. Some of what they spend goes on buying items imported into the area, but the rest goes to shopkeepers, suppliers and other producers inside the area. These people, in turn, pay their taxes, save some money and spend the rest.

From the £1000 of tourist spend, let us assume that the average rate of taxation is 20 per cent and that people are saving on average 10 per cent of their gross income, so are left to spend 70 per cent on goods and services (for this example, this would be £700). Let us further assume that, of this £700, the tourist has spent £200 on goods and services imported from other areas, while the remaining £500 is spent on locally produced goods and services, which is money that is retained within the local community. The original £1000 spent by the tourists will then circulate in the local community as shown in Figure 5.2, in the category 'First circulation', the arrows shown in black.

Of the £500 spent within the community, some will go to tourism businesses, that, in turn, will make payments to their local suppliers for such items as food. The shopkeepers or restaurateurs then pay their employees, who, in turn, shop in other shops locally, although some of what they purchase will have been brought into the region from outside.

This second circulation (The arrows shown in red) highlights the further spend by the recipients, including taxation (again at 20 per cent), savings (10 per cent) and leakages due to the purchase of imports.

Once again, the income received by employees and local businesses will circulate through the economy (third circulation, the arrows shown in blue) and so the cycle goes on, with a declining level of expenditure at each level of circulation.

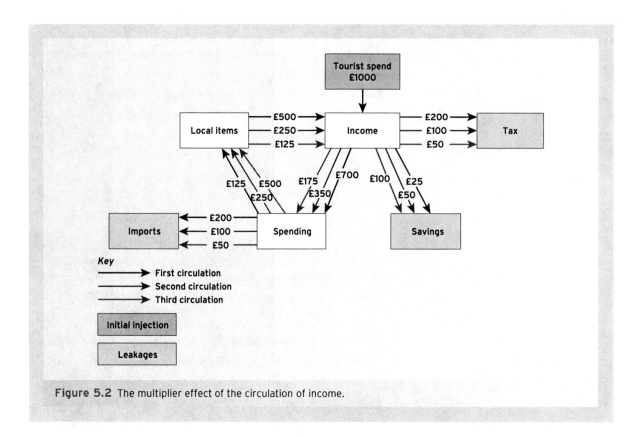

Figure 5.2 The multiplier effect of the circulation of income.

The money spent directly by tourists is considered to be the **direct income** received by a destination. This spend goes to tourism businesses, which provide tourists with the goods and services they require for their holiday (for example, accommodation, meals, guided tours). These tourism businesses will then spend some of this earned income obtaining goods and services from their suppliers, which allows them to fulfil their obligations to the tourists. For example, a tourism business providing guided tours may have to pay entry fees to an attraction or the salary for a guide. This secondary spend of income is termed **indirect income**. At this stage, some spend – such as residents spending their pay on food in a local supermarket or a visit to the cinema – may occur. Such spend is known as **induced income**, available as a result of direct or indirect tourist expenditure.

Example

The effect of leakages on the tourism income multiplier

Each time the money is circulated in this way, some will be lost to the area. For example, taxes paid are transmitted outside the area, some savings, similarly, may be removed from the area and some of the spend has gone on paying for goods imported into the area from other regions of the country or even abroad.

Expenditures that mean money is lost to other areas are known as **leakages** from the system. Leakages in this sense can therefore be regional or national, the latter being a loss of revenue to the country as a whole.

So far, how much income has been created? From Figure 5.2, we can calculate this by considering the money entering the field marked 'income'; it is £1,000 + £500 + £250 + £125 + . . . A progression is developing and, by adding up all the figures (until the circulations become so small that the additional income is negligible) or by using the appropriate mathematical formula, we will find that the total sum is £2000. The original injection of £1000 by tourists visiting the area has multiplied by a factor of 2 to produce an income of £2000.

It is possible to forecast the value of the multiplier if one knows the proportion of leakages in the local economy. In the example above, tax was 20/100ths of the original income, savings were 10/100ths of income and imports were 20/100ths of income. Total leakages, therefore, amounted to 50/100ths, or half the original income. The multiplier can be found by applying the formula:

$$\text{Multiplier} = \frac{1}{\text{Proportion of leakages}}$$

In the example given, the multiplier was 1/0.5, or, 2.

Leakages

So, in an economy with a high proportion of leakages – such as high tax rates (although we must remember that the government may choose to reinvest this tax money in the local economy, so much of it may not be lost for all time) or where many of the goods demanded by consumers are imported – the tourism income multiplier may be quite low and then the economy will not benefit greatly from tourism. Local hotels may also be foreign-owned, so profits achieved are then transmitted to the hotel chain's head office and lost to the area. This might be true of other tourist facilities in the area and even local ground-handling agents or coach operators may be owned by companies based elsewhere, leading to further losses in the multiplier effect.

If, alternatively, many firms are in the hands of locals and leakages of these kinds are minimized, the multiplier effect may be quite high and then tourism will contribute far more than the amount originally spent by the tourists themselves.

The principal reasons for leakages include:

- cost of imported goods, especially food and drink
- foreign exchange costs of imports for the development of tourist facilities
- remittance of profits abroad
- remittance of pay to expatriates
- management fees or royalties for franchises
- payments to overseas carriers and travel companies
- costs of overseas promotion
- additional expenditure on imports resulting from the earnings of those benefiting from tourism.

Example

National tourism income multiplier

Many studies have been undertaken of the tourism income multiplier in different areas, ranging from individual resorts, such as Eastbourne and Edinburgh in the UK, to entire countries, such as Barbados and Fiji. In most cases, the multiplier has varied between 1 and 2.5 (estimates have put it at about 1.7 for Britain as a whole and around 1.2–1.5 for individual towns and regions in the UK), although, in the case of some destinations in the developing world that depend heavily on outside investment and must import much of the food and other commodities demanded by tourists, the figure may be well below 1. The figure for Barbados, for instance, has been estimated at 0.60. Leakages in Western developed nations are generally estimated at around 10 per cent of tourism income, while in developing economies with strong tourism dependency, such as Fiji, the Cook Islands, Mauritius and the Virgin Islands, estimates suggest that imports consume between 36 and 56 per cent of gross tourism receipts.

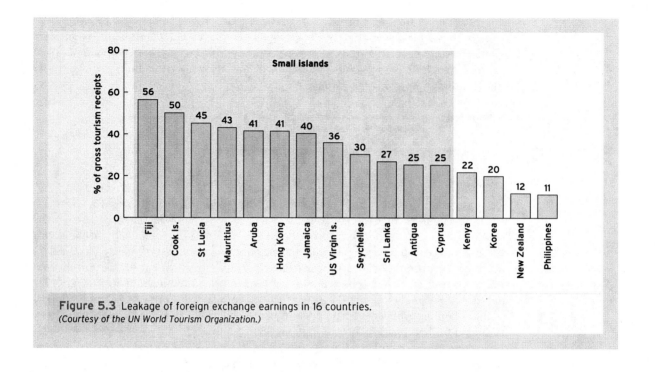

Figure 5.3 Leakage of foreign exchange earnings in 16 countries.
(Courtesy of the UN World Tourism Organization.)

Employment

The WTTC anticipates that employment in tourism will rise from 238.3 million jobs in 2008, accounting for 8.4 per cent of total employment, to more than 296 million jobs by 2018.[10] The industry's importance to many economies as a generator of employment is therefore clear.

As noted, several of the leading tourist destinations in the world are developing countries and, in some tourism-dependent economies such as the Caribbean, as many as 25 per cent of all jobs are associated with the industry. Estimates suggest that some three million tourism jobs will be created in the ten nations that joined the European Union in 2004, most of which are expected to be in Poland and Hungary.

Jobs are created in travel agencies, tour operators and other intermediaries who supply tourist services in both the generating and destination areas. Transport companies such as airlines also employ staff to serve tourists in both areas, but the bulk of employment is in the destination country. The jobs range from hotel managers to deckchair attendants, from excursion-booking clerks to cleaners employed in the stately homes that are open to the public or maintenance staff who keep the rides going at leisure centres or theme parks in the resort.

Many of these jobs are seasonal or part-time, so tourism's contribution to full-time employment is considerably less than the total employment figures may suggest. While this is a criticism of the industry in economic terms – and one that has resulted in large sums of money being spent in an effort to lengthen the tourist season in many resorts – it is important to realize that these jobs are often being created in areas where there is little alternative employment. It is also worth making the point that many of the jobs attract those who wish to work seasonally, such as students seeking jobs as resort representatives during the summer or householders who wish to open their house for summer periods only as bed-and-breakfast establishments.

For countries that are major receiving destinations or enjoy a strong domestic demand for tourism, employment figures will be far higher. On balance, tourism as a form of employment is economically beneficial, although efforts must be made to create more full-time jobs in the industry. The extent to which tourism benefits employment can be seen when it is appreciated that, given the figure quoted earlier, roughly 1 job in 12 in the world is directly ascribed to tourism. Tourism is considered by many to be the largest industry in the world and it is believed to be growing the fastest.

Just as tourism is globally important, so it is important for regions within an economy. The multiplier that affects income in a region affects employment in the same way. If tourists stay at a destination, jobs are directly created by the tourism industry there. Those workers and their families resident in the neighbourhood must also buy goods and services locally, their families require education and need medical care. This, in turn, gives rise to jobs in shops, schools and hospitals to serve their needs. The value of the employment multiplier is likely to be broadly similar to that of the tourism income multiplier, assuming that jobs with average rates of pay are created.

Recent developments in technology however, are threatening labour opportunities in tourism. For example, computer reservation systems (CRS) are rapidly replacing manual reservation systems and, as a result, many booking clerk jobs in large companies such as airlines, tour operators and hotel chains are disappearing. Similarly, the trend towards online bookings via the Internet threatens jobs in travel agencies and suppliers. Call centres are replacing branch shops and, increasingly, these are set up abroad, in countries with low levels of pay, such as India. Fortunately for the future of the industry, at the 'sharp end' – where the tourist seeks a high level of personal service at the destination – the nature of the tourist experience should ensure that technology cannot replace many jobs (although, as discussed in Chapter 18, even the key job of resort representative has been sharply curtailed in recent years). The success of tourism in a country however, will, in part, be dependent on an adequate supply of skilled labour with the right motivation towards employment in the industry and appropriate training.

Example

Tourism employment in Britain

Employment in the tourism industry in Britain is often considered to have a poor image. Turnover of labour is high (attributable to relatively poor pay and working conditions compared with many other fields of business). Training, while it has improved considerably over recent years, still lags behind that of many other countries. Also, attitudes towards working in a 'service industry', where many people in Britain still equate service with servility, make recruitment of good staff difficult. Furthermore, as many as nine out of ten tourism jobs are in small- to medium-size enterprises (SMEs), with turnover lower than £40 million. The European Commission defines these as micro enterprises if employees number fewer than 11, small if between 11 and 50, and medium-sized if between 51 and 250. Firms at the lower end of this scale tend to have fewer qualified staff, fewer training facilities and poorer management, as well as paying less, thus making careers in tourism less attractive to high-flyers and impacting on their ability to compete with other organizations.

Balance of payments

In a national context, tourism may have a major influence on a country's balance of payments. International tourists are buying tourist services in another country and those payments are noted in a country's accounts as 'invisibles'. A British resident going on holiday to Spain will be making an invisible payment to that country, which is a debit on Britain's balance of payments account and a credit to Spain's balance of payments.

Similarly, the money spent by an American visitor to Britain is credited to Britain's balance of payments, becoming an invisible receipt for Britain, while it is debited as a payment against the American balance of payments. It is important to remember at this point that, as mentioned earlier, the outflow of British money in the form of spending abroad by British residents counts as an *import*, while the inflow of foreign holidaymakers' money spent in Britain counts as an *export*.

The total value of receipts minus the total payments made during the year represents a country's **balance of payments on the tourism account**. This is part of the country's entire invisible balance, which will include other services such as banking, insurance and transport. This latter item is, of course, also important for tourism. If an American visitor to Britain decides to travel on a British airline, then a contribution is made to Britain's invisible receipts, while the fare of a Briton going on holiday to Spain flying with Iberia Airlines is credited to Spain and represents a payment on the British balance of payments account. Of course, with the demise of national airlines and the growth of global integration, it may no longer be the case that the leading airlines will in the future be so clearly identified with their country of origin and, if the majority shareholding is abroad, ultimately the profits, if not the earnings, will find their way to other countries in the form of leakages.

Some countries, particularly developing countries, cannot afford to have a negative balance of payments as this is a drain on their financial resources and, in such a case, they may be forced to impose restrictions either on the movement of their own residents or the amount of money that they may take abroad with them. Some countries may suffer severe deficiencies in their tourism balance of payments, which can be sometimes offset by manufacturing exports. Germany and Japan have in the past been examples of countries heavily in deficit on the tourism balance of payments, but which have nevertheless enjoyed a surplus overall through the sale of goods overseas. With both countries now finding it increasingly difficult to compete against low-pay economies in the industrial sector, they are now seeking to boost their own inbound tourism to compensate for this net outflow on the tourism account. By contrast, Spain and Italy both enjoy a strong surplus on their tourism balance of payments as they are popular receiving countries with fewer residents going abroad for their own holidays.

Example

Tourism balance of payments for the UK

Throughout the 1970s, Britain enjoyed a surplus on its tourism balance of payments, reaching a peak during 1977, the year of the Queen's Silver Jubilee. Since then, however, spending by British tourists travelling abroad has increased faster than receipts the country has gained from overseas tourists, with the result that, as we have seen, there has been a net, and steadily increasing, deficit since 1986 (see Figure 5.4).

For a country such as Britain, which has experienced a steady decline in terms of trade (amount of our goods sold abroad, compared with the amounts of goods that we import), it is important to try to redress the balance by a better showing on our invisible exports. As can be seen, however, tourism is not producing a net gain for Britain, which is a concern. The government has attempted to resolve this deficit by encouraging more visitors to come to Britain via the marketing efforts of the national tourist boards or more Britons to take domestic holidays. However, the lure of the sun is a strong magnet for British tourists, so the tourist boards may find it easier to attract the overseas tourist to Britain.

International Business

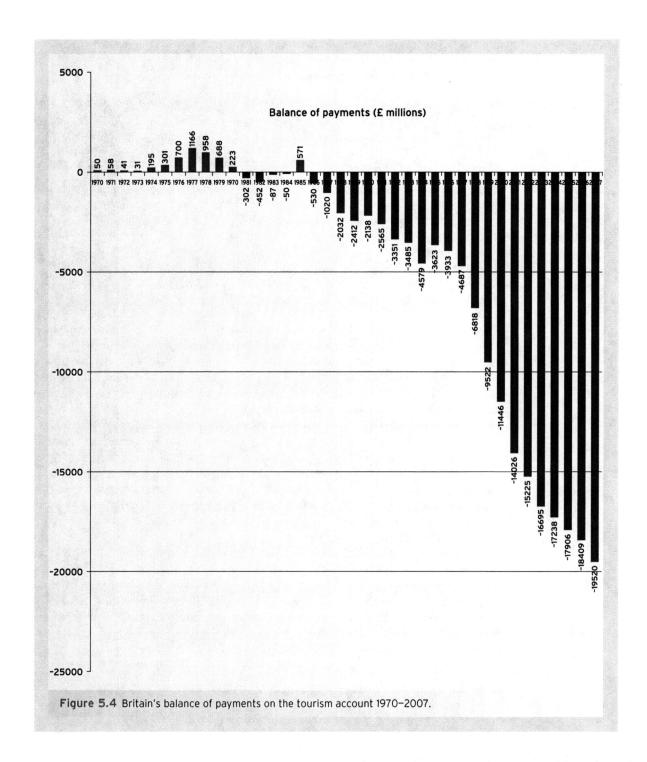

Figure 5.4 Britain's balance of payments on the tourism account 1970–2007.

Investment and development

One factor helping to determine the success or otherwise of tourism in a region is the level of investment, whether private or public, in the industry. Unfortunately, tourism – indeed, leisure generally – are seen by private investors as high-risk investments. Banks are reluctant to lend money for tourism projects and developers are not very willing to take investment risks. This often means that tourism cannot take off until the public sector is prepared to 'kick-start' the economy – that is, invest risk capital in order to encourage the development of tourism. This might take the form of grants or low-interest loans to private developers or, in some more centrally operated economies, it may mean that government itself builds and runs facilities such as hotels for tourists.

Investment is something of a chicken and egg situation. There may be an unwillingness to invest until a flow of tourists to the area can be demonstrated, but the area will attract few tourists until they can see evidence of there being sufficient facilities to attract them. Once tourism is shown to be successful, however, private developers or government agencies are often willing to invest even further in the area – in short, success breeds success. Economists refer to this as the **accelerator concept**.

Areas that have benefited from this phenomenon include Spain and the Mexican East Coast in the 1960s, Hawaii, Tunisia and the Languedoc-Roussillon region of France in the 1970s and Turkey and Greece in the 1980s and 1990s. Naturally, the attraction of these regions to tourists will also attract other industries, which will recognize the benefits to be gained from a large inflow of consumers and a pleasant working environment for staff. Resorts such as Bournemouth and Brighton in Britain or the fast-expanding resorts of Florida in the USA and the Gold Coast in Queensland, Australia, have all benefited from this phenomenon.

Unfortunately, the relationship between growth in tourism and economic development is uneven, owing to other complicating factors such as the rate of inflation, the ability of an area to diversify and attitudes to work among the local labour force. Often, key workers are brought in from outside the area in cases where the local labour force is either unwilling or unable to adapt to the needs of the tourism industry. This may lead to leakages as pay is repatriated, thus reducing the economic benefit to the area. Consequently, the risk attending investment remains high, as it does in many other areas of the economy.

Balancing economic diversification with overdependency on tourism

For some countries or even regions, such as rural areas or declining industrial areas, tourism may offer an opportunity to diversify the economy, increasing the variety of empowerment opportunities available for the local population. In addition to this, any downturn in one particular sector may be offset by an increase or stability in other sectors.

An example of this is the city of Bradford in the UK, which sought to encourage tourism to the city when it suffered a decline in the textile and engineering industries – the traditional mainstays of its economy. An initiative by the local government in the mid-1980s saw the introduction of initiatives and funding to encourage tourism to the city. By the turn of the millennium, the number of hotel bednights sold annually in the city had quadrupled, to over 370,000.[12]

In some rural areas, tourism is being amalgamated with farming businesses to provide additional income as well as new products for an area. Farm tourism, or **agritourism** (discussed at greater length in Chapter 9), is just one form of rural tourism that can help to bring income and jobs to remote areas.

Such a reliance on attracting visitors must be placed in context, however. While tourism has been used as a catalyst for expanding economies, perhaps in less developed countries or regions, a concern raised is that over-reliance on this one sector can bring difficulties. A significant downturn in the tourist demand, perhaps through no fault of the destination, or a recession in the home market, may reduce tourist numbers, leaving the destination economically vulnerable. For destinations where tourism is an important component of the economy, attracting tourists from many different source regions as well as different market segments may help to spread the risk. This will not guard against problems experienced in the local tourism area, however. An example of this was seen when foot and mouth disease effectively closed many rural areas of England for most of 2001. While cities across England could still be visited, estimates suggested that this had cost the tourism industry more than £3.3 billion.[13]

While tourism is valuable to many economies, often, as noted, acting as a catalyst for attracting inward investment, the pressures it places on the economy should also be acknowledged and it should not be relied on to the exclusion of other opportunities.

Inflationary pressures

While tourism can bring money into a tourism destination, creating job opportunities and wealth, the demand for resources (including land and labour) can push the cost of those resources higher as that very demand creates an imbalance in terms of supply. As prices of those resources rise, it can create an inflationary effect – employees seek higher levels of pay in order to be able to afford the higher costs of accessing land or property, food and entertainment and so on. Ultimately, some of the local population may be unable to afford the increased costs and become excluded from accessing their own community's resources.

Example

Is tourism to blame for inflation in Argentina?

Following devaluation of the peso in 2002, Argentina experienced growth in international tourist numbers as the depressed value of the local currency helped to make Argentina a more affordable destination than previously. By 2006, visitor numbers had increased by more than 120 per cent. This increase in demand was beneficial for the country as it provided employment, brought in foreign money and encouraged inward investment. It was estimated that more than $3.61 billion was spent by foreign tourists in 2005, amounting to 7 per cent of GDP.

Alongside this apparent success, however, was a concern – inflation. The increased demand led to price rises for products such as hotel rooms. Furthermore, the pressure on supply meant that there was a scarcity of rooms and prices went up – both of which effectively crowded out the domestic market. Furthermore, tourism businesses themselves were having to deal with the higher levels of pay demanded by their employees, as inflationary pressure eroded the purchasing power of their pesos. The outcome of this growth in tourism was a major inflationary headache for the government.

Source: Michael Casey, 'Argentina finds new inflation culprit in tourism sector', *Dow Jones International News*, 8 February 2006.

The opportunity cost of tourism

Further to the key economic impact discussed above, it is necessary also to consider that, by developing tourism, many resources (such as land, labour and capital investment) are used to support the industry, thus making them unavailable for other industries. This is termed the **opportunity cost**.

Crompton proposes that 'Opportunity costs are the benefits that would be forthcoming if the public resources committed to a tourism project were (1) redirected to other public services or (2) retained by the taxpayer.'[14] This principle acknowledges the lost opportunities as a result of using such resources for tourism development and those costs should be set against the benefits received.

A further area of opportunity cost to be considered is that of taxation. When governments tax residents, in order to be able to invest in tourism projects, they reduce the spending capability of the local population, which can impact on the multiplier effect of induced or indirect expenditure. Thus, any positive effect of the tourism project may need to be set against the negative impact on residents' spending.

Statistical measurement of tourism

Gathering data on tourism is a vital task for the government of a country. Governments need to know the contribution that tourism makes to the economy in terms of income, employment, balance of payments and investment. Sufficiently detailed figures must be available in order to know how they have affected regional as well as national economies. Governments will wish to examine trends over time, not only within the country, but also in comparison with the performance of other, competing countries. National tourist offices will use this information to forecast growth, plan for tourism in their areas and as a guide for their promotional campaigns.

Information must be both **quantitative** and **qualitative** in nature – that is, data should be provided about not only the numbers and composition of tourists but also their nature and purpose. For example, national statistics on tourism should include:

- the number of international visitors (arrivals) as well as the number of domestic tourists
- how these are distributed over the months of the year
- the countries generating the international tourists and the regions generating the domestic tourists
- the growth, year on year, of those tourists
- their spend – in absolute terms and how they distribute it between accommodation, transport, shopping, catering and so on.
- their mode of travel – that is, what form of transport they use, whether they are travelling independently or on an inclusive tour
- the duration of their visit
- the types of accommodation they use
- the purposes of their visit – whether leisure, business, VFR
- demographic profiles – age, group composition, social class
- sociographic profiles – personality, lifestyle, interests and activities
- what these tourists seek and the extent to which they are satisfied with what they find.

This is a great deal of information and relates to both inbound and domestic tourism. Data must also be gathered for outbound tourism – residents travelling abroad. Thus, the task of collecting tourism data is daunting, but it is vital that governments undertake it and, as far as is possible, the data collected are based on commonly defined criteria, so that meaningful comparisons can be made between countries.

If the collection of data allows the nation to know what trends are developing over time, what patterns of growth are taking place and how tastes and preferences are changing over time, this information will enable governments to determine where to site roads and airports, where to plan for expansion in local government plans and in what countries to increase or decrease the spend on advertising (as well as how to redirect the themes of advertisements when it is found that new types of tourists are being reached).

The private sector will benefit from this information, too, when deciding whether or not and where to invest in hotels or tourist attractions and the forms those facilities should take. Furthermore, the industry requires an understanding of the propensity to take holidays – that is, the proportion of the population choosing to take a holiday each year and, in particular, a holiday abroad or more than one holiday a year – and how that propensity is affected by a growth in disposable income.

Public-sector planners must be aware of the multiplier effect, which will call for sophisticated research techniques if the figures produced are to be accurate.

We will examine the two most commonly used measurements of tourism – international and national surveys.

International surveys

Statistics of intra-European and transatlantic tourist flows were collected even before World War II. The systematic collection of tourism data on a global scale, however, can be dated back to the early post-war years. The methods of measurement used have been gradually refined and improved in recent years, particularly in those developed countries that have seen tourism expand rapidly.

Example

The British International Passenger Survey (IPS)

In Britain, information on travel in to and out of the country is obtained in a variety of ways. Until the early 1960s, most basic data on incoming tourism were obtained from Home Office immigration statistics, but, as the purpose of gathering such data was to control immigration rather than to measure tourism, the data had major weaknesses, including a failure to distinguish the purpose of travel – obviously a key statistic when surveying tourists. The government, therefore, decided to introduce a regular survey of visitors entering and leaving the country.

The International Passenger Survey (IPS) has enabled data to be collected on tourists since 1964. It is undertaken by the Office of National Statistics for the Department for Culture, Media and Sport and the national tourist boards and over a quarter of a million international travellers are interviewed annually. Records are made of the number of visitors, purpose of their visit, geographical region visited, their expenditure, mode of travel, transport used and duration of stay. The information is based on their country of residence, so, for example, the large number of British visitors living in America and travelling to visit friends and relatives in Britain each year would be counted as American visitors. This information is published quarterly and compounded annually in the government's *Business Monitor* series (MQ6, *Overseas Travel and Tourism*).

The IPS is a random sample of all visitors travelling in to or out of the UK via the major seaports and airports and the Channel Tunnel, stratified by port of arrival or departure, time of day and mode of transport used.

Global tourism statistics – covering traffic flows, expenditure and trends over time – are collated annually by the UNWTO and the Organization for Economic Cooperation and Development (OECD). The figures are published in the UNWTO's *World Tourism Statistics Annual Report* and *Compendium of Tourism Statistics*, and in the OECD's annual *Tourism Policy and International Tourism*. These statistics are not always strictly comparable, however, as data-gathering methods vary and differences in the definitions of terms remain.

Other surveys are undertaken to provide additional data on the volume of tourists and their expenditure, although reductions in resources have led to cutbacks in the collection of data by the public-sector bodies, so supplementary information is now largely collected by private organizations. For example, IPK International undertakes more than half a million interviews each year, asking populations of more than 50 countries about their travel behaviour. The results of these interviews are published in the *World Travel Monitor* and *European Travel Monitor*. They also provide businesses with extracts of data, on request, ensuring that they can access the most relevant data for their needs. It should be mentioned that full reports as well as data extracts are often quite expensive to purchase.

National surveys

The need for data on domestic tourism is important for both national and regional governments. With this in mind, many governments invest in surveys that can provide details of the travel habits of residents. For example, in Britain, as in other countries in Europe, surveys are regularly carried out on tourism flows within the country. The most important of these is the 'United Kingdom Tourism Survey' (UKTS) on behalf of VisitBritain, VisitScotland, VisitWales and the Northern Ireland Tourist Board.

This survey was originally carried out using monthly telephone interviews, but, since 2005, over 2000 adults are now questioned face-to-face on a weekly basis. Information is collected on the volume and value of all trips involving at least one overnight stay, including

Example

Occupancy surveys for accommodation in Spain

Following an EU directive requiring the collection of tourism data, the Spanish Institute of Statistics introduced the Hotel Occupancy Survey in 1996. This survey examines the number of overnight stays and levels of occupancy of hotel establishments.

In addition, other forms of accommodation are also surveyed in order to understand more about this sector of the industry. They include:

- the Tourist Accommodation Occupancy Survey, which covers tourist apartments
- the Campsite Occupancy Survey, which provides data on tourist stays at campsites
- the Rural Tourist Accommodation Occupancy Survey, which covers establishments registered as rural tourist accommodation.

The data are reported on both a national and regional basis.

These surveys complement the expenditure, national and inbound surveys (FRONTUR and EGATUR) also undertaken by the Ministry of Industry, Tourism and Trade.

Source: Instituto Nacional de Estadística, Hotel Occupancy Survey, available online at: **www.ine.es/inebmenu/ mnu_hosteleria.en.htm**

the purpose of the trip, accommodation and transport used, activities engaged in, the method of booking and demographic details of respondents.

In the UK, information on day visitors is less widely available. A Leisure Day Visits Survey is carried out biennially in England (and a similar survey is completed in Scotland, but not currently in Wales or Northern Ireland). This survey collects data on the volume and value of leisure visits to rural areas as well as cities and towns across the country, including seaside resorts.

National tourist boards often provide the funding for surveys that provide data on tourism in their area. For example, in the UK, the national tourist boards collect information on hotel occupancy in each of their own regions.

Techniques and problems regarding measurement of tourism

From the descriptions of the methods for gathering tourist statistics outlined above, it can be seen that most research employs quantitative methods in order to provide descriptive information about issues such as when and where tourists travel, where they come from, how long they stay and how much they spend. In some cases, this information is available in considerable levels of detail. For instance, expenditure can be broken down into sectors (shopping, food, accommodation) and data on visits can be identified by tourism region within the country. Although the data collected are not above criticism, by and large there is a sufficient body of information on which to base decisions.

The demand for qualitative research

Research dealing with why people travel is far more limited, however. This situation is beginning to change, though, as organizations become more concerned with understanding the behaviour of tourists – how they choose their destinations, what they do when they arrive and why, what satisfies them, their purchasing patterns (preferences to book directly rather than through an agent or to book early rather than close to departure time).

None of these factors is easily addressed by the use of structured questionnaires – a more qualitative approach to research is needed. This can involve lengthy interviews in the home or in panels, or groups, of up to eight consumers who will talk about their behaviour under the guidance of a skilled interviewer. Some information is best obtained by observation rather than questioning. For example, watching how customers visiting a travel agency choose their brochures from the racks.

All these types of research are expensive, and time-consuming to administer. What is more, unlike quantitative methods, they cannot be subjected to tests of statistical probability in order to 'prove' the accuracy of the findings, no matter how carefully and scientifically the information is collected. Many organizations are therefore reluctant to commission research involving qualitative methods, although a growing number of research experts now recognize that they may produce richer and more complete data than the more common survey. After all, the information provided by the use of questionnaires will only be as accurate as the honesty of the answers, but it is particularly difficult to know if respondents are answering questionnaires honestly or giving sufficient thought to the questions. This problem is compounded where mailed questionnaires are used.

Some criticisms of quantitative methods

Asking questions of passengers arriving at a destination is, in reality, an *intention* survey rather than an accurate picture of what those passengers actually end up doing while in the country. Equally, surveys carried out on departing travellers require good levels of recall, so some answers will be, at best, guesswork, especially where the aim is to assess the expenditure that the tourist has incurred.

The categories or definitions used may vary by survey. For instance, the travel survey for Finnish residents limits the sample to adults aged between 15 and 74, which may effectively ignore the unique travel habits of the increasingly significant senior citizen (or grey) market. Age is not the only definitional difficulty. One of the issues that occurs when comparing data for different countries as reported by the UNWTO is that some countries may count international tourists by country of residence, while other countries use nationality (determined either by passport or based on immigration forms completed on arrival).

Even if common definitions are used, direct comparisons may be misleading. For example, an international journey may require an American resident to make a trip of several hundred kilometres or cross a stretch of water, which will usually mean forward planning, while a resident of Continental Europe may live within a couple of kilometres of an international border and think nothing of crossing it regularly to go shopping or for a meal out. In some cases, it is even difficult to think of border crossings as international. The Schengen Agreement, for example, eradicated border controls between several of the EU countries, with the result that monitoring visitors has become much harder. Another issue is that some countries still use hotel records to estimate the number of visitors – a system known to be notoriously inadequate because visitors travelling from one hotel to another are counted twice, while those visiting friends and relatives will be omitted entirely from the count.

While international standards for methods of data collection and definitions of terms have become widely accepted, particularly among the developed countries, small variations continue to make genuine comparison difficult, not only between countries but also within a country over a period of time. Above all, if specific types of tourist activity are being examined, as part of a larger sample of general tourists, limits of confidence may fall sharply. Some survey data in the past have produced results that are accurate only to within 20 per cent either way, owing to the small number of respondents in the particular category being examined.

Accurate measures of tourist expenditure are equally difficult to make. Shopping surveys have problems distinguishing between residents and tourists, and tourists frequently under- or overestimate their expenditure. Above all, much of the real tourist expenditure is not recorded at all, especially in developing countries, because it is not taken into account. This includes secondary spend by recipients of tourist monies and even direct spend by tourists in shops and other outlets. In countries where cash, rather than credit cards, is still the normal means of payment and bargaining normal for even the smallest of items, calculating spending patterns reliably is particularly difficult.

Tourism satellite accounts

In an effort to provide more accurate assessment, the UNWTO has introduced the concept of the **tourism satellite account (TSA)**. This technique attempts to include all such indirect expenditures and their resultant contribution to GDP, employment and capital investment. The technique was approved as an international standard by the United Nations Statistical Commission in 2000. It created a set of standardized procedures that aim to ensure that all countries are operating similar systems and, thus, the resulting data are comparable across nations.[15]

The creation of a TSA provides information regarding the economic importance of tourism for a national economy, as well as providing details of both the employment created by tourism and the tax revenues earned as a direct result of tourism activity. Such information can assist with planning tourism resources and may encourage greater awareness of the tourism industry and further investment in the industry.

The implementation of TSAs, however, is fraught with difficulties. It is not only expensive and time-consuming to employ, but accepts all tourism expenditure as beneficial, disregarding the question of sustainability. Neither can the results revealed in one country or region necessarily be transposed to another as each situation is unique and there is no magic formula that will allow estimates of statistical measures to be obtained without full-scale research within the area.

Example

Tourism satellite accounts for New Zealand

Since the end of the last century, the statistics office for New Zealand has worked towards the regular collection of data to provide an account of the value of tourism to its economy. The first account was provided in 1995 and these are now published annually. The reports provide details specifically on the following:

- total tourism expenditure, incuding separate figures for international and domestic tourism
- direct contribution of tourism to GDP
- indirect value of tourism
- employment in tourism, including figures for part-time employment.

Tourism satellite accounts, 2006

Tourism expenditure	NZ$ (million)	
International	8,325	
Domestic	10,264	
GDP	**NZ$ (million)**	**Contribution to GDP (%)**
Direct contribution	6,931	4.8
Indirect contribution	5,898	4.1
Tourism employment	**Persons**	**Tourism employment as percentage of total employment**
Full-time (including working proprietors)	80,600	
Part-time (including working proprietors)	55,900	
Total employment (FTE)	108,600	5.9%
Indirect employment (FTE)	74,500	4.0%

FTE = Full-time equivalent employment
Source: Statistics New Zealand, 'Tourism satellite accounts, 2006'.

Providing such details allows the tourism industry as well as government to understand its value and importance. It also allows comparisons to be made with other years, which can provide insight into changes within the industry. The full report provides a convenient source of additional data on tourism, including expenditure in different sectors of the industry, such as accommodation, air travel and so on.

Future issues

The issue of sustainability is a critical one when discussing the economic impacts of tourism. It can be argued that often far too much concern is given to measuring the economic impacts of tourism on a region at the expense of considering the social or environmental impacts. The industry's sole concern with growth in annual trends may conceal the very real danger that the number of tourists visiting a region will eventually exceed the number the region can comfortably contain. Statistics on the ratio of tourists to residents, for example, or the number of tourists per square kilometre would provide some guidance on the degree of congestion experienced by the region. The social impacts of tourism are also outcomes of many other variables, however, and statistical measurement is still a comparatively recent art that will require continual refinement in the future for the purposes of both economic and social planning. Furthermore, as awareness of the need to protect the environment grows, and media attention encourages greener travel, the need to balance economic development with environmental protection will become more significant for destinations globally.

As new destinations develop their tourism potential, greater understanding of the tourism industry will encourage destinations to maximize the potential to be gained. This will require efforts to maximize the multiplier effect, especially by reducing the leakages. This may include implementing legislation to restrict or control foreign ownership of tourism businesses or the repatriation of profits or pay to foreign employees. Managing the benefits may also include ensuring that the economic benefits of tourism are filtered down to the community rather than an elite few. Balancing the need to attract investment in order to develop the destination with the need to control their own future may be a difficult dilemma for many upcoming destinations.

Computerization has made storage, manipulation of data and, via the Internet, access to data more convenient for businesses interested in the tourism industry. As a consequence, data on many areas of the tourism industry can be used to support planning and development decisions. It needs to be recognized, however, that conflicting data may exist as different survey methodologies can all impact the accuracy of the results. Ultimately, greater information cautiously used can ensure that informed decisions lead to greater levels of business success.

Notes

1. WTTC (2008) 'Progress and priorities 2008/2009' WTTC.

2. UNWTO (2008) 'Tourism highlights', UNWTO.

3. Euromonitor (2008) 'Tourism flows domestic: world', and 'Tourist flows inbound: world', Euromonitor, 10 April.

4. Euromonitor (2008) 'Tourism flows outbound: world', Euromonitor, 22 April.

5. Euromonitor.

6. Policy Research Bureau (2005) 'Briefing paper for policy makers and service providers', Family Holiday Association.

7. Department for International Development *Developments*, Department for International Development 27, 3/2004.

8. 'Tourism tax revenues rise in 2006', Canadian Press 10 September 2007.

9. WTTC (2006) 'China, China Hong Kong and SAR and China Macau SAR: The impact of travel and tourism on jobs and the economy', WTTC p. 46.

10. WTTC (2008) 'Progress and priorities 2008/9', WTTC, p. 6.

11. Stewart, A. (1999) 'Lawmakers raise theme park doubts', *South China Morning Post*, 17 June.

12. Hope, C. A. and Klemm, M. S. (2001) 'Tourism in difficult areas revisited: the case of Bradford', *Tourism Management*, 22 (6).

13. 'Foot-and-mouth has cost English tourism 3.3 billion pounds, government says', Associated Press, 30 October 2001.

14. Crompton, John L. (2006) 'Economic impact studies: instruments for political shenanigans', *Journal of Travel Research*, 45 (1), p. 75.

15. UNWTO, 'Basic concepts of the tourism satellite account (TSA)', UNWTO, available online at: **www.unwto.org/statistics/tsa/project/concepts.pdf**

Further reading

Bull, A. (1995) *The Economics of Travel and Tourism* (2nd edn), Longman.

Lennon, J. (ed.) (2003) *Tourism Statistics: International perspectives and current issues*, Continuum.

OECD, *Tourism Policy and International Tourism in OECD Member Countries* (annual).

Sinclair, M. T. and Stabler, M. (1997) *The Economics of Tourism*, Routledge.

Tribe, J. (1999) *The Economics of Leisure and Tourism* (2nd edn), Butterworth-Heinemann.

UNWTO, *Compendium of Tourism Statistics* (annual).

UNWTO, *Yearbook of Tourism Statistics* (annual).

UNWTO, *World Tourism Barometer* (monthly).

Veal, A. J. (1997) *Research Methods for Leisure and Tourism: A practical guide* (2nd edn) Longman.

Websites

Organisation for Economic Co-operation and Development (OECD) **www.oecd.org**
UN World Tourism Organization (UNWTO) **www.unwto.org**
World Travel and Tourism Council **www.wttc.org**

Questions and discussion points

1. The UK has a significant deficit in its tourism balance of payments. To narrow the gap between receipts and expenditure, it is necessary to encourage a reduction in spend by residents abroad or an increase in spending by international visitors or residents domestically. How might the UK government achieve each of these changes? Do you think some changes may be harder to achieve than others?

2. A weak exchange rate can make a destination appear cheaper for tourists. Discuss whether this is an important factor influencing a family's decision over where to take a holiday or not.

3. Outbound data for tourists often do not correspond with arrivals data. For example, the number of outbound tourists from Australia visiting the UK reported by the Australian Bureau of Statistics does not match the number of arrivals from Australia reported by the UK Office of National Statistics. Discuss the reasons for there being a difference between these two figures.

Tasks

1. Drawing on specific examples to support your report, explain the main reasons for gathering statistics on international tourism and discuss some of the problems that are encountered in gathering and analysing such data.

2. For a country of your choice, gather statistics on outbound and domestic tourism. Using these data, calculate the gross travel propensity. What does this figure tell you about the travel habits of your selected country? How useful is that information for a tour operator selling holidays to that market?

3. Developing countries often focus on promoting tourism to their region in order to gain from the positive economic benefits of visitors. However, it has often been suggested that rich countries are better able to profit from tourism than poor ones. Explain why this may be the case and discuss the actions that a developing country may take to maximize the benefits of developing tourism.

Semester 2

International Business and the Multinational Enterprise

Section 1
FDI Theory

7

Foreign Direct Investment

■ A LOOK AT THIS CHAPTER

This chapter examines another significant form of international business: foreign direct investment (FDI). Again, we are concerned with the patterns of FDI and the theories on which it is based. We also explore why and how governments intervene in FDI activity.

Learning Objectives

After studying this chapter, you should be able to

1 Describe worldwide patterns of foreign direct investment (FDI) and reasons for these patterns.

2 Describe each of the theories that attempt to explain why foreign direct investment occurs.

3 Discuss the important management issues in the foreign direct investment decision.

4 Explain why governments intervene in the free flow of foreign direct investment.

5 Discuss the policy instruments that governments use to promote and restrict foreign direct investment.

Auf Wiedersein to VW Law

FRANKFURT, Germany — The Volkswagen Group (www.vw.com) owns eight of the most prestigious and best-known automotive brands in the world, including Audi, Bentley, Bugatti, Lamborghini, Seat, Skoda, and Volkswagen. From its 48 production facilities worldwide, the company produces and sells around 6 million cars annually. The VW Group sells cars in more than 150 countries and holds a 10 percent share of the world car market. Pictured at right, workers train at the Volkswagen plant in Puebla, Mexico.

Volkswagen, like companies everywhere, received plenty of help in getting where it is today. Since the 1960s, Volkswagen received special protection from its own legislation known as the "VW Law." The law gave the German state of Lower Saxony, which owns 20.1 percent of Volkswagen, the power to block any takeover attempt that threatened local jobs and the economy. Germany's former Chancellor Gerhard Schröder once told a cheering crowd of autoworkers in Germany, "Any efforts by the [European Union] commission in Brussels to smash the VW culture will meet the resistance of the federal government as long as we are in power."

Source: Keith Dannemiller/
CORBIS-NY.

The European Court finally struck down the VW Law in late 2007, although Lower Saxony's government did not give up the fight. Legislators introduced multiple reincarnations of the VW Law to help it avoid the wrath of European regulators, but it is unlikely to be resurrected.

Volkswagen's special treatment lies in its importance to the German economy and close ties between government and management in Germany. Volkswagen employs tens of thousands of people at home and symbolizes the resurgence of the German economy over the past 60 years. As you read this chapter, consider all the issues that can arise between companies and governments in global business.[1]

foreign direct investment
Purchase of physical assets or a significant amount of the ownership (stock) of a company in another country to gain a measure of management control.

portfolio investment
Investment that does not involve obtaining a degree of control in a company.

Many early trade theories were created at a time when most production factors (such as labor, financial capital, capital equipment, and land or natural resources) either could not be moved or could not be moved easily across national borders. But today, all of the above except land are internationally mobile and flow across borders to wherever they are needed. Financial capital is readily available from international financial institutions to finance corporate expansion, and whole factories can be picked up and moved to another country. Even labor is more mobile than in years past, although many barriers restrict the complete mobility of labor.

International flows of capital are at the core of **foreign direct investment (FDI)**—the purchase of physical assets or a significant amount of the ownership (stock) of a company in another country to gain a measure of management control. But there is wide disagreement on what exactly constitutes foreign direct investment. Nations set different thresholds at which they classify an international capital flow as FDI. The U.S. Commerce Department sets the threshold at 10 percent of stock ownership in a company abroad, but most other governments set it at anywhere from 10 to 25 percent. By contrast, an investment that does not involve obtaining a degree of control in a company is called a **portfolio investment**.

In this chapter, we examine the importance of foreign direct investment to the operations of international companies. We begin by exploring the growth of FDI in recent years and investigating its sources and destinations. We then take a look at several theories that attempt to explain foreign direct investment flows. Next, we turn our attention to several important management issues that arise in most decisions about whether a company should undertake FDI. This chapter closes by discussing the reasons why governments encourage or restrict foreign direct investment and the methods they use to accomplish these goals.

Patterns of Foreign Direct Investment

Just as international trade displays distinct patterns (see Chapter 5), so too does foreign direct investment. In this section, we first take a look at the factors that have propelled growth in FDI over the past decade. We then turn our attention to the destinations and sources of foreign direct investment.

Ups and Downs of Foreign Direct Investment

After growing around 20 percent per year in the first half of the 1990s, *FDI inflows* grew by about 40 percent per year in the second half of the decade. In 2000, FDI inflows peaked at around $1.4 trillion. Slower FDI for 2001, 2002, and 2003 reduced FDI inflows to nearly half its earlier peak. Strong economic performance and high corporate profits in many countries lifted FDI inflows to around $648 billion in 2004, $946 billion in 2005, and $1.3 trillion in 2006. Figure 7.1 illustrates this pattern and shows that changes in FDI flows are far more erratic than changes in global GDP.[2]

The main causes of decreased FDI around the year 2000 were slower global economic growth, tumbling stock market valuations, and relatively fewer privatizations of state-owned firms. Yet FDI inflows show a recovery since then. Despite the ebb and flow of FDI that we see in Figure 7.1, the long-term trend points toward greater FDI inflows worldwide. Among the driving forces behind renewed activity in FDI is an emphasis on the "offshoring" of business activities. The two main drivers of FDI flows are *globalization* and international *mergers and acquisitions*.

Globalization Recall from Chapter 6 that years ago barriers to trade were not being reduced, and new, creative barriers seemed to be popping up in many nations. This presented a problem for companies that were trying to export their products to markets around the world. This resulted in a wave of FDI as many companies entered promising markets to get around growing trade barriers. But then the Uruguay Round of GATT negotiations created renewed determination to further reduce barriers to trade. As countries lowered their trade barriers, companies realized that they could now produce in the most efficient and productive locations and simply export to their markets worldwide. This set off another

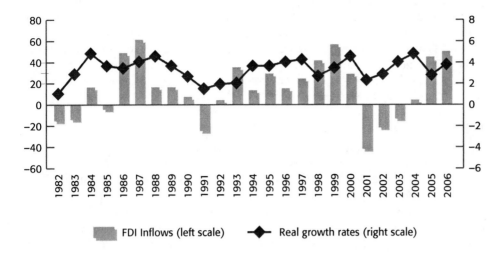

FIGURE 7.1

Growth Rate of FDI versus GDP

Source: *World Investment Report 2007* (Geneva, Switzerland: UNCTAD, September 2007), Chapter 1, Table I.4, p. 9; World Economic Outlook Database, April 2008.

wave of FDI flows into low-cost, newly industrialized nations and emerging markets.) Forces causing globalization to occur are, therefore, part of the reason for long-term growth in foreign direct investment.

Increasing globalization is also causing a growing number of international companies from emerging markets to undertake FDI. For example, companies from Taiwan began investing heavily in other nations two decades ago. Acer (www.acer.com), headquartered in Singapore but founded in Taiwan, manufactures personal computers and computer components. Just 20 years after it opened for business, Acer had spawned 10 subsidiaries worldwide and became the dominant industry player in many emerging markets.

Mergers and Acquisitions (The number of *mergers and acquisitions (M&As)* and their exploding values also underlie long-term growth in foreign direct investment. In fact, cross-border M&As are the main vehicle through which companies undertake foreign direct investment.) Throughout the past two decades the value of all M&A activity as a share of GDP rose from 0.3 percent to 8 percent. The value of cross-border M&As peaked in 2000 at around $1.15 trillion. This figure accounted for about 3.7 percent of the market capitalization of all stock exchanges worldwide. Reasons previously mentioned for the dip and later rise in FDI inflows also caused the pattern we see in cross-border M&A deals (see Figure 7.2). By 2006, the value of cross-border M&As had climbed back to around $880 billion.[3]

Many cross-border M&A deals are driven by the desire of companies to:

- Get a foothold in a new geographic market
- Increase a firm's global competitiveness
- Fill gaps in companies' product lines in a global industry
- Reduce costs of R&D, production, distribution, and so forth

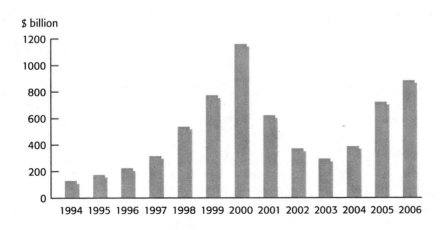

FIGURE 7.2

Value of Cross-Border M&As

Source: Based on *World Investment Report 2007* (Geneva, Switzerland: UNCTAD, 2007), Chapter 1, Figure I.3, p. 6.

Entrepreneurs and small businesses also play a role in the expansion of FDI inflows. There is no data on the portion of FDI contributed by small businesses, but we know from anecdotal evidence that these companies are engaged in FDI. Unhindered by many of the constraints of a large company, entrepreneurs investing in other markets often demonstrate an inspiring can-do spirit mixed with ingenuity and bravado. For a day-in-the-life look at a young entrepreneur who is realizing his dreams in China, see the Entrepreneur's Toolkit titled, "The Cowboy of Manchuria."

Worldwide Flows of FDI

Driving FDI growth are more than 70,000 multinational companies with over 690,000 affiliates abroad, nearly half of which are now in developing countries.[4] Developed countries remain the prime destination for FDI because cross-border M&As are concentrated in developed nations. Developed countries account for around 65 percent ($857 billion) of global FDI inflows, which were a little over $1.3 trillion in 2006. By comparison, FDI inflows to developing countries were valued at $379 billion—about 29 percent of world FDI inflows and down from a peak of a little more than 40 percent a decade earlier.

Among developed countries, European Union (EU) nations, the United States, and Japan account for the vast majority of world inflows. The EU remains the world's largest FDI recipient, garnering $531 billion in 2006 (over 40 percent of the world's total). Behind the large FDI figure for the EU is increased consolidation in Europe among large national competitors and further efforts at EU regional integration.

Developing nations had varying experiences in 2006. FDI inflows to developing nations in Asia were nearly $259 billion in 2006, with China attracting over $69 billion of that total. India, the largest recipient on the Asian subcontinent, had inflows of nearly $17 billion. FDI flowing from developing nations in Asia is also on the rise, coinciding with the rise of these nations' own global competitors.

ENTREPRENEUR'S TOOLKIT

The Cowboy of Manchuria

Tom Kirkwood, at just 28 years of age, turned his dream of introducing his grandfather's taffy to China into a fast growing business. Kirkwood's story—his hassles and hustling—provides some lessons on the purest form of global investing. The basics that small investors in China can follow are as basic as they get. Find a product that's easy to make, widely popular, and cheap to sell and then choose the least expensive, investor-friendliest place to make it.

Kirkwood, whose family runs the Shawnee Inn, a ski and golf resort in Shawnee-on-Delaware, Pennsylvania, decided to make candy in Manchuria—China's gritty, heavily populated, industrial northeast. Chinese people often give individually wrapped candies as a gift, and Kirkwood reckoned that China's rising, increasingly prosperous urbanites would have a lucrative sweet tooth. "You can't be M&Ms, but you don't have to be penny candy, either," Kirkwood says. "You find your niche because a niche in China is an awful lot of people."

Kirkwood decided early on that he wanted to do business in China. In the mid-1980s after prep school, he spent a year in Taiwan and China learning Chinese and working in a Shanghai engineering company. The experience gave him a taste for adventure capitalism on the frontier of China's economic development. Using $400,000 of Kirkwood's family money, Kirkwood and his friend Peter Moustakerski bought equipment and rented a factory in Shenyang, a city of six million people in the heart of Manchuria. Roads and rail transport were convenient, and wages were low. The local government seemed amenable to a 100 percent foreign-owned factory, and the Shenyang Shawnee Cowboy Food Company was born.

Although it's a small operation, it now has 89 employees and is growing. Kirkwood is determined to succeed selling his candies with names such as Longhorn Bars. As he boarded a flight to Beijing for a meeting with a distributor recently, Kirkwood realized he had a bag full of candy. He offered one to a flight attendant. When lunch is over, he vowed, "Everybody on this plane will know Cowboy Candy."

Source: Adapted from Roy Rowan "Mao to Now," *Fortune* (www.fortune.com), October 11, 1999; Marcus W. Brauchli, "Sweet Dreams," *Wall Street Journal*, June 27, 1996, R, 10:1.

Elsewhere, all of Africa drew in slightly more than $35 billion of FDI in 2006, or about 2.7 percent of the world's total. FDI flows into Latin America and the Caribbean declined rapidly in the early 2000s but then surged to $84 billion in 2006. Finally, FDI inflows to southeast Europe and the Commonwealth of Independent States reached an all-time high of $69 billion in 2006.

Quick Study

1. What is the difference between *foreign direct investment* and *portfolio investment*?
2. What factors influence global flows of foreign direct investment?
3. Identify the main destinations of foreign direct investment. Is the pattern shifting?

Explanations for Foreign Direct Investment

So far we have examined the flows of foreign direct investment, but we have not investigated explanations for why FDI occurs. Let's now investigate the four main theories that attempt to explain why companies engage in foreign direct investment.

International Product Life Cycle

Although we introduced the international product life cycle in Chapter 5 in the context of international trade, it is also used to explain foreign direct investment.[5] The **international product life cycle** theory states that a company will begin by exporting its product and later undertake foreign direct investment as a product moves through its life cycle. In the *new product stage*, a good is produced in the home country because of uncertain domestic demand and to keep production close to the research department that developed the product. In the *maturing product stage*, the company directly invests in production facilities in countries where demand is great enough to warrant its own production facilities. In the final *standardized product stage*, increased competition creates pressures to reduce production costs. In response, a company builds production capacity in low-cost developing nations to serve its markets around the world.

Despite its conceptual appeal, the international product life cycle theory is limited in its power to explain why companies choose FDI over other forms of market entry. A local firm in the target market could pay for (license) the right to use the special assets needed to manufacture a particular product. In this way, a company could avoid the additional risks associated with direct investments in the market. The theory also fails to explain why firms choose FDI over exporting activities. It might be less expensive to serve a market abroad by increasing output at the home country factory rather than by building additional capacity within the target market.

The theory explains why the FDI of some firms follows the international product life cycle of their products. But it does not explain why other market entry modes are inferior or less advantageous options.

international product life cycle
Theory stating that a company will begin by exporting its product and later undertake foreign direct investment as the product moves through its life cycle.

Market Imperfections (Internalization)

A market that is said to operate at peak efficiency (prices are as low as they can possibly be) and where goods are readily and easily available is said to be a *perfect market*. But perfect markets are rarely, if ever, seen in business because of factors that cause a breakdown in the efficient operation of an industry—called *market imperfections*. **Market imperfections** theory states that when an imperfection in the market makes a transaction less efficient than it could be, a company will undertake foreign direct investment to internalize the transaction and thereby remove the imperfection. There are two market imperfections that are relevant to this discussion—trade barriers and specialized knowledge.

market imperfections
Theory stating that when an imperfection in the market makes a transaction less efficient than it could be, a company will undertake foreign direct investment to internalize the transaction and thereby remove the imperfection.

Employees from quality control check plasma screens on the production line at a newly opened television assembly plant in Nymburk near Prague, Czech Republic. The plant is a foreign direct investment by a company called Chinese Changhong Europe Electric TV. The plant is Changhong's biggest foreign direct investment in recent times and produces LCD, plasma, and classic televisions. What advantages do you think the Chinese company gained by investing in the Czech Republic?
Source: Radim Beznoska/ CORBIS-NY.

Trade Barriers One common market imperfection in international business is trade barriers, such as tariffs. For example, the North American Free Trade Agreement stipulates that a sufficient portion of a product's content must originate within Canada, Mexico, or the United States for the product to avoid tariff charges when it is imported to any of these three markets. That is why a large number of Korean manufacturers invested in production facilities in Tijuana, Mexico, just south of Mexico's border with California. By investing in production facilities in Mexico, the Korean companies were able to skirt the North American tariffs that would have been levied if they were to export goods from Korean factories. The presence of a market imperfection (tariffs) caused those companies to undertake foreign direct investment.

Specialized Knowledge The unique competitive advantage of a company sometimes consists of specialized knowledge. This knowledge could be the technical expertise of engineers or the special marketing abilities of managers. When the knowledge is technical expertise, companies can charge a fee to companies in other countries for use of the knowledge in producing the same or a similar product. But when a company's specialized knowledge is embodied in its employees, the only way to exploit a market opportunity in another nation may be to undertake FDI.

The possibility that a company will create a future competitor by charging another company for access to its knowledge is another market imperfection that can encourage FDI. Rather than trade a short-term gain (the fee charged another company) for a long-term loss (lost competitiveness), a company will prefer to undertake investment. For example, as Japan rebuilt its industries following the Second World War, many Japanese companies paid Western firms for access to the special technical knowledge embodied in their products. Those Japanese companies became adept at revising and improving many of these technologies and became leaders in their industries, including electronics and automobiles.

Eclectic Theory

The **eclectic theory** states that firms undertake foreign direct investment when the features of a particular location combine with ownership and internalization advantages to make a location appealing for investment.[6] A *location advantage* is the advantage of locating a particular economic activity in a specific location because of the characteristics (natural or acquired) of that location.[7] These advantages have historically been natural resources such as oil in the Middle East, timber in Canada, or copper in Chile. But the advantage can also be an acquired one such as a productive workforce. An *ownership advantage* refers to company ownership of some special asset, such as brand recognition, technical knowledge, or management ability. An *internalization advantage* is one that arises from internalizing a business activity rather than leaving it to a relatively inefficient market. The eclectic theory states that when all of these advantages are present, a company will undertake FDI.

Market Power

Firms often seek the greatest amount of power possible in their industries relative to rivals. The **market power** theory states that a firm tries to establish a dominant market presence in an industry by undertaking foreign direct investment. The benefit of market power is greater profit because the firm is far better able to dictate the cost of its inputs and/or the price of its output.

One way a company can achieve market power (or dominance) is through **vertical integration**—the extension of company activities into stages of production that provide a firm's inputs (*backward integration*) or absorb its output (*forward integration*). Sometimes a company can effectively control the world supply of an input needed by its industry if it has the resources or ability to integrate backward into supplying that input. Companies may also be able to achieve a great deal of market power if they can integrate forward to increase control over output. For example, they could perhaps make investments in distribution to leapfrog channels of distribution that are tightly controlled by competitors.

market power
Theory stating that a firm tries to establish a dominant market presence in an industry by undertaking foreign direct investment.

vertical integration
Extension of company activities into stages of production that provide a firm's inputs (backward integration) or absorb its output (forward integration).

Quick Study

1. Explain the international *product life cycle theory* of foreign direct investment (FDI).
2. How does the theory of *market imperfections* (internalization) explain FDI?
3. Explain the *eclectic theory*, and identify the three advantages necessary for FDI to occur.
4. How does the theory of *market power* explain the occurrence of FDI?

Management Issues in the FDI Decision

Decisions about whether to engage in foreign direct investment involve several important issues regarding management of the company and its market. Some of these issues are grounded in the inner workings of firms that undertake FDI, such as the control desired over operations abroad or the firm's cost of production. Others are related to the market and industry in which a firm competes, such as the preferences of customers or the actions of rivals. Let's examine each of these important issues.

Control

Many companies investing abroad are greatly concerned with controlling the activities that occur in the local market. Perhaps the company wants to be certain that its product is being marketed in the same way in the local market as it is at home. Or maybe it wants to ensure that the selling price remains the same in both markets. Some companies try to maintain ownership of a large portion of the local operation, say, even up to 100 percent, in the belief that greater ownership gives them greater control.

Yet for a variety of reasons, even complete ownership does not *guarantee* control. For example, the local government might intervene and require a company to hire some local managers rather than bring them all in from the home office. Companies may need to prove a scarcity of skilled local managerial talent before the government will let them bring managers in from the home country. Governments might also require that all goods produced in the local facility be exported so they do not compete with products of the country's domestic firms.

Partnership Requirements   Many companies have strict policies regarding how much ownership they take in firms abroad because of the importance of maintaining control. In the past, IBM (www.ibm.com) strictly required that the home office own 100 percent of all international subsidiaries. But companies must sometimes abandon such policies if a country demands shared ownership in return for market access.

Some governments saw shared ownership requirements as a way to shield their workers from exploitation and their industries from domination by large international firms. Companies would sometimes sacrifice control to pursue a market opportunity, but frequently they did not. Most countries today do not take such a hard-line stance and have opened their doors to investment by multinational companies. Mexico used to make decisions on investment by multinationals on a case-by-case basis. IBM was negotiating with the Mexican government for 100 percent ownership of a facility in Guadalajara and got the go-ahead only after the company made numerous concessions in other areas.

Benefits of Cooperation   Many nations have grown more cooperative toward international companies in recent years. Governments of developing and emerging markets realize the benefits of investment by multinationals, including decreased unemployment, increased tax revenues, training to create a more highly skilled workforce, and the transfer of technology. A country known for overly restricting the operations of multinational enterprises can see its inward investment flow dry up. Indeed, restrictive policies of India's government hampered foreign direct investment inflows for many years.

Cooperation also frequently opens important communication channels that help firms to maintain positive relationships in the host country. Both parties tend to walk a fine line—cooperating most of the time, but holding fast on occasions when the stakes are especially high.

Cooperation with a local partner and respect for national pride in Central Europe contributed to the successful acquisition of Hungary's Borsodi brewery (formerly a state-owned enterprise) by Belgium's Interbrew (www.interbrew.com). From the start, Interbrew wisely insisted it would move ahead with its purchase only if local management would be in charge. Interbrew then assisted local management with technical, marketing, sales, distribution, and general management training. Borsodi eventually became one of Interbrew's key subsidiaries and is now run entirely by Hungarian managers.

At one time, Boeing aircraft were made entirely in the United States. But today Boeing can source its landing gear doors from Northern Ireland, outboard wing flaps from Italy, wing tip assemblies from Korea, rudders from Australia, and fuselages from Japan. Boeing sometimes undertakes foreign direct investment by buying a large portion of its suppliers' assets or traded stock in another country. Why do you think a company may want to control its suppliers through taking an ownership stake?

Source: Larry W. Smith/Getty Images.

Purchase-or-Build Decision

Another important matter for managers is whether to purchase an existing business or to build a subsidiary abroad from the ground up—called a *greenfield investment*. An acquisition generally provides the investor with an existing plant, equipment, and personnel. The acquiring firm may also benefit from the goodwill the existing company has built up over the years and, perhaps, brand recognition of the existing firm. The purchase of an existing business may also allow for alternative methods of financing the purchase, such as an exchange of stock ownership between the companies. Factors that can reduce the appeal of purchasing existing facilities include obsolete equipment, poor relations with workers, and an unsuitable location.

Mexico's Cemex, S.A. (www.cemex.com), is a multinational company that made a fortune by buying struggling, inefficient plants around the world and reengineering them. Chairman Lorenzo Zambrano has long figured the overriding principle was "Buy big globally, or be bought." The success of Cemex in using FDI has confounded, even rankled, its competitors in developed nations. For example, Cemex shocked global markets when it carried out a $1.8 billion purchase of Spain's two largest cement companies, Valenciana and Sanson.

But adequate facilities in the local market are sometimes unavailable and a company must go ahead with a greenfield investment. Because Poland is a source of skilled and inexpensive labor, it is an appealing location for car manufacturers. But the country had little in the way of advanced car-production facilities when General Motors (www.gm.com) considered investing there. So GM built a $320 million facility in Poland's Silesian region. The factory has the potential to produce 200,000 units annually—some of which are destined for export to profitable markets in Western Europe. However, greenfield investments can have their share of headaches. Obtaining the necessary permits, financing, and hiring local personnel can be a real problem in some markets.

Production Costs

Many factors contribute to production costs in every national market. Labor regulations can add significantly to the overall cost of production. Companies may be required to provide benefits packages for their employees that are over and above hourly wages. More time than was planned for might be required to train workers adequately to bring productivity up to an acceptable standard. Although the cost of land and the tax rate on profits can be lower in the local market (or purposely lowered to attract multinationals), it cannot be assumed that they will remain constant. Companies from around the world using China as a production base have witnessed rising wages erode their profits as the economy continues to industrialize. Some companies are therefore finding that Vietnam is their low-cost location of choice.

Rationalized Production One approach companies use to contain production costs is called **rationalized production**—a system of production in which each of a product's components is produced where the cost of producing that component is lowest. All the components are then brought together at one central location for assembly into the final product. Consider the typical stuffed animal made in China whose components are all imported to China (with the exception of the polycore thread with which it's sewn). The stuffed animal's eyes are molded in Japan. Its outfit is imported from France. The polyester-fiber stuffing comes from either Germany or the United States, and the pile-fabric fur is produced in Korea. Only final assembly of these components occurs in China.

Although this production model is highly efficient, a potential problem is that a work stoppage in one country can bring the entire production process to a standstill. For example, the production of automobiles is highly rationalized, with parts coming in from a multitude of countries for assembly. When the United Auto Workers (www.uaw.com) union held a strike for weeks against General Motors (www.gm.com), many of GM's international assembly plants were threatened. The UAW strategically launched their strike at GM's plant that supplied brake pads to virtually all of its assembly plants throughout North America.

rationalized production
System of production in which each of a product's components is produced where the cost of producing that component is lowest.

Mexico's *Maquiladora*   Stretching 3,200 kilometers from the Pacific Ocean to the Gulf of Mexico, the 210-kilometer-wide strip along the U.S.–Mexican border may well be North America's fastest-growing region. With 11 million people and $150 billion in output, the region's economy is larger than that of Israel's. The combination of a low-wage economy nestled next to a prosperous giant is now becoming a model for other regions that are split by wage or technology gaps. Some analysts compare the U.S.–Mexican border region to that between Hong Kong and its manufacturing realm, China's Guangdong province. Officials from cities along the border between Germany and Poland studied the U.S.–Mexican experience to see what lessons could be applied to their unique situation.

Cost of Research and Development   As technology becomes an increasingly powerful competitive factor, the soaring cost of developing subsequent stages of technology has led multinationals to engage in cross-border alliances and acquisitions. For instance, huge multinational pharmaceutical companies are intensely interested in the pioneering biotechnology work done by smaller, entrepreneurial startups. Cadus Pharmaceutical Corporation of New York determined the function of 400 genes related to so-called receptor molecules. Many disorders are associated with the improper functioning of these receptors—making them good targets for drug development. Britain's SmithKline Beecham (www.gsk.com) then invested around $68 million with Cadus in order to access Cadus's research knowledge.

One indicator of technology's significance in foreign direct investment is the amount of R&D conducted by companies' affiliates in other countries. The globalization of innovation and the phenomenon of foreign direct investment in R&D are not necessarily motivated by demand factors such as the size of local markets. They instead appear to be encouraged by supply factors, including gaining access to high-quality scientific and technical human capital.

Customer Knowledge

The behavior of buyers is frequently an important issue in the decision of whether to undertake foreign direct investment. A local presence can help companies gain valuable knowledge about customers that could not be obtained from the home market. For example, when customer preferences for a product differ a great deal from country to country, a local presence might help companies to better understand such preferences and tailor their products accordingly.

Some countries have quality reputations in certain product categories. German automotive engineering, Italian shoes, French perfume, and Swiss watches impress customers as being of superior quality. Because of these perceptions, it can be profitable for a firm to produce its product in the country with the quality reputation, even if the company is based in another country. For example, a cologne or perfume producer might want to bottle its fragrance in France and give it a French name. This type of image appeal can be strong enough to encourage foreign direct investment.

Following Clients

Firms commonly engage in foreign direct investment when the firms they supply have already invested abroad. This practice of "following clients" is common in industries in which producers source component parts from suppliers with whom they have close working relationships. The practice tends to result in companies clustering within close geographic proximity to each other because they supply each other's inputs (see Chapter 5). When Mercedes (www.mercedes.com) opened its first international car plant in Tuscaloosa County, Alabama, auto-parts suppliers also moved to the area from Germany— bringing with them additional investment in the millions of dollars.

Following Rivals

FDI decisions frequently resemble a "follow the leader" scenario in industries having a limited number of large firms. In other words, many of these firms believe that choosing not to make a move parallel to that of the "first mover" might result in being shut out of a

Surprises of Investing Abroad

The decision of whether to build facilities in a market abroad or to purchase existing operations in the local market can be a difficult one. Managers can minimize risk by preparing their companies for a number of surprises they might face.

- **Human Resource Policies.** Home country policies cannot be simply imported and they seldom address local laws and customs. Countries have differing requirements for plant operations and their own regulations regarding business operations.
- **Labor Costs.** France has a minimum wage of about $12 an hour, whereas Mexico has a minimum wage of nearly $5 a day. But Mexico's real minimum wage is nearly double that due to government-mandated benefits and employment practices.
- **Mandated Benefits.** These include company-supplied clothing and meals, required profit sharing, guaranteed employment contracts, and generous dismissal policies. These costs can exceed an employee's wages and are typically nonnegotiable.
- **Labor Unions.** In some countries organized labor is found at almost every company. Rather than dealing with a single union at plants in Scandinavian countries, managers may need to negotiate with five or six different unions, each of which represents a distinct skill or profession.
- **Economic-Development Incentives.** These incentives can be substantial and change constantly. The European Union is trying to standardize incentives based on unemployment levels, but some nations continually stretch the rules and exceed guidelines.
- **Information.** Sometimes there simply is no reliable data on factors such as labor availability, cost of energy, and national inflation rates. These data are generally high quality in developed countries and suspect in developing ones.
- **Personal and Political Contacts.** These contacts can be extremely important in developing and emerging markets and the only way to establish operations. But complying with locally accepted practices can cause ethical dilemmas for managers.

Source: Conrad de Aenlle, "China's Cloudy Investment Picture," *International Herald Tribune* (www.iht.com), June 13, 2008; "Mexico Raises Minimum Wages by 4 Percent, to around $4.85 a Day," *International Herald Tribune* (www.iht.com), December 22, 2007; U.S. Department of Labor Web site (www.dol.gov), select reports.

potentially lucrative market. When firms based in industrial countries moved back into South Africa after the end of apartheid, their competitors followed. Of course, each market can sustain only a certain number of rivals. Firms that cannot compete choose the "least damaging option." This seems to have been the case for Pepsi (www.pepsi.com), which went back into South Africa in 1994, but withdrew in 1997 after being crushed there by Coke (www.cocacola.com).

In this section we have presented several key issues managers consider when investing abroad. We will have more to say on this topic in Chapter 15, when we learn how companies take on such an ambitious goal. Meanwhile, you can read more about what managers should consider when going global in the Global Manager's Briefcase titled, "Surprises of Investing Abroad."

Quick Study

1. Why is control important to companies considering the FDI decision?
2. What is the role of production costs in the FDI decision? Define *rationalized production*.
3. Explain the need for customer knowledge, following clients, and following rivals in the FDI decision.

Government Intervention in Foreign Direct Investment

Nations often intervene in the flow of FDI to protect their cultural heritages, domestic companies, and jobs. They can enact laws, create regulations, or construct administrative hurdles that companies from other nations must overcome if they want to invest in the nation. Yet rising competitive pressure is forcing nations to compete against each other to attract multinational companies. The increased national competition for investment is causing governments to enact regulatory changes that encourage investment. As Table 7.1 demonstrates, the number of regulatory changes that governments introduced in recent years has climbed, the vast majority of which are *more favorable to FDI*.

In a general sense, a bias toward protectionism or openness is rooted in a nation's culture, history, and politics. Values, attitudes, and beliefs form the basis for much of a government's position regarding foreign direct investment. For example, South American nations with strong cultural ties to a European heritage (such as Argentina) are generally enthusiastic about investment received from European nations. South American nations with stronger indigenous influences (such as Ecuador) are generally less enthusiastic.

Opinions vary widely on the appropriate amount of foreign direct investment a country should encourage. At one extreme are those who favor complete economic self-sufficiency and oppose any form of FDI. At the other extreme are those who favor no governmental intervention and booming FDI inflows. Between these two extremes lie most countries, which believe a certain amount of FDI is desirable to raise national output and enhance the standard of living for their people.

Besides philosophical ideals, countries intervene in FDI for a host of very practical reasons. But to fully appreciate those reasons, we must first understand what is meant by a country's *balance of payments*.

Balance of Payments

balance of payments
National accounting system that records all payments to entities in other countries and all receipts coming into the nation.

A country's **balance of payments** is a national accounting system that records all payments to entities in other countries and all receipts coming into the nation. International transactions that result in payments (outflows) to entities in other nations are reductions in the balance of payments accounts, and are therefore recorded with a minus sign. International transactions that result in receipts (inflows) from other nations are additions to the balance of payments accounts, and thus are recorded with a plus sign.

For example, when a U.S. company buys 40 percent of the publicly traded stock of a Mexican company on Mexico's stock market, the U.S. balance of payments records the transaction as an outflow of capital and it is recorded with a minus sign. Table 7.2 shows the recent balance of payments accounts for the United States. As shown in the table, any nation's balance of payments consists of two major components—the *current account* and *capital account*. Let's describe each of these accounts and discuss how to read Table 7.2.

TABLE 7.1 National Regulations and FDI

	1997	1998	1999	2000	2001	2002	2003	2004	2005	2006
Number of countries that introduced changes	76	60	65	70	71	72	82	103	93	93
Number of changes	150	145	139	150	207	246	242	270	205	184
More favorable to FDI	134	136	130	147	193	234	218	234	164	147
Less favorable to FDI	16	9	9	3	14	12	24	36	41	37

Source: Based on *World Investment Report 2007* (Geneva, Switzerland: UNCTAD, September 2007), Overview, Table I.8, p. 14.

TABLE 7.2 U.S. Balance of Payments Accounts (U.S. $ millions)

Current Account		
Exports of goods and services and income receipts	1,418,568	
Merchandise	772,210	
Services	293,492	
Income receipts on U.S. assets abroad	352,866	
Imports of goods and services and income payments		−1,809,099
Merchandise		−1,224,417
Services		−217,024
Income payments on foreign assets in United States		−367,658
Unilateral transfers		−54,136
Current account balance		−444,667
Capital Account		
Increase in U.S. assets abroad (capital outflow)		−580,952
U.S. official reserve assets		−290
Other U.S. government assets		−944
U.S. private assets		−579,718
Foreign assets in the United States (capital inflow)	1,024,218	
Foreign official assets	37,619	
Other foreign assets	986,599	
Capital account balance	443,266	
Statistical discrepancy	55,537	

Source: *Survey of Current Business*, July 2001, (Washington, D.C.: U.S. Department of Commerce, 2001), p. 47.

Current Account   The **current account** is a national account that records transactions involving the import and export of goods and services, income receipts on assets abroad, and income payments on foreign assets inside the country. The *merchandise* account in Table 7.2 includes exports and imports of tangible goods such as computer software, electronic components, and apparel. The *services* account includes exports and imports of services such as tourism, business consulting, and banking services. Suppose a company in the United States receives payment for consulting services provided to a company in another country. The receipt is recorded as an "export of services" and assigned a plus sign in the services account in the balance of payments.

The *income receipts* account includes income earned on U.S. assets held abroad. When a U.S. company's subsidiary in another country remits profits back to the parent in the United States, the receipt is recorded in the income receipts account and given a plus sign. The *income payments* account includes income paid to entities in other nations that is earned on assets they hold in the United States. For example, when a French company's U.S. subsidiary sends profits earned in the United States back to the parent company in France, the transaction is recorded in the income payments account as an outflow, and it is given a minus sign.

A **current account surplus** occurs when a country exports more goods and services and receives more income from abroad than it imports and pays abroad. Conversely, a **current account deficit** occurs when a country imports more goods and services and pays more abroad than it exports and receives from abroad. Table 7.2 shows that the United States had a current account deficit in the year shown.

Capital Account   The **capital account** is a national account that records transactions involving the purchase or sale of assets. Suppose a U.S. citizen buys shares of stock in a Mexican company on Mexico's stock market. The transaction would show up on the capital accounts of both the United States and Mexico—as an outflow of assets from the

current account
National account that records transactions involving the import and export of goods and services, income receipts on assets abroad, and income payments on foreign assets inside the country.

current account surplus
When a country exports more goods and services and receives more income from abroad than it imports and pays abroad.

current account deficit
When a country imports more goods and services and pays more abroad than it exports and receives from abroad.

capital account
National account that records transactions involving the purchase or sale of assets.

Foreign Direct Investment

391

United States and an inflow of assets to Mexico. Conversely, suppose a Mexican investor buys real estate in the United States. That transaction also shows up on the capital accounts of both nations—as an inflow of assets to the United States and as an outflow of assets from Mexico. Although the balances of the current and capital accounts should be the same, there commonly is error caused by recording methods. This figure is recorded in Table 7.2 as a *statistical discrepancy*.

Reasons for Intervention by the Host Country

A number of reasons underlie a government's decisions regarding foreign direct investment by international companies. Let's now look at the two main reasons countries intervene in FDI flows—to control the *balance of payments* and *to obtain resources and benefits*.

Control Balance of Payments Many governments see intervention as the only way to keep their balance of payments under control. First, because foreign direct investment inflows are recorded as additions to the balance of payments, a nation gets a balance-of-payments boost from an initial FDI inflow. Second, countries can impose local content requirements on investors from other nations coming in for the purpose of local production. This gives local companies the chance to become suppliers to the production operation, which can help reduce the nation's imports and thereby improve its balance of payments. Third, exports (if any) generated by the new production operation can have a favorable impact on the host country's balance of payments.

But when companies repatriate profits back to their home countries, they deplete the foreign exchange reserves of their host countries. These capital outflows decrease the balance of payments of the host country. To shore up its balance of payments, the host nation may prohibit or restrict the nondomestic company from removing profits to its home country.

Alternatively, host countries conserve their foreign exchange reserves when international companies reinvest their earnings. Reinvesting in local manufacturing facilities can also improve the competitiveness of local producers and boost a host nation's exports—thus improving its balance-of-payments position.

Obtain Resources and Benefits Beyond balance-of-payments reasons, governments might intervene in FDI flows to acquire resources and benefits such as technology and management skills and employment.

A worker is shown looking up at a skyscraper being built in Beijing, China. The country's liberal economic policies have caused foreign direct investment in China to surge. The investments of multinationals brings badly needed jobs to China's 130 million migrant workers, who travel from one city and job site to another doing day labor on construction sites. How might such investments affect China's balance of payments?
Source: Michael Reynolds/ CORBIS-NY.

ACCESS TO TECHNOLOGY   Investment in technology, whether in products or processes, tends to increase the productivity and the competitiveness of a nation. That is why host nations have a strong incentive to encourage the importation of technology. For years, developing countries in Asia were introduced to expertise in industrial processes as multinationals set up factories within their borders. But today some of them are trying to acquire and develop their own technological expertise. When German industrial giant Siemens (www.siemens.com) chose Singapore as the site for an Asia-Pacific microelectronics design center, Singapore gained access to valuable technology. Singapore also accessed valuable semiconductor technology by joining with U.S.-based Texas Instruments (www.ti.com) and others to set up the country's first semiconductor production facility.

MANAGEMENT SKILLS AND EMPLOYMENT   As we saw in Chapter 4, many formerly communist nations suffer from a lack of management skills needed to succeed in the global economy. By encouraging FDI, these nations can attract talented managers to come in and train locals and thereby improve the international competitiveness of their domestic companies. Furthermore, locals who are trained in modern management techniques may eventually start their own local businesses—further expanding employment opportunities. Yet detractors argue that, although FDI may create jobs, it may also destroy jobs because less competitive local firms may be forced out of business.

Reasons for Intervention by the Home Country

Home nations (those from which international companies launch their investments) may also seek to encourage or discourage *outflows* of FDI for a variety of reasons. But home nations tend to have fewer concerns because they are often prosperous, industrialized nations. For these countries, an outward investment seldom has a national impact—unlike the impact on developing or emerging nations that receive the FDI. Nevertheless, among the most common reasons for discouraging outward FDI are the following:

- *Investing in other nations sends resources out of the home country.* As a result, fewer resources are used for development and economic growth at home. On the other hand, profits on assets abroad that are returned home increase both a home country's balance of payments and its available resources.

- *Outgoing FDI may ultimately damage a nation's balance of payments by taking the place of its exports.* This can occur when a company creates a production facility in a market abroad, the output of which replaces exports that used to be sent there from the home country. For example, if a Volkswagen (www.vw.com) plant in the United States fills a demand that U.S. buyers would otherwise satisfy with purchases of German-made autos, Germany's balance of payments is correspondingly decreased. Still, Germany's balance of payments would be positively affected when companies repatriate U.S. profits, which helps negate the investment's initial negative balance-of-payments effect. Thus an international investment might make a positive contribution to the balance-of-payments position of the country in the long term and offset an initial negative impact.

- *Jobs resulting from outgoing investments may replace jobs at home.* This is often the most contentious issue for home countries. The relocation of production to a low-wage nation can have a strong impact on a locale or region. However, the impact is rarely national, and its effects are often muted by other job opportunities in the economy. In addition, there may be an offsetting improvement in home country employment if additional exports are needed to support the activity represented by the outgoing FDI. For example, if Hyundai (www.hyundai-motor.com) of South Korea builds an automobile manufacturing plant in Brazil, Korean employment may increase in order to supply the Brazilian plant with parts.

But foreign direct investment is not always a negative influence on home nations. In fact, under certain circumstances governments might encourage it. Countries promote outgoing FDI for the following reasons:

- *Outward FDI can increase long-term competitiveness.* Businesses today frequently compete on a global scale. The most competitive firms tend to be those that conduct business in the most favorable location anywhere in the world, continuously improve their performance relative to competitors, and derive technological advantages from alliances formed with other companies. Japanese companies have become masterful at benefiting from FDI and cooperative arrangements with companies from other nations. The key to their success is that Japanese companies see every cooperative venture as a learning opportunity.

■ *Nations may encourage FDI in industries identified as "sunset" industries.* Sunset industries are those that use outdated and obsolete technologies or employ low-wage workers with few skills. These jobs are not greatly appealing to countries having industries that pay skilled workers high wages. By allowing some of these jobs to go abroad and retraining workers in higher-paying skilled work, they can upgrade their economies toward "sunrise" industries. This represents a trade-off for governments between a short-term loss of jobs and the long-term benefit of developing workers' skills.

Quick Study

1. What is a country's *balance of payments*? Briefly explain its usefulness.
2. Explain the difference between the *current account* and the *capital account*.
3. For what reasons do *host* countries intervene in FDI?
4. For what reasons do *home* countries intervene in FDI?

Government Policy Instruments and FDI

Over time, both host and home nations have developed a range of methods to either promote or restrict FDI (see Table 7.3). Governments use these tools for many reasons, including improving balance-of-payments positions; acquiring resources; and, in the case of outward investment, keeping jobs at home. Let's take a look at these methods.

Host Countries: Promotion

Host countries offer a variety of incentives to encourage FDI inflows. These take two general forms—financial incentives and infrastructure improvements.

Financial Incentives   Host governments of all nations grant companies financial incentives if they will invest within their borders. One method includes tax incentives, such as lower tax rates or offers to waive taxes on local profits for a period of time—extending as far out as five years or more. A country may also offer *low interest loans* to investors.

The downside of these types of incentives is they can allow multinationals to create bidding wars between locations that are vying for the investment. In such cases, the com-

TABLE 7.3 **Methods of Promoting and Restricting FDI**

	FDI Promotion	FDI Restriction
Host Countries	Tax incentives	Ownership restrictions
	Low-interest loans	Performance demands
	Infrastructure improvements	
Home Countries	Insurance	Differential tax rates
	Loans	Sanctions
	Tax breaks	
	Political pressure	

pany typically invests in the most appealing region after the locations endure rounds of escalating incentives. Companies have even been accused of engaging other governments in negotiations to force concessions from locations already selected for investment. The cost to taxpayers of attracting FDI can be several times what the actual jobs themselves pay—especially when nations try to one-up each other to win investment.

Infrastructure Improvements   Because of the problems associated with financial incentives, some governments are taking an alternative route to luring investment. Lasting benefits for communities surrounding the investment location can result from making local *infrastructure improvements*—better seaports suitable for containerized shipping, improved roads, and increased telecommunications systems. For instance, Malaysia is carving an enormous Multimedia Super Corridor (MSC) into a region's forested surroundings. The MSC promises a paperless government, an intelligent city called Cyberjaya, two telesuburbs, a technology park, a multimedia university, and an intellectual-property-protection park. The MSC is dedicated to creating the most advanced technologies in telecommunications, medicine, distance learning, and remote manufacturing.

Host Countries: Restriction

Host countries also have a variety of methods to restrict incoming FDI. Again, these take two general forms—ownership restrictions and performance demands.

Ownership Restrictions   Governments can impose *ownership restrictions* that prohibit nondomestic companies from investing in certain industries or from owning certain types of businesses. Such prohibitions typically apply to businesses in cultural industries and companies vital to national security. For example, as some Islamic countries in the Middle East try to protect traditional values, accepting investment by Western companies is a controversial issue between purists and moderates. Also, most nations do not allow FDI in their domestic weapons or national defense firms. Another ownership restriction is a requirement that nondomestic investors hold less than a 50 percent stake in local firms when they undertake foreign direct investment.

But nations are eliminating such restrictions because companies today often can choose another location that has no such restriction in place. When General Motors was deciding whether to invest in an aging automobile plant in Jakarta, Indonesia, the Indonesian government scrapped its ownership restriction of an eventual forced sale to Indonesians because China and Vietnam were also courting GM for the same financial investment.

Performance Demands   More common than ownership requirements are *performance demands* that influence how international companies operate in the host nation. Although typically viewed as intrusive, most international companies allow for them in the same way they allow for home country regulations. Performance demands include ensuring that a portion of the product's content originates locally, stipulating the portion of output that must be exported, or requiring that certain technologies be transferred to local businesses.

Home Countries: Promotion

To encourage outbound FDI, home country governments can do any of the following:

- Offer *insurance* to cover the risks of investments abroad, including, among others, insurance against expropriation of assets and losses from armed conflict, kidnappings, and terrorist attacks.
- Grant *loans* to firms wishing to increase their investments abroad. A home country government may also guarantee the loans that a company takes from financial institutions.
- Offer *tax breaks* on profits earned abroad or negotiate special tax treaties. For example, several multinational agreements reduce or eliminate the practice of double taxation—profits earned abroad being taxed both in the home and host countries.

- Apply *political pressure* on other nations to get them to relax their restrictions on inbound investments. Non-Japanese companies often find it very difficult to invest inside Japan. The United States, for one, repeatedly pressures the Japanese government to open its market further to FDI. But because such pressure has achieved little success, many U.S. companies cooperate with local Japanese businesses.

Home Countries: Restriction

On the other hand, to limit the effects of outbound FDI on the national economy, home governments may exercise either of the following two options:

- Impose *differential tax rates* that charge income from earnings abroad at a higher rate than domestic earnings.
- Impose outright *sanctions* that prohibit domestic firms from making investments in certain nations.

Quick Study

1. Identify the main methods host countries use to promote and restrict FDI.
2. What methods do home countries use to promote and restrict FDI?

Bottom Line FOR BUSINESS

Companies ranging from massive global corporations to adventurous entrepreneurs all contribute to FDI flows, and the long-term trend in FDI is upward. Here we briefly discuss the influence of national governments on FDI flows and flows of FDI in Asia and Europe.

National Governments and FDI

The actions of national governments have important implications for business. Companies can either be thwarted in their efforts or be encouraged to invest in a nation, depending on the philosophies of home and host governments. The balance-of-payments positions of both home and host countries are also important because FDI flows affect the economic health of nations. To attract investment, a nation must provide a climate conducive to business operations, including pro-growth economic policies, a stable regulatory environment, and a sound infrastructure, to name just a few.

Increased competition for investment by multinationals has caused nations to make regulatory changes more favorable to FDI. Moreover, just as nations around the world are creating free trade agreements (covered in Chapter 8), they are also embracing bilateral investment treaties. These bilateral investment treaties are becoming prominent tools used to attract investment. Investment pro-

visions within free trade agreements are also receiving greater attention than in the past. These efforts to attract investment have direct implications for the strategies of multinational companies, particularly when it comes to deciding where to locate production, logistics, and back-office service activities.

Foreign Direct Investment in Europe

Developing nations in Africa, Latin America, and much of Southeast Asia were hit especially hard by the lower FDI flows in the early 2000s, but are rebounding. FDI inflows into the developing (transition) nations of Southeast Europe and the Commonwealth of Independent States hit an all-time high in 2006. Countries that recently entered the European Union did particularly well. They saw less investment in areas supporting low-wage, unskilled occupations, and greater investment in higher value-added activities that take advantage of a well-educated workforce.

Yet the main reason for the fast pace at which foreign direct investment is occurring in Western Europe is regional economic integration (see Chapter 8). Some of the foreign investment reported by the European Union certainly went to the relatively less developed markets of the new central and eastern European members. But much of the activity occurring among western European companies is industry consolidation brought on by the opening of markets and the tearing down of barriers to free trade and investment. Change in the economic landscape across Europe is creating a more competitive business climate there.

Foreign Direct Investment in Asia

China attracts the majority of Asia's FDI, luring companies with a low-wage workforce and access to an enormous domestic market. Many companies already active in China are upping their investment further, and companies not yet there are developing strategies for how to include China in their future plans. The "off-shoring" of services will likely propel continued FDI in the coming years, of which India is the primary destination. India's attraction is its well-educated, low-cost, and English-speaking workforce.

An aspect of national business environments that has implications for future business activity is the natural environment. By their actions, businesses lay the foundation for people's attitudes in developing nations toward FDI by multinationals. For example, greater decentralization in China's politics has placed local Communist Party bosses and bureaucrats at the center of many FDI deals there. These individuals are often more motivated by their personal financial gain than they are worried about pollution. But China's government is increasing spending on the environment, and multinationals are helping in cleaning up the environment.

Chapter Summary

1. Describe worldwide patterns of foreign direct investment (FDI) and reasons for these patterns.
   - FDI inflows peaked in 2000 at $1.4 trillion, but then contracted through 2003. They then rebounded to around $648 billion in 2004, $946 billion in 2005, and $1.3 trillion in 2006.
   - Developed countries account for around 65 percent of global FDI inflows, and developing countries account for about 29 percent.
   - Among developed countries, the European Union (EU), the United States, and Japan account for the majority of FDI inflows. The EU garnered $531 billion of FDI in 2006 (40 percent of the world total).
   - FDI inflows to developing Asian nations were just over $259 billion in 2006, with China attracting over $69 billion and India attracting nearly $17 billion.
   - FDI inflows to all of Africa accounted for about 2.7 percent of total world FDI inflows in 2006.
   - *Globalization* and a growing number of *mergers and acquisitions* account for the rising tide of FDI flows.

2. Describe each of the theories that attempt to explain why foreign direct investment occurs.
   - The *international product life cycle theory* says that a company begins by exporting its product and later undertakes foreign direct investment as the product moves through its life cycle of three stages: new product, maturing product, and standardized product.
   - *Market imperfections theory* says that when an imperfection in the market makes a transaction less efficient than it could be, a company will undertake foreign direct investment to internalize the transaction and thereby remove the imperfection.
   - The *eclectic theory* says that firms undertake foreign direct investment when the features of a particular location combine with ownership and internalization advantages to make a location appealing for investment.
   - The *market power theory* states that a firm tries to establish a dominant market presence in an industry by undertaking foreign direct investment.

3. Discuss the important management issues in the foreign direct investment decision.
   - Although companies investing abroad often wish to *control* activities in the local market, they may be forced to hire local managers or to export all goods produced locally.
   - Acquisition of an existing business is preferred when the existing business entails updated equipment, good relations with workers, and a suitable location.
   - When adequate facilities are unavailable, a company might need to pursue a *greenfield investment*.
   - A local market presence can give a company valuable knowledge of local *buyer behavior*.
   - Firms commonly engage in FDI when it locates them close to *client* firms and *rival* firms.

4. Explain why governments intervene in the free flow of foreign direct investment.
   - *Host nations* receive a *balance-of-payments* boost from initial FDI and from any exports the FDI generates, but they see a decrease in balance of payments when a company sends profits to the home country.
   - FDI in *technology* brings in people with *management skills* who can train locals and increase a nation's productivity and competitiveness.
   - *Home countries* intervene in FDI outflows because they can lower the balance of payments, but profits sent home that are earned on assets abroad increase the balance of payments.
   - FDI outflows may replace jobs at home that were based on exports to the host country and may damage the home nation's balance of payments if they reduce prior exports.
5. Discuss the policy instruments that governments use to promote and restrict foreign direct investment.
   - Host countries can promote FDI inflows by offering companies *tax incentives* (such as lower tax rates or waived taxes), extending *low interest loans*, and making local *infrastructure improvements*.
   - Host countries can restrict FDI inflows by imposing *ownership restrictions* (prohibitions from certain industries) and by creating *performance demands* that influence how a company can operate.
   - Home countries can promote FDI outflows by offering *insurance* to cover investment risks abroad, granting loans to firms investing abroad, guaranteeing company loans from financial institutions, offering *tax breaks* on profits earned abroad, negotiating special tax treaties, and applying *political pressure* to get other nations to accept FDI.
   - Home countries can restrict FDI outflows by imposing *differential tax rates* that charge income from earnings abroad at a higher rate than domestic earnings and by imposing *sanctions* that prohibit domestic firms from making investments in certain nations.

Talk It Over

1. You overhear your superior tell another manager in the company: "I'm fed up with our nation's companies sending manufacturing jobs abroad and off-shoring service work to lower-wage nations. Don't any of them have any national pride?" The other manager responds, "I disagree. It is every company's duty to make as much profit as possible for its owners. If that means going abroad to reduce costs, so be it." Do you agree with either of these managers? Why or why not? Now step into the conversation and explain where you stand on this issue.
2. The global carmaker you work for is investing in an automobile assembly facility in Costa Rica with a local partner. Explain the potential reasons for this investment. Will your company want to exercise a great deal of control over this operation? Why or why not? In what areas might your company want to exercise control and in what areas might it cede control to the partner?
3. This chapter presented several theories that attempt to explain why firms undertake foreign direct investment. Which of these theories seems most appealing to you? Why is it appealing? Can you think of one or more companies that seem to fit the pattern described by the theory? In your opinion, what faults do the alternative theories have?

Teaming Up

1. **Research Project.** In a small group, locate an article in the business press that discusses a cross-border merger or acquisition within the past year. Gather additional information on the deal from any sources available. What reasons did each company give for the merger or acquisition? Was it a marriage of equals or did a larger partner absorb a far smaller one? Do the articles identify any internal issues managers had to deal with following the merger or acquisition? What is the current performance of the new company? Write a two- to three-page report of your group's findings.
2. **Market Entry Strategy Project.** This exercise corresponds to the *MESP* online simulation. For the country your team is researching, does it attract large amounts of FDI? Is it a major source of FDI for other nations? What is the nation's balance-of-payments position? What is its current account balance? List some possible causes for its surplus or deficit. How is this surplus or deficit affecting the nation's economic performance? What is its capital account balance? How does the government encourage or restrict trade with other nations? Integrate your findings into your completed *MESP* report.

Key Terms

balance of payments
capital account
current account
current account deficit
current account surplus

eclectic theory
foreign direct investment
  (FDI)
international product
  life cycle

market imperfections
market power
portfolio investment
rationalized production
vertical integration

Take It to the Web

1. **Video Report.** Visit this book's channel on YouTube (YouTube.com/MyIBvideos). Click on "Playlists" near the top of the page and click on the set of videos labeled "Ch 07: Foreign Direct Investment." Watch one video from the list and summarize it in a half-page report. Reflecting on the contents of this chapter, which aspects of foreign direct investment can you identify in the video? How might a company engaged in international business act on the information contained in the video?

2. **Web Site Report.** This chapter presented many reasons why companies directly invest in other nations and factors in the decision of whether and where to invest abroad.

    Research the economy of the Philippines and its neighbors. In what economic sectors is each country strong? Do the strengths of each country really complement one another, or do they compete directly with one another? If you were considering investing in the Philippines, what management issues would concern you? Be specific in your answer. (*Hint*: A good place to begin your research is the CIA's World Factbook (www.odci.gov/cia/publications/factbook).

    In this era of intense national competition to attract jobs, Southeast Asian governments fear losing ground to China in the race for investment. What do you think those governments could do to increase the attractiveness of their homelands for multinationals?

    Find an article on the Internet that describes a company's decision to relocate some or all of its business operations (goods or services). What reasons are stated for the relocation? Was any consideration given to the plight of employees being put out of work?

Ethical Challenges

1. You are the president of a major textile manufacturer in Dubai, considering the purchase of a struggling factory in Pakistan. The factory you might purchase has been accused of practicing poor environmental procedures. It is located on a major river and was recently found to be dumping waste into the river. If you do purchase the factory, you would like to completely overhaul the business by replacing the management and hiring all new employees. If you were to do this, the current workers and managers of the factory would be out of work, but the factory could potentially be more productive and adopt environment-friendly practices. What do you do? Do you purchase the factory, replace the staff, and hope that it turns a profit? Do you purchase the factory, keep the current staff, and train them to use better environmental practices? Or do you abandon the idea because of the factory's damaged reputation and current troubles?

2. You are a sales manager working in international sales for a rice distributor from Thailand. Your company wants you to sell a large shipment of rice to Japan. Your boss has instructed you to sell the rice immediately, at a price that is well below its current market value. In the office you overhear the quality assurance manager discussing with another employee the "potentially contaminated shipment headed for Japan." You are aware that your company has had problems with E. coli contamination in the past. How do you respond to your boss's request? Do you go ahead with the shipment to Japan, despite the possibility of contamination? Who should you contact --your boss or someone else inside or outside the company?

3. You are the French ambassador to Malaysia. In order to become a major export platform for the semiconductor industry, Malaysia's government has not only offered tax breaks, but also guaranteed that electronics workers would be prohibited from organizing independent labor unions. The government decreed that the goal of national development required a "union-free" environment for the "pioneers" of semiconductors. Under pressure from

U.S. labor unions, the Malaysian government offered a weak alternative to industry unions: company-by-company "in-house" unions. Yet, as soon as workers organized one at a Harris Electronics plant, the 21 union leaders were fired and the new union was disbanded. In another case, when French-owned Thomson Electronics inherited a Malaysian factory with a union of 3,000, it closed the plant and moved the work to Vietnam. Newly industrialized nations such as Malaysia feel that their future depends on investment by multinationals. Yet their governments are acutely aware that in the absence of incentives such as a "union-free" workforce, international companies can easily take their investment money elsewhere. Discuss the problems that these governments face in balancing the needs of their citizens with the long-term quest for economic development. As the ambassador, what advice would you give Malaysian business and government leaders? Find an example of another nation that can help you make the case for local unions.

Sunshine Powers Joint Venture in India

"**B**ritish Petroleum (BP) is a worldwide leader in the energy business and is involved in much more than just drilling for and refining oil. Solar power has not yet reached the point of being widely implemented around the world, but BP has an international department, BP Solar, which is devoted to making advances in and encouraging the use of solar power. The company is based in England, but has spread across the globe. One of its most successful outlets originated when BP Solar joined forces with a successful Indian company, Tata Energy. Tata BP Solar India Unlimited was born in 1989, and it has become one of the most successful and prestigious solar power companies in the world.

The main Tata BP Solar manufacturing plant is located in Bangalore, India, and it has the capability to manufacture solar cells, assemble solar modules, and balance solar power systems. It is essentially a one-stop shop for the manufacture, installation, and service of solar power systems. The solar photovoltaic and solar thermal products assembly plant is the largest assembly line of its kind in the country. Tata BP Solar provides solar power products for all of India and also provides a major supplement to BP Solar's production and manufacturing for the rest of the world. Engineers aid in developing new technologies to be produced at all BP Solar locations. Over 600 workers are employed at the three manufacturing centers and eight offices that the company owns in India.

Photovoltaic technology converts sunlight directly into electricity. Tata BP Solar is one of the worldwide leaders in manufacturing photovoltaic systems, which consist of a panel of individual solar cells bonded together electrically. Sales of these systems are on the rise, as concerns about utilizing renewable sources of energy are becoming more prevalent. Almost 60 percent of the company's sales come from exporting photovoltaic systems, mostly to high-cost markets such as Europe and the United States. They have also had some success in creating solar markets in nearby Asian and Middle Eastern countries, such as Bangladesh, Sri Lanka, Afghanistan, Nepal, Bhutan, Myanmar, and Dubai. A major solar power and communications project has been undertaken in Bhutan, linking small villages and hamlets through telecommunications. Tata BP Solar earned the contract to provide solar power for the corDECT telecom network, which now spreads all over Bhutan. Seeing Bhutan's success, the WLL telecom network in Afghanistan asked Tata BP to provide solar power for their budding network.

British Petroleum is a good example of a company that started with its original home base and expanded all over the world. BP markets its solar products in North America, Europe, Asia, and Australasia. By purchasing existing foreign energy companies, BP has become hugely successful. The purchase of existing companies is often advantageous compared with starting a new company in a foreign nation, as the existing company is already established. It takes capital to do this, but it is wise because the foreign company is already established. The original names are still used by many of the companies that BP has purchased, including Amoco, Arco, Sohio, Castrol, and Aral, all of which are major gasoline suppliers. BP has expanded its repertoire beyond the energy business, as it owns the ampm convenience store brand that is located at many of its Arco locations, as well as the Wild Bean Café brand, which sells coffee products, deli sandwiches, and desserts.

International expansion is the goal of most large businesses, but it can be extremely difficult. British Petroleum has successfully positioned itself as an international energy powerhouse through its wise investments and purchases.

Thinking Globally

1. Why do you think British Petroleum has been so success-ful in securing an international reputation? Due to the recent speculation and concern about the end of the diesel and gasoline era, do you think that BP is taking sufficient measures toward getting involved in developing and uti-lizing new forms of fuel?

2. Why might India be a good location for a company developing solar power products? Give several reasons. What other countries do you think would be a good choice for BP to develop its alternative energy manufacturing facilities? Why?

3. What do you think are the pros and cons of British Petroleum's approach to managing foreign direct investments? What might they do differently? Do you think that it is wise to allow these companies to maintain the management that is already in place and allow them to operate with some independence from BP?

4. Do you think it is an astute business decision to allow foreign companies to keep their original brand name after BP purchases them? Why or why not? In your opinion, does this reduce the credibility of the British Petroleum brand, or increase it?

Source: Based on "Tata BP Solar—Inheritors of a rich legacy," http://www.tatabpsolar.com/corporateprofile.html, Accessed December 18, 2008.

OBJECTIVES

- To offer an historical overview of consumption and consumerism
- To summarize sociological, neoclassical, and marxist views of consumption
- To analyze the geographies of consumption at multiple spatial scales
- To note the environmental impacts of mass consumption

Consumption is simultaneously a spatial as well as economic, cultural, and psychological process.

THE BASIC CIRCULAR MODEL

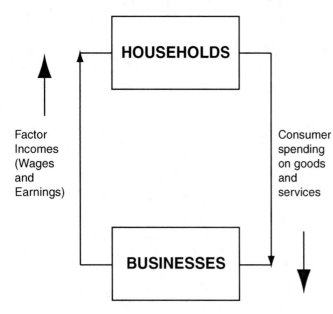

HOUSEHOLDS

Factor Incomes (Wages and Earnings)

Consumer spending on goods and services

BUSINESSES

FIGURE 11.1
Production and consumption constitute two intertwined dimensions of capitalism. Without demand, there will not be a supply. Because both production and consumption produce and are shaped by complex geographies, their interrelations across space and time are complex, contingent, and ever changing.

In contrast to production, which has been studied in exhaustive detail in economic geography, consumption has long been ignored. While consumption played a role in traditional models of space and location theory, only recently have economic geographers come to view the issue in social terms. Yet consumption is critically important to understanding how economies are stretched over the earth's surface, their impacts, and how they change. Consumption and production cannot be neatly separated and are closely intertwined: Most people work in order to consume, and consume in order to live. Thus, we can think of consumption and production as two facets of one circular process (Figure 11.1).

The term "consumption" means a variety of things: As long as there have been people, there has been consumption. The Latin word *consumere* meant "to use up," and for centuries consumption referred to the disease tuberculosis. Today, consumption is typically taken to mean the use of goods and services to satisfy individual and collective wants and needs. Consumption is a complex topic because it lays at the intersection of various spheres of social life, such as production, class, gender, the relations between state and market, and the individual and society. Far more than simply an "economic" phenomenon, consumption is also a cultural and psychological construction that reflects and affects people at both the social and personal levels. Consumption is a major interface between the individual and society.

Economically, consumption is enormously important, constituting the bulk of the economic activity of most countries. For example, roughly 55 percent of the U.S. GDP consists of consumer or household purchases of different types (Figure 11.2); in comparison, business spending (investment) is only 15 percent, foreign trade is 18 percent, and government is 12 percent.

Composition of U.S. GDP by sector

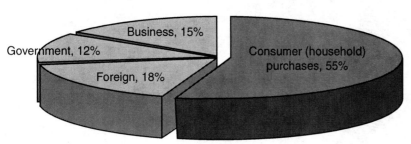

Business, 15%

Government, 12%

Foreign, 18%

Consumer (household) purchases, 55%

FIGURE 11.2
More than half of the U.S. economy consists of consumption by households and individuals. Small changes in consumer spending have enormous repercussions for the economy as a whole. For this reason, consumer confidence levels, shopping habits, changing preferences, and inclinations to spend versus save are closely monitored by social scientists and policy-making officials.

The historical context of consumption

Although it may seem "natural," consumption as a social process has a history that reflects the extent and ways in which people have consumed over time. Most of what we know of premodern consumption focuses on elites, who had the greatest purchasing power. In such societies, in which there was relatively little trade and most goods were produced and consumed locally, trade was largely confined to luxury goods that were affordable only to the wealthy. High levels of consumption were hobbled by low average spending power. In medieval Europe, there was no single word for consumption; only with the rise of taxation in the sixteenth and seventeenth centuries did diverse activities like clothes and eating come to be seen as having something in common. We may thus posit that consumption as a social category is essentially an invention of capitalism. The rise of the colonial world economy in the sixteenth century (Chapter 2) simultaneously created a class of people with significantly large incomes to spend and the ability to make available products from a wide array of places around the globe, such as sugar from the Caribbean, cod from New England, and spices from Asia.

The rise of the modern form of consumption—consumerism—occurred largely through the emergence of the Industrial Revolution in the late eighteenth century. Industrialization, inanimate energy sources, and mechanized production generated a sudden, dramatic breakthrough that significantly lowered the prices of many goods and lifted millions of people above subsistence levels. Food and clothing, for example, became affordable to the growing middle class. Simultaneously, gradually increasing incomes began to transform workers into consumers, leading to the birth of the consumer society, with enormous implications for class consciousness. In the 1830s, the first department stores appeared, in Paris, which were the retail trade version of the factory. Historically, the growth of mass production in the nineteenth century was accompanied by mass consumption. Because capitalism thrives on newness, advertising was an integral part of this process, forever generating new needs and desires and converting luxuries into necessities. In the late twentieth century, changes in the world economy, including deindustrialization and the explosive growth of producer services, induced concomitant changes in consumption, including increasingly specialized niche markets and sophisticated consumers.

It should be noted that this process was far from smooth: Consumerism threatened much older ways of looking at the world. In particularly, ideas of thrift, embodied in slogans such as "waste not, want not," gradually gave way to morals that reflected the role of money as the measure of social status and consumption as the means to obtain it. Objections to consumerism had religious overtones, often couched in a scorn for the material world and an emphasis on asceticism. Ultimately, however, the ethic of the rising bourgeois class triumphed, a process that occurred during the growth of capitalism, the Industrial Revolution, the Enlightenment, and the growing dominance of individualism. Mass consumption entailed the commodification of consciousness, in which the self is defined through want, not social obligation. Consumerism was thus an integral part of the ascendancy of modernity; if tradition is the regulation of desire, modernity tends to unleash it.

Consumerism involved not simply the purchase of goods but the entire experience of shopping, including early catalogs and mail orders made possible by the growth of postal system, as well as printed advertisements (which were useful in societies with low literacy rates). As workers fought for higher wages and lower working hours, including the eight-hour work day and the five-day work week, consumption increasingly came to be equated with leisure. In the process, everyday life changed dramatically. Child rearing, for example, increasingly included the purchase of goods to comfort children. Clean clothes became the norm expected of an increasingly larger fraction of society. By the early twentieth century, the association of romance with consumption led to the invention of dating among couples. Buying and purchasing increasingly came to be naturalized as the keys to happiness, success, relief from pain and boredom, and a positive self-image.

Consumerism started primarily in Britain and the United States, although in the nineteenth century it had engulfed Western Europe. After World War II, consumerism has spread to large parts of the world, where it displaced traditional value systems. In many ways the spread of this phenomenon reflects the enormous influence of the United States in the world economy and the diffusion of capitalism. Multinational corporations, increased international trade, rising literacy levels, and television played key roles in this process. The triumph of consumerism was uneven geographically, and often resisted, yet almost always unsuccessfully. Typically the growth of consumerism has been slowest in societies in which entrenched religious objections were difficult to overcome. As ever larger shares of the world's population embraced this lifestyle, consumerism came to be the model for many kinds of social relations, such as education, religion, and family life. As commodity relations dominate more societies, everyone, it seems, has become essentially a buyer or seller, for better or worse.

After World War II, the expansion of consumerism was closely linked to the growth of credit. In consumerist societies, credit cards can enhance many people's quality of life, and are useful for emergencies or the purchase of important luxuries. Psychologically, credit cards are often portrayed as synonymous with

Consumer using credit card.

freedom, a rite of passage for adolescents. In the United States, the size of the "credit card nation" is staggering, including 158 million Americans and 1.5 billion cards in 2001 or 9.5 per card holder. The average card has $6,648 in debt. The rising tide of credit card debt in the 1990s, including small businesses, has generated a wave of personal bankruptcies; indeed, more people go bankrupt each year than go to college. Credit card companies such as American Express make a profit by charging merchants fees and by charging consumers relatively high interest rates.

The explosion of consumer debt undermined the traditional view of credit, which was grounded in the Puritan work ethic. This perspective emphasized frugality, delayed gratification, and saving, and debt was often regarded as sinful. Consumption was morally supposed to be held in line with one's income.

This worldview was annihilated by the onslaught initiated by banks and credit card companies in the 1970s and 1980s, with marketing campaigns that centered on the commodification of fun. Credit cards were sold as a marker of social sophistication and a carefree lifestyle. In the context of the deregulation of banking,

which produced a more competitive environment, credit cards became the golden goose for many banks, earning higher rates of return than other avenues. Banks aggressively targeted many social groups that they had previously ignored, such as college students and the elderly. Moreover, consumers faced growing problems that arose with the end of the postwar boom, including deindustrialization, globalization, and stagnant incomes (Chapter 7). As spending continued to rise but incomes did not (Figure 11.3), U.S. savings rates declined steadily (in 2004, it was zero) (Figure 11.4) and many households found themselves swimming in debt they could not afford.

THEORETICAL PERSPECTIVES ON CONSUMPTION

Consumption may be viewed from several conceptual angles. Three perspectives are discussed here, the sociological, neoclassical economic, and marxist notions. There are merits as well as weaknesses to each of these.

Sociological Views

Sociologists have long examined the role of consumption in relation to individuals' and households' standard of living, class, and status. In the early twentieth century, for example, Max Weber argued that delayed gratification lay at the heart of the Protestant ethic; consumerism mutated this ethic into the unmitigated pursuit of pleasure. American sociologist Thorsten Veblen, studying the profligate consumption of the rich during the late nineteenth century era of the robber barons, coined the famous term "conspicuous consumption" to denote consumption as a social statement to others, that is, as a display of wealth and status. This line of thought led to a long series of works concerned with the relations between consumption and identity, emphasizing shopping as something much more than simply the purchase of goods but as a set of signals used to define who we are and what we mean. It is ironic, for example, that in societies such as the United States many people find their individual identities through the purchase of mass-produced commodities.

Sociologists have noted how consumption varies by social category, a phenomenon of vital importance to marketers. For example, consumption is highly gendered: men and women buy very different items, and shop in different ways. Because women are typically responsible for buying necessities for the household, they comprise the bulk of consumers, and many advertisers appeal to them. Likewise, shopping preferences vary predictably by age across the lifestyle. For example, as people age, they tend to spend more on medical care (Chapter 8). Race and ethnicity are also

Domestic consumption and consumer debt in the U.S., relative to disposable income

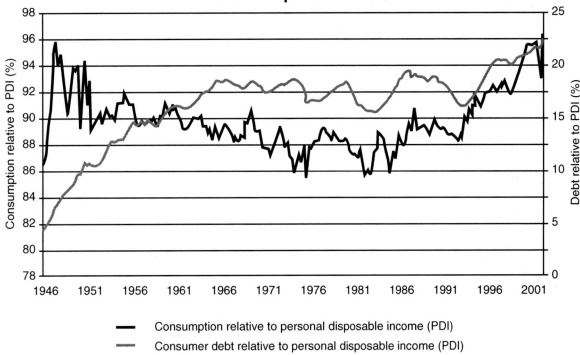

Consumption relative to personal disposable income (PDI)

Consumer debt relative to personal disposable income (PDI)

FIGURE 11.3
Faced with stagnant average real (post-inflation) incomes, rising costs, and ferocious advertising, and rising consumer debt, the U.S. savings rate has steadily declined over time. Savings forms the pool of capital necessary for investment.

critical sociological categories that are intertwined with the class and gender dimensions of consumption, as different ethnic groups have different preferences for food, clothes, automobiles, and other goods.

Critical to the sociological understanding of consumption is the role of advertising. Advertising is essentially a mechanism that funnels consciousness to the commodity, generating new wants and desires. Consumerist societies are saturated by advertising, which plays a major role in the construction of roles and role models. For example, two-thirds of newspapers typically consist of advertising. The average American child has seen 1 million television advertisements by age 20. Advertising encourages us to meet nonmaterial needs through material ends, generating a faith that commodities will impart a desired status, sexuality, physical prowess, lifestyle, and so forth.

So extensive has consumerism become that it has generated an epidemic of "affluenza," which may be variously described as the dogged pursuit of more, an obsessive quest for pleasure, materialism run amuck. Many people find themselves on an endless treadmill of permanent discontent. Ironically, never has so much meant so little to so many. To pay for this lifestyle,

FIGURE 11.4
In the face of mounting international competition, deindustrialization, and low income growth but sustained consumption, the U.S. personal savings rate has declined steadily.

U.S. Savings Rate, 1959-2006

Americans often suffer a "time famine" in which they work more hours than they did in the 1960s, and get 20 percent less sleep than they did in 1900. The average American parent spends six hours per week shopping and only 40 minutes with their children. Studies of average satisfaction levels, which peaked in the United States in the 1950s, indicate that money does not necessarily buy happiness. Even as consumption levels have risen, so have psychological markers of unhappiness such as depression and suicide. In the need to be constantly entertained by the new, many people find themselves bored as the exotic quickly becomes commonplace.

Moreover, consumerism often carries into interpersonal relationships, mutating citizens into consumers and collapsing the field of social obligations into the self. Rather than citizens, everyone becomes simply a consumer, whose sense of citizenship extends no further than their shopping cart. This process is manifested, for example, in steady, long-term declines in voting, volunteering, and disinvestment in public areas.

Neoclassical Economic Views

The historically dominant view of consumption came from neoclassical economics, which analytically privileges demand over production. Neoclassical economics, which emerged in the 1870s, detached economics from political economy, and drew upon a long tradition of utilitarianism initiated by the philosopher Jeremy Bentham (1748–1832). This school of thought, which is dominant in the United States Canada, and much of Europe, begins with the individual. Bentham offered what he called a "hedonic calculus" based on mythical units called "utils" that he suggested standardized our understanding of happiness. Arguing that people are inherently self-interested, he suggested the principle of greatest happiness, that is, people will maximize pleasure and minimize pain. In the nineteenth century, neoclassical economists began to model this process in highly simplified but powerful ways, often invoking complex mathematics.

In this perspective, individual consumers are modeled using a model of human beings, *Homo economicus,* who is all-knowing about his or her opportunities in the world and their respective costs, benefits, and consequences. The level of satisfaction that individuals experience, their utility with a particular combination of goods, is reflected in indifference curves that map the trade-offs each person is willing to make to achieve equal satisfaction (Figure 11.5). Thus, along one utility curve the person is equally happy; the higher the utility curve is, the higher the person is. The law of diminishing marginal utility holds that as a person consumes increasing quantities of a given good, the pleasure or utility they derive from it—their

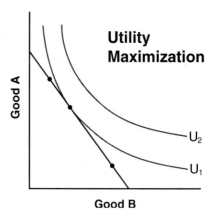

FIGURE 11.5

The conventional neoclassical economic view of consumption begins with utility maximization. Utility, or happiness, is held to be equal with different combinations of goods. With a limited income, a consumer will rationally attempt to maximize his or her utility by consuming the combination of goods and services in which the slope of the utility curve just touches the income constraint. While elegant and popular, this view takes utility as a given, ignoring the social origins of desire and demand.

utility—increases, but at a decreasing rate. Because consumption is always limited by income, each person must maximize his or her total utility or happiness by allocating their income among different goods. Since we cannot spend more than we earn (at least in the long run), the model does not allow the consumer to rise from Utility line 1 to Utility line 2. The slope of the income constraint reflects the relative prices of Good A and Good B, that is, the amount one must give up of one in order to purchase a unit of another. The optimal amount consumed (point z) occurs when the consumer maximizes utility by equating the marginal amount derived from the consumption of each good with the marginal cost as reflected in the income line. Essentially, utility curves reflect what consumers would *like* to do, income constraints depict what they *can* do, and the point of tangency explains what they *actually* do.

Aggregate consumption patterns in this model reflect the multitude of individual choices about how to spend their incomes. Because consumer demand is held to be the motor that drives the economy, this view is often equated with the notion of consumer sovereignty. Spending levels, in turn, reflect the dynamics of the labor market, unemployment rates, wage levels, prices, attitudes toward saving and spending, and the various factors that determine the shape of utility curves, such as the demographic composition of a society. Consumer tastes and preferences will be molded by a number of social issues, including fads and fashions and concerns over health and safety (e.g., beer and wine are displacing hard liquor, chicken has surpassed beef consumption in the United States). Consumption patterns will reflect how income-and price-elastic the demand for different commodities is. We noted in Chapter 8 that increased consumption of services is a driving force in the growth of retail trade and personal services.

The neoclassic view of consumption is that markets are always optimally efficient economically (and hence morally optimal as well). While the neoclassical view is internally consistent within its own terms of reference, it suffers from several problems, including the lack of any historical or social context and its inability to do justice to the rich semiotics and social dimensions of consumption. In part, this failure arises because neoclassical economics does not represent the consumer, or consumption, as a *social* act, that is, one embedded within broader relations of class, gender, ethnicity, and power, but as a purely individual one. For example, neoclassical economics offers no account of the origins of utility curves or why they assume their particular form; they are simply taken as given. "Individual" choices are always part of web of public policy choices; for example, the simple act of buying butter reflects federal subsidies to dairy farmers, health laws, the use of artificial chemicals and hormones, and so on. Social categories in neoclassical economics, if they arise at all, are defined largely by their relations to consumption: Class in conventional social analysis, for example, refers to income and socioeconomic status. Adam Smith's famous hidden hand assumes individual's choices are independent, not socially produced, and that they don't affect each other.

Finally, even when individuals act rationally, that is, maximize utility, they can lead to collective irrationalities or market failures. These occur, for example, when the market price does not reflect all of the social costs of a good. If each person at a concert stands up for a better view, for example, everyone is forced to do so and is therefore worse off. Each person's decision to drive is individually rational, but collectively these decisions create irrational traffic jams and gridlock.

Marxist Views

A third interpretation of consumption comes from marxism, which argues that social science must penetrate the veneer of outer appearances to reveal the social relations that lie beneath them. The expansion of capitalism historically has been predicated upon a widening and deepening of commodity relations, that is, the development of new markets and the transformation of goods and services that were formerly outside of the market into commodities (e.g., housing, child care, transportation, education). While marxism has

generally privileged production and labor over consumption, Karl Marx did argue that unless products are consumed in the market, firms and employers cannot realize the profits generated at the workplace.

In this vein, Marx argued that commodities are not simply *things*, but embodiments of social relations. To view commodities separately from their social origins is to commit the error of commodity fetishism, the opaqueness by which market relations obscure relations among producers is functional for capitalism. Marx argues that the social character of labor appears as objective, given the nature of products:

> The relations connecting the labour of one individual with that of the rest appear, not as direct social relations between individuals at work, but as what they really are, material relations between persons and social relations between things. . . . To [producers], their own social action takes the form of the action of objects, which rule the producers instead of being ruled by them. (1976, pp. 73, 75)

When seen in this way, commodities are not simply items on the shelf or advertised on television, they become complex combinations of labor, nature, and ideology.

Marxism drew upon classical economics to differentiate the use value of commodities—the qualitative, subjective dimensions—from their exchange value, the quantitative price they command on the market. For example, the use value of an apple is its taste and relief from hunger it offers, its exchange value is what it sells for. Critically, for marxists, labor too is a commodity whose use value to employers is less than its exchange value in wages. Class is thus defined by relations to production, not consumption.

Marxism suggests that the extraction of surplus value by employers inevitably leads to underconsumption by the working class and the tendency toward crisis. Employers, in this view, cannot by definition pay their workers the value of their output, or no profit would be generated. Thus, capitalism is perpetually faced with the problem of producing too much, which drives down prices, and ultimately profits. For marxists, this line of thought is the most severe of the internal contradictions that capitalism faces.

GEOGRAPHIES OF CONSUMPTION

Drawing upon the work of sociologists, historians, philosophers, and anthropologists, geographers have engaged in numerous lines of thought that suture commodities to their social and spatial origins. This body of work has tended to fall into three major categories.

First, drawing upon the tradition of humanistic geography, some geographers have examined the relations between consumption, the body, and individual experience. The body is the most intimate of geographies, the

Fast food preparation exemplifies standardization of production that accompanied the stanardization of consumption. The 'McDonaldization' of many forms of social activity is widespread.

site of intentionality, where mind resides and a basis of identity. Bodies appear natural but are social constructions, inscribed with social meanings. The geography of the body locates it within social relations, as a place within a network of places. A considerable literature, for example, has looked at food, its origins and cultural meanings in different geographic contexts, and its role in the unfolding of daily life. Eating is the most intimate relation between body and environment, and food consumption plays a major role in shaping bodies, such as the epidemic of obesity plaguing the United States today, in part due to the widespread consumption of fast food.

Similarly, geographers have examined the shopping mall not simply as an economic phenomenon, but as a cultural site pregnant with meanings. For many Americans, time spent in shopping centers is third only to time at home or at work or school; many prefer shopping to sex. Shopping is the nation's dominant form of public life, and the shopping mall the only remaining pedestrian space in which to congregate. Thus, the mall is not just a place to consume, but a metaphor for public life in general. For example, the West Edmonton mall in Canada, the first and largest megamall in the world, has 600 stores, 18,000 employees, and generates 1 percent of all of Canada's retail trade. Inside it contains a golf course, skating rink, fantasy-land hotel, and four submarines. Similarly, the Mall of America in Bloomington, Minnesota, has 520 stores, chapels, a roller coaster, aquarium, and rain forest. In this environment, fantasy, fun, and the commodity are merged into a seamless whole. Malls are carefully engineered to maximize throughput of people and turnover of goods, including the locations of anchor stores and minimally visible exits. Symbolically, this environment is designed to transport shoppers to a

mythologized looking glass world where the only thing that matters is commodity. All "backstage" functions involving the production, transportation, and storage of goods are carefully hidden.

Third, geographers have focused on consumption in the context of the global economy, particularly the manner in which commodities are produced, distributed, and consumed through the use of commodity chains (also called value chains). A commodity chain is a network of labor and production processes that gives rise to a commodity; it extends from the raw material to various stages in processing, delivery, and ends in consumption. For example, the coffee commodity chain begins with

West Edmonton Mall in Canada exemplifies the ways in which spaces of consumption lie at the boundary of reality and fantasy, enticing consumers into a world in which status and happiness are allegedly guaranteed by purchasing commodities.

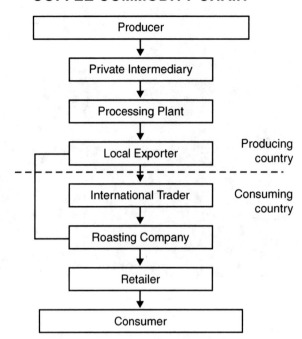

COFFEE COMMODITY CHAIN

Producer

Private Intermediary

Processing Plant

Local Exporter — Producing country

- - - - - - - - - - - - - - -

International Trader — Consuming country

Roasting Company

Retailer

Consumer

FIGURE 11.6
The coffee commodity chain represents the multiple steps involved in growing, harvesting, and roasting the bean, the various intermediaries involved in transporting and marketing it, and finally, the consumer. Different goods have different commodity chains associated with them, which stretch unevenly over time and space, suturing together producers, consumers, and those in between in complex networks of causality.

the grower, typically an impoverished farmer, and extends through the processing plant, exporters, traders, roasting companies, retailers, and, finally, the consumer (Figure 11.6). At each stage, the commodity is transformed in some way, and value is added. The same company may control one or more stages in a commodity chain depending on how vertically integrated or disintegrated the production process is. Because different nodes where these activities are carried out are spatially separated, commodity chains are geographic as well as economic and cultural phenomena.

Commodity chains are thus a means of depicting the ways economic activity reverberates through the production process, the linkages among different economic sectors, flows of value over time and space, and overcome the artificial separation between consumption and production. They allow us to see the commodity as more than just a thing, but as an embodiment of processes at different spatial scales. Essentially, commodity chains are mechanisms that allow us to trace the impacts of consumption decisions backward through the production and distribution process, broadening our scale of analysis from the local to the global. They trace the commodity through complex, contingent lines of causality linking sellers and buyers across multiple spatial scales.

Over time, with the expansion of capitalism globally, commodity chains have become longer and longer. This device allows us to understand, for example, the ways in which globalization has unleashed a tidal wave of cheap imports that has propelled the high rates of consumer spending in societies such as the United States.

By uniting consumption with production, they point to the sacrifices made by low-wage labor trapped in sweatshops in the developing world in order to provide American consumers with cheap goods. Such a perspective reveals consumption as being simultaneously an economic, cultural, psychological, and environmental act that simultaneously reproduces both the world's most abstract space, the global economy, and the most intimate, the individual subject and body.

ENVIRONMENTAL DIMENSIONS OF CONSUMPTION

In addition to its status as an economic and cultural phenomenon, consumption is also a deeply environmental one. Because consumption is linked to other domains such as transportation and production, every act of consumption imposes changes on the environment. These impacts occur through direct consumption by households and individuals and indirect consumption of resources in the production process. Often, because commodity chains are long, the environmental impacts may be felt thousands of miles away or on the other side of the world.

Traditional views of environmental destruction typically focused on the poor. With origins in Malthusianism (Chapter 3) and the high birthrates found in many developing countries, the large numbers of the world's impoverished have often been blamed for clearing forests for farms, soil erosion, and other environmental predicaments. While there is no question that rapid population growth contributes to environmental destructive, this

Large trash dump.
If consumption is the purchase of inputs to the household, this large trash dump illustrated the flip side, the enormous quantities of waste that industrialized societies generate, with significant social and environmental consequences.

perspective often overlooks the even more destructive role played by overconsumption in the economically developed world, which generates the vast bulk of the planet's environmental problems.

Inevitably, as standards of living rise, and thus consumption, a society puts increasing stress on the environment, using more resources and producing more waste. For example, in 2000, the United States consumed 14 times more raw materials than it did in 1900, but its population only tripled. In many respects, mass consumption is disastrous for the world's ecologies, with enormous repercussions. Whole ecosystems are sacrificed to support our lifestyle, including the deforestation of tropical regions to produce plywood and newspaper. Entire landscapes are ravaged by the tremendous hunger of the developed world, and, increasingly, the developing world, for minerals, water, and energy to produce houses, hamburgers, and clothes. Our demand for seafood is emptying the world's oceans: 75 percent fish stocks are overfished, and the size of the catch is not limited by our fishing technology but by reduced stocks in the seas. Pollution, deforestation, and habitat destruction are generating the greatest loss of biodiversity in the planet's history. For economically developed countries, the effects of these processes are often not experienced directly because globalization allows us to export problems.

Of the many things we consume, private transportation via the automobile is perhaps the most wasteful. Urban sprawl and long commutes have locked us into an energy-intensive lifestyle. In the United States, for example, there are more cars than drivers. Transportation consumes 40 percent of the country's total energy budget, largely due to fuel-inefficient cars. With 5 percent of the world's people, the United States consumes 25 percent of its energy. The consumption of petroleum is a primary generator of greenhouse gases such as carbon

dioxide that are a major force in the creation of the greenhouse effect and global warming (Chapter 4).

A fundamental feature of the world economy is the uneven distribution of purchasing power and resource consumption, a pattern that reflects the legacy of colonialism and the uneven development generated by capitalism. Today, roughly 20 percent of the world consumes about 80 percent of its vital materials, including 40 percent of the world's meat, 60 percent of its energy, and 80 percent of its paper and vehicles (Figure 11.7). In return, the First World generates

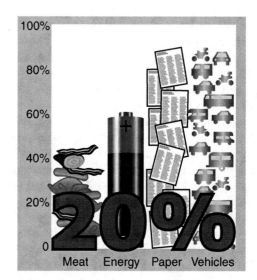

FIGURE 11.7
The economically developed world, which represents only about one-fifth of humanity, nonetheless consumes the bulk of many of the world's resources, testimony to its higher incomes and privileged position internationally. This unevenness reflects the historical dynamics of capitalism, which simultaneously produced wealthy and impoverished societies worldwide.

412

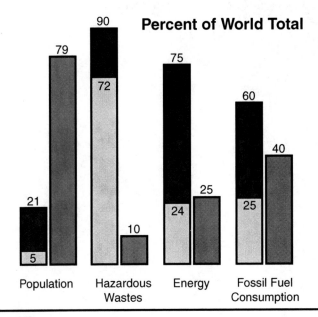

Percent of World Total

Population: 21, 5, 79
Hazardous Wastes: 90, 72, 10
Energy: 75, 24, 25
Fossil Fuel Consumption: 60, 25, 40

United States

Developed Countries

Developing Countries

FIGURE 11.8
The flip side of consumption is the production of waste. By consuming a vast share of the world's resources, the economically advanced world also generates most of its pollution.

disproportionate amounts of the world's hazardous wastes (Figure 11.8). As the consumerist lifestyle has spread to much of the developing world, their demand for energy, meat, and other materials has risen accordingly. The growing middle class in China and India, for example, is putting huge stress on their ecosystems. Many ecologists are highly doubtful that the world could generate the resources necessary to support the entire planet's population at any level approaching that of the United States today.

One way to analyze this issue is through the notion of an ecological footprint, which estimates the amount of resources necessary to support a person's lifestyle. For example, during his or her lifetime, one U.S. citizen has 200 times the environmental impact that child in Mozambique has. (Go to eco-foot.org to estimate your own footprint size, which is a function of the size of your house, your diet, mode of transportation, etc.) The economically developed world has much larger footprints than do societies in Asia, Africa, or Latin America (Figure 11.9). The global distribution of total footprints generated by each country thus reflects total population and the per capita environmental impact (Figure 11.10).

FIGURE 11.9
Ecological footprints reflect the use of the world's resources and their biophysical impacts on the planet. Their size is directly proportionate to the levels of income and consumption that occur in each society. Consumption is thus simultaneously an economic, social, psychological, geographical, and ecological phenomenon.

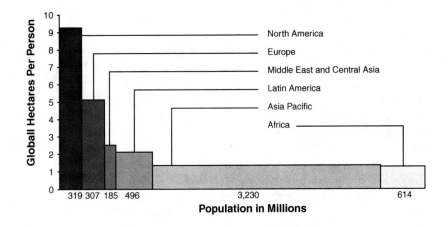

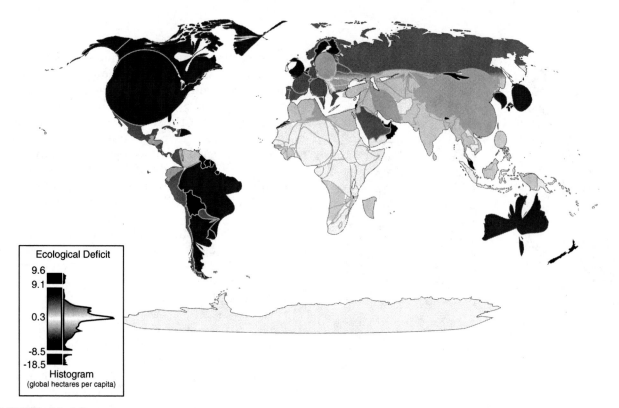

Ecological Deficit

9.6
9.1

0.3

-8.5
-18.5

Histogram
(global hectares per capita)

FIGURE 11.10
Because the First World consumes so much, it has much greater ecological footprints on the world's ecosystems than does the developing world.

SUMMARY

Consumption is a complex process with psychological, economic, cultural, political, geographic, and environmental dimensions. Consumerism arose historically on the heels of capitalism, and mass consumption accompanied the Industrial Revolution as a working class with a disposable income and sufficient free time arose. Consumerism has reached its apex in societies such as the United States, and has spread rapidly to much of the rest of the world. However, despite higher incomes and consumption levels, surveys reveal that the populations of societies such as the United States are not necessarily happier than they were a half century ago. Buying more, it seems, has not made as substantially more satisfied.

The neoclassical view of consumption, "homo economicuo," is elegant but takes the construction of demand as given. Sociological views of consumption portray it as a social act, in which individual choices are produced and constrained by their relative social status. In this view, demand does not simply appear in the individual consumer, but is generated by pressures such as advertising, which is exceptionally adept at turning luxuries into necessities. In neoclassical economics, demand is modeled using utility curves and the desolate figure of *homo economicus*. In marxism, the labor theory of value leads to the conclusion that employers always extract more value from workers than they can consume, leading to a chronic problem of overproduction and underconsumption.

Geographically, consumption can be understood at multiple spatial scales. The body, for example, reflects the networks of consumption in which people find themselves. While bodies appear natural, they are social constructions. Shoppers engage in consumption in spatial environments such as the mall that are saturated with webs of symbolic meanings, often consciously constructed to entice people to spend as much as possible. Commodity chains are a useful means of linking consumption with production, noting the various stages through which commodities pass from raw material to final product.

Consumption inevitably entails some degree of transformation of the environment, generally for the worse. While popular opinion often holds the developing world responsible for most of the world's environmental ills, statistically it is the mass consumption lifestyle of the First World that generates the bulk of environmental problems such as global warming. A relatively small proportion of the world—around 1.7 billion people or 20 percent—consume up to 80 percent of the world's resources. As consumerism has spread to much of the world, the impacts on ecosystems have multiplied accordingly. Ecological footprints are one means of analyzing the environmental costs of consumption.

STUDY QUESTIONS

1. When and where did consumerism originate historically?
2. Why don't rising levels of consumption make everyone happier?
3. What are the major theoretical perspectives on consumption?
4. How is the body a geographic locus of consumption?
5. Are most of the world's environmental problems generated in the developing world?
6. What is an ecological footprint?

KEY TERMS

affluenza
commodification
commodity chains
conspicuous consumption

consumerism
ecological footprint
exchange value
homo economicus

underconsumption
use value
utility maximization

SUGGESTED READINGS

Bell, D. and Valentine, G. 1997. *Consuming Geographies: We Are Where We Eat.* London: Routledge.

De Graaf, J., Wann, D., and Naylor, T. 2001. *Affluenza: The All-Consuming Epidemic.* San Francisco, Calif: Berrett-Koehler Publication.

Goss, J. 1993. "'The Magic of the Mall': An Analysis of Form, Function, and Meaning in the Contemporary Retail Built Environment." *Annals of the Association of American Geographers* 83:18–47.

Goss, J. 1999. "Once Upon a Time in the Commodity World: An Unofficial Guide to the Mall of America." *Annals of the Association of American Geographers* 98:45–75.

Hartwick, E. 1998. "Geographies of Consumption: A Commodity-Chain Approach." *Environment and Planning D: Society and Space* 16:423–37.

Hartwick, E. 2000. "Towards a Geographical Politics of Consumption." *Environment and Planning A* 32:1177–92.

Stearns, P. 2001. *Consumerism in World History: The Global Transformation of Desire.* London: Routledge.

WORLD WIDE WEB SITES

EARTHDAY NETWORK:
ECOFOOT.ORG
Calculate your ecological footprint or that for any part of the world.

Section 2
Market Entry Strategies

Marketing in the Global Firm

Learning Objectives

In this chapter, you will learn about:

1. Global marketing strategy
2. Standardization and adaptation of the international marketing program
3. Global branding and product development
4. International pricing
5. International marketing communications
6. International distribution
7. Ethical dimensions of international marketing

> ## Zara's Unique Model for International Marketing Success

The Spanish multinational Inditex has transformed itself into Europe's leading apparel retailer. Inditex's flagship store is Zara, the fashion chain that specializes in up-to-date clothing at affordable prices. Headquartered in northern Spain, Zara generated about $5 billion in sales in 2006 across its stores in some 60 countries. In Asia, Zara has some 40 stores from Bangkok to Tokyo, and opened its first shop in Shanghai in 2006. In the United States, the firm plans to double its store count to more than 50 by 2009.

Zara is a leader in rapid-response retailing. In-house teams produce fresh designs twice a week. While competitors typically have up to an 11–month lead time to move a garment from design to manufacturing, total turn-around time at Zara is just 2 weeks. None of its styles last in stores more than a month. Zara is fast and flexible in meeting market needs by integrating design, production, distribution, and sales within its own stores. Zara created about 20,000 different items in 2006, roughly triple what Gap produced. Because textiles are a labor-intensive business, most retailers source from low-cost shops in Asia. Zara, on the other hand, produces its most fashionable items—50 percent of all its merchandise—at a dozen company-

owned factories in Spain. Clothes with longer shelf life are outsourced to low-cost suppliers in Turkey and Asia.

Zara's supply chain is lightning fast. Once clothing is produced, it is shipped to stores in 24 to 36 hours. Using the latest information technology, garments are continuously scanned as they pass through the distribution channel. Distributors immediately know what is needed for restocking. Predetermined fabrics await design instructions, and suppliers provide other needed materials, such as thread, zippers, and buttons just-in-time. Rapid-response retailing means fashions go straight from the factory to stores. Nevertheless, the Spain-based production and distribution model has its limitations. Rapid-response retailing becomes harder to manage the farther away from Spain the firm's outlets are located.

Stores are both uncluttered and colorful, creating a high-end luxury shopping environment. Management emphasizes product innovation and value pricing. Adapted to individual markets, prices are higher in high-income countries and more competitive in low-income or low-demand countries. Much of the firm's promotional activities depend on creating buzz, generating word-of-mouth, and setting up stores in prominent locations. Zara's flashy outlets are on some of the world's priciest streets: Fifth Avenue in New York, Ginza in Tokyo, Via Condotti in Rome, and the Champs-Elysees in Paris.

Zara's positioning differentiates the firm from key competitors based on pricing (low to moderate) and fashion (slightly formal, chic). For instance, the United States-based chain Gap and Italy's Benetton are positioned as moderately high-priced but not particularly fashion-forward. Sweden's H&M offers merchandise that is casual and targeted to younger people. A key competitive advantage of Zara is that it stays at the very leading edge of fashion.

The retailer follows a unique approach to eliciting consumer feedback. Management reacts quickly to daily sales figures. Using wireless organizers, managers and salespeople in Zara's stores advise headquarters daily about constantly changing consumer tastes. Stores employ retail specialists with a strong sense of fashion who advise on which items move fastest. Fast-moving items are replicated quickly, in a myriad of colors or styles, and slow-moving items are removed. Zara's researchers also visit college campuses, clubs, and other hotspots. Magazines like Vogue as well as fashion shows provide additional inspiration.

In a fickle industry, often characterized by sluggish growth, Zara has been growing fairly rapidly. The firm is expanding in Asia and North America and penetrating deeper into Europe. Managers intend to apply the same strategies that have proven successful thus far.

Sources: *Business Week*, (2007). "Retailers Need to Boost Product Turnover," January 16. Retrieved from www.businessweek.com; *Business Week*, (2006). "Fashion Conquistador,'" September 4. Retrieved from www.businessweek.com; *Business Week*, (2006). "Zara: Taking the Lead in Fast-Fashion," April 4. Retrieved from www.businessweek.com; Echikson, William. (2000). "The Mark of Zara," *Business Week*, May 29, pp. 98–100; *Economist*, (2005). "The Future of Fast Fashion," June 18, p. 63; Fraiman, Nelson, and Medini Singh. (2002). *Zara*. Case study. New York: Columbia Business School, Columbia University; Heller, Richard. (2001). "Galician Beauty," *Forbes*, May 28, p. 98; Hoovers.com entry on Zara International, Inc.; Inditex press kit, June 2007. www.inditex.com; Inditex Press Release "Business Week Ranks Inditex as the Seventh Best Performing European Company," May 14, 2007; Maitland, Alison. (2005). "Make Sure You Have Your Christmas Stock In," *Financial Times*, December 19, p. 11.

 # Global Marketing Strategy

Marketing brings the customer focus to the firm's cross-border business. Marketing in the internationalizing firm is concerned with identifying, measuring, and pursuing market opportunities abroad. Exhibit 17.1 provides a framework for these activities and previews the topics of this chapter. The outer layer represents the cultural, social, political, legal, and regulatory environment of foreign markets. These environmental conditions constrain the firm's ability to price, promote, and distribute a product. For example, the firm will need to review prices frequently in high-inflation countries, adapt the positioning of the product to suit customer expectations, and ensure products comply with mandated government standards.

Working with the diversity of individual country markets, managers then will need to formulate a global marketing strategy. The middle layer in Exhibit 17.1 represents the **global marketing strategy**—a plan of action that guides the firm in: (1) how to position itself and its offerings in foreign markets and which customer segments to target, and (2) the degree to which its marketing program elements should be standardized and adapted.[1]

Before we turn to the second aspect of global marketing strategy (standardization/adaptation), let's discuss the first function: targeting customer segments and positioning.

Targeting Customer Segments and Positioning

Market segmentation refers to the process of dividing the firm's total customer base into homogeneous clusters in a way that allows management to formulate unique marketing strategies for each group. Within each market segment, customers exhibit similar characteristics regarding income level, lifestyle, demographic pro-

Global marketing strategy A plan of action that guides the firm in how to position itself and its offerings in foreign markets, which customer segments to target, and the degree to which its marketing program elements should be standardized and adapted.

Exhibit 17.1

Organizing Framework for
Marketing in the International Firm

The Environment of International Business
Diverse Cultural, Political, Legal, Monetary, and Financial
Environment of the Firm

Global Marketing Strategy
Targeting Customer Segments and Positioning

**International Marketing Program
Standardization and Adaptation**

Global Branding and Product Development	International Pricing
International Distribution	International Marketing Communications

file, or desired product benefits. As an example, Caterpillar targets its earthmoving equipment by applying distinct marketing approaches to several major market segments, such as construction firms, farmers, and the military. For each of these customer segments, Caterpillar devises a distinct marketing program, for example, creating value-priced tractors for farmers, moderately priced earthmoving equipment for construction firms, and high-priced, heavy-duty trucks and other vehicles for the military.

In international business, firms frequently form market segments by grouping countries together based on macrolevel variables, such as level of economic development or cultural dimensions. For example, many MNEs group the Latin American countries together based on a common language (Spanish or Portuguese), or the European countries together based on similar economic conditions. The approach has proven most effective for product categories in which governments play a key regulatory role (such as telecommunications, medical products, and processed foods) or where national characteristics prevail in determining product acceptance and usage.[2]

Today, firms increasingly target *global* customer or market segments. A global market segment represents a group of customers that share common characteristics across many national markets. Firms target these buyers with relatively uniform marketing programs. For example, MTV and Levi Strauss both target a largely homogenous youth market that exists around most of the world. In fact, consumer product

Global market segment A group of customers that share common characteristics across many national markets.

MTV has a global market segment of young adults who enjoy music. Here, members of the Mexican band, Mana, hold their MTV Legend Award at the MTV Video Music Awards Latin America 2006 in Mexico City.

companies are targeting the youth market across advanced and emerging economies. This segment generally follows global media, is quick to embrace new fashions and trends, and has significant disposable income. Another global market segment is jet-setting business executives. They have much disposable affluence and are eager consumers of premium products that represent luxury and sophisticated style.

The firm's objective in pursuing global market segments is to create a unique positioning of its offerings in the minds of target customers. *Positioning* is an aspect of marketing strategy in which the firm develops both the product and its marketing to evoke a distinct impression in the customer's mind, emphasizing differences from competitive offerings. For example, in the international construction industry, Bechtel positions itself as providing sophisticated technical solutions for major infrastructure projects worldwide. In the theme park business, Disney positions itself as standing for family values and "good, clean fun" to attract families to its theme parks around the world.[3]

Positioning may also involve the images of specific product *attributes* held by consumers. For example, Diet Coke elicits an image of someone who needs to lose or maintain weight compared to regular Coca-Cola. When Coca-Cola first entered Japan, research revealed that Japanese women do not like products labeled as "diet," nor is the population considered overweight. Thus, management altered the product's positioning in Japan by changing the name of Diet Coke to Coke Light.

Internationalizing firms aim for a *global positioning strategy,* that is, one in which the offering is positioned *similarly* in the minds of buyers worldwide. Starbucks, Volvo, and Sony are good examples of companies that successfully use this approach. Consumers around the world view these strong brands in the same way. Global positioning strategy is beneficial because it reduces international marketing costs by minimizing the extent to which management must adapt elements of the marketing program for individual markets.[4]

Standardization and Adaptation of the International Marketing Program

In addition to guiding the process of targeting and positioning, global marketing strategy also articulates the degree to which the firm's marketing program should vary across foreign markets. In the innermost layer in Exhibit 17.1, we identify the key elements of the marketing program (sometimes referred to as the *marketing mix*) that are subjected to the standardization/adaptation decision, given the international context. These elements are: global branding and product development, international pricing, international marketing communications, and international distribution. Domestic marketing strategy is concerned with the marketing program elements in a single country. In the international context, marketing strategy takes on additional complexity because of local competitors, as well as cross-national differences in culture, language, living standards, economic conditions, regulations, and quality of business infrastructure. In addition, the firm needs to keep abreast of *global* competitors and optimize its value-chain activities across its various markets. Accordingly, the firm's key challenge is how to resolve the trade-offs between standardizing the firm's marketing program elements *and* adapting them for individual international markets. Since the firm is typically involved in more than a single foreign market, management also must grapple with how best to coordinate marketing activities across national markets.

Adaptation refers to the firm efforts to modify one or more elements of its international marketing program to accommodate specific customer requirements in a particular market. In contrast, **standardization** refers to the firm efforts to make its marketing program elements uniform, with a view to targeting entire regions, or even the global marketplace, with a similar product or service.

Achieving a balance between adaptation and standardization is part of a broader corporate strategy that has the firm debating its position between *global integration* and *local responsiveness*. As we discussed in Chapter 11, global integration seeks worldwide efficiency, synergy, and cross-fertilization in the firm's value-chain activities, while local responsiveness objectives seek to meet the specific needs of buyers in individual countries. How the firm resolves the balance between global integration and local responsiveness affects how it makes standardization and adaptation decisions in its marketing program elements.

Exhibit 17.2 highlights the trade-offs between standardization and adaptation in international marketing. Let's now examine the arguments for, and advantages of, each strategy.

Standardization

Representing a tendency toward global integration, standardization is more likely to be pursued in global industries such as aircraft manufacturing, pharmaceuticals, and credit cards. Boeing, Pfizer, and MasterCard are examples of firms that use standardized marketing strategy with great success. Their offerings are largely uniform across many markets worldwide. A standardized marketing approach is most appropriate when:

Adaptation Firm efforts to modify one or more elements of its international marketing program to accommodate specific customer requirements in a particular market.

Standardization Firm efforts to make its marketing program elements uniform, with a view to targeting entire regions, or even the global marketplace, with a similar product or service.

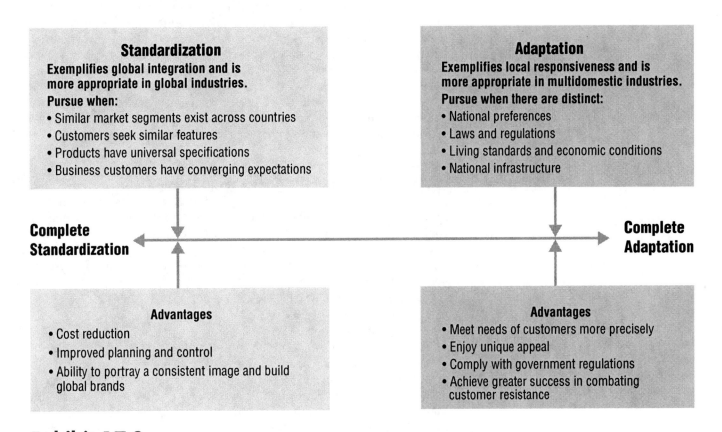

Exhibit 17.2 Tradeoffs between Adaptation and Standardization of International Marketing Program

Popular consumer electronics such as Apple's iPod can gain a worldwide following and require little adaptation from country to country.

- Similar market segments exist across countries.

- Customers seek similar features in the product or service.

- Products have universal specifications.

- Business customers have converging expectations such as quality and performance.

The viability of standardization varies across industries and product categories. For example, commodities, industrial equipment, and high-technology products lend themselves to a high degree of standardization. Popular consumer electronics (e.g., Sony's PlayStation, Apple's iPod, and Canon digital cameras) and several well-known fashion accessories (e.g., Rolex watches and Louis Vuitton handbags) are largely standardized around the world. Automotive parts, building materials, dinnerware, and basic food ingredients are other examples of products that require little or no adaptation.

When managers build on commonalities in customer preferences and attempt to standardize their international marketing program, they can expect at least three types of favorable outcomes.

- *Cost Reduction.* Standardization reduces costs by enabling economies of scale in design, sourcing, manufacturing and marketing. Offering a similar marketing program to the global marketplace or across entire regions is more efficient than having to adapt products for each of numerous individual markets. For example, the appliance manufacturer Electrolux once made hundreds of refrigerator models to accommodate the diverse tastes and regulatory requirements of each country in Europe. However, as product standards and tastes gradually harmonized across the European Union, Electrolux was able to reduce the number of its refrigerators to a few dozen models. The move allowed management to consolidate manufacturing facilities and streamline its marketing activities across the EU. The resulting consolidation saved Electrolux millions of euros. With fewer offerings, the company can better concentrate on incorporating advanced features and superior technology into its products.

- *Improved Planning and Control.* Standardization provides for improved planning and control of value-adding activities. In the case of Electrolux, for example, fewer offerings mean that management can simplify quality control and reduce the number of parts that it stocks for repairing defective products. Marketing activities are also simplified. Instead of designing a unique marketing campaign for each country in Europe, the firm is able to standardize its campaigns.

- *Ability to Portray a Consistent Image and Build Global Brands.* A *brand* is a name, sign, symbol, or design intended to identify the firm's product and differentiate it from those of competitors. A **global brand** is a brand whose positioning, advertising strategy, look, and personality are standardized worldwide. Standardization allows the firm to establish and project a globally recognized corporate or product brand that helps increase customer interest and reduces the confusion that arises from the proliferation of numerous adapted products and marketing programs.[5] Marketing is more effective and efficient because the firm can serve larger global market segments that transcend multiple countries.

Global brand A brand whose positioning, advertising strategy, look, and personality are standardized worldwide.

As an example, Gillette, the U.S. shaving products company recently acquired by Procter & Gamble, sells the same products using uniform marketing in all the countries where it does business, often engaging in a simultaneous global launch. The firm has successfully launched its line of shavers (such as Trak II, Sensor, and Fusion) across multiple countries. Results have been impressive. While achieving 70 percent market share in the world shaver market, Gillette's global approach allows management to minimize the cost of marketing and distribution.[6]

Adaptation

While standardizing where they can, firms will also engage in adaptation. Adaptation of an international marketing program exemplifies local responsiveness. It is a strategy used in *multidomestic industries*, which tailor their offerings to suit individual markets. Examples include publishing and software industries, where books, magazines, and software must be translated into the language of the target country. Adaptation may be as simple as translating labels and instructions into a foreign language, or as complex as completely modifying a product to fit the needs of unique market conditions. Local adaptation can provide the marketer with important advantages. Let's explore the major reasons why firms may adapt marketing program elements.

Differences in National Preferences. Adaptation makes the offering more acceptable to customers in individual markets. Differences in consumer behavior around the world are a major driver of local adaptation. For example, when targeting China, the dairy producer New Zealand Milk adds ginger and papaya flavoring to its milk products to suit the tastes of local customers. The Netherlands' Foremost Friesland Co. sells green tea-flavored fresh milk in Thailand. Japan's Meiji Co. is selling a pandan-flavored milk in Singapore.[7] When *The Simpsons* cartoon series was broadcast in Saudi Arabia, it was substantially adapted for language and local Islamic sensibilities. The show was renamed *Al Shamshoon*, Homer Simpson's name was changed to "Omar," and Bart Simpson became "Badr." The program aims to win coveted young viewers, who constitute a large proportion of the population in the Arab world. In addition to translating the show into Arabic, producers had to deal with the way the Simpson daughter and mother dress. Producers removed references to practices forbidden by the Qur'an or considered potentially offensive, such as consuming pork and beer. Producers changed Homer Simpson's Duff beer to soda, hot dogs to Egyptian beef sausages, and donuts to the popular Arab cookies called *kahk*. Moe's Bar was completely written out of the show. As one Arab viewer told ABC News "It's different. . . . we are a totally different culture, so you can't be talking about the same subject and in the same way."[8]

McDonald's has been able to standardize its hamburgers across most world markets, but not all. Because some people do not eat beef—for example, Hindus in India—the company substitutes lamb in its burgers in some markets, while adding to its menu additional items such as Kofte burgers (hamburger with special spices) in Turkey. In Japan, McDonald's offers shrimp burgers, as well as miso soup and rice. McDonald's outlets in Norway serve "McLaks"—a grilled salmon sandwich with dill sauce. In Berlin, consumers can savor a beer with their double cheeseburgers and fries. In some Arab countries, the "McArabia"—a flatbread, spicy chicken filet—has been a success.[9]

Differences in Laws and Regulations. The promotion of certain products is restricted in some countries. For example, laws in Europe, including Germany, Norway, and Switzerland, restrict advertising directed at children. Packaged foods in Europe are often labeled in several different languages, including English, French, German, and Spanish. In Quebec, Canada's French-speaking province, local law requires product packaging to be in both English and French. The use of some sales promotion activities—for example, coupons and sales contests—is restricted or just not customary in some markets.

Differences in Living Standards and Economic Conditions. Because income levels vary substantially around the world, firms typically adjust both the pricing and the complexity of their product offerings for individual markets. For example, Microsoft has had to lower the price of its software for some markets (e.g., Thailand, Malaysia, and Indonesia) in order to bring it in line with local purchasing power.[10] Dell sells simplified versions of its computers in developing economies to accommodate lower local spending power. Inflation and economic recessions also influence pricing policy. A recession signals a drop in consumer confidence, and the firm may need to reduce prices in order to generate sales. High inflation can rapidly erode profits, even as prices rise. Exchange rate fluctuations also necessitate adjustments. When the importing country currency is weak, the buying power of its consumers is reduced. But when the importing country currency is strong, buyers can afford to pay higher prices for imported products.

Differences in National Infrastructure. The quality of transportation networks, marketing institutions, and overall business infrastructure particularly influences the alternatives and quality of marketing communications and distribution systems that firms employ abroad. Infrastructure is especially poor in the rural parts of developing economies, which necessitates innovative approaches for getting products to customers. For example, the density of roads and rail networks in western China is underdeveloped. Firms use small trucks to reach retailers in outlying communities. Deficiencies in media require substantial adaptations to promotional activities. In rural Vietnam, most consumers cannot access television, magazines, or the Internet. Radio, billboards, and brochures are favored for targeting low-income buyers.

What can managers expect when they accommodate these differences by customizing international marketing program elements? Primary advantages of adapting an international marketing program to the individual market include the following:

- Meeting needs of customers more precisely
- Creating unique appeal for the product
- Complying with such government regulations as health and technical standards
- Achieving greater success in combating customer resistance

In addition, adaptation provides managers with an opportunity to explore alternative ways of marketing the product or service. Such knowledge of market reactions to customized offerings can guide the firm in its R & D efforts, often leading to superior products for sale abroad and at home. In fact, products developed or modified for foreign markets sometimes prove so successful that they are launched as new products in the firm's home market. For example, Toyota originally designed the Lexus for the U.S. market. After perfecting the luxury car during 15 years in the United States, the firm launched Lexus in Japan in 2005.[11]

Standardization and Adaptation: A Balancing Act

A managerial decision about the degree of standardization and adaptation is not an either/or decision, but, rather, a balancing act. There are good arguments and outcomes in favor of both standardization and adaptation; it is up to the manager to sort out the trade-offs in light of the unique circumstances of the international business environment and the firm's chosen strategy.

Perhaps the most important distinction between standardization and adaptation is that standardization helps the firm reduce its costs, while adaptation helps the firm more precisely cater to local needs and requirements, thereby increasing its revenues. While there are many reasons for firms to engage in adaptation of their international marketing program, adaptation is costly. Adaptation may require substantial redesign of products, modifications to manufacturing operations, lower pricing, and overhauled distribution and communications strategies. The costs add up when these changes simultaneously multiply in numerous national markets. Therefore, whenever possible, managers usually err on the side of standardization because it is easier and less costly than adaptation. Others adapt marketing program elements *only when necessary,* to respond to local customer preferences and mandated regulations. For instance, the Anglo-Dutch MNE Unilever streamlined the number of its brands from over 1,600 to about 400 and focused attention on a dozen or so global brands. However, the firm had to retain many local adaptations to suit individual markets. In nutrition-conscious countries, Unilever is adapting its food products by lowering the levels of sugar, salt, trans-fats, and saturated fats.

Often managers will engage in standardization and adaptation simultaneously, at varying degrees. They will make adjustments to some elements of the marketing program while keeping others intact. For example, IKEA will maintain product design uniformity across markets while making modifications to, say, the size of beds or drawers it sells in individual countries. Similarly, it will emphasize its catalog as the principal promotional tool but supplement it with TV advertising in a mass-media oriented market such as the United States.

It is also rarely feasible or practical to follow a "one offering-one world" strategy across *all* dimensions of the marketing program. For example, automotive companies tried for years to market a "world car" that meets customer preferences everywhere as well as complying with various government-imposed safety specifications. Ambitious experiments such as the Ford Mondeo failed to meet the approval of customers and regulatory bodies around the world. Flexibility and adaptability in design became necessary due to climate and geography (for example, engine specifications), government regulations (emissions standards), customer preferences (e.g., cupholders), and gas prices.

As a compromise, some firms will pursue standardization as part of a *regional* strategy, where international marketing program elements are formulated to exploit commonalities across a geographic region instead of across the world. For example, General Motors markets distinctive car models for China (e.g., Buick), Europe (Opel, Vauxhall), and North America (Cadillac, Saturn). Convergence of regional preferences, regional economic integration, harmonization of product standards, and growth of regional media and distribution channels all make regional marketing more feasible than pursuing global marketing approaches.[12]

 ## Global Branding and Product Development

Global marketing strategy poses unique challenges and opportunities for managers, particularly in the marketing program elements of global branding and global product development. Let's review these specific topics.

Global Branding

A key outcome of global positioning strategy is the development of a global brand. Well-known global brands include Hollywood movies (for example, Star Wars), pop stars (Shakira), sports figures (David Beckham), personal care products (Gillette Sensor), toys (Barbie), credit cards (Visa), food (Cadbury), beverages (Heineken), furniture (IKEA), and consumer electronics (iPod).[13] Consumers prefer globally branded products because branding provides a sense of trust and confidence in the purchase decision.[14] A strong global brand enhances the efficiency and effectiveness of marketing programs, stimulates brand loyalty, facilitates the ability to charge premium prices, increases the firm's

Well-known celebrities such as Shakira are considered global brands because they command worldwide appeal and premium value.

Exhibit 17.3

Top Global Brands, by Region, 2007

SOURCE: *Business Week* (www.businessweek.com/brand) and *Interbrand* (www.interbrand.com)

Company	Brand Value U.S.$ billions	Country of Origin	Main Product or Service
Asian Brands			
Toyota	24.8	Japan	Cars
Honda	15.8	Japan	Cars
Samsung	15.0	South Korea	Consumer electronics
Sony	10.7	Japan	Consumer electronics
Canon	9.0	Japan	Copiers, cameras
European Brands			
Nokia	26.5	Finland	Cell phones
Mercedes-Benz	20.0	Germany	Cars
BMW	17.1	Germany	Cars
Louis Vuitton	16.1	France	Fashion accessories
Nescafé	12.2	Switzerland	Coffee
U.S. Brands			
Coca-Cola	67.5	United States	Soft drinks
Microsoft	59.9	United States	Software
IBM	53.4	United States	IT services and consulting
GE	47.0	United States	Appliances, jet engines
Intel	35.6	United States	Computer chips

leverage with intermediaries and retailers, and generally enhances the firm's competitive advantage in global markets.[15] The firm can reduce its marketing and advertising costs by concentrating on a single global brand instead of a number of national brands.

The strength of a global brand is best measured by its brand equity—the market value of a brand. Exhibit 17.3 provides brand equity figures for selected global brands, as calculated by Interbrand (www.interbrand.com), a European-based company. *Business Week* devotes a special issue each year to Interbrand's list of the top 100 global brands (www.businessweek.com/brand). To qualify for Interbrand's list, a brand must first generate worldwide sales exceeding $1 billion, at least a third of which should come from outside the home market. Then, Interbrand estimates the projected brand earnings and deducts a charge for the cost of owning the tangible assets from these earnings. Finally, Interbrand calculates the net present value of future brand earnings, ending with an estimate of brand value.

You may wish to look up the entire list of 100 global brands on the *Business Week* portal. What makes these brands so successful in capturing such a worldwide following? Here are the underlying features that make these brands special:

* Some are highly visible, conspicuous consumer products, such as consumer electronics and jeans.

* Some serve as status symbols worldwide, such as cars and jewelry.

* Many have widespread appeal because of innovative features that seem to fit everyone's lifestyle, such as mobile phones, credit cards. and cosmetics.

* Some are identified with the country of origin and command a certain degree of country appeal, such as Levi's (American style) and IKEA furniture (Scandinavian style).

Still, in other cases, global brands are reaping the benefits of first-mover advantages in offering new and novel products or services. For example, in 1971 the first

Starbucks opened in Seattle, Washington, and offered freshly-brewed coffee in a comfortable setting that encouraged people to sit and relax. Nokia, originally founded as a Finnish wood-processing plant in 1865, reengineered itself in the 1990s to become one of the world's leading telephone exchange and mobile phone companies. It has distanced itself from competitors by investing in new technologies and design. Samsung Electronics, part of a larger South Korean conglomerate, also propelled itself into consumer electronics with unique design and leading-edge technology. Interestingly, Sony—a long-time leader in consumer electronics—turned to Samsung in 2004 to help it gain a foothold in the flat-panel TV market.

Developing and maintaining a global brand name is the best way for firms to build global recognition and maximize the effectiveness of their international marketing program. For example, the Eveready Battery Co. consolidated its various national brand names—such as Ucar, Wonder, and Mazda—into one global brand name, Energizer. The move greatly increased the efficiency of Eveready's marketing efforts around the world. While most managers conceive brands for a national market and then internationalize them, the preferred approach is to build a global brand from the beginning. Several firms have succeeded in this approach, including Japan's Sony Corporation. "Sony" was derived from the Latin for "sound." Another Japanese firm, Datsun, switched to Nissan worldwide to create a unified global brand.[16]

Global branding also helps the MNE compete more effectively with local brands, which are often quite popular because they appeal to buyers' sense of local tradition, pride, and preference. For example, market leaders Coca-Cola and Pepsi face many local brands around the world. In Europe, popular local brands include Virgin Cola (Britain), Afri-Cola (Germany), Kofola (Czech Republic), and Cuba Cola (Sweden). Cola Turka was developed to help retain soft drink profits in its native Turkey and challenged the dominance of Coca-Cola and PepsiCo. In Peru, Inca Kola was long a successful local brand that established itself as "Peru's Drink." But Inca Kola's experience revealed how local brands can be vulnerable to the market power of strong global brands. In 1999, Coca-Cola purchased 50 percent of the Inca Kola Corporation. Inca Cola and Coke each have about 30 percent of the Peruvian market, giving Coke an edge since it owns half of the former local brand.

Global Product Development

In developing products with multicountry potential, managers emphasize the commonalities across countries rather than the differences between them.[17] A basic product will incorporate only core features into which the firm can inexpensively implement variations for individual markets. For example, while the basic computers that Dell sells worldwide are essentially identical, the letters on its keyboards and the languages used in its software are unique to countries or major regions. Everything else in the computers is largely identical. Firms design many products using *modular architecture,* a collection of *standardized* components and subsystems that can be rapidly assembled in various configurations to suit the needs of individual markets. Honda and Toyota design models like the Accord and Corolla, respectively, around a standardized platform to which modular components, parts, and features are added to suit specific needs and tastes.

General Motors has been relying on its *Global Product Development Council* in Detroit to improve efficiency. Concerned about duplication of effort across its divisions, GM top management took authority away from regional engineering operations and charged the council with overseeing $7 billion annual spending on new model development. The council promotes company-wide use of GM's best car platforms, wherever they are developed, worldwide. For example, it adapted the Holden Monaro from its Australian subsidiary for North American use as the GTO rather than creating a totally new model. As a result, development cost was a modest $50 million instead of the $500 million it would typically cost to create a new model.

A *global team* is a group within a firm that develops common solutions and global products. As we discussed in Chapter 11, global teams are assigned to formulate best practices that a firm would implement in all of its worldwide units. Global teams assemble employees with specialized knowledge and expertise from various geographically diverse units of the MNE, who collaborate in a project to develop workable solutions to common problems.

The *Global Trend* feature highlights the increasing use of global teams in the development of global products and designs. You may wish to do a quick on-line search for creative product designs that benefited from global teams. For example, the iRobot Roomba Discovery Floorvac, designed by iRobot Corporation, performs domestic chores by navigating its way through rooms without falling down stairs. The iXi Bike was designed in Britain, France, and the United States for France's iXi Bicycle Company. The bike fits easily into the trunk of a small car. Lenovo Smartphone ET960 was designed by a team from East Asia. The lightweight telephone is an MP3 and media player, a game console, and can receive television transmissions. PerfectDraft was developed for Belgium's Inbev Company.

A special feature of global development is the opportunity for a firm to engage in global product launch—simultaneous roll-out of a new product across multiple markets. Simultaneous launch of products that cater to a global clientele has also become increasingly common because it provides scale economies in R&D, product development, production, and marketing. IT products (for example, Apple computers), software (Microsoft), pharmaceuticals (Viagra), movies (*The Matrix*), and many consumer products (Gillette's razor series) are often introduced simultaneously across several countries or geographic regions.

 International Pricing

Pricing is complex and generally subjective in domestic business. It is even more difficult in international business, with multiple currencies, trade barriers, additional cost considerations, and typically longer distribution channels. Managers readily acknowledge the critical role of prices in international markets' success.[18] After all, prices do have a measurable effect on sales and directly affect profitability. Prices often invite competitive reaction, which can drive down a price. Conversely, prices can escalate to unreasonable levels because of tariffs, taxes, and higher markups by foreign intermediaries. Price variations among different markets can lead to **gray market activity**—legal importation of genuine products into a country by intermediaries other than authorized distributors (also known as parallel imports). We discuss gray markets later in this chapter.

Pricing interacts with and affects all other marketing program elements. Prices influence customers' perception of value, determine the level of motivation to expect from foreign intermediaries, have an impact on promotional spending and strategy, and compensate for weaknesses in other elements of the marketing mix. Let's explore the unique aspects of international pricing.

Gray market activity Legal importation of genuine products into a country by intermediaries other than authorized distributors (also known as parallel imports).

Factors Affecting International Pricing

Factors that influence pricing for international customers fall into four categories. First is the *nature of the product or industry*. A specialized product, or one with a technological edge, gives a company greater price flexibility. When the firm holds a relative monopoly in a given product (such as Microsoft's operating system software), it can generally charge premium prices.

The second factor is the *location of the production facility*. Locating manufacturing in countries with low-cost labor enables a firm to charge cheaper prices. Locating factories in or near major markets cuts transportation costs and may eliminate problems created by foreign exchange fluctuations. During the 1980s, for example,

Designing Global Products with Global Teams

Until the 1990s, product development and design was a sequential process, usually based in a single country. Marketers and engineers agreed on a set of technical specifications and they developed a product and sent it to the factory for manufacturing. However, development in a single national environment meant that the product required much adaptation for selling abroad. Today, many more firms develop global products that are intended for world markets from the outset. Product designers work in virtual global teams, held together by information and communications technologies. Firms usually draw global team members from various functional areas in subsidiaries around the globe. The firm identifies members based on their comparative advantages rather than on their physical location.

Consider how Verifone develops its latest telecommunications products at its development centers in France, India, Singapore, Taiwan, and the United States. Management emphasizes a strong global culture of interpersonal communications and information sharing among the centers and team members. The firm uses international rotational assignments, ongoing training, videoconferencing, and crossnational social events to facilitate cross-fertilization of knowledge. As another example, the Boeing 777 was developed by design teams composed of

experts from Europe, Japan, and the United States. The company separated the jet design plans into tail, fuselage, wings, and other modular sections. A global team developed and designed each section. Boeing management prefers the team approach because it leverages comparative advantages provided by designers and engineers in specific countries as well as the core competencies of the best subcontractors and experienced personnel, wherever they are located worldwide.

While the global team approach requires careful cross-national coordination, it results in offerings that are both cost effective and suitable for major markets worldwide. Design and development occur simultaneously, and many companies co-opt suppliers and customers. Such teams allow firms to optimize their global resources, run their design and development operations on a 24–hour clock, and launch new products in record time.

Modern communications technology enables global teams. Groupware and Web-enabled design and product development applications allow multinational teams to seamlessly manage product development and design. Teams use computer-aided design (CAD)—which facilitates three-dimensional design on compatible computer systems—to integrate contributions from their counterparts from around the world. Sophisticated software allows the

team to pilot various product configurations at virtually no cost. Rapid prototyping means that a firm can test new designs on global customers and modify them based on market research.

How do companies organize the global design process? Best-in-class firms manage the global team effort centrally, typically from company headquarters. Success depends on obtaining and sharing the latest data on customer needs and circumstances and continuously measuring product development performance internally and with partners. International market research is critical. To continuously learn what customers are thinking, many firms use online communities and *blogs* (*weblogs*), a user-generated portal where entries are made and displayed in journal style. Blogs combine text, images, Internet links, and the ability for members to leave interactive comments.

Sources: Aberdeen Group. (2005). *The Global Product Design Benchmark Report: Managing Complexity as Product Design Goes Global,* December, Boston: Aberdeen Group; *BusinessWeek Online.* (2006). "Special Report: Innovation," April 24. Retrieved from www.businessweek.com; *Business Week,* (2005). "The Best Product Designs of 2005," July 4. Retrieved from www.businessweek.com; Galbraith, Jay. (2000). *Designing the Global Corporation.* San Francisco: Jossey-Bass; Keller, Robert. (2001). "Cross-Functional Project Groups in Research and New Product Development," *Academy of Management Journal,* 44(3), pp. 547–555; Murray, Janet, and Mike C. H. Chao. (2005). "A Cross-Team Framework of International Knowledge Acquisition on New Product Development Capabilities and New Product Market Performance," *Journal of International Marketing,* 13(3), pp. 54–73.

Toyota and Honda built car factories in the United States, their most important foreign market. But Mazda retained much of its manufacturing in Japan, exporting its cars to the United States. As the Japanese yen appreciated against the dollar, Mazda had to raise its prices, which hurt its U.S. sales.

The third factor that influences international pricing is the *type of distribution system*. Exporting firms rely on independent distributors based abroad, who occasionally modify export pricing to suit their own goals. Some distributors mark up prices substantially—up to 200 percent in some countries—which may harm the manufacturer's image and pricing strategy in the market. By contrast, when the firm internationalizes via FDI by establishing company-owned marketing subsidiaries abroad, management can maintain control over pricing strategy. Firms that make direct sales to end users also control their pricing and can make rapid adjustments to suit evolving market conditions.

The fourth factor is *foreign market considerations*. Such foreign market factors as climate and other natural conditions may require the firm to spend money to modify a product or its distribution. Food items shipped to hot climates require refrigeration, which drives up costs. In countries with many rural residents, or those with a poor distribution infrastructure, delivering products to widely dispersed customers necessitates higher pricing because of higher shipping costs. Foreign government intervention is also a critical factor. Governments impose tariffs that lead to higher prices. Many governments also impose limits on prices. For example, Canada imposes price limits on prescription drugs, which reduces the firm's pricing flexibility. Health rules, safety standards, and other regulations increase the cost of doing business locally, which necessitates higher prices.

Exhibit 17.4 provides a comprehensive list of the factors, both internal and external to the firm, that influence how firms set international prices. Ini-

Exhibit 17.4

Internal and External Factors That Affect International Pricing

---

Internal to the Firm

- Management's profit and market share expectations
- Cost of manufacturing, marketing, and other value-chain activities
- The degree of control management desires over price setting in foreign markets

External Factors

- Customer expectations, purchasing power, and sensitivity to price increases
- Nature of competitors' offerings, prices, and strategy
- International customer costs:
  - Product/package modification; labeling and marking requirements
  - Documentation (certificate of origin, invoices, banking fees)
  - Financing costs
  - Packing and container charges
  - Shipping (inspection, warehousing, freight forwarder's fee)
  - Insurance
- Landed cost
  - Tariffs (customs duty, import tax, customs clearance fee)
  - Warehousing charges at the port of import; local transportation
- Importer's cost
  - Value-added tax and other applicable taxes paid by the importer
  - Local intermediary (distributor, wholesaler, retailer) margins
  - Cost of financing inventory
- Anticipated fluctuations in currency exchange rates

---

tially, management must account for its own objectives. Most firms seek to maximize profits abroad. However, many companies focus on market share, often charging low prices in order to gain the largest number of customers. Earlier in this chapter we discussed other factors, such as control issues and the cost of production and marketing. Many countries in Europe and elsewhere charge value-added taxes (VATs) on imported products. Unlike a sales tax, which is calculated off of the retail sales price, the VAT is determined as a percentage of the gross margin—the difference between the sales price and the cost to the seller of the item sold. In the EU, for example, VAT rates range between 15 and 25 percent.

A Framework for Setting International Prices

Managers examine the suitability of prices at several levels in the international distribution channel—importers, wholesalers, retailers, and end users—and then set prices accordingly. Exhibit 17.5 presents a systematic approach for managers to use to set international prices at various levels.[19]

Let's illustrate the international pricing framework with an example. Suppose that a leading musical instrument manufacturer, Melody Corporation, wants to begin exporting electric guitars to Japan and needs to set prices. Initially, Melody will export its "John Mayer" line of guitars, which normally retail at around $2,000 in the United States. Initial research reveals that added costs of shipping, transportation insurance, and a 5 percent Japanese tariff will add a total of $300 to the price of each guitar, bringing the total landed price to $2,300. Melody has identified an importer in Japan, Aoki Music Wholesalers, which wants to add a 10 percent profit margin to the cost of each imported guitar. Thus, the total price once a

Step 1. Estimate the "landed" price of the product in the foreign market by totaling all costs associated with shipping the product to the customer's location.

Step 2. Estimate the price the importer or distributor will charge when it adds its profit margin.

Step 3. Estimate the target price range for end users. Determine:
- Floor price (lowest acceptable price to the firm, based on cost considerations)
- Ceiling price (highest possible price, based on customer purchasing power price sensitivity and competitive considerations)

Step 4. Assess the company sales potential at the price the firm is most likely to charge (between the floor price and ceiling price).

Step 5. Select a suitable pricing strategy based on corporate goals and preferences from:
- Rigid cost-plus pricing
- Flexible cost-plus pricing
- Incremental pricing

Step 6. Check consistency with current prices across product lines, key customers, and foreign markets (in order to deter potential gray market activity).

Step 7. Implement pricing strategy and tactics, and set intermediary and end-user prices. Then, continuously monitor market performance and make pricing adjustments as necessary to accommodate evolving market conditions.

Exhibit 17.5

Key Steps in International Price Setting

guitar leaves Aoki's Japan warehouse is $2,530, which is also the lowest acceptable price to Melody (the floor price), since management doesn't want Japanese earnings to dip below those in the United States.

Next, market research on per capita (per person) income levels and competitor prices reveals that Japanese musicians are willing to pay prices about 20 percent above typical U.S. prices for high-quality instruments. Given this information, Melody management believes that Japan can sustain a ceiling price for the Mayer guitar of 10 percent above the floor price—that is, $2,783. Next, management commissions a report from a Japanese market research firm that estimates Melody's sales potential at the floor price and at the ceiling price. Managers eventually decide on a suggested price of $2,560, representing a desire to get established quickly in the Japanese market. This price is also consistent with other factors in the target market, such as Japanese purchasing power, market growth, Japan's large musician population, competitors' prices, and Japanese attitudes on the relationship of price to product quality. Management also feels the price is reasonable given the Melody's pricing in other markets, such as Hawaii and Australia. Accordingly, the firm implements the price level for end users and the corresponding price for its importer, Aoki. Melody begins shipping guitars to Japan and monitors the marketplace, paying close attention to actual demand and the need to make any pricing adjustments in coming months.

Let's review the three pricing strategies in Step 5 of Exhibit 17.5. *Rigid cost-plus pricing* refers to setting a fixed price for all export markets. It is an approach favored by less experienced exporters. In most cases, management simply adds a flat percentage to the domestic price to compensate for the added costs of doing business abroad. The export customer's final price includes a mark-up to cover transporting and marketing the product, as well as profit margins for both intermediaries and the manufacturer. This method often fails to account for local market conditions, such as buyer demand, income level, and competition.

In *flexible cost-plus pricing*, management includes any added costs of doing business abroad in its final price. At the same time, management adjusts prices as needed to accommodate local market and competitive conditions, such as customer purchasing power, demand, competitor prices, and other external variables, as identified in Exhibit 17.4. This approach is more sophisticated than rigid cost-plus pricing because it accounts for specific circumstances in the target market. In the opening vignette, Zara uses this approach, adapting prices to suit conditions in each of the countries where it does business.

In highly competitive markets, the firm may set prices to cover only its variable costs, not its fixed costs. This is known as *incremental pricing*. Here, management assumes that fixed costs are already paid from sales of the product in the firm's home country or other markets. The approach enables the firm to offer very competitive prices, but must be pursued carefully because it may result in suboptimal profits.

When carried to an extreme, incremental pricing may invite competitors to accuse a firm of dumping. As discussed in Chapter 7, *dumping* is the practice of charging a lower price for exported products, sometimes below manufacturing cost—potentially driving local suppliers out of business. The seller may compensate for the low price by charging higher prices in other markets. Many national governments regard dumping as a form of unfair competition and, consequently, may impose antidumping duties or initiate legal action with the World Trade Organization.

Managing International Price Escalation

International price escalation refers to the problem of end-user prices reaching exorbitant levels in the export market caused by multilayered distribution channels, intermediary margins, tariffs, and other international customer costs (identified in Exhibit 17.4). International price escalation may mean that the retail price

International price escalation The problem of end-user prices reaching exorbitant levels in the export market caused by multilayered distribution channels, intermediary margins, tariffs, and other international customer costs.

International Business

in the export market may be two or three times the domestic price, creating a competitive disadvantage for the exporter. Managers can use five key strategies to combat export price escalation abroad.[20]

First, the exporter can attempt to *shorten the distribution channel*. The exporter can set up a more direct route to reach the final customer by bypassing some intermediaries in the channel. With a shorter channel, there are fewer intermediaries to compensate, which reduces the product's final price. Second, the *product can be redesigned* to remove costly features. For example, Whirlpool developed a no-frills, simplified washing machine that it can produce inexpensively and which it sells for a lower price in developing economies. Third, the firm can *ship its products unassembled*, as parts and components, qualifying for lower import tariffs. The firm will then perform final assembly in the foreign market, often by low-cost labor. Some firms have their product assembled in Foreign Trade Zones, where import costs are lower and government incentives may be available.[21] Fourth, some firms explore whether the product can be *re-classified using a different tariff classification* to qualify for lower tariffs. Suppose that Motorola faces a high tariff when exporting "telecommunications equipment" to Bolivia. By having the product reclassified as "computer equipment," Motorola might be able to export the product under a lower tariff. The practice is possible because imported products often fit more than one product category for determining tariffs. Finally, the firm may decide to *move production or sourcing to another country* to take advantage of lower production costs or favorable currency rates.

Managing Pricing under Varying Currency Conditions

The strength of the home-country currency vis-à-vis its trading partners affects the firm's pricing abroad. For example, when the U.S. dollar is strong, it costs Europeans more to purchase U.S. products. Conversely, when the U.S. dollar is weak, it costs Europeans relatively less to purchase U.S. products. In export markets, a strong domestic currency can deter competitiveness, while a weakening domestic currency makes the firm's pricing more competitive. Examine Exhibit 17.6 for strategies firms can use to react to either weakening or appreciating domestic currencies.[22]

Transfer Pricing

Also known as intracorporate pricing, **transfer pricing** refers to the practice of pricing intermediate or finished products exchanged among the subsidiaries and affiliates of the same corporate family located in different countries.[23] For example, when Ford's factory in South Africa sells parts and components to the Ford manufacturing plant in Spain, it charges a transfer price for this intracorporate transaction. These prices, for products transferred within the Ford corporate family, generally differ from the market prices that Ford charges its external customers.

MNEs like Ford attempt to manage internal prices primarily for two reasons. First, companies use transfer pricing to repatriate—that is, to bring back to the home country the profits from countries that restrict MNEs from taking their earnings out of the country. Occasionally, a foreign government may block the transfer of funds out of the country, often due to a shortage of its own currency. When this happens, the MNE might opt to charge high prices to its foreign affiliate as an alternative means of transferring money out of the affiliate's country. In this way, the affiliate transfers substantial funds to the parent, by paying high prices for goods imported from the parent. The strategy works because controls imposed on money transferred in this way are not normally as strict as controls imposed on straight repatriation of profits. Second, transfer pricing can serve as a vehicle for MNEs to shift profits out of a high corporate income-tax country into a low corporate

Transfer pricing The practice of pricing intermediate or finished products exchanged among the subsidiaries and affiliates of the same corporate family located in different countries.

Exhibit 17.6

Strategies for Dealing with Varying Currency Conditions

When the exporter gains a price advantage because its home-country currency is WEAKENING relative to the customer's currency, then it should:	When the exporter suffers from a price disadvantage because its home-country currency is APPRECIATING relative to the customer's currency, then it should:
Stress the benefits of the firm's low prices to foreign customers.	Accentuate competitive strengths in nonprice elements of its marketing program, such as product quality, delivery, and after-sales service.
Maintain normal price levels, expand the product line, or add more costly features.	Consider lowering prices by improving productivity, reducing production costs, or redesigning the product to eliminate costly features.
Exploit greater export opportunities in markets where this favorable exchange rate exists.	Concentrate exporting to those countries whose currencies have not weakened in relation to the exporter.
Speed repatriation of foreign-earned income and collections.	Maintain foreign-earned income in the customer's currency and delay collection of foreign accounts receivable (if there is an expectation that the customer's currency will regain strength over a reasonable time period).
Minimize expenditures in the customer's currency (for example, for advertising and local transportation).	Maximize expenditures in the customer's currency.

income-tax one and thereby increase company-wide profitability. When this occurs, the MNE may opt to maximize the expenses (and therefore minimize the profits) of the foreign-country affiliate by charging high prices for goods sold to the affiliate. MNEs typically centralize transfer pricing under the direction of the chief financial officer at corporate headquarters.

Consider Exhibit 17.7 for a simple illustration of transfer pricing. A subsidiary may buy or sell a finished or intermediate product from another affiliate at below cost, at cost, or above cost. Suppose that the MNE treats Subsidiary A as a favored unit. That is, Subsidiary A is allowed to *source at or below cost* and *sell at a relatively high price* when transacting with other subsidiaries. When consistently applied over a period of time, Subsidiary A will produce relatively more favorable financial results, at the expense of Subsidiaries B, C, and D. Why would the MNE headquarters allow this? In this scenario, the favored Subsidiary A is likely to be in a country that has:

* Lower corporate income-tax rates
* High tariffs for the product in question
* Favorable accounting rules for calculating corporate income
* Political stability
* Little or no restrictions on profit repatriation
* Strategic importance to the MNE

While the subsidiary's financial performance has been boosted in an artificial way, the earnings of the MNE as a whole are optimized. Nevertheless, this benefit

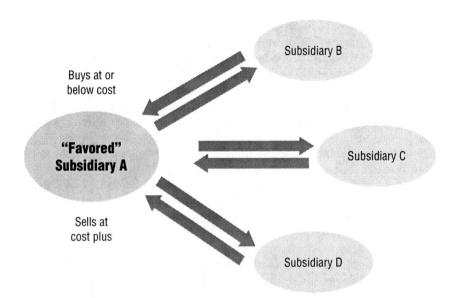

Exhibit 17.7

How Transfer Pricing Can Help
Maximize Corporate-Wide
Reported Earnings

often comes at a cost. First, there is the complication of internal control measures. Manipulating transfer prices makes it very difficult to determine the true profit contribution of a subsidiary. Second, morale problems typically surface at a subsidiary whose profit performance has been made to look worse than it really is. Third, some subsidiary managers may react negatively to price manipulation. Fourth, there is the concern about local accounting regulations. Subsidiaries, as local businesses, must abide by the rules. Legal problems will arise if the subsidiary follows accounting standards that are not approved by the host government. Indeed, many governments closely scrutinize transfer pricing practices of multinational companies to ensure that foreign companies pay their fair share of taxes by reporting accurate earnings.

Gray Market Activity (Parallel Imports)

What do companies such as Caterpillar, Duracell, Gucci, Mercedes-Benz, and Sony have in common? They are MNEs with established brand names that have been the target of gray market activity. Exhibit 17.8 illustrates the nature of flows

Exhibit 17.8 Illustration of Gray Market Activity

and relationships in a gray market activity—the legal importation of genuine products into a country by intermediaries other than authorized distributors.[24] Consider a manufacturer that produces in the source country and exports its products to another, illustrated by the green arrow between countries A and B in Exhibit 17.8. If the going price of the product happens to be sufficiently lower in Country B, then gray market brokers can exploit arbitrage opportunities—buy the product at a low price in Country B, import it into the original source country, and then sell it at a high price there, illustrated by the orange arrow.

In this scenario, the first transaction, illustrated by the green arrow, is carried out by authorized channel intermediaries. The second transaction, illustrated by the red arrow, is carried out by unauthorized intermediaries. Often referred to as *gray marketers,* the unauthorized intermediaries are typically independent entrepreneurs. Because their transactions parallel those of authorized distributors, gray market activity is also called *parallel importation.*

A recent example of gray marketing activity can be drawn from the pharmaceutical trade between the United States and Canada where, in the latter, prescription drugs are available at a lower cost. Some consumers in the United States purchase their prescription drugs from online pharmacies in Canada, at a considerable saving. The gray market opportunity arises because the Canadian provinces negotiate with pharmaceutical companies in establishing a wholesale price—often lower than the prevailing price in the United States. Though the U.S. Federal Drug Administration discourages importation of drugs from other countries since their authenticity or efficacy cannot be verified, consumers continue to fill their prescriptions through Internet pharmacies in Canada. Gray market activity is especially common among premium brands of automobiles, cameras, watches, computers, perfumes, and even construction equipment. It also occurs in international buying and selling of commodities, such as light bulbs and car parts.

You can see that the root cause of gray market activity is a sufficiently large difference in price of the same product between two countries. Such a price difference may be due to either: (1) the manufacturer's inability to coordinate prices across its markets, or (2) a conscious effort on the part of the firm to charge higher prices in some countries when competitive conditions permit. Exchange rate fluctuations may also exacerbate gray market activity by widening the price gap between products priced in two different currencies.

Manufacturers of branded products have good reason to be concerned. Substantial gray market activity complicates at least three aspects of their business. First, there is the risk of a tarnished brand image when customers realize that the product is available at a lower price through alternative channels—particularly less-prestigious outlets. Second, manufacturer-distributor relations can be strained because parallel imports result in lost sales to authorized distributors. Third, gray market activity can disrupt regional sales forecasting, pricing strategies, merchandising plans, and other marketing efforts.

In the United States, the legality of parallel imports had not been initially clarified (hence the term *gray* markets) until the U.S. Supreme Court ruled in 1988 that trademark owners cannot prevent parallel importation. By ruling in favor of the gray market brokers, the Supreme Court acted to serve the best interests of the consumer, who has access to *genuine* (not counterfeit) products at substantially lower prices. Since lobbying by the COPIAT (The Coalition to Preserve the Integrity of American Trademarks) has not produced adequate legislation to stop gray market imports, companies are now compelled to develop their own solutions to combat such activity.

Companies can pursue at least four strategies to cope with gray market imports.[25] First, they can counter through aggressive *price-cutting* in countries and regions targeted by gray market brokers. Second, they can interfere with the flow of products into markets where gray market brokers procure the product. For example, the U.S. firm Pfizer could substantially reduce the shipment of its cholesterol drug Lipitor to Canada to levels that would be just sufficient for local use by Canadian patients. Third, companies can publicize the limitations of gray market channels. Trademark owners such as pharmaceutical companies could flood the media with messages that tactfully build doubt about gray market products. Consumers who fill their prescriptions via online Canadian pharmacies have been warned that the products they receive through these channels may be counterfeits. Indeed, this is a legitimate concern, since counterfeit drugs do make their way into pharmacies in Canada and the United States.[26] Finally, firms can design products with exclusive features that strongly appeal to customers. Adding safety, luxury, or functional features that are unique to each market reduces the likelihood that products will be channeled elsewhere.

 # International Marketing Communications

Companies use *marketing communications* (also known as *promotion*) to provide information to and communicate with existing and potential customers, with the ultimate aim of stimulating demand. International marketing communications emphasize advertising and promotional activities. The nature of these activities can vary substantially around the world. Let's examine them in more detail.

International Advertising

Firms conduct advertising via *media*, which includes direct mail, radio, television, cinema, billboards, transit, print media, and the Internet. *Transit* refers to ads placed in buses, trains, and subways, and is particularly useful in large cities. *Print media* refer to newspapers, magazines, and trade journals. We can assess media availability by examining the amount of advertising spending by region. In 2006, advertising expenditures on major media (newspapers, magazines, television, radio, cinema, billboards, and Internet) amounted to approximately U.S. $100 billion in each of Western Europe and Asia-Pacific. In the United States, advertising expenditures totaled almost U.S. $200 billion.

The availability and quality of media closely determine the feasibility and nature of marketing communications. Exhibit 17.9 provides statistics on media

	Literacy Rate (percentage of population)	Percentage of Households with Television	Radio Stations per one Million People	Newspapers per one Million People
Argentina	97	97	6.5	2.7
Australia	99	96	30.0	2.4
China	91	91	0.5	0.7
India	60	37	0.2	4.8
Japan	99	99	9.2	0.9
Mexico	92	92	13.0	2.9
Netherlands	99	99	15.2	2.1
Nigeria	68	26	0.9	0.2
South Africa	86	54	13.7	0.4
United States	99	99	46.7	5.0

Exhibit 17.9

Media Characteristics in Selected Countries

SOURCES: CIA World Factbook at www.cia.gov; World Bank at www.worldbank.org

Note: Data are for the most recent year available.

Many firms use a standardized approach to international advertising. Benetton's standardized 'United Colors of Benetton' ad has enjoyed much success worldwide.

for various countries. The literacy rate indicates the number of people who can read—a critical ability for understanding most ads. Other data reveal the diversity of communication media in selected countries. Media are widely available in advanced economies. In developing economies, however, TV, radio, the Internet, and newspapers may be limited. The firm must use creative approaches to advertise in countries with low literacy rates and limited media infrastructure. Certain media selections make sense for some countries but not for others. For example, Mexico and Peru emphasize television advertising, Kuwait and Norway concentrate on print media, and Bolivia uses a lot of outdoor advertising on billboards and buildings.

At the firm level, international advertising expenditures vary depending on the size and extent of the firm's foreign operations. For instance, smaller firms often lack the resources to advertise on TV or develop a foreign sales force. Differences in culture, laws, and media availability mean that it is seldom possible to duplicate in foreign markets the type and mix of advertising used in the home market. For example, the Italian government limits television advertising on state channels to 12 percent of airtime per hour and 4 percent per week. Mexico and Peru require that firms produce commercials for the local audience in their respective countries and use local actors.

Advertising conveys a message encoded in language, symbols, colors, and other attributes, each of which may have distinctive meanings. Buyer receptiveness differs as a function of culture and language. Culture determines buyer attitudes toward the role and function of advertising, humor content, the depiction of characters (such as the role of men and women), and decency standards. In China, Nike Inc. ran an ad produced for the U.S. audience in which NBA basketball star LeBron James battles—and defeats—a computer-generated Chinese Kung Fu master. Chinese consumers were offended and China's national government banned the ad.[27]

Many MNEs succeed in applying a relatively standardized approach to international advertising. Benetton, the Italian clothing manufacturer, has run essentially the same and highly successful, "United Colors of Benetton" ad campaign, which features interracial harmony, in markets worldwide. Levi Strauss' advertising approach is similar around the world, stressing the all-American image of its jeans. One TV ad in Indonesia showed teenagers cruising around a small U.S. town in 1960s convertibles. In Japan, Levi's frequently used James Dean, the 1950s U.S. film star, as the centerpiece of its advertising. The dialogue in Levi's ads is often in English, worldwide.[28] The most effective ad campaigns are based on a full understanding of the target audience's buying motivations, values, behavior, purchasing power, and demographic characteristics.

Most MNEs employ advertising agencies to create promotional content and select media for foreign markets. The choice is usually between a home-country-based agency with international expertise, a local agency based in the target market, and a *global ad agency* that also has offices in the target market. Exhibit 17.10 identifies the leading global advertising agencies. Such agencies maintain networks of affiliates and local offices around the world. Consequently, they can create advertising that is both global and sensitive to local conditions while offering a range of additional services such as market research, publicity, and package design.

Rank	Agency	Headquarters	Parent Company
1	McCann Erickson Worldwide	U.S.	Interpublic Group, U.S.
2	Ogilvy & Mather	U.S.	WPP Group, U.K.
3	Grey Worldwide	U.S.	WPP Group, U.K.
4	Euro RSCG Worldwide	U.S.	Havas, France
5	Saatchi & Saatchi	U.S.	Publicis Groupe, France
6	BBDO Worldwide	U.S.	Omnicom Group, U.S.
7	Publicis	France	Publicis Groupe, France
8	JWT	U.S.	WPP Group, U.K.
9	Y&R Advertising	U.S.	WPP Group, U.K.
10	Lowe Worldwide	U.K.	Interpublic Group, U.S.

Exhibit 17.10 The Largest Global Ad Agencies, 2005

SOURCE: Adapted from Endicott, R. Craig. (2005). "Ad Age Global Marketing Report 2005," *Advertising Age*, Nov. 14.

International Promotional Activities

Promotional activities are short-term marketing activities intended to stimulate an initial purchase of the product, immediate purchase, or increased purchases, as well as to improve intermediary effectiveness and cooperation. They include tools such as coupons, point-of-purchase displays, demonstrations, samples, contests, gifts, and Internet interfacing. Some promotional activities (for example, couponing) are illegal or restricted abroad. For instance, Greece, Portugal, and Spain permit virtually every type of promotion, but Germany, Norway, and Switzerland forbid or restrict some. Other promotional activities, such as giveaways, may be considered unethical. Depending on the country, some consumers may be turned off by particular activities. In much of the world, promotional activities are relatively uncommon and may be misunderstood. For example, receiving a free gift is difficult to interpret in some societies. Promotional activities usually require a high level of intermediary or retailer sophistication in order to succeed.

Global Account Management

With more transparent markets, global customers demand uniform and consistent prices, quality, and customer service. **Global account management (GAM)** refers to servicing a key global customer in a consistent and standardized manner, regardless of where in the world it operates. For example, Wal-Mart is a key global account for Procter & Gamble as it purchases a substantial amount of products from P&G. Wal-Mart expects consistent service, including uniform prices for the same product from P&G regardless of where in the world they are delivered. Key accounts such as Migros, Zellers, and Wal-Mart typically purchase from a collection of preferred suppliers who meet their specifications. Suppliers target these key customers by shifting resources from national, regional, and function-based operations to GAM, whose programs feature dedicated cross-functional teams, specialized coordination activities for specific accounts, and formalized structures and processes. Private IT-based portals facilitate the implementation of such systems. Each global customer is assigned a global account manager, or team, who provides the customer with coordinated marketing support and service across various countries.[29]

Global account management (GAM) Servicing a key global customer in a consistent and standardized manner, regardless of where in the world it operates.

International Distribution

Distribution refers to the processes of getting the product or service from its place of origin to the customer. Distribution is the most inflexible of the marketing program elements—once a firm establishes a distribution channel, it may be difficult to change it. As we discussed in chapters 3 and 13, the most common approaches to international distribution include engaging independent intermediaries (for exporting firms), or establishing marketing and sales subsidiaries directly in target markets (an FDI-based approach).

For exporters, intermediaries typically include foreign distributors, agents, trading companies, and export management companies. Many exporters prefer a full stocking distributor because it possesses product knowledge, expert personnel, physical facilities (such as warehousing), and financial resources. When the firm enters a market with direct investment, it will establish a subsidiary. This implies investing directly in the market to lease, acquire, or set up a sales office, production facilities, warehouse, or an entire distribution channel. Entering a new market as a foreign direct investor provides various advantages. First, it helps ensure control over marketing and distribution activities in the target market. Second, it facilitates monitoring the performance of employees and other actors in the local market. Third, it allows the firm to get close to the market, which is especially helpful when the market is complex or rapidly changing.

Some firms bypass traditional distribution systems altogether by using *direct marketing*—selling directly to end users. To supplement direct marketing efforts, many firms use the Internet to provide detailed product information and the means for foreigners to buy offerings. Some firms, such as Amazon.com, are entirely Internet-based, with no retail stores. Others, such as Carrefour, Coles, and Tesco, combine direct marketing with traditional retailing.

The international distribution channel differs for the exporter and the foreign subsidiary. The exporter ships goods to its intermediary, who moves the product through customs and the foreign distribution channel to retail outlets or end users. By contrast, the foreign subsidiary may function as its own distributor, working directly with customers and retailers to move offerings through the channel into the local marketplace. *Channel length* refers to the number of distributors or other intermediaries that it takes to get the product from the manufacturer to the market. The longer the channel, the more intermediaries the firm must compensate, and the costlier the channel. For example, Japan is characterized by long distribution channels involving numerous intermediaries. High channel costs contribute to international price escalation, creating a competitive disadvantage for the firm.

Ethical Dimensions of International Marketing

Because of market globalization, firms' marketing activities strongly influence the buying decisions of consumers worldwide. MNEs now recognize that their customers and other stakeholders expect them to act in a socially responsible manner and display corporate citizenship in their international operations. Many MNEs are proactively developing policies aimed at meeting higher expectations of the public. An important dimension of corporate citizenship is the way firms develop and align their products and services to create greater value for society. In marketing, ensuring that suppliers earn a sustainable income, providing needed products to poor consumers, and disposing of used products responsibly are examples of issues that are high on the corporate social responsibility (CSR) agenda.

For example, in its 7,400 outlets throughout Europe, McDonald's in 2007 began selling coffee sourced only from growers certified by the Rainforest Alliance. The nonprofit organization aims to ensure a sustainable income to the world's poorest coffee growers, mostly in Africa.[30] In a similar move, Nestlé in 2005 joined the Fair Trade movement and began offering a brand of coffee that is sourced from farmers who receive a guaranteed price above world market levels.

Meanwhile, some firms are developing products to serve the needs of the world's poor, such as a bicycle rigged to carry heavy loads, and simple pumps for irrigating crops during the dry season. Such products help people who cannot afford labor-saving and technological products ordinarily targeted to customers in advanced economies. For example, Quanta Computers Inc. makes a laptop computer that is inexpensive enough—around U.S. $100—to help ensure that children in poor countries have access to the information technologies that drive the world economy. The computer is aimed at the nearly 2 billion children in developing economies who receive little or no education.[31]

Motorola has developed various initiatives to promote greater access to mobile communications in developing economies where fixed-line telecommunications are often inadequate or nonexistent, and hinder productivity and economic development. Telephone service is a critical vehicle that promotes increased entrepreneurship and improved GDP. Many countries leapfrogged into fixed-line infrastructure and developed mobile phone networks to support national telecommunication needs. Between 2006 and 2010, it is estimated that the number of mobile customers in developing economies will double, surpassing two billion users. To support this growth, Motorola delivered more than 16 million low-cost (under $30) mobile phones to more than 50 developing countries. In 2006, the firm helped develop a mobile phone-based system for disease management in Africa, where field health workers file patient reports and check drug supplies by mobile phone. Cellular connectivity helps professionals in poor areas deal more effectively with disease outbreaks, medicine shortages, and health maintenance.[32]

A critical environmental issue in marketing is the proper disposal of used products. In the United States, for example, consumers own more than three billion electronic products, ranging from cellular telephones to computers and television sets. Rapid technological changes mean that the life expectancy of these goods is growing shorter. They are usually discarded not because they are broken, but because better versions become available. Products that could be recycled instead end up in landfills, harming the natural environment. In Europe, national governments have passed legislation to deal with the problem. The Waste Electrical and Electronic Equipment (WEEE) directive of the European Union makes companies responsible for collecting and recycling unwanted electronic goods. Similar legislation has been passed in some U.S. states. European law also restricts the types of materials (e.g., harmful substances such as lead and mercury) that can be used to manufacture electronic products. Meanwhile, Cisco and other firms have created incentive programs that encourage consumers to return their old equipment, often for credit toward the purchase of new products. Cisco's program is designed as a financial incentive to prevent old equipment from piling up in landfills.[33]

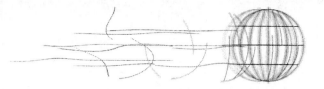

CLOSING CASE

MTV India: Balancing Global and Local Marketing

MTV Networks (www.mtv.com), a division of Viacom, has a big audience among young people in Asia, Australia, Canada, Europe, and Latin America. In total, MTV is broadcast in more than 170 countries in 32 languages. Only 20 percent of all MTV viewers live in the United States, the company's home market. There are 136 distinct MTV channels and 230 Web sites, and they are more widely viewed than any other global network, including CNN. Originally created as a basic cable channel dedicated to music, MTV now encompasses an array of media services and even licensed consumer products.

MTV first went international in 1987 when it launched MTV Europe. With the U.S. market near saturation, management decided to target the huge and growing youth market abroad. Indeed, about one in four people around the world is between 15 and 34 years old. Despite being a global media giant, MTV maintains its international strategy of "Think globally and locally, act appropriately." Management requires that about 70 percent of its programming be developed or adapted for each of the youth segments that it targets abroad. But while most MTV channels have flourished, especially in Brazil and the United Kingdom, others have struggled to find a niche, especially in Asia, and more specifically, in India.

With 470 million people between the ages of 10 and 34, India seems like a huge potential market. India's middle class is rapidly expanding, and the number of households with TV sets has skyrocketed in recent years to 100 million, half of which receive cable. Economic liberalization has made it easier for foreign businesses to enter India. Nevertheless, the Indian market poses various challenges. There are roughly 100 distinctive cable channels vying for advertising dollars. Competition for cable subscribers is intense, and profit margins are often razor thin. There is also corruption and theft, including cable cutting, piracy, and theft of subscriber fees. Indian families typically watch TV as an entire household, which makes it difficult for advertisers to isolate target audiences.

MTV first entered India through a low-risk licensing agreement with Hong Kong's Star TV. Initially MTV was responsible only for programming, while Star TV focused on negotiating deals with local cable companies and advertisers. Because individual markets remained small and undeveloped, MTV management developed a regional marketing strategy by delivering a pan-Asian music channel.

Later, Star TV was sold to the News Corporation, the media giant owned by Rupert Murdoch. News Corporation had its own music channel, known simply as [V], so Star TV ended its partnership with MTV and even hired key staffers away from MTV to develop a new music channel specifically for India. As MTV continued to fol-

low a regional marketing approach, targeting all of Asia and employing English-speaking hosts, management at [V] pursued a different approach. It decided to adapt its music channel to accommodate the preferences of customers in individual Asian markets. This approach paid off, as [V] managed to capture much of MTV's market share. Over time, as [V] flourished, MTV struggled to gain share using its more standardized programming.

MTV also committed some blunders that hurt its prospects in Asia. MTV's Indian staff initially insisted that widely popular Bollywood music (Bollywood is the Indian equivalent of the Hollywood movie industry) wasn't "cool" enough for the teen market. However, the Indian audience disagreed, and MTV's ratings suffered. Gradually, several other music channels emerged, hosted in a variety of local dialects in the population.

Finally, in the late-1990s MTV management opted for a more localized approach and began adapting its programming. It launched MTV India, based in Mumbai, and broadcast across Bangladesh, Nepal, Pakistan, Sri Lanka, and the Middle East as well. MTV India utilized new technologies, such as digital compression, to achieve its goals of increased local programming. When MTV began including more Bollywood music in its programming, ratings soared by 700 percent. Hosts began to speak a mix of both English and Hindi, dubbed "Hinglish." MTV also targeted Indian youth with cricket matches and fashion shows. As the sophistication of its strategy improved, MTV grabbed more market share and eventually surpassed its main rival, [V]. On a worldwide basis, however, MTV's Indian profitability was still low compared to the firm's other international subsidiaries, mainly due to poor advertising revenue.

MTV needed to be creative to become profitable. Initially, it established relationships with advertisers. Instead of merely selling time slots to advertisers, MTV developed programming that incorporates a particular product or brand. For example, the firm worked with Honda to develop "Roadies," a series that documents the experiences of seven young people traveling across India on Honda motorbikes. MTV also created the "World's Longest Dance Party," sponsored by Axe deodorant, and a fashion awards show, sponsored by Lycra.

Ultimately, MTV management discovered that it could not simply export U.S. programming to India. Shows that were extremely popular in the United States, such as "The Osbournes," floundered in India. MTV catered increasingly to the Indian audience, developing costly programming tailored to specific cultural traits and other characteristics.

Localization of TV programming seems to have worked well for MTV. Nevertheless, MTV managers are concerned that the firm may not be reaping the benefits of a global marketing strategy. Programming is broadcast worldwide, but many channels are highly localized, reducing potential gains from economies of scale. Thus, the latest strategic initiative is to develop uniform programming that sells in multiple countries. Therefore, MTV has greatly increased funding of international programming and has developed a jointly based team out of London and New York to develop ideas.

In addition, suspecting that it is missing out on opportunities to cater to the youth market with alternative products and services such as video games, MTV also wishes to explore the feasibility of becoming a one-stop shop for companies hoping to reach global youth markets. For instance, in an advertising relationship with Motorola, MTV aired commercials in Europe, Latin America, and Asia. To supplement revenues, MTV is also considering launching a line of consumer products—fragrances, CDs, and clothing—designed for the youth market.

MTV continues to seek international growth from emerging markets such as China and Mexico, where strong per capita income gains are expected. Management believes that international operations are capable of earning 40 percent of total revenue in the near term. Yet, the goal of sustaining a profitable organization by striking an ideal balance between local adaptation and global standardization has been very elusive.

AACSB: Reflective Thinking

Case Questions

1. What strategies and tactics in marketing program elements are most important in MTV's international operations?

2. What is MTV's main international market segment? What are the characteristics of this segment? How did management position MTV for this segment in India?

3. Describe the evolution of MTV's international marketing strategy in India. What approach did it apply in the early years compared to the later years? Has MTV been able to articulate a clear global marketing strategy in India? What other opportunities can it pursue with the youth market in addition to broadcasting music?

4. Is it feasible for MTV to reach an ideal balance between standardization of programming and local adaptation? If so, how? Thinking in terms of the marketing program elements and marketing strategy, what can management do now to make MTV succeed around the world?

This case was written by Kelly Nealis under the supervision of Dr. Gary Knight. Sources: Capell, Kerry. (2002). "MTV's World," *Business Week*, February 18, pp. 81–86; *Economist.com*, (1998). "Star Woes," April 9. Retrieved from www.economist.com/displaystory.cfm?story_id=159806; Goldsmith, Charles. (2003). "MTV Seeks Global Appeal," *Wall Street Journal*, July 21, p. B1; Gunther, Marc. (2004). "MTV's Passage to India," *Fortune*, August 9, pp.117–121; "MTV: Music Television." Retrieved from www.viacom.com; "MTV Launches Innovative Web Site in India." Retrieved from www.viacom.com; "MTV Announces International Expansion Plans for Europe, Asia, and Latin America." Retrieved from www.viacom.com; (2007). "MTV Networks India." Retrieved from www.mtvindia.com; (2007). "MTV Property Counts." Retrieved from www.viacom.com.

CHAPTER ESSENTIALS

Key Terms

adaptation

global account management (GAM)

global brand

global market segment

global marketing strategy

gray market activity

international price escalation

standardization

transfer pricing

Summary

In this chapter, you learned about:

1. Global marketing strategy

Developing a marketing strategy requires managers to assess the unique foreign market environment and then make choices about market segments, targeting, and positioning. A **global marketing strategy** is a plan of action that guides the firm in: how to position itself and its offerings in foreign markets, which customer segments to pursue, and the degree to which its marketing program elements should be standardized and adapted.

2. Standardization and adaptation of the international marketing program

How the firm balances **adaptation** and **standardization** determines the extent to which the firm must modify a product and its marketing to suit foreign markets. When possible, firms prefer to standardize their products to achieve scale economies and minimize complexity. A **global market segment** is a group of customers that share common characteristics across many national markets. *Positioning* strategy involves using marketing to create a particular image of a product or service, especially relative to competitor offerings, among the firm's customers worldwide.

3. Global branding and product development

A **global brand** is perceived similarly in all the firm's markets and increases marketing strategy effectiveness, allowing the firm to charge higher prices and deal more effectively with channel members and competitors. In developing products with multicountry potential, managers emphasize the commonalities across countries rather than the differences. The development of global products facilitates economies of scale in R&D, production, and marketing. Innovation and design in international product development are increasingly performed by *global teams*—an internationally distributed group of people with a specific mandate to make or implement decisions that are international in scope.

4. International pricing

International prices are determined by factors both internal and external to the firm, which often cause prices to inflate abroad. A special challenge for exporters in pricing is **international price escalation**—the problem of end-user prices reaching exorbitant levels in the export market, caused by multilayered distribution channels, intermediary margins, tariffs, and other international customer costs. **Transfer pricing** is the practice of pricing intermediate or finished products exchanged among the subsidiaries and affiliates of the same corporate family located in different countries. **Gray market activity**, also known as parallel imports, refers to legal importation of genuine products into a country by intermediaries other than authorized distributors.

5. International marketing communications

International marketing communications involves the management of advertising and promotional activities across national borders. Managers are often compelled to adapt their international communications due to unique legal, cultural, and socioeconomic factors in foreign markets. Firms must also accommodate literacy levels, language, and available media. In working with key business customers, firms may follow **global account management (GAM)** practices—the servicing of a key global customer in a consistent and standardized manner, regardless of where in the world they operate.

6. International distribution

Firms usually engage foreign intermediaries or foreign-based subsidiaries to reach customers in international markets. When designing the international channel, management must account for various factors, including the nature of the product and the market. Some firms bypass traditional distribution systems altogether by using *direct marketing*. *Channel length* refers to the number of distributors or other intermediaries that it takes to get the product from the manufacturer to the market. The longer the channel, the more intermediaries must be compensated, and the costlier the distribution function.

7. Ethical dimensions of international marketing

Firms increasingly recognize that their international marketing activities are closely scrutinized by the public. In response, firms put in place corporate social responsibility programs such as ensuring that suppliers earn a sustainable income, providing needed products to poor consumers, and disposing of used products responsibly. Firms are becoming more proactive in corporate citizenship, but much more remains to be accomplished.

Test Your Comprehension AACSB: Reflective Thinking, Ethical Reasoning

1. Describe the marketing program elements and how each influences sales and performance in international business.

2. Audrey Corp. has historically adapted its offerings for all its foreign markets, leading to a proliferation of product variations. Explain why Audrey Corp. might want to consider global marketing strategy. What are the benefits of global marketing strategy?

3. Distinguish between adaptation and standardization in international marketing.

4. Consider Toshiba's laptop computer division. In terms of the marketing program elements, what attributes of laptop computers does the firm need to adapt and which attributes can it standardize for international markets?

5. What is the role of market segmentation and positioning in international marketing? What is a global market segment?

6. William Corporation is a manufacturer of high-quality men and women's fashions. What steps should you take to transform William into a well-recognized global brand?

7. What are the most important factors to consider when formulating international pricing strategies? What steps would you follow in arriving at international prices?

8. Export customers of a consumer products firm tend to be highly sensitive to price. However, the firm is experiencing substantial price escalation in these markets. What factors may be causing this situation? What can management do to reduce the detrimental impact of international price escalation?

9. What are the most important factors to consider when designing strategy for international marketing communications?

10. Describe the role of distribution and logistics in international business.

11. Summarize the key ethical issues that characterize international marketing.

Apply Your Understanding AACSB: Reflective Thinking, Analytical Skills

1. One manifestation of global marketing strategy is the increased tendency of MNEs to launch new products simultaneously around the world. For example, many movies—such as *The Matrix* and *Harry Potter*—are introduced at the same time in markets worldwide, using essentially the same marketing program. Visit the Web sites of the *Matrix* and the *Harry Potter* movies. What global market segments do these movies appear to target? Describe the specific aspects of global marketing strategy that you can detect in the international marketing of these films.

2. Products must be adapted to accommodate national differences arising from customer preferences and each market's economic conditions, climate, culture, and language. Think about the following products: packaged flour, swimsuits, textbooks, and automobiles. For each of these products, describe how a firm would need to adapt different marketing program elements to suit conditions in China, Germany, and Saudi Arabia. Keep in mind that China is an emerging market with low per capita income, Saudi Arabia is an emerging market with a conservative culture rooted in Islam, and Germany is an advanced and liberal economy. In developing your answer for each product, think especially about the nature of the product, its pricing and distribution, and how a firm would promote it in the market.

3. Office Depot, the supplier of office equipment and supplies, has stores in countries throughout Asia, Europe, and Latin America. Suppose the firm has decided to launch its own line of notebook computers and wants to know how to price them in various markets. What would be the most important factors Office Depot should consider when setting prices in foreign markets? Suggest a step-by-step approach to international pricing.

AACSB: **Reflective Thinking**

Refer to Chapter 1, page 27, for instructions on how to access and use globalEDGE™.

1. Global branding is key to international marketing success. Every year *Business Week* and *Interbrand* publish a ranking of the top 100 global brands. The ranking can be accessed by searching the term "global brand" at globalEDGE™, or by entering "global brands scorecard" in a Google search. For this exercise, locate and retrieve the most current ranking and answer the following questions:

   a. What do you consider are the strengths and weaknesses of the methodology *Interbrand* uses to estimate brand equity?

   b. What patterns do you detect in terms of the countries and industries most represented in the top 100 list?

   c. *Business Week* publishes an article in conjunction with the ranking. According to *Business Week,* what managerial guidelines are helpful in order for a company to develop a strong global brand?

2. Procter and Gamble (P&G) and Unilever are the two leading firms in the consumer products industry for products such as soap, shampoo, and laundry detergent. P&G (www.pg.com) is based in the United States and Unilever (www.unilever.com) is based in Europe. What are the major regional markets of each firm? What products does each firm offer through a global marketing strategy? Structure your answer in terms of the elements of the marketing program. That is, what global strategy approaches does each firm apply for the product, its pricing, promotion, and distribution?

3. A *third-party logistics provider* (3PL) provides outsourced or "third party" logistics services to companies for part or all of their distribution activities. Examples include C.H. Robinson Worldwide, Maersk Logistics, and FedEx. Your firm needs to find a 3PL to handle its distribution efforts abroad. Your task is to locate two 3PLs online and address the following questions:

   a. What logistical services does each firm provide?

   b. What types of customers does each 3PL serve?

   c. Where are their headquarters and branch offices located?

   d. Based on the information provided, which of the two 3PLs would you most likely choose? Why?

CKR *Cavusgil Knight Riesenberger*

Management Skill Builder©

Developing a Distribution Channel in Japan

A critical step in developing international marketing operations is the creation of the foreign distribution channel. The distribution channel provides the means to convey products (and many services) from their point of production to a convenient location where they can be purchased by customers. In the absence of a well-conceived distribution channel, efforts in formulating the other marketing program elements—product, pricing, and communications—may prove fruitless.

AACSB: Reflective Thinking, Multicultural and Diversity

Managerial Challenge

The firm should establish a reliable distribution channel in the foreign market from the very beginning. Channels are often costly to set up, and once established, may be difficult to change. Because buyers may view the distributor as the originator of the product or service, the firm must use a systematic approach to choose the right distributor. In this C/K/R Management Skill Builder©, your challenge is to investigate the nature of distribution channels in Japan for a firm that manufactures medical equipment.

Background

The market in Japan for medical equipment and supplies is very promising. Japan's medical device market is the second largest in the world and is one of the few product markets that have achieved steady growth despite the sluggish performance of the Japanese economy in recent years. The value of the market exceeds $10 billion annually, and imported products are popular. Foreign firms see bright sales prospects in such product categories as pacemakers, artificial implants, and catheters, as well as software and other products used in medical information and communications systems.

Managerial Skills You Will Gain

In this C/K/R Management Skill Builder©, as a prospective manager, you will:

1. Acquire a deeper understanding of the nature of distribution channels in Japan.

2. Learn the factors to consider when making international channel arrangements for a specific industry.

3. Research critical factors to consider in the development of an international channel.

4. Learn how firms can go about finding intermediaries for international channels.

Your Task

Investigate establishing a distribution channel in Japan for a firm in your home country that makes medical equipment.

Go to the C/K/R Knowledge Portal©

www.prenhall.com/cavusgil

Proceed to the C/K/R Knowledge Portal© to obtain the expanded background information, your task and methodology, suggested resources for this exercise, and the presentation template.

Learning Objectives

In this chapter, you will learn about:

1. The nature of contractual entry strategies in international business

2. Licensing

3. Advantages and disadvantages of licensing

4. Franchising

5. Advantages and disadvantages of franchising

6. Other contractual entry strategies

7. Management of licensing and franchising

Licensing, Franchising, and Other Contractual Strategies

> ## Harry Potter: The Magic of Licensing

One of the hottest properties in merchandise licensing is Harry Potter, valued at over $1 billion. Not bad for a bespectacled 11-year-old boy. Potter has come a long way since he first appeared in the 1997 children's book by J. K. Rowling. Potter evolved from an unhappy orphan to a confident trainee wizard. The stories appeal to both children and adults. Kids love Potter because he is a fantastic combination of cool kid and good kid. Adults like the classical theme of good versus evil. Licensing deals have benefited immensely from the Warner Bros. production and release of major Harry Potter movies.

Warner Bros. purchased exclusive licensing rights for Harry Potter. Warner allows firms all over the world to use Potter images on their manufactured products—such as game software, children's furniture, and clothing—in exchange for a royalty. The royalty is a flat percentage of the sale generated by the licensed product that the manufacturer pays to the licensor. The ability to associate Potter with manufactured products greatly increases the sale of licensed products, allowing them to command high prices. Such deals have made Rowling one of the wealthiest women in England.

Warner licenses Harry Potter to a number of firms. Some firms produce *artefacts*—products seen in the films that do not have Potter's name on them. For example, Califor-

nia's Jelly Belly Candy Company creates Potter's favorite candy, Bertie Bott's Every Flavour Beans, in flavors such as earwax, sardine, and vomit. LEGO is making construction kits that allow kids to build their own Hogwarts castle, and Mattel is making Harry Potter toys.

Electronic Arts, the largest independent software game producer, paid Warner for a license to develop and market video games. The license covers games played on the Internet, video game consoles such as Sony's PlayStation 2, and cellular telephones. Fans can play a virtual version of Quidditch, which is a bit like aerial polo but with contestants flying on broomsticks. Mattel, Electronic Arts, and other licensees pay a royalty to Warner for the right to use the Potter image to sell their merchandise.

Goodwin Weavers, a home furnishings company, also has a Harry Potter license. The company produces Potter tapestry throws, wall hangings, decorative pillows, "pillow buddies," and fleece. P. J. Kids made a line of Potter loft beds that sold extremely well, despite a nearly $2,000 price tag. Such products command high prices through the magic of licensing a very popular brand.

The licensing process is self-generating—each Harry Potter book sets the stage for a film, which boosts book sales, which promotes sales of Potter-licensed products.

Globally, the first four Potter books sold over 200 million copies in 55 languages. The first two Potter movies grossed over $1.8 billion at the box office. Meanwhile, Rowling and Warner have exercised restraint. They don't want to license Potter to just anyone. Experts estimate that the hot property could have generated 200 to 300 product licenses in the United States alone. Warner wants to make sure that overexposure doesn't kill the golden goose.

One of the risks that licensors such as Warner face is intellectual property violations. These occur when a firm or individual uses the licensed item to generate profits without permission of the property's owner. For instance, over 80 percent of recorded music and business software in China is counterfeit. Pirated DVD versions of Potter movies are sold on the streets of Chinese cities for as little as one dollar, often before the film's official premiere in China. Unauthorized translations of one of the Potter books have been posted on the Internet. Such postings affect future sales because people may not bother to buy the book if an online version is available. Chinese bookstores recently released a boxed set of Harry Potter novels, but even before release, kiosks around China were selling unauthorized versions of the books. To combat counterfeiting, the official Chinese publisher printed the Potter books on special light green paper and advised the local media—newspapers, magazines, television—how to recognize the real version. Licensees hope that Harry Potter will generate the same magic in China that he has in the rest of the world.

Sources: Derrick, Stuart. (2005). "Brands Cash In on Literary Scene," *Promotions & Incentives*, July/August, pp. 13–14; *DSN Retailing Today*. (2000). "Harry Potter: Is Warner Bros. Brewing Licensing Magic," August 21, pp. A8; *Economist.com / Global Agenda*. (2003). "Harry Potter and the Publishing Goldmine," June 23, p. 1; Forney, Matt. (2000). "Harry Potter, Meet 'Ha-li Bo-te'—Children's Books Hit China, But Price and Piracy Could Put Crimp in Sales," *Wall Street Journal*, Sept 21, p. B1; Jardine, Alexandra. (2001). "Marketing Magic," *Marketing*, November 15, p. 20; O'Mara, Sheila. (2002). "Harry—Licensing's Golden Child," *Home Textiles Today*, January/February, p. 10; *Wall Street Journal*. (2000). "Electronic Arts Gets Rights to Develop Harry Potter Games," August 11, p. A4

 ## The Nature of Contractual Entry Strategies in International Business

In this chapter, we address various types of cross-border contractual relationships, including licensing and franchising. **Contractual entry strategies in international business** refer to cross-border exchanges where the relationship between the focal firm and its foreign partner is governed by an explicit contract. **Intellectual property** refers to ideas or works created by firms or individuals, such as patents, trademarks, and copyrights. It incorporates such knowledge-based assets of the firm or individuals as industrial designs, trade secrets, inventions, works of art, literature, and other "creations of the mind."[1]

Two common types of contractual entry strategies are *licensing* and *franchising*. **Licensing** is an arrangement in which the owner of intellectual property grants another firm the right to use that property for a specified period of time in exchange for royalties or other compensation. **Franchising** is an arrangement in which the firm allows another the right to use an entire business system in exchange for fees, royalties, or other forms of compensation.

Contractual relationships are fairly prevalent in international business. Manufacturers as well as service firms routinely transfer their knowledge assets to foreign partners. For example, pharmaceutical manufacturers engage in cross-licensing practices where they exchange scientific knowledge about producing specific products, as well as the rights to distribute these products in certain geographic regions. Professional service firms such as those in architecture, engineering, advertising, and consulting extend their international reach through contracts with foreign partners. Similarly, service firms in retailing, fast food, car rentals, television programming, and animation rely on licensing and franchising agreements. As an example, 7-Eleven runs the world's largest chain of convenience stores, with about 26,000 stores in 18

Contractual entry strategies in international business Cross-border exchanges where the relationship between the focal firm and its foreign partner is governed by an explicit contract.

Intellectual property Ideas or works created by firms or individuals such as patents, trademarks, and copyrights.

Licensing Arrangement in which the owner of intellectual property grants another firm the right to use that property for a specified period of time in exchange for royalties or other compensation.

Franchising Arrangement in which the firm allows another the right to use an entire business system in exchange for fees, royalties, or other forms of compensation.

countries. While the parent firm in Japan owns most of the stores, several thousand in Canada, Mexico, and the United States are operated through franchising arrangements.

Unique Aspects of Contractual Relationships

Cross-border contractual relationships share six common characteristics. They are:

* *Governed by a contract that provides the focal firm a moderate level of control over the foreign partner.* A formal agreement specifies the rights and obligations for both partners. Control refers to the ability of the focal firm to influence the decisions, operations, and strategic resources of a foreign venture and ensure that foreign partners undertake assigned activities and procedures. The focal firm also maintains ownership and jurisdiction over its intellectual property. However, as Exhibit 14.1 on page 420 relies on shows, contractual agreements do not afford the same level of control as foreign direct investment, since the focal firm relies on independent businesses abroad.

* *Typically involve exchange of intangibles (intellectual property) and services.* Examples of intangibles that firms exchange include technical assistance and know-how. (See Exhibit 3.5 on page 70 for a complete list). Along with intangibles, however, firms may also exchange products or equipment to support the foreign partner.

* *Can be pursued independently or in conjunction with other foreign market entry strategies.* Firms can engage in contractual agreements as an alternative way of responding to international opportunities. In other cases, contractual relationships may accompany and support FDI and exporting.[2] Their use is context specific; that is, a focal firm may pursue a contractual relationship with certain customers, countries, or products, but not others.

* *Provide for a dynamic, flexible choice.* Over time the focal firm may switch to another way of servicing foreign markets. For example, franchisors such as McDonald's or Coca-Cola often find it desirable to acquire some of their franchisees and bottlers. In doing so, they would be switching from a contractual to an ownership-based entry strategy.

* *Often reduce local perceptions of the focal firm as a foreign enterprise.* Since the focal firm partners with a local firm, it may attract less of the criticism often directed at foreign MNEs.

* *Generate a predictable level of earnings from foreign operations.* In comparison to FDI, contractual relationships imply reduced volatility and risk.[3]

Types of Intellectual Property

A *patent* provides an inventor with the right to prevent others from using, selling, or importing an invention for a fixed period—typically, up to 20 years.[4] It is granted to any firm or individual that invents or discovers any new and useful process, device, manufactured product, or any new and useful improvement on these. A *trademark* is a distinctive design, symbol, logo, word, or series of words placed on a product label. It identifies a product or service as coming from a common source and having a certain level of quality. Well-known trademarks include British Petroleum's "BP" acronym, McDonald's golden arches, and Nike's swoosh symbol. A *copyright* protects original works of authorship, giving the creator the exclusive right to reproduce the work, display and perform it publicly, and to authorize others to perform these activities. Copyrights cover works from music, art, literature, films, and computer software.

An *industrial design* refers to the appearance or features of a product. The design is intended to improve the aesthetics and usability of a product in order to increase its production efficiency, performance, or marketability. The thin Apple iPod with the company logo is a well-known industrial design. A *trade secret* is confidential know-how or information that has commercial value.[5] Trade secrets include information such as production methods, business plans, and customer lists. For example, the formula to produce Coca-Cola is a trade secret. A *collective mark* is a logo belonging to an association or group whose members retain the right to use the mark identifying the origin of a product or service. Typically, the members use the marks to identify themselves and their products with a level of quality or accuracy, geographical origin, or other characteristics established by the organization. For example, DIN is the collective mark for the German Institute for Standardization, typically found on home appliances in Europe.

Intellectual property rights (IPRs) refer to the legal claim through which the proprietary assets of firms and individuals are protected from unauthorized use by other parties. The availability and enforcement of these rights varies from country to country. The fundamental rationale for IPRs is to provide inventors with a monopoly advantage for a specified period of time, so that they can exploit their inventions and create commercial advantage. Such legal rights enable inventors not only to recoup investment costs, but also to acquire power and dominance in markets by granting a period of years in which the inventor need not face direct competition from competitors producing the same product. Without legal protection and the assurance of commercial rewards, most firms and individuals would have little incentive to invent.

 # Licensing

A licensing agreement specifies the nature of the relationship between the licensor (owner of intellectual property) and the licensee (the user). High-technology firms routinely license their patents and know-how to foreign companies. For example, Intel has licensed the right to a new process for manufacturing computer chips to a chip manufacturer in Germany. As revealed in the opening vignette, Warner licenses images from the Harry Potter books and movies to companies worldwide. Disney licenses the right to use its cartoon characters in the production of shirts and hats to clothing manufacturers in Hong Kong. Disney also licenses its trademark names and logos to manufacturers of apparel, toys, and watches for sale worldwide. Licensing allows Disney to create synergies with foreign partners who adapt materials, colors, and other design elements to suit local tastes. Licensing allows the licensee to produce and market a product similar to the one the licensor may already produce in its home country. By gaining an association with a famous name like Disney, the licensee can generate substantial sales.

Exhibit 15.1 illustrates the nature of the licensing agreement between the licensor and the licensee.[6] Upon signing a licensing contract, the licensee pays the licensor a fixed amount up front *and* an ongoing **royalty** of typically 2 to 5 percent on gross sales generated from using the licensed asset. The fixed amount covers the licensor's initial costs of transferring the licensed asset to the licensee, including consultation, training in how to deploy the asset, engineering, or adaptation. However, certain types of licensable assets, such as copyrights and trademarks, have much lower transfer costs.

The licensing contract typically runs from 5 to 7 years and is renewable at the option of the parties. While the licensor usually must provide technical information and assistance to the licensee, once the relationship is established and the licensee fully understands its role, the licensor has little or no additional role. The licensor typically plays an advisory role, but has no direct involvement in the mar-

Intellectual property rights (IPRs) The legal claim through which the proprietary assets of firms and individuals are protected from unauthorized use by other parties.

Royalty A fee paid periodically to compensate a licensor for the temporary use of its intellectual property; often based on a percentage on gross sales generated from using the licensed asset.

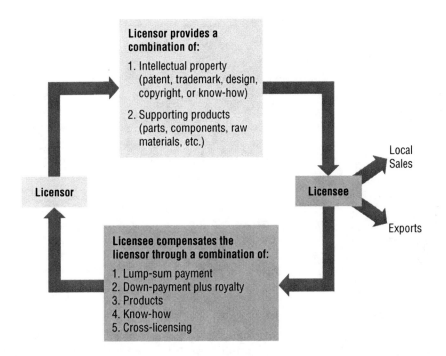

Exhibit 15.1

Licensing as a Foreign Market
Entry Strategy

SOURCE: Adapted from Welch and Welch (1996)
and personal correspondence with Lawrence Welch.

Licensor provides a combination of:

1. Intellectual property (patent, trademark, design, copyright, or know-how)
2. Supporting products (parts, components, raw materials, etc.)

Licensor

Licensee

Local Sales

Exports

Licensee compensates the licensor through a combination of:

1. Lump-sum payment
2. Down-payment plus royalty
3. Products
4. Know-how
5. Cross-licensing

ket and provides no ongoing managerial guidance. Most firms enter into *exclusive agreements*, implying that the licensee is *not* permitted to share the licensed asset with any other company within a prescribed territory. In addition to operating in its domestic market, the licensee may also be permitted to export to third countries.

If the licensor is an MNE, it may enter a licensing arrangement with its own wholly or partly-owned foreign affiliate. In this case, licensing is an efficient way to compensate the foreign affiliate and transfer intellectual property to it within a formal legal framework. Typically, the firm uses this form of licensing when the foreign affiliate is a separate legal entity, a common scenario in many countries. Multinational firms often use licensing as an innovative way to compensate or transfer intellectual property to their foreign subsidiaries or affiliates. Some firms view licensing as a supplementary strategy to other entry strategies, such as exporting or FDI.

In the fashion industry, firms with strong brands such as Bill Blass, Hugo Boss, and Pierre Cardin generate substantial profits from licensing deals for jeans, fragrances, and watches. Saks Inc., the first foreign luxury department store in China, entered the country by licensing its Saks Fifth Avenue name for a flagship department store in Shanghai. Saks generates revenue from the licensing agreement and controls which merchandise is sold there, but has no other involvement. Licensing brings greater awareness of Saks Fifth Avenue to Asia without requiring Saks itself to operate the store, thereby reducing its risk.[7]

The national origin of popular brands might surprise you. In the food industry, Peter Paul Mounds and Almond Joy are owned by the British food firm Cadbury Schweppes and produced in the United States through a licensing agreement with Hershey Foods. Planters, Sunkist, and Budweiser brands are owned by U.S. companies and sold in Britain, Japan, and Singapore through licensing agreements with local companies. Coca-Cola has a licensing agreement to distribute Evian bottled water in the United States on behalf of the brand's owner, French company Danone. Indeed, a review of annual reports from 120 of the largest multinational food companies revealed that at least half are involved in some form of international product licensing.[8]

There are two major types of licensing agreements: (1) trademark and copyright licensing, and (2) know-how licensing. Let's review each in detail.

Trademark and Copyright Licensing

Trademark licensing involves a firm granting another firm permission to use its proprietary names, characters, or logos for a specified period of time in exchange for a royalty. Trademarks appear on such merchandise as clothing, games, food, beverages, gifts, novelties, toys, and home furnishings. Organizations and individuals with name brand appeal benefit from trademark licensing, such as Coca Cola, Harley-Davidson, Laura Ashley, Disney, Michael Jordan, and even your favorite university! Playboy Enterprises successfully licensed its logo and other marketing assets to clothing manufacturers in other countries. As revealed in the opening vignette, a famous trademark like Harry Potter generates millions of dollars to the owner, with little effort. U.S. companies derive trademark-licensing revenues well in excess of $100 billion annually.

In the United States and a number of other countries, firms acquire rights to trademarks through first use and continuous usage. In other countries, however, rights to trademarks are acquired through registration with government authorities, and many countries require local use of the registered mark to maintain the registration. When a firm registers its trademark, it formally notifies government authorities that it owns the trademark and is entitled to intellectual property protection. The convention of gaining ownership to a trademark simply through registration has caused concerns for many firms. For example, when it wanted to enter South Africa in 1993, McDonald's was frustrated to learn that a local businessperson had already applied to register the McDonald's trademark for his own use and to have the company's rights to the trademark withdrawn.[9] When McDonald's protested in court to establish its ownership, the South African Supreme Court actually ruled in favor of the local entrepreneur.

Disney licenses its trademark characters to apparel and consumer products manufacturers worldwide, generating substantial licensing revenue. These girls in Tokyo, Japan are dressed like Disney princess characters Cinderella and Snow White and Minnie Mouse.

Winnie the Pooh is one of trademark licensing's biggest success stories. Developed as a children's literary character in 1926, Pooh evolved into a multi-billion dollar licensing property. Acquired by Disney in 1961, Pooh is the second-highest earning fictional character of all time, behind only Mickey Mouse. The Pooh image is licensed to many manufacturers for inclusion on a range of products, from baby merchandise to textiles to gardening products. There are roughly 1,000 Pooh licensees in Europe alone.[10]

In many countries, a *copyright* gives the owner the exclusive right to reproduce the work, prepare derivative works, distribute copies, or perform or display the work publicly. Original works include art, music, and literature, as well as computer software. The term of protection varies by country, but the creator's life plus 50 years is typical. However, because many countries offer little or no copyright protection, it is wise to investigate local copyright laws before publishing a work abroad.[11]

Know-How Licensing

Know-how agreement
Contract in which the focal firm provides technological or management knowledge about how to design, manufacture, or deliver a product or a service.

Gaining access to technology is an important rationale for licensing. A **know-how agreement** is a contract in which the focal firm provides technological or management knowledge about how to design, manufacture, or deliver a product or a service. The licensor makes its patents, trade secrets, or other know-how available to a licensee in exchange for a royalty. The royalty may be a lump sum, a *running royalty* based on the volume of products produced from the know-how, or a combination of both.

In some industries, such as pharmaceuticals, chemicals, and semiconductors, technology is acquired in reciprocal licensing arrangements between firms from the same or similar industries. This is known as *cross-licensing.* In industries where the rate of technological advances is rapid and where innovations often build on each other, technology licensing from competitors provides key advantages. It reduces the cost of innovation by avoiding duplication of research, while reducing the risk of excluding any one firm from access to new developments.

For example, AT&T once held most of the key patents in the semiconductor industry. As more firms entered the industry and the pace of R & D quickened, AT&T was at risk of being surpassed by competitors. In Europe, Japan, and the United States, thousands of semiconductor patents were eventually awarded. In such a complex network of patents, it would have been nearly impossible for any one firm to operate in the industry without licenses from competitors. Thus, AT&T, Intel, Siemens, and numerous other competitors began licensing their patents to each other. The collective licensing activities of these firms greatly accelerated innovation in semiconductors.

A similar observation can be made of the pharmaceutical industry. Because the R & D to develop a new drug can reach hundreds of millions of dollars, and new drugs require time-consuming government approval processes, pharmaceutical firms want to launch their discoveries as quickly as possible. To reduce cost and increase the speed of new drug development, pharmaceutical firms license inventions to each other.[12] In other industries, firms may license technology and know-how from competitors to compensate for insufficient knowledge, fill gaps in their product line-ups, or enter new businesses. It is often more efficient to acquire technology from other firms through licensing than to invest potentially huge sums in R & D. Typically, there is an understanding that the firm that acquires technology in this way will, in turn, license some of its own technology to others.

Who Are the Top Licensing Firms?

Exhibit 15.2 lists the world's top licensing firms by annual revenues. All but one (Sanrio) are based in the United States. Among them, the greatest amount of licensing occurs in the apparel, games, and toy industries. Licensing sales have benefited immensely from the emergence of large-scale retailers, such as Wal-Mart and Carrefour, and Internet-based selling.

 ## Advantages and Disadvantages of Licensing

Exhibit 15.3 summarizes the advantages and disadvantages of licensing from the perspective of the licensor. Let's highlight some of the key points.

Advantages of Licensing

As an entry strategy, licensing requires neither substantial capital investment nor involvement of the licensor in the foreign market. Licensing allows the firm to gain market presence without FDI. For this reason, it is a preferred strategy of small and medium-sized enterprises (SMEs), which may lack the resources to internationalize through more costly entry strategies. Licensing also allows the firm to exploit the fruits of research and development that it has already conducted. Once the licensing relationship is established, the licensor needs to invest little additional effort while it receives a stream of royalty income. Thus, unlike

Rank	Firm Name	Annual Licensing Revenues (U.S.$ billions)	Typical Deals
1	Disney Consumer Products	$21.0	Toy and apparel licensing for Disney movies such as *The Little Mermaid* and *The Lion King*, and characters such as Winnie the Pooh and Mickey Mouse
2	Warner Bros. Consumer Products	6.0	Toy and apparel licensing from movies such as *Superman Returns*, *Scooby-Doo*, and *Harry Potter*
3	Nickelodeon & Viacom Consumer Products	5.2	Toy and apparel licensing for TV programs such as *SpongeBob SquarePants*; video game licensing from *The Godfather* movie
4	Marvel Entertainment	5.0	Toy, game, and apparel licensing for *Ghost Rider*, *Fantastic Four*, *Captain America*, and *X-Men*
5	Major League Baseball	4.7	Baseball-related video games, apparel, toys
6	Sanrio (Japan)	4.2	Toys and apparel tied to the *Hello Kitty* character
7	The Cherokee Group	4.1	Apparel and shoes tied to Cherokee and Sideout brands
8	National Football League	3.5	American football-related apparel and equipment
9	General Motors	3.0	Toys and apparel based on popular car models
10	Lucasfilm Ltd.	3.0	Toys, games, and apparel based on the *Star Wars* and *Indiana Jones* movies

Exhibit 15.2

Leading Licensors Ranked by Licensing Revenues

SOURCE: Wilensky, Dawn, (2006). "101 Leading Licensors," License, April, pp.22–37, accessed at www.licensemag.com

other foreign entry strategies, the licensor bears no cost of establishing a physical presence in the market or maintaining inventory there. Meanwhile, the licensee benefits by gaining access to a key technology at a much lower cost than if it had developed the technology on its own.[13]

Licensing makes entry possible in countries that restrict foreign ownership in specific industries, such as defense and energy, that may be considered critical for national security. Licensing enables firms to enter smaller markets or those that are difficult to enter because of trade barriers, such as tariffs and bureaucratic requirements. For example, drug manufacturer Roche entered a licensing agreement with Chugai Pharmaceuticals in Japan in order to expand its presence in the Japanese patented medication market. Success in Japan requires substantial market know-how and a deep knowledge of the local drug approval process. The relationship accelerated Roche's penetration of the huge Japanese market.[14]

Licensing can also be used as a low-cost strategy to test the viability of foreign markets. By establishing a relationship with a local licensee, the foreign firm can learn about the target market and devise the best future strategy for establishing a more substantive presence there. A firm may use licensing as a strategy to pre-

Exhibit 15.3

Advantages and Disadvantages of Licensing to the Licensor

Advantages	Disadvantages
• Does not require capital investment or presence of the licensor in the foreign market	• Revenues are usually more modest than with other entry strategies
• Ability to generate royalty income from existing intellectual property	• Difficult to maintain control over how the licensed asset is used
• Appropriate for entering markets that pose substantial country risk	• Risk of losing control of important intellectual property, or dissipating it to competitors
• Useful when trade barriers reduce the viability of exporting or when governments restrict ownership of local operations by foreign firms	• The licensee may infringe the licensor's intellectual property and become a competitor
• Useful for testing a foreign market prior to entry via FDI	• Does not guarantee a basis for future expansion in the market
• Useful as a strategy to preemptively enter a market before rivals	• Not ideal for products, services, or knowledge that are highly complex
	• Dispute resolution is complex and may not produce satisfactory results

empt the entry of competitors in a target market. That is, by establishing a licensing presence in a market, the firm develops its brand name and familiarity there, hindering competitors who enter the market later.

Disadvantages of Licensing

Because royalties are based on the licensee's sales volume, the licensor depends on the licensee's sales and marketing prowess for its profits. A poor partner may be unable to generate substantial sales. As a moderate-control entry strategy, the licensor is limited in its ability to control the manner in which its asset is used. If the licensee uses the asset carelessly, such as by producing a substandard product, the licensor's reputation can be harmed. For this reason, experienced firms usually require foreign licensees to meet minimum quality standards. For example, U.S.-based Anheiser-Busch Brewing Company markets Budweiser beer in Japan through a licensing arrangement with Kirin, a strong local brewer. One of the most reputable brewers in Japan, Kirin produces Bud and other beers according to Anheiser-Busch's strict standards.

If the licensee is very successful, the licensor may wish it had entered the market through a more lucrative entry strategy. This was the case that Disney faced when it developed Disneyland Tokyo through a licensing arrangement with a Japanese partner. When the theme park proved much more successful than originally thought, Disney management wished it had developed Disneyland Tokyo itself. In Mexico, Televisa experienced the same problem. The largest producer of Spanish-language TV programming, Televisa opted for a licensing arrangement with California-based Univision to enter the U.S. market, where over 35 million people speak Spanish as their primary language. For its part, the Mexican company receives only 9 percent of Univision's advertising revenue. Licensing profits tend to be substantially lower than those possible from exporting or FDI entry. Moreover, licensing does not guarantee a basis for future expansion. The licensor's options for internationalizing by other means are usually restricted in the licensing agreement.

Can you tell the difference between these two dolls? Licensors run the risk of creating competitors, as Mattel discovered when it granted a license to a Brazilian firm to market Barbie doll. The latter firm went on to create a competitor to Barbie, the Susi doll (on the left).

A focal firm should ensure that its valued intellectual assets do not fall into the hands of individuals or companies that are likely to become competitors. Licensing is more viable in industries in which technological changes are frequent and affect many products. Rapid technological change means that the licensed technology becomes obsolete before the licensing contract expires. Otherwise, in cases where loss of the licensor's technical knowledge or other know-how to a potential competitor is the major concern, it is often best for a firm to avoid licensing as an entry strategy.

Because licensing requires sharing intellectual property with other firms, the risk of creating the future competitor is substantial.[15] The rival may go on to exploit the licensor's intellectual property for entering third countries or creating products that differ somewhat from those prescribed in the licensing contract. Licensees can leverage the licensed know-how to become strong competitors and, eventually, industry leaders. This scenario has played out in the auto, computer chip, and consumer electronics industries in Asia as Western firms have transferred process technologies to firms in China, Japan, and South Korea.

For instance, Japan's Sony originally licensed the technology associated with the transistor from inventor Bell Laboratories in the United States. Bell had advised Sony to use the transistors to make hearing aids. But instead, Sony used the technology to create small, battery-powered transistor radios. Based on this advantage, Sony and other Japanese companies soon became the global leaders in transistor radios. Bell squandered a huge opportunity. Sony subsequently became the first Japanese company listed on the New York Stock Exchange and one of the world's biggest consumer electronics firms.[16]

In another example, the U.S. toymaker Mattel licensed rights to distribute the Barbie doll to the Brazilian toymaker Estrela. Once the agreement expired, Estrela developed its own Barbie look-alike doll—"Susi"—which eclipsed Brazilian sales of Barbie dolls. Estrela then launched the Susi doll in Argentina, Chile, Paraguay, and Uruguay to great success. In Japan, Mattel entered a licensing agreement with local toymaker Takara, which adapted the doll to suit the tastes of Japanese girls. When the agreement expired, Takara continued to sell the doll under a different name, "Jenny," becoming a competitor to Mattel in the world's second biggest toy market.[17]

 Franchising

Franchising is an advanced form of licensing in which the focal firm (the *franchisor*) allows an entrepreneur (the *franchisee*) the right to use an entire business system in exchange for compensation. As with licensing, an explicit contract defines the terms of the relationship. McDonald's, Subway, Hertz, and FedEx are well-established international franchisors. Others that use franchising to expand abroad include Benetton, Body Shop, Yves Rocher, and Marks & Spencer. As these examples suggest, franchising is very common in international retailing. Nevertheless, some retailers, such as IKEA and Starbucks, have a strong preference for expanding abroad through company-owned outlets. In such a case, these companies are opting for greater control over foreign operations forgoing the possibility of more rapid expansion abroad.

Although there are various types of franchising, the most typical arrangement is *business format franchising* (sometimes called *system franchising*).[18] Exhibit 15.4 shows the nature of the franchising agreement. In this arrangement, the franchisor transfers to the franchisee a total business method, including production and marketing methods, sales systems, procedures, and management know-how, as well as the use of its name and usage rights for products, patents, and trademarks.[19] The franchisor also provides the franchisee with training, ongoing support, incentive programs, and the right to participate in cooperative marketing programs. In return, the franchisee pays some type of compensation to the franchisor, usually a royalty representing a percentage of the franchisee's revenues. The franchisee may be required to purchase certain equipment and supplies from the franchisor to ensure standardized products and consistent quality. For instance, Burger King and Subway require franchisees to buy food preparation equipment from specified suppliers. Some franchisors, such as McDonald's, also lease property (especially land) to franchisees.

While licensing relationships are often short-lived, the parties to franchising normally establish an ongoing relationship that may last many years. Accordingly, compared to licensing, franchising is usually a much more stable, long-term entry strategy. In addition, franchisors often combine franchising with other entry strategies. For instance, about 70 percent of the more than 2,000 Body Shop stores worldwide are operated by franchisees, while the rest are owned by Body Shop headquarters. Large retailers such as IKEA and Carrefour often employ both franchising and FDI when expanding abroad.

Franchising is more comprehensive than licensing because the franchisor prescribes virtually all of the business activities of the franchisee. The franchisor tightly controls the business system to ensure consistent standards. International franchisors employ globally recognized trademarks and attempt

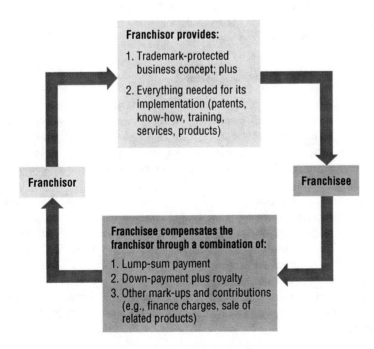

Exhibit 15.4

Franchising as a Foreign Market Entry Strategy

SOURCE: Adapted from Welch (1992) and personal correspondence with Lawrence Welch.

to guarantee the customer a uniform and consistent retail experience and product quality. Completely standardized business activities, however, are difficult to replicate across diverse markets. Differences in areas such as key ingredients, worker qualifications, and physical space may necessitate changes to the franchise formula. For example, space restrictions in Japan forced KFC to reconfigure its cooking equipment from a wide horizontal design, common in the United States, to a narrower, more vertical design that saves space. In addition, Japanese KFCs tend to be multistoried restaurants, in order to save on the high cost of land. The challenge is to strike the right balance, adapting the format to respond to local markets without affecting the overall image and service of the franchise.[20]

McDonald's is perhaps the leading example of business format franchising. Its worldwide franchisee network is remarkably successful. The opening of the first Russian McDonald's outlet in Moscow in January 1990 had political implications as well, coming soon after the collapse of the communist regime in the former Soviet Union. The store seated 700 inside, had 27 cash registers, and was enormously popular. About 80 percent of McDonald's 30,000-plus restaurants worldwide are owned and run by franchisees. These restaurants serve over 50 million customers daily and employ 1.5 million people.

Some focal firms may choose to work with a single, coordinating franchisee in a particular country or region. In this **master franchise** arrangement, an independent company is licensed to establish, develop, and manage the entire franchising network in its market. The master franchisee has the right to subfranchise to other independent businesses and thus assume the role of the local franchisor. McDonald's is organized this way in Japan. From the focal firm's perspective, the arrangement is the least capital- and time-intensive. However, the trade-off is that, by delegating the responsibilities of identifying and working with its franchisees directly, the focal firm gives up considerable control over its foreign market operations.

Franchisees prefer the arrangement because it provides an exclusive, large, predefined territory (often an entire country) and substantial economies of scale from operating numerous sales outlets simultaneously. It gains access to a proven retailing and marketing concept, and partnership with a corporate headquarters and master franchisees in other territories, which typically provide support, know-how, and the latest innovations in the field. Master franchising accounts for as much as 80 percent of international franchising deals. Sbarro, Inc., the Italian pizza chain, operates via master franchises in Belgium, Britain, Canada, Guatemala, Kuwait, and the Philippines.[21]

Master franchise

Arrangement in which an independent company is licensed to establish, develop, and manage the entire franchising network in its market and has the right to subfranchise to other franchisees, thus assuming the role of local franchisor.

Who Are the Top Franchisors?

Franchising is a global phenomenon and accounts for a large proportion of international trade in services. Many product and service categories lend themselves to international franchising. These include fast food outlets, health and fitness, professional business services, and home improvement products and services and various types of retailers.[22] (See Exhibit 3.6 on page 72 for a list of the world's top franchisors).

The United States is home to the largest number of franchisors and dominates international franchising. U.S. franchisors and their franchisees account for roughly $1 trillion in annual U.S. retail sales—an astonishing 40 percent of total U.S. retail sales. Approximately 1 in every 12 retail establishments in the United States is a franchised business.[23] Other countries are also active in franchising. For instance, annual franchised sales of fast foods in England are said to account for 30 percent of all foods eaten outside the home. The internationalization of franchising systems is a major trend that became popular beginning in the 1970s.

International Business

Information and communications technologies have accelerated the pace of international franchising. The ability to exchange information instantaneously through the Internet enhances the franchisor's ability to control international operations. Some franchisees use electronic point-of-sale equipment that links their sales and inventory data to the franchisor's central warehouse and distribution network. Information technology also allows the franchisor to serve customers or franchisees with central accounting and other business process functions.

 ## Advantages and Disadvantages of Franchising

The relationship between the franchisor and franchisee is characterized by complementary functions. While franchisors provide vital assets, franchisees perform functions in foreign markets, such as marketing and distribution, which the franchisor usually cannot perform. The franchisor possesses economies of scale, a wealth of intellectual property, and know-how about its own industry, while the franchisee has entrepreneurial drive and substantial knowledge about the local market and how to run a business there. Franchising combines centralized control over foreign operations and a standardized business approach with the skills of local entrepreneurs who have enough flexibility to deal with local market conditions. In other words, franchising provides an effective blending of skill centralization and operational decentralization.

When economic and cultural conditions in the target market vary greatly from those of the franchisor's home market, the franchisor relies much more on the franchisee's expertise in the market. A large pool of well-chosen franchisees can greatly enhance the speed and quality of the franchisor's performance abroad.[24] For example, KFC internationalized quickly and performed well worldwide by developing franchisees in 90 countries.

The Franchisor Perspective

Exhibit 15.5 highlights the advantages and disadvantages of franchising to the franchisor. Firms prefer franchising when they lack the capital or international experience to get established abroad through FDI, or when offering the product abroad through independent distributors or traditional licensing is ineffective as

Advantages	Disadvantages
• Entry into numerous foreign markets can be accomplished quickly and cost effectively	• Maintaining control over franchisee may be difficult
• No need to invest substantial capital	• Conflicts with franchisee are likely, including legal disputes
• Established brand name encourages early and ongoing sales potential abroad	• Preserving franchisor's image in the foreign market may be challenging
• The firm can leverage franchisees' knowledge to efficiently navigate and develop local markets	• Requires monitoring and evaluating performance of franchisees, and providing ongoing assistance
	• Franchisees may take advantage of acquired knowledge and become competitors in the future

Exhibit 15.5

Advantages and Disadvantages of Franchising to the Franchisor

an internationalization strategy. Foreign markets often provide greater profitability than the home market. For example, the Beijing KFC store has generated more sales than any other KFC outlet worldwide due, in part, to the novelty of the offering, absence of direct competition, and huge pedestrian traffic. Governments in host countries often encourage franchising by foreigner entrants because most of the profits and investment remain in the local economy.

For the franchisor, franchising is a low-risk, low-cost entry strategy. It offers the ability to develop new and distant international markets relatively quickly and on a larger scale than possible for most nonfranchise firms. The franchisor can generate additional profit with only small, incremental investments in capital, personnel, production, and distribution.

However, the major disadvantages to the franchisor include the need to maintain control over potentially thousands of outlets worldwide. When dealing in numerous, complex international markets, the risk of creating competitors is substantial. The franchisor must disclose business secrets and detailed knowledge. When the franchising agreement is terminated, some franchisees leverage their newly acquired knowledge to remain in business, often by slightly altering the franchisor's brand name or trademark. There is also the risk that existing franchisees will jeopardize the franchisor's image by not upholding its standards. For instance, Dunkin' Donuts experienced problems in Russia when it discovered that some franchisees were selling vodka along with donuts.

A major challenge for franchisors is to become familiar with foreign laws and regulations. As an example, the European Union has strict laws that favor the franchisee, which sometimes hamper the franchisor's ability to maintain control over franchisee operations. Laws and foreign exchange circumstances affect the payment of royalties.

Franchising emphasizes standardized products and marketing. But this does not imply 100 percent uniformity. Local franchisees exercise some latitude in tailoring offerings to local needs and tastes. For example, McDonald's offers a McPork sandwich in Spain, a spicy chicken burger in China, teriyaki burgers in Japan, and wine in France. In its Beijing outlets, KFC offers shredded carrots, fungus, and bamboo shoots instead of the coleslaw that it sells in Western countries. Also in China, Starbucks offers a Green Tea Cream Frappuccino, TCBY sells sesame-flavored frozen yogurt, and Mrs. Fields markets mango muffins.[25]

The Franchisee Perspective

Exhibit 15.6 highlights the advantages and disadvantages of franchising to the franchisee. From the perspective of the franchisee, franchising is especially beneficial to the SME. Most small firms lack substantial resources or strong managerial skills. The big advantage of franchising to the franchisee is the ability to launch a business using a tested business model. In essence, franchising amounts to cloning best practices. It greatly increases the small firm's chances for success by duplicating a tried-and-true business format.[26]

 Other Contractual Entry Strategies

In addition to licensing and franchising, there are several other types of contractual agreements in international business. These international agreements involve major construction projects, manufacturing products under contract, providing management and marketing services, or leasing major assets. We devote Chapter 16 to global sourcing, a specific form of international con-

Advantages	Disadvantages
• Gain a well-known, recognizable brand name • Acquire training and know-how; receive ongoing support from the franchisor • Operate an independent business • Increase likelihood of business success • Become part of an established international network	• Initial investment or royalty payments may be substantial • Franchisee are required to purchase supplies, equipment, and products from the franchisor only • The franchisor holds much power, including superior bargaining power • Franchisor's outlets may proliferate in the region, creating competition for the franchisee • Franchisor may impose inappropriate technical or managerial systems on the franchisee

tracting. Here, we discuss the following contracting strategies: turnkey contracting, build-operate-transfer arrangements, management contracts, and leasing.

Turnkey Contracting

Turnkey contracting refers to an arrangement where the focal firm or a consortium of firms plans, finances, organizes, manages, and implements all phases of a project abroad and then hands it over to a foreign customer after training local personnel. Contractors are typically firms in construction, engineering, design, and architectural services. In a typical turnkey project, a major facility (such as a nuclear power plant or a subway system) is built, put into operation, and then handed over to the project sponsor, often a national government. The arrangement involves construction, installation, and training, and may include follow-up contractual services, such as testing and operational support.

Among the most popular turnkey projects are extensions and upgrades to metro systems, such as bridges, roadways, and railways. Turnkey projects are also used to construct airports, harbors, refineries, and hospitals. One of the world's largest publicly funded turnkey projects is in Delhi, India. The estimated $2.3 billion project was commissioned by Delhi Metro Rail Ltd. to build roads and tunnels that run through the city's central business district. The turnkey consortium includes local firms and Skanska AB, one of the world's largest construction firms, based in Sweden.[27]

In recent years, firms in the construction, engineering, architecture, and design industries have become major players in global contract services. These firms include Hochtief AG of Germany and Skanska AB of Sweden. (See Exhibit 3.7 on page 74 for a list of leading firms). They have undertaken some of the world's most important construction projects, such as the Three Gorges Dam in China and the Chunnel linking England to France. California-based Bechtel participated in projects such as the renovation of London's 140-year-old subway, the cleanup of the Chernobyl nuclear plant in Russia, and construction of nuclear power plants in South Korea.[28] In Hong Kong, a consortium of firms, including the French giant Bouygues, signed a $550 million contract to build the main highway running from Hong Kong into mainland China.[29] Bovis Lend Lease of the United Kingdom was responsible for building the Petronas Towers in Kuala Lumpur, Malaysia.

Turnkey contracting
Arrangement where the focal firm or a consortium of firms plans, finances, organizes, manages, and implements all phases of a project abroad and then hands it over to a foreign customer after training local personnel.

Build-Operate-Transfer Arrangements (BOT)

Under a **build-operate-transfer (BOT)** arrangement, a firm contracts to build a major facility abroad, such as a dam or water treatment plant, operates the facility for a specified period, and then transfers its ownership to the project sponsor, typically the host-country government or public utility. This is a variation of turnkey contracting. Instead of turning the completed facility over to the project sponsor, in a BOT deal, the builder operates it for a number of years, sometimes a decade, before transferring ownership to the sponsor.

In a typical deal, a consortium of private multinational financiers, contractors, and advisors joins together to finance, design, construct, and operate the facility. During the time that the consortium operates the facility, it can charge user fees, tolls, and rentals to recover its investment and generate profits. Alternatively, the host-country government may pay the BOT partner for services provided by the facility, such as water from a treatment plant, at a price calculated over the life of the contract, to cover its construction and operating costs and provide a reasonable return.

Governments often grant BOT concessions to get needed infrastructure built cost-effectively. Typical projects include sewage treatment plants, highways, airports, bridges, tunnels, mass transit systems, and telecommunications networks. In Vietnam, for example, rapid growth in industry and tourism has greatly increased demand for electric power. The Vietnamese government commissioned the construction of the 720 megawatt Phu My 3 Power Plant, the country's first privately owned major energy facility. It was built as a BOT project by Siemens Power Generation (Germany) and is owned by a consortium that includes BP (Britain) and Kyushu Electric Power (Japan).[30]

Management Contracts

Under a **management contract**, a contractor supplies managerial know-how to operate a hotel, resort, hospital, airport, or other facility in exchange for compensation. In contrast to licensing or franchising, management contracts involve specialized know-how as well as actual operation of a facility. The contractor provides its unique expertise in running a facility without actually owning it.

In a management contract, the client organization receives assistance in managing local operations while the management company generates revenues without having to make a capital outlay. For instance, much of Disney's income from its theme parks in France and Japan comes from providing management services for the parks, which are largely owned by other interests. In another example, BAA Limited manages the retailing and catering operations of various airports in Europe and the United States. As an entry strategy, the use of management contracts traces back to the 1950s. Both the Marriott and Four Seasons corporations run numerous luxury hotels around the world through management contracts, without owning the hotels that they manage.

Management contracts can help foreign governments with infrastructure projects when the country lacks local people with the skills to run the projects. Occasionally the offering of a management contract is the critical element in winning a bid for other types of entry strategies, such as BOT deals and turnkey operations. A key disadvantage of management contracts is that they involve training foreign firms that may become future competitors.[31]

Leasing

International leasing is another contractual strategy, in which a focal firm (the lessor) rents out machinery or equipment to corporate or government clients abroad (lessees), often for several years at a time. International leasing plays an important role in developing economies that may lack the financial resources to purchase needed equipment. The lessor retains ownership of the property throughout the lease period and receives regular lease payments from the lessee. From the perspective of the lessee, leasing helps reduce the costs of using needed machinery and equipment. A major advantage for the lessor is the ability to gain quick access to target markets, while putting assets to use earning profits. Leasing may be more profitable for the lessor in international business than in domestic markets because of tax regulations.[32]

For example, Amsterdam-based ING Lease International Equipment Management owns and leases Boeing commercial aircraft to clients such as Brazil's Varig airlines. Dubai-based Oasis Leasing leases aircraft to Air New Zealand, Airtours, Gulf Air, Go, Virgin Express, and Macedonian Airlines. One of the leading leasing firms is ORIX. Based in Japan, ORIX leases everything from computers and measuring equipment to aircraft and ships. The firm operates over 1,300 offices worldwide and generated sales of nearly $7 billion in 2006.

One industry sector active in international leasing is composed of firms manufacturing capital goods such as elevators and escalators. Read the *Recent Grad in IB* feature on page 468 feature to learn about an international business career working for a capital goods company. The feature also illustrates that you can acquire valuable experience in international business by working for a foreign-owned company in your native country.

Leasing has become an important, contract-based internationalization strategy. ING Lease International Equipment Management of the Netherlands leases Boeing aircraft to Brazil's Varig airlines, such as this jet landing in Rio de Janeiro.

The Special Case of Internationalization by Professional Service Firms

Professional services include accounting, advertising, market research, consulting, engineering, legal counsel, and IT services. Firms in these industries have rapidly internationalized their activities over the past three decades. They use both direct investment (company-owned foreign branches) as well as independent contractors to gain a foothold in the foreign market. Some professional service firms internationalize by simply following their key clients abroad. The Internet has greatly aided the international spread of some business process services such as software engineering. As a result, their value-adding is increasingly centralized in cost-effective locations such as India and Eastern Europe.

Professional service firms encounter three unique challenges when going international. First, professional qualifications that allow firms to practice law, dentistry, medicine, or accounting in the home country are rarely recognized by other countries. For example, if you are certified as a Certified Public Accountant in the United States and would like to practice accounting in Argentina, you must earn local certification in that country. Second, professionals who work abroad for long periods generally must obtain employment visas in the countries where they are employed. Third, professional services often require intensive interaction with the local public, which necessitates language and cultural skills.[33]

What market entry strategies do professional service firms employ when going international? Typically, a mix of direct investment and contractual strategies are used concurrently. As we noted earlier, explicit contracts can coexist with other entry modes. For example, an advertising agency such as Publicis Groupe, based in France, will maintain a network of company-owned branches around the world while simultaneously entering into contractual relationships with independent

Licensing, Franchising, and Other Contractual Strategies

Jennifer Knippen's interest in international business was confirmed when she participated in a study abroad program in Valencia, Spain as an undergraduate. She returned from Spain with a renewed focus for an international career. She graduated with dual degrees in economics and international business, and immediately headed back to Spain for five months of intensive language training in Spanish. While in Spain, she traveled through various regions to broaden her education.

When Jennifer returned home, she attended a career fair, which led to a sales engineer position with the United States subsidiary of KONE, Inc., a leading manufacturer of elevators and escalators based in Finland. Her experience at KONE was incredibly challenging and uplifting. Jennifer had to learn a technical product in the demanding construction industry.

Her job description as sales engineer encompassed various tasks. She consulted architects in the design stages of a project—cost analysis, equipment specifications, building integration, and code compliance. She then generated a proposal to the general contractor working on the project. If her proposal was accepted, she would then manage the project through completion (usually more than a year). Jennifer managed multiple projects at a time while still meeting annual and quarterly sales budgets.

Managers at KONE praised Jennifer's strong presentations and relationship-building skills. She began working on high-rise projects with some of the top architectural and construction firms. Through preselling, with KONE's global support and resources, Jennifer stimulated substantial demand. Eventually she was awarded "Best in Class" for the highest-volume sales in her region.

Jennifer experienced the benefits and challenges that come with working for a local subsidiary of an international parent company. KONE has been extremely successful in Europe and other parts of the world and has applied a similar approach in the United States. One of the challenges that Jennifer faced was strict U.S. building code regulations. She also had to monitor fluctuations in the euro–dollar exchange rate, as this greatly affects the sales price of imported equipment.

Jennifer's majors: Economics and international business
Jobs held since graduating:
Sales Engineer, KONE, Inc.

What's Ahead?

The elevator business has its ups and downs, and eventually Jennifer decided to return to school to pursue an International MBA. She thought that the experience she had gained, coupled with an advanced degree in international management, would position her well for an exciting international career. Jennifer is excited about what lies ahead.

Success Factors for a Career in International Business

Foreign travel and a study abroad program in college inspired Jennifer to pursue an international career. Learning Spanish enhanced her credentials to secure an international business job. Jennifer set career goals and worked hard to achieve them.

local firms. Focal firms in professional services are likely to serve their major markets with direct investment; that is, they will opt for company-owned representative offices in these markets. In numerous small markets, however, they will enter into contractual relationships with independent partner firms in the same line of business. These independent contractors are sometimes known as *agents, affiliates,* or *representatives.* For example, PriceWaterhouseCooper, a leading international accounting firm, can contract with indigenous accounting firms in smaller markets where it chooses not to have its own offices. Those focal firms with limited international experience are also more likely to rely upon foreign partners.

Read the *Global Trend* feature to learn how a management consulting firm internationalizes.

 ## Management of Licensing and Franchising

Licensing and franchising are complex undertakings and they require skillful research, planning, and execution. The focal firm must conduct advance research on the host country's laws on intellectual property rights, repatriation of royalties, and contracting with local partners. Key challenges of the focal firm include: establishing whose national law takes precedence for interpreting and enforcing the contract, deciding whether to grant an exclusive or nonexclusive arrangement, and determining the geographic scope of territory to be granted to the foreign partner.

> GLOBAL TREND

Internationalization of Management Consulting Firms

The internationalization of U.S. management consulting firms began in the 1950s during the economic growth period following World War II. These firms were often attracted abroad by their clients. For example, IBM World Trade hired McKinsey to undertake a major reorganization study, and McKinsey launched its first international office in London in 1959. Expanding into South America and continental Europe in the 1960s, McKinsey established offices in the Netherlands, Germany, Italy, France, and Switzerland, as well as Canada and Australia. In smaller markets, the firm entered into contractual relationships with local consulting firms. Management consulting firms from the United States played a major role in the development of local management thinking and business approaches in foreign markets. For example, Unilever, an Anglo-Dutch consumer products company and one of Europe's largest firms, hired McKinsey to review its corporate structure. McKinsey recommended Unliver change from geographic divisions to product divisions.[34]

McKinsey was not the only consulting firm to internationalize. Arthur D. Little opened its first European office in Zürich in 1957. Booz Allen Hamilton broadened its reach to Europe, the Philippines, and elsewhere during the 1960s and 1970s. The Boston Consulting Group (BCG)—which developed the *growth share matrix* to assist its clients categorize their products into stars, cash cows, question marks, and dogs—had also internationalized relatively early, opening its first international office in Tokyo. Bain & Co. began its operations in London and Tokyo.

Management consulting firms faced various challenges in international expansion. Because management consulting is a knowledge-intensive business and the critical resource—experienced consultants—is scarce, opening multiple offices around the world proved difficult. In addition to opening new offices abroad, these firms pursued two other internationalization strategies. First, some consulting firms acquired local consulting firms as a means of quickly getting established in the target market. A. T. Kearney first entered Britain by acquiring a local consulting firm,

Norcross and Partners. Second, some consulting firms chose to contract with local consultancies, commissioning projects for them to fulfill. This approach—developing a contractual relationship with indigenous consulting firms—proved to be a practical strategy to serve smaller markets that did not warrant a company-owned office. Through such a contractual relationship, foreign firms transferred their standard operating procedures and best practices to local partners to ensure high-quality project fulfillment.

Today, management consulting firms are spread around the world through an international network of company-owned offices, affiliates, and contractual partners. For instance, McKinsey has more than 80 offices in 44 countries. It provides a full range of consulting services to corporations, government agencies, and foundations, including leadership training, operations analysis, and strategic planning.

SOURCES: Hoovers corporate profile of McKinsey at http://www.hoovers.com, Jones, Geoffrey and Alexis Lefort (2006), "McKinsey and the Globalization of Consultancy," Case Study 9-806-035, Boston: Harvard Business School Press; McKinsey corporate website at www.mckinsey.com

With contractual entry strategies, success also requires patience and the ability to remain in the market despite setbacks. As an example, Pizza Hut's initial entry in China failed. One early partner was the Chinese government, which lacked entrepreneurial drive and business expertise. Low-quality food and poor service initially undermined Pizza Hut's image in China. To address the problem, Pizza Hut repurchased all the licenses it had granted to local franchisees. It then revised its entry strategy by developing corporate-owned restaurants until the franchising market matured. This approach is also useful when the franchisor is not well known in the market. In this case, the franchisor invests time and money to develop its reputation and brand name before contracting with local franchisees.

Careful Selection of Qualified Partners

As with other entry strategies, the most critical success factor in contracting is often finding the right partner abroad. The focal firm should carefully identify, screen, and train potential contractors who are unlikely to become competitors in the future.

Selecting a strong partner is especially important in international franchising because it speeds up market entry and helps minimize start-up costs. The most qualified franchisees tend to have entrepreneurial drive, access to capital and prime real estate, a successful business track record, good relationships with local and national government agencies, strong links to other firms (including facilitators), a pool of motivated employees, and a willingness to accept oversight and to follow company procedures. In emerging markets, a knowledgeable, locally connected partner can help sort through various operational problems. In China and Russia, partnering with a state-owned enterprise may be necessary to gain access to key resources and navigate complex legal and political environments.

Choosing the right partner for master franchisees is critical. Master franchising contracts are of long duration (usually 10 to 20 years), resulting in ongoing problems if the master franchisor performs poorly. To ensure success, franchisors often partner with established firms abroad. For example, in Japan, KFC's franchise partner is Mitsubishi and Burger King's partner is Japan Tobacco.

For franchisors, developing capable partners in local supply chains is also a prerequisite. Franchisees need a reliable supply chain in order to obtain input products and supplies. In developing economies and emerging markets, host-country suppliers may be inadequate for providing a sufficient quantity or quality of input goods. In Turkey, Little Caesars pizza franchisees found it difficult to locate dairy companies that could produce the cheese varieties required for pizza. In other countries, KFC developed its own supply-chain network, ensuring dependable delivery of chicken and other critical inputs. In Russia and Thailand, McDonald's had to develop its own supply lines for potatoes in order to ensure the quality of its french fries. When McDonald's first entered India, management faced resistance from the government. Eventually government authorities came to understand that McDonald's would work with Indian farmers to improve the country's agricultural practices and production. Relations improved as the government recognized that McDonald's was committed to being a good corporate citizen.

Managerial Guidelines for Protecting Intellectual Property

As we noted earlier in the chapter, working with independent partners through contractual arrangements provides the focal firm with only moderate control over foreign partners. Therefore, safeguarding intellectual property and foreign operations becomes a challenge. Laws that govern contractual relations are not always clear, conflicts arise due to cultural and language differences, and contract enforcement abroad is often costly or unattainable. Thus, in addition to devising a detailed contract, the focal firm should emphasize developing a close, trusting relationship with foreign partners. Management in the focal firm can enhance the relationship by providing the foreign partner with superior resources and strong support. A satisfied partner is more likely to comply with contractual provisions and produce successful outcomes.

Infringement of intellectual property is the unauthorized use, publication, or reproduction of products and services that are protected by a patent, copyright, trademark, or other intellectual property right. Such a violation amounts to *piracy.* Infringement of intellectual assets often results in the production and distribution of *counterfeit,* or fake, products or services that imitate the original produced by the asset's owner. See Exhibit 6.10 on page 185 for a listing of losses from piracy in selected countries. For example, annual piracy losses are $177 million in Brazil in records and music, and $1,433 million in Russia in business software in a recent year.

The total value of counterfeit and pirated goods crossing borders and traded online worldwide is approximately $600 billion annually, a figure equivalent to about five percent of the United States GDP.[35] Counterfeiters create knockoffs of products that include clothing, fashion accessories, watches, medicines, and appliances. Some counterfeiters use a product name that differs only slightly from a well-known brand, but is close enough that buyers associate it with the genuine product. They alter the name or design of a product just enough so that prosecution is hampered. While firms such as Rolex and Tommy Hilfiger are well-known victims, counterfeiting is common in such industrial products as medical devices and car parts (e.g., brake pads, fan belts, and batteries). In China, counterfeiters have even produced entire fake motor vehicles.[36]

Cisco Systems sued its Chinese joint venture partner, Huawei Technologies Co., for pirating its networking software and infringing several patents. The lawsuit also cited Huawei, the largest telecommunications equipment manufacturer in China, for illegally using technical documentation that Cisco copyrighted in its own product manuals.[37] In China, fake versions of computer software are widely available for only a few dollars, while the cost of legitimate products can exceed a typical worker's monthly salary. Although Microsoft's Windows and Office products dominate the software market, the firm never gets paid when its software is copied and distributed by unauthorized parties. In Russia, up to 90 percent of computer software may be pirated. As a result, Microsoft has decided to focus on corporate customers only. The firm battles piracy even among the employees in its Russian subsidiary.[38]

The Internet has added a new dimension to international counterfeiting. In Russia, web sites sell popular music downloads for as little as 5 cents each, or less than one dollar for an entire CD. The illegal sites use low prices to attract music fans worldwide. The sites are easily accessed by shoppers in countries where they are outlawed under IPR laws.[39]

Counterfeiting and piracy are particularly troublesome in emerging markets and developing economies where intellectual property right laws are weak or poorly enforced. When piracy occurs, the firm's competitive advantage and brand equity are eroded.[40] Small and medium-sized enterprises are particularly vulnerable as they typically lack the resources to litigate intellectual property rights violators.

Infringement of intellectual property Unauthorized use, publication, or reproduction of products or services that are protected by a patent, copyright, trademark, or other intellectual property right.

In advanced economies, intellectual property is usually protected within established legal systems and methods of recourse. A firm can initiate legal action against someone who infringes its intellectual assets and will usually achieve a satisfactory remedy. In recent years, advanced economies have taken the lead in signing treaties that support the international protection of IPRs. Key international treaties include The Paris Convention for the Protection of Industrial Property, The Berne Convention for the Protection of Literary and Artistic Works, and The Rome Convention for the Protection of Performers and Broadcasting Organizations. The World Intellectual Property Organization (WIPO; www.wipo.int)—an agency of the United Nations—administers these multilateral agreements.

Recently, the World Trade Organization (WTO) created the Agreement on Trade Related Aspects of Intellectual Property Rights (TRIPS), a comprehensive international treaty that lays out remedies, dispute-resolution procedures, and enforcements to protect intellectual property. The WTO is pressuring member countries to comply with the accord, and can discipline violators through the dispute settlement mechanism. At the same time, TRIPS provides exceptions that benefit developing economies, such as the ability to access needed patent medication for ailments such as AIDS, which is widespread in Africa.

Firms that are working in countries that are not signatories to WIPO, TRIPS, or other treaties still face challenges. Rights granted by a patent, trademark registration, or copyright apply only in the country where they are obtained; they confer no protection abroad. Moreover, on top of rewarding and promoting innovation, foreign governments often have additional priorities, such as gaining access to new technologies. In each country, intellectual property protection varies as a function of local laws, administrative practices, and treaty obligations. IPR enforcement depends on the attitudes of local officials, substantive requirements of the law, and court procedures. As a result, former licensees and franchisees can launch illicit businesses using proprietary knowledge that they are no longer entitled to.

A focal firm should have a proactive and comprehensive set of strategies to reduce the likelihood of IPR violations and help avoid their adverse effects, especially in countries with weak property rights. Exhibit 15.7 illustrates such a set of strategies:[41]

- Understand local intellectual property laws and enforcement procedures, especially when exposed assets are very valuable. For each target country, determine how easily licensed assets can be replicated. Avoid countries with weak intellectual property laws.

- Register patents, trademarks, trade secrets, and copyrights with the government in each country where the firm does, or intends to do, business. Also register in countries known to be sources of counterfeit products.

- Ensure that licensing and franchising agreements provide for oversight to ensure intellectual property is used as intended.

- Include a provision in licensing contracts that requires the licensee to share any improvements or technological developments on the licensed asset with the licensor. In this way, the licensee never acquires any advantages that allow it to surpass the licensor.[42]

- Pursue criminal prosecution or litigation against those who infringe on protected assets, such as logos and proprietary processes. For example, Mead Data Central, Inc., owner of the Lexis-Nexis brand of computerized legal research services, sued Toyota when the Japanese firm began selling its new luxury automobiles under the name "Lexus." The suit failed, but shows how Mead is resolute in protecting its assets.[43]

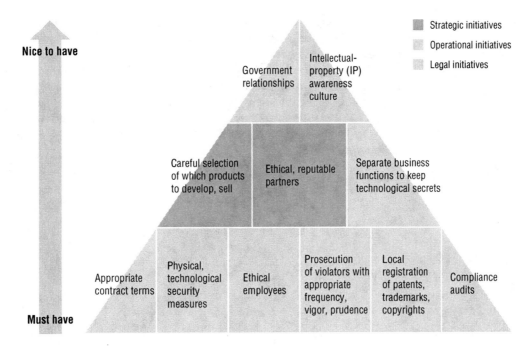

Exhibit 15.7 The Pyramid of Intellectual Property Protection

SOURCE: Meagan Dietz, Sarena Shao-Tin Lin, and Lei Yang. (2005). "Protecting Intellectual Property in China," *The McKinsey Quarterly*, number 3.

* Monitor franchisee, distribution, and marketing channels for any asset infringements. Monitor the activities of local business partners for potential leaks of vital information and assets.[44]
* Include in franchise contracts a requirement that the franchisee, suppliers, and distributors report infringements of products or processes, if discovered.
* Guard trade secrets closely. Use password-based security systems, surveillance, and firewalls to limit access to intellectual property. Intel and Microsoft release only limited information about key technologies to partner firms, especially in locations such as China, where intellectual property violations are rife.
* Train employees to use registered assets correctly and to preserve desired protection levels. In emerging markets, some firms emphasize hiring managers with international work and educational experience, as this tends to foster a healthy respect for intellectual property.
* Include noncompete clauses in employee contracts for all positions to prevent employees from serving competitors for up to three years after leaving the firm.[45]
* Use contemporary technology to minimize counterfeiting. For example, many firms include biotech tags, electronic signatures, or holograms with their products, to differentiate them from fakes.
* Continuously update technologies and products. The firm that regularly renews its technology can stay ahead of counterfeiters by offering products that counterfeiters cannot imitate fast enough. Differentiate products by emphasizing a strong brand name. When available, customers usually prefer established brands that feature the latest technology.

In the long run, the best way to cope with the consequences of infringement is to sustain competitiveness through innovation and constant technological advances. Then, even when licensing violations occur the firm is protected, as the stolen intellectual property rapidly becomes obsolete. Firms also lobby national governments and international organizations for stronger intellectual property laws and more vigilant enforcement, with limited success. Ultimately, when contractual strategies prove undesirable or ineffective, focal firms may step up to the higher-control entry strategy of acquiring ownership, which accompanies FDI.

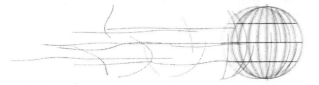

Subway and the Challenges of Franchising in China

Subway, the fast-food marketer of submarine sandwiches and salads, has roughly 28,300 shops in 86 countries and generates over $10 billion in annual revenues. The franchising chain opened its first international restaurant in Bahrain in 1984. Since then, Subway has expanded worldwide, and generates about one fifth of its annual revenues abroad. The firm expects foreign markets to contribute to much of its future growth.

In China, Subway is the third-largest U.S. fast food chain, after McDonald's and KFC. Fish and tuna salad sandwiches are the top sellers. Despite China's huge potential, however, by 2005 Subway had opened only 19 stores there. The franchise had its share of initial setbacks. Subway's master franchisor in Beijing, Jim Bryant, lost money to a scheming partner and had to teach the franchising concept to a country that had never heard of it. Until recently, there was no word in Chinese for "franchise."

According to his agreement with Subway's corporate office, Bryant is authorized to recruit local entrepreneurs, train them to become franchisees, and act as a liaison between them and Subway headquarters. For this work, he receives half of their $10,000 initial fee and one third of their 8 percent royalty fees. This kind of arrangement made a billionaire out of McDonald's master franchisor in Japan. Nevertheless, multinational franchisors face significant challenges, particularly in dealing with China's ambiguous legal environment, finding appropriate partners, and identifying the most suitable marketing, financing, and logistics strategies. Famous brands like A&W, Dunkin' Donuts, and Rainforest Cafe all stumbled in their initial forays into China.

Cultural problems are an ongoing challenge. After Bryant opened his first Subway shop, customers stood outside and watched for a few days. When they finally tried to buy a sandwich, they were so confused that Bryant had to print signs explaining how to order. They didn't believe the tuna salad was made from fish because they could not see the head or tail. They did not like the idea of touching their food, so they would gradually peel off the paper wrapping and eat the sandwich like a banana. To make matters worse, few customers liked sandwiches.

But Subway—or Sai Bei Wei (Mandarin for "tastes better than others")—is forging ahead. Bryant managed to recruit a few highly committed franchisees that he monitors closely to maintain quality. One franchisee lost about $6,000 in her first 8 months but is now profitable and recently bought a second outlet. In addition to the stores in Beijing, numerous more are under construction.

Why China for Franchising?

On the surface, franchising in China is very attractive because of its huge market, long-term growth potential, and the dramatic rise in disposable income among its rapidly expanding urban population. The market for fast food is estimated at $15 billion per year. China's urban population, the target market for casual dining, has expanded at a 5 percent compound annual growth rate over the past several years, a trend expected to continue. Increasingly hectic lifestyles also have led to an increase in meals the Chinese eat outside the home. Furthermore, surveys reveal that Chinese consumers are interested in sampling non-Chinese foods.

Market researchers have identified several major benefits to franchising in China:

- *A win-win proposition.* Restaurants were one of the first industries the government opened to private ownership in the early 1980s. Franchising in China combines the Western know-how of franchisors with the local market knowledge of franchisees. Many Chinese have strong entrepreneurial instincts and are eager to launch their own businesses.

- *Minimal entry costs.* Because much of the cost of launching a restaurant is borne by local entrepreneurs, franchising minimizes the costs to franchisors of entering the market.

- *Rapid expansion.* By leveraging the resources of numerous local entrepreneurs, the franchisor can get set up quickly. Franchising is superior to other entry strategies for rapidly establishing many outlets throughout any new market.

- *Brand consistency.* Because franchisors are required to strictly adhere to company operating procedures and policies, brand consistency is easier to maintain.

- *Circumvention of legal constraints.* Franchising allows the focal firm to avoid trade barriers associated with exporting and FDI, common barriers in China.

Challenges of Franchising in China

China's market also poses many challenges for franchisors:

- *Knowledge Gap.* Despite the likely pool of potential franchisees, realistically, few Chinese have significant knowledge about how to start and operate a business. There is still much confusion about franchising among lawmakers, entrepreneurs, and consumers. Focal firms must educate government officials, potential franchisees, and creditors on the basics of franchising, a process that consumes energy, time, and money.

- *Ambiguous Legal Environment.* Franchisors need to closely examine China's legal system regarding contracts and intellectual property rights. The Chinese government introduced regulations permitting franchising in 1997. The legal system is evolving and is full of loopholes and ambiguities. Some critical elements are not covered. The situation has led to diverse interpretations of the legality of franchising in China. Franchisors must be vigilant about protecting trademarks. A local imitator can quickly dilute or damage a trademark a focal firm has built up through much expense and effort. Branding is important to franchising success, but consumers become confused if several similar brands are present. For instance, Starbucks fought a Shanghai coffee shop, which had copied its logo and name. The fast-food hamburger chain "Merry Holiday" uses a yellow color scheme and emphasizes the letter "M" in its signage, similar to McDonald's. There have been reports about fake Burger King restaurants operating in China. Large franchisors such as KFC and Pizza Hut are struggling to root out counterfeiters.
- *Escalating Start-Up Costs.* Ordinarily, entry through franchising is cost-effective. However, various challenges, combined with linguistic and cultural barriers, can increase the up-front investment and resource demands of new entrants in China and delay profitability. Given the shortage of restaurant equipment in China, the franchisor may have to invest in store equipment and lease it to the franchisee, at least until the franchisee can afford to buy it. Franchisors must be patient. For instance, McDonald's has been in China since the early 1990s and has devoted substantial resources to building its brand. But few firms have the resources of McDonald's.

Perhaps the biggest challenge of launching franchises in China is finding the right partners. It is paradoxical that entrepreneurs with the capital to start a restaurant often lack the business experience or entrepreneurial drive, while entrepreneurs with sufficient drive and expertise often lack the start-up capital. Subway's franchise fee of $10,000 is equivalent to more than two year's salary of the average Chinese. China lacks an adequate system of banks and other capital sources for small business. Entrepreneurs often borrow funds from family members and friends to launch business ventures. Fortunately, Chinese banks are increasingly open to franchising. For example, the Bank of China established a comprehensive credit line of $12 million for Kodak franchisees.

Availability and financing of suitable real estate are major considerations as well, particularly for initial show-case stores where location is critical. According to real estate laws enacted in 1990, local and foreign investors are allowed to develop, use, and administer real estate. But in many cases, the Chinese government owns real estate that is not available for individuals to purchase. Private property laws are underdeveloped and franchisees occasionally risk eviction. Fortunately, a growing number of malls and shopping centers are good locations for franchised restaurants.

The Chinese authorities maintain restrictions on the repatriation of profits to the home country. Strict rules discourage repatriation of the initial investment, making this capital rather illiquid. To avoid this problem, firms make initial capital investments in stages to minimize the risk of not being able to withdraw overinvested funds. Fortunately, China is gradually relaxing its restrictions on repatriated profits. To alleviate the burden of these restrictions, franchisors have been reinvesting their profits back into China to continue to fund the growth of their operations. Reinvesting profits also provides a natural hedge against exchange rate fluctuations.

Learning from the Success of Others

Experience has shown that new entrants to China often benefit from establishing a presence in Hong Kong and then moving inland toward the southern provinces. Before it was absorbed by mainland China, Hong Kong was one of the world's leading capitalist economies. It is an excellent probusiness location to gain experience for doing business in China. In other cases, franchisors have launched stores in smaller Chinese cities, gaining experience there before expanding into more costly competitive urban environments such as Beijing and Shanghai.

Adapting offerings to local tastes appears to be a prerequisite. Suppliers and business infrastructure in the country are often lacking. Franchisors spend much money to develop supplier and distribution networks. They may also need to build logistical infrastructure to move inputs from suppliers to individual stores. McDonald's has replicated its supply chain, bringing its key suppliers, such as potato supplier Simplot, to China. There is no one best approach in China. For instance, TGI Friday's imports roughly three-quarters of its food supplies, which helps maintain quality. But heavy importing is expensive and exposes profitability to exchange rate fluctuations.

AACSB: Reflective Thinking, Multicultural and Diversity

Case Questions

1. Subway brings to China various intellectual property in the form of trademarks, patents, and an

entire business system. What are the specific threats to Subway's intellectual property in China? What can Subway do to protect its intellectual property in China?

2. What do you think about Subway's method and level of compensating its master franchisee and regular franchisees in China? Is the method satisfactory? Is there room for improvement?

3. What are the advantages and disadvantages of franchising in China from Jim Bryant's perspective? What can Bryant do to overcome the disadvan-

tages? From Subway's perspective, is franchising the best entry strategy for China?

4. Subway faces various cultural challenges in China. What are these challenges and what can Subway and its master franchisee do to overcome them?

Source: Adler, Carlye. (2005). "How China Eats a Sandwich," *Fortune*, March 21, pp. F210[B]–[D]; Alon, Ilan. (2001). "Interview: International Franchising in China with Kodak," *Thunderbird International Business Review*, 43(6), pp. 737–46; Bugg, James. (1994). "China: Franchising's New Frontier," *Franchising World*, 26(6) pp. 8–10; Burke, Bob, and Carol Wingard. (1997), "The Big Chill." *China Business Review*, 24(4), pp. 12–18; Clifford, Mark. (1998). "Companies: And They're Off," *Far Eastern Economic Review*, 156(48), pp. 76–79; Dayal-Gulati, A., and Angela Lee. (2004). *Kellogg on China: Strategies for Success.* Evanston, IL: Northwestern University Press; Subway corporate Web site at www.subway.com.

CHAPTER ESSENTIALS

Key Terms

build-operate-transfer (BOT)
contractual entry strategies in international business
franchising
infringement of intellectual property

intellectual property
intellectual property rights (IPRs)
know-how agreement
licensing
management contract

master franchise
royalty
turnkey contracting

Summary

In this chapter, you learned about:

1. The nature of contractual entry strategies in international business

Contractual entry strategies in international business refer to granting permission to use intellectual property to a foreign partner in exchange for a continuous stream of payments. **Intellectual property rights** refer to the legal claim through which the proprietary assets of firms and individuals are protected from unauthorized use by other parties. Firms run the risk of disclosing their intellectual property to outside parties. **Licensing** is an arrangement in which the owner of intellectual property grants a firm the right to use that property for a specified period of time in exchange for royalties or other compensation. **Franchising** is an arrangement in which the firm allows another the right to use an entire business system in exchange for fees, royalties, or other forms of compensation. A **royalty** is a fee paid to the licensor at regular intervals to compensate for the temporary use of intellectual property. Under a

know-how agreement, the focal firm provides technological or managerial knowledge about how to design, manufacture, or deliver a product or service.

2. Licensing

The agreement between the licensor and the licensee is for a specific time period, in a specific country or region. The licensor may enter an *exclusive agreement* with the licensee to minimize competition with other licensees in the same territory. Once the relationship is established and the licensee fully understands its role, the licensor has little additional input. Licensing is widely used in the fashion and toy industries.

3. Advantages and disadvantages of licensing

The main advantage of licensing to the licensor is that it does not require substantial capital investment or physical presence in the foreign market. Licensing allows the firm to gain market presence without making an equity investment. The licensor can avoid political risk, government regulations, and other risks associated with *FDI*. Licensing enables firms to enter markets that have high trade barriers or to test market viability. But licensing generates lower profits and limits the firm's ability to control its intellectual property. There is a risk that the licensee will become a competitor once the licensing agreement expires.

4. Franchising

Franchisors employ widely identifiable trademarks and attempt to guarantee the customer a consistent retail experience and product quality. A **master franchise** is an arrangement whereby a franchisee obtains the rights to, and is responsible for, developing franchised outlets to serve a country or a region. Franchising is common in international retailing, but is difficult to replicate across diverse markets.

5. Advantages and disadvantages of franchising

Franchising allows franchisees to gain access to well-known, well-established brand names and business systems, allowing them to launch successful businesses with minimal risk. The franchisor can rapidly internationalize by leveraging the drive and knowledge of local franchisees. But as with licensing, franchisors risk dissipating their intellectual property to unauthorized parties.

6. Other contractual entry strategies

Under **build–operate–transfer (BOT)** arrangements, the firm contracts to build a major facility, such as a power plant, which it operates for a period of years and then transfers to the host-country government or other public entity. **Turnkey contracting** involves one or several firms planning, financing, organizing, and managing all phases of a project which, once completed, they then hand over to a host-country customer. **Management contracts** occur when a company contracts with another to supply management know-how in the operation of a factory or service facility, such as a hotel. With *leasing*, the firm rents machinery or equipment, usually for a long period, to clients located abroad.

7. Management of licensing and franchising

Infringement of intellectual property rights takes place through counterfeiting and piracy, which cost companies billions of dollars per year. Managers must proactively safeguard their proprietary assets by registering patents, trademarks, and other assets in each country and minimize operating in major counterfeiting countries and countries with weak intellectual property laws. Firms must also train employees and licensees in the proper legal use of intellectual property and vigilantly track down and prosecute intellectual property violators. Licensors and franchisors should carefully investigate individuals or firms seeking a contractual relationship. The best franchisee candidates are trustworthy and willing to follow company procedures. They also have a successful business record and vigorous entrepreneurial spirit.

Test Your Comprehension AACSB: Reflective Thinking

1. Distinguish between the major types of intellectual property: trademarks, copyrights, patents, industrial designs, and trade secrets.

2. What are the major characteristics of licensing? What are the major characteristics of franchising?

3. What are the advantages and disadvantages of licensing?

4. What are the advantages and disadvantages of franchising from the perspective of franchisors and franchisees?

5. What industry sectors are more likely to rely on franchising to tap foreign markets?

6. Define and distinguish the following contractual entry strategies: build-operate-transfer, turnkey projects, management contracts, and leasing.

7. What are best practices in managing international contractual relationships?

8. Suppose you work for a firm that holds valuable intellectual property and is contemplating various international business projects. What strategies would you recommend to management for protecting the firm's intellectual property?

Apply Your Understanding AACSB: Communication, Reflective Thinking

1. The licensing of intellectual property is now a global business. As revealed in the opening vignette, Warner Bros. is doing a thriving business by licensing images of Harry Potter characters on its manufactured products, such as software, games, and clothing. However, safeguarding intellectual property is a big challenge in many countries. Illicit operators worldwide produce their own books, shirts, games, and other products that feature the Potter images—without entering a licensing agreement with Warner. What steps can Warner take to address this problem? That is, what types of strategies can Warner use to protect Harry Potter from intellectual property infringement around the world?

2. In addition to licensing and franchising, there are various other contractual entry strategies. Suppose upon graduation you get a job with Hitachi America, Ltd. (www.hitachi.us)—the U.S. subsidiary of the giant Japanese firm. Hitachi is involved in various contractual entry strategies in its international operations. These include build-operate-transfer and turnkey projects in the infrastructure development sector, management contracts to run nuclear power plants, and leasing of heavy earthmoving equipment to foreign governments. Suppose that Hitachi America wants to extend its reach into Latin America. Prepare a report for your senior managers in which you explain the various ways for Hitachi to implement these entry strategies.

3. Suppose you own a "flying doctor" business in Australia in which you employ physicians to travel by air to ranches and rural communities in Australia's Outback to care for the sick and wounded. Your business has thrived and you've been able to add numerous employees. You've decided that, given your success, you can extend your service to rural areas in the Asia-Pacific region beyond Australia. There are numerous nations in Southeast Asia and the South Pacific characterized by populations concentrated in remote areas, many of which are underserved by medical care. There are various ways to internationalize professional services, including *licensing, franchising,* and FDI. For the professional services sector, differentiate between these three entry strategies: (a) what are the advantages and disadvantages of each? (b) What are the main differences between franchising and FDI?

AACSB: Reflective Thinking

Refer to Chapter 1, page 27, for instructions on how to access and use globalEDGE™.

1. You have just started working in the office of the International Intellectual Property Alliance (IIPA; www.iipa.com). You learn that worldwide piracy of products is rampant. Your boss assigns you the task of drafting a brief policy memo in which you address the following questions:

   - What is the worldwide scope of piracy? What industries are most affected by piracy, and what is the financial loss from piracy in each of these industries?
   - What are the top five countries that are the greatest sources of piracy?
   - What strategies do you recommend for combating piracy?

   In addition to globalEDGE™ and the IIPA portal, other useful sites for this exercise are the Office of the United States Trade Representative (www.ustr.gov), United Nations (www.un.org), and the Business Software Alliance (www.bsa.org).

2. Suppose you are an international entrepreneur and want to open your own franchise somewhere in Europe. You decide to conduct research to identify the most appropriate franchise and to learn how to become a franchisee. Entrepreneur.com publishes an annual list of the top 200 franchisors seeking international franchisees. Visit www.entrepreneur.com for the list or search for "franchising" at globalEDGE™. Choose the franchise that interests you most (for example, Subway, ServiceMaster, Century 21), and visit its corporate Web site. Based on information from the Web site, as well as globalEDGE™ and Hoovers.com, address the following questions:

   - How many franchised operations does this firm have outside its home country?
   - What are the major countries in which the firm has franchises? Are there any patterns in terms of the countries where this firm is established?
   - According to the application information provided at the corporate site, what qualifications is the firm seeking in new franchisees?
   - What types of training and support does the firm provide for its franchisees?

3. The International Licensing Industry Merchandisers' Association (LIMA; www.licensing.org) is an organization with offices worldwide. It fosters the growth and expansion of licensing by helping members network, educating members about licensing, and establishing standards of ethical and professional conduct in intellectual property licensing. Suppose you work for a small animation company that has developed several popular cartoon characters that have licensing potential, in the same way that Disney licenses its cartoon characters. Management would like to learn more about becoming a licensor of its cartoon characters. To begin licensing the characters to interested garment makers, school supply manufacturers, and similar firms, visit the LIMA Web site and write a memo that addresses the following:

   - Who are the major members of LIMA?
   - What are the major trade shows that your firm can attend to exhibit its licensable products and learn more about licensing?
   - What types of seminars and training are available to learn more about becoming a licensor?
   - Based on the information provided at the site, what can you learn about anticounterfeiting activities and challenges in licensing?

CKR
Cavusgil Knight Riesenberger

Management Skill Builder©

Choosing the Best Entry Strategy

As firms pursue internationalization, managers must select the most suitable entry strategy from among exporting, FDI, licensing, franchising, and the other strategies described in this and previous chapters. Managers should carefully consider all the costs and benefits—especially the possible expenses and revenues—involved with each potential entry strategy. The ultimate objective of internationalization is usually to maximize profits and market share. Failure to choose the best entry strategy can lead to suboptimal performance.

AACSB: Reflective Thinking, Analytical Skills

Managerial Challenge

This C/K/R Management Skill Builder© examines the case of Gliders, a firm that makes tennis shoes with an embedded wheel that allows the wearer to skate. Gliders is facing growing competition from low-cost producers in countries such as China. In order to confront this threat and increase sales, Gliders management wants to begin selling the tennis shoes abroad and has targeted Germany as its initial market. Because Gliders is a small firm with limited human and financial resources, management must choose the best strategy to enter Germany in order to maximize company performance.

Background

Gliders's target market is primarily children. Kids love to wear Gliders to dance, play street hockey, and just glide around town. Preteens love them as alternative transportation. The firm has an established brand name and is constantly retooling and churning out upgraded wheel varieties, fashions, and comfort features. It also offers various accessories, such as helmets and kneepads, that feature the Gliders logo. The firm owns other intellectual property, such as designs, trademarks, and patents. Branding is extremely important, and management wants to maintain the shoes' image as quality and cool.

Managerial Skills You Will Gain

In this C/K/R Management Skill Builder©, as a prospective manager, you will:

1. Understand the various types of foreign market entry strategies, including the costs and benefits associated with each.

2. Learn how to improve a company's prospects for increasing sales and profits in foreign markets.

3. Appreciate an important component of international business planning and strategy.

Your Task

Assume you are a recently hired, first-line manager at Gliders. Top management wants to begin selling Gliders in Germany and has given you the task of conducting an analysis to determine the most appropriate entry strategy, choosing among exporting, licensing, FDI, and joint venture.

Go to the C/K/R Knowledge Portal©

www.prenhall.com/cavusgil

Proceed to the C/K/R Knowledge Portal© to obtain the expanded background information, your task and methodology, suggested resources for this exercise, and the presentation template.

Learning Objectives

In this chapter, you will learn about:

1. An overview of global market opportunity assessment

2. Analysis of organizational readiness to internationalize

3. Assessment of the suitability of products and services for foreign markets

4. Screening countries to identify target markets

5. Assessment of industry market potential

6. Selection of foreign business partners

7. Estimating of company sales potential

> ## Estimating Market Demand in Emerging Markets and Developing Countries

Estimating the demand for products or services in emerging markets and developing economies is a challenging task for managers. These countries have unique commercial environments and may lack reliable data, market research firms, and trained interviewers. Consumers may consider research activities an invasion of privacy, and some survey respondents may try to please researchers by telling them what they want to hear, rather than providing fully honest and accurate information.

Just three emerging markets—China, India, and Brazil—have a combined GDP of more than $15 trillion, significantly more than the United States. Africa is among the biggest worldwide markets for mobile phone sales, growing to over 100 million users in just a few years. While most Africans can't afford a cell phone, the trend illustrates an often-overlooked point: developing economies are huge markets for products and services. For instance, Unilever and Procter & Gamble are among the companies that market shampoo and other necessities in India. Narayana Hrudayalaya is an Indian firm that sells health insurance to countless customers for pennies per month.

Estimating market demand in such countries requires managers to be flexible and creative. Let's consider the case of two firms trying to estimate the demand for wallpaper and adhesive bandages (band-aids) in Morocco.

In Morocco, the wealthier people live in villas or condominiums, which are potential target markets for sales of wallpaper. Import statistics are often not very helpful, because the government usually records wallpaper imports by weight and value. Companies sell wallpaper by the roll, and different qualities and designs will have different weights. Such information is of little use in estimating the number of modern households that will buy wallpaper.

One wallpaper company used three approaches to estimate demand for wallpaper. First, managers used a recent study that reported the number of water heaters purchased in Morocco. Managers assumed that if households purchased this important, "modern" convenience, they also would likely want to purchase wallpaper. Second, managers accessed government statistics that disclosed the level of domestic wallpaper sales, discretionary income by type of household, and home construction data. Third, managers surveyed the lifestyle of a sample of local consumers. Their findings revealed that Moroccans usually shop for wallpaper as a complementary decoration to fitted carpets. Among married couples, it is generally the wife who decides the style and decoration of the home. Customers tend to be well-to-do; they include professionals, merchants, and high-ranking administrators. Each of these approaches provided this wallpaper company with separate estimates of its market size for wallpaper. The company then triangulated a single estimate. Specifically, the company was interested in the degree to which the three separate estimates converged. Researchers blended their own judgment into these findings in order to ultimately arrive at a reasonably reliable estimate of demand for wallpaper.

In the case of adhesive bandages, available data revealed that 70 percent of demand for pharmaceutical items—including adhesive bandages—was met by wholesalers concentrated in Casablanca, Morocco's capital city. The country imported all its adhesive bandages. Demand was quickly growing, due to rapid population growth, free hospitalization and medication for the needy, and reimbursement programs for medical and drug expenses. Although the government published import statistics, the information was confusing, because data on band-aid imports was mixed together with data on other types of adhesives. Moreover, the band-aid data was superficial and incomplete. Finally, widespread smuggling and gray-marketing of adhesive bandages through unofficial distribution channels complicated estimates of demand.

In an effort to gather more information, researchers interviewed band-aid sales personnel from firms such as Johnson & Johnson and Curad. Their findings revealed that consumers tend to be price sensitive when buying band-aids, and that they rely on doctors and pharmacists to recommend well-known brands. Researchers eventually arrived at a reasonable estimate of band-aid sales by assimilating data from various sources. They visited numerous retail stores to ask about sales, prevailing retail prices, competitive brands, and consumer attitudes toward prices and brands. Researchers also tallied statistics from the United Nations Development Program and other aid agencies that donate medical supplies to developing countries.

As you can see, estimating demand in foreign markets is challenging, but managers can overcome the challenges through creative use of market research. ◄

Sources: Amine, Lyn and S. Tamer Cavusgil. (1986). "Demand Estimation in a Developing Country Environment: Difficulties, Techniques, and Examples," *Journal of the Market Research Society* 28 (1): 43–65; Cavusgil, S. Tamer, P. Ghauri, and M. Agarwal. (2002). *Doing Business in Emerging Markets: Entry and Negotiation Strategies.* Thousand Oaks, CA: Sage; Prahalad, C. K. (2005). "Aid Is Not the Answer," *The Wall Street Journal* Aug 31, p. A8; Wilkes, V. (2005). "Marketing and Market Development: Dealing with a Global Issue: Contributing to Poverty Alleviation," *Corporate Governance* 5 (3): 61–69; U.S. Commercial Service and the U.S. Department of State. (2005). *Country Commercial Guide Morocco Fiscal Year 2005,* retrieved at www.buyusainfo.net.

 ## An Overview of Global Market Opportunity Assessment

The choices managers make determine the future of the firm. Making good choices depends on objective evidence and hard data about which products and services to offer, and where to offer them. The more managers know about an opportunity, the better equipped they will be to exploit it. This is particularly true in international business, which usually entails greater uncertainty and unknowns than domestic business.[1]

Central to a firm's research is identifying and defining the best business opportunities in the global marketplace to pursue. **Global market opportunity** refers to a favorable combination of circumstances, locations, or timing that offers prospects for exporting, investing, sourcing, or partnering in foreign markets. In various foreign locations, the firm may perceive opportunities to: sell its products and services; establish factories or other production facilities to produce its offerings more competently or more cost-effectively; procure raw materials, components, or services of lower cost or superior quality; or enter into collaborative arrangements with foreign partners. Global market opportunities can enhance company performance, often far beyond what the firm can normally achieve in its home market.

Global market opportunity
Favorable combination of circumstances, locations, or timing that offers prospects for exporting, investing, sourcing, or partnering in foreign markets.

In this chapter, we discuss six key tasks that the manager should perform to define and pursue global market opportunities. Exhibit 12.1 illustrates the objectives and outcomes typically associated with each task. Such a formal process is especially appropriate in pursuing a marketing or collaborative venture opportunity. As the exhibit shows, the six key tasks are:

1. Analyze organizational readiness to internationalize.

2. Assess the suitability of the firm's products and services for foreign markets.

3. Screen countries to identify attractive target markets.

4. Assess the industry market potential, or the market demand, for the product(s) or service(s) in selected target markets.

5. Select qualified business partners, such as distributors or suppliers.

6. Estimate company sales potential for each target market.

In carrying out this systematic process, the manager will need to employ objective *selection criteria* by which to make choices, as listed in the final column of Exhibit 12.1. Let's examine each task in detail.

Task One: Analyze Organizational Readiness to Internationalize

Before undertaking a substantial investment in international business, whether it is launching a product abroad or sourcing from a foreign supplier, the firm should conduct a formal assessment of its readiness to internationalize. A thorough evaluation of organizational capabilities is useful, both for firms *new* to international business and for those with considerable experience. Such a self-audit is similar to a SWOT analysis (that is, an evaluation of the firm's Strengths, Weaknesses, Opportunities, and Threats). Here, managers peer into their own organization to determine the degree to which it has the motivation, resources, and skills necessary to successfully engage in international business.

Concurrently, management also examines conditions in the *external* business environment by conducting formal research on the opportunities and threats that face the firm in the markets where it seeks to do business. Here, managers research the specific needs and preferences of buyers, as well as the nature of competing products, and the risks involved in entering foreign markets.

Management's goal in analyzing organizational readiness to internationalize is to figure out what resources the firm has and the extent to which they are sufficient for successful international operations. In this way, managers assess the firm's *readiness* to venture abroad. During this process, management considers the firm's degree of international experience, the goals and objectives that management envisions for internationalization, the quantity and quality of skills, capabilities, and resources available for internationalization, and the extent of actual and potential support provided by the firm's network of relationships. If it is discovered that the firm lacks one or more key resources, management must commit necessary personnel and time *before* allowing the contemplated venture to go forward.

As an example, consider *Home Instead, Inc.,* a small U.S. firm that provides services for the elderly who choose to live independently at home but require companionship, assistance with meal preparation, and help with shopping and housekeeping. Following an assessment of its readiness to internationalize, management perceived substantial international opportunities—particularly in Japan—but also recognized deficiencies in certain key capabilities. So, the company hired Ms. Yoshino Nakajima, who is fluent in Japanese and an expert on the Japanese market, to be vice president for international development. Ms. Nakajima

Task	Objective	Outcomes	Selection criteria
1. Analyze organizational readiness to internationalize	To provide an objective assessment of the company's preparedness to engage in international business activity.	A list of firm strengths and weaknesses, in the context of international business, and recommendations for resolving deficiencies that hinder achieving company goals.	Evaluate factors needed for international business success: • Relevant financial and tangible resources • Relevant skills and competencies • Senior management commitment and motivation
2. Assess the suitability of the firm's products and services for foreign markets	To conduct a systematic assessment of the suitability of the firm's products and services for international customers. To evaluate the degree of fit between the product or service and customer needs.	• Determination of factors that may hinder product or service market potential in each target market. • Identification of needs for the adaptations that may be required for initial and ongoing market entry.	Assess the firm's products and services with regard to: • Foreign customer characteristics and requirements • Government-mandated regulations • Expectations of channel intermediaries • Characteristics of competitors' offerings
3. Screen countries to identify target markets	To reduce the number of countries that warrant in-depth investigation as potential target markets to a manageable few.	Identification of five to six high-potential country markets that are most promising for the firm.	Assess candidate countries that the firm may enter with regard to: • Market size and growth rate • Market intensity (that is, buying power of the residents in terms of income level) • Consumption capacity (that is, size and growth rate of the country's middle class) • Country's receptivity to imports • Infrastructure appropriate for doing business • Degree of economic freedom • Political risk

Exhibit 12.1 Key Tasks in Global Market Opportunity Assessment

Task	Objective	Outcomes	Selection criteria
4. Assess industry market potential	To estimate the most likely share of industry sales within each target country. To investigate and evaluate any potential barriers to market entry.	• 3 to 5-year forecasts of industry sales for each target market • Delineation of market entry barriers in industry	Assess industry market potential in the target country by considering: • Market size, growth rate, and trends in the industry • The degree of competitive intensity • Tariff and nontariff trade barriers • Standards and regulations • Availability and sophistication of local distribution • Unique customer requirements and preferences • Industry-specific market potential indicators
5. Select qualified business partners	To decide on the type of foreign business partner, clarify ideal partner qualifications and plan entry strategy.	• Determination of value adding activities required of foreign business partners • List of attributes desired of foreign business partners • Determination of value-adding activities required of foreign business partners	Assess and select intermediaries and facilitators based on: • Manufacturing and marketing expertise in the industry • Commitment to the international venture • Access to distribution channels in the market • Financial strength • Quality of staff • Technical expertise • Infrastructure and facilities appropriate for the market
6. Estimate company sales potential	To estimate the most likely share of industry sales the company can achieve, over a period of time, for each target market.	• 3 to 5-year forecast of company sales in each target market • Understanding of factors that will influence company sales potential	Estimate the potential to sell the firm's product or service, with regard to: • Capabilities of partners • Access to distribution • Competitive intensity • Pricing and financing • Market penetration timetable of the firm • Risk tolerance of senior managers

launched the franchise in Japan, where it captured substantial market share. Next, management tapped into the global network of 1,700 trade specialists of the U.S. Commercial Service, a government agency that provided the firm with leads and contacts in countries it had identified as the best target markets. Now *Home Instead* has numerous franchises in Australia, Canada, Ireland, and Portugal. Its international operations are thriving.[2]

A formal analysis of organizational readiness to internationalize requires managers to address the following questions:

* *What does the firm hope to gain from international business?* Various objectives and goals are possible, including increasing sales or profits, following key customers who locate abroad, challenging competitors in their home markets, or pursuing a global strategy of establishing production and marketing operations at various locations worldwide.

* *Is international business expansion consistent with other firm goals, now or in the future?* The firm should manage internationalization in the context of its mission and business plan. Over time, firms have various opportunities. Managers should evaluate one venture against others that might be undertaken in the domestic market to ensure that internationalization is the best use of firm resources.

* *What demands will internationalization place on firm resources, such as management, personnel, and finance, as well as production and marketing capacity? How will the firm meet such demands?* Management must confirm that the firm has enough production and marketing capacity to serve foreign markets. Nothing is more frustrating to the management team and the international channel than not being able to fill orders due to insufficient capacity. For instance, when Cirrus Logic, Inc., a manufacturer of audio microchips, wanted to expand its ability to market chips to international customers like Bose, LG Electronics, and Sony, it had to increase its manufacturing capacity first.[3]

* *What is the basis of the firm's competitive advantage?* Here, managers evaluate the reasons for the firm's current success. Firms derive competitive advantage from doing things better than competitors. It might be based on strong R&D capabilities, sourcing of superior input goods, cost-effective or innovative manufacturing capacity, skillful marketing, or a highly effective distribution channel. It is important to understand what advantages the firm has, so that managers can apply these advantages effectively in foreign markets.

Managers can use diagnostic tools to facilitate a self-audit of the firm's readiness to internationalize. One of the best-known tools is *CORE (COmpany Readiness to Export)*, developed by Professor Tamer Cavusgil in the early 1980s (see www.globalEDGE.msu.edu). *CORE* has been adopted and used widely by individual enterprises, consultants, and the U.S. Department of Commerce. Since *CORE* has benefited from extensive research on the factors that contribute to successful exporting, it also serves as an ideal tutorial for self-learning and training.

CORE asks managers questions about their organizational resources, skills, and motivation to arrive at an objective assessment of the firm's readiness to successfully engage in exporting. It also generates assessments on both organizational readiness and product readiness. This self-assessment tool helps managers recognize the useful assets they have and the additional resources they need to make internationalization succeed. The assessment emphasizes exporting, since it is the typical entry mode for most newly internationalizing firms.

Assessing organizational readiness to internationalize is an ongoing process. Managers need to continuously verify the firm's ability to modify its products and processes to suit conditions in local markets. For example, Levi

Strauss is the world's largest manufacturer of trousers, notably denim jeans, which are sold worldwide. Countries differ in their tastes and fashions, which creates the need for firms to adapt products and services. Levi has had to assess its ability to undertake marketing adaptations in various markets. For example, in Islamic countries, women are discouraged from wearing tight-fitting attire, so Levi made a line of loose-fitting jeans. When Levi first entered Japan, local preferences and the smaller physique of many Japanese meant that the firm had to make its famous blue jeans tighter and smaller.

In addition to considering local customs, preferences, and physical makeup, Levi also adapts to local regulations. Levi often re-shot TV commercials in countries such as Australia and Brazil because local regulations insist on domestically produced commercials. Differences in climate also necessitate changes; for instance, in hot climates, customers prefer thinner denim in brighter colors, and shorts. Management has had to regularly assess the firm's capacity to accommodate the adaptations required for numerous individual markets.[4]

Levi makes tight-fit jeans to accommodate the Japanese physique and loose-fitting jeans to accommodate tastes in Islamic countries.

Task Two: Assess the Suitability of the Firm's Products and Services for Foreign Markets

Once management has confirmed the firm's readiness to internationalize, it next ascertains the degree to which its products and services are suitable for foreign markets. Most companies produce a portfolio of offerings, some or all of which may hold the potential for generating international sales.

Factors Contributing to Product Suitability for International Markets

There are various ways to gauge the viability of offerings in foreign markets. The products or services with the best international prospects tend to have the following four characteristics:

1. *Sell well in the domestic market.* Those products and services that are received well at home are likely to succeed abroad, especially where similar needs and conditions exist. The manager should examine why the product or service is received well at home and then identify foreign markets with similar demand requirements.

2. *Cater to universal needs.* For example, buyers all over the world demand personal-care products, medical devices, and banking services. International sales may be promising if the product or service is relatively unique or has important features that are hard to duplicate by foreign firms.

3. *Address a need not well served in particular foreign markets.* Potential may exist in developing countries or elsewhere, where the product or service does not currently exist, or where demand is just beginning to emerge.

4. *Address a new or emerging need abroad.* For some products and services, demand might suddenly emerge following a disaster or other largescale or emergent trend. For example, a major earthquake in Turkey can create an urgent need for portable housing. Rising AIDS cases in South Africa can create a need for pharmaceuticals and medical supplies. Growing affluence in various emerging markets can create a growing demand for restaurants and hospitality services. Managers need to monitor such trends, so they can be prepared to enter the right market at the right time.

Key Issues for Managers to Resolve in Determining Product Potential

Here are some of the key questions managers should answer to determine the international market potential of a particular product or service:

* Who initiates purchasing? For example, homemakers are usually the chief decision-makers for household products. Professional buyers make purchases on behalf of firms.

* Who uses the product or service? For instance, children consume various products, but their parents may be the actual buyers. Employees consume various products, but their company makes the purchases.

* Why do people buy the product or service? That is, what specific needs does the product or service fulfill? These needs vary around the world. For example, Honda sells gasoline-powered generators that consumers in advanced economies use for recreational purposes; consumers in developing economies may buy these for basic household heating and lighting.

* Where do consumers purchase the product or service? Once the researcher understands where the offering is typically purchased, it is useful to visit potential buyers to find out the extent of their potential interest. These store audits also provide useful information on whether the product or service must be adapted to specific market needs, as well as how to price, promote, and distribute it.

* What economic, cultural, geographic, and other factors in the target market can limit sales? Countries vary substantially in terms of buyer-income levels, preferences, climate, and other factors that can inhibit or facilitate purchasing behavior. Managers should investigate such factors and adapt their offers accordingly.

One of the simplest ways to find out if a product or service holds promise for generating international sales is to ask potential intermediaries in the target market about the potential of a product in their markets. A manager can also review importer or distributor lists, available from government sources, trade associations, or directories online or in libraries.

Data on the extent to which the target country has imported a product over time is also very useful for understanding current and future potential demand. Data may be available from various sources, such as http://export.gov, http://www.stat-usa.gov, or globalEDGE™. The level of exports should be investigated as well, because some countries, such as Singapore or Hong Kong, are used mainly as a transit point for international products and, therefore, may not actually be major users.

Another useful method for determining a product's marketability is to attend an industry trade fair in the target market or region and interview prospective customers or distributors. Since trade fairs often cover entire regions, such as Asia or Europe, this approach is efficient and cost effective for simultaneously learning about the market potential of several countries.

For successful international ventures, most firms focus on offering products and services that fit its resources and competitive advantages and can be produced from existing production facilities with minimal adaptation. The managers target those markets that are most likely to accept their offering and which have high profit and long-term potential growth.

Task Three: Screen Countries to Identify Target Markets

Screening for the best country to target is a fundamental decision in international business, whether the firm is engaged in importing, investing, or exporting. Firms that seek to source from foreign suppliers need to identify countries where capable suppliers are located. Once a firm chooses a particular country, it needs to ensure that conditions for importing from that country are favorable. For firms looking to make a direct investment in foreign markets, it is best to focus on countries that promise long-term growth and substantial returns, while posing relatively low political risk. Finally, exporting firms should target countries with low tariff barriers, steady demand, and qualified intermediaries.

Exporters typically use trade statistics that reveal exports or imports by country and product and allow the researcher to compare the size of the market among candidate countries. Statistics on how much of the product is already being exported to the target market help gauge the market's viability for accepting sales of the offering. By examining statistics over a period of years, a manager can determine which markets are growing and which are shrinking. The exporter can purchase research reports from professional market research consultants that provide descriptions, assessments, and key statistics on particular markets. For instance, the U.S. Department of Commerce conducts and publishes numerous market surveys, such as *The Water Supply and Wastewater Treatment Market in China, Automotive Parts and Equipment Industry Guide in Europe,* and the *Country Commercial Guide for Brazil.*

The choice of country markets is particularly important in the early stages of internationalization. Failure to choose the right markets will not only result in a financial loss, but the firm will incur opportunity costs as well. That is, by choosing the wrong markets, the firm ties up resources that it might have more profitably employed somewhere else. When entry is planned through *foreign direct investment (FDI)*, choosing the right market is especially critical, because FDI is very costly. As you learned in Chapter 1, FDI is an internationalization strategy in which the firm establishes a physical presence abroad through acquisition of productive assets such as capital, technology, labor, land, plant, and equipment. With FDI entry, the cost of abandoning the market and terminating relationships can easily exceed millions of dollars.

Some firms target psychically similar countries—that is, countries similar to the home country in terms of language, culture, and other factors. These countries fit management's comfort zone. For instance, Australian firms often choose New Zealand, the United Kingdom, or the United States as their first target markets abroad. Many choose the United Kingdom rather than France or Italy as their first European target. The choice is logical, because English is spoken in New Zealand, the United Kingdom, and the United States, and these cultures bear similarities to that of Australia. As their managerial experience, knowledge, and confidence increase, these firms expand into more complex and culturally distant markets, such as China or Japan.

In the contemporary era, however, firms have become more venturesome as well as more knowledgeable regarding foreign-market entry. As a result, many target nontraditional, higher-risk countries. The born-global companies exemplify this trend. Ongoing globalization tends to mitigate the foreignness of markets and—thanks to advances in communication and transportation technologies—have reduced the cost and risk of reaching out to culturally distant countries, including emerging markets.

As firms become more knowledgeable about foreign markets, they are venturing into countries with different languages and cultures. U.S.-based Motorola sells mobile phones in Vietnam. The United States imports agricultural and other products from Vietnam.

When screening countries, it is best for managers to target markets that are growing rapidly or in which the offered product or service is relatively new to the market. Markets in which there are numerous competitors or in which the product is already widely used are unattractive, because existing rivals may strongly resist the entry of newcomers.

The nature of information necessary for country screening varies by product type or industry. For example, in marketing consumer electronics, the researcher would emphasize countries with large populations of people with adequate discretionary income and ample energy production and consumption. For farming equipment, the researcher would consider countries with substantial agricultural land and farmers who enjoy relatively high incomes. For health care insurance, the researcher targets countries that have numerous hospitals and doctors.

In the process of screening for attractive country markets, managers need to monitor a range of economic, political, and cultural factors. These factors affect the international business environment in major ways, and point to various opportunities and threats that firms analyze and evaluate. Read the *Global Trend* feature to learn about a number of current trends that affect the global market environment.

Targeting Regions or Gateway Countries

Often, the firm may target a region or a group of countries rather than individual countries. Compared to targeting one country at a time, targeting a group of countries is more cost effective, particularly when the markets have similar demand conditions, business regulations, and culture. A good example is the European Union, which comprises some 27 countries that are relatively similar in terms of income level, regulations, and infrastructure. When entering Europe, firms often devise a pan-European strategy that considers many member countries of the European Union, rather than planning separate efforts in individual countries.

In other cases, the firm may target so-called *gateway countries*, or *regional hubs*, which serve as entry points to nearby or affiliated markets. For example, Singapore has traditionally served as the gateway to southeast Asian countries, Hong Kong is an important gateway to China, Turkey is a good platform for entering the central Asian republics, and Finland provides business-friendly access to the former Soviet Union. Firms base their operations in a gateway country so they can serve the larger adjacent region.

Screening Methodology for Potential Country Markets

With almost 200 countries around the world, it is neither cost effective nor practical to target all of them. Thus, management must choose markets that offer the best prospects. There are two basic methods for accomplishing this: gradual elimination and indexing and ranking.

International Business

Global Macro Trends That Affect International Business

Managers must regularly assess the long-term trends in its product markets, as well as shifting aspects of technology and globalization. Firms succeed when they ride these currents—those that swim against them usually struggle. For instance, in sectors such as banking, telecommunications, and technology, almost two-thirds of recent organic growth in western firms (that is, growth from increasing sales) has resulted from being in the right markets and regions. By identifying and analyzing key trends, it is possible to forecast long-term directional changes that affect the firm's future fortunes.

What current trends are international managers tracking that will make the future world very different from the world of today? A recent study by McKinsey, a consulting firm, identified the following macroeconomic trends as transforming the global economy.

Centers of economic activity that will undergo a major shift, not just globally, but also regionally. The locations of global economic activities are shifting due to economic liberalization, technological advances, capital market developments, and demographic shifts. Today, Asia (excluding Japan) accounts for 13 percent of world GDP, while western Europe accounts for more than 30 percent. By 2025, these proportions may reverse, as most global economic activity shifts toward Asia. Some industries and functions in Asia—manufacturing and IT services, for example—will be the major beneficiaries. Elsewhere, emerging markets are becoming centers of activity as well.

Need to increase organizational productivity. Populations are aging across the developed countries, meaning there are fewer young people to work and pay taxes. This demographic shift requires higher levels of efficiency and creativity from both the public and private sectors. Governments must perform their services less expensively and with greater efficiency. They will gradually apply private-sector approaches in the provision of social services. Otherwise, there is a risk that aging populations will reduce the overall level of global wealth. The shift is creating opportunities for firms in certain product and service sectors, such as finance and health care.

More consumers, especially in the developing economies. Almost a billion new consumers will enter the global marketplace through 2015, as economic growth in emerging markets pushes them beyond the threshold level of $5,000 in annual household income, a point when people begin to spend on discretionary goods. In the period up to 2015, consumers' spending power in emerging economies will increase to more than $9 trillion, near the current spending power of western Europe. Consumers everywhere will increasingly leverage information and communications technologies to access the same products and brands. These shifts require firms to devise new products and marketing strategies. For example, firms are increasingly employing the Internet to reach new markets and deepen relations with existing customers.

The shifting talent battlefield. The shift to knowledge-intensive industries highlights a growing scarcity of knowledge workers. Increasing integration of global labor markets (e.g., China, India, and Eastern Europe) is opening vast new talent sources. Emerging markets now have tens of millions of university-educated young professionals, more than double the number in advanced economies. To take advantage of this trend, firms increasingly leverage information and communication technologies to employ well-educated individuals located in the emerging markets and elsewhere.

Growing demand for natural resource. As economic growth accelerates, especially in emerging markets, use of natural resources will grow at unprecedented rates. Demand for oil is likely to grow by 50 percent through the year 2025. This shift portends new opportunities for firms in the global energy sector. In China, demand for copper, steel, and aluminum has tripled in recent years, suggesting new opportunities for mining companies. Meanwhile, water shortages are increasingly common in much of the world. Climate change and the gradual decay of the ozone level require attention. Addressing these challenges is costly, and will likely slow growth. Innovation in technology, regulation, and the use of resources is central to creating a world that can both drive robust economic growth and sustain environmental demands.

Widespread access to information. Knowledge is increasingly available to people worldwide. For instance, the presence of search engines such as Google makes seemingly limitless information instantly available. Knowledge production itself is growing. For example, worldwide patent applications have been rising annually at 20 percent. Companies are applying new models of knowledge production, access, distribution, and ownership.

Managers need to understand the implications of these macroeconomic trends, along with customer needs and competitive developments. In such an evolving environment, the role of market research and competitive intelligence is growing. Managers who account for these trends in their strategy development will be best placed to succeed in the global marketplace. Thinking about these trends will be time well spent for any future manager.

Sources: Davis, I., and E. Stephenson. (2006). "Ten Trends to Watch in 2006," *The McKinsey Quarterly*, retrieved January, 2006 at www.mckinsey.com; Porter, Eduardo. (2003). "Buying Power of Hispanics Is Set to Soar," *Wall Street Journal*, April 18, p. B1.

Gradual Elimination The firm that applies *gradual elimination* starts with a large number of prospective target countries and then gradually narrows its choices by examining increasingly specific information. As indicated in Exhibit 12.1 on pages 348–349, the firm aims to reduce to a manageable few the number of countries that warrant in-depth investigation as potential target markets. The objective is to identify five or six high-potential country markets that are most promising for the firm. Research can be expensive. To save time and money, it is essential to eliminate unattractive markets as quickly as possible. At the same time, it is wise to be open-minded and consider all reasonable markets. For example, targeting developing economies with a product that is not yet widely consumed may be more profitable than targeting saturated and more competitive markets in Europe, Japan, and North America.

In the early stages, market research proceeds in a stepwise manner, in which the researcher follows a funnel approach of obtaining general information first, then specific information next. The researcher initially obtains information on macro-level market-potential indicators, such as population- or income-related measures, to identify a short list of countries (perhaps five or six) that represent the most attractive markets. Such broad screening data are readily available from sources such as globalEDGE ™.

Once managers identify the most promising markets, they employ more specific and precise indicators to narrow the choices. For example, a manager may use current import statistics of the particular product to determine the potential desirability of a target market. This information is readily available, because most countries record the flow of imported and exported products to levy import duties and to determine the value of their own exports. Most countries also make these statistics available to international organizations, such as the United Nations (see www.comtrade.un.org/db/) and the Organi-

Country	Market Size		Market Growth Rate		Market Intensity		Market Consumption Capacity	
	Rank	Index	Rank	Index	Rank	Index	Rank	Index
China	1	100	1	100	25	23	12	59
Hong Kong	24	1	20	23	1	100	13	54
Singapore	27	1	18	27	9	59	11	62
Taiwan	12	5	6	57	11	57	—	—
Israel	25	1	12	45	2	79	4	82
South Korea	7	12	16	30	5	63	2	99
Czech Rep.	23	2	9	48	13	55	3	97
Hungary	26	1	24	14	3	76	1	100
India	2	44	3	63	22	37	7	77
Poland	14	5	27	1	10	58	6	80

Exhibit 12.2 Application of Indexing and Ranking Methodology: Emerging Market Potential Indicators, 2007

Note: Only top 10 countries are provided here; consult www.globaledge.msu.edu for the complete list.

Source: globalEDGE™ (www.globaledge.msu.edu/ibrd/marketpot.asp).

zation for Economic Cooperation and Development (OECD; www.oecd.org). By analyzing research data and gradually narrowing the choices, the researcher identifies the one or two most promising markets for further exploration.

Indexing and Ranking The second primary method for choosing the most promising foreign markets is *indexing* and *ranking*, in which the researcher assigns scores to countries for their overall market attractiveness. For each country, the researcher first identifies a comprehensive set of market-potential indicators and then uses one or more of these indicators to represent a variable. Weights are assigned to each variable to establish its relative importance: the more important a variable, the greater its weight. The researcher uses the resulting weighted scores to rank the countries.

This indexing and ranking method is illustrated by the *Emerging Market Potential (EMP) Indicators* methodology, developed by the senior author of this book, Tamer Cavusgil,[5] and featured at globalEDGE™.[6] Exhibit 12.2 presents the resulting index. It ranks the emerging markets—some of the world's most-promising developing countries. The Exhibit highlights a collection of variables that are useful for describing the attractiveness of countries as potential target markets. Exhibit 12.3 defines the variables and relative weights used in the Exhibit.

Among the variables in Exhibit 12.3, *market size* and *market growth rate* are especially important for measuring market potential.[7] They address the question "Is the market big enough and does it have a future?" If a country's population is large and its per–capita income is substantial, it is probably a good prospect for international sales. By itself, however, a sizable market is insufficient. The market should also be growing at a stable or substantial rate, particularly in terms of population or income. Countries with robust income growth are desirable targets. For each country, a researcher examines population,

Commercial Infrastructure		Economic Freedom		Market Receptivity		Country Risk		Overall Index	
Rank	Index	Rank	Index	Rank	Index	Rank	Index	Rank	Index
16	45	27	1	22	3	13	49	1	100
2	97	6	79	2	75	2	90	2	96
6	83	10	71	1	100	1	100	3	93
1	100	8	76	5	23	3	87	4	79
3	94	3	86	4	26	5	63	5	78
5	90	7	78	10	13	4	65	6	75
4	91	2	93	9	15	6	63	7	73
7	78	4	83	8	16	8	62	8	64
25	17	17	44	27	1	16	39	9	55
8	71	5	82	14	7	9	58	10	46

Variable	Definition	Weight (out of 100)	Example Measurement Indicators
Market size	Proportion of the country's population concentrated in urban areas	20	• Urban population
Market growth rate	Pace of industrialization and economic development	12	• Annual growth rate of commercial energy use • Real GDP growth rate
Market intensity	Buying power of the country's residents	14	• Per-capita gross national income, based on purchasing power parity • Private consumption as a percentage of GDP
Market consumption capacity	Size and growth rate of the country's middle class	10	• Percentage share of middle-class income and consumption
Commercial infrastructure	Ease of access to marketing, distribution, and communication channels	14	• Telephone mainlines (per 100 habitants) • Cellular mobile subscribers per 100 inhabitants • Paved road density • Internet hosts per million people • Population per retail outlet • Television sets per capita
Economic freedom	Degree to which the country has liberalized its economy	10	• Trade and tax policies • Monetary and banking policies • Government consumption of economic output • Capital flows and foreign investment • Property rights • Extent of black market activity
Market receptivity to imports	Extent to which the country is open to imports	12	• Per-capita imports • Trade as percentage of GDP
Country risk	Level of political risk	8	• Country risk rating
Total		100	

Exhibit 12.3 Variables Used for Country Screening in the Emerging Market Potential (EMP) Indicators Index

national income, and growth statistics for the previous 3 to 5 years. A key question is whether or not market growth has been consistent year to year. In addition to large, fast-growing markets, a researcher should identify some smaller but fast-emerging markets that may provide ground-floor opportunities. There are likely to be fewer competitors in new markets than in established ones. Countries in which the product is not currently available or in which competitors have only recently entered may also be promising targets.

As we discussed in Chapter 9 on emerging markets, the *size* and *growth rate* of the middle class are critical indicators of promising targets.

The *middle class* is measured by the share of national income available to middle-income households. These middle-class consumer households are the best prospect for a typical marketer because the wealthier class in most emerging markets is relatively small and the poorest segment has little spending capacity. The relative size of the middle class, and the pace with which it is growing, also indicate how national income is distributed in that country. If income is not equally distributed, the size of the middle class will be limited and the market will not be very attractive.

While the middle class is an important indicator for estimating the size of foreign markets, as also elaborated in Chapter 9, per capita income measure may underestimate the true potential of emerging markets due to such factors as the existence of a large, informal economy.

In Exhibit 12.2, an analysis of the rankings for each of the dimensions reveals some interesting patterns. For example, China ranks first in market size, but twenty-fifth in market intensity and last in economic freedom. It also ranks low in infrastructure. As this observation reveals, there are always trade-offs in targeting country markets. No single country is attractive on all dimensions. Along with more-desirable features, the researcher must also contend with less-desirable features. For example, both Singapore and Hong Kong are favorable targets in terms of economic freedom, but they are city-states with small populations.

The top four countries in the index in Exhibit 12.2 are all in East Asia. In recent years, East Asian economies have made tremendous strides in market liberalization, industrialization, and modernization. South Korea is a champion of economic growth, with annual per-capita GDP growth of almost 6 percent. The level of per capita GDP in the past 40 years has advanced tenfold. South Korean firms have become world leaders in many industries, such as shipbuilding, mobile communications, and flat-screen televisions. The country is the world's test market for state-of-the-art wireless and Internet services and applications. South Korean firms use pioneering technologies that are years ahead of their competitors and are poised to overtake other countries in mobile technology, broadband, and other leading communications technologies. Asia's rapid economic development is a primary factor in the current phase of globalization.[8]

Country rankings of the type indicated in Exhibit 12.2 are not static. Rankings change over time as shifts occur in each country because of macroeconomic events or country-specific developments. For example, while India ranks relatively high, it may dramatically fall if a new political regime reverses market liberalization. The recent accession of Hungary and Poland into the European Union should improve the economic prospects of these countries. The introduction of modern banking systems and legal infrastructure should increase Russia's attractiveness as an export market. Chile has achieved substantial progress in economic reforms and higher living standards. However, economic stagnation has led to a drop in Argentina's market attractiveness.

A final point relates to the rather generic and broad nature of the variables suggested by ranking indicators. They are only a general guide for identifying promising country markets. The ranking and indexing methodology is intended for use in the early stages of qualifying and ranking countries. Much more detailed analysis is needed once a firm identifies a handful of target markets. The researcher will eventually need to supplement the indicators for specific industries. Indicators to emphasize when researching soft drink markets, for example, vary substantially from those used for researching medical equipment. For medical equipment, the researcher will probably gather additional data on health care expenditures, number of physicians per capita, and number of hospital beds per-capita. Firms in the financial services sector will require specific data on commercial risk. In addition, depending on the industry, researchers may apply different *weights* to each market-potential indicator. For example, population size is relatively less important for a firm that markets yachts than for one that sells footwear. Each firm must assign appropriate weights to each indicator, depending on its specific circumstances.

Screening Countries for Direct Investment and Global Sourcing

The discussion so far has taken the perspective of a firm seeking the best country markets for exporting. However, firms internationalize through other entry modes as well—such as FDI—to set up production and assembly facilities abroad, and to source goods from foreign suppliers. While the goal of delineating a handful of prospective countries remains the same in these entry modes, the researcher may employ a different set of criteria for country screening. Let's discuss how the desirable country attributes differ for FDI and global sourcing.

Country Screening for Foreign Direct Investment FDI amounts to investing in physical assets, such as a factory, marketing subsidiary, or regional headquarters, in a foreign country. Such investments are usually undertaken for the long term. Accordingly, the types of variables to consider differ from those appropriate for export entry. For example, the availability in the target market of skilled labor and managerial talent are relatively more important to consider for FDI entry than exporting. Researchers identifying the best locations for FDI entry would normally consider the following variables:

* Long-term prospects for growth
* Cost of doing business: potential attractiveness of the country based on the cost and availability of commercial infrastructure, tax rates and wages, access to high-level skills and capital markets
* Country risk: regulatory, financial, political, and cultural barriers, and the legal environment for intellectual property protection
* Competitive environment: intensity of competition from local and foreign firms
* Government incentives: availability of tax holidays, subsidized training, grants, or low-interest loans

As in the case of screening countries for export opportunities, there are several sources of publicly accessible studies for screening countries for FDI. A useful resource is provided by the United Nations Conference on Trade and Development (UNCTAD). UNCTAD's *FDI Indices* methodology benchmarks both FDI performance and potential, ranking countries by how well they perform as recipients or originators of FDI (www.unctad.org). Another resource is provided by the consulting firm, A. T. Kearney, which prepares an annual *Foreign Direct Investment Confidence Index,* (www.atkearney.com). The index tracks how political, economic, and regulatory changes affect the FDI intentions and preferences of the world's top 1,000 firms. By surveying executives at these firms, the index captures the most important variables to consider from the 65 countries that receive more than 90 percent of global FDI investments.

Exhibit 12.4 displays the results of the A. T. Kearney Index. The index reveals that advanced economies in western Europe, as well as Australia, Japan, and the United States, possess high investor confidence. In other words, firms prefer these locations for making FDI-based investments. These locations are popular due to their relative size and business-friendly infrastructure. The advanced economies engage in substantial cross-investments in each other's markets. For example,

Europe and the United States are each others' most important partners for FDI. Their transatlantic economy represents over $2.5 trillion in total foreign affiliate sales, and it mutually supports nearly a quarter of the world's entire foreign affiliate workforce employed by MNEs abroad.

Note that of the top ten destinations in the A. T. Kearney Index, six are emerging markets: China, India, Poland, Russia, Brazil, and Hong Kong. Investors prefer China because of its huge size, fast-growing consumer market, and position as an excellent site for low-cost manufacturing. China also enjoys superior access to export markets, favorable government incentives, low-cost structure, and a stable macroeconomic climate. However, executives see India as the world's leader for business process and outsourcing IT services. India has a highly educated workforce, strong managerial talent, established rule of law, and transparent transactions and rules.

Country Screening for Global Sourcing Global sourcing and offshoring refer to the procurement of finished products, intermediate goods, and services from suppliers located abroad. Sourcing is critically important to all types of firms. As with FDI decisions, the types of screening variables managers consider in sourcing are often distinct from those they consider for exporting. When seeking foreign sources of supply, managers will examine such factors as cost and quality of inputs, stability of exchange rates, reliability of suppliers, and the presence of a work force with superior technical skills.

A. T. Kearney also prepares an annual *Offshore Location Attractiveness Index* (www.atkearney.com). This index assists managers to understand and compare the factors that make countries attractive as potential locations for offshoring of service activities such as IT, business processes, and call centers. A. T. Kearney evaluates countries across 39 criteria, categorized into three dimensions:

- *Financial structure* takes into account compensation costs (for example, average wages), infrastructure costs (for electricity and telecom systems), and tax and regulatory costs (such as tax burden, corruption, and fluctuating exchange rates).

- *People skills and availability* accounts for a supplier's experience and skills, labor-force availability, education and linguistic proficiency, and employee-attrition rates.

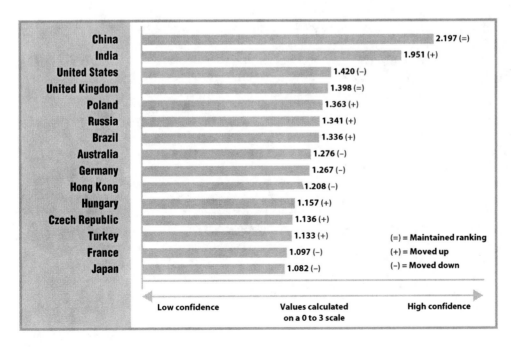

Exhibit 12.4

A. T. Kearney Foreign Direct Investment Confidence Index

- *Business environment* assesses economic and political aspects of the country, commercial infrastructure, cultural adaptability, and security of intellectual property.

Exhibit 12.5 presents the *Offshore Location Attractiveness Index*. Note that 9 of the top 10 countries in the index are emerging markets, such as India, China, and Brazil. Although important, the cost of labor is only one of several factors in the decision to source inputs from abroad. Managers also cite productivity level, technical skills, and customer service skills as important factors. The index credits India and China (and to a lesser extent Russia and the Philippines) for educational achievement. Among developed economies, the index credits New Zealand, Canada, and Ireland with other strengths, such as highly developed infrastructure, English fluency, low country risk, and high degree of global integration.

 ## Task Four: Assess Industry Market Potential

The methods for screening countries discussed so far are most useful for gaining comparative insights into individual markets and for reducing the complexity of choosing appropriate foreign locations. Once the number of potential countries has been reduced to a manageable number—say five or six—the next step is to conduct in-depth analysis of each of these country markets. Rather than examining broad, macro-level indicators, as done in earlier stages, the researcher narrows

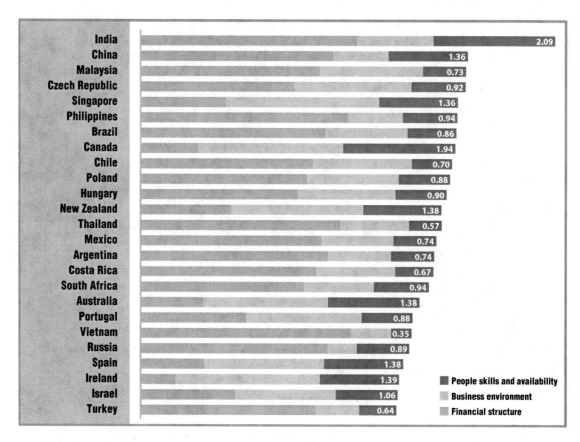

Exhibit 12.5 A. T. Kearney's Offshore Location Attractiveness Index

the focus to examine *industry-level* market potential indicators, because market potential is industry specific.

In task four, the researcher estimates the current and future levels of sales expected for the particular industry as a whole. This is termed **industry market potential**—an estimate of the likely sales that can be expected for all firms in the particular industry for a specified period of time. In other words, it is an aggregate of the sales that may be realized by all companies in the industry. Industry market potential is different from *company sales potential*, which refers to the share of industry sales the focal firm itself can expect to achieve during a given year. Most firms forecast sales at least three years into the future, of both industry market potential and company sales potential.

Estimating industry market potential enables the manager to refine the analysis and identify the most attractive countries for the firm's product or service. By examining country-level characteristics more closely at this stage, the manager is able to decide which countries to retain for subsequent analysis of company sales potential. In addition to gaining industry-specific insights into the select markets, managers will be able to formulate an understanding of the degree to which the firm needs to adapt its product and marketing approaches.

To develop an estimate of industry market potential, managers need data and insights on the following variables:

* Market size, growth rate, and trends in the specific industry
* Tariff and nontariff trade barriers to enter the market
* Standards and regulations that affect the industry
* Availability and sophistication of local distribution
* Unique customer requirements and preferences
* Industry-specific market potential indicators

In addition to generic determinants of demand, each industry sector—from fire alarms to zippers—has its own *industry-specific potential indicators* or *distinctive drivers of demand*. Marketers of cameras, for instance, examine climate-related factors such as the average number of sunny days in a typical year, given that most pictures are taken outdoors. In marketing laboratory equipment, the researcher might examine data on the number of hospitals, clinics, hospital beds, and doctors, as well as the level of governmental expenditures on health care. A manufacturer of electric generators might examine the rate of industrialization and dependence on hydroelectricity. A marketer of cooling equipment and industrial filters will consider the number of institutional buyers, such as restaurants and hotels. These are all industry-specific market potential indicators.

Managers also evaluate factors that affect the marketing and use of the product, such as consumer characteristics, culture, distribution channels, and business practices. Intellectual property rights and enforcement vary around the world. Managers should therefore evaluate regulations, trademarks, and product liability, and formulate strategies for protecting the firm's critical assets. The researcher should also ascertain the existence and nature of subsidy and incentive programs, from home and foreign governments, that the firm can access to obtain capital and to reduce the cost of foreign market entry.

A key question is whether industry market growth has been consistent from year to year. In addition to large, fast-growing markets, the researcher should identify some smaller but fast-emerging markets that may provide ground-floor opportunities. There are fewer competitors in markets that are opening for the first time. For example, most of the 60,000 pubs in the United Kingdom have recently come under the ownership of big chains, which are injecting substantial capital and trying to attract new clientele by serving food, a shift that will greatly

Industry market potential
An estimate of the likely sales that can be expected for all firms in the particular industry for a specified period of time.

More British pubs are serving food, creating a new market potential for firms in the food catering industry.

increase opportunities for firms in the restaurant food industry. The market research firm Mintel International estimated that food sales to British pubs will increase several billion dollars through the late 2000s. This represents a big change in British pub culture and a large new market for firms in the food industry.[9]

Growth rates tend to be substantially higher in new industries or those undergoing rapid innovation. For each country, the researcher should bear in mind that the product is likely to be in a different phase of its product life cycle. Countries in which the product is not currently available or in which competitors have only recently introduced the product may be especially promising targets.

Practical Methods for Managers to Assess Industry Market Potential

Managers can use a variety of practical methods to estimate industry market potential:

* *Simple trend analysis.* This method quantifies the total likely amount of industry market potential by examining aggregate production for the industry as a whole, adding imports from abroad and deducting exports. This gives a rough estimate of the size of the current industry sales in the country.

* *Monitoring key industry-specific indicators.* The manager examines unique industry drivers of market demand by collecting data from a variety of sources. For example, Caterpillar, a manufacturer of earthmoving equipment, examines the volume of announced construction projects, number of issued building permits, growth rate of households, infrastructure development, and other pertinent leading indicators as a way of anticipating countrywide sales of its construction equipment.[10]

* *Monitoring key competitors.* To gain insights into the potential of a particular country, the manager investigates the degree of major competitor activity in the countries of interest. For example, if Caterpillar is considering Chile as a potential market, he or she investigates the current involvement in Chile of its number one competitor, the Japanese firm Komatsu. Caterpillar gathers competitive intelligence to anticipate Komatsu's likely future moves.

* *Following key customers around the world.* Using this approach, the firm follows its major accounts as they enter new markets. Automotive suppliers can anticipate where their services will be needed next by monitoring the international expansion of their customers, such as Honda or Mercedes Benz. Similarly, Caterpillar follows current customers in the construction industry (such as Bechtel) as these customers bid for contracts or establish operations in specific foreign markets.

* *Tapping into supplier networks.* Many suppliers serve multiple clients and can be a major source of information about competitors. Firms can gain valuable leads from current suppliers by inquiring with them about competitor activities.

* *Attending international trade fairs.* Industry trade fairs and exhibitions are excellent venues for managers to obtain a wide range of information on potential foreign markets. By attending a trade fair in the target country, a

manager can learn a great deal about market characteristics that can help to estimate industry sales potential. Trade fairs are also helpful for identifying potential distributors and other business partners.

Data Sources for Estimating Industry Market Potential

For each target country, the manager seeks data that directly or indirectly report levels of industry sales and production, as well as the intensity of exports and imports in the product category of interest. A particularly useful information source is the National Trade Data Base (NTDB), available from the U.S. Department of Commerce's STAT-USA[11] and www.export.gov databases. Specific reports available from the NTDB include the following:

- *Best Market Reports* identify the top ten country markets for specific industry sectors.
- *Country Commercial Guides* analyze countries' economic and commercial environments.
- *Industry Sector Analysis Reports* analyze market potential for sectors such as telecommunications.
- *International Market Insight Reports* cover country and product-specific topics, providing various ideas for approaching markets of interest.

In developing market estimates of any kind, managers must be creative and must consult any resource that may shed light on the task at hand. Data and resources are rarely complete and precise in international market research. Consider the example of Teltone Inc. The firm wished to enter Mexico with its inexpensive brand of cellular telephones and needed to estimate industry-wide demand. It consulted numerous sources, including reports by the International Telecommunications Union (in Geneva, Switzerland), the *National Trade Data Bank,* and several United Nations publications. Managers researched the size of the Mexican upper class and its average income, the nature of support infrastructure for cellular systems in Mexico, and the nature and number of retail stores that could handle cell phones. Teltone managers also came across some statistics from the National Telecommunications Trade Association on the number of competitors already active in Mexico and their approximate sales volumes. From these sources, the company was able to arrive at a rough estimate of market size for telephones and prevailing prices in Mexico.

The *Recent Grad in IB* feature on the next page profiles Javier Estrada, who found exciting opportunities in his young career in international market research.

 Task Five: Select Foreign Business Partners

As we discussed in Chapter 3, business partners are critical to the success of the focal firm in international business. These partners include distribution-channel intermediaries, facilitators, suppliers, and collaborative venture partners, such as joint venture partners, licensees, and franchisees. Once a target market has been selected, the focal firm needs to decide on the type of partners it needs for its foreign-market venture. It also needs to identify suitable partner candidates, negotiate the terms of its relationship with chosen partners, and support as well as monitor the conduct of chosen partners. The firm's success depends on its ability to perform these tasks well.

There are many examples of partnering in international business. Exporters tend to collaborate with foreign-market intermediaries such as distributors and agents. Firms that choose to sell their intellectual property, such as know-how, trademarks, and copyrights, tend to work through foreign licensees. These

Javier's major: Business

Objectives: Integrating business skills with social planning in a public agency and pursuing a career in politics

Jobs held since graduating:

- United Nations World Food Programme in Guatemala and Honduras
- Director of Research, Bates Advertising, Dominican Republic
- Director of a major charity in Mexico

Javier Estrada graduated from a state university several years ago with a bachelor's degree in business. Upon graduation, Javier went to work for the United Nations World Food Programme (WFP) in Guatemala and Honduras. Fluent in Spanish, Javier was the youngest U.N. officer in Latin America. He was given the task of monitoring the functioning and execution of all WFP projects. The experience taught Javier about international management and logistics in the high-pressure environment of the various disasters the United Nations faced in Central America.

Ever adventurous, Javier next moved to the Dominican Republic, where, at the age of 24, he took a position as director of research in the local office of Bates Advertising, a global ad agency that handled accounts such as Wendy's, Purina, and Bell South. In this position, Javier investigated the local target market— how the market responded to key brands, the level of market share, and the most effective way of reaching target markets with advertising and other marketing communications tools. According to Javier, "the real challenge in international advertising is not in the large, established brands, but in the small, poorly positioned one."

A typical day for Javier included meetings with colleagues to discuss the progress of market research projects and assessing the next steps on behalf of his clients. Javier implemented consumer surveys to find out what specific benefits Latin American consumers were seeking. He used the information from this research to craft advertising campaigns ideally tailored to customer needs and attitudes. In creating surveys, Javier researched various secondary data sources on the Internet and in Bates' private library. He visited Santa Domingo to get a more authentic feel for the market and to meet with local experts. He also used a comprehensive report prepared by the United States Department of Commerce International Trade Administration (ITA) on the target market.

Javier developed Spanish-language questionnaires to gain an even deeper understanding of the market. Javier sent out questionnaires to a random sample of typical consumers throughout the Dominican Republic. He then analyzed the completed questionnaires and presented the results to his superiors. Findings from these studies helped Javier prepare reports with recommendations on the most appropriate advertising strategies for the Dominican Republic.

Success Factors

"My parents felt strongly that our lives should be influenced not only by the quality of our education, but also by our travels. . . . In school we were far from the wealthiest kids, but we were definitely among the most traveled." Javier was lucky enough to live in several countries during his teens and twenties. He comments: "You really get to know yourself when you are completely alone in a whole new culture, and reestablishing a network of friends and work contacts." International experience contributed to Javier's independent spirit and his ability to function successfully anywhere in the world.

In his market research position, Javier enjoyed going to other countries and meeting different people.

"My job provided the chance to help companies develop marketing programs that were really appropriate for their customers. If you really understand your customer, you have tremendous responsibility to use the information wisely and honestly. . . . Of course, I wouldn't have received the job if I hadn't worked hard in school. Good management training provided me with the skills to perform effectively. Sensitivity is important, since you need to be able to communicate with people who are culturally different from you. You need a strong empathy for your customers, and you need to try to identify exactly which research questions they are trying to address. . . ."

What's Ahead?

Javier has ever-higher goals for his career. He has been long concerned about poverty issues in Latin America, and his experiences with the United Nations had a profound effect on him. Javier pursued a master's degree in social policy and planning from the London School of Economics. Having worked in both business and development, Javier found his passion in integrating his business skills with social planning at the governmental level. Recently, Javier headed a major charity organization in Mexico. Eventually he wants to pursue a political career. He says, "I need to dream big."

licensing partners are independent businesses that apply intellectual property to produce products in their own country. In the case of internationalization through **franchising**, the foreign partner is a franchisee—an independent business abroad that acquires rights and skills from the focal firm to conduct operations in its own market (such as in the fast-food or car-rental industries). Alternatively, the focal firm may internationalize by initiating an **international collaborative venture**, which entails business initiatives undertaken jointly with other local or international partners. These collaborations may be project-based or may involve equity investments. Other types of international business partnerships include global sourcing, contract manufacturing, and supplier partnerships. We describe these partnerships in greater detail in Chapters 13 through 16.

Criteria for Selecting a Partner

Perhaps the most important decision for the focal firm is to identify the ideal qualifications of potential foreign partners. In general, the firm should seek a good fit in terms of both strategy (common goals and objectives) and resources (complementary core competencies and value-chain activities). It is helpful to anticipate the potential degree of synergy with the prospective partner for the intermediate-term, say 3 to 6 years into the future. Managers must be assured of a harmonious partnership in a dynamic environment.

Brunswick Corporation, a leading manufacturer of bowling equipment, considers the following criteria when screening for potential foreign distributors:

* Financially sound and resourceful, so that they can invest in the venture and ensure their future growth
* Competent and professional management, with qualified technical and sales staff
* Willing and able to invest in the focal firm's business and grow the business
* Possessing a good knowledge of the industry, and has access to distribution channels and end-users
* Known in the marketplace and well-connected with local government (as political clout is helpful especially in emerging markets)
* Committed and loyal in the long run

Firms also seek partners with complementary expertise. For example, while the focal firm may bring engineering and manufacturing expertise to the partnership, the local distributor may bring knowledge of local customers and distribution channels.

These and similarly desirable characteristics are not always available in prospective partners. If a company enters a foreign market late, then it may have to pick the second best or an even less-qualified partner. This implies that the firm should be ready and able to strengthen the partner's capabilities by transferring appropriate managerial and technical know-how over time.

Searching for Prospective Partners

The process of screening and evaluating business partners can be overwhelming. It is an ongoing task for most internationally-active firms. To identify prospective partners and gather background information, managers

Licensing Arrangement where the owner of intellectual property grants a firm the right to use that property for a specified period of time in exchange for royalties or other compensation.

Franchising Arrangement whereby the focal firm allows another the right to use an entire business system in exchange for fees, royalties, or other forms of compensation.

International collaborative venture Cross-border business alliance where partnering firms pool their resources and share costs and risks to undertake a new business initiative. Also referred to as an international partnership or an international strategic alliance.

Firms seeking a foreign business partner look for a variety of qualifications, including common goals and objectives and competent management.

consult various sources as well as conduct field research. Commercial banks, consulting firms, trade journals, and industry magazines, as well as country and regional business directories, such as *Kompass* (Europe) and *Dun and Bradstreet* are very helpful in developing a list of partner candidates. Many national governments offer inexpensive services that assist firms in finding partners in specific foreign markets. The knowledge portal globalEDGE™ (www.globalEDGE.msu.edu) provides additional resources, including several diagnostic tools, to help managers make systematic choices about alternative partner candidates.

Field research through onsite visits and gathering research from independent sources and trade fairs are crucial in the early stages of assessing a partner. Companies also find it useful to ask prospective partners to prepare a formal business plan before entering into an agreement. The quality and sophistication of such a plan provides insights into the capabilities of the prospective partner and serves as a test of the partner's commitment.

 Task Six: Estimate Company Sales Potential

Once managers have singled out several promising country markets, verified industry market potential, and assessed the availability of qualified business partners, the next step is to estimate company sales potential in each country. **Company sales potential** is an estimate of the share of annual industry sales that the firm expects to generate in a particular target market. Estimating company sales potential is often much more challenging than earlier tasks. It requires the researcher to obtain highly refined information from the market. The researcher needs to make certain fundamental assumptions about the market and project the firm's revenues and expenses for 3 to 5 years into the future. The estimates are never precise and require quite a bit of judgmental analysis.

Determinants of Company Sales Potential

In arriving at an estimate of company sales potential in the foreign market, managers will collect and review various research findings and assess the following:

- *Partner capabilities.* The competencies and resources of foreign partners, including channel intermediaries and facilitators, tend to determine how quickly the firm can enter and generate sales in the target market.

- *Access to distribution channels.* The ability to establish and make best use of channel intermediaries and distribution infrastructure in the target market determines how much sales the firm can achieve.

- *Intensity of the competitive environment.* Local or third-country competitors are likely to intensify their own marketing efforts when confronted by new entrants. Their actions are often unpredictable and not easily observed.

- *Pricing and financing of sales.* The degree to which pricing and financing are attractive to both customers and channel members is critical to initial entry and to ultimate success.

- *Human and financial resources.* The quality and quantity of the firm's resources are a major factor in determining the proficiency and speed with which success can be achieved in the market.

- *Market penetration timetable.* A key decision is whether managers opt for gradual or rapid market entry. Gradual entry gives the firm time to develop and leverage appropriate resources and strategies, but may cede some advantages to competitors in getting established in the market.

Company sales potential An estimate of the share of annual industry sales that the firm expects to generate in a particular target market.

Rapid entry may allow the firm to surpass competitors and obtain first-mover advantages, but it can tax the firm's resources and capabilities.

* *Risk tolerance of senior managers.* Results are a function of the level of resources that top management is willing to commit, which in turn depend on the extent of management's tolerance for risk in the market.
* *Special links, contacts, and capabilities of the firm.* The extent of the focal firm's network in the market—its existing relationships with customers, channel members, and suppliers—can have a strong effect on venture success.
* *Reputation.* The firm can succeed faster in the market if target customers are already familiar with its brand name and reputation.

Such a comprehensive assessment should lead to general estimates of potential sales, which managers can compare to actual sales results of incumbent firms in the market, when such data are available.

Thus, the process of estimating company sales is more like starting from multiple angles, then converging on an ultimate estimate that relies heavily on judgment. Exhibit 12.6 provides one framework managers may use to estimate company sales. Managers would combine information about customers, intermediaries, and competition, and see if such an analysis points to a reasonable estimate. Often, managers prepare multiple estimates based on best case, worst case, and most-likely case scenarios. Note also that arriving at such estimates will require assumptions from the manager as to the degree of firm effort, price aggressiveness, possible competitive reactions, degree of intermediary effort, and so on. Finally, note that sales prospects for a company hinges on factors both controllable by management (e.g., prices charged to intermediaries and customers), as well as uncontrollable factors (e.g., intensity of competition). Ultimately, the process of arriving at a sales estimate is more of an art than a science.

Exhibit 12.6

A Framework for Estimating Company Sales Potential in the Foreign Market

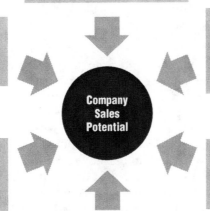

Customer characteristics
* Demographics
* Growth of demand
* Size of customer segment
* Intensity
* Purchasing power

Customer receptivity
* Perceived benefits of product
* Promotional effort directed to customers

Competitive positioning of focal brand
* Unique selling proposition of product
* What are its superior features compared to competitive offerings

Company Sales Potential

Channel effort and productivity
* Margins and incentives offered to distribution intermediaries

Competition
* Intensity
* Relative strength
* Potential reactions to market entrants

Pricing
* The cost of product landed in the foreign market (a function of international shipping costs, tariffs, etc.)
* Customary margins for distributors
* Whether the firm pursues a penetration versus skimming pricing

Practical Approaches to Estimating Company Sales Potential

It is critical for managers to begin with the factors suggested in Exhibit 12.6. In addition, experienced managers find the following activities to be especially helpful in estimating company sales potential in a foreign market:

- *Survey of end-users and intermediaries.* The firm can survey a sample of customers and distributors to determine the level of potential sales.

- *Trade audits.* Managers may visit retail outlets and question channel members to assess relative price levels of competitors' offerings and perceptions of competitor strength. In this approach, managers estimate market potential through the eyes of the trade (intermediaries) responsible for handling the product in the market. The trade audit can also indicate opportunities for new modes of distribution, identify types of alternative outlets, and provide insights into company standing relative to competitors.

- *Competitor assessment.* The firm may benchmark itself against principal competitor(s) in the market and estimate the level of sales it can potentially attract away from them. What rival firms will have to be outperformed? If key competitors in a given market are large, powerful firms, competing head-on could prove costly and lead to failure. Keep in mind, however, that even in those countries dominated by large firms, research may reveal market segments that are underserved or ignored altogether. Such market niches may be attractive, particularly for smaller firms with modest sales goals.

- *Obtaining estimates from local partners.* Collaborators such as distributors, franchisees, or licensees already experienced in the market are often best positioned to develop estimates of market share and sales potential.

- *Limited marketing efforts to test the waters.* Some companies may choose to engage in a limited entry in the foreign market—a sort of test market—as a way of gauging long-term sales potential or gaining a better understanding of the market. From these early results, it is possible to forecast longer-term sales.

In addition to these approaches, other techniques are also useful in the developing-country and emerging-market settings, where information sources are especially limited. These are *analogy* and *proxy indicators*. We illustrated these approaches in the opening vignette.

- *Analogy.* When using the *analogy* method, the researcher draws on known statistics from one country to gain insights into the same phenomenon for another, similar country. For instance, if the researcher knows the total consumption of citrus drinks in India, then—assuming that citrus-drink consumption patterns do not vary much in neighboring Pakistan—a rough estimate of Pakistan's consumption can be made, making an adjustment, of course, for the difference in population. Another illustration would be for the marketer of antibiotics. If the firm knows from experience that X number of bottles of antibiotics are sold in a country with Y number of physicians per thousand people, then it can be assumed that the same ratio (of bottles per 1,000 physicians) will apply in a similar country.

- *Proxy indicators.* By using *proxy indicators*, the researcher uses information known about one product category to infer potential about another product category. For the wallpaper marketer in the opening vignette, a useful proxy was the water heaters. This simple approach may lead to practical results especially if the two products exhibit a complementary demand relationship. For example, a proxy indicator of demand for professional hand tools in a country may be the level of construction activity in the country. Surrogate indicators of potential for a particular piece of surgical equipment in a market may include the total number of surgeries performed.

 ## In Conclusion

The decision to internationalize is never easy. Some firms are attracted to foreign markets by the promise of revenues and profits; others are drawn by the prospect to increase production efficiency; still others internationalize due to competitive pressures or to keep pace with rivals. Whatever the rationale, when companies fail in their international business ventures, it is often because they neglect to conduct a systematic and comprehensive assessment of global market opportunity.

Although we present the six tasks for global market opportunity assessment in a sequential manner, firms do not necessarily pursue them in succession. Indeed, firms often pursue two or more of the tasks simultaneously. In addition, the process is highly dynamic. Market conditions change, partner performance may fluctuate, and competitive intensity will increase. These dynamic events require managers to constantly evaluate their decisions and commitments. Management must be open to making course changes as circumstances dictate.

Of the six key tasks, some of the choices that managers will make are interrelated. For example, the choice of a business partner is very much a function of the country. The type of distributor to use is likely to vary from market to market, be it the Netherlands or Nigeria. The degree of political risk firms can expect in the latter case implies a need for a politically well-connected business partner. Similarly, in a nontraditional market such as Vietnam, the firm may opt for a partner who can serve both as a distributor and cultural adviser.

The local business partner is crucial to the success of the cross-border venture. Seasoned executives contend that even the most attractive country cannot compensate for a poor partner. While the quantity and quality of market information about individual countries have increased substantially, most managers tend to struggle in their ability to identify qualified and interested business partners. This is especially true in emerging markets that may lack an abundance of competent and professional intermediaries, suppliers, joint venture partners, or facilitators. The most qualified partners are likely to be already subscribed and representing other foreign firms. This necessitates the recruitment of second- or even third-best candidates, and then committing adequate resources to upgrade their technical and managerial skills.

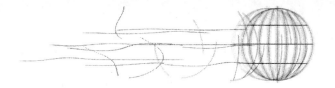

CLOSING CASE

Advanced Biomedical Devices: Assessing Readiness to Export

Advanced Biomedical Devices, Inc. (ABD), is headquartered in Maryland, and plans to initiate exporting activities. The company just completed the process of assessing its readiness to export, using CORE (**CO**mpany **Re**adiness to **E**xport). ABD was founded by Dr. Richard Bentley, a well-known British surgeon who developed a medical device that helps the wound-healing process. Dr. Bentley was so committed to the ground-breaking technology that he left his surgery practice and founded ABD in the United States. ABD's product line includes several innovative devices called Speedheal, named because of their ability to accelerate the healing rate of wounds following surgery. Speedheal also reduces post-surgery pain because it keeps the wound area from swelling. Speedheal oxygenates the wound area by pulsing electrons through the bandage covering the wound. The devices are very small and portable. Various versions exist for different types of surgeries: hand surgery, face lifts, abdominal procedures, and so on.

Dr. Bentley launched ABD with a skillful management team. The team includes managers who have worked extensively in the European market and have traveled and worked periodically in the Pacific Rim and Latin America. In addition, ABD's manufacturing director is from Germany, and another manager had lived in France and Malaysia for several years.

Substantial demand for Speedheal helped to rapidly increase sales, approaching 20 percent annual growth in some years. Over time, employment at ABD grew to 85 people and sales expanded, primarily through medical product distributors, to hospitals and clinics throughout the United States. The firm's success had stimulated the entry of competitors offering similar products, but rivals never achieved the degree of miniaturization in ABD's products. Miniaturization remains one of Speedheal's competitive advantages. ABD management's projections for future growth remain promising.

Dreams of International Expansion

Top management turned its thoughts to internationalization and generating sales outside of the United States. ABD had received unsolicited orders from abroad and had learned a great deal about handling international transactions, including foreign exchange, letters of credit, and logistics. While ABD's plan to internationalize was in its early stages, management intended to expand beyond occasional export sales. The long-term motivation was to target key world markets.

One expected benefit of internationalization was the opportunity for ABD to learn from global competitors and markets. Many trends that start in foreign markets eventually reach the United States, and often the best way to track them is to do business internationally. Management also believed it could reduce ABD's overall risks by selling to a variety of foreign markets. Finally, management believed that by internationalizing, competitors with similar products could be preempted in specific foreign markets.

International Strategic Intent

Dr. Bentley and his management team formulated some questions about ABD's internationalization decision. They knew that the answers to these questions would represent the company's first real strategic direction for going international, ABD's strategic intent. Management wanted to develop a comprehensive strategic plan that would lay the foundation for international success. Following a series of meetings, the team reached consensus on the following key elements of ABD's initial strategic direction:

- Top management will strongly commit to internationalization, and ABD will pursue foreign markets aggressively. The firm will hire a vice president for international operations within the coming year.

- ABD will invest up to 20 percent of the firm's earnings in export opportunities.

- ABD will begin building distributor relationships in a number of countries.

- ABD will establish a marketing subsidiary in at least one foreign location within three to five years, and hire sales personnel who select and manage the distributors in their market area.

- Management will take steps to ensure that all international ventures reach profitability within two years of their launch.

- Management will develop international marketing plans for each target market, each with its own budget.

- Plans call for international sales to reach 35 percent of total sales within four years.

- ABD will establish an annual budget of $220,000 to finance international activities for each of the first three years. Of that, about $60,000 will be devoted to market research to determine the best target markets and to understand competitors.

Product Readiness for Export

Following approval of the strategic intent, Dr. Bentley and his management team addressed questions about the challenges of internationalization. The first question dealt with training sales representatives in foreign markets to sell medical devices to hospitals and clinics, the primary end-markets for ABD products. Sales reps require training because they deal with doctors, nurses, and other professionals who are deeply involved in decision making about purchases of hospital supplies. Because training costs can be high in foreign markets, Dr. Bentley wanted to ensure ABD was prepared to make this investment as part of succeeding abroad.

Dr. Bentley also raised the issue of after-sales service. Because ABD's products were seldom defective, the solution for a defective product was to replace it rather than trying to make a repair. U.S. customers counted on a ready backup stock in the event of product defects. ABD planned to employ the same solution for its foreign operations, and management assumed there would be no need for a separate staff to deal with after-sales service. Because Speedheal devices are small and lightweight but valuable, per-unit transportation costs are very low. In fact, in urgent situations abroad, ABD often solved customer service complaints by shipping a replacement device by air.

Eventually, the management team came to realize that pricing for foreign markets was complex and would require substantial market research. While pricing in the United States was well understood, management realized there was much it did not know about foreign pricing. Dr. Bentley and several managers had attended trade fairs in Europe and had concluded that ABD's prices were not too expensive, particularly since no other firms offered similar wound-healing products. In fact, ABD had filled unsolicited orders from the European Union and found that customers never challenged its pricing. Nevertheless, management decided that some research was needed to refine their pricing approach.

Next, the team discussed foreign inventory management. Because the devices are cheap to transport by air freight, distributors can replenish inventories quickly and economically. This was a significant benefit to distributors, on the one hand, because they would not have to maintain much inventory to support sales. On the other hand, Speedheal devices are sensitive to changes in temperature and humidity, and function best when warehoused in climate-controlled facilities. Such warehousing is increasingly common, so ABD should have no problem locating the right warehousing in Europe and elsewhere.

ABD's management realized that the firm's flexible packaging put them in a good position to enter foreign markets, and they were prepared to modify the product in various ways that might be required for foreign markets.

Management instinctively understood the importance of designing products that meet worldwide standards and regulations. The team knew, for example, that products targeted to Europe would have to meet two standards: the CE mark, a mandatory safety mark required of toys, machinery, and low-voltage equipment; and ISO standards, aimed at making the development, manufacturing, and supply of products and services efficient, safe, and clean.

Knowledge, Skills, and Resources

In a subsequent meeting, the ABD team considered less-tangible aspects of the firm's readiness to internationalize. Management knew that critical self-assessment was vital to the long-term success of the firm. They gradually realized that internationalization would incur numerous additional costs. For example, they needed additional working capital for foreign warehousing, longer shipping times, and maintaining larger inventories abroad. While letters of credit would be used when first opening new markets, management would opt for open-account payment systems (payable in 30 or 60 days, depending on the market).

Dr. Bentley also considered the appropriate growth rate for the firm. Management knew of companies that began exporting but were interrupted when foreign demand grew too quickly, or when an imbalance developed between domestic and international sales. In some cases, a company's business could increase rapidly, demanding the firm to supply a volume of product that greatly exceeded production capacity. In other cases, the company's domestic sales dropped sharply, requiring management to divert all efforts to rescuing domestic operations, thus disrupting the export program.

Management had much to learn about the costs ABD would incur in getting into specific foreign markets. There would be costs for legal help, freight forwarding, international transportation, and customs duties. There would also be costs for bank charges, rental costs for establishing foreign offices, and expenses for getting approvals for certain regulatory issues. ABD's management was not completely clear on the amount of these costs, but they were willing to learn.

Competitive intelligence was another concern. In fact, another incentive for internationalization was to learn more about global competitors. While some of the major medical device manufacturers were marketing in the United States, others were based strictly abroad. ABD would have to research and understand the strategies and marketing practices of the important competitors. Dr. Bentley recognized the importance of getting patent coverage on his inventions around the world, and of protecting the intellectual property rights of his firm. He plans to retain legal counsel, at home and abroad, to ensure ABD's critical assets are protected from patent infringements. ABD plans to hire lawyers to develop suitable distribution and agent agreements, sales agreements, licensing, and to deal with local employment laws.

ABD's management believed the firm's initial foreign markets would be Australia, Canada, Western Europe, and Japan, because they have the largest proportion of affluent consumers with the ability to pay for sophisticated medical care. Therefore, ABD had gathered information about the markets and competition in those countries, but recognized that it needed to do much more.

Managerial Capabilities for Long-Term Internationalization

One concern was whether management would be able to cope with deepening internationalization. In the end, the ABD team recognized that, at minimum, they were right to take painstaking efforts to determine the firm's readiness to export. Extensive meetings and preliminary research provided the basis for developing initial strategies and action programs, as well as the basis for identifying improvements to make the company stronger in the coming months and years.

This case was written by Myron M. Miller, Michigan State University (retired), in association with Professor S. Tamer Cavusgil.

AACSB: Reflective Thinking, Analytical Skills
Case Questions

1. Do you believe that ABD's products are in a state of readiness to begin exporting to Europe? Why or why not? Are the products ready for exporting to emerging markets (e.g., China, Russia, Mexico) that may have little experience with the high-tech solutions afforded by Speedheal products? What factors suggest that Speedheal products might enjoy substantial demand in all types of foreign markets?

2. Does management at ABD possess the appropriate knowledge, skills, and capabilities for internationalization? Why or why not? What steps should management take to better prepare the firm, managers, and employees to internationalize?

3. Refer to Exhibit 12.1, "Key Tasks in Global Market Opportunity Assessment" on page 348. Evaluate if ABD accomplished each task well or poorly. Did ABD achieve each of the objectives set out for the tasks?

4. If you were a member of ABD's management team, what countries would you recommend that ABD target first? As a manager, you would need to justify your recommendation. Carry out an investigation by examining characteristics of specific countries to arrive at your recommendation. ◀

CHAPTER ESSENTIALS

Key Terms

company sales potential
franchising
global market opportunity

industry market potential
international collaborative venture
licensing

Summary

In this chapter, you learned about:

1. An overview of global market opportunity assessment

Global market opportunity assessment refers to a favorable combination of circumstances, locations, or timing that offer prospects for exporting, investing, sourcing, or partnering in foreign markets. The firm may perceive opportunities to sell, establish factories, obtain inputs of lower cost or superior quality, or enter collaborative arrangements with foreign partners that support the focal firm's goals. Global market opportunities help the firm improve its performance, often far beyond what it can achieve in the home market. Managers continuously seek the most relevant data and knowledge to make the most of international opportunities. This chapter discusses six key tasks that managers perform in defining and pursuing global market opportunities. See Exhibit 12.1 for a summary of these tasks.

2. Analysis of organizational readiness to internationalize

As the first task, management assesses the firm's readiness to internationalize. Similar to a SWOT analysis (that is, an evaluation of the firm's Strengths, Weaknesses, Opportunities, and Threats), management assesses the firm's strengths and weaknesses regarding its ability to do international business. Managers assess the *external* business environment by conducting formal research on the opportunities and threats that face the firm. The objective of assessing readiness to internationalize is to figure out what resources the firm has and the extent to which they are appropriate for successful international operations. The firm must develop resources that it lacks. Diagnostic tools, such as *CORE* (**CO**mpany **R**eadiness to **E**xport), facilitate a self-audit of the firm's readiness to internationalize.

3. Assessment of the suitability of products and services for foreign markets

Products and services that are good candidates for marketing successfully abroad are those that sell well in the domestic market, cater to universal needs, address a need not well served in the target market, or address a new or emergent need abroad. Management should ask specific questions to determine the product's or service's international market potential. For example, who initiates purchasing in the market? Who uses the offering? Why do people buy it? Where is the product or service purchased? What economic, cultural, geographic, and other factors can limit sales?

4. Screening countries to identify target markets

Whether the firm is engaged in importing (sourcing from abroad), investing, or exporting, the choice of country is critical, particularly in the early stages of internationalization. Failure to choose the right markets is costly not only for its own sake, but also because of opportunity costs. The best markets are those that are large and fast-growing. The nature of information necessary for country screening varies by product type and industry. There are two basic methods for screening country markets: gradual elimination and ranking and indexing.

5. Assessment of industry market potential

Once a firm reduces the number of potential country targets to a manageable number—say five or six—the next step is to conduct in-depth analyses of each of these country markets. The researcher examines industry-level market potential indicators. **Industry market potential** refers to an estimate of the likely sales that can be expected for all firms in the particular industry for a specific period of time. An estimate of industry market potential enables the manager to hone in on a few most promising countries. In addition to generic determinants of demand, each industry sector has its own *industry-specific potential indicators.* Among the methods for assessing industry market potential are simple trend analysis, monitoring key industry-specific indicators, monitoring key competitors, following key customers around the world, tapping into supplier networks, and attending international trade fairs.

6. **Selection of foreign business partners**

   International business partners include distribution channel intermediaries, facilitators, suppliers, and collaborative venture partners such as joint venture partners, licensees, and franchisees. Management in the focal firm must decide the types of partners it needs, identify suitable partner candidates, negotiate the terms of relationships with chosen partners, and support as well as monitor the conduct of chosen partners.

7. **Estimation of company sales potential**

   Company sales potential refers to the share of annual industry sales that the firm can realistically achieve. It is the best estimate of how much the firm believes it can sell in the target market over a given time period. Estimating company sales potential requires the researcher to obtain highly refined information from the market. Among the most influential determinants of company sales potential are: partner capabilities, access to distribution channels in the target market, intensity of the competitive environment, pricing and financing of sales, quality of human and financial resources, the timetable for market entry, risk tolerance of senior managers, the firm's contacts and capabilities, and being well-known in the market.

Test Your Comprehension AACSB: Reflective Thinking

1. What is a global market opportunity? What opportunities do firms seek abroad?

2. Identify and explain the six major tasks that managers undertake in global market opportunity assessment.

3. Identify the major issues that managers consider when they perform a formal analysis of organizational readiness to internationalize.

4. What are the typical characteristics of products or services that have the best prospects for selling in foreign markets?

5. Summarize the screening methodology for potential country markets.

6. What are the typical variables used in indexing and ranking method?

7. What types of variables should the researcher consider when screening for export markets, foreign direct investment, and global sourcing?

8. What is involved in assessing industry market potential?

9. What are the major issues to consider when selecting foreign business partners?

10. How can firms go about estimating company sales potential?

Apply Your Understanding AACSB: Communication, Reflective Thinking

1. Target is a large retailer with about 1,500 stores in the United States, but very few in other countries. Target has a reputation for merchandising thousands of chic yet inexpensive products for the home, including apparel, furniture, electronics, sporting goods, and toys. Management is looking to open stores in major European cities, but due to limited floor space, it is unable to offer all its usual products. Target hires you as a consultant to decide which products from the firm's U.S. product line to offer in Europe. In other words, your task is to identify Target products suitable for global business. Although a challenging task, you know of various criteria that Target can apply to identify the most appropriate products. Write a brief report in which you describe these criteria and offer some examples to back up your ideas. Be sure to justify your answer using the advice and other information included in this chapter.

2. Cuesta Corporation, an SME manufacturer of various types of scented hand and body soaps, hires Victoria Ridge to locate foreign markets. She seeks your help in deciding how to proceed. You have decided to lend Victoria a hand, before she washes out of the soap business. You advise Victoria that markets for scented soap are fairly saturated within advanced

economies. However, you are aware of numerous *emerging markets* that the industry has overlooked. Using your knowledge of Exhibit 12.2, "Emerging Market Potential Indicators," on pages 356–357 develop a list of the top five emerging markets that Victoria should target. These are the emerging markets that, based on your research, offer the greatest prospects for generating sales. Be sure to justify your choice of countries, based on indicators from this chapter such as market size, market growth rate, market intensity, and market consumption capacity.

3. Upon graduation, a company that makes and sells accessories for luxury automobiles hires you. The company hopes to expand into foreign markets. Your boss comes into your office and hands you a list of countries that he believes hold the greatest potential for international sales. You peruse the list and notice that your boss has based his analysis on per capita income levels of the target countries, reasoning that consumers with the highest incomes are most likely to own luxury cars. Nevertheless, his analysis is based on traditional per capita income, without regard to purchasing power parity. In addition, you feel that some other key indicators of demand are neglected. Mustering your courage, you decide to propose an improved methodology for picking countries. What should be the principal features of this methodology?

globalEDGE Internet Exercises
(http://globalEDGE.msu.edu)

AACSB: Reflective Thinking, Use of Information Technology

Refer to Chapter 1, page 27, for instructions on how to access and use globalEDGE™.

1. China is an attractive market partly because of its large size and growing affluence. Before they begin exporting to China, most firms conduct market research to acquire a fuller understanding of the country's market situation. Two useful sites for conducting research are the China Business Information Center (CBIC; www.export.gov/china) and UK Trade and Investment (www.uktradeinvest.gov.uk). At the CBIC, for example, firms can find out if they are "China Ready." They can access trade leads and read current news about doing business in China. Suppose you get a job with a firm that markets various products, including: (a) breakfast cereal, (b) popular music on CDs, and (c) laptop computers, and wants to begin exporting to China. For each of these three product categories, using the Web sites given above and globalEDGE™, prepare a wish list of the information that the firm should gather prior to making a decision to export to China.

2. Wal-Mart is now the largest retailer in the United States, Canada, and Mexico. However, Wal-Mart still gets only about a quarter of its sales from outside the United States. Coles Myer is the largest retailer in Australia, and gets very little of its sales from outside Australia (its main foreign market is nearby New Zealand). Assess the international retailing sector using online resources, such as globalEDGE™ and A. T. Kearney (www.atkearney.com). Based on your research: (a) What factors should these top retailers consider in choosing countries for internationalizing their operations? (b) What are the best target markets for these companies to expand to? (c) What types of questions should management at each firm ask in assessing their readiness to internationalize?

3. The U.S. Census Bureau tracks foreign trade statistics. Visit the site at www.census.gov and find the most recent versions of the report "Profile of U.S. Exporting Companies" by entering this title in the search engine. Peruse the report and address the following questions: (a) What types of companies export from the United States? That is, what is the breakdown by company type of U.S. exporters? For example, are the exporters mainly large or small firms? Do they operate mainly in the manufacturing, agricultural, or services sectors? (b) What is the role of small and medium-sized exporters in U.S. trade? What percent of U.S. exporters are these types of firms, and what proportion of total exports do they account for? (c) What countries are the three favorite targets of U.S. exporters? According to the report, what factors make these countries the top markets for U.S. firms?

Management Skill Builder©

Global Market Opportunity Assessment for Cancer Insurance

Cancer is a leading cause of premature death. Major types of cancer include skin, lung, stomach, breast, and prostate cancer. It is a life-threatening disease that is often difficult and expensive to treat, with medical bills running into the hundreds of thousands of dollars. In many countries, people buy health insurance to pay the costs of medical care. Health insurance companies such as AFLAC and American International Group (AIG) specialize in supplemental policies to cover specialized cancer care.

AACSB: Reflective Thinking, Analytical Skills

Managerial Challenge

Given limited resources, managers must identify the most appropriate countries to target with their products and services. Because decisions about which markets to enter can be very challenging, managers conduct research on the available choices. Initially, managers systematically narrow the number of potential target countries using *Global Market Opportunity Assessment*. In this exercise, your challenge is to assess markets for supplemental cancer insurance in various countries.

Background

Companies and governments often provide citizens with basic medical insurance. However, these policies may not fully cover the high cost of life-threatening ailments such as cancer. Moreover, most people lack comprehensive health insurance against cancer. Thus, people often purchase supplemental health insurance. A sizeable market for comprehensive cancer insurance exists around the world. There are numerous health insurance companies that offer cancer insurance. When seeking to sell insurance abroad, these firms need to find out what countries offer the best sales prospects. Because the choice of potential markets can be overwhelming, managers use Global Market Opportunity Assessment (GMOA).

Managerial Skills You Will Gain

In this C/K/R Management Skill Builder©, as a prospective manager, you will:

1. Learn the factors to consider when screening countries for foreign market entry.

2. Understand how these factors relate to maximizing the firm's competitive advantages.

3. Screen foreign markets to identify the most appropriate markets to target with the firm's products and services.

Your Task

In this exercise, your task is to conduct a *Global Market Opportunity Assessment* to identify the most promising country to target for sales of supplemental cancer insurance. You will examine variables that can help you estimate the size of relevant industry sales within each of four possible target countries. Your assessment of each target country will be based on industry-specific indicators of demand for cancer insurance.

Go to the C/K/R Knowledge Portal©

www.prenhall.com/cavusgil

Proceed to the C/K/R Knowledge Portal© to obtain the expanded background information, your task and methodology, suggested resources for this exercise, and the presentation template.

Section 3
Strategies and Structures

chapter

11

Global Strategy and Organization

Learning Objectives

In this chapter, you will learn about:

1. The role of strategy in international business

2. The integration-responsiveness framework

3. Distinct strategies emerging from the integration-responsiveness framework

4. Organizational structure

5. Alternative organizational arrangements for international operations

6. Building the global firm

7. Putting organizational change in motion

> ## IKEA's Global Strategy

Furniture retailer IKEA is a Swedish company that has transformed itself into a global organization over the past three decades. Ingvar Kamprad founded the firm in Sweden in 1943 when he was 17 years old. IKEA originally sold pens, picture frames, jewelry, and nylon stockings—any product that Kamprad could sell at a low price. In 1950, IKEA began selling furniture and housewares. In the 1970s, the company began expanding into Europe and North America. IKEA's philosophy is to offer quality, well-designed furnishings at low prices. The company designs "knock-down" furniture that the customer purchases and then assembles at home. Designs implement functional, utilitarian, and space-saving features, with a distinctive Scandinavian style.

IKEA Group sales for the fiscal year 2006 totaled 17.3 billion euros, making IKEA the largest furniture retailer in the world. Its stores, usually located in major cities, are mammoth, warehouse-style outlets, with each stocking approximately 9,500 items, including everything for the home—from sofas to plants to kitchen utensils.

IKEA is now owned by a Dutch-registered foundation controlled by the Kamprad family. Its corporate offices are in the Netherlands, Sweden, and Belgium.

520   International Business

Product development, purchasing, and warehousing are concentrated in Sweden. Headquarters designs and develops IKEA's global product line and branding, often in close collaboration with external suppliers. Approximately 30 percent of the merchandise is made in Asia, and two-thirds in Europe. A few items are sourced in North America to address the specific needs of that market, but 90 percent of IKEA's product line is identical worldwide. Managers at IKEA stores feed market research back to headquarters in Sweden on sales and customer preferences.

IKEA targets people all over the world, with a focus on families with limited income and limited living space. This global segment is characterized by liberal-minded, well-educated, white-collar people—including college students—who care little about status and view foreign products positively. Targeting a global customer segment allows IKEA to offer standardized products at uniform prices, a strategy that minimizes the costs of international operations. IKEA seeks scale economies by consolidating worldwide design, purchasing, and manufacturing. It distinguishes itself from conventional furniture makers that serve fragmented markets. Its designers work closely with contract suppliers around the world to ensure savings, high volume, and high standards.

Each IKEA store follows a centrally developed communications strategy. The catalogue is the most important marketing tool. In 2006, 175 million copies were printed in 27 languages, representing the largest circulation of a free publication in the world. The catalogue, also available online (www.ikea.com), is prepared in Sweden to assure conformity to the IKEA look. The catalogue conforms to IKEA's cosmopolitan style. Each product has a unique, proper name. For sofas, IKEA uses Scandinavian rivers or cities (Henriksberg, Falkenberg), women's names for fabric (Linne, Mimmi, Adel), and men's names for wall units (Billy, Niklas, Ivar).

IKEA's employees ("co-workers") across the globe are widely acknowledged as the basis for the firm's success. Corporate culture is informal. There are few titles, no executive parking spaces, and no corporate dining room. Managers fly economy class and stay in inexpensive hotels. Regional organizations are minimized so that stores maintain direct contact with IKEA in Sweden. This speeds decision making and ensures that the IKEA culture is easily globalized. Management in each store is required to speak either English or Swedish, to ensure efficient communications with headquarters.

IKEA organizes an "antibureaucratic week" each year in which managers wear sales clerks' uniforms and do everything from operating cash registers to driving forklifts. By using this system, managers stay in touch with all of IKEA's operations and remain close to suppliers, customers, and salespeople. The firm's culture emphasizes consensus-based decision making and problem solving, and managers readily share their knowledge and skills with co-workers. IKEA's distinct culture helps employees and suppliers feel they are an important part of a global organization. This culture has a strong global appeal, supporting IKEA's continued growth.

How does a company like IKEA manage its operations across 35 countries, 240 stores, more than 100,000 employees, 20 franchises, and 2,000 suppliers? Part of the complexity comes from having to adapt to local regulations on labor laws, store operations, unique supplier relationships, and shopping preferences. Among other challenges, IKEA must figure out how to:

1. Ensure valuable customer feedback (for example, design preferences) from individual markets reach decision makers at headquarters

2. Reward employees and motivate suppliers with expectations that vary from country to country

3. Achieve the real benefits of international operations—efficiency on a global scale and learning—while remaining responsive to local needs

4. Keep designs standardized across markets, yet be able to respond to local preferences and trends

5. Delegate adequate autonomy to local store managers while retaining central control

Sources: Coppola, V. (2002). "Furniture as Fashion Wins Ikea." *Adweek*, Feb. 25, pp. 12–13; Duff, M. (2003). "IKEA Eyes Aggressive Growth," *DSN Retailing Today* Jan. 27, p. 23; www.businessweek.com, "Online Extra: IKEA's Design for Growth," June 6, 2005; www.businessweek.com, "IKEA: How the Swedish Retailer became a Global Cult Brand," November 14, 2005; IKEA corporate web site at www.IKEA-group.IKEA.com; IKEA company profile at Hoovers, at *www.hoovers.com*

Globalization has increased the speed, frequency, and magnitude by which firms from diverse industries can access international markets for customers. Managers are evolving their internationalization strategies to transform their organizations into globally competitive enterprises. As the IKEA vignette shows, managers are striving to coordinate sourcing, manufacturing, marketing, and other value-adding activities on a worldwide basis. They seek to eliminate redundancy and adopt organization-wide standards and common processes. Some managers, like those at IKEA, try to nurture products that may gain the approval of a global clientele and become global brands. Nevertheless, organizing the firm on a global scale is very challenging. It requires strategic positioning, organizational capabilities, alignment of value-adding activities on a worldwide basis, a high degree of coordination and integration, attention to the needs of individual markets, and implementation of common processes.

In this chapter, we discuss the role of strategy and alternative structural arrangements in building a globally integrated enterprise. In the next chapter, we follow up with a discussion of how managers can go about identifying global market opportunities.

 ## The Role of Strategy in International Business

Strategy is a plan of action that channels an organization's resources so that it can effectively differentiate itself from competitors and accomplish unique and viable goals. Managers develop strategies based on their examination of the organization's strengths and weaknesses relative to its competition and the opportunities it faces. Managers decide which customers to target, what product lines to offer, and with which firms to compete.

Strategy in the international context is a plan for the organization to position itself positively from its competitors and configure its value-adding activities on a global scale. It guides the firm toward chosen customers, markets, products, and services in the global marketplace, not necessarily in a particular international market.[1] As a minimum, strategy in the international context should help managers to formulate a strong international vision, allocate scarce resources on a worldwide basis, participate in major markets, implement global partnerships, engage in competitive moves in response to global rivals, and configure value-adding activities on a global scale.[2]

What is the role of strategy in creating competitive advantage in international business? It has been argued that an effective international strategy begins with developing a standardized product that can be produced and sold the same way in multiple countries.[3] Kenichi Ohmae[4] argues that delivering value to customers worldwide is the overriding goal, while other observers stress achieving strategic flexibility.[5] The idea of exploiting scale economies by building global volume and deriving synergies across the firm's different activities is also relevant.[6] Managers should also build a strong worldwide distribution system and use profits from successful products and markets to subsidize the development of other products and markets.[7]

The most widely accepted prescription for building sustainable, competitive advantage in international business is that of Bartlett and Ghoshal.[8] They argue that managers should look to "develop, *at one and the same time*, global scale efficiency, multinational flexibility, and the ability to develop innovations and leverage knowledge on a worldwide basis."[9] They propose that the firm that aspires to become a globally competitive enterprise must seek simultaneously these three strategic objectives—efficiency, flexibility, and learning. Let's review each objective.

Efficiency *The firm must build efficient international supply chains.* Efficiency refers to lowering the cost of the firm's operations and activities on a global scale. Multinational enterprises with multiple value chains around the world must pay special attention to how they organize their R&D, manufacturing, sourcing product, marketing, and customer service activities. For example, automotive companies such as Toyota strive to achieve scale economies by concentrating manufacturing and sourcing activities in a limited number of locations around the world.

Flexibility *The firm must develop worldwide flexibility to manage diverse country-specific risks and opportunities.* The diversity and volatility of the international environment is a special challenge for managers. Therefore, the firm's ability to tap

Strategy A plan of action that channels an organization's resources so that it can effectively differentiate itself from competitors and accomplish unique and viable goals.

Strategy in the international context A plan for the organization to position itself positively from its competitors and configure its value-adding activities on a global scale.

local resources and exploit local opportunities is critical. For example, managers may opt for contractual relationships with independent suppliers and distributors in one country while engaging in direct investment in another. Or, the firm may adapt its marketing and human resource management practices to suit its unique country conditions (we discuss marketing and human resource management issues in chapters 17 and 18). Changing environmental circumstances, such as exchange rate fluctuations, may prompt managers to switch to local sourcing or to adjust prices.

Learning *The firm must create the ability to learn from international exposure and exploit learning on a worldwide basis.* The diversity of the global environment presents the internationalizing firm with unique learning opportunities. Even though the firm goes abroad to exploit its unique advantages, such as technology, brand name, or management capabilities, managers can add to the stock of capabilities by internalizing new knowledge gained from international exposure. Thus, the organization can acquire new technical and managerial know-how, new product ideas, improved R&D capabilities, partnering skills, and survival capabilities in unfamiliar environments. The firm's partners or subsidiaries can capture and disseminate this learning throughout their corporate network. For example, it was Procter & Gamble's research center in Brussels that developed a special capability in water-softening technology, primarily because European water contains more minerals than water in the United States. Similarly, the company learned to formulate a different kind of detergent in Japan, where customers wash their clothes in colder water than in the United States or Europe.

In the final analysis, international business success is largely determined by the degree to which the firm achieves its goals of efficiency, flexibility, and learning. But it is often difficult to excel in all three areas simultaneously. Rather, one firm may excel at efficiency while another may excel at flexibility, and a third at learning. In the 1980s, for example, many Japanese MNEs achieved international success by developing highly efficient and centralized manufacturing systems. In Europe, numerous MNEs have succeeded by being locally responsive while sometimes failing to achieve substantial economic efficiency or technological leadership. Many MNEs based in the United States have struggled to adapt their activities to the cultural and political diversity of national environments, and instead have proven to be more skillful at achieving efficiency via scale economies.

Strategy in Multidomestic and Global Industries

Companies in the food and beverage, consumer products, and clothing and fashion industries may often resort to a country-by-country approach to marketing to specific needs and tastes, laws, and regulations. Industries in which competition takes place on a country-by-country basis are known as **multidomestic industries**. In such industries, each country tends to have a unique set of competitors.

By contrast, industries such as aerospace, automobiles, telecommunications, metals, computers, chemicals, and industrial equipment are examples of **global industries**, in which competition is on a regional or worldwide scale. Formulating and implementing strategy is more critical for global industries than multidomestic industries. Most global industries are characterized by the existence of a handful of major players that compete head-on in multiple markets. For example, Kodak must contend with the same rivals—Japan's Fuji and the European multinational, Agfa-Gevaert—wherever it does business around the world. Similarly, American Standard and Toto dominate the worldwide bathroom fixtures market. In the earthmoving equipment industry, Caterpillar and Komatsu compete head-on in all major world markets.

Multidomestic industry An industry in which competition takes place on a country-by-country basis.

Global industry An industry in which competition is on a regional or worldwide scale.

The Integration-Responsiveness Framework

Since efficiency and learning objectives are often related, they are frequently combined into a single dimension, called global integration. **Global integration** refers to the coordination of the firm's value-chain activities across countries to achieve worldwide efficiency, synergy, and cross-fertilization in order to take maximum advantage of similarities between countries. The flexibility objective is also called local responsiveness. **Local responsiveness** refers to meeting the specific needs of buyers in individual countries.

The discussion about the pressures on the firm to achieve the dual objectives of global integration and local responsiveness has become known as the *integration-responsiveness (IR) framework*.[10] The IR framework, shown in Exhibit 11.1, was developed to help managers better understand the trade-offs between global integration and local responsiveness.

In companies that are locally responsive, managers adjust the firm's practices to suit distinctive conditions in each market. They adapt to customer needs, the competitive environment, and the local distribution structure. Thus, Wal-Mart store managers in Mexico adjust store hours, employee training, compensation, the merchandise mix, and promotional tools to suit conditions in Mexico. Firms in multidomestic industries such as food, retailing, and book publishing tend to be locally responsive because language and cultural differences strongly influence buyer behavior in these industries

In contrast, global integration seeks economic efficiency on a worldwide scale, promoting learning and cross-fertilization within the global network and reducing redundancy. Headquarters personnel justify global integration by citing converging demand patterns, spread of global brands, diffusion of uniform technology, availability of panregional media, and the need to monitor competitors on a global basis. Thus, designing numerous variations of the same basic product for individual markets will only add to overall costs and should be avoided. Firms in global industries such as aircraft manufacturing, credit cards, and pharmaceuticals are more likely to emphasize global integration.

Global integration
Coordination of the firm's value-chain activities across countries to achieve worldwide efficiency, synergy, and cross-fertilization in order to take maximum advantage of similarities between countries.

Local responsiveness
Meeting the specific needs of buyers in individual countries.

The need to:

■ Seek cost reduction through scale economies

■ Capitalize on converging consumer trends and universal needs

■ Provide uniform service to global customers

■ Conduct global sourcing

■ Monitor and respond to global competitors

■ Take advantage of media with cross-national reach

The need to:

■ Leverage national endowments such as local talent

■ Cater to local customer needs

■ Accommodate differences in distribution channels

■ Respond to local competition

■ Adjust to cultural differences

■ Meet host government requirements and regulations

Vertical axis: Pressures for global integration (Weak to Strong)
Horizontal axis: Weak — Pressures for local responsiveness — Strong

Exhibit 11.1

Integration-Responsiveness Framework: Competing Pressures on the Internationalizing Firm

Pressures for Local Responsiveness

There are various factors that compel the firm to become locally responsive in the countries where it conducts business.[11] These factors are:

- *Unique natural endowments available to the firm.* Each country has national endowments that the foreign firm should access.

- *Diversity of local customer needs.* Businesses, such as clothing and food, require significant adaptation to local customer needs.

- *Differences in distribution channels.* These vary considerably from market to market and may increase the need for local responsiveness. For example, small retailers in Japan understand local customs and needs, so locally responsive MNEs use them to distribute products in that country.

- *Local competition.* When competing against numerous local rivals, centrally controlled MNEs will have difficulty gaining market share with global products that are not adapted to local needs.

- *Cultural differences.* Cultural characteristics influence consumer buying decisions. The influence of cultural differences may vary considerably, depending on the type of product. For those products where cultural differences are important, such as clothing and furniture, local managers require considerable freedom from headquarters to adapt their product and marketing practices.

- *Host government requirements and regulations.* When governments impose trade barriers or complex business regulations, they can halt or reverse the competitive threat of foreign firms. The MNE may establish a local subsidiary with substantial decision-making authority to minimize the effects of protectionism.

Pressures for Global Integration

Another set of factors compels the firm to coordinate its activities across countries in an attempt to build efficient operations.[12] These are:

- *Economies of scale.* Concentrating manufacturing in a few select locations where the firm can profit from economies of mass production motivates global integration. Also, the smaller the number of manufacturing and R&D locations, the easier it is for the firm to control quality and cost.

- *Capitalize on converging consumer trends and universal needs.* Standardization is appropriate for products with widespread acceptance and whose features, quality, and cost are similar worldwide. Examples include computer chips and electronic components. Companies such as Nike, Dell, ING, and Coca-Cola offer products that appeal to consumers everywhere.

- *Uniform service to global customers.* Services are easiest to standardize when firms can centralize their creation and delivery. Multinational enterprises with operations in numerous countries particularly value service inputs that are consistent worldwide.

- *Global sourcing of raw materials, components, energy, and labor.* Firms face an ongoing pressure to procure high-quality input goods in a cost-efficient manner. Sourcing of inputs from large-scale, centralized suppliers provides benefits from economies of scale and more consistent performance outcomes. Sourcing from a few well-integrated suppliers is more efficient than sourcing from numerous loosely connected distributors.

- *Global competitors.* Competitors that operate in multiple markets threaten firms with purely domestic operations. Global coordination is necessary to monitor and respond to competitive threats in foreign and domestic markets.

* *Availability of media that reaches consumers in multiple markets.* The availability of cost-effective communications and promotion makes it possible for firms to cater to global market segments that cross different countries. For example, firms now take advantage of the Internet and cross-national television to simultaneously advertise their offerings in numerous countries.

 ## Distinct Strategies Emerging from the Integration-Responsiveness Framework

The integration-responsiveness framework presents four distinct strategies for internationalizing firms. Exhibit 11.2 illustrates these strategies. Internationalizing firms pursue one or a combination of four major types of strategies. In general, multidomestic industries favor home replication and multidomestic strategies, while global industries favor global and transnational strategies.

With a **home replication strategy** (sometimes called *export strategy* or *international strategy*), the firm views international business as separate from, and secondary to, its domestic business. Early in its internationalization process, such a firm may view international business as an opportunity to generate incremental sales for domestic product lines. Typically, products are designed with domestic customers in mind, and international business is sought as a way of extending the product life cycle and replicating its home-market success. The firm expects little knowledge flows from foreign operations.[13]

A second approach is **multidomestic strategy** (sometimes called *multilocal strategy*), whereby an internationalizing firm delegates considerable autonomy to each country manager, allowing him or her to operate independently and pursue local responsiveness. With this strategy, managers recognize and emphasize differences between national markets. As a result, the internationalizing firm allows

Home replication strategy
An approach in which the firm views international business as separate from and secondary to its domestic business.

Multidomestic strategy An approach to firm internationalization where headquarters delegates considerable autonomy to each country manager, allowing him or her to operate independently and pursue local responsiveness.

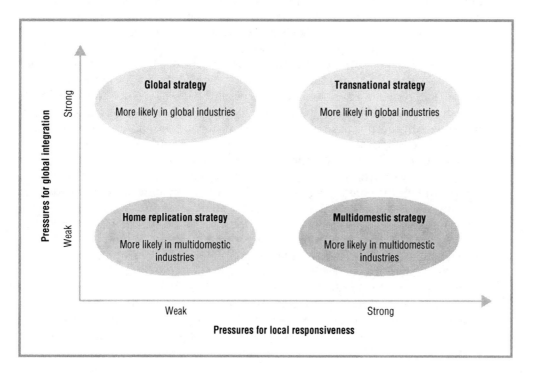

Exhibit 11.2

Four Distinct Strategies Emerging from the Integration-Responsiveness Framework

subsidiaries to vary product and management practices by country. Country managers tend to be highly independent entrepreneurs, often nationals of the host country.[14] They function independently and have little incentive to share knowledge and experience with managers in other countries. Products and services are carefully adapted to suit the unique needs of each country.

Firms that pursue a multidomestic strategy relinquish considerable autonomy to foreign subsidiaries and exercise little central control. The multidomestic approach has several advantages. If the foreign subsidiary includes a factory, locally produced goods and products can be better adapted to local markets. The approach places minimal pressure on headquarters staff because management of country operations is delegated to individual managers in each country. Firms with limited internationalization experience often find multidomestic strategy an easy option, as they can delegate many tasks to their country managers (or foreign distributors, franchisees, or licensees, where they are used).

Nevertheless, multidomestic strategy has some disadvantages. The firm's foreign subsidiary managers tend to develop strategic vision, culture, and processes that differ substantially from those of headquarters. They have little incentive to share knowledge and experience with managers in the firm's other country markets, which leads to duplication of activities and reduced economies of scale. Limited information sharing also reduces the possibility of developing a knowledge-based competitive advantage.[15] Competition may escalate between the subsidiaries for the firm's resources because subsidiary managers do not share a common corporate vision. While a multidomestic strategy results in firms having a highly responsive presence in different national markets, it leads to inefficient manufacturing, redundant operations, a proliferation of products designed to meet local needs, and generally higher cost of international operations than other strategies.[16]

These disadvantages may eventually lead management to abandon multidomestic strategy in favor of a third approach—**global strategy**. With this strategy, headquarters seeks substantial control over its country operations in an effort to minimize redundancy and achieve maximum efficiency, learning, and integration worldwide. In the extreme case, global strategy asks why not make "the same thing, the same way, everywhere?"[17] In this way, global strategy emphasizes greater central coordination and control than multidomestic strategy, with various product or business managers having worldwide responsibility. Activities such as R&D and manufacturing are centralized at headquarters, and management tends to view the world as one large marketplace.

Global strategy offers many advantages: It provides management with a greater capability to respond to worldwide opportunities, increases opportunities for cross-national learning and cross-fertilization of the firm's knowledge base among all the subsidiaries, and creates economies of scale, which results in lower operational costs. Global strategy can also improve the quality of products and processes—primarily by simplifying manufacturing and other processes. High-quality products promote global brand recognition and give rise to consumer preference and efficient international marketing programs.

The ability of firms to pursue global strategy has been facilitated by many factors, including the converging needs and tastes of consumers around the world, the growing acceptance of global brands, the increasing diffusion of uniform technology (especially in industrial markets), the integrating effects of the Internet and e-commerce, the integration of markets through economic blocs and financial globalization, and the spread of international collaborative ventures.

As in other approaches, global strategy has its limitations. It is challenging for management to closely coordinate the activities of a large number of widely dispersed international operations. The firm must maintain an ongoing communication between headquarters and its subsidiaries, as well as between the subsidiaries. When carried to an extreme, global strategy results in a loss of responsiveness and flexibility in local markets. Local managers who are stripped

Global strategy An approach where headquarters seeks substantial control over its country operations in an effort to minimize redundancy and achieve maximum efficiency, learning, and integration worldwide.

of autonomy over their country operations may become demoralized and lose their entrepreneurial spirit.

A final alternative is **transnational strategy**, a coordinated approach to internationalization in which the firm strives to be more responsive to local needs while retaining sufficient central control of operations to ensure efficiency and learning. Transnational strategy combines the major advantages of multidomestic and global strategies while minimizing their disadvantages.[18] Transnational strategy implies a flexible approach: *standardize where feasible; adapt where appropriate.* In practice, managers implement transnational strategy by:

* Exploiting scale economies by sourcing from a reduced set of global suppliers and concentrating the production of offerings in relatively few locations where competitive advantage can be maximized

* Organizing production, marketing, and other value-chain activities on a global scale

* Optimizing local responsiveness and flexibility

* Facilitating global learning and knowledge transfer

* Coordinating *competitive moves*— that is, how the firm deals with its competitors, on a global, integrated basis[19]

Transnational strategy requires planning, resource allocation, and uniform policies on a global basis. Firms standardize products as much as possible while adapting them as needed to ensure ample sales in individual markets. For example, in IKEA's case, some 90 percent of its product line is identical across more than two dozen countries. IKEA's overall marketing plan is centrally developed at company headquarters in Europe in response to convergence of product expectations. Nevertheless, the plan is implemented with local adjustments. The firm also modifies some of its furniture offerings to suit tastes in individual countries. IKEA decentralizes some of its decision making, such as the language to use in advertising, to local stores.

The British bank Standard Chartered, Procter & Gamble (P&G), Dow Chemical, and software maker Oracle are all striving for a transnational strategy. Dow Chemical created global business divisions to take charge of investment and market development. But Dow also relies on local managers to deal with regulatory issues, which can be complex in emerging markets. Procter & Gamble cut the country manager's role and handed all strategic questions about brands back to headquarters. Procter & Gamble's new model differentiates between high- and low-income countries. In high-income countries, major decisions are made at headquarters. In low-income countries, some decision making is delegated to the regional level. Local managers in these countries require more autonomy to deal effectively with difficult local issues such as sourcing and marketing.

Given the difficulty of maintaining a delicate balance between central control and local responsiveness, most firms find it difficult to implement transnational strategy. In the long run, almost all firms find that they need to include some elements of localized decision making as well, because each country has its idiosyncratic characteristics. For instance, few people in Japan want to buy a computer that has an English-language keyboard. Thus, while Dell can apply a mostly global strategy to Japan, it must incorporate some multidomestic elements as well. Even Coca-Cola,

Transnational strategy A coordinated approach to internationalization in which the firm strives to be more responsive to local needs while retaining sufficient central control of operations to ensure efficiency and learning.

This IKEA Home Furnishings store opened in Shanghai, China in April, 2003. Consistent with a global strategy, IKEA standardizes its products as much as possible.

often touted as a global brand, varies its ingredients slightly in different markets. While consumers in the United States prefer a sweeter Coca-Cola, the Chinese want less sugar.[20]

Having discussed distinct strategies that firms pursue in international expansion, let's now explore the related topic—organizational structure alternatives. While a strategy is the blueprint for action, a firm needs a structure with people, resources, and processes to implement the blueprint.

 # Organizational Structure

Organizational structure

Reporting relationships inside the firm that specify the linkages between people, functions, and processes.

Organizational structure refers to the reporting relationships inside the firm—"the boxes and lines"—that specify the linkages between people, functions, and processes that allow the firm to carry out its international operations. In the larger, more experienced MNE, these linkages are extensive and include the firm's subsidiaries and affiliates. A fundamental issue in organizational design is how much decision-making responsibility the firm should retain at headquarters and how much it should delegate to foreign subsidiaries and affiliates. This is the choice between *centralization* and *decentralization*. Let's examine this fundamental choice in more detail.

Centralized or Decentralized Structure?

A centralized approach means that headquarters retains considerable authority and control. A decentralized approach means that the MNE delegates substantial autonomy and decision-making authority to the country subsidiaries. There is no clear-cut best approach.

Exhibit 11.3 identifies the typical contributions of headquarters and subsidiaries. Generally, the larger the financial outlay or the riskier the anticipated result, the more involved headquarters will be in decision making. For example, decisions on developing new products or entering new markets tend to be centralized to headquarters. Decisions involving strategies for two or more countries are best left to headquarters managers who have a more regional or global perspective.[21] Decisions to source products from one country for export to another, or decisions on intracorporate transfer pricing are likely to be centralized. Decisions on global products that are marketed in several countries with common trademarks and brand names are usually the responsibility of headquarters. Conversely, decisions on local products that are sold only in single-

A subsidiary is the primary contributor to these activities:	Headquarters is the primary contributor to these activities:	Shared responsibility of subsidiary and headquarters:
• Sales • Marketing • Local market research • Human resource management • Compliance with local laws and regulations	• Capital planning • Transfer pricing • Global profitability	**With the subsidiary's lead:** • Geographic strategy • Local product and service development • Technical support and customer service • Local procurement **With the headquarters' lead:** • Broad corporate strategy • Global product development • Basic research and development • Global product sourcing • Development of global managers

Exhibit 11.3 Subsidiary and Headquarters Contributions

country markets should be the joint responsibility of corporate and respective country managers, with the latter taking the leadership role.

The choice between headquarters and subsidiary involvement in decision making is also a function of the nature of the product, the nature of competitors' operations, and the size and strategic importance of foreign operations. In the long run, no firm can centralize *all* its operations. Retaining some local autonomy is desirable. Companies need to effectively balance the benefits of centralization and local autonomy. The challenge is for companies to achieve these goals simultaneously.[22] The old phrase, "think globally, act locally," is an oversimplification of the true complexities of today's global competition; *"think globally and locally, act appropriately"* better describes the reality of today's marketplace.[23]

A worker inspects the first production of bottled Coca-Cola beverages during the opening of the new Coca-Cola plant in central Bacolod City, Philippines. While the headquarters organization of Coca-Cola will provide global brand support and broad marketing guidance to its bottlers in individual countries, the local bottler organization will assume responsibility for such activities as local sales promotion, labeling to meet local government requirements, retail support, and local customer research.

Planning, shared by managers at headquarters and subsidiaries, is vital to the design of effective strategies that take full advantage of existing worldwide operations. Highly centralized, top-down decision making ignores subsidiary managers' intimate knowledge of host countries. Conversely, highly decentralized, bottom-up decision making by autonomous subsidiary managers ignores the functional knowledge that managers at headquarters possess and fails to integrate strategies across countries and regions. Shared decision making necessitates negotiations between headquarters and subsidiary managers, with give-and-take on both sides. In the final analysis, however, all decisions are subject to headquarters approval. Senior corporate managers should employ various strategies to encourage positive, open-minded, collaborative relationships with country managers. These strategies include:

* Encouraging local managers to identify with broad, corporate objectives and make their best efforts
* Visiting subsidiaries to instill corporate values and priorities
* Rotating employees within the corporate network to develop multiple perspectives
* Encouraging country managers to interact and share experiences with each other through regional meetings
* Providing/establishing financial incentives and penalties to promote compliance with headquarters' goals

Alternative Organizational Arrangements for International Operations

There are four typical organizational structures for the internationalizing firm: export department/international division, decentralized structure, centralized structure, and global matrix structure. A long-established body of literature suggests that "structure follows strategy."[24] The organizational design a firm chooses for international operations is largely the result of how important managers consider international business and whether they prefer centralized or decentralized decision making. The firm's experience in international business also affects its organizational design. Organizational designs tend to follow an evolutionary pattern: As the firm's international involvement increases, it adopts increasingly more complex organizational designs. Let's explore the four types of organizational structures in detail.[25]

Export Department or International Division

Export department A unit within the firm charged with managing the firm's export operations.

International division structure An organizational design in which all international activities are centralized within one division in the firm, separate from domestic units.

For manufacturing firms, exporting is usually the first foreign market entry strategy. At first, it rarely involves much of a structured organizational response. As export sales reach a substantial proportion of the firm's total sales, however, senior managers will usually establish a separate **export department** whose manager may report to senior management or to the head of domestic sales and marketing. Exhibit 11.4 illustrates the export department structure.

The export department is the simplest form of organizational structure for controlling international operations. As the company develops extensive export operations, or as it initiates more sophisticated foreign market entry strategies, such as FDI, management will typically create an **international division structure**, a separate division within the firm dedicated to managing its international operations. Exhibit 11.5 illustrates this organizational structure. Typically, a vice president of international operations is appointed, who reports directly to the corporate CEO. The decision to create a separate international unit is usually accompanied by a significant shift in resource allocation and an increased focus on the international marketplace.[26] Managers in this division typically oversee the development and maintenance of relationships with foreign suppliers and distributors. The division typically undertakes more advanced internationalization options, such as licensing and small-scale foreign investment.

The international division structure offers several advantages. It centralizes management and coordination of international operations. It is staffed with international experts who focus on developing new business opportunities abroad and offering assistance and training for foreign operations. When a firm develops the division, it signals that management is committed to international operations. Nevertheless, the international division structure has several disadvantages. For one, a domestic versus international power struggle often occurs—for example, over the control of financial and human resources. There is likely to be little sharing of knowledge between the foreign units or between the foreign units and headquarters. R&D and future-oriented planning activities tend to remain domestically focused. Products continue to be developed for the domestic marketplace, with international needs considered only after domestic needs have been addressed. Because of these problems, many firms eventually evolve out of the international division structure.[27]

Firms at more advanced stages of internationalization tend to set up more complex organizational designs. The major rationale for firms to select a more complex structure is to reap economies of scale through high-volume production and economies of scope—that is, more efficient use of marketing and other strategic resources over a wider range of products and markets. There is greater emphasis on innovative potential through learning effects, pooling of resources, and

Exhibit 11.4

The Export Department Structure

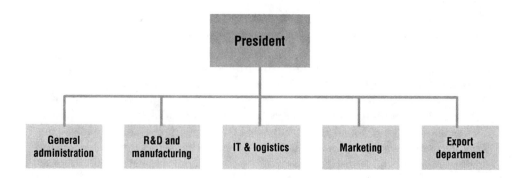

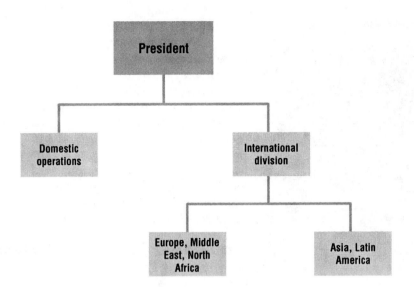

Exhibit 11.5

The International Division Structure

know-how. The integrated chain of command in this structure allows management to make rapid, cohesive decisions regarding global operations.[28]

The more complex organizational designs emphasize a decentralized structure, typically organized around geographic areas; or a centralized structure, typically organized around product or functional lines. We describe these structures next.

Multi-domestic!

Decentralized Structure (Geographic Area Division)

Geographic area division is an organizational design in which control and decision making are decentralized to the level of individual geographic regions, whose managers are responsible for operations within their region. Exhibit 11.6 illustrates this type of organizational design. Firms that market relatively uniform goods across entire regions with little adaptation requirements tend to organize their international operations geographically. The structure is decentralized because management of international operations is largely delegated to the regional headquarters responsible for each geographic area. Nestlé uses such a structure. It has organized its international divisions into a South America division, North America division, Europe division, Asia division, and so forth. The firm treats all geographic locations, including the domestic market, as equals. All areas work in unison toward a common global strategic vision. Assets, including capital, are distributed with the intent of optimal return on corporate goals—not area goals. Geographic area divisions usually manufacture and market locally appropriate goods within their own areas. Firms that use the geographic area approach are often in mature industries with narrow product lines, such as the pharmaceutical, food, automotive, cosmetics, and beverage industries.

Geographic area division An organizational design in which control and decision making are decentralized to the level of individual geographic regions, whose managers are responsible for operations within their region.

Exhibit 11.6

The Geographic Area Structure.

President

| Vice President North America | Vice President South America | Vice President Europe and Middle East | Vice President Asia Pacific | Vice President Africa |

Nestlé chocolate bars on sale in Beijing. Nestlé uses a geographic area division structure for organizing its international operations.

Product division An arrangement in which decision making and management of the firm's international operations is organized by major product line.

Functional division An arrangement in which decision making and management of the firm's international operations are organized by functional activity (such as production and marketing).

Advantages of the geographic area structure include the ability to strike a balance between global integration while achieving local adaptation on a regional basis. The area division leadership has authority to modify products and strategy. Improved communications and coordination are possible between subsidiaries within each region, but communication and coordination with *other* area divisions and corporate headquarters may be de-emphasized. The area focus may distract the regional management team from addressing *global* issues such as product development and product management.[29]

Centralized Structure (Product or Functional Division)

A **product division** is an arrangement in which decision making and management of the firm's international operations is organized by major product line. Management creates a structure based on major categories of products within the firm's range of offerings. Each product division has responsibility for producing and marketing a specific group of products, worldwide. For instance, Motorola organizes its international operations within each of its product categories, including cell phones, consumer electronics, and satellites. Exhibit 11.7 illustrates such an organization. Each of the international product divisions operates as a stand-alone profit center with substantial autonomy. Their primary goal is to achieve a high degree of worldwide coordination within each product category. Increased coordination encourages greater economies of scale and an improved flow of product knowledge and technology across borders.

The advantage of the product division structure is that all support functions, such as R&D, marketing, and manufacturing, are focused on the product. At the same time, products are easier to tailor for individual markets to meet specific buyer needs. Nevertheless, the product division structure also causes duplication of corporate support functions for each product division and a tendency for managers to focus their efforts on subsidiaries with the greatest potential for quick returns.[30] In addition, suppliers and customers may be confused if several divisions call on them.

A variation of the centralized structure is the functional division. A **functional division** is an arrangement in which decision making and management of the firm's international operations are organized by functional activity (such as production and marketing). For example, oil and mining firms, which have value-adding processes of exploration, drilling, transportation, and storing, tend to use this type of structure. Exhibit 11.8 illustrates such an arrangement. Cruise ship lines may engage in both shipbuilding and passenger cruise marketing—two very distinctive functions that require separate departments for international production and international marketing. Thus, it makes sense to delineate separate divisions for the performance of production and marketing functions worldwide. The advantages of the

Exhibit 11.7

The Global Product Structure

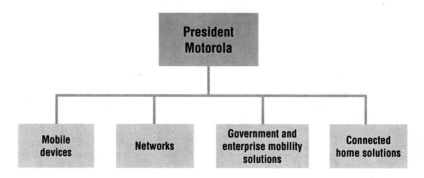

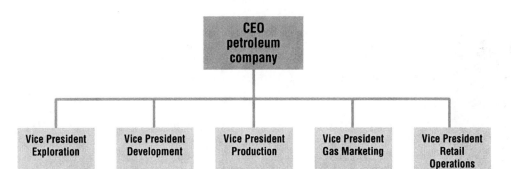

Exhibit 11.8

The Global Functional Structure

functional division are a small central staff, which provides strong central control and coordination, and a united, focused global strategy with a high degree of functional expertise. However, the functional approach may falter in coordinating manufacturing, marketing, and other functions in diverse geographic locations because the central staff lacks expertise in these areas. In addition, when the firm deals with numerous product lines, coordination can become unwieldy.[31]

Global Matrix Structure ← *Transnational*

The organizational designs described so far worked well in the 1970s and 1980s. As worldwide business moved into the early 1990s, however, a number of economic conditions began to shift. Many countries experienced increasing trade deficits and rising interest rates on foreign debt. Local governments responded by increasing restrictions on foreign companies, requiring them to invest locally, meet local content needs, and transfer technology. In some markets, local customers showed a renewed preference for local brands. Corporations began to realize that these economic forces increasingly required them to address global and local needs *simultaneously*. This realization led managers to create the global matrix structure.

A **global matrix structure** is an arrangement that blends the geographic area, product, and functional structures in an attempt to leverage the benefits of a purely global strategy and maximize global organizational learning while remaining responsive to local needs. It is an attempt to capture the benefits of the geographic area, product, and functional organization structures simultaneously while minimizing their shortcomings.

Among the four strategy alternatives we discussed so far, the global matrix structure is most closely associated with the transnational strategy. The area structure facilitates local responsiveness but can inhibit worldwide economies of scale and the sharing of knowledge and core competences among the geographic areas. The product structure overcomes these shortcomings but is weak in local responsiveness. By using the global matrix structure approach, responsibility for operating decisions about a given product is shared by the product division and the particular geographic areas of the firm. To implement the matrix approach, the firm develops a dual reporting system in which, for example, an employee in a foreign subsidiary may report on an equal basis to two managers: the local subsidiary general manager and a corporate product division manager.

In the global matrix structure, organizational capabilities and best practices are shared with all country units. This approach requires managers to think and operate along two of the following three major dimensions: geography, product, and function (cross-functional). The firm must simultaneously possess the ability to: (1) develop worldwide coordination and control, (2) respond to local needs, and (3) maximize interorganizational learning and knowledge sharing.[32]

The global matrix structure recognizes the importance of flexible and responsive country-level operations and shows firms how to link those operations to retain competitive effectiveness and economic efficiency. Managers working in this structure must make shared decisions that affect the entire organization. For most firms, the

Global matrix structure An arrangement that blends the geographic area, product, and functional structures in an attempt to leverage the benefits of a purely global strategy and maximize global organizational learning while remaining responsive to local needs.

Firms such as Unilever, which owns numerous global brands such as Lipton tea, Hellman's spreads, Slimfast, and Dove products, need to balance forces of global integration with local adaptation. Local adaptation is necessary for such marketing issues as retail distribution strategy, labeling requirements, and consumer incentives.

matrix approach represents relatively new thinking in the management of the modern MNE. How successfully firms are able to implement and maintain this approach for long-term global success remains to be seen.

Unilever—the European company with over $50 billion sales in food, beverage, cleaning, and personal care products—is an example of a firm that has benefited from a matrix organization. Originally a merger between British and Dutch firms, in recent years Unilever headquarters has moved toward coordination while retaining local responsiveness. The firm had long pursued a multidomestic approach, but this became unwieldy over time. For example, in the late 1990s, Unilever was buying more than 30 different types of vanilla for its ice cream in Europe, while its Rexona deodorant had 30 different packages and 48 distinctive formulations. Advertising and branding efforts were handled locally and often amateurishly. The firm struggled to develop global products that could compete with rivals such as Procter & Gamble and L'Oreal. These competitors, with more centralized operations, were responding faster to changing consumer tastes. They were better at coordinating their international units and had captured efficiencies by striking supplier contracts for many countries simultaneously. At the same time, giant retailers such as Wal-Mart were pressuring Unilever to cut its prices. Unilever's total sales were in line with P&G, but the firm had over 230,000 employees, twice as many as P&G. The decentralized structure of Unilever's international organization had produced needless duplication and countless obstacles to applying a more efficient global approach.

To address its problems, Unilever put in place a massive reorganization plan designed to centralize authority and reduce the power of local country bosses. To implement a global culture and organization, the firm divested hundreds of businesses, cut 55,000 jobs, closed 145 factories, and discontinued 1,200 brands. Today, Unilever has about 400 brands. The firm develops new products using global teams that emphasize the commonalities among major-country markets. Local managers are not allowed to tinker with packaging, formulation, or advertising of global brands, such as Dove soap. Unilever is well on the road to implementing a more balanced matrix approach to its international operations.[33]

As with the other organizational structures, the matrix approach has its disadvantages. For example, the chain of command from superiors to subordinates can become muddled. It is difficult for employees to receive directions from two different managers who are located thousands of miles apart and have different cultural backgrounds and business experiences. When conflict arises between two managers, senior management must offer a resolution. The matrix structure can, therefore, give rise to conflict, waste management's time, and compromise organizational effectiveness. The heightened pace of environmental change, increased complexity and demands, and the need for cultural adaptability have been overwhelming for many firms that have attempted the matrix structure.[34] For this reason, many companies that have experimented with the matrix structure have eventually returned to simpler organizational arrangements.

 Building the Global Firm

Exhibit 11.9 illustrates the requisite dimensions of a truly global firm. As highlighted earlier, management must start with an appropriate strategy and organizational structure. While critical, these dimensions by themselves are insufficient. In addition to strategy and organizational structure, management must cultivate three additional areas: visionary leadership, organizational culture, and organizational processes. We discuss these three attributes of truly global firms next.[35]

Visionary Leadership

Visionary leadership is defined as senior human capital in an organization that provides the strategic guidance necessary to manage efficiency, flexibility, and learning in an internationalizing firm.[36] Leadership is more complex in global firms than in domestic firms because valuable organizational assets—such as productive capabilities, brands, and human resources—all cross national borders. In firms with various complex international operations, visionary leadership is critical for success.

Take the example of Peter Brabeck, CEO of Nestlé. Brabeck is a keen pilot, mountain climber, and Harley-Davidson fan with a reputation for straight talking. From Nestlé's headquarters in Switzerland, he is leading Nestlé into the growing nutrition market by developing healthier, value-added products and services. Brabeck perceived a worldwide market for food products that meet consumers' growing interest in health and nutrition. To address this growing market, Nestlé recently purchased Jenny Craig, the U.S. weight management and food-products company. In Germany, Nestlé launched a nutritional institute to advise consumers on dietary issues, dispensing nutritional advice to more than 300,000 customers per month. In France, Brabeck created a nutritional home-care service, providing for patients with special dietary needs. These initiatives position Nestlé in a growing global market and generate global brand loyalty for the firm's line of healthy food products.[37]

At least four traits exemplify visionary leaders:

Global mindset and cosmopolitan values. Initially, visionary leadership requires management to acquire a **global mindset**—openness to, and awareness of, diversity across cultures. The degree of management's global outlook is critical to ultimate success.[38] Dogmatic managers—who tend to be close-minded, lack vision, and have difficulty adapting to other cultures—are likely to fail. By contrast, managers who are open minded, committed to internationalization, and adopt to other cultures are likely to succeed. Such a posture is particularly important among smaller internationalizing firms that lack substantial tangible resources.[39]

Visionary leadership Senior human capital in an organization that provides the strategic guidance necessary to manage efficiency, flexibility, and learning in an internationalizing firm.

Global mindset Openness to, and awareness of, diversity across cultures.

Exhibit 11.9

Dimensions of Truly Global Companies

Willingness to commit resources. Commitment drives visionary leaders to develop needed financial, human, and other resources to achieve their firms' international goals. The complexities of foreign markets imply that international ventures take more time than domestic ones to become profitable. Such conditions require high levels of managerial commitment and the unrelenting belief that the firm will eventually succeed. In the absence of such commitment, lower-level managers cannot respond adequately to foreign markets and perform the tasks necessary to ensure success. Highly committed firms engage in systematic international market expansion, allocate necessary resources, and empower structures and processes that ensure ultimate success.

Global strategic vision. Visionary leaders are effective in articulating a *global strategic vision*—what the firm wants to be in the future and how it will get there. As they develop their strategic vision, senior managers focus on the ideal picture of what the company should become. This ideal picture is the central rallying point for all plans, employees, and employee actions. This is akin to the concept of *strategic intent*, defined as an ambitious and compelling dream that energizes and provides emotional and intellectual energy.[40]

As an example of a firm with strategic vision, consider Synclayer, a Japanese SME whose senior managers have envisioned a large and growing market for new products for the elderly. By 2015, one in four Japanese—about 30 million people—will be over 65. The company has ambitions to take worldwide leadership in developing products for senior citizens. Synclayer has developed an IT-based system that allows older people still living at home to take basic medical measurements, such as blood pressure and temperature, and send them to a local health database. The medical service can then act if the measurements suggest a health problem. The firm's vision is to develop the products in Japan and then launch them into foreign markets with sizeable elderly populations.[41]

Willingness to invest in human assets. Visionary leaders must nurture the most critical asset of any organization—human capital. At the center of any globalization effort are a handful of managers who understand the world and are prepared to manage the complexity, uncertainty, and learning that the firm faces in the global marketplace. Leadership involves the ongoing effort to develop human capital that is capable of creating the organizational culture, strategy, structure, and processes of a global firm. In global firms, senior leaders adopt such human resource practices as the use of foreign nationals, promoting multicountry careers, and cross-cultural and language training to develop global supermanagers.[42]

Ratan Tata is chairman of India's Tata group. Tata transformed the giant Indian conglomerate into a transnational organization, with operations throughout the world.

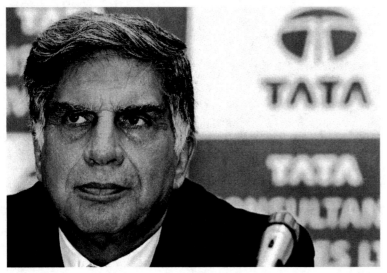

Ratan N. Tata, the chairman of the Tata Group who transformed this Indian conglomerate into a transnational organization, and Carlos Ghosn, the CEO of Nissan and Renault, featured in this chapter's Closing Case, both exemplify visionary leadership. Tata oversees a $22 billion family conglomerate whose companies market a range of products from automobiles to watches. Since 2000, his group has made numerous international acquisitions (from Tetley Tea to the London-based steel firm Corus), reflecting a change in strategic vision from local to global. Another example is Toyota CEO Fujio Cho, who has led his firm to record sales in the intensely competitive global automobile industry. In a recent year, profits rose nearly 150 percent. His leadership style emphasizes innovation, product quality, continuous improvement, and an ability to spot future-oriented opportunities, including the Prius hybrid and the youth-oriented Scion brands of Toyota cars.[43]

Organizational Culture

Organizational culture refers to the pattern of shared values, norms of behavior, systems, policies, and procedures that employees learn and adopt. Employees acquire them as the correct way to perceive, think, feel, and behave in relation to new problems and opportunities that confront the firm.[44] Organizational culture is the "personality" of the firm. Employees demonstrate organizational culture by using the firm's common language and accepting rules and norms, such as the pace and amount of work expected and the degree of cooperation between management and employees.

As seen in the case of IKEA, in the opening vignette, organizational culture usually derives from the influence of founders and visionary leaders or some unique history of the firm. The role of the founder's values and beliefs is particularly important. Visionary leaders can transform organizational culture, as Lou Gerstner and Jack Welch radically altered the fortunes of IBM and General Electric (GE), respectively—large bureaucratic organizations that had failed to adapt to changing environments.

At the Japanese electronics giant Canon, CEO Fujio Mitarai has developed an organizational culture that emphasizes science and technology. The focus extends from product development to the way goods are made on the factory floor. Recent innovations have slashed production time and costs. Canon invests billions in R&D and is the world's second largest recipient of new U.S. patents. This orientation has allowed Canon to become a world leader in digital cameras, copiers, printers, and flat-screen TVs.[45] Similarly, focus on product quality is a pillar of Toyota's organizational culture. For instance, the gap between the hood and the grille on its Lexus luxury car is not allowed to be more than an eyelash. Toyota workers in Canada receive continuous quality-oriented training in Lexus manufacturing processes, and if no one responds to computer-detected manufacturing flaws within 15 minutes, upper management is automatically notified. Toyota performs a *triple-check* on quality at every stage of Lexus production.[46]

Today, management at firms like Canon and Toyota seek to build a *global* organizational culture—an organizational environment that plays a key role in the development and execution of corporate global strategy. Companies that proactively build a global organizational culture:[47]

* Value and promote a global perspective in all major initiatives
* Value global competence and cross-cultural skills among their employees
* Adopt a single corporate language for business communication
* Promote interdependency between headquarters and subsidiaries
* Subscribe to globally accepted ethical standards

Firms aspiring to become truly global seek to maintain strong ethical standards in all the markets where they are represented. Ultimately, senior leadership of any company must be held accountable for cultivating an organizational culture that welcomes social responsibility and is deliberate about fulfilling its role. We define **corporate social responsibility** as operating a business in a manner that meets or exceeds the ethical, legal, commercial, and public expectations of stakeholders (customers, shareholders, employees, and communities). The *Global Trend* feature elaborates on the role of corporate social responsibility in the multinational firm.

Firms combine visionary leadership with organizational culture to create processes that define how the firm will carry out day-to-day activities in order to achieve company goals. Let's examine these organizational processes next.

Organizational culture The pattern of shared values, norms of behavior, systems, policies, and procedures that employees learn and adopt.

Corporate social responsibility Operating a business in a manner that meets or exceeds the ethical, legal, commercial, and public expectations of stakeholders (customers, shareholders, employees, and communities).

Global Corporate Social Responsibility Rises to the Top of the MNE Agenda

As companies internationalize, they increasingly confront the question of how to be good global citizens. Global corporate social responsibility (CSR) affects the quality of life of customers, suppliers, workers, and other stakeholders with which the firm interacts. CSR addresses issues such as workers' rights, workers' pay sufficient to ensure a reasonable living standard, company activities that disrupt traditional communities and lifestyles, and environmental damage caused by corporate activities. A study by McKinsey & Co. found that executives worldwide overwhelmingly embrace the idea that firms have societal and environmental obligations in addition to ensuring corporate profitability.

As an example, IKEA (featured in the opening vignette) has been deliberate about promoting social and environmental responsibility. The firm employs its own specially trained auditors and environmental coordinators. IKEA products must be manufactured under acceptable working conditions by suppliers who take responsibility for the environment. IKEA and its suppliers work closely with UNICEF, Save the Children, and the WWF to prevent child labor and to support responsible forestry. All work is in conjunction with the UN Convention on the Rights of the Child (1989). All suppliers must meet the standards of the Forest Stewardship Council (FSC). In addition to these activities, the IKEA Foundation supports various charitable causes through generous contributions.

Governments and stakeholders have expectations of how multinational firms should fulfill their global CSR social contract. These expecta-tions include contributing to a region's employment opportunities, protecting workers and communities from physical harm, providing good working conditions, avoiding discriminatory hiring practices and workplaces, maintaining transparency and avoiding corruption, reducing poverty and injustice, and improving access to quality health care and education.

Minding social and environmental accountability is increasingly part of how international business gets done. Firms must incorporate CSR into various activities abroad. Nevertheless, the task is complex, because when companies step onto the global stage, they encounter a wide variety of stakeholders, whose expectations often appear contradictory and overwhelming. In addition, social and environmental problems commonly encountered abroad may appear baffling to management at headquarters, who have little direct international experience. It is often country managers, rather than those at headquarters, who are at the forefront of deciding what issues to address and how to address them.

How do MNEs address global CSR? The Center for Corporate Citizenship at Boston College interviewed managers worldwide and found that they are becoming more sophisticated about identifying, balancing, and prioritizing social and environmental issues. In a world ever sensitive to social and environmental issues, managers increasingly undertake the following types of activities:

- Develop closer relations with foreign stakeholders to better understand their needs and jointly work toward solutions

- Build internal and external capabilities to enhance the firm's contribution to the local community and the global environment

- Ensure that diverse voices are heard by creating organizational structures that employ managers and workers from around the world

- Develop global CSR standards and objectives that are communicated and implemented across the firm, worldwide

- Train managers in global CSR principles and integrate these into managerial responsibilities

Global CSR has firmly inserted itself into the day-to-day agenda of the executive suite, as growing MNE activities increasingly pose environmental concerns and bring firms into daily contact with a range of international activities—such as R&D, manufacturing, sales, and marketing—that can pose a variety of ethical dilemmas. The McKinsey study found that business executives should balance their obligation to shareholders with explicit contributions "to the broader public good." Eighty percent of the executives agreed that generating high returns for investors should be accompanied by a focus on providing good jobs, supporting social causes in local communities, and going beyond legal requirements to minimize pollution and other negative effects of business.

Sources: Center for Corporate Citizenship. (2005). *Going Global: Managers' Experiences Working with Worldwide Stakeholders.* Research report. Boston: Boston College; McKinsey & Co. (2006). *The McKinsey Global Survey of Business Executives: Business and Society.* Accessed January 2006 at www.mckinseyquarterly.com

Organizational Processes

Organizational processes refer to managerial routines, behaviors, and mechanisms that allow the firm to function as intended. In an international firm, typical processes include mechanisms for collecting strategic market information, assessing and rewarding employees, and budgeting for international operations.

General Electric and Toyota have gained substantial competitive advantage by emphasizing and refining the countless processes that comprise their value chains. For example, GE digitizes all key documents and uses intranets and the Internet to automate many activities and reduce operating costs. Many processes cross functional areas within the firm. For example, the new product development process involves input from R&D, engineering, marketing, finance, and operations. In global firms, processes also cut across national borders, which increase both the urgency and complexity of devising well-functioning processes.

Organizational processes Managerial routines, behaviors, and mechanisms that allow the firm to function as intended.

Common Organizational Processes Designed to Achieve Coordination

Contemporary firms develop and implement common processes. Managers attempt to achieve global coordination and integration not just by subscribing to a particular organizational design, such as the global matrix structure, but by also implementing a variety of common processes or *globalizing mechanisms*. These common processes provide substantial interconnectedness within the MNE network and allow for meaningful cross-fertilization and knowledge. Together, they constitute important and powerful vehicles in the creation of truly global firms. These common processes include *global teams, global information systems*, and *global talent pools*.

Global teams Increasingly, global teams are charged with problem-solving and best-practice development within the company.[48] A **global team** is "an internationally distributed group of people . . . with a specific mandate to make or implement decisions that are international in scope."[49] Team members are drawn from geographically diverse units of the MNE and may interact entirely via corporate intranets and video conferencing, without meeting in person. A global team brings together employees with the experience, knowledge, and skills to resolve common challenges. It is assigned fairly complex tasks, represents a diverse composition of professional and national backgrounds, and has members that are distributed around the world. Often, global teams are charged with specific agendas and a finite time period to complete their deliberations and make recommendations.

The nature of global teams varies. *Strategic global teams* identify or implement initiatives that enhance the positioning of the firm in its global industry. *Operational global teams* focus on the efficient and effective running of the business across the whole network.[50] An example of a strategic global team is the Global Strategy Board at General Motors (GM). It includes GM executives who are leaders in processes such as labor relations, design-engineering, manufacturing, marketing, quality, human resource management, and purchasing. The team is charged with overseeing the development of common global processes, spreading best practices throughout GM's worldwide operations, and avoiding "reinventing the wheel" in individual regions.

The most successful teams are flexible, responsive, and innovative. To develop global strategies, it is important that the team involve culturally diverse managers whose business activities span the globe. Culturally diverse teams have three valuable roles:

1. Create a global view inside the firm while remaining in touch with local realities.
2. Generate creative ideas and make fully informed decisions about the firm's global operations.
3. Ensure team decisions are implemented throughout the firm's global operations.

Global team An internationally distributed group of people with a specific mandate to make or implement decisions that are international in scope.

Global information systems The desire to create a globally coordinated company is motivated by the need for world-scale efficiency and minimal redundancy. In the past, geographic distance and cross-cultural differences served as impediments to achieving an interconnected, global company. The advent of the Internet and modern information technologies now provide the means for virtual interconnectedness within the global company network. Global IT infrastructure, together with tools such as intranets and electronic data interchange, make it feasible for distant parts of the global network to share and learn from each other.

The development of Chevrolet Equinox by General Motors illustrates the effective use of modern IT and communication technologies. When GM decided in 2001 to develop a sports utility vehicle to compete with Toyota's RAV4 and Honda's CR-V, it tapped its capabilities all over the globe. The V6 engine was built in China, with cooperation from engineers in Canada, China, Japan, and the United States. From a global collaboration room in Toronto, engineers teleconferenced almost daily with counterparts from Shanghai, Tokyo, and Warren, Ohio. They exchanged virtual-reality renderings of the vehicle and collaborated on the styling of exteriors and design of components. The SUV was built in Ontario, Canada, at a factory that GM shares with its Japanese partner, Suzuki.

Global talent pools Developing managers and other members of the organization to think and behave globally is necessary for ultimate global success. International firms employ a combination of home-country personnel, host-country personnel, and expatriates. An **expatriate** is an employee who is assigned to work and reside in a foreign country for an extended period, usually a year or longer. For example, a U.S. firm might employ a German or U.S. manager in its subsidiary in France. In this example, both the German and American managers are expatriates. Sophisticated MNEs develop a pool of highly developed talent, regardless of nationality, to manage evolving international operations. The MNEs develop a database of skilled individuals within the firm and make it available on the corporate intranet. As an example, Citibank managers can search on the company intranet for the right recruit—with desirable qualifications—regardless of where that individual is located in the company's global network. In this way, Citibank identifies and uses the best talent worldwide for the task at hand.

Global firms invest in their employees to build needed capabilities, not just in technical or business terms, but in terms of language and cultural capabilities and types of international experience. The development of a *global talent pool* requires the creation of an environment that fosters and promotes cooperation across borders, the free exchange of information, and the development of creative managers capable of functioning effectively anywhere in the world.

 Putting Organizational Change in Motion

This chapter has highlighted strategies, structures, and processes that help build truly global firms. Reorganizing the firm on a global scale is not a simple task nor can it be accomplished quickly. Take the case of Procter & Gamble's "Organization 2005" program, launched in 1998.[51] The plan called for an aggressive redesign of P&G's organizational structure, work processes, culture, and pay structures worldwide. Procter & Gamble's management sought to create a global organization that could simultaneously serve specific national needs. The firm moved from four business units based on geographical regions to seven based on global product lines, thereby changing their organizational structure significantly. It established Market Development Organizations in eight world regions to tailor its global marketing to local markets. Business processes such as human resource management, order management, and accounting were to be consolidated from separate geographic regions to one corporate organization that would serve P&G operations worldwide.

Expatriate An employee who is assigned to work and reside in a foreign country for an extended period, usually a year or longer.

However, "Organization 2005" floundered in various ways. Efforts to make P&G a more nimble MNE did not go well in the firm's conservative corporate culture. Management laid off thousands of workers and abruptly transferred about 2,000 people to Geneva and about 200 to Singapore. These changes created resentment among key personnel. A reorganization of reporting structures created confusion. Some food and beverage managers at the U.S. headquarters had to report to the president of the Venezuela subsidiary. Managers in the U.S. household cleaning division reported to Brussels. Global marketing programs failed from insufficient research. In Germany, the name of P&G's dishwashing liquid suddenly changed from Fairy to Dawn, the U.S. brand. But since Dawn was unknown in Germany, sales plummeted. In short, while seemingly a promising plan, "Organization 2005" was based on inadequate research and poor implementation. Headquarters alienated managers and sowed anxiety and confusion among customers and employees alike.

As this example illustrates, firms must approach the development of global strategy with great care. For many firms, a truly global organization remains an ideal yet to be achieved. To ensure international business success, the firm should: (1) formulate a global strategy; (2) develop an appropriate organizational structure; (3) provide visionary leadership; (4) cultivate an organizational culture worldwide and (5) refine and implement organizational processes.

Internationalizing a company will not fully succeed unless all five of these organizational dimensions complement each other to support the desired outcomes. Success in international markets is not based on a single prescription or formula but a multidimensional and coherent set of actions. These include: participating in all major markets in the world, standardizing product and marketing programs wherever feasible, taking integrated, competitive moves across the country markets, concentrating value-adding activities at strategic locations across the world, and coordinating the value-chain activities to exploit the synergies of multinational operations. Superior global performance will result if all the dimensions of a global strategy are aligned with external industry globalization forces and internal organizational resources.[52]

In this chapter, we have described the essential dimensions of internationally effective firms. In all of its complexity, there are seemingly countless variables to consider when designing for international success. How should senior leaders proceed? Where does one start? With processes? Structure? Organizational culture? Hasty and highly ambitious efforts to transform an organization may fail. It is best for senior management to focus on only one or two dimensions at a time, tackling the most easily changed dimensions of the organization first in order to prepare the way for the more difficult changes.

Finally, transforming an organization into a truly global company can take years and involve many obstacles and uncertainty. Senior management needs to instill a sense of urgency to drive the organization toward the desired changes. Equally important is buy-in from employees for implementation—securing wholehearted participation of key individuals and groups toward common organizational goals. One CEO of a very large company, who was asked to resign by his board of directors after a bungled corporate turnaround, put it this way: ". . . we did not fail because we did not have a clever strategy. We did not fail because we did not have shrewd managers or talented engineers and scientists. We failed because I simply could not rally the troops."

CLOSING CASE

Carlos Ghosn and Renault-Nissan: Leading for Global Success

Nissan Motor Co., based in Tokyo, is Japan's number two automobile manufacturer. The company's 2006 sales were over 10 billion Japanese yen, with an operating profit margin of 7.4 percent. In 2007, Nissan launched 11 all-new products globally. A few years ago, Nissan was on the verge of bankruptcy. The French automaker Renault stepped in, took a 44 percent stake, and installed Carlos Ghosn as Nissan's CEO. In a dramatic turnaround, Ghosn (hard *G*, rhymes with "stone") returned Nissan to profitability and became a celebrity in Japan. Born in Brazil, raised in Lebanon, and educated in France, Ghosn is a charismatic leader who speaks four languages. He is smooth in public, works constantly, and is committed to organizational goals. He is featured in Japanese comic books, mobbed for autographs during factory tours, and adored throughout Japan for saving a car company once given up for dead.

Under Ghosn's watchful eye, Nissan evolved from a troubled carmaker to a corporate success story in just a few years. He closed inefficient factories, reduced Nissan's workforce, curbed purchasing costs, shared operations with Renault, and introduced new products. Ultimately, Nissan became one of the world's most profitable automotive companies. How did Nissan do it?

Nissan's Organizational Culture

Ghosn defied Japan's often bureaucratic and clubby business culture, for example, by reducing Nissan's steel suppliers from five to three. The CEO of NKK Steel protested that "Toyota would never act in such a way." One of Ghosn's biggest tests was overcoming the denial inside Nissan about the firm's perilous condition. In Japan, large companies are viewed as too big to fail. If the *keiretsu*'s banks don't rush to the rescue, then the government will. Ghosn cut through such antiquated thinking to save Nissan.

Corporate Japan often moves slowly and reactively. Ghosn introduced a proactive style, with fast decision making. Senior management at Nissan is now proactive, operating with a sense of urgency even when the firm is not in crisis. The culture is about anticipating problems, putting them on the table, and eliminating them before they happen. Ghosn is always in a rush, relying on decisiveness and delegation—but yielding to consensus when it is passionate. In the style of a true globalist, Ghosn notes that "It's irrelevant where you are headquartered . . . the keys are where the jobs are located and where the profits go." To reinforce his global aspirations, Ghosn has made English, not Japanese, the official language of Nissan. Managers who learn English advance faster than those who speak only Japanese.

This move puts Nissan on a clear footing to change its organizational culture and become a global firm.

Ghosn's Leadership Style

Ghosn dislikes long meetings. Instead of spending a lot of time analyzing and discussing, he prefers action. At Nissan, he pushed top staff to meet tough sales targets and promised publicly that the entire management team would resign if it didn't meet the targets. He inspires the workforce by communicating with them on the factory floor. Even the most mundane events were handled like big media shows. One Nissan earnings news conference opened with loud music and dazzling video shots of zooming cars.

Renault-Nissan

On the heels of his success, Ghosn took over as CEO of Renault in 2005. He now runs *both* companies, commuting between Paris and Tokyo in his Gulfstream jet. The unusual arrangement underscores the demand for proven leaders in the global auto industry, which has suffered from oversupply and intense competition. In a typical month, he could spend the first week in Paris, focusing solely on Renault, and the third week in Japan, focusing on Nissan. He personally oversees Nissan's North America business, where 60 percent of Nissan profits are earned. He carries two agendas: one for Nissan and one for Renault.

Innovation Is Key

Renault-Nissan's long-term strategy is to continually invest substantially in R&D for breakthrough technologies and innovative products. In the 2000s, top management increased R&D by 50 percent, reinvesting 5 percent of net sales in new technologies. At its new Mississippi plant in the United States, Nissan launched five models in less than 8 months. It rolled out a small car (the "Versa"), a re-engineered Altima midsize sedan, a heavily redesigned Nissan Quest minivan, and a redesigned Infiniti G35. Nissan established a design subsidiary in Shanghai, China, to produce cars that fit that country's growing market. The firm has developed hybrid vehicles to address a growing consumer demand triggered by high gasoline prices.

Global Production

Renault-Nissan has production plants in Britain, France, and the United States, to be close to key foreign markets. It also manufactures in China, Taiwan, and the Philippines, to profit from low-cost, high-quality labor. Nissan uses modular architecture. The Maxima and Altima, built in

Nissan's U.S. plant in Tennessee, as well as the new Quest, Titan pickup, and Armada sport-utility vehicle are put together with single modules from parts suppliers. The finished modules are then bolted into a car or truck body rolling down the assembly line. All together, buying modules built by supplier partners save up to 30 percent of the total cost of that section of the car.

Nissan consolidated its U.S. manufacturing operations, moving thousands of jobs from southern California to Tennessee. The move centralized manufacturing and made it easier for senior management to keep tabs on U.S. operations. The Tennessee plant has been the most productive factory in North America for years, producing a car in less than 16 labor hours, several hours fewer than rival carmakers.

Additional Global Strategy Elements

Senior management set up a company in Amsterdam—Renault-Nissan BV—which offers a neutral forum where both firms can map out a common strategy for product engineering, model development, and computer systems and leverage their combined size to squeeze suppliers for lower costs. Renault-Nissan's board of directors consists of four members from each organization.

Nissan is globalizing its engineering, production, and purchasing operations. It built a $45 million engineering center near Tokyo to consolidate its global production-engineering activities. Also, Ghosn is taking the Infiniti luxury brand global. Nissan makes Infiniti dealerships conform to an interior design that gives them a uniform look and global image.

The integration of Nissan with Renault went smoothly. Renault has been building its Clio compact and Scenic minivan at Nissan plants in Mexico, while Nissan makes its Frontier pickup at a Renault factory in Brazil. The ultimate goal is to reduce the number of platforms (chassis) that the group uses to a minimum. This is important because every shared platform provides $500 million in annual savings for each carmaker. Renault also shares eight engine designs with Nissan. They share engineering and parts purchases. Roughly three-quarters of the parts used by the two automakers are jointly sourced. These moves allow both firms to slash the expense and time of introducing new models, consistently driving down purchasing costs and increasing global profits, and they shave months off development time of new vehicles. One result of shared platforms is the world's most global car, called the Nissan Versa in the United States, the Renault Clio in Europe, the Nissan Tiida in Asia, and the Renault Logan in the Middle East. In total, Nissan offers seven different vehicles based on the underpinnings that go into the Versa, creating scale economies that cut costs and improve profits.

But avoiding redundancy is not the only way for Nissan to be global. It is also critical to have a presence in the most important markets. While the United States is a relatively expensive place to make cars, it is also the world's biggest market. Thus, Toyota, Honda, BMW, Mercedes, Nissan, and Hyundai all produce there, even expanding U.S. production in recent years. Nissan now exports its U.S.-made Quest minivans to China, considered to be the next big market. It exports other U.S.-made models—the Altima sedan and Infiniti QX56 SUV—to the Middle East and Latin America.

The Future of Automobile Industry Growth—Emerging Markets

In the coming decade, hundreds of millions of Indians, Chinese, Russians, Brazilians and others will join the ranks of the middle class and will have automobiles high on their list of wanted items. Estimates indicate that the market for automobiles priced under $10,000 will grow from 12 million to 18 million cars by 2012. India's car market is forecast to double to 3.3 million cars by 2014, and China's demand will grow 140 percent, to 16.5 million cars in the same period.

The One-Lakh Car

India's Tata Motors is planning to launch a new automobile in 2008 that is targeted at a retail price of one-lakh (about U.S. $25,000). The key is the low wages of engineers in India and the firm's ability to squeeze manufacturing costs to their lowest levels. Tata's prototype has four doors, achieves a top speed of 80 mph, and has a 33-horsepower engine. Renault-Nissan CEO Ghosn announced that it plans to create its own $2,500 vehicle to compete with the new Tata Motors model.

The Logan is key to Ghosn's success in emerging markets. The Logan, built in Romania, was first launched in 2004 for about $7,500. In 2006, Renault-Nissan sold 247,000 Logans, and it is forecasting sales in excess of 1 million Logans worldwide by 2010. Many of these sales will be in China and India. The company plans to build a low-cost pickup truck based on the Logan for sale in Southeast Asia, South Africa, and the Middle East. Renault-Nissan originally planned to sell the Logan only in emerging markets, but the Logan became available for sale in Western Europe in 2005. Demand has been exceedingly strong because of the high quality and low price.

Renault-Nissan in Emerging Markets

At Renault, Ghosn is charging ahead with an ambitious restructuring plan. He is expanding Renault's potential beyond Europe, especially into Eastern Europe, India, Iran, Russia, and South Korea. He aims to increase international sales of Renault to nearly half the firm's total production. Part of the rationale for the expansion is to reduce production in France, which has become costly, in part due to strong union demands. Renault also acquired full control of Samsung Motors, making South Korea an important base for both Renault and Nissan.

Renault is a market leader in Europe, Japan, China, and in the United States. Renault-Nissan is on the verge of capturing the number three spot globally, behind Toyota and General Motors.

AACSB: Reflective Thinking
Case Questions

1. In what ways is Carlos Ghosn a visionary leader? What traits does he possess that are typical of a visionary leader?

2. What is the nature of Nissan's international strategy? Is the firm following a primarily global strategy or a multidomestic strategy? What advantages does Nissan derive from the particular strategy that it pursues? In what ways does Nissan demonstrate efficiency, flexibility, and learning?

3. Describe Nissan's organizational culture. What are the characteristics of Nissan's culture? In what ways has Carlos Ghosn contributed to Nissan's culture? Elaborate.

4. Global firms pursue a relatively centralized approach to international operations. What are the characteristics of the trend toward global integration of company operations? How does Nissan demonstrate these characteristics?

5. Examine Nissan in terms of the Integration-Responsiveness Framework. What are the pressures that Nissan faces for local responsiveness? What are the pressures that Nissan faces for global integration? What advantages do each of local responsiveness and global integration bring to Nissan?

Sources: Bremner, B., G. Edmondson, and C. Dawson. (2004). "Nissan's Boss," *Business Week,* Oct 4, pp. 50–55; Flint, J. (2003). "Too Much Globalism," *Forbes,* Feb 17, p. 96; Ghosn, C., and P. Ries. (2005). *Shift: Inside Nissan's Historic Revival,* New York: Currency/Doubleday; Guthrie, A. (2005). "For Nissan, Success in Mexico Rides on Tsuru's Enduring Appeal," *Wall Street Journal,* Dec 21, p. 1; Hoovers' information web site at www.hoovers.com; Muller, J. (2006). "The Impatient Mr. Ghosn," *Forbes,* May 22, pp. 104–107; Shirouzu, N. (2006). "Ghosn's Goal for Renault: Go Global," *Wall Street Journal,* June 21, p. B3; Shirouzu, N., and N. Boudette. (2006). "What Alliance with Mr. Ghosn Could Bring GM," *Wall Street Journal,* July 7, p. B1; Welch, D. (2003). "How Nissan Laps Detroit," *Business Week,* Dec 22, p. 58; Wrighton, J. and J. Sapsford (2005), "Split Shift: For Nissan's Rescuer, Ghosn, New Road Rules Await at Renault," *Wall Street Journal,* April 26, p. A.1; www.businessweek.com. "Putting Ford In The Rearview Mirror," February 12, 2007; www.businessweek.com. "The Race To Build Really Cheap Cars," April 23, 2007; www.nissan-global.com.

CHAPTER ESSENTIALS

Key Terms

corporate social responsibility
expatriate
export department
functional division
geographic area division
global integration
global mindset
global industry
global matrix structure

global strategy
global team
home replication strategy
international division
  structure
local responsiveness
multidomestic industry
multidomestic strategy
organizational culture

organizational processes
organizational structure
product division
strategy
strategy in the international
  context
transnational strategy
visionary leadership

Summary

In this chapter, you learned about:

1. The role of strategy in international business

Strategy is a plan of action that channels an organization's resources so that it can effectively differentiate itself from competitors and accomplish unique and viable goals. **Strategy in the international context** is a plan for the organization to position itself positively from its competitors and configure its value-adding activities on a global scale.

2. The integration-responsiveness framework

The integration-responsiveness (IR) framework reduces the managerial imperatives to two key needs: the need for global integration of value-chain activities and the need for local responsiveness. **Local responsiveness** refers to meeting the specific needs of buyers in individual host countries. **Global integration** refers to the coordination of the firm's value-chain activities across countries to achieve worldwide efficiency, synergy, and cross-fertilization in order to take maximum advantage of similarities across countries. The key challenge is in deciding how locally responsive the firm should be in comparison to how far it should go in integrating its worldwide business.

3. Distinct strategies emerging from the integration-responsiveness framework

The IR framework presents four alternative strategies. Using **home replication strategy**, the firm views international business as separate from, and secondary to, its domestic business. Products are designed with domestic consumers in mind, and the firm is essentially a domestic company with some foreign activities. **Multidomestic strategy** is a more committed approach, emphasizing entry via FDI, but in which managers recognize and emphasize differences among national markets. Managers treat individual markets on a stand-alone basis, with little cross-national integration of company efforts. **Global strategy** aims to integrate the firm's major objectives, policies, and action sequences into a cohesive whole, targeted primarily to the global marketplace. Top management performs sourcing, resource allocation, market participation, and competitive moves on a global scale. Using **transnational strategy**, the firm strives to be more responsive to local needs while simultaneously retaining maximum global efficiency and emphasizing global learning and knowledge transfer. The strategy involves combining the major beneficial attributes of both multidomestic and global strategies while minimizing their disadvantages.

4. Organizational structure

Organizational structure refers to the reporting relationships in the organization between people, functions, and processes that allow the firm to carry out its international operations. Organizational structure determines where key decisions are made, the relationship between headquarters and subsidiaries, the nature of international staffing, and the degree of *centralization* and *decentralization* of decision making and value-chain activities in the firm's worldwide operations. In achieving a fine balance between the two choices, managers should recognize the unique contributions made by both headquarters and subsidiaries. The best role for corporate managers is to provide broad leadership, experience, and serve as a source of encouragement. In turn, subsidiary managers are best at dealing with customers, handling employee issues, and initiating action in the field. In this way, an ideal partnership develops and evolves.

5. Alternative organizational arrangements for international operations

There are various organizational designs for global operations. The **export department** is the simplest, in which a unit within the firm manages all export operations. Slightly more advanced is the **international division structure**, in which all international activities are centralized within one division separate from other domestic units. The decentralized structure emphasizes the **geographic area division**, in which control and decision making are decentralized to the level of individual geographic regions. The centralized structure involves either product or functional divisions. Using the **product division**, decision making and management of the firm's international operations are organized by major product line. Using the **functional division**, decision making is organized by functional activity, such as production and marketing. The **global matrix structure** blends the geographic area, product, and functional structures in an attempt to leverage the benefits of a purely global strategy and maximize global organizational learning while remaining responsive to local needs.

6. Building the global firm

Managers who exhibit **visionary leadership** possess a **global mindset**, cosmopolitan values, and a globally strategic vision. They engage in strategic thinking, committing resources and human assets to realizing a global approach to business. **Organizational culture** is the pattern of shared values, norms, systems, policies, and procedures that employees learn and adopt. Advanced international firms value global competence and cross-cultural skills, adopt a single corporate language, and promote interdependency among headquarters and the firm's subsidiaries. They subscribe to globally accepted ethical standards and responsible citizenship. **Organizational processes** refer to managerial routines, behaviors, and mechanisms that allow the firm to function as intended. International organizational processes include **global teams**, global talent pools, and global information systems.

7. Putting organizational change in motion

As a minimum, managers should formulate a global strategy, develop a suitable organizational structure, provide visionary leadership, cultivate an organizational culture worldwide, and refine and implement organizational processes. Highly ambitious efforts to rapidly transform an organization may falter. Instead, focusing on one or two dimensions at a time is prudent. It is best to tackle the most easily changed dimensions of the organization first, in order to prepare the way for the more difficult changes. Senior management needs to instill a sense of urgency to drive the organization forward.

Test Your Comprehension AACSB: Reflective Thinking

1. What are the primary strategic objectives in international business?

2. Describe the integration-responsiveness framework. What are the pressures for local responsiveness? What are the pressures for global integration?

3. What is the difference between global strategy and multidomestic strategy? Visit the web site of Dell Computer (www.dell.com). Does Dell generally apply a global strategy or a multidomestic strategy? How can you tell?

4. Define transnational strategy. Give examples of firms that apply a transnational strategy.

5. What is the difference between a centralized and a decentralized organizational structure? Why do firms often prefer to have a centralized structure?

6. What are different organizational arrangements for global operations? Which arrangement is most associated with global strategy?

7. Define visionary leadership. What are the traits of a manager who has visionary leadership?

8. Define organizational culture. What kind of organizational culture is needed to become a global firm?

9. Define organizational processes. Give and elaborate on several examples of organizational processes. What organizational processes are most salient to achieving a global approach to international business?

Apply Your Understanding AACSB: Communication, Reflective Thinking

1. Visit online sites for Toyota (www.toyota.com) and Procter & Gamble (www.pg.com). From what you can gather, how do these two firms organize their international activities? Do they seem to be applying multi-domestic strategy or global strategy in sourcing, manufacturing, product development, and marketing activities? Would you expect a firm to change its approach to internationalization over time?

2. AlumCo is a large producer of aluminum products. AlumCo now handles international operations through its export department. But top management believes this arrangement is no longer suited to the firm's growing international activities and wants to adopt a more sophisticated approach. What alternative organizational structures (international division, geographic area structure, etc.) should the firm consider? Make a recommendation to top management as to the most appropriate international structure that AlumCo should employ. For reference, check out the website of Alcan, the well-known Canadian aluminum firm, at www.alcan.com.

3. Firms with a global organizational culture have several common characteristics. They seek a global identity, value a global perspective in all undertakings, adopt a common language, promote interdependency between headquarters and subsidiaries, value input from foreign units, and subscribe to globally accepted ethical standards. Recall the opening vignette in this chapter on IKEA, the giant furniture retailer. Based on your reading, outline the various ways that IKEA exhibits these characteristics.

4. Multinational firms that apply a coordinated global strategy see the world as one large production and marketing platform and develop standardized products that are then marketed worldwide using a uniform marketing approach. In reality, however, most firms do not apply a purely global strategy. At the same time, a strictly multidomestic approach is inefficient. While a few large countries (e.g., China, Japan, and the United States) might warrant individual treatment, many firms strike a compromise by dividing the world into regions. Usually these firms apply a geographic area strategy for their international operations. What is the rationale for using a regional approach when thinking about, and devising strategy for, international business?

globalEDGE Internet Exercises

AACSB: Reflective Thinking, Analytical Skills, Use of Information Technology

Refer to Chapter 1, page 27, for instructions on how to access and use globalEDGE™.

1. Multinational firms play a key role in globalization. Various news organizations prepare classifications and rankings of MNEs (e.g., *Business Week, Forbes, Fortune, Financial Times*). Find two such rankings and identify the criteria used to rank the top global firms. What countries are home to the great majority of MNEs on these lists? For each list, how "global" are the top three firms? That is, in what countries do they operate? Conduct a search for 'rankings.'

2. You work for an MNE that makes and markets cellular telephones. Senior managers want to begin selling the phones in Latin America. To pursue a transnational strategy, management wants to minimize adaptation of the phones. They have asked you for a briefing. Focusing on three Latin American countries, prepare a report that identifies the *common* features of Latin American markets that management should consider when developing the cell phones that the firm will sell there. For example, what language should be used in the cell phones? What pricing should management use? You may wish to consult the country commercial guides, Country Insights, and market research reports available through globalEDGE™. In addition, the Area Studies (http://www.psr.keele.ac.uk/area.htm), and the U.S. Department of Commerce (http://www.export.gov) portals are useful resources.

3. Global strategy is characterized by various elements. First, at its most basic level, managers who use global strategy seek to *centralize* the firm's value-chain activities around the world. Centralization helps the firm achieve economies of scale, thereby cutting the costs of operations. Second, the firm attempts to *standardize* its marketing activities by offering relatively standardized (that is, largely unadapted) products and services worldwide. Standardization is possible because world markets are being homogenized by advances in communication and transportation technologies. Customers worldwide increasingly exhibit similar preferences and demand for the same products. Finally, firms that pursue global strategy locate manufacturing and marketing subsidiaries at numerous locations around the world in order to leverage the comparative advantages of specific countries and operate on a truly global basis. globalEDGE™ is home to a large collection of articles that describe the global strategy approaches of numerous firms. Conduct a search at globalEDGE™ by entering the keyword *global strategy* to find articles on this topic. Find and describe examples of companies that apply global strategy. Based on your reading of these articles, and on the previous summary of global strategy elements, describe specific ways in which the example firms that you found employ global strategy in practice.

The Critical Role of Negotiations in International Business

Negotiations are a cooperative process in which two parties commit to reach an agreement via communication and interaction. Negotiations are critical in international business. In any negotiation, cultural differences between the negotiators will play a significant role in how the participants think and act. It is critical to understand the negotiating culture, customs, and other characteristics of the other party before negotiations commence. In numerous cultures, for example, it is essential to get acquainted with each other and to establish a "comfort level" before initiating the negotiation process.

AACSB: Communication, Multicultural and Diversity, Analytical Skills

Managerial Challenge

Miscommunication is a key cause of failure in the negotiation process. Miscommunication arises from various sources, but perhaps the most important is a failure to understand the mindsets and motives of the negotiating parties. A critical managerial challenge is to develop an understanding of negotiators from a variety of national and cultural backgrounds. In order to succeed, a negotiator must conduct substantial advance research.

Background

Negotiations are an essential component of all international business transactions, whether they are the sale of a product or service to a buyer, the formation of a joint venture, the acquisition of a firm, or the licensing of a technology. Communication is the lifeblood of negotiations. The potential for cross-cultural misunderstandings is ever present. Differing circumstances dictate different approaches to negotiations. Goals of the parties may differ; they may even be diametrically opposed. The parties employ a number of techniques, such as persuasion, coercion, and even manipulation. Developing skills in international negotiations can determine the success of a wide range of collaborations, contractual relations, and everyday encounters in international business.

Managerial Skills You Will Gain

In this C/K/R Management Skill Builder©, as a prospective manager, you will:

1. Learn how to increase company performance by acquiring knowledge of negotiation skills.

2. Learn to recognize important cultural dimensions, negotiating styles, and other factors in international negotiations.

3. Acquire research skills to access the information needed to prepare for and to optimize international negotiations.

Your Task

Assume you are the team leader at an international firm that will engage in negotiations with businesspeople from Mexico and Saudi Arabia. To ensure success, you are to perform advance research on the cultural characteristics of the people with whom you will be negotiating.

Go to the C/K/R Knowledge Portal©

www.prenhall.com/cavusgil

Proceed to the C/K/R Knowledge Portal© to obtain the expanded background information, your task and methodology, suggested resources for this exercise, and the presentation template.

Section 4
International Collaborations

CHAPTER THIRTEEN

International Strategic Alliances

AFTER STUDYING THIS CHAPTER YOU SHOULD BE ABLE TO:

- Compare joint ventures and other forms of strategic alliances.
- Characterize the benefits of strategic alliances.
- Describe the scope of strategic alliances.
- Discuss the forms of management used for strategic alliances.
- Identify the limitations of strategic alliances.

© Grapheast/Alamy

554

International Business

> ## "[Gulfjet's] strategic alliances are aimed not only at expansion, but also to create a higher profile in a highly competitive market."

Gulfjet

Gulfjet came into existence in November 2005 and manages a broad range of business aircraft that operate out of Dubai International Airport. The business provides aircraft charter, management, and air ambulance services.

Gulfjet is a joint venture between the Al Mulla Business Group and Leader Capital. The majority of Gulfjet's customers lease the jets for a few months, paying on average between $4,000 and $6,500 an hour for each plane. The booming economy of the Gulf region is ideal for an operation such as Gulfjet and the strategic alliances are aimed not only at expansion, but also to create a higher profile in a highly competitive market. Catering to the cash-rich but time-poor clients, Gulfjet, as Yousef Al Ghareeb describes, aims to utilize a relatively simple concept, excellent service and efficiency. The business is committed to not sacrificing customer comfort in pursuit of profit. Mirroring the demands of their clientele, Gulfjet's goal was to ensure a pleasant and productive experience for all customers.

In 2007 Gulfjet decided to become the sponsor of the Middle East Business Aviation (MEBA), an exhibition of jets and aircraft-related services under the patronage of the Chairman of Dubai Department of Civil Aviation, Sheikh Ahmed bin Saeed Al Maktoum. Gulfjet had certainly put a marker down in the aviation industry in the Middle East to become a major contender in the growing business. The managing director of Gulfjet, Yousef Al Ghareeb, recognized the value of Gulfjet choosing to sponsor the MEBA 2007 exhibition. It was an opportunity for Gulfjet to increase its visibility at a time when the industry was enjoying a fast growth rate. The global market was still extremely competitive and the Middle East was forecasted to account for 8 percent of the $9 billion global private jet market, amounting to 600 aircraft. The exhibition brought together experts who were able to share their views and concerns about the airline business, an industry that is a primary revenue generator for a number of emerging economies around the world.

The exhibition was to prove to be a major event for Gulfjet. They were already using some of the most up-to-date aircraft in the world, including the Bombardier Challenger, which could fly 7,400 km non-stop. Gulfjet is able to fly its passengers for more than seven hours non-stop. The jets operate from the Jet Aviation Terminal at Dubai

International Airport. The terminal has its own dedicated customs and immigration facilities, along with a VIP lounge.

Gulfjet signed a number of partnership agreements at the exhibition. The first was with the German company, ADAC-Ambulance Service, experts in air rescue. The second was with Cedar Jet Centre, a Beirut-based company that was part of Middle East Airlines ground handling, and the third alliance was with PrivatSea, an exclusive membership club for luxury yachting and lifestyle services. The idea was to begin to boost Gulfjet's range of services and visibility in the region. Gulfjet's managing director was delighted with the positive results of their involvement in the MEBA 2007 exhibition. They had been able to consolidate their position in the Middle East region by entering into partnerships with ADAC-Ambulance Service, Cedar Jet Centre, and PrivatSea. The intention was to be able to offer a broader range of services to Gulfjet's customers using reliable and established partners.

Robert Glueck, the marketing manager of ADAC-Ambulance Service, confirmed the importance of the strategic alliance. He was certain that their partnership with Gulfjet would aid them in their goal of being able to deploy a large fleet of Medivac aircraft across the region. This would allow efficient medical repatriation from all of the Gulf Cooperation Council countries, including Bahrain, Qatar, Kuwait, Oman, Saudi Arabia, and the United Arab Emirates. This would ensure that patients from the Middle East region would be able to be routed to the most advanced medical treatment in Europe by using chartered Gulfjet and ADAC flights. The intention was for ADAC to deal with all of the medical and organizational activities and ensure that the highest quality of service was provided by experienced medical and flight personnel.

ADAC-Ambulance Service has a reputation as one of the most expert at worldwide medical repatriation. Under the new partnership agreement, Gulfjet committed itself to purchasing Medivac aircraft that would be based in the United Arab Emirates. In exchange, ADAC would provide the necessary medical and technical backup.

The strategic alliance with Cedar Jet Centre would focus primarily on handling. Yousef Al Ghareeb explained that the partnership with Cedar Jet Centre would allow Cedar Jet Centre to handle the operational and service issues for Gulfjet flights into and out of Beirut, including overflying and landing permits and access to the VIP lounges.

The general manager of Middle East Airlines ground handling, the parent company of Cedar Jet Centre, Richard Mujais, was equally enthusiastic about the partnership. They could now provide a broad range of services for Gulfjet passengers en route to Beirut, paying particular attention to the premium services that were expected.

Middle East Airlines ground handling was established in 1999 and now offers 24-hour airport services to 26 major airlines. They handle around 80 percent of the traffic at Rafic Hariri International Airport in Beirut. This company, too, has pushed forward in terms of striking strategic alliances and in August 2008 announced new agreements with Lebanon's national airline and with the Lebanese Canadian Bank to upgrade their fleet.

The final strategic alliance that Gulfjet signed at the exhibition was with PrivatSea. The airline would now be able to offer access to a fleet of super yachts. Yousef Al Ghareeb was able to announce that through the PrivatSea Club, Gulfjet would now be able to offer the very best in yachting, which would add to their existing portfolio of luxury air and sea chartered services.

The agreement would allow both Gulfjet and PrivatSea to share one another's customer databases and contacts and to allow them to cross-promote one another's products and services.

Strategic alliances such as those that Gulfjet have forged are essential in a growing Gulf and West Asian market, particularly given the fact that European operators are interested in the region as the European sector is already saturated.

Globalization can be a very expensive process, particularly when a firm must perfectly coordinate R&D, production, distribution, marketing, and financial decisions throughout the world in order to succeed. A firm may discover that it lacks all the necessary internal resources to effectively compete against its rivals internationally. The high costs of researching and developing new products alone may stretch its corporate budget. Thus a firm may seek partners to share these costs. Or a firm may develop a new technology but lack a distribution network or production facilities in all the national markets it wants to serve. Accordingly, the firm may seek out other firms with skills or advantages that complement its own and negotiate agreements to work together. Such factors motivated Mast Industries, Courtaulds, and MAS Holdings to team together, as the opening case indicated.

International Corporate Cooperation

Cooperation between international firms can take many forms, such as cross-licensing of proprietary technology, sharing of production facilities, cofunding of research projects, and marketing of each other's products using existing distribution networks. Such forms of cooperation are known collectively as **strategic alliances,** business arrangements whereby two or more firms choose to cooperate for their mutual benefit. The partners in a strategic alliance may agree to pool R&D activities, marketing expertise, and/or managerial talent. For example, in the early 1990s, Kodak and Fuji—two fierce competitors in the film market—formed a strategic alliance with camera manufacturers Canon, Minolta, and Nikon to develop a new standard for cameras and film, the Advanced Photo System, to make picture taking easier and more goof-proof.[1]

A **joint venture (JV)** is a special type of strategic alliance in which two or more firms join together to create a new business entity that is legally separate and distinct from its parents. Joint ventures are normally established as corporations and are owned by the founding parents in whatever proportions they negotiate. Although unequal ownership is common, many are owned equally by the founding firms. Gulfjet represents this type of alliance.

A strategic alliance is only one method by which a firm can enter or expand its international operations. As Chapter 12 discussed, other alternatives exist: exporting, licensing, franchising, and FDI. In each of these alternatives, however, a firm acts alone or hires a second individual or firm—often one further down the distribution chain—to act on its behalf. In contrast, a strategic alliance results from cooperation among two or more firms. Each participant in a strategic alliance is motivated to promote its own self-interest but has determined that cooperation is the best way to achieve its goals.

Some means is required for managing any cooperative agreement. A joint venture, as a separate legal entity, must have its own set of managers and board of directors. It may be managed in any of three ways. First, the founding firms may jointly share management, with each appointing key personnel who report back to officers of the parent. Second, one parent may assume primary responsibility. And third, an independent team of managers may be hired to run it. The third approach is often preferred, because independent managers focus on what is best for the joint venture rather than attempting to placate bosses from the founding firms.[2] Other types of strategic alliances may be managed more informally—for example, by a coordinating committee, composed of employees of each of the partners, which oversees the alliance's progress.

A formal management organization allows a joint venture to be broader in purpose, scope (or range of operations), and duration than other types of strategic alliances. A non–joint venture strategic alliance may be formed merely to allow the partners to overcome a particular hurdle that each faces in the short run. A joint venture will be more helpful if the two firms plan a more extensive and long-term relationship. A typical non–joint venture strategic alliance has a narrow purpose and scope, such as marketing a new videophone system in Canada. A joint venture might be formed if firms wanted to cooperate in the design, production, and sale of a broad line of telecommunications equipment in North America. Non–joint venture strategic alliances are often formed for a specific purpose that may have a natural ending. For example, the agreement among the camera manufacturers Canon, Minolta, and Nikon and the film manufacturers Fuji and Kodak to jointly create the Advanced Photo System for cameras and film terminated in 1996, after the new standards were developed. Each participant then marketed the resulting products on its own: Kodak called its new film Advantix; Minolta labeled its new cameras Vectis; and Nikon chose the name Nuvis.[3] But because joint ventures are separate legal entities, they generally have a longer duration. A venture such as Gulfjet has an indefinite time horizon in that it will continue to function so long as its three owners are satisfied with its performance.

Because of their narrow mission and lack of a formal organizational structure, non–joint venture strategic alliances are relatively less stable than joint ventures. For example, in 1988 United Airlines and British Airways entered into an agreement to form a strategic marketing alliance involving their North American and European routes. At the time, United was offering limited service to Europe and was losing market share to archrivals Delta and American Airlines, both of which offered more extensive service there. To solve its problem, United agreed to coordinate its flight schedules with British Airways, thereby making it more convenient for a Europe-bound U.S. traveler to board a domestic United flight and then transfer to a transatlantic British Airways flight. United and British Airways both prominently described the arrangement in their marketing campaigns and in the visits of their marketing reps to U.S. and European travel agencies. Within a year, however, Pan Am's routes to London were placed on the auction block. United quickly purchased those routes from Pan Am and severed relations with its strategic ally. British Airways was of little use to United once United could operate in London on its own. Needing a transatlantic partner, British Airways then entered into a similar strategic alliance with US Air in 1993. Three years later American Airlines and British Airways agreed to form a separate strategic alliance. US Air, believing that it would be the weakest partner in a three-way alliance, promptly sued British Airways and terminated their alliance.

 ## Benefits of Strategic Alliances

Firms that enter into strategic alliances usually expect to benefit in one or more ways.[4] As summarized in Figure 13.1, international business may realize four benefits from strategic alliances: ease of market entry, shared risk, shared knowledge and expertise, and synergy and competitive advantage.[5]

FIGURE 13.1

**Benefits of Strategic
Alliances**

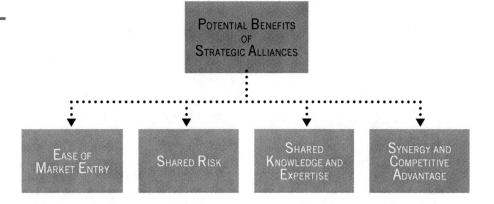

Ease of Market Entry

A firm wishing to enter a new market often faces major obstacles, such as entrenched competition or hostile government regulations. Partnering with a local firm can often help it navigate around such barriers. In other cases, economies of scale and scope in marketing and distribution confer benefits on firms that aggressively and quickly enter numerous markets.[6] Yet the costs of speed and boldness are often high and beyond the capabilities of a single firm. A strategic alliance may allow the firm to achieve the benefits of rapid entry while keeping costs down.

For example, Warner Brothers, the movie studio subsidiary of Time Warner, recently targeted China as an important growth market for branded merchandise. To speed its entry, it entered into a joint venture with Hutchison Whampoa Ltd., one of Hong Kong's oldest trading companies, to own and operate a chain of 200 stores in China, Hong Kong, and Macau to sell movie-related merchandise.[7] A similar meshing of strengths motivated a joint venture between Cigna, the U.S. insurance giant, and Banco Excel Economico, one of Brazil's largest privately owned banks, to sell personal insurance in Brazil. Cigna provides expertise in selling life, accident, and credit insurance to consumers, while Banco Excel supplies its knowledge of the Brazilian financial services industry, as well as access to its existing retail customer base. Each partner contributed half the $19 million invested in the new company, Excel Cigna Seguradora.[8]

Regulations imposed by national governments also influence the formation of joint ventures. Many countries are so concerned about the influence of foreign firms on their economies that they require MNCs to work with a local partner if they want to operate in these countries.[9] For example, the government of Namibia, an African nation, requires foreign investors operating fishing fleets off its coast to work with local partners (see Map 13.1). At other times governments strongly encourage foreign companies to participate in joint ventures in order to promote other policy goals. A case in point is China, which required foreign automobile companies to partner with local firms as a means of transferring technology to its automobile industry.

Shared Risk

Today's major industries are so competitive that no firm has a guarantee of success when it enters a new market or develops a new product. Strategic alliances can be used to either reduce or control individual firms' risks. For example, Boeing established a strategic alliance with several Japanese firms to reduce its financial risk in the development and production of the Boeing 777 jet. Researching, designing, and safety-testing a new aircraft model costs billions of dollars, much of which must be spent before the manufacturer can establish how well the airplane will be received in the marketplace. Even though Boeing has enjoyed much success as a manufacturer of

Namibia's government has promoted development of the country's fishing industry by requiring foreign companies who wish to fish its waters to join with local partners in establishing onshore fish-processing plants. As a result, joint ventures have created jobs, both onshore and offshore, for some 10,000 Namibians.

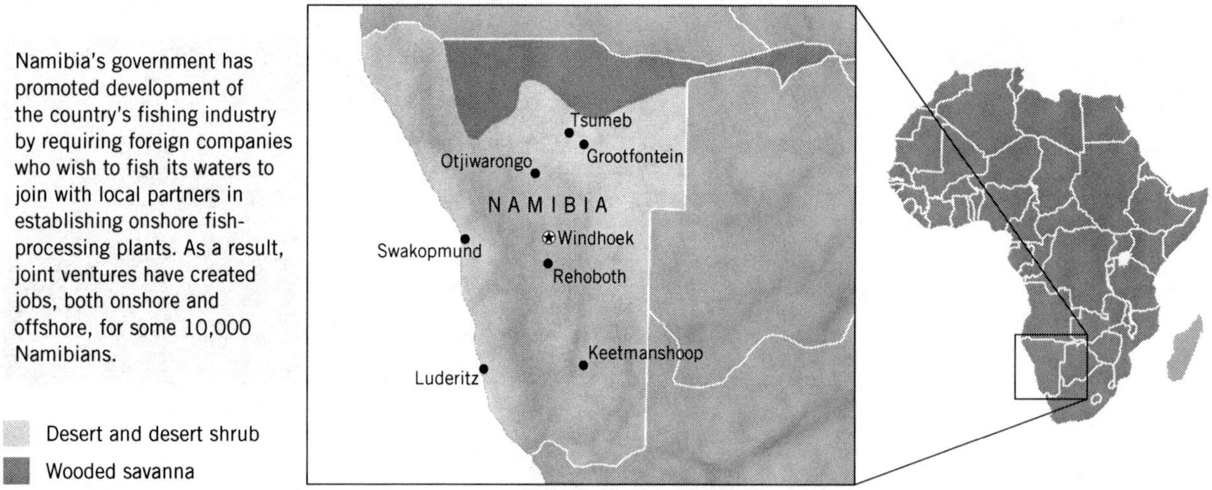

Desert and desert shrub

Wooded savanna

MAP 13.1

Namibia and Joint Ventures

commercial aircraft, it wanted to reduce its financial exposure on the 777 project. Thus it collaborated with three Japanese partners—Fuji, Mitsubishi, and Kawasaki—agreeing to let them build 20 percent of the 777 airframe. Boeing, the controlling partner in the alliance, also hoped its allies would help sell the new aircraft to large Japanese customers such as Japan Air Lines and All Nippon Airways. The arrangement proved so successful that Boeing utilized it as well in designing and producing its latest jet, the 787 Dreamliner.

Or consider the strategic alliance involving Kodak and Fuji and three Japanese camera firms discussed previously. At face value, it might seem odd for Kodak to agree to collaborate with Fuji, its biggest competitor, to develop a new film that both now make and sell. Closer scrutiny, however, suggests that the arrangement reduced Kodak's risks considerably. Kodak managers realized that if they developed the film alone, Fuji would aggressively fight the innovation in the marketplace and Kodak would have to work hard to gain consumer acceptance of its new standard for film. Still worse, Fuji might have decided to develop its own new film standard, thereby jeopardizing Kodak's R&D investment should the Japanese-dominated camera-manufacturing industry adopt Fuji's approach rather than Kodak's. Mindful of the financial losses incurred by Sony when VHS rather than Betamax became the standard format for VCRs, Kodak chose to include Fuji in the deal. Through this strategic alliance, Kodak perhaps reduced its potential profits but also substantially reduced its risks. It was then free to compete on a playing field of its own choosing, able to harness its marketing clout, distribution networks, and formidable brand name against the efforts of its rivals.

Shared risk is an especially important consideration when a firm is entering a market that has just opened up or that is characterized by much uncertainty and instability. "Emerging Opportunities" discusses how one international business, Otis Elevator, uses joint ventures to slash its risks in such situations.

Shared Knowledge and Expertise

Still another common reason for strategic alliances is the potential for the firm to gain knowledge and expertise that it lacks. A firm may want to learn more about how to produce something, how to acquire certain resources, how to deal with local governments' regulations, or how to manage in a different environment—information that a partner often can offer.[10] The firm can then use the newly acquired information for other purposes. For instance, in 2006, Moody's entered into a joint venture with

The Ups and Downs of Market Entry

Entering a new market is always a risky proposition, but when a firm is the first foreigner to enter, its risks are even greater. That's why many foreign firms who try to be first often look for a local partner for help. A good case in point is Otis Elevator.

A division of United Technologies, Otis has a strategy of trying to be the first foreign elevator manufacturer to enter emerging markets. For example, the firm entered China in 1984. The morning after the Berlin Wall fell, Otis executives began negotiating with prospective local partners in Central and Eastern Europe. And more recently, it was among the very first U.S. companies to announce plans to enter Vietnam when President Clinton lifted the trade embargo with that country.

Otis always looks for one or more local partners to ease its entry and reduce its risks. For example, the firm has 10 different joint ventures in China (see Map 13.2), employing over 8,000 people. These partners know the local landscape and can help the company avoid problems. They also aid the marketing of Otis's products. For example, Otis won the lucrative contract to provide 158 escalators for the Shanghai metro system thanks in part to its Chinese partners. It also was chosen to install 110 elevators and escalators for Tianjin's new subway system, as well as those for the Beijing Transit Center, which served thousands of visitors arriving for the 2008 Summer Olympics. On the other hand, Otis also often has to work hard to get its partners "up to speed." For example, it took Otis three years to get its first Chinese partner to phase out its own antiquated product line and replace it with newer Otis equipment. And convincing the partner about the benefits of customer service took even longer. To instill the service-oriented spirit vital to its success, Otis now spends over $2 million a year training its Chinese managers and employees.

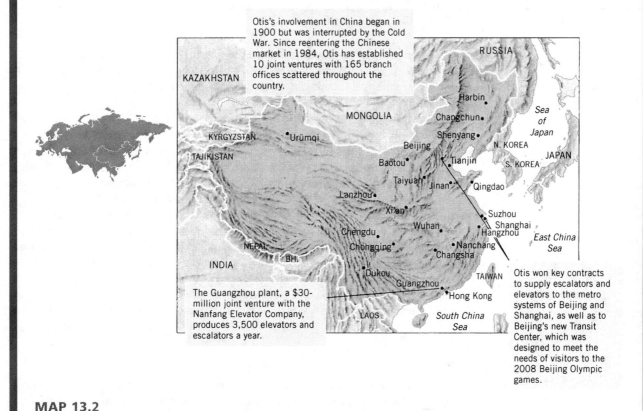

Otis's involvement in China began in 1900 but was interrupted by the Cold War. Since reentering the Chinese market in 1984, Otis has established 10 joint ventures with 165 branch offices scattered throughout the country.

The Guangzhou plant, a $30-million joint venture with the Nanfang Elevator Company, produces 3,500 elevators and escalators a year.

Otis won key contracts to supply escalators and elevators to the metro systems of Beijing and Shanghai, as well as to Beijing's new Transit Center, which was designed to meet the needs of visitors to the 2008 Beijing Olympic games.

MAP 13.2

Otis Elevators' Joint Ventures in China (Shown in Red)

Otis Elevators has relied on local joint venture partners to ease and speed its entry into the Chinese market. Otis's Beijing venture was chosen to outfit the elevators and escalators for the Beijing Transit Center, the new Number Ten subway line, and 30 sporting venues used for the 2008 Beijing Olympic games.

Otis's strategy seems to be a sound one. Providing its local partner with cutting-edge technology, equipment, and training often yields high returns. Yet often low-tech solutions are equally as valuable. For example, the simple act of providing its new Russian workforce with vans boosted productivity; previously, these workers often transported spare parts by carrying them on the Moscow subway. Otis now services over 118,000 elevators throughout Russia and Ukraine. All told, 81 percent of Otis's $11.8 billion in revenues in 2007 were earned outside the United States. Perhaps more important, the company is perfectly positioned to benefit from the elevated growth prospects of many large emerging markets.

Sources: United Technologies Annual Report 2007; www.otis.com, various press releases; "The Pioneers," *Wall Street Journal*, September 26, 1996, pp. R1, R14; "Overseas, Otis and Its Parent Get In on the Ground Floor," *Wall Street Journal*, April 21, 1995, p. A6.

China Cheng Xin International Credit Rating Company to allow them to offer joint credit ratings for participants in cross-border financings; the Chinese company will provide credit ratings for domestic firms, while Moody's will provide ratings on international companies.[11]

One of the more successful joint ventures in the United States has been that between Toyota and GM. In 1982 GM closed an old automobile manufacturing plant in Fremont, California, because it had become too costly and inefficient to run. In 1984 Toyota agreed to reopen the plant and manage it through a joint venture called NUMMI (New United Motor Manufacturing, Inc.). Although NUMMI is owned equally by the two partners, Toyota manages the facility and makes automobiles for both. Each firm entered into the deal primarily to acquire knowledge. Toyota wanted to learn more about how to deal with labor and parts suppliers in the U.S. market; GM wanted to observe Japanese management practices firsthand.[12] Toyota used its newly acquired information when it opened its own manufacturing plant in Georgetown, Kentucky, in 1988. GM used lessons learned from NUMMI in developing and operating its newest automotive division, Saturn, and in organizing its newest European assembly plant in Eisenach, Germany. As a result, productivity in this plant is double that of GM's plants in the United States.

Synergy and Competitive Advantage

Firms may also enter into strategic alliances in order to attain synergy and competitive advantage. These related advantages reflect combinations of the other advantages discussed in this section: the idea is that through some combination of market entry, risk sharing, and learning potential, each collaborating firm will be able to achieve

The New United Motor Manufacturing, Inc. (NUMMI) joint venture between Toyota and General Motors will celebrate its 25th birthday in 2009. Located in a former GM assembly plant in Fremont, California, but managed by Toyota executives, NUMMI was created to allow each partner to acquire knowledge necessary to implement its future strategy.

Gary Reyes/Jose Reyes/San Jose Mercury News/Newscom

more and to compete more effectively than if it had attempted to enter a new market or industry alone.[13]

For example, creating a favorable brand image in consumers' minds is an expensive, time-consuming process, as is creating efficient distribution networks and obtaining the necessary clout with retailers to capture shelf space for one's products. These factors led PepsiCo, the world's second-largest soft drink firm, to establish a joint venture with Thomas J. Lipton Co., a division of Unilever, to produce and market ready-to-drink teas in the United States. Lipton, which has a 50 percent share of the $400-million worldwide market for ready-to-drink teas, provided the joint venture with manufacturing expertise and brand recognition in teas. PepsiCo supplied its extensive and experienced U.S. distribution network.[14] Similarly, Siemens and Motorola established a joint venture to produce DRAM computer chips. Motorola teamed with Siemens in part to help finance the new $1.5 billion factory the partners agreed to build, while Siemens sought to benefit from Motorola's manufacturing expertise and to improve its access to the U.S. market, which typically accounts for 40 percent of the worldwide market for DRAM memory chips.[15] "Venturing Abroad" provides another example of this phenomenon.

Venturing Abroad

South Korea in the Middle East

In May 2007 His Highness Sheikh Mohammed Bin Rashid Al Maktoum, the Vice President and Prime Minister of the United Arab Emirates and the ruler of Dubai, visited South Korea. During his visit the Dubai-based Al Fattan Properties and the Sungwon Corporation signed a Memorandum of Understanding to forge their strategic alliance. Signing for Al Fattan Properties was Phillip Fusco and for Sungwon was the president, Hae Shick Cho. Sungwon Corporation, being one of the largest construction and property development companies in South Korea, would market and sell Al Fattan Properties' projects in South Korea.

The key Al Fattan projects included the Jumeirah Al Fattan Palm Resort, a $245 million development at one of the most renowned landmarks in Dubai. The project incorporates service apartments, a marina, spar, beach club, and five star hotel. Another major project is the Al Fattan Currency House, a $258 million development consisting of a modern office block, retail and leisure facilities, and private residences.

In order to make full use of the marketing opportunities, Sungwon renamed its Dubai showroom, in Samsungdong in Seoul, the Dubai Experience Center. The idea was to showcase Dubai's property developments and to build longer-term relationships between South Korea and the United Arab Emirates.

Al Fattan Properties has also struck other key strategic alliances to market, sell, and finance apartments in the Dubai marina area, such as the Al Fattan Marina Towers. In June 2008, Al Fattan Properties entered into a strategic alliance with the Jumeirah Group, a Dubai-based luxury international hospitality management group, to manage the Jumeirah Al Fattan Palm Resort, consisting of over 200 rooms and suites and other facilities, which is due to open in late 2009.

Sources: Al Fattan Properties (www.alfattan.ae), Sungwon Corporation (www.sungwon.co.kr), Santevill Dubai (www.dubai-sungwon.com), and Arabian Business (www.arabianbusiness.com).

Scope of Strategic Alliances

The scope of cooperation among firms may vary significantly, as Figure 13.2 illustrates. For example, it may consist of a comprehensive alliance, in which the partners participate in all facets of conducting business, ranging from product design to manufacturing to marketing. Or it may consist of a more narrowly defined alliance that focuses on only one element of the business, such as R&D. The degree of collaboration will depend on the basic goals of each partner.

FIGURE 13.2

The Scope of Strategic Alliances

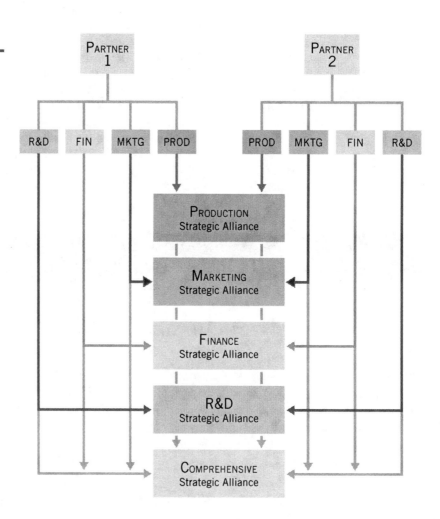

Comprehensive Alliances

Comprehensive alliances arise when the participating firms agree to perform together multiple stages of the process by which goods or services are brought to the market: R&D, design, production, marketing, and distribution. Because of the broad scope of such alliances, the firms must establish procedures for meshing such functional areas as finance, production, and marketing for the alliance to succeed. Yet integrating the different operating procedures of the parents over a broad range of functional activities is difficult in the absence of a formal organizational structure. As a result, most comprehensive alliances are organized as joint ventures. As an independent entity, the joint venture can adopt operating procedures that suit its specific needs, rather than attempting to accommodate the often incompatible procedures of the parents, as might be the case with another type of strategic alliance.

Moreover, by fully integrating their efforts, participating firms in a comprehensive alliance are able to achieve greater synergy through sheer size and total resources. For example, General Mills and Nestlé created a comprehensive joint venture, Cereal Partners Worldwide, to market cereal in Europe in the face of fierce, entrenched competition from Kellogg. General Mills contributed its cereal-making technology to the joint venture, while Nestlé added its European distribution network and name recognition. Cereal Partners Worldwide would have had a major uphill battle in the European cereal market if the joint venture had covered only a single function, such as marketing. But a complete meshing of each firm's relative strengths resulted in a business unit that has emerged as a formidable competitor for Kellogg. Similarly, Dow Chemical and the Saudi Arabian Oil Co. (Aramco) agreed to build and operate a $22 billion petrochemical complex near Ras Tanura that is scheduled to begin operation in 2012. Aramco will provide the feedstock for the plant, while Dow Chemical will contribute its technology and expertise in manufacturing petrochemicals.[16]

Functional Alliances

Strategic alliances may also be narrow in scope, involving only a single functional area of the business. In such cases, integrating the needs of the parent firms is less complex. Thus functionally based alliances often do not take the form of a joint venture, although joint ventures are still the more common form of organization. Types of functional alliances include production alliances, marketing alliances, financial alliances, and R&D alliances.

PRODUCTION ALLIANCES. A **production alliance** is a functional alliance in which two or more firms each manufacture products or provide services in a shared or common facility. A production alliance may utilize a facility one partner already owns. For example, as we discussed earlier, the NUMMI joint venture between Toyota and GM is housed in a former GM assembly plant in California, which the company had closed down. Alternatively, the partners may choose to build a new plant, as is the case for a new $3.5 billion joint venture between Sony and Sharp to manufacture liquid crystal display panels for high-definition televisions in western Japan.[17]

MARKETING ALLIANCES. A **marketing alliance** is a functional alliance in which two or more firms share marketing services or expertise. In most cases, one partner introduces its products or services into a market in which the other partner already has a presence. The established firm helps the newcomer by promoting, advertising, and/or distributing its products or services. The established firm may negotiate a fixed price for its assistance or may share in a percentage of the newcomer's sales or profits. Alternatively, the firms may agree to market each others' products on a reciprocal basis. For example, U.S. toymaker Mattel and its Japanese rival Bandai established a strategic marketing alliance in 1999. Bandai agreed to distribute Mattel products like Barbie dolls, Hot Wheels, and Fisher Price toys in Japan, while Mattel agreed to market Bandai's Power Rangers and Digimon in Latin America, where Mattel's distribution network is strong but Bandai's nonexistent.[18] Marketing alliances are also very common in the international airline industry, as "Venturing Abroad" indicates. However, when forming a marketing alliance, partners must take care to ensure that their expectations and needs are mutually understood.

Alliances in the Sky

Marketing alliances are usually ad hoc in nature, established to remedy some problem a firm has in a specific market. In the international airline industry, however, mega-marketing alliances now dominate competition within the industry. Three mega-alliances together account for about 69 percent of the world's air revenue passenger-miles. The Star Alliance, established in 1997, was the first of the mega-alliances to form and is the industry's largest. Its 21 members include United, USAir, Lufthansa, SAS, Air Canada, Air China, South African Airways, and Singapore Airlines. The Star Alliance provides service to 975 airports in 162 countries. The eleven-member SkyTeam alliance includes Air France, KLM, Northwest, Delta, Continental, Aeromexico, Korean Air Lines, and Aeroflot. This alliance serves 841 cities in 162 countries. The One World alliance, whose 10 members include American Airlines, British Airways, Qantas, Cathay Pacific, and Japan Airlines, is the third largest alliance. This alliance flies to 675 cities in 130 countries.

Alliances have become a critical component of competition in the international airline industry because of decisions made at the International Civil Aviation Conference held in Chicago in 1944. The Chicago Conference, like the Bretton Woods Conference of 1944, was convened to structure a portion of the post–World War II economic environment—in this case, that of the civil aviation industry. The Chicago conferees decided to grant each government control over international airline service to and from its country. Most countries chose to grant commercial airline rights on a reciprocal basis: Country A would grant country B the right to designate a carrier from country B to fly between a city in B and a city in A if country B granted country A the right to designate a carrier from country A to fly between a city in A and a city in B. Moreover, very few nations allowed cabotage—the carrying of passengers by a foreign carrier from one city in the host country to another city in the host country (e.g., Delta Airlines carrying a passenger from Vancouver to Montreal).

Thus an airline like Delta could develop an elaborate hub-and-spoke system in Atlanta that would allow it to pick up a passenger in a U.S. city like Buffalo, transport her to Atlanta, and transfer her to a Delta flight going to Albuquerque. Using a hub-and-spoke system, Delta could provide convenient

The Star Alliance is the largest of the three major consortia formed by international airlines to improve the service offered to travelers around the world. Among its newest members are Air China and Shanghai Airlines, whose entry into the Star Alliance led to this ceremony in Beijing.

Photo by Hu Xuebai/JHSB/ChinaFotoPress, Newscom

service to Buffalo-Albuquerque travelers, even though only a few passengers might wish to fly from Buffalo to Albuquerque on any given day. This advantage, however, stopped at the water's edge. Because of the Chicago Conference, Delta could not create a similar hub in Europe or Asia. However, by joining the SkyTeam Alliance, Delta can take advantage of Air France's hub in Paris, KLM's hub in Amsterdam, Aeroflot's hub in Moscow, and Korean Airlines' hub in Seoul. Thus Delta and any other member of the SkyTeam alliance can advertise and offer service on over 16,000 flights a day to 841 cities in 162 countries even though it physically flies only a small percentage of these flights itself.

Besides offering customers more flights and more destinations, these marketing alliances make it easier for customers to transfer between alliance members' flights and allow customers to use frequent flyer miles earned on one carrier to fly free on the flights of other members of the alliance. The alliances also strive to maintain uniformly high standards of service and to promote consistent customer service policies. The SkyTeam alliance, for instance, coordinates its in-flight video offerings so that passengers flying different SkyTeam carriers on a given day see different movies on each leg of their journey.

Sources: www.staralliance.com; www.skyteam.com; www.oneworld alliance.com.

FINANCIAL ALLIANCES. A **financial alliance** is a functional alliance of firms that want to reduce the financial risks associated with a project. Partners may share equally in contributing financial resources to the project, or one partner may contribute the bulk of the financing while the other partner (or partners) provides special expertise or makes other kinds of contributions to partially offset its lack of financial investment. The strategic alliance between Boeing and its three Japanese partners was created primarily for financial purposes—Boeing wanted the other firms to help cover R&D and manufacturing costs. Those firms, in turn, saw a chance to gain valuable experience in commercial aircraft manufacturing as well as profits. And 20th Century Fox and Paramount Pictures were financial allies in producing *Titanic,* one of the most successful movies in history.

RESEARCH AND DEVELOPMENT ALLIANCES. Rapid technological change in high-technology industries and the skyrocketing cost of staying abreast of that change have prompted an increase in functional alliances that focuses on R&D. In an **R&D alliance,** the partners agree to undertake joint research to develop new products or services. An example of a typical R&D alliance is one formed in 2000 among Intel, Micron Technology, Samsung, Hyundai, NEC, and Siemens to develop the next generation of DRAM chips.[19] Similarly, Bayer AG formed R&D alliances with smaller biotechnology companies like Millenium Pharmaceuticals and Morphosys to strengthen their joint search for new miracle drugs.[20]

Such alliances are usually not formed as joint ventures, since scientific knowledge can be transmitted among partners through private research conferences, the exchange of scientific papers, and laboratory visits. Moreover, forming a separate legal organization and staffing it with teams of researchers drawn from the partners' staffs might disrupt ongoing scientific work in each partner's laboratory. Instead each partner may simply agree to cross-license whatever new technology is developed in its labs, thereby allowing its partner (or partners) to use its patents at will. Each partner then has equal access to all technology developed by the alliance, an arrangement that guarantees the partners will not fall behind each other in the technological race. Partners also are freed from legal disputes among themselves over ownership and validity of patents. For example, the alliance among Kodak, Fuji, and the three Japanese camera makers focused solely on R&D. Both Kodak and Fuji are licensed to make the new film they developed; the three camera makers are free to market the cameras to use it.

Because of the importance of high-tech industries to the world economy, many countries are supporting the efforts of R&D consortia as part of their industrial policies. An **R&D consortium** is a confederation of organizations that band together to research and develop new products and processes for world markets. It represents a special case of strategic alliance in that governmental support plays a major role in its formation and continued operation.[21] Japanese firms have successfully practiced this type of arrangement for many years. For example, more than two decades ago the Japanese government, Nippon Telephone and Telegraph, Mitsubishi, Matsushita, and three other Japanese firms agreed to work together to create new types of high-capacity memory chips. They were so successful that they dominated this market for many years. Similarly, the EU has developed a wide array of joint research efforts with clever acronyms—such as ESPRIT, RACE, BRITE, EURAM, JOULE, and SCIENCE—to ensure that its firms can compete against U.S. and Japanese firms in high-tech markets.

Implementation of Strategic Alliances

The decision to form a strategic alliance should develop from the firm's strategic planning process, discussed in Chapter 11. Having made this decision, its managers must then address several significant issues, which set the stage for how the arrangement will be managed.[22] Some of the most critical of these issues are the selection of partners, the form of ownership, and joint management considerations.

Selection of Partners

The success of any cooperative undertaking depends on choosing the appropriate partner(s). Research suggests that strategic alliances are more likely to be successful if the skills and resources of the partners are complementary—each must bring to the alliance some organizational strength the other lacks.[23] A firm contemplating a strategic alliance should consider at least four factors in selecting a partner (or partners): (1) compatibility, (2) the nature of the potential partner's products or services, (3) the relative safeness of the alliance, and (4) the learning potential of the alliance.

COMPATIBILITY.   The firm should select a compatible partner that it can trust and with whom it can work effectively. Without mutual trust, a strategic alliance is unlikely to succeed. But incompatibilities in corporate operating philosophies may also doom an alliance. For example, an alliance between General Electric Corporation (a U.K. firm unrelated to the U.S. firm of the same name) and the German firm Siemens failed because of incompatible management styles. The former firm is run by financial experts and the latter by engineers. General Electric Corporation's financial managers continually worried about bottom-line issues, short-term profitability, and related financial considerations. Siemens' managers, in contrast, cared little about financial issues and paid more attention to innovation, design, and product development.[24] In contrast, a key ingredient in Cereal Partners Worldwide's success is the high level of compatibility between General Mills and Nestlé.

NATURE OF A POTENTIAL PARTNER'S PRODUCTS OR SERVICES.   Another factor to consider is the nature of a potential partner's products or services. It is often hard to cooperate with a firm in one market while doing battle with that same firm in a second market. Under such circumstances, each partner may be unwilling to reveal all its expertise to the other partner for fear that the partner will use that knowledge against the firm in another market.

Most experts believe a firm should ally itself with a partner whose products or services are complementary to but not directly competitive with its own. The joint venture between General Mills and Nestlé is an example of this principle in action: Both are food-processing firms, but Nestlé does not make cereal, the product on which it is collaborating with General Mills. Similarly, PepsiCo and Lipton complement but do not compete with one another, thus raising the likelihood of success for their joint venture to market ready-to-drink tea in the United States.

THE RELATIVE SAFENESS OF THE ALLIANCE.   Given the complexities and potential costs of failed agreements, managers should gather as much information as possible about a potential partner before entering into a strategic alliance. For example, managers should assess the success or failure of previous strategic alliances formed by the potential partner. Also, it often makes sense to analyze the prospective deal from the other firm's side. What does the potential partner hope to gain from the arrangement? What are the partner's strengths and weaknesses? How will it contribute to the venture? Does the proposed arrangement meet its strategic goals? The probability of success rises if the deal makes good business sense for both parties.[25]

For example, Corning, Inc., created a joint venture—Asahi Video Products Company—by integrating its television glass production with the operations of Asahi Glass, a producer of large television bulbs. Corning believed this joint venture would be a sound one for several reasons:

- Asahi Glass's expertise in large television bulb technology complemented Corning's strength in other bulb sizes.
- The joint venture would benefit from Asahi Glass's ongoing business connections with the increasing number of Japanese television manufacturers that were establishing North American facilities.
- The combined strengths of the two firms would help both keep abreast of technological innovations in the video display industry.
- Asahi Glass would benefit from Corning's technology and marketing clout in the U.S. market.
- Corning had successfully operated another joint venture with Asahi Glass since 1965.

In fact, Corning is so good at developing joint ventures that almost half its profits are generated by joint ventures with PPG, Dow Chemical, Samsung, Siemens, Ciba-Geigy, IBM, and, of course, Asahi Glass.

THE LEARNING POTENTIAL OF THE ALLIANCE.   Before establishing a strategic alliance, partners should also assess the potential to learn from each other. Areas of learning can range from the very specific—for example, how to manage inventory more efficiently or how to train employees more effectively—to the very general—for example, how to modify corporate culture or how to manage more strategically. At the same time, however, each partner should carefully assess the value of its own information and not provide the other partner with any that will result in competitive disadvantage for itself should the alliance dissolve—a point we revisit in the next section.[26]

Form of Ownership

Another issue in establishing a strategic alliance is the exact form of ownership that is to be used. A joint venture almost always takes the form of a corporation, usually incorporated in the country in which it will be doing business. In some instances, it may be incorporated in a different country, such as one that offers tax or legal advantages. The Bahamas, for example, are sometimes seen as a favorable tax haven for the incorporation of joint ventures.

The corporate form enables the partners to arrange a beneficial tax structure, implement novel ownership arrangements, and better protect their other assets. This form also allows the joint venture to create its own identity apart from those of the partners. Of course, if either or both of the partners have favorable reputations, the new corporation may choose to rely on those, perhaps by including the partners' names as part of its name.

A new corporation also provides a neutral setting in which the partners can do business. The potential for conflict may be reduced if the interaction between the partners occurs outside their own facilities or organizations. It may also be reduced if the corporation does not rely on employees identified with either partner and instead hires its own executives and workforce whose first loyalty is to the joint venture. For example, a joint venture formed by Corning and Genentech was not performing as well as expected. Corning soon discovered one source of the difficulties: Managers contributed by Genentech to the joint venture were actually on leave from Genentech. To ensure that these managers' loyalties were not divided between Genentech and the joint venture, Corning requested that they resign from Genentech. Once they did, the performance of the joint venture improved rapidly.[27]

In isolated cases, incorporating a joint venture may not be possible or desirable. For example, local restrictions on corporations may be so stringent or burdensome that incorporating is not optimal. The partners in these cases usually choose to operate under a limited partnership arrangement. In a limited partnership, one firm, the managing partner, assumes full financial responsibility for the venture, regardless of the amount of its own investment. The other partner (or partners) has liability limited to its own investment. Obviously, such arrangements are riskier for the managing partner.

PUBLIC-PRIVATE VENTURE.   A special form of joint venture, a **public-private venture**, is one that involves a partnership between a privately owned firm and a government. Such an arrangement may be created under any of several circumstances.

When the government of a country controls a resource it wants developed, it may enlist the assistance of a firm that has expertise related to that resource. For example, South American countries have used several foreign lumber firms, such as Weyerhaeuser, to assist in the development of their rain forests and surrounding lands. A similar pattern exists in the discovery, exploration, and development of oil fields. National governments that control access to and ownership of oil fields may lack the technical expertise to drill for and manage the extraction of crude oil reserves. International oil firms, on the other hand, possess the requisite knowledge and expertise but may lack the necessary drilling rights. A common result is a joint venture for which the government grants drilling rights and private oil firms provide capital and expertise. For example, in 2006 Exxon Mobil entered into a joint venture with the Abu Dhabi government, receiving a 28 percent interest in Abu Dhabi's Upper Zakum field; as part of the deal, the company agreed to establish a technology institute in Abu Dhabi and boost the field's production by 50 percent using advanced drilling and reservoir management techniques.[28]

Similarly, a firm may pursue a public-private venture if a particular country does not allow wholly owned foreign operations. If the firm cannot locate a suitable local partner, it may invite the government itself to participate in a joint venture, or the government may request an ownership share. Public-private ventures are typical in the oil industry. In assessing the opportunities and drawbacks of such a venture, a firm should consider the various aspects of the political and legal environment it will be facing. Foremost among these is the stability of the government. In a politically unstable country, the current government may be replaced with another, and the firm may face serious challenges. At best, the venture will be considered less important by the new government because of its association with the old government. At worst, the firm's investment may be completely wiped out, its assets seized, and its operation shut down. However, if negotiations are handled properly and if the local government is relatively stable, public-private ventures can be quite beneficial. The government may act benignly and allow the firm to run the joint venture. It may also use its position to protect its own investment—and therefore that of its partner—by restricting competing business activity.

A firm entering public-private partnerships should ensure that it thoroughly understands the expectations and commitments of both the host country's government and its prospective business partner. These concerns are most obvious in China. Because of the vast size and growth prospects of the Chinese market, many firms are interested in investment opportunities there, and joint ventures with state-owned firms are a common mode of entry for MNCs. Many Western firms have prospered through such arrangements. For example, Alcatel's joint venture with the Ministry of Post and Telecommunications, Shanghai Bell, has captured more than half the market for switching equipment in the booming Chinese telecommunications market, much to the chagrin of its traditional rivals, Siemens and Nortel.

However, other Western firms have had their share of troubles with these arrangements, prompting a bitter joke among expatriates in China: "What qualities should you look for in a joint-venture partner?" "One who never comes to the office." For example, Unilever's joint venture partner in Shanghai not only continued to sell its own brand of detergent, White Cat, in competition with the Unilever product (Omo) produced by the joint venture, but it also began to copy Omo's formula and packaged its detergent in a box that looked almost identical to that of Omo. Similarly, Daimler-Benz signed an agreement in 1995 to establish a joint venture with state-owned Nanfang South China Motor Corporation to build minivans. Two years later, nothing had been done as the two partners bickered over a variety of issues. Nanfang, for example, wanted to assemble the minivans at two plant sites, while Daimler-Benz officials fought for a single plant so as to capture economies of scale.[29] Similarly, in 2002 New Balance discovered that its Chinese manufacturing partner was making counterfeit sneakers and selling them directly to discounters in England and Australia in addition to those it was legally making for New Balance itself.[30]

Joint Management Considerations

Further issues and questions are associated with how a strategic alliance will be managed.[31] Three standard approaches are often used to jointly manage a strategic alliance (see Figure 13.3): shared management agreements, assigned arrangements, and delegated arrangements.

Under a **shared management agreement,** each partner fully and actively participates in managing the alliance. The partners run the alliance, and their managers regularly pass on instructions and details to the alliance's managers. The alliance managers have limited authority of their own and must defer most decisions to managers from the parent firms. This type of agreement requires a high level of coordination and near-perfect agreement between the participating partners. Thus it is the most difficult to maintain and the one most prone to conflict among the partners. An example of a joint venture operating under a shared management agreement is one formed by Coca-Cola and France's Groupe Danone to distribute Coke's Minute Maid orange juice in Europe and Latin America. This joint venture combines Danone's distribution network and production facilities—Danone supplies between 15 and 30 percent of the dairy products sold by supermarkets in these countries—with the Minute Maid brand name. The joint venture operates under a shared management

FIGURE 13.3

Managing Strategic Alliances

SHARED-MANAGEMENT AGREEMENT

PARTNER 1 — Both partners participate actively — PARTNER 2 — ALLIANCE

ASSIGNED ARRANGEMENT

PARTNER 1 — One partner takes primary responsibility — PARTNER 2 — ALLIANCE

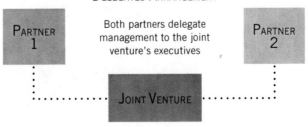

DELEGATED ARRANGEMENT

PARTNER 1 — Both partners delegate management to the joint venture's executives — PARTNER 2 — JOINT VENTURE

arrangement: Each company supplies three members of the JV's board of directors. Danone is responsible for the JV's operations, while Coke controls its marketing and finance.[32]

Under an **assigned arrangement,** one partner assumes primary responsibility for the operations of the strategic alliance. For example, GM, with a 67 percent stake in a joint venture with Raba, a Hungarian truck, engine, and tractor manufacturer, has assumed management control over the venture's operations.[33] Boeing controls the overall operations of its strategic alliance with Fuji, Mitsubishi, and Kawasaki for the design and production of its 777 and 787 commercial aircraft. Under an assigned arrangement, management of the alliance is greatly simplified because the dominant partner has the power to set its own agenda for the new unit, break ties among decision makers, and even overrule its partner(s). Of course, these actions may create conflict, but they keep the alliance from becoming paralyzed, which may happen if equal partners cannot agree on a decision.

Under a **delegated arrangement,** which is reserved for joint ventures, the partners agree not to get involved in ongoing operations and so delegate management control to the executives of the joint venture itself. These executives may be specifically hired to run the new operation or may be transferred from the participating firms. They are responsible for the day-to-day decision making and management of the venture and for implementing its strategy. Thus they have real power and the autonomy to make significant decisions themselves and are much less accountable to managers in the partner firms. For example, both American Motors and the Beijing Automotive Works contributed experienced managers to the operation of Beijing Jeep so that its management team could learn both modern automobile assembly operations and operating conditions in China. Moreover, these managers were given responsibility for the joint venture's operations.

Pitfalls of Strategic Alliances

Regardless of the care and deliberation a firm puts into constructing a strategic alliance, it still must consider limitations and pitfalls. Figure 13.4 summarizes five fundamental sources of problems that often threaten the viability of strategic alliances: incompatibility of partners, access to information, conflicts over distributing earnings, loss of autonomy, and changing circumstances.

Incompatibility of Partners

Incompatibility among the partners of a strategic alliance is a primary cause of the failure of such arrangements. At times, incompatibility can lead to outright conflict, although typically it merely leads to poor performance of the alliance. We noted earlier in the chapter the example of the conflict between Siemens's engineering-oriented management and General Electric Corporation's financially-oriented management. Incompatibility can stem from differences in corporate culture, national culture, goals and objectives, or virtually any other fundamental dimension linking the two partners. For instance, General Motors' $340-million joint venture with Russian auto manufacturer OAO Avtovaz, which was established to build Chevrolet-branded compact sports utility vehicles designed by Avtovaz, has struggled as a result of disagreements between the partners over parts pricing, product design, market development, and adjustments in the joint venture's strategic direction.[34]

FIGURE 13.4

Pitfalls of Strategic Alliances

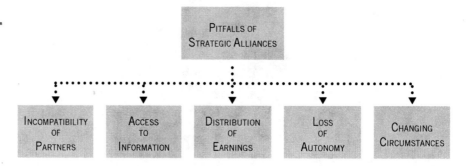

In many cases, compatibility problems can be anticipated if the partners carefully discuss and analyze the reasons why each is entering into the alliance in the first place. A useful starting point may be a meeting between top managers of the two partners to discuss their mutual interests, goals, and beliefs about strategy. The manner in which the managers are able to work together during such a meeting may be a critical clue to their ability to cooperate in a strategic alliance. Obviously, if the partners cannot agree on such basic issues as how much decision-making power to delegate to the alliance's business unit, what the alliance's strategy should be, how it is to be organized, or how it should be staffed, compromise will probably be difficult to achieve and the alliance is unlikely to succeed. For example, a marketing alliance between AT&T and Italy's Olivetti announced with great fanfare in the mid-1990s quickly failed after the firms could not reach agreement on a marketing strategy, what they wanted the alliance to accomplish, and how they planned to work together.

Access to Information

Limited access to information is another drawback of many strategic alliances. For a collaboration to work effectively, one partner (or both) may have to provide the other with information it would prefer to keep secret. It is often difficult to identify such needs ahead of time; thus a firm may enter into an agreement not anticipating having to share certain information. When the reality of the situation becomes apparent, the firm may have to be forthcoming with the information or else compromise the effectiveness of the collaboration.[35]

For example, Unisys, a U.S. computer firm, negotiated a joint venture with Hitachi, a Japanese electronics firm. Only after the venture was well underway did Unisys realize that it would have to provide Hitachi with most of the technical specifications it used to build computers. Although Unisys managers reluctantly gave Hitachi the information, they feared they were compromising their own firm's competitiveness. And an alliance between Ford and Mazda to work on the design of a new Ford sedan almost stalled when Mazda officials would not allow their Ford counterparts to visit their research laboratory. After several weeks of arguing, a compromise was eventually reached whereby Ford engineers could enter the facility but only for a limited time.

Conflicts over Distributing Earnings

An obvious limitation of strategic alliances relates to the distribution of earnings. Because the partners share risks and costs, they also share profits. For example, General Mills and Nestlé split the profits from their European joint venture on a 50/50 basis. Of course, this aspect of collaborative arrangements is known ahead of time and is virtually always negotiated as part of the original agreement.

However, there are other financial considerations beyond the basic distribution of earnings that can cause disagreement. The partners must also agree on the proportion of the joint earnings that will be distributed to themselves as opposed to being reinvested in the business, the accounting procedures that will be used to calculate earnings or profits, and the way transfer pricing will be handled. For example, in the 1990s Rubbermaid ended its joint venture to manufacture and distribute rubber and plastic houseware products throughout Europe, North Africa, and the Middle East because its local partner, the Dutch chemical company DSM Group NV, resisted reinvesting profits to develop new products to expand the joint venture's sales as Rubbermaid preferred.[36]

Loss of Autonomy

Another pitfall of a strategic alliance is the potential loss of autonomy. Just as firms share risks and profits, they also share control, thereby limiting what each can do. Most attempts to introduce new products or services, change the way the alliance does business, or introduce any other significant organizational change first must be discussed and negotiated. To overcome such problems, FedEx chose to buy out its Chinese joint venture partner, Tianjin Datian W Group, for $400 million. The 2006 purchase freed FedEx to better integrate the joint venture's 90 parcel-processing facilities and its 3,000 workers into FedEx's global distribution network.[37] Conversely, as part of its contract with General Mills, Nestlé had to agree that if the joint venture is ever terminated, Nestlé cannot enter the North American cereal market for at least 10 years.

At the extreme, a strategic alliance may even be the first step toward a takeover. In the early 1980s, the Japanese firm Fujitsu negotiated a strategic alliance with International Computers, Ltd. (ICL), a British computer firm. After nine years of working together, Fujitsu bought 80 percent of ICL. One survey of 150 terminated strategic alliances found that more than three-fourths ended because a Japanese firm had taken over its non-Japanese partner.[38] In other cases, partners may accuse each other of opportunistic behavior, that is, trying to take unfair advantage of each other. For example, a joint venture between the Walt Disney Company and Sky Television, a British pay-TV channel operator, broke down after Sky accused Disney of deliberately delaying the supply of promised programming. Disney, in turn, accused Sky of proceeding too hastily and without consulting it.[39]

Changing Circumstances

Changing circumstances may also affect the viability of a strategic alliance. The economic conditions that motivated the cooperative arrangement may no longer exist, or technological advances may have rendered the agreement obsolete. For example, in 2008, Siemens announced it wished to terminate its joint venture with Fujitsu, Fujitsu Siemens Computers (FSC). Although FSC has been one of Europe's leading personal computer manufacturers since its creation in 1999, Siemens believed that the future profitability of the joint venture was unpromising due to increased competition from Hewlett-Packard, Dell, and Apple.[40] Similarly, the joint venture between Corning and Asahi Glass, Asahi Video Products Company, was terminated in 2003 due to declining demand for the venture's product, cathode ray tubes for TV sets.

CHAPTER REVIEW

Summary

Strategic alliances, in which two or more firms agree to cooperate for their mutual benefit, are becoming increasingly popular in international business. A joint venture, a common type of strategic alliance, involves two or more firms joining together to create a new entity that is legally separate and distinct from its parents.

Strategic alliances offer several benefits to firms that use them. First, they facilitate market entry. Second, they allow the partners to share risks. Third, they make it easier for each partner to gain new knowledge and expertise from the other partner(s). Finally, they foster synergy and competitive advantage among the partners.

The scope of strategic alliances can vary significantly. Comprehensive alliances involve a full array of business activities and operations. Functional alliances involving only one aspect of the business, such as production, marketing, finance, or R&D, are also common.

The decision to form a strategic alliance needs to be based on a number of different considerations. Selecting a partner is, of course, critically important and must take into account compatibility, the nature of the potential partner's products or services, the relative safety of the alliance, and the learning potential of the alliance. Selecting a form of organization is also very important to the success of the alliance. A special form of strategic alliance involves public and private partners. The management structure of the strategic alliance must also be given careful consideration.

Partners in a strategic alliance must be aware of several pitfalls that can undermine the success of their cooperative arrangement. These include incompatibility of the partners, access to information, conflicts over distributing earnings, loss of autonomy, and changing circumstances.

Review Questions

1. What are the basic differences between a joint venture and other types of strategic alliances?
2. Why have strategic alliances grown in popularity in recent years?
3. What are the basic benefits partners are likely to gain from their strategic alliance? Briefly explain each.

4. What are the basic characteristics of a comprehensive alliance? What form is it likely to take?
5. What are the four common types of functional alliances? Briefly explain each.
6. What is an R&D consortium?
7. What factors should be considered in selecting a strategic alliance partner?

8. What are the three basic ways of managing a strategic alliance?
9. Under what circumstances might a strategic alliance be undertaken by public and private partners?
10. What are the potential pitfalls of strategic alliances?

Questions for Discussion

1. What are the relative advantages and disadvantages of joint ventures compared to other types of strategic alliances?
2. Assume you are a manager for a large international firm, which has decided to enlist a foreign partner in a strategic alliance and has asked you to be involved in the collaboration. What effects, if any, might the decision to structure the collaboration as a joint venture have on you personally and on your career?
3. What factors could conceivably cause a sharp decline in the number of new strategic alliances formed?
4. Could a firm conceivably undertake too many strategic alliances at one time? Why or why not?
5. Can you think of any foreign products you use that may have been marketed in this country as a result of a strategic alliance? What are they?
6. What are some of the issues involved in a firm's trying to learn from a strategic alliance partner without giving out too much valuable information of its own?

7. Why would a firm decide to enter a new market on its own rather than using a strategic alliance?
8. What are some of the similarities and differences between forming a strategic alliance with a firm from your home country and forming one with a firm from a foreign country?
9. Gulfjet is a joint venture between the Al Mulla Business Group and Leader Capital. What are the benefits of this joint venture to each of these companies? Why did each choose to participate in the joint venture rather than operate its own wholly owned subsidiary? From the perspective of each of the partners, are there any potential pitfalls to joining this joint venture?
10. Otis Elevator has sought to obtain first-mover advantages by quickly entering emerging markets with the help of local partners. This strategy has proven very successful for Otis. Should all firms adopt this strategy? Under what conditions is this strategy most likely to be successful?

Building Global Skills

Break into small groups of four to five people. Assume your group is the executive committee (that is, the top managers) of Resteaze, Inc. Resteaze is a large manufacturer of mattresses, box springs, and waterbeds. The publicly traded firm is among the largest in the U.S. bedding market. It operates 15 factories, employs over 10,000 people, and last year generated $20 million in profits on sales of $380 million. Resteaze products are sold through department stores, furniture stores, and specialty shops and have the reputation of being of good quality and medium-priced.

Your committee is thinking about entering the European bedding market. You know little about the European market, so you are thinking about forming a joint venture. Your committee has identified three possible candidates for such an arrangement.

One candidate is Bedrest. Bedrest is a French firm that also makes bedding. Unfortunately, Bedrest products have a poor reputation in Europe and most of its sales stem from the fact that its products are exceptionally cheap. However, there are possibilities for growth in Eastern Europe. The consultant who recommended Bedrest suggests that your

higher-quality products would mesh well with Bedrest's cheaper ones. Bedrest is known to be having financial difficulties because of declining sales. However, the consultant thinks the firm will soon turn things around.

A second candidate is Home Furnishings, Inc., a German firm that manufactures high-quality furniture. Its line of bedroom furniture (headboards, dressers, chests, and so on) is among the most popular in Europe. The firm is also known to be interested in entering the U.S. furniture market. Home Furnishings is a privately owned concern that is assumed to have a strong financial position. Because of its prices, however, the firm is not expected to be able to compete effectively in Eastern Europe.

Finally, Pacific Enterprises, Inc., is a huge Japanese conglomerate that is just now entering the European market. The firm does not have any current operations in Europe but has enormous financial reserves to put behind any new undertaking it might decide to pursue. Its major product lines are machine tools, auto replacement parts, communications equipment, and consumer electronics.

Your task is to assess the relative advantages and disadvantages of each of these prospective partners for Resteaze. The European market is important to you, this is your first venture abroad, and you want the highest probability for success. After assessing each candidate, rank the three in order of their relative attractiveness to your firm.

1. How straightforward or ambiguous was the task of evaluating and ranking the three alternatives?
2. Determine and discuss the degree of agreement or disagreement among the various groups in the class.

Closing Case

Danone v. Wahaha—a Clash of Giants

In April 2007, the French food giant Danone announced that it was considering taking legal action against its joint venture partner in China, Wahaha, the largest producer of beverages in the country. The reason for the proposed action was breach of contract.

Danone's joint venture with Wahaha gave them a 51 percent share in the business. Danone had been investing in China since the 1980s and had also entered into joint ventures with China Huiyuan Juice and Mengniu Dairy, among other local beverage producers. Between 2006 and 2007, Danone's sales in China had risen 21 percent and it had become the market leader in bottled water and the second largest biscuit manufacturer in China.

At the centre of the dispute was the contention that Wahaha, or more specifically, the Chinese multimillionaire Zong Quinghos had been bottling and selling drinks independently, which was in violation of the joint venture agreement in which he had agreed not to compete with Danone or joint venture products directly. Danone had now taken legal action as it had sent a letter to Zong in early April and given him thirty days to resolve the dispute.

At the end of May the stakes were increased when China's General Administration of Quality Supervision, Inspection, and Quarantine (AQSIQ) seized five containers (118,000 litres) of Evian water due to concern over bacteria found in the bottles. Another dispute was inevitable, as the Chinese water standards apply to treated water and not natural mineral water, which has higher levels of bacteria. Many linked the decision about the water to the legal dispute with Wahaha.

Meanwhile, the dispute was passed on to arbitration in Stockholm. Zong had claimed that the non-competition and exclusivity agreements were unfair. He was waging a media battle against Danone, partially appealing to Chinese nationalism.

Zong Qinghou resigned as the chairman of the joint venture between Danone and Wahaha. He accused Danone of harming his reputation, and Danone said the vice chairman of Wahaha Joint Ventures, Emmanuel Faber, would temporarily replace him. Zong accused Danone of "bullying and slander." He was adamant that he would make sure that "Danone won't win for sure and we won't lose for sure."

By mid-June, Hangzhou Arbitration Commission accepted Wahaha's arbitration application. Hangzhou Wahaha Group signed an agreement in 1996 to transfer the Wahaha brand to Hangzhou Wahaha Food Co., a joint venture with Danone, but the agreement failed to get the approval from China's state trademark office.

By the end of the month, it was Wahaha that was on the offensive and threatening to sue Danone for $6 billion. The argument was that Danone's investments in several major Chinese drinks companies had hurt Wahaha's performance, and Wahaha wanted compensation for the impact.

The dispute continued throughout the year until in November, Danone announced that it had secured a court order freezing the assets of 10 companies connected to its former partner Wahaha.

Danone had lodged complaints against the businesses in which Wahaha were major shareholders; all of the businesses, claimed Danone, were manufacturing Wahaha products without permission.

Despite offers by Danone to negotiate a peaceful settlement to the dispute, in December workers of China's Wahaha Group announced that they had won local court orders freezing some of Danone's joint venture assets in the country. A court at Weifang froze the assets of two of the joint ventures (Danone had 39 joint ventures with Wahaha in China, with assets valued at 7.9 billion yuan [$1.1 billion] in 2007).

By mid-December 2007, it seemed that Danone's appetite for joint ventures in China was waning. Danone and China Mengniu Dairy Co., a major producer of milk in China's Inner Mongolia, announced that they had failed to agree the terms of a joint venture with the French company. Two months earlier, Danone had pulled out of another joint venture in China by selling its 20 percent share of Shanghai's Bright Dairy & Food Co.

By the end of the year, a temporary halt to legal action was agreed to by Danone and Wahaha, but the conflict was not yet over. The companies were still unable to reach a settlement by the end of March 2008 when the temporary truce was due to run out. Danone had proposed that their joint venture, along with the businesses at the centre of the dispute, be listed as one entity. Further, that Wahaha guaranteed the value of Danone's share of the listed firm would not fall below 50 billion yuan ($7 billion). Zong's reaction was that he could not guarantee the value of shares, as that was for the market to decide. Instead he proposed that Danone buy his share of the joint ventures, or that it be bought by a third party, but Danone rejected those options.

In the past 20 years, Danone had purchased shares of many of the top ten beverage companies in China: 51 percent of shares of the 39 companies owned by Wahaha Group, 98 percent of Robust Group, 50 percent of Shanghai Maling Aquarius Co., Ltd., 54.2 percent of Shenzhen Yili Mineral Water Company, and 22.18 percent of China Huiyuan Group. It also purchased 50 percent of Mengniu and 20.01 percent of Bright Dairy. However, after the purchase of Robust, Danone sacked the original management and replaced them. As a result, the fortunes of the company faded, having posted sales of RMB2 billion in 1999 and in 2006 a loss of RMB150 million.

The market share of Shanghai Aquarius Co. Ltd. similarly plunged after the takeover. Many of the takeovers had been hostile ones, and it transpired that Danone had attempted a hostile takeover of Wahaha and this had been the catalyst that had started the dispute between the two companies.

The accusations against Danone were that they were determined to oust Zong, as they saw him as a major block in their attempt to seize control of the joint ventures. They launched a public relations offensive against him and the company, but Chinese consumers rallied around and against Danone.

Whatever the truth, the dispute continues. Whether Danone will ultimately prove its case and compel Wahaha to conform to their joint venture agreement is doubtful. International decisions may be one thing, but whether the Chinese court, the market, or the consumers will comply is another question. As to the rights and wrongs of the situation, perhaps no one will ever know the full truth of it.

Case Questions

1. Why was the joint venture approach to breaking into the Chinese market so popular and what has changed?
2. From the perspective of each of the partners, are there any potential pitfalls to joining this joint venture?
3. What is at the heart of the argument over the joint venture between Danone and Wahaha?
4. One of the problems may have been the weak legality of the joint venture agreement and the transfer of the trademark. What were the implications of this aspect?

Sources: China Daily (www.chinadaily.com); Flex News – News for the Food Industry (www. flex-news-food.com); Danone (www.danone.com); Wahaha (www.en.wahaha.com.cn); China Business Review (www. chinabusinessreview.com); China Law Blog (www.chinalawblog.com); Industry Week (www.industryweek.com); China Economic Review (www.chinaeconomicreview.com).

Section 5

International Production Networks

Organizational Participants that Make International Business Happen

Learning Objectives

In this chapter, you will learn about:

1. Three types of participants in international business

2. Participants organized by value-chain activity

3. Focal firms in international business

4. Foreign market entry strategies of focal firms

5. Distribution channel intermediaries in international business

6. Facilitators in international business

> Born Global Firms

Established in 1989, Geo Search Ltd. is a Japanese company that develops high-technology equipment to help engineers survey ground surfaces for cavities and build safe roads, highways, airports, and underground utility lines. At the request of the United Nations, Geo Search designed the world's first land mine detector, called Mine Eye, in 1997. The firm had an immediate international market because of millions of mines buried in countries like Kuwait, Cambodia, Afghanistan, and Lebanon. The firm works with non-governmental organizations (NGOs) to search for mines worldwide. Removing land mines is a risky undertaking, particularly plastic mines that cannot be found with metal detectors. Geo Search's electromagnetic radar can distinguish between mines and other objects buried underground. Images appear in three dimensions on a liquid crystal display, and there is no need to touch the ground surface.

Geo Search is one example of an increasing number of small- and medium-sized enterprises (SMEs) that are active in international business. SMEs make up the majority of all firms in a typical country and account for about 50 percent of economic activity. Compared to large multinational enterprises (MNEs) that historically

were the most common types of international firms, the typical SME has far fewer financial and human resources. In the past, international business was beyond the reach of most SMEs. But globalization and technological advances have made venturing abroad much less expensive, and created a global commercial environment in which there are many more small firms doing international business than ever before. Since the 1980s, companies that internationalize at or near their founding, *born-global firms*, have been springing up all over the world.

Despite the scarce resources that characterize most SMEs, managers in born globals tend to see the world as their marketplace from or near the firm's founding. The period from domestic establishment to initial foreign market entry is often three years or less. By internationalizing as early and rapidly as they do, born globals develop a borderless corporate culture. Management targets products and services to a dozen or more countries within a few years after launching the firm. Compared to MNEs, smaller size provides born globals with a high degree of flexibility, which helps them serve their foreign customers better. Born globals usually internationalize through exporting.

Some firms internationalize early for various reasons. Management may perceive big demand for the firm's products abroad. Management may also have a strong international orientation, and push the firm into foreign markets. In addition, firms sometimes specialize in a particular product category for which demand in the home market is too small. When this happens, management must seek markets abroad. For example, Neogen Corporation is a born global in the United States that manufactures chemicals that kill harmful bacteria and toxins in food crops. The fact that certain toxins are more common in foreign locations led Neogen to internationalize shortly after its founding.

The widespread emergence of born global firms is an exciting trend because it shows that *any* company, regardless of its size, age, or resource base, can participate actively in international business. We therefore need to revisit the traditional view of the large multinational corporation as the dominant player in international business. Today, born globals and other SMEs that are fairly active exporters make up a sizable proportion of internationally active firms. Their relative inexperience and limited financial resources no longer prevent them from succeeding in foreign markets. The trend is particularly relevant to college students who specialize in international business, because SMEs provide many new job opportunities as they aggressively pursue international ventures.

Sources: da Costa, Eduardo. (2001). *Global E-Commerce Strategies for Small Businesses*. Cambridge, MA: The MIT Press; Knight, G., and S. T. Cavusgil. (2004). "Innovation, Organizational Capabilities, and the Born-Global Firm." *Journal of International Business Studies* 35(2): 124–41; Mambula, C. J. (2004). "Relating External Support, Business Growth and Creating Strategies for Survival: A Comparative Case Study Analysis of Small Manufacturing Firms (SMFs) and Entrepreneurs." *Small Business Economics* 22:83–109; Oviatt, B., and P. McDougall. (1994). "Toward a Theory of International New Ventures," *Journal of International Business Studies* 25 (1): 45–64; OECD. (1997). *Globalization and Small and Medium Enterprises (SMEs)*. Paris: Organisation for Economic Co-operation and Development; McDougall, P., and B. Oviatt. (2000). "International Entrepreneurship: The Intersection of Two Research Paths." *Academy of Management Journal* 43 (5): 902–6; Rahman, Bayan. (1999). "Extra Eye on Land Mines." *Financial Times* (July): 19; Rennie, M. (1993). "Born Global." *McKinsey Quarterly* (4): 45–52.

In Chapter 2, we learned that market globalization is the growing integration of the world economy through the activities of firms. Factors that drive globalization include falling trade and investment barriers and technological advances. In this chapter, we discuss the people and organizations that make globalization happen and their role in the value chain.

Three Types of Participants in International Business

International business is a complex undertaking and requires numerous organizations to work together as a coordinated team. These organizations, or participants, contribute various types of expertise and inputs that facilitate international business. The participants vary in terms of their motives for going international, modes of entry, and types of operations. There are three major categories of participants:

1. A **focal firm** is the initiator of an international business transaction, including MNEs and SMEs, that conceives, designs, and produces the offerings intended for consumption by customers worldwide. Focal firms take the center stage in international business. They include large multinational enterprises (MNEs; also known as Multinational Corporations or MNCs) and small- and medium-sized enterprises (SMEs). Some are privately owned companies, others are public, stock-held firms, and still others are state enterprises owned by governments. Some focal firms are manufacturing businesses, while others are in the service sector.

2. A **distribution channel intermediary** is a specialist firm that provides a variety of logistics and marketing services for focal firms as part of the international supply chain, both in the home country and abroad. Intermediaries such as dis-

Focal firm The initiator of an international business transaction, including MNEs and SMEs, that conceives, designs, and produces the offerings intended for consumption by customers worldwide.

Distribution channel intermediary A specialist firm that provides a variety of logistics and marketing services for focal firms as part of the international supply chain, both in the home country and abroad.

tributors and sales representatives are typically located in foreign markets and provide distribution and marketing services on behalf of focal firms. Intermediaries are independent businesses in their respective markets, and work for focal firms on a contractual basis.

3. A **facilitator** is a firm or an individual with special expertise in legal advice, banking, customs clearance, or related support services, that assists focal firms perform international business transactions. Facilitators include logistics service providers, freight forwarders, banks, and other support firms that assist focal firms perform specific functions. A **freight forwarder** is a specialized logistics service provider that arranges international shipping on behalf of exporting firms, much like a travel agent for cargo. Facilitators are found in both home and foreign markets.

International business transactions require the participation of numerous focal firms, intermediaries, and facilitators, all working closely together. The activities of the three groups of participants overlap to some degree. The focal firm performs certain activities internally and delegates other functions to intermediaries and facilitators when their special expertise is needed. In other words, the focal firm becomes a client of intermediaries and facilitators who provide services on a contractual basis.

While these three types of participants make up the international business landscape, keep in mind that international business transactions take place within political, legal, and regulatory environments. Nations also have a strong influence over their own economic development and the progress of their industries and firms. Governments create commercial environments that encourage the development of strong industries and technological prowess. Most nations have a trade infrastructure that consists of industry associations, chambers of commerce, universities, and helpful government agencies. For example, Japan registered exemplary economic growth (what was labeled an "economic miracle") during the 1980s through careful planning and a strong partnership between government and industry that skillfully mobilized technology, capital, and skilled labor.

While the focal firms, intermediaries, and facilitators represent the supply side of international business transactions, customers or buyers make up the demand side. Customers constitute the ultimate target of international business activity. For the most part, customers comprise individual *consumers and households*, *retailers* (businesses that purchase finished goods for the purpose of resale), and *organizational buyers* (businesses, institutions, and governments that purchase goods and services as inputs to a production process, or as supplies needed to run a business or organization). Governments and nonprofit organizations such as CARE and UNICEF are among major international customer groups.

Participants Organized by Value-Chain Activity

It is useful to think of the three categories of participants in terms of the firm's value chain we discussed in Chapter 2. The focal firms, intermediaries, and facilitators all are involved in one or more critical value-adding activities such as procurement, manufacturing, marketing, transportation, distribution, and support—configured across several countries. The value chain can be thought of as the complete business system of the focal firm. It comprises all of the activities that the focal firm performs.

In international business, the focal firm may retain core activities such as production and marketing within its own organization and delegate distribution and customer service responsibilities to independent contractors, such as foreign-market based distributors. Therefore, the resulting business system is subject to

Facilitator A firm or an individual with special expertise in legal advice, banking, customs clearance, or related support services, that assists focal firms in the performance of international business transactions.

Freight forwarder A specialized logistics service provider that arranges international shipping on behalf of exporting firms, much like a travel agent for cargo.

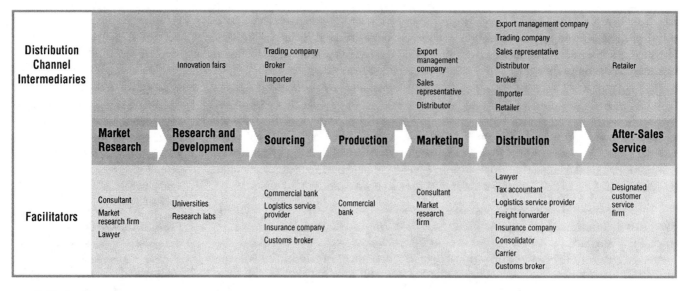

Distribution Channel Intermediaries		Innovation fairs	Trading company Broker Importer			Export management company Sales representative Distributor	Export management company Trading company Sales representative Distributor Broker Importer Retailer	Retailer
	Market Research	**Research and Development**	**Sourcing**	**Production**	**Marketing**	**Distribution**		**After-Sales Service**
Facilitators	Consultant Market research firm Lawyer	Universities Research labs	Commercial bank Logistics service provider Insurance company Customs broker	Commercial bank	Consultant Market research firm	Lawyer Tax accountant Logistics service provider Freight forwarder Insurance company Consolidator Carrier Customs broker		Designated customer service firm

Exhibit 3.1

Typical Positions of Intermediaries and Facilitators in the International Value Chain

internationalization; that is, individual value-adding activities can be configured in multiple countries. Exhibit 3.1 shows the stages in the value chain where channel intermediaries and facilitators typically operate. It also identifies intermediaries and facilitators critical to the functioning of international business transactions that we discuss in this chapter.

In exporting firms, much of the value chain is concentrated within one nation—the home country. In highly international firms, management may perform a variety of value-chain activities—production, marketing, distribution—within several countries. In highly internationalized focal firms, the value chain is configured in numerous countries and often from multiple suppliers. Multinational enterprises strive to rationalize their value chain by locating each activity in a country with the most favorable combination of cost, quality, logistical considerations, and other criteria.

Exhibit 3.2 illustrates the national and geographic diversity of suppliers that provide content for an automobile. When General Motors redesigned the Chevrolet Malibu for the 2004 model year, it purchased key components from several dozen primary (so-called *tier one*) suppliers, such as alternators from Valeo, transmission chains from BorgWagner, door panels from Johnson Controls, and tires from Bridgestone/Firestone. These suppliers are headquartered in such countries as Germany, Japan, France, Korea, and the United Kingdom, in addition to the United States, but the components they sell are manufactured in typically low-cost countries and then shipped to the General Motors plant in Fairfax, Kansas. As you can see, manufacturing of products such as automobiles involves a truly international value chain.

An Illustration of an International Value Chain: Dell Inc.

Dell makes a variety of products, each with its own value chain. Depending on the number of products offered and the complexity of operations, companies may develop and manage numerous value chains. Exhibit 3.3 illustrates the value chain for the production and marketing of Dell notebook computers. Let's take the example of Tom, a Dell customer who placed an order for a notebook. Such orders can be placed online at Dell.com or by telephone with a Dell sales representative. After Tom placed his order, the representative input it into Dell's order management system, verified his credit card through Dell's work-flow connection with Visa, a global financial services facilitator, and released the order into Dell's production system.

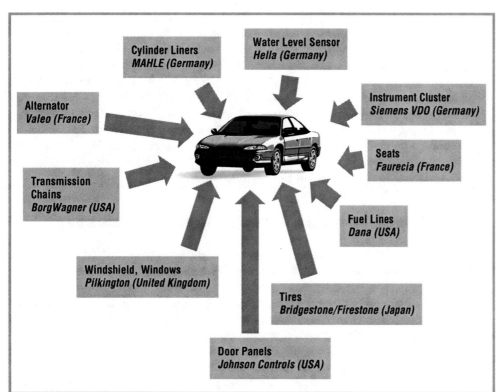

Exhibit 3.2

Sample Suppliers of Components for the Chevrolet Malibu

SOURCE: *Automotive News.*

Tom's order was processed at the Dell notebook factory in Malaysia, where the employees access parts that comprise the 30 key components of Dell notebooks from nearby suppliers. The total supply chain for Tom's computer, including multiple tiers of suppliers, involves about 400 companies, primarily in Asia, but also in Europe and the Americas.

Exhibit 3.3

Dell's International Value Chain

SOURCES: Adapted from Friedman, Thomas (2005). *The World Is Flat.* New York: Farrar, Straus, & Giroux; Lashinsky, A. (2004). "Where Dell is Going Next," *Fortune*, October 18, pp. 115–20.

Upstream Value-Chain Activities				Downstream Value-Chain Activities		
Market Research	**R&D**	**Sourcing**	**Production**	**Marketing**	**Distribution**	**After-Sales Service**
Dell conducts continuous market research, through direct interaction with thousands of customers everyday, worldwide.	R&D allows Dell to develop new notebook models and improve existing ones. Notebooks are completely redesigned every twelve months. Dell engineers in the United States conduct R&D jointly with specialized notebook designers in Taiwan.	The parts for the notebook are sourced worldwide, but mainly from suppliers in Asia. For example, Intel microprocessors are sourced from Intel factories in China, Costa Rica, and Malaysia; LCD displays are sourced from factories in South Korea, Japan, and Taiwan.	The notebook is assembled and software installed at one of Dell's six factories in Brazil, China, Ireland, Malaysia, or the United States.	Dell sells computers to buyers worldwide, but especially in the United States, where it holds one-third of the PC market, and online sales are common. Outside the United States, Dell has about 12 percent of total market share.	For its U.S. sales, Dell uses air transport to ship notebooks from its factories to the express delivery firm UPS, in Nashville, Tennessee. UPS then ships the notebooks to final customers. For sales in other countries, Dell uses local express delivery firms. The time period from order submission to final order delivery is typically less than two weeks.	Dell performs service and technical support in its major markets, especially Europe, Japan, and the United States. It employs technical support personnel in Europe, India, Japan, and the United States.

On a typical day, Dell processes orders for 150,000 computers, which are sold and distributed to customers around the world. Although based in Texas, non-U.S. sales account for roughly 40 percent of Dell's total sales (about $56 billion in 2006). As growth in U.S. sales flattens over time, the proportion of non-U.S. sales will grow. Shipping is handled via air transport. For instance, from the Dell Malaysia factory to the United States, Dell charters a China Airlines 747 that flies to Nashville, Tennessee six days a week. Each jet carries 25,000 Dell notebooks that weigh a total of 110,000 kilograms, or 242,500 pounds.

One of the hallmarks of Dell's value chain is collaboration. CEO Michael Dell and other members of top management constantly work with their suppliers to make process improvements in Dell's value chain.

 # Focal Firms in International Business

Imagine a typical theatrical production on Broadway in New York or on London's West End. There are script writers, stage managers, lighting technicians, musicians, set directors, business managers, and publicity staff, in addition to performing actors. Each participant contributes to the production in different ways. Much coordination among the players is required. Advance planning, preparation, timeliness, and synchronization are critical to ultimate success. Fulfillment of international business transactions similarly requires the participation of many specialist organizations, exact timing, and precision.

As we saw early in this chapter, focal firms initiate an international business transaction by conceiving, designing, and producing offerings intended for consumption by customers worldwide. Focal firms are the most prominent international players, partly because they include well-known multinational enterprises and small- and medium-sized exporting firms, including contemporary organizations such as the born globals discussed in the opening vignette. Let's learn more about each of these key actors in international business.

The Multinational Enterprise

Multinational enterprise (MNE) Is a large company with substantial resources that performs various business activities through a network of subsidiaries and affiliates located in multiple countries.

A **Multinational enterprise (MNE)** is a large company with substantial resources that performs various business activities through a network of subsidiaries and affiliates located in multiple countries. Leading MNEs are listed on the *Fortune Global 500* (www.fortune.com). Examples include well-known companies like Nestlé, Sony, Unilever, Nokia, Ford, Citibank, ABB, and Shell Oil. Although such firms employ a range of foreign market entry modes, MNEs are best known for their direct investment activities. They operate in multiple countries, especially in Asia, Europe, and North America, by setting up production plants, marketing subsidiaries, and regional headquarters. MNEs such as Exxon, Honda, and Coca-Cola derive a substantial portion of their total sales and profits, often more than half, from cross-border operations. Exhibit 3.4 highlights a sample of MNEs and illustrates the diverse industry sectors these focal firms represent.

Some focal firms operate in the services sector, including airlines, construction companies, and management consultancies. Examples include Citibank in banking, CIGNA in insurance, Bouygues in construction, Accor in hospitality, Disney in entertainment, Nextel in telecommunications, and Best Buy in retailing. Although retailers are usually classified as intermediaries, some large ones such as IKEA, Wal-Mart, and Gap are considered focal firms themselves. In addition, nontraditional *Internet*-mediated businesses that deliver knowledge-based offerings like music, movies, and software online have joined the ranks of global focal firms. Amazon and Netflix are examples.

International Business

Sector	2005 Market Value (U.S. $ billions)	Percentage of World Total	Representative Firms
Financials	$ 5,832	24.3%	Capital One, Danske Bank, Royal Bank of Scotland
Consumer discretionary	2,667	11.1	Coach, Adidas, Salomon, Matsushita Electric
Information technology	2,635	11.0	Microsoft, Oracle, Hoya, Taiwan Semiconductor Manufacturing
Industrials	2,431	10.1	Landstar Systems, Shenzhen Expressway, Haldex
Energy	2,316	9.7	Mobil, Total, China Oilfield Services
Health care	2,274	9.5	GlaxoSmithKline, Novartis, Baxter International
Consumer staples	2,134	8.9	Procter & Gamble, Unilever, China Mengniu Dairy, Honda
Telecom services	1,394	5.8	AT&T, China Mobile, Royal KPN
Materials	1,316	5.5	Dow Chemical, Alcan, Vitro SA
Utilities	956	4.0	Duke Energy, Empresa Nacional de Electricidad SA, Hong Kong and China Gas, Ltd.
Total	**23,955**	100.0	

Exhibit 3.4

Multinational Enterprises as Focal Firms (Ranked by Industry Sector Size)

SOURCES: Business Week Global 1200, www.businessweek.com, "Breaking It Down by Industry".

Not all focal firms are private businesses. In developing countries and centrally planned economies, some focal firms are partly or wholly owned by the government. For example, Lenovo Group is China's leading computer maker. It owns the former PC business of IBM and is 50 percent government-owned. CNOCC is a huge oil company that tried to buy Unocal in the United States in 2005. It is 71 percent government-owned. Numerous other leading Chinese MNEs—Sinopec and PetroChina in oil, China Mobile and China Netcom in telephony, First Auto Works and Shanghai Automotive in cars, China Minmetals in mining, and China Life in insurance—are wholly or partially owned by the Chinese government.

MNEs have played a major role in the current phase of globalization. In the years following World War II, most multinationals, typically from the United States and the United Kingdom, went abroad in search of raw materials, production efficiencies, and foreign-based customers. Today, these firms undertake sourcing, manufacturing, servicing, and marketing activities that span all areas of the world.

A typical MNE, and one whose products you may have sampled, is Sodexho, a French firm that is the world's second-largest contract foodservice provider. Its 300,000 employees provide cafeteria-style food to universities, hospitals, corporations, and public institutions in more than 75 countries. Typical Sodexho customers include the United Kingdom's Unilever, Germany's Ministry of Foreign Affairs, and the U.S. Marine Corps. Sodexho is the food source for numerous college cafeterias in Australia, Canada, and the United States. Chances are, if you eat in a university cafeteria, it is a Sodexho operation. In the 1990s, Sodexho expanded into Japan, Africa, Russia, and Eastern Europe.

Small and Medium-Sized Enterprises

Small and medium-sized enterprise (SME) A company with 500 or fewer employees in the United States, although this number may need to be adjusted downward for other countries

Another type of focal firm that initiates cross-border business transactions is the **small and medium-sized enterprise (SME)**. SMEs are typically small (with 500 or fewer employees in the United States) manufacturers or service providers and now comprise the majority of firms active in international business. Nearly all firms, including the large MNEs, started out small. Compared to the large multinationals, SMEs can be more flexible and quicker to respond to global business opportunities if they have less bureaucracy and fewer fixed assets tied up in foreign markets. SMEs can also be more innovative, more adaptable, and more entrepreneurial. They are often seen as the backbone for entrepreneurship and innovation in national economies.

Being smaller organizations, SMEs are constrained by limited financial and human resources. This explains why most smaller firms choose exporting as their major international business mode. Their limited resources prevent them from undertaking direct investment, which is an expensive entry mode. To compensate, SMEs leverage the services of intermediaries and facilitators to succeed abroad. As their operations grow, some gradually establish company-owned sales offices or subsidiaries in their key target markets.

Because of their size and relative inexperience, SMEs often target specialized products to market niches that MNEs consider too small to service. Smaller firms increasingly serve neglected global market segments because they have access to direct marketing, globe-spanning logistics specialists such as FedEx and DHL, and local distributors. Internationally active SMEs are typically avid users of information and communications technologies that allow management to segment customers into narrow global market niches and efficiently serve highly specialized needs of buyers around the world. As a result, SMEs are gaining equal footing with large multinationals in the marketing of sophisticated products for sale around the world.

In Eastern Europe, the development of emerging market countries is driven increasingly by the rise of small and midsize fast-growth firms. These firms range from Latvian coffee shop chain Double Coffee to Hungarian employment recruiter CVO Group. Many of Eastern Europe's small firms are not in manufacturing, but in intellectual, knowledge-intensive industries, such as software and consulting. The rise of small firms in Eastern Europe is the result of two trends: recent, growing access to the affluent markets of the European Union, and the interest on the part of foreign direct investors in such liberalizing economies.[1]

Born Global Firms

Born global firm A young entrepreneurial company that initiates international business activity very early in its evolution, moving rapidly into foreign markets.

Born global firms, such as Geo Search Ltd., featured in the opening vignette, represent a relatively new breed of the international SME—those that undertake early and substantial internationalization. Despite the scarce resources typical of most small businesses, born globals achieve considerable foreign sales early in their evolution. One example is History and Heraldry, a born global in England that specializes in gifts for history buffs and those with English ancestry. In its first five years, the firm expanded its sales into 60 countries, exporting about 70 percent of total production. The firm's biggest markets include France, Germany, Italy, Spain, and the Americas. It recently opened a North American subsidiary in Florida.[2] Indeed, some successful born globals grow large enough to be considered an MNE.

Another example is QualComm. Founded in California in 1985, the firm eventually grew to become a major MNE on the strength of substantial international sales. QualComm initially developed and launched the e-mail software, Eudora. The firm's early international success was OmniTRACS, a two-way satellite message and position reporting system used in the global transportation industry. QualComm's first international launch was to Europe, just four years after founding. The firm was soon exporting to Europe, Brazil, China, India, Indonesia, and Japan. QualComm's founders were entrepreneurs who, from the beginning, made little distinction between domestic and international markets. Technological prowess and managerial vision were strong factors in making the firm an early international success.

ERG Group is an Australian-born global firm that produces fare management systems for the public transit industry worldwide.

The born-global phenomenon represents a new reality in international business. In such diverse countries as Australia, Denmark, Ireland, and the United States, born globals account for a substantial proportion of national exports. In many cases, born globals offer leading-edge products with substantial potential for generating international sales. They are typically avid users of the Internet and modern communications technologies, which further facilitate early and efficient international operations.

The emergence of born globals is associated with *international entrepreneurship*, in which innovative, smaller firms increasingly pursue business opportunities everywhere, regardless of national borders. Communications and transportation technologies, falling trade barriers, and the emergence of niche markets worldwide make it possible for many contemporary entrepreneurial firms to view the world as their marketplace. Entrepreneurial managers are creative, proactive, have a strong feel for the business environment, and are ready to pursue new opportunities. They are comfortable dealing with risk and have the flexibility to make changes to company strategies as circumstances evolve. The appearance of born globals is heartening because it implies that any firm, regardless of size or experience, can succeed in international business.[3]

Foreign Market Entry Strategies of Focal Firms

One way to analyze focal firms in international business is in terms of the entry strategies that they typically use to expand abroad. Earlier, we noted that the larger MNEs tend to expand abroad through foreign direct investment. Smaller firms, including born globals, tend to be exporters. Both MNEs and SMEs rely on contractual relationships such as franchising and licensing.

A Framework for Classifying Market Entry Strategies

Exhibit 3.5 shows the array of foreign market entry modes that focal firms use and the foreign partners they seek. The exhibit helps us understand the diversity of foreign market entry strategies.

The first column in Exhibit 3.5 lists three categories of international business transactions: transactions that involve the trade of products, transactions that involve contractual exchange of services or intangibles; and transactions based on investing equity ownership in foreign-based enterprises. Therefore, firms are generally involved in one or more of three major types of cross-border transactions: buying or selling products, buying or selling services, and producing or selling products or services abroad by establishing a foreign presence through direct investment.

Nature of International Transaction	Types of Focal Firm	Foreign Market Entry Strategy	Location of Major Activities	Typical Foreign Partners
Trade of products	Small manufacturer	Exporting	Home country	Distributor, agent, or other independent representative
	Large manufacturer	Exporting	Mainly abroad	Company-owned office or subsidiary
	Manufacturer	Importing (e.g., sourcing)	Home	Independent supplier
	Importer	Importing	Home	Trader or manufacturer
	Trading company	Exporting and Importing	Home	Trader or manufacturer
Contractual exchange of services or intangibles	Service provider	Exporting	Usually abroad	Agent, branch, or subsidiary
	Supplier of expertise or technical assistance	Consulting services	Abroad (temporarily)	Client
	Licensor with patent	Licensing	Home	Licensee
	Licensor with know-how	Licensing (technology transfer)	Home	Licensee
	Franchisor	Franchising	Home	Franchisee
	Service contractor	Management/Marketing service contracting	Abroad	Business owner or sponsor
	Construction/Engineering/ Design/ Architectural Firm	Turnkey contracting or Build-Own-Transfer	Abroad (temporarily)	Project owner
	Manufacturer	Non-equity, project-based, partnerships	Home or abroad	Manufacturer
Equity ownership in foreign-based enterprises	MNE	FDI via greenfield investment	Abroad	None
	MNE	FDI via acquisition	Abroad	Acquired company
	MNE	Equity joint venture	Abroad	Local business partner(s)

Exhibit 3.5 International Business Transactions, Types of Focal Firms, and Foreign Market Entry Strategies

Licensor A firm that enters a contractual agreement with a foreign partner that allows the latter the right to use certain intellectual property for a specified period of time in exchange for royalties or other compensation.

Franchisor A firm that grants another the right to use an entire business system in exchange for fees, royalties, or other forms of compensation.

Turnkey contractors Focal firms or a consortium of firms that plan, finance, organize, manage, and implement all phases of a project and then hand it over to a foreign customer after training local personnel.

The second column in Exhibit 3.5 identifies the types of focal firms engaged in international business. Some focal firms are manufacturing businesses such as Ford, Sharp, and John Deere. They use manufacturing processes to produce tangible products that they sell in foreign markets. Trading companies are brokers of goods and services. Service providers are firms in the services sector, such as insurance companies and theme parks. Some services firms, suppliers of expertise, provide purely intangible offerings such as advice and teaching, often one-on-one, to clients. Examples include lawyers, teachers, and consulting firms.

The second column also identifies licensors of various types of intellectual property, including patents and know-how. A **licensor** is a firm that enters a contractual agreement with a foreign partner that allows the latter the right to use certain intellectual property for a specified period of time in exchange for royalties or other compensation. A **franchisor** is a firm that grants another the right to use an entire business system in exchange for fees, royalties, or other forms of compensation. Franchisors are sophisticated licensors that provide an entire business system to a foreign franchisee, such as McDonald's and Hertz Car Rental. In addition, many firms in the construction, engineering, design, or architectural industries provide their offerings via turnkey contracting. **Turnkey contractors** are focal firms or a consortium of firms that plan, finance, organize, manage, and implement all phases of a project and then hand it over to a foreign customer after training local personnel.

The third column in Exhibit 3.5 identifies the foreign market entry strategy, or the mode of internationalization. A foreign market entry strategy refers to the manner in which the focal firm internationalizes, whether through exporting, importing, licensing, or FDI. The type of entry mode depends on the nature of the

International Business

business as well as the nature of the focal firm, its products, and goals. When the nature of business is dealing in intangibles, such as professional services, the focal firm may enter into agency relationships with a foreign partner. This is common among banks, advertising agencies, and market research firms. Licensing and franchising are common in the international transfer of intangibles. A franchisor makes a contract with a foreign franchisee; a supplier of expertise makes a contract with a foreign client, and so forth.

In undertaking international business, firms have the option of serving customers either through foreign investment, or relying upon the support of independent intermediaries located abroad. In the former case, the company will set up *company-owned* manufacturing and distribution facilities. Accordingly, another key characteristic of focal firms is whether the firm maintains a physical presence in the market of interest. The fourth column in Exhibit 3.5 identifies the location of major activities. For example, most exporters carry out major activities—manufacturing, marketing, and sales—in their home country; they produce goods at home and ship them to customers abroad. MNEs and other large firms, however, tend to carry out major activities in multiple countries; they produce goods and sell them to customers primarily located abroad.

The last column in Exhibit 3.5 identifies the nature of the foreign partner. In almost all cases, the focal firm will rely upon intermediaries as well as support firms located in foreign markets. Significant activities are typically delegated to these foreign partners, including marketing, distribution, sales, and customer service. MNEs have seen a strong trend in recent years away from fully integrated operations toward the delegation of certain noncore functions to outside vendors, a practice known as *outsourcing*. Outsourcing involves the firm in a variety of foreign partnerships. For example, Nike maintains its design and marketing operations within the firm, but outsources production to independent suppliers located abroad. We explore outsourcing and offshoring more fully in Chapter 16.

Focal Firms other Than the MNE and SME

Let's develop a full understanding of focal firms other than the MNEs and SMEs that are highlighted in Exhibit 3.5. Some focal firms expand into foreign markets by entering into contractual relationships with foreign partners. Licensing and franchising are examples of contractual relationships. Occasionally, the licensor sells essential components or services to the licensee as part of their ongoing relationship. Licensing allows companies to internationalize rapidly while remaining in their home market. For instance, Anheuser-Busch signed a licensing agreement with the Japanese beer brewer Kirin, under which Kirin produces and distributes Budweiser beer in Japan. The agreement has substantial potential, given Japan's $30 billion-a-year beer market.[4] In another example, Canadian toymaker Mega Bloks signed an agreement with Disney that gives the SME the right to produce toys that feature Disney characters such as Winnie the Pooh and the Power Rangers. The toys are aimed at preschoolers and boys aged 4 to 7.[5]

Like licensors, the franchisor remains in its home market and permits its foreign partners to carry on local activities. The franchisor assists the franchisee in setting up its operation, and then maintains ongoing control over aspects of the franchisee's business, such as operations, procurement, quality control, and marketing. The franchisee benefits by gaining access to a proven business plan and substantial expertise.

Franchising is well accepted around the world and is popular among many types of service industry firms. For many successful service firms such as Subway or KFC, it is a relatively practical way to expand into many foreign markets. Exhibit 3.6 profiles some of the leading global franchisors. In China, Subway is the third-largest U.S. fast food chain, where its fish and tuna salad sandwiches are top sellers. Other

Organizational Participants that make International Business Happen

Franchisor	Type of Business	International Profile	Major International Markets
Subway	Submarine sandwiches and salads	24,838 shops in 82 countries	Canada, Australia, UK, New Zealand, China
Curves	Women's fitness and weight loss	9,000 centers in 17 countries	Canada, Mexico, Australia, Ireland, UK
UPS Store/Mail Boxes Etc.	Postal, business, and communications services	13 million packages in 200 countries	Canada, Germany, China
Pizza Hut	Pizza	12,500 outlets in 90 countries	China, Brazil
WSI Internet	Internet services	1,700 franchises in 87 countries	Canada, UK
KFC	Chicken	13,000 outlets in 90 countries	China, UK
RE/MAX	Real estate	100,000 agents in 50 countries	Canada, Australia, UK, New Zealand
Jani-King	Commercial cleaning	9,000 franchisees in 16 countries	Canada, Australia, Brazil, France, Turkey, New Zealand, Malaysia
McDonald's	Fast food restaurant	30,000 restaurants in 119 countries	Canada, France, UK, Australia, China
GNC	Vitamin and nutrition stores	5,000 stores in 38 countries	Canada, Mexico, Puerto Rico, Australia

Exhibit 3.6 Examples of Leading International Franchisors

SOURCES: Entrepreneur.com; Hoovers.com; company web sites and reports.

firms, such as The Athlete's Foot and Century 21, have been steadily growing in foreign markets through franchising. China recently passed its first laws that require franchisees to adhere closely to contractual obligations in the franchisor agreement.[6]

Turnkey contractors specialize in international construction, engineering, design, and architectural projects, typically involving airports, hospitals, oil refineries, and campuses. In a typical turnkey contract, the contractor plans, finances, organizes, manages, and implements all phases of a construction project. The contractors provide hardware and know-how to build a factory, power plant, railway, or some other integrated system that is capable of producing the products or services that the project sponsor requires. Hardware includes buildings, equipment, and inventory that comprise the tangible aspects of the system. Know-how is the knowledge about technologies, operational expertise, and managerial skills that the contractor transfers to the customer during and upon completion of the project.

These projects are typically awarded on the basis of open bidding, in which many potential contractors participate. Some contracts are highly publicized megaprojects, such as the European Channel Tunnel, the Three Gorges Dam in China, and the Hong Kong Airport. Typical examples of turnkey projects include upgrades to public transportation networks such as bridges, roadways, and rail systems. Financed largely from public budgets, most metro projects are in Asia and Western Europe, where demand is driven by intensifying urbanization and worsening congestion. One of the world's largest publicly funded heavy rail projects is underway in Delhi, India. Delhi Metro Rail Ltd. commissioned the estimated $2.3 billion turnkey project to build roads and tunnels that run through the city's central business district. The turnkey consortium includes numerous local firms as well as Skanska AB, Stockholm, one of the world's largest construction companies.[7] In Hong Kong, a private toll road operator awarded a $550-million turnkey contract to a French and Japanese joint venture for a new highway running into China. The team includes the Hong Kong subsidiary of the French giant Bouygues SA.[8] Bouygues has over 40 subsidiaries and affiliates in 80 countries.

ABB and Alstom are among the international construction contractors that have built the Three Gorges Dam on the Yangtze River in China's Hubei province. The project, which aims to control the country's mighty Yangtze River and tame the floods, is thought to have cost more than any other single construction project in China's history, with unofficial estimates as high as $75 billion.

An increasingly popular type of turnkey contract in the developing economies is the *build-own-transfer* venture. In this arrangement, the contractors acquire an ownership in the facility for a period of time until it is turned over to the client. In addition to owning a stake in the project, the contractors provide ongoing service in the form of advice, training, and assistance navigating regulatory requirements and obtaining needed approvals from government authorities. At some point after a successful period of operation, the contractors will divest their interest in the project.

Exhibit 3.7 identifies the top construction contractors in the world based on contracting revenues from projects outside their home countries. A quick perusal of the list reveals the highly global nature of the large-scale construction industry. The top firms in this industry come from various European countries, Japan, China, and the United States. These firms derive a considerable share of their total revenues from international projects. Many have established reputations in specialized project areas such as airports, steel plants, refineries, high-speed rail, and environmental projects.

International collaborative ventures represent a cross-border business alliance where partnering firms pool their resources and share the costs and risks of the new venture. Collaborative ventures are a middle ground between FDI-based foreign market entry and home country-focused operations such as exporting. In effect, a collaborative arrangement allows the focal firm to *externalize* some of its value-chain activities. Collaborative arrangements help the focal firm increase international business, compete more effectively with rivals, take advantage of complementary technologies and expertise, overcome trade barriers, connect with customers abroad, configure value chains more effectively, and generate economies of scale in production and marketing.

Joint ventures (JV) and project-based, nonequity ventures are both examples of international collaborative ventures. A **joint venture partner** is a focal firm that creates and jointly owns a new legal entity through equity investment or pooling of assets. Partners form JVs to share costs and risks, gain access to needed resources, gain economies of scale, and pursue long-term strategic goals.

As an example, Hitachi formed a joint venture with MasterCard to promote a smart card system for banking and other applications. The Japanese electronics giant invested $2.4 million to take an 18 percent stake in the JV established in San Francisco. The firms created the venture to manage the brand and other operations of the *Multos* smart card worldwide. [9]In another instance, British Petroleum (BP) entered a joint venture in India in one of several deals intended to boost energy output in the Asian subcontinent. BP partnered with

Joint venture partner A focal firm that creates and jointly owns a new legal entity through equity investment or pooling of assets.

Rank Based on 2006 Revenues	Contractor	2006 Revenue (U.S.$ millions)		Example of a Recently Completed Mega-Construction Project
		International	*Total*	
1	Hochtief AG, Essen, Germany	$17,598	$19,795	Berlin's new mega-airport at the Schönefeld site, Germany
2	Skanska AB, Solna, Sweden	12,347	15,722	Øresund Bridge, Denmark
3	Vinci, Rueil-Malmaison, France	11,065	32,699	Channel Tunnel, France-Great Britain
4	Strabag SE, Vienna, Austria	10,799	13,502	Xiaolangdi Multi-Purpose Dam, China
5	Bouygues, Paris, France	9,576	24,960	Groene Hart Tunnel, The Netherlands
6	Bechtel, San Francisco, CA, U.S.A.	8,931	15,367	Hong Kong Airport, China
7	Technip, Paris-La Dèfense, France	8,084	8,245	Hong Kong New Airport Passenger Terminal Building, China
8	KBR, Houston, Texas, U.S.A.	7,426	8,150	The Great Man-Made River Project (GMRP), Libya
9	Bilfinger Berger AG, Mannheim, Germany	6,553	9,967	Taipei–Kaohsiung High Speed Railway, Taiwan
10	Fluor Corp., Irving, Texas, U.S.A.	6,338	11,273	Shell Rayong Refinery, Thailand

Exhibit 3.7 Top International Construction Contractors. Based on Contracting Revenues from Projects Outside Home Country.

SOURCE: Reprinted from Engineering News-Record. Copyright © McGraw-Hill Companies, Inc. August 20, 2007. All rights reserved.

Project-based, nonequity venture partners Focal firms that collaborate through a project, with a relatively narrow scope and a well-defined timetable, without creating a new legal entity.

the state-controlled Hindustan Petroleum Corporation. The new venture built a $3 billion refinery in Punjab and established a joint marketing business, including a network of retail service stations around India. BP is developing similar ventures in China.[10]

Partners in a project-based, nonequity venture are focal firms that collaborate through a project, with a relatively narrow scope and a well-defined timetable, without creating a new legal entity. In contrast to JVs, which involve equity investment by the parent companies, project-based partnerships are less formal nonequity ventures, and are intended for a fixed duration. The partners pool their resources and expertise to perform some mutually beneficial business task, such as joint R&D or marketing, but they do not invest equity to form a new enterprise. Firms often form project-based ventures to share the enormous fixed costs involved in knowledge-intensive research and development projects. Partners may share know-how and intellectual property to develop a new technological standard.

Cisco Systems is the worldwide leader in Internet networking technology, and has expanded much of its operations through strategic alliances with key foreign players. It formed an alliance with Japan's Fujitsu to jointly develop routers and switches that enable clients to build Internet protocol networks for advanced telecommunications. In Italy, Cisco teamed with the telecommunications company Italtel to jointly develop network solutions for the convergence of voice, data, and video to meet growing global demands. In China, Cisco formed an alliance with telecommunications company ZTE to tap the Chinese and Asian markets. The two companies are collaborating to provide equipment and services to telecommunications operators in the Asia-Pacific region.[11]

Distribution Channel Intermediaries in International Business

A second category of international business participant is the distribution channel intermediary. Intermediaries are physical distribution and marketing service providers in the value chain for focal firms. They move products and services in the home country and abroad, and perform key downstream functions in the target market on behalf of focal firms, including promotion, sales, and customer service. They may organize transportation of goods and offer various logistics services such as warehousing and customer support. Intermediaries are of many different types, ranging from large international companies to small, highly specialized operations. For most exporters, relying on an independent foreign distributor is a low-cost way to enter foreign markets. The intermediary's intimate knowledge, contacts, and services in the local market can provide a strong support system for exporters that are inexperienced in international business or too small to undertake market-based activities themselves. There are three major categories of intermediaries: those based in the foreign target market, those based in the home country, and those that operate through the Internet.

Intermediaries Based in the Foreign Market

Most intermediaries are based in the exporter's target market. They provide a multitude of services, including market research, appointing local agents or commission representatives, exhibiting products at trade shows, arranging local transportation for cargo, and clearing products through customs. Intermediaries also orchestrate local marketing activities, including product adaptation, advertising, selling, and after-sales service. Many intermediaries finance sales and extend credit, facilitating prompt payment to the exporter. In short, intermediaries based in the foreign market can function like the exporter's local partner, handling all needed local business functions.

A **foreign distributor** is a foreign market-based intermediary that works under contract for an exporter, takes title to, and distributes the exporter's products in a national market or territory, often performing marketing functions such as sales, promotion, and after-sales service. Foreign distributors are essentially independent wholesalers that purchase merchandise from exporters (at a discount) and resell it after adding a profit margin. Because they take title to the goods, foreign distributors are often called *merchant distributors*. The distributor promotes, sells, and maintains an inventory of the exporter's products in the foreign market. The distributor typically maintains substantial physical resources and provides financing, technical support, and after-sales service for the product, relieving the exporter of these functions abroad. Distributors may carry a variety of noncompeting complementary products, such as home appliances and consumer electronics. For consumer goods, the distributor usually sells to retailers. For industrial goods, the distributor sells to other businesses and/or directly to end users. Compared to sales representatives, distributors are usually a better choice for firms that seek a more stable, committed presence in the target market. A key advantage of using a foreign distributor is that they typically have substantial knowledge of the exporter's products and the nature of the local market.

An **agent** is an intermediary (often an individual or a small firm) that handles orders to buy and sell commodities, products, and services in international business transactions for a commission. Also known as a *broker*, an agent may act for either buyer or seller but does not assume title or ownership of the goods. The typical agent is compensated by commission, expressed as a percentage of the price of the product sold. In economic terms, the agent brings buyers and sellers

Foreign distributor A foreign market-based intermediary that works under contract for an exporter, takes title to, and distributes the exporter's products in a national market or territory, often performing marketing functions such as sales, promotion, and after-sales service.

Agent An intermediary (often an individual or a small firm) that handles orders to buy and sell commodities, products, and services in international business transactions for a commission.

together. Agents operate under contract for a definite period of time (often as little as one year), which is renewable by mutual agreement. The contract defines territory, terms of sale, compensation, as well as grounds and procedures for terminating the agreement.[12]

The function of the agent is especially important in markets made up of many small, widely dispersed buyers and sellers. For example, brokers on the London Metal Exchange (LME) deal in copper, silver, nickel, and other metals sourced from mining operations worldwide. The volume of metal buying and selling is huge (around $5 billion per year) and the suppliers are widely dispersed worldwide. The LME greatly increases the efficiency with which manufacturing firms access the metal ingredients they need to conduct manufacturing operations. Agents are common in the international trade of commodities, especially food products and base minerals. In the services sector, agents often transact sales of insurance and securities.

Manufacturer's representative An intermediary contracted by the exporter to represent and sell its merchandise or services in a designated country or territory.

A **manufacturer's representative** is an intermediary contracted by the exporter to represent and sell its merchandise or services in a designated country or territory. Manufacturer's representatives go by various names, depending on the industry in which they work—agents, sales representatives, or service representatives. In essence, they act as contracted sales personnel in a designated target market on behalf of the exporter, but usually with broad powers and autonomy. Manufacturer's representatives may handle various noncompetitive, complementary lines of products or services. They do not take title to the goods they represent and are most often compensated by commission. With this type of representation, the exporter usually ships merchandise directly to the foreign customer or end user. Manufacturer's representatives do not maintain physical facilities, marketing, or customer support capabilities, so these functions must be handled primarily by the exporter.

In consumer markets, the foreign firm must get its products to end users through *retailers* located in the foreign market. A retailer represents the last link between distributors and end-users. Some national retail chains have expanded abroad and are now providing retail services in multiple countries. For example, Seibu, Carrefour, Royal Ahold, Tesco and Sainsbury are major retail store chains based in Japan, France, the Netherlands, and the United Kingdom, respectively. Rolex and Ralph Lauren sell their products directly to these retailers. This type of transaction has emerged from the international growth of major retail chains. Often, a traveling sales representative facilitates such transactions. Large international retailers such as Carrefour and Wal-Mart maintain purchasing offices abroad. Wal-Mart and Toys "R" Us have opened hundreds of stores around the world, especially in Mexico, Canada, Japan, China, and Europe. IKEA, a Swedish company, is the world's largest furniture retailer. Dealing directly with foreign-based retailers is efficient because it results in a much shorter distribution channel and reduced channel costs.

Retailer Tesco's delivery vans distribute products to end-users throughout Britain.

Intermediaries Based in the Home Country

In contrast to those intermediaries located abroad, a select group of intermediaries are domestically based. For one, a variety of wholesaler *importers* bring in products or commodities from foreign countries for the purpose of selling them in the home market, re-exporting them, or for use in the manufacture of finished products. Manufacturers and retailers are also important importers. Manufacturers import a range of raw materials, parts, and components used in the production of higher value-added products. They may also import a complementary collection of products and services to supplement or augment their own product range. Retailers such as department stores, specialized stores, mail order houses, and catalogue firms import many of the products that they sell. A trip to retailers such as Best Buy, Home Depot, or Staples, for instance, quickly reveals that most of their offerings are sourced from abroad, especially low labor-cost countries. (You can learn more about the world's largest retailers from various studies, including those by PriceWaterhouseCoopers: www.pwc.com).

Wholesalers import input goods that they in turn sell to manufacturers and retailers. A typical importer in this category is Capacitor Industries Inc., an SME in Chicago that imports low-cost electronic components from China and sells them to motor makers and other manufacturers in the United States and other countries. Capacitors are tiny devices that store electrical charges, keep motors running, and protect computers from surges. Capacitor Industries' strategy is simple—buy from a low-cost country and sell at a profit in an advanced economy. Importing from China and other low-cost suppliers means that the prices of domestic suppliers can be undercut by up to 30 percent.

For exporting firms that prefer to minimize the complexity of selling internationally, a **trading company** serves as an intermediary that engages in import and export of a variety of commodities, products, and services. A trading company assumes the international marketing function on behalf of producers, especially those with limited international business experience. Large trading companies operate much like agents and may deal in thousands of products that they sell in markets worldwide. Typically, they are high-volume, low-margin resellers, and are compensated by adding profit margins to what they sell.

Trading company An intermediary that engages in import and export of a variety of commodities, products, and services.

Trading companies are very common in commodities and agricultural goods such as grain. Companies such as Minneapolis, Minnesota-based Cargill provide a useful service as international resellers of agricultural goods. With annual sales of more than $50 billion, Cargill is often listed as the largest private firm in the United States. The company employs roughly 150,000 employees in more than 60 countries. Cargill controls about 25 percent of U.S. grain exports and one-fifth of the corn-milling capacity. It buys, sorts, ships, and sells a wide range of commodities, including coffee, sugar, cotton, oil, hemp, rubber, and livestock. Most of its profits come from turning these commodities into value-added products, including oils, syrups, and flour. The company also processes all the ingredients that many food companies use to produce cereal, frozen dinners, and cake mixes.

Exhibit 3.8 provides a list of the largest trading companies in the world. What strikes you about these firms? First, note that these companies work with remarkably low margins in international trading; they tend to be high-volume, low-margin resellers. This is due to the trading companies' dealing largely in commodities such as grains, minerals, coal, and metals. Second, note that five of the ten largest trading companies are based in Japan. This is because trading companies have historically played a very important role in Japan's external trade. Being an island economy and lacking most raw materials needed for industrialization, Japan has to import them. Trading companies are also more common in South Korea, India, and Europe.

In Japan, large trading companies are known as *sogo shosha*. The sogo shosha are usually involved in both exporting and importing, and are specialists in low-margin, high-volume trading. They may also supply a range of manufacturing, financial, and logistical services. To stay close to foreign markets, managers of the sogo shosha use extensive networks of local offices, travel, and participate in trade shows, and establish business relationships with agents and distributors worldwide.

Organizational Participants that make International Business Happen

Exhibit 3.8

World's Largest Trading Companies

SOURCE: "Ten Largest companies by revenue" FORTUNE Global 500, July 24, 2006 issue, FORTUNE. Copyright © 2006 Time, Inc. All rights reserved.

Rank Based on Annual Revenues	Company (Home Country)	Revenues (U.S.$ millions)	Profits (U.S.$ millions)	Profits as Percentage of Total Revenues
1	Mitsubishi (Japan)	$42,633	$3,092	7.3%
2	Mitsui (Japan)	36,349	1,788	4.9
3	Marubeni (Japan)	27,732	652	2.4
4	Sumitomo (Japan)	22,800	1,415	6.2
5	Sinochem (China)	21,089	260	1.2
6	Itochu (Japan)	19,592	1,282	6.5
7	SHV Holdings (Netherlands)	18,826	444	2.4
8	Samsung (South Korea)	15,114	77	0.5
9	COFCO (China)	14,654	199	1.4
10	SK Networks (South Korea)	14,571	467	3.2

The sogo shosha include giant firms that are little known in the West, such as Mitsui, Mitsubishi, Sumitomo, Itochu, and Marubeni, all firms on the Fortune magazine Global 500. In the 1990s, total trade of the nine top sogo shosha averaged about 25 percent of Japan's total GDP. They typically have extensive global operations. For instance, Marubeni has 23 corporate subsidiaries and a total of 121 offices in 72 countries. It owns 502 companies, of which 285 are outside Japan. The firm has about 27,000 employees, of which roughly 14,000 are overseas. Marubeni is consistently ranked in the upper end of the Global 500 and had recent annual sales of about $28 billion.

In the United States, trading companies have had a relatively negligible impact on the volume of export activity. The U.S. Congress passed the Export Trading Company (ETC) Act in 1982, providing firms with two important incentives to engage in joint exporting through the formation of export trading companies. First, immunity from antitrust legislation could allow firms to collaborate for export marketing purposes without the fear of being prosecuted for collusion. Second, U.S. bank holding companies could hold equity interest in ETCs and facilitate the formation of financially strong trading companies like the Japanese sogo shosha. This represented a significant departure from the longstanding policy of separating banking from commercial activities. Despite these incentives, trading companies are not forming to act on behalf of a group of manufacturers with limited international business experience. One of the deterrents has been the preference of U.S. firms to pursue international business expansion independently of other firms.[13]

In the United States, a more common type of domestically based intermediary is the **export management company (EMC)**, which acts as an export agent on behalf of a (usually inexperienced) client company. In return for a commission, an EMC finds export customers on behalf of the client firm, negotiates terms of sale, and arranges for international shipping. While typically much smaller than a trading company, some EMCs have well-established networks of foreign distributors in place that allow exported products immediate access to foreign markets. EMCs are often supply driven, visiting the manufacturer's facilities regularly to learn about new products and even to develop foreign-market strategies. But because of

Export management company (EMC) An intermediary that acts as an export agent on behalf of (usually inexperienced) a client company.

the indirect nature of the export sale, the manufacturer runs the risk of losing control over how its products are marketed abroad, with possible negative consequences for its international image.

Online Intermediaries

The Internet has triggered much disintermediation—the elimination of traditional intermediaries. Some focal firms now use the Internet to sell products directly to customers rather than going through traditional wholesale and retail channels. By eliminating traditional intermediaries, companies can sell their products cheaper and faster. This benefits SMEs in particular because they typically have limited resources for international operations.[14]

Just when people thought disintermediation would be an important consequence of the Internet, another trend emerged: reintermediation. This occurs when a new firm—usually an online intermediary—injects itself between buyers and suppliers in the online buying and selling environment.[15] For example, consumers can buy high-definition TVs directly from Sony at its Web site or from an online intermediary, such as CompUSA.com or Tesco.com.

Today, countless online intermediaries are brokering transactions between myriad buyers and sellers worldwide. Intermediaries survive by adding value in the distribution process. If changes in the marketplace render an intermediary's role less valuable, then the intermediary must adapt. Emergent technologies offer—and sometimes require—new roles that intermediaries have not taken previously. Many traditional retailers establish Web sites or link with online service providers to create an electronic presence. The electronic sites of stores like Tesco and Wal-Mart complement existing physical distribution infrastructure and bring more customers into retail outlets. In total, countless intermediaries and support services provide a wide range of buyer-seller functions online. They have shifted the landscape of retailing and intermediation in the global marketplace. Read more about the new Internet-based international intermediaries in the *Global Trend* feature on the next page.

More broadly, intermediaries as well as focal firms and facilitators employ the Internet and information technology (IT) tools to achieve various tasks. The Internet and IT provide enormous opportunities to transform, manage, and communicate within value chains. The technologies have triggered fundamental changes in core aspects of global business processes, including supply-chain management, procurement, and manufacturing. Information systems, electronic data interchange networks, shared databases, and other electronic links connect firms with suppliers and buyers in unprecedented ways. These links are particularly beneficial to multinational firms, whose customers may be spread around the globe. The Internet allows suppliers to be more in touch with buyers, in more direct ways.

Nevertheless, easy accessibility of the Internet has also led many shady online marketers to cause harm to unsuspecting consumers. For example, a recent *Business Week* investigation has found that only 11 percent of Web pharmacies require a prescription.[16] An astounding 89 percent, scattered largely in developing countries, appear to operate illegally. By sending billions of spam e-mail messages a day for pharmaceuticals, unscrupulous companies generate millions of dollars of drug sales. Unfortunately, these drugs are often fake products with foreign substances that may cause serious harm to users. Phony Viagra made in Thailand was found to contain vodka; bogus Tamiflu has been manufactured with vitamin C and lactose; and sometimes a medication contains lethal amounts of dangerous chemicals. Even though the pharmaceutical industry, together with various governments have been actively identifying and pursuing these companies, they seem to be elusive and often out of the reach of legal prosecution.

Online Retailers: Contemporary Global Intermediaries

Online retailing is experiencing explosive growth. The leading online auctioneer, eBay, is attracting some 70 million buyers and sellers to its Web site in a typical month. Amazon.com is a leading online retailer with 40 million visitors. Offerings at eBay and Amazon resemble online versions of vast department stores. Amazon now sells more consumer electronics than books. The Web sites of conventional retailers—once considered stuck in the bricks-and-mortar era of retailing—are growing fast. The number of shoppers using Wal-Mart's Web site now exceeds those visiting Amazon. In the United Kingdom, popular e-retailers include Argos, a catalogue merchant, and Tesco, Britain's biggest supermarket chain. The hottest online products include toys, computer games, clothing, and jewelry.

Consumers like e-retailing because they can compare products and prices, and save time. For retailers, laws and restrictions that apply to retail stores are not as strict online, and selling online is cheap. Wal-Mart and Tesco use the Web to test the market for new products before offering them in their stores. Such advantages explain why traditional retailers have made the move to become major online sellers.

EBay's cross-border business is surging, with more than 30 sites straddling the globe, from Brazil to Germany. International transactions now generate half of eBay's overall trading revenues and are growing twice as fast as domestic operations. Roughly half of eBay's 125 million registered users are located outside the United States. EBay shoppers buy a soccer jersey every five minutes in Britain, a bottle of wine every three minutes in France, a garden gnome every six minutes in Germany, and a skincare product every 30 seconds in China. EBay has managed to rapidly transplant its business model around the world. Local managers adapt to local conditions without losing the core competencies at the heart of eBay. Germany is by far the biggest international site, generating roughly one-third the sales of the U.S. market. Germany boasts a far higher percentage of active users than any other country, with roughly three-quarters of registered users trading regularly.

The internationalization of online selling indicates an interesting trend: Most of the business of international online retailers occurs *within* individual countries. At eBay's Germany site, nearly all the products, information, and chat boards are created by local buyers and sellers. The site and conversations are nearly all in German, and virtually all the users are German citizens. The same is true for India and Italy. Only about 12 percent of eBay's total gross merchandise sales involve cross-border transactions. In most countries, eBay has acquired a strong local flavor as buyers and sellers create a local community. Each country is a self-contained marketplace.

Yet international online retailers must adapt to local conditions. A big challenge is getting global markets to accept online payment systems, such as PayPal. In much of Asia, electronic payment systems remain a mystery, and online deals often require face-to-face cash payments. Cultural differences play a role, too. Asians are typically reluctant to buy used goods. Even among siblings, it is uncommon to pass down clothing. Nevertheless, more and more Asians are acquiring online trading habits. With more than 90 million Internet users, China is a fast-growing market. Within a few years, more people will be surfing the Web in China than in the United States.

One challenge for online retailers is the fact that most of the world lacks access to the Internet. The success of international online retailers depends on the availability of IT infrastructure. Countries can be ranked in terms of *electronic readiness (e-readiness)*, the degree to which its citizens can participate in the advantages and opportunities of a knowledge-based economy. By this measure, Denmark is the most e-ready country in the world, followed by the United States, Sweden, Switzerland, the United Kingdom, Hong Kong, Finland, and the Netherlands. By contrast, countries such as Russia, China, Indonesia, and India score relatively low on e-readiness. In such places, online retailers can target only a small portion of the local population. In Africa and parts of South Asia, poverty is prevalent and the level of e-readiness is even lower.

Sources: *Economist.* (2005). "E-readiness," May 7, p. 98; *Economist.* (2005). "Clicks, Bricks and Bargains," December 3, pp. 57–58; Schonfeld, Erick. (2005). "The World According to eBay," *Business 2.0* (January/February): 77–84.

Facilitators in International Business

The third category of participant in international business is the facilitator. While focal firms take center stage in global business, facilitators make it possible for international business transactions to occur efficiently, smoothly, and in a timely manner. They are independent individuals or firms that assist the internationalization and international operations of focal firms. Examples include banks, international trade lawyers, freight forwarders, customs brokers, and consultants. The number and role of facilitators have grown in recent years due to the complexity of international business operations, intense competition, and technological advances. Facilitators provide many useful services, ranging from conducting market research to identifying potential business partners and providing legal advice. They typically rely heavily on IT and the Internet to carry out their facilitating activities.

Some facilitators are supply-chain management specialists, responsible for physical distribution and logistics activities of their client companies. In the *Recent Grad in IB* feature on the next page, read about Cynthia Asoka, who is developing a career in global supply-chain management.

An important facilitator of international trade is the logistics service provider. A **logistics service provider** is a transportation specialist that arranges for physical distribution and storage of products on behalf of focal firms, also controlling information between the point of origin and the point of consumption. Companies such as DHL, FedEx, UPS, and TNT provide a cost-effective means for delivering cargo virtually anywhere in the world. They also increasingly provide traditional distributor functions such as warehousing, inventory management, and order tracking. FedEx, a leading express shipping company, delivers several million packages per day and offers supply-chain management services. The firm delivers to more than 210 countries and territories, covering virtually the entire planet with its fleet of over 640 aircraft and nearly 50,000 cars, trucks, and trailers. FedEx's business in Brazil, China, and India has grown rapidly.

Recently Red Wing, a U.S. shoe manufacturer, has taken advantage of UPS's supply chain services to bypass its own Salt Lake City distribution center, which is normally used to consolidate and repackage goods for shipment to retail stores. Red Wing produces some of its shoes in China, and sorts and repackages them at a UPS facility in southern China. Shoes are then delivered directly to Red Wing retail stores around the United States. By using outside express delivery firms, Red Wing gets its product to market faster and at lower cost. To serve the international distribution needs of companies like Red Wing, UPS has built over 50 warehouses in China.

Red Wing and countless other international manufacturers use *common carriers*, companies that own the ships, trucks, airplanes, and other transportation equipment used to transport goods around the world. Common carriers play a vital role in international business and global trade. A *consolidator* is a type of shipping company that combines the cargo of more than one exporter into international shipping containers for shipment abroad.

Most exporters utilize the services of freight forwarders because they are a critical facilitator in international business. Usually based in major port cities, freight forwarders arrange international shipments for the focal firm to a foreign entry port, and even to the buyer's location in the target foreign market. They are experts on transportation methods and documentation for international trade, as well as the export rules and regulations of the home and foreign countries. They arrange for clearance of shipments through customs on the importing side of the transaction. Freight forwarders are an excellent source of advice on shipping requirements such as packing, containerization, and labeling.

Logistics service provider
A transportation specialist that arranges for physical distribution and storage of products on behalf of focal firms, also controlling information between the point of origin and the point of consumption.

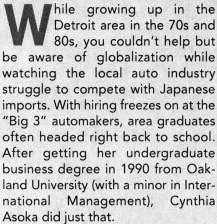

While growing up in the Detroit area in the 70s and 80s, you couldn't help but be aware of globalization while watching the local auto industry struggle to compete with Japanese imports. With hiring freezes on at the "Big 3" automakers, area graduates often headed right back to school. After getting her undergraduate business degree in 1990 from Oakland University (with a minor in International Management), Cynthia Asoka did just that.

After a semester in Vienna as an exchange student piqued an interest in language learning, Cynthia began a graduate program in linguistics studying Chinese and Spanish. She interrupted her studies to serve as a Peace Corps microenterprise development volunteer in the Dominican Republic, working on community projects funded by the Agency for International Development and teaching English in the evenings. She returned to graduate school to complete coursework in teaching English as a second language, then worked for Samsung for two years as a corporate trainer.

When Cynthia returned from Korea, she spent 18 months working for the Korean government's Trade Promotion Organization (KOTRA) in its Chicago office, sourcing Korean products for U.S. importers as well as promoting U.S. exports to Korea. Hoping to sharpen her skills so she could open her own trading com-

pany one day, she once again returned to graduate school to pursue her MBA degree in Supply-Chain Management.

Cynthia graduated in 1999 and was recruited by International Business Machines (IBM) to join its Supply Chain Leadership Training program. After completion of the two-year program, Cynthia sourced memory chips from Korean, German, and Taiwanese manufacturers, and then managed buyers of IT equipment and software. Acknowledging her company's increased emphasis on services, Cynthia switched to sourcing services for IBM's internal use in 2004, and now uses that expertise to source for IBM's customers who have outsourced that function to her firm's Business Transformation organization.

Cynthia's Advice for an International Business Career

Constantly seek out opportunities to learn new global skills. In multinational corporations, all solutions or processes you design should be applicable across many countries, forcing you to think and act globally, as well as work in teams (most often virtually) across the world. Although my dream was to open my own trading company, the skills and experience I have acquired working at a multinational corporation have served as an education I could never have acquired on my own.

Cynthia's major: Business
Internships during college: GM auto plants in Argentina and Brazil

Jobs held since graduating:

* Peace Corps volunteer in the Dominican Republic
* Samsung in Korea
* Trade Promotion Organization (KOTRA) of Korea, Chicago office
* IBM

Success Factors

Don't be afraid to be the trainee. When I found myself as an intern working at the GM auto plants in Argentina and Brazil, I struggled to carry on a conversation in my mediocre Spanish and practically non-existent Portuguese. After graduation the next year, I again spent two years as a trainee, moving every six months to work in different roles in various IBM plants across the United States and Canada. While your former classmates may already have become managers and directors at their companies, try to focus on skill acquisition rather than titles. Ultimately, a broad understanding of issues will help you identify better solutions and put global processes in place that will last.

Governments typically charge tariffs and taxes and devise complex rules for the import of products into the countries that they govern. **Customs brokers** are specialist enterprises that arrange clearance of products through customs on behalf of importing firms. They prepare and process the required documentation to get goods cleared through customs. They are to importing what freight forwarders are to exporting, specializing in getting goods cleared through customs in the country to which the goods are shipped. Also known as *customs house brokers*, customs brokers are specifically licensed to transact customs clearance procedures, with substantial expertise in navigating complex import procedures. They understand the regulations of the national customs service, as well as other governmental agencies that affect the import of products. Usually, the freight forwarder, based in the home country, works with a customs house broker based in the destination country in handling importing operations.

Various other players facilitate the financial operations of international business. *Commercial banks* are an important player in the international activities of all firms by facilitating the exchange of foreign currencies and providing financing to buyers and sellers who usually require credit to finance transactions. The process of getting paid usually takes longer in international than in domestic transactions, so a focal firm may need a loan from a commercial bank. Commercial banks can also: transfer funds to individuals or banks abroad, provide introduction letters and *letters of credit* to travelers, supply credit information on potential representatives or foreign buyers, and collect foreign invoices, drafts, and other foreign receivables. Within each country, large banks located in major cities maintain correspondent relationships with smaller banks spread around the nation. Large banks also maintain correspondent relationships with banks throughout the world, or operate their own foreign branches, thus providing a direct channel to foreign customers.

Banking is one of the most multinational sectors. Barclays, Citicorp, and Fuji Bank have as many international branches as any of the largest manufacturing MNEs. These banks frequently provide consultation and guidance, free of charge, to their clients since they derive income from loans to the exporter and from fees for special services. They may be knowledgeable about particular countries and their business practices or industries.

When it comes to SMEs, however, banks are often reluctant to extend credit, as these smaller firms usually lack substantial collateral and experience a higher failure rate than large MNEs. When this occurs, smaller firms in the United States can turn to the *Export Import Bank* (Ex-IM Bank; www.exim.gov), a federal agency that assists exporters in financing sales of their products and services in foreign markets. The Ex-Im Bank provides direct loans, working capital loans, loan guarantees, and other financial products aimed at supporting the exporting activities of smaller firms.

In other countries, particularly in the developing world, it is commonplace for governments to provide financing, often through public *development banks* and agencies. Money is routinely available in developing countries to finance the construction of infrastructure projects such as dams and power plants. Government bank loans are

Customs brokers Specialist enterprises that arrange clearance of products through customs on behalf of importing firms.

Commercial banks such as this one at the Mall of the Emirates in Dubai are key facilitators in international commercial transactions.

generally offered at very favorable rates, and therefore attract various types of borrowers. Host governments provide loans, even to foreign firms, to the extent the incoming investment is likely to result in new jobs, technology transfer, or substantial foreign exchange. Governments in Australia, Canada, Ireland, France, Spain, the United Kingdom, and numerous other countries similarly provide financing to MNEs for the construction of factories and other large-scale operations in their countries. In the United States, several state development agencies have provided loans to MNE automakers such as BMW, Honda, Mercedes, and Toyota to establish plants in their regions.

Focal firms and other participants also use the services of *international trade lawyers* to help navigate international legal environments. The best lawyers are knowledgeable about their client's industry, the laws and regulations of target nations, and the most appropriate means for international activity in the legal/regulatory context. Foreign lawyers are familiar with the obstacles involved in doing business with individual countries, including import licenses, trade barriers, intellectual property concerns, and government restrictions in specific industries.

Firms need international trade lawyers to negotiate contracts for the sales and distribution of goods and services to customers, intermediaries, or facilitators. Lawyers play a critical role when negotiating joint venture and strategic alliance agreements, or for reaching agreement on international franchising and licensing. International trade lawyers also come into play when disputes arise with foreign business partners. When the firm needs to hire foreign employees, a good lawyer can explain labor law and employment rights and responsibilities. Internationalizing firms often apply for patents for their products and register their trademarks in the countries where they do business, which requires the services of a patent attorney. In addition, lawyers can help to identify and optimize tax benefits that may be available from certain entry modes or within individual countries.

Insurance companies provide coverage against commercial and political risks. Losses tend to occur more often in international business because of the wide range of natural and man-made circumstances to which the firm's products are exposed as they make their way through the value chain. For example, goods shipped across the ocean are occasionally damaged in transit. Insurance helps to defray the losses that would otherwise result from such damage.

International business *consultants* advise internationalizing firms on various aspects of doing business abroad and alert them to foreign market opportunities. Consultants help companies improve their performance by analyzing existing business problems and helping management develop future plans. Particularly helpful will be *tax accountants,* who can advise companies on minimizing tax obligations resulting from multicountry operations. *Market research firms* are a potential key resource for identifying and targeting foreign buyers. They possess or can gain access to information on markets, competitors, and the methods of international business.

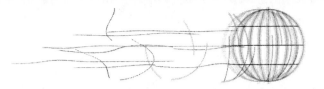

DHL International: An Ambitious Competitor in Global Logistics Services

When Adrian Dalsey, Larry Hillbolm, and Robert Lynn founded DHL as a door-to-door express service between San Francisco and Honolulu in 1969, no one could have imagined the business evolving into a cross-border express delivery group linking 120,000 destinations in more than 220 countries and territories. Now owned by the German company Deutsche Post World Net, DHL offers express services, international air and ocean freight, contract logistics, and value-added services. While DHL is the market leader for courier express delivery in Europe and Asia, the brand struggled to develop a reputation for quality service in the United States.

Global Supply Chain and Logistics Industry

To address the needs of customers who want simple and convenient solutions at competitive prices, the supply-chain and logistics industry has changed dramatically since the early seventies. The industry includes companies that move raw materials, finished goods, packages, and documents throughout the world. Four trends are affecting the industry: globalization, deregulation, digitization, and outsourcing. Growing cross-border trade has increased the complexity of the supply chain, creating demand for professional management of the logistics activities of a focal firm. Focal firms clearly recognize the benefits of moving goods through a supply chain faster and more efficiently. As a result, specialized logistic service providers such as DHL, UPS, and FedEx have emerged to organize, coordinate, and control supply chains through technological advancements and a global presence. These facilitating firms developed global networks of offices and warehouses, acquired trucks and aircraft, and invested in extensive information tracking systems.

DHL's Internationalization

DHL entered the international express arena in 1971 with services to the Philippines. The next year, DHL initiated services to Japan, Hong Kong, Singapore, and Australia. The Asia-Pacific focus was further developed in 1980, when DHL entered China through an agency agreement with Sinotrans that was later upgraded to a 50/50 joint venture in 1986, making it the first international joint venture express company in China. In 1973 DHL expanded into Europe, with later entry in the Middle East and Africa. DHL was the first company to offer international air express services to Eastern European countries in the 1980s. To support customers worldwide, DHL established hub operations in Brussels, Cincinnati, and Manila from 1985 to 1995. Strategically positioned facilities were located in Athens, Bombay, Hong Kong, Kuala Lumpur, Moscow, Osaka, Sydney, and Bahrain. DHL formed alliances with Japan Airlines, Lufthansa, and trading company Nissho Iwai.

In 2002, the German-based company Deutsche Post acquired 100 percent ownership of DHL for $2.7 billion. Deutsche Post AG, formerly owned and operated by the German government, became a publicly traded company in 2000. Deutsche Post provides national and international services in four corporate divisions (mail, express, logistics, and financial services) under three brand names—Deutsche Post, DHL, and Postbank. Since 2002, Deutsche Post has focused on integrating its express delivery and logistics units, which include Euro Express and Danzas, under the DHL umbrella. DHL maintains five main brands: DHL Exel Supply Chain, DHL Express, DHL Freight, DHL Global Forwarding, and DHL Global Mail.

Global Positioning

In the courier, express, and parcel market, DHL International is ahead of competitors in Europe due to its efficient national express networks. With a 35 percent share of the international express segment in the Asia Pacific region, DHL is the market leader in Japan and China. A major advantage in China is its dedicated air network of more than 20 aircraft in dedicated freighter operations. DHL is investing heavily on upgrading capabilities in the China area, committing close to $1 billion dollars since 2002 to upgrade ground and air capabilities. DHL's 2005 acquisition of 81 percent of the Indian express company Blue Dart strengthens the company's ability to offer customers domestic and international express services in the key Asian markets of China and India.

In the growing logistics industry, the DHL brand has experienced double-digit increases in volume. It is the global leader in airfreight ahead of Nippon Express. DHL is able to offer airfreight in regions not served by competitors through its internal freight carrier and air fleet. It is also the leading provider of ocean freight and contract logistics.

As the express delivery service is traditionally low margin, DHL focuses on bundling services with the more lucrative, value-added contract logistics management in automotive, pharmaceutical, healthcare, electronics, telecommunications, consumer goods, and textiles/fashion sectors. These contracts are long term, an average of three years. With the acquisition of Exel, DHL has been able to extend a great majority of its existing agreements. Client companies that have recently awarded contracts to DHL include Standard Chartered Bank, Deutsche Telekom, Philips, PepsiCo, Ford, BMW, Sun Microsystems, Unisys, and Electrolux.

The Importance of the U.S. Market for DHL

The United States is an important strategic market for DHL as a global logistics service provider offering customers a global network. North American express traffic accounts for nearly half the worldwide total with highly attractive margins, reaching $46.9 billion in 2004. In 2004, 20 percent of DHL express volumes flowed into the United States or moved from there around the globe. More than one third of all global Fortune 500 companies are headquartered in the United States, where decisions on logistics and transport orders are increasingly made.

The courier service market in the United States is highly competitive and relatively consolidated, with the top five companies in the market accounting for about 47 percent of the total market value. The largest sector is ground courier service, accounting for 61 percent of sales and worth about $30 billion. The U.S. Postal Service, with a monopoly on delivering all nonurgent letters in the United States, remains the largest provider. The U.S. Postal Service and FedEx continue to broaden their range of nondelivery services, including logistics, supply-chain management, and e-commerce. By 2005, FedEx and UPS together commanded 78 percent of the U.S. parcel market, with DHL obtaining only a 7 percent share of the express delivery market. With the acquisition of Exel, DHL is the market leader of logistics in the United States.

Challenges in the U.S. Market

DHL has performed well in two other NAFTA (North American Free Trade Agreement) markets. In Canada, DHL purchased a national business to complement international activities and was able to reach break even in less than two years. In Mexico, DHL is number one in the overall express and parcel market, with a strong market position. Yet it faces considerable challenges in the United States market.

In the United States, DHL's ambition is to be a strong number three in the market after UPS and FedEx. Focusing on the small and medium-sized U.S. businesses that are increasingly involved in cross-border trade, the company aims to raise its market share. A significant move

towards that goal began with the $1.1 billion acquisition in 2003 of Airborne Express, the nation's number three express service. However, the parcel market in the United States is shifting toward ground transport, due to high fuel prices making air shipment costly. DHL's limited ground network has hurt its ability to attract domestic customers who want to send parcels overland. DHL announced plans to invest $1.2 billion in its North American network to expand the company's ground delivery capacity by 60 percent. These efforts resulted in losses of $630 million in 2004 and $380 million in 2005.

DHL is facing various challenges in its operations as well. It experienced start-up difficulties when opening a central air hub in Wilmington, Ohio, that led to delivery delays and lost customers. In November of 2005, the company was responsible for losing a computer tape with the personal information of two million ABN AMRO residential mortgage customers. Although the tape later turned up in the Ohio facility, the damage to DHL's reputation was widespread. After extensive media coverage, and incurring the cost of providing all customers access to credit reporting services, ABN announced plans to use a "secure courier system" by FedEx, in which drivers stay with the computer tape the entire time.

DHL is also experiencing challenges by FedEx and UPS on regulatory grounds. These competitors have repeatedly contested Deutsche Post's operation in the United States by petitioning the U.S. Department of Transportation to cancel DHL's registration as a foreign-owned freight forwarder. UPS argued that Deutsche Post would use its monopoly profits to engage in predatory pricing in the United States. FedEx and UPS also called for a formal enforcement investigation of DHL Airways' citizenship, alleging that foreign nationals, including Germany's postal system Deutsche Post, would control DHL Airways. Under U.S. law, citizens of the United States must own at least 75 percent of the voting stock of a U.S. airline, and U.S. citizens must manage the operations. These debates generated much discussion regarding competition in the parcel delivery market. After years of motions and hearings, regulators denied the petitions and ruled in favor of DHL.

Marketing strategy in the United States includes spending $150 million in an identity rollout with a yellow and red logo. DHL had to repaint more than 17,000 trucks, purchase 20,000 worker uniforms, paint 467 service centers, replace 16,000 drop boxes and create the packaging, envelopes, and air bills used by employees and clients. These efforts coincided with the launch of an ad campaign intended to reintroduce the company to potential customers, attacking UPS and FedEx directly. The new look contributed to a 1 percent rise in market share in the United States, about $600 million in revenue.

AACSB: **Reflective Thinking**

Case Questions

1. DHL is integrating international express and logistic services. What value-added services does DHL provide? How do the services tie in to an organization's value chain activities? Can you anticipate changes to the supply chain that would further alter the express and logistic industry?

2. Who are the target clients for a company like DHL? What factors would influence the customer to choose a particular express courier and logistics provider?

3. Given the importance of the U.S. market to the global express industry, what would you recommend to DHL for changing its position in the United States? Do you feel that DHL's current strategies will be successful?

4. It appears that DHL needs to focus on improved customer satisfaction through better service quality and a more customer-friendly workforce. In this increasingly competitive industry, personalized service and investment in a trained sales force seems to be critical in attracting clients. Would customers in the United States be willing to risk critical shipping activities to a fledgling operation? Will patience run out for the parent company Deutsche Post?

Note: This case was written by Tracy Gonzalez-Padron, under the supervision of Professor S. Tamer Cavusgil.

Sources: Berman, J. (2006). "Survey Indicates DHL Is Closing the Gap on U.S. competitors." Retrieved September 15, 2006, from www.logisticsmgmt.com; Boyd, J. (2006). "Deutsche Post Ag." (2006), in Hoover's company records, retrieved April 1, 2007, at <proquest.umi.com/pqdweb?index=0&did=168275191&SrchMode=1&sid=1&Fmt=3&VInst=PROD&VType=PQD&RQT=309&VName=PQD&TS=1177706376&clientId=20174>; "Couriers in the USA." *Euromonitor International* (October 2005); "Deutsche Post AG." (June 2006) Retrieved from www.datamonitor.com; Deutsche Post Worldwide Net. (2005). Annual Report. Retrieved from www.dpwn.de; "DHL International Limited." (June 2006). Retrieved from www.datamonitor.com; "DHL Parent DPWN Restructures." *Traffic World* 1; "DHL Worldwide Network S.A./N.V.," (2006). Hoover's company records, retrieved April 1, 2007, at <proquest.umi.com/pqdweb?index=4&did=168173401&SrchMode=1&sid=2&Fmt=3&VInst=PROD&VType=PQD&RQT=309&VName=PQD&TS=1177706548&clientId=20174>; Ewing, Jack, Dean Foust, and Michael Eidam. "DHL's American Adventure," *Business Week* November 29, 2004, 126; Introduction to the Transportation and Logistics Industry. Retrieved October 15, 2006, from Plunkett Research, Ltd. Web site: www.plunkettresearch.com; Mucha, T. (2005). "Pouring It On to Compete with UPS and FedEx, DHL Underwent a Corporate Makeover, with New Colors, New Commercials, and 17,000 Newly Painted Trucks." *Business 2.0*, 6 (2):60; Yerak, B. (2005). "USA Finance: Shipper Locates Missing Tape with Mortgage Data." *Chicago Tribune* (December 21, 2005); Zumwinkel, Klaus. (2006). Speech presented at the annual general meeting of Deutsche Post AG on May 10, 2006, in Cologne, Germany. Retrieved from www.dpwn Media Relations.

CHAPTER ESSENTIALS

Key Terms

agent

born global firm

customs brokers

distribution channel
   intermediary

export management company
   (EMC)

facilitator

focal firm

foreign distributor

franchisor

freight forwarder

joint venture partner

licensor

logistics service provider

manufacturer's representative

multinational enterprise (MNE)

project-based, nonequity venture
   partners

small and medium-sized
   enterprise

trading company

turnkey contractors

Summary

In this chapter, you learned about:

1. Three types of participants in international business

International business transactions require the participation of numerous focal firms, intermediaries, and facilitators. A **focal firm** is the initiator of an international business transaction that conceives, designs, and produces the offerings for customers worldwide. A **distribution channel intermediary** is a specialist firm that provides a variety of logistics and marketing services for focal firms as part of the international supply chain, both in the home country and abroad. A **facilitator** is a firm or individual with special expertise such as legal advice, banking, and customs clearance that assists focal firms in the performance of international business transactions. The three types of participants bring various types of expertise, infrastructure, and inputs that make international business take place.

2. Participants organized by value-chain activity

Focal firms, intermediaries, and facilitators all make up participants in global value chains. The value chain is the complete business system of the focal firm. It comprises all of the focal firm's activities, including market research, R&D, sourcing, production marketing, distribution, and after-sales service. Channel intermediaries and facilitators support the focal firm by performing value-adding functions. In focal firms that export, most of the value chain is concentrated in the home country. In highly international firms, value-chain activities may be performed in various countries.

3. Focal firms in international business

Focal firms include MNEs, large global corporations such as Sony and Ford. MNEs operate in multiple countries by setting up production plants, marketing subsidiaries, and regional headquarters. SMEs now comprise the majority of internationally active firms. They are relatively flexible firms that tend to emphasize exporting and leverage the help of intermediaries and facilitators to succeed in international business. **Born globals** are a category of international SMEs that internationalize at or near the firm's founding.

4. Foreign market entry strategies of focal firms

Focal firms include a **licensor**, a firm that enters a contractual agreement with a foreign partner that allows the latter the right to use certain intellectual property for a specified period of time in exchange for royalties or other compensation. A **franchisor** is a firm that grants another the right to use an entire business system in exchange for fees, royalties, or other forms of compensation. A **turnkey contractor** is a focal firm or a consortium of firms that plans, finances, organizes, manages, and implements all phases of a project, and then hands it over to a foreign customer after training local personnel. A **joint venture partner** is a focal firm that creates and jointly owns a new legal entity through equity investment or pooling of assets. **Project-based, nonequity venture partners** are focal firms that collaborate through a project with a relatively narrow scope and a well-defined timetable, without creating a new legal entity.

5. Distribution channel intermediaries in international business

Distribution channel intermediaries move products and services across national borders and eventually to end-users. They perform key downstream functions in the target market on behalf of focal firms, including marketing. A **foreign distributor** is a foreign market-based intermediary that works under contract for an exporter, takes title to, and distributes the exporter's products in a national market or territory, often performing marketing functions such as sales, promotion, and after-sales service. An **agent** is an intermediary that handles orders to buy and sell commodities, products, and services in international business transactions for a commission. A **manufacturer's representative** is an intermediary contracted by the exporter to represent and sell its merchandise or services in a designated country or territory. A **trading company** is an intermediary that engages in import and export of a variety of commodities, products, and services. An **export management company (EMC)** is an intermediary that acts as an export agent on behalf of client companies.

6. Facilitators in international business

Facilitators assist with international business transactions. A **logistics service provider** is a transportation specialist that arranges for physical distribution and storage of products on behalf of focal firms, also controlling information between the point of origin and the point of consumption. A **freight forwarder** is a specialized logistics service provider that arranges international shipping on behalf of exporting firms, much like a travel agent for cargo. A **customs broker** is a specialist enterprise that arranges clearance of products through customs on behalf of importing firms. Other facilitators include *banks, lawyers, insurance companies, consultants,* and *market research firms.*

Test Your Comprehension

1. Identify and briefly define the three major categories of participants in international business.

2. In the stages of a typical international value chain, what role does each of the three categories of participants typically play?

3. What are the specific characteristics of focal firms? Distinguish the characteristics of international MNEs, SMEs, and born-global firms.

4. What is unique about such focal firms as franchisors, licensors, and turnkey contractors?

5. What role do distribution channel intermediaries provide?

6. What are major distribution channel intermediaries based in the home country and those based abroad?

7. What are online intermediaries? How do focal firms use the Internet to carry out international activities?

8. What are the characteristics of facilitators? List and define the major types of facilitators.

Apply Your Understanding AACSB: Reflective Thinking, Communication

1. The international business landscape is occupied by focal firms, distribution channel intermediaries, and facilitators. Each group of participants assumes a different and critical role in the performance of international business transactions. Think about the degree of interdependency that exists among the three groups. What would happen if distribution channel intermediaries could not provide competent services to the focal firm? What if adequate facilitators were not available to the focal firm? To what degree would the focal firm's international business performance be hampered? Under what circumstances would the focal firm choose to internalize its value-chain activities in international business rather than delegate them to channel intermediaries and facilitators? What would be the consequences of retaining distribution and support activities within the firm?

2. Think about a company for which you would like to work following graduation. Perhaps it is in one of the following industries: music (such as Virgin), banking (Citibank), engineering (Skanska AB), food (Kraft), automobiles (BMW), or another. Next, using the framework outlined in Exhibit 3.1 on page 64, sketch out the value chain that your chosen firm most likely uses in a particular product or service category. To complete this exercise, do library research or visit the Web site of this firm. Your value chain should include all of the major international business activities in which the firm is engaged. Next, develop a list of the intermediaries and facilitators that your company is likely to engage to configure its value chain. Indicate along your value chain where these participants are most likely to be located.

3. Following graduation, assume that you get a job at Kokanee Corporation, an SME that manufactures collars, leashes, grooming supplies, and other products for dogs and other household pets. Your boss, Mr. Eugene Kimball, wants to begin exporting Kokanee's products to foreign markets. Prepare a memo for Mr. Kimball in which you briefly describe the kinds of intermediaries and facilitators with whom Kokanee is likely to consult and work to maintain successful export operations.

globalEDGE Internet Exercises

(http://globalEDGE.msu.edu)

AACSB: Reflective Thinking, Use of Information Technology

Refer to Chapter 1, page 27, for instructions on how to access and use globalEDGE™.

1. Visit the government agency or ministry in your country responsible for supporting international business. For example, in the United States, visit, the Department of Commerce (www.doc.gov). In Canada, visit Industry Canada (www.ic.gc.ca). In Denmark, visit the Ministry of Economic and Business Affairs (www.oem.dk). Identify and describe the most important support functions that the agency provides to companies that do international business. One approach is to sketch out a typical value chain, and then systematically identify the support services that the agency offers. For example, for the distribution link in the value chain, numerous governments provide "matchmaker" services, trade missions, and commercial services that link manufacturing firms with appropriate distributors located abroad.

2. Visit the Whirlpool Corporation (www.Whirlpool.com) and click on "International Sites" (under "Corporate Information"). Whirlpool has a complex value chain. Based on the information provided at the Web site address the following questions: What types of upstream value-chain activities does Whirlpool perform? What types of downstream value-chain activities does Whirlpool perform? Identify the types of participants (mainly intermediaries and facilitators) that Whirlpool is likely to use at each stage of the value chain.

3. Your company is about to initiate export activities in a country of your choice. You will need to identify distribution channel intermediaries and freight forwarders in order to have your products reach end-users in this country. Now visit the Resource Desk and Diagnostic Tools directories of globalEDGE™. What sources of information are especially helpful to you in identifying suitable foreign distributors and freight forwarders? What do you learn from these sources?

610

International Business

CKR Cavusgil Knight Riesenberger
Management Skill Builder©

Finding and Evaluating Freight Forwarders

As you learned in the chapter, a freight forwarder is a company that organizes the shipment of cargo via transportation modes including ships, airplanes, trucks, and railroads for manufacturers that export products. Freight forwarders do not ship cargo themselves but instead arrange for its transport by common carriers. Freight forwarders also prepare and process the documentation required for international shipments and arrange for transportation insurance and clearance through foreign customs. Freight forwarders charge a fee for their services that covers the total transport cost. Transportation is arranged from the exporter's factory or from a port in the exporter's country, to the customer's destination abroad, typically involving two or more transportation modes. UPS and DHL Worldwide Forwarding are two of the largest freight forwarders.

AACSB: Reflective Thinking, Use of Information Technology

Managerial Challenge

Evaluating and selecting a qualified freight forwarder is a critical strategic decision for managers in international operations. Freight forwarders are concentrated in large cities, and port cities, typically close to port facilities, transportation companies, and customs operations. By looking in the telephone directory of any such city, a manager can find dozens or even hundreds of freight forwarders. Freight forwarders vary widely in terms of their resources, capabilities, experience, and knowledge.

Background

It is estimated that more than 90 percent of all exporting firms have used the services of a freight forwarder. Roughly 75 percent of all international shipments involve the services of a freight forwarder. The rise of internationally active SMEs makes the services and expertise of freight forwarders even more important because smaller firms usually lack the resources or knowledge to conduct international shipping themselves.

Increased competition in both domestic and foreign markets has made the services of freight forwarders more important to exporters. First, on-time delivery can put an exporter ahead of many others. Second, firms exporting to emerging markets and developing economies need third parties with experience in these new markets or ports. Finally, parent companies that have increased trade with their foreign affiliates need reliable freight forwarders that facilitate timely trans-

portation services, helping to ensure that production lines operate smoothly.

Managerial Skills You Will Gain

In this C/K/R Management Skill Builder©, as a prospective manager, you will:

1. Learn about freight forwarders and their role in international trade.

2. Learn the most important criteria for evaluating freight forwarders.

3. Research information to find the most appropriate freight forwarder for company needs.

Your Task

Assume that you are a manager in a small or medium-sized manufacturing firm. You are about to begin exporting your firm's products abroad. Choose a product category such as machinery or musical instruments to be shipped to foreign customers. Your task is to gather information on three different freight forwarders and then choose the best forwarder for your company.

Go to the C/K/R Knowledge Portal©

www.prenhall.com/cavusgil
Proceed to the C/K/R Knowledge Portal© to obtain the expanded background information, your task and methodology, suggested resources for this exercise, and the presentation template.

chapter

16

Global Sourcing

Learning Objectives

In this chapter, you will learn about:

1. Trends toward outsourcing, global sourcing, and offshoring

2. Evolution of global sourcing

3. Benefits and challenges of global sourcing for the firm

4. Implementing global sourcing through supply-chain management

5. Risks in global sourcing

6. Strategies for minimizing risk in global sourcing

7. Implications of global sourcing for public policy and corporate citizenship

> ## Global Sourcing of Pharmaceutical Drug Trials

Nearly 40 percent of clinical trials for new drugs in the pharmaceutical industry are now conducted in emerging markets such as China and Russia. It is estimated that by 2010, some two million people in India will take part in clinical trials. Where drug testing was once conducted mostly in developed economies, pharmaceutical firms such as Pfizer increasingly prefer emerging markets because they offer clear advantages: (1) lower costs for recruitment of physicians and patients, (2) large potential patient populations, (3) diversity of patient populations and medical conditions, and (4) less likelihood of patients taking other medicines that could interact with the drug under study.

It costs an average of $900 million to develop and bring a new drug to market in the United States. More than half the cost relates to confirming drug safety and effectiveness in trial phases on humans, as required by the U. S. Food and Drug Administration (FDA) and similar agencies worldwide. Recruiting patients accounts for 40 percent of the trial budget. Testing in emerging markets greatly reduces recruitment costs. According to GlaxoSmithKline, a drug trial costs about $30,000 on a per-patient basis in the United States and about $3,000 in Romania.

612

International Business

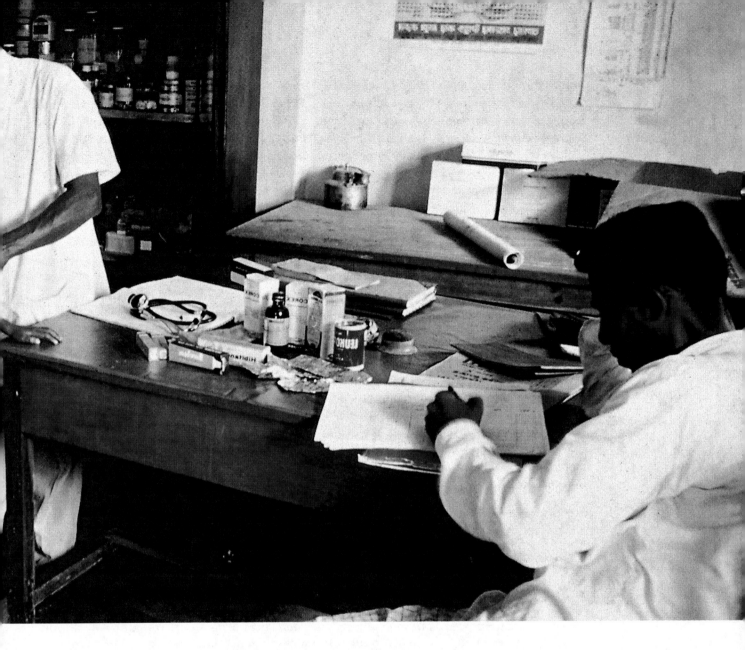

Firms typically outsource the trials to contract research organizations, which in turn hire physicians in local communities and hospitals to find patients. For example, subcontractors tested Merck's Vioxx and Zocor drugs and many of Pfizer's billion-dollar drugs in Russia and other developing countries before gaining approval in the United States. Almost every major Western pharmaceutical firm is conducting clinical trials in hospitals across Russia. In a poor country with a dysfunctional medical system, patients often consider the trials a way to access medical treatment. Russia's centralized hospital system recruits patients for trials quickly, which shaves millions of dollars and several months off the drug development process.

Nevertheless, offshoring of clinical trials raises questions about ethics and oversight of this critical stage in the development of new medications. While the vast majority of trials in emerging markets have been conducted without problems, some breakdowns in ethical and scientific processes have occurred. For example, Pfizer was sued for testing a meningitis drug on Nigerian children without their parents' consent, resulting in five deaths. Some trials endangered patients or were conducted without proper ethical review. Better oversight of this critical stage in the development of new medications is warranted, but conducting drug trials properly can be challenging. Emerging markets may lack the resources the FDA normally requires. One official asks "How do you meet procedures required by the FDA in settings where electricity is going off two hours a day?"

In one case, the Nigerian trial for an antiretroviral drug was shut down amid concerns that researchers did not store the drugs or handle the scientific data properly. Where physicians in Russia normally earn $200 per month, a trial investigator there can make 10 times that amount by recruiting patients into trials. This financial incentive raises potential conflicts for doctors, some of whom may bribe patients to ensure their participation in trials.

In emerging markets, some drug trials do not receive adequate attention from ethics review committees. One study found that a quarter of all trials in developing economies did not receive any local official review. Still, the U.S. approval process places a great burden on local review. The FDA is required to inspect a certain proportion of trial sites. Nevertheless, in a recent year, despite more than 500 drug trials in Russia alone at some 3,000 sites, the FDA inspected only about 100 sites worldwide. Of the international sites inspected, the FDA criticized more than 30 percent for failure to follow protocol, and cited nearly 10 percent for failure to report adverse patient reactions to trial drugs.

While the FDA is working closely with local governments with hopes that world ethical standards will catch up with its regulations, pharmaceutical firms are increasing their outsourcing of drug trials abroad. Trials will continue to shift to emerging markets in search of more patients with faster recruitment at lower cost. ◄

Sources: Bloch, M., A. Dhankhar, and S. Narayanan. (2006). "Pharma Leaps Offshore," *McKinsey Quarterly*, July, p. 12; Engardio, Pete. (2006). "The Future of Outsourcing: How It's Transforming Whole Industries and Changing the Way We Work," *Business Week*, January 30, p. 58; *Economist Intelligence Unit*. (2007). "U.K. Regulations: Tougher on Drugs," April 11. Retrieved from www.viewswire.com; A. T. Kearney. (2007). *Country Attractiveness Index for Clinical Trials*, A. T. Kearney Company. Retrieved from www.atkearney.com; Lustgarten, Abrahm. (2005). "Drug Testing Goes Offshore," *Fortune*, August 8, pp. 66–71; PhRMA. (2007, March). *Pharmaceutical Industry Profile 2007*. March.

 ## Trends Toward Outsourcing, Global Sourcing, and Offshoring

As noted in the opening vignette, companies in the pharmaceutical industry cut product development costs and hasten speed to market by sourcing drug-testing processes from emerging markets. Focal firms shop around the world for inputs or finished products to meet efficiency and strategic objectives and remain competitive.

The search for the best sources of products and services is an ongoing task for managers. In some cases, firms have moved entire value-chain activities such as manufacturing to foreign locations. Nike Inc., along with competitors Reebok and Adidas in the athletic shoe industry, contracts out nearly all of its athletic shoe production to foreign suppliers. These firms are best described as brand owners and marketers today, not as manufacturers. Similarly, Apple Inc. sources some 70 percent of its production abroad while focusing its internal resources on improving its operating system and other software platforms. This approach allows Apple to optimally utilize its limited capital resources and focus on its core competences. Dell Inc. is another firm that relies extensively on a global manufacturing network, composed largely of independent suppliers. See Exhibit 16.1 to learn how Dell assembles components from suppliers in numerous locations for its Dell Inspiron notebook computer.[1]

Global sourcing is the procurement of products or services from independent suppliers or company-owned subsidiaries located abroad for consumption in the home country or a third country. Also called *global procurement* or *global purchasing*, global sourcing amounts to *importing*—an inbound flow of goods and services. It is an entry strategy that involves a contractual relationship between the buyer (the

Global sourcing The procurement of products or services from independent suppliers or company-owned subsidiaries located abroad for consumption in the home country or a third country.

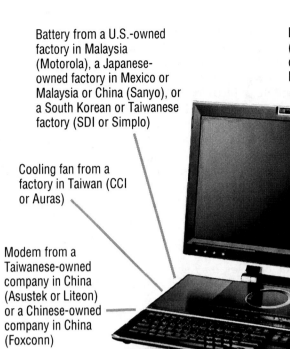

Battery from a U.S.-owned factory in Malaysia (Motorola), a Japanese-owned factory in Mexico or Malaysia or China (Sanyo), or a South Korean or Taiwanese factory (SDI or Simplo)

LCD display from a factory in South Korea (Samsung or LG Phillips LCD), Japan (Toshiba or Sharp), or Taiwan (Chi Mei Optoelectronics, Hamstar Display, or AU Optronics)

Cooling fan from a factory in Taiwan (CCI or Auras)

Keyboard from a Japanese-owned factory (Alps) or a Taiwanese-owned factory (Sunrex or Darfon), all in China

Modem from a Taiwanese-owned company in China (Asustek or Liteon) or a Chinese-owned company in China (Foxconn)

Intel microprocessor from an Intel factory in China, Malaysia, the Philippines, or Costa Rica

Hard disk drive from a U.S.-owned factory in Singapore (Seagate), a Japanese-owned company in Thailand (Hitachi or Fujitsu), or a Japanese-owned factory in the Philippines (Toshiba)

Motherboard from a Korean-owned factory in China (Samsung), a Taiwanese-owned factory in China (Quanta), or a Taiwanese-owned factory in Taiwan (Compal or Wistron)

Memory from a factory in Japan (Elpida), South Korea (Samsung), Taiwan (Nanya), or Germany (Infineon)

Exhibit 16.1 Sourcing for the Dell Inspiron Notebook Computer

SOURCE: Adapted from Friedman, Thomas. (2005). *The World is Flat*, New York: Farrar, Straus, & Giroux

focal firm) and a foreign source of supply. Global sourcing involves subcontracting the performance of specific manufacturing or services tasks to the firm's own subsidiaries or independent suppliers. As illustrated in Exhibit 14.1 on page 420, global sourcing is a low-control strategy in which the focal firm sources from independent suppliers through contractual agreements, as opposed to buying from company-owned subsidiaries.

Although global sourcing has been an established international business activity since the 1980s, it has gained new momentum in the current phase of globalization. Four key drivers are especially responsible for the growth of global sourcing in recent years:

* Technological advances, including instant Internet connectivity and broadband availability

* Declining communication and transportation costs

* Widespread access to vast information, including growing connectivity between suppliers and the customers that they serve

* Entrepreneurship and rapid economic transformation in emerging markets

While firms had their early experience with the sourcing of merchandise goods, in recent years they have increasingly subcontracted the performance of business processes and other services to subsidiaries and independent suppliers located worldwide.[2] For example, contractors such as Softtek in Mexico help U.S. banks to develop customized software, manage their IT systems, and perform support and maintenance for commercial finance operations. Softtek has 3,500 employees, mostly engineers, and outsourcing facilities in Brazil, Colombia, Peru, and Venezuela. Argentina, which boasts one of the best-educated workforces in Latin America, is aggressively promoting software development centers. The low salaries of software engineers (typically less than $12,000 a year) has persuaded such companies as Walt Disney, Peugeot, and Repsol to have web site design and software development performed in Argentina.

In undertaking global sourcing, managers face two key decisions: (1) which value-chain activities should be outsourced; and (2) where in the world these activities should be performed. Let's consider these two managerial choices.

Decision 1: Outsource or Not?

Managers must decide between *internalization* and *externalization*—whether each value-adding activity should be conducted in house or by an external, independent supplier. In business, this is traditionally known as the *make or buy* decision: "Should we make a product or perform a particular value-chain activity ourselves, or should we source it from an outside contractor?" Firms usually internalize those value-chain activities that they consider part of their *core competence*, or which involve the use of proprietary knowledge and trade secrets that they want to control. For example, Canon uses its core competencies in precision mechanics, fine optics, and microelectronics to produce some of the world's best cameras, printers, and copiers. Canon usually internalizes value-chain activities such as R&D because they yield improvements in these competencies. By contrast, firms will usually source from *external* suppliers those products or services that are peripheral to the firm's main offerings, have a lower cost, or when the supplier specializes in providing the specific offerings. By contrast, firms will usually source from *external* suppliers when the sourced products or services are peripheral to the firm's main offerings, can be obtained at lower cost, or can be provided by suppliers specialized in providing the specific offerings.

By contrast, firms will usually source from external suppliers, products, or services that: are peripheral to the firm's main offerings; can be obtained at lower cost; or can be provided by suppliers specialized in providing the specific offerings. More formally, **outsourcing** refers to the procurement of selected value-adding activities, including production of intermediate goods or finished products, from external independent suppliers. Firms outsource because they generally are not superior at performing *all* primary and support activities. Most value-adding activities—from manufacturing to marketing to after-sales service—are candidates for outsourcing.

Historically, outsourcing involved the acquisition of raw materials, parts, and components from independent suppliers. More recently, outsourcing has extended to include the procurement of services as well.[3] The typical firm will outsource services such as accounting, payroll, and some human resource functions, as well as travel services, IT services, customer service, and technical support. This type of outsourcing is known as **business process outsourcing (BPO)**.[4] Firms contract with third-party service providers to perform specific business tasks, usually as a means of reducing the cost of performing tasks that are not part of the firm's core competencies or critical to maintaining the firm's competitive position in the marketplace. BPO can be divided into two categories: *back-office activities*, which includes internal, upstream business functions such as payroll and billing, and *front-office activities*, which includes downstream, customer-related services such as marketing or technical support.

Today in Europe, North America, Japan, and other advanced economies, few firms produce an entire product. Most firms contract out their peripheral activities to outside suppliers.

Outsourcing The procurement of selected value-adding activities, including production of intermediate goods or finished products, from independent suppliers.

Business process outsourcing (BPO) The outsourcing of business functions to independent suppliers, such as accounting, payroll, human resource functions, IT services, customer service, and technical support.

Decision 2: Where in the World Should Value-Adding Activities Be Located?

For each value-adding activity, managers have the choice of either keeping the activity at home or locating it in a foreign country. **Configuration of value-adding activity** refers to the pattern or geographic arrangement of locations where the firm carries out value-chain activities.[5] For instance, to run its global network of package shipping, DHL established offices in countries and cities worldwide. It also set up high-tech tracking centers in Arizona, Malaysia, and the Czech Republic. This configuration allows DHL staffers to track the locations of shipments worldwide, 24 hours a day. DHL management chose these specific locations for shipment tracking because, in a world of 24 time zones, they are each about 8 hours distant from each other.

Instead of concentrating value-adding activities in their home country, many firms configure these activities across the world to save money, reduce delivery time, access factors of production, and extract maximal advantages relative to competitors. This helps explain the migration of manufacturing industries from Europe, Japan, and the United States to emerging markets in Asia, Latin America, and Eastern Europe. Depending on the firm and the industry, management may decide to concentrate certain value-adding activities in just one or a handful of locations, while dispersing others to numerous countries.

For example, the German automaker Bayerische Motoren Werke AG (BMW) employs 70,000 factory personnel at 23 sites in 13 countries to manufacture sedans, coupes, and convertibles. Workers at the Munich plant build the BMW 3 Series and supply engines and key body components to other BMW factories abroad. In the United States, BMW has a plant in South Carolina that makes over 500 vehicles daily for the world market. In northeast China, BMW makes cars in a joint venture with Brilliance China Automotive Holdings Ltd. In India, BMW has a manufacturing presence to serve the needs of the rapidly growing South Asia market. However, BMW's profits have suffered in recent years due to higher cost of raw materials such as plastics and steel. Management must configure BMW's sourcing at the best locations worldwide in order to: minimize costs (for example, by producing in China), access skilled personnel (by producing in Germany), remain close to key markets (by producing in China, India, and the United States), and succeed in the intensely competitive global car industry.

Global Sourcing from Subsidiaries versus Independent Suppliers

The two strategic choices we just discussed lead us to the framework in Exhibit 16.2. The focal firm can source from independent suppliers, from company-owned subsidiaries and affiliates, or from both. In the Exhibit, Cells C and D represent the global sourcing scenarios. While global sourcing implies procurement from foreign locations, in some cases the focal firm may source from its own wholly owned subsidiary or an affiliate jointly owned with another firm (Cell C). This is known as **captive sourcing**, which refers to sourcing from the firm's own production facilities located abroad. In this scenario, production is carried out at a foreign facility that the focal firm owns through direct investment. For example, Genpact (formerly Gecis Global) was a captive sourcing unit of General Electric (GE). With annual revenues of about $500 million and more than 19,000 employees worldwide, Genpact is one of the largest providers of business-process outsourcing services. GE sold Genpact in 2005, and the supplier became an independent firm. While maintaining its work for GE, Genpact is now free to seek other customers worldwide.[6]

Configuration of value-adding activity The pattern or geographic arrangement of locations where the firm carries out value-chain activities.

Captive sourcing Sourcing from the firm's own production facilities located abroad.

Exhibit 16.2

The Nature of Outsourcing and Global Sourcing

	Value-adding activity is internalized	Value-adding activity is externalized (outsourced)
Value-adding activity kept in home country	*A* Keep production in-house, in home country	*B* Outsource production to third party provider at home
Value-adding activity conducted abroad (global sourcing)	*C* Delegate production to foreign subsidiary or affiliate (captive sourcing)	*D* Outsource production to a third-party provider abroad (contract manufacturing or global sourcing from independent suppliers)

Alternatively, the focal firm can procure intermediate goods or finished products from independent suppliers (Cell D), an increasingly likely scenario. The firm externalizes its production to foreign partners to harness their capabilities. Global sourcing requires the firm to identify qualified suppliers, develop necessary organizational and technological capabilities to relocate specific tasks, and coordinate a geographically dispersed network of activities.

Contract Manufacturing: Global Sourcing from Independent Suppliers

The typical relationship between the focal firm and its foreign supplier (Cell D in Exhibit 16.2) may take the form of **contract manufacturing**, an arrangement in which the focal firm contracts with an independent supplier to manufacture products according to well-defined specifications. Often, an explicit contract spells out the terms of the relationship. The supplier is responsible for production and adheres to the focal firm's specifications. Once the products are manufactured, the supplier turns them over to the focal firm, which then markets, sells, and distributes them. In essence, the focal firm "rents" the manufacturing capacity of the foreign contractor.

In a typical scenario, the focal firm approaches several suppliers with product designs or specifications and asks for quotations on the cost to produce the merchandise, accounting for cost of labor, processes, tooling, and materials. Once the bidding process is complete, the focal firm contracts with the most qualified manufacturer. Contract manufacturing is especially common in the apparel, shoe, furniture, aerospace, defense, computer, semiconductor, energy, medical, pharmaceutical, personal care, and automotive industries.

Patheon is one of the world's leading contract manufacturers in the pharmaceutical industry. The company provides drug development and manufacturing services to pharmaceutical and biotechnology firms worldwide. Patheon operates 11 production facilities in North America and Europe, producing over-the-counter drugs and several of the world's top-selling prescription drugs on contract for most of the world's 20 largest pharmaceutical firms. Patheon generates about half its sales in North America and the other half in Europe.[7] Benetton employs contract manufacturers to produce clothing, and IKEA uses contract manufacturers to produce furniture. Contract manufacturing also allows firms to enter target countries quickly, especially when the market is too small to justify significant local investment.

You have probably never heard of Taiwan's Hon Hai Precision Industry Co., a leading contract manufacturer in the global electronics industry. Hon Hai works

Contract manufacturing An arrangement in which the focal firm contracts with an independent supplier to manufacture products according to well-defined specifications.

under contract for well-known companies, churning out iPods and iPhones for Apple, PlayStations for Sony, printers and PCs for Hewlett-Packard, and thousands of other products. In 2007, Hon Hai's sales surpassed $40 billion. The firm employs some 360,000 people in scores of contract factories worldwide, from Malaysia to Mexico.[8]

One advantage of contract manufacturing is that the focal firm—for example, Apple, Hewlett-Packard, or Sony—can concentrate on product design and marketing while transferring manufacturing responsibility to an independent contractor. The contract manufacturer is likely to be located in a low-wage country and have strengths in terms of scale economies, manufacturing prowess, and specific knowledge about the engineering and development processes of products that it handles for its clients.[9] A major drawback of contract manufacturing is that the focal firm has limited control over the supplier. Lack of direct ownership implies limited influence over the manufacturing processes of the supplier, potential vulnerability to the supplier's acting in bad faith, and limited ability to safeguard intellectual assets.

Offshoring

Offshoring is a natural extension of global sourcing. **Offshoring** refers to the relocation of a business process or entire manufacturing facility to a foreign country. Large multinational companies are particularly active in shifting production facilities or business processes to foreign countries to enhance their competitive advantage. Offshoring is especially common in the service sector, including banking, software code writing, legal services, and customer-service activities. For example, large legal hubs have emerged in India that provide services such as drafting contracts and patent applications, conducting research and negotiations, as well as performing paralegal work on behalf of Western clients. With lawyers in North America and Europe costing $300 an hour or more, Indian firms can cut legal bills by 75 percent.[10]

Firms generally offshore certain tasks or subactivities of business functions. In each of the business functions—human resources, accounting, finance, marketing, and customer service—certain tasks are routine and discrete. These functions are candidates for offshoring, as long as their performance by independent suppliers does not threaten or diminish the focal firm's core competencies or strategic assets. Examples of successful offshoring to foreign providers include billing and credit card processing in finance, creating customer databases and recording sales transactions in marketing, and payroll maintenance and benefits administration in human resources.

India receives the bulk of advanced economies' relocated business services. This sector in India has grown by as much as 50 percent per year during the 2000s. The country's emergence as a major offshoring destination results from its huge pool of qualified labor who work for wages as little as 25 percent of comparable workers in the West, combined with the worldwide economic downturn of the early 2000s, which triggered multinational firms to seek ways to shave costs.[11] But India is not the only destination of substantial outsourcing work. Firms in Eastern Europe perform support activities for architectural and engineering firms from Western Europe and the United States. Accountants in the Philippines perform support work for major accounting firms. Accenture has back-office operations and call centers in Costa Rica. Many IT support services for customers in Germany are actually based in the Czech Republic

Offshoring The relocation of a business process or entire manufacturing facility to a foreign country.

Workers at a call center in Bangalore support international customers. India has received the bulk of outsourced business process services in recent years.

and Romania. Boeing, Motorola, and Nortel do much of their R&D in Russia. South Africa is the base for technical and user-support services for English, French, and German-speaking customers throughout Europe.[12]

Limits to Global Sourcing

Not all business activities or processes lend themselves to offshoring. Jobs most conducive to being offshored tend to be in industries with the following characteristics:

- Large-scale manufacturing industries whose primary competitive advantage is efficiency and low cost
- Industries such as automobiles that have uniform customer needs and highly standardized processes in production and other value-chain activities
- Service industries that are highly labor intensive, such as call centers and legal transcription
- Information-based industries whose functions and activities can be easily transmitted via the Internet, such as accounting, billing, and payroll
- Industries such as software preparation, whose outputs are easy to codify and transmit over the Internet or by telephone, such as routine technical support and customer service activities.

In contrast, many jobs in the services sector cannot be separated from their place of consumption. This limits the types of service jobs that firms can move abroad. Personal contact is vital at the downstream end of virtually all value chains. Other services are consumed locally. For example, people normally do not travel abroad to see a doctor, dentist, lawyer, or accountant.[13] Consequently, many service jobs will never be offshored. For example, through 2005, only about 3 percent of jobs in the United States that require substantial customer interaction (for example, those in the retailing sector) have been transferred to low-wage economies. By 2008, less than 15 percent of all service jobs have moved from advanced economies to emerging markets.[14]

In addition, many companies, such as Harley-Davidson in the United States, have their own reasons to keep production at home. A great proportion of the value added by Harley-Davidson is local. Harley-Davidson both assembles its motorcycles and procures key components such as the engine, transmission, gas tank, brake system, and the headlight assembly in the United States.[15] Harley's customers view the product as an American icon and tend to not tolerate production abroad. Another factor is labor union contracts, which limit management's ability to transfer core production abroad without union consent.

Strategic Implications of Outsourcing and Global Sourcing

Exhibit 16.3 explains the strategic implications of the two choices firms face: whether to perform specific value-adding activities themselves or to outsource them, *and* whether to concentrate each activity in the home country or disperse it abroad. The Exhibit portrays a typical value chain, ranging from R&D and design, to customer service. The first row indicates the degree to which management considers each value-adding activity a strategic asset to the firm. The second row indicates whether the activity tends to be internalized inside the focal firm or outsourced to a foreign supplier. The third row indicates where management typically locates an activity.

These decisions depend largely on the strategic importance of the particular activity to the firm. For example, companies typically consider R&D and design activities central to their competitive advantage. As a result, they are more likely to internalize these functions and less likely to outsource. In con-

	R&D Design	Component Manufacturing	Manufacturing or Assembly	Marketing and Branding	Sales, Distribution and Logistics	Customer Service
Importance of this activity to the firm as a strategic asset	Very important	Low importance	Low to medium importance	Very important	Medium importance	Medium importance
Likelihood of internalizing rather than outsourcing this activity	High	Low	Low to Medium	High	Low to Medium	Low to Medium
Geographic configuration: Overall tendency to locate activity at home or abroad	Usually concentrated at home	Usually dispersed across various markets	Usually concentrated in a few markets	Branding concentrated at home; Marketing concentrated or dispersed to individual markets	Dispersed to individual markets	Dispersed to individual markets, except call centers, which are often concentrated

Exhibit 16.3 Typical Choices of Outsourcing and Geographic Dispersion of Value-Chain Activities among Firms

trast, manufacturing, logistics, and customer service activities tend to be more readily outsourced and geographically dispersed. The decision will also be a function of the firm's experience with international business and availability of qualified suppliers.

 # Evolution of Global Sourcing

Global sourcing by the private sector now accounts for more than half of all imports by major countries.[16] Global sourcing has changed the way companies do business in all kinds of industries. For example, Steinway procures parts and components from a dozen foreign countries to produce its grand pianos. Similarly, retailers do extensive global sourcing: Most of the products sold by Best Buy, Target, Wal-Mart, and Carrefour are sourced from suppliers in emerging markets. These retailers benefit by importing good-quality consumer products at low prices.

Phases in the Evolution: From Global Sourcing of Inputs to Offshoring Value-Adding Activities

The first major wave of global sourcing emphasized the *manufacturing* of input *products* and began in the 1960s with the shift of European and United States manufacturing to low-cost countries as geographically diverse as Mexico and Spain. Early observers pointed to the emergence of the *modular* corporation and the *virtual* corporation in the context of global sourcing.[17] Eventually, managers began to realize that tasks within most functions and value-chain activities are subject to externalization if such a move serves to facilitate efficiency, productivity, quality, and higher revenues.

The next wave of global sourcing began in the 1990s with offshoring, in which firms began to outsource specific value-adding activities in the services sector to locations such as India and Eastern Europe. In addition to IT services (software, applications, and technical support) and customer-support activities (technical support, call centers), many other service sectors became part of the offshoring trend. For example, in the health care sector, procedures such as CT scans and radiology evaluation are conducted in offshore locations. Consumers also are engaged in so-called *medical tourism,* in which they travel to countries such as India and Thailand for such medical procedures as bypass surgery or appendix removal.

Today, business-process outsourcing in product development, human resources, and finance/accounting services has become very common.[18] For example, Microsoft has invested billions in India to add to its existing R&D and technical-support operations there. Both Intel and Cisco Systems have invested billions to develop R&D operations in India as well. JP Morgan, a large investment bank, has several thousand employees in India who have evolved from performing simple back-office tasks, such as data entry to set-tling structured-finance and derivative deals—highly sophisticated banking transactions. India has reached a more mature stage in its development than other emerging countries. It first served as a center for software application development and maintenance. Subsequently, Indian firms and local captive operations of numerous MNEs began offering low-cost back-office services. Most recently, India has developed a strong industrial base of its own in IT and other high value-added business processes. Wipro, Infosys, and Tata Consultancy are among the most prominent players in global sourcing in the business services, software development, and call center industries. Note India's prominence in this activity is in addition to that of the United States. While many of the firms are headquartered in the United States, much of their work is actually performed in India or other emerging markets.

Magnitude of Global Sourcing

The magnitude of global sourcing is considerable. In 2005, India alone booked $22 billion worth of business in answering customer phone calls, managing far-flung computer networks, processing invoices, and writing custom soft-ware for MNEs from all over the world.[19] Global sourcing has created more than 1.3 million jobs during the past decade for India. Meanwhile, between 2000 and 2004, the United States outsourced some 100,000 service jobs each year.[20] In 2006, information-technology and business-process outsourcing exceeded $150 billion worldwide.

Diversity of Countries That Initiate and Receive Outsourced Work

Clearly, China and India are major players in global sourcing. The *Global Trend* feature highlights the ongoing rivalry between these two countries as they compete to be the world's leading destinations for global sourcing. Nevertheless, as noted in the opening vignette, numerous other countries are active players as well. In terms of buyer countries, global sourcing is prac-ticed by firms all around the world. U.S. firms have led the trend with nearly two-thirds of total offshore service projects. In 2003, firms in the United States offshored $87 billion of business services. In the same year, companies in other nations offshored to the United States $134 billion of business services. This insourcing supported a variety of relatively high-skilled U.S. jobs in engineering, management consulting, banking, and legal services.

China: Rivaling India in the Global Sourcing Game

For services, India is perhaps the world's leading offshoring destination. India is a popular destination for software development and back-office services, such as telephone call centers and financial accounting activities. India is one of the world's leading centers in the IT industry, thanks in part to the emergence of indigenous MNEs such as Infosys and Wipro. Infosys rivals Microsoft as one of the top software development firms worldwide.

Compared to India, however, China's history as a supplier to the world is longer. China is the center of manufacturing for countless Western firms. For example, the U.S. firm Keurig manufactures single-serving coffee machines. After Keurig management found that its coffeemakers were overpriced at $250 each because of high manufacturing costs, the firm outsourced manufacturing to a partner in China. The move allowed Keurig to begin offering new models for as little as $99. As a result, Keurig has greatly increased its sales.

China aims to surpass India in services outsourcing, and the Chinese government is making huge investments to upgrade worker training and the quality of its universities. China has three major advantages. First, the country is home to a large amount of skilled, low-cost labor. It produces 350,000 graduate engineers every year, almost four times that of the United States. Second, China has a huge domestic market with rapid and sustainable economic growth. Third, the attitude of the Chinese government, long an obstacle to foreign firms, is increasingly probusiness. The government has been developing a range of policies that favor foreign firms that manufacture in China.

Nevertheless, China still has numerous pitfalls. The country is weak in intellectual property protection, has a language and culture that foreign firms find challenging, and lacks quality infrastructure. Dealing with the Chinese government is complicated because of substantial bureaucracy and infighting among its various agencies. The resulting chaos hampers the ability of Chinese entrepreneurs to launch and manage companies.

By contrast, India has better intellectual property protection, a workforce with English language skills, and infrastructure that, although poor by advanced-economy standards, is often superior to that of China. India is likely to remain the global-sourcing leader in the services sector for some time to come.

Sources: *Economist*. (2005b). "The Myth of China Inc.," September 3, pp. 53–54; Farrell, Diana, Noshir Kaka, and Saacha Sturze. (2005). "Ensuring India's Offshoring Future," *The McKinsey Quarterly*, Special Edition: Fulfilling India's Promise; Hagel, John. (2004). Offshoring Goes on the Offensive: Cost Cutting is Only the First Benefit, *The McKinsey Quarterly*, no. 2, online journal; *Inc. Magazine*. (2006). "Singling Out a New Market," January, p. 46; Overby, Stephanie. (2005). "It's Cheaper in China," *CIO Magazine*, September 15. Retrieved from www.cio.com/archive/091505/nypro.html, December 10, 2005.

In Europe, forty percent of large firms report that they have outsourced services to other countries. The biggest European outsourcing deal of 2005—a $7 billion, 10-year contract to manage 150,000 computers and networking software for the British military—was awarded to a consortium led by EDS, a Texas-based company.[21] In Japan's IT industry, 23 percent of firms have outsourced services abroad.

Exhibit 16.4 identifies key players in global sourcing by four geographic regions. For example, Cairo-based Xceed Contact Center handles calls in Arabic and European languages for Microsoft, General Motors, Oracle, and Carrefour. Russia is aiming at high-end programming jobs. With its strong engineering culture, Russia has an abundant pool of underemployed talent available at wages about one-fifth those of the United States.

Singapore and Dubai have declared that their safety and advanced legal systems give them an edge in handling high-security and business-continuity services. The Philippines draws on longstanding cultural ties and solid English skills to attract call-center work. Central and South American countries use their Spanish skills to seek call-center contracts for the Hispanic market in the United States.[22]

	Central and Eastern Europe	China and South Asia	Latin America and the Caribbean	Middle East and Africa
Top-Ranked Countries	Czech Republic, Bulgaria, Slovakia, Poland, Hungary	India, China, Malaysia, Philippines, Singapore, Thailand	Chile, Brazil, Mexico, Costa Rica, Argentina	Egypt, Jordan, United Arab Emirates, Ghana, Tunisia, Dubai
Up-and-Comers	Romania, Russia, Ukraine, Belarus	Indonesia, Vietnam, Sri Lanka	Jamaica, Panama, Nicaragua, Colombia	South Africa, Israel, Turkey, Morocco
Emerging Local Providers	Luxoft (Russia), EPAM Systems (Belarus), Softline (Ukraine), DataArt (Russia)	NCS (Singapore), Bluem, Neusoft Group, BroadenGate Systems (China)	Softtek (Mexico), Neoris (Mexico), Politec (Brazil), DBAccess (Venezuela)	Xceed (Egypt), Ness Technologies (Israel), Jeraisy Group (Saudi Arabia)

Exhibit 16.4

Key Players in Global Sourcing by Region

SOURCE: Engardio, Pete. (2006). "The Future of Outsourcing: How It's Transforming Whole Industries and Changing the Way We Work," *Business Week*, January 30, p. 58.

In addition to low labor costs, other attractions of offshoring include the ability to increase productivity, improve service, and access superior technical skills. Recently, Vietnam has attracted considerable offshored business. With Europe as its largest export market, outscored production in Vietnam doubled in the early 2000s because it offers modern but low-cost operations, skilled but less expensive labor, and access to local sources unencumbered by trade restrictions.

A.T. Kearney's Global Services Location Index (www.atkearney.com) is topped by emerging markets only, including: India, China, Malaysia, Thailand, Brazil, Indonesia, Chile, and the Philippines. The United States is the only advanced economy ranked in the top 21 destinations. To help firms identify countries for outsourcing value-chain activities, the index emphasizes various criteria: the country's financial structure (compensation costs, infrastructure costs, tax and regulatory costs), the availability and skills of people (cumulative business-process experience and skills, labor force availability, education and language, and worker attrition rates), and the nature of the business environment (the country's political and economic environment, physical infrastructure, cultural adaptability, and security of intellectual property).

 ## Benefits and Challenges of Global Sourcing for the Firm

As with other international entry strategies, global sourcing offers both benefits and challenges for the firm. Exhibit 16.5 provides an overview of these benefits and challenges.

In terms of challenges, firms should pay special attention to the seven concerns mentioned in Exhibit 16.5. Many of these challenges arise if the focal firm is sourcing from independent suppliers abroad. The low-control nature of global sourcing implies that the issues of identifying, screening, negotiating, and monitoring partner activities become highly critical to the success of the firm. We elaborated on these issues earlier in the book, in Chapters 13 through 15. An additional challenge is the vulnerability to adverse currency fluctuations. Potential cost savings from global sourcing can be offset by a weakening home currency. In this scenario, foreign-sourced products cost more to import. For example, if China allowed its currency to appreciate, then its exports are

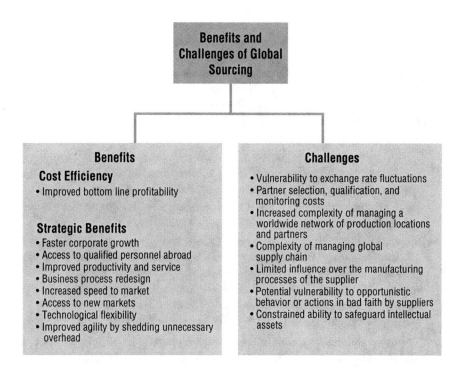

Exhibit 16.5

Benefits and Challenges of Global
Sourcing

likely to slow down, as it will be relatively more expensive for customers to continue to source from China.

In terms of benefits of global sourcing to the focal firm, there are two primary reasons to pursue global sourcing: cost efficiency and the achievement of strategic goals. Let's consider these in turn.

Cost Efficiency

Cost efficiency is the traditional rationale for sourcing abroad. The firm takes advantage of "labor arbitrage"—the large wage gap between advanced economies and emerging markets. One study found that firms expect to save an average of more than 40 percent off baseline costs as a result of offshoring.[23] These savings tend to occur particularly in R&D, product design activities, and back-office operations such as accounting and data processing. For example, a programmer in the United States with an IT-related college degree and five years of JAVA programming experience can expect to earn over $60,000 a year, plus benefits. In Bangalore, the salary is likely to be around $6,000 including benefits. A Ph.D. statistician in India earns up to $40,000 annually, compared with $200,000 in the United States. Most of the work that such Indian information workers perform can be transmitted instantly over the Internet. This wage discrepancy explains why firms like IBM, HP, Accenture, Dell, HSBC, Citicorp, and JP Morgan have been growing their India operations by 30 to 50 percent a year during the 2000s.[24]

Achievement of Strategic Goals

In addition to helping save the firm money, global sourcing can also help it achieve longer-term goals. This strategic view of global sourcing—called *transformational outsourcing*—suggests that a firm can achieve gains in efficiency, productivity, quality, and revenues much more effectively by leveraging offshore talent.[25] Global sourcing can provide the means to speed up innovation, fund development projects that are otherwise unaffordable, or turn around failing businesses. Firms leverage global sourcing to free expensive analysts, engineers, and sales personnel from routine tasks so they can spend more time innovating and working with customers.[26] Global sourcing can be a catalyst to overhaul outdated office operations and prepare for new competitive battles.

Often, both types of rationale—cost efficiency and achieving strategic goals—are present and are not mutually exclusive in a particular global sourcing activity. Whatever the primary motivation, the firm engaged in global sourcing can expect a variety of specific benefits, including:

* *Faster corporate growth.* By outsourcing various peripheral activities to external suppliers, firms can focus their resources on performing more profitable activities such as R&D or building relationships with customers. For example, global sourcing enables companies to expand their staff of engineers and researchers while keeping constant their cost of product development as a percentage of sales.[27]

* *Access to qualified personnel abroad.* Countries such as China, India, the Philippines, and Ireland offer abundant pools of educated engineers, managers, and other specialists. The ability to access a larger pool of talented individuals, wherever they are located, helps firms achieve their goals. For example, Disney has much of its animation work done in Japan because some of the world's best animators are located there.

* *Improved productivity and service.* Manufacturing productivity and other value-chain activities can be improved by global sourcing to suppliers that specialize in these activities. For example, Penske Truck Leasing improved its efficiency and customer service by outsourcing dozens of business processes to Mexico and India. Global sourcing enables firms to provide 24/7 coverage of customer service, especially for customers who need around-the-clock support.

* *Business process redesign.* By reconfiguring their value-chain systems or reengineering their business processes, companies can improve their production efficiency and resources utilization. Multinational firms see offshoring as a catalyst for a broader plan to overhaul outdated company operations.[28]

* *Increased speed to market.* By shifting software development and editorial work to India and the Philippines, the U.S.-Dutch publisher Walters Kluwer was able to produce a greater variety of books and journals and publish them faster. As the opening vignette describes, big pharmaceutical firms get new medications to market faster by global sourcing of clinical drug trials.

* *Access to new markets.* Firms can tap emerging markets and technologies in other countries, which not only helps them better understand foreign customers, but also facilitates their marketing activities there. Firms can also use global sourcing to service countries that may be otherwise closed due to protectionism. For example, by moving much of its R&D operations to Russia, the telecommunications firm Nortel gained an important foothold in a market that desperately needs telephone switching equipment and other communications infrastructure.

* *Technological flexibility.* By switching suppliers at a time when new, less expensive technology becomes available, firms are no longer as tied to specific technologies as they would be if they produced the technology themselves. Sourcing provides greater organizational flexibility and faster responsiveness to evolving consumer needs.

* *Improved agility by shedding unnecessary overhead.* Unburdened by a large bureaucracy and administrative overhead, companies can be more responsive to opportunities and adapt more easily to environmental changes, such as new competitors.

Combined, these benefits give firms the ability to continuously renew their strategic postures. For example, Genpact, Accenture, and IBM Services are outsourcing specialists that dispatch teams to meticulously dissect the workflow of other firms' human resources, finance, or IT departments. This helps the specialists build new IT platforms, redesign all processes, and administer programs, acting as a virtual subsidiary to their client firms. The contractor then disperses work among global networks of staff from Asia to Eastern Europe and elsewhere.[29]

Industries that particularly benefit from global sourcing include those in labor-intensive sectors such as garments, shoes, and furniture, those that use relatively standardized processes and technologies such as automotive parts and machine tools, and those that make and sell established products with a predictable pattern of sales, such as components for consumer electronics. For example, diamond processing is a labor-intensive industry that uses standardized processes that result in diamond rings and equipment used for fine cutting. The diamond cutting industry has been concentrated in Antwerp, Belgium, for the past five centuries. Recently, however, diamond cutting is being outsourced to firms in India that perform the work more cost-effectively and provide other advantages. China is also emerging as an important participant in diamond cutting.

Implementing Global Sourcing through Supply-Chain Management

A major reason why sourcing products from distant markets has become a major business phenomenon today is the efficiency with which goods can be physically moved from one part of the globe to another. This efficiency is due to the sophisticated processes and strategies involved in moving products from one point—such as from manufacturer to intermediaries—to another point—such as intermediaries to customers.

Global supply chain refers to the firm's integrated network of sourcing, production, and distribution, organized on a worldwide scale and located in countries where competitive advantage can be maximized. Global supply-chain management involves both upstream (supplier) and downstream (customer) flows.

Note that the concepts of the supply chain and the value chain are related but distinct. Recall that the value chain is the collection of activities intended to design, produce, market, deliver, and support a product or service. The supply chain is the collection of logistics specialists and activities that provides inputs to manufacturers or retailers. Skillful supply-chain management serves to optimize value-chain activities. Sourcing from numerous suppliers scattered around the world would be neither economical nor feasible without an efficient supply-chain system. Even as a casual observer, one has to be impressed when seeing the vast collection of products in a supermarket or department store that originated from dozens of different countries. The speed with which these products are delivered to end users is equally impressive.

Consider a striking example of how global supply-chain management is making global sourcing feasible and, at the same time, contributing to firm competitiveness. The roll-out of the first Boeing 787 Dreamliner jet in Everett, Washington, in July, 2007, marked a new beginning for this aircraft maker. Several features of the new aircraft are unique. It is a fuel-saving, medium-sized passenger jet that uses carbon composite for the fuselage (instead of aluminum). It is lightweight and has spacious interiors and higher cabin pressure than other models—for a more comfortable journey. However, the most remarkable aspect of the Boeing 787 Dreamliner jet is the extent of outsourcing. Boeing itself is responsible for only about 10 percent of the value added of this new aircraft—the tail fin and final assembly. Some 40 suppliers worldwide contribute the

Global supply chain The firm's integrated network of sourcing, production, and distribution, organized on a worldwide scale and located in countries where competitive advantage can be maximized.

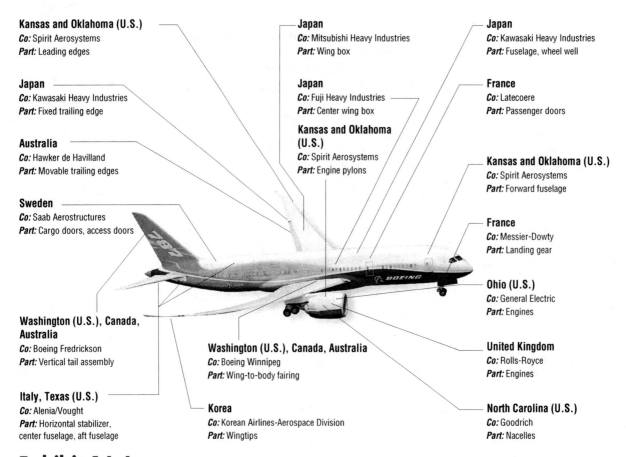

Kansas and Oklahoma (U.S.)
Co: Spirit Aerosystems
Part: Leading edges

Japan
Co: Kawasaki Heavy Industries
Part: Fixed trailing edge

Australia
Co: Hawker de Havilland
Part: Movable trailing edges

Sweden
Co: Saab Aerostructures
Part: Cargo doors, access doors

Washington (U.S.), Canada, Australia
Co: Boeing Fredrickson
Part: Vertical tail assembly

Italy, Texas (U.S.)
Co: Alenia/Vought
Part: Horizontal stabilizer, center fuselage, aft fuselage

Japan
Co: Mitsubishi Heavy Industries
Part: Wing box

Japan
Co: Fuji Heavy Industries
Part: Center wing box

Kansas and Oklahoma (U.S.)
Co: Spirit Aerosystems
Part: Engine pylons

Washington (U.S.), Canada, Australia
Co: Boeing Winnipeg
Part: Wing-to-body fairing

Korea
Co: Korean Airlines-Aerospace Division
Part: Wingtips

Japan
Co: Kawasaki Heavy Industries
Part: Fuselage, wheel well

France
Co: Latecoere
Part: Passenger doors

Kansas and Oklahoma (U.S.)
Co: Spirit Aerosystems
Part: Forward fuselage

France
Co: Messier-Dowty
Part: Landing gear

Ohio (U.S.)
Co: General Electric
Part: Engines

United Kingdom
Co: Rolls-Royce
Part: Engines

North Carolina (U.S.)
Co: Goodrich
Part: Nacelles

Exhibit 16.6 Where Boeing Company Sources the Components for its New 787 Aircraft

SOURCE: Tatge, Mark (2006), "Global Gamble," Forbes, (April 17), pp. 78–80.

remaining 90 percent of the value. For example, the wings are built in Japan, the carbon composite fuselage is made in Italy, and the landing gear is manufactured in France. As illustrated in Exhibit 16.6, components for the new 787 originate from distant parts of the world. The global dispersion of manufacturing responsibility allows Boeing to transform itself into a systems integrator and focus on its core capabilities—design, marketing, and branding. Boeing also reduces the chance of a bottleneck at one plant holding up production of the aircraft. It is no longer at the mercy of the weakest link in the chain, which was often one of Boeing's own plants.[30]

Networks of supply-chain hubs and providers of global delivery service are an integral part of global supply chains. Many focal firms delegate supply-chain activities to such independent logistics service providers as DHL, FedEx, TNT, and UPS. Consulting firms that manage the logistics of other firms are called *third party logistics providers (3PLs)*. Using a 3PL is often the best solution for international logistics, especially for firms that produce at low volumes or lack the resources and the expertise to create their own logistics network.

A good example of how global supply-chain management has evolved can be taken from the ongoing European Union integration. The removal of border controls allowed supply-chain managers to redraw the maps of their sourcing and distribution activities throughout Europe. Warehousing and distribution centers were consolidated and centralized. Intel reduced shipping costs by at least 7 percent by consolidating its worldwide freight expenditures into four transportation firms. As a result, from its 14 manufacturing sites around the world, Intel improved on-time delivery and customer-service performance substantially.[31]

A global supply-chain network consolidates a firm's sourcing, manufacturing, and distribution in a few strategic locations worldwide so the firm can *concentrate* these activities in countries where it can maximize its competitive advantages. Exhibit 16.7 illustrates the stages, functions, and activities in the supply chain. It reveals how suppliers interact with the focal firm and how these, in turn, interact with distributors and retailers. Each stage in the global supply chain encompasses functions and activities that involve the focal firm in sourcing and distribution. When the focal firm deals with multiple products and demanding customers spread around the world, managing supply chains becomes more complex.

Costs associated with physically delivering a product to an export market may account for as much as 40 percent of the total cost. Skillful supply-chain management reduces this cost while increasing customer satisfaction. Experienced firms make optimal use of information and communications technology (ICT), which streamlines supply chains, reducing costs and increasing distribution efficiency. For example, managers use *Electronic Data Interchange (EDI)*, which passes orders directly from customers to suppliers automatically through a sophisticated ICT platform. The UK-based supermarket chain Tesco greatly reduced inventory costs by using an EDI system to link point-of-sale data to logistics managers. Technology allows Tesco to track product purchases down to the minute. Many canned foods that used to sit in Tesco's warehouses for days or weeks are now received directly from suppliers.[32]

Supply-chain applications software enhances information sharing and improves efficiency by helping the manufacturer and focal firm track international shipments and clear customs. Many firms digitize key documents such as customs declarations and invoices, which improves speed and reduces order processing costs and shipping procedures. Spain-based retailer Zara is a good example of firms that use EDI technology to optimize supply-chain management, inventory management, and responsiveness to consumer demands. The firm uses

Exhibit 16.7

Stages, Functions, and Activities in the Global Supply Chain

	Suppliers	Focal Firm	Intermediaries and/or Retailers
Stage in supply chain	Sourcing, from home country and abroad	Inbound materials; outbound goods and services	Distribution to domestic customers or foreign customers (exports)
Major functions	Provide raw materials, parts, components, supplies, as well as business processes and other services to focal firms	Manufacture or assemble components or finished products, or produce services	Distribute and sell products and services
Typical activities	Maintain inventory, process orders, transport goods, deliver services	Manage inventory, process orders, manufacture or assemble products, produce and deliver services, distribute products to customers, retailers, or intermediaries	Manage inventory, place or process orders, produce services, manage physical distribution, provide after-sales service

wireless personal digital assistants (PDAs) and instantaneous communications with its stores to carry out ongoing market research. These technologies have allowed Zara to become a leader in rapid-response retailing. Like Zara's, the best global supply chains consist of reliable, capable partners all connected through automated, real-time communications. In an efficient global supply chain, the focal firm and its supply-chain partners continuously communicate and share information in order to meet the demands of the marketplace.

Logistics and Transportation

Logistics involves physically moving goods through the supply chain. It incorporates information, transportation, inventory, warehousing, materials handling, and similar activities associated with the delivery of raw materials, parts, components, and finished products. Managers seek to reduce moving and storage costs by using just-in-time inventory systems. Internationally, logistics are complex due to greater geographic distance, multiple legal and political environments, and the often inadequate and costly nature of distribution infrastructure in individual countries. The more diverse the firm's global supply chain, the greater the cost of logistics.

Competent logistics management is critical. For example, the California ports of Los Angeles and Long Beach handle over 40 percent of imports into the United States. Although the two California ports process over 24,000 containers per day, infrastructure deficiencies and increasing demand combine to result in long delays, which translate into longer transit times and higher costs for U.S. importers. Because of delays, Toys "Я" Us had to build 10 extra days into its supply chain, and MGA Entertainment lost $40 million in revenues when it could not deliver its bestselling Bratz dolls on time to retailers.[33] As a result of poor supply-chain planning, Microsoft's Xbox 360 games console sold out soon after launch. Their scarcity led to high prices in unofficial channels. On eBay, Xbox consoles sold for as much as $1,000, compared with the official price of about $400.[34]

Transportation Modes

International logistics typically involves multiple *transportation modes*. Land transportation is conducted via highways and railroads. Ocean transportation is handled through large container ships. Air transportation involves commercial or cargo aircraft. Ocean and air transport are common in international business because of long shipping distances. Ships are the most common transportation mode, even among countries connected by land bridges. Sea transport was revolutionized by the development of 20- and 40-foot shipping containers, the big boxes that sit atop ocean-going vessels. Sea transportation is very cost effective because one ship can carry thousands of these containers at a time.

The transportation modes involve several trade-offs. There are three considerations in choosing a particular mode: *transit time* is the amount of time it takes for the goods to be delivered, *predictability* is the reliability of anticipated transit time versus actual transit time, and the *cost* of transportation. For example, ocean transport is far slower, but also far cheaper, than air transport. Air transport is fast and extremely predictable, but costly. Given its high cost, air transport is the preferred transportation mode in three common situations: to transport perishable products, such as food and flowers, to transport goods with a high value-to-weight ratio, such as jewelry and laptop computers, and to make emergency shipments, such as when a foreign customer urgently needs a missing part.

The use of air freight has increased dramatically since the 1970s, as the cost of air transport has declined. Air freight accounts for only about one percent of the total volume but more than a third of the total value of international shipments.

Land transport is usually more expensive than ocean transport but cheaper than air freight. Ocean shipping from, for example, China to the United States, or from East Asia to Europe, takes two to four weeks, including customs clearance. While timeconsuming, the cost of ocean freight is quite low, often accounting for less than one percent of a product's final price.

Risks in Global Sourcing

Global sourcing is carried out by small and large firms alike. In many firms, initial involvement in international business takes the form of global sourcing (which, for such firms, can be viewed as *inward internationalization*). Based on the experience gained through global sourcing, a firm may then progress to exporting, direct investment, or collaborative ventures (*outward internationalization*). Global sourcing often leads to increased company awareness of international opportunities. In this way, global sourcing expands managers' horizons by showing the way to expand sales and other activities.

However, as with other business activities, global sourcing also involves unexpected complications. In fact, studies reveal that as many as half of all outsourcing arrangements are terminated earlier than planned. Specifically, global sourcing involves seven major risks.[35]

1. *Less-than-expected cost savings.* International transactions are often more complex and costly than expected. Conflicts and misunderstandings arise because of differences in the national and organizational cultures between the focal firm and foreign supplier. Such factors give rise to cost savings that are less than what management had originally anticipated.

2. *Environmental factors.* Numerous environmental challenges confront focal firms, including exchange rate fluctuations, labor strikes, adverse macroeconomic events, high tariffs and other trade barriers, as well as high energy and transportation costs. Firms sometimes find that the cost to set up a foreign outsourcing facility is far greater than planned, due to the need to upgrade poor infrastructure or because the facility must be located in a large city to attract sufficient skilled labor. As noted in the opening vignette, for example, inadequate energy systems and other infrastructure problems in Africa compromised the testing of new medications developed by big pharmaceutical firms.

3. *Weak legal environment.* Many of the popular locations for global sourcing (for example, China, India, and Russia) have weak laws and enforcement regarding intellectual property, which can lead to the erosion of key strategic assets. Many countries are characterized by inadequate legal systems, red tape, convoluted tax systems, and complex business regulations that complicate local operations.

4. *Risk of creating competitors.* As the focal firm shares its intellectual property and business-process knowledge with foreign suppliers, it also runs the risk of creating future rivals. For example, Schwinn, long the leader in the global bicycle industry, created competitors by transferring much of its production and core expertise to foreign suppliers. The suppliers acquired sufficient knowledge, became lower-cost competitors, and eventually forced Schwinn into bankruptcy (from which it eventually recovered).

Firms that undertake global sourcing may encounter problematic environmental factors, such as poor infrastructure in transportation systems, as suggested by this street scene in India.

5. *Inadequate or low-skilled workers.* Some foreign suppliers may be staffed by employees who lack appropriate knowledge about the tasks with which they are charged. Other suppliers suffer rapid turnover of skilled employees, who find jobs with more desirable firms. For instance, typical Indian operations in business processing lose 20 percent or more of their workers each year and good managers are often in short supply. Customer complaints about the quality of service led Dell to move its corporate call center from India back to the United States in 2003.

6. *Over-reliance on suppliers.* Unreliable suppliers may put earlier work aside when they gain a more important client. Suppliers occasionally encounter financial difficulties or are acquired by other firms with different priorities and procedures. When such events occur, management at the focal firm may find itself scrambling to find alternative suppliers. Overreliance can shift control of key activities too much in favor of the supplier. As more and more tasks are performed by the supplier, the focal firm may lose control of important value-chain tasks. Focal firm management should strive to maintain an appropriate balance of power between itself and foreign suppliers.

7. *Erosion of morale and commitment among home-country employees.* Global sourcing can create a situation in which employees are caught in the middle between their employer and their employer's clients. At the extreme, workers find themselves in a psychological limbo, unclear about who their employer really is. When outsourcing causes retained and outsourced staff to work side by side, tensions and uncertainty may arise, evolving into a sort of "us-versus-them" syndrome and diminished employee commitment and enthusiasm.

One firm that experienced problems in its early phases of global sourcing is the London-based bank HSBC. Starting with one software-development center in Pune, a satellite city of Bombay, the bank established development centers in China and Brazil. When departments with tech needs at HSBC headquarters would order large jobs from India, the outsourcing staff in Pune would comply but occasionally realize they had bitten off more than they could chew. While the center had technical skills, it lacked specific knowledge in the banking industry. For instance, HSBC asked the Pune staff to build an insurance product but soon discovered the staff was unfamiliar with the insurance industry. HSBC management solved the problems by requiring bank experts from London to sit alongside the technical experts in Pune during project development.

 ## Strategies for Minimizing Risk in Global Sourcing

The experience of firms with global sourcing so far reveals six managerial guidelines for strategic global sourcing.

1. *Go offshore for the right reasons.* The best rationale is strategic. The vast majority of companies cite cost-cutting as the main reason for global sourcing. After the first year, however, most firms encounter diminishing returns in the amount of money saved. Cost-cutting is often a distraction from more beneficial, long-term goals such as enhancing the quality of offerings, improving overall productivity, and freeing up knowledge workers and other core resources that can be redeployed to improve long-term performance. To maximize returns, management should engage in substantive planning that examines tasks and subactivities in each of the firm's value chains. The analysis should aim to outsource those tasks in which the firm is relatively weak, that offer relatively little value to the bottom line, or that can be performed more effectively by others, yet are not critical to the firm's core competencies.

2. *Get employees on board.* Global sourcing tends to invite opposition from employees and other organizational stakeholders. Disaffected middle managers can undermine projects and other goals that offshoring seeks to achieve. Poorly planned sourcing projects can create unnecessary tension and harm employee morale. Thus, management should seek to gain employee support for outsourcing projects. The decision to outsource should be based on reaching a consensus of middle managers and employees throughout the firm. Management should be diligent about developing alternatives for redeploying laid-off workers, and involve employees in selecting foreign partners. Where labor unions are involved, management should seek their counsel and incorporate their views. For example, when management at Dutch bank ABN Amro decided to offshore numerous accounting and finance functions, it took great pains to prepare the firm's large base of employees in advance. The bank set up a full-time communications department to explain the move to middle managers and staff. Senior executives held town hall meetings with employees and involved unions in managing the shift.[36]

3. *Choose carefully between a captive operation and contracting with outside suppliers.* Managers should be vigilant about striking the right balance between the organizational activities that it retains inside the firm and those that are sourced from outside suppliers. An increasing number of firms are establishing their own sourcing operations abroad. By owning the offshored facility, management maintains complete control of outsourced activities and retains control of key technologies and processes. For example, when Boeing wanted to outsource key value-chain tasks, management established a company-owned center in Moscow where it employs 1,100 skilled but relatively low-cost aerospace engineers. The Russian team is working on a range of projects, including the design of titanium parts for the new Boeing 787 Dreamliner jet.[37]

4. *Emphasize effective communications with suppliers.* A common reason for global sourcing failure is that both buyers and suppliers tend not to spend enough time up front to get to know each other well. They rush into a deal before clarifying partner expectations, which can give rise to misunderstandings and inferior results. Partners need to maintain active communication and oversight. For instance, because production quality in an emerging market may vary over time, managers at the focal firm may need to closely monitor manufacturing processes. When partners do not share necessary information with each other, vagueness and ambiguity emerge, followed by misunderstanding and frustration in outsourcing projects.[38] Poor cultural fit is also a potential problem. Guided by different business philosophies and practices, partners tend to approach the same issue differently. Effective communication is necessary to minimize misunderstandings that can diminish relationships between buyers and suppliers.

5. *Invest in supplier development and collaboration.* When a business function is delegated to a supplier, the parties need to exchange information, transfer knowledge, troubleshoot, coordinate, and monitor. Over the long haul, various benefits emerge when the focal firm adjusts its processes and product requirements to match the capabilities of foreign suppliers. Management should collaborate closely with suppliers in codevelopment and codesign activities. Close supplier cooperation also enables the focal firm to tap into a stream of ideas for new products, processes, technologies, and improvements. Efforts to build strong relationships help create a moral contract between the focal firm and the supplier, which is often more effective than a formal legal contract.

6. *Safeguard interests.* The focal firm should take specific actions to safeguard its interests in the supplier relationship. First, it can encourage the supplier to refrain from engaging in potentially destructive acts that jeopardize the firm's reputation. Second, it can escalate commitments by making partner-specific investments (such as sharing knowledge with the supplier) on an *incremental* basis, allowing for ongoing review, learning, and adjustment. Third, it can share costs and revenues by building a stake for the supplier so that, in case of failure to conform to expectations, the supplier also suffers costs or foregoes revenues. Fourth, it can maintain flexibility in selecting partners by keeping options open to find alternative partners in case a particular supplier does not work out. Finally, the focal firm can hold the partner at bay by withholding access to intellectual property and key assets in order to safeguard the firm's interests for the long term. If conflicts with the supplier become an ongoing problem, unresolved by negotiations, one option for the firm is to acquire full or partial ownership of the supplier.

Implications of Global Sourcing for Public Policy and Corporate Citizenship

Global sourcing is controversial. The business community sees global sourcing as a way of maintaining or increasing business competitiveness. Others view it negatively, focusing on the loss of jobs. After IBM workers in Europe went on strike against offshoring, shareholders at IBM's annual meeting argued for an anti-offshoring resolution. If the resolution had passed, it would have limited IBM's options to manage the firm, threatening company performance.

The general public is equally likely to be critical of offshoring. When the state of Indiana awarded a $15 million IT services contract to a supplier that planned to use technicians from India to do some of the work, the Indiana Senate intervened and cancelled the deal. Indiana is one of many public sector players that are contracting out services to foreign vendors in order to save tax dollars. The state recently leased the management of the Indiana Toll Road to an Australian-Spanish partnership for 75 years for $3.8 billion.

Global sourcing has sparked protests in many countries. Here, a union member protests IBM's policies of job outsourcing.

Concerns about outsourcing and offshoring are not new. In the 1970s and 1980s, when manufacturing jobs were outsourced, labor unions protested about "runaway corporations." Fortunately, bleak forecasts of job losses proved wrong as a result of economic expansion and job growth in the 1990s. In the United States, the proportion of jobs outsourced abroad each year is still less than 0.1 percent of total U.S. employment.

Potential Harm to Economies from Global Sourcing

Concerns about the consequences of global sourcing deserve serious attention. Critics of global sourcing point to three major problems. Global sourcing can result in (1) job losses in the home country, (2) reduced national competitiveness, and (3) declining standards of living. Regarding the last two concerns, critics worry that, as more tasks are performed at lower cost with comparable quality in other countries, high-wage countries will eventually lose their national competitiveness. Critics fear that long-held knowledge and skills will eventually drain away to other countries, and the lower wages paid abroad to perform jobs that were previously done in high-wage countries will eventually pull down wages in the latter countries, leading to lower living standards.

The biggest worry is job losses. For example, the number of U.S. jobs in the legal industry outsourced to foreign contractors now exceeds 25,000 jobs per year.[39] Some estimate that more than 400,000 jobs in the IT industry that were previously performed in the United States have moved offshore.[40] One study predicts that by the year 2017, 3.3 million U.S. service jobs—with a value of $136 billion—will be sent abroad.[41] Critics say all of this amounts to exporting jobs.

Moreover, job losses result when companies increase their sourcing of input and finished goods from abroad. For instance, Wal-Mart sources as much as 70 percent of its merchandise from China. This has led public officials and concerned citizens to form a protest group called Walmartwatch.com. The group claims that millions of U.S. jobs have been lost due to Wal-Mart's sourcing from foreign instead of U.S. suppliers.[42] In addition to the advanced economies, however, job losses are occurring in developing economies as well. For instance, El Salvador, Honduras, Indonesia, Morocco, and Turkey are restructuring as jobs in the textile industry are gradually transferred to China, India, and Pakistan, where multinational clothiers can operate more efficiently.[43]

Consider the potentially devastating effect of wholesale job losses on a small community. Recently, Electrolux, one of the world's largest household-appliance manufacturers, closed its factory in Michigan and moved production to Mexico. The company had been producing refrigerators in Greenville, Michigan, for nearly 40 years, providing 2,700 jobs. From the company's viewpoint, closing the plant made economic sense. Once the world's largest refrigerator factory, it had developed weak financial performance and costly labor. By establishing a *maquiladora* plant in Juarez, Mexico, Electrolux sought to profit from low wages and take advantage of the El Paso Foreign Trade Zone just across the border in Texas. Management believed it was acting in the firm's best interest and strengthening its global competitiveness.

From the local community's standpoint, however, the decision was devastating. How could so many jobs be replaced in such a small community? What would happen to the town's social and economic landscape? Assistance from labor unions and the State of Michigan were to no avail. Concessions in terms of lower wages by the labor union, and over $100 million from Michigan to Electrolux in tax breaks and grants were insufficient for Electrolux to change its mind. It did not help that Electrolux is a foreign-owned company headquartered in Sweden. Residents perceived the company had little loyalty to their community. In 2007, the Greenville plant was demolished. The town hopes to redevelop the site for mixed usage, as riverfront condominiums, commercial space, and parkland. Most former workers found other jobs in the service sector, although typically for less pay.[44]

Also recall the Boeing 787 Dreamliner aircraft. In the process of transforming itself from a manufacturer into a systems integrator, the company shed about 38,000 jobs in the United States. It was also criticized for transferring technology to foreign partners.

From these examples, it is easy to see the clash of interests between MNEs and local communities. Proponents of global sourcing argue that workers who lose their jobs due to offshoring can find new work. But this may be overly optimistic. It takes considerable time for laid-off workers to find new jobs. According to one estimate, as much as one-third of U.S. workers who have been laid off cannot find suitable employment within a year.[45] Older workers are particularly vulnerable. Compared to younger workers, they find it more difficult to learn the skills needed for new positions. The rate of redeployment is likely to be even lower in Europe, where unemployment rates are already high, and in Japan, where employment practices are less flexible. In Germany, the percentage of

Workers at a Nike factory in Vietnam, where Nike is the largest private employer. Following charges that its foreign contract factories were run like "sweatshops," Nike took steps to improve working conditions.

workers who are not reemployed within a year of losing their jobs is as high as 60 percent. Under such circumstances, global sourcing may increase the overall unemployment rate, reduce overall income level, and harm the national economy. Even workers who do find new jobs may be unable to achieve wages and work levels that equal those of their former positions.

Ethical and Social Implications of Global Sourcing

The prevalence of global sourcing has also raised public debate about the role of MNEs in protecting the environment, promoting human rights, and improving labor practices and working conditions. In other words, the bar for global corporate citizenship has been raised. Consider, for example, the case of foreign suppliers that operate *sweatshops*—factories in which people may work long hours for very low wages, often in harsh conditions.[46] Sweatshops may employ child labor, a practice that has been outlawed in much of the world. Those who defend moving production to low-wage facilities abroad point to a lower standard of living as an explanation for the low wages, and argue that their operations benefit the community by providing needed jobs. They point out that the choice for local workers is often between low-paying work or no work at all. Others argue that the alternatives available to such workers are even less desirable, such as poverty, prostitution, and social problems.

Opponents of sweatshops argue that corporations that sell their products in wealthy countries have a responsibility to pay their workers according to basic Western standards, especially when their products command high prices in advanced-economy markets. Another argument is that the foreign companies that establish factories destroy the preexisting agricultural market that may have provided a better life for laborers. In response to public pressure, some companies have reduced or ended their use of such cheap labor. For example, apparel makers Gap, Nike, and New Balance are notable for changing their policies after intense pressure from campus anti-sweatshop groups.

Potential Benefits to National Economy

Those in favor of global sourcing call attention to the benefits that it provides to the national economy. Proponents advance four key arguments. First, by reconfiguring value chains to the most cost-efficient locations, companies reduce their production costs and enhance their performance in an increasingly competitive global marketplace. For example, Roamware Inc., a U.S. firm that sells computer systems to cell phone providers, saved thousands of dollars on a project to create an electronic database by hiring Pangea3, an Indian firm, to do the job instead of relying on a nearby supplier.[47] As individual firms enhance their competitiveness, the national economy should strengthen as well.

Second, cost reductions and enhanced competitiveness allow firms to reduce the prices that they charge their customers. This benefits not only buyers but also the firms themselves, which become more price-competitive and enjoy greater market demand, which in turn stimulates job creation, offsetting much of the employment lost to outsourcing.

Third, by leveraging a flexible labor market and strong economic growth, countries that outsource may be able to shift their labor force to higher-value activities. This transformation has the effect of boosting the nation's productivity and industrial efficiency. By concentrating resources in higher-value activities, firms create better jobs. Large software firms Microsoft and Oracle have simultaneously increased both outsourcing and their domestic payrolls for higher-value jobs.[48]

Finally, declining wages may be offset by lower prices secured for outsourced products or services. Hence global sourcing tends to indirectly increase consumers' purchasing power and lift their living standards.[49] For instance, Wal-Mart has been roundly criticized for sourcing most of its merchandise from China. But the practice allows Wal-Mart to resell the goods at low prices, which translates into higher living standards for Wal-Mart customers.

Public Policy toward Global Sourcing

The consequences of global sourcing for the national economy and workers are not yet fully known. A recent comprehensive study, carried out for the United States, argues that the official statistics understate the impact of offshoring on the national economy.[50] Digging deeper into the statistics, the study finds that import growth, adjusted for inflation, is faster than the official numbers show. The author concluded that more of the gain in living standards in recent years has come from cheap imports, less from an increase in domestic productivity. This suggests that real GDP (gross domestic product) may be overstated. In contrast, the benefits that U.S. consumers gain from trade are actually understated. An implication is that the United States' living standards depend in part on the ability of foreign factories to boost output and cut costs.

In short, the findings suggest that U.S. consumers may enjoy an even better deal from imports than previously thought. From a public-policy standpoint, it is simply impractical for a nation to prohibit global sourcing. A more enlightened approach is to mitigate the harm that global sourcing can cause.[51] Offshoring amounts to a process of *creative destruction*, a concept first proposed by Austrian economist Joseph Schumpeter.[52] According to this view, over time, firms' innovative activities tend to make mature products obsolete. For example, the introduction of personal computers essentially wiped out the typewriter industry, the DVD player eliminated the VCR industry, and so on. Similarly, just as offshoring results in job loss and adverse effects for particular groups and economic sectors, it also creates new advantages and opportunities for firms and consumers alike. New industries created through the process of creative destruction will create new jobs and innovations.

If the loss of certain jobs is inevitable as a result of offshoring, public-policy makers are better off guiding employment toward higher value-added jobs by stimulating innovation, for example. Admittedly, this implies greater government intervention and is likely to produce positive outcomes only in the long run. The public sector can reduce the unfavorable consequences of global sourcing. One of the best ways would be to keep the cost of doing business relatively low. Governments can use economic and fiscal policies to encourage the development of new technologies by helping entrepreneurs reap the financial benefits of their work and keeping the cost of capital needed to finance R&D relatively low. Another useful policy is to ensure that the nation has a strong educational system, including technical schools and well-funded universities that supply engineers, scientists, and knowledge workers. A strong educational system helps to ensure that firms can draw from a high-quality pool of qualified labor. As firms restructure through global sourcing efforts, increased worker flexibility ensures that many who lose jobs can be redeployed in other positions.

Good Hopes for Global Outsourcing

Good Hope Hospitals of California, Inc. ("Good Hope") is a chain of nine hospitals in or near Los Angeles, San Diego, and San Francisco. Founded in 1976, Good Hope is run on a for-profit basis and management continuously strives for efficient operations. Andy Delgado is Good Hope's Vice President for Finance and Accounting, and Joy Simmons is the senior manager in Information Technology. The two executives needed to make significant cuts in operational costs in their respective areas. Extremely reluctant to lay off workers, they mutually agreed on a plan to outsource some work now done by contractors in California to suppliers located abroad.

Delgado and Simmons believed that some of Good Hope's ongoing business processes could be outsourced, including data processing for accounts receivable and accounts payable, certain customer service applications, transcription of medical records, and some data processing. Both managers had heard about the benefits of global sourcing but neither knew how to proceed. So, they began to research their options.

The Downside of Global Sourcing

In the course of their research, Delgado and Simmons also learned that services are frequently more challenging to outsource than manufacturing. This is partly because it is usually more difficult to judge the quality of services than that of manufactured products. Firms that use global sourcing sign legal contracts with suppliers binding themselves to deliver promised levels of service. In reality, there is much variation in the quality of services delivered. To achieve satisfactory outcomes, the contracting firm should emphasize developing trust and understanding with the supplier, especially critical in cross-cultural settings. Delgado and Simmons wondered about the enforceability of legal agreements in different country settings.

Another potential concern was the quality of workers. Some foreign suppliers cannot hire a sufficient number of skilled managers to oversee the work performed by their staffs. Workers must be trained, supervised, and properly motivated. Could Good Hope provide such support and technical assistance?

Delgado and Simmons also read troubling stories about firms whose offshore operations proved to be more costly than originally planned. They read about firms that lost customers and jeopardized their reputations because of poor customer service received from abroad. Delgado and Simmons also worried about breach of confidentiality—to what extent could they rely on foreign organizations to keep patient data confidential? The various risks implied that Good Hope would need to interact closely and frequently with the external supplier, which would add substantial costs in terms of negotiating, transacting, and monitoring, as well as international travel. Delgado and

Simmons realized they would need to approach global sourcing very carefully.

Offshoring Destinations

Delgado and Simmons next focused their research on identifying the most promising foreign locations for offshoring. Their investigation revealed that India was the most popular choice for many types of services. The country's outsourcing sector had been growing at 25 to 50 percent per year. India's labor costs are 25 to 40 percent of those in the United States and English is widely spoken. The team learned that reputable firms such as IBM, Dell, and Citicorp had offshored numerous service operations to India.

Their investigation revealed that China was also a potential destination. The country has millions of suitable workers and soon is expected to rival India as a provider of services such as insurance underwriting and back-office operations. Outsourcing costs are currently lower in China than in India. However, a concern is China's reputation for excessive regulation and bureaucracy. Delgado and Simmons wondered if they could develop sufficient trust and understanding with partners in an unfamiliar and distant culture with language differences.

Eastern Europe also emerged as a promising location. The region is culturally similar to the United States, and wages in much of the region are on par with those in India. For example, while Indian accountants earn roughly $10 an hour, wages are substantially lower in Bulgaria and Romania. The Czech Republic is a popular location and is the site of business-process centers for firms such as DHL, Siemens, and Lufthansa. One expert claimed the quality of work in the Czech Republic sometimes surpasses the best available in India. Even Infosys, the giant Indian IT firm, has major support operations in the Czech Republic. But Eastern European countries sometimes have a shortage of qualified labor, particularly among middle managers. As the region's economies develop, social and health insurance costs are also increasing. Taxes can be high and bureaucratic governments hinder efficient business operations. Corruption is a problem in some countries.

Delgado and Simmons also considered sites in Latin America such as Chile, Mexico, and Costa Rica. Latin America offered various attractions. In addition to being cost effective, it is much closer to the United States and generally in the same time zone. Outsourcing customer service to Latin America also makes sense to Californians, many of whom speak Spanish as their first language. But Latin America's outsourcing infrastructure is still young, and Delgado and Simmons worried about whether they could find an appropriate supplier. Numerous other outsourcing locations were possible around the world. For Delgado and Simmons, the number of options was bewildering. Somehow they had to reach a decision.

Help from an Outsourcing Broker

The executives sought the assistance of an outsourcing broker, a consultant with expertise in finding subcontractors and services suppliers abroad. Brokers are especially useful for firms new to outsourcing or those that lack the resources to find foreign suppliers on their own. Eventually the broker found a supplier in India that appeared well suited to meet Good Hope's needs. For example, for transcribing doctor's notes and other medical documents, Simmons learned that Good Hope would pay 12 cents per word, 5 cents less than charged by the firm's current supplier in California. Simmons determined that Good Hope would save about $640,000 a year on medical transcriptions alone. When the accounting and customer service work were added to the mix, the executives discovered that Good Hope would save roughly $1.4 million annually. Delgado was elated: "How else could we shave so much from our expenses with so little effort? And best of all, we don't have to lay off any of our own workers."

The Supplier Firm

To meet all their outsourcing needs, Delgado and Simmons settled on a firm in Bangalore, India, known as BangSource. According to the outsourcing broker, BangSource had a good reputation and was already handling accounting, data processing, transcription, and customer service operations for several large U.S. hospitals. BangSource expects to pick up many new accounts in Australia, Canada, and Europe. BangSource is located in one of the fastest-growing areas of Bangalore and buses in workers from all around the region. The outsourcing broker confided that although BangSource's employee turnover rate was 25 percent, this was consistent with the rate at other outsourcing firms.

The consultant put Good Hope in touch with Mr. Singh, a manager at BangSource and recent graduate of one of India's numerous MBA programs. Mr. Singh explained that BangSource had been in business for about 4 years and had quickly achieved considerable expertise in various business processes. BangSource had recently begun to hire computer engineers and marketing personnel, as the firm was planning to increase its outsourcing capabilities to include software development and telemarketing.

The Situation One Year Later

In the year following the signing of a contract with Bang-Source, Good Hope encountered various problems. The cost of BangSource's services proved to be significantly higher than what Mr. Singh had originally forecast. Processing of accounting and other data was more complex than anticipated, so costs had escalated. Also, BangSource proved less efficient in addressing Good Hope's customer service queries, and required more telephone time and phone calls to address customer needs. Although the Indian customer service workers generally spoke perfect English, some had hard-to-understand accents and a few of Good Hope's customers had complained. Various misunderstand-

ings arose between BangSource and Good Hope as management at the respective firms attempted to refine activity processing. The problem was exacerbated by recent fluctuations in the rupee-dollar exchange rate, which sometimes inflated the cost of BangSource's services even further.

In addition, while BangSource's business had increased substantially in the previous year, provision of electrical power by the local energy utility had not kept pace, and BangSource occasionally experienced power outages and downtime of computer systems. Growing demand for workers in the Bangalore area delayed hiring efforts, and BangSource was sometimes late in performing promised services due to a shortage of skilled workers. BangSource also faced problems hiring enough qualified managers, which further impaired the quality of its accounting and call-center services.

Delgado and Simmons were disappointed and unsure whether Good Hope was better off today than a year earlier. Top management was pressing the team to solve the problems. As the pair prepared to fly to India to meet with BangSource management, they knew that outsourcing could succeed but they had to figure out how to overcome the various challenges.

AACSB: Reflective Thinking, Ethical Reasoning

Case Questions

1. What motives and specific strategic goals can Good Hope achieve by outsourcing to India? Identify strategic goals that Good Hope could potentially achieve in the future.

2. What are the specific risks that Good Hope faced and potentially faces in outsourcing the activities to India?

3. What specific guidelines should management at Good Hope have taken into account as it ventured into global sourcing? What should Good Hope do now to resolve the problems it faces in outsourcing to BangSource?

4. Suppose that thousands of additional firms in California decided to outsource their back-office activities (such as accounting, finance, and data analysis) to India. What would be the implications of such a trend to California's workers and economy? What steps could California take to reduce the potential harm to its citizens of widespread global sourcing?

Sources: Dahl, Darren. (2005). "Outsourcing the Outsourcing," *Inc. Magazine*, December, pp. 55–56; *Economist*. (2004). "A World of Work: A Survey of Outsourcing," November 13, special section; *Economist*. (2005). "The Rise of Nearshoring," December 3, pp. 65–67; *Economist*. (2005). "India: The Next Wave," December 17, pp. 57–58; Engardio, Pete. (2006). "The Future of Outsourcing: How It's Transforming Whole Industries and Changing the Way We Work," *Business Week*, January 30, p. 58; Ewing, Jack, and Gail Edmondson. (2005). "The Rise of Central Europe," *Business Week*, December 12, pp. 50–56; Human Resources Outsourcing Association Europe. (2007). "Outsourcing's Future Holds Major Surprises for Global Providers," April 13, at www.hroaeurope.com.

Key Terms

business process outsourcing (BPO)

captive sourcing

configuration of value-adding activity

contract manufacturing

global sourcing

global supply chain

offshoring

outsourcing

Summary

In this chapter, you learned about:

1. Trends toward outsourcing, global sourcing, and offshoring

Global sourcing refers to the procurement of products or services from suppliers or company-owned subsidiaries located abroad for consumption in the home country or a third country. **Outsourcing** is the procurement of selected value-adding activities, including production of intermediate goods or finished products, from external independent suppliers. **Business process outsourcing** refers to the outsourcing of business functions such as finance, accounting, and human resources. Procurement can be from either independent suppliers or via company-owned subsidiaries or affiliates. **Offshoring** refers to the relocation of a business process or entire manufacturing facility to a foreign country. Managers make two strategic decisions regarding value-adding activities: whether to *make or buy* inputs and where to locate value-adding activity—that is, the geographic **configuration of value-adding activity**. **Contract manufacturing** is an arrangement in which the focal firm contracts with an independent supplier to have the supplier manufacture products according to well-defined specifications.

2. Evolution of global sourcing

Today much of the growth in global sourcing is in the services sector, in areas such as IT, customer support, and professional services. India has received the bulk of outsourced business services, while China is favored for manufacturing. But other countries, mostly emerging markets, are viable outsourcing destinations as well. Hundreds of billions of dollars of business services are outsourced to foreign suppliers annually. The potential for global sourcing remains huge. Certain conditions make countries popular recipients of outsourced activity, including workers' mastery of English, a skilled labor force, low labor costs, and strong intellectual-property protections.

3. Benefits and challenges of global sourcing for the firm

Global sourcing aims to reduce the cost of doing business or to achieve other strategic goals. For some entrepreneurs, global outsourcing has provided the means to turn around failing businesses, speed up the pace of innovation, or fund development projects that are otherwise unaffordable. Other benefits of global sourcing include faster corporate growth, the ability to access qualified personnel, improved productivity and service, redesigned business processes, faster foreign market entry, access to new markets, and technological flexibility. Global sourcing also allows firms to focus on their core activities and continuously renew their strategic assets.

4. Implementing global sourcing through supply-chain management

The efficiency with which goods can be physically moved from one part of the globe to another makes global sourcing feasible. **Global supply chain** refers to the firm's integrated network of sourcing, production, and distribution, organized on a world scale, and located in countries where competitive advantage can be maximized.

5. Risks in global sourcing

Global sourcing involves business risks, including failure to realize anticipated cost savings, environmental uncertainty, the creation of competitors, engaging suppliers with insufficient training, overreliance on suppliers, and eroding the morale of existing employees. Firms should approach global sourcing very carefully, with meticulous planning.

6. Strategies for minimizing risk in global sourcing

Firms should develop a strategic perspective in making global sourcing decisions. Although cost cutting is usually the first rationale, global sourcing is also a means to create customer value and improve the firm's competitive advantages. It is a tool to enhance the quality of offerings, improve productivity, and free up resources that can be redeployed to improve long-term performance. To make global sourcing succeed, management should gain employee cooperation, emphasize strong supplier relations, safeguard its interests in the supplier relationship, and choose the right foreign suppliers.

7. **Implications of global sourcing for public policy and corporate citizenship**

Global sourcing is a means to sustain or enhance firm competitiveness, but can also contribute to job losses and declining living standards. Some firms outsource to suppliers that employ sweatshop labor. But attempts to prohibit global sourcing are impractical. Governments should enact policies in the home country that encourage job retention and growth by reducing the cost of doing business and by encouraging entrepreneurship and technological development. Public policy should aim to develop a strong educational system and upgrade the modern skills of the population.

Test Your Comprehension AACSB: Reflective Thinking, Ethical Reasoning

1. What are the differences between outsourcing, global sourcing, and offshoring?

2. What is business process outsourcing? What are its implications for company strategy and performance?

3. What are the two strategic decisions that managers face regarding the firm's international value chain, and what are their implications for company performance?

4. Identify the various benefits that companies receive from global sourcing. Why do firms outsource to foreign suppliers?

5. What two countries are the most important global sourcing destinations today? What are the basic differences between these two countries, and what activities are typically outsourced to each?

6. What are the characteristics that make countries attractive as global sourcing destinations?

7. In what service industries are jobs commonly outsourced to foreign suppliers?

8. What are the risks that firms face in global sourcing?

9. What steps can managers take to minimize the risks of global sourcing?

10. What are the major guidelines for strategic global sourcing? What actions can management take to make global sourcing succeed?

11. What are the advantages and disadvantages of global sourcing to the nation? What public policy initiatives are likely to reduce the disadvantages of global sourcing?

Apply Your Understanding AACSB: Reflective Thinking, Ethical Reasoning

1. Revisit the opening vignette at the beginning of this chapter. Assume you have started a new job as a junior manager at a pharmaceutical firm. Management is considering outsourcing some of the firm's value chain to suppliers located abroad. Which activities is the firm most likely to outsource? Identify the benefits that your firm can obtain and the specific strategic goals that it could potentially achieve by undertaking global sourcing.

2. Suppose your new job is at Intel, the world's largest semiconductor company and the inventor of the microprocessors found in many personal computers. Intel combines advanced chip design capability with a leading-edge manufacturing capability. The firm is well known for advanced R&D and innovative products. Intel has much of its manufacturing done in China, to take advantage of low-cost labor and an educated workforce capable of producing Intel's knowledge-intensive products. Intel has been stepping up its R&D activity in China and collaborates with Chinese firms in new-technology development. Identify the risks that Intel faces in its operations in China. What strategies and proactive measures can Intel management take to safeguard its interests? What long-term strategic goals does Intel achieve by offshoring from China?

3. Global sourcing helps firms increase their business competitiveness. But it also contributes to job losses in the home country. Some firms outsource to suppliers that employ sweatshop labor. Attempts to prohibit global sourcing are impractical, so governments take other steps to reduce its limitations. What policies should a government adopt to minimize the harm of global sourcing? What can governments in advanced-economy countries do to minimize job loss or encourage job retention and growth? What can such governments do to reduce the problems associated with sweatshops?

AACSB: Reflective Thinking, Ethical Reasoning, Use of Information Technology, Analytical Skills

Refer to Chapter 1, page 27, for instructions on how to access and use globalEDGE™.

1. You work for a software company that aims to outsource some of its software development to a foreign supplier. At present, you are considering three countries: Hungary, Mexico, and Russia. You need to learn more about the capabilities of these countries as sites for the outsourcing of software development and production. One approach is to visit the research section of the World Bank (www.worldbank.org). At the World Bank Web site, go to Topics, then on Information & Communication Technologies (ICT), then on Tables. For each of the three countries, find and examine variables that indicate the quality of the local software and IT environment. Based on your findings, which country appears strongest for meeting the needs of your firm?

2. International labor standards are complex and closely related to global sourcing. In particular, the use of sweatshops has attracted much attention. A sweatshop is a factory characterized by very low wages, long hours, and poor working conditions. Some sweatshops employ children in unsafe conditions. Various prolabor groups advocate for minimum labor standards in foreign factories. Suppose your future employer wants to outsource a portion of its production to certain developing countries, but is concerned about the possibility of employing sweatshop labor. Visit the Web sites of groups that encourage minimum standards in labor conditions (for example, www.sweatshopwatch.org, www.aworldconnected.org, www.corpwatch.org, or enter the keywords "labor conditions" at globalEDGE™) and prepare a memo to your employer that discusses the major concerns of those who advocate minimum labor standards.

3. Your firm just decided to outsource to India such back-office operations as accounting and basic finance functions. Unclear on how to proceed, management has asked you to find candidate suppliers in India. As a first step, you decide to check the online Yellow Pages (such as yahoo.com or superpage.com) and search for appropriate Indian firms. Find three firms in India that specialize in business-process outsourcing and examine their Web sites. Describe and compare the business-process services that each firm provides. What selection criteria should you use? Which firm seems most qualified and reputable for providing outsourcing of business-process services?

CKR Cavusgil Knight Riesenberger
Management Skill Builder©

A Smarter Approach to Global Sourcing

Firms now increasingly outsource many of their service activities in much the same way as manufacturing firms outsource parts and components production. While the main motive for global sourcing is to reduce costs, other motives include the ability to achieve strategic goals and concentrate on the firm's core competencies, allowing management to redirect resources to the most profitable uses.

AACSB: Reflective Thinking

Managerial Challenge

Undertaking global sourcing is risky and potentially expensive. Choosing the wrong sourcing partner can lead to unexpected costs and complications. Management at the focal firm must deal with foreign legal systems, tax laws, and bureaucratic regulations. In some countries corruption is commonplace, and the firm may struggle to protect its core technologies and know-how.

Background

The top global sourcing locations include major cities in India, China, the Philippines, and Eastern Europe. But these locations increasingly suffer from shortcomings, particularly shortages of qualified workers, which are pushing up wages. High demand is straining local infrastructure and has led to severe traffic congestion, frequent power outages, and communications blackouts. Other locations—such as Turkey, Thailand, South Africa, Brazil, Mexico, Botswana, and Indonesia—are increasingly attractive outsourcing destinations. Many companies are now seeking new foreign locations to outsource their value-chain activities.

Managerial Skills You Will Gain

In this C/K/R Management Skill Builder©, as a prospective manager, you will:

1. Learn the factors to consider when evaluating countries as potential locations for global sourcing.

2. Understand how these factors relate to maximizing corporate competitive advantages.

3. Use the methodology of screening countries for sourcing potential.

4. Build research skills for planning company operations.

Your Task

Assume that you work for a large investment brokerage firm, such as Merrill Lynch, AIG, Goldman Sachs, or UBS Financial Services. Your firm performs various business process activities (such as accounting, financial analysis, account reconciliation, data entry) that result in substantial ongoing expenses. To reduce costs, management has decided to outsource some of these activities to a foreign business-process subcontractor. Management sought the advice of a global sourcing consultant, who advised that two countries—Russia and Mexico—are particularly good locations for meeting the firm's needs. Your task is to complete the final stages of the analysis by researching Russia and Mexico and recommending which country better meets the brokerage's sourcing needs.

Go to the C/K/R Knowledge Portal©

www.prenhall.com/cavusgil
Proceed to the C/K/R Knowledge Portal© to obtain the expanded background information, your task and methodology, suggested resources for this exercise, and the presentation template.

Chapter 10

PRODUCTION STRATEGY

Contents

Introduction

Research, development, and innovation

Generation of goods and services

International logistics

Different kinds of global production systems

Strategic management and production strategy

■ **Active Learning Case**

The GE production process and Six Sigma

■ **International Business Strategy in Action**

Gap Inc.: a successfully "Hollow Corporation"

Greening the supply chain

■ **Real Cases**

Flextronics

Nike

Objectives of the chapter

Production strategy is critical to effective international operations. Most goods and services have very limited lives, so MNEs must continually provide new offerings, which can be accomplished only through a well-formulated production strategy. This chapter examines how MNEs carry out this process. In doing so, we will focus on the entire range of production strategies from research and development to manufacturing, shipment, and the final international destination. We will look at the most current approaches, including speed-to-market, concurrent engineering, and continuous cost reduction.

The specific objectives of this chapter are to:

1 *Examine* the role of research, development, and innovation in production strategy.
2 *Relate* some of the most critical steps in generating goods and services, including global sourcing, costing techniques, quality maintenance, effective materials handling, inventory control, and the proper emphasis on service.
3 *Describe* the nature and importance of international logistics in production strategy.
4 *Review* some of the major production strategies being used by MNEs, including strategic alliances and acquisitions.

The GE production process and Six Sigma

General Electric is a multibillion-dollar multinational corporation whose products range from 65 cent light bulbs to billion-dollar power plants. Based on revenues, assets, profits, and market value, the company was listed by *Fortune* magazine as number six in the world in 2007. One reason for GE's annual revenue of more than $168 billion is its ability to manage a diverse multiproduct-line operation, handling such products as major appliances, lighting, medical diagnostic imaging equipment, motors, and commercial and military aircraft engines and engineering materials. GE also provides a range of services, including those related to electricity provision, media (GE owns NBC in the United States), and multimedia programming and distribution. Much of the company's success can be attributed to the production-related concepts it has employed over the last two decades. During the 1980s, work-out, process mapping, and best practices were GE's applied concepts.

Work-out is a training program designed to empower employees to implement their problem-solving ideas. A group of 40 to 100 people, picked by management from all ranks and functional areas, attend a three-day meeting. The first day consists of a manager leading the group in roughing out an agenda addressing areas in which productivity can be increased. Then the manager leaves and for the next $1\frac{1}{2}$ days the group breaks into teams to tackle the agenda. On the last afternoon the manager returns and one by one the team members make their proposals for improved productivity. The manager can make only three responses: agree, disagree, or ask for more information; in the last case, an individual manager must empower a team to get the information by an agreed-upon date. These work-out sessions have proved extremely successful. In one case, a group of workers convinced management to allow their factory to bid against an outside vendor for the right to build new protective shields for grinding machines. As a result, the GE group completed the job for $16,000 versus $96,000 for the vendor.

The second method, *process mapping*, is to create a flowchart that shows all the steps, no matter how small, involved in making or doing something. The map is analyzed for ways to eliminate steps and save time and money. One work group was able to reorganize production, cut manufacturing time in half, and reduce inventory by $4 million.

The third method, *best practices*, consists of finding companies that do things better than GE does and emulating them. GE personnel try to answer the question: what is the

secret of this other company's success? Quite often the answer includes such things as getting products to market faster than anyone else, treating suppliers like partners, or having superior inventory management. As a result of best practices, GE is now keeping executives in their jobs for longer periods of time rather than rotating them quickly through new jobs; the best practices process revealed that frequent changes create problems in new product introductions. The company also learned how to use continuous improvement processes more effectively to bring a new product into the market ahead of the competition and then work on introducing new technologies. In the past the firm would try to perfect all technologies first and then introduce the final product version.

In the 1990s, the dominant production concept was Six Sigma, a name that originates from a statistical method for deriving near-perfect quality, equal to 3.4 defects per million operations. The Six Sigma process allows GE to measure how many "defects" there are in a given process and then systematically work to eliminate them to approximate "zero defects." Six Sigma recognizes three elements: the customer, the process, and the employee. The customer is the key to defining quality. GE uses the term "Delighting Customers" to generate a mentality whereby customer expectations of performance, reliability, competitive price, on-time delivery, service, clear and correct transaction processing, and other customer needs become a key factor in all processes. The second element, the process, promotes "Outside-In Thinking Quality." GE must understand the transaction life cycle from the customer's point of view and identify significant value and improvement from that same perspective. Under the banner "Leadership Commitment People," the third element of Six Sigma, the employee, requires that all personnel use their talents and energies to satisfy customers. All employees are trained in Six Sigma, including statistical tools, strategy, and techniques of Six Sigma quality. At the core of the process is a workforce mentality on customer quality expectations, defect reduction, process capability, variation (the customer reacts to the variance rather than the average results), stability of operations, and designing processes to meet customer expectations.

GE's advantage over failing conglomerates is its ability to transfer knowledge over the whole company. This can be attributed to former CEO Jack Welch, who oversaw GE's transformation from a mainly manufacturing firm to a service-oriented, knowledge-based company. He defined

GE's culture by creating a workforce that can identify opportunities and implement changes.

Despite GE's firm-specific advantages (FSAs) in production, its competitive edge has not been transferred equally to other parts of the world, especially not other triad nations that have significant domestic competitors. The company derives approximately 59.8 percent of its revenues from the United States alone. If its revenues from Canadian and Latin American operations are added in, the number rises to almost 63.7 percent. Europe, its largest foreign regional market, accounts for only 18.5 percent of revenues, whereas countries in the Pacific Basin account for a mere 9.1 percent. The remaining 8.7 percent are accounted for by other regions (3 percent) and non-segmented US exports to other countries (5.7 percent).

In October 2000, GE, as the world's largest producer of jet engines, and Honeywell, a manufacturer of aircraft electronics, agreed to a $42 billion merger. The two US-based companies secured antitrust authorities' approval in the United States and Canada, but the deal came to a halt because of the European Union. This was the first time the EU had blocked a merger between two US companies. The European competition commissioner claimed that such a merger would have closed the market to competitors and asked GE to divest itself of GE Capital Aviation Services by selling it to one of its main rivals. GE offered to sell the company privately, but the EU countered that a friendly transaction might not result in true divestiture. US politicians, frustrated by the European stand, threatened to retaliate if the EU did not approve the merger. Republican Senator Phil Gramm went as far as to accuse the EU of enacting policies to protect its companies. The EU rejected US government intervention in the matter and the merger did not materialize.

Website: www.ge.com.

Sources: Thomas A. Stewart, "GE Keeps Those Ideas Coming," *Fortune*, August 12, 1991, pp. 40–49; "The World's Super Fifty," *Forbes*, July 27, 1998, p. 118; www.ge.com; General Electric, *10K SEC Filing*, 2002; "EU Rejects Latest GE Offers," *BBC.co.uk*, June 29 2001; "EU Blocks GE/Honeywell Deal," BBC.co.uk, July 3, 2001; "US Senators Lash Out at EU Over GE Deal," BBC.co.uk, June 15, 2001; "The Fortune Global 500," *Fortune*, 2007, at http://money.cnn.com/galleries/2007/fortune/.

1 How did GE use work-out to increase speed-to-market?

2 How has GE used Six Sigma to reduce cost and improve quality in consumer goods? In each case, give an example.

3 In what way could best practices help GE develop more effective international strategies? Explain.

INTRODUCTION

Production management has been responsible for many new goods and services. Examples are as varied as Palm's handhelds, Apple's iPod, Honda's hybrid cars, HP's digital cameras, eBay's Internet auctions, and five-star hotel operations at the Ritz-Carlton. The nature of production management in the MNE is similar in many respects to that in domestic firms. Both are concerned with the efficient use of labor and capital. Both are also interested in investing in research and development (R&D) and in organizing operations to generate successful new product lines and increase production and service efficiency.

Like domestic firms, MNEs need to organize their production management so they can minimize operating costs through the use of logistics and inventory control. Canon, for example, relocates production to China only if labor accounts for over 5 percent of production costs.[1] Acer, the successful upstart from Taiwan, makes sure that computer parts with short product life cycles are shipped by air, and those with long product life cycles are shipped by sea (see Active Learning Case in Chapter 19). However, pressures from host-country governments or special interest groups can affect a multinational's decision making in these areas. For example, host governments often criticize resource-based MNEs for their backward, forward, and horizontal integration. **Backward integration**, which is the ownership of equity assets used earlier in the production cycle (such as an auto firm acquiring a steel company), is criticized for doing little for employment or development in

Backward integration
The ownership of equity assets used earlier in the production cycle, such as an auto firm that acquires a steel company

Forward integration
The purchase of assets or facilities that move the company closer to the customer, such as a computer manufacturer that acquires a retail chain that specializes in computer products

Horizontal integration
The purchase of firms in the same line of business, such as a computer chip firm that acquires a competitor

the host nation. **Forward integration**, which is the purchase of assets or facilities that move the company closer to the customer (such as a computer manufacturer that acquires a retail chain that specializes in computer sales), is criticized on the basis that MNEs use the strategy to homogenize consumer tastes to the detriment of national identities. **Horizontal integration**, which is the acquisition of firms in the same line of business (such as a computer chip manufacturer that buys a competitor), is attacked for introducing similar product lines on a worldwide basis and undercutting the existence of local firms, most of which lack the economies of scale that can be achieved by MNEs.[2]

There are similar challenges in the industrial relations area, where MNEs must take into account different labor practices and wage rates. For example, multinationals are often under pressure from host governments to use local sourcing for their supplies, hire local workers, train home-country managers and supervisors, and help improve the production environment in the host nation. These decisions can sometimes result in higher production costs, although most international auto firms, for example, use local suppliers and workers to offset this problem.

The financing of operations is another production-related challenge. The choice between local and international borrowing and the use of internally generated funds to minimize the cost of capital is complicated by foreign exchange risk, international tax laws, and government controls on capital (see Chapter 14). Additionally, MNEs need to know where they are on their production cost curves in each country, as well as globally, so as to exploit any cost advantages with an appropriate organization structure. For example, as Toyota's worldwide market share began to stabilize, the firm found it needed to become increasingly more efficient.[3]

The above examples illustrate some of the common production-related problems facing international firms. However, experienced MNEs have learned how to deal with these challenges. In doing so, they employ a wide gamut of production strategies that address research, development, innovation, global sourcing, costing techniques, and inventory control.[4] The following sections examine each of these production strategies.

RESEARCH, DEVELOPMENT, AND INNOVATION

Production strategies do *not* begin with manufacturing. In the past many MNEs focused most heavily on this aspect of operations, failing to realize that an effective production strategy begins with new product development. This conclusion gains in importance when one considers that many of today's best-selling products and services were unavailable a short while ago. Examples include laptops, cellular phones, satellite navigation devices, DVD players, broadband DSL lines, and specialized discount stores that cater to selective product lines such as home-related goods or office supplies. Many other products and services have been greatly improved over the last decade or so. Examples include antidepressant medication, automobiles, facsimile machines, hazardous waste treatment services, home-delivery food services, medical diagnostic equipment, pacemakers, personal computers, photocopiers, telephones, and televisions. MNEs have come to realize that if they are not developing new goods and services, they must be improving their current offerings. In either case the focus is on R&D and innovation.

Innovation can be broadly divided into product/service development and process development. The former refers to activities that support the creation of new products and services that customers want, or improvements to existing products/services that make more customers want them instead of those of rival firms. The latter refers to innovation activities that improve the way products/services are produced, making them quicker, cheaper, or better quality. Continuous innovation lies at the heart of sustained competitive advantage, and managing it effectively has a strong international business component.

Most large firms are involved in all of these activities. Sony, for example, is continually coming up with new technology platforms (CDs, DVDs, minidisks, and so on) and new products based around these platforms. But it also invests in improving current product lines, with new models and new features, and it strives to make them cheaper through economies of scale and continuous improvement in manufacturing.

For us, concerned with the international strategy and organization of innovation and R&D, there are several key issues. The first is the question of how far products, services, and the processes that create them should be standardized across all locations, as opposed to customizing these to suit local markets. This lies at the heart of the "integration-responsiveness" theme that runs through this book. Despite the highly standardized nature of their products, even firms like McDonald's and Coca-Cola customize these for particular markets. Like all firms they have to manage a natural tension between country market managers who would like more customization to suit their local customer needs and head-office managers in the marketing, operations, human resource management, R&D, and strategy departments which would prefer to standardize across all markets.

A related issue is: where should firms locate different innovation-related activities? The answer to this depends on the industry and often the product or service in question. It is worth examining this by looking at the factors that influence the organization of R&D around the firm.

MNEs tend to operate several types of R&D networks, as shown on Figure 10.1. There is an innovation hierarchy from basic, long-term, or blue-sky R&D, which is often based around finding scientific breakthroughs, to applied, near-market, or demand-led innovation:

- Blue-sky or basic R&D centers are often linked to universities or government research institutes to tap into highly specialized expertise, wherever it is in the world.

- Technical design and development centers focus on more practical, near-market R&D and may be separate or co-located with regional headquarters or major business units.

- Applied technical development and customization departments, often situated within manufacturing centers, will focus on incremental improvements to production processes or minor adaptations to products to suit local markets.

Home country-based central R&D often sets the overall R&D strategy across a firm, but funding and other resources may partly come from country market managers who will

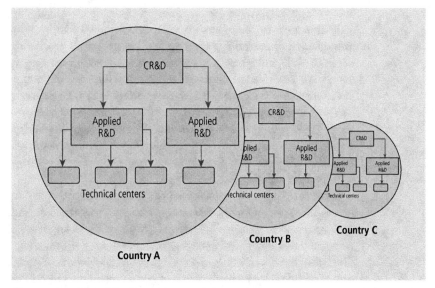

Figure 10.1 Global R&D: markets and hierarchies

push for more applied R&D activities to adapt products and services for their markets. For a large MNE, a few key locations may have R&D units, the firm's main markets may all have one or more applied R&D centers, and production locations will have technical centers. The complexity of managing strategy and implementation up and down the innovation hierarchy and across the different country locations should not be underestimated.

In terms of both product and process development, MNEs need to prioritize country locations according to both (1) local market requirements in terms of adaptation, design and development, and engineering support and (2) local technological resources, expertise, contract companies, universities, and so on, often called the "national system of innovation."

Hewlett-Packard (HP) is a good example of these kinds of structures. It has six basic R&D centers in Palo Alto, California; Cambridge, Massachusetts; Bristol, England; Grenoble, France; Haifa, Israel; and Tokyo, Japan. These explore a wide range of technologies more or less linked to its product range. Its Advanced Studies Research Labs include a subgroup doing information theory research, linking the Mathematical Science Group based in Bristol with experts at the US universities at Stanford and Berkeley. Grenoble specializes in business PC design and development and Israel in image and document processing, among other areas.

These centers of research excellence are linked to HP's global product divisions, mainly headquartered in the United States, and its national subsidiaries around the world, which encompass most of its 85,500 employees.

The Palo Alto center pioneered HP's thermal ink-jet technology, for example. Its Consumer Products group headquartered in San Diego, California, designed, developed, and led the manufacturing of a range of imaging products using this technology. The firm's subsidiary in Singapore customizes the design and produces thermal inkjet printers for the Japanese and Asian markets.

The R&D structure of the firm evolved a step further when the Singaporean subsidiary took the lead from San Diego for the design, development, and manufacturing of a new range of portable inkjet printers. It had built up a range of specialist capabilities, through learning from other parts of the internal network and through local Asian technical partnerships and subcontractors that made it the best place to lead innovation efforts in this area for the firm as a whole.[5]

The above organization structures are important because they affect how well firms leverage their R&D efforts for competitive advantage. The efficiency with which specialist knowledge inputs from experts around the firm are coordinated is paramount. For example, firms have to focus new product development (NPD) efforts at the point where technological opportunities meet market opportunities. Marketing departments and subsidiaries, distributors and retailers in country markets understand customer needs, whereas the central R&D department and technical design and development centers around the firm understand the potential of various technologies. These areas of specialist knowledge have to combine efficiently to direct NPD, and this is often done within cross-functional teams. NPD project teams are continually created and disbanded in manufacturing and service firms in response to the ever-changing technological and market opportunities they are faced with, and the strength of internal and external networks determines how well firms manage this process.[6]

Large MNEs that are good at managing knowledge networks are in a better position to leverage the scale and scope advantages that put them ahead of smaller or domestic market firms in terms of their innovativeness. They can afford large (scale) and specialist (scope) centers of excellence and can manage joint ventures with other big players to pool resources and spread the risk of R&D projects. They can then link these R&D centers to their markets around the world, prioritizing areas of development on which to focus their efforts to reap the most rewards in terms of sales of new and improved products.

International Business

Global innovation management and knowledge management are seen to be increasingly important to the long-run performance of all firms. Nohria and Ghoshal use the terms *distributed innovation* and *differentiated networks* to characterize how firms should learn globally and exploit this learning globally to improve production processes and products in all markets.[7] Other studies also emphasize the internal processes, within multinational structures, that constrain or facilitate this kind of global capability.[8]

Speed-to-market

One of the major manufacturing challenges facing MNEs is the speed with which they develop and get new products to market.[9] In recent years, many firms have found that a "speed-to-market" strategy can be extremely profitable. Table 10.1 provides some data to support this statement. Notice that a company that enters the market one month ahead of the competition can increase annual gross profits by $150,000 on a product that generates $25 million and $600,000 on a product that generates $100 million. Simply put, by carefully designing the product and getting it out of the door fast, the company can dramatically increase profitability.

MNEs have taken a number of steps to ensure early delivery of their products. For example, Cisco Systems has outsourced the production of routers and switches to Flextronics, a contract electronics manufacturer. Flextronics receives an electronic order from Cisco, manufactures the product under the Cisco brand, and then delivers it directly to the customers.[10] BMW has combined engineering, development, and production planning in bringing new cars to market in record time.[11]

The strategic emphasis is on increasing speed by developing **time-to-market accelerators**, which are factors that help reduce bottlenecks and errors and ensure product quality and performance. These accelerators vary from firm to firm, but they all produce the same results. For example, in 2000, Pirelli, the Italian tire maker, unveiled its **modular integrated robotized system (MIRB)**, which enables the entire production system to be robotized. Small and flexible, MIRB allows smaller batches to be produced in different locations, potentially locating them next to Pirelli's industrial customers.[12]

In the past, many MNEs placed the bulk of their production attention on the manufacturing side of the operation. However, recent research shows that the best way to reduce defective products and speed delivery is by placing the greatest attention on product design and planning of operations. This is accomplished through what is known as **concurrent engineering**, which involves design, engineering, and manufacturing people working

Time-to-market accelerators
Factors that help reduce bottlenecks and errors and ensure product quality and performance

Modular integrated robotized system (MIRB)
A software-based production process that relies entirely on robots

Concurrent engineering
The process of having design, engineering, and manufacturing people working together to create a product, in contrast to working in a sequential manner

Table 10.1 **The cost of arriving late to market (and still be on budget)**

	If the company is late to market by:					
6 months	5 months	4 months	3 months	2 months	1 month
Gross potential profit is reduced by:						
233%	225%	218%	212%	27%	23%
If time-to-market is improved profit will go up by:						
11.9%	9.3%	7.3%	5.7%	4.3%	3.1%
For revenues of $25 million, annual gross profit will increase by:						
$400,000	$350,000	$300,000	$250,000	$200,000	$150,000
For revenues of $100 million, annual gross profit will increase by:						
$1,600,000	$1,400,000	$1,200,000	$1,000,000	$800,000	$600,000

Source: Academy of Management Executive, "The New Competitors: They Think in Terms of 'Speed-to-Market'," by Joseph T. Vesey. Copyright © 1991 The Academy of Management (NY).

together to create and build the product. Concurrent engineering is useful for two reasons. First, if the product is carefully designed, fewer changes are needed later on and the good can be brought to market swiftly. Second, the costs associated with changes increase as the product gets closer to completion; that is, it is almost twice as expensive to correct a problem during production than during product design.

Once a product or service has been planned out, the MNE's attention turns to production. This strategy is focused very heavily on minimizing costs and increasing quality and productivity.

 Active learning check

Review your answer to Active Learning Case question 1 and make any changes you like. Then compare your answer to the one below.

1 How did GE use work-out to increase speed-to-market?

The primary way GE used work-out to increase speed-to-market was by looking for ways to eliminate production bottlenecks and streamline operations. The strategy of work-out asked the participants: how can we change the operation to get more done in less time? The workers who were familiar with the operations often had a wealth of information to share, and this was sometimes the first time anyone had asked them for their opinions. They were delighted to offer suggestions and recommendations. As a result, the company produced more products in less time than ever before.

GENERATION OF GOODS AND SERVICES

Most people think of the production process as one in which physical goods are produced. However, the process can also be used in generating services, and the two are quite often interlinked.[13] For example, GM manufactures cars but also offers auto maintenance and repair services [14] whereas Boeing both builds and services aircraft. In other cases, services are primary, such as the Hilton Corporation offering hotel accommodations, Hertz and Avis leasing cars, and CNN providing international news coverage.

Sometimes goods and/or services are provided directly by the MNE; other times the MNE has an arrangement with outside firms or suppliers (some of them being direct competitors) to assist in this process. For example, other firms make some of the HP printers, but HP has its name put on the units and assumes responsibility for marketing them. [15] Service organizations follow a similar strategy. Some airlines purchase their in-flight food from companies like Marriott, and some rely on aircraft maintenance firms such as Ryder to service their craft. Many motels subcontract their food service to companies that specialize in this area, including fast-food franchisors such as McDonald's and Burger King. So there is often a mix of product/service strategies at work when generating goods and services. The following discussion examines some of the most important functions that are carried out in this process. The production of goods is emphasized most heavily because some of the areas under discussion do not lend themselves to services—although one that does is global sourcing, a primary area of consideration in production strategy.

 ## Global sourcing

Global sourcing
The use of suppliers anywhere in the world, chosen on the basis of their efficiency

Sometimes MNEs produce all the goods and services they need. However, they often use **global sourcing** by calling upon those suppliers which can provide the needed output more efficiently regardless of where they are geographically located.[16]

Global sourcing has become important for a number of reasons. The most obvious one is cost. If GM wants to be price competitive in the European Union, one strategy is to build and ship cars from Detroit to Europe at a price equal to, or less than, that charged by EU competitors. Because this is not possible, GM uses overseas suppliers and assembly plants to build much of what it sells in Europe. In deciding who will provide these parts and supplies, the company uses global sourcing, as do other MNEs.

Not all global sourcing is provided by outside suppliers. Some MNEs own their own source of supply or hold an equity position in a supplier. This relationship does not guarantee that the supplier will get the MNE's business on every bid. However, if the supplier is unable to match the cost or quality performance of competitive suppliers, the MNE will eventually terminate the relationship. So there is a great deal of pressure on the supplier to develop and maintain state-of-the-art production facilities. Additionally, because the supplier works closely with the MNE, the company knows how its multinational client likes things done and is able to operate smoothly with the MNE's design and production people.

In recent years some giant MNEs have taken equity positions in a number of different suppliers. Japanese multinationals are an excellent example. These firms often have a network of parts suppliers, subcontractors, and capital equipment suppliers they can call on.

At the same time these suppliers often provide goods and services to other firms. This helps them to maintain their competitive edge by forcing them to innovate, adapt, and remain cost effective. If these suppliers are in similar or complementary industries, as in the case of NEC's suppliers, then technological innovations or revolutionary changes in manufacturing processes will be quickly accepted or copied by others. So the close proximity of the suppliers coupled with their business relationships helps to ensure that they attain and hold positions as world-class suppliers, and this advantage carries over to the customers, who gain both innovative ideas and high-quality, low-cost supplies.[17]

A good example is the leather footwear industry in Italy. Manufacturers regularly interact with leather suppliers, designers, and producers of other leather goods. As a result, the manufacturers are extremely knowledgeable about industry technology, production techniques, fashion trends, and supply sources.

These advantages also help explain why many US suppliers are going international. By setting up operations near world-class competitors, these suppliers find it easier to monitor developments, remain alert to changes in technology and production processes, and maintain state-of-the-art facilities.[18] In fact, when manufacturers expand operations to another country, it is common to find their major suppliers setting up operations nearby in order to continue serving the manufacturers. The other reason is to prevent local competitors from capturing some of this business, which often happens when the supplier attempts to compete from the home country.

The global clothing industry provides a good example of these trends. The production of clothing sits within a broader value chain, which includes textiles and fibers for a range of both household and industrial goods. Upstream, the textile industry relies on access to sources of natural fibers, a "natural" factor endowment in Porter's Diamond of Advantage, compared to the "acquired" factor endowments associated with the chemicals industry for the production of artificial fibers. Clearly, each has favored different countries at different stages of the industry's development. Downstream, distribution and retailing and, in particular, branding and marketing have remained predominantly within the major markets of industrially advanced countries (and under their ownership). The case International Business Strategy in Action: Gap Inc. illustrates these patterns.

The clothing industry itself can be subdivided into three activities: design, preparation, and production. The last two have remained relatively labor intensive, which is why most preparation and production are done in cheap-labor locations. China's share of world

Gap Inc.: a successfully "Hollow Corporation"

In 1999, after 28 years, founders Don and Doris Fisher still owned 24 percent of Gap Inc. and still played a leading role in managing the operations of this $2 billion clothing firm. By 2006 Gap's revenue had grown to $15.9 billion and the Fisher family was still very much involved. As with other high-street clothing firms, its competitive advantage stemmed from linking cheap manufacturing in contract production facilities in around 45 countries, with design and fashion expertise and huge distribution and sales chains in the United States and Europe.

Source: Alamy Images/Niall McDiarmid

Just 1 percent of its own employees have any production-related role: 600 quality control employees in eight shipment processing facilities in North America, Europe, and Asia. Gap is essentially a distribution, retailing, sales, and, particularly, marketing firm—a specialty retailer operating over 3,100 stores selling casual apparel, personal care products, and accessories. Its brands include Gap, GapKids, BabyGap, Banana Republic, Old Navy, and Piperlime. Gap measures its own success on its sales and its expansion rate, in terms of new stores, so in part it is also a real estate business. These provide an indication of its ongoing performance, its multinationality at any point in time, and its international expansion or retrenchment over time. In the late 1990s it was opening over 100 stores per year. More recently its overall growth and its international expansion have slowed (see table below). Despite Gap being a well-known brand in Europe, it is heavily reliant on its North American

sales, with less than 10 percent of its stores situated outside in other parts of the triad. Gap's product development offices are based in New York City, where product managers, designers, and graphic artists monitor (and create) customer trends in its main consumer markets.

The Sourcing and Logistics Group, together with buying agents around the globe, draw up production schedules and place orders with the approved third-party clothes plants located around the world. Like other mid-range department stores, such as Neiman-Marcus or Macy's in the United States, Marks & Spencer in the UK or Karstadt in Germany, Gap's higher-quality, higher-priced garments are sourced from countries like South Korea, Taiwan, Hong Kong, Singapore, Turkey, Brazil, Mexico, and parts of India and China. In terms of the global clothing value chain, these garments sit "below" fashion designer clothing from Armani, Donna Karan, Boss, or Gucci, which is manufactured in small, high-quality batches in Italy and high-capability locations in South-East Asia. But they sit "above" the discount chains like Wal-Mart and Kmart in the United States, Asda and Matalan in the UK, and Carrefour in France which source in bulk from lower-cost and lower-quality locations such as Malaysia, Indonesia, Vietnam, China, India, Mexico, Chile, Hungary, Kenya, and Pakistan. The value hierarchy in clothing is mirrored by a global hierarchy of locations, ordered by virtue of their cost base and local endowments that underpin quality, and speed of delivery, from related infrastructure to relevant expertise.

Each Gap brand has its own marketing team based in the San Francisco Bay area, which creates advertising posters, in-store design and graphics, and magazine and TV commercials. Distribution centers receive goods from overseas production plants, check the quality, sort the goods and

Gap Inc. store count by brand and country, 2007

GAP	
United States	1,188
Canada	90
Banana Republic	
United States	519
Canada	30
Old Navy	
United States	997
Canada	65
Forth & Towne	
United States	0
International	
United Kingdom	139
France	33
Japan	130
Total	**3,191**

Source: http://www.gapinc.com/public/documents/Store_Count_Brand.pdf.

redistribute them to retail outlets in each of the country markets, the United States, Canada, Japan, the UK, and the Netherlands. The subcontracting arrangement with overseas manufacturers sometimes involves financial and technical support but mainly relies on imposing strict quality and cost limitations which independent suppliers must adhere to in order to maintain their contracts.

There are clear similarities in this strategy with Nike (see Real Case: Nike, below). Nike, however, has closer ties with its first-tier suppliers often including some equity-share, technology transfer, management, and design training. Nike is also well known for its poor record on ethical labor practices, through well-publicized studies of its South-East Asian "sweatshops." These triggered damaging reprisals from shareholders and customers, sending out a warning sign to many consumer goods manufacturers which relied on a strong brand that exploitation of cheap labor can sometimes be highly unprofitable.

Websites: http://www.gap.com; http://www.gapinc.com.

Sources: P. Dicken, *Global Shift: Reshaping the Global Economic Map in the 21st Century*, 4th ed. (London: Sage, 2003). OECD, "A New World Map in Textiles and Clothing: Adjusting to Change," Paris (210 pp.), at http://www.oecd.org/.

exports in clothing grew from 4 percent in 1980 to over 18 percent in 2000, and it is now the world's dominant exporter. Over 2 million Chinese are employed in the sector. By contrast the United States has the biggest trade deficit in clothing ($48 billion in 2004). Scotland and Italy, two dominant forces in textiles and clothing at one time, for example, have shifted upmarket to specialize in design and high-quality/fashion items. Employment has fallen drastically in these countries as a result and the patterns of trade have also reversed.

When MNEs turn to global sourcing, there is typically a hierarchical order of consideration. The company gives first preference to internal sources, such as having subassemblies produced by the manufacturing department or the subsidiary that specializes in this work. However, if a review of outside sources reveals a sufficient cost/quality difference that would justify buying from an external supplier, this is what the company will do. In fact, sometimes an MNE will not attempt to make a particular part or product because it lacks the expertise to do so efficiently. The firm will simply solicit bids from outside suppliers and award the contract based on predetermined specifications (price, quality, delivery time, etc.). Over time the MNE will learn which suppliers are best at providing certain goods and services and will turn to them immediately. When this process is completed, attention will then focus on the actual manufacture of the goods.

Recently, environmentalists have reviewed the global supply chains of MNEs. They argue that all suppliers to an MNE should follow environmentally sensitive policies—in other words, be "green." The case International Business Strategy in Action: Greening the supply chain examines this issue.

Manufacturing of goods

MNEs face a variety of concerns in manufacturing goods and services. Primary among these are cost, quality, and efficient production systems.

Cost

Multinationals seek to control their costs by increasing the efficiency of their production processes. Often this means using new, improved technology such as state-of-the-art machinery and equipment. Although these purchases can be expensive, they may be the best way to raise productivity and lower costs, thus maintaining competitive advantage. A good example is provided by the automobile industry in Brazil, which is the heart of the South American automobile market. The country is host to 13 auto makers, including DaimlerChrysler, Volkswagen, and Ford, which are investing over $20 billion to update Brazilian plants to modular manufacturing. **Modular manufacturing** allows suppliers of parts to take on some of the assembly. Dana Corporation, which has set up shop near a

Modular manufacturing
A manufacturing process that consists of modules that can be easily adapted to fit changing demand

Greening the supply chain

The supply chain is an important part of the production process and overall strategy in the automobile sector, where most Tier One auto parts suppliers have adopted ISO 9000 quality standards over the last decade in order to remain key suppliers to the OEMs. Less well known is that the supply chain has also been used to introduce environmentally friendly "green" standards. This occurs through the implementation of ISO 14000.

A successful example of this is in Mexico. Despite many NGOs arguing that Mexico is a pollution haven, research by Rugman et al. shows that the use of ISO 14000 green processes has unambiguously raised Mexico's environmental standards. When both auto suppliers and assemblers have to change their engineering processes to meet ISO 14001 standards in the United States and Canada, these new manufacturing processes raise overall environmental performance in Mexico, even if the government is lagging in enforcing the standards. The "foreign-owned" firms bring in new technologies to poorer countries, including green technologies.

This also occurs in the retail/food sector. A study of the UK retail sector in 2001 found that all along the supply chain firms engage in green purchasing. This occurred across at least three sectors: grocery retailing, furniture, and building materials. The green purchasing was helped by EU environmental regulations, which have led to basic changes in environmental management systems of retail companies. These management systems are closely linked to the Denning model of continuous process improvements of quality standards.

The supply chain, or Porter's value chain, typically consists of supplier management, purchasing, materials management, production scheduling, facilities planning, logistics, and consumer services.

Best practices in UK retail were B&Q (part of the Kingfisher Group) and The Body Shop. Both of these retailers require their suppliers to meet EU environmental standards.

In general, UK grocery retailers (like Sainsbury's, Safeway, and Asda) were more engaged in green purchasing than UK furniture and building material retailers, although both B&Q and The Body Shop had also developed some green capabilities.

Websites: www.kingfisher.co.uk; www.the-body-shop.com; www.sainsbury.co.uk; www.safeway.com; www.asda.co.uk.

Sources: Linnett M. Mabuku, "Green Purchasing and Corporate Strategy: A Case Study of UK Retail Firms and their International Supply Chains," MSc Dissertation, Environmental Change Institute, University of Oxford, September 2001; Alan M. Rugman, John Kirton and Julie Soloway, *Environmental Regulations and Corporate Strategy* (Oxford: Oxford University Press, 1999); Michael Porter, *Competitive Advantage* (New York: Free Press, 1985).

Chrysler factory in the city of Curitiba, is now responsible for the assembly of the Dakota's basic skeleton, which represents approximately 30 percent of the total cost of production. Once this skeleton reaches Chrysler, it is mounted with an engine and a body. Entire assembly lines had to be rebuilt to accommodate this process. Volkswagen, Ford, and General Motors are also developing similar assembly plants to test their efficiency for future implementation to their other factories.[19]

A second approach is to tap low-cost labor sources. A good example is the *maquiladora* industry (as discussed in Chapter 6) that has sprung up in Mexico just across the US border. Hundreds of US plants have been established in this area. Examples include TRW Inc., which has a factory where workers assemble seat belts, and Mattel, which has a plant where workers turn out Barbie-doll houses and Disney teething rings.[20] Labor costs in these facilities are less than 20 percent of those of similar workers in the United States. Also, because this is a free trade zone, US duties are levied on the imports only to the extent of the value added in Mexico, so low wage rates in Mexico help keep down the import duty.

A third approach is the development of new methods used to cut costs.[21] For example, in the United States, it is typical for a firm to calculate selling price after a new product is developed. If the price is judged to be too high, the product is sent back to the drawing board to be reworked, or the company accepts a smaller profit on the product. A different system has been introduced in Japan, where firms begin by determining the target cost of the product *before* going into design, engineering, and supplier pricing, and the latter

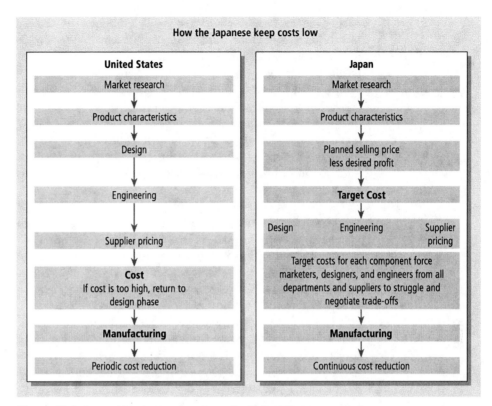

How the Japanese keep costs low

United States	Japan
Market research	Market research
↓	↓
Product characteristics	Product characteristics
↓	↓
Design	Planned selling price less desired profit
↓	↓
Engineering	**Target Cost**
↓	↓
Supplier pricing	Design Engineering Supplier pricing
↓	Target costs for each component force marketers, designers, and engineers from all departments and suppliers to struggle and negotiate trade-offs
Cost If cost is too high, return to design phase	
↓	↓
Manufacturing	**Manufacturing**
↓	↓
Periodic cost reduction	Continuous cost reduction

Figure 10.2 Cost reduction approaches: the United States versus Japan

Source: Ford S. Worthy, "Japan's Smart Secret Weapon," *Fortune*, August 12, 1991, p. 73.

groups then work to bring the product in at the desired price. This unique cost management system has helped Japanese firms cut costs for some time (Figure 10.2).[22]

A fourth method that is gaining popularity with MNEs is that of costing products not on an individual basis but as part of a portfolio of related goods. Instead of evaluating the expenses of developing one new soft drink, for example, a company looks at the costs and revenues associated with the entire line of beverages. Coca-Cola of Japan provides an example. Every year it introduces more than 1,000 new soft drinks, fruit drinks, and cold coffees into the Japanese market. Ninety percent of them fail, but this does not stop Coke from introducing approximately one new product a month. From a cost accounting standpoint this is not a profitable strategy. However, as one Coke executive in Japan puts it, "We know that some of these products will survive only a month or two, but our competitors have them, so we have to have them."[23] As a result, Japan is Coke's most profitable market and the company sells a variety of non-carbonated drinks to complement its main brand.[24]

Quality

For well over a decade, quality has been one of the major criteria for business success.[25] As the president of an international consulting firm puts it, "Products are expected to be nearly perfect."[26] Nowhere is this more clearly reflected than in the auto industry, where the Japanese have garnered a large share of the international market by using what is called ***kaizen***, or continuous improvement.[27] A good example is Toyota Motors, which has continually worked to reduce costs and improve quality. One way Toyota has achieved this goal is partly through large R&D expenditures. Another is through meticulous design, engineering, and production processes that ensure a proper fit of all parts and overall durability of the unit.[28] In recent years US auto manufacturers have also succeeded in improving their

Kaizen
A Japanese term that means continuous improvement

quality, gaining market share as a result. European car makers today are also heavily focused on quality, aware that the Japanese are a major threat to their markets.[29]

Other excellent examples of MNEs that have succeeded because of a strong focus on quality include such lesser-known firms as Stanley Works, the WD-40 Co., and A. T. Cross. Stanley Works manufactures tape measures in Asia, then has the accuracy of samples checked by sophisticated laser computers back in New Britain, Connecticut, before selling them worldwide. Stanley has also developed a host of other high-quality products, from double-toothed saws that cut on both the upstroke and the downstroke for the Asian market, to hammers without claws for carpenters in Central Europe (who prefer to use pliers to pull out bent nails), to levels shaped like elongated trapezoids, which the French market prefers.

The WD-40 Co. of San Diego manufactures WD-40, a water-displacing lubricant that fights rust, cleans heel marks from linoleum and walls, and provides a variety of other services around the house. Car mechanics use it to loosen sticky valves and remove moisture from balky carburetors; odd jobbers apply it to frozen locks and screws. Today the blue-and-yellow spray can is found in stores throughout the world, where it enjoys fanatical customer loyalty. WD-40 is a best-seller in the UK and is rapidly gaining market share throughout Europe and Asia.[30]

A. T. Cross of Providence, Rhode Island, has been manufacturing mechanical pens and pencils for almost 150 years. The units are assembled by hand and "every one of the company's hourly employees is a quality control expert who is responsible for checking the tolerances of the engraved grooves to within one ten-thousandth of an inch and for detecting nearly microscopic scratches or the slightest clotting of ink on a pen ball."[31] A. T. Cross's product quality is so high that, despite a lifetime guarantee, less than 2 percent of its products are ever returned for repair. Today these pens and pencils are one of the most popular US-made gifts in Japan.[32]

Production systems

A **production system** is a group of related activities designed to create value. In the generation of goods and services this system includes location, layout, and material handling.

Location

Location is important because of its impact on production and distribution costs. Many MNEs have found that governments (national and local) are willing to provide tax breaks or other financial incentives to encourage them to set up operations. Accompanying considerations include the availability and cost of labor, raw materials, water, and energy as well as the development of the country's transportation and communication systems. As noted earlier, many suppliers set up operations near their major customers. So Ford has built up an integrated production network in Western Europe (see the map on the Ford Fiesta production network). Ford suppliers are part of this production network so as to maintain their business relationship. Location is also important to service enterprises because they usually require face-to-face contact with their customers. Hotels and airlines are typical examples. Personal service firms such as those of accountants, lawyers, and management consultants also fall into this category.[33]

Layout

Plant layout is important because of its impact on efficiency. For example, most auto producers use an assembly line layout in which the workers remain at their station and, as the cars move past them, perform the necessary functions such as installing radios, air-conditioners, interior trim, and so on. In the case of Volvo, the employees work in small teams to build an entire car and the plant is laid out to accommodate this work flow.[34] In other manufacturing settings, however, worldwide competitive firms tend to use U-shaped-cell flow lines, which

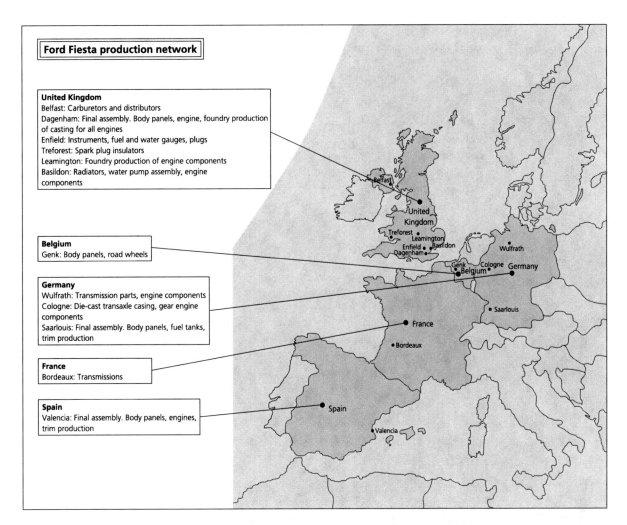

Ford Fiesta production network

United Kingdom
Belfast: Carburetors and distributors
Dagenham: Final assembly. Body panels, engine, foundry production of casting for all engines
Enfield: Instruments, fuel and water gauges, plugs
Treforest: Spark plug insulators
Leamington: Foundry production of engine components
Basildon: Radiators, water pump assembly, engine components

Belgium
Genk: Body panels, road wheels

Germany
Wulfrath: Transmission parts, engine components
Cologne: Die-cast transaxle casing, gear engine components
Saarlouis: Final assembly. Body panels, fuel tanks, trim production

France
Bordeaux: Transmissions

Spain
Valencia: Final assembly. Body panels, engines, trim production

are more efficient. Schonberger, an internationally known manufacturing expert, has noted that U-shaped production designs enable one person to tend several workstations and increase the speed at which materials can be delivered and defective parts can be reworked.[35] Finally, Maytag has chosen to combine different layouts to cater to each production line in just one factory. A traditional long conveyer belt assembly line makes its standardized models. A second area makes more sophisticated models in smaller production cells instead of a long line. The third area makes the most sophisticated machines. In this setting, workers are craftworkers putting together a substantial part of the machine.[36]

Layout varies widely in service organizations, although it appears to be universal in use. Most hotels, regardless of the country, have the check-in and check-out areas in the same place as such support groups as the bellhops, concierge, and cashier. In fast-food units, the food preparation area is situated so that the personnel can quickly serve both in-unit and drive-through customers. In movie theaters, the concession area is located in the lobby and the projection room at the back of the theater.

Material handling

Material handling involves the careful planning of when, where, and how much inventory will be available to ensure maximum production efficiency. Part of this is resolved through careful inventory control processes. Part of it is handled when the production layout is determined. For example, General Electric uses **process mapping**, a flowchart that shows every small step in producing a product. As a result, the company is able to study every part of an

Material handling
The careful planning of when, where, and how much inventory will be available to ensure maximum production efficiency

Process mapping
A flowchart of every step that goes into producing a product

Production Strategy

659

operation and determine those that are redundant or that can be streamlined. Consequently, the company has been able to reduce work time on some jobs by as much as 50 percent.[37]

Inventory control

Just-in-time inventory (JIT)
The delivery of parts and supplies just as they are needed

Inventory control has received a great deal of attention in recent years because a well-designed inventory strategy can have dramatic effects on the bottom line.[38] One of the most popular concepts has been **just-in-time inventory (JIT** for short), which is based on delivering parts and supplies just as they are needed. If this concept were carried to the extreme, it would mean that manufacturers would not need to store materials because suppliers would be delivering them just in time for shipment to the factory floor.

JIT is an important concept that has been adopted by MNEs throughout the world. However, the degree of use varies based on the product and the company's production strategy. For example, the Big Three US auto makers use JIT to keep inventory to a minimum. In Japan, firms like Toyota have taken the concept even further and apply it the same way airlines handle reservations: supply is matched directly to demand. Dealers order directly from the factory, which means that customers can get their built-to-order car in 7 to 10 days.

One of the major problems with JIT is that its success rests heavily on the quality and reliability of the suppliers. In Japan, where MNEs often have an equity position in these companies, suppliers will go out of their way to meet partners' demands. However, in the United States and Europe, most suppliers are independent businesses that work under a contract relationship, so the bonds are often not as strong between the two parties. This helps explain why Toyota, which buys US-made parts for cars made in the United States, also keeps Japanese-made parts on hand as insurance against defective US materials.[39]

A second problem with JIT is that, although it works well in managing delivery of parts to the assembly line, few firms have been able to apply the concept to the entire production process. Most firms still manufacture and ship their output to dealers to sell, in contrast to Toyota's approach of matching supply and demand before producing.

One of the most important things to remember about JIT is that it needs strong support from the workers and the suppliers. Everyone must be operating in unison. If the workers are slow, there will be excess inventory on hand; if the supplier is late, the workers will be sitting by idly.

Demand-Flow™ Technology (DFT)
A production process that is flexible to demand changes

Demand-Flow™ Technology (DFT) is a production process that allows for flexible changes in the middle stages of production. Typically used to produce standardized assembly products, such as computers, DFT permits quick reactions to changes in demand and technology. A surge of demand for Pentium IV computers, for instance, would immediately shift inputs from other computers to be combined with Pentium IV chips to respond to demand. This virtually eliminates inventories.[40] Intermec, a company that makes bar code scanners, mobile computers, and related products, reduced inventory by 50 percent after implementing DFT. It was also able to consolidate five different printer lines into one flexible mixed-model line, decreasing the amount of required manufacturing floor space by 20 percent.[41]

Developing a strong service orientation

As noted earlier, many products have a service element associated with them. Sometimes this element is more important than the product itself. For example, many people will not purchase a car or home appliance unless it can be serviced easily. Service is also important when choosing a bank, insurance agent, lawyer, or doctor. Many of the ideas we have discussed in this section, including sourcing, cost, and quality, are also key factors in shopping for services. In addressing this area, MNEs will do two things: (1) consider whether their strategy needs to be oriented toward a product, a service, or a combination of the two; and (2) determine the ideal degree of service to provide.

Product-dominated businesses	Equally balanced	Service-dominated businesses
Farm produce (corn, wheat, etc.)	Aircraft manufacturing	Advertising agency
Home construction	Fast-food unit	Theater production
Auto production	TV network	Teaching

Figure 10.3 Product- and service-dominated businesses

Determining the product/service balance

Some outputs lend themselves to a strong production orientation, whereas others require much more attention to service. Figure 10.3 offers an illustration. Designed more as a point of reference than as a factual source that addresses every firm in the respective industry, the figure nonetheless shows that some MNEs need to have a strong product-dominated focus whereas others benefit most from a service orientation. A good example is offered by aircraft manufacturers that must be concerned with both ends of the continuum. Olympus and Pentax, both manufacturers of flexible endoscopic equipment, provide another example. To develop their brand names in Latin America, these companies offer medical professionals the surgical training necessary to use their equipment. Because after-sales service is also an important consideration for prospective buyers, including hospitals, all major endoscope manufacturers have service stations in the region.

On the other hand, some manufactured products require far less service than they used to need. A good example is photocopiers. Manufacturers of these machines have improved product quality so substantially that many units are now sold on the basis of price. Service is no longer a major factor because everyone's product is of such high quality.

Knowing whether to sell on the basis of product or service (or a combination of the two) is critical to the success of many MNEs. A mistake at this point can result in emphasis on the wrong sales factors.

Providing the right amount of service

Once the MNE has determined the proper balance of product and service domination, it evaluates the specific type of service warranted. This is particularly important because many MNEs find that the strategy used in their own country does not work overseas. A good example is the Japanese approach to retail services.[42] The amount of personal service provided in Japan would surprise many Westerners. For example, auto dealers typically provide pick-up and delivery for repair service customers and make new car sales calls to customers' homes. In department stores, it is common to find executives and sales clerks alike lined up to bow to the first customers in the store. Japanese banks often help their customers sell or buy homes, find distributors for merchandise, and provide them with tax advice.

Although these services help Japanese companies maintain customer satisfaction, research has found that they are of little value to doing business in other countries. For example, Japanese banks in the United States have discovered that US customers want only a limited amount of quality service; they prefer quantity and efficiency in the form of a variety of different services offered at low prices. As a result, Japanese banks here offer the same types of services as do other US banks. Would they be more successful if they changed this strategy and tried to emulate the approach used back home? Given the nature of the US market, they believe this would be a mistake. The lesson is clear: when competing in terms of service, one must match the competition but not exceed it unless the customer is willing to pay for this service. In the United States, the banking customer is not willing.[43]

Active learning check

Review your answer to Active Learning Case question 2 and make any changes you like. Then compare your answer to the one below.

2 **How has GE used Six Sigma to reduce cost and improve quality in consumer goods? In each case, give an example.**

Six Sigma allows GE to use process mapping to reduce cost by identifying those activities that can be eliminated or combined in the production process. For example, can an individual who is performing one assembly line task take on other tasks and thus reduce the number of people needed to produce the product? Can inventory be ordered and delivered in smaller amounts, thus making greater use of just-in-time? Consideration of these types of questions can help reduce cost. In improving product quality, the work group can examine how well all parts of the product fit together, examine the durability of the unit, and look for additional ways of testing the product to ensure that it measures up to quality standards.

INTERNATIONAL LOGISTICS

International logistics
The designing and managing of a system to control the flow of materials and products throughout the organization

International logistics is the designing and managing of a system to control the flow of materials and products throughout the firm. This includes the inflow of materials, movement through the production process, and outflow to the wholesale/retail firm or final consumer. International logistics is an important area of strategic consideration because these expenses can account for 10 percent of the total costs.[44] The material management aspect of international logistics has already been addressed. The following discussion examines three other key topics: transportation, packaging, and storage.

Transportation

In examining international logistics, we focus on the primary modes of transportation: ocean and air. The others—rail, pipeline, and motor carrier—are of importance in some regions (such as the European Union), but they are not as commonly used in moving goods from an MNE's plant to their final destination. Moreover, their use is highly dependent on the infrastructure of the country—that is, the extensiveness and quality of the nation's road system and rail network. In many non-triad countries the infrastructure is poor and the MNE's use of them is greatly limited.

Ocean shipping

Container ships
Vessels used to carry standardized containers that can be simply loaded onto a carrier and then unloaded at their destination without any repackaging of the contents of the containers

Unconventional cargo vessels
Vessels used for shipping oversized and unusual cargoes

Roll-on–roll-off (RORO) vessels
Ocean-going ferries that can carry wheeled cargo such as automobiles, trailers, and trucks that drive onto built-in ramps and roll off at the point of debarkation

Lighter aboard ship (LASH) vessel
Barges stored on a ship and lowered at the point of destination

International firms can choose from a fairly wide variety of ocean carriers. The three most common carriers are conventional container ships, cargo vessels, and roll-on–roll-off (RORO) vessels. **Container ships** are used to carry standardized containers that can be simply loaded onto the carrier and then unloaded at their destination, without any repackaging of the contents of the containers. **Unconventional cargo vessels** are used for shipping oversized and unusual cargoes. **Roll-on–roll-off (RORO) vessels** are ocean-going ferries that can carry wheeled cargo such as automobiles, trucks, semi-trailer trucks, trailers, or railroad cars that drive onto built-in ramps and roll off at the point of debarkation. A carrier similar to the RORO is the **lighter aboard ship (LASH) vessel**, which consists of barges that are stored on the ship and lowered at the point of destination. These individual barges can then operate on inland waterways.

One of the major problems in planning an ocean shipping strategy is the limitations caused by the lack of ports and port services. In developing countries, for example, seaports sometimes lack the equipment necessary to load or unload container cargo, thus limiting the country's ability to export and import. In recent years a number of Third World countries have been working to improve their ports so they can become more active in the international trade arena.

Air shipping

Most countries have airports that can accommodate air freight. The problem with this mode of transportation is its high cost. Thus, although international air freight has grown dramatically over the last 30 years, it still accounts for less than 1 percent of the total volume of international shipments. It is used in trade more commonly among industrialized nations than any others, and it is usually restricted to high-value items that must reach their destination quickly.

Several developments have occurred over the past couple of decades that have helped increase the use of air shipments. These include more efficient ground facilities, larger aircraft, and better marketing of these services to shippers. In particular, the development by aircraft manufacturers of jumbo cargo jet planes and combination passenger and cargo aircraft has helped immensely.

Choice criteria

In deciding the best transportation mode to use, MNEs tend to focus on four important criteria: time, predictability, cost, and non-economic factors.

Time

The period between departure and arrival of a carrier can vary significantly between an ocean freighter and an aircraft. So one of the questions a firm must answer is: how quickly is delivery needed? A number of factors can influence the answer. One is the perishability of the product. Exotic flowers from South America are flown to the United States because they would not survive a sea voyage. A second factor is how soon the goods are needed to replenish current stocks. Autos from Japan are brought into the United States by ship because the length of the trip does not hurt the supply of cars on hand at local dealerships.

In businesses where speed is critical, companies are now coordinating their worldwide supply chains in order to reduce the amount of time needed to get the goods through the production cycle and to the customer. Victor Fung, CEO of Li & Fung, Hong Kong's largest export trading company and an innovator in the development of supply-chain management, has provided an example of how this is being done:

> Say we get an order from a European retailer to produce 10,000 garments. It's not a simple matter of our Korean office sourcing Korean products or our Indonesian office sourcing Indonesian products. For this customer we might decide to buy yarn from a Korean producer but have it woven and dyed in Taiwan. So we pick the yarn and ship it to Taiwan. The Japanese have the best zippers and buttons, but they manufacture them mostly in China. Okay, so we go to YKK, a big Japanese zipper manufacturer, and we order the right zippers from their Chinese plants. Then we determine that, because of quotas and labor conditions, the best place to make the garments is Thailand. So we ship everything there. And because the customer needs quick delivery, we may divide the order across five factories in Thailand. Effectively, we are customizing the value chain to best meet the customer's needs. Five weeks after we have received the order, 10,000 garments arrive on the shelves in Europe, all looking like they came from one factory, with colors, for example, perfectly matched.[45]

Predictability

Although both air and water transportation are basically reliable, they are subject to the vagaries of nature. Bad weather can close an airport; inadequate seaport facilities can slow the loading and unloading of cargo. Because of the great difference in delivery time between the two modes, the choice is often obvious. If a company needs to have a package delivered tomorrow, it will come by air; if the firm wants to clear merchandise out of the warehouse today but the international customer does not need it for 90 days, it will be sent by water. However, certain carriers are more reliable than others, and the MNE will use its experience in determining which companies to choose for delivery. Reliability is particularly important for air shipments, where a difference of one day could significantly influence the salability of the product.

Cost

The expense associated with shipping is a major consideration when choosing an international transportation mode. Because air freight is significantly more costly than shipment by water, the cost must be economically justifiable. Typically, an MNE will use air shipments only when time is critical and/or the product has high value. For example, if the company has purchased expensive watches in Zurich for its specialty outlets in New York and San Francisco, the watches will be flown to the retailers. Similarly, if a London-based MNE has bought a US-made supercomputer for the home office and wants it installed immediately, the unit will be flown over from the United States. On the other hand, if the merchandise is bulky or the cost of air freight is a significant portion of the value of the product, it will be sent by water. Autos are exported by ship, as are bulk commodities and resources such as oil and coal.

Non-economic factors

Sometimes non-economic factors influence the choice of transportation mode. For example, in the United States all government cargo must use national flag carriers when available, so there is seldom a question of how to send these goods. Similarly, other governments own or subsidize their carriers, and there is pressure on MNEs to use these transportation modes when doing business with those countries. Such political considerations must be taken into account when formulating the transportation strategy.

Packaging

Packaging is important in ensuring that a product is shipped in a safe container and arrives undamaged. When goods are transported a long distance or to areas with climates different from the one where they are manufactured, the container can prevent spoilage or leakage. Chemicals, for example, must be carefully sealed in containers that can withstand impact and will not crack open if tipped over or dropped. Machines, such as personal computers, must have interior packing that prevents damage during transit.

Packaging is also important because of its direct effect on cost. If units must be shipped in odd-shaped containers, fewer of them can be loaded into the hold of the transport than if they are shipped in square or rectangular containers and can be loaded atop and alongside each other. The weight of the packing material is also important, especially when goods are being shipped by air and costs are based on both distance and weight.

Intermodal containers
Large metal boxes that fit on trucks, railroad trains, and aircraft and help reduce handling costs and theft losses by placing the merchandise in a tightly sealed, easy-to-move unit

Packaging is also important in reducing loading and unloading costs and minimizing theft and pilferage. In recent years many shippers have begun using **intermodal containers**, which are large metal boxes that fit on trucks, railroad trains, and aircraft and help cut handling costs and theft losses by placing the merchandise in an easy-to-move unit that is tightly sealed.

As more goods are shipped internationally, packaging will continue to be a focal point of attention. Such considerations can help an MNE maximize shipping space and minimize transportation costs.

Storage

In some cases, goods that are shipped internationally have to be stored before being moved to their final destinations. In the United States, public storage is widely available. In other countries, including Japan, warehousing facilities are in short supply. Additionally, the configuration of many warehouses is different from that in the United States. Ceilings are often lower and there is little automation for handling such common chores as loading and unloading packages or stacking containers on top of each other. In such cases, the MNE must decide whether to invest in warehouse facilities or ship goods only when needed, thus eliminating the warehouse function.

Foreign trade zones
Areas where foreign goods may be held and processed and then re-exported without incurring customs duties (same as a free trade zone)

As discussed in Chapter 6, some countries have **foreign trade zones**, which are areas where foreign goods may be held and processed and then re-exported without incurring customs duties (same as a free trade zone). These zones are usually found at major ports of entry (including international air terminals). Their effective use can help an MNE: (1) temporarily store its goods while breaking a large shipment into smaller ones to be shipped to other locales; (2) combine small shipments into larger ones and then reship them; (3) process the goods and perform a host of value-added activities before repackaging them for the market; and (4) give those goods that will remain in the local market a "made in" status so that they can be sold as locally produced products.

An effective storage strategy can be particularly helpful in carrying out the final stages of an MNE's production plan. The strategy can also help minimize overall product cost, reduce delivery time, and increase customer satisfaction.[46]

DIFFERENT KINDS OF GLOBAL PRODUCTION SYSTEMS

Location is a key factor in deciding the global structure of firms' production systems. But it needs to be considered alongside other factors which vary considerably by industry.

Companies tend to focus on the functions and innovation activities where they have the major advantage and often outsource activities, or parts of the value chain where they add less value. This determines the "boundaries" of the firm, what activities are internalized, and what are externalized or left to other firms to provide on a contract basis. Figure 10.4 shows a number of example industries and firms that have very different global production systems, determined by the functions and activities that add the most value.

Although Intel does a lot of marketing, its main competitive advantage lies in the continual development of new semiconductors, the heart of PCs and other IT and electronic devices. Product and process development are internalized and highly centralized because this suits the type of technology and product that the firm focuses on. It alone accounts for

Production system / Where is the value added?	Internalized (within the firm's hierarchy)	Mixed	Externalized (to other firms in the market)
R&D/technology	Example: semiconductors (Intel)		Example: telecoms (Ericsson)
Manufacturing		Example: autos (Toyota)	
Marketing			Example: clothing (Gap)

Figure 10.4 Global production systems: where is the value added?

Source: Adapted from UNCTAD, *World Investment Report 2002.*

around 25 percent of all R&D investment in the semiconductor industry. Much of its high-value manufacturing, particularly wafer production and fabrication, is done in the United States, where 75 percent of its manufacturing workforce is based. Other production sites are in Israel and Ireland. Much of its labor-intensive assembly and testing takes place in Malaysia, the Philippines, China, and Costa Rica, but is owned by Intel (internalized).

Ericsson also keeps much of its research, design, and development activities within the firm but not so long ago decided to let other firms make many of the components that make up its telecom systems. In 2001 Flextronics, a $14.5 billion Singaporean firm, took over much of Ericsson's manufacturing and supply-chain activities in Brazil, Malaysia, Sweden, and the UK. It externalized these activities because it decided they were not part of its core competencies, and it could safely contract other firms to supply these components. (See Real Case: Flextronics at the end of this chapter.)

Gap Inc. and other clothing firms have externalized the manufacturing function for many years now. Their focus is clothing design, marketing, branding, and real estate management. There are enough producers in cheap labor locations (such as China, which exports more garments than any other country by far) for Gap to use the market to contract out this activity to the cheapest and/or best. Intermediaries in this industry, like Flextronics in telecoms, include Mast Industries, which works with 400 factories in 37 countries, and Li & Fung, a $5 billion Hong Kong company that connects around 700 US and European brand owners with a network of 7,500 suppliers (1.5 million workers) around the world (of which 2,000 are active at any one time).

Toyota lies in the middle of these two extremes. Because manufacturing, and particularly maintaining continuous improvement in manufacturing, is so central to its competitive advantage, Toyota is partly vertically integrated down the supply chain. New product development (new car models and features) and process development (improving price and quality) are closely linked and involve good relationships with (and/or ownership of some) component suppliers. It cannot externalize car production because it is the source of many of its core competitive advantages.

Finally, for diversified or multiproduct firms, configuring the right kind of global production system can get complicated. Philips, for example, makes semiconductors, like Intel, but also has large consumer electronics and consumer products divisions. It has to manage both technology-driven and market-driven innovation and production activities.

STRATEGIC MANAGEMENT AND PRODUCTION STRATEGY

MNEs are currently focusing on a number of areas in improving their production strategies. Three that are getting particular attention include (1) technology and design, (2) continuous improvement of operations, and (3) the use of strategic alliances and acquisitions.

Technology and production design

MNEs are now spending more money on R&D than they have in the past. For example, Aventis, Eli Lilly, AstraZeneca, and Pfizer spend over 15 percent of their revenues on R&D, which provides the backroom for the introduction of new pharmaceutical products.[47] Yet, R&D is not only developing new products, but also helping firms find alternative parts as well as production techniques.

A second current trend is the use of concurrent engineering, which was discussed earlier in the chapter. Many MNEs are now realizing that a team approach to product development, which combines the talents of research, design, and manufacturing people as well as customers and clients, results in a more successful product. Ford Motors is an excellent example. Ford put together a group called Team Taurus to develop its Taurus and Sable automobile lines. Team members were drawn from designing, engineering, and production and were brought together with customers. Collectively the group discussed how to build the new cars and replaced the sequential approach to manufacturing autos (first design the cars, then produce them, then market them) with a concurrent approach that involved addressing the design, production, and marketing issues all at the same time. The result of this strategy was a Taurus that captured a significant market niche and helped Ford close the gap between itself and the competition.[48]

Coupled with these strategies are innovative human resource development programs that are designed around the concept of **empowerment**, which involves giving employees greater control over their work. This strategy is particularly effective because it creates a feeling of pride and ownership in the job and makes employees feel they are important assets. The use of empowerment is not limited to the research and design areas; it is important in all phases of production, beginning with product creation. Additionally, if things go smoothly at this early stage of the production cycle, there are likely to be fewer problems later on.

Empowerment
The process of giving employees increased control over their work

Continuous improvement

Due to the success of Japanese MNEs, *kaizen* (continuous improvement) has been emulated by MNEs worldwide. No matter what the good or service is, every day the company tries to do the job better. Some consultants have referred to this strategy as "rapid inch-up,"[49] which certainly captures the essence of the concept. US firms in particular have benefited from this idea. A good example can be found in the automotive industry. In the 1980s and 1990s, Toyota and Honda were able to offset the rising value of the yen with cost saving in their factories, thus allowing them to hold the price line on many of their new cars. These innovations were exported to US plants. By the early 2000s, however, US firms had successfully fought back by imitating and improving Japanese production techniques. In 2004, four of the five most efficient auto plants in the United States were owned by GM.[50]

A large number of firms helped account for these results. One is Xerox, internationally known for its photocopiers. At the beginning of the 1980s the company was losing market share to overseas competitors. However, the firm then began implementing a production strategy for dramatically improving quality and reducing cost. Today Xerox is again a world leader in copiers.

Another example is TPG, which services Ford's Toronto factory by arranging for 800 deliveries a day from 300 parts makers. The parts arrive at 12 different stages of production within 10 minutes of scheduled time to decrease the amount of parts inventory in the plant.[51]

As discussed in an earlier section, JIT is a related concept that the MNEs are using to achieve continuous improvement. In the past JIT was used almost exclusively for managing inventory, but now the concept is being employed in other ways. For example, Toyota's use of JIT helps it assemble a car in 13 labor-hours, compared to 19 to 22 labor-hours for Honda, Nissan, and Ford.

Alliances and acquisitions

Another current strategic production trend is the development of alliances and acquisitions. Many MNEs are finding they cannot compete effectively without entering into joint ventures or other alliances with MNEs that can complement their production strategy. For example, Compaq is well known for its personal computers, but many of the components in these machines are purchased from outside suppliers or are developed by these firms under an alliance agreement. When Compaq needed a hard disk drive for its first laptops, it financed Conner Peripherals, a Silicon Valley start-up with a disk drive already underway, rather than develop the machine inhouse. More recently, Compaq has ventured into the market for powerful desktop workstations used primarily by scientists and engineers. Instead of going head-to-head with market leaders such as Sun Microsystems and HP, the company assembled a dozen hardware and software firms, including these two computer giants, and put together an alliance aimed at defining a new technical standard for high-speed desktop computing. The objective of the alliance is to develop a standard that will suit any workstation, thus allowing customers the freedom to buy the latest, fastest machine without fear of being tied to any single manufacturer.

Compaq's approach is not unique; the Japanese *keiretsu* system has been using it for years.[52] In fact, some researchers claim that industry alliances account for more of the success of Japanese firms than does JIT or any other manufacturing technique. Working in unison with each other, *keiretsu* companies have been able to wield a great deal of power. Many have monthly meetings in which they exchange information and ideas. Table 10.2 provides a brief overview of two of the country's major *keiretsu* members. Looking closely at the table, we see that it illustrates how valuable cooperation among the members can be. The idea has not been lost on US firms, among others, which are now beginning to put together their own "mini-*keiretsus*." For example, Eastman Kodak has acquired a number of distributors in Japan and has taken small stakes in some 50 suppliers and customers, and

Table 10.2 The Mitsubishi and Mitsui *keiretsu* in Japan

	Mitsubishi	Mitsui
Financial services and insurance	BOT Lease	Mitsui & Co. Financial Services Ltd.
	DC Cash One	Mitsui Leasing & Development
	kabu.com Securities	P.T. Bussan Auto Finance
	MEIJI Dresdner Asset Management	
	Mitsubishi Auto Leasing Corporation	
	Mitsubishi Corporation Capital	
	Mitsubishi Corporation Futures & Securities	
	Mitsubishi Electric Credit	
	Mitsubishi UFJ Asset Management	
	Mitsubishi UFJ Capital	
	Mitsubishi UFJ Financial Group	
	Mitsubishi UFJ Lease & Finance	
	Mitsubishi UFJ NICOS	
	Mitsubishi UFJ Personal Financial Advisers	
	Mitsubishi UFJ Securities	
	Mitsubishi UFJ Trust and Banking	
	MMC Diamond Finance	
	The Bank of Tokyo-Mitsubishi UFJ	
	The Mitsubishi UFJ Factors	
	Union Bank of California N.A.	
Computers, electronics, and electrical equipment	DIA Instruments	
	Meiryo Technica	
	Meldas System Engineering	
	Mitsubishi Electric Business Systems	
	Mitsubishi Electric	
	Mitsubishi Electric Engineering	
	Mitsubishi Electric Lighting	
	Mitsubishi Electric OSRAM	
	Mitsubishi Electric Plant Engineering	
	Mitsubishi Electric System & Service	
	Mitsubishi Precision	
	Ryoden Koki Engineering	

	Mitsubishi	Mitsui
Motor vehicles	Mitsubishi Motors	Asahi Tec Corporation
	Mitsubishi Automotive Engineering	Japan Automobile Auction Inc.
	Mitsubishi Fuso Truck & Bus	Komatsu Australia Pty. Ltd.
		Mitsui Automotive Europe B.V.
		MMK CO., LTD.
		P.T. Bussan Auto Finance
		Penske Automotive Group, Inc.
		PT Yamaha Indonesia Motor Manufacturing
		Toyota Canada Inc.
		Toyota Chile S.A.
Food and beverages	Dai-Nippon Meiji Sugar	Dai-Ichi Broiler Co., Ltd.
	Kirin Beverage	Hokushuren Company Limited
	Kirin Brewery	Kadoya Sesame Mills Incorporated
	Kirin Holdings Company Limited	Mcm Foods B.V.
	Kirin Yakult NextStage	Mikuni Coca-Cola Bottling Co., Ltd.
	Koiwai Dairy Products	Mitsui Foods Co., Ltd.
	KOIWAI FARM	Mitsui Norin Co., Ltd.
	Nagano Tomato	Mitsui Sugar Co., Ltd.
	Ryoshoku	San-Ei Sucrochemical Co., Ltd.
		Vendor Service Co., Ltd.
		Wilsey Foods, Inc.
Construction	Hiroshima Ryoju Kousan	Mitsui Bussan Construction Materials Co.
	Kakoki Plant & Environment Engineering	
	Kinki Ryoju Estate	
	The Kodensha	
	KOIWAI FARM	
	Mitsubishi Cable Industries	
	Mitsubishi Chemical Engineering	
	Mitsubishi Chemical Functional Products	
	Mitsubishi Electric Building Techno-Service	
	Mitsubishi Estate	
	Mitsubishi Estate Home	
	Mitsubishi Materials Techno	
	Mitsubishi Rayon Engineering	
	P.S. Mitsubishi Construction	
	Ryoju Estate	
	Ryoken Kiso	
Metals, mining, and forestry	Metal One Corporation	Mitsui Bussan Construction Materials Co., Ltd.
	Mitsubishi Corporation Technos	Nippon Steel Trading Co., Ltd.
	Mitsubishi Nagasaki Machinery Mfg.	Regency Steel Asia Pte Ltd.
	Mitsubishi Steel Mfg.	Seikei Steel Tube Corp.
	Ryoko Lime Industry	Shanghai Bao-Mit Steel Distribution Co., Ltd.
	Mitsubishi Aluminum	Sintsuda Corporation
	Mitsubishi Materials	Thai Tinplate Manufacturing Co., Ltd.
	Mitsubishi Materials Natural Resources Dev.	Tokyo Kohtetsu Co., Ltd.
	Mitsubishi Nuclear Fuel	
	Mitsubishi Shindoh	
	Onahama Smelting and Refining	
	Ryotec	
	Sambo Copper Alloy	
Real estate	Chitose Kosan	Bussan Community Company
	Hiroshima Ryoju Kousan	Bussan Real Estate Co., Ltd.
	IMS	Mbk Real Estate Europe Limited
	Kinki Ryoju Estate	Sumisho & Mitsuibussan Kenzai Co., Ltd.

Table 10.2 (Continued)

	Mitsubishi	Mitsui
	Marunouchi Yorozu	
	Mitsubishi Electric Life Service	
	Mitsubishi Estate Building Management	
	Mitsubishi Estate	
	Mitsubishi Estate Home	
	Mitsubishi Jisho Property Management	
	Mitsubishi Jisho Retail Property Mgmt.	
	Mitsubishi Jisho Towa Community	
	Mitsubishi Real Estate Services	
	Mitsubishi UFJ Real Estate Services	
	Ryoju Estate	
	Sotsu Corporation	
	Tamachi Building	
	Yokohama Sky Building	
Resources and energy	Astomos Energy Corporation	BHP Mitsui Coal Pty. Ltd.
	Marunouchi Heat Supply	Japan Australia LNG (MIMI) Pty. Ltd.
	Mitsubishi Chemical Functional Products	Kokusai Oil & Chemical Co., Ltd.
	Mitsubishi Gas Chemical Company	Kyokuto Petroleum Industries, Ltd.
	Mitsubishi Heavy Industries	MitEnergy Upstream LLC
	Nippon Oil	Mitsui Coal Holdings Pty. Ltd.
	Nippon Petroleum Refining	Mitsui E&P Australia Pty Limited
		Mitsui E&P Middle East B.V.
		Mitsui Gas Development Qatar B.V.
		Mitsui Liquefied Gas Co., Ltd.
		Mitsui LNG Nederland B.V.
		Mitsui Oil Co., Ltd.
		Mitsui Oil Exploration Co., Ltd.
		Mitsui Sakhalin Holdings B.V.
		Mittwell Energy Resources Pty., Ltd.
		United Petroleum Development Co., Ltd.
Chemicals	Asahi Glass	Advanced Composites, Inc.
	DIA Instruments	Agro Kanesho Co., Ltd.
	Kirin Pharma	Bussan Chemicals Co.,Ltd.
	Mitsubishi Chemical America	Daito Chemical Co., Ltd.
	Mitsubishi Chemical	Honshu Chemical Industry Co., Ltd.
	Mitsubishi Chemical Functional Products	Japan-Arabia Methanol Company Ltd.
	Mitsubishi Chemical Holdings	Mitsui AgriScience International SA/NV
	Mitsubishi Chemical Medience	Mitsui Bussan Agro Business Co., Ltd.
	Mitsubishi Chemical MKV	Mitsui Bussan Plastics Co., Ltd.
	Mitsubishi Engineering-Plastics	Mitsui Bussan Solvent & Coating Co., Ltd.
	Mitsubishi Gas Chemical Company	Mitsui Electronics Asia Pte. Ltd.
	Mitsubishi Pharma	Nippon Trading Co., Ltd.
	Mitsubishi Plastics	Novus International, Inc.
	Mitsubishi Polyester Film	P.T. Kaltim Pasifik Amoniak
	Mitsubishi Rayon America	Salt Asia Holdings Pty. Ltd
	Mitsubishi Rayon	Sanko Gosei Ltd.
	Mitsubishi Shoji Plastics	Soda Aromatic Co., Ltd.
	Nippon Polypenco	Tensho Electric Industries Co., Ltd.
	Tokyo Shokai	TG Missouri Corporation

Sources: The individual websites of each business group (www.mitsubishi.co.jp and www.mitsui.co.jp).

IBM is investing venture capital in a host of small European computer-related firms. Motorola has not taken equity positions, but it uses a *keiretsu* approach by developing extremely close ties with suppliers.

✔ Active learning check

Review your answer to Active Learning Case question 3 and make any changes you like. Then compare your answer to the one below.

 In what way could best practices help GE develop more effective international strategies? Explain.

Best practices could help GE develop more effective international strategies by encouraging it to identify those MNEs that are most successful and then discover how they accomplish that feat. Do these firms manage to develop more new products than do their competitors? Or are they best at getting their new goods into the marketplace quickly? Do they produce the highest-quality goods? Or are they lowest-cost producers? What accounts for their ability to achieve such an excellent performance? By asking and answering these questions, GE can gain insights into how it needs to change its own production processes in order to emulate those MNEs successfully.

KEY POINTS

1 Many of today's goods and services will be replaced in the future with faster, more efficient, and cheaper substitutes. For this reason, MNEs need to continually research, develop, and bring new offerings to the marketplace. One way this is being done is through the use of time-to-market accelerators. A good example is concurrent engineering.

2 The generation of goods and services entails a number of specific functions. One is obtaining materials or supplies. Many MNEs have found that global sourcing is the best strategy because it helps keep down costs while providing a number of other benefits, including ensuring an ongoing source of supply and helping the company penetrate overseas markets.

3 In the production of goods and services, MNEs focus on a number of key factors, including cost, quality, and well-designed production systems. While these three factors are often interrelated, each merits specific attention. Multinationals have also developed very effective inventory control systems that help minimize carrying costs and increase productivity. Attention is also focused on gaining the proper balance between production and service domination. Figure 10.3 illustrates this point.

4 International logistics is the designing and managing of a system to control the flow of materials and products throughout the firm. In addition to inventory control, this involves transportation, packaging, and storing.

5 MNEs are currently focusing on a number of areas in improving their production strategies. Three approaches that have been receiving particular attention include (a) technology and design, (b) continuous improvement of operations, and (c) the use of strategic alliances and acquisitions. These approaches are helping multinationals meet new product and service challenges while keeping costs down and quality up.

Key terms

- backward integration
- forward integration
- horizontal integration
- time-to-market accelerators
- modular integrated robotized system (MIRB)
- concurrent engineering
- global sourcing
- modular manufacturing
- *kaizen*
- production system
- material handling
- process mapping
- just-in-time inventory (JIT)
- Demand-Flow™ Technology (DFT)
- international logistics
- container ships
- unconventional cargo vessels
- roll-on–roll-off (RORO) vessels
- lighter aboard ship (LASH) vessels
- intermodal containers
- foreign trade zones
- empowerment

Review and discussion questions

1 Why are MNEs so interested in new product development? Why do they not simply focus on improving their current offerings?

2 Why is speed-to-market such an important production strategy? Explain.

3 What are time-to-market accelerators? In what way is concurrent engineering one of these accelerators?

4 Why do many MNEs use global sourcing? Why do they not produce all the parts and materials in-house? Be complete in your answer.

5 Why are world-class suppliers often located next to world-class manufacturers? What forms of synergy often exist between the two groups?

6 How do MNEs try to cut production costs? Identify and describe three steps.

7 In what way is the continuous reduction cost method used by Japanese manufacturers different from the periodic cost reduction method employed by many US firms? Compare and contrast the two.

8 Some MNEs use a production strategy that involves costing a portfolio of related goods rather than just costing each individually. What is the logic behind this strategy?

9 How does *kaizen* help bring about increased quality? Is this approach limited to Japanese firms or are other MNEs using it as well?

10 What types of issues does an MNE confront when it seeks to improve its production system? Identify and describe three.

11 How does JIT help an MNE control its inventory? Give two examples.

12 How is employee training an important factor in implementing JIT and DFT production processes?

13 Why would an MNE want to determine the degree to which its primary business was product dominated and service dominated? Explain.

14 Why are MNEs concerned with international logistics? How does this help the companies increase their competitiveness?

15 In recent years MNEs have been focusing on a number of areas in improving their production strategies. What are two of these? Identify and describe each.

Flextronics

You wouldn't think that company rivals such as Sony and Phillips, or Ericsson, Alcatel, and Motorola, would choose to share the same factories to build competing products, but that is just what has been happening since the emergence of electronic manufacturing service providers (EMSPs). Contract manufacturing has become a sweeping trend in electronics manufacturing. Companies unknown to the public, such as Flextronics, Sanmina-SCI, Celestica, and Jabil, among others, now make such well-known products as IBM PCs, the Microsoft Xbox video console, Web TV set-top boxes for Phillips and Sony, and portable phones for Ericsson, Alcatel, and Motorola. In 2006, EMSP industry revenues were estimated at over $200 billion. In 2007 two of the largest EMSP companies, Flextronics and Solectron, combined when Flextronics, with revenues of $18.854 billion, acquired Solectron, with revenues of $10.561 billion.

Flextronics, the largest EMSP, is one of the *Fortune* Global 500 companies, but most end-customers who use its products have never heard of it. Incorporated in Singapore in 1990, the company has design, engineering, and manufacturing operations in 29 countries across the world. Though officially headquartered in Singapore, the company has strong ties to the US market and most of its customers are US companies.

Flextronics specializes in handheld electronic devices, IT infrastructure, communications infrastructure, and computer and office automation. Over the years it has expanded by purchasing smaller EMSP contractors and factories from its customers. In 2001, Flextronics purchased half of Xerox's office equipment-making operations for $220 million. The deal came with a five-year outsourcing contract for Flextronics to manufacture Xerox products. Currently its 10 largest customers, including Sony–Ericsson, Motorola, and Hewlett-Packard, account for about 64 percent of net sales from continuing operations.

In 2003, only 35.9 percent of Flextronics revenues originated in its home-region market of Asia. More specifically, China is the company's largest market; 18 percent of all revenues originate there. Another 15 percent of its sales originate in Malaysia, while Mexico and Hungary account for 12 percent and 11 percent, respectively. No other country accounts for more than 10 percent of Flextronics's revenues.

Because of lower transportation costs as a percentage of total value, electronics can be transported by air, whereas cars are always transported by sea. This is one main reason why contract manufacturing has been so

Source: Cobris/Thomas White/Reuters

successful in the electronics industry, where parts might travel the world over before the product is finished.

Prior to the merger with Solectron, Flextronics had six industrial parks in low-cost regions near each large triad market. In Asia, two industrial parks in China and a network of regional manufacturing facilities supply printers, cell phones, telephone switching boards, and PDAs, among other products. In the Americas, products from its two industrial parks (one in Mexico, one in Brazil) and its network of manufacturing facilities include automotive, telecommunications, networking equipment, and hardware products, among others. In Eastern Europe, Poland and Hungary host two industrial parks that are also supported by nearby manufacturing facilities and that produce telecommunications infrastructure, electronics for automotives, printers, and disposable cameras, among others.

The choice of location for production facilities is determined by the quality of the labor force, the cost of producing in the country, and the proximity to a triad market. Mexico, for example, is the low-cost region in the North American market. Brazil has the best industrial capabilities among countries in South America and strong ties to large international firms from Europe and North America. China has abundant labor, high expected economic growth, and proximity to the large Japanese market where international firms like Canon, NEC, and Sony are headquartered. Eastern Europe is the low-cost production area for West European markets. It is no surprise that the Flextronics industrial park in Poland is located near a university from which it can acquire skilled labor.

EMSPs do much more than provide cost-effective manufacturing. They help in the design of products to make them easier to manufacture; they also provide logistics services, such as material procurement, inventory management, vendor management, packaging and distribution, and automation of key components of the supply chain through advanced IT. In addition, they offer after-market services such as repair and warranty services.

Today's electronic manufacturers have come a long way from the cheap labor-based contractors that used to dominate the industry. Robotic automation is now a significant part of the production process and is handled mostly by specialists. It is their manufacturing expertise that makes for lower costs, but EMSPs provide many more advantages to OEMs. They decrease the risk of manufacturing because OEMs no longer need to make large investments in a new factory to create a new product that might or might not be successful. EMSPs can also purchase inputs at lower prices because they are making cell phones not only for Alcatel, but also for Motorola and Ericsson, increasing their purchasing power.

Contract manufacturing accounts for less than one-fourth of electronic manufacturing; however, there are reasons to believe that EMSP companies will dominate the industry in the future. This process will redefine the role of OEMs in the electronics industry to one of design and marketing.

Sources: Karyn McCormack, "Flextronics Adds a Key Part," *Business Week*, June 4th, 2007; http://www.businessweek.com/investor/; "Have Factory, Will Travel," *The Economist*, February 10, 2000; "Let the Bad Times Roll," *The Economist*, April 5, 2001; Jonathan Sprague, "Invasion of the Factory Snatchers," *Fortune*, August 15, 2002; "Xerox Sells Half Its Plants for $220 Million," BBC.co.uk, October 2, 2001; Flextronics, *Annual Report*, 2002; www.flextronics.com/en/.

1 Keeping in mind that Flextronics does not sell to end-customers, how does that change your interpretation of the regional sales data presented in this case?

2 What effect does the emergence of EMSPs have for new entrants into the electronics industry?

3 Why should OEMs be concerned about using EMSPs?

Real Case

Nike

One of the rules of international production strategy is: manufacture the highest-quality product and the world is likely to beat a path to your door. A number of firms help illustrate this rule. One is Nike, the sports shoe producer. Making a wide variety of high-quality shoes, Nike catalogues more than 800 models for use in approximately 25 sports. In 1999 it had 35 percent of the world's market for training shoes (and 45 percent in the United States). In 2007 its sales were over $16 billion. In an effort to keep ahead of the competition, Nike updates each shoe at least every six months. Most of these ideas are generated by Nike's R&D center in Beaverton, near Portland, Oregon, where physiologists and mechanical engineers study the stresses on an athlete's feet and collaborate with stylists on new shoe ideas.

The aim of the takeover of Umbro in 2007 was to extend these scale advantages.

Although Nike sells its products in over 140 countries and produces in more than 50, it is really a triad MNE. Over 92 percent of its sales are in the triad markets of the United States, the European Union, and Asia. In 2000 there was a 15 percent growth of sales in the EU, due mainly to a new distribution facility in Belgium and a new design house in Holland. Nike is still strong in its home market, with 40 percent of all sales in the US athletic footwear market and more than 65 percent of the basketball footwear market. About 60 percent of its sales are still in its US home base.

Nike's high-quality production is matched by superb marketing skills. The world might be beating a path to Nike's door, but the company makes sure the world knows where it is. It spends 11 percent of its revenue on marketing, and its "swoosh" brand is recognized the world over. The company continues to use sports stars to endorse its products. Besides American stars like Tiger Woods and Andre Agassi, it has used European soccer players and cricket players in India, and has gone to China for the 2008 Olympic Games in Beijing. The idea is: if you can make the "cool" guys wear your products, the rest will follow.

Perhaps the only thing Nike does not like to be remembered for is the bad publicity around its labor practices in Asia. Nike has outsourced all of its production to low-wage areas. In 2004, China produced 36 percent of its footwear, Vietnam 24 percent, Indonesia 22 percent, and Thailand 16 percent. The remainder is manufactured in other developing countries. In addition, all its apparel is produced in 35 host countries by contract manufacturers. NGOs have criticized the poor working conditions in some of its Asian factories, from Pakistani children stitching Nike's soccer balls to Vietnamese working in unsafe conditions. NGOs in the Western world started campaigns to boycott Nike, and demonstrators protested in front of Nike's stores. Allegations of long working hours, bad ventilation, and physical abuse of a mostly young female workforce have tarnished Nike's reputation.

Nike's industry dominance was a main reason for its being severely targeted. Many of its competitors were found to have the same labor practices, but were not subjected to the same level of criticism. More recently Nike has acknowledged its corporate responsibility to improve working conditions in its own factories and help influence its suppliers.

Website: www.nike.com.

Sources: Adapted from Dylan Jones, "No More Mr. Nike Guy," *Sunday Times Magazine*, August 23, 1998; David Shook, "Why Nike is Dragging its Feet," *Business Week*, March 19, 2001; Sydney H. Schanberg, "On the Playgrounds of America, Every Kid's Goal Is to Score: In Pakistan, Where Children Stitch Soccer Balls for Six Cents an Hour, the Goal Is to Survive," *Life*, June 1996; Harry Dunphy, "Nike to Improve Conditions," *Associated Press*, May 12, 1998; Tom Braithwaite, "Nike Moves Closer to Deal for Umbro," *Financial Times*, December 21, 2007; Nike, *Annual Report*, 2000; www.nike.com.

1 What is the key to Nike's production strategy? Explain.

2 What are the advantages of frequent design changes in Nike's sneakers?

3 Why was it important for Nike to clean up its labor practices in Asia? What more should the company do?

ENDNOTES

1 "(Still) Made in Japan," *The Economist*, April 7, 2004.

2 Also see Emily Thornton, "Mazda Learns To Like Those Intruders," *Business Week*, September 14, 1998, p. 172.

3 Alex Taylor III, "How Toyota Copes with Hard Times," *Fortune*, January 25, 1993, pp. 78–81; and Joah Muller and Katie Kerwin, "Detroit Is Cruising for Quality," *Business Week*, September 3, 2001.

4 For a good example of these challenges, see Ferdinand Protzman, "Daimler's Quest Collides with Slump," *New York Times*, August 3, 1993, pp. C1, C5.

5 C. W. L. Hill, *International Business: Competing in the Global Marketplace*, 3rd ed. (New York: McGraw-Hill, 2000); and http://www.hp.com.

6 Simon C. Collinson, "Knowledge Management Capabilities in R&D: A UK-Japan Company Comparison," *R&D Management*, vol. 31, no. 3 (2001), pp. 335–347.

7 Nohria, N. and Ghoshal, S. *The Differentiated Network: Organizing Multinational Corporations for Value Creation* (San Francisco: Jossey-Bass, 1997).

8 Malnight, T. W. "Emerging Structural Patterns within Multinational Corporations: Toward Process-based Structures," *Academy of Management Journal*, vol. 44, no. 6 (2001); and Hansen, M. T. and Løvås, B. "How Do Multinational Companies Leverage Technological Competencies? Moving from Single to Interdependent Explanations," *Strategic Management Journal*, vol. 25, no. 8/9 (2004).

9 See Don Clark, "Intel to Ship Its Next-Generation Chip in 1995, Boosts Outlay for Production," *Wall Street Journal*, January 28, 1994, p. B5.

10 Gene Bylinsky, "Heroes of US Manufacturing," *Fortune*, March 20, 2000.

11 Also see C. K. Prahalad and Kenneth Lieberthal, "The End of Corporate Imperialism," *Harvard Business Review*, July/August 1998, pp. 69–79.

12 Joseph T. Vesey, "The New Competitors: They Think in Terms of 'Speed-to-Market'," *Academy of Management Executive*, May 1991, pp. 23–33; and "Re-inventing the Wheel," *The Economist*, April 20, 2000.

13 Saul Hansell, "Is This the Factory of the Future?" *New York Times*, July 26, 1998, Section 3, pp. 1, 12.

14 Rebecca Blumenstein, "GM Is Building Plants in Developing Nations to Woo New Markets," *Wall Street Journal*, August 4, 1997, pp. A1, 5.

15 Gene Bylinsky, "Heroes of US Manufacturing," *Fortune*, March 20, 2000.

16 Larry Holyoke, William Spindle and Neil Gross, "Doing the Unthinkable," *Business Week*, January 10, 1994, pp. 52–53; and Andrew Pollack, "Nissan Plans to Buy More American Parts," *New York Times*, March 26, 1994, pp. 17, 26.

17 Michael E. Porter, *The Competitive Advantage of Nations* (New York: Free Press, 1990), p. 103.

18 For more on this, see Earl Landesman, "Ultimatum for US Auto Suppliers: Go Global or Go Under," *Journal of European Business*, May/June 1991, pp. 39–45.

19 "The Modular T," *The Economist*, September 3, 1998; and David Welch, "Why Detroit is Going to Pieces," *Business Week*, September 3, 2001.

20 Larry Reibstein et al., "A Mexican Miracle?" *Newsweek*, May 20, 1991, p. 42.

21 Ernest Beck, "Why Foreign Distillers Find It So Hard to Sell Vodka to the Russians," *Wall Street Journal*, January 15, 1998, pp. A1, 8.

22 Ford S. Worthy, "Japan's Smart Secret Weapon," *Fortune*, August 12, 1991, pp. 72–75.

23 Ibid., p. 75.

24 Suh-kyung Yoon, "Working Up a Thirst to Quench Asia," *Far Eastern Economic Review*, February 1, 2001.

25 See Louis Kraar, "Korea Goes for Quality," *Fortune*, April 13, 1994, pp. 153–159; and Gale Eisenstodt, "Sullivan's Travels," *Forbes*, March 28, 1994, pp. 75–76.

26 Erick Calonius, "Smart Moves by Quality Champs," *Fortune*, Spring/Summer 1991, p. 24.

27 See, for example, Christopher Palmeri, "A Process That Never Ends," *Forbes*, December 21, 1992, pp. 52–54.

28 "The Car Company in Front," *Economist.com*, January 27, 2005.

29 Richard A. Melcher and Stewart Toy, "On Guard, Europe," *Business Week*, December 14, 1992, pp. 54–55.

30 Louis S. Richman, "What America Makes Best," *Fortune*, Spring/Summer 1991, p. 80.

31 Ibid., p. 81.

32 Michael Shari and Pete Engardio, "The Sweet Sound of Success," *Business Week*, September 8, 1997, p. 56.

33 See Michael E. McGrath and J. Gordon Stewart, "Professional Service Firms in Europe Move Toward Integrated European Practices," *Journal of European Business*, May/June 1991, pp. 26–30.

34 Steven Prokesch, "Edges Fray on Volvo's Brave New Humanistic World," *New York Times*, July 7, 1991, p. F5.

35 Richard J. Schonberger, *Building a Chain of Customers* (New York: Free Press, 1990), pp. 50–51.

36 "A Long March," *Economist.com*, July 12, 2001.

37 Thomas A. Stewart, "GE Keeps Those Ideas Coming," *Fortune*, August 12, 1991, p. 48.

38 Lucinda Harper, "Trucks Keep Inventories Rolling Past Warehouses to Production Line," *Wall Street Journal*, February 7, 1994, p. B3.

39 Alex Taylor III, "Why Toyota Keeps Getting Better and Better and Better," *Fortune*, November 19, 1990, p. 79.

40 Gene Bylinsky, "Heroes of U.S. Manufacturing," *Fortune*, March 20, 2000.

41 "Intermec Recognized for Its Use of Demand Flow™ Technology," *Intermec News Release*, May 21, 1997.

42 David A. Aaker, "How Will the Japanese Compete in Retail Services?" *California Management Review*, Fall 1990, pp. 54–67.

43 For still other examples of service-related problems in Japan, see Jon Woronoff, *The Japanese Management Mystique: The Reality Behind the Myth* (Chicago: Probus, 1992), pp. 120–124.

44 "A Moving Story," *Economist.com*, December 5, 2002.

45 Joan Magretta, "Fast, Global, and Entrepreneurial: Supply Chain Management, Hong Kong Style: An Interview with Victor Fung," *Harvard Business Review*, September/October 1998, pp. 105–106.

46 See, for example, Hellene S. Runtagh, "GE Tracks Transportation and Distribution Opportunities in the EC," *Journal of European Business*, September/October 1990, pp. 22–25.

47 See Alan M. Rugman and Cecilia Brain, "Regional Strategies of Multinational Pharmaceutical Firms," *Management International Review*, vol. 44, no. 3 (2004), pp. 7–25.

48 Vesey op. cit.

49 Ibid.

50 "Fighting Back," *The Economist*, September 2, 2004.

51 "A Moving Story," *Economist.com*, December 5, 2002.

52 See "Breaking Japan's *Keiretsu*," *The Economist*, March 20, 2003.

ADDITIONAL BIBLIOGRAPHY

Adler, Paul S. and Cole, Robert E. "Designed for Learning: A Tale of Two Auto Plants," *Sloan Management Review*, vol. 34, no. 3 (Spring 1993).

Ambos, Björn and Schlegelmilch, Bodo B. "The Use of International R&D Teams: An Empirical Investigation of Selected Contingency Factors," *Journal of World Business*, vol. 39, no. 1 (February 2004).

Bellak, Christian and Cantwell, John. "Revaluing the Capital Stock of International Production," *International Business Review*, vol. 13, no. 1 (February 2004).

Bhappu, Anita D. "The Japanese Family: An Institutional Logic for Japanese Corporate Networks and Japanese Management," *Academy of Management Review*, vol. 25, no. 2 (April 2000).

Brouthers, Lance Eliot, Werner, Steve and Matulich, Erika. "The Influence of Triad Nations' Environments on Price-Quality Product Strategies and MNC Performance," *Journal of International Business Studies*, vol. 31, no. 1 (Spring 2000).

Cantwell, John. "Innovation and Information Technology in the MNE," in Alan M. Rugman and Thomas Brewer (eds.), *The Oxford Handbook of International Business* (Oxford: Oxford University Press, 2001).

Collins, R. and Schmenner, R. "Taking Manufacturing Advantage of Europe's Single Market," *European Management Journal*, vol. 13, no. 3 (May/June 1995).

Collinson, Simon C. "Organising Knowledge to Manage R&D: A UK-Japan Company Comparison," *R&D Management*, vol. 31, no. 3 (2001).

Cusumano, Michael A. "Manufacturing Innovation: Lessons from the Japanese Auto Industry," *Sloan Management Review*, vol. 30, no. 1 (Fall 1988).

Douglas, Susan P. and Wind, Yoram. "The Myth of Globalization," *Columbia Journal of World Business*, vol. 22, no. 4 (Winter 1987).

DuBois, Frank L., Toyne, Brian and Oliff, Michael D. "International Manufacturing Strategies of US Multinationals: A Conceptual Framework Based on a Four-Industry Study," *Journal of International Business Studies*, vol. 24, no. 2 (Second Quarter 1993).

Flaherty, M. Therese. "Global Sourcing Strategy: R&D, Manufacturing, and Marketing Interfaces," *Journal of International Business Studies*, vol. 24, no. 1 (First Quarter 1993).

Frost, Tony S. and Zhou, Changhui. "R&D Co-Practice and 'Reverse'; Knowledge Integration in Multinational Firms," *Journal of International Business Studies*, vol. 36, no. 6 (November 2005).

Griffith, David A. and Myers, Matthew B. "The Performance Implications of Strategic Fit of Relational Norm Governance Strategies in Global Supply Chain Relationships," *Journal of International Business Studies*, vol. 36, no. 3 (2005).

Hagedoorn, John, Cloodt, Danielle and Kanenburg, Hans van. "Intellectual Property Rights and the Governance of International R&D Partnerships," *Journal of International Business Studies*, vol. 36, no. 2 (2005).

Hansen, Morten T. and Løvås, Bjorn. "How Do Multinational Companies Leverage Technological Competencies? Moving from Single to Interdependent Explanations," *Strategic Management Journal*, vol. 25, nos. 8/9 (2004).

Hodgetts, Richard. *Measures of Quality and High Performance: Simple Tools and Lessons from America's Most Successful Firms* (New York: Amacom, 1998).

Kotabe, Masaaki. "The Relationship Between Offshore Sourcing and Innovativeness of US Multinational Firms: An Empirical

Investigation," *Journal of International Business Studies*, vol. 21, no. 4 (Fourth Quarter 1990).

Kotabe, Masaaki and Murray, Janet Y. "Linking Product and Process Innovations and Modes of International Sourcing in Global Competition: A Case of Foreign Multinational Firms," *Journal of International Business Studies*, vol. 21, no. 3 (Third Quarter 1990).

Kotabe, Masaaki and Omura, Glenn S. "Sourcing Strategies of European and Japanese Multinationals: A Comparison," *Journal of International Business Studies*, vol. 20, no. 1 (Spring 1989).

Levy, David L. "Lean Production in an International Supply Chain," *Sloan Management Review*, vol. 38, no. 2 (Winter 1997).

Malnight, Thomas W. "Emerging Structural Patterns within Multinational Corporations: Toward Process-based Structures," *Academy of Management Journal*, vol. 44, no. 6 (2001).

Nohria, Nitin and Ghoshal, Sumantra. *The Differentiated Network: Organizing Multinational Corporations for Value Creation* (San Francisco: Jossey-Bass, 1997).

Ojah, Kalu and Monplaisir, Leslie. "Investors' Valuation of Global Product Design and Development," *Journal of International Business Studies*, vol. 34, no. 5 (September 2003).

Patel, Pari and Pavitt, Keith. "Large Firms in the Production of the World's Technology: An Important Case of 'Non-Globalization'," *Journal of International Business Studies*, vol. 22, no. 1 (First Quarter 1991).

Quinn, James Brian and Hilmer, Frederick G. "Strategic Outsourcing," *Sloan Management Review*, vol. 35, no. 4 (Summer 1994).

Reddy, Prasada. "New Trends in Globalization of Corporate R&D and Implications for Innovation Capability in Host Countries: A Survey from India," *World Development*, vol. 25, no. 11 (November 1997).

Rehder, Robert R. "Building Cars as if People Mattered: The Japanese Lean System vs. Volvo's Uddevalla System," *Columbia Journal of World Business*, vol. 27, no. 2 (Summer 1992).

Rondinelli, Dennis and Berry, Michael, "Multimodal Transportation, Logistics, and the Environment: Managing Interactions in a Global Economy," *European Management Journal*, vol. 18, no. 4 (August 2000).

Rugman, Alan M. and Bennett, Jocelyn. "Technology Transfer and World Product Mandating," *Columbia Journal of World Business*, vol. 17, no. 4 (Winter 1982).

Rugman, Alan M. and Brain, Cecilia. "Regional Strategies of Multinational Pharmaceutical Firms," *Management International Review*, vol. 44, Special Issue 3 (2004).

Rugman, Alan M. and Verbeke, Alain. "Subsidiary-specific Advantages in Multinational Enterprises," *Strategic Management Journal*, vol. 22, no. 3 (March 2001).

Serapio, Manuel G., Jr. "Macro-Micro Analyses of Japanese Direct R&D Investments in the US Automotive and Electronics Industries," *Management International Review*, vol. 33, no. 3 (Third Quarter 1993).

Sobek, Durward K. II, Ward, Allen C. and Liker, Jeffrey K. "Toyota's Principles of Set-Based Concurrent Engineering," *Sloan Management Review*, vol. 40, no. 2 (Winter 1999).

Swamidass, Paul M. and Kotabe, Masaaki. "Component Sourcing Strategies of Multinationals: An Empirical Study of European and Japanese Multinationals," *Journal of International Business Studies*, vol. 24, no. 1 (First Quarter 1993).

Vandermerwe, Sandra. "Increasing Returns: Competing for Customers in the Global Market," *Journal of World Business*, vol. 32, no. 4 (Winter 1997).

Yip, George S. "Global Strategy. In a World of Nations?" *Sloan Management Review*, vol. 31, no. 1 (Fall 1989).

Section 6
International Knowledge Networks and Technology

Chapter 1
Innovation management: an introduction

Introduction

There is extensive scope for examining the way innovation is managed within organisations. Most of us are well aware that good technology can help companies achieve competitive advantage and long-term financial success. But there is an abundance of exciting new technology in the world and it is the transformation of this technology into products that is of particular concern to organisations. There are numerous factors to be considered by the organisation, but what are these factors and how do they affect the process of innovation? The Apple case study at the end of this chapter illustrates how difficult decisions still remain even after the launch of a successful product.

Chapter contents

The importance of innovation
The study of innovation
    Recent and contemporary studies
The need to view innovation in an organisational context
    Individuals in the innovation process
Problems of definition and vocabulary
    Entrepreneurship
    Design
    Innovation and invention
    Successful and unsuccessful innovations
    Different types of innovation
    Technology and science
Popular views of innovation
Models of innovation
    Serendipity
    Linear models
    Simultaneous coupling model
    Interactive model
Innovation as a management process
    A framework for the management of innovation
    Open innovation and the need to share and exchange knowledge
        (network models)
    Innovation and new product development
Case study: The success of the iPod raises the licensing question for
    Apple . . . again

Learning objectives

When you have completed this chapter you will be able to:

- recognise the importance of innovation;

- explain the meaning and nature of innovation management;

- provide an introduction to a management approach to innovation;

- appreciate the complex nature of the management of innovation within organisations;

- describe the changing views of innovation over time;

- recognise the role of key individuals within the process; and

- recognise the need to view innovation as a management process.

Corporations must be able to adapt and evolve if they wish to survive. Businesses operate with the knowledge that their competitors will inevitably come to the market with a product that changes the basis of competition. The ability to change and adapt is essential to survival.

Today, the idea of innovation is widely accepted. It has become part of our culture – so much so that it verges on becoming a cliché. But even though the term is now embedded in our language, to what extent do we fully understand the concept? Moreover, to what extent is this understanding shared? A scientist's view of innovation may be very different from that of an accountant in the same organisation.

The Apple Inc. story in Illustration 1.1 puts into context the subject of innovation and new product development. In this case Apple's launch of a new product in the mobile phone market will help Apple generate increases in revenue and grow the firm. Innovation is at the heart of many companies' activities. But to what extent is this true of all businesses? And why are some businesses more innovative than others? What is meant by innovation? And can it be managed? These are questions that will be addressed in this book.

'. . . not to innovate is to die,' wrote Christopher Freeman (1982) in his famous study of the economics of innovation. Certainly companies that have established themselves as technical and market leaders have shown an ability to develop successful new products. In virtually every industry, from aerospace to pharmaceuticals

Illustration 1.1

Apple branches out with iPhone and set-top boxes

Apple yesterday laid out ambitious plans to broaden its early lead in the digital entertainment business, announcing an iPod mobile phone and an Apple TV set-top box that together could extend the US technology company's reach into big new consumer electronics markets.

Speaking at Apple's annual MacWorld trade show in San Francisco, Steve Jobs, chief executive, claimed the widely anticipated cellular device, the iPhone, represented a breakthrough.

'Apple is going to reinvent the phone,' he declared, showing off a thin, handheld device with a 3.5-inch screen that displays touch-screen controls.

Describing the gadget as 'the ultimate digital device,' Mr Jobs said it would play music and video, display emails and act as a handset for web browsing.

The iPhone will cost from $499 (£257) and will go on sale in the US in June, with European sales to begin in the second half of this year and Asia in 2008, Apple said.

The Apple TV set-top box, with a 40Gb hard drive, will be available in February for $299.

Mr Jobs said Apple hoped to corner 1 per cent of the global handset market by 2008, a goal that would mean sales of 10m iPhone units.

The new products, which come as Mr Jobs continues to face scrutiny for his role in options backdating at the company, sent shares in Apple up 6.4 per cent to $91.12 by mid-afternoon in New York.

In a further sign of the company's transition, Mr Jobs announced that Apple Computer would henceforth be known simply as 'Apple'.

Source: *Financial Times*, 10 January 2007. Reprinted with permission.

and from motor cars to computers, the dominant companies have demonstrated an ability to innovate (*see* Table 1.1). Furthermore, in *Business Week*'s 2006 survey of the world's most innovative companies these same firms are delivering impressive growth and/or return to their shareholders (*see* Table 1.2).

A brief analysis of economic history, especially in the United Kingdom, will show that industrial technological innovation has led to substantial economic benefits for the innovating *company* and the innovating *country*. Indeed, the industrial revolution

Table 1.1 **Market leaders in 2007**

Industry	Market leaders	Innovative new products and services
Cell phones	Nokia	Design and new features
Internet-related industries	eBay; Google	New services
Pharmaceuticals	Pfizer; GlaxoSmithKline	Impotence; ulcer treatment drug
Motor cars	Toyota; BMW	Car design and associated product developments
Computers and software development	Intel; IBM and Microsoft; SAP	Computer chip technology, computer hardware improvements and software development

Table 1.2 **World's most innovative companies**

2006 Rank	Company	Margin growth 1995–2005 %	Stock returns 1995–2005 %
1	Apple	7.1	24.6
2	Google	NA	NA
3	3M	3.4	11.2
4	Toyota	10.7	11.8
5	Microsoft	2.0	18.5
6	General Electric	5.7	13.4
7	Procter & Gamble	4.4	12.6
8	Nokia	0.0	34.6
9	Starbucks	2.2	27.6
10	IBM	−0.7	14.4
11	Virgin	NA	NA
12	Samsung	−4.5	22.7
13	Sony	−11.0	5.1
14	Dell	2.0	39.4
15	IDEO	NA	NA
16	BMW	9.1	14.2
17	Intel	−0.3	13.8
18	eBay	13.0	NA
19	IKEA	NA	NA
20	Wal-Mart	1.9	16.2

Source: *Business Week*, 24 April 2006.

Table 1.3 Nineteenth-century economic development fuelled by technological innovations

Innovation	Innovator	Date
Steam engine	James Watt	1770–80
Iron boat	Isambard Kingdom Brunel	1820–45
Locomotive	George Stephenson	1829
Electromagnetic induction dynamo	Michael Faraday	1830–40
Electric light bulb	Thomas Edison and Joseph Swan	1879–90

of the nineteenth century was fuelled by technological innovations (*see* Table 1.3). Technological innovations have also been an important component in the progress of human societies. Anyone who has visited the towns of Bath, Leamington and Colchester will be very aware of how the Romans contributed to the advancement of human societies. The introduction over 2,000 years ago of sewers, roads and elementary heating systems is credited to these early invaders of Britain.

Pause for thought

Not all firms develop innovative new products, but they still seem to survive. Do they thrive?

The study of innovation

Innovation has long been argued to be the engine of growth. It is important to note that it can also provide growth almost regardless of the condition of the larger economy. Innovation has been a topic for discussion and debate for hundreds of years. Nineteenth-century economic historians observed that the acceleration in economic growth was the result of technological progress. However, little effort was directed towards understanding *how* changes in technology contributed to this growth.

Schumpeter (1934, 1939, 1942) was among the first economists to emphasise the importance of *new products* as stimuli to economic growth. He argued that the competition posed by new products was far more important than marginal changes in the *prices* of existing products. For example, economies are more likely to experience growth due to the development of products such as new computer software or new pharmaceutical drugs than to reductions in prices of existing products such as telephones or motor cars. Indeed, early observations suggested that economic development does not occur in any regular manner, but seemed to occur in 'bursts' or waves of activity, thereby indicating the important influence of external factors on economic development.

This macro view of innovation as cyclical can be traced back to the mid-nineteenth century. It was Marx who first suggested that innovations could be associated with waves of economic growth. Since then others such as Schumpeter (1934, 1939), Kondratieff (1935/51), and Abernathy and Utterback (1978) have

A review of the history of economic growth

The classical economists of the eighteenth and nineteenth centuries believed that technological change and capital accumulation were the engines of growth. This belief was based on the conclusion that productivity growth causes population growth, which in turn causes productivity to fall. Today's theory of population growth is very different from these early attempts at understanding economic growth. It argues that rising incomes slow the population growth because they increase the rate of opportunity cost of having children. Hence, as technology advances, productivity and incomes grow.

Joseph Schumpeter was the founder of modern growth theory and is regarded as one of the world's greatest economists. In the 1930s he was the first to realise that the development and diffusion of new technologies by profit-seeking entrepreneurs formed the source of economic progress. Robert Solow, who was a student of Schumpeter, advanced his professor's theories in the 1950s and won the Nobel Prize for economic science. Paul Romer has developed these theories further and is responsible for the modern theory of economic growth, sometimes called neo-Schumpeterian economic growth theory, which argues that sustained economic growth arises from competition among firms. Firms try to increase their profits by devoting resources to creating new products and developing new ways of making existing products. It is this economic theory that underpins most innovation management and new product development theories.

Source: Adapted from M. Parkin *et al.* (1997) *Economics*, 3rd edn, Addison-Wesley, Harlow.

argued the long-wave theory of innovation. Kondratieff was unfortunately imprisoned by Stalin for his views on economic growth theories, because they conflicted with those of Marx. Marx suggested that capitalist economies would eventually decline, whereas Kondratieff argued that they would experience waves of growth and decline. Abernathy and Utterback (1978) contended that at the birth of any industrial sector there is radical product innovation which is then followed by radical innovation in production processes, followed, in turn, by widespread incremental innovation. This view was once popular and seemed to reflect the life cycles of many industries. It has, however, failed to offer any understanding of *how* to achieve innovative success.

After the Second World War economists began to take an even greater interest in the causes of economic growth (Harrod, 1949; Domar, 1946). One of the most important influences on innovation seemed to be industrial research and development. After all, during the war, military research and development (R&D) had produced significant technological advances and innovations, including radar, aerospace and new weapons. A period of rapid growth in expenditure by countries on R&D was to follow, exemplified by US President Kennedy's 1960 speech outlining his vision of getting a man on the moon before the end of the decade. But economists soon found that there was no *direct* correlation between R&D spending and national rates of economic growth. It was clear that the linkages were more complex than first thought (this issue is explored more fully in Chapter 8).

There was a need to understand *how* science and technology affected the economic system. The neo-classical economics approach had not offered any explanations.

A series of studies of innovation were undertaken in the 1950s which concentrated on the internal characteristics of the innovation process within the economy. A feature of these studies was that they adopted a cross-discipline approach, incorporating economics, organisational behaviour and business and management. The studies looked at:

- the generation of new knowledge;
- the application of this knowledge in the development of products and processes;
- the commercial exploitation of these products and services in terms of financial income generation.

In particular, these studies revealed that firms behaved differently (*see* Simon, 1957; Woodward, 1965; Carter and Williams, 1959). This led to the development of a new theoretical framework that attempted to understand how firms managed the above, and why some firms appeared to be more successful than others. Later studies in the 1960s were to confirm these initial findings and uncover significant differences in organisational characteristics (Myers and Marquis, 1969; Burns and Stalker, 1961; Cyert and March, 1963). Hence, the new framework placed more emphasis on the firm and its internal activities than had previously been the case. The firm and how it used its resources was now seen as the key influence on innovation.

Neo-classical economics is a theory of economic growth that explains how savings, investments and growth respond to population growth and technological change. The rate of technological change influences the rate of economic growth, but economic growth does not influence technological change. Rather, technological change is determined by chance. Thus population growth and technological change are exogenous. Also, neo-classical economic theory tends to concentrate on industry or economy-wide performance. It tends to ignore differences among firms in the same line of business. Any differences are assumed to reflect differences in the market environments that the organisations face. That is, differences are not achieved through choice but reflect differences in the situations in which firms operate. In contrast, research within business management and strategy focuses on these differences and the decisions that have led to them. Furthermore, the activities that take place within the firm that enable one firm seemingly to perform better than another, given the same economic and market conditions, has been the focus of much research effort since the 1960s.

The Schumpeterian view sees firms as different – it is the way a firm manages its resources over time and develops capabilities that influences its innovation performance. The varying emphasis placed by different disciplines on explaining how innovation occurs is brought together in the framework in Figure 1.1. This overview of the innovation process includes an economic perspective, a business management strategy perspective and organisational behaviour which attempts to look at the internal activities. It also recognises that firms form relationships with other firms and trade, compete and cooperate with each other. It further recognises that the activities of individuals within the firm also affect the process of innovation.

Each firm's unique organisational architecture represents the way it has constructed itself over time. This comprises its internal design, including its functions and the relationships it has built up with suppliers, competitors, customers, etc. This framework recognises that these will have a considerable impact on a firm's innovative performance. So too will the way it manages its individual functions and its

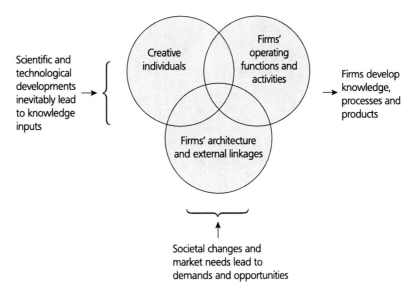

Scientific and technological developments inevitably lead to knowledge inputs

Creative individuals

Firms' operating functions and activities

Firms develop knowledge, processes and products

Firms' architecture and external linkages

Societal changes and market needs lead to demands and opportunities

Figure 1.1 **Overview of the innovation process**

employees or individuals. These are separately identified within the framework as being influential in the innovation process.

Recent and contemporary studies

As the twentieth century drew to a close there was probably as much debate and argument concerning innovation and what contributes to innovative performance as a hundred years ago. This debate has, nonetheless, progressed our understanding of the area of innovation management. It was Schumpeter who argued that modern firms equipped with R&D laboratories have become the central innovative actors. Since his work others have contributed to the debate (Chandler, 1962; Nelson and Winter, 1982; Cohen and Levinthal, 1990; Prahalad and Hamel, 1990; Pavitt, 1990; Patel and Pavitt, 2000). This emerging Schumpeterian or evolutionary theory of dynamic firm capabilities is having a significant impact on the study of business and management today. Success in the future, as in the past, will surely lie in the ability to acquire and utilise knowledge and apply this to the development of new products. Uncovering how to do this remains one of today's most pressing management problems.

The importance of uncovering and satisfying the needs of customers is the important role played by marketing and these activities feed into the new product development process. Recent studies by Hamel and Prahalad (1994) and Christensen (2003) suggest that listening to your customer may actually stifle technological innovation and be detrimental to long-term business success. Ironically, to be successful in industries characterised by technological change, firms may be required to pursue innovations that are not demanded by their current customers. Christensen (2003) distinguishes between 'disruptive innovations' and 'sustaining innovations' (radical or incremental innovations). Sustaining innovations appealed to existing customers, since they provided improvements to established products. For example, the introduction of new computer software usually provides improvements for existing customers in terms of added features. Disruptive innovations tend to provide improvements greater than those demanded. For example, while the introduction of 3.5-inch disk drives to replace 5.25-inch drives provided an enormous improvement in performance, it also created problems for users who were familiar with the previous format. These disruptive innovations also tended to create new markets, which eventually captured the existing market (see Chapter 15 for much more on this).

The need to view innovation in an organisational context

During the early part of the nineteenth century manufacturing firms were largely family oriented and concentrated their resources on one activity. For example, one firm would produce steel from iron ore, another would roll this into sheet steel for use by, say, a manufacturer of cooking utensils. These would then be delivered to shops for sale. Towards the latter part of the century these small enterprises were gradually replaced by large firms that would perform a much wider variety of activities. The expansion in manufacturing activities was simultaneously matched by an expansion in administrative activities. This represented the beginnings of the development of the diversified functional enterprise. The world expansion in trade during the early part of the twentieth century saw the quest for new markets by developing a wide range of new products (Chandler, 1962).

Unfortunately, many of the studies of innovation have treated it as an artefact that is somehow detached from knowledge and skills and not embedded in know-how. This inevitably leads to a simplified understanding, if not a misunderstanding, of what constitutes innovation. This section shows why innovation needs to be viewed in the context of organisations and as a process within organisations.

The diagram in Figure 1.1 shows how a number of different disciplines contribute to our understanding of the innovation process. It is important to note that firms do not operate in a vacuum. They trade with each other, they work together in some areas and compete in others. Hence, the role of other firms is a major factor in understanding innovation. As discussed earlier, economics clearly has an important role to play. So too does organisational behaviour as we try to understand what activities are necessary to ensure success. Studies of management will also make a significant contribution to specific areas such as marketing, R&D, manufacturing operations and competition.

As has been suggested, in previous centuries it was easier in many ways to mobilise the resources necessary to develop and commercialise a product, largely because the resources required were, in comparison, minimal. Today, however, the resources required, in terms of knowledge, skills, money and market experience, mean that significant innovations are synonymous with organisations. Indeed, it is worthy of note that more recent innovations and scientific developments, such as significant discoveries like cell phones or computer software and hardware developments, are associated with organisations rather than individuals (see Table 1.4). Moreover, the increasing depth of our understanding of science inhibits the breadth of scientific study. In the early part of the twentieth century, for example, ICI was regarded as a world leader in chemistry. Now it is almost impossible for chemical companies to be scientific leaders in all areas of chemistry. The large companies have specialised in particular areas. This is true of many other industries. Even

Table 1.4 **More recent technological innovations**

Date	New product	Responsible organisation
1930s	Polythene	ICI
1945	Ballpoint pen	Reynolds International Pen Company
1950s	Manufacturing process: float glass	Pilkington
1970/80s	Ulcer treatment drug: Zantac	GlaxoSmithKline
1970/80s	Photocopying	Xerox
1980s	Personal computer	Apple Computer
1980/90s	Computer operating system: Windows 95	Microsoft
1995	Impotence drug: Viagra	Pfizer
2000s	Cell phones	Motorola/Nokia
2005	MP3 players	Creative; Apple

university departments are having to concentrate their resources on particular areas of science. They are no longer able to offer teaching and research in all fields. In addition, the creation, development and commercial success of new ideas require a great deal of input from a variety of specialist sources and often vast amounts of money. Hence, today's innovations are associated with groups of people or companies. Innovation is invariably a team game. This will be explored more fully in Chapters 3, 6 and 15.

Pause for thought

If two different firms, similar in size, operating in the same industry spend the same on R&D, will their level of innovation be the same?

Individuals in the innovation process

Figure 1.1 identifies individuals as a key component of the innovation process. Within organisations it is individuals who define problems, have ideas and perform creative linkages and associations that lead to inventions. Moreover, within organisations it is individuals in the role of managers who decide what activities should be undertaken, the amount of resources to be deployed and how they should be carried out. This has led to the development of so-called key individuals in the innovation process such as inventor, entrepreneur, business sponsor, etc. These are discussed in detail in Chapter 3.

Problems of definition and vocabulary

While there are many arguments and debates in virtually all fields of management, it seems that this is particularly the case in innovation management. Very often these centre on semantics. This is especially so when innovation is viewed as a single event. When viewed as a *process*, however, the differences are less substantive. At the heart of this book is the thesis that innovation needs to be viewed as a process. If one accepts that inventions are new discoveries, new ways of doing things, and that products are the eventual outputs from the inventions, that process from new discovery to eventual product is the innovation process. A useful analogy would be education, where qualifications are the formal outputs of the education process. Education, like innovation, is not and cannot be viewed as an event.

Arguments become stale when we attempt to define terms such as new, creativity or discovery. It often results in a game of semantics. First, what is new to one company may be 'old hat' to another. Second, how does one judge success in terms of commercial gain or scientific achievement? Are they both not valid and justified goals in themselves? Third, it is context dependent – what is viewed as a success today may be viewed as a failure in the future. We need to try to understand how to encourage innovation in order that we may help to develop more successful new products (this point is explored in Chapters 11 and 12).

Entrepreneurship

In the United States the subject of innovation management is often covered in terms of 'entrepreneurship'. Indeed, there are many courses available for students in US business schools on this topic. In a study of past and future research on the subject of entrepreneurship, Low and MacMillan (1988) define it as 'the process of planning, organising, operating, and assuming the risk of a business venture'.

It is the analysis of the role of the individual entrepreneur that distinguishes the study of entrepreneurship from that of innovation management. Furthermore, it is starting small businesses and growing them into large and successful businesses that is the focus of attention of those studying entrepreneurship. For example, the *Sunday Times* reported how the founder of *The Source*, Daniel Mitchell, developed and grew his business from zero to sales of £35 million. Mitchell argues that 'success is about customers, but it is also about the people you employ' (*Sunday Times*, 2004). Illustration 1.3 shows the remarkable entrepreneurial skills of an 8-year-old boy.

Design

The definition of design with regard to business seems to be widening ever further and encompassing almost all aspects of business (*see* the Design Council, www.Designcouncil.com). For many people design is about developing or creating something; hence we are into semantics regarding how this differs from innovation. Hargadon and Douglas (2001: 476) suggest design is concerned with the emergent arrangement of concrete details that embody a new idea. A key question, however, is how design relates to research and development. Indeed, it seems that in most cases the word *design* and the word *development* mean the same thing. Traditionally design referred to the development of drawings, plans and sketches. Indeed, most dictionary definitions continue with this view today and refer to a designer as a 'draughtsman who makes plans for manufacturers or prepares drawings for clothing or stage productions' (*Oxford English Dictionary*, 2005). In the aerospace industry engineers and designers would have previously worked closely together for many years, developing drawings for an aircraft. Today the process is dominated by

Penny apples – selling them thrice over

In his autobiography the Irish entrepreneur Billy Cullen (2003) tells the story of how, as an 8-year-old boy, he demonstrated sharp entrepreneurial skills. In a poverty stricken area of Dublin young Billy would buy wooden crates of apples for a shilling and then sell the apples on a Saturday afternoon to the hundreds of local people who would flock to watch their local football team play. This provided Billy with a healthy profit of a shilling if he could sell all the apples. But, his entrepreneurial skills did not stop there. He would then take the wooden apple boxes to the football ground and sell them for a penny to people at the back of the crowds so that they could stand on the box for a better view. And finally,

when the match had finished Billy would collect up the wooden boxes, break them up and sell them in bundles for firewood.

computer software programmes that facilitate all aspects of the activity; hence the product development activities and the environments in which design occurs have changed considerably. Figure 1.2 shows, along the horizontal axis, the wide spectrum of activities that design encompasses from clothing design to design within

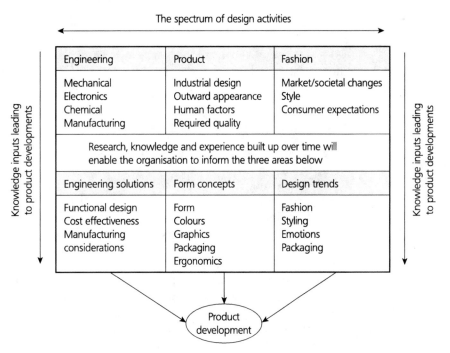

Figure 1.2 **The interaction between development activities and design environment**

electronics. The vertical axis shows how the areas of design feed into outputs from choice of colour to cost effectiveness; all of which are considered in the development of a product. The view taken by this book is to view design as an applied activity within research and development, and to recognise that in certain industries, like clothing for example, design is the main component in product development. In other industries, however, such as pharmaceuticals, design forms only a small part of the product development activity.

Innovation and invention

Many people confuse these terms. Indeed, if you were to ask people for an explanation you would collect a diverse range of definitions. It is true that innovation is the first cousin of invention, but they are not identical twins that can be interchanged. Hence, it is important to establish clear meanings for them.

Innovation itself is a very broad concept that can be understood in a variety of ways. One of the more comprehensive definitions is offered by Myers and Marquis (1969):

> *Innovation is not a single action but a total process of interrelated sub processes. It is not just the conception of a new idea, nor the invention of a new device, nor the development of a new market. The process is all these things acting in an integrated fashion.*

It is important to clarify the use of the term 'new' in the context of innovation. Rogers and Shoemaker (1972) do this eloquently:

> *It matters little, as far as human behaviour is concerned, whether or not an idea is 'objectively' new as measured by the lapse of time since its first use or discovery . . . If the idea seems new and different to the individual, it is an innovation.* [emphasis added]

Most writers, including those above, distinguish innovation from invention by suggesting that innovation is concerned with the *commercial and practical application* of ideas or inventions. Invention, then, is the conception of the idea, whereas innovation is the subsequent translation of the invention into the economy (US Dept of Commerce, 1967). The following simple equation helps to show the relationship between the two terms:

Innovation = theoretical conception + technical invention + commercial exploitation

However, all the terms in this equation will need explanation in order to avoid confusion. The *conception* of new ideas is the starting point for innovation. A new idea by itself, while interesting, is neither an invention nor an innovation; it is merely a concept or a thought or collection of thoughts. The process of converting intellectual thoughts into a tangible new artefact (usually a product or process) is an *invention*. This is where science and technology usually play a significant role. At this stage inventions need to be combined with hard work by many different people to convert them into products that will improve company performance. These later activities represent *exploitation*. However, it is the *complete* process that represents *innovation*. This introduces the notion that innovation is a process with a number of distinctive features that have to be managed. This is the view taken by this book. To summarise, then, innovation depends on inventions but inventions need to be harnessed to commercial activities before they can contribute to the growth of an organisation. Thus:

Illustration 1.4

An example of an invention

Scientists and development engineers at a household cleaning products company had been working for many months on developing a new lavatory cleaning product. They had developed a liquid that when sprayed into the toilet pan, on contact with water, would fizz and sparkle. The effect was to give the impression of a tough, active cleaning product. The company applied for a patent and further developments and market research were planned.

However, initial results both from technical and market specialists led to the abandonment of the project. The preliminary market feedback suggested a fear of such a product on the part of consumers. This was because the fizz and sparkle looked too dramatic and frightening. Furthermore, additional technical research revealed a short shelf-life for the mixture. This is a clear example of an invention that did not progress beyond the organisation to a commercial product.

Innovation is the management of all the activities involved in the process of idea generation, technology development, manufacturing and marketing of a new (or improved) product or manufacturing process or equipment.

This definition of innovation as a management process also offers a distinction between an innovation and a product, the latter being the output of innovation. Illustration 1.4 should help to clarify the differences.

It is necessary at this point to cross-reference these discussions with the practical realities of managing a business today. The senior vice-president for research and development at 3M, one of the most highly respected and innovative organisations, recently defined innovation as:

Creativity: the thinking of novel and appropriate ideas. Innovation: the successful implementation of those ideas within an organisation.

Successful and unsuccessful innovations

There is often a great deal of confusion surrounding innovations that are not commercially successful. A famous example would be the Kodak Disc Camera or the Sinclair C5. This was a small, electrically driven tricycle or car. Unfortunately for Clive Sinclair, the individual behind the development of the product, it was not commercially successful. Commercial failure, however, does not relegate an innovation to an invention. Using the definition established above, the fact that the product progressed from the drawing board into the marketplace makes it an innovation – albeit an unsuccessful one.

Pause for thought

Apple's iPhone looks set to be as successful as the iPod, but Apple has experienced similar success before with its Apple Mac computer and eventually lost out to Microsoft. Will history repeat itself?

Different types of innovation

Industrial innovation not only includes major (radical) innovations but also minor (incremental) technological advances. Indeed, the definition offered above suggests that successful commercialisation of the innovation may involve considerably wider organisational changes. For example, the introduction of a radical, technological innovation, such as digital cameras by Kodak and Fuji, invariably results in substantial internal organisational changes. In this case substantial changes occurred with the manufacturing, marketing and sales functions. Both of these firms decided to concentrate on the rapidly developing digital photography market. Yet both Fuji and Kodak were the market leaders in supplying traditional 35mm film cartridges. Their market share of the actual camera market was less significant. Such strategic decisions forced changes on all areas of the business. For example, in Kodak's case the manufacturing function underwent substantial changes as it began to substantially cut production of 35mm film cartridges. Opportunities existed for manufacturing in producing digital cameras and their associated equipment. Similarly, the marketing function had to employ extra sales staff to educate and reassure retail outlets that the new technology would not cannibalise their film-processing business. While many people would begin to print photographs from their PCs at home, many others would continue to want their digital camera film processed into physical photographs. For both Fuji and Kodak the new technology has completely changed the photographic industry. Both firms have seen their revenues fall from film cartridge sales, but Kodak and Fuji are now market leaders in digital cameras whereas before they were not.

Hence, technological innovation can be accompanied by additional managerial and organisational changes, often referred to as innovations. This presents a far more blurred picture and begins to widen the definition of innovation to include virtually any organisational or managerial change. Table 1.5 shows a typology of innovations.

Innovation was defined earlier in this section as the application of knowledge. It is this notion that lies at the heart of all types of innovation, be they product,

Table 1.5 **A typology of innovations**

Type of innovation	**Example**
Product innovation	The development of a new or improved product
Process innovation	The development of a new manufacturing process such as Pilkington's float glass process
Organisational innovation	A new venture division; a new internal communication system; introduction of a new accounting procedure
Management innovation	TQM (total quality management) systems; BPR (business process re-engineering); introduction of SAPR3*
Production innovation	Quality circles; just-in-time (JIT) manufacturing system; new production planning software, e.g. MRP II; new inspection system
Commercial/marketing innovation	New financing arrangements; new sales approach, e.g. direct marketing
Service innovation	Internet-based financial services

Note: SAP is a German software firm and R3 is an enterprise resource planning (ERP) product.

process or service. It is also worthy of note that many studies have suggested that product innovations are soon followed by process innovations in what they describe as an industry innovation cycle (*see* Chapter 12). Furthermore, it is common to associate innovation with physical change, but many changes introduced within organisations involve very little physical change. Rather, it is the activities performed by individuals that change. A good example of this is the adoption of so-called Japanese management techniques by automobile manufacturers in Europe and the United States.

It is necessary to stress at the outset that this book concentrates on the management of product innovation. This does not imply that the list of innovations above are less significant; this focus has been chosen to ensure clarity and to facilitate the study of innovation.

Technology and science

We also need to consider the role played by *science and technology* in innovation. The continual fascination with science and technology at the end of the nineteenth century and subsequent growth in university teaching and research have led to the development of many new strands of science. The proliferation of scientific journals over the past 30 years demonstrates the rapidly evolving nature of science and technology. The scientific literature seems to double in quantity every five years (Rothwell and Zegveld, 1985).

Science can be defined as systematic and formulated knowledge. There are clearly significant differences between science and technology. Technology is often seen as being the application of science and has been defined in many ways (Lefever, 1992). It is important to remember that technology is not an accident of nature. It is the product of deliberate action by human beings. The following definition is suggested:

Technology is knowledge applied to products or production processes.

No definition is perfect and the above is no exception. It does, however, provide a good starting point from which to view technology with respect to innovation. It is important to note that technology, like education, cannot be purchased off the shelf like a can of tomatoes. It is embedded in knowledge and skills.

In a lecture given to the Royal Society in 1992 the former chairman of Sony, Akio Morita, suggested that, unlike engineers, scientists are held in high esteem. This, he suggested, is because science provides us with information which was previously unknown. Yet technology comes from employing and *manipulating science* into concepts, processes and devices. These, in turn, can be used to make our life or work more efficient, convenient and powerful. Hence, it is technology, as an *outgrowth of science*, that fuels the industrial engine. And it is *engineers* and not scientists who make technology happen. In Japan, he argued, you will notice that almost every major manufacturer is run by an engineer or technologist. However, in the United Kingdom, some manufacturing companies are led by chief executive officers (CEOs) who do not understand the technology that goes into their own products. Indeed, many UK corporations are headed by chartered accountants. With the greatest respect to accountants, their central concerns are statistics and figures of *past* performance. How can an accountant reach out and grab the future if he or she is always looking at *last* quarter's results (Morita, 1992)?

The above represents the personal views of an influential senior figure within industry. There are many leading industrialists, economists and politicians who would concur (Hutton, 1995). But there are equally many who would profoundly disagree. The debate on improving economic innovative performance is one of the most important in the field of political economics.

Illustration 1.5

Theory and practice

Too much of a good thing: innovation increases in a competitive market – but only up to a point, says a new study

'Competition good, market power bad' is as close as popular economics gets to a religious belief.

The faith is perhaps best articulated in Adam Smith's *Wealth of Nations* (1776), the bible of free-market economists.

'To widen the market and to narrow the competition is always the interest of the dealers . . . The proposal of any new law or regulation of commerce which comes from this order, ought always to be listened to with great precaution, and ought never to be adopted, till after having been long and carefully examined, not only with the most scrupulous, but with the most suspicious attention.'

But if competition so clearly works wonders by reducing costs, providing incentives for efficient production and eliminating vested interests, it has generated a surprising number of powerful critics over the years.

The main complaint, echoed in work from Joseph Schumpeter, one of the most famous economists of the last century, to Bill Gates, chairman of Microsoft, is that these notions fail to take account of the dynamic forces in markets.

If entrepreneurs cannot protect their ideas and inventions from competitors, innovation will be stifled and the progress of capitalism undermined.

Adam Smith's suspicion of laws or regulations that are in the interests of 'the dealers' still dominates the thrust of competition policy.

But the disbelievers have had success in transforming theory into competition policy in some areas. Politicians have created patents to protect new ideas; trademarks outlaw the copy-ing of brands, designs, words and phrases; and copyright laws protect the original way an idea is expressed, for example in books, cinema or music.

In each case, the idea was to encourage innovation, to ensure that the benefits of progress accrue to those with the original idea, not to those who are good at reproducing it. Restrictions on all-out competition have been tolerated in the hope of generating innovation and a more dynamic economy.

So who is right, Smith or Schumpeter? In the mid-1990s, a serious problem emerged with the Schumpeterian view so beloved by drugs companies and Bill Gates: many studies found little connection between more innovative industries and markets where competition was restricted.

This work has now been extended by an international team of academic economists who have developed a theory from evidence relating innovation to competition. The study* concludes that innovation is least likely in the most and the least competitive industries.

Where competition is rife, companies refuse to spend money on innovation for fear that they will not be able to profit from their ideas. And where companies have lots of market power, they become lazy and do not bother to innovate.

Rachel Griffith, one of the authors, says: 'The theory appeals to common sense and fits the evidence well.'

It is probably in its painstaking use of data that the research itself is most innovative. The team collected information on a panel of 461 companies listed on the London Stock Exchange

---

between 1968 and 1996, from which they measured the degree of competition each company faced. They combined this data with information from the US patent office to determine how innovative each company had been. Because some patents are trivial, the team considered not just the number of patents received by a company but also how often it was subsequently cited in other successful patents.

The results are striking. Companies in highly competitive and monopolistic industries were much less innovative than companies in the middle. Using profit margins as a proxy for competition, companies with margins of about 10 per cent on average produced 40 per cent more patents than companies with margins of 3 per cent or 20 per cent.

The research also evaluated the importance of other details of market structure on innovation. Where companies were neck and neck – for example Procter & Gamble and Unilever in the soap powder market – more innovation would occur than if one company was a clear leader, with many laggards. The research concludes that in neck-and-neck markets, the advantages of getting ahead (and so achieving a quieter life)

encourages more innovation in all companies, while less innovation occurs overall if one company has a clear advantage.

These results seem to give rather awkward policy prescriptions for competition authorities: try to encourage competition, particularly if companies are evenly matched, but only up to a point – after which it can become counter-productive.

But Dr Griffith says it is possible to draw a more subtle conclusion. 'You must strive to encourage competition to drive down profits in the absence of innovation, while allowing companies just enough protection to profit in the future from their current ideas.'

The moral is that, as long as the cost of innovation can be recovered, competition should be encouraged. It suggests that existing protection of innovative ideas that generate large profit margins, for example in software and pharmaceuticals, has gone too far and is encouraging laziness not dynamism. Adam Smith would be pleased.

*Note: Aghion et al. (2002) 'Competition and innovation: an inverted U relationship', IFS Working Papers, W02/04, 2 February 2002.

Source: C. Giles, 'Theory and practice', Financial Times, 14 May 2002. Reprinted with permission.

Popular views of innovation

Science, technology and innovation have received a great deal of popular media coverage over the years, from Hollywood and Disney movies to best-selling novels (see Figure 1.3). This is probably because science and technology can help turn vivid imaginings into a possibility. The end result, however, is a simplified image of scientific discoveries and innovations. It usually consists of a lone professor, with a mass of white hair, working away in his garage and stumbling, by accident, on a major new discovery. Through extensive trial and error, usually accompanied by dramatic experiments, this is eventually developed into an amazing invention. This is best demonstrated in the blockbuster movie Back to the Future. Christopher Lloyd plays the eccentric scientist and Michael J. Fox his young, willing accomplice. Together they are involved in an exciting journey that enables Fox to travel back in time and influence the future.

Cartoons have also contributed to a misleading image of the innovation process. Here, the inventor, an eccentric scientist, is portrayed with a glowing lightbulb above his head, as a flash of inspiration results in a new scientific discovery. We have all seen and laughed at these funny cartoons.

Figure 1.3 **The popular view of science**

This humorous and popular view of inventions and innovations has been reinforced over the years and continues to occur in the popular press. Many industrialists and academics have argued that this simple view of a complex phenomenon has caused immense harm to the understanding of science and technology.

Models of innovation

Traditional arguments about innovation have centred on two schools of thought. On the one hand, the social deterministic school argued that innovations were the result of a combination of external social factors and influences, such as demographic changes, economic influences and cultural changes. The argument was that *when* the conditions were 'right' innovations would occur. On the other hand, the individualistic school argued that innovations were the result of unique individual talents and such innovators are born. Closely linked to the individualistic theory is the important role played by serendipity; more on this later.

Over the past 10 years the literature on what 'drives' innovation has tended to divide into two schools of thought: the market-based view and the resource-based view. The market-based view argues that market conditions provide the context which facilitate or constrain the extent of firm innovation activity (Slater and Narver, 1994; Porter, 1980, 1985). The key issue here, of course, is the ability of firms to recognise opportunities in the marketplace. Cohen and Levinthal (1990) and Trott (1998) would argue that few firms have the ability to scan and search their environments effectively.

The resource-based view of innovation considers that a market-driven orientation does not provide a secure foundation for formulating innovation strategies for markets which are dynamic and volatile; rather a firm's own resources provide a much more stable context in which to develop its innovation activity and shape its markets in accordance to its own view (Penrose, 1959; Wernerfelt, 1984; Wernerfelt, 1995; Grant, 1996; Prahalad and Hamel, 1990; Conner and Prahalad, 1996; Eisenhardt and Martin, 2000). The resource-based view of innovation focuses on the firm and its resources, capabilities and skills. It argues that when firms have resources that are valuable, rare and not easily copied they can achieve a sustainable competitive advantage – frequently in the form of innovative new products. Chapter 6 offers a more detailed overview of the resource-based theory of the firm.

Serendipity

Many studies of historical cases of innovation have highlighted the importance of the unexpected discovery. The role of serendipity or luck is offered as an explanation. As we have seen, this view is also reinforced in the popular media. It is, after all, everyone's dream that they will accidentally uncover a major new invention leading to fame and fortune.

On closer inspection of these historical cases, serendipity is rare indeed. After all, in order to recognise the significance of an advance one would need to have some prior knowledge in that area. Most discoveries are the result of people who have had a fascination with a particular area of science or technology and it is following extended efforts on their part that advances are made. Discoveries may not be expected, but in the words of Louis Pasteur, 'chance favours the prepared mind'.

Linear models

It was US economists after the Second World War who championed the linear model of science and innovation. Since then, largely because of its simplicity, this model has taken a firm grip on people's views on how innovation occurs. Indeed, it dominated science and industrial policy for 40 years. It was only in the 1980s that management schools around the world began seriously to challenge the sequential linear process. The recognition that innovation occurs through the interaction of the science base (dominated by universities and industry), technological development (dominated by industry) and the needs of the market was a significant step forward (*see* Figure 1.4). The explanation of the interaction of these activities forms the basis of models of innovation today.

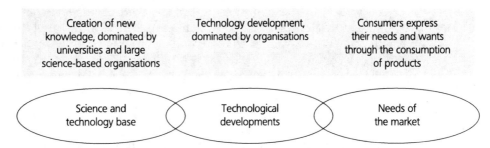

Figure 1.4 **Conceptual framework of innovation**

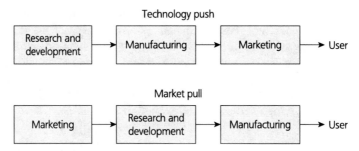

Figure 1.5 **Linear models of innovation**

There is, of course, a great deal of debate and disagreement about precisely what activities influence innovation and, more importantly, the internal processes that affect a company's ability to innovate.

Nonetheless, there is broad agreement that it is the linkages between these key components that will produce successful innovation. Importantly, the devil is in the detail. From a European perspective an area that requires particular attention is the linkage between the science base and technological development. The European Union (EU) believes that European universities have not established effective links with industry, whereas in the United States universities have been working closely with industry for many years.

As explained above, the innovation process has traditionally been viewed as a sequence of separable stages or activities. There are two basic variations of this model for product innovation. First, and most crudely, there is the technology-driven model (often referred to as 'technology push') where it is assumed that scientists make unexpected discoveries, technologists apply them to develop product ideas and engineers and designers turn them into prototypes for testing. It is left to manufacturing to devise ways of producing the products efficiently. Finally, marketing and sales will promote the product to the potential consumer. In this model the marketplace was a passive recipient for the fruits of R&D. This technology-push model dominated industrial policy after the Second World War (*see* Figure 1.5). While this model of innovation can be applied to a few cases, most notably the pharmaceutical industry, it is not applicable in many other instances; in particular where the innovation process follows a different route.

It was not until the 1970s that new studies of actual innovations suggested that the role of the marketplace was influential in the innovation process (von Hippel, 1978). This led to the second linear model, the 'market-pull' model of innovation. The customer need-driven model emphasises the role of marketing as an initiator of new ideas resulting from close interactions with customers. These, in turn, are conveyed to R&D for design and engineering and then to manufacturing for production. In fast-moving consumer goods industries the role of the market and the customer remains powerful and very influential. The managing director of McCain Foods argues that knowing your customer is crucial to turning innovation into profits:

> *It's only by understanding what the customer wants that we can identify the innovative opportunities. Then we see if there's technology that we can bring to bear on the opportunities that exist. Being innovative is relatively easy – the hard part is ensuring your ideas become commercially viable.* (Murray, 2003)

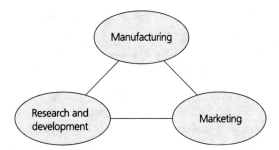

Figure 1.6 **The simultaneous coupling model**

Simultaneous coupling model

Whether innovations are stimulated by technology, customer need, manufacturing or a host of other factors, including competition, misses the point. The models above concentrate on what is driving the downstream efforts rather than on *how* innovations occur (Galbraith, 1982). The linear model is only able to offer an explanation of *where* the initial stimulus for innovation was born, that is, where the trigger for the idea or need was initiated. The simultaneous coupling model shown in Figure 1.6 suggests that it is the result of the simultaneous coupling of the knowledge within all three functions that will foster innovation. Furthermore, the point of commencement for innovation is not known in advance.

Interactive model

The interactive model develops this idea further (*see* Figure 1.7) and links together the technology-push and market-pull models. It emphasises that innovations occur as the result of the interaction of the marketplace, the science base and the organisation's capabilities. Like the coupling model, there is no explicit starting point. The use of information flows is used to explain how innovations transpire and that they can arise from a wide variety of points.

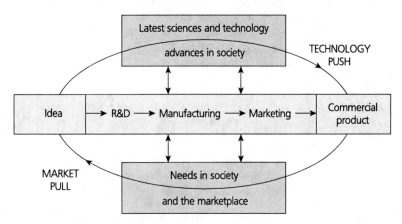

Figure 1.7 **Interactive model of innovation**

Source: Adapted from B. Rothwell and W. Zegveld (1985) *Reindustrialisation and Technology*, Longman, London.

Table 1.6 The chronological development of models of innovation

Date	Model	Characteristics
1950/60s	Technology-push	Simple linear sequential process; emphasis on R&D; the market is a recipient of the fruits of R&D
1970s	Market-pull	Simple linear sequential process; emphasis on marketing; the market is the source for directing R&D; R&D has a reactive role
1980s	Coupling model	Emphasis on integrating R&D and marketing
1980/90s	Interactive model	Combinations of push and pull
1990s	Network model	Emphasis on knowledge accumulation and external linkages
2000s	Open innovation	Chesbrough's (2003) emphasis on further externalisation of the innovation process in terms of linkages with knowledge inputs and collaboration to exploit knowledge outputs

Source: Based on R. Rothwell (1992) 'Successful industrial innovation: critical factors for the 1990s', *R&D Management*, Vol. 22, No. 3, 221–39.

While still oversimplified, this is a more comprehensive representation of the innovation process. It can be regarded as a logically sequential, though not necessarily continuous, process that can be divided into a series of functionally distinct but interacting and interdependent stages (Rothwell and Zegveld, 1985). The overall innovation process can be thought of as a complex set of communication paths over which knowledge is transferred. These paths include internal and external linkages. The innovation process outlined in Figure 1.7 represents the organisation's capabilities and its linkages with both the marketplace and the science base. Organisations that are able to manage this process effectively will be successful at innovation.

At the centre of the model are the organisational functions of R&D, engineering and design, manufacturing and marketing and sales. While at first this may appear to be a linear model, the flow of communication is not necessarily linear. There is provision for feedback. Also, linkages with the science base and the marketplace occur between all functions, not just with R&D or marketing. For example, as often happens, it may be the manufacturing function which initiates a design improvement that leads to the introduction of either a different material or the eventual development by R&D of a new material. Finally, the generation of ideas is shown to be dependent on inputs from three basic components (as outlined in Figure 1.4): organisation capabilities; the needs of the marketplace; the science and technology base.

Table 1.6 summarises the historical development of the dominant models of the industrial innovation process.

Innovation as a management process

The preceding sections have revealed that innovation is not a singular event, but a series of activities that are linked in some way to the others. This may be described as a process and involves (Kelly and Kranzberg, 1978):

1 a response to either a need or an opportunity that is context dependent;
2 a creative effort that if successful results in the introduction of novelty;
3 the need for further changes.

Usually, in trying to capture this complex process, the simplification has led to misunderstandings. The simple linear model of innovation can be applied to only a few innovations and is more applicable to certain industries than others. The pharmaceutical industry characterises much of the technology-push model. Other industries, like the food industry, are better represented by the market-pull model. For most industries and organisations innovations are the result of a mixture of the two. Managers working within these organisations have the difficult task of trying to manage this complex process.

A framework for the management of innovation

Industrial innovation and new product development have evolved considerably from their early beginnings outlined above. However, establishing departmental functions to perform the main tasks of business strategy, R&D, manufacturing and marketing does not solve the firm's problems. Indeed, as we have seen, innovation is extremely complex and involves the effective management of a variety of different activities. It is precisely how the process is managed that needs to be examined. Over the past 50 years there have been numerous studies of innovation attempting to understand not only the ingredients necessary for it to occur but also what levels of ingredients are required and in what order. Furthermore, a recent study by *Business Week* and Boston Consulting Group (2006) of over 1,000 senior managers revealed further explanations as to what makes some firms more innovative than others. The key findings from this survey are captured in Table 1.7. While these headline-grabbing bullet points are interesting, they do not show us what firms have to do to become excellent in design (BMW) or to improve cooperation with suppliers (Toyota). Table 1.8 captures some of the key studies that have influenced our understanding.

A framework is presented in Figure 1.8 that helps to illustrate innovation as a management process. This framework does not pretend to any analytical status, it is simply an aid in describing the main factors which need to be considered if innovation is to be successfully managed. It helps to show that while the interactions of the functions inside the organisation are important, so too are the interactions of those functions with the external environment. Scientists and engineers within the firm will be continually interacting with fellow scientists in universities and other

Table 1.7 **Explanations for innovative capability**

Innovative firm	Explanation for innovative capability
Apple	Innovative chief executive
Google	Scientific freedom for employees
Samsung	Speed of product development
Procter & Gamble	Utilisation of external sources of technology
IBM	Share patents with collaborators
BMW	Design
Starbucks	In-depth understanding of customers and their cultures
Toyota	Close cooperation with suppliers

Table 1.8 **Studies of innovation management**

	Study	Date	Focus
1	Carter and Williams	1957	Industry and technical progress
2	Project Hindsight – TRACES (Isensen)	1968	Historical reviews of US government-funded defence industry
3	Wealth from knowledge (Langrish *et al.*)	1972	Queens Awards for technical innovation
4	Project SAPPHO (Rothwell *et al.*, 1974)	1974	Success and failure factors in chemical industry
5	Minnesota Studies (Van de Ven)	1989	14 case studies of innovations
6	Rothwell	1992	25-year review of studies
7	Sources of innovation (Wheelwright and Clark)	1992	Different levels of user involvement
8	MIT studies (Utterback)	1994	5 major industry-level cases
9	Project NEWPROD (Cooper)	1994	Longitudinal survey of success and failure in new products
10	Radical innovation (Leifer *et al.*)	2000	Review of mature businesses
11	TU Delft study (Van der Panne *et al.*)	2003	Literature review of success and failure factors

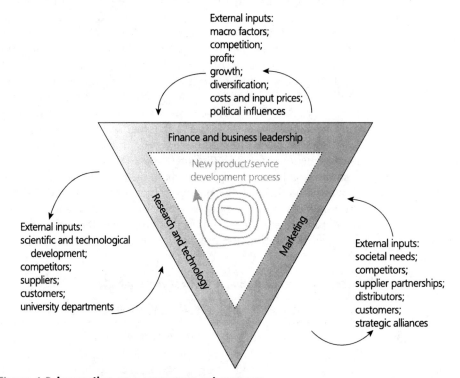

Figure 1.8 **Innovation as a management process**

firms about scientific and technological developments. Similarly, the marketing function will need to interact with suppliers, distributors, customers and competitors to ensure that the day-to-day activities of understanding customer needs and getting products to customers are achieved. Business planners and senior management will likewise communicate with a wide variety of firms and other external institutions, such as government departments, suppliers and customers. All these information flows contribute to the wealth of knowledge held by the organisation. Recognising this, capturing and utilising it to develop successful new products forms the difficult management process of innovation.

Within any organisation there are likely to be many different functions. Depending on the nature of the business, some functions will be more influential than others. The framework shown in Figure 1.8 identifies three main functions: marketing, research and manufacturing, and business planning. Historical studies have identified these functions as the most influential in the innovation process. Whether one lists three or seven functions misses the point, which is that it is the interaction of these internal functions and the flow of knowledge between them that needs to be facilitated (Trott, 1993). Similarly, as shown on the framework, effective communication with the external environment also requires encouragement and support (Mason *et al.*, 2004).

Pause for thought

Surely all innovations start with an idea and end with a product; does that not make it a linear process?

Open innovation and the need to share and exchange knowledge (network models)

The framework in Figure 1.8 emphasises the importance placed on interaction (both formal and informal) within the innovation process. Indeed, innovation has been described as an information–creation process that arises out of social interaction. In effect, the firm provides a structure within which the creative process is located (Nonaka and Kenney, 1991).

These interactions provide the opportunity for thoughts, potential ideas and views to be shared and exchanged. However, we are often unable to explain what we normally do; we can be competent without being able to offer a theoretical account of our actions (Polanyi, 1966). This is referred to as 'tacit knowledge'. A great deal of technical skill is know-how and much industrial innovation occurs through on-the-spot experiments, a kind of action-oriented research with *ad hoc* modifications during step-by-step processes, through which existing repertoires are extended. Such knowledge can only be learned through practice and experience. This view has recently found support from a study of Japanese firms (Nonaka, 1991) where the creation of new knowledge within an organisation depends on tapping the tacit and often highly subjective insights, intuitions and hunches of individual employees and making those insights available for testing and use by the organisation as a whole. This implies that certain knowledge and skills, embodied in the term 'know-how', are not easily understood; moreover they are less able to be communicated. This would suggest that to gain access to such knowledge one may have to be practising in this or related areas of knowledge. Cohen and Levinthal (1990: 130) refer to this condition as 'lockout', suggesting that failure to invest in research and technology will limit an organisation's ability to capture technological opportunities: 'once off the technological escalator it's difficult to get back on'.

In addition to informal interactions, the importance of formal interactions is also highlighted. There is a substantial amount of research stressing the need for a 'shared language' within organisations to facilitate internal communication (Allen, 1977; Tushman, 1978). The arguments are presented along the following lines. If all actors in the organisation share the same specialised language, they will be effective in their communication. Hence, there needs to be an overlap of knowledge in order for communication to occur. Such arguments have led to developments in cross-functional interfaces, for example between R&D, design, manufacturing and marketing. Concurrent engineering is an extension of this; in this particular case a small team consisting of a member from each of the various functional departments manages the design, development, manufacture and marketing of a product (*see* Chapter 16 for more on concurrent engineering).

More recently, Chesbrough (2003), adopting a business strategy perspective, presents a persuasive argument that the process of innovation has shifted from one of closed systems, internal to the firm, to a new mode of open systems involving a range of players distributed up and down the supply chain. Significantly, it is Chesbrough's emphasis on the new knowledge-based economy that informs the concept 'open innovation'. In particular it is the use of cheap and instant information flows which places even more emphasis on the linkages and relationships of firms. It is from these linkages and the supply chain in particular that firms have to ensure that they have the capability to fully capture and utilise ideas.

Furthermore, the product innovation literature, in applying the open innovation paradigm, has recently been debating the strengths and limitations of so-called 'user toolkits' which seem to ratchet up further this drive to externalise the firm's capabilities to capture innovation opportunities (von Hippel, 2005).

Recently authors such as Thomke (2003), Schrange (2000) and Dodgson *et al.* (2005) have emphasised the importance of learning through experimentation. This is similar to Nonaka's work in the early 1990s which emphasised the importance of learning by doing in the 'knowledge creating company'. However, Dodgson *et al.* argue that there are significant changes occurring at all levels of the innovation process, forcing us to reconceptualise the process with emphasis placed on the three areas that have experienced most significant change through the introduction and use of new technologies. These are: technologies that facilitate creativity, technologies that facilitate communication and technologies that facilitate manufacturing. For example, they argue that information and communication technologies have changed the way individuals, groups and communities interact. Cell phones, email and websites are obvious examples of how people interact and information flows in a huge osmosis process through the boundaries of the firm. When this is coupled with changes in manufacturing and operations technologies, enabling rapid prototyping and flexible manufacturing at low costs, the process of innovation seems to be undergoing considerable change (Dodgson *et al.*, 2005; Chesbrough, 2003; Schrange, 2000). Models of innovation need to take account of these new technologies which allow immediate and extensive interaction with many collaborators throughout the process from conception to commercialisation. The innovation systems and firm performance model presented in Chapter 1 emphasises how these considerable external environment changes impact on the innovativeness of the firm and hence firm performance.

More recently Berkhout's cyclic innovation model captures this cyclical nature of knowledge creation and development of business opportunities. It considers innovation processes as coupled 'cycles of change', connecting science with business, and technology with markets, in a cyclic manner (Berkhout, 2000; Berkhout *et al.*, 2006; Berkhout and van der Duin, 2007).

Innovation and new product development

Such thinking is similarly captured in the framework outlined in Figure 1.8. It stresses the importance of interaction and communication within and between functions and with the external environment. This networking structure allows lateral communication, helping managers and their staff unleash creativity. This framework emphasises the importance of informal and formal networking across all functions (Pittaway *et al.*, 2004).

This introduces a tension between the need for diversity, on the one hand, in order to generate novel linkages and associations, and the need for commonality, on the other, to facilitate effective internal communication.

Finally, the centre of the framework is represented by the process of new product development. The purpose of this book is to illustrate the interconnections of the subjects of innovation management and new product development. Indeed, some may argue they are two sides of the same coin. By directly linking together these two significant areas of management the clear connections and overlaps between the subjects can be more fully explored and understood.

It is hoped that this framework will help to provide readers with a visual reminder of how one can view the innovation process that needs to be managed by firms. The industry and products and services will determine the precise requirements necessary. It is a dynamic process and the framework tries to emphasise this. It is also a complex process and this helps to simplify it to enable further study. Very often product innovation is viewed from a purely marketing perspective with little, if any, consideration of the R&D function and the difficulties of managing science and technology. Likewise, many manufacturing and technology approaches to product innovation have previously not taken sufficient notice of the needs of the customer.

Case study

The success of the iPod raises the licensing question for Apple . . . again

Introduction

This case study explores the rise of the Apple Corporation. The Apple iPod is one of the most successful new product launches of recent years, transforming the way the public listens to music, with huge ramifications for major record labels. More than 50 million MP3 players are expected to be sold in 2005, over a third more than in 2004. Cell phones have long been regarded as the most credible challenger to

MP3 players and iPods. The launch of digital download services via cell phones illustrates the dramatic speed of convergence between the telecoms and media industries, which many observers expect to usher in a new era of growth for cell phones. Users are willing to pay more for additional services and many analysts predict that cell phone handsets will eventually emerge as the dominant technology of the age, combining personal organisers, digital music players and games consoles in a single device. Indeed, Microsoft founder Bill Gates in May 2006 predicted that cell phones will supersede the iPod as the favoured way of listening to digital music.

Apple and the iPod

For those not yet fully plugged into digital music listening, MP3 is an acronym for MPEG layer 3, which is a compressed audio format. A compression ratio of up to 12 to 1 compression is possible, which produces high sound quality. Layer 3 is one of three coding schemes (layer 1, layer 2 and layer 3) for the compression of audio signals. It reduces the amount of data required to represent audio, yet still sound like a faithful reproduction of the original uncompressed audio to most listeners. It was invented by a team of German engineers of the Fraunhofer Society, and it became an ISO/IEC standard in 1991. This format of compression facilitates the transfer of audio files via the Internet and storage in portable players, such as the iPod, and digital audio servers.

The remarkable success of the iPod music player has propelled Apple back into the FT500 ranking of global companies. This marks a return of the technology company to the ranks of the world's top companies after falling out of the list in 2001. Its shares have risen fivefold in the past two years, valuing the company at $34 billion (£19 billion). Apple, founded (in 1975) 30 years ago by Steven Jobs, who is now chief executive, has seen its fortunes ebb and flow. Mr Jobs has achieved a transformation since his

Photo: A. Harrison/Pearson

return to the company in 1997 after leaving some ten years earlier following a dispute with John Sculley, who was then chief executive (Coggan, 2005).

Historically Apple is a computer company and its core customer base today is only about 8 million active users; in a world of 400 million Windows users. Apple has always understood that its core franchise was very closely connected to the core computer franchise. Consumer electronics products, for example, are sold through different channels and they have different product life cycles. Making the transition has been extremely hard. What made the iPod transition easier is that the iPod began as a PC peripheral, even though it is ultimately a consumer electronics product. Eventually, Apple recognised that the iPod could not be limited to the Mac and it had to become a PC peripheral as well. The move into the PC market enabled Apple to access a much broader market than its core customer base.

Apple's iTune Music Store website

Apple's success with its iPod is helped by its iTune Music Store website (www.Apple.com/itunes), which offers consumers the ability to digitise all their CDs as well as download new music at 79p per song. This site has sold over 50 million songs since its launch in April 2003, bringing considerable revenue to Apple (Durman, 2005). However, downloads from the iTunes Music Store will only play on Apple's iPods (Webb, 2007). The site is universally regarded as being simple and fun; it is also offers a legal way to add music to your library. To import songs into iTunes, you simply insert a CD into your computer and click 'Import CD'. iTunes also compresses and stores music in AAC – a format that builds upon state-of-the-art audio technology from Dolby Labs. It also offers users the ability to select different audio formats. iTunes lets you convert music to MP3 at high bit-rate at no extra charge. Using AAC or MP3, you can store more than 100 songs in the same amount of space as a single CD. iTunes also supports the Apple Lossless format, which gives you CD-quality audio in about half the storage space.

The rise and fall and rise of Apple

Apple computers began in 1977 when Steven Wozniak and Steven Jobs designed and offered the Apple I to the personal computer field. It was designed over a period of years, and was only built in printed circuit-board form. It debuted in April 1976 at the Homebrew Computer Club in Palo Alto, but few took it seriously. Continual product improvements and wider technological developments including microprocessor improvements led to the launch of the Apple Macintosh in 1984.

The Macintosh computer was different because it used a mouse driven operating system; all other PCs used the keyboard driven system known as MS DOS (Microsoft disc operating system). Early in the 1980s Microsoft licensed its operating system to all PC manufacturers, but Apple decided against this approach, opting instead to stay in control of its system. The 1980s was a period of dramatic growth for personal computers as virtually every office and home began to buy into the PC world. Slowly Microsoft became the market leader, not because its technology was better, but largely because its system became the dominant standard. As people bought PCs, so with it they would buy the operating system: MS Windows; hence it became the de-facto dominant standard. The Apple operating system was only available if you bought an Apple PC. Consequently Apple's market share plummeted. This was also the time when Steven Jobs quit Apple after disagreements with other members of the board. Interestingly in 1986 Steven Jobs became involved in another new venture, Pixar Animation Studios, of which he is now chairman and chief executive officer (see Illustration 1.6). By the mid-1990s Apple had grown to a $12 billion company, twice the size of Microsoft; but Microsoft was powering ahead on the back of the launch of Windows and it would soon become the $40 billion firm it is today (Schofield, 2005).

In 1993 Apple launched the Newton, its first completely new product in many years. Indeed, it represented Apple's entry into (and perhaps creation of) an entirely new market: personal digital assistants (PDAs). The PDA market was barely present when the Newton was released, but other companies were working on similar devices. The Newton Message Pad featured a variety of personal-organisation applications, such as an address book, a calendar and notes, along with communications capabilities such as faxing and

Illustration 1.6

Pixar Animation Studios

Pixar Animation Studios eventually became the Academy Award winning computer animation pioneer. The northern California studio has created six of the most successful and beloved animated films of all time: *Toy Story* (1995); *A Bug's Life* (1998); *Toy Story 2* (1999); *Monsters, Inc.* (2001); *Finding Nemo* (2003); and *The Incredibles* (2004). Pixar's six films have earned more than $3 billion at the worldwide box office to date. *Cars* was Pixar's new film in 2006.

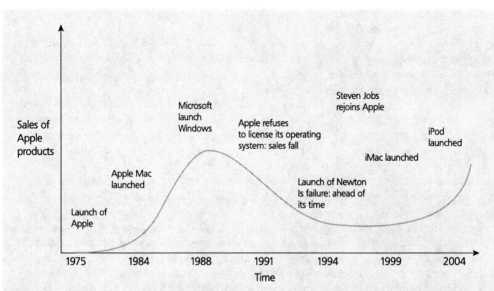

Figure 1.9 **The rise and fall and rise of Apple**

email. It featured a pen-based interface, which used a word-based, trainable handwriting recognition engine. Unfortunately this engine had been developed by a third party, and was notoriously difficult to use and was partly responsible for the product's failure.

In the mid-1990s Apple's future in the computer technology industry looked bleak, with a diversified product portfolio and a low market share within the PC market of only 3 per cent. Many were therefore surprised when Steven Jobs returned to the company as chief executive in 1997. He quickly set about culling many product lines and much of its operations and decided to focus on only a few products including the new looking iMac. This coincided with the economic boom in the late 1990s and allowed Apple to generate cash very quickly. This provided revenue for the development of the iPod, which was launched in 2003 (*see* Figure 1.9).

iPod dominates MP3 market, but competition is fierce

In 2005 triple-digit sales growth for Apple's iconic digital music player sent the company's share price soaring more than 200 per cent over 2004. The challenge for Apple, however, is how to maintain the success of the iPod, especially with its indirect impact on sales of its PCs: most notably the iMac and its Notebook range of portable PCs. Apple could continue to cut prices, but this would mean smaller mar-

gins. Another option would be product developments such as iPods with new capabilities and functions, such as a handheld computer, satellite radio, wireless email capability and a phone. Such a move, however, would seem counter-intuitive for Apple, which has a reputation for simply designed and easy-to-use products (Morrison, 2005). In actual fact Apple began fighting the competition in the MP3 market by cutting prices and improving the product. In 2005 it launched lower-priced versions of its best selling iPod digital music player, the Shuffle, with significantly improved battery performance, plus an ultra thin iPod Nano. However, at the same time a potential big threat in the form of Sony Electronics announced a new, low-price, high-performance digital music player under its Walkman brand. Since October 2001, when Apple first launched its iPod, it has slowly reduced the price and improved the performance of the product. The design and styling have significantly contributed to Apple's success with its 50 per cent market share for MP3 players. Competitors including Dell, Creative Technologies and Rio have launched many rival players, most cheaper and offering better battery performance. Yet it seems the iPod has an iconic status that is proving difficult to attack.

iPod patent battles

Despite the success of the iPod, Apple continues to fend off challenges to the propriety of its technology.

In August 2005 Creative Technology, the Singapore maker of the Zen digital music player, suggested it was considering a legal battle with several digital music manufactures including Apple Computer, alleging that the US company's popular iPod and iPod mini music players use Creative's recently patented technology. Creative was one of the first companies to market digital music players in 2000, but the company's devices have been overshadowed by Apple's popular iPod product line. Apple has shipped over 40 million units since introducing the iPod in 2001, dominating the US market.

Apple has extensive experience of fighting patent infringement cases and understands that such legal battles can take many years to settle. Its own battle with Microsoft over infringement of its operating system technology was eventually settled after eight years without a satisfactory outcome. It may be better for Creative to seek royalties from Apple, as patent cases can drag out for many years and are highly unpredictable.

An interesting twist to the patent fraud case is the increasing use of Apple iPods by industrial fraudsters who use them to download vast quantities of corporate information either to sell to rivals or to support their own start-up operations. Anti-fraud experts have warned that the machines, along with other music players that boast hard drives with up to 20Gb of memory (allowing users to store over 10,000 songs), could become widely used by employees to fool security officials and breach data security rules. In one case a recruitment agency found much of its client database had been copied to an iPod's memory and used to defraud the firm. Staff who have been given the sack or missed out on promotions are the most likely to turn to this type of fraud. They may be supported by criminal gangs who use employees as insiders to extract information, but in these cases they are more likely to be disgruntled employees who want to punish their employer. The National Criminal Intelligence Service points out that fraud cost £14 billion last year (Inman, 2005).

The rise of Apple as a lifestyle brand

At the centre of Apple's recent success is the emergence of Apple as a lifestyle brand rather than as a technology company. Apple is very keen, for instance, to reinforce its California heritage (the person credited with designing the iPod is Johnathan Ive, a graduate from Newcastle Polytechnic and now Apple's vice president for design). Every iPod comes with the words 'Designed in California'. Also, it may have been a subtle move, but remaining friendly – not just user-friendly but friendly, as opposed to the unfriendly giant Microsoft – may be helping to increase the brand's appeal. It may be that people at last have become tired of Microsoft and efficiency and effectiveness and now are searching for something different. If Apple can capitalise on the success of the iPod and translate this into increased market share of the PC market, this will truly signify a dramatic turnaround for the firm in the PC industry.

To reinforce the idea of a lifestyle brand one need look no further than the huge increase in accessories for the iPod. It seems cool-conscious iPod buyers cannot get enough of carrying cases, adaptors, microphones or software; these accessories give consumers the edge as they take their iPods on the road, into classrooms and on to the street. Indeed, the road provides a big growth opportunity for Apple and the iPod. The challenge for Apple is whether it can establish the iPod in the in-car entertainment market by becoming the product of choice for those wishing to move effortlessly from *'home-to-car-to-sidewalk'* without any interruptions to listening, simply by plugging and unplugging your digital music player. Apple has already worked with BMW to offer an in-car adapter that allows users to plug their iPod into the car stereo. Car stereo makers Pioneer, Alpine and Clarion have all unveiled adaptors that will allow iPod owners to wire music players directly to their car stereos and to use the stereo controls to play iPod-stored music. Furthermore, Japan's Nissan and a handful of European luxury car makers said they would begin selling cars with iPod-compatible stereo systems. Still notably absent from the iPod club are the big automotive players: Japan's Honda and Toyota, as well as the big three US groups: DaimlerChrysler, GM and Ford.

The licensing question returns to haunt Apple

Since Apple launched the iPod in 2001, doubters have said it was only a matter of time before Microsoft and its hardware partners developed a cheaper industry-standard music player that would relegate Apple to the fringes of the market; just like Microsoft did with Windows. Few forget how Apple's refusal to license its technology contributed to its demise in the personal computer market and critics say the company appears determined to make the same mistake again. A key issue for Apple is whether it can sustain the huge premiums that it earns with the iPod when Dell and others begin entering the market with much lower priced product offerings. Also, Apple is running into the same challenge as it experienced with the Mac of selling a proprietary solution. That is, music on the iPod cannot play on non-Apple devices. This time around, however, Apple is allowing HP to resell iPod. It's their first small step into trying to get into the mass market. It could be a fundamental change in strategy, if they were to pursue it aggressively. On the other hand, if they pursue their iPod licensing strategy like they pursued their computer operating system licensing strategy, which means selective licences to a small number of players, then they will still run the risk that they will continually get downward pressure on price by competitors like Dell, and greater availability of options by customers using Microsoft software, leading to a repeat of the Mac problem. Essentially, just like the mid-1980s, there is a standards war; just as there was between VHS and Betamax. There is a proprietary standard with iTunes, and there will be alternative standards pushed by Microsoft, Real Networks, and others. One can still detect an Apple orientated approach to growth rather than one driven by absolute growth. For example, iTunes, was initially available only on the Mac. This was meant to drive Macintosh sales, and then six or nine months later Apple would bring out a Windows version. The problem is that it gave competitors six to nine months to bring out Window's products, which creates a more competitive environment. Some analysts argue that if Apple had really been thinking in terms of breaking away from Apple users and its heritage, it would have started out on Windows and come to Macintosh later like everybody else in the world. But, critics argue that is not the way Apple thinks. There are clearly advantages when developing a new product to target the 400 million market and then target the total Apple user and ex-user market of 25 million. But there are also advantages of doing it the Apple way.

If Apple doesn't open itself up and make sure that it becomes the dominant standard, it could end up becoming the niche product again that makes it a little bit less attractive for users. Apple may be able to learn from Sony's experiences, for although Sony lost the VCR industry standards battle it did win huge market shares with its Walkman. Sony drove the Walkman into a mass audience by drastically bringing down the price. Apple may be able to do this successfully with the iPod, but it has never been very good at very high volume manufacturing at very low costs. But, it may be that the iPod is becoming the dominant platform in MP3 players just like Microsoft did with its Windows operating system.

Cell phones: the new threat

In 2005 Vodafone and Orange introduced their own downloading services. Sony Ericsson has also launched its first Walkman cell phone, and Nokia and others are producing their own music phones. At present most music phones have limited stereo capacity, but this will inevitably change. The key question is whether consumers prefer their music on their cell phone or their iPod. Consumers can already download music to their cell phone, but the cost is almost twice that compared to Apple's iTunes. There are other limitations too. A song bought from Orange Media Player will be lost if the consumer switches to another network provider or changes SIM card. Nor can the song be played from a computer. Nonetheless, the inexorable shift from separate devices to a single handheld device appears to be gathering momentum (see Figure 1.10). In particular third-generation (3G) cell phones will also offer the capability to download high-speed data over the airwaves including television pictures. The 3G handsets may be destined to become mini-TVs, allowing consumers to watch sporting highlights and other entertainment, and game consoles.

To try to combat the threat from cell phones Apple has established a strategic alliance with its long-time partner Motorola, which will enable Motorola cell phones to incorporate iTunes technology. Late in 2005 Motorola put its new model phone (ROKR E1) in the shops, announcing it as the first cell phone compatible with iTunes.

Conclusions

The success of the Apple iPod has been remarkable by any measure. It has surprised Apple's competitors but, moreover, it has surprised market analysts and investors, who had largely believed Apple was a niche player in the computer world. To be successful

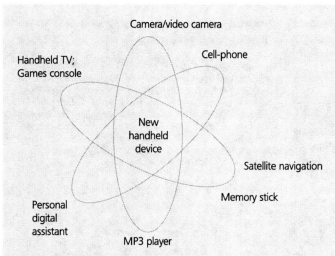

Camera/video camera

Handheld TV;
Games console

Cell-phone

New
handheld
device

Satellite navigation

Memory stick

Personal
digital
assistant

MP3 player

Figure 1.10 **The future handheld device will probably incorporate many separate devices**

in the mainstream mass market is unusual for Apple. Many people recognise the Apple brand, but far fewer buy its products. Take the iMac; this iconic stylish PC was universally praised for making the desktop PC an attractive product rather than a dull grey box. Yet, when one analyses sales of the iMac they are tiny compared to other PC manufacturers such as Dell and Hewlett-Packard. The iMac is clearly different from other PCs and customers have to pay a price premium for this, but few are willing to pay twice as much for a machine that ends up doing much the same as any other PC (Mac users would understandably argue at this point, saying that the Mac operating system is far superior to Microsoft's Windows, but to most consumers who are not computer literate a PC is a PC). Profit margins are extremely small for PCs; this is why it is difficult for Apple to produce any revenue from the iMac despite its success. Indeed, it is the iPod that has delivered the cash for Apple. Apple has been here before, twenty years ago in fact. The success of the Apple Mac in 1984 delivered piles of cash for Apple and a rising market share of the growing PC market, yet it was Microsoft that emerged the winner largely because it licensed its operating system to all PC manufacturers, whereas Apple decided against this approach, opting instead to stay in control of its system. Microsoft has gone on to be the dominant software company in the world. In 2005 Apple's iPod is the leading digital music player, but should it

license its successful iPod technology? There are certainly lots of automobile manufacturers that would like to offer in-car iPod music players. There are cell phone handset manufacturers that would like to incorporate iPod music players into their products. And there are many electronic companies such as Sony, Sharp, Cannon and others that would be able to develop digital music players using iPod technology. It may be that Apple feels the technology, in this case the software, is an integral part of the physical product and that to separate the aesthetics of the music player from the software would damage the iPod brand, leading to a commoditisation of the digital music player market and an overall decline in the iPod. Furthermore, margins are relatively good for Apple and licensing the technology would surely mean increased competition and reduced margins.

Apple, perhaps best known for its Macintosh computers, has relied on the iPod and sales of music from its iTune online Music Store to make up for its lack of market gains in the highly competitive PC market. It is necessary to remind students of business that ultimately this is about money and Apple was twice the size of Microsoft in 1995 and since then has largely failed to deliver growth for its shareholders. Indeed, Apple has not performed well compared to the overall stock market and a dollar invested in 1992 would only be worth 79 cents today. It made a lot of cash during the last years of the technology boom (2000), and because Mr Jobs did such a good job of streamlining the company it was able to hold on to that cash. But fundamentally, the growth is flat. The core business of PCs continues to shrink, with iPod and iTunes driving its current revenue growth. While eye-catching, the iPod still has only a relatively small impact on Apple's overall fortunes. But the rapid growth in the portable music business means that the iPod contributed around 40 per cent of the revenue growth in 2003, compared with the same period a year before, and offers huge growth potential.

Sources: Coggan, P. (2005) 'iPod's popularity fires Apple back into FT500 ranks', *Financial Times*, 11 June; Durman, P. (2005) 'A second bite of Apple', *Sunday Times*, Business, 25 September, p. 5; Inman, P. (2005) 'Fraudsters use iPods to steal company information', *Guardian*, 14 June; Morrison, S. (2005) 'Wall St wants Apple to raise iPod volume', FT.com, 12 July; Schofield, J. (2005) 'Microsoft gets creative to stave off its midlife crisis', *Technology Guardian*, 29 September, p. 9; Webb, A. (2007) 'The end of the road for DRM', *Technology Guardian*, 8 February, p. 10.

Questions

1 Explain how the iPod is helping Apple achieve increased PC sales.

2 What are the potential benefits and limitations of licensing the iPod software to other MP3 manufacturers?

3 The iPod is facing fierce competition from all quarters: Sony, Dell and other electronics firms as well as cell phone makers who are incorporating MP3 players into their devices. How can Apple compete?

4 What about longer-term success? How can Apple influence future technology developments or establish strategic alliances to ensure it is a dominant force in the new handheld device that will incorporate both cell phone and MP3 player?

5 Can Apple adopt a 'BMW strategy' (BMW strategy is to target high-premium segments) for the PC market and MP3 market?

6 What are the advantages and disadvantages of the Apple approach to launching a new product at Apple users first and then the larger Microsoft Windows users second?

7 The launch of the iPhone in 2007 helps answer Apple's strategy decision on competing with cell phones, but what about licensing, can it license the iPhone? Should it?

Chapter summary

This initial chapter has sought to introduce the subject of innovation management and place it in context with the theory of economic growth. One can quickly become ensnarled in stale academic debates of semantics if innovation is viewed as a single event, hence the importance of viewing it as a process. The chapter has also stressed the importance of understanding how firms manage innovation and how this can be better achieved by adopting a management perspective.

The level of understanding of the subject of innovation has improved significantly over the past half century and during that time a variety of models of innovation have emerged. The strengths and weaknesses of these were examined and a conceptual framework was presented that stressed the linkages and overlaps between internal departments and external organisations.

1 Many innovations today are associated with companies as opposed to individuals. Why is this, and what does it tell us?

2 What is wrong with the popular view of innovation in which eccentric scientists develop new products?

3 Explain how technology differs from science, yet still does not equal innovation.

4 What is the difference between an unsuccessful innovation and an invention?

5 To what extent do you agree with the controversial view presented by the chairman of Sony?

6 To what extent are industry standards (such as the VHS format) beneficial?

7 Explain McCain Foods managing director's view that invention is easy but innovation is difficult.

Key words and phrases

Economic growth

Organisational architecture

Innovation as a management process

Network models of innovation

Resource-based theory of the firm

Open innovation

Websites worth visiting

Advice for inventors from the UK Government **www.innovation.gov.uk**

Alternative resource for innovation **www.Innovationzen.com**

Association for University Research and Industry Links **www.auril.org.uk/**

Business Dynamics **www.businessdynamics.org.uk/gen/default.aspx**

Business Link **www.businesslink.gov.uk**

Chemical Industries Association **www.cia.org.uk**

Confederation of British Industry **www.cbi.org.uk**

Crazy ideas and inventions **www.halfbakery.com**

Design Council **www.design-council.org.uk/**

DTI Innovation Site **www.innovation-point.com/resources.htm**

The Engineering Council (EC UK) **www.engc.org.uk**

European Community information service **http://cordis.europa.eu/en/home.html**

European Industrial Research Management Association (EIRMA) **www.eirma.asso.fr**

European Union, Enterprise and Innovation **www.europa.eu.int/comm/enterprise/innovation**

European Union, Innovation Directorate **www.cordis.lu/fp6/innovation.htm**

The Global Entrepreneurship Monitor **http://www.gemconsortium.org/**

IBM's global innovation outlook **Global Innovation Outlook**

Ideas, innovations **www.abettermousetrap.co.uk/links.htm**

Innovation in education **www.innovation-unit.co.uk/**

Innovation Internet links **www.innovationlinks.com**

Innovation tools, resources and strategies **www.Innovationtools.com**

Institute of Directors (IOD) **www.iod.com**

Intellectual Property Office **www.ipo.gov.uk/**

Intellect UK **www.intellectuk.org**

National Council for Graduate Entrepreneurship **http://ncge.com/content/page/85**

Patent Office **www.patent.gov.uk**

Quoted Companies Alliance (QCA) **www.qcanet.co.uk**

The R&D Society **www.rdsoc.org**

The Royal Academy of Engineering **www.raeng.org.uk**

Stanford University, explaining innovation **www.Manufacturing.Stanford.edu**

UK Government, Department of Trade and Industry **www.Dti.gov.uk/innovation**

Young Enterprise **www.young-enterprise.org.uk/pub/**

References

Abernathy, W.J. and Utterback, J. (1978) 'Patterns of industrial innovation', in Tushman, M.L. and Moore, W.L. *Readings in the Management of Innovation*, 97–108, HarperCollins, New York.

Allen, T.J. (1977) *Managing the Flow of Technology*, MIT Press, Cambridge, MA.

Berkhout, A.J. (2000) *The dynamic role of knowledge innovation: An integrated framework of cyclic networks for the assessment of technological change and sustainable growth*, Delft University Press, Delft, Netherlands.

Berkhout, A.J., Hartman, D., van der Duin, P. and Ortt, R. (2006) 'Innovating the innovation process', *International Journal of Technology Management*, Vol. 34, No. 3/4, 390–404.

Berkhout, A.J. and van der Duin, P. (2007) 'New ways of innovation: an application of the cyclic innovation model to the mobile telecom industry', *International Journal of Technology Management*.

Berkhout, A.J., van der Duin, P., Hartmann, D. and Ortt, R. (eds) (2007) 'The cyclic nature of innovation: Connecting hard sciences with soft values', *Advances in the Study of Entrepreneurship, Innovation and Economic Growth*, Vol. 17.

Burns, T. and Stalker, G.M. (1961) *The Management of Innovation*, Tavistock, London.

Business Week (2006) 'The world's most innovative firms', 24 April.

Carter, C.F. and Williams, B.R. (1957) 'The characteristics of technically progressive firms', *Journal of Industrial Economics*, March, 87–104.

Chandler, A.D. (1962) *Strategy and Structure: Chapters in the History of American Industrial Enterprise*, MIT Press: Cambridge, MA.

Chesbrough, H. (2003) *Open Innovation: The new imperative for creating and profiting from technology*, Harvard Business School Press, Boston, MA.

Christensen, C.M. (2003) *The Innovator's Dilemma: When New Technologies Cause Great Firms to Fail*, 3rd edn, HBS Press, Cambridge, MA.

Cohen, W.M. and Levinthal, D.A. (1990) 'A new perspective on learning and innovation', *Administrative Science Quarterly*, Vol. 35, No. 1, 128–52.

Conner, K.R. and Prahalad, C.K. (1996) 'A resource-based theory of the firm: knowledge versus opportunism', *Organisation Science*, Vol. 7, No. 5, 477–501.

Cooper, R. (1994) 'Third generation new product processes', *Journal of Product Innovation Management*, Vol. 11, No. 1, 3–14.

Coyne, W.E. (1996) Innovation lecture given at the Royal Society, 5 March.

Cullen, B. (2003) *It's a long way from penny apples*, Coronet, London.

Cyert, R.M. and March, J.G. (1963) *A Behavioural Theory of the Firm*, Prentice-Hall, Englewood Cliffs, NJ.

Dodgson, M., Gann, D. and Salter, A. (2005) *Think, Play, Do*, Oxford University Press, Oxford.

Domar, D. (1946) 'Capital expansion, rate of growth and employment', *Econometra*, Vol. 14, 137–47.

Eisenhardt, K.M. and Martin, J.A. (2000) 'The knowledge-based economy: from the economics of knowledge to the learning economy', in Foray, D. and Lundvall, B.-A. (eds) *Employment and Growth in the Knowledge-Based Economy*, OECD, Paris.

European Commission (2001) European Innovation Scoreboard 2001, Cordis Focus supplement, document SEC 1414.

European Commission (2003) European Innovation Scoreboard, Technical Paper No. 1: Indicatives and Definitions, 11 November 2003.

Freeman, C. (1982) *The Economics of Industrial Innovation*, 2nd edn, Frances Pinter, London.

Galbraith, J.R. (1982) 'Designing the innovative organisation', *Organisational Dynamics*, Winter, 3–24.

Grant, R.M. (1996) 'Towards a knowledge-based theory of the firm', *Strategic Management Journal*, Summer Special Issue, Vol. 17, 109–22.

Hamel, G. and Prahalad, C.K. (1994) 'Competing for the future', *Harvard Business Review*, Vol. 72, No. 4, 122–8.

Hargadon, A. and Douglas, Y. (2001) 'When innovations meet institutions: Edison and the design of the electric light', *Administrative Science Quarterly*, Vol. 46, 476–501.

Harrod, R.F. (1949) 'An essay in dynamic theory', *Economic Journal*, Vol. 49, No. 1, 277–93.

Hutton, W. (1995) The State We're In, Jonathan Cape, London.

Isenson, R. (1968) 'Technology in retrospect and critical events in science' (Project Traces), Illinois Institute of Technology/National Science Foundation, Chicago IL.

Kelly, P. and Kranzberg, M. (eds) (1978) *Technological Innovation: A Critical Review of Current Knowledge*, San Francisco Press, San Francisco, CA.

Kondratieff, N.D. (1935/51) 'The long waves in economic life', *Review of Economic Statistics*, Vol. 17, 6–105 (1935), reprinted in Haberler, G. (ed.) *Readings in Business Cycle Theory*, Richard D. Irwin, Homewood, IL (1951).

Langrish, J., Gibbons, M., Evans, W.G. and Jevons, F.R. (1972) *Wealth from Knowledge*, Macmillan, London.

Lefever, D.B. (1992) 'Technology transfer and the role of intermediaries', PhD thesis, INTA, Cranfield Institute of Technology.

Leifer, R., Colarelli O'Connor, G., Peters, L.S. (2000) *Radical Innovation*, Harvard Business School Press, Boston, MA.

Low, M.B. and MacMillan, I.C. (1988) 'Entrepreneurship: past research and future challenges', *Journal of Management*, June, 139–59.

Mason, G., Beltram, J. and Paul, J. (2004) 'External knowledge sourcing in different national settings: a comparison of electronics establishments in Britain and France', *Research Policy*, Vol. 33, No. 1, 53–72.

Morita, A. (1992) ' "S" does not equal "T" and "T" does not equal "I" ', paper presented at the Royal Society, February 1992.

Murray, S. (2003) 'Innovation: A British talent for ingenuity and application', www.FT.com, 22 April.

Myers, S. and Marquis, D.G. (1969) 'Successful industrial innovation: a study of factors underlying innovation in selected firms', National Science Foundation, NSF 69–17, Washington, DC.

Nelson, R.R. and Winter, S. (1982) *An Evolutionary Theory of Economic Change*, Harvard University Press, Boston, MA.

Nonaka, I. (1991) 'The knowledge creating company', *Harvard Business Review*, November–December, 96–104.

Nonaka, I. and Kenney, M. (1991) 'Towards a new theory of innovation management: a case study comparing Canon, Inc. and Apple Computer, Inc.', *Journal of Engineering and Technology Management*, Vol. 8, 67–83.

Oxford English Dictionary (2005), Oxford University Press, London.

Parkin, M., Powell, M. and Matthews, K. (1997) *Economics*, 3rd edn, Addison-Wesley, Harlow.

Patel, P. and Pavitt, K. (2000) 'How technological competencies help define the core (not the boundaries) of the firm', in Dosi, G., Nelson, R. and Winter, S.G. (eds) *The Nature and Dynamics of Organisational Capabilities*, Oxford University Press, Oxford, 313–33.

Pavitt, K. (1990) 'What we know about the strategic management of technology', *California Management Review*, Vol. 32, No. 3, 17–26.

Penrose, E.T. (1959) *The Theory of the Growth of the Firm*, Wiley, New York.

Pittaway, L., Robertson, M., Munir, K., Denyer, D. and Neely, A. (2004) 'Networking and innovation: a systematic review of the evidence', *International Journal of Management Reviews*, Vol. 5/6, Nos 3&4, 137–68.

Polanyi, M. (1966) *The Tacit Dimension*, Routledge & Kegan Paul, London.

Porter, M.E. (1980) *Competitive Strategy*, The Free Press, New York.

Porter, M.E. (1985) *Competitive Strategy*, Harvard University Press, Boston, MA.

Prahalad, C.K. and Hamel, G. (1990) 'The core competence of the corporation', *Harvard Business Review*, Vol. 68, No. 3, 79–91.

Rogers, E. and Shoemaker, R. (1972) *Communications of Innovations*, Free Press, New York.

Rothwell, R. and Zegveld, W. (1985) *Reindustrialisation and Technology*, Longman, London.

Rothwell, R. (1992) 'Successful industrial innovation: critical factors for the 1990s', *R&D Management*, Vol. 22, No. 3, 221–39.

Rothwell, R., Freeman, C., Horlsey, A., Jervis, V.T.P., Robertson, A.B. and Townsend, J. (1974) 'SAPPHO updated: Project SAPPHO phase II', *Research Policy*, Vol. 3, 258–91.

Schrange, M. (2000) *Serious Play – How the world's best companies stimulate to innovate*, Harvard Business School Press, Boston, MA.

Schumpeter, J.A. (1934) *The Theory of Economic Development*, Harvard University Press, Boston, MA.

Schumpeter, J.A. (1939) *Business Cycles*, McGraw-Hill, New York.

Schumpeter, J.A. (1942) *Capitalism, Socialism and Democracy*, Allen & Unwin, London.

Simon, H. (1957) *Administrative Behaviour*, Free Press, New York.

Slater, S.F. and Narver, J. (1994) 'Does competitive environment moderate the market orientation performance relationship?' *Journal of Marketing*, Vol. 58 (January), 46–55.

Sunday Times (2004) 'Quick learner who staked his claim in computer insurance', Business Section 3, 18 January.

Thomke, S.H. (2003) *Experimentation Matters: Unlocking the potential of new technologies for innovation*, Harvard Business School Press, Boston, MA.

Trott, P. (1993) 'Inward technology transfer as an interactive process: a case study of ICI', PhD thesis, Cranfield University.

Trott, P. (1998) 'Growing businesses by generating genuine business opportunities', *Journal of Applied Management Studies*, Vol. 7, No. 4, 211–22.

Tushman, M.L. (1978) 'Task characteristics and technical communication in research and development', *Academy of Management Review*, Vol. 21, 624–45.

Utterback, J. (1994) *Mastering the Dynamics of Innovation*, Harvard Business School Press, Boston, MA.

Van de Ven, A.H. (1999) *The Innovation Journey*, Oxford University Press, New York.

von Hippel, E. (1978) 'Users as innovators', *Technology Review*, Vol. 80, No. 3, 30–4.

von Hippel, E. (2005) *Democratizing Innovation*, MIT Press, Cambridge, MA.

Wernerfelt, B. (1984) 'A resource based view of the firm', *Strategic Management Journal*, Vol. 5, No. 2, 171–180.

Wernerfelt, B. (1995) 'The resource-based view of the firm: ten years after', *Strategic Management Journal*, Vol. 16, No. 3, 171–4.

Wheelwright, S. and Clark, K. (1992) *Revolutionising Product Development*, The Free Press, New York.

Woodward, J. (1965) *Industrial Organisation: Theory and Practice*, 2nd edn, Oxford University Press, Oxford.

Further reading

For a more detailed review of the innovation management literature, the following develop many of the issues raised in this chapter:

Adams, R., Bessant, J. and Phelps, R. (2006) 'Innovation management measurement: A review', *International Journal of Management Reviews*, Vol. 8, No. 1, 21–47.

Byron, K. (1998) 'Invention and innovation', *Science and Public Affairs*, Summer, Royal Society.

Evans, H. (2005) 'The Eureka Myth', *Harvard Business Review*, 83, June, 18–20.

Shavinina, L.V. (ed.) (2003) *The International Handbook on Innovation*, Elsevier, Oxford.

Sundbo, J. and Fuslang, L. (eds) (2002) *Innovation as Strategic Reflexivity*, Routledge, London.

Tidd, J. (2000) *From Knowledge Management to Strategic Competence: Measuring technological, market and organisational innovation*, Imperial College Press, London.

Tidd, J., Bessant, J. and Pavitt, K. (2005) *Managing Innovation*, 3rd edn, John Wiley & Sons, Chichester.

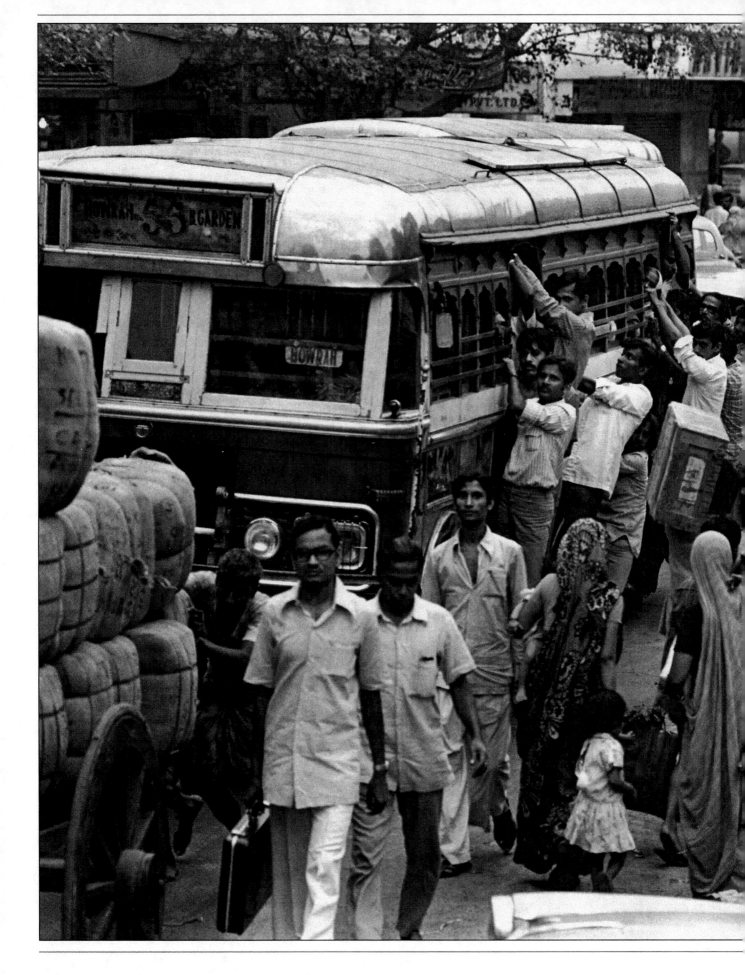

TRANSPORTATION AND COMMUNICATIONS

OBJECTIVES

- To develop an understanding of modern transportation and communication systems
- To point out the historically specific nature of these systems
- To illustrate the nature of cost-space and time-space convergence
- To demonstrate the relationship between transport and economic development
- To emphasize the critical role of transportation policy.
- To consider recent innovations in transport development of U.S. metropolitan areas
- To examine communications innovations and online computer networks
- To summarize the social and economic impacts of the Internet
- To speculate realistically on likely future impacts of telecommunications technology

Traffic in Calcutta, India.

For most of human existence, people occupied narrowly circumscribed areas that were mostly isolated from other groups of people. Gradually, improvements in the efficiency of transportation systems changed patterns of human life. Control and exchange became possible over wider and wider areas and facilitated the development of more elaborate social structures such as far-flung empires. The course of human history, and people's relations to space and time, changed dramatically when capitalism conquered over the globe. From the sixteenth century onward, there were great revolutions in science and trade, great voyages of discovery and conquest, and a consequent increase in the amount of productive, commodity, and financial capital. During the Industrial Revolution of the late eighteenth and nineteenth centuries, the speed with which people, goods, and information crossed the globe accelerated exponentially when inanimate energy was applied to transportation. Capitalism required a world market for its goods; hence, it broke the isolation of preindustrial economies.

The engine that drove this economic expansion was capital accumulation, that is, production for the sake of profit. In an effort to increase the rate of accumulation, all forms of capital had to be moved as quickly and cheaply as possible between places of production and consumption. To annihilate space by time, some of the resulting profits of commerce were devoted to developing the means of transportation and communication. "Annihilation of space by time" does not simply imply that better transportation and communication systems diminish the importance of geographic space; instead, the concept poses the question of how and by what means space can be used, organized, created, and dominated to facilitate the circulation of capital. Time and space appear to us as "natural," that is, as somehow existing outside of society, but a historical perspective on how capitalism has changed our experience of them reveals time and space to be social constructs. Different societies experience and give meaning to time and space in different ways, and the changes unleashed by capitalism reconfigured these experiences worldwide.

The steady integration of production systems around the globe does not change their absolute location (*site*), but it does dramatically alter their relative location (*situation*). If we measure the distances between places in terms of the time or cost needed to overcome them (the friction of distance), then those distances have steadily shrunk over the last 500 years, particularly over the last 100. Transport improvements thus increase the importance of relative space. The progressive integration of absolute space into relative space means that economic development becomes less dependent on relations with nature (e.g., resources and environmental constraints) and more dependent on social relations across space.

Improvements in transportation promote spatial interaction; consequently, they spur specialization of location. The formation of local comparative advantages is facilitated by declines in transport costs (Chapter 12). By stimulating specialization, better transportation leads to increased land and labor productivity as well as to more efficient use of capital. As societies abandon self-sufficiency for dependency on trade, their wealth and incomes generally rise, although not equally for everyone.

In today's world, almost nothing is consumed where it is produced; therefore, without transport services, most goods would be worthless. Part of their value derives from transport to market. Transport costs, then, are not a constraint on productivity; rather, efficient transportation increases the productivity of an economy because it promotes specialization of location.

Transportation and communications are keys for understanding economic geography. How does the geographic pattern of transport routes affect development? How do changing transport networks shape and structure space? What is the impact of transport costs and transit time on the location of facilities? How is information technology (IT) changing the way we live, work, and conduct business? This chapter provides answers to these questions in discussions on transport costs and networks, transport development, transportation and communications innovation, and metropolitan concerns in transportation policy. It explores the historical development of modern transport systems, some general properties of transport costs, and the central role played by the state. Later, it turns to telecommunications and their impacts.

TRANSPORTATION NETWORKS IN HISTORICAL PERSPECTIVE

Prior to the development of railroads, overland transportation of heavy goods was slow and costly. Movement of heavy raw materials by water was much cheaper than by land. For this reason, most of the world's commerce was carried by water transportation, and the important cities were maritime or riverine cities.

To bring stretches of water into locations that needed them, canals were constructed in Europe beginning in the sixteenth century, with the height of technology represented by the pound lock developed in the Low Countries and northern Italy. Until the nineteenth century, canals were the most advanced form of transportation and were built wherever capital was available. Road building was the cheap alternative where canals were physically or financially impractical.

The most active period of canal building coincided with the early Industrial Revolution in the eighteenth century. The vast increase in manufacturing and trade fostered by the canals paved the way for the Industrial

Revolution. The canals were financed by central governments on the Continent and by business interests in England, where a complex network was built during the last 40 years of the eighteenth century and the first quarter of the nineteenth century. Somewhat later, artificial waterways were constructed in North America (e.g., the Erie Canal). They supplemented the rivers and Great Lakes, the principal arteries for moving the staples of timber, grain, preserved meat, tobacco, cotton, coal, and ores.

At sea, efforts before the Industrial Revolution concentrated on expanding the known seas and on improving ships (e.g., better hulls and sails) to allow for practical transport over increasing distances. By 1800, or a few decades later in the case of the technology of sail, the traditional technology of transport reached its ultimate refinement. Subsequently, the rapid expansion of commerce and industry overtaxed existing facilities. The canals were crowded and ran short of water in dry periods, and the roads were clogged when traffic in wet periods. These problems contributed to a general crisis of profitability by the late eighteenth century. The result was an effort to utilize mechanical energy as the motivating power.

The invention of the steam engine by James Watt in 1769 paved the way for technical advances in transportation. Its application to water in 1807 and to land in 1829, through the development of the steamship and locomotive, respectively, heralded the era of cheap transportation. In Europe, an expanding network of railways helped to create markets and provided urban populations with an excellent system of freight and passenger transportation (Figure 9.1). In the United States, the railroad was an instrument of national development; it preceded virtually all settlement west of the Mississippi, helped to establish centers such as Kansas City and Atlanta, and integrated regional markets. Today the Amtrak system (Figure 9.2) forms the passenger rail system in the United States. However, relatively low demand and public subsidies have rendered the U.S. rail network very poorly developed compared with the high-speed trains of Europe. In developing countries, railroads linked export centers to the economies of Europe and North America.

Until the 1880s, cities were mainly pedestrian centers requiring business establishments to agglomerate in close proximity to one another. This usually meant about a 30-minute walk from the center of town to any given urban point; hence, cities were extremely compact. The transformation of the compact city into the modern metropolis depended on the invention of the electric traction motor by Frank Sprague. The first electrified trolley system opened in Richmond, Virginia, in 1888. The innovation, which increased the average speed of intraurban transport from 5 to more than 15 miles per hour, diffused rapidly to other North American and European cities, as well as to Australia, Latin America, and Asia. Electric trolleys were the primary form of urban commuting until the widespread adoption of the automobile in the 1920s.

FIGURE 9.1
Europe's planned new rail network. As part of a worldwide mission to encourage more travelers onto rail from other modes, railway companies are developing improved passenger and freight information services. Real-time information at stations and on trains is now a reality in some quarters, with more services to come. High-speed passenger transport applications are driving technology innovation in the rail industry. The focus is now on extensions into eastern Europe.

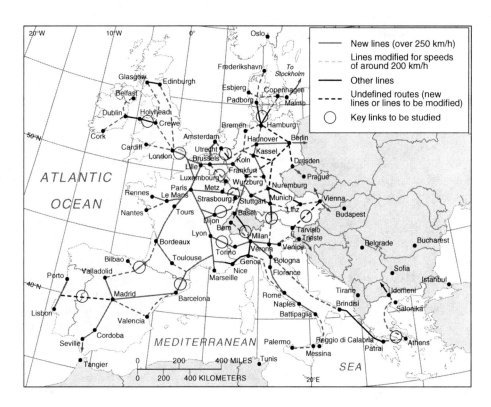

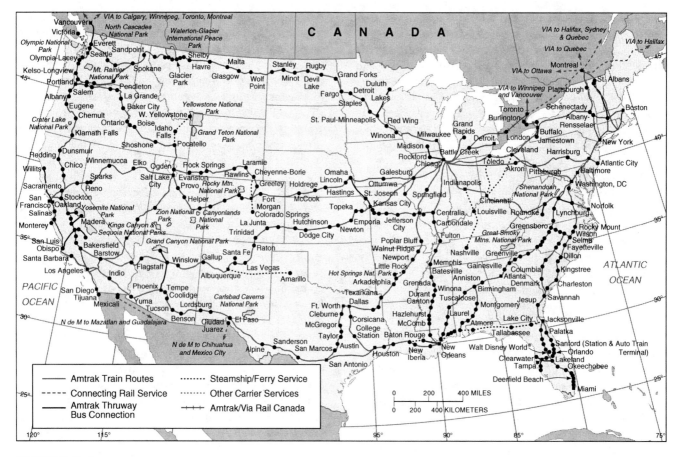

FIGURE 9.2
Amtrack's network.

The nineteenth century was a time when roads were reduced to feeders for the railroads. Road improvements awaited the arrival of the automobile. In the United States, heavy reliance on the automobile is a cross between a love affair with the passenger car and a lack of alternatives. In most cities, roughly 90 percent of the working population travels to and from work by car; in the less auto-dependent cities like New York, cars still account for two-thirds of all work-related trips. Public transportation is relatively rare, and confined to a few large cities. By comparison, in Europe, where cities are less extensively suburbanized and average commuting distances are half those of North America, only 40 percent of urban residents use their cars. In Tokyo, a mere 15 percent of the population drives to work. In these cases, commuting trains and buses are the norm.

In the developing world, insufficient capital investments in transportation have created a crisis—the result of a mismatch between inadequate budgets for the transportation infrastructure, services, and the need for vast mobility of the majority of the population. Governments that favor private car ownership by a small but affluent and politically influential elite distort their country's development priorities and promote inefficient transportation systems that do not serve the bulk of the

population. Importing fuels, car components, or already assembled cars consumes foreign revenues and negatively impacts trade balances. Similarly, building and maintaining an elaborate highway system devours enormous resources. The twentieth century saw a road-building boom in many LDCs, to the detriment of railroads and other forms of transport. With insufficient resources for maintenance, many roads in LDCs are in disrepair. In cities, bus systems and other means of public transportation are often also in a poor state, meeting only a small proportion of transportation needs; crowded buses and trains are symptoms of underinvestment in this sector. Often, the poor cannot afford public transportation at all. Walking still accounts for two-thirds of all trips in large African cities like Kinshasa and for almost one-half the trips in Bangalore, India. Pedestrians and traditional modes of transportation are increasingly being marginalized in the developing countries.

Transport networks are constructed to facilitate *spatial interaction*, the movement of goods, people, and information among countries and cities as well as within cities. These networks range greatly in their degree of complexity and connectivity among nodes (Figure 9.3). These flows represent the exchange of supplies and demands at different locations. The term *distance decay*

International Business

Five Simplified Networks

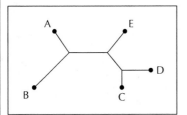

(a) BRANCHING NETWORK: shortest total interpoint connections, lowest construction costs; poor connections for nearby points (e.g., developing country road or rail system).

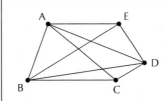

(b) CIRCUIT NETWORK: shortest connection between points; lowest user costs (e.g., developed country road or air network).

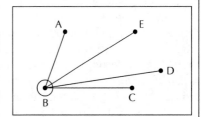

(c) HIERARCHY NETWORK: the shortest set of connections between a central point and all other points; the hub-and-spoke system of airlines (e.g., connection to primate city).

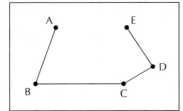

(d) PAUL REVERE'S RIDE: the shortest path between a beginning point and all other points; a minimum distance solution to pipeline placement or energy transmission lines.

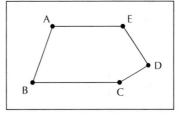

(e) TRAVELING SALESMAN NETWORK: the shortest route around a set of points; the most efficient shopping trip pattern (e.g., truck delivery pattern).

FIGURE 9.3
Five simplified transport networks.

An Amtrak conventional passenger train at Harper's Ferry, West Virginia. New magnetic levitated trains will shuttle passengers between American cities at over 300 mph. Using far less energy and time than automobile and air travel, one will go by train from Los Angeles to San Francisco in an hour and a half, or between Washington, D.C., and Boston in less than an hour.

describes the attenuation or reduction in the flow or movement among places with increasing distance between them. Most food shipments, passenger trips, natural resource flows, and commodity movements occur within regions and within countries, rather than between them. The underlying principle of distance decay is the *friction of distance*. There are time and cost factors associated with extra increments of distance for all types of flow or movement. Figures 9.4 and 9.5 illustrate the distance decay for the movements of goods and people, respectively, in the United States, indicating that most trips occur over a relatively short distance. For individuals, the out-of-pocket costs of operating a vehicle or truck are combined with the cost of a person's time. With longer distance, it is more expensive to ship

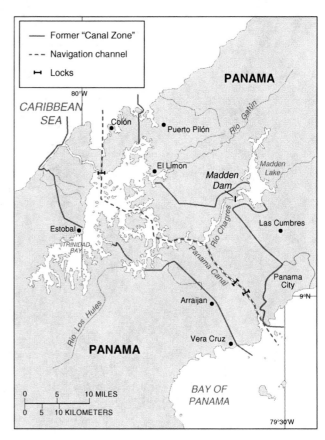

FIGURE 9.5
The Panama Canal, with 14,000 transits in 2004, has enormous strategic and commercial importance. The government of Panama now controls the canal after 85 years of operation by the U.S. government.

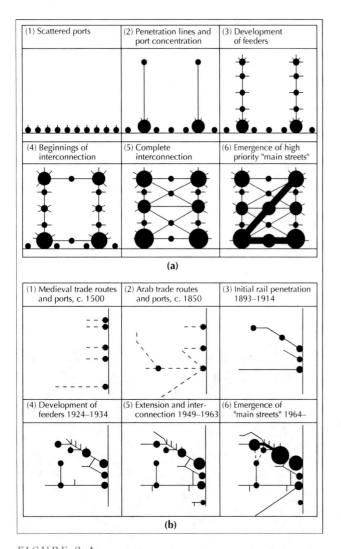

FIGURE 9.4
An idealized sequence of transportation development: (a) the Taaffe, Morrill, and Gould model, 1963; and (b) an adaptation to East Africa by Hoyle, 1973.

commodities because of labor rates of drivers and operators, as well as over-the-road costs of vehicle operation. Telephone calls and parcel deliveries, likewise, are generally more expensive for more distant locations.

Historically, the development of transport networks has reflected and induced settlement, industrialization, and urbanization. The impact of transport networks on regional economic development is demonstrated in a famous stage model of network change in underdeveloped countries created by Taaffe, Morrill, and Gould (1963). This model illustrates how the interplay between the evolution of a transport network and urban growth is self-reinforcing (see Figure 9.4). The ideal-typical sequence begins the first stage when early colonial conquest creates a system of settlements and berthing points along the seacoast. Gradually, a second stage evolves with the construction of penetration routes that link the best-located ports to the inland mining, agricultural, and population centers. Export-based development stimulates growth in the interior, and a number of intermediate centers spring up along the principal access routes. This process results in the third stage of transport evolution—the growth of feeder

Commuter traffic in Bejing. For half of the world's population, the bicycle is a principal means of transportation. In China, less than one person in 1000 owns an automobile. Public buses are cheap and moderately efficient, but human power is still very important for intraurban movement by foot and bicycle. Pedestrian movement dominates urban areas in terms of the number of trips. If the price of gasoline or the price of parking doubled, would you be willing to travel by bicycle to get to work or school?

routes and links from the inland centers. By the fourth stage, lateral route development enhances the competitive position of the major ports and inland centers. A few nodes along the original lines of inland penetration (i.e., N_1 and N_2) become focal points for feeder networks of their own, and they begin to capture the hinterlands of smaller centers on each side. The fifth stage evolves when a transport network interconnects all the major centers. In the sixth and last stage, the development of high-priority linkages reinforces the advantages of urban centers that have come to dominate the economy.

The idealized model of network change describes one typical sequence of development. It shows that a transport network has the short-run purpose of facilitating movement but that its fundamental effect is to influence the subsequent development and structure of the space economy through the operation of cumulative causation. *Cumulative causation* refers to the process by which economic activity tends to concentrate in an area with an initial advantage. The stage model, therefore, illustrates how a space economy roots itself ever more firmly as initial locational decisions that shaped the system are subsequently reinforced by other decisions. The result is a concentrated and polarized pattern of development.

Transport changes in the last 175 years have not been confined to railroads and roads. At sea, ships equipped first with steam turbines and then diesel engines facilitated the rapid expansion of international trade. In addition, the opening of the Suez Canal in 1869 and the Panama Canal in 1914 dramatically reduced the distance of many routes (see Figure 9.5), reconfiguring

trade networks and changing the geography of port cities. In ocean shipping, containerships, which use standardized containers that can be efficiently stacked and easily switched between ships and trucks, have become the basic transoceanic carrier. Planes have ousted passenger liners and trains as the standard travel mode for long-distance passengers. The shipment of cargo by air, however, is still in its infancy; while heavy, bulky, and low-valued goods are always shipped by water (e.g., oil, flour), only perishable, high-value, or urgently needed shipments are sent by air freight (e.g., pharmaceuticals).

COST-SPACE AND TIME-SPACE CONVERGENCE

If geography is the study of how human beings are stretched over the earth's surface, a vital part of that process is how we know and feel about space and time. Although space and time appear as "natural" and outside of society, they are in fact social constructions; every society develops different ways of dealing with and perceiving them. In this reading, time and space are socially created, plastic, mutable institutions that profoundly shape individual perceptions and social relations. Transport improvements have resulted in what geographers call *cost-space* and *time-space convergence* or *time-space compression*—that is, the progressive reduction in cost of travel and travel time among places. Similarly, if we measure transport costs in terms of the cost of overcoming the friction of distance, ever-cheaper movement of people and goods leads to *cost-space convergence*.

Transport improvements have brought significant cost reductions to shippers, creating a cost-space compression that altered the geographies of centrality and peripherality of different places. For example, the opening of the Erie Canal in 1825 reduced the cost of transport between Buffalo and Albany from $100 to $10 and, ultimately, to $3 per ton. Railroad freight rates in the United States dropped 41 percent between 1882 and 1900. Between the 1870s and 1950s, improvements in the efficiency of ships reduced the real cost of ocean transport by about 60 percent.

Cheaper, more efficient modes of transport widened the range over which goods could be shipped economically and contributed to the growth of cities. They enabled cities to obtain food products from distant places and facilitated urban concentration by stimulating large-scale production and geographic division of labor. Furthermore, transportation improvements changed patterns of urban accessibility. North American cities have grown from compact walking- and horse-car cities (pre-1800–1890), to electric streetcar cities (1890–1920), and, finally, to dispersed automobile cities in the recreational automobile era (1920–1945), the freeway era (1945–1970), the edge city era (1970–1990), and the exurban era (1990–present) (Figure 9.6).

Developments in transportation have also cut travel times extensively. For example, the travel time between Edinburgh and London, a distance of 640 kilometers, decreased from 20,000 minutes by stagecoach in 1658 to less than 60 minutes by airplane today (Figure 9.7). Time-space convergence was marked during the period of rapid transport development; for example, in the 1840s, travel time between Edinburgh and London was longer than 2,000 minutes by stagecoach, but by the 1850s, with the arrival of the steam locomotive, the travel time had been reduced by two-thirds, to 800 minutes. By 1988, the rail journey between Edinburgh and London took 275 minutes. When the line was electrified in 1995, travel time was reduced to less than 180 minutes. In communications, the steadily declining cost of long-distance telephone calls increased the interactions among cities such as New York and San Francisco (Figure 9.8).

Air transportation provides spectacular examples of time-space convergence. In the late 1930s, it took a DC-3 between 15 and 17 hours to fly the United States from coast to coast. Modern jets now cross the continent in about 5 hours. In 1934, planes took 12 days to fly between London and Brisbane. Today the Boeing 747 SP is capable of flying any commercially practicable route nonstop. The result is that any place on earth is within less than 24 hours of any other place, using the most direct route.

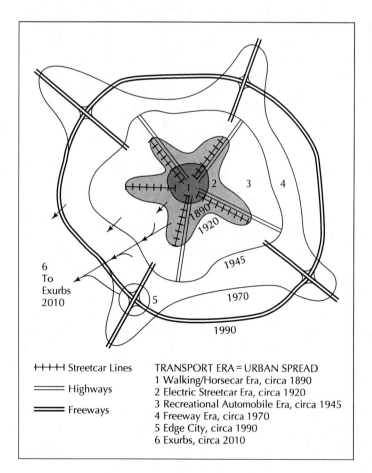

FIGURE 9.6
Stages of metropolitan growth and transport development in a North American city.

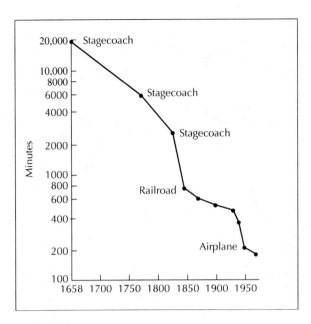

FIGURE 9.7
Time-space convergence between London and Edinburgh.

TRANSPORTATION INFRASTRUCTURE

Transportation and communication infrastructures allow countries to specialize in production and trade. This regional division of labor is comparable to the task division of labor among its workers. The transportation and communications infrastructure of a country influences its internal geography. In some countries, transportation and communications are slow and difficult. Some regions are totally inaccessible (Figure 9.9). Much of the developing world has poorly developed infrastructures.

Fast and efficient transportation systems release capital for productive investment and allow the development of natural resources, regional specialization of production, and internal trade among regions. Even though India appears to be well connected, it is a country whose economic growth is harnessed by an inadequate transportation and communications infrastructure. Passenger and commodity traffic on India's roads has increased 30-fold since independence in 1948. Roads are overcrowded, and 80 percent of villages lack all-weather roads. Improved accessibility would allow regional specialization of production and cash crop farming, especially of high-value crops such as fruits and vegetables that spoil quickly.

Conversely, the well-developed infrastructures of North America and Europe bespeak their level of economic development. However, most countries of the world have simple transport networks penetrating the interior from ports along the ocean. These railroads and highways are called tap routes. Tap routes are the legacy of colonialism or the product of neocolonialism. Such routes facilitate getting into and out of a country, but they do not allow for internal circulation or circulation between countries in the same region.

GENERAL PROPERTIES OF TRANSPORT COSTS

Transportation costs appear deceptively simple but are far more complex upon further scrutiny. They can be categorized as either *terminal costs* or *line-haul costs* (Figure 9.10). Terminal costs must be paid regardless of the distance involved. They include the cost of loading and unloading, capital investment, and line maintenance. Line-haul costs, in contrast, are strictly a function of distance. For example, fuel costs are proportional to the distance a load must be moved.

The most recent development has been the provision of container-handling facilities and roll-on/roll-off terminals. The world's first containerized service tied trucks and ships together in 1956. By the early 1970s, numerous carriers entered into the containership business. At first, the greatest appeal of the containership was its speed and economy in port. Moreover, it facilitated the multimodal transport of goods. For example, commodities from Japan and other Pacific Rim countries could be transported economically to Europe via North America. Later, container operations sped up the ocean voyage as well—top usable speeds increased from 15 knots in the 1950s to 33 knots in the 1970s.

With the emergence of a new international division of labor, ports continue to modernize their methods of handling cargo as they compete with each other for shares of global commodity traffic. In developed countries served by many ports, competition has decreased the relevance of the traditional concept of the port hinterland (i.e., the area served by the port). On the West Coast of the United States, for example, ports in

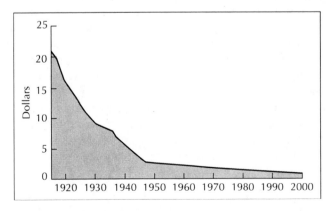

FIGURE 9.8
Cost-space convergence in telephone calls between New York and San Francisco, 1915–2000.

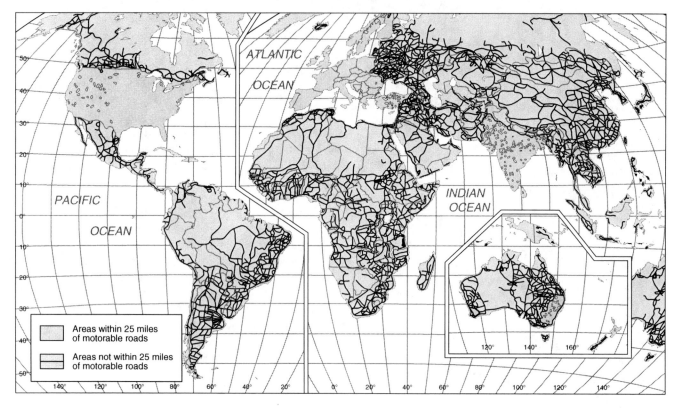

FIGURE 9.9

Major world roads and highways. Note areas within the United States, Europe, India, Southeastern Australia, and New Zealand are virtually all within 25 miles of roads and highways. Only a few exceptions exist in the Western mountain regions of the United States.

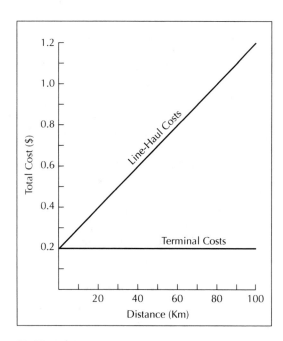

FIGURE 9.10

Terminal and line-haul costs. Terminal costs are also fixed costs. Line-haul costs incurred "over the road" are also variable costs.

California, Oregon, and Washington compete fiercely for the mounting trade with East Asia.

Carrier Competition

Competitive differences in terminal and line-haul costs among various transport modes lead firms to use different forms over different distances (Figure 9.11). Trucks have low terminal costs partly because they do not have to provide and maintain their own highways and partly because of their flexibility. However, trucks are not as efficient in moving freight on a ton-kilometer basis as are railroad and water carriers. Of the three competing forms of transport, trucks involve the least cost only out to distance D_1. Railroad carriers have higher terminal costs than truck carriers, but lower than water carriers, and a competitive advantage through the distance D_1–D_2. Water carriers, such as barges, have the highest terminal costs, but they achieve the lowest line-haul costs, giving them an advantage over longer distances.

Elasticity of Demand

The *elasticity of demand* for transportation is the degree of responsiveness of a good or service to changes in its

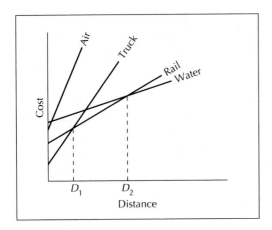

FIGURE 9.11
Variations in terminal and line-haul costs for
air, truck, rail, water, and pipeline.

Container cargo handling at the Maersk Line Terminal,
Port Newark, New Jersey. Containerization has greatly
improved the operation, management, and logistics of
conventional oceangoing freight. The impact of the
container evolution has gone far beyond shipping and
international trade alone. Newly designed cellular vessels
have much faster ship turnaround times in ports as well as
improved cargo-handling productivity at ports. An
expanded interface between water and land transportation
has occurred. Container trains have also enhanced the
economy and scale of rail transportation.

price (i.e., the percentage change in demand that a percentage change in price causes). Carriers generally charge
what the market will bear. Goods with a very high value
per unit of weight, such as televisions, are able to bear a
higher transportation rate than goods with a very low
value per unit of weight, such as coal (Figure 9.12). The
left-hand graph illustrates transportation price inelastic-
ity for television sets. An increase in the rate from P_1 to
P_2 produces only a slight change in the quantity of shipments. Coal, however (in the right-hand graph), exhibits
a great change in the quantity of shipments, with only
slight change in the transportation rate (P_1 to P_2).

Freight Rate Variations and Traffic Characteristics

An absence of competition between transport modes
means a carrier can set rates between points to cover
costs, and in the absence of government intervention,
a carrier may set unjustifiably high rates. Intermodal
competition or government regulation reduces the likelihood of such practices. Competition among carriers
reduces rate differences among them. For example, the
opening of the St. Lawrence Seaway in 1959 resulted
in lower rail freight rates on commodities affected by
low water-transport rates.

Many carriers face heavy demand only in a specific
direction. Consider the large volume of produce
shipped from Florida to New York. Trucks must often
return empty for the next load. The cost of the total
trip, however, is used to determine the transportation
rate. Because carriers must make return trips anyway,
they are willing to charge very low rates on the backhaul. Any revenue on backhaul is preferred to returning empty. Rates are higher where there is little or no
possibility of backhauling; most such runs occur in the
transportation of raw materials from resource points to
production points. An example is the railroad that

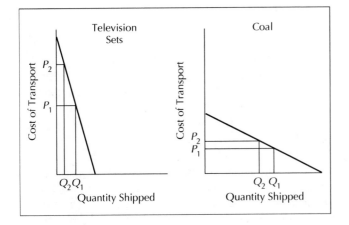

FIGURE 9.12
Demand elasticity for transportation. Higher-valued television
sets are more valuable and less elastic than quantities of coal.
A large price increase to ship television sets results in a small
reduction in the quantity shipped. A small price increase to
ship coal results in a large reduction in the quantity shipped.

carries iron ore pellets from Labrador to the port of Sept Iles, Quebec. This railroad may be likened to a huge conveyor belt that operates in one direction only. By contrast, the distribution of finished products generally involves traffic among many cities, creating a reciprocal flow and lower rates.

Regimes for International Transportation

In the international arena, transport rates and costs are affected by the nature of the regime governing the transport mode. To illustrate, consider the contrasting regimes of civil aviation and shipping. The international regime for aviation is dominated by nation-states; in contrast, the international regime for shipping has been shaped by large shipping corporations. The regime for shipping evolved over more than 500 years and has been more concerned with facilitating commerce than with national security. The regime for civil aviation developed in the early twentieth century and primarily reflects a concern for national security.

The fundamental principle governing international aviation is that states have sovereign control over their own air space. From this principle, rules and procedures have developed that permit countries to regulate their routes, fares, and schedules. As a result, many countries, developed and developing, have secured a market share that is more or less proportional to their share of world airline traffic. Developing countries have been able to compete with companies based in the industrialized world on an equal footing; for example, Air India, Avianca, and Korean Air Lines can challenge Delta, Air France, and British Airways.

The international regime for shipping has left many developing countries in a weak position with regard to establishing and nurturing their own merchant fleets. In a world of markets, few underdeveloped countries have much influence when it comes to setting commodity rate structures. Lack of control over international shipping is an important area of concern in the Third World's quest for development.

Although the regime for shipping is dominated by firms, the market is inherently unfair—it favors developed countries over developing countries. Hence, LDCs are faced with rate structures that work against them, inadequate transport services, a perpetuation of center-periphery trade routes, and a lack of access to decision-making bodies. Those LDCs generating cargoes such as petroleum, iron ore, phosphates, bauxite/alumina, and grains cannot penetrate the bulk-shipping market, which is dominated by the vertically integrated MNCs based in developed countries. Cartels of ship owners called liner conferences set the rates and schedules for liners (freighters that ply regularly scheduled routes).

Developing countries have attempted to change the international rules of shipping. They want to generate fleets of a size proportional to the goods generated by their ports. Their accomplishments have been limited, however. The United Nations Commission on Trade and Development (UNCTAD) Code of Conduct for Liner Conferences, which was adopted in 1974, was rejected by the United States. The Liner Code gives developing country carriers a presumptive right to a share of the market; however, proposals to eliminate flags of convenience have not been accepted. Flags of convenience assume little or no real economic link between the country of registration and the ship that flies its flag. They inhibit the development of national fleets, but for ship owners they offer a number of advantages, including low taxation and lower operating costs. Liberia and Panama are the most important open-registry, or flags-of-convenience, countries. Flags of convenience are used mainly by oil tankers and bulk-ore carriers controlled by MNCs.

The global pattern of container ports reflects the geography of production and trade. Traditionally, the largest ports were located in Europe and North America. For many years, Rotterdam, at the mouth of the Rhine River in the Netherlands, was Europe's primary port and the largest in the world. Up until the 1980s, the largest ports in the United States were located on the Atlantic coast (e.g., New York), as most American trade was with Europe. The rapid economic growth of East Asia, however, changed these patterns. Today, the world's largest ports are located in Hong Kong and Singapore (Figure 9.13). Because most U.S. trade is across the Pacific Ocean, West Coast ports such as Los Angeles, Oakland, and Seattle have surpassed East Coast ports in trade volume. These changing patterns reflect the ways in which globalization is changing the domestic economic geography of the United States.

Transit Time and Location

Transport costs are of crucial importance for industries that are raw material seekers and market seekers, but they are of little importance for industries dealing in materials and final products that are of very high value in relation to their weight. This is especially so for high-tech firms.

High-tech firms rely on input materials from a variety of domestic and foreign sources; thus the advantages of locating a plant near any one supplier are often neutralized by the distance separating them from other suppliers. Their markets also tend to be scattered. Transport is a factor of some locational significance for these firms, but transit time is more crucial than cost. High-technology firms require access to high-level rapid-transport facilities to move components and final products, as well as specialized and skilled personnel. For this reason, they are often attracted to sites near

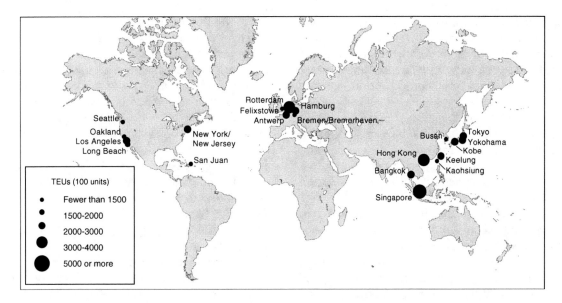

FIGURE 9.13
Most of the world's container ports are located in East and Southeast Asia and in Europe. New York, Los Angeles, and Vancouver represent major container ports in North America. Such ports are "hub ports" and act as major centers where container traffic splits into feeder flows to and from centers within the hub's respective hinterland.

major airports with good national and international passenger and air-cargo facilities. Concentrations of high-tech firms and research and development facilities are located in Silicon Valley near San Francisco, along the M4 motorway in Britain to the west of London, and in Tsukuba Science City, situated northeast of Tokyo.

Transport Improvements and Location

Transport innovations have reduced circulation costs and fostered the new international division of labor. They have encouraged the decentralization of manufacturing processes in industrialized countries, both from major cities toward suburbs and smaller towns, and from central regions to those more peripheral. They have also encouraged the decentralization of manufacturing processes to those LDCs with an abundance of weakly unionized, low-wage labor.

The "container revolution" and bulk-air cargo carriers enabled MNCs based in the United States, Japan, and Europe to locate low-value-added manufacturing and high-pollution manufacturing processes "offshore" in more than 80 Third World free-trade zones. Almost one-half of these zones are in Asia, including Hong Kong, Taiwan, Malaysia, and South Korea. Free-trade zones are areas where goods may be imported free of duties for packaging, assembling, or manufacturing and then exported. These global workshops are geared to export markets, often with few links to the national economy or the needs of local consumers. They tend

to be located near ports (e.g., La Romana, Dominican Republic), near international airports (e.g., San Bartola, El Salvador), and in areas virtually integrated into global centers of business (e.g., Mexico's northern border or maquilla zone) in Tijuana–San Diego.

TRANSPORTATION POLICY

Well-established national transportation policies and regulation were the norm until the 1970s. The purpose of regulation of airlines and rail carriers was to ensure quality control, protect companies and customers, and establish quality and safety control standards throughout the industry. During this period, providers not only provided basic transportation services but also met a social obligation, such as providing service to low-income, unprofitable areas. For example, Britain's Road Traffic Act of 1930 introduced a system of licenses and rates that effectively regulated the sporadic and unsafe market for bus services in that country.

Deregulation and Privatization

By the late 1970s, with the growth of conservative neoliberalism, international trade regulators required that there be free entry of new transportation operators into the market to ensure efficiency and welfare maximization. The move toward *privatization* had begun. Regulation was criticized by advocates of markets as creating inefficiency, limiting competition, and raising prices to consumers. The Swedish railways, for example, were deregulated by 1968, and British trucking also was deregulated in that year. In Great Britain, in 1980, the Transport Act removed all controls on bus service and express service between cities; the 1985 Transportation Act deregulated local bus service inside and outside greater London; and the British government sold nationalized transportation companies and many municipally owned companies. In the United States, deregulation included the Airline Deregulation Act of 1978 and the Motor Carriers Act of 1980.

Privatization and *deregulation* have been hampered in developing countries because of a lack of foreign exchange to purchase necessary spare parts and replacement equipment. Sri Lanka, for example, deregulated all bus routes, while China deregulated long-distance coach service, and fares are now allowed to vary. Nigeria followed suit by privatizing Nigeria Airways and its National Shipping Line, while Singapore privatized Singapore Airlines and started to privatize its mass transit corporation.

Deregulation of the U.S. Airlines

The Civil Aeronautics Board (CAB) of the United States regulated the U.S. airline industry from 1938 until recently. During most of this period, the CAB's goal was to preserve the 16 trunk line airlines that existed in 1938 and to provide good service at fair prices with a high level of quality control. More recently, the 16 companies were reduced to 11 companies by mergers.

Air passenger traffic increased 1000% between 1950 and 1970. Airfares remained almost constant because of the lower cost of operating more efficient planes. However, the oil embargos of 1973–1974 and 1978 increased operating costs, leading to a crisis of profitability and leading airlines to pressure the federal government for deregulation of domestic air services. In 1978, the United States Airline Deregulation Act limited the CAB's route licensing powers (eventually phasing them out) and its fare controls.

Domestic U.S. airlines are now open to any carrier that might venture into the market. The most important result of airline deregulation has been more competitive fares and survival of the most efficient companies (as well as bankruptcies of others). The development of a hub-and-spoke network has been a cost-saving measure. Most direct flights have been reduced, and now air service requires at least one stopover in an airline hub city, unless the city pair are very large American cities. Service from smaller cities is directed into larger city airports or hubs and then linked to final destinations by direct flights.

Privatization and deregulation have kept fares down. In 1976, only 15 percent of passengers on domestic air routes used discount fares; today, 90 percent of passengers use discounted tickets. However, as average fares have fallen on long-haul routes, fares on short routes have risen. Load factors have increased substantially with a hub-and-spoke system, and the number of flights has declined, leading to lower overall costs.

Hub-and-Spoke Networks

In order to remain competitive, the airlines that survived the shake-out following deregulation restructured their networks so that they could reduce direct flights between most city pairs. They made their operations more efficient and cost-effective by using a hub-and-spoke network model. Hubs serve central locations that collect and redistribute passengers between sets of original cities. Extremely large passenger volumes are funneled through hubs, and this allows the airlines to fly larger and more efficient aircraft and to offer more frequent flights between major hubs, increasing load factors (Figure 9.14).

Delta Airlines' network has hubs in Atlanta and Cincinnati.

International Business

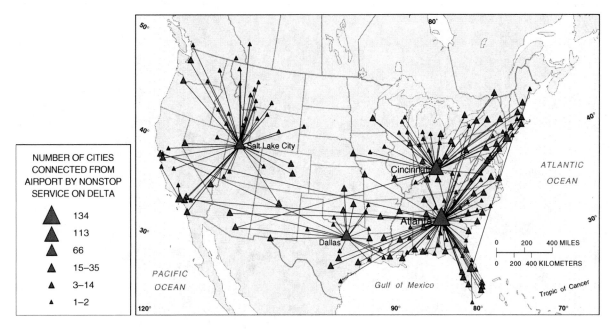

FIGURE 9.14
Hub-and-spoke networks for two major U.S. air carriers. (These figures were first published in the *Journal of Transport Geography* Vol. 1, no. 1 [March 1993]: pp 51–54, and are reproduced here with the permission of Butterworth-Heinemann, Oxford, U.K.)

However, *hub-and-spoke networks* can provide disadvantages, especially to the travelers who find the number of links in their trips increased, frequently with a change of planes, and fewer direct flights available. Also, congestion is created at the main hub cities, and this affects efficiency both in the air and on the ground. It is important for airlines to make careful decisions as to the location and exact number of hubs so that their operation is competitive with other airlines. There are a large number of optimum hub location studies in the literature. These mathematical optimization approaches attempt to capture the real-world realities of air passenger networks and the design problems that face most airlines.

Not all cities have fared equally well. Some airports showed a precipitous decline in traffic after deregulation began. Resulting from this mad scramble to reduce fares and elevate efficiency for megahubs, Atlanta, Chicago, Dallas, and Denver surfaced as major hubs for two or more airlines; Salt Lake City, Minneapolis–St. Paul, Memphis, and Detroit have also emerged. Different airlines use different cities in their respective hub-and-spoke networks (Table 9.1).

Transportation of Nuclear Wastes

Nuclear wastes produced during the fission process include reactor metals, such as fuel rods and assemblies, coolant fluids, and gases found in the reactor. Fuel rods are the most highly radioactive waste found on earth today, and their dangerous level of

Table 9.1
Major U.S. Airlines and Their Hubs

American	Dallas–Fort Worth, Chicago
Continental	Houston, New York, Denver, Cleveland
Delta	Atlanta, Cincinnati, Dallas
Northwest	Detroit, Memphis, Minneapolis –St. Paul
United	Chicago
U.S. Air	Pittsburgh, Charlotte

radioactivity requires that they be transported to a special site for storage. The storage site must be located so that the radioactive material will not contaminate the groundwater or the biosphere in any way. Geologic stability is a must. Most experts support deep underground geologic disposal in salt domes or other rock formations. Presently, the United States has 100 sites where radioactive waste has been temporarily stored. These include Hanford, Washington; Livermore, California; Beatty and Las Vegas, Nevada; Idaho Falls, Idaho; Los Alamos and Albuquerque, New Mexico; Amarillo, Texas; Weldon Springs, Missouri; Sheffield, Illinois; Paducah, Kentucky; Oakridge, Tennessee; Aiken and Barnwell, South Carolina; and Niagara Falls and West Valley, New York. Recently, however, the federal government

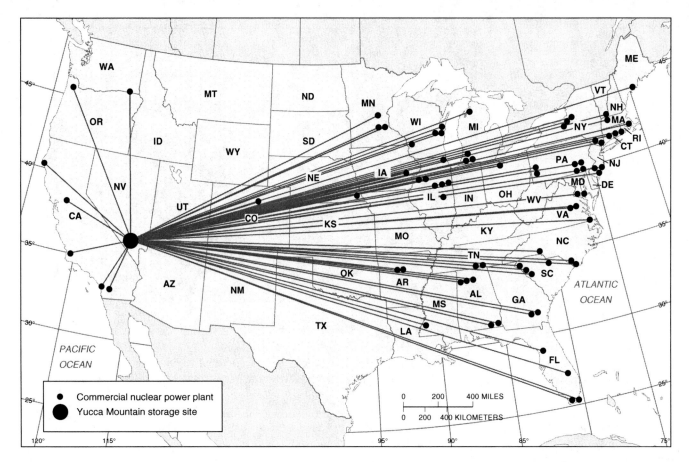

FIGURE 9.15
High-level nuclear waste from commercial power plants will be transported to Yucca Mountain, Nevada.

selected Yucca Mountain, Nevada, as a permanent facility for the storage of high-level nuclear wastes from commercially operated power plants in America (Figure 9.15).

Special containers on rail and truck will be used, and the routes will avoid high population areas. One of the factors responsible for the selection of Yucca Mountain is the so-called *NIMBY* ("not in my backyard") effect. The problem with nuclear waste deposition is that, because no official or engineer can assure that each site will be completely safe, local residents want no possibility of an accident. Politicians are quite sensitive to their constituencies' pleas and concerns for safety and usually vote to remove nuclear wastes and power plants from their districts.

PERSONAL MOBILITY IN THE UNITED STATES

One important dimension of urban transportation concerns changes in the personal mobility in the United States. Personal mobility in the United States is at its highest point in history, with individuals making more and longer trips and owning more vehicles. Three factors account for this greater level of mobility in general.

The first is the overall increased performance of the national economy. When more people have more money to spend on transportation, greater automobile ownership and greater travel distances result. The second factor is the increasing growth of cities and their spread over the surrounding countryside through low-density exurban expansion. On the average, distances between home and job have increased, leading to longer commutes. A third major reason for increased mobility is the changing role of women in the workforce. Many more women own their own vehicles, have entered the workforce full time, and have increased their travel demands during the last 40 years.

Because of increased mobility, individuals have benefited in the social and economic sense, but society as a whole suffers the negative consequences. New concerns about rising levels of air pollution, congestion on the freeways, and the movement of goods are being posed. The new levels of mobility have created a set of problems that are very difficult to address. Two techniques to address the issue of greater congestion and slower average speeds are being forwarded. One is to increase volumes on present roadways through *intelligent vehicle highway systems* (IVHS), and the other is to reduce travel demand by planning a land-use mix in localities so that trip origins and destinations are less

Rush-hour traffic fills the northbound lanes of the San Diego freeway in California. Rapid growth of automobile ownership in Western cities in the second half of the twentieth century has been met by unparalleled congestion. Greater levels of wealth in Western countries, more drivers, more auto ownership, and more women entering the labor force have contributed to high levels of car ownership. In California, auto ownership approaches one car for every person, whereas in cities worldwide the figure rarely exceeds 10 per 100, and the figures are much lower figures than that for rural areas.

separated. This approach is called *transit-oriented development* (TOD). However, before we discuss these two measures of reducing congestion and increasing the greater volumes of flow, we first examine trends occurring in personal mobility in the United States.

In the late twentieth century, the number of households, drivers, vehicles, vehicle trips, vehicle miles traveled (VMT), person trips, and the person miles of travel all increased at a much faster rate than did the population. In addition, the number and percentage of households that did not own a vehicle dropped. However, the number of households with three or more vehicles increased dramatically.

The *journey-to-work trip,* both in terms of total miles of travel and in terms of number of trips, continued to account for the largest proportion of travel by U.S. households. Both annual vehicle miles traveled and annual number of vehicle trips per household increased from 1970 to 2004 (Figure 9.16). The average home-to-work trip was 12 miles, while social and recreation trips averaged just over 11 miles per trip. Other family or personal business trip lengths averaged 7 miles, and shopping trips averaged 5.6 miles. The declines in vehicle occupancy are explained partially by the increased number of vehicles per household and the decrease in average household size during this period.

Because of the escalation in average vehicle price, Americans retain their vehicles for a longer period. For example, in 1969, 42% of household automobiles were two years old or less; by 2005, only 14 percent were two years old or less. The number of automobiles that were 10 or more years in age increased from 6 percent in 1969 to 37 percent by 2005. The usage of older vehicles, which have been shown to burn energy less efficiently and cleanly than newer vehicles, contributes to energy and air pollution problems.

Intelligent Vehicle Highway Systems (IVHS)

During the next 30 years, traffic volume in the United States is expected to double. Yet each year, some 135 million drivers spend about 2 billion hours stuck in highway traffic. An estimated $46 billion is lost by American drivers trapped in traffic delays, by detours, and by wrong turns. However, IVHS could greatly ameliorate this situation. "Smart" cars are equipped with microcomputers, video screens, and other technologies that reduce the frustration of driving. Through the use of in-vehicle computers and navigation systems, drivers are guided step-by-step to their destinations. Fast, accurate

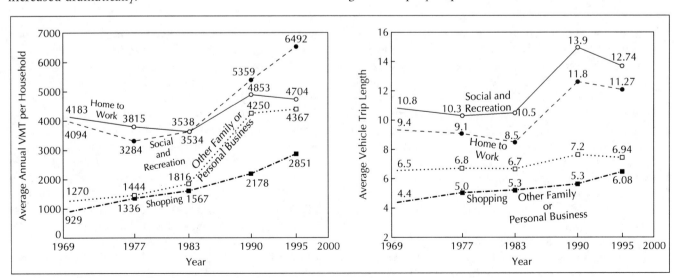

FIGURE 9.16
Vehicle miles traveled (VMT) and average vehicle length in the United States, 1970–1995.

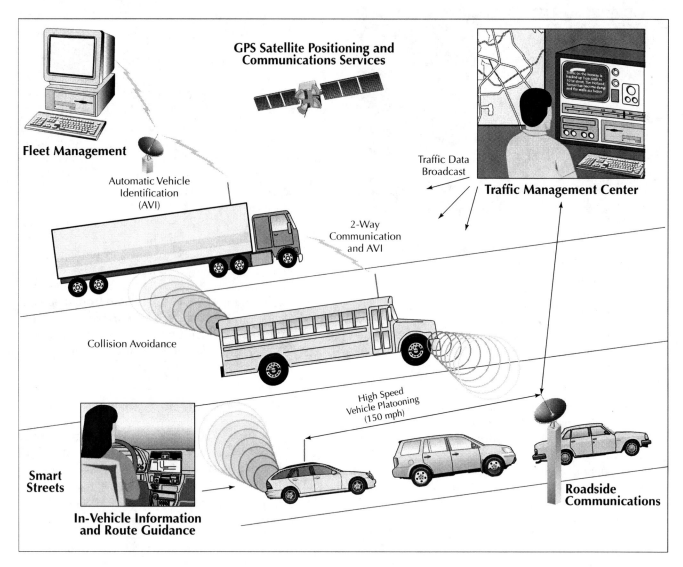

Elements of IVHS.

information allows drivers to avoid accidents and congestion while simultaneously offering information on restaurants, hotels, attractions, and emergency services.

"Smart" highways are created by installing vehicle sensing systems. These sensing systems monitor traffic volume, speed, and vehicle weights. This information helps traffic engineers and transportation planners regulate signals to control traffic flow and plan new roads. The radar-based collision warning systems will automatically signal a car to brake to avoid collisions. If successful, cars could someday safely travel faster and closer together, thus allowing more vehicles to use the road at the same time.

The current challenge that IVHS faces is the translation of these ideas into applications that are practical, cost-effective, and user friendly (Figure 9.17). IVHS will offer drivers much more data than previously available with paper maps and atlases, including data that can

be updated on a continuous basis, such as status reports on traffic and environmental conditions.

Currently, freeways in the developed world can handle about 2000 vehicles per lane per hour. More traffic than this per freeway lane causes stop-and-go traffic, which leads to accidents and gridlock. If the average vehicle is traveling 60 miles per hour on a freeway, then the average density of automobiles per lane is one every 135 feet. If the vehicle is 16 feet long, then 118 feet of freeway is going to waste. One concept behind IVHS is to increase the number of vehicles traveling at high speeds, packing together into a platoon, so that up to 7000 vehicles per lane per hour could exist on a modern freeway—one car every half-second. If this could be accomplished, the present freeway system could be used in a much more efficient way, preventing the addition of extra freeway lanes and the double-deckering of freeways through the

The dashboard in a smart car.

and German governments have spent approximately $1 billion each on magnetic levitation research. In the future, *maglevs* may transfer passengers between U.S. cities separated by up to 300 miles, at over 300 miles per hour, using far less energy and time than automobiles, Amtrak, or even air carriers. One could shuttle between Boston and Washington, or Chicago and Minneapolis, or Los Angeles and San Francisco in less than an hour. Maglevs presently are twice as fuel efficient as automobiles and four times as efficient as airliners, producing little or no air pollution. In the future, maglevs may be built alongside highways and will occupy far less room than airports (the Dallas–Fort Worth airport consumes as much land as a 65-foot-wide right-of-way coast to coast).

In the meantime, high-speed conventional rail systems have been improved to include *tilting train technology* (TTT). An example of this technology is found in the Swedish X2000 train that can travel up to 150 miles per hour and give service in the northeast corridor of the United States. The passenger car carriage tilts inward on curves, allowing increased speeds on existing track curvatures. Amtrak, the national railroad passenger corporation train service, is presently making heavy investments in tilting train technology. ISTEA, the Intermodal Surface Transportation Efficiency Act of 1991, has identified five existing rail corridors selected for development of high-speed trains. These

most congested urbanized areas. Double-deckering in a variety of U.S. cities, including San Francisco, Seattle, and New York, has always been met with strong environmental opposition.

IVHS technologies range from real-time routing and congestion information being broadcast to the auto driver via radio to allowing the car to drive by itself on an automated roadway. New electronics associated with IVHS provide real-time information on accident, congestion, and roadway incidents. Traffic controllers, which have information, beam it to motorists, who can select new routing strategies or use roadside services. Collision avoidance systems using radar, lane tracking technologies that platoon or stack vehicles at high density, and readout terminals on the dashboard that display a map of the city, as well as locations of accidents and the shortest route between two points based on real-time traffic flow information, will be given.

High-Speed Trains and Magnetic Levitation

Magnetic levitation technology eliminates mechanical contact between a vehicle and the roadbed, thus eliminating wear, noise, and alignment problems. The vehicle floats on a cushion of air one-half foot above the guideway supported by magnetic forces. The Japanese

TGV Express Train in France. In 1983, the Trans Grande Vitesse was introduced by the French Railway with service between Paris and Lyon at speeds of up to 200 mph on an entirely new track. It soon captured millions of new passengers from the highways and from domestic airlines. Proposed high-speed trains from Naples to Milan, from Lisbon to Marseille, from Bordeaux to Glasgow via the Channel Tunnel, and from Geneva to Amsterdam are to be opened by the year 2005. Despite these advances, interurban rail will continue to occupy a subordinate role in the United States. But in China, Russia, and India, where private car ownership is low, the railway still carries the bulk of interurban traffic.

include SanDiego–LosAngeles–San Francisco, Dallas–Houston–San Antonio, Miami–Orlando–Jacksonville, Pittsburgh–Chicago–Minneapolis, and Washington–New York–Boston.

TELECOMMUNICATIONS

The transmission of information is every bit as important as the movement of people and goods. An abundance of information availability facilitates and accompanies economic development and political liberty. Modernization of transportation has integrated the economic world, but equally important are technical developments in communication. Communications is the invisible layer of transport supplementing the physical transport links among and within cities, regions, and countries. Because the circulation of information is critical to the operation and success of large, complex economies, the history of capitalism has been accompanied by wave after wave of innovations in communications (Figure 9.18).

Telecommunications are not a new phenomenon. Starting in 1844, the first form of telecommunications began with Samuel Morse's invention of the telegraph, which allowed communications to become detached from transportation. The telegraph made possible the worldwide transmission of information concerning commodity needs, supplies, prices, and shipments—information that was essential if international commerce was to be conducted on an efficient basis. Telegraphy grew rapidly in the United States, from 40 miles of cable in 1844 to 23,000 miles by 1852. Starting with the first transcontinental telegraph wire in 1861, the telegraph

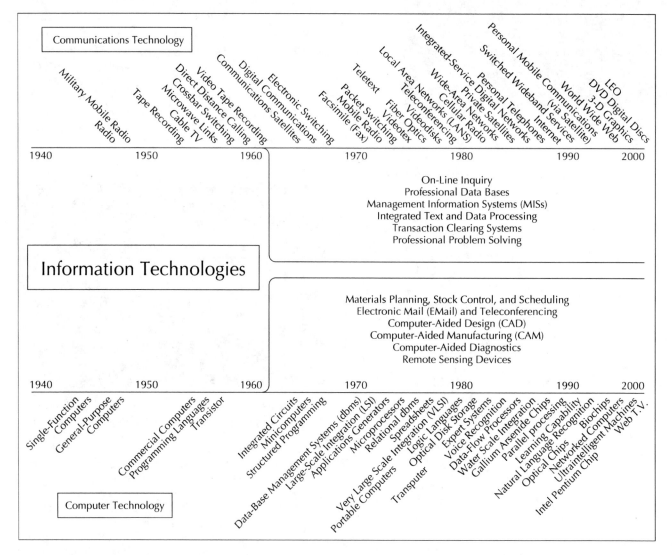

FIGURE 9.18
Innovations in the history of computer and communication technologies.

was important in the American colonization of the West, where it displaced the Pony Express, and helped to form a national market by allowing long-distance circulation of news, prices, stocks, and other information. In 1868, the first successful trans-Atlantic telegraph line was laid, part of the round of international time-space compression that accompanied the Industrial Revolution.

For decades after the invention of the telephone in 1876, telecommunications was synonymous with simple telephone service. Just as the telegraph was instrumental to the colonization of the American West, in the late nineteenth century the telephone became critical to the growth of the American city-system, allowing firms to centralize their headquarters functions while they spun off branch plants to smaller towns. Growing multiestablishment corporations utilized the telephone to coordinate production and shipments. In the 1920s, the telephone, like the automobile and the single-family home, became a staple of the growing middle class, with significant social effects on friendship networks, dating, and other ties. In the 1950s, direct dialing eliminated the need for shared party lines, and the first international phone line was laid across the Atlantic Ocean. Even today, despite the proliferation of several new forms of telecommunications, the telephone remains by far the most commonly used form of telecommunications for businesses and households.

From 1933 to 1984, the American Telegraph and Telephone Company (AT&T) enjoyed a monopoly over the U.S. telephone industry. Congress exempted AT&T from antitrust laws in return for its commitment to guarantee universal access among the population, eventually resulting in a 98 percent penetration rate among U.S. households. The widespread deregulation of industry extended to telecommunications, and in 1984, AT&T was broken up into one long-distance and several local service providers ("Baby Bells"). New firms such as MCI and Sprint entered the field. Faced with mounting competition, telephone companies have steadily upgraded their copper cable systems to include fiber-optic lines, which allow large quantities of data to be transmitted rapidly, securely, and virtually error free.

The provision of telephones is a common measure of a nation's communications infrastructure (Figure 9.19). Telephone penetration rates—the availability per 1000 people—are highest in the economically developed world. Africa has less than 1 percent of the world's telephones and comprises 15 percent of the world's population. One-half of the world's population has never made a telephone call. Landlines, however, are rapidly being supplemented or replaced by wireless technologies; indeed, there are more cell phones today than landlines. For developing countries, wireless technologies offer the possibility of "leapfrogging," that is moving directly into newer, lower cost forms of technology.

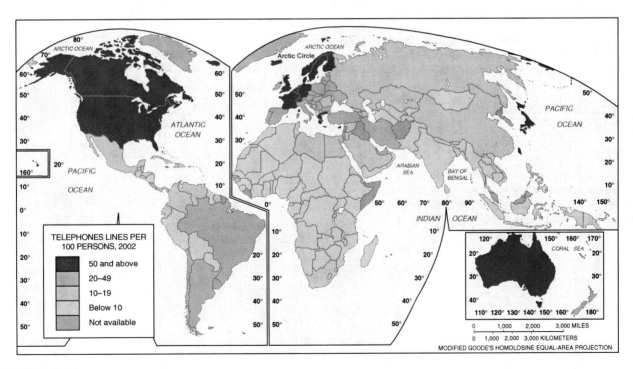

FIGURE 9.19
Telephones per 1000 people worldwide, 2002. (See Color Insert for more illustrative map.)

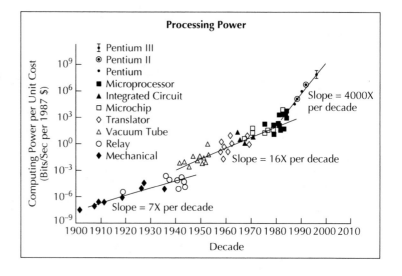

A shopkeeper in Ivory Coast has steady customers for mobile phones.

The microelectronics revolution of the late twentieth century was particularly important in the telecommunications industry, which is arguably the world's most rapidly expanding and dynamic sector today. Innovations in processing power have led to exponential increases in the ability of computerized systems to analyze and transmit data (Figure 9.20). The ability to transmit vast quantities of information in real time over the planetary surface is crucial to "digital capitalism." No large corporation can operate in multiple national markets simultaneously, coordinating the activities of thousands of employees within highly specialized corporate divisions of labor, without access to sophisticated channels of communications. Thus telecommunications are important to understanding broader issues pertaining to globalization and the world economy, including the complex relations between firms and nation-states.

Today, two technologies—satellites and fiber-optic lines—form the primary technologies deployed by the global telecommunications industry. The transmission capacities of both of these grew rapidly in the late twentieth century as the microelectronics revolution began to unfold. Multinational corporations, banks, and media conglomerates typically employ both technologies, often simultaneously, either in the form of privately owned facilities or leased circuits from shared corporate networks. Roughly 1000 fiber optic and two dozen public and private satellite firms provide international telecommunications services. The network of fiber lines linking the world constitutes the nervous system of the global financial and service economy, linking cities, markets, suppliers, and clients around the world (Figure 9.21).

Although they overlap to a great extent, satellite and fiber-optic carriers exhibit market segmentation. Fiber is heavily favored by large corporations for data transmission and by financial institutions for electronic funds transfer systems. Satellites tend to be used more often by international television carriers. Telephone and Internet traffic use both. These two types of carriers are differentiated geographically as well: Because their transmission costs are unrelated to distance, satellites are optimal for low-density areas (e.g., rural regions and remote islands), where the relatively high marginal costs of fiber lines are not competitive. Fiber-optic carriers prefer large metropolitan regions, where dense concentrations of clients allow them to realize significant economies of scale in cities where frequency transmission congestion often plagues satellite transmissions. Satellites are ideal for point-to-area distribution networks, whereas fiber-optic lines are preferable for

FIGURE 9.20
Computer processing power per unit cost has increased exponentially (note the vertical axis is logarithmic). The application of new software that links manufacturing, inventory, and other functions is dramatically increasing industrial and office efficiency.

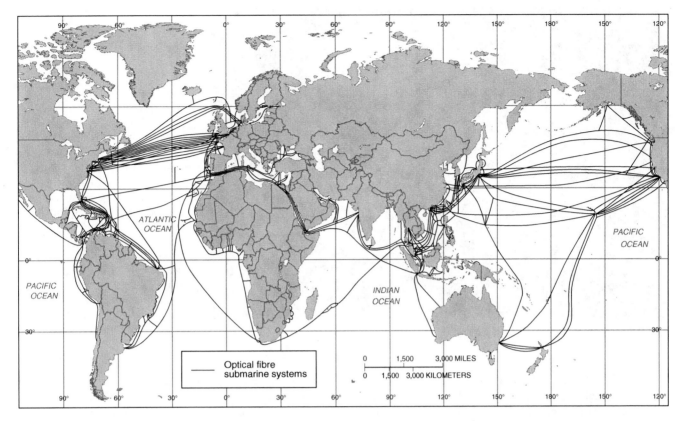

FIGURE 9.21
The global network of fiber optic lines. Starting in the 1980s across the Atlantic, many telecommunications giants have laid an expanding grid of fiber optics with exponentially increasing power to transmit enormous quantities of data.

point-to-point communications, especially when security is of great concern.

Historically, the primacy of each technology has varied over time. From 1959 to 1980 (i.e., before the invention of fiber optics), satellites enjoyed limited competition from transocean copper cable lines with low-capacity rates. From the 1970s onward, the microelectronics revolution allowed fiber-optic lines to erode the market share of traffic held by satellites (Figure 9.22). New techniques of data transmission, such as the so-called frame delay format, raise speeds of transmission nearly 30-fold over the 1990s technology.

However, more recently the growth of wireless and cellular phone traffic has led to a resurgence of low-orbiting satellites. Large scale, *low earth orbit* (LEO) satellite systems provide telephone communications to and from anyplace on earth and are ideal for the rapidly expanding cell phone market. These private, global satellite constellations transmit television, radio, fax, computer, and voice images.

Telecommunications and Geography

There exists considerable popular confusion about the real and potential impacts of telecommunications on

One of the satellites in the tracking and data relay satellite system in orbit around the earth is the TDRSS satellite. The system provides advanced tracking and telemetry services for a number of other satellites, as well as commercial telecommunications services.

An important improvement in global communications has been the development of satellite technology. The first communication satellites date from 1965, with the launching of Early Bird, able to carry 250 telephone conversations or two television channels simultaneously. Since then, more advanced communication satellites carry 100,000 circuits of simultaneous telephone communications or television channeling.

spatial relations, in part due to the long history of ex-aggerated claims made in the past. We keep read, for example, that telecommunications means "the end of geography." Often such views hinge on a simplistic, utopian technological determinism that ignores the complex relations between telecommunications and local economic, social, and political circumstances. For example, repeated predictions that telecommunications would allow everyone to work at home via telecommuting, dispersing all functions and spelling

the obsolescence of cities, have fallen flat in the face of the persistent growth in densely inhabited urbanized places and global cities. In fact, telecommunications are usually a poor substitute for face-to-face meetings, the medium through which most sensitive corporate inter-actions occurs, particularly when the information in-volved is irregular, proprietary, and unstandardized in nature. Most managers spend the bulk of their working time engaged in face-to-face contact, and no electronic technology can yet allow for the subtlety and nuances critical to such encounters. It is true that networks such as the Internet allow some professionals to move into rural areas, where they can conduct most of their busi-ness online, gradually permitting them to escape from their longtime reliance on large cities where they needed face-to-face contact. Yet the full extent to which these systems facilitate decentralization is often countered by other forces that promote the centralization of activity.

For this reason, a century of telecommunications, from the telephone to fiber optics, has left most high-wage, white-collar, administrative command and control functions clustered in downtown areas. In contrast, telecommunications are ideally suited for the transmis-sion of routinized, standardized forms of data, facilitat-ing the dispersal of functions involved with their processing to low-wage regions. In short, there is no par-ticular reason to believe that telecommunications in-evitably lead to the dispersal or deconcentration of functions; by allowing the decentralization of routinized ones, information technology actually enhances the com-parative advantage of inner cities for nonroutinized, high-value-added functions that are performed face to face. Thus telecommunications facilitate the simultaneous con-centration and deconcentration of economic activities.

FIGURE 9.22

Global telecommunications capacity. Fiber-optic and satellite transmission have surpassed copper wire and the coaxial cable. The increase has been an exponential one regarding voice circuitry.

Thus, popular notions that "telecommunications will render geography meaningless" are simply naïve. While the costs of communications have decreased, as they did with transportation, other factors have risen in importance, including local regulations, the cost and skills of the local labor force, government policies, and infrastructural investments. Economic space, in short, will not evaporate because of the telecommunications revolution. Exactly how telecommunications are deployed is a contingent matter of local circumstances, public policy, and local niche within the national and world economy.

Within cities, digital networks have contributed to an ongoing reconstruction of urban space. Telecommunications networks tend to be largely invisible to policy makers and planners and receive little attention. While many city governments are willing to invest in new roads or water control projects, urban planners and economic development officials have often overlooked or ignored altogether the role that telecommunications can play in stimulating economic growth. For example, only 5 percent of U.S. municipalities have explicit plans for telecommunications. One reason is that there is no statistical correlation between local investment in telecommunications and economic growth; the idea that "if you build it, they will come" is not necessarily true. However, while the telecommunications industry per se is relatively small and capital intensive, generating few jobs, and while telecommunications do not guarantee economic development, such systems have become necessities for many firms. In short, telecommunications are necessary but not sufficient to induce economic growth.

Teleworking is often touted as the answer to reduced transportation costs, easing demands on energy and reducing environmental impacts. There is a growing trend toward wireless terminals because the wiring of computers and peripherals to networks is costly. Wireless terminals include computers and other devices that can communicate with machines with infrared or electromagnetic signals. This allows computers to function within company or international networks. The first generation of wireless terminals is now popular in the form of desktop and laptop PCs. Palmtop units can send large data files or e-mail using satellite communications technology, and will eventually replace pagers and cellular phones. The trend toward wireless terminals is significant because it allows more portability and eliminates the need to be connected and disconnected from local area networks.

Although large cities typically have much better developed telecommunications infrastructures, the technology has rapidly diffused through the urban hierarchy into smaller towns and is becoming increasingly equalized among regions. In the future, therefore, the marginal returns from investments in this infrastructure are bound to diminish, minimizing competitive advantages based on information systems infrastructure alone and

forcing competition among localities to occur on other bases, such as the cost and quality of labor, taxes, and regulatory framework. Regions with an advantage in telecommunications generally succeed because they have attracted firms for other reasons.

A growing set of impacts of information systems on urban form concerns transportation informatics, including a variety of improvements in surface transportation such as smart metering, electronic road pricing, synchronized traffic lights, automated toll payments and turnpikes, automated road maps, information for trip planning and navigation, travel advisory systems, electronic tourist guides, remote traffic monitoring and displays, and computerized traffic management and control systems, all of which are designed to minimize congestion and optimize traffic flow (particularly at peak hours), enhancing the efficiency, reliability, and attractiveness of travel. Wireless technologies such as cellular phones allow more productive use of time otherwise lost to congest. Such systems do not so much comprise new technologies as the enhancement of existing ones.

Among U.S. cities, telecommunications have accelerated the spatial reorganization of financial services. By relying on economies of scale, large firms can combine services in a few centralized database management systems. American Express, for example, shifted its credit card processing to three facilities, and Aetna Insurance consolidated 55 claims adjustment centers to 22 metropolitan regions. Allstate Insurance consolidated 28 processing centers into three (Charlotte,

Teleworking has allowed busy parents to juggle professional and domestic responsibilities by working at home either full time or part time.

Dallas, and Columbus); CNA centralized theirs in Reading, Pennsylvania; and Travelers Insurance established two in Knoxville, Tennessee, and Albany, New York. Other insurers are developing online marketing via the Internet. Among telecommunications carriers, AT&T has six megacenters, and Sprint opted for low-cost places such as Jacksonville, Florida, Dallas, Texas, Kansas City, Missouri, Phoenix, Arizona, and Winona, Minnesota. Meanwhile, local sales offices in small towns have experienced a steady decline. This phenomenon exemplifies the manner in which telecommunications can simultaneously centralize as well as decentralize different economic activities.

With the digitization of information, telecommunications steadily merged with computers to form integrated networks (Figure 9.23). New technologies such as fiber optics have complemented and at times substituted for telephone lines. Fax services and 800 number free toll calls are now standard for virtually all companies, and even newer technologies such as Electronic Data Interchange and wireless services are becoming increasingly popular. Like the railroad system of the nineteenth century and the interstate highway system of the twentieth century, the information highway of fiber-optic cables, satellites, and wireless grids links billions of computers, telephones, faxes, and other electronic products all over the world.

GEOGRAPHIES OF THE INTERNET

Among the various networks that comprise the world's telecommunications infrastructure, the largest and most famous is the Internet, a vast web of electronic networks nicknamed the *information superhighway*. This system delivers large amounts of services to homes, offices, and factories, including e-mail, telephone calls, TV programs and other video images, text, and music. The system enables students at rural schools to use computers to tap resources at distant universities or researchers in small colleges to use supercomputers at located far away. The superhighway allows doctors to check patients from their homes, and it permits doctors in several remote cities to collaborate on a patient's care by immediately sharing multimedia computer screens.

Origins and Growth of the Internet

The Internet originated in the 1960s under the U.S. Defense Department's Defense Agency Research Projects Administration (DARPA), which designed it to withstand a nuclear attack. Much of the durability of the current system is due to the enormous amounts of federal dollars dedicated toward research in this area. In the 1980s, control of the Internet was transferred to the

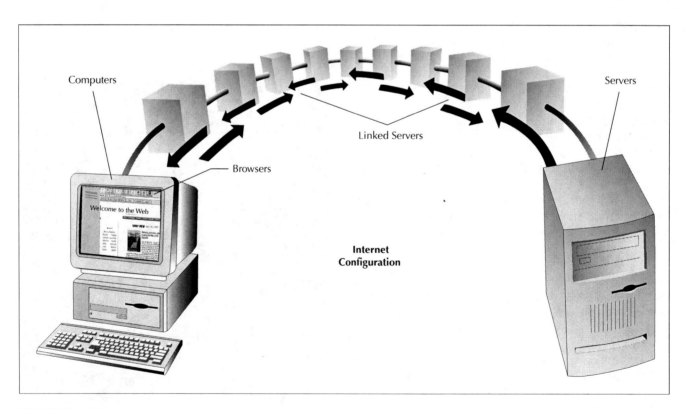

FIGURE 9.23
The convergence of computer technology and communications technology yields information technologies (IT). Two initially distinct technologies have now combined to impact the world economy. Communications technology is concerned with the transmission of information, while computer technology is concerned with the processing of information.

National Science Foundation, and in the 1990s, control was privatized via a consortium of telecommunications corporations. The Internet emerged on a global scale through the integration of existing telephone, fiber-optic, and satellite systems, which was made possible by the technological innovation of packet switching, TCP/IP (Transmission Control Protocol/Internet Protocol), and *Integrated Services Digital Network* (ISDN), in which individual messages may be decomposed, the constituent parts transmitted by various channels, and then reassembled, virtually instantaneously, at the destination. In the 1990s, graphical interfaces developed in Europe greatly simplified the use of the Internet, leading to the creation of the World Wide Web.

The growth of the Internet has been phenomenal (Figure 9.24); indeed, it is arguably the most rapidly diffusing technology in world history. By the end of 2005, penetration was 50 percent of U.S. households and 63 percent of the population. Like the automobile 80 years ago—which inspired the development of the moving assembly line, a fundamental and far-reaching innovation in manufacturing practice—the Internet has significantly changed the ways we work, consume, and live. The Internet is well on its way to becoming an indispensable mass communications technology for the average American.

Technological changes will further increase the utility and popularity of the Internet in the future. Mobile phones make it possible for consumers to access the Internet from any location, not just in the home or at the

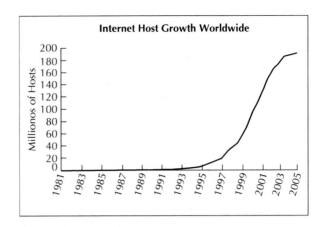

FIGURE 9.24
The growth of the Internet, 1981–2005. Roughly 1 billion people, or 15 percent of the planet, use the Internet today.

office. Broadband connectivity is becoming increasingly mainstream, allowing for innovations such as on-demand television. This next phase of Internet expansion will produce the real information revolution for everyday consumers. TV-quality video and voice-activated commands will enjoy the Internet as a practical home appliance, useful for entertainment, communication, and shopping.

In 2005, an estimated 1018 million people, or roughly 15 percent of the world's population (including 185 million in the United States) in more than 200 countries, were connected to the Internet (Figure 9.25).

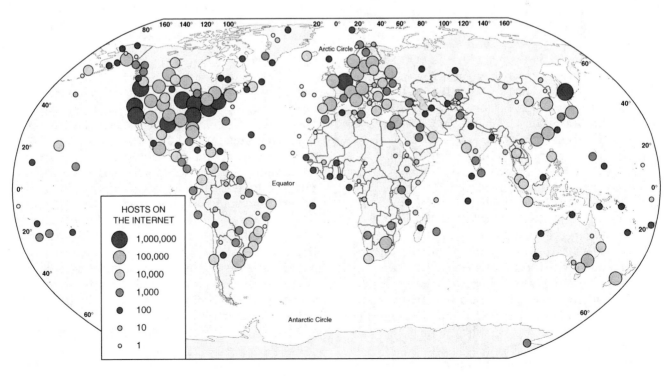

FIGURE 9.25
The geography of Internet hosts, 2003.

Transportation and Communications

Table 9.2

Estimated Internet Usage by World Region, 2005

Region	Internet Users (Millions)	Penetration Rate (%)
Africa	22.7	0.9
Asia	364.2	5.9
Europe	290.1	27.6
Middle East	18.2	4.6
North America	225.8	63.2
Latin America	79.0	6.6
Oceania	17.7	47.9
World	1,018.0	15.7

Source: Internet World Statistics, www.internetworldstats.com.

Table 9.3

Largest 20 Internet Users, 2005

	Users	Penetration Rate
United States	184.5	63.2
China	68.0	5.2
Japan	59.2	46.4
Germany	44.1	53.9
United Kingdom	34.4	58.2
South Korea	26.3	56.1
France	22.0	37.2
Italy	19.2	34.2
Canada	16.8	53.1
India	16.6	1.6
Brazil	14.3	8.0
Spain	14.0	33.7
Australia	12.8	64.2
Taiwan	11.6	49.1
Netherlands	10.3	63.7
Malaysia	24.0	32.5
Sweden	8.9	75.8
Russia	6.0	4.2
Turkey	4.9	6.7
Thailand	4.8	7.6

Source: Internet World Statistics, www.internetworldstats.com.

However, there are large variations in the Internet penetration rate (percentage of people with access) among the world's major regions (Table 9.2), ranging from as little as 0.9 percent in Africa to as high as 63 percent in North America. Inequalities in access to the Internet internationally reflect the long-standing bifurcation between the First and Third Worlds. While virtually no country is utterly without Internet access (although portions of Africa come close), the variations among and within nations in accessibility are huge. Given its large size, the United States—with more than 185 million users—dominates when measured in terms of absolute number of Internet hosts.

Internet use rates vary considerably by country (Table 9.3). The highest penetration rate is in Sweden (75.8%). In Europe, the greatest connectivity is in relatively wealthy nations such as the Netherlands (63.7%), Britain (58.2%), and Germany (53.9%); Eastern Europe lags considerably behind, and in Russia a mere 4.2 percent of the population uses the Internet. In Asia, access is by greatest in Taiwan (49.1%) and Japan (46.4%); about 5 percent of China is hooked up, although the numbers there are growing rapidly. In Latin America, the largest numbers of users are found in Brazil (8%) and Mexico (4.6%). The Internet in the African continent is essentially confined to South Africa. In all cases, per capita incomes are the key; the Internet can only be used by people with resources sufficient to own computers and learn the essential software. In many developing countries, where most people cannot afford their own computers, Internet cafés are popular. Variations in the number of users is also reflected in the geography of Internet flows (although flow data are much harder to come by than are place-specific attribute data): 80 percent of all international traffic on the Internet is either to or from the United States (Figure 9.26), fueling fears among some people that the Internet is largely a tool for the propagation of American culture.

Social and Spatial Discrepancies in Internet Access

Significant discrepancies exist in terms of access to the Internet, largely along the lines of wealth, gender, and race. While 40 percent of U.S. households have personal computers, only 20 percent have modems at home. Access to computers linked to the Internet, either at home or at work, is highly correlated with income; wealthier households are far more likely to have a personal computer at home with a modem than are the poor. In the United States, white households use networked computers more frequently than do African American or Latino ones. The elderly likewise often find access to the Internet to be intimidating and unaffordable, although they comprise the fastest-growing demographic group of users. American Internet users thus tend to be white and middle class, well educated, younger than average, and employed in professional occupations demanding college degrees.

Social and spatial differentials in access to the skills, equipment, and software necessary to get onto the electronic highway threaten to create a large, predominantly

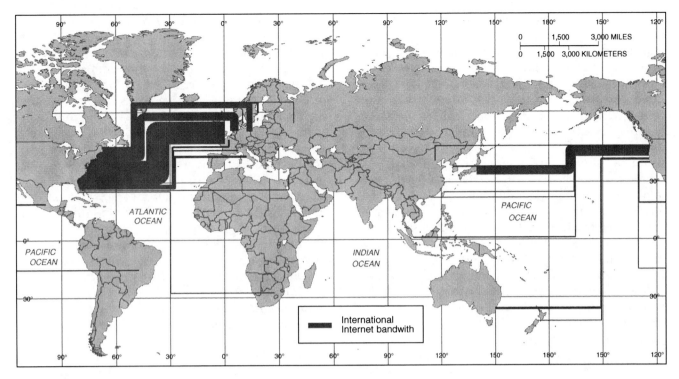

FIGURE 9.26
International information flows on the Internet. Eighty percent of all traffic is to or from the United States.

minority underclass deprived of the benefits of cyberspace. This phenomenon must be viewed in the broader context of the growing inequalities throughout industrialized nations generated by labor market polarization (i.e., deindustrialization and growth of low-income, contingent service jobs). Modern economies are increasingly divided between those who are comfortable and proficient with digital technology and those who neither understand nor trust it, disenfranchising the latter group from the possibility of citizenship in cyberspace. Despite the falling prices for hardware and software, basic entry-level machines for Internet access cost roughly $1000, an exorbitant sum for low-income households. Internet access at work is also difficult for many. For employees in poorly paying service jobs (the most rapidly growing category of employment) that do not offer access to the Internet at their place of employment, the obstacles to access are formidable.

The public educational system cannot offer an easy remedy to the problem of the digital divide. Even in the United States, the wide discrepancies in funding and the quality of education among school districts, particularly between suburban and central city schools, may reproduce this inequality rather than reduce it. Some public libraries offer free access to the Internet; mounting financial constraints in many municipalities, moreover, have curtailed the growth of these systems.

Even within the most digitized of cities there remain large pockets of "offline" poverty. Those who need the Internet the least, already living in information-rich environments with access through many non-Internet channels (e.g., newspapers and cable TV), may have the most access to it, while those who may benefit the most (e.g., through electronic job banks) may have the smallest chance to log on.

Internationally, access to the Internet is deeply conditioned by the density, reliability, and affordability of national telephone systems. Most Internet communications occurs along lines leased from telephone companies, some of which are state regulated (in contrast to the largely unregulated state of the Internet itself), although the global wave of privatization is ending government ownership in this sector. Prices for access vary by length of the phone call, distance, and the degree of monopoly. In nations with telecommunications monopolies, prices are higher than in those with deregulated systems, and hence usage rates are lower. The global move toward deregulation in telecommunications will lead to more use-based pricing (the so-called pay-per revolution), in which users must bear the full costs of their calls, and fewer cross-subsidies among different groups of users (e.g., between commercial and residential ones), a trend that will likely make access to cyberspace even less affordable to low-income users.

In an age in which more and more people's social life is increasingly mediated through computer networks, the reconstruction of interpersonal relations around the digitized spaces of cyberspace is of the utmost significance. However, the fact that cybercontacts differ from face-to-face ones serves as a useful reminder that telecommunications change not only what we know about the world, but also how we know and experience it.

Many of the Internet's uses revolve around entertainment, personal communication, research, downloading files, and online games. However, the Internet can also be used to challenge established systems of domination and legitimate and publicize the political claims of the relatively powerless and marginalized. The Internet has given voice to countless groups with a multiplicity of political interests and agendas, including civil and human rights advocates, sustainable development activists, antiracist and antisexist organizations, gay and lesbian rights groups, religious movements, those espousing ethnic identities and causes, youth movements, peace and disarmament parties, nonviolent action and pacifists, animal rights groups, and gays living in homophobic local environments. By facilitating the expression of political positions that otherwise may be difficult or impossible, the Internet allows for a dramatic expansion in the range of voices heard about many issues. In this sense, it permits the local to become global. Within the Internet itself one finds all the diversity and contradictions of human experience. Cyberpolitics mirrors those of its nonelectronic counterparts, although the boundaries between the two realms are increasingly fuzzy. Indeed, in a sociopsychological sense, cyberspace may allow for the reconstruction of "communities without propinquity," groups of users who share common interests but not physical proximity.

Finally, there is also what may be called the "dark side" of the Internet, in which it is deployed for illegal or immoral purposes. Hackers, for example, have often wreaked havoc with computer security systems. Such individuals are typically young men playing pranks, although others may unleash dangerous computer viruses and worms. Most hacks—by some estimates as much as 95 percent—go unreported, but their presence has driven up the cost of computer firewalls. The dark side also includes unsavory activities such as identity theft of counterfeit drivers' licenses, passports, Social Security cards, identities, securities swindles, and adoption scams. Credit card fraud is a mounting problem; 0.25 percent of Internet credit card transactions are fraudulent, compared with 0.08 percent for non-Internet transactions. Some Internet sites even offer credit card "marketplaces," where people who hack into merchant accounts may steal large numbers and sell them wholesale.

The impacts of telecommunications on businesses include a varieties of activities often lumped together under the term *e-commerce,* which may include both business-to-business transactions, as well as those linking firms to their customers. In general terms, information technology lowers the transaction costs among corporations, which helps to spur productivity. Moreover, it has been argued that such systems were instrumental in the restructuring of many corporations in response to mounting global competition, as they downsized in favor of flatter corporate hierarchies. Many firms sought improved productivity by accelerating information flows within the firm and lower costs by reducing intermediaries and distribution costs.

One important version of ecommerce concerns electronic data interchange (EDI) systems, which are generally used in business-to-business (B2B) contacts. Common uses of EDI include up-to-date advertising, online product catalogs, the sharing of sales and inventory data, submissions of purchase orders, contracts, invoices, payments, delivery schedules, product updates, and labor recruitment. E-commerce reduces delays and marketing and delivery costs and has led to a greater emphasis on connectivity, ideas, creativity, speed, and customer service. In the same vein, "e-tailing" or electronic retailing, reveals the growing commercialization of the Internet. In 1993, 2 percent of all Web sites were commercial (i.e., "dot com") sites; by 2005, 60 percent were so categorized. Shopping by the Internet requires only access (e.g., a modem), a credit card, and a parcel delivery service, and allows effortless comparison shopping. The most successful example perhaps is Amazon.com, started by Seattle entrepreneur Jeff Bezos, which now is responsible for 60 percent of all books sold online. Other examples include online auctions (e.g., eBay), Internet-based telephony (e.g., Skype), and Internet music (e.g., downloading of MP3 music files), which has provoked a firestorm of opposition from music companies complaining about infringement of their intellectual property rights and declining over-the-counter music sales.

Internet sales have also provoked worries about tax evasion and sales of illegal goods (e.g., pharmaceuticals from abroad). Despite predictions that "click and order" shopping would eliminate "brick and mortar" stores, e-tailing has been slow to catch on, however, comprising only 3 percent of total U.S. retail sales, perhaps because it lacks the emotional content of shopping. Shoppers using this mode tend to be above average in income and relatively well educated. Web-based banking has experienced slow growth, even though it is considerably cheaper for banks than automatic teller machines, as have Internet-based bill payments, mortgages, and insurance. Internet-based sales of stocks (e.g., E. Schwab, E* Trade) now comprise 15 percent of all trades. One particularly successful application has been in the travel reservation and ticketing business, where Web-based purchases of hotel rooms and airline seats (e.g., through services such as Travelocity and Priceline.com) have caused a steady decline in the number of travel agents. Electronic publishing, including more than 700 newspapers worldwide, has been extended to e-books and e-magazines, which, unlike printed text, can be complemented with sound and graphics. Other services offer Internet searches of databases and classified ads. Webcasting, or broadcasts over the Internet (typically of sports or entertainment events), demands high-bandwidth capacity but comprises a significant share of Internet traffic today. Web-logs, or "blogs," have become increasingly important sources of personal, social, and political commentary, alternatives to the mainstream media and a voice for independent views.

Internet advertising has proven to be difficult, in part because the Internet reaches numerous specialized markets rather than mass audiences. Cyberspace does allow specialized companies to reach global niche markets. E-advertising comprises only 1 percent of total revenues in the United States and is overwhelmingly focused on computer and software firms. Indeed, many users are now wary of "spam" e-mail (unwanted commercial messages), which constitute an ever-larger, and increasingly annoying, share of e-mail traffic (by some estimates as high as 75%).

Another version of e-commerce concerns universities, many of which have invested heavily in Web-based distance learning courses. Although such programs are designed to attract nonlocal and nontraditional students, many of whom may not be able to take lecture-based courses in the traditional manner, they also reflect the mounting financial constraints and declining public subsidies that many institutions face, which may see distance learning as a means of attracting additional students, and tuition, at relatively low marginal costs. The largest example of Web-based teaching is the University of Phoenix, based in Arizona but with students located around the world; with more than 100,000 students, it is now the largest university in the world. Distance learning has provoked fears that it opens the door to the corporatization of academia and the domination of the profit motive, while others have questioned whether the chat rooms that form an important part of its delivery system are an effective substitute for the face-to-face teaching and learning that classrooms offer. It remains unclear whether Web-based learning is an effective complement or substitute for traditional forms of instruction. Others suggest that distance-learning programs may be better suited to professional programs in business or engineering than in the liberal arts.

More morally ambiguous is the growing role of Internet-based gambling systems, which include a variety of betting services, especially concerning sports events, and even online slot machines in which gamblers may use their credit cards. (Some complain that online gambling doesn't adequately substitute for the heady experience of a gaudy casino in Las Vegas, Nevada, or Atlantic City, New Jersey). Because the geography of legal gambling is highly uneven, the existence of such systems challenges the laws of communities in which gambling is illegal. Offshore gambling centers have grown quickly, particularly in the Caribbean, which started when Antigua licensed its first Internet casino in 1994. By 2004, an estimated 700 online casinos, mostly in the Caribbean, attracted roughly 8 million users. In the United States, gambling is permitted in some states (e.g., Nevada and Mississippi) but not others; oddly, running an online casino in the United States is legal but using one is not.

Electronic Data Interchange

EDI can be defined as the electronic movement of standard business documents between and within firms. EDI uses a structured machine-retrievable data format that permits data to be transferred between networked computers without rekeying. Like e-mail, EDI enables the sending and receiving of messages between computers connected by a communication link such as a telephone line.

However, EDI has some special characteristics:

1. *Business transaction messages.* EDI is used primarily to transfer repetitive business transactions. These include purchase orders, invoices, approvals of credit, shipping notices, and confirmations. In contrast, e-mail is used mainly for nonstandard correspondence.
2. *Data formatting standards.* Because EDI messages are repetitive, it is sensible to use some formatting standards. In contrast, there are no data formatting standards for e-mail because it is usually not formatted.
3. *EDI translators.* The conversation of data sent into standard formats is done by special EDI translators.
4. *EDI uses Value Added Networks (VAN).* In contrast to e-mail, which uses regular telephone lines, EDI uses value-added networks, specialized companies with expertise in maintenance that help customers develop the necessary interfaces.

The major advantages of EDI are as follows:

1. EDI enables a company to send and receive large amounts of information around the world in real time.
2. Companies have the ability to access partners' computers to retrieve and store standard transactions.

3. EDI fosters a true partnership because it involves a commitment to a long-term investment and refinement of the system over time.
4. EDI creates a paperless environment, saving money and increasing efficiency.
5. The time for collecting payments can be shortened by several weeks.

FUTURE IMPACTS OF INFORMATION TECHNOLOGIES

For all that telecommunications technology has provided, the biggest changes are still ahead. The coming digital revolution will redefine lives, work, education, commerce, and leisure. Whole industries will vanish, and new ones will spring up overnight. The restraints of time and space, long the adhesive that has held many communities together, will be reconstructed dramatically.

Today, the "virtual transportation network" of computers and cables promises to remake cities and nation-states yet again. Communities unprepared for these changes risk being consigned to geopolitical obsolescence. In the process, they are likely to suffer a fate similar to that of many of the great industrial cities of the past, becoming "electronic ghost towns" on the virtual frontier, abandoned by corporate and human citizens seeking a more electronically hospitable environment.

Smart Cities

Linking parts and functions of a city through networked computers may be one answer to urban decline. Such computer-networked cities are known as *smart cities*. In the past, cities prospered as geopolitical entities because of their importance as transportation crossroads or as centers of industrial production. But telecommunications developments like telephones, fax machines, and electronically linked computers weakened the once inextricable connections between transportation systems and mobility.

The new telecommunications network made it possible for businesses to produce, consumers to purchase, and workers to interact with one another without the need for a common physical location, allowing corporate and human citizens to choose where to reside based on a wide array of factors beyond mere physical convenience. Worse, communities suddenly found themselves competing for these residents not just with neighboring municipalities, but with cities across the country—or around the globe.

At the same time, telecommunications advances are transforming a world of discrete local and national economic spheres into a single global economy, placing local businesses and workers alike into direct competition with their counterparts on distant shores. Government and business leaders watched helplessly as they began to lose control over their communities' economic destinies even as shifting business and population patterns eroded their economic base and their place in the urban hierarchy. As a result, economic and social institutions ranging from governments to economic development agencies to local schools, whose increasingly time-worn practices already were proving insufficient to the rapid technological changes and complex social and economic challenges of the late twentieth century, were left with neither adequate resources nor adequate responses for solving the very difficult problems within their midst, further loosening their hold on the people and businesses who remain.

Government

Placing government and social service information (office locations, departmental telephone numbers, city council minutes, government documents, and so on) online is a valuable first step toward building an Internet-savvy community—but only a first step. Increasing people's access to such information serves the important function of creating a more well-informed citizenry.

Information technology's greatest potential in the government arena may lie in transforming the very nature of local government, making it possible to reconfigure traditionally monolithic, downtown City Halls into a network of small, neighborhood-based "branches" linked electronically to a slimmed-down city "headquarters." Under this scenario, almost all government and social services would be dispensed in the neighborhood—either from kiosks or in small, multifunction neighborhood service centers. Such structural reengineering could further reduce government staffing, operational, and office costs; minimize traffic congestion and pollution; and increase people's access to government officials and services while creating a government more institutionally sensitive to neighborhood concerns.

E-government takes a variety of forms, ranging from simple broadcasting of information to integration (i.e., allowing user input) to integration, in which network integration minimizes duplication of efforts. E-government allows, for example, for the digital collection of taxes, voting, and provision of some public services, particularly the provision of information. Such steps boost the efficiency and effectiveness of public services, allowing, for example, online registration of companies and automobiles; electronic banking; utility bill payments; applications for government programs, universities, and licenses; access to census data; and reducing the waiting time as paperwork filters through government bureaucracies.

Business

Hundreds of thousands of companies, from small start-ups to the *Fortune* 500, use the Internet to promote their businesses. Web sites are a passive form of advertising, and potential customers often do not encounter a particular company's site unless they happen to be looking for it—turning the World Wide Web into something of a high-tech Yellow Pages. In an effort to reach a broader Web audience, therefore, many companies have taken a cue from the television advertising model and have begun to sponsor high-profile, Web-based news, information, and entertainment sites where they can gain exposure to customers that they otherwise might never reach.

For all their promotional potential, however, information networks are more than effective advertising and marketing vehicles. They can, in fact, change the very nature of work. In much the same way that government telecommunications networks may allow government agencies to distribute their workforces among communities, large businesses can establish dedicated neighborhood *telework centers* that give them access to potential employees, such as rural residents, home-makers, people with disabilities, or individuals without transportation, whom they otherwise might not be able to attract. By moving operations out of congested and high-priced central cities, telework centers simultaneously can increase workers' productivity while reducing companies' rent, transportation, and labor costs.

Telecommuting, of course, is an idea that has been around for decades, and the practice has not yet taken off in the way many of its advocates forecast. This has been due in part to business's lack of interest in telecommuting and to its reliance on traditional, fixed-site management practices. But the growing number of home-office, temporary, and contract workers makes telework not only feasible but increasingly necessary. With workers demanding more flexible schedules, shorter commutes, and relief from traffic congestion, companies may find that telecenters are a powerful tool for retaining or attracting high-quality workers. What's more, with videoconferencing, e-mail, and high-speed computer networks, telecommuting finally has become technologically practical in a wide range of job categories and work situations.

Education

Information technology's most obvious potential in education lies in giving students access to computers and the Internet. That is, in fact, the substance of most of the smart community educational initiatives now taking place at local and federal levels. Bringing computers into the classroom will increase young people's access to information, help to equalize educational resources among poorer and wealthier school districts,

and better prepare today's students for tomorrow's workforce.

Indeed, technology is forcing educational planners to reevaluate the entire concept of mass-produced, discipline-based education, in which students are herded around schools to assigned classrooms according to fixed schedules and one-size-fits-all curricula. In the smart communities, students—adults as well as young people—will learn when they want to, how they want to, and at their own pace. Already, predominantly rural states like Montana and Iowa are using telecommunications to link schools in sparsely populated areas into a statewide educational network, allowing instructors and students to interact from around the state within the confines of a single "virtual classroom." Similarly, library systems are remaking themselves into comprehensive information and research centers, while others are being planned from the start as "smart libraries," relying on multimedia, virtual reality, and global networks.

Health Care

Escalating health care costs have severely strained the nation's health care system. Much of this cost increase is due to an enormous volume of recordkeeping and data transfer—a problem well suited to a technological solution. In the United States alone, billions of dollars per year could be saved by using advanced communications technology for the routine transfer of laboratory tests and more orderly collection, storage, and retrieval of patient information. Thus telemedicine, in which physicians at one location use remote viewing techniques to diagnose and provide advice to patients located somewhere else, has grown in popularity, particularly in rural areas with inadequate access to health care. In some cases, such technologies facilitate the training of physicians engaged in virtual surgeries. The Internet has also become an important source of medical information, dramatically changing the traditional doctor-patient relationship: two-thirds of everyone online have searched for health-related information there, although much of it is inaccurate or misleading.

SUMMARY

This chapter examined two major systems of circulation—transportation of people and goods and communication of information—that are critical to the ever-changing structure of global capitalism. We considered some of the factors other than distance that play a role in determining transport costs—the nature of commodities, carrier and route variations, and the regimes governing transportation. Transport costs remain critical for material-oriented and market-oriented firms, but they are of less importance for firms that produce items for which transport costs are but a small proportion of total costs. For these firms, transit time is more crucial than cost. Modernized means of transport and reduced costs of shipping commodities have also made it possible for economic activities to decentralize. Multinationals have taken full advantage of transport developments to establish "offshore" branch-plant operations.

Movements of goods and people take place over and through transport networks. We focused on the historical development of transportation and explained how improvements over the centuries have resulted in time-space and cost-space convergence. Improved transport and communications systems integrated isolated points of production into a national or a world economy. Although the friction of distance has diminished over time, transport remains an important locational factor. Only if transportation were instantaneous and free would economic activities respond solely to aspatial forces such as economies of scale. The chapter also considered the role of the state in transportation policy, which has varied around the world and among different sectors (rail, airlines, trucking, etc.).

Innovation in urban transportation systems is necessary because of the tremendous increase in travel demand in large cities of the developed world. For example, in the United States, vehicle miles traveled, automobile ownership, and total vehicle trips are increasing rapidly.

Communications and information technology (IT) are transforming the world economy at rates never before thought possible. Profound implications, even many that the world cannot yet measure, accompany this IT explosion. At the center of this information explosion are the microprocessor, networked computers, and the Internet, which connected more than 1 billion people worldwide in 2005, about 15 percent of the planet. The chapter explored the origins, growth, and size of the Internet; noted the uneven access to it that people around the world and within the United States have; and touched on some of its many consequences, including the growth of cybercommunities. It pointed out that the social divisions that exist offline are replicated online. It also explained the nature and impacts of e-commerce.

The telecommunications revolution may only be starting to have its real impacts. The chapter noted a number of ways the IT revolution may carry forward into the future, including employment, health care, and government services.

STUDY QUESTIONS

1. What are curvilinear and stepped freight costs?
2. What are terminal and line-haul costs?
3. How do transport costs enter into location theory?
4. What network accessibility and connectivity?
5. What is the Taaffe, Morrill, and Gould model of transportation and urban development?
6. What is the gravity model?
7. What are cost-space and time-space convergence?
8. How did deregulation affect the structure of airline networks?
9. When did telecommunications begin?
10. How did the microelectronics revolution affect telecommunications?
11. What are fiber optics and what role to they play in international telecommunications?
12. Do telecommunications mean the end of geography?
13. How did the internet begin?
14. How does access to the Internet reflect social divisions?
15. What are some social impacts of the Internet?
16. What is e-commerce and why do many firms like it?
17. What is electronic data interchange?
18. What are some likely future impacts of information technology?

KEY TERMS

accessibility index
artificial intelligence
backhaul
break-of-bulk point
connectivity
cost-space convergence
deregulation
distance learning
distance-decay effect
elasticity of demand for transportation
electronic data interchange
expert systems

friction of distance
global office
gravity model
hub-and-spoke networks
information warehouse
intelligent vehicle highway systems (IVHS)
Internet
ISDN
journey to work
line-haul costs
Maglev

multimedia
networked computers
outsourcing
privatization
smart cars
smart highways
spatial interaction
stepped freight rates
telepresence
terminal costs
time-space compression or convergence
transport costs

SUGGESTED READINGS

Cairncross, F. *The Death of Distance*. 1997. Boston, Mass. Harvard Business School Press.

Crang, M., Crang, P., and May, J. 1999. *Virtual Geographies: Bodies, Space and Relations*. London: Routledge.

Dodge, M. and Kitchin, R. 2001. *Mapping Cyberspace*. London: Routledge.

Graham, S. and Marvin, S. 2001. *Splintering Urbanism: Networked Infrastructures, Technological Mobilities and the Urban Condition*. London: Routledge.

Kitchin, R. 1998. *Cyberspace: The World in the Wires*. New York: John Wiley.

Standage, T. *The Victorian Internet*. 1998. New York: Walker and Company.

Warf, B. 2006. "International Competition between Satellite and Fiber Optic Carriers: A Geographic Perspective." *The Professional Geographer* 58:1–11.

WORLD WIDE WEB SITES

ATLAS OF CYBERSPACE

http://www.cybergeography.org/atlas/

Most comprehensive collection of maps of the Internet around.

INFOSPACE

http://www.infospace.com

Search for addresses, phone numbers, e-mail addresses. Also a "My Town" profile that, using phone book data, gives you a personal profile of any town in the United States. Want to know the names of Chinese restaurants in Boise? Click. Want to see them on a map? Click. Want written directions on how to get there? Click.

MAPQUEST

http://www.mapquest.com

Type in an address and get a clickable, zoomable map of that location.

TRIPQUEST

http://www.tripquest.com

Type in a starting location and an ending location. The program provides door-to-door or city-to-city directions.

ETRADE

http://www.etrade.com

Flat rate broker allows buying or selling of stock for a flat $14.95 fee for 5000 shares or less, a penny a share more above that.

INTERNET WORLD STATS

http://www.internetworldstats.com/stats2.htm

Up-to-the-minute data on Internet users internationally.

EARTHCAM

http://www.earthcam.com

The locations of nearly every live camera on the Internet. Spy on a classroom, watch people work, check out a live skyline.

RAND MCNALLY

http://www.randmcnally.com/home/

Good travel site enhanced by a searchable index of major road construction projects all over the United States.

AMERICAN TELECOMMUTING ASSOCIATION
http://www.knowledgetree.com/ata.html

TELECOMMUTING JOBS WEB PAGE
HTTP://WWW.TJOBS.COM/

Chapter 5
Managing intellectual property

Introduction

Intellectual property concerns the legal rights associated with creative effort or commercial reputation. The subject matter is very wide indeed. The aim of this chapter is to introduce the area of intellectual property to the manager of business and to ensure that they are aware of the variety of ways that it can affect the management of innovation and the development of new products. The rapid advance of the Internet and e-commerce has created a whole new set of problems concerning intellectual property rights. All these issues will be discussed in this chapter. Finally, the case study at the end of this chapter explains how the pharmaceutical industry uses the patent system to ensure it reaps rewards from the drugs that it develops.

Intellectual property
Trade secrets
An introduction to patents
  Novelty
  Inventive step
  Industrial applications
Exclusions from patents
The patenting of life
Human genetic patenting
The configuration of a patent
Patent harmonisation: first to file and first to invent
Some famous patent cases
Patents in practice
Expiry of a patent and patent extensions
  Patent extensions
The use of patents in innovation management
Do patents hinder or encourage innovation?
Trademarks
  Should satisfy the requirements of section 1(1)
  Distinctive
  Non-deceptive
  Not confusing
Brand names
Using brands to protect intellectual property
  Exploiting new opportunities
  Brands, trademarks and the Internet
Duration of registration, infringement and passing off
Registered designs
Copyright
Remedy against infringement
  Damages
  Injunction
  Accounts
Counterfeit goods and IP
Case study: Pricing, patents and profits in the pharmaceutical industry

Learning objectives

When you have completed this chapter you will be able to:

- examine the different forms of protection available for a firm's intellectual property;
- identify the limitations of the patent system;
- explain why other firms' patents can be a valuable resource;
- identify the link between brand name and trademark;
- identify when and where the areas of copyright and registered design may be useful; and
- explain how the patent system is supposed to balance the interests of the individual and society.

Intellectual property

The world of intellectual property changes at an alarming rate. The law, it seems, is always trying to keep up with technology changes that suddenly allow firms to operate in ways previously not considered. Illustration 5.1 shows how legal events over the past few years have fundamentally affected the activities of so-called grey marketers and the subsequent powers granted to the owners of a range of branded marks including famous lucrative names such as Levi's, Nike and Calvin Klein. The pronouncements from the European Court of Justice, together with national court decisions, have created a degree of confusion. The landmark Silhouette Case has proved immensely controversial with regard to the operation of trademark law throughout the European Union. The decision seems to prohibit the importation into the European Union of branded goods or services, unless such activity has been specifically consented to by the brand owner.

This chapter will explore this dynamic area of the law and illustrate why firms need to be aware of this increasingly important aspect of innovation.

If you just happen to come up with a novel idea, the simplest and cheapest course of action is to do nothing about legal protection, just keep it a secret (as with the recipe for Coca-Cola). While this in theory may be true, in reality many chemists and most ingredients and fragrance firms would argue that science can now detect

Illustration 5.1

Levi sings the blues over jeans in Tesco

Levi Strauss, the clothing company, will today tell the European Court of Justice that its jeans should not be sold in supermarkets because sales staff need special training to explain the different styles to customers. 'Customers need advice on what's on offer and the difference between loose and baggy, straight and slim,' said Mark Elliott at Levi. 'We're not saying you need a university degree to sell jeans, but if a person is cutting bacon and filling shelves one minute, it's not possible for them to sell jeans as well.'

The company is bringing the case against Tesco, the UK retailer, which imported Levi's from outside the EU to sell at knock-down prices. The European Court will hear arguments from both companies today in an important case that could challenge rules on so-called grey-market imports of designer goods from outside the European Union. But a judgement is not expected for up to another year.

Tesco says Levi will not supply it so it buys from cheaper markets such as the US and eastern Europe. 'It's not rocket science to sell jeans . . . we don't think giving five minutes extra training than our staff get justifies an extra 20 pounds on the price and neither do our customers,' said Simon Soffe, a Tesco spokesman.

'British customers are losing out . . . because the brands are trying to protect Fortress Europe and keep lower prices out,' a Tesco statement said.

Levi says Tesco has never met the standard to become a licensed outlet, and lack of training is one of the main reasons. 'Staff have to explain how one blue is different from another blue. These things are important to jeans aficionados,' Mr Elliott said.

Source: D. Hargreaves, 'Levi sings the blues over jeans', *Financial Times*, 16 January 2001. Reprinted with permission.

Table 5.1 An overview of the main types of intellectual property

	Type of intellectual property	Key features of this type of protection
1	Patents	Offers a 20-year monopoly
2	Copyright	Provides exclusive rights to creative individuals for the protection of their literary or artistic productions
3	Registered designs	As protected by registration, is for the outward appearance of an article and provides exclusive rights for up to 15 years
4	Registered trademarks	Is a distinctive name, mark or symbol that is identified with a company's products

a droplet of blood in an entire swimming pool, and to suggest that science cannot analyse a bottle of cola and uncover its ingredients is stretching the bounds of reason. The keep-it-secret approach prevents anyone else seeing it or finding it. Indeed, the owner can take their intellectual property to their grave, safe in the knowledge that no one will inherit it. This approach is fine unless you are seeking some form of commercial exploitation and ultimately a financial reward, usually in the form of royalties.

One of the dangers, of course, with trying to keep your idea a secret is that someone else might develop a similar idea to yours and apply for legal protection and seek commercial exploitation. Independent discovery of ideas is not as surprising as one might first think. This is because research scientists working at the forefront of science and technology are often working towards the same goal. This was the case with Thomas Edison and Joseph Swan, who independently invented the light bulb simultaneously either side of the Atlantic. Indeed, they formed a company called Ediswan to manufacture light bulbs at the end of the nineteenth century.

Table 5.1 shows an overview of the different forms of intellectual property and rights available for different areas of creativity.

The issues of intellectual property are continually with us and touch us probably more than we realise. Most students will have already confronted the issue of intellectual property, either with recording pre-recorded music or copying computer software. The author is always the owner of his or her work and the writing of an academic paper entitles the student to claim the copyright on that essay. Indeed, the submission of an academic paper to a scientific journal for publication requires the author to sign a licence for the publisher to use the intellectual property. Patenting is probably the most commonly recognised form of intellectual property, but it is only one of several ways to protect creative efforts. Registered designs, trademarks and copyright are other forms of intellectual property. These will be addressed in the following sections.

Pause for thought

Given the impressive advances made in science over the past 50 years, especially in the area of detecting substances and ingredients, scientists now claim to be able to detect one drop of blood in a swimming pool full of water. Does anyone still believe that the ingredients in Coca-Cola, for example, are secret and unknown?

Trade secrets

There are certain business activities and processes that are not patented, copyrighted or trademarked. Many businesses regard these as trade secrets. It could be special ways of working, price costings or business strategies. The most famous example is the recipe for Coca-Cola, which is not patented. This is because Coca-Cola did not want to reveal the recipe to their competitors. Unfortunately, the law covering intellectual property is less clear about the term *trade secret*. Indeed, Bainbridge (1996) argues there is no satisfactory legal definition of the term.

An introduction to patents

Illustration 5.2 dramatically illustrates the importance of patents to the business world. A patent is a contract between an individual or organisation and the state. The rationale behind the granting of a temporary monopoly by the state is to encourage creativity and innovation within an economy. By the individual or

---

Illustration 5.2

Pfizer sues rivals to protect Viagra patent

Pfizer, the world's largest drugs group, filed a patent infringement suit on Tuesday against rivals Bayer AG, GlaxoSmithKline and an Eli Lilly joint venture, seeking to protect its blockbuster male impotence drug Viagra from competition in the US.

The three defendants are on the verge of launching two rival treatments for male erectile dysfunction in the US that are not prohibited by Viagra's main patent, valid until 2011.

The company said US patent authorities on Tuesday granted it a broad patent until 2019 to use oral PDE-5 inhibitors – drugs that act on the body's PDE-5 enzyme and thus treat impotence. This patent does not cover Viagra's active ingredient, sildenafil.

Pfizer subsequently filed a lawsuit in federal court in Delaware claiming the three companies' potential products infringed its patent. The rival products threaten to cut into pricing power and revenues of one of the best known drugs in the world with about $1.7 billion sales this year.

The lawsuit to preserve its 100 per cent market share in the US comes one day after President George W. Bush announced a new regulatory rule to speed generic competition.

The proposal seeks to keep brand-name drug groups from using extraneous patents to delay inexpensive generic rivals. Pfizer's Viagra patent case, however, does not involve generics.

The UK High Court struck down a similar broad patent Pfizer is invoking in the US enabling Viagra competition overseas.

The court ruled in November 2000 that scientific literature had widely reported the effects of inhibiting PDE-5 on male impotence before Pfizer filed for the patent in 1993.

'Pfizer's goal is to delay competitive entry for Viagra as long as possible, and if the patent were actually to stick, that would simply be gravy for Pfizer in our opinion,' said Anthony Butler, analyst at Lehman Brothers.

Source: C. Bowe, 'Pfizer sues rivals to protect Viagra patent', www.FT.com; 23 October 2002. Reprinted with permission.

Plate 5.1 UK Intellectual Property Office is an operating name of the Patent Office
Source: UK Intellectual Property Office.

organisation disclosing in the patent sufficient detail of the invention, the state will confer the legal right to stop others benefiting from the invention (Derwent, 1998). The state, however, has no obligation to prevent others benefiting from it. This is the responsibility of the individual or organisation who is granted the patent. And herein lies a major criticism of the patent system. The costs of defending a patent against infringement can be high indeed. This point is explored later.

The UK Patent Office was set up in 1852 to act as the United Kingdom's sole office for the granting of patents of invention. From 2 April 2007 the UK Patent Office changed its name to the UK Intellectual Property Office. This is to reflect that patents now represent only part of its activities along with Registered Designs and Trademarks (*see* Plate 5.1). The origins of patent system stretch back a further 400 years. The word patent comes from the practice of monarchs in the Middle Ages (500–1500) conferring rights and privileges by means of 'open letters', that is, documents on which the royal seal was not broken when they were opened. This is distinct from 'closed letters' that were not intended for public view. Open letters were intended for display and inspection by any interested party. The language of government in medieval England was Latin and the Latin for open letters is 'litterae patentes'. As English slowly took over from Latin as the official language the documents became known as 'letters patent' and later just 'patents'.

- *Monopoly for 20 years.* Patents are granted to individuals and organisations that can lay claim to a new product or manufacturing process, or to an improvement of an existing product or process, which was not previously known. The granting of a patent gives the 'patentee' a monopoly to make, use or sell the invention for a fixed period of time, which in Europe and the United States is 20 years from the date the patent application was first filed. In return for this monopoly, the patentee pays a fee to cover the costs of processing the patent, and, more importantly, publicly discloses details of the invention.
- *Annual fees required.* The idea must be new and not an obvious extension of what is already known. A patent lasts up to 20 years in the United Kingdom and Europe, but heavy annual renewal fees have to be paid to keep it in force.
- *Patent agents.* The role of a patent agent combines scientific or engineering knowledge with legal knowledge and expertise and it is a specialised field of work. Many large companies have in-house patent agents who prepare patents for the company's scientists. They may also search patent databases around the world on behalf of the company's scientists.

The earliest known English patent of invention was granted to John of Utynam in 1449. The patent gave Mr Utynam a 20-year monopoly for a method of making stained glass that had not previously been known in England. For a patent to benefit from legal protection it must meet strict criteria:

- novelty;
- inventive step; and
- industrial application.

Novelty

The Patent Act 1977, section 2(1), stipulates that 'an invention shall be taken to be new if it does not form part of the state of the art'. A state of the art is defined as all matter, in other words, publications, written or oral or even anticipation (*Windsurfing International* v. *Tabar Marine*, Court of Appeal, 1985), will render a patent invalid.

Inventive step

Section 3 of the Patent Act states that 'an invention shall be taken to involve an inventive step if it is not obvious to a person skilled in the art'.

Industrial applications

Under the Patent Act an invention shall be taken to be capable of industrial application if it can be a machine, product or process. Penicillin was a discovery which was not patentable but the process of isolating and storing penicillin clearly had industrial applications and thus was patentable.

> **Pause for thought**
>
> If states and governments in particular are determined to outlaw monopolistic practices in industry and commerce, why do they offer a 20-year monopoly for a patent?

Exclusions from patents

Discoveries (as opposed to inventions), scientific theory and mathematical processes are not patentable under the 1988 Patent Act. Similarly, literary artistic works and designs are covered by other forms of intellectual property such as trademarks, copyright and registered designs.

The patenting of life

The rapid scientific developments in the field of biology, medical science and biotechnology has fuelled intense debates about the morality of patenting life forms. Until very recently there was a significant difference between the US patent system, which enabled the granting of patents on certain life forms, and the European patent system, which did not. Essentially the US system adopted a far more liberal approach to the patenting of life. This difference was illustrated in the 'Harvard oncomouse' case (Patent No. 4,581,847). The Harvard Medical School had its request for a European patent refused because the mouse was a natural living life form and, hence, unpatentable. This European approach had serious implications for the European biotechnology industry. In particular, because the R&D efforts of the biotechnology industry could not be protected, there was a danger that capital in the form of intellectual and financial could flow from Europe to the United States, where protection was available. The other side of the argument is equally compelling: the granting to a company of a patent on certain genes may restrict other companies' ability to work with those genes. On 27 November 1997 the European Union agreed to Directive 95/0350(COD) and COM(97)446 which permits the granting of patents on certain life forms. This had a particular significance in the area of gene technology.

The subject of cloning a new life form from existing cells stirs the emotions of many. When Dolly, the first large mammal to be created from cells taken from other sheep, was announced it generated enormous controversy and publicity. This was especially so for the group of scientists from the Roslin Institute, a publicly funded institute, and PPL Therapeutics, a biotechnology company that developed Dolly. The debate about the ethics of the science continues and related to this is the intellectual property of the gene technology involved (*see Financial Times*, 1997 and Rowan, 1997, for a full discussion of this debate).

Human genetic patenting

Five years ago this industry barely existed: today it is worth £30 billion. Across Europe there are now 800 small and medium-sized enterprises in the business of making something new from life itself. Public institutions and private enterprises have filed claims on more than 127,000 human genes or partial human gene sequences. All are seeking wealth from DNA. These organisations are searching for tests, treatments, cures and vaccines for thousands of diseases; they are looking for new ways of delivering and new ways of making medicines.

There are many, of course, who take a more pessimistic view of this new science and argue that scientists should not play with nature and even that it is a threat to the future of mankind. A brighter view is that science is on the edge of a new frontier and the future will be one where human suffering is relieved and where incurable illnesses are treated. Whichever view you take, it is worthy of note that many of these firms are small start-ups headed by one or two scientists who have staked the future of the firm on several patent applications. Indeed, the firms' capitalisation is often based on the future predictions of patent applications. This is a very precarious situation for investors. This raises the issue of whether the patent developed all those years ago is suitable for this type of industry or the twenty-first century in general.

In 1998 the European Union harmonised patent law to give European scientists and investors the chance to make one application for one big market, rather than separate applications to member states. It also gave European entrepreneurs the right to patent genes or life. In the past few years the biotechnology firms have been making numerous patent applications for genes or partial human gene sequences. This, of course, leads to the argument that human genes are being turned into intellectual property and licensed to the highest bidders. The key question is, will this property then be made widely available to help the hungry, the sick and the desperate? Or will a few rich firms profit from many years of publicly funded science and exploit the poor and vulnerable? These are clearly difficult ethical questions that you may wish to debate among yourselves, but at the heart of this is patent law. This is illustrated in the case study at the end of this chapter. The purpose of any patent system is to strike a balance between the interests of the inventor and the wider public. At present many believe that US patent law is too heavily biased towards the needs of inventors and investors and does not take into account the poor and developing countries of the world.

The configuration of a patent

For a patent to be granted, its contents need to be made public so that others can be given the opportunity to challenge the granting of a monopoly. There is a formal registering and indexing system to enable patents to be easily accessed by the public. For this reason patents follow a very formal specification. Details concerning country of origin, filing date, personal details of applicant, etc., are accompanied by an internationally agreed numbering system for easy identification (*see* Appendix). The two most important sources of information relating to a patent are the *patent specification* and the *patent abstract*. Both of these are classified and indexed in various ways to facilitate search.

The specification is a detailed description of the invention and must disclose enough information to enable someone else to repeat the invention. This part of the document needs to be precise and methodical. It will also usually contain references to other scientific papers. The remainder of the specification will contain claims. These are to define the breadth and scope of the invention. A patent agent will try to write the broadest claim possible as a narrow claim can restrict the patent's application and competitors will try to argue that, for example, a particular invention applies only to one particular method. Indeed, competitors will scrutinise these claims to test their validity.

The patent abstract is a short statement printed on the front page of the patent specification which identifies the technical subject of the invention and the advance that it represents (*see* Appendix). Abstracts are usually accompanied by a drawing. In addition these abstracts are published in weekly information booklets.

It is now possible to obtain a patent from the European Patent Office for the whole of Europe, and this can be granted in a particular country or several countries. The concept of a world patent, however, is a distant realisation. The next section explores some of the major differences between the two dominant world patent systems.

Patent harmonisation: first to file and first to invent

Most industrialised countries offer some form of patent protection to companies operating within their borders. However, while some countries have adequate protection, others do not. Moreover, different countries are members of different conventions and some adopt different systems. The European and the US patent systems have many similarities, for example a monopoly is granted for 20 years under both systems. There is, however, one key difference. In the United States the patent goes to the researcher who can prove they were the first to invent it, not – as in Europe – to the first to file for a patent.

The implications of this are many and varied but there are two key points that managers need to consider.

1 In Europe, a patent is invalid if the inventor has published the novel information before filing for patent protection. In the United States there are some provisions which allow inventors to talk first and file later.
2 In Europe, patent applications are published while pending. This allows the chance to see what monopoly an inventor is claiming and object to the Patent Office if there are grounds to contest validity. In the United States the situation is quite different – applications remain secret until granted.

The issue of patent harmonisation has a long history. The Paris Convention for the Protection of Industrial Property was signed in 1883, and since then it has received many amendments. At present its membership includes 114 countries. European countries have a degree of patent harmonisation provided by the European Patent Convention (EPC) administered by the European Patent Office.

The sheer size of the US market and its dominance in many technology-intensive industries means that this difference in the patent systems has received, and continues to receive, a great deal of attention from various industry and government departments in Europe and the United States.

Some famous patent cases

- *1880: Ediswan*. It is rare that identical inventions should come about at the same time. But that is what happened with the electric light bulb, which was patented almost simultaneously on either side of the Atlantic by Thomas Edison and Joseph Swan. To avoid patent litigation the two business interests combined in England to produce lamps under the name of 'Ediswan', which is still registered as a trademark.
- *1930: Whittle's jet engine*. While Frank Whittle was granted a patent for his jet engine, his employers, the RAF, were unable to get the invention to work efficiently and could not manufacture it on an industrial scale. It was left to the US firms of McDonnell Douglas and Pratt and Witney to exploit the commercial benefits from the patents.
- *1943: Penicillin*. Alexander Fleming discovered penicillin in 1928 and 13 years later, on 14 October 1941, researchers at Oxford University filed Patent No. 13242. The complete specification was accepted on 16 April 1943 (*see* Illustration 5.3).

Illustration 5.3

BTG

Penicillin was discovered in a London hospital by Alexander Fleming in 1928. It was to take another 12 years (1940) before a team working at Oxford University discovered a method of isolating and storing the drug. However, as a result of the Second World War, which drained Britain of much of its financial resources, Britain did not have the capability to develop large-scale fermentation of the bacteria. Help was sought from the United States and the success of the technology is well known.

The UK government was concerned that it gave away valuable technology. By way of a response to this, following the end of the Second World War, it established the National Research Development Corporation (NRDC) in 1948 to protect the intellectual property rights of inventors' efforts which had been funded by the public sector. For example, this included research conducted in universities, hospitals and national laboratories.

From its very beginning the NRDC soon began generating funds. Oxford University developed a second generation of antibiotics called cephalosporins. They were patented worldwide and the royalties secured the financial base of the NRDC for many years.

The NRDC changed its name to the British Technology Group (BTG) and has continued to be successful in arranging and defending patents for many university professors. In 1994 BTG became an independent public limited company.

Historically BTG was involved only in UK intellectual property issues, but its activities have expanded. It was recently involved in litigation with the US Pentagon for patent infringement on the Hovercraft as well as another case concerning Johnson and Johnson, the US healthcare group. BTG was so successful in this case that Johnson and Johnson asked BTG to manage a portfolio of nearly 100 inventions to try to generate royalties.

Patents in practice

There are many industrialists and small business managers who have little faith in the patent system. They believe, usually as a result of first-hand experience, that the patent system is designed primarily for those large multinational corporations that have the finances to defend and protect any patents granted to them. The problem is that applying and securing a patent is only the beginning of what is usually an expensive journey. For example, every time you suspect a company may be infringing your patent you will have to incur legal expenses to protect your intellectual property. Moreover, there are some examples of large corporations spending many years and millions of dollars in legal fees battling in the courts over alleged patent infringement. One of the most well-known cases was *Apple Computer Inc.* v. *Microsoft*, where Apple alleged that Microsoft had copied its Windows operating system. The case lasted for many years and cost each company many millions of dollars in legal fees.

Many smaller firms view the patent system with dread and fear. Indeed, only 10 per cent of the UK patents are granted to small firms. Yet small firms represent 99 per cent of companies (*The Guardian*, 1998).

Illustration 5.4

Effective patents are dependent on the depth of your pocket!

James Dyson is now a household name across much of Europe and is responsible for designing and developing the bagless vacuum cleaner. He is, however, critical of the patent system. He has personal experience of the system and argues that it is prohibitively expensive. He explains that when he was filing for patents for his vacuum cleaner he did not have enough money to patent all the features of his product. Also, the costs of taking patents out in several countries is very expensive. Many of the costs involved are hidden. For example, there are translation fees to pay for different countries and languages. According to Mr Dyson the cost of taking out a patent in five countries is between £50,000 and £60,000. In addition, there are renewal fees to pay.

Source: N. Graham (1998) 'Inventor cleans up with profits', *Sunday Times*, 1 March.

In theory it sounds straightforward – £225 to apply for a UK patent. In practice, however, companies should be considering £1,000–£1,500 to obtain a UK patent. Furthermore, protection in a reasonable number of countries is likely to cost more like £10,000. Illustration 5.4 highlights many of the limitations of the patent system.

In some industries it seems the rules of intellectual property may need to change. Some have argued that reforming the intellectual property law may help to stimulate more innovation and that a growing part of the economy (e.g. services, information technology) is only weakly protected under current intellectual property law. One possible way to encourage innovation is by extending coverage to these products and broadening legal protection to cover new product ideas for a short period. Small companies and individual entrepreneurs would benefit most from this broader but shorter protection (Alpert, 1993).

Expiry of a patent and patent extensions

There is much written on the subject of patent application and the benefits to be gained from such a 20-year monopoly. There is, however, much less written about the subject of the effects of patent expiry. In other words, what happens when the patent protecting your product expires? A glance at the pharmaceutical industry reveals an interesting picture. Illustration 5.5 shows the reality for a firm when its patent expires.

For any firm operating in this science-intensive industry, the whole process of developing a product is based around the ability to protect the eventual product through the use of patents. Without the prospect of a 20-year monopoly to exploit many years of research and millions of dollars of investment, companies would be less inclined to engage in new product development. (The case study at the end of Chapter 9 explores new product development in the pharmaceutical industry.) On expiry of a patent competitors are able to use the technology, which hitherto had been protected, to develop their own product. Such products are referred to as generic drugs (a generic sold on its chemical composition). When a generic drug is launched, the effect on a branded drug which has just come off-patent can be

FDA gives approval for generic versions of Eli Lilly's Prozac

Washington – Federal regulators approved several generic versions of Eli Lilly & Co's popular antidepressant Prozac, ushering in one of the biggest generic-drug launches in history. The Food and Drug Administration approved Barr Laboratories Inc., of Pomona, NY, to market a 20-milligram capsule, the most common dosage. The FDA also approved an oral solution made by Teva Pharmaceutical Industries Ltd., of Jerusalem; a 40 mg capsule from Dr. Reddy's Laboratories Ltd, of Hyderabad, India; a 10 mg capsule from Geneva Pharmaceutical, of Broomfield, CO; and 10 mg and 20 mg tablets from Pharmaceutical Resources Inc., of Spring Valley, NJ. Barr started shipping its version yesterday, when Prozac's patent and market protection expired. Because it was the first to file for approval with the FDA, Barr will be the only company allowed to offer the 20 mg for 180 days. Afterwards, others with FDA approval can market the drug in that form. Barr said its version will be widely available by next week, and as early as today for those who placed orders ahead of time. Barr wouldn't say

precisely how much its version would cost, but said it would be between 25% and 40% less than Prozac, which runs about $2.50 a day. Two other forms of Prozac – a weekly pill and one for women – remain under patent protection. Sales of the blockbuster drug, known generically as fluoxetine hydrochloride, totaled about $2.5 billion last year, according to Lilly, of Indianapolis. 'Millions of American consumers will immediately begin to benefit from savings, and millions more who might otherwise have had to forgo this medicine because of its high cost will have access to a more affordable version of Prozac,' said Barr Chairman Bruce L. Downey. The generic approvals come one year after Barr won a court victory that cut nearly three years off Lilly's Prozac patent. At the time, Lilly predicted a significant drop in sales when generic versions hit the market.

Source: From 'Generic drug makers get FDA clearance for versions of Prozac', *Wall Street Journal*, 3 August 2001. (Carroll, J.), reprinted by permission of *The Wall Street Journal*, copyright © 2001 Dow Jones & Company, Inc. All rights reserved worldwide. Licence no. 1804210008771.

considerable. For example, Takeda is expecting a drop in sales of 90 per cent when its $4 billion anti-ulcer treatment drug Prevacid comes off-patent in 2009 (*see* Figure 5.1). Remarkably, market share falls of 85 per cent are typical (*Chemistry*

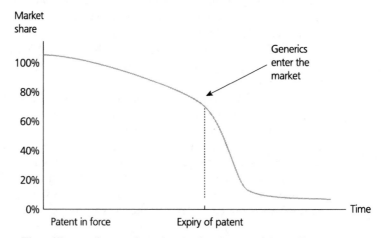

Figure 5.1 **The effect on its market share of a drug coming off-patent**

& *Industry News*, 1995; Nakamoto and Pilling, 2004). A generic drug is cheap to produce as no extensive research and development costs are incurred and pharmaceutical drugs are relatively easy to copy. It is in effect a chemical process. The principal forms of defence available to manufacturers are brand development and further research.

Pause for thought

If you obtain a patent for an invention and pay all the necessary fees, what happens if one day you see your invention in a shop window? Can you call in at the local police station and report it? Who will pay to bring a case against the retailer and manufacturer?

Developing a brand requires long-term development. Pharmaceutical companies with a product protected by patents will usually have between 10 and 20 years to develop a brand and brand loyalty, the aim being that even when the product goes off-patent customers will continue to ask for the branded drug as opposed to the generic drug. In practice, companies adopt a combination of aggressive marketing to develop the brand, and technical research on existing drugs to improve the product still further and file for additional patents to protect the new and improved versions of the product.

Patent extensions

Patent extensions are known in Europe as Supplementary Protection Certificates, usually abbreviated to 'SPC'. They were introduced in Europe in the mid-1990s to compensate patent owners for regulatory delays in approving their pharmaceuticals and agrochemicals. The approvals sometimes took so long that the patent had reached the end of its 20-year life, thus opening the invention to all comers, before the inventor had had much chance to commercialise it.

The SPC was designed to provide a level playing field for all pharmaceuticals/agrochemicals patent owners that had suffered regulatory delay exceeding five years, to restore to them an effective 15-year term of protection. The SPC takes effect at the instant of patent expiry, and then lasts for the length of time by which regulatory approval exceeded five years. Each SPC therefore has its own fixed duration, but, to protect the public, the maximum duration is five years' effect.

The United States achieves a similar result by a different route, namely by directly extending the lifetime of those individual patents where the applicant can show regulatory delay in getting the product on to the market. Japan has been considering legislation to achieve broadly similar results (BTG, 2004).

Every month of patent extension can mean hundreds of millions of dollars in additional revenues for blockbuster products. A number of companies, including Bristol Myers Squibb, AstraZeneca, GlaxoSmithKline and Schering-Plough have been accused of using such tactics to boost profits. However, a Federal Trade Commission report found only eight instances of suspect patent extensions between 1992 and 2000 (Bowe and Griffith, 2002).

The use of patents in innovation management

Patent offices for each country house millions of patents. In the United Kingdom there are over 2 million British patents and all this information is available to the public. Each publication, because of the legal requirement that details of patents be disclosed, is a valuable source of technological knowledge. Indeed, the information provision activities of the Patent Office have increased in their function. For example, scientists working in a particular field will often search patent databases to see how the problems they face have been tackled in the past. They will also use previous patents to identify how their current area of work fits in with those areas of science and technology that have been developed and patented previously. Very often patents can provide a valuable source of inspiration.

In addition, many firms also use the patent publication register to find out what their competitors are doing. For example, a search of the worldwide patent data-bases may reveal that your major competitor has filed a series of patents in an area of technology that you had not considered previously. Armed with prior knowledge of the industry and the technology it may be possible to uncover the research direc-tion in which your competitor is heading, or even the type of product line that it is considering developing. All this industrial intelligence can help research teams and companies to develop and modify their own strategy or to pursue a different approach to a problem.

Do patents hinder or encourage innovation?

According to Professor William Haseltine, the rush for patents did not hamper AIDS research. In the 1980s he worked for a team that deciphered the DNA of the HIV virus, worked out the sequences of its genes, and discovered some of the proteins those genes made. His name is on more than a dozen patents on the AIDS virus, but the patents are held by the cancer institute he then worked for at the Harvard Medical School. He makes a very strong case in favour of the patent system for fostering innovation. Indeed, he thinks the patents speeded up the assault on the virus itself.

> I would guess there may be 1000 patents filed by now (for HIV tools), each one build-ing on the other. You would be very hard pressed to make the case that a patent on the virus, a patent on the genome sequence, a patent on individual sequences, is in any way inhibiting rather than stimulating of productive research, both in academia and in companies. I can think of no case in which a patent has ever inhibited an academic scientist. (Professor W. Haseltine, *The Guardian*, 2000)

There is, however, another school of thought: Andrew Brown (2007) argues that submarine patents – those that surface only after the technologies they protect have come into wide use – are obviously dangerous. But even ordinary, open, honest patents now function as a brake on innovation. He uses the illustration of the French company Alcatel suing Microsoft for infringing its patents on the MP3 compression scheme. This he argues is an example of firms abusing intellectual property law. The patents arising from the MP3 technology joint venture (between

Table 5.2 Reasons why firms patent

	Products %	Processes %
Prevent copying	96	78
Patent blocking	82	64
Prevent suits	59	47
Use in negotiations	48	37
Enhance reputation	48	34
Licensing revenue	28	23
Measure performance	6	5

Source: Cohen, W.M. (2002) *Patents: Their Effectiveness and Role*, Carnegie Mellon University & National Bureau of Economic Research. With permission from Wesley Cohen.

Bell Labs, US telephone company, and the Fraunhofer Institute, Germany), were thought by everyone to belong to the German Research Organisation, which duly licensed them, and made a reasonable amount of money from this. Microsoft, for example, paid $16 million to incorporate MP3 support into Windows Media Player. But when Alcatel bought the remains of Bell Labs, now known as Lucent Technologies, it behaved as any modern company would, and tried to squeeze maximum value from the patents it had acquired. It asserted that these covered some of the MP3 technology that everyone assumed Fraunhofer owned, and sued two PC companies – Dell and Gateway – for selling computers equipped to play MP3s. Microsoft promised to fight the suit on their behalf and so the case came eventually to court.

Table 5.2 shows the reasons why firms patent. It is clear from this that most firms use the patent system to prevent other firms copying their technology and blocking. Blocking here refers to owners of a patent preventing others from using the technology. It is this area that is a growing concern for firms and governments around the world. For the aim of the patent system is to encourage innovation and yet there is increasing evidence that it is now being used to prevent other firms developing technology.

The European Federal Trade Commission (2006) investigated the role of patents to see whether the balance between protection for the intellectual property owners and stimulating innovation had now shifted too much in favour of protection. Their investigation revealed that patents can indeed impair competition, innovation and the economy. In particular the EFTC found that there was an increasing use of patent thickets in software and Internet-related industries. A patent thicket is a form of defensive patenting where firms unnecessarily increase the number of patents to increase complexity. This forces competing companies to divert resources from original R&D into paying to use the patents of other firms. Patent thickets make it more difficult to commercialise new products and raise uncertainty and investment risks for follow-on firms. Specifically patents deter innovation by:

1 denying follow-on innovators access to necessary technologies (EULA);
2 increasing entry barriers;
3 the expense required to avoid patent infringement;
4 the issuance of questionable patents.

This view was confirmed in March 2007 when the Commission accused Microsoft of demanding excessive royalties from companies wishing to license technical information about its Windows operating system. The EU fined Microsoft €800 million.

The case study at the end of this chapter examines whether the pharmaceutical industry is generating supra industry profits as a result of the patent system.

Trademarks

Trademarks have particular importance to the world of business. For many companies, especially in the less technology-intensive industries where the use of patents is limited, trademarks offer one of the few methods of differentiating a company's products. The example of Coca-Cola is a case in point. Trademarks are closely associated with business image, goodwill and reputation. Indeed, many trademarks have become synonymous with particular products: Mars and chocolate confectionery, Hoover and vacuum cleaners and Nestlé and coffee. The public rely on many trademarks as indicating quality, value for money and origin of goods. Significant changes have been made to trademark law in the United Kingdom. The Trade Marks Act (1994) replaced the Trade Marks Act (1938), which was widely recognised as being out of touch with business practices today. The United Kingdom now complies with the EC directive on the approximation of the laws of member states relating to trademarks and ratified the Madrid Convention for the international registration of trademarks. The law relating to trademarks is complex indeed. For example, what is a trademark? Bainbridge (1996) offers a comprehensive review of law surrounding intellectual property. The following section offers a brief introduction to some of the key considerations for product and business managers.

The Trade Marks Act (1994, section 1(1)) defines a trademark as:

being any sign capable of being represented graphically which is capable of distinguishing goods or services of one undertaking from those of other undertakings.

This can include, for example, Apple Computers, the Apple logo and Macintosh, all of which are registered trademarks. Some of the first trademarks were used by gold- and silversmiths to mark their own work. The first registered trademark, No. 1, was issued to Bass in 1890 for their red triangle mark for pale ale. Illustration 5.6 on the Mr Men offers an example of the effective and successful use of trademarks.

There are certain restrictions and principles with the use of trademarks. In particular, a trademark should:

- satisfy the requirements of section 1(1);
- be distinctive;
- not be deceptive; and
- not cause confusion with previous trademarks.

Should satisfy the requirements of section 1(1)

The much wider definition of a trademark offered by the 1994 Act opened the possibility of all sorts of marks that would not have previously been registrable. Sounds, smells and containers could now be registered. A number of perfume

Illustration 5.6

Mr Hargreaves and the Mr Men

Many of you have probably seen Mr Happy before or one of his companions. If not, he is Mr Happy and is part of the Mr Men collection. Since 1973 Mr Happy and colleagues have appeared on everything from yoghurt pots to a Japanese commercial for a gas company. That is not including the TV series or the millions of books sold. All the characters are registered trademarks. After all, if you want to stop someone stealing your ideas it is an advantage if you can prove that you own them. That's why Roger Hargreaves registered his drawings with the UK Patent Office. To date, Mr Hargreaves has received over £1.5 million ($2 million).

Source: Patent Office, *Financial Times* (1988).

manufacturers have applied to register their perfumes as trademarks. Coca-Cola and Unilever have applied to register their containers for Coca-Cola and Domestos respectively.

Distinctive

A trademark should be distinctive in itself. In general this means that it should not describe in any way the product or service to which it relates. Usually words that are considered generic or descriptive are not trademarked. In addition, it should not use non-distinctive expressions which other traders might reasonably wish to use in the course of a trade. For example, to attempt to register the word beef as a trademark for a range of foods would not be possible since other traders would reasonably want to use the word in the course of their trade. It would, however, be acceptable to use beef in association with a range of clothing because this would be considered distinctive. Laudatory terms are not allowed, for example the word heavenly for a range of cosmetics would not be possible since it is a laudatory term. The law, however, concerning this aspect of distinctiveness looks set to change following a recent ruling in the European courts. Illustration 5.7 explains why famous people may at last be able to trademark their own surname.

Non-deceptive

A trademark should also not attempt to deceive the customer. For example, to attempt to register Orlwoola, as happened in 1900, as an artificial fibre would not be possible, since the very word could persuade people to believe the material was made of wool.

Not confusing

Finally, a trade or service mark will not be registered if it could be confused with the trademark of a similar product that has already been registered. For example,

Illustration 5.7

Trademark view likely to allow sports stars to play own brand of name games

FT

Sports personalities, entertainers and other public figures could find it easier to assert monopoly rights over their surnames after a European Court of Justice opinion, said lawyers yesterday.

Applications to register surnames have become increasingly frequent, particularly in sport where personalities have either been keen to launch own-brand merchandise or – as in the case of footballer David Beckham – prevent others from exploiting their fame.

Last year, there was even an unsuccessful attempt to trademark the name Jesus to sell jeans. Other names to have raised intellectual property issues in the past have included Elvis Presley and Paul McCartney.

But the UK Trade Marks Registry has consistently refused to 'register' ordinary surnames if there is a large number of operators in the market for the goods or services designated.

Its guidelines recommend that the 'commonness' of the surname should be a factor in deciding whether a trademark can be approved, with telephone directories providing a yardstick. Any name that appears more than 200 times in the London directory is usually classed as common, for example.

But now, in the context of a British case referred to the Luxembourg court for guidance, Dámaso Ruiz-Jarabo Colomer, an advocate-general, says there is no reason to treat surnames differently from any other trademark.

'There is nothing in the [trademark] directive to justify treating surnames differently,' he said in an opinion released last week.

The legal opinion came in the case of Nichols, a British company that wanted to trademark the surname for automatic vending machines, food and drinks.

The UK registry granted the vending machine application, but refused it for the other two categories.

Photo: © M. Thomsen/zefa/Corbis

It said the surname was common and that, in a market with a large number of operators, it would be difficult for consumers to identify the commercial origin of the products from a common surname.

Advocate-generals' opinions are not binding on the ECJ but they are followed in most cases. If that happens here, lawyers say that trademark applicants are likely to benefit.

'I think it's a very sensible decision, and could result in change to UK Trade Mark Registry procedure,' said Geoff Steward, partner at the Macfarlanes law firm.

Mr Steward pointed to the case of Wayne Rooney, the footballer, who is believed to have been applying to trademark his surname in respect of football merchandise, clothing and the like. 'This decision means he will probably succeed,' he said.

Source: N. Tait, 'Trademark view likely to allow sports stars to play own brand of name games', *Financial Times*, 19 January 2004. Reprinted with permission.

'Velva-Glo' was refused as a trademark for paints because it was judged to be too near the word 'Vel-Glo' which was already registered.

Brand names

Increasingly the link between the brand name and the trademark is becoming closer and stronger. The literature tends to separate the two, with brands remaining in the sphere of marketing and trademarks within the sphere of law. In terms of a property right that is exploitable, however, brand names and trademarks are cousins. They both serve to facilitate identity and origin. That origin in turn indicates a certain level of quality, as reflected in the goods. Indeed, it is worthy of note that many brands have been registered as trademarks.

Like other capital assets owned by a firm such as manufacturing equipment or land, a brand can also be considered an asset, and a valuable one at that. 'Brand equity' is the term used to describe the value of a brand name. Accountants and marketers differ in their definitions and there have been a variety of approaches to define the term (Feldwick, 1996):

- the total value of a brand as a separable asset – when it is sold, or included on a balance sheet;
- a measure of the strength of consumers' attachment to a brand; and
- a description of the associations and beliefs the consumer has about the brand.

Brand equity creates value for both customers and the firm. The customers can clearly use brand names as simplifying heuristics for processing large amounts of information. The brand can also give customers confidence in the purchasing situation. Firms benefit enormously from having strong brand names. Investment in a brand name can be leveraged through brand extensions and increased distributions. High brand equity often allows higher prices to be charged; hence it is a significant competitive advantage.

A firm may decide to purchase a brand from another company rather than to develop a brand itself. Indeed, this may be less expensive and less risky. IKEA, for example, purchased the Habitat brand. Habitat had a strong UK presence in the furniture and household products market and enabled IKEA to increase its presence in the UK furniture market.

Using brands to protect intellectual property

Product managers, product designers and R&D managers all recognise that despite their best efforts sometimes the success of a product can be dependent on the brand. In the cigarette market, for example, over 70 per cent of consumers are loyal to a particular brand (Badenhausen, 1995), and this makes entry to this market very difficult. Brands help buyers to identify specific products that they like and reduce the time required to purchase the product. Without brands, product selection would be random and maybe more rational, based on price, value and content of the product. It would certainly force consumers to select more carefully. If all the products in a store had the same plain white packaging but information was made available on ingredients, contents and details of the manufacturing process, consumers would spend an enormous amount of time shopping. Brands symbolise a certain quality level and this can be transferred to other product items. For example, Unilever extended the Timotei shampoo name to skin-care products. This clearly enabled the company to develop a new range of products and use the benefits of brand recognition of Timotei.

An area of branding that is growing rapidly is that of the licensing of trademarks. Using a licensing agreement, a company may permit approved manufacturers to use its trademark on other products for a licensing fee. Royalties may be as low as 2 per cent of wholesale revenues or as high as 10 per cent. The licensee is responsible for all manufacturing and marketing and bears the cost if the product fails. Today the licensing business is a huge growth industry. The All England Tennis and Croquet Club license their brand to a small group of companies each year. During the summer those companies use the association with Wimbledon to promote their products. Products such as Robinson's soft drinks, Wedgwood pottery, Slazenger sports goods and Coca-Cola have all signed licence agreements with the All England Club. For an organisation like the All England Club the advantages are obvious: increased revenue and, to a lesser extent, increased promotion of the tournament. To other firms like JCB, Jaguar Cars and Harley-Davidson, all of whom license their trademarks to clothing manufacturers, it clearly provides increased revenues, but also raises opportunities for diversification. The major disadvantages are a lack of control over the products, which could harm the perception and image of the brand. The All England Club, for example, have numerous committee meetings to consider very carefully the type of organisation and product that will bear its trademark.

Exploiting new opportunities

Product and brand managers must continually be vigilant about changes in the competitive market. This will help to realise new development opportunities for the brand. Some companies have developed reputations for exploiting the latest technology developments; indeed, some of these firms are responsible for the breakthroughs. The following list of examples illustrates how pioneering firms have exploited opportunities and developed their brands:

* *New technology*. Sony and Rank Xerox are examples of firms that over the past 20 years have continually exploited new technology.
* *New positioning*. First Direct and The Body Shop uncovered and developed unique positions for themselves in the market. First Direct was one of the pioneers of telephone banking and continued to build on this position. Similarly The Body Shop was a pioneer of 'green' cosmetics and has exploited this position.
* *New distribution*. Direct Line and Argos Stores developed new channels of distribution for their products and services. Direct Line exploited the concept of telephone insurance and later expanded into other financial services, and Argos Stores developed the concept of warehouse-catalogue shopping.

Frequently, rival firms will develop generic products and services to rival the brand. Nowhere is this more apparent than in the pharmaceutical industry, as the previous section illustrated. One of the key issues for brand managers is whether the brand can sustain its strong market position in the face of such competition. It is possible to defend a brand through effective marketing communications, but this is rarely enough. Usually the brand will need to innovate in one or more of the areas listed above. Some brands have failed to innovate and have then struggled in the face of fierce competition. One example is the Kellogg's brand. Over the past 10 years Kellogg's has seen its market share of the cereal market gradually decline in the face of strong competition from store brands. Critics of Kellogg's argue that its brand managers have failed to innovate and develop the brand.

Pause for thought

Intellectual property does not just lie in physical products, it can also reside in services and ways of operating. What role does the brand play in service-based industries such as airlines?

Brands, trademarks and the Internet

Nowhere is the subject of trademarks and brands more closely intertwined than on the Internet. Individuals and firms are linked up and identified through so-called 'domain names'. These are essentially an address, comprising four numbers, such as 131.22.45.06. The numbers indicate the network (131), an Internet protocol address (22 and 45) and a local address (06). Numeric addresses, however, are difficult to remember. Internet authorities assigned and designated an alphanumeric designation and mnemonic which affords the consumer user-friendly information with regard to identity and source – the 'domain name' (for example, microsoft.com and ports.ac.uk).

It can be seen then that domain names act as Internet addresses. They serve as the electronic or automated equivalent to a telephone directory, allowing web browsers to look up their intended hits directly or via a search engine such as Alta Vista. One may argue at this point that domain names act as electronic brand names. Moreover, the characteristics of a domain name and a trademark are considerable. A recent US judgment has pronounced that domain names are protectable property rights in much the same way as a trademark (www.webmarketingtoday.com).

Duration of registration, infringement and passing off

Under the new Trade Marks Act (1994) the registration of a trademark is for a period of 10 years from the date of registration which may be renewed indefinitely for further 10-year periods. Once accepted and registered, trademarks are considered to be an item of personal property.

The fact that a trademark is registered does not mean that one cannot use the mark at all. In the case of *Bravado Merchandising Services Ltd* v. *Mainstream Publishing Ltd*, the respondent published a book about the pop group Wet Wet Wet under the title *A Sweet Little Mystery – Wet Wet Wet – The Inside Story*. Wet Wet Wet was a registered trademark and the proprietor brought an injunction against the use of the name. The court decided that the trademark had not been infringed because the respondent was using the mark as an indication of the main characteristic of the artefact which, in this instance, was a book about the pop group (Bainbridge, 1996).

Where a business uses a trademark that is similar to another or takes unfair advantage of or is detrimental to another trademark, infringement will have occurred. This introduces the area of passing off and is the common law form of trademark law. Passing off concerns the areas of goodwill and reputation of the trademark. In *Consorzio de Prosciutto di Parma* v. *Marks & Spencer plc* (1991) Lord Justice Norse identified the ingredients of a passing off action as being composed of:

- the goodwill of the plaintiff;
- the misrepresentation made by the defendant; and
- consequential damage.

Illustration 5.8 highlights many of the concerns expressed by businesses in what they see as unfair competition. This area of law has many similarities to trademark

---

Illustration 5.8

Copycats or competition

For many years now consumer goods manufacturers in the UK have been fighting to stop retailers selling own-label products that look almost identical to well-known brands.

They say own-label products are being designed deliberately to resemble manufacturers' brands – using similar bottles or packs, colours and typography, even similar names. But while manufacturers spend millions of pounds on research, development and marketing of brands, it costs retailers very little to copy them.

The issue, says Michael Mackenzie, director-general of the Food and Drink Federation, which represents manufacturers, is not so much that consumers might mistake the own-label product for the manufacturer's brand. Rather, look-alike brands may 'give the impression that the manufacturer of the proprietary brand has made the own-label product'.

Brand manufacturers may have contributed to the confusion in the past by actually making own-label products for supermarkets, but most no longer do so. Kellogg ran an advertising campaign based on the fact that it does not make cereal for anyone else.

While the big brand names believe the problem has worsened, they have nevertheless been reluctant to speak out. This is because their relations with retailers are delicate and they don't want to pick a fight with their biggest customers.

Manufacturers want protection against look-alike brands which imitate the overall appearance of their own brands, without directly copying logos or designs. The UK is out of line with most of Europe in not giving brands proper statutory protection. Germany has a statute on 'protection of get-up', and there are similar laws in France, Benelux and Greece.

The problem of look-alikes is particularly sensitive in the UK because supermarkets have worked hard to change consumers' perceptions of own-label products from inferior imitations to quality alternatives. Retailers make much higher margins on own-label products because they do not bear the same development costs as manufacturers. The big three UK grocers – Sainsbury's, ASDA and Tesco – have pushed own-label sales to more than 50 per cent of turnover, far higher than elsewhere in Europe.

The British Retail Consortium, which represents more than 200 retailers, argues that manufacturers are attempting to restrict shops' ability to introduce own-label products. The Consumers Association have found in surveys that shoppers showed a preference for many own-label products in blind tastings. It warns that tighter restrictions on own-label products could lead to narrower choice for consumers and reduced competition.

Source: N. Buckley, 'On the prowl for copycats', *Financial Times*, 3 March 1994. Reprinted with permission.

---

law and is considered to be a useful supplement to it (*see* Bainbridge, 1996, for a full explanation of the law of passing off).

Registered designs

A new product may be created which is not sufficiently novel or contain an inventive step so as to satisfy the exacting requirements for the granting of a patent. This was the situation faced by Britain's textile manufacturers in the early nineteenth century. They would create new textile designs but these would be later copied by foreign competitors. The Design Registry was set up in the early 1800s in response to growing demands from Britain's textile manufacturers for statutory protection for the designs of their products. Today, designs that are applied to articles may be protected by design law (*see* Illustration 5.7). There are two systems of design law in the United Kingdom. One is similar to that used for patent law and requires registration. The other system of design protection is design right and is provided along copyright lines. There is a large area of overlap between the two systems.

The registered designs system is intended for those designs intended to have some form of aesthetic appeal. For example, electrical appliances, toys and some forms of packaging have all been registered.

A design as protected by registration is the *outward appearance of an article*. Only the appearance given by its actual shape, configuration, pattern or ornament can be protected, not any underlying idea. The registered design lasts for a maximum of 15 years. Initially the proprietor is granted the exclusive right to a design for a fixed term of five years. This can be renewed for up to five further five-year terms.

To be registered a design must first be new at the date an application for its registration is filed. In general a design is considered to be new if it has not been published in the United Kingdom (i.e. made available or disclosed to the public in any way whatsoever) and if, when compared with any other published design, the differences make a materially different appeal to the eye. For example, if a company designed a new kettle that was very different from any other kettle, the company could register the design. This would prevent other kettle manufacturers from simply copying the design. Clearly, the kettle does not offer any advantage in terms of use, hence a patent cannot be obtained, but a good design is also worth protecting.

Copyright

This area of the law on intellectual property rights has changed significantly over the past few years, mainly because it now covers computer software. Computer software manufacturers are particularly concerned about the illegal copying of their programs. The music industry has also battled with this same problem for many years. It is common knowledge that this was an exceptionally difficult area of law to enforce and new technology may at last provide copyright holders with an advantage. Up to now they have fallen prey to copying technology, but Waldmeir (2002) suggests that compact discs will begin to include technology that prevents them from being copied. The impact of this may be to hinder creativity in the long term (*see* Illustration 5.9).

Illustration 5.9

If technology switches to the side of copyright

FT

Moves to stop music copying could leave copyright owners with far more power than was ever intended under US law

The recording industry has vowed to make 2002 the year of the copyright.

If the industry has its way, this will be the year when we all begin purchasing music in forms that cannot be stolen. Compact discs will begin to include technology that prevents them being copied (the first discs have already started to appear in music stores). And online, music will be sold through subscription services that stop unauthorised reproduction. 2002 could become the year when copyright fights back.

If the technology works, it could transform the fortunes of copyright holders. Up to now, they have fallen easy prey to any teenager who could type the characters 'MP3' into a search engine: the theft of copyrighted music online has been virtually effortless.

But if technology switches sides, if it now facilitates not theft but the perfect control of who listens to what, when, on the internet, US copyright owners could find themselves wielding far more power than was ever intended under US copyright law, or the constitution that inspired it.

Courts and lawmakers are facing that old question with new urgency: how much copyright is too much? How can copyright law reward creators without allowing them to monopolise their creation in ways that would chill future innovation?

Even the US Supreme Court, which intervenes only rarely in matters of intellectual property law, is this month considering the question of copyright. The justices are expected to announce shortly, perhaps next week, whether they will hear a case that challenges the ascendancy of copyright.

That case argues that the existing American social and legal bargain over copyright is flawed even without the intervention of technologies that could destabilise it even further.

Lawrence Lessig, Stanford University law professor and theorist of the digital society, has seized on the case to challenge the whole recent course of US copyright law, which has consistently expanded the scope and duration of copyright at the expense of public access to copyright works.

He filed the lawsuit on behalf of Eric Eldred, who wanted to compile an electronic archive of unusual and out-of-print works online but was prevented from posting some works by a 1998 law extending the term of copyright protection.

Prof Lessig argues that Congress has exceeded its constitutional authority by repeatedly extending the term of copyrights – 11 times in the past 40 years. The 1998 law alone extended copyright by 20 years: works copyrighted by individuals since 1978 were granted a term of 70 years beyond the life of the author; works made by or for corporations were protected for 95 years. The extension applied to existing works even if the author was dead or the work long out of print.

For Prof Lessig, these extensions violate the constitution's command to Congress that it 'promote the Progress of Science and useful Arts, by securing for limited Times to Authors and Inventors the exclusive Right to their respective Writings and Discoveries'.

Copyrights of such length are no longer 'limited', he argues; and Congress can scarcely claim to 'promote the Progress of Science and the useful Arts' when it extends the copyright of dead authors. Copyrights are meant not to reward authors but to serve as an incentive to creation. No incentive can make a dead writer resume production.

The problem is not just that, for example, Mickey Mouse gets 20 years' more copyright protection under the 1998 law. The issue is larger; as Prof Lessig wrote recently in *Wired* magazine: 'Our trend in copyright law has been to enclose as much as we can: the consequence of this enclosure is a stifling of creativity and innovation.'

Shakespeare would have known exactly what he meant: even the greatest creators build on previous creation. Many of Shakespeare's plays might never have been written if he had had to pay royalties to those inferior authors who wrote the dramas on which they were based.

So, Prof Lessig argues, every time Congress extends copyright it inexcusably impoverishes the public domain. Creativity builds on itself: without reasonable public access to copyrighted works, it has nothing to build on.

But if that situation is bad, how much worse a world in which copyrights are not just long but unlimited? Copy Protection technology can stop creative material from entering the public domain, not just until its copyright expires but for ever. Locked CDs may theoretically lose their copyright but that will not unlock them. Such technologies risk giving copyright owners an absolute monopoly over content for ever – a far cry from the limited monopoly outlined by the constitution.

US lawmakers have begun to ask whether record companies can guard against digital copying without violating US copyright law.

Last week Rick Boucher, who heads the Congressional internet caucus, sent a letter to record company executives asking whether anti-piracy technology might override consumers'

legal right to copy music they had purchased for use in car tape-players or other devices.

These are early days but at least the issue of copyright ascendancy is on the table. Technologies of copyright control will almost certainly transform that debate beyond all recognition, if not this year, then some time very soon afterwards. At that point, tinkering with the existing legal regime may well not be enough.

In his recent book *The Future of Ideas*, Prof Lessig recommends a radical revision of copyright law: copyright protection should be cut to five years, renewable 15 times. Where copyrights were not renewed, the work would enter the public domain.

'The benefit for creativity from more works falling into the commons would be large,' he argues. 'If a copyright isn't worth it to an author to renew for a modest fee, it isn't worth it to society to support through an array of criminal and civil statutes.'

US lawmakers may not like his suggestion but they ignore the looming copyright crisis at society's peril. Technology has precipitated the crisis; law cannot long ignore it.

Source: P. Waldmeir, 'If technology switches to the side of copyright', *Financial Times*, 10 January 2002. Reprinted with permission.

For the author of creative material to obtain copyright protection it must be in a tangible form so that it can be communicated or reproduced. It must also be the author's own work and thus the product of his or her skill or judgement. Concepts, principles, processes or discoveries are not valid for copyright protection until they are put in a tangible form such as written or drawn. It is the particular way that an idea is presented that is valid for copyright. This particular point, that ideas cannot be copyrighted, often causes confusion. If someone has written an article, you cannot simply rephrase it or change some of the words and claim it as your own. You are, however, entitled to read an article, digest it, take the ideas from that article together with other sources and weave them into your own material without any copyright problems. In most instances common sense should provide the answer.

Copyright is recognised by the symbol © and gives legal rights to creators of certain kinds of material, so that they can control the various ways in which their work may be exploited. Copyright protection is automatic and there is no registration or other formality.

Mickey Mouse is now past 75 and was to be out of copyright

This issue of copyright is currently causing great concern for one of the most famous organisations in the world and certainly the most famous cartoon character. In the USA copyright lasts for 75 years (for creations prior to 1978) and Mickey Mouse in 2003 was 75 years old. At this point, the first Mickey Mouse cartoon was to be publicly available for use by anyone. *Plane Crazy* was released in May 1928 and was to slip from the Disney empire in 2003. In the autumn of 1928 Disney released *Steam Boat Willie*, the world's first synchronised talking cartoon and soon after Disney copyrighted the film.

At first glimpse one may be tempted to have some sympathy for the Disney organisation. However, Walt Disney wisely registered Mickey Mouse as a trademark, recognising from an early date that Mickey Mouse had value far beyond the screen. Hence, the use by others of the character on numerous products produces large licensing revenues for the Disney Corporation.

The Disney Corporation managed to secure a twenty-year extension from Congress under the 1998 Copyright law.

Source: James Langton, *Sunday Telegraph*, 15 February 1998; *Financial Times*, 10 January 2002.

Copyright may subsist in any of nine descriptions of work and these are grouped into three categories:

1 original literary, dramatic, musical and artistic works;
2 sound recordings, films, broadcasts and cable programmes; and
3 the typographical arrangement or layout of a published edition.

Each of these categories has more detailed definitions. For example, films in category 2 include videograms; and 'artistic work' in category 1 includes photographs and computer-generated work.

The duration of copyright protection varies according to the description of the work. In the United Kingdom for literary, dramatic, musical and artistic works copyright expires 70 years after the death of the author, in other cases 50 years after the calendar year in which it was first published. The period was for 75 years in the United States (but is now 50 years for all works created after 1978), but this issue is currently causing a great deal of concern for one of the most well-known organisations in the world (*see* Illustration 5.10).

Remedy against infringement

There are some forms of infringement of a commercial nature such as dealing with infringing copies that carry criminal penalties. Indeed, HM Customs have powers to seize infringing printed material. Also a civil action can be brought by the plaintiff for one or more of the following:

- damages;
- injunction; and
- accounts.

Damages

The owner of the copyright can bring a civil case and ask the court for damages, which can be expected to be calculated on the basis of compensation for the actual loss suffered.

Injunction

An injunction is an order of the court which prohibits a person making infringing copies of a work of copyright.

Accounts

This is a useful alternative for the plaintiff in that it enables access to the profits made from the infringement of copyright. This is useful especially if the amount is likely to exceed that which might be expected from an award of damages.

Counterfeit goods and IP

The production and sale of counterfeit products is big business in the international economy. The value of counterfeit products marketed annually in the world is estimated to be over US$1 trillion. Counterfeiters are serving a market as willing to buy their illicit wares as they are to sell them. Nowhere is this more evident than in China (Hung, 2003; Naim, 2005). The massive expansion of the Chinese economy has led to a huge increase in foreign direct investment (FDI) and international technology transfer (ITT) and has brought the issue of intellectual property to the fore. The extent of product counterfeiting operations in China is astounding; estimates range from 10 per cent to 20 per cent of all consumer goods manufactured in the country. The Quality Brands Protection Committee (QBPC), for example, an anti-piracy body under the auspices of the China Association of Enterprises with Foreign Investment, claims that government statistics show that counterfeit products outnumber genuine products in the Chinese market by 2:1. Indeed, in a review of the intellectual property system in China, Yang and Clarke (2004) concluded that the emerging IP system requires improvements in legislation, administration and enforcement, in order to create a secure IP environment in line with the international standard. Enforcement efforts are made even more futile by popular acceptance of piracy in China. Rising incomes have created an enthusiasm for foreign goods and brands, but Chinese consumers have become so accustomed to cheap, pirated goods that they are unwilling to pay full prices for the real thing. It almost seems like imitation in modern China is a way of life. Many argue that authentic manufacturers have contributed to the problem of counterfeiting due to their unyielding self-interest of pursuing lowest possible manufacturing cost (McDonald and Roberts, 1994; Tom *et al.*, 1998). Even in the face of increased counterfeiting these firms have continued to seek production opportunities in developing countries where counterfeiting is a known problem. It may be that given the short-term gains of lower production costs, firms may be either lacking in risk management or even willing to risk the loss of intellectual property with its potential long-term damage of loss of competitive advantage for the sake of short-term gains. If this is the case then the risk of losing intellectual property is the cost of doing business in China (Naim, 2005).

Furthermore, the effectiveness of the current approaches towards counterfeiting is questionable. Indeed, in fast moving technology intensive industries legal remedies tend to be too slow and too costly for regulating complex technological developments and their associated intellectual property and ownership rights (Deakin and Wilkinson, 1998; Liebeskind and Oliver, 1998). Furthermore, Thurow has argued that the whole approach to the defence of the intellectual property rights is simplistic because it applies the same rule to all types of products in all types of industries. He argues that, for example, the 'Third World's need to get low-cost pharmaceuticals is not equivalent to its need for low-cost CDs. Any system that treats such needs equally, as our current system does, is neither a good nor a viable system' (Thurow, 1997; Vaidhyanathan, 2001). This view is shared by other economists (e.g. Sachs, 1999). Moreover, we should acknowledge that society seems content with a system that only provides protection for rich owners. It was more than 25 years ago that the Advisory Council for Applied Research and Development (ACARD, 1980) in the UK noted that if society wanted to treat intellectual property like tangible property, the state would prosecute alleged offenders at public expense. Since this time little has changed and it remains that if intellectual property is stolen, responsibility generally rests with the owner to prosecute.*

Pause for thought

Who owns the copyright on your essays that you write? What can you do if you find sections of one of your essays in a newspaper or in a book?

Case study

Pricing, patents and profits in the pharmaceutical industry

This case study explains how the pharmaceutical industry uses the patent system to ensure it reaps rewards from the drugs that it develops. Increasingly, however, there is alarm at the high costs of these drugs to the underdeveloped world, especially against a backcloth of the AIDS epidemic in Southern Africa. While the pharmaceutical industry has responded with several concessions, the case against the industry is that it enjoys a privileged position partly due to the patent system.

Introduction

There is a story about a pharmaceutical executive on a tour of the US National Mint who inquired how much it cost to produce each dollar bill. On hearing the answer, the man smiled. Making pills, it seemed, was even more profitable than printing money. Whether true or not, the three most profitable businesses in the world are reputed to be narcotics, prostitution and ethical pharmaceuticals. A recent Oxfam report showing the scale of the AIDS problem in

---

* UK IP law does contain some criminal provisions (e.g. S 92 TM Act 1994, and S 107 Copyright Patents and Designs Act 1988). Some European countries have criminal provisions relating to patent infringement as well, though that is less common. Nonetheless, the target of criminal law relating to IP is usually deliberate counterfeiters rather than inadvertent infringers or those who might legitimately argue they are not infringing. See the National Intellectual Property (IP) Enforcement Report (2005), 1–139.

Table 5.3 The scale of the AIDS epidemic in Southern Africa (% of adult population infected)

Botswana	35.8
Lesotho	23.5
Malawi	15.9
Mozambique	13.2
Namibia	19.5
South Africa	9.9
Swaziland	25.2
Tanzania	8.9
Zambia	19.9
Zimbabwe	25.6

Source: UNAIDS (2000). Reproduced by kind permission of UNAIDS, www.UNAIDS.org.

Southern Africa has brought the pharma companies into the spotlight. The allegation is that these companies exploit the poor in the developing world. With a median 35 per cent return on equity, pharmaceuticals is far and away the world's most profitable major industry. With profits of more than $6 billion, pharma companies such as Pfizer and GlaxoSmithKline dwarf the likes of Unilever, BT or Coca-Cola. Yet every year in the developing world millions of people die from diseases, such as malaria and tuberculosis, which the rich developed world has eradicated. Table 5.3 shows the scale of the problem.

In the past the pharmaceutical industry has maintained that many of the drugs that could benefit the suffering in the underdeveloped world are expensive and have taken years to research and develop. The only way the pharmaceutical industry can claw back its expenditure on research and development is by patenting their drugs, thereby providing them with a 20-year monopoly in which to generate sales and profits. The social contract underlying the patents system is based on an agreement that in return for such investment – and for publishing through patents the details of the research results – a company is entitled to an exclusive right to the sale of the resulting product for a limited period of time: 20 years.

The case against the pharmaceutical industry

Most drug prices bear no relation to the very small cost of production because the industry has a contract with society, enshrined in the patent system. For a limited period (usually 10 years not allowing for clinical trials, etc.) pharmaceutical companies charge monopoly prices for patented medicines. In return, they invest huge amounts of research dollars in pursuit of the next innovation.

At a time when the AIDS epidemic appears to have stabilised in most advanced countries, thanks largely to the use of sophisticated drugs, the disease is continuing to spread at an ever more alarming rate through developing countries (*see* Table 5.3).

Yet those countries now suffering the most from the disease are also those least able to afford the drugs necessary to control it. The issue, of course, challenges the whole patenting system.

It is not just the underdeveloped countries that are experiencing difficulties with intellectual property laws and medicine. A 30-year-old London woman contacted Bristol-Myers Squibb, a US pharmaceutical company, begging help to obtain Taxol. This drug could have controlled her breast cancer, but her National Health Service region did not prescribe it because of its exorbitant cost. There is no patent on Taxol as the US government discovered it. But Bristol-Myers Squibb, because it performed minor work calculating dosage levels, holds the intellectual property rights on dose-related data, even though the data was originally collected by the government. Ultimately, the company was shamed into offering her free medicine if she moved to the United States. However, doctors concluded that the offer was probably too late.

In AIDS and breast cancer, the stricken North and South share a horrific commonality as the new landless peasantry in the apartheid of intellectual property rights. (*The Guardian*, 27 July, 2000)

The developing countries are demanding changes. They argue that patent laws should be relaxed, allowing, for example, either for their own companies to produce cheaper generic versions of the expensive anti-AIDS drugs, or for the import of such generic copies from other countries. In February 2001 the Indian company Cipla offered to make a combination of AIDS drugs available at about one-third of the price being asked by companies in developing countries. This price is already less than those in the West. If ever there was a good example of profiteering here it is. Worst of all, it seems to be profiteering at the expense of the poor. The charge of unethical behaviour seems to be ringing loudly. But for how long will the legal systems and courts in the world tolerate thousands of deaths before one of them decides enough is enough? The pharmaceutical industry is aware of the strength of public opinion and the mounting pressure it is under and has made significant concessions, including cutting the price of many of its drugs to the developing world. Will this, however, be enough? The whole industry, it seems, is now under pressure to justify the prices it charges for its drugs. If it fails to convince governments, it may see the introduction of legislation and price controls.

The case for the pharmaceutical industry

The pharmaceutical industry can claim that it has been responsible for helping to rid many parts of the world of dreadful diseases. It is able to claim that the enormous sums of money that it spends each year on research and development is only possible because of the patent system. Any change in the system will put at risk the billions of dollars that are spent on research into heart disease, cancer and other killers. This is usually enough for most governments and others to back away from this very powerful industry. Not surprisingly, the drugs industry is appalled at the prospect of price controls. Sidney Taurel, chief executive of the US drugs company Eli-Lilly, has warned, 'If we kill free markets around the world, we'll kill innovation.'

The industry clearly has a unique structure and differs markedly from many others, but whether there is evidence for supra-normal profits is questionable. Professor Sachs, director of the Center for International Development at Harvard University, argues that if price controls were introduced, companies would simply scale back their investments in research. This is often seen by many as a 'threat' that the industry uses against governments. Once again there is limited evidence to suggest this would necessarily happen. Sachs suggests, 'This is an extremely sophisticated, high cost, risky business with very long lead-in times and an extremely high regulatory hurdle,' he says. 'My sense is that every rich country that has said, "You're making too much money" and has tried to control prices has lost the R&D edge.'

The pharmaceutical industry has a powerful voice. It is a large employer, invests large sums of money in science and technology and is without doubt an industry that will grow in this century. Most governments would like to have a thriving pharmaceutical industry and hence try to help and not hinder their efforts. Moreover, there are thousands of people in the developed world whose lives are being saved and extended by new sophisticated drugs that are being developed every month. The industry has many advocates and supporters.

Price cuts

In June 2001 Britain's biggest drugs company, GlaxoSmithKline, reduced the cost to the developing world of drugs for treating malaria, diarrhoea and infectious diseases. Merck and Bristol-Myers Squibb, two of the world's largest drugs companies, had already announced earlier in the year that they were supplying AIDS drugs at cost price or less to all developing countries. Bristol-Myers Squibb also announced that it would not be enforcing its patent rights in Southern Africa.

The field of pricing pharmaceutical products is complicated because in most countries prices are determined by what governments, the main buyers in the industry, are prepared to pay. The same pill made by the same company may cost half in Canada of what it does in the United States. In Mexico, it may cost still less. Such differential pricing is fundamental to the pharmaceutical industry. Because consumers are not paying for raw materials, but rather for intellectual property, drug companies charge what they can get away with and governments pay what they deem affordable. The United States, however, is the exception, as here prices are determined on the open market. However, it seems things are about to change, for the US upper house, the Senate, has challenged the existing market arrangements. It argues that US citizens should not be paying substantially more for patented drugs, while citizens in other countries get the same drugs at much lower prices because their government is only willing to pay a certain price. The Senate's amendment would allow drugs to be imported from any foreign factory approved by the Food and Drug Administration. As there are plenty of those in India and China, Senators are effectively demanding that US citizens get medicine at developing world prices. Clearly, social and economic pressures are mounting on the industry. In December 2003 the National Health Service (NHS) in the United Kingdom launched a £30 million lawsuit, which accuses seven firms of price-fixing by controlling and manipulating the market in penicillin-based antibiotics (Meikle, 2003).

Conclusions

It is the unique structure of the industry and the patent system that is at the crux of the problem. Europe, the United States and Japan account for virtually all the profits of the pharmaceutical companies. In most other markets profits are driven down by the power and price sensitivity of customers. But in pharmaceuticals, neither the patient who consumes the drugs nor the doctor who prescribes them is price sensitive. Customers for medicines are not price sensitive because they do not pay for them. In Europe it is the taxpayer who foots the bill.

Whereas most companies have profits capped by aggressive industry buyers, the pharmaceutical firms have to negotiate only with civil servants, and, argues Professor Doyle, 'when taxpayers' money is available, commercial disciplines frequently disappear' (Doyle, 2001). But, even in the United States where a free market exists, the pharmaceutical companies are able to charge even higher prices, hence the US Senate's proposed changes. Once again this is because the pharmaceutical companies are frequently selling to private health insurers. Many US employers offer health insurance as part of the employment package.

Competition is another key force that drives down prices in most industries. In electronics – an industry even more innovative than pharmaceuticals – excess profits from a new product soon disappear as competitors bring out copies. But, in the pharmaceutical business, it is the patent system that ensures high profits continue for an average of 10 years. The consequence of this ability to negotiate very high prices and the absence of competitive threat is that the giant pharmaceuticals have no incentive to compete on price. It also helps to explain why the pharma companies have been unwilling to sell cheap medicines to the poor in Africa and Asia. The real worry is that dropping prices to the developing world would undermine the enormous margins being received in Europe and the United States. Buyers would soon be reimporting medicines at a fraction of the official price, which may be the case soon in the United States.

The industry's justification for its high prices and patent monopolies is that it encourages innovation, but to what extent is this true? In most other industries it is intense competition and a fight to survive and win market share that drives forward innovation. Without new and better products companies such as Hewlett-Packard and Canon know they will not maintain growth and market share. As we have seen in Chapters 1, 2 and 3, innovation is dependent on a collection of factors and the patent system alone cannot stimulate innovation. It is necessary but not sufficient.

The industry's most popular argument to defend the patent system is that it has unusually high cost structures due to the enormous sums of money it has to invest in science and technology. Increasingly, however, the industry is spending more on marketing existing products than it is on developing new ones. Professor Doyle argues that marketing costs are now typically almost double the R&D spend. GlaxoSmithKline, for example, has 10,000 scientists but 40,000 salespeople! Even this well-rehearsed argument is now beginning to sound hollow.

The pharmaceutical industry has enjoyed 50 years of substantial growth and substantial profits and many people have benefited. The patent system is intended to balance the interests of the individual and society; increasing numbers of people are questioning this balance. The pharmaceutical companies need to consider every step carefully for they surely do not want to become the unacceptable face of globalisation.

Questions

1 Explain how the pricing of drugs contributes to the acquisition of supra-normal profits in the pharmaceutical industry.

2 It is because drugs are absolutely essential to life that the pharmaceutical industry is able to justify large profits. Discuss the merits of this argument. Consider also that bread and milk companies do not make huge profits.

3 Explain why drugs are not price-sensitive.

4 Explain why the patent system may not be working as originally intended.

Chapter summary

This chapter has explored the area of intellectual property and the different forms of protection available to a firm. This is a dynamic area of business. The operation of trademark law throughout the European Union is now controversial, as is the area of patents. It seems that the pharmaceutical industry is preparing itself for significant changes. This chapter also made it clear that the patent system has fierce critics, largely due to the associated costs involved with defending a patent against infringement. The patent system, however, was also highlighted as a valuable source of technological knowledge that is used by many companies.

Discussion questions

1 Explain why many research organisations are against the patenting of life forms.

2 Discuss the main forms of intellectual property protection available to companies.

3 Explain why discoveries are not patentable.

4 Discuss some of the limitations of the patent system.

5 Is the pharmaceutical industry the unacceptable face of globalisation (consider the anti-capitalist demonstrations of recent years)?

6 Explain with the use of examples when it would be appropriate to use trademarks and copyright to protect a firm's intellectual property.

Key words and phrases

Patent	Brands as intellectual property
Copyright	Trademark
Registered Design	Generic products
Patent extension	Infringement of intellectual property

Websites worth visiting

BTG www.BTGPLC.com

European Union, Enterprise and Innovation www.europa.eu.int/comm/enterprise/innovation

Intellect UK www.intellectuk.org

Inventions, designs, patents www.iacllc.com

National Endowment for Science and Technology www.NESTA.org.uk

Patent agents www.patent-faq.com

Patent Office www.patent.gov.uk

Pilkington PLC technology management **www.pilkington.com**

Thomson Derwent patents directory **www.Thomsonderwent.com**

UK Government, Department of Trade and Industry **www.Dti.gov.uk/innovation**

References

ACARD, *Exploiting Invention*, report to the Prime Minister, London, December 1980.

Alpert, F. (1993) 'Breadth of coverage for intellectual property law: encouraging product innovation by broadening protection', *Journal of Product and Brand Management*, 2, 2.

Badenhausen, K. (1995) 'Brands: the management factor', *Financial World*, 1 August, 50–69.

Bainbridge, D.I. (1996) *Intellectual Property*, 3rd edn, Financial Times Pitman Publishing, London.

Bowe, C. and Griffith, V. (2002) 'Proposal on patents set to hit revenues', *Financial Times*, 22 October.

Brown, A. (2007) 'Beware the backwards-looking patents that can stifle innovation' *The Guardian*, 1 March, www.guardian.co.uk/technology.

BTG (2004) 'About patents', www.BTGPLC/info/patents.

Chemistry & Industry News (1995) ci.mond.org/9521/952107.html.

Court of Appeal (1985) Reports of Patent, Design and Trade Mark Cases (RPC), No. 59.

Deakin, S. and Wilkinson, F. (1998) 'Contract law and the earning of inter-organisational trust', in Lane, C. and Bachmann, R. (eds) *Trust within and between organisations: Conceptual issues and empirical applications*, Oxford University Press, Oxford, 146–72.

Derwent (1998) Derwent World Patents Index, Derwent Scientific and Patent Information: www.Derwent.com.

Doyle, P. (2001) 'AIDS and the pharmaceutical industry', *The Guardian*, 10 March.

European Federal Trade Commission (2006). See European Union (2006).

European Union (2006) *European Innovation Scoreboard: Comparative analysis of innovation performance*, Brussels, retrieved 3 February 2007 from European Union website: www.proinno-europe.eu/doc/EIS2006_final.pdf.

Feldwick, P. (1996) 'Do we really need brand equity?' *Journal of Brand Management*, Vol. 4, No. 1, 9–28.

Financial Times (1997) 'Gene is out of the bottle', 30 October, 15.

Graham, N. (1998) 'Inventor cleans up with profits', *Sunday Times*, 1 March, 4, 16.

The Guardian (1998) 'Keep your ideas to yourself', 17 February, 22.

The Guardian (2000) 'Patenting life', 15 November, 4.

Hargreaves, D. (2001) *Financial Times*, 16 January.

http://www.webmarketingtoday.com.

Hung, C.L. (2003) 'The business of product counterfeiting in China and the post-WTO membership environment', *Asia Pacific Business Review*, Vol. 10, No. 1, 58–77.

Liebeskind, J. and Oliver, A. (1998) 'From handshake to contract: intellectual property, trust and the social structure of academic research', in Lane, C. and Bachmann, R. (eds) *Trust within and between organisations: Conceptual issues and empirical applications*, Oxford University Press, Oxford, 118–45.

McDonald, G.M. and Roberts, C. (1994) 'Product piracy: The problem will not go away', *Journal of Product & Brand Management*, Vol. 3, No. 4, 55–65.

Meikle, J. (2003) 'NHS seeks £30m from drug firms in price fixing claim', *The Guardian*, 23 December, 6.

Naim, M. (2005) *Illicit*, William Heinemann, London.

Nakamoto, M. and Pilling, D. (2004) 'Tough tasks ahead at Takeda', *Financial Times*, 23 August.

National Intellectual Property Enforcement Report (2005) The Patent Office, London. (www.ipo.gov.uk).

Rowan, D. (1997) 'Signing up to a patent on life', *The Guardian*, 27 November, 19.

Sachs, J. (1999) 'Helping the world's poorest', *The Economist*, 14 August, 16–22.

Thurow, L.C. (1997) 'Needed: A new system of intellectual property rights'.

Tom, G., Garibaldi, B., Zeng, Y. and Pilcher, J. (1998) 'Consumer demand for counterfeit goods', *Psychology and Marketing*, Vol. 15, No. 5, 405–21.

Vaidhyanathan, S. (2001) *Copyrights and Copywrongs*, New York University Press, New York.

Waldmeir, P. (2002) 'If technology switches to the side of copyright', *Financial Times*, 10 January, 15.

Yang, D. and Clarke, P. (2004) 'Review of the current intellectual property system in China', *International Journal of Technology Transfer and Commercialisation*, Vol. 3, No. 1, 12–37.

Further reading

For a more detailed review of the intellectual property literature, the following develop many of the issues raised in this chapter:

Borg, Eric A. (2001) 'Knowledge, information and intellectual property: implications for marketing relationships', *Technovation*, Vol. 21, 515–24.

The Economist (2000) 'The knowledge monopolies: patent wars', 8 April, 95–9.

Naim, M. (2005) *Illicit*, William Heinemann, London.

Shavinina, L. (2003) *The International Handbook on Innovation*, Elsevier, Oxford.